FINANCIAL ACCOUNTING

ACCOUNTING TEXTBOOKS FROM WILEY

Arpan and Radebaugh: INTERNATIONAL ACCOUNTING AND MULTINATIONAL
    ENTERPRISES, 2nd

Burch and Grudnitski: INFORMATION SYSTEMS: THEORY AND PRACTICE, 5th

Defliese, Jaenicke, O'Reilly, and Hirsch: MONTGOMERY'S AUDITING 11TH, REVISED COLLEGE
    VERSION

Delaney, Adler, Epstein, and Foran: GAAP, INTERPRETATION AND APPLICATION 1990 EDITION

Delaney and Gleim: CPA EXAMINATION REVIEW—AUDITING

Delaney and Gleim: CPA EXAMINATION REVIEW—BUSINESS LAW

Delaney and Gleim: CPA EXAMINATION REVIEW—THEORY AND PRACTICE

Gleim and Delaney: CPA EXAMINATION REVIEW—VOLUME I OUTLINES AND STUDY GUIDES

Gleim and Delaney: CPA EXAMINATION REVIEW—VOLUME II PROBLEMS AND SOLUTIONS

Guy and Carmichael: AUDIT SAMPLING: AN INTRODUCTION TO STATISTICAL SAMPLING IN
    AUDITING, 2nd

Haried, Imdieke, and Smith: ADVANCED ACCOUNTING, 5th

Helmkamp: MANAGERIAL ACCOUNTING, 2nd

Helmkamp, Imdieke, and Smith: PRINCIPLES OF ACCOUNTING, 3rd

Imdieke and Smith: FINANCIAL ACCOUNTING, 2nd

Kam: ACCOUNTING THEORY, 2nd

Kell, Boynton, and Ziegler: MODERN AUDITING, 4th

Kemp and Phillips: ADVANCED ACCOUNTING

Kieso and Weygandt: INTERMEDIATE ACCOUNTING, 6th

Lere: MANAGERIAL ACCOUNTING

Moriarity and Allen: COST ACCOUNTING, 3rd

Moscove, Simkin and Bagranoff: ACCOUNTING INFORMATION SYSTEMS, 4th

Newell and Kreuze: COLLEGE ACCOUNTING, CHAPTERS 1–10, 1–15, 1–27

Davis, Alderman and Robinson: ACCOUNTING INFORMATION SYSTEMS, 3rd

Romney, Cherrington, and Hansen: CASEBOOK IN ACCOUNTING INFORMATION SYSTEMS

Schroeder, McCullers, and Clark: ACCOUNTING THEORY: TEXT AND READINGS, 4th

Taylor and Glezen: AUDITING: INTEGRATED CONCEPTS AND PROCEDURES, 5th

Taylor, Glezen, and Ehrenreich: CASE STUDY IN AUDITING

Weygandt, Kieso, and Kell: ACCOUNTING PRINCIPLES, 2nd

Wilkinson: ACCOUNTING AND INFORMATION SYSTEMS, 3rd

Wilkinson: ACCOUNTING INFORMATION SYSTEMS: ESSENTIAL CONCEPTS AND
    APPLICATIONS

FINANCIAL ACCOUNTING

SECOND EDITION

LEROY F. IMDIEKE
RALPH E. SMITH
Arizona State University

WILEY

JOHN WILEY & SONS, INC.
NEW YORK · CHICHESTER · BRISBANE · TORONTO · SINGAPORE

Library of Congress Cataloging in Publication Data:

Imdieke, Leroy F.
    Financial accounting / Leroy F. Imdieke, Ralph E. Smith, — 2nd
  ed.
        p. cm.
    Includes index.
    ISBN 0-471-50419-X
    1. Accounting.   I. Smith, Ralph Eugene. 1941– . II. Title.
  HF5835.I43   1991
  657—dc20   90-24398
                                                      CIP

Printed in the United States of America

10 9 8 7 6 5 4 3 2 1

TO OUR FAMILIES

Lorraine, Arlene, Brian, Gary, Julie, Lynda, and Marla Imdieke
Mary, Alison, and Tucker Smith

PREFACE

Financial Accounting presents a comprehensive, straightforward description of modern-day principles of financial accounting and reporting. It is a blend of the preparation and use of financial accounting information, designed for those who have not previously studied accounting. Special care has been taken to provide a realistic balance between the procedures used in accounting and the theory and concepts upon which they are based. As such, we have emphasized both the "how" and "why" aspects of accounting.

Our primary objective is to describe financial accounting fundamentals as they relate to today's business environment, as we believe that this text is almost as much an introduction to business as it is to accounting. We have carefully selected the subject matter, its organization, and its description to ensure that the book fits the needs of all beginning business students. Consequently, the coverage is relevant for students interested in any type of business career. The book is intended for use in a one-semester or one-quarter accounting course at the undergraduate or MBA level.

WHY STUDY ACCOUNTING?

Practically every business administration program requires principles of financial accounting as an important prerequisite to other business courses and as an integral part of the preparation for a business career. During the twentieth century, accounting has become essential to the needs of our society. Every person and organization uses financial accounting information to make decisions. Many times we use accounting concepts and procedures without even realizing it. On a personal level, individuals maintain bank accounts, account for their income, and prepare income tax returns. Examples of other areas in which financial accounting information is useful are:

- Investors evaluate alternative investments such as bonds, stocks, and money market funds to decide how to invest their money.
- Individuals must often prepare personal financial statements to support applications for personal loans or home mortgages.
- Businesses need financial accounting information to determine if they are successful financially.

- Businesses must decide how to allocate scarce resources among their various activities.
- Boards of directors and owners use financial accounting information to evaluate management's performance.
- Creditors use financial accounting information to decide whether to lend money or to extend credit to a business.
- Governments use accounting procedures to plan and control the receipts and expenditures of public funds.

Accounting is often thought of as an information processing system because it is a means of social communication that involves a flow of information about a business. Like any form of communication, accounting has its own specialized terminology, concepts, procedures, and standards. Because of its essential role in our society, accounting as a means of communication must be continually modified and updated to satisfy the changing needs of the business world.

ORGANIZATION OF THE BOOK

The text is organized into five parts. Part I includes Chapters 1 and 2 consisting of an introduction to and overview of financial statements. Chapters 3, 4, and 5 constitute Part II and describe the data processing cycle. Part III discusses accounting for and control of assets (Chapters 6 through 10). Accounting for liabilities and owners' equity are described in Part IV, consisting of Chapters 11 through 13. Part V includes Chapters 14 through 17, where other financial accounting issues are discussed. The seventeen chapters represent a comprehensive, modern version of principles of financial accounting.

BASIC FEATURES OF THE BOOK

1. Each chapter begins with a concise description (overview) of the coverage of the chapter and a list of the learning objectives involved. The learning objectives are also repeated in the margins of the text next to the relevant subject material to assist the students through the chapters.
2. A glossary of key terms is presented at the end of each chapter. Each definition is keyed to a page within the chapter where the term is identified in boldface color.
3. A summary of the main points developed in the chapter concludes the textual material in each chapter.
4. Each chapter includes a review problem to reinforce understanding of the basic concepts and procedures.
5. Discussion questions are included at the end of every chapter to emphasize major points.
6. Exercises pertaining to the chapter topics are presented in compact form.
7. Problems are included for more comprehensive homework assignment.

8. Each exercise and problem has a brief description of the topic(s) covered. The intent is to focus the student's attention on the main consideration being addressed.

9. Each chapter contains a multiple-choice self-test.

10. Most chapters include a case requiring students to refer to the annual report of BF Goodrich Company, which is located in appendix at the end of the text.

11. Illustrations of and references to real-world accounting applications are presented throughout the text.

12. Authoritative and informative references are made in nontechnical language throughout the text to such sources as the Accounting Principles Board, Financial Accounting Standards Board, Accounting Trends & Techniques, and specific firms' financial statements.

13. A comprehensive discussion of the time value of money is presented as Part II of chapter 11 (covering the general topic of accounting for liabilities).

CHANGES IN THE SECOND EDITION

We appreciate the response to the first edition of this textbook. At the same time, we realize that any book has room for improvement to meet the ever-changing needs of instructors and students. We have listened carefully and responded to comments and suggestions made by adopters, reviewers, and students. As a result, the second edition contains adjustments and refinements recommended to us, as well as some we have chosen on the basis of our own experience. Writing a beginning accounting text is a difficult task because there are often acceptable alternative ways to handle certain transactions. What is considered the best treatment is often a matter of personal choice. We have attempted to present the alternative we believe is the most pedagogically sound for student learning. Other alternatives are generally included in related chapter appendices so instructors can use the alternative they feel most comfortable with. The following is a partial list of the changes in the second edition that we feel are most important from a teaching perspective.

1. We have introduced the topic of income statement gains and losses in Chapter 1, along with the income statement equation.

2. An eight- to ten-question multiple-choice self-test has been added to each chapter, with answers given a few pages later.

3. The fundamental accounting framework in Chapter 2 has been reorganized into basic assumptions, basic principles, and modifying conventions.

4. Changes in tax law have been incorporated in appropriate chapters throughout the text.

5. All exercises and problems have been updated and revised.

6. Special income statement items, i.e., disposal of a segment and extraordinary gains and losses, are discussed briefly in Chapter 13 along with a brief discussion of net-of-tax reporting.

7. Reference to international variations in accounting standards has been incorporated in the discussion of appropriate topics throughout the text. Examples are the discussions concerning the stable-dollar assumption, cost principle, and conservatism convention in Chapter 2.

8. There are more flowcharts, graphs, and real-world examples used to enhance student understanding and interest.

9. The package of supporting materials has been polished and enhanced. We have added a number of computerized supplements as aids to both students and instructors.

10. We have tried to improve our writing style, the description of accounting principles, and the relevancy of end-of-chapter material wherever users of the first edition or reviewers have pointed out the need for change.

SUPPLEMENTARY MATERIALS FOR THE STUDENT

Study Guide

Written by Bruce Baldwin, the Study Guide contains learning objectives, study tips, and chapter reviews organized by learning objectives, as well as matching questions, true-false questions, completion questions, multiple-choice questions, short-answer exercises, and crossword puzzles.

Practice Sets

Both manual and computerized practice sets are available to provide the student with opportunities to apply accounting concepts and procedures to specific situations.

Workpapers

Workpapers designed to minimize the ''pencil-pushing'' aspect of accounting for the student are available. The workpapers should also assist students in learning proper formats and procedures.

FOR THE INSTRUCTOR

Solutions Manual

The Solutions Manual, prepared by the authors, provides answers to discussion questions, and provides answers (as well as the procedures used to determine them) for all exercises and problems in the textbook.

Instructor's Manual

This manual identifies chapter learning objectives; keys discussion questions, exercises, and problems to the learning objectives; gives time for completion and difficulty level of problems; and contains chapter outlines with detailed teaching hints and examples.

Test Bank/Microtest

Available in traditional and computerized formats, the Test Bank consists of multiple-choice questions, true-false questions, completion questions, and problems and exercises for each chapter.

Checklist of Key Figures

These are available in quantity for instructors to distribute as learning aids to students.

Overhead Transparencies

The transparency package contains transparencies for all exercises and problems as well as for certain text material.

Solutions to Practice Sets

Solutions are available for both the traditional and computerized practice sets.

ACKNOWLEDGMENTS

Any textbook is the product of numerous efforts and contributions. We are indebted to many people for their assistance. The following faculty members assisted us in many ways during the development of this book. We thank them very much for their suggestions and constructive criticism:

Larry P. Bailey
Rider College

Roy Baker
University of Missouri at Kansas City

Francis Bird
University of Richmond

Suzanne Busch
California State University—Hayward

Gyan Chandra
Miami University of Ohio

Paul Chaney
Vanderbilt University

Richard L. Cross
Bentley College

Dennis Daly
University of Minnesota

Charles Fazzi
Bucknell University

Walker E. Fesmire
University of Michigan at Flint

Dan Hines
Eastern Carolina University

Richard Houser
Northern Arizona University

Douglas F. Hyde, ret.
Temple University

Kumen Jones
Arizona State University

Pat Kemp
Oregon State University

Malcolm Lathan
University of Virginia

Robert Parry
Indiana University

Vickie Rymer
George Mason University

Ronald Savey
Western Washington University

Mayda Shorney
University of Lowell

T. Sterling Wetzel
Oklahoma State University

Thomas S. Wetzel
Northern Illinois University

Kay Pitt
Ron Pitt
Northern Arizona University

We also wish to express a special thanks to the many people on the John Wiley & Sons staff who gave so much of themselves to this book. Lucille Sutton initiated the project and Karen Hawkins brought the second edition to completion. Linda Muriello and Katie Rubin effectively directed the production process. Terry Ann O'Shea worked closely with us to ensure a much improved supplemental package, and Amy Zelse provided administrative support throughout.

Leroy F. Imdieke
Ralph E. Smith

ABOUT THE AUTHORS

Leroy F. Imdieke, PhD, CPA, is Professor of Accounting at Arizona State University. He received his PhD in accounting from the University of Illinois. He has instructed graduate and undergraduate courses in financial accounting and reporting and has conducted many professional development seminars during his thirty-year career. Professor Imdieke's articles on financial accounting and reporting topics have appeared in *The Accounting Review*, the *Journal of Accountancy*, and other academic and professional journals. He is a member of the American Accounting Association and the Arizona State Society of Certified Public Accountants. He has served on several committees of the American Accounting Association and most recently served as a member of the Board of Directors of the Arizona Society of Certified Public Accountants. He has served as a consultant to a number of business firms and state agencies.

Ralph E. Smith, PhD, CPA, is Professor of Accounting at Arizona State University. He has instructed graduate and undergraduate courses and seminars in financial accounting theory and problems. He has also been active in developing and conducting a number of professional development seminars. Professor Smith received his PhD in accounting from the University of Kansas. He is a CPA in the state of Kansas and is a member of the American Accounting Association and the American Institute of Certified Public Accountants. He has served on several committees of the American Accounting Association and also holds membership in Beta Gamma Sigma and Beta Alpha Psi. He has written a number of articles that have appeared in *The Accounting Review*, the *Journal of Accountancy*, the *Journal of Financial and Quantitative Analysis*, and other professional and academic journals.

CONTENTS

PART I
**INTRODUCTION TO FINANCIAL
STATEMENTS**   1

CHAPTER 1
**THE NATURE OF FINANCIAL
ACCOUNTING AND REPORTING**   2
CHAPTER OVERVIEW AND OBJECTIVES   2
ACCOUNTING—AN INFORMATION
PROCESSING SYSTEM   3
CHARACTERISTICS OF ACCOUNTING
INFORMATION   3
RECORDING AND REPORTING ACCOUNTING
INFORMATION   4
USING ACCOUNTING INFORMATION   4
SOURCES OF ACCOUNTING PRINCIPLES AND
PRACTICES   5
ACCOUNTING AS A PROFESSION   7
PUBLIC ACCOUNTING   8
PRIVATE ACCOUNTING   9
GOVERNMENTAL (NOT-FOR-PROFIT)
ACCOUNTING   10
FORMS OF BUSINESS ORGANIZATION   10
COMMUNICATING ACCOUNTING
INFORMATION THROUGH FINANCIAL
STATEMENTS   11
EXTERNAL FINANCIAL STATEMENTS—AN
OVERVIEW   12
BALANCE SHEET   12
INCOME STATEMENT   14
RETAINED EARNINGS STATEMENT   16
STATEMENT OF CASH FLOWS   17
SUMMARY   18
SELF-TEST   19
REVIEW PROBLEM/GLOSSARY/DISCUSSION
QUESTIONS/EXERCISES/PROBLEMS/CASE

CHAPTER 2
**ORGANIZATION OF FINANCIAL
STATEMENTS AND ACCOUNTING
CONCEPTS**   33
CHAPTER OVERVIEW AND OBJECTIVES   33
CLASSIFICATION WITHIN EXTERNAL FINANCIAL
STATEMENTS   33
THE INCOME STATEMENT   34
THE BALANCE SHEET   36
THE RETAINED EARNINGS STATEMENT   40
STATEMENT OF CASH FLOWS (SCF)   41
OTHER DISCLOSURE METHODS   42
FUNDAMENTAL ACCOUNTING ASSUMPTIONS,
PRINCIPLES, AND MODIFYING
CONVENTIONS   43
BASIC ASSUMPTIONS   44
THE ENTITY ASSUMPTION   44
THE GOING CONCERN ASSUMPTION   44
MONETARY UNIT ASSUMPTION   45
THE STABLE-DOLLAR ASSUMPTION   45
THE TIME PERIOD ASSUMPTION   45
BASIC PRINCIPLES   46
THE OBJECTIVITY PRINCIPLE   46
THE COST PRINCIPLE   46
THE REVENUE PRINCIPLE   47
THE MATCHING PRINCIPLE   47
THE CONSISTENCY PRINCIPLE   47
THE FULL DISCLOSURE PRINCIPLE   48
MODIFYING CONVENTIONS   48
MATERIALITY CONVENTION   48
CONSERVATISM CONVENTION   48
INDUSTRY PECULIARITIES CONVENTION   49
SUMMARY   49
SELF-TEST   50
REVIEW PROBLEM/GLOSSARY/DISCUSSION
QUESTIONS/EXERCISES/PROBLEMS/CASE

PART II
DATA PROCESSING CYCLE   69

CHAPTER 3
**ANALYZING BUSINESS
   TRANSACTIONS**   70
CHAPTER OVERVIEW AND OBJECTIVES   70
CHARACTERISTICS OF ACCOUNTING
   INFORMATION   71
PREPARATION OF SOURCE DOCUMENTS   71
THE EFFECTS OF TRANSACTIONS ON THE
   ACCOUNTING EQUATION   72
TRANSACTION ANALYSIS   73
ACCRUAL ACCOUNTING   76
DOUBLE ENTRY ACCOUNTING   76
PREPARATION OF FINANCIAL STATEMENTS   76
THE ACCOUNTING DATA PROCESSING CYCLE   77
STEP 1: TRANSACTIONS OCCUR AND SOURCE
   DOCUMENTS ARE PREPARED   78
STEP 2: TRANSACTIONS ARE ANALYZED AND
   RECORDED IN A JOURNAL   80
STEP 3: JOURNAL ENTIRES ARE POSTED TO THE
   LEDGER   86
STEP 4: PREPARATION OF A TRIAL BALANCE   88
ILLUSTRATIVE PROBLEM   89
DISCOVERY AND CORRECTION OF ERRORS   97
SUMMARY   98
SELF-TEST   99
REVIEW PROBLEM/GLOSSARY/DISCUSSION
   QUESTIONS/EXERCISES/PROBLEMS/CASE

CHAPTER 4
**MEASURING NET INCOME AND
   PREPARING ADJUSTING ENTRIES**   125
CHAPTER OVERVIEW AND OBJECTIVES   125
MEASURING NET INCOME   126
CASH BASIS METHOD OF MEASURING NET
   INCOME   126
ACCRUAL BASIS METHOD OF MEASURING NET
   INCOME   127
WHY ADJUSTING ENTRIES ARE NEEDED   132
CLASSIFYING ADJUSTING ENTRIES   133
ADJUSTING ENTRIES ILLUSTRATED   134
PREPAID EXPENSES (ASSET TRANSFERRED TO
   EXPENSE ADJUSTMENTS)   135
UNEARNED REVENUES (LIABILITY TRANSFERRED
   TO REVENUE ADJUSTMENTS)   139
ACCRUED (UNRECORDED) EXPENSES (LIABILITY
   AND EXPENSE ADJUSTMENTS)   140

ACCRUED (UNRECORDED) REVENUE (ASSET
   AND REVENUE ADJUSTMENTS)   144
ADJUSTED TRIAL BALANCE   145
SUMMARY   147
SELF-TEST   149
REVIEW PROBLEM/GLOSSARY/DISCUSSION
   QUESTIONS/EXERCISES/PROBLEMS/CASE

CHAPTER 5
**PREPARATION OF A WORKSHEET AND
   COMPLETION OF THE
   ACCOUNTING DATA PROCESSING
   CYCLE—SERVICE FIRM**   175
CHAPTER OVERVIEW AND OBJECTIVES   175
THE COMPLETE ACCOUNTING CYCLE   176
STEP 4: PREPARATION OF A WORKSHEET   178
PREPARATION OF THE WORKSHEET ILLUSTRATED   178
STEP 5: PREPARATION OF FINANCIAL
   STATEMENTS   183
STEP 6: RECORDING AND POSTING
   ADJUSTING ENTRIES   183
STEP 7: RECORDING AND POSTING CLOSING
   ENTRIES   183
CLOSING ENTRIES ILLUSTRATED   187
STEP 8: THE POST-CLOSING TRIAL BALANCE   191
PREPARING INTERIM STATEMENTS WITHOUT
   CLOSING THE ACCOUNTS   191
REFINEMENTS TO A MANUAL ACCOUNTING
   SYSTEM   192
SUMMARY   192
SELF-TEST   192
REVIEW PROBLEM   194
APPENDIX: AN ALTERNATIVE METHOD OF
   RECORDING DEFERRALS   198
PAYMENTS FOR PREPAID EXPENSES RECORDED
   IN EXPENSE ACCOUNTS   199
REVENUES COLLECTED IN ADVANCE
   RECORDED IN REVENUE ACCOUNTS   200
APPENDIX: REVERSING ENTRIES   200
REVERSING ADJUSTMENTS OF DEFERRALS
   RECORDED IN TEMPORARY ACCOUNTS   201
REVERSING ENTRIES RELATED TO ADJUSTMENTS
   FOR ACCRUALS   202
SELF-TEST   205
GLOSSARY/DISCUSSION QUESTIONS/
   EXERCISES/PROBLEMS/CASE

PART III
**ACCOUNTING FOR AND CONTROL
   OF ASSETS**   227

CHAPTER 6
ACCOUNTING FOR MERCHANDISING OPERATIONS 228
CHAPTER OVERVIEW AND OBJECTIVES 228
MERCHANDISING FIRM OPERATIONS 229
INCOME STATEMENT FOR A MERCHANDISING FIRM 229
ACCOUNTING FOR SALES TRANSACTIONS 230
RECORDING GROSS SALES 231
CONTROL ACCOUNTS AND SUBSIDIARY LEDGERS 231
SALES RETURNS AND ALLOWANCES 232
CREDIT TERMS 232
FREIGHT-OUT 234
METHODS OF ACCOUNTING FOR INVENTORY AND COST OF GOODS SOLD 235
PERPETUAL INVENTORY SYSTEM 235
PERIODIC INVENTORY SYSTEM 236
ILLUSTRATION OF A PERPETUAL INVENTORY SYSTEM 236
PHYSICAL INVENTORY 238
END-OF-PERIOD PROCESS 239
ILLUSTRATION OF PERIODIC INVENTORY SYSTEM 239
PERPETUAL AND PERIODIC INVENTORY SYSTEMS CONTRASTED 242
DETERMINING THE COST OF INVENTORY 242
END-OF-PERIOD PROCESS—PERIODIC INVENTORY SYSTEM 244
ILLUSTRATION OF A WORKSHEET FOR A MERCHANDISING FIRM 245
COMPLETION OF THE ACCOUNTING CYCLE 247
INCOME STATEMENT FOR A MERCHANDISING FIRM 249
SUMMARY 249
SELF-TEST 251
REVIEW PROBLEM 253
APPENDIX: AN ALTERNATIVE METHOD FOR CLOSING ACCOUNTS—PERIODIC INVENTORY SYSTEM 256
GLOSSARY/DISCUSSION QUESTIONS/ EXERCISES/PROBLEMS/CASE

CHAPTER 7
ACCOUNTING CONTROLS AND SYSTEMS 280
CHAPTER OVERVIEW AND OBJECTIVES 280
OPERATION OF AN ACCOUNTING SYSTEM 281
THE FOREIGN CORRUPT PRACTICES ACT 282
INTERNAL CONTROL 283

ADMINISTRATIVE CONTROLS AND ACCOUNTING CONTROLS 283
DEVELOPMENT OF AN ACCOUNTING SYSTEM 287
SYSTEMS ANALYSIS 287
SYSTEMS DESIGN 288
SYSTEMS IMPLEMENTATION 288
REFINEMENTS TO A MANUAL ACCOUNTING SYSTEM 289
SUBSIDIARY LEDGERS AND CONTROL ACCOUNTS 289
THE IMPACT OF DATA PROCESSING EQUIPMENT ON ACCOUNTING 290
ELECTRONIC DATA PROCESSING 291
THE IMPACT OF MICROCOMPUTERS ON ACCOUNTING 292
INTERNAL CONTROL OF MICROCOMPUTERS 293
COMPUTERIZED ACCOUNTING SYSTEMS 294
SUMMARY 295
SELF-TEST 296
REVIEW PROBLEM 296
APPENDIX: PROCESSING OF REPETITIVE TRANSACTIONS IN A MANUAL SYSTEM 298
SPECIAL JOURNALS 298
SALES JOURNAL 299
PURCHASES JOURNAL 302
CASH RECEIPTS JOURNAL 302
CASH DISBURSEMENTS JOURNAL 306
GLOSSARY/DISCUSSION QUESTIONS/ EXERCISES/PROBLEMS/CASE

CHAPTER 8
CASH; MARKETABLE SECURITIES, AND RECEIVABLES 328
CHAPTER OVERVIEW AND OBJECTIVES 328
CASH 328
INTERNAL CONTROL OF CASH 329
THE PETTY CASH FUND 330
CASH SHORT AND OVER 332
BANK CHECKING ACCOUNTS 332
RECONCILING THE BANK ACCOUNT 334
TEMPORARY INVESTMENTS IN MARKETABLE SECURITIES 338
REPORTING TEMPORARY INVESTMENTS IN MARKETABLE SECURITIES 338
ACCOUNTING FOR MARKETABLE SECURITIES PORTFOLIOS 339
TEMPORARY INVESTMENTS IN EQUITY SECURITIES 339
TEMPORARY INVESTMENTS IN DEBT SECURITIES 341
RECEIVABLES 342

CLASSIFICATION OF RECEIVABLES   342
ACCOUNTS RECEIVABLE   342
NOTES RECEIVABLE   347
SUMMARY   350
SELF-TEST   351
REVIEW PROBLEM/GLOSSARY/DISCUSSION
   QUESTIONS/EXERCISES/PROBLEMS/CASE

CHAPTER 9
INVENTORY COSTING METHODS   377
CHAPTER OVERVIEW AND OBJECTIVES   377
DETERMINING THE INVENTORY ON HAND   378
TRANSFER OF OWNERSHIP   379
GOODS ON CONSIGNMENT   379
ALLOCATION OF INVENTORY COST BETWEEN
   ENDING INVENTORY AND COST OF GOODS
   SOLD   380
PERIODIC INVENTORY SYSTEM   381
SPECIFIC IDENTIFICATION METHOD   382
FIRST-IN, FIRST-OUT (FIFO) METHOD   383
LAST-IN, FIRST-OUT (LIFO) METHOD   383
WEIGHTED AVERAGE METHOD   384
COMPARISON OF COSTING METHODS   385
WHICH METHOD TO SELECT   389
CONSISTENCY IN USING A COSTING METHOD   389
THE LOWER OF COST OR MARKET RULE   390
NET REALIZABLE VALUE   391
PERPETUAL INVENTORY SYSTEMS   391
SPECIFIC IDENTIFICATION METHOD   392
FIRST-IN, FIRST-OUT METHOD   392
LAST-IN, FIRST-OUT METHOD   393
MOVING AVERAGE METHOD   394
COMPARISON OF COSTING METHODS   395
COMPARISON OF THE PERPETUAL AND
   PERIODIC INVENTORY SYSTEMS   395
INVENTORY ERRORS   397
ESTIMATING INVENTORIES   399
RETAIL INVENTORY METHOD   399
GROSS PROFIT METHOD   400
PRESENTATION IN FINANCIAL STATEMENTS   401
SUMMARY   403
SELF-TEST   403
REVIEW PROBLEM/GLOSSARY/DISCUSSION
   QUESTIONS/EXERCISES/PROBLEMS/CASE

CHAPTER 10
OPERATING ASSETS   428
CHAPTER OVERVIEW AND OBJECTIVES   428
DETERMINING THE ACQUISITION COST OF
   OPERATING ASSETS   429

APPORTIONING THE COST OF A LUMP-SUM
   ACQUISITION   430
ALLOCATING ACQUISITION COST TO EXPENSE   431
NATURE OF DEPRECIATION   431
DEPRECIATION METHODS   432
DEPRECIATION FOR PART OF A YEAR   437
DEPRECIATION FOR INCOME TAX PURPOSES   437
REVISION OF DEPRECIATION ESTIMATES   438
DEPRECIATION AND CASH FLOW   438
ACCOUNTING FOR EXPENDITURES AFTER
   ACQUISITION   439
REVENUE EXPENDITURE—ORDINARY REPAIRS
   AND MAINTENANCE   440
CAPITAL EXPENDITURE—EXTRAORDINARY
   REPAIRS   440
ACCOUNTING FOR DISPOSITION OF
   OPERATING ASSETS   440
DISCARDING OPERATING ASSETS   441
SALE OF OPERATING ASSETS   441
EXCHANGING OPERATING ASSETS   442
INTANGIBLE ASSETS   444
AMORTIZATION   445
NATURAL RESOURCES   448
DEPLETION   449
SUMMARY   450
SELF-TEST   451
REVIEW PROBLEM/GLOSSARY/DISCUSSION
   QUESTIONS/EXERCISES/PROBLEMS/CASE

PART IV
ACCOUNTING FOR LIABILITIES AND
   OWNERS EQUITY   471

CHAPTER 11
LIABILITIES AND THE TIME VALUE OF
   MONEY   472
CHAPTER OVERVIEW AND OBJECTIVES   472
PART I. LIABILITIES   472
CURRENT LIABILITIES   473
ACCOUNTS PAYABLE   473
SHORT-TERM NOTES PAYABLE   473
ACCRUED EXPENSES   476
UNEARNED REVENUES   477
PAYROLL LIABILITIES   477
LONG-TERM LIABILITIES   480
LEASE OBLIGATIONS   481
PENSION PLANS   482
DEFERRED INCOME TAX LIABILITY   483
PART II. THE TIME VALUE OF MONEY   485

SIMPLE AND COMPOUND INTEREST **486**
CASE I FUTURE VALUE OF A SINGLE AMOUNT **487**
CASE II FUTURE VALUE OF AN ORDINARY
   ANNUITY **489**
CASE III PRESENT VALUE OF A SINGLE
   AMOUNT **491**
CASE IV PRESENT VALUE OF AN ORDINARY
   ANNUITY **493**
SUMMARY **495**
SELF-TEST **496**
REVIEW PROBLEM **497**
APPENDIX: CONTROLLING LIABILITIES AND
   CASH DISBURSEMENTS WITH A VOUCHER
   SYSTEM **499**
PLACING ORDERS **499**
RECEIPT OF GOODS **501**
VERIFICATION OF THE ACCURACY OF
   INVOICES AND APPROVAL OF PAYMENT **502**
THE VOUCHER **502**
THE VOUCHER REGISTER **504**
THE CHECK REGISTER **505**
GLOSSARY/DISCUSSION QUESTIONS/
   EXERCISES/PROBLEMS/CASE

CHAPTER 12
ACCOUNTING FOR LONG-TERM
   BONDS PAYABLE **523**
CHAPTER OVERVIEW AND OBJECTIVES **523**
PART I. CHARACTERISTICS AND
   FUNDAMENTALS OF ACCOUNTING FOR
   AND REPORTING BONDS PAYABLE **524**
BONDS PAYABLE **524**
PAR VALUE OF BONDS **524**
WHO ISSUES THE BONDS? **525**
THE BOND INDENTURE **525**
SELLING EXISTING BONDS **526**
THE ADVANTAGES OF DEBT FINANCING **526**
COMPARISON OF DEBT FINANCING AND
   EQUITY FINANCING **527**
TYPES OF BONDS ISSUED **528**
FINANCIAL STATEMENT DISCLOSURES **530**
ACCOUNTING FOR BONDS ISSUED AT PAR
   VALUE **531**
THE EFFECT OF MARKET INTEREST RATES ON
   BOND PRICES **532**
DETERMINING THE ISSUE PRICE OF A BOND **533**
ACCOUNTING FOR BONDS ISSUED AT A
   DISCOUNT **536**
AMORTIZING THE BOND DISCOUNT—
   STRAIGHT-LINE METHOD **537**

ACCOUNTING FOR BONDS ISSUED AT A
   PREMIUM **538**
AMORTIZING THE BOND PREMIUM—STRAIGHT-
   LINE METHOD **540**
PART II. OTHER ISSUES RELATED TO
   ACCOUNTING FOR BONDS PAYABLE **542**
BONDS ISSUED BETWEEN INTEREST PAYMENT
   DATES **542**
YEAR-END ADJUSTING ENTRY FOR BOND
   INTEREST EXPENSE **543**
RETIREMENT OF BONDS BEFORE MATURITY **544**
CONVERSION OF BONDS INTO CAPITAL
   STOCK **545**
BOND SINKING FUND **546**
EFFECTIVE-INTEREST METHOD OF
   AMORTIZATION **547**
AMORTIZATION OF A DISCOUNT: EFFECTIVE-
   INTEREST METHOD **547**
AMORTIZATION OF A PREMIUM: EFFECTIVE-
   INTEREST METHOD **549**
LONG-TERM NOTES PAYABLE **550**
COMPREHENSIVE ILLUSTRATION OF
   REPORTING LIABILITIES **551**
SUMMARY **551**
SELF-TEST **552**
REVIEW PROBLEM/GLOSSARY/DISCUSSION
   QUESTIONS/EXERCISES/PROBLEMS/CASE

CHAPTER 13
ACCOUNTING FOR OWNERS' EQUITY
   AND SPECIAL INCOME STATEMENT
   ITEMS **572**
CHAPTER OVERVIEW AND OBJECTIVES **572**
CORPORATION DEFINED **573**
TYPES OF CORPORATIONS **573**
ADVANTAGES OF THE CORPORATE FORM **574**
FORMING A CORPORATION **575**
MANGING THE CORPORATION **575**
THE STOCKHOLDERS **575**
THE BOARD OF DIRECTORS **577**
THE CORPORATE OFFICERS **577**
CORPORATE CAPITAL **578**
AUTHORIZED CAPITAL STOCK **579**
OUTSTANDING STOCK **580**
ISSUING COMMON STOCK **580**
CASH DIVIDENDS **582**
PREFERRED STOCK **583**
DIVIDEND PREFERENCE **583**
CALLABLE PREFERRED STOCK **585**
CONVERTIBLE PREFERRED STOCK **585**

TREASURY STOCK   586
STOCK DIVIDENDS   587
STOCK SPLITS   590
SPECIAL INCOME STATEMENT ITEMS AND
    RETAINED EARNINGS   590
NET-OF-TAX REPORTING   591
DISCONTINUED OPERATIONS—DISPOSAL OF A
    BUSINESS SEGMENT   592
EXTRAORDINARY ITEMS   592
CHANGE IN ACCOUNTING PRINCIPLES   593
RETAINED EARNINGS STATEMENT   594
RETAINED EARNINGS RESTRICTIONS   595
BOOK VALUE PER SHARE OF COMMON STOCK   595
SUMMARY   596
SELF-TEST   597
REVIEW PROBLEM/GLOSSARY/DISCUSSION
    QUESTIONS/EXERCISES/PROBLEMS/CASE

CONSOLIDATED INCOME STATEMENT   639
PURCHASE VERSUS POOLING OF INTERESTS   640
LIMITATIONS OF CONSOLIDATED FINANCIAL
    STATEMENTS   641
SUMMARY   642
SELF-TEST   643
REVIEW PROBLEM   644
APPENDIX: ACCOUNTING FOR FOREIGN
    TRANSACTIONS AND TRANSLATION OF
    FOREIGN FINANCIAL STATEMENTS   646
EXCHANGE RATES—TRANSLATION   646
ACCOUNTING FOR IMPORT AND EXPORT
    TRANSACTIONS   647
REALIZED VERSUS UNREALIZED EXCHANGE
    GAINS AND LOSSES   649
TRANSLATION OF FOREIGN FINANCIAL
    STATEMENTS   650
TRANSLATION ILLUSTRATION   650
A MOVE TOWARD UNIFORM INTERNATIONAL
    ACCOUNTING STANDARDS   652
GLOSSARY/DISCUSSION QUESTIONS/
    EXERCISES/PROBLEMS/CASE

PART V
OTHER ISSUES

619

CHAPTER 14
LONG-TERM INVESTMENTS, CONSOLIDATED FINANCIAL STATEMENTS, AND INTERNATIONAL ACCOUNTING

LONG-TERM INVESTMENTS,
    CONSOLIDATED FINANCIAL
    STATEMENTS, AND INTERNATIONAL
    ACCOUNTING   620
CHAPTER OVERVIEW AND OBJECTIVES   620
PART I. ACCOUNTING FOR LONG-TERM
    INVESTMENTS   621
ACCOUNTING FOR LONG-TERM INVESTMENTS
    IN BONDS   621
BONDS PURCHASED AT A PREMIUM—
    STRAIGHT-LINE AMORTIZATION   622
BONDS PURCHASED AT A DISCOUNT—
    STRAIGHT-LINE AMORTIZATION   624
RECORDING THE SALE OF BOND INVESTMENTS   624
EFFECTIVE INTEREST METHOD OF
    AMORTIZATION   625
ACCOUNTING FOR LONG-TERM INVESTMENTS
    IN EQUITY SECURITIES   627
THE COST METHOD   627
THE EQUITY METHOD   630
PART II. CONSOLIDATED FINANCIAL
    STATEMENTS   632
PRINCIPLES OF CONSOLIDATION   633
CRITERIA FOR THE PREPARATION OF
    CONSOLIDATED FINANCIAL STATEMENTS   634
CONSOLIDATED BALANCE SHEET   634
PURCHASE OF STOCK FOR MORE OR LESS
    THAN BOOK VALUE   637

CHAPTER 15
STATEMENT OF CASH FLOWS

STATEMENT OF CASH FLOWS   672
CHAPTER OVERVIEW AND OBJECTIVES   672
BRIEF HISTORY OF THE DEVELOPMENT OF
    THE SCF   672
PURPOSE OF THE SCF   673
CONCEPT OF CASH   673
CLASSIFICATION WITHIN THE SCF   674
CONTENT AND FORM OF THE SCF   675
CASH FLOW FROM OPERATING ACTIVITIES   675
DIRECT METHOD OF REPORTING CASH FLOW
    FROM OPERATING ACTIVITIES   675
INDIRECT METHOD OF REPORTING CASH FLOW
    FROM OPERATING ACTIVITIES   679
RECONCILIATION OF NET INCOME TO NET
    CASH FLOW FROM OPERATING ACTIVITIES   681
CASH FLOWS FROM INVESTING ACTIVITIES   682
CASH FLOWS FROM FINANCING ACTIVITIES   683
DIRECT EXCHANGE (NONCASH)
    TRANSACTIONS   683
PREPARING THE SCF—AN EXTENDED
    ILLUSTRATION   684
SUMMARY   688
SELF-TEST   688
REVIEW PROBLEM/GLOSSARY/DISCUSSION
    QUESTIONS/EXERCISES/PROBLEMS/CASE

CHAPTER 16
ANALYSIS OF FINANCIAL
  STATEMENTS AND ACCOUNTING
  FOR CHANGING PRICES   710
CHAPTER OVERVIEW AND OBJECTIVES   710
PART I. ANALYSIS OF FINANCIAL STATEMENTS   710
SOURCES OF FINANCIAL INFORMATION   711
PUBLISHED FINANCIAL REPORTS   711
REPORTS FILED WITH THE SEC   711
ADVISORY SERVICES AND FINANCIAL
  PUBLICATIONS   711
NEED FOR ANALYTICAL TECHNIQUES   712
OBJECTIVES OF FINANCIAL STATEMENT
  ANALYSIS   712
PERCENTAGE ANALYSIS   713
HORIZONTAL ANALYSIS   713
TREND ANALYSIS   716
VERTICAL ANALYSIS   717
RATIO ANALYSIS   717
RATIOS TO ANALYZE PROFITABILITY   718
RATIOS TO ANALYZE LIQUIDITY   723
RATIOS TO ANALYZE THE USE OF FINANCIAL
  LEVERAGE   727
LIMITATIONS OF FINANCIAL ANALYSIS   728
PART II. EFFECTS OF INFLATION   730
REPORTING THE EFFECTS OF INFLATION   731
CONSTANT DOLLAR ACCOUNTING   731
CURRENT VALUE ACCOUNTING   737
FASB RECOMMENDATIONS   740
SUMMARY   741
SELF-TEST   742
REVIEW PROBLEM/GLOSSARY/DISCUSSION
  QUESTIONS/EXERCISES/PROBLEMS/CASE

CHAPTER 17
INCOME TAXES: AN OVERVIEW   768
CHAPTER OVERVIEW AND OBJECTIVES   768
PART I. INTRODUCTION TO THE FEDERAL TAX
  SYSTEM AND TAX CONSIDERATIONS FOR
  INDIVIDUALS   769
SOME FEATURES OF THE FEDERAL TAX SYSTEM   770

CLASSIFICATION OF TAXABLE ENTITIES   770
RELATIONSHIP OF TAX LAW TO GENERALLY
  ACCEPTED ACCOUNTING PRINCIPLES   771
THE ROLE OF TAX PLANNING   771
THE CHOICE OF ACCOUNTING METHODS   772
TAX CONSIDERATIONS FOR INDIVIDUAL
  TAXPAYERS   773
FILING A FEDERAL INCOME TAX RETURN   773
INCOME, EXCLUSIONS, AND GROSS INCOME   774
DEDUCTIONS FROM GROSS INCOME   774
DEDUCTIONS FROM ADJUSTED GROSS
  INCOME   776
EXEMPTIONS   779
COMPUTING THE TAX LIABILITY   779
TAX CREDITS   781
TAX PREPAYMENTS   781
THE IMPORTANCE OF THE MARGINAL TAX RATE   781
CAPITAL GAINS AND LOSSES   783
COMPUTATION OF INCOME TAX FOR A JOINT
  RETURN   784
PART II. TAX CONSIDERATIONS FOR
  CORPORATIONS   784
TOTAL REVENUES AND EXCLUSIONS   786
DEDUCTIONS FROM GROSS INCOME   786
COMPUTING THE TAX LIABILITY   787
TAX PLANNING AND BUSINESS DECISIONS   788
TAX IMPLICATIONS OF THE CHOICE OF
  BUSINESS ORGANIZATION   788
CHOICE OF FINANCING METHODS   790
OPERATING A BUSINESS   791
SUMMARY   791
SELF-TEST   793
REVIEW PROBLEM/GLOSSARY/DISCUSSION
  QUESTIONS/EXERCISES/PROBLEMS/CASE

APPENDIX: CONSOLIDATED
  FINANCIAL STATEMENTS   A1
BFGOODRICH COMPANY 1989 ANNUAL
  REPORT   A2

INDEX   i1

PART 1

INTRODUCTION TO FINANCIAL STATEMENTS

1

THE NATURE OF FINANCIAL ACCOUNTING AND REPORTING

CHAPTER OVERVIEW AND OBJECTIVES

This chapter presents an overview of the purpose and nature of financial accounting. When you have completed the chapter, you should understand:

1. What accounting information is.
2. The difference between recording and reporting accounting information.
3. The basic uses of accounting information.
4. The sources of accounting principles and practices.
5. The main fields of accounting and the type of work involved in each.
6. The different forms of business organization.
7. The names and functions of the basic financial statements.
8. The meaning of the terms *asset, liability, owners' equity, revenues, gains, expenses,* and *losses.*

Accounting is a service activity. It provides financial information about economic activity that is intended to be useful in making economic decisions.[1] Business firms, governmental agencies, charitable foundations, nonprofit organizations, families, and individuals are all economic units engaged in economic activity. Most economic activity involves decisions about how to allocate available resources effectively among alternative needs. People need relevant information to make sound decisions. In our complex society, decision-makers rely on data supplied by specialists in various fields. For example, lawyers provide information about the effects of existing and proposed legislation, medical professionals offer advice about the possible effects of different health-care decisions, and accountants supply information about the effects of business activities.

[1]Accounting Principles Board, "Basic Concepts and Accounting Principles Underlying Financial Statements of Business Enterprises," APB Statement No. 4 (New York: AICPA, October, 1970), par. 9.

ACCOUNTING—AN INFORMATION PROCESSING SYSTEM

Accounting is a means of social communication and involves a flow of information. To be effective, the information's recipient must understand the message that is being conveyed. Accounting uses words and numbers to communicate financial information to managers, investors, creditors, and other decision-makers.[2] As you study accounting, you must learn the meanings of the concepts and procedures used by accountants so that you can understand the messages contained in financial summaries and reports. Everyone involved in business, from the trainee to the top manager, eventually uses some accounting information.

The importance of understanding accounting information is not limited to those engaged directly in business. Lawyers, for example, must often understand the meaning of accounting information if they are to represent their clients effectively, and engineers and architects must consider cost data in their work. In fact, most adults must deal with their personal finances, thereby giving accounting a significant role in society.

Although accounting procedures and techniques can be used in accounting for all types of economic units, this book will concentrate on accounting for a business. Business managers need information provided by the accounting system to plan and control their business activities. In addition, investors, creditors, and governmental agencies need financial information to make investing, lending, regulatory, and tax-related decisions.

CHARACTERISTICS OF ACCOUNTING INFORMATION

Accounting is the process of measuring, recording, classifying, and summarizing financial information that is used in making economic decisions. Accounting information is financial data about business transactions expressed in terms of money. Business transactions are the economic activities of a business. Accountants classify these business transactions into two types, external and internal. External transactions are those exchange events between two or more independent firms. Internal transactions are those economic events that take place entirely within one firm. Accountants use the term *"transaction"* to refer to both internal and external transactions that constitute the inputs of the accounting information system. Recording these historical events is one important function of accounting.

Before the effects of transactions can be recorded, however, they must be *measured*. If accounting information is to be useful, it must be expressed in terms of a common denominator so the effects of transactions can be combined. Unlike items such as apples and oranges cannot be combined unless they are expressed in terms of a common measuring unit. In our economy, business activity is measured by prices expressed in terms of money. *Money* serves as both a medium of exchange and a measure of value, thus allowing us to (1) compare the value or worth of diverse objects and (2) add and subtract the economic effects of various transactions.

Simply measuring and recording transactions, however, provides information of limited use. To be useful in making decisions, the recorded data must be classified and summarized. *Classification* reduces the effects of thousands of transactions into useful groups or categories. For example, all transactions involving the sale of merchandise can be grouped into one total sales figure and all transactions involving cash can be grouped into one single net cash figure. *Summarization* of financial data is

Objective 1: Nature of accounting information

[2]Ibid, par. 40.

achieved by reports and financial statements, which are provided for the use of both management and outside users of accounting information. These reports usually summarize the effects of all business transactions occurring during some time period such as a month, a quarter, or a year.

RECORDING AND REPORTING ACCOUNTING INFORMATION

Objective 2: Recording vs. reporting accounting information

Accounting is often viewed as being limited to the recording process. No distinction between the recording and reporting of accounting data is perceived. The *recording* or *bookkeeping* process involves measuring and recording business transactions. The process may take the form of handwritten records, records produced by mechanical or electronic devices, or records produced by magnetic marks on cards or on magnetic tape in a computerized system.

The *reporting* function is much broader. It consists of classifying and summarizing accounting data into financial statements as well as preparing any other interpretive disclosures necessary to make the data understandable. The process is highly technical, and requires an accountant with extensive training, experience, and professional judgment. In addition to recording and reporting, accounting also includes the design of accounting systems, the audit of financial statements, cost studies, and the preparation of tax returns.

USING ACCOUNTING INFORMATION

Objective 3: Uses of accounting information

As stated earlier, accounting provides techniques and procedures for accumulating and reporting financial data. The ultimate goal of accounting is to provide internal and external decision-makers with usable financial information. Accountants themselves may or may not be required to analyze or interpret the data.

Decision-makers generally follow a five-step process in making and executing decisions:

1. Establish goals;
2. Consider various alternatives for reaching the goals;
3. Make decisions;
4. Implement these decisions; and
5. Evaluate the results of decisions; revise goals as needed.

Thus, the decision-making process may be illustrated as in Figure 1-1.

Internal decision-makers, for example, business managers, generally need financial accounting data for both planning (i.e., goal setting) and controlling business operations (i.e., evaluation and feedback). External decision-makers (for example, creditors, stockholders, and government agencies) need financial accounting information for evaluating alternatives concerning the granting of credit, the purchase of shares of stock, and compliance with tax laws and other regulatory standards. External de-

Figure 1-1
Decision-Making
Process

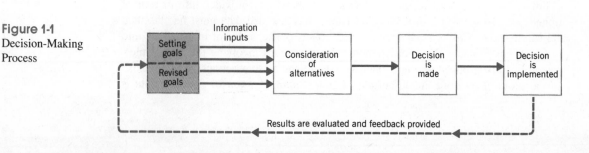

cision-makers generally need answers to questions such as: Will the business be able to repay money lent to it? What are the company's earnings prospects? Is the business financially sound?

Reports prepared for external users to aid them in answering these and similar questions are called **financial statements.** Financial statements generally consist of a balance sheet (sometimes called a statement of financial position), an income statement, a retained earnings statement, and a statement of cash flows. Some firms combine the income statement and retained earnings statement into a single statement of income and retained earnings. These statements are often called *general purpose financial statements* because they provide general information for use by all external users. General purpose financial statements also are used, along with various internal reports, by management. Figure 1-2 illustrates the relationship between accounting reports and users of accounting information.

SOURCES OF ACCOUNTING PRINCIPLES AND PRACTICES

Accounting changes along with society's needs. As new types of transactions occur in trade and commerce, accountants develop rules and practices for recording them. These accounting practices, which are called **Generally Accepted Accounting Principles (GAAP),** consist of the rules, practices, and procedures used in the preparation of financial statements. Their authority stems from their general acceptance by the accounting profession. Three formal organizations—the American Institute of Certified Public Accountants (AICPA), the Financial Accounting Standards Board (FASB), and the Securities and Exchange Commission (SEC)—predominate in the development of accounting practices and procedures. Knowing their historical and continuing roles in the development of accounting practices will help in understanding the overall accounting process. In addition, there are other U.S. and international organizations that affect accounting practice.

Objective 4:
Sources of
accounting prin-
ciples

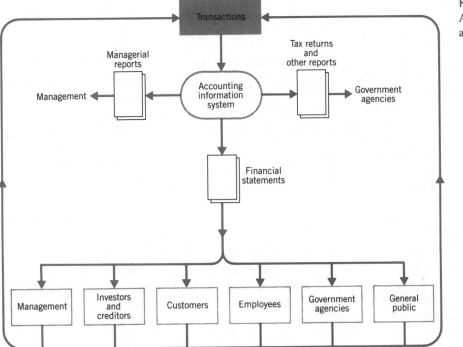

Figure 1-2
Accounting Reports
and Users

THE AICPA

The AICPA is a national professional organization of certified public accountants that has been particularly active in describing and defining GAAP. Between 1939 and 1959, the AICPA's Committee on Accounting Procedure issued 51 *Accounting Research Bulletins (ARBs)* containing recommendations on a wide variety of accounting problems. These recommendations, however, were not mandatory. As a result, different companies often developed different practices for accounting and reporting identical transactions.

In recognition of the need for a more formal process in the development of GAAP, in 1959 the AICPA replaced the Committee on Accounting Procedure with the Accounting Principles Board (APB). The APB was asked to establish principles that would narrow the areas of difference and inconsistency in accounting. Between 1959 and 1973, the APB issued 31 *APB Opinions* dealing with specific accounting problems. (In 1973, the APB was replaced by the FASB.) The AICPA publishes a monthly journal, *The Journal of Accountancy,* which serves as a medium by which accountants share their experiences and research results.

THE FASB

The APB consisted of part-time, nonsalaried members from accounting firms, industry, and universities. These individuals maintained their affiliations with their respective firms or educational institutions. As a result, the APB was frequently charged with being unduly influenced by the wishes of clients and management.

Because of the part-time nature of its members' appointments, the APB was also attacked for moving too slowly in solving accounting problems. To avoid such criticism as well as the possibility of having a governmental body take over the accounting rule-making activities, the APB was terminated in 1973 and a new board, the **Financial Accounting Standards Board (FASB),** was created.

The FASB has seven members, all of whom work full time, receive substantial salaries, and have severed their relationships with prior employers. The FASB is an independent, autonomous body whose members are appointed by the Financial Accounting Foundation. Appointments are for five-year terms with a maximum of two terms. The foundation receives its financial support from the private sector (i.e., from public accounting and industrial firms). The FASB is responsible for establishing accounting standards that will be responsive to the needs of the entire business community, not just the accounting profession. It provides a forum in open hearings, discussion memoranda, and exposure drafts through which all interested parties may express their views concerning proposed accounting standards. After considering the views of all parties, the FASB issues *Statements of Financial Accounting Standards* which, like APB Opinions, must be followed by accountants. Both APB Opinions and FASB Statements will be referred to frequently in this book.

THE SEC

The **Securities and Exchange Commission (SEC)** is a regulatory agency established by Congress to oversee enforcement of the Securities Acts of 1933 and 1934. It has the authority to establish accounting standards for the financial reports required of companies that list their securities for sale through one of the national securities exchanges. It has published accounting guidelines, particularly Regulation S-X, that contain specific reporting standards for the financial statements that must be filed annually with the SEC.

The SEC has played a significant role in setting accounting standards since its inception. It has accomplished this through both its published regulations and by working closely with the FASB in the development of accounting standards.

OTHER U.S. ORGANIZATIONS

Four other U.S. organizations, the American Accounting Association (AAA), the National Association of Accountants (NAA), the Government Accounting Standards Board (GASB), and the Financial Executives Institute (FEI), also contribute to the development of accounting standards. The AAA membership consists mainly of accounting educators. It encourages the improvement of accounting instruction and sponsors various types of accounting research, the results of which are often published in its quarterly publication, *The Accounting Review*. Its committees work with the FASB on a wide range of accounting problems. Several of its members have served on the APB and FASB.

The NAA consists primarily of accountants working in industrial firms and educators who are interested in cost and managerial accounting. It supports research in various cost and managerial accounting areas. *Management Accounting* is its monthly publication.

The GASB is the formal body responsible for establishing financial accounting and reporting standards for state and local governmental units. Formed in 1984, it consists of five members appointed by the Financial Accounting Foundation for five-year terms.

The FEI is made up primarily of chief financial officers of large businesses. It is responsible for a significant amount of accounting research. It works actively with the FASB in promoting acceptable accounting standards.

INTERNATIONAL ORGANIZATIONS

Two international organizations, the International Accounting Standards Committee (IASC) and the International Federation of Accountants (IFAC) encourage worldwide cooperation in the development of accounting practices. The IASC was formed in 1973 through an agreement among the leading accounting organizations of Australia, Canada, France, Germany, Japan, Mexico, the Netherlands, the United Kingdom and Ireland, and the United States. The IASC issues Statements of International Accounting Standards. Although they do not replace local practices, the hope is that local practices will eventually conform to the international standards, thereby harmonizing accounting standards at the international level.

The IFAC consists of a federation of 63 professional accounting organizations from 49 countries. It was established in 1977 to promote international agreement on accounting issues.

ACCOUNTING AS A PROFESSION

Over the past century, accountancy as a profession has attained a status similar to that of law and medicine. Individual states license **Certified Public Accountants (CPAs)** just as they license lawyers and doctors.

State requirements for the CPA license vary. Most states require a college degree with a specified minimum number of college credits in accounting and business. All states require the candidate to pass a nationally uniform examination. The exam, prepared and graded by the AICPA, is a rigorous, two-and-a-half-day examination covering accounting theory, accounting practice, auditing, and business law. A minimum grade of 75 is required on each part of the examination. The test is administered by each state on the same dates in May and November.

Most states also require that a candidate have one or two years of working experience in a CPA office—or equivalent experience—before the license is issued. With a few exceptions only those accountants who have passed the CPA examination, met certain state-set education and experience requirements, and received a license may use the Certified Public Accountant designation.

Because of the increasing complexity of business transactions and the related accounting requirements, many states have enacted continuing-education laws. These laws require CPAs to take a minimum number of additional education hours each year to retain their licenses. Students interested in the specific requirements of individual states can write to the State Board of Accountancy of the state in question.

There are three general areas of accounting: public accounting, private accounting, and governmental accounting. Accountants usually specialize in one area.

PUBLIC ACCOUNTING

Objective 5: Fields of accounting & types of work

Public accountants practice in firms that offer their professional services to the public. These vary from small, single-office firms to large international organizations with several thousand employees. Because of the complexity of many business transactions and increasing governmental regulation, members of public accounting firms tend to specialize in either auditing, taxation, or management advisory services.

Auditing

Auditing is a service offered by most public accounting firms. An **audit** is an independent examination of a firm's financial statements, supporting documents, and records in order to give an opinion about the fairness and general reliability of the financial statements. Independent CPA audits are often required by banks and other lending agencies before making business loans. Companies intending to offer their securities for public sale through a national securities market or exchange must have independent CPA audits. Creditors and investors who use financial statements in decision-making place considerable reliance on the CPA's audit report.

Tax Services

Another service offered by public accountants is advice concerning the tax consequences of business decisions. Few business decisions are made without considering such consequences. To offer such services, accountants must be thoroughly familiar with federal and state tax laws and regulations. They must also keep up-to-date on court decisions and changes in tax law. Accountants are often hired to aid in tax planning in order to minimize the tax liability of the business, consistent with the rules and regulations established by taxing agencies. Accountants are also often called upon to prepare the state and federal tax returns required by law.

Management Advisory Services

Although audit and tax services have traditionally been the mainstay of public accountants, another area, generally called *management advisory services,* has experienced rapid growth in recent years. Services provided include advice on such things as mergers with other companies, installation or modification of accounting systems, financial planning models, inventory control systems, and advice regarding budgeting, forecasting, and general planning.

PRIVATE ACCOUNTING

An accountant working for a single industrial company is employed in private accounting. The firm's chief accounting officer, the **controller,** has overall responsibility for directing the activities of the accounting personnel. In a large company, the controller may have several assistant controllers, each with assigned responsibility for various accounting functions such as cost accounting, tax accounting, or internal auditing. Private accountants, who do not have to be CPAs, often specialize in a single phase of the accounting process.

General Accounting

Private accounting functions include recording the company's transactions, preparing reports for management, and classifying and summarizing transaction data for the preparation of financial statements. It is difficult to distinguish clearly between general accounting and other private accounting activities because the accounting data recorded from transactions forms the basic data base from which other phases draw relevant information.

Cost Accounting

Cost accounting deals with the collection, allocation, and control of the cost of producing specific products and services. It is important to know the cost of each business operation and manufacturing process in order to make sound business decisions. For example, if management wants to determine whether a particular product is profitable, it must know that product's production and sales costs. Large manufacturing companies employ many accountants in their cost accounting departments.

Budgeting

Budgeting is the phase of accounting that deals with the preparation of a plan or forecast of future operations. Its primary function is to provide management with a projection of the activities necessary to reach established goals. Budgets are generally prepared for the business as a whole as well as for subunits such as individual departments. They also serve as control devices and as a means of measuring the efficiency of operations. Both cost accounting and budgeting are topics that are generally covered in the second semester of accounting.

Tax Accounting

Businesses are assessed a variety of taxes—including income tax, payroll tax, and excise tax—all of which require the preparation of periodic reports to taxing agencies. Management must consider the tax effects of every investment and financing decision. Although many businesses rely on public accountants for some tax-planning advice and tax-return preparation, most large companies also maintain a tax accounting department to deal with day-to-day tax problems encountered in operating a business.

Internal Auditing

The primary function of an internal auditing staff is to conduct ongoing reviews to make certain that established procedures and policies are being followed. Any deficiencies can be identified and corrected quickly. Many companies also maintain an internal audit staff because an internal audit process can reduce the time required by the CPA firm conducting the annual audit. Often, significant cost savings are realized.

GOVERNMENTAL (NOT-FOR-PROFIT) ACCOUNTING

Many accountants are employed in governmental accounting. Cities, counties, states, and the federal government collect and spend huge amounts of money annually. Governmental accounting is concerned with the identification of the sources and uses of resources consistent with the provisions of city, county, state, and federal laws.

Many of the problems and decisions faced by governmental officials are the same as those encountered in private industry, but governmental accounting requires a different approach in some respects because of the absence of a profit motive.

Other not-for-profit organizations (e.g., churches, hospitals, charities, and public educational institutions) follow accounting procedures similar to those used in governmental accounting. These institutions are also concerned with compliance with the law and the efficient use of scarce resources.

As indicated earlier in this chapter, accounting is applicable to all types of economic entities, including governmental and nonprofit units. The rest of this book, however, will concentrate on accounting methods used by business entities that have a profit motive.

FORMS OF BUSINESS ORGANIZATION

Objective 6:
Forms of business organization

Business organizations may be in the form of proprietorships, partnerships, or corporations (see Figure 1-3). A **proprietorship** is a business owned by one person. Many small service enterprises, retail stores, and professional practices are operated as proprietorships. The owner of a proprietorship is the legal owner of its assets, is legally liable for its debts, and is entitled to the proprietorship's earnings. From an

Figure 1-3
Business Entities

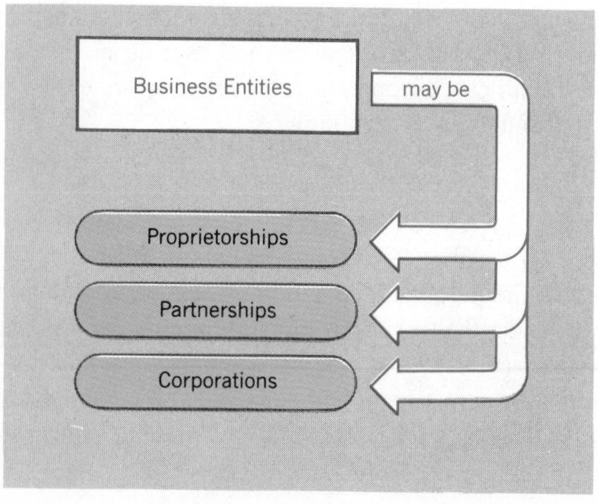

accounting standpoint, however, the business is treated as an entity separate from its owner.

A **partnership** is a business owned by two or more people who generally share profits and management responsibilities. No special legal requirements need be met to form a partnership. All that is necessary is an agreement among the persons joining together as partners. Although the partnership agreement may be oral, a written agreement is preferred in order to minimize partnership disagreements.

Partnerships are not separate legal entities. Consequently, in a general partnership each partner is personally liable for partnership debts. From an accounting viewpoint, however, partnerships are treated as entities separate from their owners. Like proprietorships, partnerships are widely used for small service firms, retail stores, and professional practices.

A **corporation** is a separate legal entity formed under the incorporation laws of individual states or the federal government. Its owners are called **stockholders** or **shareholders** because their ownership interests are represented by shares of the corporation's stock. Since a corporation is a separate legal entity, its stockholders are not personally liable for the corporation's debts; that is, each stockholder is liable for the debts of the corporation only to the extent of his or her investment therein. Separate legal entity status enables a corporation to conduct its business affairs in its own name as a legal person. Thus, a corporation can (1) buy, own, and sell property, (2) sue and be sued in its own name, and (3) enter into contracts with others. In essence, a corporation is treated as a legal person with all the rights, duties, and responsibilities of that person.

Corporate stockholders are free to sell all or part of their shares at any time. The ease of transferability of ownership, coupled with the lack of personal liability for corporate debts, generally adds to the attractiveness of investing in corporate stock. It also enhances the corporation's ability to raise large amounts of capital. Thus, corporations conduct the majority of business activity in the United States.

The corporate form will be emphasized in this book. Remember, however, that accounting concepts, procedures, and standards also apply to the other forms of business organization.

COMMUNICATING ACCOUNTING INFORMATION THROUGH FINANCIAL STATEMENTS

As we have seen, accounting is an information system designed to provide financial data to interested parties for decision-making purposes. The final result of the accounting process is the preparation of various financial statements that serve as important communication devices. These financial statements are generally classified into two types: internal statements and external statements. **Internal statements** are prepared at the request of management for the sole use of managers within the firm. Consequently, they are not intended for use by external users.

Objective 7: Purpose of financial statements

External statements, however, are designed and prepared specifically for use by outside parties such as creditors and stockholders. Because these outside parties are unable to specify the content and procedures to be followed in the preparation of external statements, GAAP serve as guides in the preparation of the statements. External financial statements must be prepared in accordance with GAAP.

Internal financial statements are generally covered in a managerial accounting course. Thus, the emphasis in this book is on the accounting principles followed in the preparation of external financial statements.

EXTERNAL FINANCIAL STATEMENTS—AN OVERVIEW

Some knowledge of the content of external financial statements (hereafter simply called financial statements) and the types of information they are designed to communicate will help you better understand the underlying concepts and measurement processes followed in accounting. The twofold purpose of such financial statements is to communicate to users (1) the effect of operating activities during a specified time period and (2) the business' financial position at the end of the period. The four main financial statements prepared for use by external decision-makers are:

1. Balance sheet;
2. Income statement;
3. Retained earnings statement; and
4. Statement of cash flows.

In this chapter, we will discuss and illustrate these statements for a relatively simple business situation. Chapter 2 contains a comprehensive discussion of a more complex case.

Balance Sheet

The **balance sheet** reports the financial position of a business at a specific point in time. Consequently, it is often called the "statement of financial position." Financial position is reflected by the amount of the business' assets (resources), the amount of its liabilities (debts owed), and the amount of its owners' equity (assets minus liabilities). Figure 1-4 shows a balance sheet for Ace Repair, Inc. on December 31, 1992, the end of the first year of operations.

Figure 1-4
Balance Sheet

ACE REPAIR, INC.
Balance Sheet
December 31, 1992

Assets			Liabilities		
Cash		$ 15,885	Accounts payable	$ 6,340	
Accounts receivable		4,920	Income tax payable	2,000	
Repair supplies		5,130	Mortgage payable (12%)	54,000	
Repair equipment	$40,000		Total liabilities		$ 62,340
Less: Accumulated			Stockholders' Equity		
depreciation	4,000	36,000	Paid-in capital:		
Land		20,000	Capital stock (10,000		
Building	65,000		shares, $2 par value)	20,000	
Less: Accumulated			Paid-in capital in		
depreciation	1,625	63,375	excess of par value	40,000	
			Retained earnings	22,970	
			Total stockholders'		
			equity		82,970
			Total liabilities and		
Total assets		$145,310	stockholders' equity		$145,310

The balance sheet heading indicates the name of the business, the name of the statement, and the date of the statement. In the balance sheet format illustrated in Figure 1-4 (called the account form), the assets of the business are listed on the left side and the liabilities and owners' equity are listed on the right side. Note that the totals on each side of the balance sheet are equal. This equality must exist because the left side lists the assets of the business and the right side shows the sources of the assets. Of the total assets owned by the business ($145,310), $62,340 were provided by creditors and the remainder, $82,970, was provided by the owners (the stockholders) or business earnings.

The basic accounting model (accounting equation) is:

$$\text{Assets} = \text{Liabilities} + \text{Owners' Equity}$$

All transactions of a business could be analyzed using this basic model, although we will see later that better analysis can be made by expanding the equation to include the effect of the income statement. Note that the balance sheet is divided into three main sections: assets, liabilities, and stockholders' equity.

Assets are the cash and noncash resources owned by a business. They may be tangible assets (such as land, buildings, and equipment) or intangible assets (such as legal claims, accounts receivable, patent rights, or rights to use leased assets.) Assets have economic value because they contain service benefits that can be used in future operations or sold to another entity. Note that each asset in the balance sheet has an assigned dollar amount. Under the *cost principle* in accounting, the assigned dollar amount represents the cost of the asset. Cost is determined by the cash or cash equivalent given in exchange for the asset. Even though the current value of the asset may be greater, it is still reported at its cost. For example, the land may have a current value of $25,000, but is reported at its cost of $20,000. We will have more to say about this important principle in Chapter 2 and later chapters.

Objective 8: Meaning of assets, liabilities, and owners' equity

Liabilities are the debts owed by a business to outside parties (called *creditors*). Liabilities include such things as amounts owed to suppliers for goods or services purchased on credit (accounts payable), amounts borrowed from banks or other lenders (notes payable), amounts owed to employees for salaries and wages, and amounts owed to tax agencies for taxes incurred but not yet paid. They result from past business transactions. Cancellation of liabilities requires either an outlay of assets, generally cash, or the performance of future services.

Liabilities may also be thought of as creditors' claims against the assets of the business. The dollar amounts assigned to liabilities generally represent the amounts initially established by the parties to the transactions from which they arose, less amounts that have already been paid.

Owners' equity is the owners' interest in the assets of the business. It may be thought of as the owners' claims against those assets. The basic accounting model introduced earlier (Assets = Liabilities + Owners' Equity) indicates that the total assets of the business equal the total claims against those assets by creditors and owners. Creditors' claims take legal precedence over owners' claims; if the assets are sold, creditors must be paid before the claims of the owners are recognized. Thus, owners' equity is considered a residual claim, and the basic accounting model is sometimes expressed as

$$\text{Assets} - \text{Liabilities} = \text{Owners' Equity}$$

Other terms used for owners' equity are *proprietorship,* and *capital.* Preferred terminology, however, is (1) owner's equity for a proprietorship, (2) partners' equity for a partnership, and (3) stockholders' equity for a corporation. The two main sources of owners' equity are direct investment by the owner(s) and earnings that are retained in the business. For a corporation, the two types are called ''paid-in capital'' and ''retained earnings.'' **Paid-in capital** represents the amounts of cash or other assets invested by the owners. **Retained earnings** represent the owners' interest in the accumulated business earnings that have not yet been distributed. Distributions of earned assets are called *withdrawals* by proprietorships and partnerships and *dividends* by corporations.

Note that the stockholders' equity of Ace Repair, Inc. (Figure 1-4) consists of paid-in capital ($60,000) and retained earnings ($22,970). Paid-in capital is subclassified into amounts representing par value (explained further in Chapter 13) and amounts paid-in in excess of par value. The retained earnings amount represents the net income of Ace Repair, Inc. for 1992 ($42,970) less a dividend paid to stockholders during 1992 in the amount of $20,000 (see Figure 1-6).

Income Statement

The **income statement** is designed to report the results of earning activities (operations) for a specific time period such as a month, quarter, or year. **Net income** for the period is the excess of revenues and gains over expenses and losses for that time. If expenses and losses for the period exceed revenues and gains, a **net loss** is incurred. Figure 1-5 shows an income statement for Ace Repair, Inc. for the first year of its operations. Ace Repair earns its revenue by repairing and servicing various types of heavy equipment.

The heading of the income statement indicates the name of the business, the name of the statement, and the time period covered by the statement. Identification of the time period covered is particularly important because it indicates the length of time it took to earn the reported net income. (In Figure 1-5, the period is one year.) Without a clear indication of the period covered, the data in the income statement would have little if any meaning to a user of the statement. Note that there are three main sections in the income statement: revenues, expenses, and other revenue and expense.

Objective 8: Meaning of revenues, gains, expenses, and losses.

Revenues are inflows of assets to an entity resulting from the sale and delivery of goods or the rendering of services by the entity.[3] Expressed another way, revenue for a period is the total selling price of goods or services that is transferred to customers during that period. Revenues are measured by the amount of cash or other assets received. Although revenue often consists of cash, it may consist of any asset received, such as a customer's promise to pay in the future (an account receivable) or the receipt of property from a customer. Regardless of the type of asset received, to represent revenue it must reflect compensation for the sale of goods or the performance of services.

Gains are net inflows of assets from incidental transactions (i.e., from transactions not related to the primary business activity of the firm) that are not revenue or owner investment transactions. For example, the firm may sell an asset, such as equipment, that is normally used in business operations. The excess of the selling price of the equipment over its value as recorded on the books is a gain on sale of equipment. If Ace Repair, Inc. sells for $5,000 equipment that is recorded on the books at $4,000, a $1,000 gain is reported. Gains are normally reported in the income statement under the caption ''Other revenue and expense'' as shown in Figure 1-5.

[3]Statement of Financial Accounting Concepts No. 6 (FASB: Stamford, Conn., 1985), par. 78.

Figure 1-5
Income Statement

ACE REPAIR, INC.
Income Statement
For the Year Ended December 31, 1992

Revenues:		
Repair revenue		$ 89,640
Service revenue		46,300
Total revenue		135,940
Expenses:		
Advertising expense	$ 6,320	
Depreciation expense: Equipment	4,000	
Building	1,625	
Interest expense	6,480	
Repair supplies used	8,650	
Salaries and wages expense	44,560	
Utilities expense	9,915	
Total expenses		81,550
Operating income		54,390
Other revenue and expense:		
Rent revenue	200	
Gain on sale of equipment	1,000	
Loss on sale of land	(500)	700
Income before income tax		55,090
Income tax expense ($55,090 × 22%)		12,120
Net Income		$ 42,970

Expenses are outflows or other uses of assets resulting from the sale or delivery of goods or the provision of services by the entity during a specific time period.[4] In other words, expense is the total purchase price of goods or services used to earn revenues. Expenses are measured by the amount of assets consumed or liabilities incurred. They may be accompanied by immediate cash payments (e.g., current wages and salaries) or promises to pay cash in the future for services already received (e.g., advertising).

In some cases, cash may be paid or a liability incurred to acquire an asset that will be expensed in the future (e.g., purchase of equipment or a building). A portion of the cost of these assets becomes an expense each year as the assets gradually wear out or become obsolete. In accounting, this expense is called *depreciation*. For example, Ace Repair, Inc. purchased repair equipment at the beginning of 1992 at a cost of $40,000. The equipment was estimated to have a useful life of 10 years. Thus, the depreciation expense each year is $4,000 ($40,000/10 years). In a similar manner, depreciation on the building acquired at the beginning of 1992 for $65,000 and having an estimated useful life of 40 years is $1,625 ($65,000/40 years). Note that depreciation expense on both the equipment and the building is reported in the income statement and the cumulative amount of depreciation is deducted from the related asset's cost in the balance sheet (Figure 1-4).

[4]Ibid., par. 80.

Losses are net outflows of assets from incidental transactions that are not expenses or dividend distributions. For example, the firm may sell land that is normally used in business operations. The excess of the land's recorded value on the books over the selling price is reported as a loss on sale of land. If Ace Repair, Inc. sells land for $3,500 that is recorded on the books at $4,000, a $500 loss is reported. Similar to gains, losses are reported in the income statement under the ''Other revenue and expense'' caption.

Net income, which is sometimes referred to as *earnings* or *profit,* is the excess of revenues (and gains) over expenses (and losses), including income tax expense. Thus, the income statement equation might be expressed as

$$\text{Net Income} = \text{Revenues (and gains)} - \text{Expenses (and losses)}$$

Note that (assuming no gains or losses)

1. Revenues are defined as inflows of assets either from the sale of goods or the performance of services,
2. Expenses are defined as outflows or other uses of assets to produce revenue, and
3. Net income is defined as the excess of revenues over expenses; consequently, net income must also represent an increase in assets.

Since the assets earned belong to the company's owners, net income also represents an increase in owners' equity. The element of owners' equity used to accumulate the effect of earnings is retained earnings.

Retained Earnings Statement

The retained earnings statement shows the changes taking place in retained earnings for the period. The most common changes in retained earnings come from net income (or net losses) and dividend distributions. Net income increases retained earnings, whereas net losses and dividends decrease retained earnings. A retained earnings statement for Ace Repair, Inc. for the year ended December 31, 1992 is presented in Figure 1-6.

Figure 1-6
Retained Earnings
Statement

ACE REPAIR, INC. Retained Earnings Statement For the Year Ended December 31, 1992	
Retained earnings, January 1	$ –0–
Add: Net income for 1992	42,970
Total	42,970
Less: Dividends distributed to stockholders	20,000
Retained earnings, December 31	$22,970

The heading shows the name of the company, the name of the statement, and the time period covered. Since this was the first year of operations, Ace Repair, Inc. had no beginning retained earnings balance. Thus, the December 31, 1992 balance represents net income for 1992 minus dividends paid during the year. Note that the December 31 balance of retained earnings ($22,970) is reported as part of stockholders' equity in the balance sheet (Figure 1-4).

Statement of Cash Flows

The main purpose of the **statement of cash flows (SCF)** is to provide information about the cash receipts and cash payments of a firm for a specific time period. A second purpose is to disclose information summarizing the net cash flows related to operating, investing, and financing activities of the firm (i.e., the sources of cash and the uses to which cash was put during the period). A SCF for Ace Repair, Inc. for the year ended December 31, 1992 is shown in Figure 1-7.

ACE REPAIR, INC.
Statement of Cash Flows
For the Year Ended December 31, 1992

Cash flows from operating activities:		
Cash received from customers		$131,220
Less cash expenses		79,705
Net cash flows from operating activities		51,515
Cash flows from investing activities:		
Purchase of repair supplies	$(5,130)	
Sale of equipment and land	8,500	
Purchases of equipment, land, and buildings	(133,000)	
Net cash used by investing activities		(129,630)
Cash flows from financing activities:		
Proceeds from long-term borrowing	54,000	
Proceeds from issuing capital stock	60,000	
Dividends paid	(20,000)	
Net cash provided by financing activities		94,000
Net increase in cash		$ 15,885

Figure 1-7
Statement of Cash Flows

The SCF and how the numbers in it are determined will be discussed in detail in Chapter 15. Note that the SCF in Figure 1-7 has three main sections, one identifying the effect of net cash flows from operating activities, one identifying the net cash flows from investing activities, and one identifying the net cash flows from financing activities. Because most users of financial statements are interested in future cash flows, knowledge of current period cash flows is useful in projecting future cash flows.

The SCF is prepared by analyzing changes in balance sheet amounts and the data in the income and retained earnings statements. For example, the revenues of $136,140 (including rent revenue of $200) reported in the income statement (Figure 1-5) less the accounts receivable balance of $4,920 in the balance sheet (Figure 1-4) equals the cash received from customers of $131,220. Cash paid for expenses is computed by subtracting noncash expenses from total expenses (including income taxes) as follows:

Total expenses ($81,550 + $12,120)		$93,670
Less noncash expenses:		
Depreciation expense ($4,000 + $1,625)	$5,625	
Increase in accounts payable	6,340	
Increase in income taxes payable	2,000	
Total noncash expenses		13,965
Cash expenses		$79,705

The difference between cash received from customers and cash paid for expenses equals net cash inflow from operating activities.

Cash flows from investing activities resulted in a total outflow of cash of $129,630, consisting of $5,130 paid for the purchase of repair supplies and $133,000 for the purchase of plant assets (equipment, land, and building) less $8,500 received from the sale of equipment and land. Net cash flows from financing activities came from borrowings ($54,000) and the issue of capital stock ($60,000) less dividends paid ($20,000). Subtracting total net cash outflows from investing activities ($129,630) from total net cash inflows from operating and financing activities ($51,515 + $94,000) results in an increase in cash of $15,885. Since this is the first year of operations for Ace Repair, Inc., and assuming no cash was invested initially, the increase in cash for the year is also the cash balance at year-end (Figure 1-4).

SUMMARY

In this chapter, we have presented an overview of the purpose and nature of financial accounting as well as the importance of accounting information in decision-making. Accounting is important for all types of economic units, including business firms, governmental agencies, and nonprofit organizations. Each of these units is an accounting entity for which financial information is accumulated and reported. Accountants work in three main areas, public accounting (public accounting firms), private accounting (industrial firms), and governmental accounting (various governmental agencies and not-for-profit organizations).

Generally accepted accounting principles (GAAP), which are the basic guidelines followed in the preparation of financial statements, were developed through the joint efforts of various professional accounting groups (FASB, APB, AAA), and governmental agencies (primarily the SEC). Future chapters of this book will develop these principles in greater detail. GAAP apply to all forms of business organization—proprietorships, partnerships, and corporations.

Financial information is communicated through four basic financial statements:

Balance sheet. The balance sheet reports financial position in terms of assets, liabilities, and owners' equity at a specific point in time.

Income statement. The income statement reports revenues, gains, expenses, losses, and net income for a specific time period.

Retained earnings statement. The retained earnings statement reports changes in the retained earnings amount for a period.

Statement of cash flows. The SCF reports net cash flows from operating, investing, and financing activities for a period of time.

Thus, the balance sheet is a status statement whereas the other three are flow statements (that is, they report the input and output activity in terms of resources or changes in balance sheet amounts during some time period.) They are, therefore, all related to the balance sheet and the basic accounting equation of

$$\text{Assets} = \text{Liabilities} + \text{Owners' Equity}$$

SELF-TEST

Test your understanding of the chapter by selecting the best answer for each of the following. (Answers are provided in each chapter after the review problem answer.)

1. Which process involves the classification and summarization of accounting data into financial statements as well as the preparation of other interpretive disclosures necessary to make accounting data understandable?
   a. Recording process
   b. Data collection process
   c. Reporting process
   d. Data analysis process
2. Generally accepted accounting principles (GAAP) consist of the rules, practices, and procedures used in the preparation of financial statements. GAAP are determined primarily by the
   a. Internal Revenue Service.
   b. U.S. Congress.
   c. Financial Accounting Standards Board and Securities and Exchange Commission.
   d. National Association of Accountants.
3. The chief accounting officer for a single industrial firm is called the
   a. Chief executive officer.
   b. Cashier.
   c. Auditor.
   d. Controller.
4. A form of business organization where the owners are not personally liable for the debts of the organization.
   a. Partnership
   b. Corporation
   c. Proprietorship
   d. Owners are personally liable in all the above business organizations.
5. Which of the following financial statements reports the results of the earnings activities for a specific time period?
   a. Income statement
   b. Balance sheet
   c. Retained earnings statement
   d. Statement of cash flows
6. At the end of an accounting period a firm had $25,000 in its bank account. Machinery and other assets totaled $15,000. The firm's unpaid bills to suppliers totaled $10,000. What was the owners' equity in the business?
   a. $40,000
   b. $ 5,000
   c. $15,000
   d. $30,000
7. Which of the following financial statements shows the dividends paid by a corporation?
   a. Income statement
   b. Retained earnings statement
   c. Statement of cash flows
   d. Balance sheet

8. A certified public accountant (CPA) in public practice
    a. Is concerned primarily with the design and installation of accounting systems.
    b. Is licensed by the federal government after passing a professional examination and satisfying specific experience requirements.
    c. Is generally an employee or a stockholder of the firm whose financial statements he or she audits and expresses an opinion on.
    d. Is involved in a variety of accounting-related services, but his or her primary function is to conduct an audit to express an opinion as to the fairness of the company's financial statements.

REVIEW PROBLEM

At the end of each chapter, a review problem and a suggested solution are presented for you to use as a tool to test your comprehension of the chapter material. To make the best use of this material, try to solve the problem before studying the suggested solution. The review problem for this chapter follows.

While attending college, Gary Karlson knew that he would need to supplement his savings with a part-time job. After an extensive search of the opportunities available in the small city where he attended college, Gary decided he could probably make more money and have more flexible working hours if he opened his own business. Because he had worked for his father's painting business part-time during high school, Gary decided to open a painting business.

He incorporated the business under the name G.K. Painters, Inc. He then issued to himself 1,000 shares of $1 par value capital stock, which he paid for by withdrawing $1,000 from his savings account. Gary decided not to keep a full set of accounting records, at least initially. Instead, he would deposit all receipts from the business in a separate checking account in the corporation's name and make all payments by check from the account. Gary also decided to enter the dates worked on painting jobs, the price charged, and the date paid in a log book. Gary's business officially opened on October 1, 1991.

On May 1, 1992, Gary decided to analyze his checkbook in order to determine whether to continue to operate the business over the summer or look for another job. A review of the checkbook and other records disclosed the following:

1. Total cash deposited from October 1, 1991 to April 30, 1992 (including the initial $1,000 from the sale of stock) was $6,528.
2. Checks were written for the following:
    a. Paint and related materials of $2,618. No painting materials were on hand on May 1.
    b. Painting equipment, brushes, rollers, and so on, of $450; these were about 60% used up on May 1.
    c. Advertising circulars, flyers, and newspaper advertisements of $300.
    d. Gasoline and repair costs on his pickup of $660.
3. Gary's log book revealed that customers owed him $600 for work he had completed. He expected to collect all of this money during May.
4. In addition to the above, Gary found an unpaid bill to a paint supplier in the amount of $383 in his wallet.

Required:

A. Prepare an income statement for G.K. Painters, Inc., for the seven-month period from October 1, 1991 to April 30, 1992.

B. Prepare a balance sheet, retained earnings statement, and a statement of cash flows.

C. What other information will Gary need to make a decision on his future choice of employment?

ANSWER TO REVIEW PROBLEM

A.

G.K. PAINTERS, INC.
Income Statement
For the Period October 1, 1991 to April 30, 1992

Painting revenues ($6,528 − $1,000 + $600)		$6,128
Expenses:		
Paint and materials ($2,618 + $383)	$3,001	
Equipment used up ($450 × 60%)	270	
Advertising	300	
Gasoline and repair costs	660	
Total expenses		4,231
Net income		$1,897

B.

G.K. PAINTERS, INC.
Balance Sheet
April 30, 1992

Assets

Cash*		$2,500
Accounts receivable		600
Painting equipment	$450	
Less: Accumulated depreciation	270	180
Total assets		$3,280

Liabilities

Accounts payable		$ 383

Stockholders' Equity

Capital stock, $1 par value, 1,000 shares issued and outstanding	$1,000	
Retained earnings	1,897	
Total stockholders' equity		2,897
Total liabilities and stockholders' equity		$3,280

*Cash Summary:

Initial investment		$1,000
Collections from customers ($6,528 − $1,000)		5,528
Total		6,528
Less cash payments for:		
Paint and related materials	$2,618	
Equipment, brushes, etc.	450	
Advertising	300	
Gasoline and truck repairs	660	
Total payments		4,028
Cash balance, April 30, 1992		$2,500

G.K. PAINTERS, INC.
Retained Earnings Statement
For the Period October 1, 1991 to April 30, 1992

Retained earnings, October 1, 1991	$ –0–
Add net income for the period	1,897
Retained earnings, April 30, 1992	$1,897

G.K. PAINTERS, INC.
Statement of Cash Flows
For the Period October 1, 1991 to April 30, 1992

Cash flows from operating activities:	
Cash received from customers	$5,528
Less cash expenses ($2,618 + $300 + $660)	3,578
Net cash flows from operating activities	$1,950
Cash flows from investing activities:	
Purchase of painting equipment	(450)
Cash flows from financing activities:	
Proceeds from issuing capital stock	1,000
Net increase in cash	$2,500

C.

Among the items of information that Gary may find useful in making the decision to continue to operate his painting business or look for another job are:

1. The types of jobs available and the amount of pay involved.
2. The satisfaction received from operating his own business compared to the potential satisfaction of working in another job.
3. The estimated amount Gary will earn from operating the painting business during the summer.
4. What costs are needed to replace equipment or purchase expansion equipment if needed.
5. The long-run outlook for operating the business throughout his college career.

ANSWERS TO SELF-TEST

1. c   **2.** c   **3.** d   **4.** b   **5.** a   **6.** d   **7.** c   **8.** d

GLOSSARY

ACCOUNTING. The process of measuring, recording, classifying, and summarizing financial information that is used in making economic decisions (p. 3).

ASSETS. The resources owned by a business (p. 13).

AUDIT. An independent examination of a firm's financial statements, supporting documents, and records (p. 8).

BALANCE SHEET. A statement describing the financial position of a business in terms of its assets, liabilities, and owners' equity as of a specific date (p. 12).

BUDGETING. The phase of accounting that deals with the preparation of a plan or forecast of future operations (p. 9).

BUSINESS TRANSACTIONS. The economic activities of a business that can be expressed in money terms (p. 3).

CERTIFIED PUBLIC ACCOUNTANT (CPA). An accountant who has met the qualifications and received a license to practice public accounting (p. 7).

CONTROLLER. A company's chief accounting officer (p. 9).

CORPORATION. A separate legal entity formed under the incorporation laws of individual states or the federal government (p. 11).

COST ACCOUNTING. The phase of accounting that deals with the collection, allocation, and control of the cost of producing a product or serivce (p. 9).

EXPENSES. Outflows or other uses of assets during a period that result from the sale or delivery of goods or the provision of services (p. 15).

EXTERNAL STATEMENTS. Statements designed and prepared specifically for use by outside parties (p. 11).

EXTERNAL TRANSACTIONS. Transactions that involve economic exchanges between two or more independent firms (p. 3).

FINANCIAL ACCOUNTING STANDARDS BOARD (FASB). The body currently responsible for establishing accounting standards for the accounting profession (p. 6).

FINANCIAL STATEMENTS. Statements prepared primarily for external users of accounting information (p. 5).

GAINS. Net inflows of assets from incidental transactions that are not revenue or owner investment transactions (p. 14).

GENERALLY ACCEPTED ACCOUNTING PRINCIPLES (GAAP). The rules, practices, and procedures followed in the preparation of financial statements. Their authority stems from their general acceptance by the accounting profession (p. 5).

INCOME STATEMENT. A statement designed to report the results of earning activities (operations) for a specific time period (p. 14).

INTERNAL STATEMENTS. Statements prepared at the request of management and specifically for the use of managers within the firm (p. 11).

INTERNAL TRANSACTIONS. Those economic events that take place entirely within one firm (p. 3).

LIABILITIES. The debts owed by a business to outside parties (p. 13).

LOSSES. Net outflow of assets from incidental transactions that are not expenses or dividend distributions (p. 16).

NET INCOME. The excess of revenues (and gains) over expenses (and losses) for a period (p. 14).

NET LOSS. The excess of expenses (and losses) over revenues (and gains) for a period (p. 14).

OWNERS' EQUITY. The interest of the owners in the assets of the business (p. 13).

PAID-IN CAPITAL. The portion of owners' equity representing amounts invested by the owners (stockholders) of a corporation (p. 14).

PARTNERSHIP. An unincorporated business owned by two or more people acting as partners (p. 11).

PROPRIETORSHIP. An unincorporated business owned by one person (p. 10).

RETAINED EARNINGS. The accumulated earnings of a corporation that have not yet been distributed to owners (p. 14).

RETAINED EARNINGS STATEMENT. A statement showing the changes taking place in retained earnings during a period (p. 16).

REVENUES. Inflows of assets to an entity resulting from the sale and delivery of goods or the rendering of services by the entity (p. 14).

SECURITIES AND EXCHANGE COMMISSION (SEC). An agency established by Congress to regulate the reporting practices of companies that list their securities for sale through one of the national securities exchanges (p. 6).

STATEMENT OF CASH FLOWS (SFC). A statement designed to provide information about net cash flows from operating, investing, and financing activities for a period of time (p. 17).

STOCKHOLDERS (SHAREHOLDERS). Those who own a corporation by owning shares of the corporation's stock (p. 11).

DISCUSSION QUESTIONS

1. What is the definition of accounting?
2. Why is accounting thought of as an information processing system?
3. Explain and give an example of the two types of business transactions: external transactions and internal transactions.
4. Distinguish between the recording and reporting processes in accounting. Which process occurs first?
5. Who are the primary users of accounting information?
6. Who are internal decision-makers? Who are external decision-makers?
7. List five examples of business decisions requiring the use of accounting information.
8. What is the Financial Accounting Standards Board? What is its function?
9. What is the Securities and Exchange Commission? What is its function?
10. How does an individual become a Certified Public Accountant?
11. What are the three main services offered by public accountants?
12. What is an audit and what is its purpose?
13. What are some services provided by accountants which are classified as management advisory services?
14. What are the main areas of private accounting?
15. How does the work of an internal auditor differ from the audit work performed by a public accountant?
16. What are the primary concerns of governmental accounting?

17. Define the following terms relating to the forms of business organization:
    a. Proprietorship;
    b. Partnership;
    c. Corporation;
    d. Partner;
    e. Stockholder.
18. What is the basic purpose of external financial statements?
19. What are the four primary external financial statements?
20. Give two forms of the accounting equation.
21. Define assets and liabilities and give four examples of each.
22. Define owners' equity.
23. What is the purpose of the balance sheet? By what other name is it frequently called?
24. Define revenues and expenses and give an example of each.
25. What is the purpose of the income statement?
26. On which external financial statement do you find assets, liabilities, and owners' equity?
27. On which external financial statement do you find revenues and expenses?
28. Define net income.
29. Define net loss.

EXERCISES

Exercise 1-1   Matching Terms and Definitions

A list of general accounting terms is given in Column I, along with a list of definitions in Column II:

Column I	Column II
1. Accounting	_____ Process of measuring and recording business transactions.
2. Business transactions	_____ Rules, practices and procedures used to prepare financial statements.
3. External transactions	_____ Expressing items in terms of a common denominator.
4. Internal transactions	_____ Service activity that provides financial information about a firm's economic activities.
5. Measuring	_____ Process of classifying and summarizing accounting data into financial statements.
6. Classification	_____ The economic activities of a business.
7. Bookkeeping	_____ Exchange events between two or more independent firms.
8. Reporting	_____ Economic events taking place entirely within one firm.
9. Generally accepted accounting principles	_____ Placing transaction results into useful groups or categories

Required:

Match the term with its definition by placing the term number from Column I in the blank preceding each definition in Column II.

Exercise 1-2 Matching Terms and Definitions

A list of general accounting related terms is given in Column I, along with a list of definitions in Column II:

Column I	Column II
1. AICPA	_____ A business owned by one person.
2. FASB	_____ A firm's chief accounting officer.
3. SEC	_____ Plan or forecast of future operations.
4. AAA	_____ Phase of accounting dealing with the collection, allocation, and control of the cost of producing goods and services.
5. Audit	_____ National professional organization of certified public accountants.
6. Controller	_____ Separate legal entity formed under laws of a specific state or the federal government.
7. Cost accounting	_____ Organization having primary duty for establishing accounting standards.
8. Budget	_____ Professional organization concerned primarily with promoting improvements in accounting education and research.
9. Internal audit	_____ Independent examination of a firm's financial statements and supporting documents.
10. Proprietorship	_____ Legal organization having authority to establish accounting standards for financial reports required by companies that list securities on a national exchange.
11. Partnership	_____ Internal, ongoing review to assure that established procedures and policies are being followed.
12. Corporation	_____ A business owned by two or more people who generally share profits and management duties.

Required:

Match the term with its definition by placing the term number from Column I in the blank preceding each definition in Column II.

Exercise 1-3 Characteristics of Business Organizations

A list of some characteristics of the three forms of business organization follows:

1. Not a separate legal entity.
2. Owners are called stockholders or shareholders.
3. Owned by two or more persons who generally share profits and management responsibilities.
4. An organization with all the rights, duties, and responsibilities of a person.
5. Owned by one person.
6. Has the ability to raise large amounts of money.
7. Ownership is easily transferred.
8. A separate legal entity formed under laws of individual states or the federal government.
9. Owner is legally liable for its debts.
10. For accounting purposes, the business is an entity separate from its owners.
11. Owners are not personally liable for the debts of the organization.

Required:
Set up the following columnar headings and indicate with an "X" which form or forms of business organization the characteristic applies to. Item one is completed as an example.

Characteristic	Proprietorship	Partnership	Corporation
1.	X	X	

Exercise 1-4   Matching Financial Statements Terms and Definitions

A list of terms related to financial statements is given in Column I, followed by a list of definitions in Column II:

Column I	Column II
1. Balance sheet	_____ The owners' interest in the accumulated, undistributed business earnings.
2. Assets	_____ Statement showing the changes taking place in retained earnings during a period
3. Liabilities	_____ Excess of revenues (and gains) over expenses (and losses).
4. Owners' equity	_____ A report showing the receipts (sources) and payments (uses) of cash.
5. Paid-in capital	_____ Assets consumed or used in the process of earning revenues.
6. Retained earnings	_____ Reports the financial position of a firm at a specific point in time.
7. Income statement	_____ Inflows of assets from the sale of goods or performance of services.
8. Net income	_____ Cash and noncash resources owned by a firm.
9. Net loss	_____ Owners' interest in the assets of a business.
10. Revenues	_____ Debts owed by a business to outside parties.
11. Expenses	_____ Amount of cash or other assets invested in a firm by its owners.
12. Retained earnings statement	_____ Reports the results of operating activities for a specific time period.
13. Statement of cash flows	_____ Excess of expenses (and losses) over revenues (and gains).

Required:
Match the term with its definition by placing the term number from Column I in the blank preceding each definition in Column II.

Exercise 1-5   Preparation of a Balance Sheet

Balance sheet items for Mida Company are presented in alphabetical order below:

Accounts payable	$ 5,785
Accounts receivable	5,675
Accumulated depreciation—building	5,950
Building	49,500
Capital stock	26,085
Cash	2,450
Income tax payable	800
Interest payable	1,468
Land	25,000
Mortgage payable	35,960
Office supplies	265
Retained earnings	5,542
Salaries payable	1,300

Required: .

Use the items listed above to prepare a balance sheet in good form for Mida Company as of December 31, 1992.

Exercise 1-6 Preparation of an Income Statement

Ron's Lawn Service, Inc., has the following income statement items:

Depreciation expense	$ 70
Income tax expense	5,590
Other expenses	180
Salaries expense	19,600
Service revenues	46,500
Supplies expense	1,200

Required:

Prepare an income statement for Ron's Lawn Service, Inc., for the year ended December 31, 1992.

Exercise 1-7 Preparation of a Retained Earnings Statement

The following items relate to the retained earnings statement for Excel Company for the year ended December 31, 1992.

Dividends declared and paid	$32,000
Net income for 1992	68,000
Retained earnings, January 1, 1992	95,000

Required:

Prepare a retained earnings statement for the year ended December 31, 1992 for Excel Company.

Exercise 1-8 Asset Valuation

Singer Company started operations on January 1, 1992. Equipment costing $25,000 was purchased during the year. Other assets purchased during 1992 included land at a cost of $30,000 and a building at a cost of $90,000.

On December 31, 1992, management of Singer Company believes the equipment, land, and building could be sold for the following amounts:

Equipment	$26,000
Land	31,300
Building	98,600

Management estimates that the equipment is 20% used up and the building is 3% used up.

Required:

At what amount should the equipment, land, and building be reported on Singer Company's December 31, 1992 balance sheet? What accounting principle serves as a guideline in determining the amounts reported on the balance sheet for assets?

Exercise 1-9 Revenue Recognition

Greely Appliance Repair Service billed customers $134,900 for services performed during 1992. Of this amount, only $114,030 was collected by December 31, 1992. Greely's accounts receivable had a balance of $18,650 on January 1, 1992. During 1992, Greely collected $18,100 of this amount.

Required:
How much revenue should Greely Appliance Repair Service report on its 1992 income statement?

Exercise 1-10 Expense Determination

During 1992, Smith Carpet Cleaning, Inc., purchased cleaning supplies on account at a total cost of $5,650. Of this amount, $830 remains unpaid at December 31, 1992, the end of Smith's accounting period. A physical count of supplies on hand on December 31, 1992 shows $475 of unused supplies. Smith had no cleaning supplies on hand on January 1, 1992.

Required:
What amount should Smith Carpet Cleaning, Inc., report on its 1992 income statement for cleaning supplies expense?

Exercise 1-11 Analysis of Income Statement Items

West Corporation was organized on January 1, 1992, to repair computers and office machines. At the end of 1992, the following income statement was prepared:

WEST CORPORATION
Income Statement
For the Year Ended December 31, 1992

Revenues:		
Service sales (cash)	$342,600	
Service sales (credit)	87,900	
Total revenues		$430,500
Expenses:		
Advertising expense	78,000	
Depreciation expense	6,000	
Interest expense	27,000	
Rent expense	4,800	
Salaries and wages	174,000	
Supplies used	40,200	
Utilities expense	48,000	
Total expenses		378,000
Income before income tax		52,500
Income tax expense		10,500
Net income		$ 42,000

Required:
A. What was the average monthly revenue amount?
B. What average amount did West Corporation spend each month for rent?
C. Why is "Supplies used, $40,200" reported as an expense?
D. Explain why "Interest expense, $27,000" is an expense.
E. Explain what is meant by "Depreciation expense, $6,000."
F. What is the income tax rate for West Corporation for 1992?

Exercise 1-12 Analysis of Financial Accounting Data

Sample Company, Inc., is a small company that repairs household appliances. The following report was prepared for the month of July 1992:

Service Revenue, Expense, and Income

Service revenues:		
Cash collected from customers for services rendered	$38,000	
Services rendered on credit, cash not yet collected	4,500	
Total revenues		$42,500
Expenses:		
Advertising (appeared in July newspaper, paid by check)	1,500	
Estimated wear and tear on truck during the month of July	700	
Repair supplies used (taken from stock, paid for in June)	7,000	
Salaries and wages (paid by checks)	9,700	
Wages for July not yet paid	600	
Other expenses (paid by checks)	3,000	
Total Expenses		22,500
Income before income tax		20,000
Income tax expense (not yet paid)		4,000
Net Income for July		$16,000

Required:

A. The owner of Sample Company would like to know the "amount of net cash flows from operations of the company during July 1992." Prepare a report showing net cash flows from operating activities.

B. What was the income tax rate for the month of July?

C. Reconcile the "Net increase or decrease in cash from operations" computed in Requirement A with net income for July 1992.

PROBLEMS

Problem 1-1 Preparation of a Balance Sheet

Black Company had the following balance sheet items on December 31, 1992:

Accounts payable	$17,600
Building (net of depreciation)	36,000
Capital stock ($10 par value)	48,000
Cash	37,240
Land	24,000
Other assets	7,200
Retained earnings	42,760
Supplies on hand	3,920

Required:
Prepare a balance sheet as of December 31, 1992.

Problem 1-2 Preparation of Income Statement and Retained Earnings Statement

Valley Apartments, Inc., had the following income statement and retained earnings statement items in their records on December 31, 1992:

Apartment maintenance expense	$ 1,140
Depreciation expense	26,900
Dividends paid to stockholders	8,000
Income tax expense	5,700
Insurance expense	950
Interest expense	24,550
Miscellaneous expense	1,615
Property tax expense	2,565
Rent revenues	126,125
Retained earnings, December 31, 1991	20,900
Salary and wage expense	11,175
Utilities expense	22,230

Required:
Prepare an income statement and retained earnings statement for the year ended December 31, 1992.

Problem 1-3 Preparation of Income Statement, Retained Earnings Statement, and Balance Sheet

Baker Realty Company's financial records showed the following amounts on December 31, 1992:

Accounts payable	$ 4,900
Accounts receivable	90,240
Accumulated depreciation—automobiles	7,200
Accumulated depreciation—office equipment	1,800
Automobiles	10,800
Capital stock ($10 par value, 5,400 shares)	54,000
Cash	61,800
Depreciation expense (on automobiles and office equipment)	900
Dividends declared and paid during 1992	17,500
Income tax expense	15,300
Income tax payable	15,300
Interest expense	3,100
Note payable, long-term	36,000
Office equipment	3,600
Office supplies on hand	960
Other operating expenses	74,600
Paid-in capital in excess of par value	10,800
Retained earnings, December 31, 1991	9,000
Salaries and commissions payable	1,800
Sales commissions revenue	138,000

Required:
Prepare an income statement, retained earnings statement, and balance sheet for Baker Realty Company for the year ended December 31, 1992.

Problem 1-4   Determining Missing Elements in Accounting Equations

Five independent cases are presented below:

Case	Total Assets	Total Liabilities	Owners' Equity	Total Revenue	Total Expenses	Net Income (Loss)
1	$132,000	$ 44,000	?	$163,200	?	$ 18,240
2	97,000	?	$ 60,000	99,600	$ 74,680	?
3	?	50,000	60,000	158,000	?	8,500
4	169,400	?	92,100	?	86,800	(12,400)
5	?	156,000	258,000	?	418,000	46,500

Required:

Compute the missing elements in each independent case.

Problem 1-5   Preparation of Statement of Cash Flows

Kerns Corporation is preparing the annual financial statements. The following data about cash flows were developed for the year ended December 31, 1992:

Cash inflow from operating revenues	$324,000
Cash expended for operating expenses	216,000
Sale of capital stock for cash	41,000
Cash dividends declared and paid	24,000
Payments on long-term mortgage	49,000

During the year, a tract of land was sold for $14,000 cash (the same price that Kerns had paid for the land in 1989), and two new machines were purchased for a total of $49,200.

Required:

Prepare a statement of cash flows for the year ended December 31, 1992. Follow the format illustrated in the chapter.

CASE 1-1   Annual Report Analysis

Refer to the financial statements and related footnotes of BFGoodrich Company in the appendix and answer the following questions. Indicate the appendix page number on which you found the answer.

1. What is the amount of total assets on December 31, 1989?
2. What is the amount of total stockholders' equity on December 31, 1989?
3. What is the amount of total liabilities on December 31, 1989?
4. What were total revenues (sales) for the year ended December 31, 1989?
5. How much were income taxes for the year ended December 31, 1989?
6. How much was net income for the year ended December 31, 1989?

ORGANIZATION OF FINANCIAL STATEMENTS AND ACCOUNTING CONCEPTS

CHAPTER OVERVIEW AND OBJECTIVES

This chapter discusses underlying accounting concepts and their relationship to the organization of financial statements. When you have completed the chapter, you should understand:

1. The content of the income statement and its organization.
2. The nature of extraordinary items in the income statement.
3. The content of the balance sheet and its organization.
4. The meaning of current assets, current liabilities, and working capital.
5. The meaning of the operating cycle of a business.
6. The objectives of financial accounting.
7. The basic assumptions and principles of accounting.

Chapter 1 introduced the basic elements of the income statement, the balance sheet, the retained earnings statement, and the statement of cash flows for a relatively simple case. This chapter extends that discussion to a more complex case including the detail of organization and classification within the financial statements. In addition, the basic underlying financial accounting principles, assumptions, and conventions are presented.

CLASSIFICATION WITHIN EXTERNAL FINANCIAL STATEMENTS

As mentioned in Chapter 1, the primary function of accounting is to provide financial information about economic activity in order to facilitate economic decisions. Because of their different educational backgrounds, experiences, objectives, and goals, external users of financial accounting information, including investors, creditors, regulators, and employees, have somewhat different needs than internal users. The financial statements prepared to meet these external needs are often called **general purpose financial statements** because they provide general information intended for use by all external users. Relatively standard classification schemes have evolved over time. The general guidelines that have evolved are discussed in this chapter. If the structure and content of the financial statements are based on the general needs of users, and if that structure is followed consistently, then the information most user groups want should be available.

We will use the financial statements of Microdata, Inc., a retailer of computer software, as a basis for discussion. Microdata, Inc. was formed early in 1985 and has grown steadily since then. Our emphasis is on the content of and classification within the various financial statements rather than on the determination of dollar amounts. You are not expected to learn and understand all facets of financial statements in this chapter, but you should understand their main features so that you can understand better the content of later chapters where many of the items presented in financial statements, including the determination of dollar amounts, are discussed in detail. Our order of presentation will be (1) the income statement, (2) the balance sheet, (3) the retained earnings statement, and (4) the statement of cash flows.

THE INCOME STATEMENT

Objective 1: Content and organization of the income statement

An income statement for Microdata, Inc. for the year ended December 31, 1992 is presented in Figure 2-1. In contrast with the **single-step income statement** used in Chapter 1, which contained only two major categories (revenues and expenses), Figure 2-1 illustrates a **multiple-step income statement**. It has several groups (steps) of data with a balance shown after each group.

Revenues were defined earlier as inflows of assets resulting from either the sale and delivery of goods or the rendering of services. Some additional descriptive term is often used to identify the type of revenue. For example,,revenue of a business performing service is generally called **service revenue** and revenue of a business that sells a product is called **sales revenue**.

Most businesses permit dissatisfied customers to either return unsatisfactory goods or keep the goods but pay a reduced price. These returns and allowances are treated as reductions in sales revenue. They are subtracted directly from sales revenue on the income statement as a **contra.** (In accounting, the term ''contra'' means a direct offset or reduction in a related amount.) Note that in Figure 2-1 gross sales revenue is reduced directly for sales returns and allowances to produce net sales revenue.

Expenses were defined earlier as outflows or other uses of assets to earn revenues during an accounting period. On the income statement, expenses are generally classified into several groups that vary somewhat depending upon the type of business. For a merchandising company that purchases goods ready for sale to customers, the normal classifications are:

> *Cost of goods sold.* **Cost of goods sold** shows the total cost of the merchandise that was sold during the period. Cost of goods sold is subtracted from sales to arrive at an intermediate income amount called either **gross margin** or **gross profit** on sales. Note that Microdata, Inc. had net sales revenues of $6,358,000 during 1992. When the cost of goods sold ($3,942,000) is subtracted, the result is a gross margin of $2,416,000. The amount of gross margin must exceed the total of all operating expenses if the business is to report operating income for the year.

MICRODATA, INC.
Income Statement
For the Year Ended December 31, 1992

Gross sales revenue		$6,420,000
Less: Sales returns and allowances		62,000
Net sales revenue		6,358,000
Less: Cost of goods sold		3,942,000
Gross margin		2,416,000
Operating expenses:		
Selling expenses:		
Advertising	$328,500	
Depreciation	174,600	
Insurance	49,400	
Repairs and maintenance	84,700	
Sales salaries	645,500	
Miscellaneous	29,300	
Total selling expenses	$1,312,000	
Administrative expenses:		
Administrative salaries	288,000	
Bad debts	31,400	
Depreciation and amortization	42,500	
Insurance	32,600	
Repairs and maintenance	28,300	
Miscellaneous	18,200	
Total administrative expenses	441,000	
Total operating expenses		1,753,000
Operating income		663,000
Other revenue and expense:		
Interest expense	82,000	
Interest and investment revenue	(49,000)	
Net other expense		33,000
Income before income tax		630,000
Income tax expense		276,000
Income before extraordinary items		354,000
Extraordinary item: Gain on condemnation of		
property ($96,000 less income tax of		
$24,000)		72,000
Net Income		$ 426,000
Earnings per share:		
Income before extraordinary items		$3.54
Extraordinary gain		.72
Net Income		$4.26

Figure 2-1
Multiple-Step Income Statement

Operating expenses. **Operating expenses** are those expenses normally incurred in operating the business during the period. Operating expenses are often subclassified by function into selling expenses and administrative expenses.

Selling expenses are those expenses, other than cost of goods sold, incurred to perform the sales activity. **Administrative expenses** are those expenses incurred for operating activities other than sales activity, including such items as administrative salaries and the cost of maintaining an accounting department.

Deducting total operating expenses from gross margin produces another interim income figure, **operating income**. Operating income shows the amount of income produced by the primary activities of the business.

Other revenue and expense. Many firms report interest expense in a separate category called **other revenue and expense**. These firms normally subtract interest revenues (from credit granting or investing activities), thereby showing a net cost (or net gain) from the financing activities of the business. Adding or subtracting the net other revenue and expense from operating income produces **income before income tax**.

Income tax expense. **Income tax expense** is the amount that must be paid to federal and other governmental units that levy a tax on business income. The corporation is the only form of business organization that is subject to income taxes. The other forms of business organization (i.e., partnerships and proprietorships) are not subject to income taxes. Rather, the income must be included in the owners' individual tax returns.

**Objective 2:
Extraordinary
items**

Accounting rules provide that total income tax expense should be allocated to operating income and to extraordinary items. **Extraordinary items** are gains and losses resulting from events that are so unusual that they are reported separately on the income statement in order to distinguish them from the results of normal operating activities. Extraordinary items are relatively rare because they must be both unusual in nature and infrequent in occurrence.

Note that the total income tax expense for Microdata, Inc. is $300,000, of which $276,000 is assigned to pretax income before extraordinary items and $24,000 assigned to the extraordinary gain. Extraordinary items are reported net of their income tax effect. A more detailed discussion of income taxes is presented in Chapter 17.

Earnings per share amounts, which must be reported on corporate income statements (but not those of proprietorships or partnerships), are computed by dividing the appropriate income amount by the number of shares of capital stock outstanding. Current accounting standards require that earnings per share amounts be reported both for income before extraordinary items and for net income. In Figure 2-2, the balance sheet for Microdata, Inc., reference to the stockholders' equity section shows that there are 100,000 shares of capital stock outstanding. Thus, the earnings per share amounts shown on the income statement were derived by dividing the appropriate income amounts by 100,000 shares. External users, particularly stockholders and their advisors, are especially interested in the earnings per share figures as they relate to the market price of the stock.

THE BALANCE SHEET

**Objective 3:
Content and
organization of
the balance sheet**

The **report form** balance sheet reporting the assets, liabilities, and owners' equity of Microdata, Inc. on December 31, 1992 is presented in Figure 2-2. It lists assets, liabilities, and owners' equity amounts in vertical columns. This format is commonly used when the balance sheet is presented on one page. In contrast, the **account form**,

MICRODATA, INC.
Balance Sheet
December 31, 1992

Assets

Current assets:
Cash		$ 187,500
Marketable securities		103,000
Accounts receivable	$ 346,000	
Less: Allowance for bad debts	9,400	336,600
Merchandise inventory		870,900
Prepaid expenses		31,000
Total current assets		1,529,000

Long-term investments:
In stocks of other companies	294,000	
In bonds of other companies	360,000	
Total long-term investments		654,000

Property, plant, and equipment:
Land		122,700
Buildings	$764,000	
Less: Accumulated depreciation	213,000	551,000
Store equipment	317,800	
Less: Accumulated depreciation	106,500	211,300
Total property, plant, and equipment		885,000

Intangible assets:
Trade-marks and trade names		216,000

Other assets:
Land held for expansion		250,000
Total Assets		$3,534,000

Liabilities

Current liabilities:
Accounts payable		$ 113,000
Short-term notes payable		200,000
Income taxes payable		84,000
Salaries and wages payable		102,000
Current portion of mortgage note payable		32,000
Total current liabilities		531,000

Long-term liabilities:
Mortgage note payable	$ 480,000	
Bonds payable, 12%, due 1998	500,000	
Total long-term liabilities		980,000
Total Liabilities		1,511,000

Stockholders' Equity

Paid-in capital:
Capital stock, $5 par value, 100,000 shares outstanding	500,000	
Paid-in capital in excess of par value	300,000	
Total paid-in capital	800,000	
Retained earnings	1,223,000	
Total stockholders' equity		2,023,000
Total Liabilities and Stockholders' Equity		$3,534,000

Figure 2-2
Classified Balance Sheet

which was illustrated in Chapter 1, shows the assets on the left side and the liabilities and owners' equity on the right side.

The three major categories in the balance sheet with their subclassifications are:

Assets	**Liabilities**
Current assets	Current liabilities
Long-term investments	Long-term liabilities
Property, plant, and equipment	**Stockholders' equity**
Intangible assets	Paid-in capital
Other assets	Retained earnings

These subclassifications facilitate the evaluation of financial data. They are arranged in the balance sheet so that important relationships between two subcategories are shown. For example, the liquidity of a firm—that is, its ability to satisfy short-term obligations as they become due—is of primary concern to most statement users. To facilitate the evaluation of a firm's liquidity, assets and liabilities are subclassified as current (or short-term) and long-term.

Classification of Assets

Objective 4:
Current assets,
current liabilities,
and working
capital

Objective 5:
Nature of the
normal operating
cycle

Current assets are cash and other types of assets, such as marketable securities and accounts receivable, that are reasonably expected to be converted into cash, sold, or used up during the normal operating cycle or within one year after the balance sheet date, whichever is longer. The normal operating cycle varies for different types of businesses. For a merchandising concern it is the average length of time that it takes to acquire inventory, sell that inventory to customers, and collect cash for the sale.

The length of the operating cycle tends to vary for different businesses and is dependent on factors such as the length of the credit period extended to customers. The type of inventory involved and the nature of the firm's operations also affect the length of the cycle. For example, a grocery store should have a shorter cycle than a jewelry store because it sells its inventory faster. The cash collected from customers is used to pay for the inventory purchased and for other operating activities of the firm. The cycle keeps repeating itself. The normal operating cycle is depicted graphically in Figure 2-3.

Figure 2-3
Normal Operating
Cycle for a
Merchandising Firm

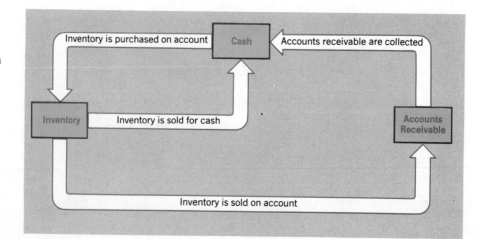

The operating cycle for a service company involves using cash to acquire supplies and services, using these supplies and services to perform services for customers, and then collecting cash from the customers. For many merchandising and service firms, the operating cycle is one year or less. For others, such as firms involved in long-term construction projects, distilling products, and lumbering operations, the cycle is longer. The specific operating cycle of such firms, rather than the one-year criterion, is used to classify assets between current and long-term.

Current assets are normally listed in order of their liquidity. The term *liquidity* refers to the average period of time it takes to convert a noncash asset into cash. In addition to cash, current assets include marketable securities, accounts and notes receivable, merchandise inventory, and prepaid expenses.

Marketable securities are current assets representing temporary investments of excess cash. They are expected to be sold for cash within the next year or operating cycle.

Accounts receivable are amounts due from customers who have been extended short-term credit. Therefore, they are expected to be collected within the near future. An estimated amount of bad debts (uncollectible accounts) is deducted as a contra to accounts receivable. The amount of uncollectible accounts is estimated, based on an analysis of the company's past experience.

Merchandise inventory is a current asset because it is expected to be sold within the near future. When the inventory is sold, its cost is transferred to cost of goods sold and deducted from sales revenue on the income statement.

Prepaid expenses represent payment for services to be received in the future, such as insurance premiums or rent paid in advance. As time passes, a portion of the prepaid insurance or prepaid rent becomes expense. Some prepaid expenses may expire over several years. Their inclusion as current assets is supported on the grounds that they are, in a sense, cash equivalents since, if an advance payment was not made, a cash outflow would be required in the next period to acquire the services. For reporting purposes, it is common practice to combine the prepaid expenses into one account rather than list them separately.

Long-term investments are those assets held for investment purposes rather than for use in normal operations. That is, they are investments that are expected to be held for a period in excess of either one year or the normal operating cycle, whichever is longer. Long-term investments normally consist of stocks and bonds of other companies, land held for speculative purposes, and cash or other assets set aside for specific long-term purposes such as a retirement fund for the firm's employees.

Property, plant, and equipment (sometimes called plant assets or *fixed assets*) consist of tangible assets that are used in the normal operations of the firm to produce and sell goods or perform services for customers. Plant assets are expected to be used by the business for a number of years and are not, therefore, held for resale. Examples include land, buildings, equipment, furniture, fixtures, and patterns and dies used in operating the business.

Plant assets (except for land) have limited useful lives. Their cost is assigned to expense over their estimated useful lives. This assignment of cost is called *deprecia-tion,* and the depreciation recorded to date is shown as *accumulated depreciation.* Accumulated depreciation is deducted from the cost of the related asset in the balance sheet to derive the asset's *book value.*

Intangible assets are those assets that have no physical substance but that are expected to provide benefits to the firm for several years. Intangible assets derive their value from the rights that possession and use confer to their owners. Like plant assets, the cost of intangibles is assigned to future periods over their estimated useful lives.

Examples of intangibles are patents, trademarks, copyrights, franchise fees, secret processes, and trade names.

Other assets is a category used to report those assets that do not fit readily into one of the categories described earlier. Some examples are plant and equipment items being held for future sale and land being held for future expansion.

Classification of Liabilities

Current liabilities are obligations of the firm that are reasonably expected to be paid or settled in the next year or the normal operating cycle, whichever is longer. Most current liabilities require the payment of cash in the near future. Examples include short-term notes payable, accounts payable, salaries and wages payable, income taxes payable, and other types of accrued liabilities for services received but not yet paid for. Also included as a current liability is that portion of long-term debt due within the next year or operating cycle, if longer than one year, for example, the portion of a mortgage note due next year.

Generally, current liabilities are those that are expected to be paid out of the current assets listed on the balance sheet. The excess of current assets over current liabilities is called **working capital.** In Figure 2-2, Microdata, Inc. has current assets of $1,529,000 and current liabilities of $531,000; consequently, the dollar amount of working capital is $998,000 ($1,529,000 − $531,000). Expressed in the form of a ratio, Microdata, Inc.'s ratio of current assets to current liabilities is 2.88 ($1,529,000/ $531,000). This means that Microdata, Inc. is in a relatively good position to settle its short-term debts.

Long-term liabilities are those obligations that do not require payment within the next year or the normal operating cycle, whichever is longer. In other words, liabilities not classified as current are reported in the long-term liability section of the balance sheet. Thus, if a firm's normal operating cycle is one year or less, obligations that mature more than one year beyond the balance sheet date are reported as long-term. Microdata, Inc. has two liabilities classified as long-term (a mortgage note payable in installments over several years after the balance sheet date and bonds payable that become due in 1998).

Stockholders' Equity

Stockholders' equity represents the owners' interest in the assets of the company. There are two main sources of stockholders' equity: (1) amounts invested in the business by the owners (paid-in capital), and (2) amounts earned by the company but not yet distributed to the owners (retained earnings). Microdata, Inc. has stockholders' equity of $2,023,000, consisting of paid-in capital of $800,000 and retained earnings of $1,223,000.

THE RETAINED EARNINGS STATEMENT

Retained earnings represent the interest of the stockholders in the assets earned by the corporation but not yet distributed to them. The retained earnings statement shows the changes taking place in retained earnings for the period being reported on. A retained earnings statement for Microdata, Inc. is presented in Figure 2-4.

Microdata, Inc. began the year with a retained earnings balance of $1,002,000. The only changes in retained earnings during the year came from net income for 1992 of $426,000 and the declaration and payment of dividends amounting to $205,000.

Figure 2-4
Retained Earnings
Statement

MICRODATA, INC.
Retained Earnings Statement
For the Year Ended December 31, 1992

Retained earnings, January 1	$1,002,000
Add: Net income for 1992	426,000
Total	1,428,000
Less: Dividends declared during 1992	205,000
Retained earnings, December 31	$1,223,000

Note that the retained earnings balance of $1,223,000 on December 31, 1992 is also reported as part of stockholders' equity in the balance sheet shown in Figure 2-2.

STATEMENT OF CASH FLOWS (SCF)

The statement of cash flows (SCF) was introduced and discussed briefly in Chapter 1. The primary purpose of the SCF is to provide information about the cash receipts and cash payments of an entity during a period. In addition, the SCF provides information about the investing and financing activities of the entity during the period. A SCF for Microdata, Inc. for the year ended December 31, 1992 is presented in Figure 2-5.

Figure 2-5
Statement of Cash
Flows

MICRODATA, INC.
Statement of Cash Flows
For the Year Ended December 31, 1992

Cash flows from operating activities:		
Cash received from customers		$6,310,000
Less cash expenses		5,630,000
Net cash flows from operating activities		680,000
Cash flows from investing activities:		
Purchases of investment securities	$(600,000)	
Purchases of property, plant and equipment	(260,000)	
Purchase of land for future expansion	(250,000)	
Proceeds from the sale of property	340,000	
Net cash used by investing activities		(770,000)
Cash flows from financing activities:		
Proceeds from short-term borrowing	150,000	
Proceeds from issuing capital stock	200,000	
Dividends paid	(205,000)	
Net cash provided by financing activities		145,000
Net increase in cash		$ 55,000

As mentioned earlier in this chapter, the derivation of the numbers in the SCF will be covered in Chapter 15. However, several important items of information are contained within the statement as discussed briefly here:

1. Cash receipts from customers ($6,310,000) exceeded cash payments for operating expenses ($5,630,000), producing a net cash inflow from operating activities of $680,000. This is an important item to users of financial statements because it is normally expected to continue into the future.

2. Net cash inflow from operating activities ($680,000) plus net cash inflows from financing activities ($145,000) exceeded net cash outflows for investing activities ($770,000), thereby producing a $55,000 increase in cash for the year.

3. A large portion of the net investments made during the year were financed internally, i.e., by net cash inflow from operations.

4. Of the total cash invested during the year, a significant amount ($600,000) was invested in securities of other companies. In addition, approximately 48% ($205,000/$426,000) of the income earned during 1992 was distributed to the stockholders as dividends.

OTHER DISCLOSURE METHODS

ANNUAL REPORTS

In addition to the information contained within the bodies of the financial statements discussed above, companies disclose information in several other ways. In an **annual report,** which is a complete set of financial statements issued to outside parties once a year, additional disclosures may be made in (1) the summary of significant accounting policies, (2) footnotes to the financial statements, and (3) the auditor's report. In order to briefly review these other disclosure methods, refer to the financial statements of BFGoodrich for the year ended December 31, 1989, which are contained in Appendix A.

Later chapters of this book explore the many acceptable alternative methods for measuring revenues, expenses, assets, and liabilities. For example, there are several acceptable methods of assigning the total cost of merchandise between inventory in the balance sheet and cost of goods sold in the income statement, and there are several acceptable methods for assigning the cost of plant assets to depreciation expense. Because these different methods can produce significantly different operating results (net income) and balance sheet totals, financial statement users must know which alternative methods were used if they are to properly interpret the data. Consequently, the methods used in the preparation of the financial statements are disclosed either immediately following the financial statements or as the first footnote. For example, see the Notes to Consolidated Financial Statements in BFGoodrich's annual report on page A7, which contains a summary of accounting policies.

The dollar amounts and terminology used in the financial statements often require additional narrative explanation to make them more meaningful to financial statements users. This additional explanation is generally presented in the *notes to the financial statements* immediately following the financial statements. For example, notes are used to explain the composition and terms of long-term debt, to report the components of inventory, and to disclose the provisions of employee's retirement plans.

AUDITOR'S REPORT

In addition to a summary of significant accounting policies and additional disclosures in notes to the financial statements, annual reports of corporations whose stock is widely held will also contain an *auditor's report.* The auditor's report is prepared by the Certified Public Accounting (CPA) firm that is hired to express an independent opinion on the financial statements.

The auditor's report generally consists of (1) an introductory paragraph, (2) a scope paragraph, and (3) an opinion paragraph. The introductory paragraph identifies the company and statements audited as well as the responsibilities of management and the auditor relative to the financial statements. The scope paragraph states that the audit was conducted in accordance with generally accepted auditing standards and discusses the nature and any limitations of the audit. The opinion paragraph contains the CPA firm's opinion as to the fairness of the data presented in the financial statements and whether those statements were prepared in accordance with generally accepted accounting principles. For an example of specific wording, see the auditor's report for BFGoodrich on page A2.

FUNDAMENTAL ACCOUNTING ASSUMPTIONS, PRINCIPLES, AND MODIFYING CONVENTIONS

The objective of financial reporting is to provide financial information for use in making economic decisions. Investors, creditors, governmental agencies, and other outside parties use accounting information to make rational investment, credit, and similar decisions that affect the allocation of scarce resources.[1] These decisions have a significant effect on all of society since they impact the form and direction of our economy. The effectiveness of decision-makers is enhanced if they have information that is relevant, reliable, and understandable.

Objective 6: Objectives of financial accounting

In addition, decision-making requires information about a business that is comparable with prior periods as well as with other businesses. In other words, accountants need standards to guide them in preparing financial reports that contain information that is relevant, reliable, understandable, and comparable over time and between businesses when used by decision-makers.[2] These standards and practices developed over time by the accounting profession are called *Generally Accepted Accounting Principles (GAAP).* They include the assumptions, principles and modifying conventions that serve as general guidelines in the preparation of financial statements.

Principles or standards become "generally accepted" by obtaining the "substantial authoritative support" of the accounting profession. As noted in Chapter 1, the most active authoritative bodies are the American Institute of Certified Public Accountants (AICPA), the Financial Accounting Standards Board (FASB), and the Securities and Exchange Commission (SEC). These organizations, with the help of extensive research staffs, study reporting alternatives for various transactions and then select the one that results in the most useful presentation of financial information. The selection

---

[1]For a more complete discussion of the objectives of financial reporting see *Statement of Financial Accounting Concepts No. 1,* "Objectives of Financial Reporting by Business Enterprises" (Stamford, Conn.: FASB, 1978).

[2]For a more detailed discussion of the qualitative characteristics of accounting information see *Statement of Financial Accounting Concepts No. 2,* "Qualitative Characteristics of Accounting Information" (Stamford, Conn.: FASB, 1980).

process came about gradually. In some areas, it has not yet been completed. Accounting standards are continually reviewed and revised to keep abreast of the increasing complexity of business operations. Accounting principles are not fundamental natural laws like those of the physical sciences; they are man-made guidelines that attain their status when they are accepted by the accounting profession.

There are several broad assumptions, principles, and modifying conventions that serve as basic guides in the selection of specific accounting rules and practices. Knowing them helps us to understand better the general framework within which accounting standards are developed and applied.

BASIC ASSUMPTIONS

Accounting principles rest on five basic assumptions:

1. The entity assumption.
2. The going concern assumption.
3. The monetary unit assumption.
4. The stable-dollar assumption.
5. The time period assumption.

THE ENTITY ASSUMPTION

Objective 7:
Accounting
assumptions and
principles

If the transactions of a business are to be recorded, classified, and summarized into financial statements, the accountant must be able to identify clearly the boundaries of the unit being accounted for. Under the **entity assumption,** the business (Microdata, Inc., for example) is considered a separate entity distinguishable from its owners and from all other entities. Each entity is assumed to own its assets and incur its liabilities. The business' assets, liabilities, and activities are kept completely separate from those of the owners of the business as well as from those of other businesses owned by the same owners. A separate set of accounting records is maintained for each business, and the prepared financial statements represent the financial position and results of operations of that business only.

THE GOING CONCERN ASSUMPTION

Unless there is evidence to the contrary, accounting reports are prepared under the assumption that the business will continue to operate in the future. Because it is not possible to predict how long a business will exist, an assumption must be made. It is assumed that the business will not be sold or liquidated in the near future, but will continue to use its resources in operating activities at least long enough to carry out its existing commitments. This assumption is called either the **going concern assumption** or the **continuity assumption.**

Adoption of the going concern assumption has important implications in accounting. For example, it provides justification for the use of the cost principle (discussed later in this chapter) in accounting for plant assets and for the allocation of their cost to depreciation over their useful lives. Because it is assumed that these assets will not be sold in the near future but will continue to be used in operating activities, current market values are of little importance.

Although the going concern assumption is followed in most cases, it should not be applied when there is conclusive evidence that the business will not continue. If management intends to liquidate the business, for example, the going concern assumption should be set aside and the financial statements prepared on the basis of expected liquidation values. In such circumstances, assets should be reported at their expected sales values and liabilities at the amount needed to settle them immediately.

MONETARY UNIT ASSUMPTION

Money is used in accounting as the common denominator by which economic activity is measured and reported. Accountants assume that data expressed in terms of money are useful in making economic decisions—the monetary unit assumption—and that the monetary unit (the dollar) represents a realistic unit of value that can be used to measure net income, financial position, and changes in financial position.

THE STABLE-DOLLAR ASSUMPTION

Another underlying assumption of accounting is the stable-dollar assumption, under which changes in the purchasing power of money are ignored. In the United States, accounting transactions are recorded and reported in terms of dollars that are assumed to have a constant value. As a result, 1992 dollars are combined with 1986 and 1980 dollars as though they all represented the same purchasing power.

Unfortunately, this is not realistic. When the general purchasing power of the dollar changes, the value of money also changes. As inflation occurs, for instance, the purchasing power of money declines. Although accountants recognize this fact, changes in the value of the measuring unit are often ignored. As a result, gains are often reported on the disposal of assets when, in fact, there has been little or no gain in purchasing power. For example, assume that (1) land was purchased for $75,000 when the general price level (the average of prices in our economy) was 100 and (2) the land was sold for $150,000 when the general price level was 200. The doubling of the general price level reflects a decrease in the purchasing power of the dollar from 100 cents to 50 cents. Current accounting practice reports a $75,000 gain on the sale of the land even though the company is no better off from a purchasing-power standpoint because it would take $150,000 on the date of sale to buy the same amount of goods and services that could have been purchased for $75,000 on the date the land was purchased.

When inflation rates are high, serious doubts exist about the wisdom of ignoring changes in the purchasing power of money. In many countries, particularly those with historically high inflation rates such as Chile and Brazil, the reported financial data are adjusted for price level changes. Methods of reporting these changes, as well as the problems and benefits involved, are discussed in Chapter 16.

THE TIME PERIOD ASSUMPTION

A complete report of the degree of success achieved by a business cannot be obtained until the business is liquidated. Only then can net income be determined precisely. Users of financial information, however, need timely information for decision-making purposes. Thus, accountants must prepare periodic reports on the results of operations, financial position, and changes in financial position. To do so, accountants have adopted the time period assumption—that is, they assume that economic activity can be associated realistically with relatively short time intervals.

Because of the many estimates, professional judgments, and assumptions required, dividing the continuous economic activity of a business into time periods such as months, quarters, and years creates many problems for accountants. The shorter the time period, the more inaccurate are the cost allocations needed to determine net income. As a result, monthly net income is generally a less reliable figure than quarterly net income, which, in turn, is less reliable than annual net income. Since cost allocations affect asset and retained earnings amounts, the shorter the reporting period, the more inaccurate the balance sheet amounts.

Periodic measurements of net income and financial position *are only estimates, and therefore tentative*. Users of financial statements should be fully aware of the tentative nature of the statement amounts when making decisions.

BASIC PRINCIPLES

Six basic principles constitute the basis for the development of accounting practices and procedures:

1. The objectivity principle.
2. The cost principle.
3. The revenue principle.
4. The matching principle.
5. The consistency principle.
6. The full disclosure principle.

THE OBJECTIVITY PRINCIPLE

The **objectivity principle** holds that, if possible, accounting information should be reliable, that is, verifiable, and free from personal bias. Verifiable means that the validity of the data is supported by adequate evidence. If information is objective and verifiable, essentially similar measures and results would be produced if two or more qualified persons examined the same data. For example, the price agreed upon in an exchange transaction is objective because it is based upon negotiation between independent parties. The price is also verifiable if it is supported by an invoice, contract, cancelled check, or other document. Accountants rely on various types of evidence to support the figures presented in accounting reports. Business documents such as contracts, purchase orders, invoices, paid checks, and physical counts of inventory and other assets provide objective, verifiable evidence in accounting.

Although accountants seek the most objective evidence available, accounting data cannot be completely objective because there are many cases in which estimates must be made on the basis of personal judgments and observations. For example, the cost of a plant asset may be highly objective, but the amount of depreciation charged to each accounting period is affected by an estimate of its useful life. However, as long as estimates are based on data and methods that can be verified by outside parties, the information is considered basically objective and verifiable.

THE COST PRINCIPLE

Resources of a business are recorded initially at their cost under the **cost principle** because of the need for objective, verifiable data. Cost is determined by the exchange price agreed upon by the parties to the exchange and is measured by the amount of cash given in exchange for the resource received. If the consideration given is something other than cash, cost is measured by the fair market value of what is given or the fair market value of the asset or service received, whichever is more clearly evident. Changes in the market value of the resources are generally ignored and the costs of the resources are allocated to the periods that benefit from their use. Thus, the income statement shows the cost of resources used as expenses and the balance sheet reports the unallocated cost of the resources. In reading a balance sheet, for example, *it is important to remember that the dollar amounts reported do not show the amounts that would be received if the assets were sold, but the unallocated cost of the assets.*

As with some of the other assumptions and principles used in the United States, the cost principle is not used universally. For example, most major companies on the stock exchange in the Netherlands report financial data using current value accounting. Current value accounting methods are discussed in Chapter 16.

THE REVENUE PRINCIPLE

An important accounting function is the determination of periodic net income—that is, the process of identifying and measuring revenues and expenses for a specified time period. Revenue for a period is determined by applying the **revenue principle,** which requires that revenue be recognized in the period when goods are sold or when services are rendered and become billable. This principle will be discussed fully in Chapter 4.

THE MATCHING PRINCIPLE

Revenue is an inflow of assets from either the sale of goods or the performance of services. Expenses are assets used up in the process of producing revenue. In general terms, revenues are recognized when they are earned and expenses are recognized (that is, matched against revenue) as assets are used. Just as the revenue principle was developed to guide in the timing of reporting revenue, the **matching principle** was developed to guide the timing of expense recognition. The application of this principle will be discussed more fully in Chapter 4.

THE CONSISTENCY PRINCIPLE

As mentioned earlier, there are many acceptable alternative methods for measuring revenues, expenses, assets, and liabilities. The methods adopted have a significant effect on (1) the amount of net income reported for a period and (2) the financial position at the end of the period. Although financial statements for any given period may be useful in themselves, they are more useful if they can be compared with similar statements of prior periods.

To improve the comparability of accounting data, accountants follow the **consistency principle,** which requires that once a particular accounting method is adopted, it will be followed from period to period. An arbitrary change in the accounting methods could result in large changes in net income and financial position—changes not reflective of true changes in business conditions or general managerial effectiveness.

The principle of consistency does not mean that a company's accounting methods can never be changed. A change to a new method should be made if the new method provides more useful information than the previous method. If a company changes an accounting method, however, the nature of and justification for the change and its effect on net income must be disclosed in the financial statements of the period in which the change is made. The justification should explain clearly why the new method is preferable. Changes in accounting methods are generally disclosed in footnotes to the financial statements and in the auditor's report.

THE FULL DISCLOSURE PRINCIPLE

The **full disclosure principle** requires that all relevant information affecting net income and financial position must be reported in the financial statements or in footnotes to the financial statements. This information need not be reported in great detail. In fact, too much detailed information may even decrease the usefulness of information. For example, a list of all of the hundreds of customers who owe money to a company and the amount owed by each would probably overwhelm most statement users. However, if a single customer owes a large portion, say 60%, of the total accounts receivable or if an important customer is having financial difficulty that may affect payment, these facts usually should be disclosed. In general, the goal is to disclose information in sufficient detail to permit the knowledgeable reader to make an informed decision.

MODIFYING CONVENTIONS

Because practical considerations sometimes require the modification of basic principles, three broad modifying conventions are followed in accounting:

1. Materiality convention.
2. Conservatism convention.
3. Industry peculiarities convention.

MATERIALITY CONVENTION

In accounting, **materiality** refers to the relative size or importance of an item or event. Although accountants generally apply the most theoretically sound treatment to transactions and events, they sometimes deviate from that practice because the effect of a transaction or event is not significant enough to affect decisions: that is, the effect is not relevant. For example, small expenditures for plant assets, such as wastepaper baskets, are often expensed immediately rather than depreciated over their useful lives. This practice saves the clerical costs involved in recording depreciation. It is allowable because the effects on the financial statements over their useful lives are not large enough to affect business decisions. Another example of the application of materiality is the common, large-company procedure of rounding amounts to the nearest thousand dollars in their financial statements.

Materiality is a relative matter: what is material for one company may be immaterial for another. A $20,000 error in the financial statements of a multimillion-dollar company may not be important. However, the same error may be critical to a small company. The materiality of an item may depend not only upon its relative size but also on its nature. For example, the discovery of a $10,000 bribe is a material event even for a large company.

Judgments as to the materiality of an item or event are not always easy to make. Accountants make them based on their knowledge of the company and on past experience. Users of financial statements must generally rely on the accountants' judgment. The rule of thumb is that an item is considered material if there is a reasonable expectation that knowledge of it would influence the decisions of financial statement users.

CONSERVATISM CONVENTION

Accountants must make many difficult judgments and estimates when determining the proper treatment of business transactions. In reaching a decision, they try to make a fair presentation of the factual effects of the transactions. When doubt still exists, accountants apply the convention of conservatism, which says, in essence: *When in doubt, choose the solution that is least likely to overstate assets and income for the current period.* For example, it is very difficult to determine how many future periods will benefit from research and development expenditures. Consequently, such expenditures are expensed in the period incurred.

Conservatism is a useful accounting approach, but it should be applied only when uncertainty prevents the reporting of factual results. Nothing in the convention of conservatism suggests that accountants should understate income or assets. An over-application of conservatism produces incorrect results in both the current and future accounting periods. Some accountants in the United States criticize U.S. GAAP for being too conservative, but many countries have even more conservative accounting rules. For example, it is allowable in Switzerland to expense property, plant, and equipment in the period it is purchased. Those companies electing to do so generally report their property, plant, and equipment at a value of only one Swiss franc.

INDUSTRY PECULIARITIES CONVENTION

The industry peculiarities exception recognizes that some industries have unique characteristics that may require the use of methods or procedures that deviate from normally accepted methods in order to produce useful information. For example, finance companies may report their investments in securities at market value rather than at cost. The special methods used are explained in the summary of significant accounting policies, which is normally the first footnote to the financial statements. This summary, which is required by GAAP, consists of a description of the accounting methods followed by the company for such things as the recognition of revenue and the recognition of expenses.

SUMMARY

This chapter has presented the normal classifications used to report accounting information in the financial statements. Subclassifications within the income statement are used for revenues, expenses, various levels of income, and earnings per share. Several subclassifications of assets, liabilities, and owners' equity are used in the balance sheet. Assets and liabilities are generally classified as current or long-term in order to facilitate the evaluation of a firm's liquidity. Liquidity is the ability to satisfy short-term obligations as they become due. Classification also aids users in analyzing relationships between subcategories. The classification of assets and liabilities as current assets and current liabilities depends on a firm's operating cycle, the average length of time that it takes to acquire inventory, sell the inventory, and collect for the sale.

Stockholders' equity is subclassified to show amounts invested by stockholders (paid-in capital) and amounts earned by the firm and not distributed to stockholders (retained earnings). The statement of cash flows classifies net cash flows into three types of activities: (1) operating; (2) investing; and (3) financing.

In studying the content of and classification in financial statements in this chapter, we emphasized the importance of concentrating on the nature of the financial statements and their components rather than on the dollar amounts assigned to various items. Details and measurement methods will be covered in later chapters.

This chapter also presented an overview of the fundamental accounting assumptions and principles that constitute the general framework within which accounting standards are developed and applied. Exceptions to the application of generally accepted methods were identified, discussed, and justified. As you study future chapters and topics, you may wish to return to this chapter to review underlying concepts.

SELF-TEST

Test your understanding of the chapter by selecting the best answer for each of the following:

1. What basic assumption of accounting indicates that operations can be broken down into yearly or monthly segments for reporting purposes through the matching of expenses and revenues?
   a. Going concern assumption.
   b. Entity assumption.
   c. Monetary unit assumption.
   d. Time period assumption.

2. Which of the following statements best describes the operating cycle concept?
   a. Any twelve-month period that a firm uses for its fiscal year.
   b. The time between the purchase of inventory and the conversion of that inventory back into cash.
   c. The average number of days required to sell inventory.
   d. The average number of days required to collect receivables.

3. Charging off a wastepaper basket with an estimated life of ten years as an expense of the period when purchased is an example of the application of the
   a. Consistency principle.
   b. Matching principle.
   c. Cost principle.
   d. Materiality convention.

4. Financial information exhibits the characteristic of consistency when
   a. expenses are reported as charges against revenues of the period in which the expenses are paid.
   b. extraordinary gains and losses are not included on the same income statement.
   c. accounting procedures are adopted that give a consistent rate of net income.
   d. an accounting entity gives identical accountable events the same accounting treatment from period to period.

5. From an accounting standpoint, which of the following are considered separate business entities?
   a. Corporations
   b. Partnerships
   c. Proprietorships
   d. All of the above

6. The assumption that an accounting entity will be in existence for an undefined period of time is the
   a. going concern assumption.
   b. stable-dollar assumption.
   c. business entity assumption.
   d. time period assumption.

7. The book value of a plant asset is defined as
   a. current market value of the asset.
   b. cost of the asset (amount paid to acquire the asset).
   c. cost of the asset less accumulated depreciation.
   d. residual value of the asset.

8. An accounting entity has $175,000 of assets, of which $55,000 are classified as current assets. Liabilities of the entity totaled $145,000, of which $30,000 are classified as current liabilities. What is the working capital of the entity?
   a. $30,000
   b. $25,000
   c. $145,000
   d. $55,000
   e. None of the above
9. A financial statement that provides information about the cash receipts and cash payments of a business during a period is the
   a. Statement of cash flows.
   b. Income statement.
   c. Retained earnings statement.
   d. Balance sheet.

REVIEW PROBLEM

This problem is a continuation of the review problem in Chapter 1.

   After analyzing his performance for the first seven months of operations and assessing the business opportunities for the summer of 1992, Gary Karlson decided to continue operating his painting business. A review of the checkbook and other records for the year May 1, 1992 to April 30, 1993, disclosed the following:

1. Total cash deposited was $32,500, which included the collection of the $600 owed by customers on May 1, 1992, and the proceeds of a $6,000 loan he received from the bank on May 1, 1992.
2. Gary's log book showed that customers owed him $750 for work completed during the year. He expected to collect all this money in May 1993.
3. Checks were written for:
   a. Paint and related materials of $12,133, which included the $383 owed to the paint supplier on April 30, 1992. (Remember, the $383 was charged to expense last year.)
   b. Painting equipment of $3,400. The painting equipment on hand on May 1, 1992, was used up and discarded during the year. The new equipment purchased was approximately 40% used up by April 30, 1993.
   c. Advertising expenses of $600.
   d. Gasoline and repair costs on the pickup, $2,025.
   e. Wages paid to a helper during June, July, and August, $900.
   f. Beginning May 1, Gary paid himself a monthly salary of $475.
   g. The purchase of a pickup truck on May 1 for $7,500. Gary estimates he can use the truck for four years at which time it should be worth about $1,500.
   h. Cash dividends of $1,000, which were paid on March 10, 1993.
4. On May 1, 1992, Gary borrowed $6,000 from a bank to help pay for the pickup truck purchased. The note is for two years with annual interest of 12% payable on each May 1. (Thus, interest of $720 should be recognized in the income statement as expense and in the balance sheet as interest payable.)
5. On April 30, 1993, Gary owed $615 for paint. No paint was on hand on April 30, 1993.

Required:

Prepare an income statement, retained earnings statement, balance sheet, and statement of cash flows for the year ended April 30, 1993.

ANSWER TO REVIEW PROBLEM

G.K. PAINTERS, INC.
Income Statement
For the Year Ended April 30, 1993

Painting revenues ($32,500 − $600 − $6,000 + $750)		$26,650
Expenses:		
Paint and materials ($12,133 − $383 + $615)	$12,365	
Depreciation expense—painting equipment ($1,360 + $180)	1,540	
Depreciation expense—pickup ($7,500 − $1,500 = $6,000/4)	1,500	
Advertising expense	600	
Salaries expense [($475 × 12) + $900]	6,600	
Gas and repair expense	2,025	
Interest expense	720	
Total expenses		25,350
Net income		$ 1,300
Earnings per share		$1.30

G.K. PAINTERS, INC.
Retained Earnings Statement
For the Year Ended April 30, 1993

Retained earnings, May 1, 1992	$ 1,897
Add: Net income for the year	1,300
Total	3,197
Less: Dividends declared during the year	1,000
Retained earnings, April 30, 1993	$ 2,197

G.K. PAINTERS, INC.
Balance Sheet
April 30, 1993

Assets			
Current assets:			
Cash			$ 1,742
Accounts receivable			750
Total current assets			2,492
Property, plant, and equipment:			
Pickup	$7,500		
Less: Accumulated depreciation	1,500	$6,000	
Painting equipment	3,400		
Less: Accumulated depreciation	1,360	2,040	
Total property, plant, and equipment			8,040
Total assets			$10,532

Liabilities

Current liabilities:	
Accounts payable	$ 615
Interest payable	720
Total current liabilities	1,335
Long-term liabilities:	
Notes payable	6,000
Total liabilities	7,335

Stockholders' Equity

Capital stock, $1 par value, 1,000 shares issued		
and outstanding	$1,000	
Retained earnings	2,197	
Total stockholders' equity		3,197
Total liabilities and stockholders' equity		$10,532

G.K. PAINTERS, INC.
Statement of Cash Flows
For the Year Ended April 30, 1993

Cash flows from operating activities:		
Cash received from customers (1)		$ 26,500
Less cash expenses (2)		21,358
Net cash flows from operating activities		5,142
Cash flows from investing activities:		
Purchase of pickup and painting equipment		(10,900)
Cash flows from financing activities:		
Proceeds from long-term borrowing	$ 6,000	
Dividends paid	(1,000)	
Net cash flows from financing activities		5,000
Net decrease in cash		$ 758
(1) Painting revenues (from the income statement)		$ 26,650
Plus beginning balance of accounts receivable		600
Less ending balance of accounts receivable		(750)
Cash received this period from customers		$ 26,500
(2) Total expenses (from the income statement)		$ 25,350
Adjustments for:		
Depreciation expense ($1,540 + $1,500)		(3,040)
Beginning balance of accounts payable		383
Ending balance of accounts payable		(615)
Ending balance of interest payable		(720)
Cash expenses for this period		$ 21,358

ANSWERS TO SELF-TEST

1. d **2.** b **3.** d **4.** d **5.** d **6.** a **7.** c **8.** b
9. a

GLOSSARY

ADMINISTRATIVE EXPENSES. Expenses incurred for operating activities other than sales activity (p. 36).

ANNUAL REPORT. A complete set of financial statements issued by a company to outside parties once a year (p. 42).

CONSERVATISM. An accounting convention which provides that when in doubt, choose the solution least likely to overstate assets and income for the current period (p. 49).

CONSISTENCY PRINCIPLE. Once a particular accounting method is adopted it should not be changed from period to period unless a different method provides more useful information (p. 47).

CONTRA. A direct offset or reduction in a related amount (p. 34).

COST OF GOODS SOLD. The total cost of merchandise that was sold during the year (p. 34).

COST PRINCIPLE. Resources and the allocation of resources are accounted for at their cost. Changes in the market value of resources are not recognized (p. 46).

CURRENT ASSETS. Cash and other types of assets that are reasonably expected to be converted into cash, sold, or used up during the normal operating cycle or within one year after the balance sheet date, whichever is longer (p. 38).

CURRENT LIABILITIES. Obligations of the firm that are reasonably expected to be paid or satisfied within one year of the balance sheet date or the normal operating cycle, whichever is longer (p. 40).

EARNINGS PER SHARE. Net income divided by the number of shares of capital stock outstanding (p. 36).

ENTITY ASSUMPTION. The notion that a business is a separate entity distinguishable from its owners and from all other entities (p. 44).

EXTRAORDINARY ITEMS. Events that are so unusual and infrequent in occurrence that any gain or loss resulting is reported separately on the income statement in order to distinguish them from the results of normal operating activities (p. 36).

FULL DISCLOSURE PRINCIPLE. All relevant information affecting net income and financial position must be reported in the financial statements or in footnotes to the financial statements (p. 48).

GOING CONCERN ASSUMPTION (CONTINUITY ASSUMPTION). The assumption that a business will continue in the future and use its assets in operations rather than sell them (p. 44).

GROSS MARGIN (GROSS PROFIT). An intermediate income amount determined by subtracting cost of goods sold from sales revenues (p. 34).

INCOME TAX EXPENSE. The amount that must be paid to federal and other governmental units that levy a tax on business income (p. 36).

INDUSTRY PECULIARITIES CONVENTION. Deviations from GAAP made to recognize the unique characteristics of some industries (p. 49).

INTANGIBLE ASSETS. Assets that have no physical substance but that are expected to provide future benefits to the firm for several years (p. 39).

LIQUIDITY. The ability to settle short-term obligations as they become due (p. 38).

LONG-TERM INVESTMENTS. Assets expected to be held for longer than one year or the operating cycle as investments rather than for use in normal operations (p. 39).

LONG-TERM LIABILITIES. Obligations of the firm that do not require payment within one year of the balance sheet date or the normal operating cycle, whichever is longer (p. 40).

MATCHING PRINCIPLE. The guidelines developed to guide the timing of expense recognition (p. 47).

MATERIALITY. The relative size or importance of an item or event. An item or event is considered material if knowledge of it would affect a user's decision (p. 48).

MONETARY UNIT ASSUMPTION. The assumption that data expressed in terms of money are useful in making economic decisions and that the monetary unit (the dollar) represents a realistic unit of measure (p. 45).

NORMAL OPERATING CYCLE. The average length of time that it takes to acquire inventory, sell the inventory to customers, and collect cash for the sale (p. 38).

OBJECTIVITY PRINCIPLE. If possible, accounting information should be factual (free from bias) and verifiable (p. 46).

OPERATING EXPENSES. Those expenses normally incurred in operating the business during the period (p. 36).

OPERATING INCOME. An intermediate income amount determined by subtracting operating expenses from gross margin (p. 36).

OTHER ASSETS. A balance sheet category used to report those assets that do not fit readily into one of the other asset categories (p. 40).

PROPERTY, PLANT, AND EQUIPMENT (PLANT ASSETS). Tangible (physical) assets that are used in the normal operations of the business and not held for resale (p. 39).

REVENUE PRINCIPLE. Provides that revenue should be recognized when goods are sold or when services are rendered (p. 47).

SELLING EXPENSES. Expenses incurred, other than cost of goods sold, to perform the sales activity (p. 36).

STABLE-DOLLAR ASSUMPTION. The assumption that the purchasing power of money does not change (p. 45).

STOCKHOLDERS' EQUITY. The owners' interest in or claims against the assets of the firm (p. 40).

TIME-PERIOD ASSUMPTION. The assumption that economic activity can be associated realistically with relatively short time intervals (p. 45).

WORKING CAPITAL. The excess of current assets over current liabilities (p. 40).

DISCUSSION QUESTIONS

1. What are the four classifications of expenses normally found on an income statement?
2. What is cost of goods sold? How is it determined?
3. Give examples of five operating expenses commonly found on an income statement.
4. Define extraordinary items.
5. How are earnings per share calculated?
6. What are the five asset classifications normally found on a balance sheet?
7. Define current assets. Why is the operating cycle important in asset classification on the balance sheet?
8. What is the difference between marketable securities and long-term investments?

9. What assets are shown in the property, plant, and equipment section on the balance sheet?
10. What are intangible assets? Give two examples.
11. If a firm owns a building that is not being used currently, where should its cost be shown on the balance sheet?
12. Define current liabilities. Why is the operating cycle important with respect to the classification of liabilities?
13. Give four examples of liabilities normally classified as current and two examples of liabilities normally classified as long-term.
14. What are the two main sources of owners' equity?
15. What does the retained earnings statement show?
16. What is the purpose of the statement of cash flows?
17. Why is it important to know the accounting principles used in the preparation of financial statements?
18. What are notes to the financial statements and why are they important?
19. What is the main objective of financial reporting?
20. What are generally accepted accounting principles?
21. Explain the entity assumption. Why is it important?
22. What is the relationship between the going concern assumption and the cost principle?
23. What is meant by the stable-dollar assumption?
24. A company owns land worth $180,000, but it is reported on the balance sheet at $115,000. What principle is illustrated by this example?
25. What is the revenue principle?
26. What is meant by the matching principle?
27. What is the materiality convention?

EXERCISES

Exercise 2-1 **Preparation of an Income Statement**

Sadsac Corporation's accounting records show the following for the year ended December 31, 1992: sales revenues, $320,000; cost of goods sold, $180,000; operating expenses, $45,000; interest expense, $6,000. The effective tax rate is 20% and Sadsac Corporation has 15,000 shares of capital stock outstanding.

Required:
Prepare an income statement for 1992.

Exercise 2-2 **Preparing an Income Statement and a Retained Earnings Statement**

Clean-All Corporation finished calendar year 1992 with the following balances: cleaning service revenue, $480,000; salaries expense, $160,000; supplies expense, $32,460; utilities expense, $9,675; automobile expense, $38,150; interest expense, $25,600; insurance expense, $10,750; store rent expense, $36,000. The effective income tax rate is 25% and Clean-All has 25,000 shares of capital stock outstanding.

Required:

A. Prepare a detailed income statement for 1992.

B. Prepare a retained earnings statement for 1992. The beginning balance in retained earnings was $76,340. Dividends of $25,000 were declared and paid in 1992.

Exercise 2-3   Income Statements from Incomplete Data

Three income statements with some information missing are shown below.

	A	B	C
Revenues	$400,000	$?	$425,800
Cost of goods sold	?	190,000	100,600
Gross margin	240,000	300,000	?
Operating expenses	?	?	100,200
Other expenses	10,000	15,600	?
Income before income tax	157,500	?	200,000
Income tax expense	?	88,200	?
Net income (loss)	126,000	120,000	?
Earnings per share	?	$6	$5
Shares of capital stock outstanding	42,000	?	25,000

Required:

Compute the missing numbers for each independent case.

Exercise 2-4   Income Determined from an Analysis of Changes in Retained Earnings

Baker Corporation's retained earnings increased by $140,000 from January 1, 1992 to December 31, 1992. Cash dividends of $25,000 were declared and paid during calendar year 1992.

Required:

A. Compute Baker's net income for 1992.

B. Assuming total revenues were $575,000 for the year, compute the expenses incurred during 1992.

Exercise 2-5   Ordering Income Statement Items

Following is a list of the major sections of an income statement in random order.

_____ Operating expenses

_____ Earnings per share

_____ Gross margin

_____ Income before income tax

_____ Revenues

_____ Other revenues and expenses

_____ Income tax expense

_____ Cost of goods sold

_____ Net income

Required:

Number the items in the order in which they normally appear on the income statement.

Exercise 2-6 Ordering Balance Sheet Items

Following is an alphabetical listing of the major classifications and subclassifications on a balance sheet:

_____ Property, plant, and equipment

_____ Current liabilities

_____ Other assets

_____ Assets

_____ Retained earnings

_____ Long-term investments

_____ Liabilities

_____ Stockholders' equity

_____ Current assets

_____ Paid-in capital

_____ Long-term liabilities

_____ Intangible assets

Required:

Number the items in the order in which they normally appear on a report form balance sheet.

Exercise 2-7 Preparing a Balance Sheet

Balance sheet items for Shutterbugs, Inc., on October 31, 1992, are presented below in alphabetical order:

Accounts payable	$ 7,200	Income taxes payable	$ 5,720
Accounts receivable	4,985	Land	20,000
Accumulated depreciation—buildings	9,500	Mortgage payable	65,300
Accumulated depreciation—furniture and equipment	3,180	Notes payable (due December 10, 1992)	17,000
Allowance for bad debts	635	Notes receivable (due February 26, 1993)	1,600
Buildings	96,250	Patents	5,000
Capital stock	25,000	Retained earnings	35,600
Cash	20,850	Salaries payable	3,250
Marketable securities	13,930	Supplies	485
Furniture and equipment	10,140	Utilities payable	855

Required:

Prepare a balance sheet as of October 31, 1992, using the three main balance sheet classifications (assets, liabilities, stockholders' equity).

Exercise 2-8 Balance Sheets with Missing Data

Balance sheet data for four independent cases are presented below:

	A	B	C	D
Cash	$?	$15,000	$33,000	$ 6,000
Accounts receivable	8,000	33,000	43,000	17,000
Plant and equipment	60,000	75,000	85,000	64,000
Accounts payable	5,000	17,000	8,000	7,000
Mortgage payable	30,000	?	70,000	31,000
Capital stock	20,000	30,000	25,000	?
Retained earnings	26,000	40,000	?	28,000

Required:
For each case, compute the missing number represented by the question mark.

Exercise 2-9 Preparation of a Balance Sheet

Three consecutive month-end balance sheet amounts for Bakers, Inc., are presented below. All the information is included except for the balance in retained earnings. (Amounts in brackets represent contra amounts.)

	1992		
	April 30	May 31	June 30
Cash	$21,600	$27,800	$28,500
Accounts receivable	32,860	31,210	39,420
Allowance for bad debts	(660)	(510)	(720)
Supplies	700	400	500
Land	15,000	15,000	19,000
Building	84,500	84,500	84,500
Accumulated depreciation—building	(20,000)	(21,500)	(23,000)
Equipment	47,100	47,100	47,100
Accumulated depreciation—equipment	(4,400)	(4,900)	(5,400)
Accounts payable	19,800	18,300	29,600
Wages payable	10,200	10,800	10,100
Short-term notes payable	6,600	4,800	3,000
Mortgage payable	53,600	53,200	52,800
Capital stock	30,000	30,000	30,000
Retained earnings	?	?	?

Required:
A. Determine the retained earnings balance at the end of each month.
B. Assuming no dividends were paid during the three months, compute net income for May and June.
C. Prepare a properly classified balance sheet as of June 30, 1992.

Exercise 2-10 Statement of Cash Flows

Following is a summary of the cash account for the Baxter Corporation for its fiscal year ended December 31, 1992.

Cash Inflows:	
Cash revenues	$3,680,000
Issue of capital stock	500,000
Borrowed by issuing a short-term note	50,000
Borrowed by issuing a long-term note	270,000

Cash Outflows:	
Cash operating expenses	2,950,000
Payment of cash dividends	300,000
Cash paid for purchase of a building	800,000
Cash paid for purchase of equipment	260,000
Cash paid for purchase of land	140,000

Required:
Prepare a statement of cash flows for the year ended December 31, 1992.

PROBLEMS

Problem 2-1 Preparation of Income Statement and Balance Sheet

Financial data for Southern Trails Corporation as of December 31, 1992 follow:

Accounts receivable	$208,550	Building	$880,000
Capital stock, 40,000 shares	300,000	Cash	78,790
Allowance for bad debts	2,250	Accounts payable	136,000
Depreciation expense—		Revenues	624,600
equipment	30,250	Mortgage payable	442,000
Accumulated depreciation—		Telephone expense	9,500
building	210,000	Supplies	1,400
Advertising expense	121,000	Land	165,000
Notes payable—long term	190,000	Utilities expense	34,700
Retained earnings, January 1	144,800	Wages expense	216,250
Depreciation expense—		Equipment	302,500
building	22,000	Supplies expense	8,600
Accumulated depreciation—		Income tax expense	54,210
equipment	84,700	Bad debts expense	1,600

Required:

Prepare an income statement for the year ended December 31, 1992 and a classified balance sheet as of December 31, 1992.

Problem 2-2 Preparation of Financial Statements

Brightmore Industries began operations early in January 1990. The company's records showed the following asset, liability, owners' equity, revenue, and expense amounts as of December 31, 1992. The amount for retained earnings is given as of January 1, 1992.

Capital stock, 15,000 shares	$ 50,000	Accounts receivable	$ 55,840
Retained earnings, January 1	37,440	Cash	28,500
Accumulated depreciation—		Accounts payable	17,600
equipment	58,400	Supplies on hand	14,300
Advertising expense	19,350	Telephone expense	7,300
Income taxes payable	32,010	Insurance expense	6,000
Notes payable—long-term	30,000	Equipment	201,500
Income tax expense	32,010	Service revenues	386,600
Depreciation expense—		Supplies expense	24,090
equipment	7,700	Rent expense	30,000
Wages expense	168,800	Utilities expense	16,660

Required:

A. Prepare an income statement and retained earnings statement for the year ended December 31, 1992. No dividends were paid during 1992.

B. Prepare a classified balance sheet as of December 31, 1992.

Problem 2-3 Preparing an Income Statement

Severn Rent-All Corporation is preparing the annual financial statements for 1992. The following amounts have been tabulated for the revenues and expenses: equipment rental revenues, $295,640; selling expenses, $103,410; interest revenue, $2,690; administrative expenses, $88,170; extraordinary loss, before tax, $18,000; interest expense, $6,000; service revenues, $17,650.

Required:
Prepare a multiple-step income statement for the year ended December 31, 1992. The income tax rate for all items is 30%. Severn Corporation had 8,000 shares of capital stock outstanding during the entire year.

Problem 2-4 Preparing an Income Statement
The bookkeeper for Bank Company has prepared the following list of financial data in order to prepare the 1992 financial statements:

Capital stock, 6,000 shares	$ 60,000	Cash	$ 4,540
Service fee revenues	88,000	Consulting revenues	201,400
Transportation expense	28,600	Utilities expense	17,300
Depreciation expense	2,300	Interest revenue	10,400
Advertising expense	31,200	Accounts payable	18,310
Salaries expense	220,400	Interest expense	5,900
Retained earnings, 1/1/92	97,760	Supplies expense	9,100
Accounts receivable	22,800		

Required:
Prepare a multiple-step income statement for the year ended December 31, 1992. (*Hint:* Not all the information will be used.) Assume a tax rate of 20%.

Problem 2-5 Preparing a Multiple-Step Income Statement
T & W Wholesalers, Inc., is preparing its annual financial statements for 1992. Following is a list of relevant income statement data:

Investment revenue	$ 1,700
Insurance on sales facilities	6,400
Depreciation expense on sales facilities	24,000
Depreciation expense on office building	2,100
Interest expense	1,000
Cost of goods sold	185,000
Sales returns and allowances	6,500
Advertising expense	17,000
Bad debt expense	7,200
Sales revenues	400,000
Extraordinary loss (net of $1,120 income tax benefit)	4,800
Miscellaneous administrative expenses	400
Administrative salaries	19,000
Insurance on office building	800
Salaries (sales personnel)	11,000
Other selling expenses	5,700

Required:
Prepare a multiple-step income statement for the year ended December 31, 1992. T & W Wholesalers, Inc., had 32,000 shares of common stock outstanding throughout 1992. Assume an income tax rate of 20%.

Problem 2-6 Classification of Financial Statement Items

Listed below on the left are financial statement items normally found in the accounting records of a business enterprise. In the right-hand column are income statement and balance sheet classifications.

Financial Statement Items
_____ Accounts Payable
_____ Office Supplies
_____ Interest revenue
_____ Equipment
_____ Prepaid insurance
_____ Unearned legal fees
_____ Rent expense on store building
_____ U.S. Treasury Bill, three-month maturity
_____ Income tax payable
_____ Long-term investment in IBM capital stock
_____ Patents
_____ Accumulated depreciation, delivery trucks
_____ Land
_____ Capital stock
_____ Interest payable
_____ Insurance expense on delivery trucks
_____ Cost of merchandise sold during the year
_____ Mortgage payable
_____ Equipment awaiting disposal
_____ Rent expense, office building
_____ Utilities payable
_____ Trademarks
_____ Depreciation expense on delivery trucks
_____ Material fire loss
_____ Total of all past net incomes less dividends paid
_____ Utilities expense for the office building
_____ Delivery trucks
_____ Cash
_____ Sales
_____ Accounts receivable
_____ Advertising expense
_____ Allowance for bad debts
_____ Short-term notes receivable

Financial Statement Classifications
Income Statement:
1. Revenues
2. Cost of goods sold
3. Selling expenses
4. Administrative expenses
5. Other revenue and expense
6. Income tax expense
7. Extraordinary items
8. Earnings per share
Balance Sheet:
9. Current assets
10. Long-term investments
11. Plant and equipment
12. Intangible assets
13. Other assets
14. Current liabilities
15. Long-term liabilities
16. Paid-in capital
17. Retained earnings

Required:
Match the financial item to its proper statement classification by placing the financial statement classification code number on the blank preceding the financial statement item.

Problem 2-7 Accounting Assumptions, Principles, and Modifying Conventions

A list of accounting assumptions, principles, and modifying conventions is given below followed by a list of statements describing specific accounting practices.

1. Full disclosure principle	8. Time period assumption
2. Industry peculiarities convention	9. Objective principle
3. Consistency principle	10. Stable-dollar assumption
4. Conservatism convention	11. Cost principle
5. Matching principle convention	12. Monetary unit assumption
6. Materiality convention	13. Entity assumption
7. Revenue principle	14. Going concern assumption

_____ A. The cost of a wastebasket is treated as a period expense rather than allocating its cost over its useful life.

_____ B. Revenue is recognized on the books when the service is performed even though the fee has not yet been collected.

_____ C. Footnotes are included in annual financial reports to describe additional economic facts not included in the financial statements.

_____ D. Action least likely to overstate assets and income for the current period.

_____ E. Land is shown on the balance sheet at $40,000, its cost 20 years ago, although its current value is $350,000.

_____ F. Financial records report the economic activities of the enterprise and exclude the economic activities of its owners.

_____ G. Expenses are recognized in the same period as the revenues which resulted from the incurrence of the expenses.

_____ H. Unless evidence indicates otherwise, a business is assumed to have an indefinite life.

_____ I. The monetary unit used to measure accounting transactions is assumed to maintain its purchasing power over time.

_____ J. Once a particular accounting method is adopted, it is not changed from one period to the next.

_____ K. Accounting reports are prepared for shorter time intervals than the natural life of the business.

_____ L. Certain industries follow accounting principles that deviate from the normally accepted methods used in other industries.

_____ M. A common denominator is used to measure and report economic activity.

_____ N. Accounting information should be free from personal bias and should be verifiable.

Required:

Match the appropriate principle, assumption, and convention to the practice described by placing the code number in the blank preceding each practice described.

Problem 2-8 Violations of Accounting Assumptions, Principles, and Conventions

Several independent situations are presented below. Each situation is a violation of one or more generally accepted accounting assumptions, principles or conventions.

1. The firm's fleet of automobiles is reported on the balance sheet at a Blue Book value of $420,000, instead of its undepreciated cost of $300,000. The difference between the two values is shown as an extraordinary gain on the income statement.

2. A business records revenue upon receipt of the customer's purchase order instead of when the goods are delivered.
3. The company is a defendent in a lawsuit which its attorney believes there is a possibility of losing. The damage amount requested equals 60% of the company's owners' equity, yet no mention of the lawsuit appears on the financial statements.
4. A business reports all its assets at a value approximating what they could be sold for within 180 days.
5. The owner of a company includes his family's personal auto expenses on the company's income statement.
6. Depreciation expense was not recorded for the current year because management did not want to show a net operating loss.
7. A firm changes its inventory valuation method each year. The method selected is the one which allows management to report its desired net income.
8. Land purchased from the president's brother was recorded at $160,000, the president's estimate of its worth, even though the purchase price was only $130,000.

Required:
For each situation, indicate the accounting assumption, principle, and/or convention violated and the correct procedure that should be followed.

Problem 2-9 Balance Sheet Analysis
The amounts below are taken from the 1992 and 1991 balance sheets of Pitboro Corporation:

	1992	1991
Cash (1)	$ 72,410	$ 89,550
Accounts receivable (1)	195,400	161,250
Allowance for bad debts (2)	(6,100)	(5,030)
Inventory (1)	815,800	883,400
Land	220,500	220,500
Buildings	855,000	855,000
Accumulated depreciation—buildings	(142,750)	(108,550)
Equipment	618,300	585,700
Accumulated depreciation—equipment	(286,800)	(223,100)
Accounts payable (1)	82,400	120,850
Salaries payable (1)	40,600	38,100
Short-term notes payable (1)	100,000	100,000
Income taxes payable (1)	86,340	63,800
Long-term notes payable	300,000	400,000
Mortgage payable	750,000	765,000
Capital stock	400,000	400,000
Retained earnings	582,420	570,970

(1) Classified as current asset or current liability.
(2) Amounts in parentheses are contra amounts.

Required:
A. Compute total assets at the end of 1991 and 1992.
B. Compute total stockholders' equity at the end of 1991 and 1992.
C. Prove the equality of net assets (assets minus liabilities) to stockholders' equity at the end of 1991 and 1992.
D. Compute the amount of working capital at the end of each year.

E. Compute the ratios of current assets to current liabilities for 1991 and 1992. What do these ratios indicate?

F. Assuming no dividends were paid in 1992, compute the 1992 net income or loss.

G. Assuming $50,000 of dividends were paid in 1992, compute the 1992 net income or loss.

Problem 2-10 Using the Statement of Cash Flows

Presented below is the 1992 SCF of Treadway Company:

TREADWAY COMPANY
Statement of Cash Flows
For the Year Ended December 31, 1992

Cash flows from operating activities:		
Cash received from customers		$4,850,000
Less cash expenses		5,075,000
Net cash flows from operating activities		(225,000)
Cash flows from investing activities:		
Purchase of equipment	$(290,000)	
Purchase of land for expansion	(300,000)	
Proceeds from the sale of used equipment	170,000	
Net cash flows from investing activities		(520,000)
Cash flows from financing activities:		
Proceeds of short-term debt	100,000	
Proceeds of long-term borrowing	600,000	
Payments on long-term debt	(200,000)	
Proceeds from the issue of capital stock	600,000	
Dividends paid	(450,000)	
Net cash flows from financing activities		650,000
Net decrease in cash		$ 95,000

Required:

A. What were the main sources of cash during 1992?

B. What were the main uses of cash during 1992?

C. What was the net increase or decrease in total debt of Treadway Company during 1992? On what other statement could you find this information?

D. If net income for 1992 was $785,000, what percent of net income was paid out in dividends? Does this percentage appear too high, too low, or about right? Why?

E. Does the information given imply the company is expanding, contracting, or maintaining its size?

F. What percent of cash receipts, including net cash receipts (payments) from operating activities, came from borrowing? Is this a healthy sign?

G. In the long-run, what must be the primary source of cash for the firm? Why?

CASE 2-1 Annual Report Analysis

Refer to the financial statements and related footnotes of BFGoodrich Company in the appendix and answer the following questions. Indicate the page number where you found the answer.

1. How much were total current assets on December 31, 1989?
2. How much were total current liabilities on December 31, 1989?
3. How much was working capital on December 31, 1989? By how much did it increase or decrease from December 31, 1988?
4. Did operating income increase or decrease from 1988 to 1989? By how much?
5. How much was the net cash provided by operating activities for the year ended December 31, 1989?
6. Did cash and cash equivalents increase or decrease during 1989? By how much?
7. What is the name of the accounting firm that performed the audit for the year ended December 31, 1989?

POR

DAN - POR -

DATA
PROCESSING
CYCLE

3

ANALYZING BUSINESS TRANSACTIONS

CHAPTER OVERVIEW AND OBJECTIVES

This chapter describes the basic procedures used to record the effects of transactions on a firm's financial position. When you have completed the chapter, you should understand:

1. The nature of accounting transactions.
2. The effects of transactions on the accounting equation.
3. Double-entry accounting and its relationship to the accounting equation.
4. A basic accounting model used to record, classify, and summarize transactions.
5. The use of accounts to summarize accounting data.
6. The rules of debit and credit and how to apply them to analyzing transactions.
7. How to record transactions in the general journal.
8. How to transfer data from the general journal into the general ledger.
9. How to verify the equality of debit and credit account balances by preparing a trial balance.
10. How to locate and correct errors.

Chapter 2 contained a detailed description of the content and classification of external financial statements. It also introduced (1) the objectives of financial accounting and (2) the assumptions, principles, and modifying conventions underlying the financial statements. The information that appears in the financial statements is the final result of what is often called the accounting data processing cycle. The *accounting data processing cycle* (or the *accounting cycle*) consists of the various steps that relate to the processing of accounting data. The occurrence of a business transaction is the initial step in the accounting cycle. The financial statements are the final result of the accounting process.

This chapter begins with a discussion of the economic activity that affects a firm and that is recorded in its accounting system. It then examines the basic procedures used in a manual accounting system to execute the accounting cycle. (In many firms, the recording and summarizing functions are performed by machines, as we shall see in Chapter 7, but the data gathered and stored in an automated system are based on an analysis quite similar to the one in this chapter.) You must have an understanding of the underlying accounting framework to be an effective user of financial reports. Knowledge is most easily acquired by studying and actually performing the procedures used in a manually operated system.

This chapter focuses on businesses that perform a service for their customers. Accounting for businesses that engage in merchandising operations will be examined in Chapter 6.

CHARACTERISTICS OF ACCOUNTING INFORMATION

As explained briefly in Chapter 1, accounting is the process of measuring, recording, classifying, summarizing, and reporting the financial information that is used in making economic decisions. Accounting information is financial data about business transactions expressed in terms of money. Business transactions are the economic activities of a business expressible in monetary terms. The term *transaction* is often used to refer to all events that are given accounting recognition. Accountants classify these business transactions into external transactions and internal transactions. *External transactions* are exchange events between two independent firms. When a business purchases merchandise from a supplier, borrows money from a bank, or sells merchandise to customers, it participates in an external transaction. In an external transaction there is an exchange of economic resources and/or obligations between the firm and one or more outside parties. For example, when a business purchases merchandise for cash it gives up one resource (cash) in exchange for another resource (inventory).

Internal transactions are those events that take place entirely within one firm. The conversion of wheat into flour, the use of supplies by an employee, and the use over time of machinery and equipment are internal transactions. Such business activities do not involve any transactions with outside parties, but are recorded in the accounting system because they affect the relationships among the firm's assets, liabilities, and owners' equity.

Some events of importance to the firm are not recorded because there has not been an exchange of goods or services—for example, receiving an order from a customer, entering into a commitment to purchase an asset in the future, the hiring or retiring of an employee, or changes in market interest rates. In other words, such events do not initially affect the firm's recorded assets, liabilities, and owners' equity. Such events will be given accounting recognition in the future if an exchange takes place, for example, when goods are delivered to customers, an asset is received that was ordered, an employee is paid for services performed, or money is borrowed at the market rate of interest. Other events that do not involve an exchange of resources, such as the destruction of an office building by fire or the city's donation of land to a company, are given accounting recognition because assets and owners' equity are decreased or increased.

Financial accounting is based on a framework of rules for determining which events constitute accounting transactions. Two difficulties encountered in the study of accounting are determining which events to record and deciding when to give an event accounting recognition. Unfortunately, there are no simple rules to follow.

PREPARATION OF SOURCE DOCUMENTS

A business record called a **source document** is prepared for most transactions that are recorded in the accounting system. This document, which provides written evidence that a transaction has occurred, contains information about the nature of the

Objective 1: Nature of transactions

transaction and the dollar amount involved. Source documents prepared for external transactions take the form of sales invoices (credit sales), purchases invoices (purchases of supplies), and cash register tapes (cash sales). The recording of internal transactions, such as depreciation on equipment used, supplies used by employees, and the conversion of raw materials into a finished product, is based on special schedules or other supporting documentation prepared internally.

The arrival of a source document in the accounting department generally initiates the recording process. Once received, the source document is analyzed to determine the amount and the effect of the transaction on the firm's financial position. Thus, it is important that a firm establish procedures to ensure that the effects of all transactions are recorded.

Source documents are also important during an audit. For example, when a firm's financial statements are audited by an independent certified public accountant (CPA), the source documents provide evidence of the underlying transaction that was processed by the accounting department.

THE EFFECTS OF TRANSACTIONS ON THE ACCOUNTING EQUATION

The basic accounting model or accounting equation is:

$$\text{Assets} = \text{Liabilities} + \text{Owners' Equity}$$

Objective 2: Effects of transactions on the accounting equation

The sum of the assets of a business is always equal to the total sources from which those assets came—that is, liabilities plus owners' equity. For a corporation, the accounting equation may be expanded as follows:

Assets	=	Liabilities	+	Paid-in Capital	+	Retained Earnings
Resources owned by a business.	=	Debts owed to outside parties.	+	Amounts invested by the owners.	+	Amounts earned by a business and not distributed to the owners.

Retained Earnings = Beginning balance + Revenues − Expenses − Dividends

As indicated in the equation, revenues increase owners' equity and expenses and dividends decrease owners' equity.

As discussed in Chapter 2, each component of the accounting equation is made up of a number of elements. For example, a firm's assets may consist of cash, accounts receivable, inventory, and equipment. Its liabilities may consist of individual short- and long-term obligations. The owners' equity component may consist of paid-in capital and retained earnings, which, in turn, is composed of the various types of revenues, expenses, and dividend distributions to the owners. Part of the accounting function is classifying the effects of transactions into meaningful categories and summarizing the results in the firm's financial statements.

To facilitate the accumulation of financial data, transactions are recorded in accounts. An account is a device used to provide a record of increases and decreases in each item that appears in a firm's financial statements. Thus, firms typically maintain a separate account for each kind of asset, liability, and owners' equity as part of their accounting system. For example, a firm will maintain a separate account to record increases and decreases in cash, a separate account to record increases and decreases in accounts receivable, a separate account for accounts payable, and still another account for capital investment.

Business transactions result in changes in individual assets, liabilities, and owners' equity. Even though the elements of the accounting equation change as a result of the transactions, its basic equality remains unchanged. Figure 3-1 shows the effects on the accounting equation of transactions undertaken during the month of January by Union Cleaners, a new business entity formed as a corporation. The type of transaction, external or internal, is identified in the list below in parentheses.

1. Sam Drew and two of his friends each purchased 2,000 shares of $10 par value stock for $10 per share. (External transaction, because under the business entity concept, the business is a separate entity distinguishable from its owners.)
2. Cleaning equipment purchased for $30,000 cash. (External transaction.)
3. Cleaning supplies purchased from Adams Supply Co. on account for $5,700. (External transaction.)
4. Performed cleaning and laundry services for customers in the amount of $6,000 which was received in cash. (External transaction.)
5. Performed cleaning of draperies for a local hotel and sent the customer a bill for $1,100. (External transaction.)
6. Paid cash in the amount of $3,400 for employees' wages and $300 for advertising. (External transaction.)
7. Collected the $1,100 account receivable recognized in transaction (5). (External transaction.)
8. Paid the amount due Adams Supply Co. for the purchase of cleaning supplies in transaction (3). (External transaction.)
9. Paid a cash dividend of $200 to each of the stockholders. (External transaction.)
10. A count of the cleaning supplies showed that $4,400 in cleaning supplies were on hand. Thus, $1,300 in supplies were used during the period, as shown here. (Internal transaction.)

Supplies on hand–January 1	$ –0–
Supplies purchased during the month	5,700
Supplies available for use	5,700
Supplies on hand–January 31	4,400
Supplies used during the month	$1,300

11. Depreciation on the cleaning equipment assigned to this period is $500. (Internal transaction.)

TRANSACTION ANALYSIS

A source document would be prepared for each transaction. Once the document is received in the accounting department, someone must analyze the source document to determine the following:

1. What are the individual accounts affected by the transaction?
2. By what amount is each account to be changed?
3. Is each account affected to be increased or decreased as a result of the transaction?

These transactions are analyzed and recorded in Figure 3-1. In this accounting system, a separate column is used for each kind of asset and liability. All owners' equity transactions are summarized in one column and are identified as either investment by the owners, dividends paid to the owners, revenue, or expense.

	Cash	+	Accounts Receivable	+	Cleaning Supplies	+	Cleaning Equipment	=	Accounts Payable	+	Stockholders' Equity	
					Assets				**= Liabilities +**		**Owners' Equity**	
(1)	+60,000										+60,000	Capital Investment
	30,000										60,000	
(2)	−30,000						+30,000					
	30,000	+					30,000	=			60,000	
(3)					+5,700				+5,700			
	30,000	+			5,700	+	30,000	=	5,700	+	60,000	
(4)	+ 6,000										+ 6,000	Revenue
	36,000	+			5,700	+	30,000	=	5,700	+.	66,000	
(5)			+1,100								+ 1,100	Revenue
	36,000	+	1,100	+	5,700	+	30,000	=	5,700	+	67,100	
(6)	− 3,700										− 300	Advertising expense
											− 3,400	Wages expense
	32,300	+	1,100	+	5,700	+	30,000	=	5,700	+	63,400	
(7)	+ 1,100		−1,100									
	33,400			+	5,700	+	30,000	=	5,700	+	63,400	
(8)	− 5,700								−5,700			
	27,700			+	5,700	+	30,000	=			63,400	
(9)	− 600										− 600	Dividends
	27,100			+	5,700	+	30,000	=			62,800	
(10)												Cleaning supplies expense
					−1,300						− 1,300	
	27,100			+	4,400	+	30,000	=			61,500	
(11)							− 500				− 500	Depreciation expense
	27,100			+	4,400	+	29,500	=			61,000	
				61,000							61,000	

Figure 3-1
Effects of Transactions on the Accounting Equation

ACCOUNTS AFFECTED

Transaction (1) in Figure 3-1 can be used to develop the process of transaction analysis from a source document. In this phase of the process, the cash and owners' equity accounts affected by the transaction are identified, and the amount of the checks received from the investors is determined ($60,000). In this case, both accounts are increased.

Revenue Principle

The revenue principle states that revenue should be recognized when it is earned rather than when it is collected. Transactions (4), performed services for cash; (5), performed services on account; and (7), collected cash for services performed and billed in transaction (5), will be analyzed here to illustrate this principle.

In Chapter 2, we defined income as the excess of revenues over expenses for a specific time period. Revenues for Union Cleaners are earned by charging a fee for the performance of cleaning and laundry services for its customers. Because the assets received as revenues belong to the owners, revenues increase owners' equity. Expenses for Union Cleaners consist of wages and salaries paid to employees, newspaper advertising, cleaning supplies used, and depreciation on the equipment. Just as revenues increase owners' equity, expenses decrease owners' equity. The excess of revenues over expenses therefore results in an increase in the net assets of the business and a net increase in owners' equity. An excess of expenses over revenues (i.e., net loss) has the opposite effect.

The effects of revenue transactions on the accounting equation are indicated in transactions (4) and (5). The effect of transaction (4) is to increase the asset cash—which represents revenue received for the performance of services—and the owners' equity by equal amounts. In accordance with the revenue principle, revenue is recognized in transaction (5) when the earning process is completed by the rendering of services rather than when cash is received. The revenue is represented by the receipt of an asset, in this case an account receivable, which represents the right to collect cash in the future. Thus, in transaction (7), the effect of the collection of the account receivable is to increase one asset (cash) and decrease another asset (accounts receivable).

Expense Recognition

Expenses are recorded when assets are used or services are received in the process of earning revenue rather than when they are paid for. Transactions (2), (3), (6), (10), and (11) illustrate this concept. Transactions (6), (10), and (11) show the effect of expenses on the accounting equation. Note that the expenses decrease assets and owners' equity—an effect opposite to the recognition of revenue.

In some cases, services are received before they are paid for. In transaction (6), the employees performed services ($3,400) and newspaper advertising ($300) was completed prior to the time payment was made. Because the services received are related to the earnings process, they are accounted for as expenses that reduced the asset cash as well as owners' equity by equal amounts ($3,700).

In other cases, assets may be acquired in advance of their use in the earnings process. For example, in transaction (3) Union Cleaners acquired cleaning supplies in the amount of $5,700 that will be used later in the earnings process. Since the purchase was on account, the transaction is recorded by increasing both an asset (Cleaning Supplies) and a liability (Accounts Payable). In transaction (10), the $1,300 cost of the supplies used during the period is accounted for as an expense by decreasing cleaning supplies and decreasing owners' equity; the cost of the supplies on hand on January 31 ($4,400) is an asset because the supplies are available for use in future periods.

Similarly, the equipment purchased in transaction (2) for $30,000 is recorded as an asset, because it is expected to be used for a number of years. The cost of the equipment is allocated to expense over its estimated useful life. In this example, depreciation expense for the month of January is estimated to be $500 and is recorded in transaction (11).

Note that in transaction (9) the cash dividends of $600 paid to the owners are recorded as a reduction in the asset cash and owners' equity. Dividends, however, are not expenses, but are distributions of income to the owners.

ACCRUAL ACCOUNTING

The combination of recognizing revenue when it is earned rather than when it is collected and the recognition of expenses when assets or benefits are used rather than when they are paid for is referred to as **accrual accounting.** We will have more to say about this important concept later in the book.

As an alternative to the accrual basis of accounting, some companies may use the cash basis of accounting. Under the cash basis, revenues are recorded in the period in which cash is received and expenses are recorded in the period in which cash is paid. On a strict cash basis, net income is the excess of cash received from revenue transactions over cash paid for expenses. This method does not recognize revenue from the sale of goods or the performance of services on credit until the receivable is collected. In addition, the cost of goods and services used to produce revenue during the current period are recognized as expenses during the period in which they are paid.

Although the cash basis approach is used by small businesses and professional people who conduct most of their activities in cash, *it is not generally accepted for use by businesses that conduct a significant portion of their business on credit.* The cash basis system is simple to operate and, when transactions are primarily in cash, produces essentially the same results as those produced by accrual accounting.

When the cash method is used, it is often modified and the accrual method is used to account for costs of inventory and plant and equipment. Thus, under the modified cash method, inventory costs are expensed when the inventory is sold and plant and equipment costs are allocated to the period in which the asset is used.

DOUBLE-ENTRY ACCOUNTING

Objective 3:
Double-entry
accounting

A review of Figure 3-1 brings out two important facts. First, every recorded transaction affected at least two accounts. This dual effect is known as **double-entry accounting**. Note, however, that the term "double-entry" does not mean that a transaction must affect each side of the equation. For example, transaction (2) affected only the left side of the equation by increasing one asset account (Cleaning Equipment) and decreasing another asset account (Cash). As a result, the totals of each side of the equation ($60,000) remained the same. Second, after the effects of each transaction were recorded, the equation remained in balance, with the sum of the assets equal to the sum of the liabilities plus owners' equity.

Note that the stockholders' equity is $61,000 after all transactions are recorded. This represents the $60,000 invested at the inception of the business plus $1,600 net income, that is, the excess of revenues ($7,100) over expenses ($5,500) for the period minus the $600 in dividends paid to the stockholders. Since Union Cleaners owes no liabilities, the assets increased by $1,000 during the period.

PREPARATION OF FINANCIAL STATEMENTS

After the effects of the above transactions are taken into account, the financial statements for Union Cleaners look like those in Figure 3-2.

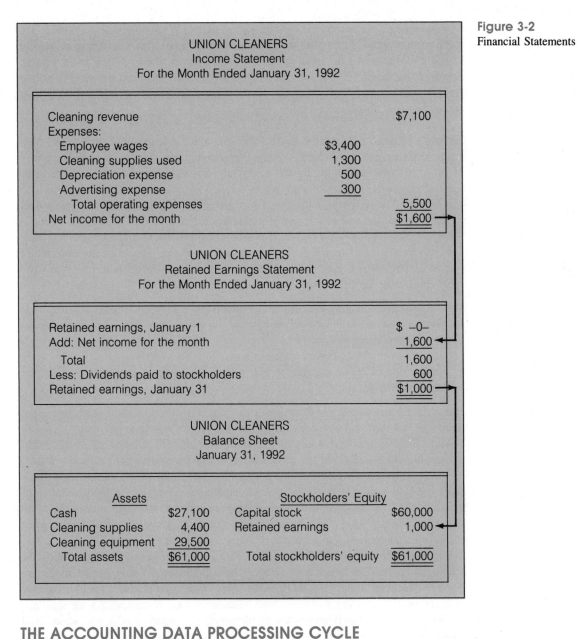

Figure 3-2
Financial Statements

UNION CLEANERS
Income Statement
For the Month Ended January 31, 1992

Cleaning revenue		$7,100
Expenses:		
Employee wages	$3,400	
Cleaning supplies used	1,300	
Depreciation expense	500	
Advertising expense	300	
Total operating expenses		5,500
Net income for the month		$1,600

UNION CLEANERS
Retained Earnings Statement
For the Month Ended January 31, 1992

Retained earnings, January 1	$ –0–
Add: Net income for the month	1,600
Total	1,600
Less: Dividends paid to stockholders	600
Retained earnings, January 31	$1,000

UNION CLEANERS
Balance Sheet
January 31, 1992

Assets		Stockholders' Equity	
Cash	$27,100	Capital stock	$60,000
Cleaning supplies	4,400	Retained earnings	1,000
Cleaning equipment	29,500		
Total assets	$61,000	Total stockholders' equity	$61,000

THE ACCOUNTING DATA PROCESSING CYCLE

In Figure 3-1, a columnar format was used to record transactions and accumulate data in a form from which the firm's financial statements were prepared. In accordance with the time period assumption, the life of a firm is divided into a series of time periods of equal length called accounting periods. Accounting periods of approximately equal length are established to enable the users of the financial statements to make meaningful comparisons of operating results of the current period with those of prior periods. A complete set of financial statements is issued to interested parties at least once a year as part of a firm's annual report.

A firm may select any 12 consecutive months for reporting. This period is called a fiscal year. If a firm's annual period ends on December 31, it is referred to as a calendar year firm. Many firms select a natural business year as a reporting period.

A *natural business year* is a 12-month period that ends when business activities are at their lowest level during the year. For example, a retail firm's inventory is usually lowest after the post-Christmas sales. Thus, retail firms often select a fiscal year of February 1 to January 31 because the employees generally have more time to complete the year-end accounting and there is less inventory to count. An added plus is that accounting cost is reduced.

Annual reports are used by creditors, investors, and other interested parties to assess the firm's progress from year to year. Although the basic accounting period for which financial statements are presented is one year, quarterly statements are commonly issued to external parties to provide timely information on the operation of the firm. Generally, quarterly statements are not as detailed as annual reports. Many firms also prepare monthly or weekly statements for internal use by management. Statements prepared before the end of the annual period are called interim statements.

During each fiscal year, a sequence of accounting procedures called the accounting data processing cycle (or accounting cycle) is completed. The columnar accounting system illustrated in Figure 3-1 provides an overview of the accounting cycle. The cycle consists of the following:

Objective 4: Accounting model

1. Transactions affecting the firm are identified and source documents are prepared.
2. Transactions are analyzed on the basis of the source documents and are recorded in the accounting system.
3. Results of the transactions are summarized in the accounts.
4. At the end of the accounting period, financial statements are prepared from the accumulated data.

The financial statements are then issued to creditors, investors, and other interested parties so that they can assess the firm's progress from year to year.

Although the columnar accounting system is useful for illustrating double-entry accounting and the fact that the accounting equation must always remain in balance, it is not practical for most firms that engage in a large number of transactions. Such firms need an accounting system that is capable of processing a large number of transactions. To accomplish this, several steps are added to the basic accounting cycle to increase its efficiency. The accounting data processing cycle is completed at least once each fiscal period; the sequence of steps is diagrammed in Figure 3-3.

The first three steps of the accounting cycle are carried out continuously during the accounting period as transactions occur. These three steps, diagrammed in Figure 3-4, are described in detail in this chapter. Step 4, the preparation of a trial balance to check on the accuracy of the account balances is also discussed. As we shall see in Chapter 5, this step is completed as part of the preparation of a worksheet. The remaining part of the cycle (steps 5 through 8), which is completed at the end of the period, is discussed in Chapters 4 and 5.

STEP 1: TRANSACTIONS OCCUR AND SOURCE DOCUMENTS ARE PREPARED

As discussed earlier, the accounting process begins when a transaction occurs. A source document is prepared which contains information about the nature of the transaction and the dollar amount involved. The identification, measurement, and recording of the economic effects of each transaction are based on an analysis of the source document.

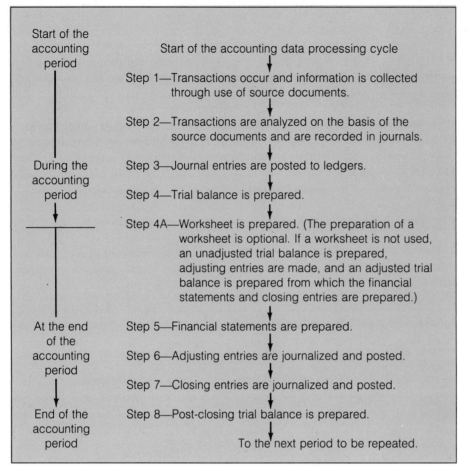

Figure 3-3
Accounting Data
Processing Cycle

Figure 3-4
The Accounting Cycle Performed During the Accounting Period

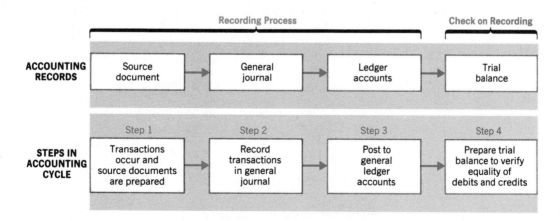

STEP 2: TRANSACTIONS ARE ANALYZED AND RECORDED IN A JOURNAL

In Figure 3-1, Union Cleaners' transactions were analyzed and then recorded in columnar form in terms of the accounting equation. To do this, we had to determine which accounts were affected by the transaction and the amount by which each account was to be increased or decreased. Accountants, however, do not refer to the changes in the accounts as increases or decreases. Instead, the terms "debits" and "credits" are used. We must be careful to note, however, that a debit does not mean an increase in the account balance, nor does a credit mean that an account is decreased. To show you how accountants use these terms, it is helpful at this point to examine accounts which are used for the efficient processing of large amounts of accounting data.

THE USE OF ACCOUNTS AS A RECORD

Objective 5:
Use of accounts

As defined earlier, an account is a device used to provide a record of increases and decreases in each item that appears in a firm's financial statements. Although an account may take various forms, each form contains three parts.

1. A title that is descriptive of the nature of the items being recorded in the account.
2. A place for recording increases.
3. A place for recording decreases.

Also, accounts typically provide space for recording an account number, the date of the transaction, an explanation of the transaction, and a posting reference. One simplified format, called a T account because of its similarity to the letter T, is shown below.

Account Title

Left side or **debit** side	Right side or **credit** side
(Abbreviation–Dr.)	(Abbreviation–Cr.)

A T account has a left side and a right side, respectively called the debit side and the credit side. An account is debited when an amount is entered on the left side and credited when an amount is entered on the right side. A debit is also called a charge to the account. Whether a debit or a credit is an increase to the account balance depends on whether the account is an asset, a liability, or an owners' equity account.

To illustrate the mechanics involved, assume that the transactions affecting the Cash account of Union Cleaners (see Figure 3-1) were recorded in a T account as follows.

Cash

Debit (Dr.)	Credit (Cr.)
(1) 60,000	(2) 30,000
(4) 6,000	(6) 3,700
(7) 1,100	(8) 5,700
	(9) 600
67,100	40,000
Balance 27,100	

Cash receipts (increases) are recorded on the debit side of the account and cash payments (decreases) are entered on the credit side.

Recording the receipts and payments on different sides of the account facilitates the determination of the account balance. The account balance is the difference between the sum of its debits and the sum of its credits. If the sum of the debits exceeds the sum of the credits, the account has a debit balance. A credit balance results when the sum of the credits is greater than the sum of the debits. An account has a zero balance if the sum of the debits equals the sum of the credits. In the Cash account above, the cash receipts of $67,100 exceeded the payments of $40,000, resulting in a debit balance of $27,100.

In a T account format, the totals, called footings, are sometimes written smaller or in a different color than the postings so that the totals will not be interpreted as additional debits and credits. The footings are often omitted with just the balance entered after a single rule. The debit balance of $27,100 in the Cash account is inserted on the debit side of the account. A balance sheet prepared at this time would report $27,100 in cash as an asset.

Balance Sheet Accounts

Increases and decreases are recorded in the three categories of balance sheet accounts in the T account format, as follows:

Objective 6:
Rules of debit
and credit

Assets		=	Liabilities		+	Owners' Equity	
Example: Cash			Example: Accounts Payable			Example: Capital Stock	
Debit to increase +	Credit to decrease −		Debit to decrease −	Credit to increase +		Debit to decrease −	Credit to increase +

An increase to an asset account is recorded as a debit; an increase in a liability or owners' equity account is recorded as a credit. The fundamental logic behind these rules lies in the fact that external transactions or exchanges involve two components, that which is received (the debit) and that which is given (the credit). In other words, a receipt of an asset increases that asset and giving up or consuming an asset correspondingly decreases it. With respect to liabilities, a promise to pay later increases the debt and the payment of the debt decreases it. In the case of owners' equity, the credit to increase it shows the entity's acknowledgment to the owners of their increased interest in the firm. The debit to owner's equity shows that the entity has received a release from further accountability to owners for their interest because the owners' interest has been reduced or eliminated by unprofitable operations and/or dividends.

Note the relationship of the debit/credit rules to the accounting equation. Assets are on the left side of the equation and are increased on the left side of the T account (the debit side); liabilities and owners' equity accounts are on the right side of the equation and are increased on the right side of the T account (the credit side). Decreases are recorded opposite of increases. Thus, a decrease in an asset is recorded as a credit; a decrease in a liability or an owners' equity account is recorded as a debit.

The recording of increases to asset accounts on the debit side and increases to liability and owners' equity accounts on the credit side permits an additional check for accuracy. Not only must the accounting equation be in balance, but the dollar amounts of the debits must equal the dollar amounts of the credits for each transaction. Therefore, since each transaction must balance, the sum of the accounts with debit balances must equal the sum of the accounts with credit balances.

Owners' Equity. The owners' equity component of the accounting equation can be classified into paid-in capital and retained earnings. Paid-in capital is increased by the amount invested by the owners. Retained earnings represents the amount of assets earned by the business and not yet distributed.

Debit and credit rules for owners' equity accounts are shown below in T account format:

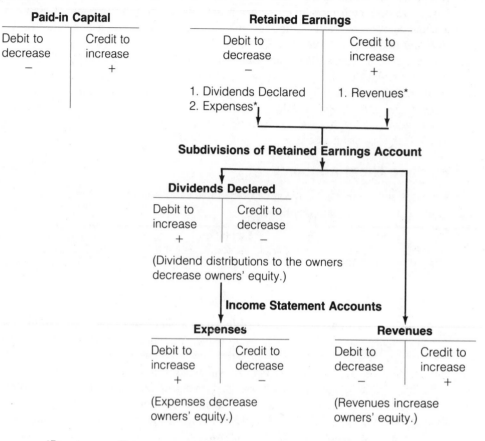

*Revenues − Expenses = net income or net loss. As shown in Chapter 5, the net effect of revenues and expenses is transferred to retained earnings.

Paid-in Capital An investment of cash or other assets in the business by an owner increases the owners' interest in the business and is recorded as a credit in a paid-in capital account. For example, when cash is invested in a corporation, Cash is debited (increased) and Capital Stock, a paid-in capital account, is credited (increased). A reduction in the Capital Stock account is made as a debit.

Dividends Declared Dividends are distributions of assets to the owners and reduce their interest in the business. Since dividend distributions decrease the owners' interest in the business, they are recorded as a debit to an owners' equity account. Although dividends could be debited directly to the Retained Earnings account, it is preferable to establish a separate account, called Dividends Declared, in order to provide an individual record of the total distributions made during the period. Thus, Dividends Declared is a subclassification of the Retained Earnings account. A dividend paid to the owners is a distribution of income, not an expense related to the production of revenue. Therefore, dividend distributions are not reported in the income statement.

Revenues and Expenses Revenues and expenses are changes in the owners' equity that are recorded in separate accounts. Thus, revenue and expense accounts are subclassifications of the Retained Earnings account. A separate account is established to account for each major source of revenue and each major expense to facilitate the preparation of the income statement.

Revenues increase owners' equity and expenses decrease owners' equity. An increase in a Revenue account is recorded as a credit consistent with the recording of an increase in owners' equity; an increase in an Expense account is recorded on the debit side of that account because expenses decrease owners' equity. Note that a debit to an expense account increases the balance in that account, but is a reduction in owners' equity.

The debit/credit rules can be illustrated by reviewing the transactions of Union Cleaners recorded in Figure 3-1. Transaction (1), the owners invest $60,000 cash in the business, is recorded as an increase (a debit) to an asset account, Cash, while at the same time owners' equity is increased (a credit). The other transactions are analyzed in a similar fashion in Figure 3-5.

NORMAL ACCOUNT BALANCES

The **normal balance** of an account is the side on which increases to the account are recorded. Knowing the normal account balance for an account can help find errors.

Account	Side Increases Recorded On	Normal Balance
Assets	Debit	Debit
Liabilities	Credit	Credit
Owners' Equity:		
Paid-in Capital	Credit	Credit
Dividends	Debit	Debit
Revenues	Credit	Credit
Expenses	Debit	Debit

If an account has a balance different from its normal balance, it is likely that an error has been made. For example, a credit balance should not be found in the Land account, nor should a debit balance be in a revenue account. However, if a bank account has been overdrawn, the Cash account will have a credit balance.

Understanding the rules of debit and credit is fundamental to understanding the material in the rest of this book. Thus, these rules should be mastered now. Here are some easy rules to help:

- Remember that to debit an account simply means to enter an amount on the left side of the account.
- To credit an account simply means to enter an amount on the right side of the account.
- A debit may increase or decrease the account balance, depending on whether the account is on the left or right side of the accounting equation. The same is true for a credit.
- Do not think of a debit or credit as an increase or decrease but simply as an entry on the left or right side.

When analyzing a transaction, think in terms of which accounts are affected by the transaction: Given the type of account, should it be debited or credited to properly reflect the change in the account?

Transaction	Amount	Assets			=	Liabilities + Owners' Equity		
		Account	+ or −*	Debit or Credit =		Account	+ or −*	Debit or Credit
(1) Owners invest in business.	$60,000	Cash	+	Debit	=	Owners' Equity	+	Credit
(2) Purchase equipment for cash.	30,000	Cleaning Equipment Cash	+ −	Debit Credit				
(3) Purchase supplies on account.	5,700	Cleaning Supplies	+	Debit	=	Accounts Payable	+	Credit
(4) Perform services for cash.	6,000	Cash	+	Debit	=	Revenue	+	Credit
(5) Perform services on account.	1,100	Accounts Receivable	+	Debit	=	Revenue	+	Credit
(6) Paid wages and advertising expenses.	3,700	Cash	−	Credit	=	Expense	+	Debit**
(7) Collected amount due from customers.	1,100	Cash Accounts Receivable	+ −	Debit Credit				
(8) Paid cash on accounts payable.	5,700	Cash	−	Credit	=	Accounts Payable	−	Debit
(9) Paid a cash dividend.	600	Cash	−	Credit	=	Owners' Equity	−	Debit
(10) Supplies used.	1,300	Cleaning Supplies	−	Credit	=	Expense	+	Debit
(11) Depreciation on equipment.	500	Cleaning Equipment	−	Credit	=	Expense	+	Debit

* + Account is increased. − Account is decreased.
** Debit increases an expense but decreases owners' equity.

Figure 3-5
Analysis of Transaction

STANDARD ACCOUNT FORMATS

The T account format described above is a convenient way to show the effects of transactions on individual accounts and is used primarily in accounting textbooks and in classroom illustrations. In practice, however, accounts generally take one of the formats shown in Figure 3-6.

TRANSACTIONS ARE RECORDED IN JOURNALS

Objective 7: Recording transactions in the journal

In the typical manual accounting system, the first record of a transaction is in a book called a **journal**. Since this is the initial recording of a transaction, journals are referred to as **books of original entry**. The transactions are then entered in the individual accounts in the general ledger as discussed on page 86.

Although the transactions could be entered directly to the accounts in the general ledger, it is more convenient in a manual system to record them first in a journal. The debit and credit amounts can then be transferred to the proper ledger accounts at a convenient time.

The journal provides a complete chronological record of all transactions. That is, the journal contains the title and dollar amounts of each account (or accounts) to be debited or credited for each transaction. Since each transaction is recorded in two or more accounts, no single account will contain a complete record of a transaction. However, the journal makes it possible to review the full effect of a particular transaction on the business. It is a useful device both for reducing errors and for providing a record for later tracing and locating errors.

Three-Column or Balance Column Format

Account   Cash   Account No.   100

Date		Explanation	Post. Ref.*	Debit	Credit	Balance
1992						
Jan.	2		GJ 1	60,000		60,000
	4		GJ 1		30,000	30,000
	8		GJ 1	6,000		36,000
	13		GJ 1		3,700	32,300
	18		GJ 2	1,100		33,400
	24		GJ 2		5,700	27,700
	28		GJ 2		600	27,100

Four-Column Format

Account   Cash   Account No.   100

Date		Explanation	Post. Ref.*	Debit	Credit	Balance Debit	Credit
1992							
Jan.	2		GJ 1	60,000		60,000	
	4		GJ 1		30,000	30,000	
	8		GJ 1	6,000		36,000	
	13		GJ 1		3,700	32,300	
	18		GJ 2	1,100		33,400	
	24		GJ 2		5,700	27,700	
	28		GJ 2		600	27,100	

*The numbers in the Posting Reference column refer to the pages in the general journal on which the transactions were recorded.

Figure 3-6
Examples of Two Account Formats

Recording Transactions in a Journal

The number of journals used and the design of each journal varies from firm to firm, depending on the nature of the firm's operations and the frequency of a particular type of transaction. This chapter is concerned with the general or two-column journal, so called because it contains two columns for entering dollar amounts. Often, when large numbers of transactions of the same type occur, a firm establishes special journals to reduce the clerical work involved in recording and posting the transactions. Special journals are discussed in Chapter 7.

The standard form of a general journal and the conventional format used to enter transactions in the journal are shown in Figure 3-7. Recording transactions in a journal is called journalizing. Each transaction recorded is a separate journal entry. Before a journal entry is prepared, it is necessary to analyze the transaction to determine which accounts are affected and the amount by which each account is to be changed. In recording a transaction, the date that each occurs is entered in the Date column. The year and month are not repeated until the start of a new page or a new month. The title of the account or accounts to be debited is entered against the left margin of the Accounts and Explanation column. The amount to be debited to each account is

Figure 3-7
Example of a
General Journal

General Journal				Page 64
Date	Accounts and Explanation	Post. Ref.	Debit	Credit
1992 July 5	Cash		14,000	
	Appraisal Fees Revenue			14,000
	To record service performed in exchange for cash.			
10	Office Supplies on Hand		12,000	
	Cash			5,000
	Accounts Payable			7,000
	Purchased office supplies for cash and on account.			

entered in the Debit column on the same line as the account title. Next, the account or accounts to be credited are entered and are indented to set them apart from the debits. An explanation of the transaction may be entered on the line immediately below the journal entry. Unless a transaction is unusual, this step is often omitted because the nature of transaction is obvious. At the time that the entry is made, the Posting Reference column (discussed in the next section) is left blank.

Two journal entries are illustrated in Figure 3-7. The first entry shows that the Cash account is to be debited for $14,000 and a revenue account (Appraisal Fees Revenue) is to be credited for the same amount. The second entry records the purchase of office supplies (debit) with a partial payment in cash (credit) and the balance purchased on credit, called accounts payable (credit).

The entry on July 10 is called a compound journal entry because it involves more than two accounts. Note that the rules of double entry accounting are observed for each transaction:

1. Two or more accounts are affected by each transaction;
2. The sum of the debit amount(s) for every transaction equals the sum of the credit amount(s); and
3. The equality of the accounting equation is maintained.

STEP 3: JOURNAL ENTRIES ARE POSTED TO THE LEDGER

Objective 8:
Transferring data
from the journal
to the ledger

The general ledger (or *ledger*) is a collection of the complete set of accounts established by a specific firm. In a manual system, each account is usually maintained on a separate card or a separate sheet in a looseleaf binder. The card file or the looseleaf binder with all of its pages is, collectively, the general ledger.

SEQUENCE AND NUMBERING OF ACCOUNTS IN THE LEDGER

Accounts are normally contained in the ledger in the order they appear in the balance sheet and the income statement, making them easier to find when preparing financial statements. Each account has an identification number that is useful for reference and as a means for cross-referencing the transactions entered in a specific account. A **chart of accounts** is a listing of the complete account titles and their related numbers.

When analyzing transactions, one refers to the chart of accounts to identify specific accounts to be increased or decreased. If an appropriate account title is not listed in the chart of accounts, an additional account may be added. A flexible numbering system permits the addition of accounts as necessary. For example:

Type of Account	Account Numbers
Assets	100–199
Liabilities	200–299
Owners' equity	300–399
Revenues	400–499
Expenses	500–599

Some numbers would not be assigned within each classification of accounts to permit the insertion of new accounts as they are needed.

A chart of accounts used in this and later chapters to illustrate the accounting for the Quality Real Estate Office, Inc. is shown in Figure 3-8.

QUALITY REAL ESTATE OFFICE, INC.
Chart of Accounts

Balance Sheet Accounts		Income Statement Accounts	
Account Title	Acct. No.	Account Title	Acct. No.
Assets		**Revenues**	
Cash	100	Commissions Revenue	400
Accounts Receivable	104	Management Fees	
Prepaid Insurance	110	Revenue	402
Office Supplies On Hand	111	**Expenses**	
Land	150	Salaries Expense	500
Building	160	Commissions Expense	505
Accumulated Depreciation–		Utilities Expense	510
Building	161	Advertising Expense	520
Office Equipment	170	Insurance Expense	521
Accumulated Depreciation–		Office Supplies	
Office Equipment	171	Expense	530
Liabilities		Depreciation Expense	540
Accounts Payable	200	Interest Expense	560
Salaries Payable	210	Income Tax Expense	590
Commissions Payable	211		
Interest Payable	215		
Utilities Payable	216		
Unearned Management			
Fees	220		
Income Taxes Payable	225		
Mortgage Note Payable	230		
Owners' Equity			
Capital Stock	300		
Retained Earnings	310		
Dividends Declared	320		
Income Summary	350		

Figure 3-8
Chart of Accounts

TRANSFERRING DATA FROM
THE JOURNAL TO THE LEDGER ACCOUNTS

The process of transferring amounts entered in the journal to the proper ledger accounts is called posting. The objective of posting is to classify the effects of transactions on each individual asset, liability, owners' equity, revenue, and expense account. Posting is done periodically, for example at the end of each day or each week. The steps involved in the posting process are:

1. Locate in the ledger the account to be debited.
2. Enter the date that the transaction occurred, as shown in the journal.
3. Enter the debit amount in the Debit column of the ledger account.
4. Enter in the Posting Reference column of the ledger account, the journal and page number from which the entry is being posted.
5. Enter in the Posting Reference column of the journal the account number to which the debit amount was posted.
6–10. Repeat steps 1 through 5 for the credit part of the entry.

The posting of one journal entry from Figure 3-7 with one debit and one credit is shown in Figure 3-9. The three-column account format is illustrated here. The debit is posted in the top half of the figure and the credit is posted in the bottom half.

In Figure 3-9, the posting reference (GJ64) in the general ledger account indicates that the entry was posted from page 64 of the general journal. This provides a convenient means for tracing an amount recorded in an individual account back to the general journal when additional information is needed about the posting. The account number, entered in the Posting Reference column of the general journal in Step 5, tells the account number to which the amount was posted in the general ledger. A number in this column indicates that the amount has been posted. Thus, the use of posting references allows one to trace any recorded transaction either from the ledger account to the journal or from the journal to the ledger accounts.

When the ledger is kept in T account format, the date (Step 2) and the debit (Step 3) are entered on the left side of the account; the credit part of the transaction is entered in a similar manner on the credit side of the account. The posting reference in the ledger may be inserted as shown here:

	Cash		100
1992			
7/5 GJ64	14,000		

Often, however, the posting reference is omitted from T accounts when they are used for illustration purposes and in preparing solutions to exercises and problems.

STEP 4: PREPARATION OF A TRIAL BALANCE

**Objective 9:
Preparing a trial
balance**

One aspect of a double-entry accounting system is that for every transaction there must be equal dollar amounts of debits and credits recorded in the accounts. The equality of debits and credits posted to the ledger accounts is verified by preparing a trial balance, that is, a list of all of the general ledger accounts in the order in which they appear in the ledger with their current balances. The dollar amounts of accounts with debit balances are listed in one column, and the dollar amounts of accounts with credit balances are listed in a second column. The sum of the two columns should be equal. When this occurs, the ledger is said to be "in balance." A trial balance may be prepared at any time during the accounting period to test the equality of debits and credits in the ledger.

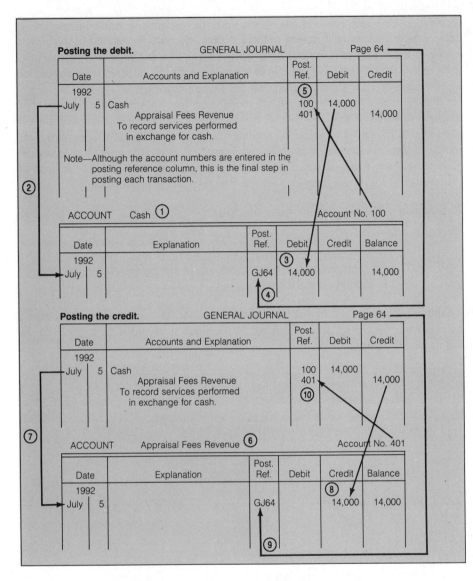

Figure 3-9
Posting from the
General Journal to
the General Ledger

ILLUSTRATIVE PROBLEM

The June transactions for the Quality Real Estate Office, Inc. are used to illustrate the analysis of transactions and the sequence of steps to be followed in recording and summarizing the transactions. Each transaction is stated below followed by an analysis of the transaction and a journal entry. In practice, the journal entries would appear sequentially in the general journal and would be uninterrupted by the analysis.

Recall that in transaction analysis each transaction is analyzed to determine:

1. Which accounts are affected. (See the chart of accounts in Figure 3-8.)
2. Whether each account affected is to be increased or decreased.
3. Whether, given the nature of each account affected, the account should be debited or credited to record the change.
4. By what amount each account is changed.

Note that each transaction affects two or more accounts with equal debits and credits recorded. Also, although it is not shown here, the accounting equation must be in balance after each entry is posted to the accounts. Because the analysis explains the nature of the transaction, explanations, which may appear in the general journal after each entry, are omitted. For illustrative purposes, accounts affected by a transaction are shown after each journal entry using the T account format.

After the transactions are journalized, the information is posted to the firm's general ledger (presented in Figure 3-10). The information accumulated in the accounts is then used in Chapter 4 to adjust the accounts and prepare financial statements for the month of June. A time period of one month is used for illustrative purposes. However, as noted earlier, financial statements may be prepared at other intervals desired by management (e.g., every quarter), but must be prepared at least annually.

Transaction: Capital stock is issued for cash.

> June 1 Steve Mandell and two of his friends file articles of incorporation and receive their authorization to operate a corporation in the state. The corporation issues them 4,500 shares of $10 par value common stock in exchange for $45,000.

Analysis: The asset cash is increased by a debit. At the same time the investment by the owners increases their equity in the firm and is recorded by a credit to the Capital Stock account.

GENERAL JOURNAL					Page 1
Date	Accounts and Explanation		Post. Ref.	Debit	Credit
1992 June 1	Cash		100	45,000	
		Capital Stock	300		45,000

Cash		**100**	**Capital Stock**		**300**
6/1	45,000			6/1	45,000

Transaction: Signed an agreement to manage an apartment complex.

> June 1 Signed an agreement for the firm to manage an apartment complex for a monthly fee of $875 to be paid on the fifth day of the following month.

Analysis: Initially, signing the agreement does not create a recordable asset or revenue and, therefore, is not given accounting recognition. That is, the signing of the agreement does not constitute an accounting transaction. In the future, as the service is performed, the fee is earned by the firm and becomes recordable.

Transaction: Purchased land and a building for cash and on credit.

> June 1 Purchased land and office building for $90,000. The terms of the agreement provided for a cash payment of $10,000, the remainder to be financed with a 20-year mortgage, bearing interest at 12% per year. The purchase price is allocated $20,000 to land and $70,000 to the building.

Analysis: The land and building are both assets that are increased by debits. The decrease in cash is recorded by a credit. The unpaid portion of the purchase price is a liability of the firm called a mortgage notes payable. A liability is increased by a credit. Although this transaction involves more than two accounts (a compound entry), the sum of the dollar amounts of the accounts debited equals the sum of the dollar amounts of the accounts credited.

June	1	Land		150	20,000	
		Building		160	70,000	
		Cash		100		10,000
		Mortgage Note Payable		230		80,000

	Cash		**100**		**Land**		**150**
6/1	45,000	6/1	10,000	6/1	20,000		

	Building		**160**		**Mortgage Note Payable**		**230**
6/1	70,000					6/1	80,000

Transaction: Paid for a 24-month insurance policy.

June 1 Cash payment of $1,200 was made for a 24-month fire and business liability insurance policy.

Analysis: The advance cash payment is recorded as a debit to an asset account, Prepaid Insurance. The asset acquired is insurance protection for 24 months, which will subsequently be expensed at some regular interval as insurance protection benefits are received and as a portion of the premium expires. Entries needed to adjust asset and liability accounts are covered in Chapter 4. A payment of cash decreases the Cash account and is recorded as a credit.

June	1	Prepaid Insurance		110	1,200	
		Cash		100		1,200

	Cash		**100**		**Prepaid Insurance**	**110**
6/1	45,000	6/1	10,000	6/1	1,200	
		6/1	1,200			

Transaction: Purchased office supplies on account.

June 5 Purchased office supplies for the amount of $940 on credit.

Analysis: This transaction increases both an asset and a liability by the same amount. Increases in assets are recorded by debits and increases in liabilities are recorded by credits. As the supplies are consumed, their cost will be transferred to an expense account, as discussed in Chapter 4.

June	5	Office Supplies On Hand		111	940	
		Accounts Payable		200		940

Office Supplies On Hand	**111**		**Accounts Payable**	**200**
6/5	940		6/5	940

Transaction: Purchased office equipment for cash and on credit.

June 5 Purchased office furniture and equipment for a total price of $12,000. Paid $5,000 in cash, with the balance due in 60 days.

Analysis: The account Office Equipment is debited for $12,000 to record the purchase of the asset. At the same time, Cash is decreased by a credit of $5,000 and Accounts Payable, a liability, is increased by a credit of $7,000 to recognize a debt of the firm.

June	5	Office Equipment	170	12,000	
		Cash	100		5,000
		Accounts Payable	200		7,000

Cash		100	Office Equipment	170		Accounts Payable	200
6/1 45,000	6/1	10,000	6/5 12,000			6/5	940
	6/1	1,200				6/5	7,000
	6/5	5,000					

Transaction: Hired employees.

June 6 Hired two sales agents and an office secretary.

Analysis: The hiring of employees is an important event but is not given accounting recognition since there are no effects at this time on the firm's accounting equation.

Transaction: Paid for advertising expense.

June 6 Paid $240 for radio commercials aired on June 3 and 4.

Analysis: Advertising is an expense. The benefits were considered to be received when the commercial announcements were made. The Advertising Expense account is increased by a debit. Expenses decrease owners' equity (a debit), but a separate account, Advertising Expense, is established to facilitate preparation of the income statement. The Cash account is decreased by a credit.

June	6	Advertising Expense	520	240	
		Cash	100		240

Cash		100	Advertising Expense		520
6/1	45,000	6/1 10,000	6/6	240	
		6/1 1,200			
		6/5 5,000			
		6/6 240			

Transaction: Earned revenue by performing a service.

June 15 Sold a residence that had been listed with the firm. A commission of $5,200 was earned on the sale, to be received when title to the property is transferred to the buyer.

Analysis: Under accrual accounting, this is a revenue transaction, even though no cash was received. Accounts Receivable is increased (a debit) to recognize the right to receive cash in the future. When the cash is received, Cash will be debited and Accounts Receivable credited. Revenues increase owners' equity (a credit), but a separate account, Commissions Revenue, is established to facilitate preparation of the income statement.

| June | 15 | Accounts Receivable | 104 | 5,200 | |
| | | Commissions Revenue | 400 | | 5,200 |

Accounts Receivable	**104**		**Commissions Revenue**	**400**
6/15	5,200		6/15	5,200

Transaction: Received cash for services to be performed in the future.

June 15 Signed an agreement to manage three single-unit rentals for a real estate investor. It is the policy of the business that management fees for single units are to be prepaid three months in advance. Received $300 management fee for the period June 15 through September 15.

Analysis: Cash is increased. Since the service has not yet been performed, the revenue has not yet been earned. Therefore, a liability, Unearned Management Fees, is recorded to show that the firm has an obligation to perform a service in the future.

| June | 15 | Cash | 100 | 300 | |
| | | Unearned Management Fees | 220 | | 300 |

	Cash		**100**	**Unearned Management Fees**	**220**
6/1	45,000	6/1	10,000	6/15	300
6/15	300	6/1	1,200		
		6/5	5,000		
		6/6	240		

Transaction: Earned revenue by performing a service.

June 19 Sold a residence that had been listed with the firm. A commission of $6,800 was earned on the sale, to be received when title to the property is transferred to the buyer.

Analysis: Same as for the revenue transaction on June 15.

	GENERAL JOURNAL			Page 2	
Date	Accounts and Explanation	Post. Ref.	Debit	Credit	
1992					
June 19	Accounts Receivable	104	6,800		
	Commissions Revenue	400		6,800	

Accounts Receivable	**104**		**Commissions Revenue**	**400**
6/15	5,200		6/15	5,200
6/19	6,800		6/19	6,800

Transaction: Paid salaries.

June   22   Paid salaries of $2,500 to the secretary, part-time employees, and sales staff for services rendered during the last two weeks.[1] Withholdings from the employees' salaries for taxes are ignored for now.

Analysis: Analysis is similar to the advertising expense transaction on June 6. However, the transactions differ as to the kind of expense involved. A separate expense account is established for each significant expense category.

June	22	Salaries Expense		500	2,500	
		Cash		100		2,500

Cash			100	Salaries Expense		500
6/1	45,000	6/1	10,000	6/22	2,500	
6/15	300	6/1	1,200			
		6/5	5,000			
		6/6	240			
		6/22	2,500			

Transaction: Paid a cash dividend to stockholders.

June   23   Declared and paid a cash dividend of $600 to the stockholders.

Analysis: A cash dividend is a distribution of profits from the corporation to its stockholders. The distribution is recorded by reducing both owners' equity (a debit) and cash (a credit) by the amount of the dividend. The debit may be recorded directly to the Retained Earnings account. However, companies that normally declare several dividends within a fiscal year often accumulate the amount of the dividends paid in a separate account called Dividends Declared. Dividends are considered a distribution of profits rather than an expense incurred for the purpose of producing revenue. Therefore, the Dividends Declared account is reported as a reduction in the retained earnings balance.

June	23	Dividends Declared (or Retained		320	600	
		Earnings)		100		600
		Cash				

Cash			100	Dividends Declared		320
6/1	45,000	6/1	10,000	6/23	600	
6/15	300	6/1	1,200			
		6/5	5,000			
		6/6	240			
		6/22	2,500			
		6/23	600			

[1]The term salary is usually used to refer to fixed compensation paid on a regular basis for services received from employees. The term wage is commonly used to refer to compensation stated in terms of an hourly rate or a similar basis. Here, for convenience, the term salary applies to both.

Transaction: Paid cash on accounts payable.

June   27   Paid $940 to creditors for office supplies purchased on credit.

Analysis: The payment reduced the entity's debt to a creditor. A decrease in liabilities is recorded by a debit and the asset Cash is decreased by a credit.

June	27	Accounts Payable		200	940	
		Cash		100		940

	Cash		100		Accounts Payable		200
6/1	45,000	6/1	10,000	6/27	940	6/5	940
6/15	300	6/1	1,200			6/5	7,000
		6/5	5,000				
		6/6	240				
		6/22	2,500				
		6/23	600				
		6/27	940				

Transaction: Paid telephone bill for the month.

June   30   Paid telephone bill in the amount of $90.

Analysis: Analysis is similar to the advertising expense transaction on June 6.

June	30	Utilities Expense		510	90	
		Cash		100		90

	Cash		100		Utilities Expense		510
6/1	45,000	6/1	10,000	6/30	90		
6/15	300	6/1	1,200				
		6/5	5,000				
		6/6	240				
		6/22	2,500				
		6/23	600				
		6/27	940				
		6/30	90				

Transaction: Received cash as payment on account.

June   30   A check for $5,200 was received for commissions earned on the residence sold on June 15.

Analysis: The increase in cash is recorded by a debit. The receipt also reduced the firm's claim against a debtor. A decrease in the asset Accounts Receivable is recorded by a credit. Note that this transaction increases one asset and decreases another. Recall that revenue was recorded on June 15 when it was earned. That is, the revenue was earned when the residence was sold for the client, rather than when the cash was collected.

June	30	Cash		100	5,200	
		Accounts Receivable		104		5,200

Cash		100		Accounts Receivable		104
6/1 45,000	6/1	10,000	6/15 5,200	6/30		5,200
6/15 300	6/1	1,200	6/19 6,800			
6/30 5,200	6/5	5,000				
	6/6	240				
	6/22	2,500				
	6/23	600				
	6/27	940				
	6/30	90				

The general ledger for the Quality Real Estate Office, Inc. showing the effects of the above transactions on the accounts maintained by the firm is presented in Figure 3-10. The accounts are shown in T account format. In an actual accounting system,

Figure 3-10
General Ledger

QUALITY REAL ESTATE OFFICE, INC.

Assets = Liabilities + Owners' Equity

Cash 100
6/1 45,000	6/1 10,000
6/15 300	6/1 1,200
6/30 5,200	6/5 5,000
	6/6 240
	6/22 2,500
	6/23 600
	6/27 940
	6/30 90
Bal. 29,930	

Accounts Receivable 104
6/15 5,200	6/30 5,200
6/19 6,800	
Bal. 6,800	

Prepaid Insurance 110
| 6/1 1,200 | |

Office Supplies On Hand 111
| 6/5 940 | |

Land 150
| 6/1 20,000 | |

Building 160
| 6/1 70,000 | |

Office Equipment 170
| 6/5 12,000 | |

Accounts Payable 200
6/27 940	6/5 940
	6/5 7,000
	Bal. 7,000

Unearned Management Fees 220
| | 6/15 300 |

Mortgage Note Payable 230
| | 6/1 80,000 |

Capital Stock 300
| | 6/1 45,000 |

Dividends Declared 320
| 6/23 600 | |

Commissions Revenue 400
	6/15 5,200
	6/19 6,800
	Bal. 12,000

Salaries Expense 500
| 6/22 2,500 | |

Utilities Expense 510
| 6/30 90 | |

Advertising Expense 520
| 6/6 240 | |

each account would be a separate page in the ledger. A trial balance taken from the ledger of Quality Real Estate Office, Inc. (see Figure 3-10) is presented in Figure 3-11. The trial balance is used in Chapters 4 and 5 to illustrate the completion of the accounting cycle.

DISCOVERY AND CORRECTION OF ERRORS

The fact that the sum of the debit column equals the sum of the credit column in the trial balance does not ensure that errors have not been made. The trial balance is simply a verification that (1) equal debits and credits have been recorded in the accounts and (2) the account balances were computed correctly, based on the recorded data. However, errors can be made that do not affect the equality of debits and credits. For example, a correct amount can be posted to the wrong account, a journal entry may be omitted, or an incorrect amount can be posted to the correct accounts. The possibility of making such errors should serve to emphasize the need to exercise due care in journalizing and posting transactions.

Objective 10: Correction of errors

A trial balance that does not balance is a clear indication that either there are one or more errors in the accounts or there was an error in preparing the trial balance. Once an error is located, it must be corrected. An error in a journal entry discovered before the amount is posted is corrected by crossing out the wrong amount with a single line and inserting the correct amount immediately above it. An error in an amount posted to a correct ledger account is corrected in the same way. Errors should never be erased because erasures can give the impression that something is being concealed.

Journal entries that have been posted in the wrong accounts should be corrected by

Figure 3-11
Trial Balance

Account Title	Debit	Credit
Cash	$ 29,930	
Accounts Receivable	6,800	
Prepaid Insurance	1,200	
Office Supplies On Hand	940	
Land	20,000	
Building	70,000	
Office Equipment	12,000	
Accounts Payable		$ 7,000
Unearned Management Fees		300
Mortgage Note Payable		80,000
Capital Stock		45,000
Dividends Declared	600	
Commissions Revenue		12,000
Salaries Expense	2,500	
Utilities Expense	90	
Advertising Expense	240	
Totals	$144,300	$144,300

QUALITY REAL ESTATE OFFICE, INC.
Trial Balance
June 30, 1992

a journal entry. For example, assume that the following entry was made in the journal to record the receipt of cash for the performance of a service for a customer and was posted in the ledger.

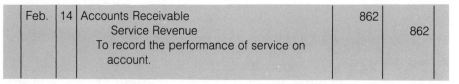

Feb.	14	Accounts Receivable	862	
		Service Revenue		862
		To record the performance of service on account.		

A correcting entry is needed to cancel the incorrect debit to Accounts Receivable and to record a correct debit to the Cash account.

Mar.	10	Cash	862	
		Accounts Receivable		862
		To correct an entry recorded on Feb. 14 in which a cash receipt was debited to Accounts Receivable.		

SUMMARY

In this chapter, the nature of transactions was discussed. Then, a basic accounting system that analyzes, records, and summarizes the effects of the transactions on the financial position of a business entity was introduced. The steps in the processing of transactions, called the accounting data processing cycle, are:

1. Recordable transactions occur and a source document is prepared to capture the essence of the transaction on paper.
2. Transactions are analyzed to determine the dollar amount involved, the accounts affected by the transaction, and the change in the accounts involved. Transactions are recorded in the journal that chronologically lists each transaction.
3. Journal entries are posted to the accounts in the general ledger. The general ledger is a collection of the complete set of accounts.
4. A trial balance is taken to determine that the sum of the accounts with a debit balance is equal to the sum of the accounts with a credit balance.

Accounts are used as a device to accumulate and summarize information related to each item appearing in the financial statements. In T account format, each account has a debit (left) side and a credit (right) side. Whether an account is increased on the debit or credit side depends on the type of account. The debit and credit rules are summarized as follows:

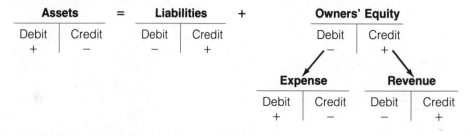

SELF-TEST

Test your understanding of the chapter by selecting the best answer for each of the following.

1. Which of the following is an example of an internal transaction?
   a. The purchase of inventory for cash.
   b. Borrowing cash from a bank.
   c. Using computer equipment to develop the firm's financial statements.
   d. Paying a utility bill.

2. In the accounting process:
   a. Posting refers to taking financial statements to the post office so that they reach stockholders in time.
   b. Journalizing means entering information into source documents.
   c. Transactions are journalized in the ledger.
   d. Journalizing comes before posting.

3. The left (debit) side of the ledger accounts is used for
   a. increases in assets and liabilities.
   b. decreases in assets and liabilities.
   c. decreases in liabilities and owner's equity.
   d. increases in liabilities and owner's equity.

4. Of the following accounts, the one that normally has a credit balance is
   a. Cash,
   b. Dividends Declared.
   c. Salaries Payable.
   d. Salaries Expense.

5. The general journal is used to record
   a. Accounting transactions and is sometimes called the "final book of entry."
   b. Accounting transactions in chronological order.
   c. Posting from the general ledger.
   d. Account balances after postings have been made to the general ledger.

6. The purchase of office equipment at a cost of $3,200 by an immediate payment of $700 and an agreement to pay the balance in 60 days is recorded by

   a. Office Equipment   700
      Accounts Receivable   2,500
          Accounts Payable   3,200

   b. Office Equipment   700
          Accounts Payable   700

   c. Office Equipment   3,200
          Cash   700
          Accounts Payable   2,500

   d. None of the above.

7. Connie Baldwin invested $10,000 cash in a business in exchange for stock. This transaction is recorded by the business as
   a. Debit to Cash, credit to Capital Stock.
   b. Debit to Capital Stock, credit to Cash.
   c. Debit to Cash, credit to Revenue.
   d. None of the above.

8. If a transaction causes an asset account to increase, which of the following related effects may occur?
   a. A decrease of equal amount in an owner's equity account.
   b. An increase in a liability account.
   c. An increase of equal amount in another asset account.
   d. A decrease of equal amount in a liability account.

9. Which of the following describes the classification and normal account balance of the Accounts Payable account?
   a. Asset, credit.
   b. Liability, debit.
   c. Asset, debit.
   d. Liability, credit.

10. A trial balance will disclose which one of the following errors?
    a. Entering a transaction twice.
    b. Entering an amount in the wrong account.
    c. Entering a debit to an account as a credit.
    d. Omitting the recording of a transaction

REVIEW PROBLEM

Mary Johnson and a friend established an interior decorating service, to be operated out of her home, called the Johnson Decorating Service, Inc. During the first month of operation, the firm completed the following transactions.

1992
July 1 The corporation issued 400 shares of $10 par value capital stock to the investors for $4,000.
1 Purchased office equipment on credit for $1,200.
2 Purchased a used automobile for $4,200, paying $1,200 cash and signing a 12% note for the balance.
2 Paid $180 cash for a one-year insurance policy on the automobile.
8 Purchased office supplies on account for a total of $140.
15 Completed a decorating assignment for a client and received $280 cash.
17 Received a deposit from a customer for services to be performed in July and August, $80.
28 Billed a client $240 for services completed in July.
30 Paid a cash dividend of $100 to the stockholders.
31 Paid $30 for advertising that appeared in the newspaper last week.

Required:

A. Set up a general ledger in T account format using the following titles and numbers:

Cash	100	Notes Payable	200
Accounts Receivable	105	Accounts Payable	210
Office Supplies on Hand	120	Unearned Service Fees	220
Prepaid Insurance	131	Capital Stock	300
Automobile	160	Dividends Declared	350
Office Equipment	180	Service Fees Revenue	400
		Advertising Expense	520

B. 1. Journalize the above transactions.
  2. Post the entries to the T accounts.
  3. Prepare a trial balance as of July 31.

ANSWER TO REVIEW PROBLEM

B. 1. Recording transactions in the general journal. The posting reference column of the journal would be completed as the entries are posted in part B.2.

GENERAL JOURNAL				Page 1
Date	Accounts and Explanation	Post. Ref.	Debit	Credit
1992				
July 1	Cash	100	4,000	
	Capital Stock	300		4,000
	The owner invested cash in the business.			
1	Office Equipment	180	1,200	
	Accounts Payable	210		1,200
	Purchased office equipment on account.			
2	Automobile	160	4,200	
	Cash	100		1,200
	Notes Payable	200		3,000
	Purchased an automobile for $1,200 cash and signed a $3,000 note.			
2	Prepaid Insurance	131	180	
	Cash	100		180
	Purchased a one-year insurance policy on the automobile.			
8	Office Supplies On Hand	120	140	
	Accounts Payable	210		140
	Purchased office supplies on account.			
15	Cash	100	280	
	Service Fees Revenue	400		280
	Earned revenue by completing an assignment.			
17	Cash	100	80	
	Unearned Service Fees	220		80
	Received an advance payment for services not yet performed.			
28	Accounts Receivable	105	240	
	Service Fees Revenue	400		240
	Billed customers for services performed.			

	30	Dividends Declared	350	100	
		Cash	100		100
		Paid a dividend to stockholders.			
	31	Advertising Expense	520	30	
		Cash	100		30
		Paid for newspaper ads.			

A. and **B.** 2.

JOHNSON DECORATING SERVICE, INC.
General Ledger

Assets

Cash			100		Accounts Receivable		105
7/1	4,000	7/2	1,200	7/28	240		
7/15	280	7/2	180				
7/17	80	7/30	100				
		7/31	30				
Bal.	2,850						

Office Supplies On Hand	120		Prepaid Insurance	131
7/8	140		7/2	180

Automobile		160		Office Equipment	180
7/2	4,200			7/1	1,200

Liabilities

Notes Payable		200		Accounts Payable		210
	7/2	3,000		7/1	1,200	
				7/8	140	
				Bal.	1,340	

Unearned Service Fees		220
	7/17	80

Owner's Equity

Capital Stock		300		Dividends Declared	350
	7/1	4,000	7/30	100	

Service Fees Revenue		400		Advertising Expense	520
	7/15	280	7/31	30	
	7/28	240			
	Bal.	520			

B. 3. Preparation of trial balance on July 31.

JOHNSON DECORATING SERVICE, INC.
Trial Balance
July 31, 1992

Account Title	Debit	Credit
Cash	$2,850	
Accounts Receivable	240	
Office Supplies On Hand	140	
Prepaid Insurance	180	
Automobile	4,200	
Office Equipment	1,200	
Notes Payable		$3,000
Accounts Payable		1,340
Unearned Service Fees		80
Capital Stock		4,000
Dividends Declared	100	
Service Fees Revenue		520
Advertising Expense	30	
Totals	$8,940	$8,940

ANSWERS TO SELF-TEST

1. c   **2.** d   **3.** c   **4.** c   **5.** b   **6.** c   **7.** a   **8.** b
9. d   **10.** c

GLOSSARY

ACCOUNT. A device used to record increases and decreases for each item that appears in a financial statement (p. 72).

ACCOUNT BALANCE. The difference between the dollar amounts of debits and credits recorded in a particular account (p. 80).

ACCOUNTING DATA PROCESSING CYCLE (ACCOUNTING CYCLE). The sequence of accounting procedures that takes place during each accounting period (p. 78).

ACCOUNTING PERIOD. A period of time covered by a set of financial statements (p. 77).

ACCRUAL ACCOUNTING. Recognizing revenue when it is earned rather than when it is collected and recognizing expenses when assets or benefits are used rather than when they are paid for (p. 76).

CALENDAR YEAR FIRM. A firm whose annual period begins on January 1 and ends on December 31 (p. 77).

CHARGE. A debit to an account (p. 80).

CHART OF ACCOUNTS. A schedule listing the titles of all accounts contained in the ledger (p. 87).

COMPOUND JOURNAL ENTRY.   A journal entry involving three or more accounts (p. 86).

CREDIT.   An amount entered on the right side of an account (p. 80).

DEBIT.   An amount entered on the left side of an account (p. 80).

DOUBLE-ENTRY ACCOUNTING.   An accounting system in which every transaction affects two or more items in the accounting equation (p. 76).

FISCAL YEAR.   An accounting or reporting period of any 12 consecutive months (p. 77).

FOOTING.   Adding a column of figures (p. 81).

GENERAL JOURNAL (TWO-COLUMN JOURNAL).   A book containing a chronological listing of transactions (p. 85).

GENERAL LEDGER.   A collection of a group of accounts for a firm, with each account appearing on a separate page (p. 86).

INTERIM STATEMENTS.   Financial statements prepared between the annual reports for a period of less than one year (monthly, quarterly, and so on) (p. 78).

JOURNAL (BOOK OF ORIGINAL ENTRY).   A book in which transactions are first recorded (p. 84).

JOURNAL ENTRY.   The format in which a transaction is entered in the general journal (p. 85).

JOURNALIZING.   The process of recording a transaction in the journal (p. 85).

NORMAL BALANCE.   The side of the account on which increases are recorded (p. 83).

POSTING.   The process of transferring information recorded in the journal to the individual accounts in the ledger (p. 88).

SOURCE DOCUMENT.   A business form that provides evidence that a transaction has occurred (p. 71).

T ACCOUNT.   An account format shaped like the letter T, in which the left side of the account is the debit side and the right side is the credit side (p. 80).

TRIAL BALANCE.   A statement listing all of the accounts in the general ledger and their debit or credit balances. A trial balance is prepared to verify the equality of debits and credits made to the accounts (p. 88).

DISCUSSION QUESTIONS

1. Tell whether each of the following events is an internal transaction, an external transaction, or not a recordable business transaction.
   a. Purchase of equipment for cash.
   b. Supplies are used by an employee.
   c. Received payment from a customer on account.
   d. Hired a new employee at a monthly salary of $1,200.
   e. Borrowed $30,000 from First National Bank.
   f. Mailed a purchase order to Stensen Office Supplies.
   g. Paid monthly salaries to employees.
   h. Purchased equipment on credit.
2. What are the two basic purposes of business documents?
3. The term "accrual accounting" encompasses two fundamental accounting principles. What are they?

4. What is the accounting data processing cycle?
5. Explain the purpose of an account. Explain the purpose of the ledger.
6. Explain the following terms as they pertain to a T account.
   a. Debit.
   c. To debit.
   b. Credit.
   d. To credit.
7. On what side of the account are increases recorded for
   a. assets
   d. revenues, and
   b. liabilities,
   e. expenses?
   c. owners' equity,
8. Why is an expense account increased on the debit side of the account, when a debit decreases an owners' equity account?
9. Identify the normal balance of the following types of accounts:
   a. Assets.
   d. Revenues.
   b. Liabilities.
   e. Expenses.
   c. Capital Stock.
10. What is the purpose of the general journal?
11. Explain what is meant by "posting."
12. What is the purpose of the posting references?
13. What is a trial balance? What is the purpose of the trial balance?
14. If the total debits equal the total credits on a trial balance, can errors still exist? Explain?

EXERCISES

Exercise 3-1 **Effects of Transactions on the Accounting Equation**
Valley International Travel began operations on June 1 and completed the following transactions during the first month.

1. Capital stock in the amount of $40,000 was issued.
2. Office equipment was purchased at a cost of $36,000, of which $5,000 was paid in cash. A note payable was given for the remainder.
3. Collected $4,600 from customers for travel services performed.
4. Rent was paid for the month of June, in the amount of $1,400.
5. Office supplies in the amount of $750 were purchased on account.
6. Salaries of $1,200 were paid, as well as a utility bill for June amounting to $450.
7. Paid for the office supplies purchased.
8. Office supplies used during June amounted to $300.
9. Depreciation on the office equipment for the month of June is estimated to be $300.

Required:
A. Prepare a schedule similar to that on page 74. List the following assets, liabilities, and owners' equity accounts as column headings: Cash, Office Supplies on Hand, Office Equipment, Notes Payable, Accounts Payable, Stockholders' Equity.
B. Show the effects of each of the transactions on the accounts listed. Indicate totals after each transaction and complete the schedule.
C. Prepare an income statement, a retained earnings statement, and a balance sheet.

Exercise 3-2 Effect of Transactions on the Accounting Equation

A series of transactions is given below.

Transactions:

1. The corporate charter is received.
2. Capital stock is issued for $60,000 cash.
3. Paid $3,000 for the current month's office rent.
4. Purchased office supplies for $450 cash.
5. Purchased $10,000 in office equipment. Paid $4,000 of the purchase price in cash; signed a 12-month, 14% note for the remaining unpaid amount.
6. Performed services and received $3,750 in cash.
7. Purchased $275 additional office supplies on account.
8. Performed services in the amount of $820 and billed customers.
9. Paid $1,350 in salaries to employees for work they had performed during the last two weeks.
10. Declared and paid a $2,000 cash dividend.
11. Paid for the office supplies purchased in (7).
12. Paid telephone bill for the first month in the amount of $195.
13. Received and recorded a $280 advertising bill for first month's advertising done by the local newspaper. The bill *was not paid*.

Required:

Set up headings across a piece of paper as follows:

Transaction	Assets	=	Liabilities	+	Stockholders' Equity

For each of the transactions, indicate its effect on the accounting equation by placing a + (increase), − (decrease), or 0 (no effect) below the elements of the accounting equation. Beside each symbol indicate the dollar amount of the transaction. Transactions (1) and (2) are given below as examples.

Transaction	Assets	=	Liabilities	+	Stockholders' Equity
1.	0		0		0
2.	+$60,000		0		+$60,000

Exercise 3-3 Effect of Transactions on Account Balances

Transactions entered into by Micro Company during its first month of operation are given below.

Transactions:

1. Issued capital stock for cash.
2. Purchased office supplies on account.
3. Paid rent expense for current month.
4. Mailed bills to customers for services performed.
5. Paid for office supplies purchased in (2).
6. Purchased land. Paid 20% of the purchase price in cash; signed a nine-month, 14% note for the unpaid amount.
7. Received and paid advertising bill for first month's advertising.
8. Collected one-half of the amount billed in (4).
9. Paid salaries to employees.
10. Borrowed money from the bank for 90 days at 12% interest.

11. Performed services for cash.
12. Received and recorded first month's utility bill. The bill *was not paid.*
13. Purchased office equipment. Signed a two-year note with a 14% annual interest rate. Interest is paid annually.
14. Declared and paid cash dividends.

Required:
Set up headings across a piece of paper as follows:

Transaction	Account(s) Increased	Account(s) Decreased	Account(s) Debited	Account(s) Credited

For each of the transactions listed, indicate its effect on the proper account by writing the names of the accounts in the proper columns. Transaction (1) is given as an example.

Transaction	Account(s) Increased	Account(s) Decreased	Account(s) Debited	Account(s) Credited
1.	Cash Capital Stock		Cash	Capital Stock

Exercise 3-4 Identification of Debit or Credit
A list of events with two columns headed debit and credit are given below.

	Debit	Credit
1. Cash is increased.	————	————
2. An account payable is increased.	————	————
3. An account receivable is decreased.	————	————
4. Capital stock is increased.	————	————
5. Rent expense is increased.	————	————
6. Service revenue is increased.	————	————
7. Dividends Declared account is increased.	————	————
8. Notes payable is decreased.	————	————
9. An account receivable is increased.	————	————

Required:
For each event listed, indicate whether the account should be debited or credited by placing a √ in the proper column.

Exercise 3-5 Determining Missing Elements in Accounting Equation
Following are various financial data for a series of independent cases.

Case	Total Assets	Total Liabilities	Stockholders' Equity	Total Revenue	Total Expenses	Net Income (Loss)
1	$ 90,000	$ 33,000	$ (a)	$ 97,000	$ (b)	$13,000
2	(c)	55,000	45,000	115,000	(d)	10,000
3	73,000	(e)	40,000	65,000	38,000	(f)
4	(g)	110,000	228,000	(h)	120,000	19,000
5	650,000	(i)	380,000	(j)	70,000	(30,000)

Required:
Compute the two missing elements for each independent case.

Exercise 3-6 Identification of Type of Account

The chart of accounts for Bent Legal Services contained the accounts listed below.

1. Notes Receivable
2. Prepaid Rent
3. Unearned Legal Fees
4. Retained Earnings
5. Cash
6. Consulting Fees Revenue
7. Rent Expense
8. Interest Revenue
9. Capital Stock
10. Legal Fees Revenue
11. Accounts Payable
12. Land
13. Income Taxes Payable
14. Mortgage Payable

Required:

A. For each account listed, indicate whether it is an asset, a liability, an owners' equity, a revenue, or an expense.

B. For each of the accounts listed

    1. Indicate whether an increase in the account balance is recorded as a debit or a credit, and

    2. Indicate whether the normal balance is a debit or a credit.

Exercise 3-7 Matching of Terms to Definitions

A number of new terms and concepts are introduced in this and previous chapters. A list of terms or concepts is given below followed by a list of definitions.

Terms or Concepts

1. General journal
2. Trial balance
3. Debit side
4. Compound journal entry
5. Double entry accounting
6. Chart of accounts
7. Accounting cycle
8. General ledger
9. Normal account balance
10. Accrual accounting
11. Source document
12. Interim statements
13. Posting
14. Journalizing

Definitions

_____ **A.** A schedule listing the titles of all accounts contained in the ledger.

_____ **B.** The left side of an account when the account is in T account format.

_____ **C.** The act of recording transactions in a journal.

_____ **D.** A collection of a complete set of accounts. In a manual system each account is on a separate page.

_____ **E.** A business record prepared for most transactions that provides evidence that a transaction occurred.

_____ **F.** A sequence of accounting procedures completed each fiscal year.

_____ **G.** Statements prepared between the end of two annual periods.

_____ **H.** A journal entry that affects more than two accounts.

_____ **I.** The side of an individual account on which increases are recorded.

_____ **J.** A journal containing two columns for entering dollar amounts. Sometimes called a two-column journal.

_____ **K.** A system of accounting in which every recorded transaction affects at least two accounts.

_____ **L.** The process of transferring amounts entered in a journal to the appropriate ledger accounts.

_____ **M.** A statement prepared to verify that the sum of the accounts with debit balances is equal to the sum of the accounts with credit balances.

_____ **N.** An accounting system whereby revenues are recognized when earned and expenses are recognized when assets are used.

Required:
Match each term or concept with the definition by placing the number of the term or concept in the blank before the corresponding definition.

Exercise 3-8   Types of Accounts Affected by Transactions

A series of transactions entered into by a firm that provides accounting services are given below.

	Debit	Credit
1. Received cash and issued capital stock to stockholders.	Asset	Owners' Equity
2. Purchased equipment and signed a note for the purchase price.		
3. Paid salaries to employees for work performed last week.		
4. Billed customers for services performed.		
5. Received cash from customers in payment on their account receivable.		
6. Purchased office supplies on account.		
7. Used office supplies to perform services for customers.		
8. Declared and paid cash dividends to stockholders.		
9. Paid for a three-year insurance policy.		

Required:
For each transaction given, indicate what types of accounts (asset, liability, owners' equity, revenue, or expense) would be debited and credited. The first transaction is analyzed for you as an example.

Exercise 3-9   Fill in the Blank

A list of incomplete statements is given below.

1. Dividing the economic life of a firm into time periods of equal length for financial reporting purposes is called the _____ _____ assumption.
2. A firm whose annual period ends on December 31, is called a _____ year firm.
3. A _____ _____ is prepared to provide written evidence that a transaction has occurred.
4. An entry on the left side of an account is called a _____ .
5. The right side of the account is called the _____ side.
6. When an asset account is _____ , its balance is reduced.
7. Credit entries increase the _____ accounts, the _____ _____ accounts, and the _____ accounts.
8. A transaction which increases an account payable will require a _____ to that account.
9. The normal balance of an asset account is a _____ .
10. Transactions are initially recorded in a book called the general _____ .
11. The process of transferring debits and credits from the general journal to the general ledger is called _____ .

Required:
Complete the statements by entering a word in the blank space that will make the statement a valid statement.

Exercise 3-10 Transaction Analysis

During the first year of operations, Always Balance Accounting Service entered into the following transactions.

1. Received cash from the issue of capital stock.
2. Purchased office supplies on account.
3. Purchased office equipment for cash.
4. Billed clients for services performed.
5. Paid rent on the office for the first month of operations.
6. Borrowed money from a bank and signed a note payable.
7. Paid salaries earned during the first month of operations.
8. Received cash due from customers billed in (4) above.
9. Paid the amount due for supplies purchased in (2) above.
10. Paid a cash dividend to the stockholders.
11. Purchased a 2-year fire insurance policy on the office equipment.
12. Collected cash from clients for services performed. The customers had not been previously billed.

The possible effects of a transaction on the accounts are listed below.

a. Debit an asset.   f. Credit owners' equity.
b. Credit an asset.   g. Debit revenue.
c. Debit a liability.   h. Credit revenue.
d. Credit a liability.   i. Debit expense.
e. Debit owners' equity.   j. Credit expense.

Required:

For each transaction, indicate the types of accounts to be debited and credited. The first transaction is done for you as an example.

	Debit	Credit
1. Received cash from the issue of stocks.	a	f

Exercise 3-11 Transaction Analysis

The following transactions were entered into by Frost Company.

1. Purchased supplies on account.
2. Issued shares of stock to stockholders in exchange for cash.
3. Performed services for customers and received cash.
4. Billed customer for a service performed.
5. Purchased land for cash and a note payable.
6. Paid cash to a creditor.
7. Paid a cash dividend to the stockholders.
8. Purchased a 36-month insurance policy for cash.
9. Received and paid an advertising bill for an ad that appeared in last week's newspaper.
10. Received payment on an account receivable.

Required:

Analyze each transaction using the form shown below. Indicate the type of account to be debited first.

Example:

Paid the rent for the current month.

Increase an expense (debit), decrease an asset (credit).

Exercise 3-12   Recording Transactions in General Journal

A number of transactions entered into by Garrett Physical Therapists are listed here.

1. Cash in the amount of $3,000 was received for capital stock to be issued to stockholders.
2. A new employee was hired at an annual salary of $24,000.
3. The company performed services and billed the customers $600.
4. Garrett purchased office equipment for $11,200. The company paid $4,400 in cash and signed a note payable for the balance.
5. Garrett signed an agreement with a football team to deliver a seminar next month for a fee of $500 to be paid after completion of the seminar.
6. Garrett purchased office supplies on account in the amount of $450.
7. The company paid $500 for the current year's property taxes.
8. Dividends in the amount of $2,000 were paid to stockholders.
9. Garrett paid $150 for newspaper advertising that appeared in the paper yesterday.
10. Received $200 from clients billed in (3) above.
11. Paid $450 to creditors for supplies purchased on account in (6) above.
12. Received a bill for $250 from a janitorial service. The bill will be paid next month.

Required:

Prepare the general journal entries that are needed to record the transactions.

Exercise 3-13   Recording Transactions in the General Journal

Campbell Company began operations on March 1, 1992. Following are the transactions for the first two weeks of operations.

March	2	Stockholders invested $50,000 in the business and received shares of capital stock.
	3	Paid rent of $1,200 for the month of March.
	3	Purchased office supplies for $540 on account.
	3	Purchased office equipment for $8,500. Paid $3,500 in cash and signed a note payable for the balance.
	6	Billed customers $4,800 for the first week's services performed on account.
	10	Performed services for $560 cash.
	12	Paid a bill for the first week's advertising in the amount of $1,850.
	13	Paid $340 of the amount due on the office supplies purchased on March 3.
	13	Collected $2,850 of the services billed to customers on March 6.

The chart of accounts for the company was as follows:

Cash	100	Notes Payable	201
Accounts Receivable	101	Capital Stock	300
Office Supplies On Hand	102	Service Revenue	400
Office Equipment	140	Rent Expense	500
Accounts Payable	200	Advertising Expense	501

Required:

Prepare a general journal and record each of the above transactions in the journal.

Exercise 3-14   Posting to T Accounts and Preparing a Trial Balance

Use the data developed in Exercise 3-13.

Required:

A. Prepare T accounts for the accounts listed in Exercise 3-13 and post the journal entries from the general journal to the general ledger. Allow two lines for each ledger account except Cash. Allow five lines for the Cash account. Enter the posting references in the general journal.

B. Prepare a trial balance.

Exercise 3-15 Preparation of a Trial Balance

The ledger account balances for Educational Consulting as of December 31, 1992 are shown below in alphabetical order. Each account contains a normal balance.

Accounts Payable	$ 5,950	Insurance Expense	$ 535
Accounts Receivable	1,700	Land	54,000
Building	123,250	Mortgage Note Payable	62,500
Capital Stock	122,400	Prepaid Insurance	400
Cash	76,500	Retained Earnings	34,000
Computer Instruction Revenue	18,700	Salary Expense	76,500
Consulting Fees Revenue	157,250	Unearned Consulting Fees	2,635
Equipment	21,250	Utilities Expense	49,300

Required:

Prepare a trial balance for Educational Consulting. The accounts should be listed in the sequence in which they would appear in the ledger.

Exercise 3-16 Effect of Errors on Trial Balance

Below are listed seven errors which occurred during the accounting period on the books of a business enterprise. The errors affect the accounting records in various ways.

1. A $275 credit to Service Revenue was posted as a $257 credit.
2. Receipt of a payment on account from a customer was recorded as a debit to Cash for $135 and a credit to Accounts Payable for $135.
3. A purchase of supplies on account for $674 was recorded as a debit to Supplies on Hand for $764 and a credit to Accounts Payable for $674.
4. A $450 credit to Accounts Receivable was not posted.
5. A $2,000 dividend payment was debited to the Capital Stock account and credited to Cash.
6. A $540 debit to Rent Expense was posted as a credit.
7. A payment of $980 for prepaid insurance was debited to Rent Expense and credited to the Cash account in the general journal.

Required:

A. For each of the errors listed above:
   1. Indicate if the error would cause the trial balance to have unequal totals.
   2. Determine the amount by which the trial balance totals would differ.
   3. Determine if the error would cause the debit total or the credit total to be larger.

B. Describe how each error should be corrected. Prepare the correcting journal entry where appropriate.

Example:

A $650 debit to accounts payable was posted as a $605 debit.

Example Solution:

A. **1.** The trial balance totals would be unequal.

2. The difference would be $45.

3. The credit total would be larger.

B. The incorrect posting of $605 would be crossed out and the correct amount of $650 inserted above it. The Accounts Payable ledger account balance would be decreased by $45 to reflect the correct balance. No journal entry is needed because the error occurred in the posting process.

PROBLEMS

Problem 3-1   Recording Transactions and Preparing Financial Statements

Account balances for Lincoln Company on June 1 are given below in accounting equation form similar to a chapter illustration.

	Assets				= Liabilities +	Owners' Equity	
		Accounts	Office		Accounts	Capital	Retained
	Cash +	Receivable +	Supplies +	Equipment =	Payable +	Stock +	Earnings
Bal.	34,000 +	18,600 +	1,800 +	42,000 =	14,200 +	80,000 +	2,200

During June, Lincoln Company entered into the following transactions.

1. Collected $12,400 of accounts receivable.

2. Paid $8,900 on accounts payable.

3. Billed customers for services performed in the amount of $13,500.

4. Purchased equipment for $8,000 cash.

5. Paid expenses in cash. (Employee salaries, $5,860; utilities, $1,550; advertising, $900).

6. Purchased office supplies on account, $480.

7. Used supplies in the amount of $740 during the period.

8. Paid a cash dividend of $2,800.

9. Depreciation on the equipment for June is estimated to be $700.

Required:

A. Prepare a schedule with a column for each account as shown above. Enter the June 1 balance for each asset, liability, and owners' equity account in the schedule.

B. Record the effects of each transaction. Show the total of each column after recording each transaction.

C. Prepare an income statement and retained earnings statement for June, and a balance sheet as of June 30 for Lincoln Company.

Problem 3-2   Recording Transactions and Preparing Financial Statements

Account balances for English Company on June 30 are given below in accounting equation form similar to a chapter illustration.

	Assets				=	Liabilities		+	Owners' Equity	
		Accounts	Office			Accounts	Notes		Capital	Retained
	Cash +	Receivable +	Supplies +	Equipment =		Payable +	Payable +		Stock +	Earnings
Bal.	24,000 +	16,000 +	1,450 +	35,000 =		9,500 +	15,000 +		50,000 +	1,950

During July, English Company entered into the following transactions.

1. Collected $12,500 of accounts receivable.
2. Paid $4,000 on accounts payable.
3. Billed customers for services performed in the amount of $11,400.
4. Purchased equipment for $8,000. Paid $2,000 in cash and signed a note payable for the balance.
5. Paid expenses of $7,800 in cash (advertising, $800; rent, $3,000; employees' wages, $4,000).
6. Paid $3,000 on notes payable.
7. Used office supplies in the amount of $890 during the month.
8. Collected $9,200 of accounts receivable.
9. Paid a $600 cash dividend to the stockholders.
10. Depreciation on the equipment for July is computed to be $1,000.
11. On July 31, paid interest for July in the amount of $225.

Required:

A. Prepare a schedule with a column for numbering the transactions, a column for each account listed above, and a column for identifying the capital transactions. Enter the June 30 balance for each asset, liability, and owners' equity account in the schedule.
B. Record the effects of each transaction. Show the total of each column after recording each transaction.
C. Prepare an income statement and retained earnings statement for the month of July, and a balance sheet as of July 31 for English Company.

Problem 3-3   Identification of Type of Account and Normal Balance

Listed here are the ledger accounts of Jones Real Estate.

1. Cash.
2. Equipment.
3. Notes Payable.
4. Commissions Revenue.
5. Depreciation Expense.
6. Building.
7. Mortgage Notes Payable.
8. Capital Stock.
9. Accounts Payable.
10. Sales Tax Payable.
11. Supplies On Hand.
12. Insurance Expense.
13. Notes Receivable.
14. Deposits with Utility Company.
15. Service Fee Revenue.
16. Rent Receivable.
17. Salaries Payable.
18. Prepaid Rent.
19. Advertising Expense.
20. Maintenance Equipment.
21. Unearned Commissions Revenue.
22. Retained Earnings.
23. Salaries Expense.
24. Rent Expense.
25. Accounts Receivable.
26. Rent Revenue.

Required:

For each account listed:

1. Identify the account as either an asset, liability, stockholders' equity, revenue, or expense.
2. Indicate on which side of a T account increases are recorded.
3. Indicate which side of a T account is the normal balance.

The first account is completed for you in the suggested solution format.

Account	Type of Account	Increases	Normal Balance
1. Cash (List remaining accounts.)	Asset	Debit	Debit

Problem 3-4 Journal Entries—Debit and Credit Analysis

Listed below are a series of transactions for Vetter Janitorial Services, Inc., which has been operating for two years. Preceding the transactions are a list of the accounts used by Vetter. For each of the transactions that are coded by a letter, indicate the account(s) to be debited and credited by entering the appropriate account number(s) to the right of the transaction in the proper column.

1. Cash
2. Accounts Receivable
3. Office Supplies On Hand
4. Cleaning Supplies On Hand
5. Prepaid Insurance
6. Office Equipment
7. Accumulated Depreciation, Office Equipment
8. Cleaning Equipment
9. Accumulated Depreciation, Cleaning Equipment
10. Trucks
11. Accumulated Depreciation, Trucks
12. Accounts Payable
13. Notes Payable
14. Wages Payable

15. Income Taxes Payable _(LIAB)_
16. Capital Stock
17. Retained Earnings
18. Dividends Declared
19. Cleaning Service Revenue
20. Salaries Expense
21. Interest Expense
22. Gas and Oil Expense
23. Repair and Maintenance Expense
24. Rent Expense
25. Cleaning Expense Uniforms
26. Utilities Expense
27. Income Tax Expense
28. Property Tax Expense
29. Miscellaneous Expense

ASSETS (brace for 1–11)
LIAB (brace for 12–14)

Transactions:

Transaction	Debit	Credit
Example:—Issued capital stock for cash	1	16
a. Performed services this period on credit.	2	19
b. Paid salaries for previous two-week period.	20	1
c. Collected cash for services performed last period (i.e., billed last period).	1	2
d. Purchased cleaning equipment. Paid part cash and gave a note payable for the balance.	8	1 13
e. Paid part of an account payable.	12	1
f. Purchased office supplies on credit.	3	12
g. Paid the local cleaners for cleaning work done on employees' uniforms. The transaction was not previously recorded.	25	1
h. Received and paid the monthly gas bill for the trucks.	22	1
i. Performed services this period for cash.	1	19
j. Declared and paid a cash dividend.	18	1
k. Collected cash for services performed this period that were previously recorded.	1	2
l. Paid monthly rent on office space.	24	1
m. Received and paid property tax assessment on equipment and trucks.	28	1

exp act onets, exp, rec
LIAB. CAP, SALES

DEBIT   CREDIT

n. Made a payment on the equipment note from transaction (d) above; the payment was part principal and part interest.

13 21   1 ✓

o. On the last day of the period, paid cash for a two-year insurance policy.

5   1 ✓

p. Recorded income taxes for the period. None of the taxes were paid. They will be paid during the next period.

27   15 ✓

Problem 3-5 Journal Entries, Entering Beginning Account Balances, Posting to T Accounts, and Preparing a Trial Balance

The November 30, 1992 trial balance of Pawnee County Medical Center is shown below.

PAWNEE COUNTY MEDICAL CENTER
Trial Balance
November 30, 1992

Account Title	Account Number	Debit	Credit
Cash	100	$ 5,260	
Accounts Receivable	110	44,200	
Allowance for Bad Debts	120		$ 1,640
Office Supplies on Hand	130	790	
Medical Supplies on Hand	140	53,460	
Prepaid Insurance	150	8,300	
Office Furniture and Equipment	160	35,900	
Accumulated Depreciation—Office Furniture and Equipment	165		17,950
Medical Equipment	170	268,000	
Accumulated Depreciation—Medical Equipment	175		49,300
Accounts Payable	200		26,400
Utilities Payable	210		4,600
Insurance Refunds Due Patients	220		3,830
Notes Payable	230		45,000
Capital Stock	300		100,000
Retained Earnings	310		97,190
Medical Service Revenues	400		313,940
Salaries Expense	500	210,540	
Utilities Expense	510	33,400	
Totals		$659,850	$659,850

The following transactions occurred during December.

December   3 Collected $11,000 of accounts receivable.
           4 Paid November utilities of $4,600 previously recorded (see trial balance).
           7 Performed medical services for $17,000 cash.

9 Purchased medical supplies on credit for $6,000.
11 Paid $3,000 of accounts payable.
15 Paid employee salaries of $15,000.
18 Collected $14,000 of accounts receivable.
22 Purchased new office furniture at a total cost of $6,000. Paid
$1,000 cash; signed a 60-day 12% note for the remainder.
31 Billed patients for December services of $26,000.
31 Recorded utilities due but unpaid of $1,300.
31 Paid employee salaries of $14,000.

Required:
A. Prepare journal entries to record each transaction.
B. **1.** Open T accounts for the accounts shown in the November 30 trial balance.
  2. Enter the November 30 balance in each account.
  3. Post the December journal entries to the T accounts.
C. Prepare a trial balance at December 31, 1992.

Problem 3-6 Recording Transactions, Posting to T Accounts, and Preparing a Trial Balance

H.T. Painters, Inc. began operations May, 1992. The following transactions were entered into during May, the first month of operations:

May 1 Issued capital stock for $7,000.
  4 Paid one month's office rent of $450.
  5 Purchased painting equipment for $4,500 on account.
  11 Purchased paint on account for $1,700.
  12 Gave electric company a $100 check as a service deposit. A service
deposit is refundable when the service is terminated if all payments
are made to the utility company.
  13 Purchased a pickup for use in the business for $9,000. Paid $1,000
down; financed the remainder over 36 months at 14.5% interest.
  15 Received $3,000 for painting work completed during the first half of
the month.
  15 Billed customers $1,600 for painting work completed during the first
half of the month.
  18 Paid $2,500 to creditors for painting equipment purchased on
May 5.
  27 Made a cash payment on account in the amount of $1,200 for paint
purchased previously.
  28 Paid May utility bills of $400.
  29 Received $1,200 from customers in payment on account.
  29 Painting revenues were $2,300 for cash and $300 on account for
painting services performed during the last half of the month.
  29 Paid salaries for the month in the amount of $4,000.

Use the following account titles and numbers:

100 Cash	220 Notes Payable
101 Accounts Receivable	300 Capital Stock
106 Paint Supplies on Hand	310 Retained Earnings
110 Equipment	400 Painting Revenues
111 Trucks	501 Salary Expense
130 Utility Deposits	502 Utility Expense
200 Accounts Payable	505 Rent Expense—Office

Required:

A. Prepare a general journal and record each of the above transactions in the journal.

B. Prepare T accounts for the accounts listed above and post the journal entries to the T accounts. Allow 10 lines for Cash. All other T accounts need only three lines.

C. Prepare a trial balance as of May 31.

Problem 3-7 Journal Entries, Posting to a Three-column Ledger, and Preparation of Trial Balance for Two Consecutive Months

Fairlawn Bowling began business on October 1, 1992, and entered into the following transactions during October.

October	1	Sold capital stock at par for $40,000.
	1	Paid October rent of $1,800.
	1	Paid $600 for a 12-month insurance policy with an effective starting date of October 1.
	5	Purchased bowling equipment for $10,000 in cash and a $31,000 long-term note payable.
	7	Purchased supplies on account for $500.
	16	Paid salaries to employees in the amount of $600.
	30	Recorded cash revenues for October of $4,400.
	30	Paid $310 for advertising expense for the month of October.

Following is the chart of accounts for Fairlawn Bowling.

100 Cash
101 Supplies on Hand
102 Prepaid Insurance
150 Bowling Equipment
200 Accounts Payable
220 Long-term Notes Payable

300 Capital Stock
301 Retained Earnings
302 Dividends Declared
400 Bowling Revenues
500 Rent Expense
501 Salaries Expense
502 Advertising Expense

Required:

A. Prepare general journal entries to record the October transactions.

B. Post the journal entries to a three-column ledger. Use posting reference numbers.

C. Prepare a trial balance as of October 31, 1992.

The following transactions were completed during November.

November	2	Paid employees' salaries of $900.
	2	Paid November rent of $1,800.
	2	Paid $250 on account for supplies previously purchased on credit.
	9	Purchased supplies for cash in the amount of $500.
	16	Paid employees' salaries of $1,050.
	16	Recorded cash revenues for the first half of November in the amount of $1,910.
	20	Paid $360 for newspaper advertisements that appeared last week.
	23	Paid a $450 cash dividend to stockholders.
	30	Cash revenues for the second half of November were $2,550.

Required:

D. Prepare general journal entries to record the November transactions.

E. Post the journal entries to the general ledger.

F. Prepare a trial balance as of November 30, 1992.

Problem 3-8 Journalizing, Posting, and Preparation of a Trial Balance

Donna Lott recently opened the Lott Advertising Agency. A trial balance as of March 31, 1992 is shown below:

LOTT ADVERTISING AGENCY
Trial Balance
March 31, 1992

Account Title	Account No.	Debit	Credit
Cash	100	$ 3,640	
Accounts Receivable	110	3,230	
Allowance for Bad Debts	120		$ 360
Office Supplies on Hand	130	420	
Prepaid Insurance	140	180	
Equipment	150	20,000	
Accumulated Depreciation—Equipment	155		750
Accounts Payable	200		2,610
Notes Payable (due June 15, 1994)	210		8,000
Capital Stock (1,000 shares)	300		15,000
Retained Earnings	310		–0–
Dividends Declared	320	–0–	
Professional Fees Revenue	400		12,680
Wage Expense	500	9,390	
Rent Expense	510	2,000	
Office Supplies Expense	520	80	
Cleaning Expense	530	460	
Totals		$39,400	$39,400

The following transactions occurred during April:

April 2 Paid April rent of $500.
  3 Received $1,500 from clients as payments on account.
  6 Purchased supplies for cash in the amount of $300.
  8 Billed clients $5,000 for work completed during the week.
  10 Paid wages of $1,000.
  17 Received $2,000 from clients as payments on account.
  20 Paid janitorial service $110 for cleaning the office.
  24 Paid creditors $800.
  27 Purchased a microcomputer for $2,000 on account.
  30 Paid $120 for a three-month insurance policy.

Required:
A. Prepare journal entries to record the April transactions.
B. 1. Open T accounts for the accounts shown in the March 31 trial balance.
  2. Enter the March 31 balance in each account.
  3. Post the April journal entries to the T accounts.
C. Prepare a trial balance at April 30.

Problem 3-9 Preparation of a Corrected Trial Balance

The accountant for Young Corporation prepared the following trial balance.

YOUNG CORPORATION
Trial Balance
June 30, 1992

Account Title	Debit	Credit
Cash	$16,340	
Accounts Receivable	5,030	
Office Supplies on Hand	140	
Equipment	17,400	
Accumulated Depreciation—Equipment		$ 1,000
Accounts Payable		5,220
Salaries Payable	3,240	
Capital Stock		12,000
Retained Earnings		2,400
Dividends Declared	1,500	
Service Revenues		37,400
Salaries Expense	10,200	
Rent Expense	6,400	
Utilities Expense	4,600	
Totals	$64,850	$58,020

An examination of the general journal and the general ledger revealed the following information:

1. An entry that contained a debit to Accounts Payable and a credit to Cash for $800 was not posted to either account.
2. A cash receipt for $540 was posted to the Cash account as a $450 debit.
3. A purchase of office supplies for $480 in cash was erroneously recorded as a purchase on account.
4. The debits and credits to Accounts Receivable totaled $19,100 and $13,800 respectively.
5. A $1,580 payment for salaries was not posted to the Cash account.
6. The Taxes Expense account with a debit balance of $780 was left out of the trial balance.
7. In totaling the Accounts Payable account the credits were overstated by $90.

Required:
Using the information given above, prepare a corrected trial balance.

Problem 3-10 **Correction of Errors**
Upon accepting a job as an accountant, your first assignment was to determine why the December 31, 1992 trial balance did not balance. In reviewing the accounting records, you discovered the errors listed below:

1. A $2,354 debit to Cash was posted as $2,534.
2. A rent payment for $42,000 was posted twice to the Rent Expense account. The credit to Cash was posted correctly.
3. A $3,450 credit to be made to the Sales account was credited to the Accounts Receivable account instead.

4. A cash collection of $2,800 from customers in partial settlement of their accounts was posted twice to both the Cash account and the Accounts Receivable account.
5. The Accounts Receivable account balance for $36,894 was listed in the trial balance as $36,849.
6. A $4,200 debit to Accounts Receivable was posted as a credit.
7. A truck purchased for $14,500 and paid for in cash was posted as a debit to the Cash account and a credit to the Equipment account.
8. A purchase of supplies for $489 on account was recorded as a debit to Supplies on Hand for $489 and a credit to Accounts Payable for $498.
9. A $2,000 payment to the newspaper for advertising was posted twice to the expense account. The credit to the Cash account was posted only once.
10. The Prepaid Insurance account with a balance of $2,450 was omitted from the trial balance.
11. A $250 credit to Service Revenue was not posted.
12. A purchase of insurance for $1,300 was posted as a debit to the Cash account and as a debit to the Prepaid Insurance account.
13. A sale of capital stock for $25,000 was posted correctly to the Cash account, but was not posted to the Capital Stock account.
14. The Unearned Rent account with a balance of $460 was listed as a debit balance in the trial balance.

Required:

A. Use the solution format shown below to indicate how each error would effect the trial balance totals. If the error does not cause the trial balance to be out of balance, place a ✓ in the third column (No) and write "none" in the Difference Between Trial Balance Totals column. Each error is to be considered independently of the others. The first error is analyzed for you as an example.

SOLUTION FORMAT

Error	Would the Error Cause the Trial Balance to be Out of Balance		Difference Between Trial Balance Totals	Column Having Largest Total	
	Yes	No		Debit	Credit
1.	✓		$180	✓	
2. through 14.					

B. Prepare journal entries, if needed, to correct the first five errors.

Problem 3-11 Comprehensive Review Problem

On January 1, 1992, Curtis Archer began a new business that was incorporated under the name Archer Enterprises, Inc. The fiscal year of the corporation is January 1 through December 31. The company was formed to provide TV and radio repair services. Following are the first year's transactions in summary form.

1. On January 1, Curtis Archer invested $30,000 in the business and received 3,000 shares $10 par value capital stock as evidence of ownership.
2. A van was purchased for the business on January 1, and paid for in cash at a cost of $15,000.

3. On January 1, various tools and equipment were purchased for cash at a cost of $4,000.

4. Rent on the building used by the business in the amount of $7,200 was paid on January 1. The payment covers the period January 1, 1992 through December 31, 1993.

5. During the first three months of the year, repair supplies costing $23,500 were purchased on account.

6. On January 1, insurance policies costing $2,400 were purchased. The policies cover the period January 1, 1992 through December 31, 1993.

7. Repair revenues for the year totaled $94,000, of which $16,000 was on credit.

8. Paid $13,500 on account for repair supplies purchased on credit in item (5).

9. The following expenses were incurred and paid in cash: Salaries $45,500, Auto $3,500, Advertising $4,500, and Utilities $2,500.

10. Received $10,500 from clients as payment on their accounts for services provided (7).

11. On November 1, the company received $1,800 from Desert Sam Hospital. The payment was for a six-month service contract on the hospital's television sets. The contract period is from November 1, 1992 to May 1, 1993.

12. Cash dividends in the amount of $1,700 were declared and paid to stockholders.

The chart of accounts for Archer Enterprises is given below:

Account Number	Account Title	Account Number	Account Title
	Assets		**Stockholders' Equity**
100	Cash	300	Capital Stock
104	Accounts Receivable	310	Retained Earnings
111	Repair Supplies On Hand	320	Dividends Declared
120	Prepaid Insurance		**Revenues**
121	Prepaid Rent	400	Repair Revenues
153	Vans		**Expenses**
154	Accumulated Depreciation—Vans	500	Salaries Expense
		502	Auto Expense
155	Tools and Equipment	503	Advertising Expense
156	Accumulated Depreciation—Tools and Equipment	504	Utilities Expense
		506	Rent Expense
	Liabilities	507	Insurance Expense
200	Accounts Payable	509	Repair Supplies Expense
201	Operating Expenses Payable	511	Income Tax Expense
206	Income Taxes Payable	554	Depreciation Expense—Vans
207	Unearned Repair Revenues	556	Depreciation Expense—Tools and Equipment

Required:

A. Prepare a T account for each account listed in the chart of accounts.

B. Prepare general journal entries to record transactions (1) through (12).

C. Post the journal entries to the T accounts.

D. Prepare a trial balance as of December 31, 1992.

Problem 3-12 Revenue and Expense Recognition Principles— An Introduction to Chapter 4

Dan Alden, Connie Batch, Edna Chadwick, and Sandy Day formed a corporation to provide personal financial planning. Each investor invested $10,000 in the business and the company began business on January 2, 1992. The company adopted the accrual method of accounting and a December 31 year-end. A select number of transactions are described below.

Part A. Revenue Principle

During December of 1992, the company billed clients $18,000 for services performed during the month. Of this amount, $12,000 was received in cash. The balance of $6,000 was received in January 1993.

Required:

A. Explain the revenue principle.
B. Based on the information given for December, how much revenue should be reported in December? in January?
C. What type of account is debited when revenue is recorded? What type of account is credited? Prepare the journal entry to record the services performed in December.
D. Prepare the entry to record the receipt of cash from clients in January.

Part B. Expense Recognition

On December 4, the company purchased office supplies for use in the business. The supplies were purchased on credit for $1,200 and were paid for on January 31, 1993. A physical count of the inventory on December 31 showed that supplies costing $350 were still on hand.

Required:

A. Describe the expense recognition principle.
B. Applying the expense recognition principle when should the office supplies be expensed? How much expense should be reported in 1992?
C. Prepare the journal entries needed to account for the supplies during 1992 and 1993.
D. How much will be reported as an asset in the balance sheet prepared on December 31, 1992?

CASE 3-1 Accrual Basis of Accounting and the Effect of Transactions on the Accounting Equation

Tina Flake and Ty Brown formed the Double T Advertising Agency as a corporation. Each organizer invested $20,000 in the business and each received 10,000 shares of capital stock. All arrangements were made and the two began business on January 2, 1992. The following summarized transactions were completed during 1992.

1. Issued 20,000 shares of capital stock for $40,000 cash.
2. Purchased equipment that cost $20,000; paid $10,000 cash and issued a note that matures in five years for the balance.
3. Revenue of $50,000 was earned of which $30,000 was received in cash.
4. Incurred expenses of $42,000 of which $20,000 were paid for in cash.
5. Received $12,000 from clients for services performed on account in item (3).
6. Declared and paid a cash dividend of $1,000 to each stockholder.
7. Paid $18,000 of the accounts payable recorded in item (4).
8. Depreciation on the equipment for the year is estimated to be $2,000.

Required:

A. Prepare a schedule similar to that on page 74. Include a separate column for each of the following accounts.

Cash	Accounts Payable
Accounts Receivable	Note Payable
Equipment	Stockholders' Equity

Show the effects of each of the transactions on the accounts listed. Indicate totals for each account after each transaction.

B. For each transaction, the sum of accounts debited must be equal to the sum of the accounts credited. Also, the accounting equation must balance after every transaction. Verify that the accounting equation is in balance after the last transaction is recorded. Explain why these checks have been provided for in an accounting system.

C. Explain how transactions (3) and (5) affect total revenues.

D. Compute the total expenses for the year and compute the amount of net income for the year.

E. Assuming a $40,000 beginning balance in stockholders' equity, compute the change in stockholders' equity for the year. Explain why your answer is the same as or different from your net income answer to requirement D.

F. Assuming a $40,000 beginning balance in the Cash account, compute the change in the Cash account. Explain why your answer is the same as or different from your net income answer to requirement D.

G. Explain how cash dividends paid to stockholders should be reported in the financial statements.

MEASURING NET INCOME AND PREPARING ADJUSTING ENTRIES

CHAPTER OVERVIEW AND OBJECTIVES

This chapter describes the preparation of adjusting entries and the effect of year-end adjustments on financial statements. The adjusting process, Step 6 in the accounting data processing cycle, is completed at the end of the period. When you have completed the chapter, you should understand:

1. The accrual basis of accounting.
2. The need for adjusting entries.
3. How to classify adjusting entries into the two broad categories of deferrals and accruals.
4. How to prepare entries to adjust for prepaid expenses.
5. How to prepare entries to adjust unearned revenues.
6. How to prepare entries to adjust for accrued expenses.
7. How to prepare entries to adjust for accrued revenues.
8. The preparation of an adjusted trial balance.

Chapter 3 covered the four steps in the accounting cycle carried out during an accounting period. During the period, journal entries are made to record the effects of business transactions on a firm's financial statements at the time the transactions occur (external transactions). Many transactions recorded during a period affect the current period's financial statements as well as those prepared in future periods. For example, the cost of a 24-month insurance policy purchased in the current period should be allocated as an expense to all accounting periods receiving the protection. At the end of each period, the account balances may need to be updated for changes that have occurred since the initial entry. There are other events that affect the firm, such as the increase in interest revenue earned on a bank savings account, which are often unrecorded at the end of the current period.

As part of the accounting cycle completed at the end of the accounting period, the accounts and source documents are analyzed, and entries, called *adjusting entries* are made to adjust the accounts. Failure to make the adjusting entries will result in misstatement of both income statement and balance sheet accounts. The other steps in the accounting cycle completed at the end of the period are discussed in the next chapter. As we shall see, accountants often use a special form, called a *worksheet*, to accumulate the information needed to complete the accounting cycle at the end of the period.

This chapter begins with a discussion of the concept of measuring net income. To comprehend the income statement and adjusting entries, the concept of *accrual basis net income*, as it is measured by accountants, must be understood. Although all revenues and expenses eventually involve cash receipts and cash payments, the timing of cash receipts and sales and cash payments and expenses are often different. For example, a firm may pay for equipment before it is used in the business to produce revenue and, therefore, eventually be expensed. Next, the need for making adjusting entries is related to the use of the accrual basis of accounting. The account balances developed in the last chapter for the Quality Real Estate Office, Inc. are used as a basis for illustrating the analysis and preparation of both adjusting entries and the adjusted trial balance.

MEASURING NET INCOME

A major objective of a business is to earn a profit (called net income). As discussed in Chapter 2, in order to provide timely information to statement users, the operating life of a business is divided into relatively short intervals of equal length called accounting periods. One important accounting function is measuring the net income earned or the net loss incurred during an accounting period. The amount of net income or loss is the difference between revenues and expenses. Revenues and expenses may be measured either on a cash basis or an accrual basis.

CASH BASIS METHOD OF MEASURING NET INCOME

Under the cash basis of accounting, revenues are recorded in the period in which cash is received and expenses are recorded in the period in which cash is paid. On a strict cash basis, net income is the excess of cash inflow from revenues over cash outflow for expenses. This method does not recognize revenue from the sale of goods or the performance of a service on credit until the receivable is collected. In addition, the costs of goods and services used to produce revenue during the current period are recognized as expenses during the period in which they are paid. The payment could have been made in the current period, but may have been made in a previous period or may be made in a future period. Thus, the cash basis method of measuring net income does not properly match the efforts of the firm to produce revenue with the revenues earned.

Although the cash basis approach is used by small businesses and professional people who conduct most of their activities in cash, *it is not generally accepted for use by businesses that conduct a significant portion of their business on credit* or hold a significant amount of inventory (goods bought for resale). The cash basis system is simple to operate and, when transactions are primarily in cash, produces essentially the same results as those produced by accrual accounting.

When the cash method is used, it is often modified to use the accrual method to account for costs of inventory and plant and equipment. Thus, under the modified cash method, inventory costs are expensed when the inventory is sold and plant and equipment costs are expensed through depreciation as the asset is used.

ACCRUAL BASIS METHOD OF MEASURING NET INCOME

Under the accrual basis of accounting, revenues are recognized in the period in which they are earned—that is, when goods are sold or services are performed—rather than when cash is received. Expenses are recognized when they are incurred—that is, during the period in which goods are used or services are received—rather than when they are paid for. The accrual basis net income for an accounting period is determined by subtracting expenses incurred during the period from revenues earned during the period, in accordance with the revenue principle. The process of associating expenses with revenues generated during the period is called matching.

Objective 1:
Accrual Basis
of Accounting

Thus, the process of determining periodic net income involves identifying and measuring the revenues earned during a specific accounting period. Next, expenses associated with producing those revenues are identified and measured. As a result, both revenues earned and the cost of assets used up in the process of producing those revenues (i.e., expenses) are reported in the same income statement. In order to fully understand accrual accounting, the important concepts of revenue and expenses must be thoroughly understood.

Accrual Basis Revenues

Revenues are the inflow of assets resulting from the sale of goods or the performance of services. As noted in Chapter 2, revenues for a period are determined by applying the revenue principle. Essentially, the revenue principle asserts that revenue should be recognized under accrual accounting when it is earned, rather than when the actual cash is received. Consequently, it is important to understand what is meant by *earning revenue*.

Some revenue, such as interest revenue and rent revenue, is earned with the passage of time and, therefore, is not difficult to associate with specific time periods. However, revenue such as sales revenue is earned in a continuous process as the operating activities that give rise to revenue take place. For example, the earning process (or earning cycle) for a manufacturing firm involves the acquisition of goods and services, the production of a product, and the sale of the finished product. Each of these steps contributes to the earning process, but it is difficult to objectively determine how much revenue is earned at each step.

Accountants have adopted the revenue principle as a practical guide. Thus, revenue is recognized when (1) the earning process is complete or essentially complete and (2) an exchange has taken place. According to this principle, then, most revenue is recognized when goods are sold (which normally means when they are delivered) or when services are rendered and thus can be billed to the customer. At this point, the earning process is considered essentially completed. The only remaining part of the earning cycle is the collection of the sales price, which is considered relatively assured in today's credit-oriented society. The sales price provides the necessary objective evidence of the amount of revenue to be recognized.

The sales price is normally received in cash or as a customer's promise to pay cash at a set time in the future (an account receivable). Occasionally, however, a firm may receive either property or services in payment. In such cases, the amount of revenue recorded is the fair value of the asset or services received. Thus, for a given accounting period, revenue earned is the sum of cash, accounts receivable, and the fair value of other assets received from customers for the sale of goods or performance of services during that period.

Although most revenue is recognized at the time of sale, two major exceptions are the percentage-of-completion method and the installment sales method.

The Percentage-of-Completion Method.
Businesses often undertake projects that may take two or more years to complete. For example, assume that a company signed a contract to construct a major section of interstate highway, which is expected to take four years to finish. If the basic revenue principle were followed, net income on the project would not be recognized until the end of construction. Such accounting is called the completed contracts method. Under that method, annual income statements would clearly be of little use to investors and other users who must make timely decisions. As a result, a departure from the revenue principle is required for long-term projects when estimates of cost to complete and the extent of progress toward completion are reasonably dependable.[1] Estimates are made of the percentage of the project completed each year and gross profit is recognized in proportion to the work completed. This approach is called the percentage-of-completion method of accounting for long-term contracts. This method works as follows.

1. An estimate is made of the total cost expected to be incurred on the project. The difference between the contract price and the total estimated cost is the company's estimated gross profit.
2. At the end of each year, the percentage of the project completed during the year is estimated. This may be done by comparing the actual project costs incurred during the year to the most recent estimate of the total cost of the project, or an estimate may be made by engineers or other qualified personnel.
3. The estimated gross profit on the project, as computed in Step 1, is multiplied by the percentage determined in Step 2 to determine the amount of gross profit for the year.
4. In the final year of the project, no estimate is needed, because total costs are known. The difference between the actual gross profit and the cumulative amount of gross profit recognized in prior years constitutes the gross profit for the final year.

Assume that Cress Company signed a contract to construct a section of interstate highway at a price of $20,000,000. The project is expected to take three years to complete at an estimated cost of $14,000,000. Therefore, estimated gross profit on the project is $6,000,000. The actual costs incurred and the amount of gross profit recognized each year are as follows.

[1]"Long-term Construction-type Contracts." *Accounting Research Bulletin No. 45* (New York: AICPA, 1955), par. 15.

Year	Actual Costs Incurred	÷	Estimated Total Costs	=	Percent Completed	×	Estimated Gross Profit	=	Gross Profit for the Year
1	$ 4,900,000	÷	$14,000,000	=	35%	×	$6,000,000	=	$2,100,000
2	5,600,000	÷	14,000,000	=	40%	×	6,000,000	=	2,400,000
3	3,700,000		Balance to complete the contract*						1,300,000
Total	$14,200,000								$5,800,000

*Balance to complete the contract:

Contract price	$20,000,000
Actual costs	14,200,000
Actual gross profit	5,800,000
Gross profit recognized in first two years ($2,100,000 + $2,400,000)	4,500,000
Remaining gross profit	$ 1,300,000

In Year 1, the actual cost incurred represented 35% of the estimated total cost of the project. The percentage-of-completion method assumes that incurring costs represents a valid reflection of progress toward completion of the project. Thus, 35% of the estimated gross profit is recognized in Year 1. Similarly, 40% of the total estimated cost was incurred in Year 2 and, thus, 40% of the estimated gross profit is recognized. In Year 3, gross profit is recognized in an amount equal to the actual total gross profit on the contract, minus the cumulative amount of gross profit recognized in Years 1 and 2.

The percentage-of-completion method is based on estimates and, therefore, introduces an element of subjectivity into the determination of net income. In spite of this, the financial statements are considered more useful than they would be if none of the profit were recognized until the end of the project.

Although the percentage-of-completion method is appropriate in accounting for long-term contracts expected to produce a profit, it is not appropriate if a loss is expected. When it becomes apparent that a loss will occur, the estimated loss must be recognized immediately under the ***conservatism convention***.

The Installment Method.   It is common practice in some businesses to make sales on an installment basis. The purchaser normally makes a down payment and agrees to pay the remainder of the purchase price in equal installments at specified times. The seller often retains title to the property until final payment is received, or instead makes other arrangements to permit the repossession of the property in the event that the purchaser defaults on payment. Even though the sales price is received over an extended period, installment sales ordinarily should be accounted for in the same manner as regular sales on account, and revenue should be recognized at the time of sale.[2] As will be discussed in a later chapter, an appropriate provision should be made for estimated uncollectible accounts. In the relatively rare situations in which collection of the sales price is not reasonably assured, the installment method of accounting may be used.[3]

Under the installment method, gross profit (sales price − cost of item sold) is deferred and recognized when payment is received. Each cash receipt consists of a

[2]Accounting Principles Board, "Omnibus Opinion—1966," *APB Opinion No. 10* (New York: AICPA, 1966), par. 12.

[3]The Internal Revenue Code allows the use of the installment method; it is often used because it permits the deferral of income tax payments until the cash is received.

partial recovery of the cost of the property sold and part of gross profit. For example, if the gross profit rate on an installment sale is 40%, each cash receipt is considered to consist of 40% gross profit and 60% recovery of cost of the property sold.

To illustrate, assume that on July 1, 1992, Franklin Company sold land for $60,000 that had cost $36,000. The gross profit rate is 40% [($60,000 − $36,000)/$60,000]. The purchaser made a down payment of $12,000 and agreed to pay the remaining $48,000 at the rate of $2,000 per month for 24 months, beginning on August 1.[4] The collection of the sales price is not reasonably assured. The amount of gross profit from installment sales recognized in each period, assuming all payments are received when due, is as follows.

Year	Amount Collected	×	Gross Profit Rate	=	Gross Profit
1992	$22,000*	×	40%	=	$ 8,800
1993	24,000	×	40%	=	9,600
1994	14,000	×	40%	=	5,600
Total	$60,000				$24,000

*The $22,000 collected in 1992 consists of the down payment of $12,000 plus five monthly payments of $2,000 each.

Accrual Basis Expenses

Costs are incurred as a necessary part of the revenue-generating process. The portion of the cost that is expected to be used in the production of revenue in the future is reported as an asset and is called an **unexpired cost**. The purchase price (cost) of a delivery truck is an example of an unexpired cost. The cost of the truck is debited to an asset account. The asset account is then reduced when the cost of the asset can be identified or matched with the revenue earned during each period. The amount of the reduction is reported in the income statement as an expense (sometimes called an **expired cost**). Expired costs are deducted from revenue in the determination of net income.

The cost can be diagrammed as follows below, assuming that a firm paid $3,000 for equipment to be used for 10 years.

Asset (Unexpired Cost)	Activity	Expense (Expired Cost)
Cost incurred to acquire economic resources. ($3,000)	Equipment is used during the period to produce revenue.	Associate cost of asset used with revenue earned (matching). ($300)

The firm computed the cost of the asset to be matched against revenues of the current period to be $300. The remaining unexpired cost ($2,700) is a measure of the costs of future economic services. Put another way, the $2,700 is an asset to be utilized in future periods to earn revenue. The $2,700 is expensed in future periods as the asset is used. Thus, assets are the resources owned by the firm, and expenses are the dollar amount of these resources consumed during the period to produce revenue.

---

[4]Installment sales contracts generally provide for interest on the unpaid balance. Although ignored in our illustration, the amount of each payment representing interest is recognized as interest revenue when received.

Matching Expenses Incurred With Revenues Earned

As noted in the preceding paragraph, the cost of assets must be allocated to both current and future periods in order to provide proper matching of expenses incurred with revenues earned. Some costs, such as the cost of a refrigerator sold by an appliance store, can be directly associated with the revenues of a specific accounting period. Other costs cannot be as directly associated with revenues (e.g., officers' salaries). Still other costs can be associated with revenues of more than one accounting period (e.g., the cost of an office building).

Just as the revenue principle was developed to serve as a guide in the timing of revenues, the matching principle was developed to guide the timing of expense recognition. A hierarchy of three basic rules—associating cause and effect, systematic and rational allocation, and immediate recognition—specify the bases for recognizing expenses.

Associating Cause and Effect.   Some expenses, such as the cost of a computer sold by a computer store and the sales commission earned by the salesperson making the sale, are recognized as having a relatively direct cause and effect association with revenues earned. Therefore, these expenses are recorded in the same period in which the revenues associated with them are recognized. For example, the sale of the computer, the cost of the computer, and the sales commission are all recorded in the same period.

Systematic and Rational Allocation.   Many expenses cannot be associated directly with revenue-producing transactions but *can* be associated with specific accounting periods. For example, the cost of purchasing a building should be allocated to each period the building is used. Although there is no direct association between the specific revenues produced and the use of the building, a portion of its cost should be expensed because the building contributed to revenue. Such a cost is allocated to specific accounting periods in a systematic and rational way. Some examples are: depreciation of plant assets and allocation of rent and insurance paid for in advance.

Accounting principles require that the method used to allocate costs to specific accounting periods must be systematic and rational. "Systematic" means that the allocation is based on a prescribed method or formula. "Rational" means that there is some logical relationship between the cost allocated and the benefits received in the current period. For example, a building that is expected to produce equal benefits each year should have an equal amount of its cost expensed each year.

Immediate Recognition.   Some expenses are associated with the current accounting period because

1. They cannot be directly associated with revenue transactions,
2. They have no discernible benefits for future accounting periods, or
3. Their allocation among several accounting periods serves no useful purpose.

According to this rule, costs, such as officers' salaries, advertising expenses, and research and development expenditures, are charged as expenses in the period in which payment is made or liability is incurred. In addition, items carried as assets that are determined to have no discernible benefit for future periods are charged as expenses or losses. One example of such an item is equipment that has become obsolete before the end of its original useful life.

As we shall see throughout the remainder of the book, applying the accrual basis of accounting involves the use of estimates, professional judgment, and assumptions.

For example, allocating the cost of long-term assets (such as a building) must be based on estimates because accountants are simply unable to predict with certainty the length of time a building will be used. However, the need for timely information (the *time period assumption*) takes precedence over the lack of precision. Although the estimates should be as accurate as possible, they are only tentative, and the actual results can be determined only when the firm ends operations. Thus, although the information reported in the financial statements appears to be precise, it can only be considered reasonably accurate. The information is made more meaningful by the explanations presented in the notes immediately following the statements. An effective user of financial statements should be aware of the limits of the statements and understand the basis on which they are prepared.

WHY ADJUSTING ENTRIES ARE NEEDED

Objective 2: Need for adjusting entries

During the accounting period, the accountant records many external transactions relative to the receipt or payment of cash. In some cases, the period in which the cash flow is recorded coincides with the period in which the revenue is earned or the expense is incurred. However, some cash receipts or payments that are recorded in the current period will affect the firm's net income and financial position for two or more accounting periods. For example, a firm that purchases a 36-month insurance policy pays for the policy in advance of receiving the protection. Although the protection expires on a daily basis over several accounting periods, the accountant does not make a series of daily entries to expense the cost of the protection because such a procedure requires too much clerical effort. Although the current account balances are not correct, this is of little concern to the accountant until financial statements are to be prepared. At that time, entries are made to adjust the accounts to their proper balances. For example, an entry is made at the end of the period to expense the cumulative total cost of the protection that has expired during that period. Failure to do so will result in assets being overstated and expenses understated, resulting in net income being overstated.

There are also cases in which revenues and expenses are reported in the current period, even though the cash for them may not be received or paid until the next period. For example, interest on a bank savings account is earned on a daily basis. Cash receipt for the interest earned on the account is received after the interest is earned rather than received in advance. All interest earned between the last accrual and the end of the accounting period should be reported in the current period's financial statements. Again, rather than making a journal entry daily to record the interest earned, one entry will be made at the end of each accounting period to record the accumulation of interest from the last accrual up to the end of the period. As you review the examples that follow, you should note that many adjustments are needed because the firm engaged in activities that occur continuously during the period.

Whatever the situation, it is important to recognize that under the accrual basis of accounting, the recognition of revenues and expenses often does not occur in the same accounting period as the cash flow. At the end of the period, the account balances may not include the proper amount of revenues earned or expenses incurred during the period or an accurate measure of the asset and liability balances on the last day of the accounting period. Thus, account balances must be adjusted to reflect the transactions that are unrecorded as of the last day of the accounting period. These journal entries are called adjusting entries.

The adjusting process involves an analysis of the accounts and supporting source documents to determine whether entries are needed to adjust account balances to their proper amounts for financial reporting purposes. Once this analysis is completed, adjusting entries are recorded in the journal and posted to the accounts.

CLASSIFYING ADJUSTING ENTRIES

Adjusting entries normally are classified into two major categories with two types of adjustments within each category. The two major categories of adjusting entries are deferrals and accruals. A deferral is either (1) the prepayment of an expense or (2) the receipt of revenue in advance of the related earning activities. An accrual is the recognition of either (1) a revenue that has been earned but for which cash has not yet been received or (2) an expense for benefits received before the cash payment is made. Thus, in the case of a deferral, the cash flow precedes the recognition of an expense or a revenue. The payment or receipt of cash necessitates the recording of a deferral. Conversely, in the case of an accrual, the recognition of revenue or of an expense precedes the receipt or payment of cash, and thus the transactions have not been recorded.

Objective 3: Classification of adjusting entries

DEFERRALS (PREPAID OR UNEARNED ITEMS)

Prepaid expenses are the costs of resources acquired by a firm before they are used to produce revenue. Prepaid expenses are assets until they are used or consumed in the earning process. They must be allocated to the periods in which they are used to properly match expenses with revenues. Examples include a payment for rent in advance of occupancy of a building and insurance premiums paid for protection to be received in the future. At the end of the period, an adjusting entry is needed to allocate the cost of the resource between an asset and an expense account.

Unearned revenues are cash receipts for the sale of goods or the performance of services before the goods are produced or the services performed. Advance receipts of revenues are liabilities until they are earned by the firm. Examples include the receipt of cash by a publishing company for a two-year magazine subscription and a rent payment received from a tenant before the occupancy period occurs. At the end of an accounting period, an adjusting entry is needed to allocate the advance receipt between a liability and a revenue account.

ACCRUALS (UNRECORDED ITEMS)

Accrued expenses are expenses that have been incurred during the current period but have not been recorded or paid for by the firm. To properly match expenses with revenues, expenses should be recognized in the period incurred regardless of when the cash payment is made. Examples include unpaid wages earned by the firm's employees and interest expense that has accumulated on an outstanding note payable. Because the goods or services received have not been paid for, an adjusting entry is made at the end of the period to record a liability and an expense.

Accrued revenues are revenues that have been earned for services performed or for goods that have been delivered in advance of collecting the payment from the customers. Under the accrual basis of accounting, revenues should be reported in the period earned, even though the cash has not been received. Examples include sales commissions earned but not yet received and interest revenue accumulated on a note receivable. An adjusting entry is made at the end of the period to record both a receivable from the customer and a revenue item.

The four types of adjusting entries are summarized in Figure 4-1. Note that every

Type of Adjustment	Original Entry		Adjusting Entry		Effect on Accounts
Deferrals:					
Prepaid expense— e.g., rent paid in advance.	Asset Cash	XX XX	Expense Asset For the cost of the asset consumed.	XX XX	Increase expense Decrease asset
Unearned revenue— e.g., rent received from tenant before occupancy.	Cash Liability	XX XX	Liability Revenue For the amount earned.	XX XX	Decrease liability Increase revenue
Accruals:					
Accrued expense— e.g., salaries earned by employees but not paid.	None		Expense Liability For the amount incurred.	XX XX	Increase expense Increase liability
Accrued revenue— e.g., commission earned from selling a product but not received.	None		Asset Revenue For the amount earned.	XX XX	Increase asset Increase revenue

Figure 4-1
Summary of the Types of Adjusting Entries

adjusting entry affects one balance sheet account and one income statement account. Also note that the Cash account is never affected by an adjusting entry.

ADJUSTING ENTRIES ILLUSTRATED

To demonstrate each of these four types of adjusting entries, the illustration of the Quality Real Estate Office, Inc. will be continued from the previous chapter. Adjusting entries are illustrated first, assuming that deferrals are initially recorded in an asset or a liability account. An alternative approach is to record deferrals in income statement accounts. The latter approach is discussed in an appendix to Chapter 5.

In determining whether an adjusting entry is needed, the accountant must examine the appropriate source documents (for example, an insurance policy or the billing from the insurance company to verify the cost of the policy and its term). The account balances listed in a trial balance are reviewed to compute the amount of the adjustment needed.

The trial balance prepared on June 30 (Figure 3-11) for the Quality Real Estate Office, Inc. is shown again in Figure 4-2 for convenience. Such a trial balance is called an **unadjusted trial balance** because it is prepared from the general ledger before the adjusting entries are posted. For illustrative purposes, it is assumed that monthly financial statements are to be prepared and that monthly adjusting entries are made in the general journal. However, it is common accounting practice to prepare formal adjusting journal entries at the end of the fiscal period only. If more frequent reports are prepared, the adjusting entries are entered on a worksheet only, as illustrated in Figure 5-2 in Chapter 5.

Figure 4-2
Unadjusted Trial
Balance

QUALITY REAL ESTATE OFFICE, INC.
Unadjusted Trial Balance
June 30, 1992

Account Title	Debit	Credit
Cash	$ 29,930	
Accounts Receivable	6,800	
Prepaid Insurance	1,200	
Office Supplies On Hand	940	
Land	20,000	
Building	70,000	
Office Equipment	12,000	
Accounts Payable		$ 7,000
Unearned Management Fees		300
Mortgage Notes Payable		80,000
Capital Stock		45,000
Dividends Declared	600	
Commissions Revenue		12,000
Salaries Expense	2,500	
Utilities Expense	90	
Advertising Expense	240	
Total	$144,300	$144,300

Figure 4-2
Unadjusted Trial
Balance

ADJUSTMENTS FOR DEFERRALS

In this section, the two types of adjusting entries related to deferrals are discussed. Recall that in the case of deferrals, a previously recorded asset is reduced and an expense account is increased for the amount consumed during the period, or a previously recorded unearned revenue account (a liability) is reduced and a revenue account is increased for the amount of revenue earned during the period.

PREPAID EXPENSES (ASSET TRANSFERRED TO EXPENSE ADJUSTMENTS)

A business often pays for some expense items (such as rent, insurance, and supplies) in advance of the items' use. Goods and services, such as the purchase of office supplies, which are paid for in advance and are expected to benefit several periods, are normally recorded as assets (unexpired costs) at the time of payment. At the end of the accounting period, the portion of the asset's cost associated with the goods that have been used or with services that have been received is transferred to an expense account. The remaining unexpired or unused portion of the asset is reported in the balance sheet. Thus, before the financial statements are prepared, the balance in the asset account is analyzed and is apportioned between an asset and an expense.

In many cases, however, the prepayment and expiration of the asset occurs in the same accounting period. While the costs of such goods and services are considered assets at the time of payment, such payments are charged directly to expense accounts if the items will be consumed in the current period. For example, the payment of one month's rent in advance on the first of the month is debited to Rent Expense.

Objective 4:
Adjusting pre-
paid expenses

Prepaid Insurance

On June 1 a 24-month fire and insurance policy was purchased by the Quality Real Estate Office, Inc, for $1,200. Insurance coverage began on June 1. The transaction was recorded as follows.

June	1	Prepaid Insurance	1,200	
		Cash		1,200

The balance in the Prepaid Insurance account remains the same until the end of the month, at which time the cost of the insurance protection for the month of June is computed. The cost of the insurance protection per month is $50 ($1,200/24 months). The following adjusting entry is made on June 30 to record Insurance Expense and to reduce the Prepaid Insurance account.

(a) June	30	Insurance Expense	50	
		Prepaid Insurance		50
		(The adjusting entries are identified by letters in this illustration for reference purposes only.)		

After the adjusting entry is posted, the account balances are:

Prepaid Insurance				Insurance Expense		
6/1	1,200	6/30	50	6/30	50	
6/30 Bal.	1,150					

The adjusting entry reduced the Prepaid Insurance account balance to $1,150, which is the unexpired portion of the cost applicable to future periods and which is reported as an asset. The portion of the cost that expired in this period ($50) is properly matched as an expense with the revenue reported in June. If the adjusting entry were not made, net income, assets, and owners' equity would all be overstated.

In future periods, the $1,150 balance is reduced by $50 each month as insurance protection is received by the firm. The costs of additional policies purchased are debited to the Prepaid Insurance account and allocated to expense by following similar procedures.

Office Supplies on Hand

Quality Real Estate Office, Inc. made the following journal entry on June 5 to record the purchase of office supplies.

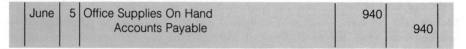

June	5	Office Supplies On Hand	940	
		Accounts Payable		940

The cost of unused office supplies is reported as an asset in the balance sheet. As the office supplies are used, their cost is transferred to an expense account. The recognition of the expense is normally deferred until the end of the accounting period. In other words, no journal entry is made during the period to record the cost of supplies consumed because this information is not needed on a day-to-day basis. Before financial statements are prepared, an adjusting entry is made to remove the cost of the supplies used from the asset account and increase an expense account.

For control purposes, firms generally keep supplies in a central location. Employees are required to fill out a requisition form which identifies the supplies they have taken or used. The total cost of the supplies is determined for each requisition. The total of these requisitions is the cost of the supplies used during the period. If a requisition system is not used, the cost of the supplies on hand is determined at the end of the period by counting and pricing them, which in turn allows for computation of the cost of supplies used.

Assume that the cost of the supplies Quality Real Estate Office, Inc. had on hand at the end of June was determined to be $780. Therefore, the cost of supplies used during this period was $160, as shown here.

Supplies on hand, June 1	$–0–
Supplies purchased during the month	940
Supplies available for use	940
Supplies on hand, June 30	780
Supplies used during the month	$160

The following adjusting entry is made to record the supplies used.

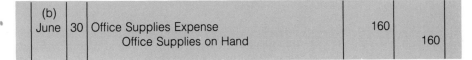

| (b) June | 30 | Office Supplies Expense | 160 | |
| | | Office Supplies on Hand | | 160 |

After this entry is posted, the accounts will appear as follows:

Office Supplies On Hand				**Office Supplies Expense**	
6/5	940	6/30	160	6/30	160
6/30	780				

The $780 balance left in the Office Supplies On Hand account is the cost of supplies available for use in future periods (an asset). The $160 balance in the Office Supplies Expense account is the cost of supplies used during June, which is matched with revenue earned during June in the income statement.

In future periods, the cost of additional purchases of supplies is debited to the Office Supplies On Hand account. The same analysis and process described above is performed at the end of each subsequent accounting period.

Depreciation of Equipment and Building

Assets such as office equipment, buildings, automobiles, store fixtures, and machines are acquired by a business for use in performing operating activities. Thus, the firm is buying future service benefits from such assets. Because such assets are used by a business (i.e., the benefits are received) over more than one accounting period, their cost is allocated to the accounting periods that benefit from their use. The portion of the asset's cost assigned to expense in the current period is called depreciation or depreciation expense.

The adjusting entry to record depreciation is similar to the entries described previously for the allocation of the cost of the insurance policy and office supplies. That is, as an asset is used, an expense account is increased for the portion of the cost allocated to the current period and an asset account is decreased for the same amount. However, unlike the the purchase of the insurance policy and the office supplies, which are generally consumed during one or two fiscal periods, items of equipment and buildings are frequently used for extended periods of time, sometimes up to 30 years or longer. The use of an asset for an extended time period results in an inability to determine precisely what portion is consumed in a given accounting period. Depreciation expense must therefore be computed as an estimate based on the following three factors.

1.   **Cost of the asset.** The cost of an asset is the amount paid to purchase the asset.
2.   **Estimated useful life.** The estimated useful life is the time period during which the asset is expected to be used.
3.   **Estimated residual value.** The estimated residual value is the amount expected to be received at the end of the asset's useful life.

Given these three factors, there are several systematic methods used by accountants to compute depreciation expense. A more complete discussion of computing depreciation is contained in Chapter 10. Until then, the *straight-line method* is used to compute depreciation. This method allocates an equal amount of depreciation to each full accounting period of the asset's useful life. The amount of depreciation for each period is computed as follows.

$$\frac{\text{Cost} - \text{Residual value}}{\text{Useful life}} = \frac{\text{Depreciation expense for}}{\text{the period}}$$

To illustrate, assume that the office equipment purchased by Quality Real Estate Office for $12,000 has an eight-year (96-month) estimated useful life and a zero residual value at the end of eight years. The building that cost $70,000 has an estimated useful life of 25 years (or 25 years × 12 months = 300 months), at which time it is expected to have a residual value of $4,000. The monthly depreciation expense for each asset is computed as follows.

Office Equipment	**Building**
$\dfrac{\$12,000}{96 \text{ months}} = \$125 \text{ per month}$	$\dfrac{\$70,000 - \$4,000}{300 \text{ months}} = \$220 \text{ per month}$

In making the adjusting entry for depreciation, a separate account, entitled **Accumulated Depreciation,** is credited for the cost associated with the period. This is done instead of making a direct credit to the asset account. The Accumulated Depreciation account is called a **contra account**. A contra account is reported as an offset to or a deduction from a related account. Thus, in the balance sheet, the Accumulated Depreciation account is reported as a deduction from the original cost reported in the related asset account. The use of the contra account preserves the original cost of the asset, while the balance in the Accumulated Depreciation account shows the portion of the cost that has been assigned to expense since the item was purchased. This provides useful information about the age of the asset to statement users.

The adjusting entries to record depreciation for June are:

(c)					
June	30	Depreciation Expense		125	
		Accumulated Depreciation—Office Equipment			125
(d)					
June	30	Depreciation Expense		220	
		Accumulated Depreciation—Building			220

The depreciation expense is reported as an expense in the income statement. The accumulated depreciation accounts are subtracted from the cost of the appropriate asset in the balance sheet. The difference between the original cost of the asset and its accumulated depreciation is called the book value of the asset and represents the unexpired cost of the asset.

As long as the assets are in use, the same adjusting entries are made for every accounting period until the cost less residual value is fully assigned to expense. Thus, in successive balance sheets, the Accumulated Depreciation—Office Equipment account will increase $125 each month and the Accumulated Depreciation—Building account will increase $220 each month. The original cost of the two assets remains in the Office Equipment and Building accounts and does not change.

UNEARNED REVENUE (LIABILITY TRANSFERRED TO REVENUE ADJUSTMENTS)

A firm may receive payment in advance for services that are to be performed or goods that are to be delivered in the future. Until the service is performed or the goods are delivered, a liability, called unearned revenue, equal to the amount of the advance payment is reported in the balance sheet. Thus, the firm's obligation to perform future services is reported. That is, recognition of the revenue is postponed until the earning cycle is completed by performance of the services or delivery of the goods. If services are not performed, it is assumed that the balance in the account is the amount that would be refunded to settle the account.

Objective 5: Adjusting unearned revenues

Unearned Management Fees

As an example of unearned revenue, Quality Real Estate Office, Inc. received a $300 advance payment on June 15 to manage three single-unit rentals for the period June 15 through September 15. The following entry was made to record the receipt of cash.

| June | 15 | Cash | 300 | |
| | | Unearned Management Fees | | 300 |

Since the management fee will be earned over a three-month period, the credit is made to an ***unearned revenue*** account (a liability) at the time the cash is received. Assuming that the management fee is earned evenly over the three-month period, an adjusting entry to transfer the earned portion of the advance payment to revenue is made on June 30. The adjusting entry is as follows.

(e)				
June	30	Unearned Management Fees	50	
		Management Fees Revenue		50

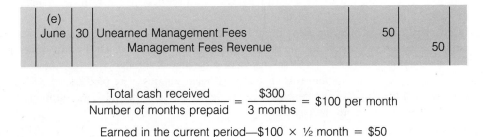

$$\frac{\text{Total cash received}}{\text{Number of months prepaid}} = \frac{\$300}{3 \text{ months}} = \$100 \text{ per month}$$

Earned in the current period—$100 × ½ month = $50

After the entry is posted, the accounts will appear as follows.

Unearned Management Fees				Management Fees Revenue	
6/30	50	6/15	300	6/30	50
		Bal.	250		

The balance in the Unearned Management Fees account shows that Quality has an obligation to perform a service in the future. An adjusting entry is made in future months to recognize the $250 balance as revenue as it is earned ($100 each in July and August, $50 in September). This results in the revenue being recognized as the service is performed, instead of all of it being reported as revenue in June when the cash is received.

The Quality Real Estate Office illustration contains one example of adjusting an unearned revenue account. Some other common unearned revenue items include rent received in advance, magazine subscriptions and advertising fees received in advance by a publisher, and deposits received from customers before merchandise is delivered.

ADJUSTMENTS FOR ACCRUALS

The two types of adjustments for accrued items are discussed in this section. Adjusting entries for accruals are needed to record expenses that were incurred during the period, but were unrecorded, and revenues that were earned during the period, but were unrecorded.

ACCRUED (UNRECORDED) EXPENSES (LIABILITY AND EXPENSE ADJUSTMENTS)

Objective 6: Adjusting accrued expenses

Most operating expenses are recorded during the period in which they are paid. However, at the end of the accounting period, there are usually some expenses that have been incurred but not recorded because payment has not been made. Such expenses include unpaid employee salaries, utilities, and interest on notes payable.

An adjusting entry is needed to assign the expense to the period in which it is incurred, rather than to the period of payment. A credit is made to a liability account to record the firm's obligation to pay for the goods or services that were received. These items are called *accrued expenses* or *accrued liabilities*. A separate liability account, such as Salaries Payable and Utilities Payable, may be established for each type of accrued expense.

Accrued Payroll Expense

Employees normally are not paid until they perform a service for the firm. Although an expense is incurred each hour that they work, the expense is generally not recognized until it is paid. Quality Real Estate Office, Inc. follows the practice of paying employees every two weeks for the preceding two weeks of service. On Friday, June 22, the employee payroll for the service period of June 8 through June 22 totaled $2,500. No particular problem was encountered when salaries were paid on June 22 because both the payment and the expense occurred in the same period. The following entry was made to record the payment.

June	22	Salaries Expense	2,500	
		Cash		2,500
		(Withholdings from the employees' salaries for taxes are ignored for now.)		

A diagram of the salaries earned between this payment and July 6 is presented in Figure 4-3. This pay period does have special problems, however, because the end of the period (June 30) occurs before the next salary payment date (July 6). An adjusting entry is required to provide (1) a proper matching of expenses incurred in June with revenues earned in June and (2) a record of the firm's liabilities at the end of June. Even though the employees are not paid until July 6, a portion of the $2,300 payment is for employees' services that were received in June. Employee time cards showed that $1,250 in salaries were earned between June 22 and June 30. The entry to accrue the unpaid wages up to June 30 is:

(f)				
June	30	Salaries Expense	1,250	
		Salaries Payable		1,250

The accounts after the adjusting entry is posted are as follows:

Salaries Payable			Salaries Expense	
	6/30 1,250	6/22	2,500	
		6/30	1,250	
		6/30 Bal.	3,750	

The adjusting entry records an expense of $1,250 for the services received in June. The total salaries expense of $3,750 is reported in the June income statement. The credit of $1,250 in the Salaries Payable account shows the amount owed to the em-

Figure 4-3
Diagram of Salaries Paid and Accrued

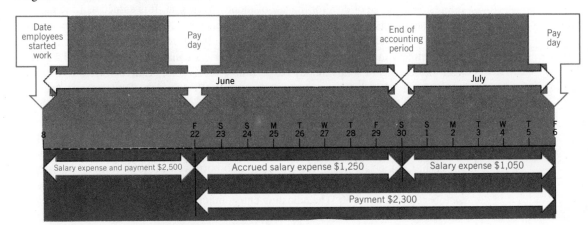

The total salaries vary each pay period because some employees work part-time.

ployees for services performed up to June 30. It is reported as a liability in the balance sheet. Failure to make the June 30 adjusting entry will result in an understatement of expenses and an overstatement of net income for June. In the balance sheet, liabilities will be understated and owners' equity will be overstated.

The $1,250 liability is eliminated on July 6, when the $2,300 employee payroll is paid. The $1,050 earned by the employees in July is recorded as an expense, as shown in the following entry:

July	6	Salaries Payable	1,250	
		Salaries Expense	1,050	
		Cash		2,300

The effect of these entries is to recognize the expense and liability during the period in which the expense was incurred rather than during the period when payment is made to the employees.

Accrued Commissions Expense

Employees on the sales staff of Quality Real Estate Office, Inc. are paid their commissions on the tenth day of the month following the month in which a sale is made. At the end of June, $5,500 in sales commissions were owed on the two residences that had been sold. Since this expense is directly associated with the revenue earned in June, the following adjusting entry is needed to provide proper matching.

(g)				
June	30	Commissions Expense	5,500	
		Commissions Payable		5,500

The expense is reported as a deduction from revenues in the income statement, and the payable is shown as a liability in the balance sheet.

Adjusting Entries Needed For Interest

Interest is a charge or cost for the use of money over time. It is earned as time passes, regardless of when the actual cash is paid or received. A business can either receive interest (a revenue) or pay interest (an expense). It will receive interest when it makes an investment in an interest paying security (e.g., a bank savings account or a certificate of deposit) or loans money (e.g., a note receivable). Conversely, the firm will pay interest when it borrows money (e.g., a note payable). Thus interest accruals must be evaluated carefully, because, unlike other adjustments, they can be either a revenue or an expense adjustment.

To illustrate the accrual of interest revenue and interest expense, assume that on May 1, Basic Company received a $10,000 note receivable from a client in exchange for cash. On the same date, the company also borrowed $10,000 from a bank giving a note payable. Interest on both notes in the amount of $600 is due twice a year on October 30 and April 30. The adjusting entry, number (3) in the first column of Figure 4-4, is necessary to record the amount of interest earned and the right to receive cash, an asset (Interest Receivable). The interest receivable will be settled on April 30 when the full six months' interest is received. Note that the right to receive cash for the

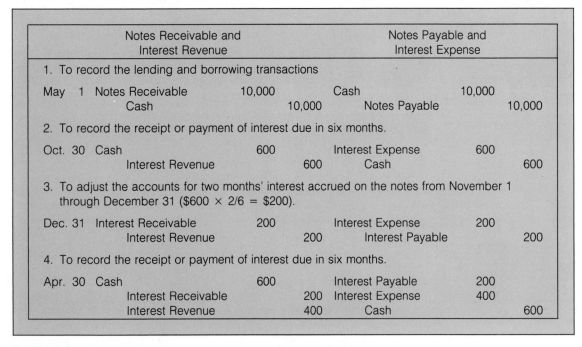

Figure 4-4
Accounting for Interest

interest is different from the right to receive cash for the $10,000 loaned, as reflected by the Note Receivable account.

The adjusting entry in the second column, related to the Notes Payable, recognizes that the unpaid interest on December 31 must be recorded to bring the expense and liability accounts up to date. The interest payable will be settled on April 30 when the six months' interest ($600) is paid.

In the case of the Quality Real Estate Office, Inc., the company financed a portion of the June 1 land and building purchase with a 20-year $80,000, 12% mortgage. An annual payment of $4,000 plus accrued interest is to be made on June 1 of each subsequent year. Therefore, an adjusting entry must be recorded to recognize interest expense incurred in June and a liability for the unpaid interest. The amount of the accrued interest is computed using the following formula.

$$\text{Principal} \times \text{Rate} \times \text{Time} = \text{Interest}$$
$$\$80,000 \times 12\% \times 1/12 = \$800$$

The entry is:

(h)					
June	30	Interest Expense		800	
		Interest Payable			800

Note that only the $800 additional liability for the accrued interest is recorded on June 30. The Mortgage Note Payable account is already on the books as a result of making the June 1 entry to record the asset purchase. Interest expense is shown as an expense in the income statement for June, and interest payable is reported as a liability on the June 30 balance sheet.

Accrued Utilities Expense

A utility company usually bills its customers after the service has been provided. Assume that on July 5 Quality Real Estate Office, Inc. received a bill in the amount of $240 for electricity used in June. The adjusting entry to record the expense in June is:

(i) June	30	Utilities Expense	240	
		Utilities Payable		240

This entry increases expenses and liabilities by equal amounts. Note that although the bill was not received until July 5, the journal entry is dated June 30 so that the expense and liability are properly reflected in the June financial statements. However, in practice, when the amounts are immaterial, companies often follow the cash basis for utility expenses and recognize the expense in the period in which the cash is paid.

Accrued Income Tax Expense

Corporations are separate taxable entities. They must file tax returns and pay state and federal tax on their taxable income in accordance with the Internal Revenue Code and the applicable state tax laws. The federal tax laws and some states require that a corporation estimate its tax liability at the beginning of the year and pay the tax in quarterly installments. Some of the more commonly applicable provisions of the tax code are discussed in more detail in Chapter 17. For now, however, a simplified tax computation is used for illustrative purposes. Income taxes are accounted for as an expense of doing business. They are matched against the income to which the tax relates. In the case of Quality Real Estate Office, Inc. assume that the income tax on the taxable income earned this period was computed to be $435. Since the amount is unpaid, the following adjusting entry is made to accrue the expense and related liability:

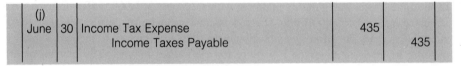

(j) June	30	Income Tax Expense	435	
		Income Taxes Payable		435

ACCRUED (UNRECORDED) REVENUE (ASSET AND REVENUE ADJUSTMENTS)

Objective 7: Adjusting accrued revenue

In most cases, when a service is completed, the firm makes an entry to recognize the transaction. Even if cash is not immediately received, an account receivable is established in order to maintain a record of amounts owed to the firm and to recognize revenue earned. No entry is required at the end of a period since the receivable and the revenue have been recorded.

There are occasions in many firms, however, when revenue has been earned but not recorded. Examples of this include the portion of revenue earned on a partially completed service contract and interest accrued on a note receivable. Earned revenue that is unrecorded at the end of the period must be included in the accounting records by debiting a receivable and crediting a revenue account.

Consider the following illustration. Quality Real Estate Office, Inc. signed an agreement on June 1 to manage an apartment complex for a monthly fee of $875. Although the service fee is earned by the firm in one month, the agreement provides for payment to be made on the fifth day of the following month. No entry was made on June 1, when the agreement was made, because there was no exchange of goods or services and none of the fee was earned at that time. However, as services are performed, a portion of the fee is earned from day to day. By June 30, the full monthly fee of $875 is earned and is recorded by the following entry.

(k)				
June	30	Accounts Receivable	875	
		Management Fees Revenue		875

Receivables for partially completed service contracts are generally recorded in the Accounts Receivable account. Separate receivable accounts, such as Interest Receivable, may be established for other types of accrued revenues. The Accounts Receivable account is shown in the balance sheet as an asset; the revenue account is reported in the income statement.

ADJUSTED TRIAL BALANCE

As stated above, the adjusting entries must be journalized and posted to the ledger accounts. An **adjusted trial balance** is a trial balance taken from the ledger after the adjusting entries have been posted. It is taken to verify the equality of debits and credits in the adjusted ledger accounts. The ledger accounts for Quality Real Estate Office, Inc. are shown after the adjusting entries were posted in T account form in Figure 4-5. Adjusting entries are shown in color for illustration only. An adjusted trial balance taken from the ledger of Quality Real Estate Office, Inc. as of June 30 is presented in Figure 4-6. Financial statements as illustrated in Figures 2-1 and 2-2 in Chapter 2 can be prepared from the adjusted trial balance.

Objective 8: Preparing an adjusted trial balance

Assets

Cash			100
6/1	45,000	6/1	10,000
6/15	300	6/1	1,200
6/30	5,200	6/5	5,000
		6/6	240
		6/22	2,500
		6/23	600
		6/27	940
		6/30	90
6/30 Bal.	29,930		

Accounts Receivable			104
6/15	5,200	6/30	5,200
6/19	6,800		
6/30 (k)	875		
6/30 Bal.	7,675		

Prepaid Insurance			110
6/1	1,200	6/30 (a)	50
6/30 Bal.	1,150		

Office Supplies On Hand			111
6/5	940	6/30 (b)	160
6/30 Bal.	780		

Land			150
6/1	20,000		

Building			160
6/1	70,000		

Figure 4-5
General Ledger After Adjusting Entries Are Posted

Figure 4-5
(Continued)

Accumulated Depr.—Bldg.   161

		6/30 (d)	220

Office Equipment   170

6/5		

Accumulated Depr.— Off. Equip.   171

		6/30 (c)	125

Liabilities

Accounts Payable   200

6/27	940	6/5	940
	—	6/5	7,000
		6/30 Bal.	7,000

Salaries Payable   210

		6/30 (f)	1,250

Commissions Payable   211

		6/30 (g)	5,500

Interest Payable   215

		6/30 (h)	800

Utilities Payable   216

		6/30 (i)	240

Unearned Management Fees   220

6/30 (e)	50		
			250

Income Taxes Payable   225

		6/30 (j)	435

Mortgage Note Payable   230

		6/1	80,000

Stockholders' Equity

Capital Stock   300

Dividends Declared   320

Revenues

Commissions Revenue   400

		6/15	5,200
		6/19	6,800
		6/30 Bal.	12,000

Management Fees Revenue   402

		6/30 (e)	50
		6/30 (k)	875
			925

Expenses

Salaries Expense   500

6/22	2,500		
6/30 (f)	1,250		
6/30 Bal.	3,750		

Commissions Expense   505

6/30 (g)	5,500		

Utilities Expense   510

6/30	90		
6/30 (i)	240		
6/30 Bal.	330		

Advertising Expense   520

6/6	240		

Insurance Expense   521

6/30 (a)	50		

Office Supplies Expense   530

6/30 (b)	160		

Depreciation Expense   540

6/30 (c)	125		
6/30 (d)	220		
6/30 Bal.	345		

Interest Expense   560

6/30 (h)	800		

Income Tax Expense   590

6/30 (j)	435		

Figure 4-6
Adjusted Trial
Balance

QUALITY REAL ESTATE OFFICE, INC.
Adjusted Trial Balance
June 30, 1992

Account Title	Debit	Credit
Cash	$ 29,930	
Accounts Receivable	7,675	
Prepaid Insurance	1,150	
Office Supplies On Hand	780	
Land	20,000	
Building	70,000	
Accumulated Depreciation–Building		$ 220
Office Equipment	12,000	
Accumulated Depreciation–Office Equipment		125
Accounts Payable		7,000
Salaries Payable		1,250
Commissions Payable		5,500
Interest Payable		800
Utilities Payable		240
Unearned Management Fees		250
Income Taxes Payable		435
Mortgage Note Payable		80,000
Capital Stock		45,000
Dividends Declared	600	
Commissions Revenue		12,000
Management Fees Revenue		925
Salaries Expense	3,750	
Commissions Expense	5,500	
Utilities Expense	330	
Advertising Expense	240	
Insurance Expense	50	
Office Supplies Expense	160	
Depreciation Expense	345	
Interest Expense	800	
Income Tax Expense	435	
Totals	$153,745	$153,745

SUMMARY

Two approaches to measuring net income—cash basis and accrual basis—were examined in this chapter. The cash basis focuses on cash flows with revenues recorded in the accounting period cash is received and expenses recorded in the period cash is paid. The cash basis is defective when a company conducts much of its business on credit because it neither reports revenue in the period of economic activity nor properly matches expenses incurred with revenues earned. Under the accrual basis, revenues are recorded in the period services are performed and expenses are recorded when they are incurred (i.e., when goods are consumed or services are received) in the revenue-generating process. The process of associating expenses incurred with revenues earned is called matching. The three matching rules of associating cause and effect, systematic and rational allocation, and immediate recognition were discussed.

The accountant records many types of transactions, including all cash receipts and cash payments, during the accounting period. The receipt of cash or the payment of cash may precede the earning of revenue or incurring of an expense. In other cases, revenue may be earned before cash is received and expenses may be incurred before they are paid for. As a result, at the end of each accounting period, adjusting entries must be made so that the accounts will properly reflect revenues earned and expenses incurred rather than cash receipts and payments. The four categories of adjusting entries are summarized in Figure 4-7.

Figure 4-7
Summary of Adjusting Entries

Type of Adjustment	Original Entry	Adjusting Entry	Errors in Financial Statements If Adjusting Entry is Not Made (– = unaffected; O = overstated; U = understated) Income Statement: Rev.	Income Statement: Exp.	Income Statement: NI	Balance Sheet: Asset	Balance Sheet: Liab.	Balance Sheet: O.E.
DEFERRALS Prepaid Expense—expense paid in advance; e.g., rent paid in advance of occupancy.	Asset Cash	Expense (for the amount used) Asset	–	U	O	O	–	O
Unearned Revenue—revenue received before earned; e.g., rent received from a tenant before occupancy occurs.	Cash Liability	Liability (for the amount earned) Revenue	U	–	U	–	O	U
ACCRUALS Accrued Expense—expense incurred but not paid for; e.g., salaries earned by employees but not paid for.	None	Expense (for the amount incurred) Liability	–	U	O	–	U	O
Accrued Revenue—revenue earned but not yet received; e.g., interest earned on notes receivable but not yet received.	None	Asset (for the amount earned) Revenue	U	–	U	U	–	U

SELF-TEST

Test your understanding of the chapter by selecting the best answer for each of the following.

1. Journal entries made at the end of the accounting period to ensure that all revenues and expenses are recorded in the proper period are called:
   a. adjusting entries.
   b. temporary entries.
   c. correcting entries.
   d. compound entries.

2. Which of the following is not one of the three basic rules applied in the allocation of expenses?
   a. Systematic and rational allocation.
   b. Associating cause and effect.
   c. Allocation that maximizes income in the current period.
   d. Immediate recognition

3. Which of the following adjusting entries could cause an increase in assets at the end of the period?
   a. The entry to record the earned portion of rent received in advance.
   b. The entry to accrue unrecorded interest revenue.
   c. The entry to accrue unrecorded interest expense.
   d. The entry to record expiration of recorded prepaid insurance.

4. How does the failure to record accrued revenue distort the financial statements?
   a. It understates revenue, net income, and current assets.
   b. It understates net income, stockholders' equity, and current liabilities.
   c. It overstates net income, stockholders' equity, and current liabilities.
   d. It overstates net income and current assets, and overstates stockholders' equity.

5. Delivery Company received $5,000 from Store Company for services to be performed. On receipt of the cash, a credit entry was made to Unearned Service Revenue. Assuming that 40% of the revenue was earned in the current period, what adjusting entry (if any) is necessary at the end of the current accounting period?
   a. Debit Cash, $2,000; Credit Service Revenue, $2,000.
   b. Debit Service Revenue, $2,000; Credit Unearned Service Revenue, $2,000.
   c. Debit Unearned Service Revenue, $2,000; Credit Service Revenue, $2,000.
   d. No adjusting entry is required since cash was recorded when received.

6. Two years' rent was paid in advance and debited to Prepaid Rent on January 1, 1991, in the amount of $24,000. The adjusting entry required on December 31 is

a.	Rent Expense	12,000	
	Prepaid Rent		12,000
b.	Rent Expense	12,000	
	Cash		12,000
c.	Prepaid Rent	12,000	
	Cash		12,000
d.	Prepaid Rent	12,000	
	Rent Expense		12,000

7. Before an adjusting entry is made, an accrued expense can best be described as an amount:
   a. paid and currently matched with revenue.
   b. paid and not currently matched with revenue.
   c. not paid and not currently matched with revenue.
   d. not paid and currently matched with revenue.
8. Employees of Armchair Manufacturing Company work a five-day week from Monday through Friday. The daily payroll is $12,000 and the company pays its employees weekly on Friday for the days of the current week worked. Wednesday was the last day of the fiscal year. The year-end adjusting entry will contain:
   a. a debit to Salaries Payable for $36,000.
   b. a credit to Salaries Payable for $36,000.
   c. a credit to Salaries Expense for $36,000.
   d. a debit to Salaries Expense for $24,000.

REVIEW PROBLEM

The unadjusted trial balance prepared for the Johnson Decorating Service, Inc. on July 31, the end of the first month of operations is as follows:

JOHNSON DECORATING SERVICE, INC.
Unadjusted Trial Balance
July 31, 1992

Account Title	Debit	Credit
Cash	$2,850	
Accounts Receivable	240	
Office Supplies On Hand	140	
Prepaid Insurance	180	
Automobile	4,200	
Office Equipment	1,200	
Notes Payable		$3,000
Accounts Payable		1,340
Unearned Service Fees		80
Capital Stock		4,000
Dividends Declared	100	
Service Fees Revenue		520
Advertising Expense	30	
Totals	$8,940	$8,940

Other information available at the end of July is as follows:

a. Depreciation on the automobile for one month is $100 and on the office equipment for one month is $20.
b. Interest accrued on the notes payable is $30.

c. Received a $48 invoice from Jayhawk Oil Company for gasoline used in the business and charged on a credit card.

d. Office supplies of $85 were determined by a physical count.

e. The balance in the Prepaid Insurance account is the cost of a 12-month policy paid for on July 2 that was effective from July 1.

f. Utilities used in July but not paid for, $165.

g. At the end of July, the company had rendered services in the amount of $70 that had not been billed and hence not yet recorded.

h. Earned $25 of the $80 advance payment received from customers and recorded in the Unearned Service Fees account.

i. Income taxes estimated for the month, $40.

Required:

A. Journalize the required adjusting entries. The posting reference column of the journal would be completed as the entries are posted in part B. The following account titles are to be added to those listed in the trial balance:

Account Title	Account Number
Accumulated Depreciation—Automobile	165
Accumulated Depreciation—Office Equipment	185
Interest Payable	265
Income Taxes Payable	270
Automobile Expenses Payable	275
Utilities Payable	280
Depreciation Expense	521
Automobile Expense	522
Insurance Expense	523
Office Supplies Expense	530
Utilities Expense	540
Interest Expense	550
Income Tax Expense	560

B. Add the accounts above to the ledger developed in the review problem at the end of Chapter 3. Post the adjusting entries to the ledger and compute an adjusted balance for each account.

C. Prepare an adjusted trial balance.

ANSWER TO REVIEW PROBLEM

A.

Date		Accounts and Explanation	Post. Ref.	Debit	Credit
July	31	Depreciation Expense	521	120	
		Accumulated Depreciation— Automobile	165		100
		Accumulated Depreciation— Office Equipment	185		20
		To record depreciation for the month of July.			
	31	Interest Expense	550	30	
		Interest Payable	265		30
		To record interest on notes payable.			
	31	Automobile Expense	522	48	
		Automobile Expenses Payable	275		48
		To record unpaid gasoline bills.			
	31	Office Supplies Expense	530	55	
		Office Supplies On Hand	120		55
		To record office supplies used in July.			
	31	Insurance Expense	523	15	
		Prepaid Insurance	131		15
		To record expired insurance.			
	31	Utilities Expense	540	165	
		Utilities Payable	280		165
		To record accrued expense.			
	31	Accounts Receivable	105	70	
		Service Fees Revenue	400		70
		To record fees earned but not collected.			
	31	Unearned Service Fees	220	25	
		Service Fees Revenue	400		25
		To record fees earned that were paid for in advance.			
	31	Income Tax Expense	560	40	
		Income Taxes Payable	270		40
		To record accrued expense.			

B.

JOHNSON DECORATING SERVICE, INC.
General Ledger

Assets

Cash			100		Accounts Receivable		105
7/1	4,000	7/2	1,200	7/28	240		
7/15	280	7/2	180	7/31	70		
7/17	80	7/30	100	7/31 Bal.	310		
		7/31	30				
7/31 Bal.	2,850						

Office Supplies On Hand			120		Prepaid Insurance		131
7/8	140	7/31	55	7/2	180	7/31	15
7/31 Bal.	85			7/31 Bal.	165		

Automobile			160		Accumulated Depreciation–Automobile		165
7/2	4,200					7/31	100

Office Equipment			180		Accumulated Depreciation–Office Equipment		185
7/1	1,200					7/31	20

Liabilities

Notes Payable			200		Accounts Payable		210
		7/2	3,000			7/1	1,200
						7/8	140
						7/31 Bal.	1,340

Unearned Service Fees			220		Interest Payable		265
7/31	25	7/17	80			7/31	30
		7/31 Bal.	55				

Income Taxes Payable			270		Automobile Expenses Pay.		275
		7/31	40			7/31	48

Utilities Payable			280
		7/31	165

Stockholders' Equity

Capital Stock			300		Dividends Declared		350
		7/1	4,000	7/30	100		

Service Fees Revenue			400
		7/15	280
		7/28	240
		7/31	70
		7/31	25
		7/31 Bal.	615

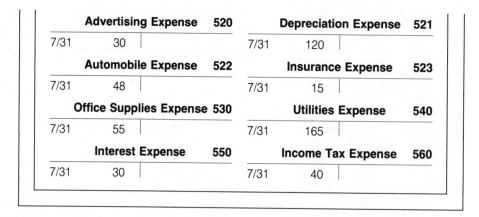

C.

JOHNSON DECORATING SERVICE, INC.
Adjusted Trial Balance
July 31, 1992

Account Title	Debit	Credit
Cash	$2,850	
Accounts Receivable	310	
Office Supplies On Hand	85	
Prepaid Insurance	165	
Automobile	4,200	
Accumulated Depreciation–Automobile		$ 100
Office Equipment	1,200	
Accumulated Depreciation–Office Equipment		20
Notes Payable		3,000
Accounts Payable		1,340
Unearned Service Fees		55
Interest Payable		30
Income Taxes Payable		40
Automobile Expenses Payable		48
Utilities Payable		165
Capital Stock		4,000
Dividends Declared	100	
Service Fees Revenue		615
Advertising Expense	30	
Depreciation Expense	120	
Automobile Expense	48	
Insurance Expense	15	
Office Supplies Expense	55	
Utilities Expense	165	
Interest Expense	30	
Income Tax Expense	40	
Totals	$9,413	$9,413

ANSWERS TO SELF-TEST

1. a   **2.** c   **3.** b   **4.** a   **5.** c   **6.** a   **7.** c   **8.** b

GLOSSARY

ACCRUAL. Expense that has been incurred but not recorded or revenue that has been earned but not recorded (p. 133).

ACCUMULATED DEPRECIATION. The amount of depreciation that has been recorded on an asset since it was acquired (p. 138).

ADJUSTED TRIAL BALANCE. A trial balance taken from the general ledger after the adjusting entries have been posted (p. 145).

ADJUSTING ENTRIES. Journal entries made at the end of an accounting period to update the balance sheet account balances and to record income effects in the proper period (p. 132).

BOOK VALUE. The original cost of an asset less its accumulated depreciation (p. 139).

COMPLETED CONTRACTS METHOD. A method of accounting for long-term contracts under which gross income is recognized in full in the year the project is completed (p. 128).

CONTRA ACCOUNT. An account that is deducted from a related account (p. 138).

DEFERRAL. The postponement of the recognition of expense or revenue that has been paid for or received during the period (p. 133).

DEPRECIATION (DEPRECIATION EXPENSE). That portion of the cost of a plant asset that is assigned to current expense over the estimated useful life of an asset in a systematic and rational manner (p. 137).

EXPIRED COST. The cost of an asset used to produce revenue; an expense (p. 130).

INSTALLMENT METHOD. A method of accounting for installment sales under which gross profit is recognized in proportion to the amount of cash collected. Its use is permitted for financial reporting purposes only when collection of the sales price is not reasonably assured (p. 129).

MATCHING. The process of associating expenses with revenues earned during the accounting period (p. 127).

PERCENTAGE-OF-COMPLETION METHOD. A method of accounting for long-term contracts under which gross profit is recognized in proportion to the work completed during the period (p. 128).

RESIDUAL VALUE. The estimated value of a plant asset at the end of its useful life (p. 138).

UNADJUSTED TRIAL BALANCE. A trial balance taken from the general ledger before the adjusting entries are posted (p. 134).

UNEXPIRED COST. A cost that has not yet been used to produce revenue but represents future economic benefit to the firm. Unexpired costs are reported as assets (p. 130).

USEFUL LIFE. The period of time a plant asset is expected to be used by the firm owning the asset (p. 138).

DISCUSSION QUESTIONS

1. Explain the cash basis accounting system and how net income is determined when it is used.
2. Explain the accrual basis accounting system and how net income is determined when it is used.
3. What generally accepted accounting principles are the bases for accrual accounting?
4. A company receives a machine as full payment for services rendered. The machine has a fair value of $2,200 and a book value of $1,500 on the customer's books. How much revenue should the company receiving the machine recognize?
5. A corporation experiences cash inflows of $500,000 and makes cash payments of $400,000 during a fiscal year. Its income statement shows a net income of $50,000. Explain the possible reasons for this difference.
6. What is an unexpired cost? How is it shown on the financial statements?
7. Explain the "systematic and rational allocation procedure" as it relates to expense recognition.
8. What are the objectives of making adjusting entries?
9. Define the terms "deferral" and "accrual."
10. When prepaid expenses are reduced during the adjusting entry process, what kind of account is *always* debited?
11. Explain why the purchase of office supplies is usually recorded in an asset account rather than an expense account.
12. What is a contra account? Give an example.
13. When recording accrued expenses at year-end, what types of accounts are *always* debited and credited?
14. A neighbor reading a balance sheet is puzzled by the account "accumulated depreciation." Explain the purpose of the account and what is represented by its balance.
15. Why is the Cash account never debited or credited in an adjusting entry?

EXERCISES

Exercise 4-1   Cash Versus Accrual Basis of Accounting

At the end of the first year of operations, Martin Cooper, office manager of Legal Advisors, Inc., contacts you to prepare the 1992 financial statements on the accrual basis. Following is a summary of the transactions occurring during 1992.

1. Legal fees of $405,000 were collected for services performed during the year.
2. Receivable from clients at year-end totaled $33,800.
3. Cash payments of $329,000 were made for salaries, utilities, rent, insurance, and other operating expenses.
4. An $8,000 retainer was received at year-end from a major client for services to be performed in 1993.
5. Expenses of $8,600 (part of the $329,000) were prepaid as of December 31, 1992.
6. The firm owed $4,000 interest on a note payable to the bank.

Required:
Prepare the 1992 income statement in accordance with the accrual basis of accounting.

Exercise 4-2 Adjusting a Cash Basis Income Statement to the Accrual Basis

Shown below is a cash basis income statement prepared for Silver Company at the end of its first year of operations.

SILVER COMPANY
Income Statement
For the Year Ended September 30, 1992

Revenues:		
Service revenues		$192,000
Expenses:		
Salaries expense	$96,800	
Utilities expense	6,300	
Supplies expense	1,500	
Advertising expense	2,500	
Rent expense	16,500	
Total Expenses		123,600
Net Income		$ 68,400

Below is additional information about the firm at year-end:

1. Customers owed Silver Company $4,500 for services performed during the year.
2. Salaries earned by employees but not paid by Silver totaled $5,200.
3. A telephone bill for $640 and a gas bill for $220 were received on September 30, and had not been paid at year-end.
4. Advertising costing $500 was run by the local newspaper in September. It has not been paid for.
5. September's rent of $1,500 has not been paid.
6. $700 of interest is owed on a note payable.
7. The income taxes for the year are $12,828. No taxes have been prepaid.

Required:
Prepare an income statement in accordance with the accrual basis for Silver Company for the year ended September 30, 1992.

Exercise 4-3 Revenue Recognition

Case I
Construction equipment with a cost of $215,000 was sold for $250,000. A $40,000 down payment was received in 1991 and the purchaser agreed to pay the balance in eight equal quarterly installments during 1992 and 1993. Collection of the full sales price is not reasonably assured.

Required:
Determine the amount of gross profit that should be recognized in 1991, 1992, and 1993.

Case II

Earth-movers Construction Company signed a contract to construct an office complex at a contract price of $8,000,000. The project is expected to take three years to complete, at an estimated total cost of $6,000,000. Actual costs incurred on the project during 1992 were $2,100,000. Estimates of cost to complete and the extent of progress toward completion are reasonably dependable. Estimated total costs remained $6,000,000 during 1992.

Required:

Determine the amount of gross profit that should be recognized in 1992.

Exercise 4-4   Accounting for Long-term Contracts

Boulder Construction Company signed a contract to construct a dam on the Colorado River for $40,000,000. The project is expected to take four years to complete at an estimated cost of $28,000,000. Actual costs incurred each year were:

Year	Costs Incurred
1	$ 6,160,000
2	8,400,000
3	9,800,000
4	4,140,000
Total	$28,500,000

Assume that the estimated total cost of the project remained at $28,000,000 through the end of the third year.

Required:

A. Determine the amount of gross profit that should be recognized each year under the percentage-of-completion method.
B. Determine the amount of gross profit that should be recognized each year assuming that all revenues and expenses are recognized in the year the construction is completed.
C. Which method would you recommend to the management of Boulder Construction Company?

Exercise 4-5   Adjusting Entries—Types of Accounts Affected

Complete the chart presented below by filling in the combinations of accounts debited and credited in preparing adjusting entries. The adjustment for prepaid expenses is completed for you as an example.

	Type of Account Debited	Type of Account Credited
Deferrals:		
Prepaid Expenses	Expense	Asset
Unearned Revenues		
Accruals:		
Accrued Revenues		
Accrued Expenses		

Exercise 4-6   Adjusting Entry for Prepaid Expense

Johnson Company purchased a two-year insurance policy on September 1, 1992 for $33,600.

Required:
A. Assuming the entire premium cost was debited to Prepaid Insurance, prepare the journal entry on September 1, 1992 to record the transaction.
B. Prepare the required adjusting entry on December 31, 1992.
C. What should be the balance in the Prepaid Insurance account on the December 31, 1992 balance sheet?
D. If the December 31, 1992 adjusting entry is not made, by how much will net income and total assets be overstated or understated?
E. Prepare the required December 31, 1993 adjusting entry.

Exercise 4-7 Adjusting Entry for Unearned Revenue
Bulwark Corporation engages in constructing and renting office space to various businesses. On November 1, 1992, one tenant gave Bulwark Corporation a $12,000 check for six months' rent. Bulwark credited Unearned Rental Fees to record the receipt.

Required:
A. Prepare the journal entry on November 1, 1992 to record the transaction.
B. Prepare the required adjusting entry on December 31, 1992.
C. If the December 31, 1992 adjusting entry is omitted, what will be the impact on the financial statements?
D. Prepare the entry to be made in 1993 to recognize the remaining portion of the rental fees earned.
E. Compute the balance in the Unearned Rental Fees account on the December 31, 1992 balance sheet.

Exercise 4-8 Adjusting Entry for Accrued Expense
Meyer Corporation pays its employees weekly on Friday for the days of that week. The weekly payroll for salaried employees, based on a five-day work week, is $70,000.

Required:
A. Assuming that December 31, the last day of the fiscal year, falls on a Tuesday, prepare the year-end adjusting entry.
B. Assuming January 1 is a paid holiday, prepare the entry to pay the employees on January 3.
C. If the adjusting entry on December 31 was omitted, what would be the effect on:
   1. Net income?
   2. Total assets on the year-end balance sheet?
   3. Total liabilities on the year-end balance sheet?
   4. Total owners' equity on the year-end balance sheet?

Exercise 4-9 Adjusting Entry for Accrued Revenue
Phase Company frequently performs services on credit. Customers with poor credit ratings are required to sign an interest-bearing note receivable for the value of the services received. On November 1, 1992, Phase performed $12,000 of services for Atwater Corporation and Atwater signed a $12,000, three-month note at an annual interest rate of 12 percent.

Required:

For Phase Company:

A. Prepare the journal entry on November 1, 1992 to record the transaction.
B. Prepare the adjusting entry required on December 31, 1992.
C. What is the financial statement classification for each account affected by this adjusting entry?
D. Assuming Atwater pays the note on the due date, prepare the journal entry to record collection of the note.

Exercise 4-10 Adjusting Entries

Clay's Computer Company provides computer services to other businesses on a credit basis. The company's fiscal year-end is May 31, at which time the following information is available:

1. The Company provided computer services for $3,200 during the last week of May that have not been recorded or collected.
2. A telephone bill for $160 and an electric bill for $315 were received on May 30. Neither bill has been recorded or paid.
3. Office supplies on hand June 1 of the preceding year totaled $4,200. During the year supplies in the amount of $23,400 were purchased and debited to the asset account. Office supplies on hand at year-end total $1,860.
4. The employees had worked a total of 750 hours since their last pay date. The pay rate is $6 an hour. Employees are paid on the 5th and the 20th of each month.
5. Computer equipment costing $32,000 and having a four-year life with no residual value was used throughout the entire year.

Required:

Prepare the necessary adjusting entries.

Exercise 4-11 Adjusting Entries—Missing Information

Below in general journal format is a series of incomplete adjusting entries.

GENERAL JOURNAL				
Date		Accounts	Debit	Credit
1992				
May	30			
		Interest Revenue		950
	30	Depreciation Expense—Building	14,000	
	30			
		Prepaid Rent		400
	30	Unearned Service Revenue	4,650	
	30	Interest Expense	3,100	
	30			
		Wages Payable		18,000
	30	Unearned Legal Fees	2,400	

	30	Rent Receivable	1,800
	30		
		Income Taxes Payable		38,300
	30	Legal Fees Receivable	800
	30	Unearned Subscription Revenue	6,400
	30	Insurance Expense	1,100
	30	Utilities Expense	115
	30		
		Office Supplies On Hand		2,800

Required:

Complete each journal entry by entering the proper account title to be debited or credited and the dollar amount.

Exercise 4-12   Adjusting Entries

Listed below are several independent situations.

1. Equipment with a cost of $200,000 is depreciated by the straight-line method over 10 years. Expected residual value at the end of 10 years is $15,000.
2. Repair service revenues earned but not yet billed to customers is $1,800.
3. Salaries earned by employees in December to be paid January 3, 1993 total $18,700.
4. All subscription fees received in advance in the amount of $42,000 were credited to a liability account. The amount remaining unearned at December 31, 1992 is $12,600.
5. Automobile depreciation is computed based on a five-year useful life and a zero residual value. Total cost of the automobiles is $120,000; balance in the Accumulated Depreciation—Automobiles account on January 1, 1992 is $36,000.
6. On November 1, 1992, $30,000 was borrowed from the bank for four months at 16%. Interest and principal will be paid on the maturity date.

Required:

Prepare annual adjusting entries on December 31, 1992.

Exercise 4-13   Adjusting Entries—Ledger Account Analysis

Selected T accounts and partial information on each one is shown below. The adjusting entries for the period have been recorded and posted.

Prepaid Insurance			
Dec. 31 Balance	1,450		

Supplies On Hand			
Dec. 31 Balance	420		

Insurance Expense			
Dec. 31 Adjusting Entry	1,050		

Supplies Expense			
Dec. 31 Adjusting Entry	520		

Rent Receivable			Interest Payable		
Jan. 1			Jan. 1.		
Balance	−0−		Balance		−0−
Dec. 31			Dec. 31		
Balance	−0−		Balance		1,500

Unearned Rent Revenue			Interest Expense		
	Jan. 1.		Dec. 31		
	Balance	−0−	Balance	4,000	
	Dec. 31				
	Balance	1,400			

Rent Revenue		
	Dec. 31	
	Balance	8,000

Required:

A. Prepaid Insurance had a balance on January 1 of $1,500. Determine the total cash payments made during the year for insurance premiums.

B. Supplies costing $680 were purchased during the year. Compute the January 1 balance in the Supplies On Hand account.

C. Calculate the total rental fees received in cash during the year.

D. Calculate the amount of cash interest paid during the year.

 Exercise 4-14 Determination of Adjusting Entries from Differences in Trial Balance and Adjusted Trial Balance Account Balances

Presented below are the trial balances prepared before and after the adjusting entries were made at year-end.

Account Title	Unadjusted Trial Balance		Adjusted Trial Balance	
	Debit	Credit	Debit	Credit
Cash	$ 23,000		$ 23,000	
Accounts Receivable	46,000		46,000	
Office Supplies On Hand	3,200		1,800	
Prepaid Insurance	1,800		1,000	
Prepaid Advertising	6,100		5,600	
Equipment	30,000		30,000	
Accumulated Depreciation—Equipment		28,700		32,800
Accounts Payable		3,600		3,600
Salaries Payable		−0−		8,200
Interest Payable		−0−		400
Notes Payable		10,000		10,000
Capital Stock		20,000		20,000
Retained Earnings		18,000		18,000
Service Revenues		250,000		250,000
Salaries Expense	190,200		198,400	
Advertising Expense	−0−		500	
Rent Expense	30,000		30,000	
Office Supplies Expense	−0−		1,400	
Depreciation Expense—Equipment	−0−		4,100	
Insurance Expense	−0−		800	
Interest Expense	−0−		400	
Totals	$330,300	$330,300	$343,000	$343,000

Required:

From an analysis of the two trial balances, prepare in general journal form the adjusting entries that were made.

Exercise 4-15 Multiple Choice—Accrual-basis Accounting and Adjusting Entries Concepts

Select the best answer to each of the following questions.

1. Under the accrual basis of accounting,
    a. revenues are recognized when the cash is received.
    b. net income is the excess of cash inflows over cash outflows.
    c. revenues are generally recognized at the point of sale.
    d. expenses are recognized when the cash is paid.
2. Immediate recognition of expenses is appropriate when:
    a. they cannot be directly associated with revenue transactions.
    b. they have no discernible benefits to future accounting periods.
    c. their allocation over several accounting periods serves no useful purpose.
    d. All of the above.
3. Which of the following accounts would never be affected by an adjusting entry?
    a. Office Supplies On Hand
    b. Cash
    c. Accumulated Depreciation
    d. Prepaid Insurance
4. Which of the following statements about adjusting entries is true?
    a. Adjusting entries are prepared at the end of every month.
    b. Adjusting entries are not required when a company uses the accrual basis of accounting.
    c. Adjusting entries are required to update account balances, even if a company uses the accrual basis of accounting.
    d. Adjusting entries are voluntary.
5. Failure to record prepaid insurance expired during a period would have what effect on the following accounts?

	Assets	Liabilities	Owner's Equity
a.	understate	overstate	overstate
b.	overstate	no effect	overstate
c.	understate	understate	understate
d.	overstate	no effect	no effect

6. The entry to record prepaid insurance expired during the period would include which of the following adjustments?
    a. A credit to Cash.
    b. A debit to Insurance Expense.
    c. A debit to Prepaid Insurance.
    d. A credit to Insurance Expense.
7. If salaries due and payable were not accrued at a company's fiscal year end, it would have which of the following effects on the financial statements?
    a. Expenses would be understated.
    b. Net income would be understated.
    c. Retained earnings would be understated.
    d. Assets would be overstated.

8. Office supplies of $200 were on hand at the beginning of the year and purchases were $700. If supplies on hand at the end of the year were $250, the adjusting entry to record supplies used during the year would include:
    a. a credit to Cash for $700.
    b. a debit to Office Supplies On Hand of $650.
    c. a debit to Office Supplies Expense of $650.
    d. a debit to Office Supplies Expense of $700.
9. The adjusted trial balance:
    a. ensures that all adjusting entries have been posted correctly.
    b. verifies the equality of debits and credits in the adjusted ledger accounts.
    c. is taken before the adjusting entries have been posted.
    d. ensures that there are no errors in the accounting system.
10. What type of account is Accumulated Depreciation?
    a. An asset.
    b. A stockholder's equity account.
    c. An expense.
    d. A contra asset account.

PROBLEMS

Problem 4-1 Cash versus Accrual Accounting—Account Analysis

Cork Corporation uses the accrual basis of accounting. Presented below is selected financial data regarding their 1992 calendar year operations.

	Beginning of Year	End of Year	During the Year
Cash Received:			
Interest			$ 1,000
Cash sales			4,000
Collection on accounts receivable			12,000
Cash Paid:			
Interest			4,000
Payments on operating expenses			12,000
Account Data:			
Accounts Receivable	$6,000	$3,000	
Interest Receivable	750	500	
Interest Payable	200	250	
Accrued Operating Expenses	800	1,000	
Prepaid Operating Expenses	1,200	1,500	

Required:

Using the information above, compute the following. Show supporting calculations.

1. Interest revenue.
2. Interest expense.
3. Service revenue.
4. Operating expenses.

Problem 4-2   Adjusting Entries

The trial balance of the Pinewood Service Company on December 31, 1992 is shown below:

PINEWOOD SERVICE COMPANY
Trial Balance
December 31, 1992

Account Title	Debit	Credit
Cash	$ 5,700	
Investment in 12%, U.S. Treasury Notes	40,000	
Chemicals on Hand	160,000	
Prepaid Insurance	3,200	
Land	9,000	
Buildings	50,000	
Accumulated Depreciation—Buildings		$ 10,000
Equipment	560,000	
Accumulated Depreciation—Equipment		105,200
Notes Payable, 8%		24,000
Unearned Service Revenues		105,000
Capital Stock		200,000
Retained Earnings		227,700
Service Revenues		414,000
Utilities Expense	30,000	
Salaries Expense	220,000	
Gas and Oil Expense	8,000	
Totals	$1,085,900	$1,085,900

Additional information is as follows:

1. The U.S. Treasury notes were purchased on November 1, 1992 when no interest was accrued thereon. Interest is paid on November 1 and May 1.
2. Chemicals used during the year totaled $150,000.
3. The debit balance in prepaid insurance resulted from the cash purchase of a four-year insurance policy on April 1, 1992.
4. The building has an expected life of 50 years. The equipment has an expected life of ten years. Straight-line depreciation is used for both assets. Assume a zero residual value for both assets.
5. The note payable is the result of a bank loan received December 1, 1992.
6. Eighty percent of the Unearned Service Revenues is earned by the end of 1992.

Required:
Prepare in general journal form the needed adjusting entries on December 31, 1992.

Problem 4-3   Year-end Adjusting Entries

Below are a series of statements concerning the adjusting entry process and certain account balances for the Freeman Corporation for 1992.

1. On January 1, 1992, the account Prepaid Rent had a balance of $6,000. Its balance on December 31, 1992, before the adjusting entries were made, was $18,000. On the 1992 income statement, the amount shown for Rent Expense was $10,000.
    Prepare the adjusting entry that was made on December 31, 1992.

2. On August 1, 1992, a 14%, six-month bank loan was taken out in the amount of $30,000. Interest is to be paid at maturity.

   Prepare the required adjusting entry on December 31, 1992.

3. Five automobiles were purchased on October 31, 1992 at a total cost of $50,000. Straight-line depreciation is used. The automobiles have an expected useful life of 5 years and a salvage value of $1,000 per auto.

   Prepare the required adjusting entry on December 31, 1992.

4. On January 1, 1992, the balance in the Unearned Rent account was $90,000 for the period January 1 through September 30. On October 1, $144,000 was received for a 12-month period beginning October 1, 1992.

   Calculate the amount of rent revenue to be reported in the 1992 income statement.

5. The balance in the Interest Receivable account on January 1, 1992 was zero. During 1992, cash received from customers for interest on outstanding notes receivable amounted to $1,100. The 1992 income statement showed Interest Revenue in the amount of $1,400.

   Prepare the adjusting entry that was made on December 31, 1992.

6. On January 1, 1992, the balance in the Office Supplies On Hand account was $1,000. During 1992, purchases of $25,000 were made and debited to Office Supplies On Hand. On the 1992 income statement, the amount in the Office Supplies Expense account is $25,400.

   Prepare the adjusting entry that was made on December 31, 1992 and compute the amount of supplies on hand on December 31.

Required:

Supply the information requested in each statement. Consider each statement independently of the others.

Problem 4-4 Multiple Choice—Adjusting Entry Concepts

Select the best answer to each question.

1. Services were paid for by a customer, but have not yet been provided to that customer by the firm that received the cash. From the point of view of the firm receiving the cash, the advance is called a(an):
   a. accrued expense.
   b. accrued revenue.
   c. prepaid expense.
   d. unearned revenue.
2. An item that represents services that have been paid for but have not yet been received by that firm is called a(an):
   a. accrued expense.
   b. accrued revenue.
   c. prepaid expense.
   d. unearned revenue.
3. An item that represents services received by the firm for which it will pay for in the future is called an:
   a. accrued expense.
   b. accrued revenue.
   c. prepaid expense.
   d. unearned revenue.

4. An item that represents services provided by a firm for which it will receive payment in the future is called an:
   a. accrued expense.
   b. accrued revenue.
   c. prepaid expense.
   d. unearned revenue.
5. Accrued revenues:
   a. decrease assets.
   b. increase liabilities.
   c. decrease liabilities.
   d. increase assets.
6. Accrued expenses:
   a. decrease assets.
   b. increase liabilities.
   c. decrease liabilities.
   d. increase assets.
7. Adjusting entries are necessary to:
   a. update and correct the accounts at the end of the fiscal period.
   b. balance the books at the end of the fiscal period.
   c. record the sales for the period.
   d. ensure the equality of the debits and credits.
8. The journal entry to record an accrued expense results in which of the following types of accounts being debited and credited?

	Debited	Credited
a.	asset	revenue.
b.	asset	liability.
c.	expense	asset.
d.	expense	liability.

9. The journal entry to record an accrued revenue results in which of the following types of accounts being debited and credited?

	Debited	Credited
a.	asset	revenue.
b.	asset	liability.
c.	expense	asset.
d.	expense	liability.

10. The word "Accrued" implies which of the following?
    a. Money has been paid but no services have been provided.
    b. Money has been received and the services have been performed.
    c. Money has not been paid or received but the service has been performed or received.
    d. Money has been paid and the service has been provided.

Problem 4-5   Adjusting Entries

The following transactions were entered into by Keith Lavery, a local real estate broker, during July, 1992, the last month of his fiscal year.

July   1   Purchased a computer for $4,500. The computer will be depreciated over five years on the straight-line basis. Assume a zero residual value.

1   Purchased a 12-month fire insurance policy for $1,176.

1   Borrowed $10,000 from First National Bank by signing a 90-day note at an annual interest rate of 15%.

6   Purchased office supplies for $290. On July 31, supplies worth $174 remained unused. There were no supplies on hand at the beginning of the month.

15 Paid $840 for one month's rent covering the period July 15 to August 15.

20 Received a check from a client for $800 in prepayment of work to be performed. On July 31, 1992, 25% of the work had been completed.

24 Hired a secretary at a weekly salary of $350. The secretary started work on Monday, July 27. As of July 31, her first week's salary was unpaid.

30 Received a bill from the County Treasurer's office for $185 of accrued property taxes.

Required:

Prepare the journal entries to record each transaction and prepare the adjusting entries necessary on July 31, the end of the fiscal year.

Problem 4-6 Adjusting Entries and Effect on Financial Statements

Part I.

The information below is available for Sparkle Florists, Inc., which uses a fiscal year ending June 30.

a. On April 15, Sparkle Florists borrowed $10,000 from National Bank at 12% interest. The principal and interest are payable October 15.

b. Property taxes of $1,500 for the six-month period ending September 30 are due in October.

c. Equipment depreciation for the fiscal year ended June 30 is $6,000. The balance in the Accumulated Depreciation—Equipment account on July 1 of the previous year was $21,500.

d. On May 1 of the previous year Sparkle Florists purchased a one-year insurance policy for $504. A three-year policy was purchased on March 1 of the current year for $1,746. An asset account was debited to record both purchases. The proper adjusting entry was made at the end of the last fiscal year.

e. Sparkle Florists has four employees; two earn $50 a day each and two earn $25 a day each. They have not been paid for the last three days they worked in June.

f. On April 1, the Ultimate Experience restaurant paid Sparkle Florists $900 in advance for cut flower arrangements to be provided through September. Unearned Floral Revenues was credited to record the transaction. The revenue is earned equally each month.

g. June utilities of $500 are unrecorded and unpaid.

h. The Greenhouse Supplies On Hand account had a debit balance of $510 on July 1. Supplies costing $1,685 were purchased during the year. A physical count indicates $281 of supplies remain unused on June 30.

Required:

Use the information presented to prepare the necessary adjusting entries at year-end.

Part II.

All adjusting entries impact one balance sheet account and one income statement account. Below is a schedule listing some of Sparkle Florists' accounts.

Entry	Account	Balance in Account Before Adjustment	Balance In Account on June 30 Balance Sheet	Balance Sheet Classification	Effect of Adjusting Entry on Net Income Increase (Decrease)
a	Interest Payable	$–0–	10000. 12% × 2.5/12 $250	Current Liability	$ (250)
b	Property Taxes Payable	0	750	Current Liability	Decrease 750
c	Accumulated Depreciation	28,500	27500	Contra Asset	Decrease (6000)
d	Prepaid Insurance	420	278	Plant Asset	614 Decrease
e	Wages Payable	0	450	Current Liability	450 Decrease
f	Unearned Floral Revenues	900	450	Current Liability	450 Increase
g	Utilities Payable	0	500	Liability	500 Decrease
h	Greenhouse Supplies On Hand	2195	281	Expense	1194 Decrease

Required:
Based on the adjusting entries you prepared in Part I, complete the schedule. The first entry is shown as an example.

Problem 4-7 Adjusting Entries for Prepaid Insurance, Unearned Revenue, and Prepaid Rent

Three independent situations are described below.

Insurance:
On July 1, 1991, Prepaid Insurance had a $3,870 debit balance, allocable to the period July 1, 1991 through March 31, 1992. On October 15, 1991, a 24-month policy starting October 15, 1991 was purchased for $10,800.

Subscriptions:
On July 1, 1991, Unearned Subscriptions Revenue had a $21,900 credit balance; $5,500 of which expires on September 30, 1991 and $16,400 of which expires on April 30, 1992.

The following subscriptions were received during the year:

1. October 1, 1991 ——— $4,220 for 6 months.
2. February 1, 1992 ——— 8,640 for 24 months.
3. May 1, 1992 ——— 5,580 for 12 months.
4. June 1, 1992 ——— 8,220 for 6 months.

Rent:
On July 1, 1991, Prepaid Rent had a $4,225 debit balance, allocable to the period July 1 through November 30, 1991. On December 1, 1991, nine months rent of $6,975 was paid.

Required:
For each situation, prepare the necessary adjusting entry at June 30, 1992, the fiscal year-end. (You may wish to use T accounts to help you keep track of the data.)

Problem 4-8   Impact of Errors in the Adjusting Entry Process on the Income Statement and Balance Sheet

Below are listed nine errors that were made during the adjusting entry process for a firm.

Error	Total Revenues	Total Expenses	Net Income	Total Assets	Total Liabilities	Total Stockholders' Equity
1. Did not record depreciation for the period.	0	−	+	+	0	+
2. Did not record cost of supplies used during the period.	0	−	+	+	0	+
3. Failed to accrue interest on note payable.	0	−	+	0	−	+
4. Did not accrue salaries owed to employees at year-end.	0	−	+	0	−	+
5. Failed to recognize portion of unearned revenue earned during the period.	−	0	−	0	+	−
6. Debited cash instead of interest receivable when recording accrued interest on notes receivable.	0	0	0	0	0	0
7. Did not record the expired portion of prepaid insurance.	0	−	+	+	0	+
8. Failed to record income tax expense and liability at year-end.	0	−	+	0	−	+
9. Utilities expense included amounts paid for previous year.	0	+	−	0	+	−

Required:

For each situation, indicate the effect of the error on: total revenues, total expenses, net income, total assets, total liabilities, and stockholders' equity by placing a " − " for understate, " + " for overstate, and "0" for no effect.

Problem 4-9   Preparation of Adjusting Entries from Narrative Descriptions of Events

Descriptions of several independent situations are given below.

1. The Office Supplies On Hand account on the unadjusted trial balance had a $1,200 balance. The income statement showed office supplies expense of $925.
2. Cash wages paid during the year for the current-year's work totaled $750,000. Salaries expense on the income statement had a balance of $768,250.

3. The Prepaid Rent account balance at the beginning of the period was $3,250. During the year rent payments of $23,000 were made and debited to the asset account. Rent expense on the income statement was $22,500.

4. The Prepaid Insurance account had a beginning balance of $1,020. During the period $8,600 was paid for insurance and debited to the Prepaid Insurance account. At year-end, $550 of the insurance was unexpired.

5. The Interest Expense account on the unadjusted trial balance was $4,455; on the adjusted trial balance it was $5,225.

6. The Accumulated Depreciation—Equipment account on the unadjusted trial balance was $31,000 and on the adjusted trial balance it was $34,660.

7. Interest revenue on the income statement was $5,760; on the unadjusted trial balance it was $5,180.

8. Rent revenue of $25,000 was reported on the income statement; on the unadjusted trial balance it was $19,800.

9. Utilities expense on the income statement was $1,970. The Utilities Payable account had a balance of $–0– on the unadjusted trial balance and $150 on the adjusted trial balance.

10. The Unearned Legal Fees account had a balance of $2,700 on the unadjusted trial balance and an $800 balance on the adjusted trial balance.

Required:
For each situation, prepare the adjusting entry that was made at year-end during the adjusting entry process.

Problem 4-10   Original and Adjusting Entries
The following transactions of Bates' Carpet Cleaners, Inc. occurred during the month of September which is the last month of the fiscal year.

September 1 Purchased a 24-month insurance policy for $5,616.
           1 Borrowed $15,000 from the First National Bank. The principal, plus 14% annual interest, is due in six months. Bates' Carpet Cleaners, Inc., signed a note payable as evidence of the loan.
           1 Purchased a personal computer for $6,000 cash. The computer will be depreciated over an estimated useful life of four years at which time it is expected to have a zero residual value.
           8 Purchased office supplies for $325 on account. On September 30, supplies costing $130 remained on hand.
          15 Prepaid $2,910 rent for the period ending December 15.
          29 Received $1,350 as prepayment for carpet cleaning to take place in October.

Required:
Prepare the journal entries to record each transaction and the adjusting entries for September 30, the year-end. All prepayments are recorded in balance sheet accounts.

Problem 4-11   Comprehensive Review Problem
Refer to Problem 3-11. Below is information relating to needed adjusting entries on December 31, 1992.

a. The van purchased on January 1, 1992 has an expected useful life of five years with no residual value.

b. The tools and equipment purchased on January 1, 1992 have an expected life of four years with no residual value.

c. The building rent prepayment made on January 1, 1992 was for the period January 1, 1992 through December 31, 1993.
d. $4,800 of the repair supplies were on hand on December 31, 1992.
e. $1,200 of the insurance was expired by December 31, 1992.
f. Salaries owed to employees on December 31, 1992 were $1,800.
g. The following bills had been received by December 31, 1992 but were unrecorded and unpaid

Utilities ——————— $275
Advertising ——————— 400 (completed during December 1992)
Gas for autos ——————— 220

h. The six-month contract with Desert Sam Hospital covers the period from November 1, 1992 to May 1, 1993.
i. The income tax expense for the year is $468.

Required:

A. Prepare the required adjusting entries on December 31, 1992.
B. Post the adjusting entries to the T accounts.
C. Prepare an adjusted trial balance as of December 31, 1992.

CASE

Case 4-1 Discussion Case

On his 35th birthday Jerry Snyder received a $70,000 trust fund inheritance that had been established by his grandfather. Jerry invested $50,000 of the money in a new business he started on May 1, 1992 called Snyder's Caterers, Inc. Business was better than Jerry anticipated and on August 1 he hired an assistant to allow him more time to solicit new business. Jerry hired a bookkeeping service to maintain his financial records since he had neither the time nor the training to do so himself. At year-end, April 30, 1993, the bookkeeping service prepared the following statements based on the information Jerry gave them.

SNYDER'S CATERERS, INC.
Income Statement
For the Year Ended April 30, 1993

Revenues:		
Catering revenues		$118,300
Expenses:		
Food expense	$47,600	
Salary expense	32,000	
Advertising expense	5,500	
Auto expense	4,600	
Utilities expense	2,300	
Rent expense	12,000	
Table supplies expense	2,430	
Accounting fees expense	900	
Total Expenses		107,330
Net Income		$ 10,970

SNYDER'S CATERERS, INC.
Balance Sheet
April 30, 1993

Assets		Liabilities	
Cash	$ 1,600	Accounts payable	$ 3,920
Accounts receivable	23,250	Notes payable	30,000
Prepaid insurance	2,800	Total Liabilities	33,920
Office supplies on hand	620	**Stockholders' Equity**	
Kitchen equipment	29,250	Capital stock	50,000
Cooking utensils	3,870	Retained earnings	10,970
Delivery van	28,900	Total Stockholders'	
Office equipment	4,600	Equity	60,970
		Total Liabilities and	
Total Assets	$94,890	Stockholders' Equity	$94,890

Jerry was quite upset with the low net income and could not understand why his cash balance is less than the net income number. Knowing that you are currently enrolled in an accounting course, Jerry showed the statements to you and asked you to recalculate net income and to explain the low cash balance.

In discussing the firm's operations with Jerry, you learn the following facts. Jerry rented a building on May 1, 1992 for $1,000 per month. The building is used for both his office and kitchen. Jerry had remodeled the building's interior and installed the kitchen equipment. He officially opened for business on May 1, 1992, the date he acquired the delivery van and office equipment. He estimates the kitchen equipment will last six years, the cooking utensils three years, the delivery van four years, and the office equipment ten years. The expected residual values of these items at the end of their useful lives is zero except for the delivery van, which Jerry thinks will be worth $1,900. To purchase these assets Jerry paid $36,620 in cash and borrowed $30,000 from the bank on May 1, 1992. The interest rate on the note is 14 percent. Interest and $6,000 of the principal are due each May 1. If the business is successful, Jerry plans to buy the building.

Jerry pays himself a salary of $2,000 per month, which is a reasonable charge for the services he performs, and pays his assistant $1,000 per month. The assistant's salary for April is unpaid.

Jerry had questions about four items on the balance sheet. He collected $9,000 of the accounts receivable and paid $3,000 of the accounts payable during the first week in May, 1993. He wants to know why these transactions should not be represented on the April 30, 1993 balance sheet since he did not receive the statements until May 14. He also cannot understand why office supplies shows a balance of $620 when there was only $180 worth of supplies on hand when he counted them April 30. Also, he explained that one-fourth of the insurance policy had expired by April 30, 1993—so how could the balance be $2,800?

From a stack of bills and invoices on Jerry's desk, you determined that Jerry had performed $14,500 worth of catering in April that was unbilled at month-end. In addition, he had received the following bills for April activities that *he had not yet taken* to the bookkeeping service: food supplies ($600), utilities ($210), gasoline company credit card billings ($300), and advertisements ($300). The income tax expense for Jerry's business is $871.

Required:

A. Using accrual accounting procedures, prepare a revised income statement and classified balance sheet for the fiscal year. Round all numbers to the nearest dollar.

B. Answer the questions Jerry has asked as contained in the case.

C. Explain to Jerry how a company with profits could have a cash reduction during the year.

5

PREPARATION OF A WORKSHEET AND COMPLETION OF THE ACCOUNTING DATA PROCESSING CYCLE —SERVICE FIRM

CHAPTER OVERVIEW AND OBJECTIVES

This chapter completes our discussion of the accounting data processing cycle. It also introduces a worksheet that is commonly used by accountants to assist in accumulating the information needed to complete the cycle. When you have completed this chapter, you should understand:

1. How to prepare and use a worksheet.
2. How to prepare financial statements from the worksheet.
3. Journalizing adjusting entries using information from the worksheet.
4. The closing process and how to prepare closing entries using information from the worksheet.
5. How to prepare a post-closing trial balance.
6. An alternative approach used to record deferrals: Appendix.
7. The purpose of reversing entries: Appendix.

In this chapter, we complete the steps in the accounting cycle for service-type firms. As defined in Chapter 3, the *accounting cycle* is a series of steps completed at least once each fiscal period. The complete cycle is discussed and diagrammed in the first section of this chapter.

In Chapter 4, (1) an unadjusted trial balance was prepared, (2) account balances were analyzed and adjusting entries were made directly in the journal and then posted to the ledger, after which (3) an adjusted trial balance was prepared. It was noted that financial statements could be prepared from the adjusted trial balance. However, accountants often prepare a worksheet to organize this information. The **worksheet** is a columnar business form designed so the account balances needed to complete the accounting cycle at the end of the period can be presented in one place. As part of completing a worksheet, an unadjusted trial balance is prepared, adjusting entries are entered first in the worksheet before they are recorded in the journal, and an adjusted trial balance is prepared. The data developed in Chapters 3 and 4 for the Quality Real Estate Office, Inc. will be used in this chapter to illustrate (1) the preparation of a worksheet; and (2) the use of a worksheet to complete the steps in the accounting cycle.

In Chapter 3, the prepayment of an expense or the advance receipt of revenue (deferrals) were recorded initially in balance sheet accounts. An alternative approach to recording deferrals is covered in the Appendix to this chapter. An optional step in the accounting process, the preparation of *reversing entries*, is also discussed.

THE COMPLETE ACCOUNTING CYCLE

The accounting cycle is completed at least once each fiscal year. The steps in the accounting cycle are diagrammed in Figure 5-1 and are as follows.

Steps Performed during the Period

Step 1   **Transactions occur.** Transactions occur and source documents are prepared to collect information related to the transactions.

Step 2   **Journalize transactions.** Source documents are analyzed to determine accounts affected and the dollar amounts involved. The transactions are recorded in the general journal (or special journals as discussed in Chapter 6).

Step 3   **Post journal entries to ledger accounts.** Debits and credits are transferred to the proper accounts in the ledger.

Steps Performed at the End of the Period

Step 4   **Prepare a worksheet.** An unadjusted trial balance is prepared as part of the worksheet and the worksheet is completed.

Step 5   **Prepare financial statements.** Using the information in the worksheet, the following financial statements are prepared.
1. Income statement.
2. Retained earnings statement.
3. Balance sheet.

A statement of cash flows is also prepared. Preparation of this statement is covered in Chapter 15.

Step 6   **Journalize and post adjusting entries.** Using the information in the worksheet, adjusting entries are journalized and posted to the ledger.

Step 7   **Journalize and post closing entries.** Using the information in the worksheet, closing entries are journalized and posted to the ledger.

Step 8   **Prepare post-closing trial balance.** A post-closing trial balance is prepared to verify that accounts are in balance after the adjusting and closing entries have been posted.

Optional step   **Journalize and post reversing entries.** Reversing entries are dated the first day of the next accounting period. Reversing entries are made to facilitate the recording of routine transactions in the next period.

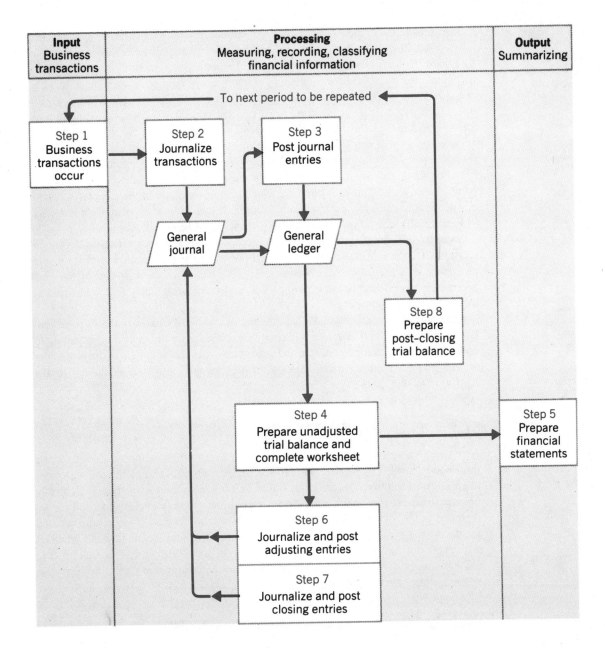

Figure 5-1
Steps in the Accounting Cycle

The first three steps in the accounting cycle, which are carried out during an accounting period as transactions occur, were discussed in Chapter 3. Although preparing a trial balance is not shown as a separate step, one may be prepared at any time during the period to verify that the ledger accounts are in balance. The structure and content of the financial statements were covered in Chapters 1 and 2. The preparation of adjusting entries (Step 6) was discussed in detail in Chapter 4. The remaining steps in the cycle are discussed in this chapter, with an emphasis on the closing process, a step in the cycle not previously discussed. When the steps in the cycle are completed, the process starts over again and is completed in the next accounting period.

The steps in the cycle can be completed without using a worksheet. If a worksheet is not used, the cycle is completed using an adjusted trial balance, as discussed in Chapter 4. However, because of the volume of work and the amount of detail involved in completing the cycle, accountants for most firms prepare a worksheet to help organize their work and minimize errors. When a worksheet is used (Step 4), an unadjusted trial balance is prepared as part of the worksheet format, adjusting entries are first entered on the worksheet before they are recorded in the journal, and an adjusted trial balance is developed as part of the worksheet. Financial statements are prepared (Step 5) and adjusting entries *are recorded* in the general journal (Step 6) based on the information developed on the worksheet. The worksheet is also used to complete the closing process (Step 7), which is discussed later in this chapter. A post-closing trial balance (Step 8) is taken from the ledger to verify that the accounts are in balance after the adjusting and closing entries have been posted.

Some companies perform an optional step, which is the preparation of reversing entries, after the closing entries have been posted to the ledger and the post-closing trial balance is prepared. A **reversing entry** is dated as of the first day of the next accounting period and is the opposite of a related adjusting entry that was made at the end of the current period.

Reversing entries are made to facilitate the recording of entries in the next period. Because they are optional and a thorough knowledge of them is not essential to understanding accounting concepts and procedures, they are not made in the remainder of this text. A more complete discussion of reversing entries is contained in the Appendix to this chapter.

STEP 4: PREPARATION OF A WORKSHEET

Objective 1:
Preparation of a
Worksheet

As noted earlier, a worksheet is a device designed to bring together in one place the information needed to prepare formal financial statements (except for the statement of cash flows) and to record the adjusting and closing entries. A worksheet is generally prepared in pencil so that errors can be erased and corrected before the entries are recorded in the journal. Here are some facts about a worksheet: (1) it is not prepared for use by the owners or management of the firm; (2) it replaces neither the financial statements nor the necessity to journalize and post the adjusting and closing entries; (3) it is simply a tool used to gather and organize the information needed to complete the accounting cycle.

PREPARATION OF THE WORKSHEET ILLUSTRATED

The basic format of a worksheet is shown in Figure 5-2. The heading contains the usual three parts: the name of the firm; the title of the form; and the period covered. The first column is used for the account titles. This column is followed by five sets of debit and credit columns provided for: (1) the unadjusted trial balance; (2) the adjusting entries; (3) the adjusted trial balance; (4) the income statement; and (5) the balance sheet. Each set consists of a debit column and a credit column, making a total of 10 columns for entering dollar amounts.

The Unadjusted Trial Balance, Adjustments, and Adjusted Trial Balance columns have been completed in Figure 5-2 based on the data developed in Chapters 3 and 4 for the Quality Real Estate Office, Inc. The steps followed in preparing a worksheet will be illustrated and described by using this information.

QUALITY REAL ESTATE OFFICE, INC.
Worksheet
For the Month Ended June 30, 1992

Account Title	Unadjusted Trial Balance Debit	Credit	Adjustments Debit	Credit	Adjusted Trial Balance Debit	Credit	Income Statement Debit	Credit	Balance Sheet Debit	Credit
Cash	29,930				29,930					
Accounts Receivable	6,800		(k) 875		7,675					
Prepaid Insurance	1,200			(a) 50	1,150					
Office Supplies on Hand	940			(b) 160	780					
Land	20,000				20,000					
Building	70,000				70,000					
Accumulated Depr.– Building		–0–		(d) 220		220				
Office Equipment	12,000				12,000					
Accumulated Depr.– Office Equipment		–0–		(c) 125		125				
Accounts Payable		7,000				7,000				
Unearned Management Fees		300	(e) 50			250				
Mortgage Note Payable		80,000				80,000				
Capital Stock		45,000				45,000				
Retained Earnings		–0–				–0–				
Dividends Declared	600				600					
Commissions Revenue		12,000				12,000				
Salaries Expense	2,500		(f) 1,250		3,750					
Utilities Expense	90		(i) 240		330					
Advertising Expense	240				240					
Totals	144,300	144,300								
Insurance Expense			(a) 50		50					
Office Supplies Expense			(b) 160		160					
Depreciation Expense			(c) 125							
			(d) 220		345					
Management Fees Revenue				(e) 50						
				(k) 875		925				
Salaries Payable				(f) 1,250		1,250				
Commissions Expense			(g) 5,500		5,500					
Commissions Payable				(g) 5,500		5,500				
Interest Expense			(h) 800		800					
Interest Payable				(h) 800		800				
Utilities Payable				(i) 240		240				
Income Tax Expense			(j) 435		435					
Income Taxes Payable				(j) 435		435				
Totals			9,705	9,705	153,745	153,745				

Figure 5-2
Worksheet Format—Unadjusted Trial Balance Entered, Adjusting Entries Entered, and Account Balances Extended to the Adjusted Trial Balance Columns (Steps 1–3 in the preparation of a worksheet.)

Step 4-1. Enter the ledger account titles and dollar amounts in the Account Title and Unadjusted Trial Balance columns. After all of the transactions that occurred during the period have been posted, a trial balance is prepared to verify the equality of debit and credit account balances, as shown in Figure 5-2. The trial balance is taken directly from the general ledger (see Figure 3-10 on page 96).

Note that every account with a balance at the end of the period is listed in this trial balance. Also listed are the two accumulated depreciation accounts and the retained earnings account that currently have zero balances at this stage in the cycle. Since these accounts normally report a balance in all periods except the first, they are listed here to illustrate how they are extended in the worksheet. In the next period, these zero-balance accounts will carry forward credit balances as a result of the adjusting and closing process.

Step 4-2.   Enter the necessary adjusting entries in the Adjustments columns. The adjusting entries are entered first on the worksheet in the Adjustments columns. After the worksheet is completed, the adjusting entries are recorded in the general journal. To aid in journalizing the entries and locating errors, each adjusting entry is identified by a separate letter so that the debit part of the entry can be cross-referenced to the credit part of the entry. The adjustments made in Figure 5-2 are the same as those explained in detail in Chapter 4. Adjustments were required for the following items.

Entry (a)   Prepaid insurance expired, $50.
Entry (b)   Office supplies used, $160.
Entry (c)   Depreciation on office equipment, $125.
Entry (d)   Depreciation on the building, $220.
Entry (e)   Management fees earned, $50.
Entry (f)   Salaries earned by employees but not yet paid, $1,250.
Entry (g)   Commissions earned by employees but not yet paid, $5,500.
Entry (h)   Accrued interest on mortgage notes payable, $800.
Entry (i)   Utilities used but not yet paid, $240.
Entry (j)   Unpaid income taxes at the end of the period, $435.
Entry (k)   Revenue earned from management of apartment complex but not yet received, $875.

When entering the adjustments, if an account already has a balance in the Unadjusted Trial Balance columns, the adjusting amount is entered on the same line. The account titles required by adjusting entries that were not listed in the Unadjusted Trial Balance columns are added on lines immediately below the unadjusted trial balance.

After all of the adjustments are entered, the two Adjustments columns are added to prove that the total debit adjustments equal the total credit adjustments. Adding the amounts entered in a vertical column is called footing the column.

Step 4-3.   Prepare an adjusted trial balance. In this step, each account balance in the Unadjusted Trial Balance columns is combined with the corresponding adjustments, if any, in the Adjustments columns and the resulting balance is extended on the same line to the proper Adjusted Trial Balance column, as shown in Figure 5-2. The combined amounts entered in these two columns will be the same as the ledger account balances after the adjusting entries are recorded in the journal and posted to the ledger. (To verify this, refer back to the adjusted trial balance of Quality Real Estate Office, Inc., Figure 4-6 on page 147.) Combining the amounts entered on each line—that is, adding or subtracting across the worksheet horizontally—is called **cross-footing**.

For those accounts unaffected by the adjustments, such as Cash, Accounts Payable, and Commissions Revenue, the balance is simply extended directly to the appropriate debit or credit column in the Adjusted Trial Balance columns. If an account has a debit balance in the Unadjusted Trial Balance column, a debit adjustment will increase the balance (see the Salaries Expense account), whereas a credit adjustment will decrease the balance (see the Prepaid Insurance account). An account with a credit balance is increased by a credit adjustment and decreased by a debit adjustment. In some cases, an account may not have a balance in the Unadjusted Trial Balance columns, but an adjustment is made to the account. In such cases, the amount of the adjustment is extended directly to the appropriate Adjusted Trial Balance column. Examples are those accounts added below the unadjusted trial balance. After all adjusted account balances have been determined, the equality of debits and credits is verified by footing the two Adjusted Trial Balance columns.

Step 4-4.   Extend every account balance listed in the Adjusted Trial Balance columns to its proper financial statement column. Every account balance listed in the Adjusted Trial Balance columns is extended to either the Balance Sheet columns or the Income Statement columns, as shown in Figure 5-3. Asset, liability, and stockholders' equity accounts are extended to the proper Balance Sheet debit or credit column. Revenue accounts are extended to the Income Statement credit column. Expense accounts are extended to the Income Statement debit column. In other words, in this part of the process, accounts are sorted on the basis of their financial statement classification.

Note that the Dividends Declared account is extended to the Balance Sheet debit column, rather than to the Income Statement debit column, because it is a decrease in retained earnings rather than an expense. The balance sheet columns will eventually contain all data needed to prepare both the statement of retained earnings and the balance sheet.

Step 4-5.   Add the two Income Statement columns and the two Balance Sheet columns. Compute the difference between the totals of the two Income Statement columns and enter this as a balancing amount in both the Income Statement and Balance Sheet columns. Add the four columns again with the balancing amount included. After all the amounts have been extended to either the Income Statement or the Balance Sheet columns, the four columns are added and their total entered at the bottom of each column. The net income or net loss for the period is determined by computing the difference between the totals of the two Income Statement columns, as shown in Figure 5-3. The computation in this illustration is:

Total of the credit column (revenues)	$12,925
Total of the debit column (expenses)	11,610
Difference (net income)	$ 1,315

In this illustration, the revenues earned ($12,925) exceeded the expenses incurred ($11,610), resulting in a net income of $1,315. This difference is entered in the Income Statement debit column to balance the two columns.

The net income is also entered on the same line in the Balance Sheet credit column to balance the debit and credit subtotals. The balance sheet subtotals are not equal because net income for the period is an increase in owners' equity that has not been transferred to the Retained Earnings account at this stage in the accounting cycle. Stated another way, except for the Retained Earnings account, which shows the balance at the beginning of the period, all of the account balances extended to the Balance Sheet columns are end-of-period balances. Extending the net income amount to the Balance Sheet credit column recognizes that operations increased stockholders' equity this period; extending the revenue and expense transactions to the Income Statement columns determines the net income for the period. The other change in retained earnings (a decrease due to the distribution of a cash dividend to the stockholders) is

QUALITY REAL ESTATE OFFICE, INC.
Worksheet
For the Month Ended June 30, 1992

Account Title	Unadjusted Trial Balance Debit	Credit	Adjustments Debit	Credit	Adjusted Trial Balance Debit	Credit	Income Statement Debit	Credit	Balance Sheet Debit	Credit
Cash	29,930				29,930				29,930	
Accounts Receivable	6,800		(k) 875		7,675				7,675	
Prepaid Insurance	1,200			(a) 50	1,150				1,150	
Office Supplies on Hand	940			(b) 160	780				780	
Land	20,000				20,000				20,000	
Building	70,000				70,000				70,000	
Accumulated Depr.—Building		–0–		(d) 220		220				220
Office Equipment	12,000				12,000				12,000	
Accumulated Depr.—Office Equipment		–0–		(c) 125		125				125
Accounts Payable		7,000				7,000				7,000
Unearned Management Fees		300	(e) 50			250				250
Mortgage Note Payable		80,000				80,000				80,000
Capital Stock		45,000				45,000				45,000
Retained Earnings		–0–				–0–				–0–
Dividends Declared	600				600				600	
Commissions Revenue		12,000				12,000		12,000		
Salaries Expense	2,500		(f) 1,250		3,750		3,750			
Utilities Expense	90		(i) 240		330		330			
Advertising Expense	240				240		240			
Totals	144,300	144,300								
Insurance Expense			(a) 50		50		50			
Office Supplies Expense			(b) 160		160		160			
Depreciation Expense			(c) 125 / (d) 220		345		345			
Management Fees Revenue				(e) 50 / (k) 875		925		925		
Salaries Payable				(f) 1,250		1,250				1,250
Commissions Expense			(g) 5,500		5,500		5,500			
Commissions Payable				(g) 5,500		5,500				5,500
Interest Expense			(h) 800		800		800			
Interest Payable				(h) 800		800				800
Utilities Payable				(i) 240		240				240
Income Tax Expense			(j) 435		435		435			
Income Taxes Payable				(j) 435		435				435
Totals			9,705	9,705	153,745	153,745	11,610	12,925	142,135	140,820
Net income for the period							1,315			1,315
Totals							12,925	12,925	142,135	142,135

Figure 5-3

Worksheet—Account Balances Extended to Financial Statement Columns and Totals Computed (Steps 4 and 5 in the preparation of the worksheet.)

reported in the Balance Sheet debit column. The ending retained earnings balance to be reported in the balance sheet ($715) can now be determined directly from the worksheet by adding the net income ($1,315 credit) to and subtracting the dividends declared ($600 debit) from the beginning retained earnings balance ($–0–).

The four columns are added again with the net income of $1,315 included as a balancing amount in the columns. If the debit and credit columns under Balance Sheet are not equal, there is an error in extending the amounts from the Adjusted Trial Balance columns.

If the Income Statement debit column had exceeded the Income Statement credit column, a net loss for the period would be indicated. In that case, the difference between the two columns would be captioned ''Net Loss for the Period'' and that difference entered in the Income Statement credit column and the Balance Sheet debit column.

Adding the debit and credit columns to verify the equality of debits and credits as work proceeds across the worksheet does not ensure that no errors have been made. For example, an adjustment may have been omitted entirely or the wrong adjusting amount may have been entered on the worksheet. In Step 4-4, an amount may be extended to the wrong column (e.g., the credit balance in the Management Fees account, a liability, may have been extended to the Income Statement credit column). This will not destroy the equality of debits and credits, but it will result in (1) an overstatement of revenues in the income statement, and (2) an understatement of liabilities and an overstatement of stockholders' equity in the balance sheet.

The worksheet is now completed. It is used to prepare the financial statements, journalize the adjusting entries, and journalize the closing entries.

STEP 5: PREPARATION OF FINANCIAL STATEMENTS

Because the worksheet format provides for sorting account balances between the income statement and the balance sheet, preparation of the formal financial statements, such as the income statement, the retained earnings statement, and the balance sheet is a relatively easy step. However, as noted earlier, the worksheet is not designed to accumulate information to be used in the preparation of a statement of cash flows.

Objective 2: Using worksheet to prepare financial statements

The income statement in Figure 5-4 is prepared from account balances listed in the two Income Statement columns in Figure 5-3. The retained earnings statement, illustrated in Figure 5-5, and the balance sheet, illustrated by Figure 5-6, are prepared from items contained in the Balance Sheet columns of Figure 5-3. Note that in the retained earnings statement, the beginning retained earnings balance is zero since this was the first year of operations for the company. The beginning balance in the next period is $715, which is the ending balance of the current period.

STEP 6: RECORDING AND POSTING ADJUSTING ENTRIES

The adjusting entries are entered in the general journal as shown in Figure 5-7. The necessary information is available directly from the Adjustments columns of the worksheet. Note that the entries are dated on the last day of the accounting period. After the adjusting entries are posted, the ledger account balances should agree with the balances reported in the Adjusted Trial Balance columns of the worksheet.

Objective 3: Using worksheet to record adjusting entries

STEP 7: RECORDING AND POSTING CLOSING ENTRIES

The income statement reports revenues earned and expenses incurred to earn those revenues during a single accounting period. Data needed to prepare the income statement are accumulated in the individual revenue and expense accounts. Once the income statement has been prepared for the current period, the revenue and expense accounts have served their intended purpose, and they are closed or cleared (i.e., reduced to a zero balance) by transferring their balances to another account, called

Objective 4: Preparing closing entries

Figure 5-4
Income Statement

QUALITY REAL ESTATE OFFICE, INC.
Income Statement
For the Month Ended June 30, 1992

Revenues:		
Commissions		$12,000
Management fees		925
Total Revenues		12,925
Expenses:		
Commissions expense	$5,500	
Salaries expense	3,750	
Interest expense	800	
Depreciation expense	345	
Utilities expense	330	
Advertising expense	240	
Office supplies expense	160	
Insurance expense	50	
Total Expenses		11,175
Income Before Income Taxes		1,750
Income tax expense		435
Net Income		$ 1,315
Earnings Per Share ($1,315/4,500 shares)		$.29

Figure 5-5
Retained Earnings
Statement

QUALITY REAL ESTATE OFFICE, INC.
Retained Earnings Statement
For the Month Ended June 30, 1992

Retained earnings, June 1	$ –0–
Add: Net income for the month of June	1,315
Total	1,315
Less: Dividends paid to stockholders	600
Retained earnings, June 30	$ 715

the Income Summary account, as discussed below. This step in the accounting cycle is referred to as the closing process, and journal entries made to close the accounts are called closing entries. The closing process results in each revenue and expense account beginning the next period with a zero balance. Because the revenue and expense accounts are reduced to a zero balance at the end of each fiscal period, they are called temporary accounts or nominal accounts.

Balance sheet accounts are not closed. Their ending balances of one period are carried forward to become the beginning balances of the next period. Balance sheet accounts are called permanent accounts or real accounts.

A new temporary account, called the Income Summary account, is normally established to summarize the balances in the revenue and expense accounts. For a service firm, this is the only time in the accounting process when this account is used. Closing entries are generally made in the following sequence:

Figure 5-6
Balance Sheet

QUALITY REAL ESTATE OFFICE, INC.
Balance Sheet
June 30, 1992

Assets

Current Assets:			
Cash			$29,930
Accounts receivable			7,675
Prepaid insurance			1,150
Office supplies on hand			780
Total Current Assets			39,535
Property, Plant, and Equipment:			
Land		$20,000	
Building	$70,000		
Less: Accumulated depreciation	220	69,780	
Office equipment	12,000		
Less: Accumulated depreciation	125	11,875	
Total Property, Plant, and Equipment			101,655
Total Assets			$141,190

Liabilities and Stockholders' Equity
Liabilities

Current Liabilities:		
Accounts payable		$ 7,000
Commissions payable		5,500
Salaries payable		1,250
Interest payable		800
Income taxes payable		435
Unearned management fees		250
Utilities payable		240
Current portion of mortgage notes payable		4,000
Total Current Liabilities		19,475
Long-term Liabilities:		
Mortgage note payable		76,000
Total Liabilities		95,475

Stockholders' Equity

Capital stock, $10 par value	$45,000	
Retained earnings	715	
Total Stockholders' Equity		45,715
Total Liabilities and Stockholders' Equity		$141,190

1. All revenue accounts are closed by debiting each revenue account for the balance in the account and crediting the Income Summary account for the sum of the individual debits. The effect of this entry is to reduce each revenue account to a zero balance and transfer the sum of the balances in the revenue accounts to the credit side of the Income Summary account.

2. All expense accounts are closed by crediting each expense account for the balance in the account and debiting the Income Summary account for the sum of the

Figure 5-7
Recording of Adjusting Entries

	Date	Accounts and Explanation	Post. Ref.	Debit	Credit
		GENERAL JOURNAL Page 3			
		Adjusting Entries			
June	30	Insurance Expense	521	50	
		Prepaid Insurance	110		50
		To record insurance expense for June.			
	30	Office Supplies Expense	530	160	
		Office Supplies On Hand	111		160
		To record office supplies used in June.			
	30	Depreciation Expense	540	125	
		Accumulated Depreciation–Office Equipment	171		125
		To record depreciation for June on office equipment.			
	30	Depreciation Expense	540	220	
		Accumulated Depreciation– Building	161		220
		To record depreciation for June on the building.			
	30	Unearned Management Fees	220	50	
		Management Fees Revenue	402		50
		To record fees earned for services performed during June.			
	30	Salaries Expense	500	1,250	
		Salaries Payable	210		1,250
		To record unpaid salaries at the end of June.			
	30	Commissions Expense	505	5,500	
		Commissions Payable	211		5,500
		To record unpaid commissions at the end of June.			
	30	Interest Expense	560	800	
		Interest Payable	215		800
		To record accrued interest on mortgage notes payable at the end of June.			
	30	Utilities Expense	510	240	
		Utilities Payable	216		240
		To record unpaid utilities at the end of June.			
	30	Income Tax Expense	590	435	
		Income Taxes Payable	225		435
		To record income taxes accrued on net income earned during June.			
	30	Accounts Receivable	104	875	
		Management Fees Revenue	402		875
		To record revenue earned but not yet billed for management of apartment complex during June.			

individual credits. The effect of this entry is to reduce each expense account to a zero balance and transfer the sum of the balances in the expense accounts to the debit side of the Income Summary account.

3. After the first two closing entries have been posted, the balance in the Income Summary account will be equal to the net income or net loss for the period. The balance in the account is transferred to the Retained Earnings account.

4. The Dividends Declared account is closed by crediting the Dividends Declared account and debiting the Retained Earnings account. The effect of this entry is to reduce the Dividends Declared account to a zero balance and transfer its balance to the debit side of the Retained Earnings account.

CLOSING ENTRIES ILLUSTRATED

Closing entries for Quality Real Estate Office, Inc. are illustrated in Figures 5-8 and 5-9. The related postings are shown in T account format. The information needed to prepare the closing entries is conveniently available from the Income Statement columns of the worksheet (see Figure 5-3 on page 182). For illustrative purposes only, the closing entries are identified by a reference number in the date column of the ledger and in the T accounts.

The first two entries to close the revenue and expense accounts are shown in Figure 5-8. After these two closing entries are posted, the balances formerly reported in the individual revenue and expense accounts are summarized in the Income Summary account. If revenues exceed expenses, a net income is earned and the Income Summary account will contain a credit balance. If expenses exceed revenues, a net loss is incurred and the account will have a debit balance. In either case, the balance is transferred to the Retained Earnings account. In other words, stockholders' equity, specifically the Retained Earnings account, is increased by revenues and decreased by expenses. However, because they are recorded in separate temporary accounts rather than directly to the Retained Earnings account, journal entries are needed at the end of the period to transfer the net effect of the revenues and expenses to the Retained Earnings account.

The Quality Real Estate Office, Inc. earned a net income during June. The credit balance of $1,315 in the Income Summary account is closed to the Retained Earnings account as shown by entry (3) in Figure 5-9. The effect of this entry is to recognize that the net assets (i.e., assets minus liabilities) of the company increased $1,315 this period due to profitable operations. This increase in net assets adds to the owners' interest in the firm. Conversely, if a net loss is reported, the Income Summary account is credited to reduce the account to a zero balance and the Retained Earnings account is debited to reflect a decrease in stockholders' equity from operations.

The debit balance in the Dividends Declared account ($600) represents a reduction in stockholders' interest due to the distribution of a cash dividend to them during the period. The balance in the account is transferred directly to the Retained Earnings account (see entry 4 in Figure 5-9). Note that the Dividends Declared account is not closed to the Income Summary account, because the distribution of assets to the owners is not an expense of doing business.

A complete ledger in T account format after the closing entries have been posted is presented in Figure 5-10 for Quality Real Estate Office, Inc. Note in Figure 5-10 that after the closing process is complete, all of the revenue, expense, income summary, and dividends declared accounts have zero balances and are ready for recording transactions in the next period. As a result, the retained earnings balance of $715 is equal to the ending balance reported in the balance sheet in Figure 5-6.

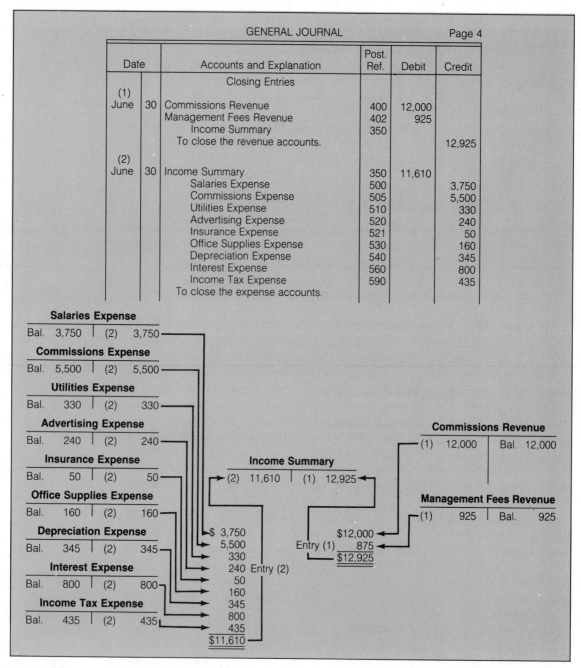

GENERAL JOURNAL				Page 4	
Date		Accounts and Explanation	Post. Ref.	Debit	Credit
		Closing Entries			
(1) June	30	Commissions Revenue	400	12,000	
		Management Fees Revenue	402	925	
		Income Summary	350		
		To close the revenue accounts.			12,925
(2) June	30	Income Summary	350	11,610	
		Salaries Expense	500		3,750
		Commissions Expense	505		5,500
		Utilities Expense	510		330
		Advertising Expense	520		240
		Insurance Expense	521		50
		Office Supplies Expense	530		160
		Depreciation Expense	540		345
		Interest Expense	560		800
		Income Tax Expense	590		435
		To close the expense accounts.			

Salaries Expense

Bal. 3,750 | (2) 3,750

Commissions Expense

Bal. 5,500 | (2) 5,500

Utilities Expense

Bal. 330 | (2) 330

Advertising Expense

Bal. 240 | (2) 240

Insurance Expense

Bal. 50 | (2) 50

Office Supplies Expense

Bal. 160 | (2) 160

Depreciation Expense

Bal. 345 | (2) 345

Interest Expense

Bal. 800 | (2) 800

Income Tax Expense

Bal. 435 | (2) 435

Income Summary

(2) 11,610 | (1) 12,925

Commissions Revenue

(1) 12,000 | Bal. 12,000

Management Fees Revenue

(1) 925 | Bal. 925

$ 3,750
5,500
330
240 Entry (2)
50
160
345
800
435
$11,610

$12,000
Entry (1) 875
$12,925

Figure 5-8
Closing the Revenue and Expense Accounts

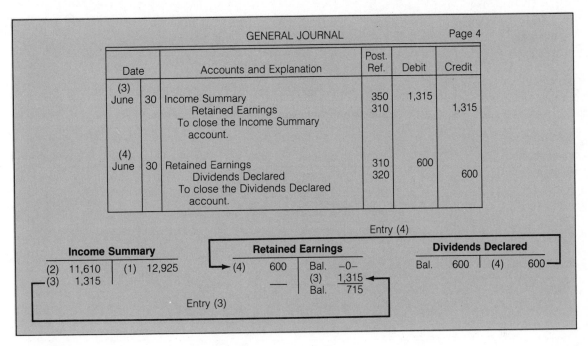

Figure 5-9
Closing the Income Summary and Dividends Declared Accounts

Figure 5-10
General Ledger
After Closing En-
tries Are Posted

Assets

		Cash		**100**		Accounts Receivable		**104**
6/1	45,000	6/1	10,000		6/15	5,200	6/30	5,200
6/15	300	6/1	1,200		6/19	6,800		
6/30	5,200	6/5	5,000		6/30 (k)	875		
		6/6	240		6/30 Bal.	7,675		
		6/22	2,500					
		6/23	600					
		6/27	940					
		6/30	90					
6/30 Bal.	29,930							

	Prepaid Insurance		**110**		Office Supplies On Hand		**111**
6/1	1,200	6/30 (a)	50	6/5	940	6/30 (b)	160
6/30 Bal.	1,150			6/30 Bal.	780		

	Land	**150**		Building	**160**
6/1	20,000		6/1	70,000	

Accumulated Depr.—Bldg.		**161**		Office Equipment	**170**
	6/30 (d)	220	6/5	12,000	

Accumulated Depr.—Off. Equip.		**171**
	6/30 (c)	125

Figure 5-10
(continued)

Liabilities

Accounts Payable				200
6/27	940	6/5	940	
		6/5	7,000	
		6/30 Bal.	7,000	

Salaries Payable		210
	6/30 (f)	1,250

Commissions Payable		211
	6/30 (g)	5,500

Interest Payable		215
	6/30 (h)	800

Utilities Payable		216
	6/30 (i)	240

Unearned Management Fees				220
6/30 (e)	50	6/15	300	
		6/30 Bal.	250	

Income Taxes Payable		225
	6/30 (j)	435

Mortgage Note Payable		230
	6/1	80,000

Stockholders' Equity

Capital Stock		300
	6/1	45,000

Retained Earnings				310
6/30 (4)	600	6/30 (3)	1,315	
		6/30 Bal.	715	

Dividends Declared				320
6/23	600	6/30 (4)	600	

Income Summary				350
6/30 (2)	11,610	6/30 (1)	12,925	
6/30 (3)	1,315			
6/30 Bal.	–0–			

Revenues

Commissions Revenue				400
6/30 (1)	12,000	6/15	5,200	
		6/19	6,800	
		6/30 Bal.	–0–	

Management Fees Revenue				401
6/30 (1)	925	6/30 (e)	50	
		6/30 (k)	875	
		6/30 Bal.	–0–	

Expenses

Salaries Expense				500
6/22	2,500	6/30 (2)	3,750	
6/30 (f)	1,250			
6/30 Bal.	–0–			

Commissions Expense				505
6/30 (g)	5,500	6/30 (2)	5,500	
6/30 Bal.	–0–			

Utilities Expense				510
6/30	90	6/30 (2)	330	
6/30 (i)	240			
6/30 Bal.	–0–			

Advertising Expense				520
6/6	240	6/30 (2)	240	
6/30 Bal.	–0–			

Insurance Expense				521
6/30 (a)	50	6/30 (2)	50	
6/30 Bal.	–0–			

Office Supplies Expense				530
6/30 (b)	160	6/30 (2)	160	
6/30 Bal.	–0–			

Depreciation Expense				540
6/30 (c)	125	6/30 (2)	345	
6/30 (d)	220			
6/30 Bal.	–0–			

Interest Expense				560
6/30 (h)	800	6/30 (2)	800	
6/30 Bal.	–0–			

Income Tax Expense				590
6/30 (j)	435	6/30 (2)	435	
6/30 Bal.	–0–			

STEP 8: THE POST-CLOSING TRIAL BALANCE

After the closing entries have been posted, a trial balance is prepared to verify the equality of debits and credits in the ledger. Because the trial balance is taken from the ledger after the revenue and expense accounts have been closed, it is called a **post-closing trial balance**. At this point, only the balance sheet accounts (i.e., the permanent accounts) should have balances. A post-closing trial balance for the Quality Real Estate Office, Inc. is presented in Figure 5-11.

Objective 5: Preparing a post-closing trial balance

PREPARING INTERIM STATEMENTS WITHOUT CLOSING THE ACCOUNTS

It is common practice for a firm to prepare monthly financial statements for use by management. In addition, most large firms issue quarterly statements to external statement users. Such statements are called *interim statements* because they are prepared between the annual reports issued at the fiscal year-ends. The preceding illustration of Quality Real Estate Office, Inc. assumed that (1) monthly financial statements were to be prepared and (2) the accounting cycle, including journalizing and posting both adjusting and closing entries, was completed at the end of the month. However, most firms adjust and close their accounts at the end of the fiscal period only. Information needed to prepare interim financial statements is accumulated on the worksheet only.

Figure 5-11
Post-Closing Trial Balance

QUALITY REAL ESTATE OFFICE, INC.
Post-Closing Trial Balance
June 30, 1992

Account Title	Account Balance	
	Debit	Credit
Cash	$ 29,930	
Accounts Receivable	7,675	
Prepaid Insurance	1,150	
Office Supplies On Hand	780	
Land	20,000	
Building	70,000	
Accumulated Depreciation–Building		$ 220
Office Equipment	12,000	
Accumulated Depreciation–Office Equipment		125
Accounts Payable		7,000
Salaries Payable		1,250
Commissions Payable		5,500
Interest Payable		800
Utilities Payable		240
Unearned Management Fees		250
Income Taxes Payable		435
Mortgage Note Payable		80,000
Capital Stock		45,000
Retained Earnings		715
Total	$141,535	$141,535

In other words, most accountants make adjustments on the worksheet, but do not enter them in the accounting records or close the accounts until the end of the fiscal period.

REFINEMENTS TO A MANUAL ACCOUNTING SYSTEM

In these early chapters, we have limited our consideration to a manually operated accounting system in order to introduce basic accounting procedures. Such a system may be satisfactory for a small business with a limited number of transactions. In most cases, however, a more sophisticated accounting system is required. In Chapter 7, some refinements to the manual system to make the processing of data more efficient are discussed.

SUMMARY

This chapter completes the discussion of the steps in the accounting data processing cycle. There are two phases to the cycle: the first phase (Steps 1-3) is carried out during the accounting period and the second phase (Steps 4-8) is completed at the end of the period.

In this chapter, a worksheet was prepared to assist in the completion of the cycle at the end of the period. A worksheet is an optional form that may be used to facilitate the preparation of financial statements, the recording of adjusting entries, and the recording of closing entries.

Closing entries are journal entries made at the end of the period to reduce the revenue, expense, and dividends declared accounts to a zero balance and transfer the net effect of these changes in stockholders' equity to the Retained Earnings account. These temporary accounts are then ready to accumulate information for the next accounting period.

After the adjusting and closing entries are posted to the ledger, a post-closing trial balance is prepared to verify the equality of debits and credits. As a final step in the cycle, some firms prepare reversing entries. Reversing entries are optional journal entries made to facilitate the recording of certain entries in the subsequent period.

SELF-TEST

Test your understanding of the chapter by selecting the best answer for each of the following.

1. A worksheet assists in accomplishing all the following steps in the accounting cycle of an enterprise except one. Which step does not belong in this listing?
   a. Journalizing transactions.
   b. Preparing adjusting entries.
   c. Preparing closing entries.
   d. Preparing financial statements.

2. In the worksheet as it is described in this chapter, a net income for the period is entered in which of the following columns?
   a. Income Statement Credit; Balance Sheet Credit.
   b. Income Statement Debit; Balance Sheet Credit.
   c. Income Statement Debit; Balance Sheet Debit.
   d. Income Statement Credit: Balance Sheet Debit.

3. At the end of the accounting period:
   a. the balances in the permanent accounts are reported in the income statement.
   b. the balances in the temporary accounts are reported in the balance sheet.
   c. all the permanent accounts are closed.
   d. the balances in the temporary accounts are closed to the Retained Earnings account.

4. Examples of accounts that are closed at the end of the accounting period include:
   a. Accumulated Depreciation, Unearned Revenue, and Income Summary.
   b. Income Summary, Dividends Declared, and Interest Receivable.
   c. Salary Expense, Service Revenue, Income Summary.
   d. Salary Expense, Salary Payable, and Utilities Expense.

5. Assume the following trial balance accounts and amounts:

Cash	$10 debit	Wages Payable	$10 credit
Equipment	50 debit	Revenues	80 credit
Accounts Payable	20 credit	Unearned Revenue	30 credit
Wages Expense	30 debit	Other Expenses	40 debit

   One necessary closing entry would require that Income Summary be:
   a. debited, $110.
   b. credited, $70.
   c. debited, $80.
   d. credited, $80.

6. In a worksheet, the Dividends Declared account is extended to the:
   a. Income Statement Debit column.
   b. Income Statement Credit column.
   c. Balance Sheet Debit column.
   d. Balance Sheet Credit column.

7. Adjusting entries are not recorded in a journal since they are entered in the worksheet.
   a. True.
   b. False.

8. The entry to close an Income Summary account with a credit balance will contain:
   a. a debit to the Retained Earnings account.
   b. a credit to the Capital Stock account.
   c. a credit to the Income Summary account.
   d. a debit to the Income Summary account.

9. The balance in the Dividends Declared account is:
   a. closed to the Retained Earnings account.
   b. carried forward since the account is not an expense.
   c. closed to the Income Summary account.
   d. none of the above.

10. Which of the following accounts will not appear in a post-closing trial balance?
    a. Retained Earnings.
    b. Unearned Rent Revenue.
    c. Rent Revenue.
    d. Salaries Payable

REVIEW PROBLEM

The unadjusted trial balance for Robinson and Parkinson, Inc., a legal corporation, on October 31, 1992, the end of the fiscal year is presented below.

ROBINSON AND PARKINSON, INC.
Unadjusted Trial Balance
October 31, 1992

Account Titles	Debits	Credits
Cash	$ 38,750	
Marketable Securities	70,000	
Accounts Receivable	7,520	
Prepaid Rent	13,500	
Prepaid Insurance	12,000	
Office Supplies On Hand	6,200	
Office Equipment	48,000	
Accumulated Depreciation–Office Equipment		$ 14,400
Automobiles	32,000	
Accumulated Depreciation–Automobiles		16,000
Accounts Payable		4,520
Notes Payable, due March 1, 1993		8,000
Unearned Legal Fees		3,980
Notes Payable, due March 1, 1995		16,000
Capital Stock		40,000
Retained Earnings		59,400
Dividends Declared	8,000	
Legal Fees Revenue		449,000
Salaries Expense	283,400	
Rent Expense	49,500	
Utility Expense	4,200	
Research Expense	10,600	
Travel Expense	22,800	
Gas, Oil, and Repair Expense	3,460	
Miscellaneous Expense	1,370	
Totals	$611,300	$611,300

Information available on October 31 for the preparation of the adjusting entries is as follows:

a. The balance in the Prepaid Rent account is for the three-month period, October, November, and December, 1992.
b. Insurance expired during the period is $6,500.
c. The amount of office supplies on hand determined by physical count is $1,600.
d. Interest earned but not yet received on the marketable securities is $4,200.
e. The office equipment is depreciated over 10 years with no residual value. The automobiles are depreciated over four years with no residual value.
f. $720 interest is accrued on the notes payable.
g. Unpaid salaries earned by employees are $24,000.
h. $2,700 of the balance in the Unearned Legal Fees account has been earned by the end of the year.
i. Travel expenses incurred by employees but unpaid are $1,420.
j. The income tax expense for the period is $5,206.

The following account titles are included in the chart of accounts.

Interest Receivable	Interest Revenue
Interest Payable	Insurance Expense
Salaries Payable	Office Supplies Expense
Travel Expense Payable	Depreciation Expense
Income Taxes Payable	Interest Expense
	Income Taxes Expense

Required:
A. Prepare a 10-column worksheet.
B. Prepare the closing entries.

ANSWER TO REVIEW PROBLEM

A.

ROBINSON AND PARKINSON, INC.
Worksheet
October 31, 1992

Account Titles	Unadjusted Trial Balance Debit	Credit	Adjustments Debit	Credit	Adjusted Trial Balance Debit	Credit	Income Statement Debit	Credit	Balance Sheet Debit	Credit
Cash	38,750				38,750				38,750	
Marketable Securities	70,000				70,000				70,000	
Accounts Receivable	7,520				7,520				7,520	
Prepaid Rent	13,500			(a) 4,500	9,000				9,000	
Prepaid Insurance	12,000			(b) 6,500	5,500				5,500	
Office Supplies On Hand	6,200			(c) 4,600	1,600				1,600	
Office Equipment	48,000				48,000				48,000	
Accumulated Depreciation— Office Equipment		14,400		(e) 4,800		19,200				19,200
Automobiles	32,000				32,000				32,000	
Accumulated Depreciation— Automobiles		16,000		(e) 8,000		24,000				24,000
Accounts Payable		4,520				4,520				4,520
Notes Payable, due March 1, 1993		8,000				8,000				8,000
Unearned Legal Fees		3,980	(h) 2,700			1,280				1,280
Notes Payable, due March 1, 1995		16,000				16,000				16,000
Capital Stock		40,000				40,000				40,000
Retained Earnings		59,400				59,400				59,400
Dividends Declared	8,000				8,000				8,000	
Legal Fees Revenue		449,000		(h) 2,700		451,700		451,700		
Salaries Expense	283,400		(g) 24,000		307,400		307,400			
Rent Expense	49,500		(a) 4,500		54,000		54,000			
Utility Expense	4,200				4,200		4,200			
Research Expense	10,600				10,600		10,600			
Travel Expense	22,800		(i) 1,420		24,220		24,220			
Gas, Oil, and Repair Exp.	3,460				3,460		3,460			
Miscellaneous Expense	1,370				1,370		1,370			
Totals	611,300	611,300								
Insurance Expense			(b) 6,500		6,500		6,500			
Office Supplies Expense			(c) 4,600		4,600		4,600			
Interest Receivable			(d) 4,200		4,200				4,200	
Interest Revenue				(d) 4,200		4,200		4,200		
Depreciation Expense			(e) 12,800		12,800		12,800			
Interest Expense			(f) 720		720		720			
Interest Payable				(f) 720		720				720
Salaries Payable				(g) 24,000		24,000				24,000
Travel Expense Payable				(i) 1,420		1,420				1,420
Income Taxes Expense			(j) 5,206		5,206		5,206			
Income Taxes Payable				(j) 5,206		5,206				5,206
Totals			66,646	66,646	659,646	659,646	435,076	455,900	224,570	203,746
Net income							20,824			20,824
Totals.							455,900	455,900	224,570	224,570

Determination of amounts for adjusting entries:

a. Because the Prepaid Rent account balance covers three months and one of the three months is October, one-third of the amount ($4,500) has expired and must be recognized as an expense.

b. Insurance Expense is the amount listed as expired in the problem.

c. If $6,200 is shown as the Office Supplies On Hand account balance on the trial balance, but only $1,600 is on hand at year-end, then the difference between the two amounts ($4,600) has been used up and must be recognized as an expense and a reduction in the balance in office supplies on hand.

d. Interest earned but not received must be recognized as both a receivable and a revenue for the amount earned.

e. Depreciation on the office equipment is calculated as follows:

$$\$48,000/10 \text{ years} = \$4,800 \text{ per year}$$

Depreciation on the automobiles is calculated as follows:

$$\$32,000/4 \text{ years} = \$8,000 \text{ per year}$$

f. Accrued interest on the notes payable constitutes an expense which has not been recognized and a liability which is not yet due. Therefore, the adjusting entry must recognize both the expense and the liability.

g. Salaries earned by employees but not yet paid must be recognized as both an expense and a liability for the amount earned.

h. The Unearned Legal Fees account shows a balance of $3,980. Of this amount, $2,700 has been earned. Therefore, the $2,700 is transferred to the Legal Fees Revenue account with a concurrent reduction in the balance of the Unearned Legal Fees account.

i. Travel expenses incurred but not yet paid must be recognized as an expense and a liability.

j. Income tax expense is the amount listed. The adjusting entry recognizes both an expense and liability for the unpaid taxes.

B. Closing Entries:

The information needed to close the revenue and expense accounts is available from the Income Statement columns of the worksheet. Accounts entered in the Income Statement debit column are closed by crediting them in the closing entries, and accounts entered in the Income Statement credit column are closed by debiting them in the closing entries. The closing entries for the revenue and expense accounts are as follows:

Oct.	31	Legal Fees Revenue	451,700	
		Interest Revenue	4,200	
		Income Summary		455,900
	31	Income Summary	435,076	
		Salaries Expense		307,400
		Rent Expense		54,000
		Utility Expense		4,200
		Research Expense		10,600
		Travel Expense		24,220
		Gas, Oil, and Repair Expense		3,460
		Miscellaneous Expense		1,370
		Insurance Expense		6,500
		Office Supplies Expense		4,600
		Depreciation Expense		12,800
		Interest Expense		720
		Income Taxes Expense		5,206
	31	Income Summary	20,824	
		Retained Earnings		20,824

The information needed to close the Dividends Declared account is available from the Balance Sheet columns of the worksheet. The Dividends Declared account is credited to reduce its balance to zero, and the Retained Earnings account is debited. The closing entry for the Dividends Declared account appears below.

	31	Retained Earnings	8,000	
		Dividends Declared		8,000

After the above journal entries have been posted to the ledger, all temporary accounts will have zero balances, and the closing entry process will have been completed.

ANSWERS TO SELF-TEST

1. a **2.** b **3.** d **4.** c **5.** d **6.** c **7.** b **8.** d
9. a **10.** c

APPENDIX: AN ALTERNATIVE METHOD OF RECORDING DEFERRALS

Objective 6: Alternative approach to record deferrals

In the preceding chapters, a prepaid expense was initially recorded in a prepaid asset account. Likewise, a revenue collected in advance was initially recorded in an unearned revenue account. In the case of a prepaid expense, an adjusting entry was made at the end of the period to transfer the portion of the asset consumed this period to an expense account. Similarly, an adjusting entry was made to transfer earned revenue from the liability account to a revenue account.

However, another approach is sometimes used to record the initial transaction related to the prepayment of an expense or the receipt of unearned revenue. Some businesses find it more convenient to initially record all payments for goods or services in expense accounts, regardless of whether a particular cost will benefit the current period only or several accounting periods. If this procedure is used, the ***unused portion of the prepaid expense*** must be transferred at the end of the period to an asset account. Consistent with this approach, the receipt of cash for services to be performed in the future is recorded directly in a revenue account, not a liability account, as in the method used in Chapter 4. Thus, at the end of the period, an adjusting entry is prepared to transfer the still ***unearned revenue*** from the revenue account to a liability account in the balance sheet.

PAYMENTS FOR PREPAID EXPENSES RECORDED IN EXPENSE ACCOUNTS

To illustrate recording prepaid expenses in expense accounts, assume that the policy of Quality Real Estate Office, Inc. is to record payments for insurance policies in an Insurance Expense account. The entry on June 1 to record the payment of $1,200 for a 24-month insurance policy that is effective June 1 is:

June	1	Insurance Expense	1,200	
		Cash		1,200

The monthly cost for the insurance protection is $50 ($1,200/24 months). One month of the coverage expired during June leaving 23 months prepaid. The unexpired portion at June 30 is:

$$\text{Prepaid insurance} = 23 \text{ months} \times \$50$$
$$= \$1,150$$

At the end of the period an adjusting entry is needed to remove the unexpired portion of the insurance coverage from the expense account and transfer it to an asset account.

(a) June	30	Prepaid Insurance	1,150	
		Insurance Expense		1,150

After these entries are posted, the two accounts appear as follows:

Prepaid Insurance			Insurance Expense			
6/30	1,150		6/1	1,200	6/30	1,150
			6/30 Bal.	50		

The June 30 balances are the same (Prepaid Insurance, $1,150; Insurance Expense, $50) as when the insurance premium payment was initially made to the Prepaid Insurance account (see page 136 in Chapter 4).

REVENUES COLLECTED IN ADVANCE RECORDED IN REVENUE ACCOUNTS

To illustrate the adjustment of unearned revenue when the receipt is recorded initially in a revenue account, assume that Quality Real Estate Office, Inc. received $300 on June 15 to manage three rental units for the period June 15 through September 15 and made the following entry on June 15.

June	15	Cash	300	
		Management Fees Revenue		300

On June 30, an adjusting entry is needed to transfer the unearned portion of the revenue from the Management Fees Revenue account to a liability account. The amount of the adjusting entry is computed as follows.

$$\$300/3 \text{ months} = \$100 \text{ of revenue earned per month}$$
$$\$100 \times 2\frac{1}{2} \text{ months unearned} = \$250 \text{ unearned at the end of June}$$

The adjusting entry is:

June	30	Management Fees Revenue	250	
		Unearned Management Fees		250

After the entries are posted, the accounts will show:

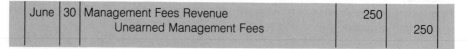

Unearned Management Fees		**Management Fees Revenues**		
	6/30　250	6/30　250	6/15	300
			6/30 Bal.	50

Note again that the results are the same as those that existed when the cash receipt was recorded initially in the liability account (see page 140).

APPENDIX: REVERSING ENTRIES

Objective 7: Preparing reversing entries

In the Quality Real Estate Office, Inc. illustration, the preparation of a post-closing trial balance was the last step in the accounting cycle. However, some firms add another step, reversing entries, to the cycle. A reversing entry is a journal entry that is the opposite of a related adjusting entry that was made at the end of the current period. It is dated as of the first day of the next accounting period. The reversing process *is a bookkeeping technique made to simplify the recording of regular transactions in the next accounting period*.

A discussion of reversing entries is presented here because they are used in practice by some companies. It should be emphasized that reversing entries are optional and are made only to facilitate the recording of routine transactions in future periods. Furthermore, all accruals, but only deferrals initially recorded in income statement (temporary) accounts, are reversed. Reversing entries are not made for deferrals initially recorded in balance sheet (permanent) accounts. As a general rule, a *reversing entry should be made for any adjusting entry that increased an asset or liability account*.

REVERSING ADJUSTMENTS OF DEFERRALS RECORDED IN TEMPORARY ACCOUNTS

In the first section of this Appendix, expenses paid in advance and revenues collected in advance were originally recorded in temporary accounts. When this method is used, adjusting entries are normally reversed on the first day of the next accounting period. In the case of the prepaid insurance, the following reversing entry is made on July 1 to restore the prepaid portion of the premium of $1,150 to the Insurance Expense account.

July	1	Insurance Expense	1,150	
		Prepaid Insurance		1,150

After this entry is posted, the Prepaid Insurance account balance is zero and the Insurance Expense account balance is $1,150 (the $50 balance as of June 30 was closed to the Income Summary). Additional payments for insurance premiums are then added to the balance in the Insurance Expense account. At the end of the next reporting period, the account is analyzed and the prepaid portion is removed, as was done in entry (a) on page 199.

Compare this reversing entry to the adjusting entry on June 30. Note that the debit and credit amounts are the same in both entries, but the account debited (Prepaid Insurance) in the adjusting entry is credited in the reversing entry, whereas the account credited (Insurance Expense) in the adjusting entry is debited in the reversing entry. In other words, the reversing entry is the opposite of the adjusting entry.

The adjusting entry for the unearned revenue is reversed by the following entry.

July	1	Unearned Management Fees	250	
		Management Fees Revenue		250

The accounts would appear as follows after this entry is posted.

Unearned Management Fees

7/1	250	6/30	250

Management Fees Revenue

6/30	250	6/15	300
6/30	50		
	300		300
		7/1	250

Additional receipts for management fees in the next fiscal period are credited to the Management Fees Revenue account. This results in bookkeeping consistency as all receipts for management fees are recorded in this one account. The unearned fees are adjusted out at the end of the next period.

REVERSING ENTRIES RELATED TO ADJUSTMENTS FOR ACCRUALS

Adjusting entries for accruals of revenues and expenses are often reversed to permit the recording of a routine entry in the next accounting period when the cash is received or paid. To illustrate reversing entries for an accrued expense, we will use the same accrued salaries adjustment that was used in Chapter 4.

1. Salaries paid on June 22 were $2,500.
2. Unpaid salaries of $1,250 were accrued on June 30.
3. Salaries earned for the period June 23 to July 6 in the amount of $2,300 are to be paid on July 6.

The journal entries to record these transactions are:

June	22	Salaries Expense	2,500	
		Cash		2,500
		To record payment of salaries.		
	30	Salaries Expense	1,250	
		Salaries Payable		1,250
		To record unpaid salaries at the end of June.		
	30	Income Summary	3,750	
		Salaries Expense		3,750
		To close the Salaries Expense account.		
July	6	Salaries Payable	1,250	
		Salaries Expense	1,050	
		Cash		2,300
		To record payment of salaries for the period June 23 to July 6.		

Because the $2,300 payment is for salaries earned during two different accounting periods, the payment must be divided into two elements. First, the $1,250 debit settles the liability for the salaries earned by employees in June that were reported as an expense in June. Second, the $1,050 debit to the expense account properly recognizes as an expense that portion of the payment made for salaries incurred in July.

After posting the entry, the Salaries Expense and Salaries Payable accounts appear as follows:

Salaries Payable					**Salaries Expense**			
7/6	1,250	6/30	1,250	6/22	2,500	6/30	3,750
				6/30	1,250		
					3,750		3,750
				7/6	1,050		

Note that the entry to record the payment on July 6 requires two debits—a variation from the normal entry of one debit to the Salaries Expense account. Thus, a change from the normal procedures is necessary. The adjusting entry or the Salaries Expense account in the general ledger must be referred to in order to divide the payment between the two accounts. To simplify the July 6 entry, a reversing entry may be made to reverse the effects of the adjusting entry as follows.

July	1	Salaries Payable	1,250	
		Salaries Expense		1,250
		To reverse the adjusting entry to accrue unpaid salaries.		

The reversing entry transfers the balance in the liability account to an expense account. This produces a temporary credit balance of $1,250 in the expense account (however, it is still a liability) on July 1 since it had a zero balance before the reversing entry as a result of the closing process. This permits making the normal entry to record the payment on July 6 as follows.

July	6	Salaries Expense	2,300	
		Cash		2,300
		To record payment of salaries for the period June 23 to July 6.		

The accounts after this entry is posted are as follows:

Salaries Payable				Salaries Expense			
7/1	1,250	6/30	1,250	6/22	2,500	6/30	3,750
				6/30	1,250		
					3,750		3,750
				7/6	2,300	7/1	1,250
				Bal.	1,050		

The debit of $2,300 is partially offset by the credit of $1,250 made in the reversing entry. This leaves a balance of $1,050 in the Salaries Expense account, which is the expense for July.

A comparison of the account balances reveals that the two approaches produce identical results. Salaries expense for June and July are $3,750 and $1,050, respectively, and a liability for $1,250 is reported in the June 30 balance sheet.

Reversing entries are also useful when many similar transactions involve the computation of accruals. For example, a bank may have thousands of outstanding notes receivable. At the end of the period, interest earned but not received must be accrued in order to properly report interest revenue and interest receivable in the financial statements. If a reversing entry is not made, then each time that an interest payment is received in the next period, an employee must refer back to the list of accruals. This is necessary in order to divide the amount of the payment between the reduction in the receivable balance and the interest earned in the current period. If the adjusting entry is reversed, the receipt of cash for interest is simply recorded as a debit to Cash and a credit to Interest Revenue. In this case, reversals will result in saving a great deal of time since an employee will not have to allocate each interest payment between two periods. An illustration of a reversing entry related to a revenue transaction is presented in Figure 5-12.

To illustrate the reversal of the accrual of revenue, assume that a company loaned a client $100,000 and that at December 31, the fiscal year-end, unpaid interest of $2,000 had accrued on the note.

Without Reversing Entries	With Reversing Entries

1. December 31, 1992–Adjusting entry to accrue interest revenue and interest receivable.

Dec. 31	Interest Receivable	2,000		Interest Receivable	2,000	
	Interest Revenue		2,000	Interest Revenue		2,000

2. December 31, 1992–Closing entry assuming that the Interest Revenue account contained a $10,000 balance before the adjusting entry.

Dec. 31	Interest Revenue	12,000		Interest Revenue	12,000	
	Income Summary		12,000	Income Summary		12,000

3. January 1, 1993–Entry to reverse the effects of the adjusting entry.

Jan. 1	No entry is made.			Interest Revenue	2,000	
				Interest Receivable		2,000

4. May 1, 1993–Record the receipt of the interest payment in the amount of $6,000.

May 1	Cash	6,000		Cash	6,000	
	Interest Receivable		2,000	Interest Revenue		6,000
	Interest Revenue		4,000			

Without Reversing Entries

Interest Receivable				Interest Revenue					Cash		
12/31	2,000	5/1	2,000	12/31	12,000	Bal.	10,000	5/1	6,000		
						12/31	2,000				
					12,000		12,000				
						5/1	4,000				

With Reversing Entries

Interest Receivable				Interest Revenue					Cash		
12/31	2,000	1/1	2,000	12/31	12,000	Bal.	10,000	5/1	6,000		
						12/31	2,000				
					12,000		12,000				
				1/1	2,000	5/1	6,000				
						Bal.	4,000				

Figure 5-12
Illustration of Reversing Entries Revenue Transaction

SELF-TEST

Test your understanding of the Appendix by selecting the best answer for each of the following.

1. If the rent was paid on October 1, 1991 for one year and the entry to record that payment was a debit to Rent Expense and a credit to Cash for $4,000, which of the following adjustments would need to be made on December 31, 1991?

   a. Rent Expense   1,000
         Prepaid Rent   1,000

   b. Prepaid Rent   3,000
         Rent Expense   3,000

   c. Rent Expense   3,000
         Prepaid Rent   3,000

   d. Prepaid Rent   1,000
         Rent Expense   1,000

2. Reversing entries are:
   a. normally prepared for all prepaid and accrued adjusting entries.
   b. necessary to achieve a proper matching of revenue and expenses.
   c. made to facilitate the recording of routine transactions in future periods.
   d. made for any adjusting entry that decreased an asset or a liability account.

3. Reversing entries are made by journalizing the exact opposite of a previous adjusting entry. They are:
   a. used to facilitate routine bookkeeping but are not required by accounting principles.
   b. required by accounting principles and must be made at the end of the accounting period.
   c. used to ensure that all account balances are correct before the books are closed.
   d. needed if it is desired to avoid making closing entries.

4. At December 31, unpaid wages amounted to $6,000. What is the reversing entry?

   a. Wages Expense   6,000
         Wages Payable   6,000

   b. Prepaid Wages   6,000
         Wages Expense   6,000

   c. Wages Expense   6,000
         Prepaid Wages   6,000

   d. Wages Payable   6,000
         Wages Expense   6,000

ANSWERS TO SELF-TEST

1. b   **2.** c   **3.** a   **4.** d

GLOSSARY

CLOSING ENTRIES. Journal entries made at the end of an accounting period to reduce temporary accounts to a zero balance and transfer the net balance to the Retained Earnings account (p. 184).

CROSSFOOTING. Adding or subtracting horizontally across a worksheet (p. 180).

PERMANENT (REAL) ACCOUNTS. Balance sheet accounts are called permanent accounts, because they are not closed at the end of the period (p. 184).

POST-CLOSING TRIAL BALANCE. A trial balance taken after the adjusting and closing entries have been posted to the accounts (p. 191).

REVERSING ENTRIES. Entries made to record the opposite effects of certain adjusting entries (p. 178).

TEMPORARY (NOMINAL) ACCOUNTS. The revenue, expense, and dividends declared accounts are called temporary accounts, because they are reduced to a zero balance (closed) at the end of an accounting period (p. 184).

WORKSHEET. A form used by accountants to gather and organize the information needed to complete the accounting cycle (p. 176).

DISCUSSION QUESTIONS

1. List the steps in the accounting cycle that are completed at the end of an accounting period. Prepare a diagram.
2. Why do accountants prepare a worksheet?
3. In which columns of the worksheet is the Dividends Declared account entered?
4. On a worksheet the totals of the debit and credit columns of the income statement and the balance sheet will not balance. What is this difference called?
5. In which columns of the worksheet is the net income for the period entered? the net loss?
6. What will be the effect on the worksheet and the financial statements if the Unearned Revenue account is erroneously entered as a credit in the income statement columns instead of the balance sheet columns?
7. Why are the adjusting entries recorded in the journal and posted to the ledger even though they are entered on the worksheet?
8. What is a nominal or temporary account? a real or permanent account? Which accounts are closed?
9. Explain the process and the purpose of closing entries.
10. List the four sequential steps in the closing entry process.
11. Why are the balance sheet accounts not closed?
12. Why is the Dividends Declared account not included with expenses in the closing entry process?
13. What is the purpose of the post-closing trial balance?

14. Most large firms issue interim quarterly statements, but only formally adjust and close the books annually. Explain the process used to prepare interim statements.

15A. If a company debits Supplies Expense when supplies are purchased, what accounts will be debited or credited in the end-of-period adjusting entry?

16A. What are reversing entries?

17A. What types of adjusting entries are normally reversed?

EXERCISES

Exercise 5-1 Accounting Process
Listed below in alphabetical order are the steps in the accounting cycle.

_____ Adjusting entries are entered on the worksheet.
_____ Adjusting entries are posted to the ledger.
_____ Adjusting entries are recorded in the journal.
_____ Analysis of the event takes place.
_____ Closing entries are posted to the ledger.
_____ Closing entries are recorded in the journal.
_____ Financial statements are prepared.
_____ Journal entries are posted to the ledger.
_____ Occurrence of the event.
_____ Post-closing trial balance is prepared.
_____ Transactions are recorded in the journal.
_____ Unadjusted trial balance is entered on the worksheet.
_____ Worksheet is completed.

Required:
In the blanks preceding each step, number the process in its chronological order.

Exercise 5-2 Extension of Account Balances to Proper Worksheet Columns
Listed below are the ledger accounts appearing in the adjusted trial balance columns of a worksheet.

_3_ Cash	_____ Interest Expense
_____ Dividends Declared	_____ Interest Revenue
_____ Buildings	_____ Unearned Revenues
_____ Wage Expense	_____ Office Supplies On Hand
_____ Mortgage Payable	_____ Property Tax Expense
_____ Prepaid Insurance	_____ Interest Payable
_____ Equipment	_____ Accumulated Depreciation—
_____ Utilities Expense	Buildings
_____ Land	_____ Rent Expense
_____ Service Revenues	_____ Retained Earnings
_____ Wages Payable	_____ Marketable Securities
_____ Accounts Receivable	_____ Accounts Payable
_____ Capital Stock	_____ Income Tax Expense

Required:

Indicate in the blank provided in which column of the worksheet the amount in each account would be extended by entering the following code numbers:

> 1 = income statement, debit
> 2 = income statement, credit
> 3 = balance sheet, debit
> 4 = balance sheet, credit

The first account is completed as an example.

Exercise 5-3 Completion of Worksheet and Preparation of Financial Statements

The following unadjusted trial balance was prepared from the general ledger account balances of the Clarke Company on December 31, 1992. (All 000s have been omitted.)

Account Titles	Debit	Credit
Cash	$ 10	
Accounts Receivable	32	
Prepaid Insurance	4	
Office Supplies On Hand	8	
Equipment	60	
Accumulated Depreciation—Equipment		$ 18
Accounts Payable		9
Notes Payable, Long-term		15
Capital Stock		30
Retained Earnings		14
Service Revenues		95
Salaries Expense	31	
Utilities Expense	10	
Rent Expense	20	
Miscellaneous Expense	6	
Totals	$181	$181

Required:

A. Enter the above trial balance on a ten-column worksheet. Add the following account titles to those listed in the above trial balance: Insurance Expense, Office Supplies Expense, Depreciation Expense, Interest Expense, Interest Payable, Salaries Payable, and Rent Payable.

B. Record the adjusting entries on the worksheet using the following information:
  a. Unexpired insurance on December 31, 1992 is $2.
  b. Office supplies used during 1992 are $4.
  c. Annual depreciation on the equipment is $6.
  d. Accrued interest on the note is $3.
  e. Unpaid salaries at December 31, 1992 are $3.
  f. The December, 1992 rent of $4 is unpaid as of December 31, 1992.

C. Complete the worksheet.

D. Prepare an income statement and a classified balance sheet.

Exercise 5-4   Completion of Worksheet with Missing Numbers

Following is a partially completed worksheet for the Baxter Consulting Company.

BAXTER CONSULTING COMPANY
Worksheet
December 31, 1992

Account Titles	Unadjusted Trial Balance Debit	Credit	Adjustments Debit	Credit	Income Statement Debit	Credit	Balance Sheet Debit	Credit
Cash	1,200						(q)	
Accounts Receivable	(a)						(r)	
Prepaid Rent	520			(h)			200	
Office Supplies On Hand	200			(i)			120	
Equipment	6,000						(s)	
Accumulated Depreciation— Equipment		(b)		240				960
Accounts Payable		400						(v)
Capital Stock		(c)						(w)
Retained Earnings		1,100						1,100
Dividends Declared	600						(t)	
Consulting Revenues		9,160				(o)		
Salaries Expense	5,200		300		(l)			
Utilities Expense	260		(d)		320			
Rent Expense	400		(e)		(m)			
	14,980	14,980						
Office Supplies Expense			(f)		80			
Depreciation Expense			(g)		240			
Salaries Payable				(j)				(x)
Utilities Payable				(k)				60
			1,000	1,000	6,860	(p)	8,720	(y)
Net Income					(n)			(z)
					9,160	9,160	(u)	8,720

Required:

Compute the missing amounts (indicated by letters) and complete the worksheet. All adjustments are usual and routine. The letters *do not* indicate the order in which the missing amounts should be computed.

Exercise 5-5   Closing Accounts and Preparation of the Retained Earnings Statement

On January 1, 1992, Bailey Company had capital stock of $250,000 and retained earnings of $700,000. During the period $80,000 of cash dividends were declared and paid. The income statement reported revenues of $2,500,000 and operating expenses of $2,475,000.

Required:
A. Prepare closing entries using summary revenue and expense account balances.
B. Prepare a retained earnings statement for the year ended December 31, 1992.
C. At December 31, 1992, how much equity in the corporation's assets do the stockholders have?
D. During 1992 Bailey Company paid dividends in excess of net income. How were they able to do this?

Exercise 5-6 **Closing Entries**
The following T accounts were taken from the ledger of Lily, Inc.

Capital Stock	Retained Earnings
12/31 Bal. 50,000	12/31 Bal. 22,000

Dividends Declared	Income Summary
12/31 Bal. 8,000	

Service Revenue	Salaries Expense
12/31 Bal. 45,000	12/31 Bal. 16,000

Rent Expense	Utilities Expense
12/31 Bal. 14,000	12/31 Bal. 5,000

Required:
A. Set up the T accounts and their balances.
B. Prepare the closing entries in general journal format.
C. Post the closing entries to the T accounts.
D. Compute the balance in the Retained Earnings account.

Exercise 5-7 **Closing Entries**
The following information is from the adjusted trial balance of the Mountain Corporation as of July 31, 1992.

Account Title	Debit	Credit
Cash	$178,000	
Accounts Receivable	80,520	
Office Supplies On Hand	600	
Prepaid Insurance	1,000	
Equipment	80,000	
Accumulated Depreciation—Equipment		$ 18,700
Accounts Payable		52,000
Wages Payable		10,000
Notes Payable		50,000
Capital Stock		120,000
Retained Earnings		74,660
Dividends Declared	10,000	
Backpacking Revenue		198,200
Interest Revenue		1,360
Miscellaneous Revenue		800
Salaries Expense	108,110	

Rent Expense	32,000	
Depreciation Expense—Equipment	15,800	
Supplies Expense	4,840	
Insurance Expense	14,800	
Miscellaneous Expense	50	
Totals	$525,720	$525,720

Required:
Use the relevant information from the trial balance to prepare the appropriate closing entries.

Exercise 5-8 Closing Entries

The income statement and retained earnings statement of Conglomerate Rentals, Inc., are presented below:

CONGLOMERATE RENTALS, INC.
Income Statement
For the Year Ended August 31, 1992

Revenues:		
Equipment rental revenues	$62,810	
Automobile rental revenues	45,100	
Furniture rental revenues	59,230	
Total Revenues		$167,140
Expenses:		
Salaries expense	42,380	
Depreciation expense	23,510	
Insurance expense	21,250	
Maintenance expense	11,830	
Utilities expense	5,600	
Supplies expense	5,400	
Advertising expense	4,220	
Property tax expense	2,450	
Income tax expense	15,150	
Total Expenses		131,790
Net Income		$ 35,350

CONGLOMERATE RENTALS, INC.
Retained Earnings Statement
For the Year Ended August 31, 1992

Retained earnings, September 1, 1991	$230,420
Add: Net income	35,350
Total	265,770
Deduct: Dividends declared and paid	20,000
Retained earnings, August 31, 1992	$245,770

Required:
Prepare the closing entries for Conglomerate Rentals, Inc., for the year ended August 31, 1992.

Exercise 5-9A Deferred Expense Recorded in an Expense Account

Valet Company purchased a three-year insurance policy on November 1, 1992 for $32,400.

Required:

A. Assuming the entire premium cost was debited to Insurance Expense, prepare the journal entry on November 1, 1992 to record the transaction.
B. Prepare the adjusting entry on December 31, 1992.
C. What will be the balance in the Prepaid Insurance account on December 31, 1992? What will be the balance in the Insurance Expense account on December 31, 1992?
D. If reversing entries are made by Valet Company, prepare the entry that would be made on January 1, 1993 to reverse the adjusting entry.

Exercise 5-10A Deferred Revenue Recorded in a Revenue Account

Wren Corporation engages in constructing and renting office space to various businesses. On August 1, 1992, one tenant gave Wren Corporation a $9,000 check for eight months' rent. Wren credited Rental Fees Revenue to record the receipt.

Required:

A. Prepare the journal entry on August 1, 1992 to record the transaction.
B. Prepare the adjusting entry on December 31, 1992.
C. If the December 31, 1992 adjusting entry is omitted, what will be the impact on the financial statements?
D. Compute the balance in the Rental Fees Revenue account on December 31, 1992.
E. Assuming that Wren Corporation makes reversing entries, prepare the reversing entry on January 1, 1993, if needed.

Exercise 5-11A Reversing Entries—Accrued Expense

On September 1, 1992, Ashok, Inc., purchased a computer from Byte Electronics for $8,000. Ashok paid $3,000 in cash and gave a $5,000, six-month note with an annual interest rate of 12% for the remainder of the purchase price. The note principal and interest are due on March 1, 1993.

On December 31, 1992, the end of Ashok's fiscal year, $200 of interest had accrued on the note. On March 1, 1993, Ashok paid the note principal plus $300 of interest to Byte Electronics.

Required:

A. Prepare the required adjusting entry on December 31, 1992 with respect to this note.
B. Prepare the closing entry related to this note on December 31, 1992.
C. Prepare the reversing entry with respect to this note on January 1, 1993.
D. Prepare the journal entry to record payment of this note and interest on March 1, 1993, assuming:
   1. a reversing entry was made on January 1, 1993.
   2. no reversing entry was made on January 1, 1993.
E. Refer to requirement (D). Does the preparation of a reversing entry on the first day of a new fiscal year make subsequent entries to record payments of accrued expenses as of the end of the previous fiscal period easier or more difficult? Explain.

Exercise 5-12A   Reversing Entries—Accrued Revenue

Barbara Healey operates an interior design service for restaurants, shopping malls, professional offices, and other similar businesses. Barbara bills her clients quarterly on January 15, April 15, July 15, and October 15. Payments are due by the first of the month following the billing month. On December 31, 1992, Barbara's year-end, revenues of $21,420 were accrued but not yet billed or recorded.

Required:
A. Prepare the adjusting entry needed on December 31, 1992. The chart of accounts contains an Accounts Receivable account and a Service Revenues account.
B. Prepare the closing entry related to this transaction.
C. Prepare the reversing entry on January 1, 1993.
D. Prepare the journal entry on January 22, 1993 to record receipt of a client's payment of $1,000 for services performed in 1992:
    1. assuming a reversing entry was made on January 1, 1993.
    2. assuming no reversing entry was made on January 1, 1993.
E. Prepare the journal entry on February 8, 1993 to record receipt of a new client's payment of $500 for the months of December and January at a monthly fee of $250:
    1. assuming a reversing entry was made on January 1, 1993.
    2. assuming no reversing entry was made on January 1, 1993.

Exercise 5-13A   Reversing Entries—Unearned Revenue

Charles Horne, an attorney, has several clients who pay a monthly fee. The amount received is credited to the Legal Fees Revenue account when received by Horne. On September 30, 1992, the end of Horne's fiscal year, an analysis of the revenue account reflected $7,810 was unearned on that date.

Required:
A. Prepare the adjusting entry needed on September 30, 1992.
B. Prepare the reversing entry on October 1, 1992.
C. If the reversing entry is not made on October 1, 1992, how and when will the balance in the liability account be removed?

Exercise 5-14   Multiple Choice—Preparation of a Worksheet and Completion of the Accounting Cycle

Select the best answer to each of the following questions.

1. A worksheet is prepared:
    a. to facilitate preparation of financial statements.
    b. instead of financial statements.
    c. as part of the corporate annual report.
    d. only by manufacturing firms.
2. Worksheets are prepared for use by:
    a. stockholders.
    b. banks and other financial institutions.
    c. the management of the firm.
    d. the accountant only.

3. Which of the following is a temporary account?
   a. Cash.
   b. Unearned Revenue.
   c. Taxes Payable.
   d. Interest Revenue.

4. Which of the following accounts is not closed at a company's fiscal year end?
   a. Salaries Expense.
   b. Service Revenue.
   c. Accumulated Depreciation.
   d. Depreciation Expense.

5. Which of the following type(s) of accounts is (are) closed in the year-end closing process?
   a. Real accounts.
   b. Asset accounts.
   c. Contra accounts.
   d. Temporary accounts.

6. Reversing entries are:
   a. always required.
   b. required only when a worksheet is prepared.
   c. required only for interim financial statements.
   d. not required.

7. If a company had revenues of $1,200, salaries expense of $600, operating expenses of $200, and dividends declared of $100, its closing entries would include:
   a. a debit to Income Summary of $1,200.
   b. a credit to Income Summary of $1,200.
   c. a debit to Dividends Declared of $100.
   d. a credit to Income Summary of $800.

8. Which of the following is not an expense?
   a. Depreciation Expense.
   b. Dividends Declared.
   c. Telephone Expense.
   d. Insurance Expense.

9. The post-closing trial balance includes:
   a. only permanent accounts.
   b. income statement accounts.
   c. nominal accounts.
   d. all accounts.

PROBLEMS

Problem 5-1 **Preparation of a Worksheet**

The trial balance for the Santa Fe Hair Company on December 31, 1992 is presented below.

SANTA FE HAIR COMPANY
Trial Balance
December 31, 1992

Account Title	Debit	Credit
Cash	$ 22,870	
Accounts Receivable	4,280	
Office Supplies on Hand	1,850	
Beauty Supplies on Hand	15,800	
Prepaid Insurance	3,600	
Equipment	56,000	
Accumulated Depreciation—Equipment		$ 8,000
Accounts Payable		3,480
Notes Payable, Due September 30, 1995		20,000
Capital Stock		25,000
Retained Earnings		15,620
Dividends Declared	2,000	
Service Revenues		146,800
Salaries Expense	65,700	
Rent Expense	44,000	
Advertising Expense	2,800	
Totals	$218,900	$218,900

Required:

A. Enter the above trial balance on a 10-column worksheet. The following account titles are included in the chart of accounts.

Office Supplies Expense	Beauty Supplies Expense
Insurance Expense	Interest Expense
Depreciation Expense—Equipment	Income Taxes Expense
Interest Payable	Salaries Payable
	Income Taxes Payable

B. Complete the worksheet using the following information in preparing the adjusting entries.

a. Office supplies used during the year totaled $950.

b. Beauty supplies on hand were determined to be $2,790.

c. Unexpired prepaid insurance amounted to $560.

d. The equipment is depreciated over ten years and is expected to have a zero residual value.

e. Accrued interest on the notes payable is $900.

f. December salaries of $3,540 have not been paid or recorded.

g. Unpaid income taxes at the end of the year were $2,820.

Problem 5-2 **Preparation of a Worksheet, Financial Statements, and Closing Entries**

The unadjusted trial balance of Reliable Moving Company at the end of their fiscal year is shown below.

RELIABLE MOVING COMPANY
Trial Balance
October 31, 1992

Account Title	Debit	Credit
Cash	$ 67,800	
Accounts Receivable	45,700	
Office Supplies on Hand	1,280	
Prepaid Advertising	4,300	
Moving Vans	210,000	
Accumulated Depreciation—Vans		$ 72,000
Office Equipment	48,000	
Accumulated Depreciation—Equipment		12,000
Accounts Payable		36,480
Unearned Moving Fees		4,520
Capital Stock		120,000
Retained Earnings		33,200
Moving Revenues		331,000
Insurance Expense	24,320	
Salaries Expense	145,240	
Advertising Expense	4,560	
Maintenance Expense	15,200	
Gas Expense	42,800	
Totals	$609,200	$609,200

A year-end analysis of the accounting records disclosed the following information.

a. A physical inventory of the office supplies showed $500 of office supplies on hand October 31, 1992.

b. Annual depreciation on the moving vans is $42,000.

c. Annual depreciation on the office equipment is $6,000.

d. The balance in the Unearned Moving Fees account includes $3,020 received in September for moving services provided in October. The remaining portion has not been earned.

e. Salaries earned but not paid amount to $2,100.

f. Gas purchased on account for $1,700 and used during the last half of October has not been paid for or recorded.

g. The October insurance premium of $2,500 is past due and has not been recorded.

h. The Prepaid Advertising account balance includes $1,000 prepayment for an advertising campaign beginning in November. Advertising services for the remaining balance had been performed.

Required:

A. Prepare a 10-column worksheet for the year ended October 31, 1992. Add accounts as needed during the adjusting entry process. The following account titles are included in the chart of accounts:

Office Supplies Expense
Depreciation Expense—Vans
Depreciation Expense—Equipment
Salaries Payable
Accrued Expenses Payable

B. Prepare an income statement, retained earnings statement, and a balance sheet.
C. Journalize the closing entries.

Problem 5-3 End of Period Analysis of Financial Information

Cedar Hills Corporation began operations January 2, 1992. The following two trial balances were prepared at the end of the first year of operations, December 31, 1992. All amounts are in thousands of dollars.

Account Titles	Unadjusted Trial Balance		Adjusted Trial Balance	
	Debit	Credit	Debit	Credit
Cash	$ 52		$ 52	
Accounts Receivable	65		65	
Prepaid Insurance	10		5	
Rent Receivable	0		4	
Equipment	80		80	
Accumulated Depreciation—				
Equipment		$ 0		$ 16
Accounts Payable		22		22
Salaries Payable		0		6
Income Taxes Payable		0		4
Unearned Rent Revenue		12		6
Notes Payable, 14%, dated				
April 1, 1992		50		50
Capital Stock, $5 par value		100		100
Retained Earnings		0		0
Dividends Declared	5		5	
Revenues (total)		186		196
Expenses (including interest and				
depreciation)	158		185	
Income Tax Expense	0		4	
Totals	$370	$370	$400	$400

Required:
A. Based upon an analysis of the two trial balances, prepare the 1992 adjusting entries in general journal form.
B. Based upon the above information, prepare the 1992 closing entries. Note: You may complete a worksheet, but it is not required.
C. Using the information contained within the two trial balances and that which you developed in requirements (A) and (B), answer the following questions. Show your computations.
  1. How many shares of capital stock were outstanding at year-end?
  2. What is the balance in the retained earnings account to be reported on the 1992 balance sheet?
  3. Assuming no residual value and straight-line depreciation, what is the estimated useful life of the equipment?
  4. What is the amount of depreciation expense included in the total expenses for 1992?

5. What was the interest expense included in the total expenses for 1992?
6. Assuming the insurance policy was purchased on June 30, 1992, for what period of time is the coverage?
7. Explain how the amount of cash could increase by $52,000 during the year, when the net income for the period is relatively small.

Problem 5-4 Preparation of Worksheet, Financial Statements, and Closing Entries

Telephone Express Service had the following unadjusted trial balance prepared on September 30, 1992, the end of the fiscal year.

TELEPHONE EXPRESS SERVICE
Trial Balance
September 30, 1992

Account Title	Debit	Credit
Cash	$ 9,600	
Accounts Receivable	2,870	
Prepaid Rent	1,200	
Office Supplies on Hand	505	
Office Equipment	28,640	
Accumulated Depreciation—Equipment		$ 7,795
Accounts Payable		4,120
Note Payable—Due March 31, 1993		7,100
Capital Stock		3,940
Retained Earnings		4,310
Dividends Declared	2,000	
Fees Earned		70,340
Rent Expense	19,655	
Wages Expense	31,840	
Utilities Expense	1,295	
Totals	$97,605	$97,605

Use the following information to make year-end adjustments. The following accounts are included in the chart of accounts.

Office Supplies Expense	Depreciation Expense
Interest Payable	Interest Expense

a. Rent of $1,200 for the four month period from September 1 to December 31 was paid in advance.
b. A physical count of office supplies shows $100 on hand as of September 30, 1992.
c. Depreciation on the office equipment is $3,000.
d. Interest accrued on the note payable is $500.

Required:

A. Prepare a 10-column worksheet for the year ended September 30, 1992.
B. Prepare an income statement and a retained earnings statement for the year ended September 30, 1992 and a balance sheet as of September 30, 1992.
C. Journalize the closing entries.

Problem 5-5   Mini-Comprehensive Review Problem

The March 31, 1992 trial balance of Fidelity Company is shown below.

FIDELITY COMPANY
Trial Balance
March 31, 1992

Acct. No.	Account Title	Debit	Credit
101	Cash	$ 12,600	
102	Accounts Receivable	7,480	
111	Office Supplies on Hand	6,450	
113	Prepaid Insurance	6,400	
151	Equipment	84,000	
152	Accumulated Depreciation—Equipment		$ 21,000
201	Accounts Payable		7,490
202	Salaries Payable		–0–
203	Income Taxes Payable		–0–
204	Interest Payable		–0–
221	Notes Payable, Due July 1, 1995, 12%		20,000
301	Capital Stock		30,000
302	Retained Earnings		16,300
303	Dividends Declared	3,000	
310	Income Summary		–0–
401	Beach Tour Revenues		61,500
501	Salaries Expense	25,860	
502	Rent Expense	9,900	
503	Income Tax Expense	–0–	
511	Office Supplies Expense	–0–	
513	Insurance Expense	–0–	
514	Interest Expense	600	
551	Depreciation Expense—Equipment	–0–	
	Totals	$156,290	$156,290

Transactions completed during April 1992, in summary form, are as follows.

1. Beach tour revenues were $12,000 of which $5,000 was received in cash.
2. Collected $4,000 of accounts receivable.
3. Purchased office supplies on account for $420.
4. Paid $4,820 of accounts payable.
5. Declared and paid a cash dividend of $1,000.
6. Paid rent for the month of April in the amount of $890.
7. Paid salaries for the first half of the month of $1,150.

Fidelity Company ends its fiscal year on April 30. Information for the year-end adjusting entries is as follows.

a. A physical count of office supplies showed $2,820 on hand at April 30.
b. Prepaid insurance in the amount of $2,200 expired by April 30.
c. Unpaid salaries for the second half of April are $1,200.
d. The equipment is depreciated over 12 years with no residual value.

e. Interest on the note payable was last paid on July 1, 1991.

f. Income taxes in the amount of $2,370 are due as of April 30.

Required:

A. Prepare the company's general ledger by opening T accounts for the accounts listed on the March 31, 1992 trial balance.

B. Enter the March 31, 1992 account balances in the ledger accounts.

C. Prepare journal entries to record the April transactions.

D. Post the journal entries to the ledger.

E. Prepare an unadjusted trial balance on April 30, 1992 in the first two columns of a 10-column worksheet.

F. Complete the worksheet.

G. Prepare an income statement and a retained earnings statement for the period ended April 30, 1992 and a classified balance sheet as of April 30, 1992.

H. Journalize and post the adjusting entries.

I. Journalize and post the closing entries.

J. Prepare a post-closing trial balance.

Problem 5-6 Adjusting and Closing Entries

A partially completed worksheet for the Quad Cities Janitorial Service is presented below.

QUAD CITIES JANITORIAL SERVICE
Worksheet
For the Year Ended December 31, 1992

	Unadjusted Trial Balance		Adjustments		Adjusted Trial Balance		Income Statement		Balance Sheet	
	Debit	Credit	Debit	Credit	Debit	Credit	Debit	Credit	Debit	Credit
Cash	3,600				3,600					
Accounts Receivable	4,615				5,175					
Office Supplies on Hand	875				410					
Prepaid Rent	600				200					
Office Equipment	19,300				19,300					
Accumulated Depreciation		3,600				4,450				
Accounts Payable		2,915				2,915				
Unearned Revenue		1,050				380				
Capital Stock		12,000				12,000				
Retained Earnings		7,000				7,000				
Dividends Declared	4,000				4,000					
Fees Revenue		38,205				39,435				
Salary Expense	20,650				20,865					
Utility Expense	8,350				8,480					
Property Tax Expense	780				780					
Rent Expense	2,000				2,400					
Totals	64,770	64,770								
Utilities Payable						130				
Salaries Payable						215				
Depreciation Expense					850					
Supplies Expense					465					
Totals					66,525	66,525				

Required:
A. Based on the above information:
1. Prepare the adjusting entries in general journal format and indicate the type of adjusting entry (prepaid expense, accrued expense, unearned revenue, or accrued revenue).
2. Compute the net income for the period.
3. Prepare the closing entries.
4. Compute the ending retained earnings balance.

B. In completing the worksheet, each account balance in the Unadjusted Trial Balance columns is extended to one of the following four columns.

Income Statement Debit
Income Statement Credit
Balance Sheet Debit
Balance Sheet Credit

Indicate to which column the accounts listed below would be extended.

Dividends Declared	Capital Stock
Salaries Payable	Rent Expense
Fees Revenue	Accumulated Depreciation
Prepaid Rent	Supplies Expense

Problem 5-7 Impact of Errors in Closing Entry Process on Financial Statements

Steve Harrison was hired as the new bookkeeper by Robert's Motors on December 18, 1992. This was Steve's first job as a bookkeeper. While preparing the closing entries for 1992, Steve overlooked and failed to close the following three accounts: Dividends Declared of $18,000; Investment Revenue of $7,500; and Contributions Expense of $4,200. These three accounts remained open throughout 1992. They were closed in the 1993 closing entry process when their balances were $40,000, $18,800, and $8,100 respectively.

Because these three accounts still had a balance at the 1992 year-end, Steve included them on the 1992 balance sheet. The dividends declared was classified as a contra stockholder's equity, the investment revenue as a current liability, and the contributions expense as an other asset.

Required:
Ignoring income taxes, calculate the impact of these errors on the following financial statement items.

1. Total liabilities at December 31, 1992.
2. Net income for 1992.
3. Retained earnings at December 31, 1992.
4. Total stockholders' equity at December 31, 1992.
5. Working capital (current assets − current liabilities) at December 31, 1992.
6. Total assets at December 31, 1993.
7. Total liabilities at December 31, 1993.
8. Net income for 1993.
9. Retained earnings at December 31, 1993.
10. Total stockholders' equity at December 31, 1993.
11. Working capital at December 31, 1993.

Problem 5-8 Account Classification and Analysis

Below is a list of 40 accounts that could be found on the books of a business enterprise.

Accounts

1.	Marketable Securities	21.	Customer Deposits
2.	Sales Revenue	22.	Insurance Expense
3.	Dividends Payable	23.	Copyrights
4.	Delivery Expense	24.	Freight-in Expense
5.	Interest Receivable	25.	Dividends Declared
6.	Utilities Expense	26.	Interest Expense
7.	Capital Stock	27.	Land for Future Plant Site
8.	Interest Revenue	28.	Gain on Sale of Investments
9.	Prepaid Rent	29.	Accounts Receivable
10.	Loss on Sale of Building	30.	Income Taxes Payable
11.	Property Tax Expense	31.	Building Under Construction
12.	Maintenance Expense	32.	Office Supplies On Hand
13.	Cost of Goods Sold (an expense)	33.	Retained Earnings
14.	Investments in Capital Stock of IBM	34.	Depreciation Expense
15.	Mortgage Payable	35.	Notes Payable
16.	Income Tax Expense	36.	Miscellaneous Expense
17.	Investment Revenue	37.	Interest Payable
18.	Office Equipment	38.	Payroll Tax Expense
19.	Excise Tax Expense	39.	Unearned Revenue
20.	Accumulated Depreciation—Building	40.	Income Summary

Format

Account	Temporary or Permanent	Income Statement or Balance Sheet	Closed or Open	Closed by Debit or Credit
Cash	Permanent	Balance Sheet	Open	—
Salaries Expense	Temporary	Income Statement	Closed	Credit
1. through 40.				

Required:

For each of the accounts listed, use the format shown after the accounts to:

1. classify the account as temporary or permanent;
2. classify the account as an income statement or a balance sheet account;
3. indicate whether the account is closed or remains open at year-end; and
4. if the account is closed, indicate if it is debited or credited in the closing entry.

Two examples are provided using the Cash account and the Salaries Expense account.

Problem 5-9A Reversing Entries and Unearned Revenue

During its 1992 fiscal year, Business Publications, Inc., received $528,000 for magazine subscriptions.

Part I:

Assume Unearned Subscriptions Revenue is credited when the subscriptions are received. An analysis of the liability account on December 31, 1992 reveals that $68,500 of the subscriptions are for magazines to be published in 1993.

Required:

A. What amount should be reported:
    1. on the 1992 income statement for Subscriptions Revenue?
    2. on the 1992 balance sheet for Unearned Subscriptions Revenue?
B. Prepare the adjusting entry needed on December 31, 1992.
C. Prepare the reversing entry, if needed, on January 1, 1993.

Part II:

Assume Subscriptions Revenue is credited when the subscriptions are received. An analysis of the revenue account on December 31, 1992 reveals that $68,500 of the subscriptions are for magazines to be published in 1993.

Required:

A. What amount should be reported:
    1. on the 1992 income statement for Subscriptions Revenue?
    2. on the 1992 balance sheet for Unearned Subscriptions Revenue?
B. Prepare the adjusting entry needed on December 31, 1992.
C. Prepare the reversing entry, if needed, on January 1, 1993.
D. Compare the amounts calculated for Subscriptions Revenue and for Unearned Subscriptions Revenue in Part I, requirement A, to those calculated in Part II, requirement A. Are they the same or are they different? If they are the same, explain why.

Problem 5-10A   Reversing Entries and Prepaid Expenses

During 1992, Red Rock Corporation purchased $3,300 of office supplies. An expense account was debited to record the purchase. On July 1, 1992, $4,200 was paid for a two-year comprehensive liability insurance policy. The account Prepaid Insurance was debited to record the transaction. Red Rock's fiscal year ends on December 31, at which time a physical count of office supplies showed $820 of supplies on hand.

Required:

A. Journalize the purchase of the office supplies.
B. Prepare the required adjusting entry with respect to the office supplies on December 31, 1992.
C. Prepare a reversing entry, if needed, on January 1, 1993.
D. Journalize the purchase of the insurance policy.
E. Prepare the required adjusting entry with respect to the insurance on December 31, 1992.
F. Prepare a reversing entry, if needed, on January 1, 1993.
G. Comment on the confusion resulting from using two different methods to record the acquisition of prepaid items during the year. Which method do you prefer? Why?

Problem 5-11A   Adjusting and Reversing Entries

The following information regarding selected transactions of Meadows Apartments, Inc., is available on August 31, 1992, the end of the fiscal year.

1. Received $2,200 from a tenant on August 1, 1992. The rental receipt covers the four-month period August through November. A revenue account was credited to record the transaction.
2. Unpaid salaries to employees on August 31, 1992 are $1,550.
3. Accrued interest receivable on investments is $950.

4. Utility bills received but not paid or recorded are $375.
5. Prepaid insurance was debited for $1,050 on June 29 to record the cost of a six-month policy beginning July 1.

Required:

A. Prepare the required adjusting entry for each item.
B. Prepare reversing entries where appropriate.

Problem 5-12 The Complete Accounting Cycle

Paul Hooke owns Answer and Message Center. The post-closing trial balance as of December 31, 1991 is shown below.

ANSWER AND MESSAGE CENTER
Post-closing Trial Balance
December 31, 1991

Account Title	Debit	Credit
Cash	$ 960	
Accounts Receivable	2,860	
Prepaid Insurance	620	
Supplies On Hand	225	
Truck	12,700	
Accumulated Depreciation—Truck		$ 4,250
Accounts Payable		780
Interest Payable		220
Payable on Truck Loan		8,350
Capital Stock		4,000
Retained Earnings		765
Dividends Declared	1,000	
Totals	$18,365	$18,365

Transactions for the year are given below in summary form. Numbers, rather than dates, are used to identify transactions since they are in summary form.

1 Phone answering fees were $13,000 in cash and $3,000 on account for the year.
2 Message service fees totaled $14,000 for the year; $8,000 of that was in cash and the remainder was on account.
3 Supplies costing $100 were purchased on account.
4 On June 20, 1992 the company paid $2,400 on the truck loan and $400 on accrued interest. Of the $400, $220 was for accrued interest in 1991 and the remainder was for interest accrued during the first half of 1992.
5 $2,400 in gas and oil for the truck was purchased on account.
6 Prepaid a six month insurance premium on the truck in the amount of $200.
7 Telephone expenses of $500 were paid.
8 Accounts receivable of $2,000 were collected.
9 A cash dividend of $500 was declared and paid to stockholders.
10 Paid $2,000 on accounts payable.

The following information should be used for making adjusting entries.

a. A physical count of the supplies showed that $140 had been used during the year.
b. Accrued interest on the truck loan is $100.
c. Insurance costing $240 expired during the year.
d. Depreciation on the truck was $1,000.
e. The December telephone bill of $123 has not been paid or recorded.

Required:
A. Open T accounts for each of the accounts listed below. Insert beginning balances from the post-closing trial balance.

100 Cash	301 Retained Earnings
101 Accounts Receivable	302 Dividends Declared
102 Prepaid Insurance	310 Income Summary
103 Supplies On Hand	400 Answering Service Fees
104 Truck	401 Message Service Fees
105 Accumulated Depreciation—Truck	500 Gas and Oil Expense
200 Accounts Payable	501 Telephone Expense
201 Interest Payable	502 Supplies Expense
202 Telephone Expense Payable	503 Insurance Expense
203 Payable on Truck Loan	504 Depreciation Expense
300 Capital Stock	505 Interest Expense

B. Prepare journal entries to record the transactions completed in 1992.
C. Post the entries to the T accounts.
D. Prepare a 10-column worksheet.
E. Prepare an income statement, a retained earnings statement, and a balance sheet. Of the ending balance payable on the truck loan, $2,400 is due next year.
F. Journalize and post the adjusting entries.
G. Journalize and post the closing entries.
H. Prepare a post-closing trial balance.

CASE

Worksheets are used extensively by accountants for a variety of tasks. Presented below are some statements and questions relating to worksheets. Answer the questions.

1. Why are worksheets generally prepared in pencil?
2. Why are worksheets not distributed to the owners or the management of a firm?
3. Discuss the primary purpose of the worksheet presented and discussed in this chapter.
4. After a worksheet is prepared, it is still necessary to journalize and post the adjusting entries and the closing entries in the accounting records. Why must these procedures be completed when the information is already on the worksheet?
5. Could worksheets like the ones illustrated in this chapter be expanded to 12 columns with the additional two columns comprising the retained earnings statement? If yes, what advantages do you see in this expanded version of the worksheet?

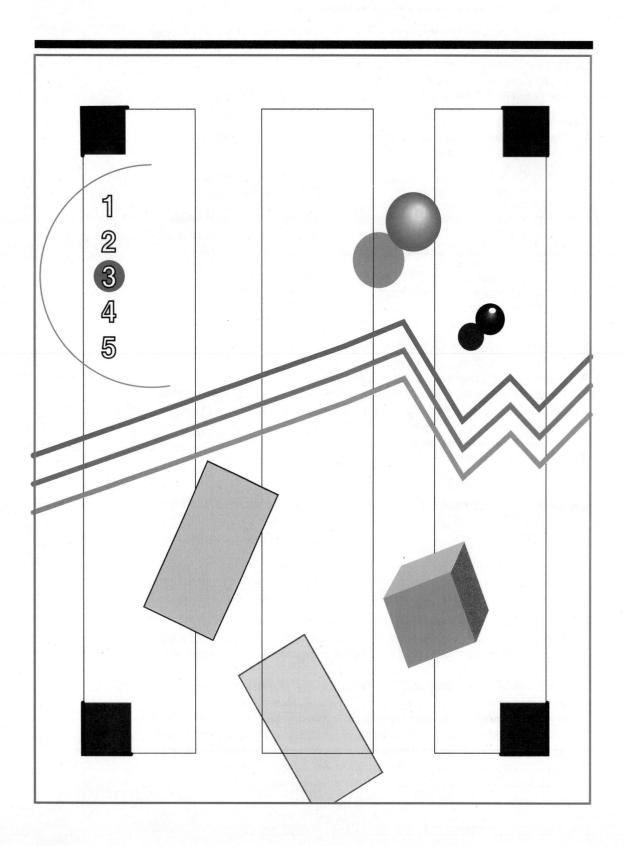

PART 3

ACCOUNTING FOR AND CONTROL OF ASSETS

6

ACCOUNTING FOR MERCHANDISING OPERATIONS

CHAPTER OVERVIEW AND OBJECTIVES

This chapter describes accounting procedures for businesses that buy and sell merchandise inventory. When you have completed the chapter, you should understand:

1. The nature of merchandise inventory.
2. The basic format of an income statement prepared for a merchandising firm.
3. How to record transactions related to the sale of inventory.
4. The various credit terms related to the sale of inventory.
5. Busines practices as they relate to freight cost and the transfer of title to inventory.
6. The difference between perpetual and periodic inventory systems.
7. How to record inventory transactions for a firm using a perpetual inventory system.
8. How to record inventory transactions for a firm using a periodic inventory system.
9. How to prepare a worksheet and complete the closing process for both inventory systems.
10. The format of a multiple-step income statement.
11. An alternative method for closing the accounts when the periodic inventory system is used: Appendix.

The preceding chapters used a service business to illustrate the accounting cycle. Service firms make up a significant part of our nation's economy. Service firms include law firms, accounting firms, motels, management consulting firms, equipment repair firms, barber and beauty shops, airlines, advertising agencies, golf courses, theaters, and photography studios. The primary business activity of many other firms centers on selling merchandise to earn revenue. *Manufacturing firms* purchase raw materials and component parts for conversion into finished products for sale to their customers.

Accounting for these firms is covered in the *Managerial Accounting* volume to this series. *Merchandising* or *trading firms*, which may distribute at the wholesale and/ or retail levels, purchase goods in substantially the same form in which they are sold. A merchandising operation uses the term **merchandise inventory** or simply **inventory** to designate tangible assets held for sale in the normal course of business. Other assets held for future disposition but not normally sold as part of the regular business activities, such as unused office equipment, are not included in the inventory category.

This chapter discusses accounting for a merchandising firm. Although the accounting principles and methods described in earlier chapters apply to merchandising firms, a number of additional accounts and procedures are used to record inventory transactions. This chapter begins with a discussion of the operations of a merchandising firm with an emphasis on the accounting concepts involved in recording the operations. This is followed by an examination of an income statement prepared for a merchandising firm. Finally, accounting for the sale of inventory is described, along with the two inventory systems (perpetual and periodic) that are used to account for inventory costs.

Objective 1: Nature of merchandise inventory

MERCHANDISING FIRM OPERATIONS

As described in Chapter 2, the normal operating cycle for a merchandising firm is the average length of time it takes for the firm to acquire inventory, sell that inventory to its customers, and collect cash from the sale. At the time of purchase, inventory is recorded at its acquisition price in accordance with the cost principle described in Chapter 2. *Cost* is defined as all expenditures needed to acquire and prepare the inventory for sale to customers. Thus, inventory cost should include the invoice price plus such costs as freight charges paid on the goods purchased and costs incurred to assemble the product. The cost of inventory available for future sale is reported in the balance sheet as a current asset because it is expected to be sold within the normal operating cycle or one year, whichever is longer. Inventories are usually listed after receivables because they are one step further removed from cash.

When a sale is made, an asset account is debited and a revenue account is credited for an amount equal to the sales price. In the income statement, the cost of inventory sold is matched with the revenue received from selling it. Proper *matching* of costs and revenues is, in fact, a major objective of accounting for inventory. It involves determining the amount of the total inventory cost to be deducted from sales in the current period's income statement and the amount to be carried forward as an asset to be expensed in some future period.

Inventory-related transactions are among the most common transactions for a merchandising firm. Inventory is continually being acquired, sold, and replaced, and makes up a significant part of a firm's total assets. The cost of goods sold for a given period is frequently the firm's largest expense, sometimes exceeding the sum of all operating expenses. For these reasons, the control and safeguarding of inventory is essential for efficient and profitable operations. The establishment of such controls is discussed in Chapter 7.

INCOME STATEMENT FOR A MERCHANDISING FIRM

Figure 6-1 compares the major parts of an income statement for Scotch Records and Tapes, a merchandising firm, to the income statement for Quality Real Estate Office, Inc. developed in the last chapter.

Objective 2: Income statement for a merchandising firm

SCOTCH RECORDS AND TAPES Income Statement For the Year Ended December 31, 1992			QUALITY REAL ESTATE OFFICE, INC. Income Statement For the month ended June 30, 1992	
Net sales		$344,000	Revenues	$12,925
Less: Cost of goods sold		206,000	Less: Expenses*	11,175
Gross profit on sales		138,000	Income before income taxes	1,750
Less: Operating expenses			Less: Income tax expense	435
Selling expenses	$52,000		Net income	$ 1,315
Administrative expenses	36,000			
Total operating expenses		88,000	*Individual expenses are listed.	
Income before income taxes		50,000		
Less: Income tax expense		20,000		
Net income		$ 30,000		

Figure 6-1
Comparison of Income Statements

A comparison of the two income statements reveals several differences:

1. Revenue earned is the first item reported in both cases, but, for a merchandising firm, revenue is called *sales*.

2. The income statement for Scotch Records and Tapes contains a cost of goods sold section that shows the total cost of the inventory ($206,000) that was sold during the period. The cost of goods sold is an expense that is subtracted from sales to arrive at an intermediate income amount called *gross profit* or *gross margin on sales*. The gross profit is calculated to show the amount of markup on the goods sold during this period. The relationship between gross profit and sales is of interest to statement users because companies must sell their inventory at an adequate markup if they are to cover operating expenses and produce a desirable profit.

3. Operating expenses and income taxes are subtracted from gross profit on sales to determine the net income (or net loss) for the period. Operating expenses, which are normally separated by function, are those expenses related to the major activities of the firm.

Although many of the operating expenses incurred by service firms are also incurred by merchandising firms, merchandising firms incur additional expenses that relate to buying and selling inventory. Selling expenses result from efforts to market the inventory and include advertising, sales salaries and commissions, and the cost of delivering goods to customers. Administrative expenses are management costs associated with the general administration of the company's operations. These expenses include those incurred to operate such subdivisions of the firm as the general office, accounting, personnel, and credit and collection departments. Income before income taxes for a merchandising firm results if the revenue from sales exceeds the cost of the goods sold and the operating expenses incurred.

ACCOUNTING FOR SALES TRANSACTIONS

Objective 3:
Recording sale
transactions

In Figure 6-1, the first item in the income statement for Scotch Records and Tapes is net sales. Income statements prepared for use by parties outside the firm often begin with net sales because the details of the computation are not relevant to external users.

Net sales is computed as follows and is included in the income statement in this format when the detail is reported.

Revenue from sales:		
Gross sales		$363,000
Less: Sales returns and allowances	$14,000	
Sales discounts	5,000	19,000
Net sales		$344,000

The determination of these amounts is discussed in the following section.

RECORDING GROSS SALES

A sales transaction is generally recorded by the seller when the ownership of the inventory is transferred from the business to the customer. To record the sale, an asset account is debited and the Sales account is credited for an amount equal to the sales price. Usually, the asset recorded in exchange for the inventory is cash or accounts receivable. The entry to record a credit sale of $300 is as follows.

Oct.	10	Accounts Receivable		300	
		Sales			300
		Sold merchandise to John Reeves on account.			

The Cash account would be debited if this were a cash sale. At year's end, the balance in the Sales account shows the total amount of cash and credit sales made during the accounting period.

CONTROL ACCOUNTS AND SUBSIDIARY LEDGERS

In the preceding entry, it was assumed that one Accounts Receivable account is used to record the sale of inventory on account. A firm that sells inventory on credit may have hundreds or even thousands of customers. In order to efficiently provide detailed information concerning the amount of sales to, the amount collected from, and the balance due from each customer, firms often establish a separate receivable account for each customer. However, rather than including a large number of individual receivable accounts in the general ledger, the firm establishes one Accounts Receivable account, called a **control account**, in the general ledger to summarize the transactions with all the customers.

The Accounts Receivable control account in the general ledger takes the place of the individual receivable accounts which are contained in a separate record called the **subsidiary ledger**. The accounts receivable subsidiary ledger contains an individual account for each customer and provides the detailed information about the control account in the general ledger. The sum of the individual account balances in the subsidiary ledger should be equal to the balance in the general ledger control account.

A subsidiary ledger is established when a large amount of detailed information about a certain general ledger account must be kept. Companies often use a separate subsidiary ledger and a control account for a number of general ledger accounts such as accounts receivable, accounts payable, merchandise inventory, marketable securities, plant assets, and operating expenses. Control accounts and subsidiary ledgers are discussed further in Chapter 7.

SALES RETURNS AND ALLOWANCES

To maintain good customer relations and honor warranty agreements, most businesses permit a customer to return unsatisfactory goods. Alternatively, the customer may agree to keep the goods in exchange for a reduction in the sales price. The return of goods (sales return), or an adjustment to the sales price (sales allowance) is a reduction in the amount of recorded sales, and either a cash refund is made or the customer's account receivable is reduced. In either case, once a return or allowance is authorized, the seller issues a source document, called a **credit memorandum** or **credit memo**, to the customer, and forwards a copy to the accounting department so that the transaction can be properly recorded. The document is called a credit memorandum because the seller is informing the customer that the customer's account is being reduced (credited) on the seller's books.

Handling returned merchandise is time-consuming and results in increased costs. For these reasons, management must look for the cause of excessive returns and correct the problem whenever possible. To provide information on the volume of returns and allowances, a contra sales account called Sales Returns and Allowances is debited as follows:

Oct.	15	Sales Returns and Allowances	50	
		Accounts Receivable*		50
		John Reeves returned unsatisfactory merchandise sold on Oct. 10 for credit. (Making only one entry at this time assumes use of the periodic inventory system discussed in a later section of this chapter.)		

*Cash is credited if a cash refund is given.

As shown on page 231, sales returns and allowances are subtracted from sales (a contra account) in the income statement.

CREDIT TERMS

Objective 4:
Credit terms

The parties involved in a sale/purchase transaction may agree that payment is to be made immediately upon transfer of the goods (a cash sale). Sometimes the sale is made on credit and payment is delayed for a specific length of time called the **credit period**. The length of the credit period varies among firms, but 30 to 60 days is typical.

When merchandise is sold on credit, the terms of payment, called the **credit terms**, should be clear as to the amount due and the credit period. The terms of payment normally appear in a source document called the **sales invoice** by the seller and the **purchase invoice** by the buyer. The credit period is usually abbreviated in the following form: ''n/10 EOM'' or ''n/30.'' In the first case, the invoice price is due 10 days after the end of the month in which the sale occurred. In the second case, the invoice price is due within 30 days after the invoice date.

Cash Discounts

To provide an incentive for the buyer to make payment before the end of the credit period, the seller may grant a cash discount called a **sales discount** by the seller and a **purchase discount** by the buyer. A **cash discount** entitles the buyer to deduct a specified percentage of the sales price if payment is made within a given time span, called the **discount period**. The terms are normally quoted in a format such as "2/10, n/30" (verbally the terms are stated "two ten, net thirty"). This notation means that the buyer has two payment options. If payment is made within 10 days of the invoice date, the buyer may deduct 2% from the amount of the invoice. If payment is not made within the 10-day discount period, the full price is due 30 days from the invoice date.

To illustrate, assume that the credit terms were 2/10, n/30 on the $300 sale to John Reeves recorded earlier. The entry to record the collection within the discount period, net of the $50 return, is:

Oct.	20	Cash	245	
		Sales Discounts	5	
		Accounts Receivable		250
		Received payment from John Reeves within		
		the discount period.		

Note that the sales discount of $5 is computed on the sales price less the merchandise returned by the customer [($300 − $50) × 2% = $5].

Two methods, the net invoice method or the gross invoice method, may be used to record the purchase and sale of merchandise inventory. Entries in this text are based on use of the gross invoice method. The gross invoice method is illustrated because it is commonly used in practice and it avoids the problem of allocating the discount to individual units when a physical inventory is taken or when the amounts are entered on individual inventory cards. (The use of inventory cards is discussed later in the chapter.) In addition, the discount amounts are often immaterial.

Under the **gross invoice method**, sales and accounts receivable are recorded at the gross invoice price (see the October 10 entry on page 231). In other words, under this method, sales discounts are not recorded unless the customer takes advantage of the cash discount as shown in the October 20 transaction above. If the customer pays within the discount period, the sales discount is recorded in a separate account in order to provide information to management on the amount of sales discount taken. A sales discount is considered a reduction in the sales price of the goods. It is reported as a subtraction from gross sales (i.e., a contra sales account) in the income statement.

From the seller's point of view, the purpose of granting cash discounts is to induce the customer to pay the receivable earlier. Hence, the firm will have the cash available for use before the end of the credit period. The earlier payment also tends to reduce losses from uncollectible accounts receivable.

When a cash discount is included in the credit terms, the buyer must decide whether to pay the account payable within the discount period. Usually, the annual cost of forgoing cash discounts is quite high. This can be shown by converting the discount rate to an annual rate. For example, assume that an agreement for the purchase of $250 in goods contained the terms 2/10, n/30. To obtain the maximum benefit of the credit terms granted by the seller, the buyer should pay the invoice on the last possible date. Thus, the buyer will either (1) pay $245 within 10 days after the invoice date or (2) pay the full invoice price of $250 within 30 days after the invoice date. By not paying within the 10-day discount period, the buyer has the use of the $245 for an additional 20 days. The additional $5 that must be paid in 30 days is an interest charge for extending the credit period 20 days. The effective annual yield is computed as follows.

$$\text{Effective rate for the 20-day period} = \$5/\$245$$
$$= 2.04\%$$
$$\text{Effective annual rate} = (360 \text{ days}/20) \times 2.04\%$$
$$= 36.7\%$$

The effective rate of 36.7% is quite high. A company should compare this rate to the rate it would have to pay to other sources of credit such as banks, savings and loans, or other lending institutions. The buyer should take advantage of the discount even if the firm has to borrow the money provided that it can borrow the money at a lower interest rate.

Trade Discounts

A **trade discount** is a percentage reduction granted to a customer from a suggested list price. In contrast to a cash discount, a trade discount is not related to early payment. Instead, it is used to determine the actual invoice price to a particular class of customer. Trade discounts enable the firm to print one price list or catalog but still vary prices for different customer groups, such as retailers or wholesalers, or to grant quantity discounts.

Trade discounts are not normally recorded in the accounts by either the buyer or the seller. For example, assume that a wholesaler quotes a list price of $350 per item but grants retailers a trade discount of 20% on the purchase of five or more items. The entry to record the sale of 10 units is:

June	16	Accounts Receivable	2,800	
		Sales		2,800
		To record the sale of inventory on credit		
		subject to a 20% quantity discount.		

The computation is as follows.

List price $350 × 10 units	$3,500
Less: 20% quantity discount	700
Invoice price	$2,800

The buyer records a purchase of inventory in the amount of $2,800.

If included in the terms of the sale, a cash discount is computed on the $2,800 sales price less any subsequent returns or allowances. That is, if three of the 10 items are later returned, then the cash discount is computed on $1,960 (7 units × $280 per unit).

FREIGHT-OUT

Objective 5: Transfer of title

The sales invoice will normally indicate which party to the transaction must pay the cost of shipping the goods. If the goods are sold **FOB (free on board) shipping point**, the buyer takes title at the seller's shipping dock. Therefore, freight costs incurred from the point of shipment are paid by the buyer. Conversely, the term **FOB destination** indicates that the title changes when the goods reach the buyer's receiving dock. Hence, the seller is responsible for paying the freight cost. The point at which the title transfers, and the party responsible for the freight cost, are summarized below.

Shipping Terms	Point Title Transfers	Party Responsible for Freight Costs
FOB Shipping point	At shipping dock of seller	Buyer
FOB Destination	At receiving dock of buyer	Seller

When terms of the sale are FOB destination, the seller normally records the payment of freight costs as a debit to a *Freight-Out* or *Delivery Expense* account. The entry to record a $35 freight payment on goods sold is

Aug.	10	Freight-out	35	
		Cash		35

Freight-out is an expense and should be reported in the selling expense category of the income statement. Freight charges *paid by the seller on goods sold* should not be confused with freight charges *paid on goods purchased*, which is discussed later in the chapter.

METHODS OF ACCOUNTING FOR INVENTORY AND COST OF GOODS SOLD

As noted earlier, the cost of inventory sold during the year is matched against sales revenue. The cost of unsold inventory is reported as a current asset in the balance sheet. Two distinctly different inventory systems—perpetual and periodic—are used to determine the amounts reported for the ending inventory and the cost of goods sold. The system adopted by a firm is largely determined by the type of inventory held.

Objective 6: Perpetual vs. periodic inventory system

A perpetual inventory system involves keeping a current and continuous record of all increases and decreases of each item of inventory. Under this system, purchases are recorded in an asset account called the Merchandise Inventory account. As goods are sold, their cost is determined, and an entry is made to reduce the Merchandise Inventory account. A corresponding increase is made in an expense account called Cost of Goods Sold. That is, the cost of inventory purchased is accounted for as an asset until it is sold and produces revenues, at which time the cost is transferred to an expense account to be matched against earned revenue. Thus, on any given date, the total dollar value of inventory held by the firm and the cost of goods sold to that date can be determined from the two accounts.

A perpetual inventory system is used because it provides more timely information to management for use in planning and controlling inventory costs. Because the maintenance of perpetual inventory records involved more clerical work than the periodic system, it was usually used by firms that sold a limited number of items with a high unit cost (e.g., automobiles, heating and air conditioning units, works of art, pianos, television sets, stereo equipment, computers, and home appliances). In recent years, however, the introduction of computers and other electronic business machines has made the perpetual inventory system feasible for many firms (e.g., drug stores, variety stores, hardware stores, and grocery stores) dealing in low unit cost items.

The development of on-site computers, in particular, has been a real breakthrough for the perpetual inventory system. For example, many grocery stores now use optical-scan cash registers that not only record the sales price of the item but also enter the item for inventory purposes. Firms that adopt the perpetual inventory system do so because they believe the benefits of improved managerial planning and control obtained from a current record of inventory on hand outweigh the additional cost of maintaining the system.

PERIODIC INVENTORY SYSTEM

Firms that sell a large number of items with a low cost per unit may find the maintenance of perpetual inventory records too costly and time-consuming. This type of business often uses the **periodic inventory system**, in which the cost of goods sold for the period is determined at the end of the accounting period. A store operating with a high volume of sales may conveniently record the amount of each sale, but would find it difficult to trace the cost of each item sold back to the inventory records. Thus, a day-to-day record of goods on hand or cost of goods sold is not maintained.

ILLUSTRATION OF A PERPETUAL INVENTORY SYSTEM

Objective 7: Using a perpetual inventory system

When the perpetual inventory method is used, a single Merchandise Inventory account is maintained in the general ledger to record all inventory transactions. Supporting details are entered on individual inventory cards which serve as a subsidiary ledger. One card is maintained for each type of inventory item held. Each inventory card shows the quantity, unit cost, and total cost for each purchase, each sale, and the inventory balance. When every item is different, as with automobiles where each unit has different options and cost, a separate inventory card is maintained for each item. The balance in the general ledger control account (the Merchandise Inventory account) should equal the sum of the dollar amounts shown on the inventory cards in the subsidiary ledger. Generally, the maintenance of such detailed inventory cards for each item of inventory requires a great deal of clerical effort. Consequently, most firms use some type of electronic equipment to process the data more efficiently and accurately than can be done in a manual system. The electronic processing of inventory records is very similar to the manual operations shown below.

Figure 6-2 is an example of an inventory card kept for a (Model DP93) personal computer. The cost of the merchandise on hand at the beginning of the period ($2,400), called the **beginning inventory,** consisted of two units at a unit cost of $1,200. The other data entered on the card are based on the following transactions:

1. July 12 Purchased six units of inventory for $1,200 per unit on account from Datapoint Inc.
2. July 14 Sold four units on account for $2,500 per unit; cost $1,200 per unit.
3. July 17 Returned a defective unit to Datapoint, Inc. which cost $1,200.
4. July 18 A unit sold on July 14 is returned by a customer for credit on account. Because the unit was suitable for resale, it was returned to stock.

The entries to record the transactions above and the postings to the inventory related accounts for a perpetual inventory system are shown in Figure 6-3. The operations of the system may be summarized as follows:

1. The inventory on hand at the beginning of the period is reported in the Merchandise Inventory control account and on the inventory card.
2. Purchases of inventory are added to the beginning inventory balance in the Merchandise Inventory control account and to the inventory card.

		Purchases			Cost of Goods Sold			Balance		
Date	Explanation	Units	Unit Cost	Total Cost	Units	Unit Cost	Total Cost	Units	Unit Cost	Total Cost
7/1	Beginning balance							2	1,200	2,400
7/12	Purchase	6	1,200	7,200				8	1,200	9,600
7/14	Sales				4	1,200	4,800	4	1,200	4,800
7/17	Purchase returns	(1)	1,200	(1,200)				3	1,200	3,600
7/18	Sales returns				(1)	1,200	(1,200)	4	1,200	4,800

Item Personal Computer Code DP93
Location 1 unit showroom Remainder—Warehouse
Minimum Stock 2 Maximum Stock 10

Figure 6-2
Inventory Card

Figure 6-3
Entries to Record Inventory Transactions Under the Perpetual Inventory System

Merchandise Inventory

Beg. Bal.	2,400	

1. Purchased six computers on credit.

| July | 12 | Merchandise Inventory | 7,200 | |
| | | Accounts Payable | | 7,200 |

2. Sold four computers on account.

July	14	Accounts Receivable	10,000	
		Sales		10,000
	14	Cost of Goods Sold	4,800	
		Merchandise Inventory		4,800

3. Returned one computer to supplier for credit on account.

| July | 17 | Accounts Payable | 1,200 | |
| | | Merchandise Inventory | | 1,200 |

4. Customer returned one computer for credit on account.

July	18	Sales Returns and Allowances	2,500	
		Accounts Receivable		2,500
	18	Merchandise Inventory	1,200	
		Cost of Goods Sold		1,200

General ledger account balances at the end of the period.

Merchandise Inventory

Beg. Bal.	2,400	7/14	4,800
7/12	7,200	7/17	1,200
7/18	1,200		
End Bal.	4,800		

Cost of Goods Sold

| 7/14 | 4,800 | 7/18 | 1,200 |
| End. Bal. | 3,600 | | |

3. When goods are sold, an entry is made to record the sale (the revenue aspect of the transaction) and another entry is made to reduce (credit) the Merchandise Inventory control account and increase (debit) Cost of Goods Sold (the expense aspect of the transaction). The number of units, unit cost, and total cost of those sold are also entered on the inventory card.

4. To provide a continuous record of inventory on hand, units returned to the manufacturer and units suitable for resale that are returned by customers are recorded in the Merchandise Inventory control account, and are either subtracted from or added to the balance on hand on the inventory card.

5. Assuming that this is the only item of inventory held, the cost of the ending inventory is the balance in the Merchandise Inventory control account ($4,800); the cost of goods sold for the period ($3,600) to be matched against revenues in the income statement is the balance in the Cost of Goods Sold account. The ending inventory is merchandise on hand at the end of the period that is available for sale in the next period, and is reported as an asset in the balance sheet.

Note that every entry made to the Merchandise Inventory control account requires that the units, unit cost, and total cost also be entered on the appropriate inventory card in the subsidiary ledger, as shown in Figure 6-2.

PHYSICAL INVENTORY

Note that the balance in the Merchandise Inventory account agrees with the balance on the inventory card (see Figure 6-2). Keeping a continuous inventory record makes it unnecessary to take a physical count of the inventory on hand to determine the ending balance. Nevertheless, firms using a perpetual inventory system should take a physical inventory once a year to verify the accuracy of the inventory records.

A physical inventory involves (1) counting all inventory units on hand, (2) determining the unit cost of each type of item on hand from purchase invoices or inventory cards, and (3) multiplying the unit cost of each item by the appropriate number of units to determine the dollar cost of that particular item. The dollar cost of the entire inventory is the sum of the individual costs determined for each item.

Differences between the physical count and the inventory records could result from clerical error, theft of goods, breakage, and obsolescence. In some cases, the difference may result from natural causes such as evaporation or shrinkage. Causes of large discrepancies should be identified and eliminated if at all possible. Taking a physical inventory is discussed in more detail in Chapter 9.

When the physical inventory and the Merchandise Inventory account balance differ, a journal entry is made to bring the account balance into agreement with the physical count. For example, an entry to reduce the Merchandise Inventory account by $247 would be:

Dec.	31	Inventory Loss	247	
		Merchandise Inventory		247
		To adjust the inventory account to the		
		physical count.		

The Inventory Loss account is for management information only. The account balance is normally included in cost of goods sold in the income statement.

END-OF-PERIOD PROCESS

At the end of the accounting period, a worksheet can be used to organize the information needed to prepare financial statements, adjusting entries, and closing entries. Except for the new accounts introduced in this chapter, the preparation of the worksheet and the closing process for a merchandising business are similar to that illustrated for a service firm in Chapter 5.

When a perpetual inventory system is used to account for the flow of goods, the balance in the Merchandise Inventory account is the ending inventory amount. This balance is an asset and, accordingly, it is extended to the Balance Sheet debit column. The balance in the Cost of Goods Sold account is the cost of inventory sold this period. Since it is an expense account, it is extended to the Income Statement debit column and is closed along with the other expense accounts to the Income Summary account. Because there is little difference when the perpetual system is used from that illustrated in Chapter 5, a worksheet is not prepared here. The end-of-period process related to a periodic inventory system is more complex and is discussed at the end of this chapter.

ILLUSTRATION OF A PERIODIC INVENTORY SYSTEM

In a periodic inventory system, the cost of the merchandise on hand at the beginning of the period is reported in the Merchandise Inventory account. The balance in the account is not changed, except to correct errors, until the end of the accounting period.

Objective 8:
Using a periodic inventory system

Inventory purchases made during the period are recorded in a Purchases account. At the end of the period, the balance in the Purchases account is added to the beginning inventory balance to determine the **cost of goods available for sale** during the period. The goods available for sale either were sold during the period or should still be on hand.

When inventory is sold, an entry is made to record the sale only. Unlike the perpetual inventory system, no record of the cost of goods on hand or the cost of goods sold is maintained during the period. Instead, they are computed at the end of each accounting period. The cost of goods on hand is determined by taking a physical inventory. Cost of goods sold is then computed by subtracting the cost of goods on hand (i.e., the *ending inventory*) from the cost of goods available for sale, as shown below based on the data shown in Figure 6-2. Note that the ending inventory and the cost of goods sold are the same as under the perpetual inventory system.

Cost of beginning merchandise inventory	$2,400
Add: Cost of goods purchased during the current period	6,000
Cost of goods available for sale	8,400
Less: Cost of ending merchandise inventory (per physical count)	4,800
Cost of goods sold	$3,600

The cost of the ending inventory for the current period of $4,800 becomes the beginning inventory amount for the next period. The process of adjusting the inventory account to its end-of-year balance is discussed later in this chapter.

A periodic inventory system is illustrated below. To facilitate a comparison between a periodic system and a perpetual system, the illustration is based on the same data used in the perpetual illustration. In practice, remember, the periodic system would normally be used when selling a high volume of low priced items. The Merchandise

Inventory account at the beginning of the period is:

Merchandise Inventory

7/1 Beg. Bal.	
(2 units @ $1,200) 2,400	

The beginning inventory of $2,400 is the ending inventory determined by a physical inventory conducted on the last day of the preceding period.

July   12   Purchased 6 units of inventory at $1,200 per unit on account from Datapoint, Inc.

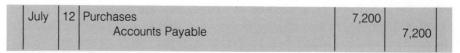

July	12	Purchases	7,200	
		Accounts Payable		7,200

The Purchases account is a temporary account used to accumulate the cost of all inventory acquired for resale during the period. This account is used to record inventory purchases only. (Acquisitions of other assets are recorded in appropriate asset accounts.) Because the balance in the Purchases account is closed at the end of each accounting period, the accumulated account balance reflects the purchases for the current period only.

July   14   Sold 4 units for $2,500 per unit to customers on account.

July	14	Accounts Receivable	10,000	
		Sales		10,000

At the time of sale, one entry is made to record the revenue earned from the sale of merchandise. A second entry to record the cost of goods sold is not made.

July   17   Returned a defective unit that cost $1,200 to the manufacturer for credit on account:

The buyer and seller may agree that an item is to be returned or that the item is to be kept and an adjustment made to the purchase price for a number of reasons, such as that the goods were damaged when received. A source document that contains the information needed to record the transaction, called a **debit memorandum** or **debit memo** is prepared. It is called a debit memorandum because the supplier's account payable is debited on the buyer's books. The return of goods to Datapoint, Inc. is recorded as follows.

July	17	Accounts Payable	1,200	
		Purchases Returns and Allowances		1,200

There is a cost to the firm to order merchandise, receive and inspect the merchandise, and to repack it for return to the manufacturer. To provide relevant information to management concerning the total amount of goods returned, the return is recorded in a contra purchases account called Purchases Returns and Allowances, rather than directly as a credit to the Purchases account. The entry is the same if the goods are kept by the buyer and an adjustment is made to the invoice price.

July   18   A unit that was sold for $2,500 was returned by a customer for credit
             on account.

July	18	Sales Returns and Allowances	2,500	
		Accounts Receivable		2,500

When a periodic inventory system is used, only one entry is needed to record the
merchandise returned. A second entry, to credit the cost of goods sold, is not needed
here because the cost of goods sold was not recorded on the date of sale.

Based on these transactions, a partial income statement is prepared in Figure 6-4.
It is assumed that a physical inventory count taken at the end of the period confirmed
that four units were on hand. The dollar amount is computed to be $4,800 (4 units
× $1,200).

Some relationships shown in statement format for the periodic inventory system are
summarized below:

1. Gross profit on sales = Net sales − Cost of goods sold
2. Cost of goods purchased = Purchases − Purchases returns and allowances
3. Cost of goods available for sale = Cost of beginning inventory + Cost of goods
    purchased
4. Cost of goods sold = Cost of goods available for sale − Cost of ending inventory;
    or Cost of goods sold = Cost of beginning inventory + Cost of goods purchased
    − Cost of ending inventory

Familiarity with these relationships will aid in understanding the characteristics of the
periodic inventory system and make it easier to determine the effect of inventory
errors.

Note that under the periodic inventory system, the cost of goods sold is a residual
amount that is left after deducting the ending inventory from the cost of goods available
for sale. As a result, losses of inventory from causes such as theft, shrinkage, breakage, and clerical error are difficult to identify. Techniques used to determine large
inventory losses are examined in Chapter 9.

Figure 6-4
Partial Income
Statements—Periodic
Inventory System

CAMPUS COMPUTERS Income Statement For the Month Ended July 31, 1992			
Sales			$10,000
Less: Sales returns and allowances			2,500
Net Sales			7,500
Cost of Goods Sold:			
Cost of beginning merchandise inventory		$2,400	
Add: Purchases	$7,200		
Less: Purchases returns and allowances	1,200		
Cost of goods purchased		6,000	
Cost of goods available for sale		8,400	
Less: Cost of ending merchandise inventory		4,800	
Cost of Goods Sold			3,600
Gross Profit on Sales			$ 3,900

PERPETUAL AND PERIODIC INVENTORY SYSTEMS CONTRASTED

The perpetual and periodic inventory systems are contrasted with the entries shown in Figure 6-5. There are several basic differences between the two systems.

1. Under the perpetual inventory system, the cost of units purchased and sold is recorded in the Merchandise Inventory account, thus providing management with a continuous and current record of inventory on hand. The periodic inventory system does not provide this useful information to management.
2. A perpetual system provides for an accumulation of the cost of goods sold during the period. When a periodic inventory system is used, a physical inventory must be taken to determine the inventory on hand and the cost of goods sold. A physical count is taken under the perpetual system only to verify the accuracy of the ending inventory.
3. A Purchases account is maintained with a periodic system, whereas a Cost of Goods Sold account is maintained with a perpetual system.

As shown in Figure 6-5, the two systems should produce approximately the same financial statements.

DETERMINING THE COST OF INVENTORY

As with the accounting for other assets, cost is the primary basis of accounting for inventory. Applied to inventory, cost means the sum of all direct and indirect expenditures incurred to acquire the inventory and bring it to its existing location in salable condition.

Conceptually, the invoice price, freight charges, insurance on the goods while in transit, special handling costs, adjustments and assembly costs incurred in preparing the goods for sale, costs incurred to operate a purchasing department, costs associated with receiving and inspecting the goods, and storage costs incurred before the goods are sold are among the costs that may be properly identified and allocated to inventory. For example, this means that freight costs incurred on a shipment of merchandise should be allocated to each unit and recorded as a cost of the inventory. Under the periodic system, such costs should be included in the cost of goods available for sale, and, at the end of the period should be allocated between the units of the ending inventory and the units sold during the period. If a perpetual inventory system is in use, freight charges should be debited to the inventory account. The invoice price plus the freight cost should be expensed as each unit is sold to be matched against revenue as part of the cost of goods sold.

In practice, however, freight costs are normally not allocated between units on hand and units sold because of the practical problem of allocating them to individual units when several types of inventory are acquired in one shipment. Furthermore, in most cases the allocation of freight costs does not significantly change the firm's financial statements. As a result, freight costs are often expensed in the period incurred rather than added to the cost of inventory, which is the conceptually preferred treatment.

If the seller includes the freight charges in the list price, it is not separated on the invoice and becomes a part of the inventory cost when the entry is made to record the purchase transaction. If the seller pays the freight and charges the buyer, it will normally be listed separately on the invoice and is generally debited to an account called either Freight-in or Transportation-in. This account is also used to record freight

DATA: Unit cost $500
        Unit sales price   800
        Beginning inventory   4 units @ $500 per unit = $2,000
        Ending inventory   8 units @ $500 per unit = $4,000

Perpetual	Periodic
Merchandise Inventory	**Merchandise Inventory**
Beg. Bal. 2,000		Beg. Bal. 2,000	

Transaction 1: Purchased six units on credit.

Perpetual			Periodic		
Merchandise Inventory	3,000		Purchases	3,000	
Accounts Payable		3,000	Accounts Payable		3,000

Transaction 2: Sold two units to customers on account.

Perpetual			Periodic		
Accounts Receivable	1,600		Accounts Receivable	1,600	
Sales		1,600	Sales		1,600
Cost of Goods Sold	1,000		(No entry required to		
Merchandise Inventory		1,000	record the cost of units sales.)		

Transaction 3: Returned one unit to supplier for credit on account.

Perpetual			Periodic		
Accounts Payable	500		Accounts Payable	500	
Merchandise Inventory		500	Purchases Returns and Allowances		500

Transaction 4: Customer returned one unit for credit on account.
Returned unit was suitable for resale and was returned to stock.

Perpetual			Periodic		
Sales Returns and Allowances	800		Sales Returns and Allowances	800	
Accounts Receivable		800	Accounts Receivable		800
Merchandise Inventory	500		(No entry required to		
Cost of Goods Sold		500	record the cost of returned unit.)		

General ledger account balances at the end of the period.

Merchandise Inventory				**Merchandise Inventory**	
Beg. Bal.	2,000	(2)	1,000	Beg. Bal. 2,000	
(1)	3,000	(3)	500		
(4)	500				
End. Bal.	4,000				

Cost of Goods Sold				**Purchases**	
(2)	1,000	(4)	500	(1) 3,000	
End. Bal.	500				

Purchases Returns and Allowances	
	(3) 500

Computation of cost of goods sold.

Balance in the Cost of Goods Sold account, $500.		
Beginning inventory		$2,000
Add: Purchases	$3,000	
Less: Purchases returns and allowances	500	
Cost of goods purchased		2,500
Cost of goods available for sale		4,500
Less: Ending inventory		4,000
Cost of goods sold		$ 500

Figure 6-5
Comparison of Perpetual and Periodic Inventory Systems

costs paid by the buyer when the terms of the sale are FOB shipping point. For example, assume that the terms of a purchase of inventory were FOB shipping point and freight costs of $825 were incurred. The entry to record payment of the freight is:

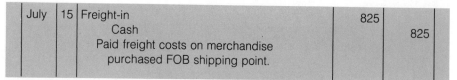

July	15	Freight-in	825	
		Cash		825
		Paid freight costs on merchandise purchased FOB shipping point.		

In the income statement, freight-in is added to purchases (periodic inventory system) or is combined with the amount reported for the cost of goods sold (perpetual inventory system).

The allocation of other incidental costs, such as storage costs and costs related to operating a purchasing and receiving department, also requires an arbitrary allocation method. This procedure does not produce enough benefits to justify the additional cost of making the allocation. Many inventory costs are thus expensed in the period incurred rather than added to the cost of inventory. As a result, only the invoice price is normally used in computing a unit cost of goods purchased.

END-OF-PERIOD PROCESS—PERIODIC INVENTORY SYSTEM

Objective 9: Using a worksheet to complete the closing process

At the end of the accounting period, a worksheet may be used to organize the information for completing the accounting cycle for a merchandising firm. The preparation of a worksheet along with financial statements and the completion of the adjusting and closing process for a merchandising business are similar to those given for a service firm in Chapter 5, except for a few differences associated with inventory related accounts.

For a merchandising firm using the periodic inventory system, the accounts that enter into the determination of cost of goods purchased and both the beginning and ending inventory balances are needed to compute the cost of goods sold. Thus, in addition to recording such adjusting and closing entries as illustrated in previous chapters, it is necessary to do the following.

1. Remove the beginning inventory balance from the Merchandise Inventory account and transfer it to the Income Summary account.
2. Enter the ending inventory balance in the Merchandise Inventory account and the Income Summary account.
3. Close the balances in the accounts that enter into the cost of goods purchased and transfer the balances to the Income Summary account.

Several approaches can be used to enter the ending inventory in the Inventory account and close the balances in the purchases-related accounts. Some accountants prefer to do this as part of the adjusting process. Others adjust the Inventory account and close the purchases-related accounts as part of the closing process. We use the second approach because it requires making fewer journal entries. (An alternative approach to closing the accounts is shown in the Appendix to this chapter.) Although the preparation of the worksheet and the adjusting and closing entries differ with the various approaches, the end results are the same. Selecting which approach to use is just a matter of personal preference.

ILLUSTRATION OF A WORKSHEET FOR A MERCHANDISING FIRM

A worksheet for Educational Software, Inc., a firm that has adopted the periodic inventory system, is presented in Figure 6-6. In the figure, the Unadjusted Trial Balance columns contain a listing of the account balances taken from the general ledger of the company. The next two columns are for the end-of-year adjustments

Figure 6-6
Worksheet When the Periodic Inventory System Is Used

EDUCATIONAL SOFTWARE, INC.
Worksheet
For the Year Ended December 31, 1992

Account Title	Unadjusted Trial Balance Debit	Unadjusted Trial Balance Credit	Adjustments Debit	Adjustments Credit	Adjusted Trial Balance Debit	Adjusted Trial Balance Credit	Income Statement Debit	Income Statement Credit	Balance Sheet Debit	Balance Sheet Credit
Cash	47,050				47,050				47,050	
Accounts Receivable	91,620				91,620				91,620	
Merchandise Inv.–1/1	52,560				52,560		52,560	57,480	57,480	
Prepaid Insurance	1,720			(d) 550	1,170				1,170	
Store Equipment	64,800				64,800				64,800	
Acc. Depr.–Store Equip.		41,940		(b) 6,840		48,780				48,780
Office Equipment	23,760				23,760				23,760	
Acc. Depr.–Office Equip.		11,970		(c) 2,880		14,850				14,850
Accounts Payable		59,630				59,630				59,630
Notes Payable		50,000				50,000				50,000
Capital Stock		45,000				45,000				45,000
Retained Earnings		32,400				32,400				32,400
Dividends Declared	9,000				9,000				9,000	
Sales		638,860				638,860		638,860		
Sales Returns & Allow.	19,250				19,250		19,250			
Sales Discounts	2,940				2,940		2,940			
Purchases	425,360				425,360		425,360			
Freight-in	5,120				5,120		5,120			
Purchases Ret. & Allow.		12,130				12,130		12,130		
Purchases Discounts		2,570				2,570		2,570		
Sales Salaries and Commissions	52,950		(a) 1,980		54,930		54,930			
Delivery Expense	6,060				6,060		6,060			
Advertising Expense	9,980				9,980		9,980			
Bad Debts Expense	6,380				6,380		6,380			
Rent Expense	26,100				26,100		26,100			
Office Salaries Exp.	43,010		(a) 1,320		44,330		44,330			
Income Tax Expense	8,100		(e) 1,100		9,200		9,200			
Interest Expense	900				900		900			
Rent Revenue		2,160				2,160		2,160		
Totals	896,660	896,660								
Salaries Payable				(a) 3,300		3,300				3,300
Depreciation Expense– Store Equipment			(b) 6,840		6,840		6,840			
Depreciaton Expense– Office Equipment			(c) 2,880		2,880		2,880			
Insurance Expense			(d) 550		550		550			
Income Taxes Payable				(e) 1,100		1,100				1,100
Totals			14,670	14,670	910,780	910,780	673,380	713,200	294,880	255,060
Net income for the period							39,820			39,820
Totals							713,200	713,200	294,880	294,880

Beginning inventory balance

Enter ending inventory balance

Cost of goods purchased

based on the following information.

(a)	Accrued salaries:	Sales	$1,980
		Administrative	1,320
(b)	Depreciation:	Store equipment	6,840
(c)	Depreciation:	Office equipment	2,880
(d)	Prepaid insurance expired during the year		550
(e)	Unpaid income taxes at the end of the period		1,100

Based on a physical inventory taken December 31 of each year, the ending merchandise inventory was determined to be $57,480 at the end of the current period and was $52,560 at the end of the prior period. Completion of the worksheet proceeds as illustrated in Chapter 5.

Income Taxes in the Worksheet

An Income Tax Expense balance of $8,100 is included in the Unadjusted Trial Balance debit column. (As noted in Chapter 4, corporate income is subject to state and federal income taxes.) In this illustration, $8,100 in taxes has been paid during the year. At the end of the period, the income subject to tax and the resulting tax expense is computed on forms provided by the Internal Revenue Service. It is assumed that the total tax expense for Educational Software, Inc. is $9,200. To recognize the unpaid portion of the taxes of $1,100 ($9,200 − $8,100), the following adjusting entry is made in the Adjustments column.

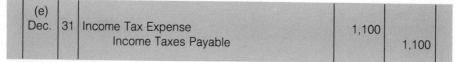

(e)					
Dec.	31	Income Tax Expense		1,100	
		Income Taxes Payable			1,100

The adjusted Income Tax Expense account balance of $9,200 ($8,100 balance in the account + $1,100 adjusting entry) is extended to the Income Statement Debit column, and the Income Taxes Payable balance of $1,100 is extended to the Balance Sheet Credit column.

Merchandise Inventory in the Worksheet

Under a periodic inventory system, the merchandise inventory balance of $52,560 listed in the Unadjusted Trial Balance Debit column is the beginning inventory amount. This amount is extended to the Income Statement Debit column because it is added to the cost of goods purchased to determine the cost of goods available for sale. The accounts that enter into the cost of goods purchased—Purchases ($425,360 debit), Freight-in ($5,120 debit), Purchases Returns and Allowances ($12,130 credit), and Purchases Discounts ($2,570 credit)—are also extended to the appropriate Income Statement columns.

The ending merchandise inventory of $57,480 does not appear in the accounts and must be entered on the worksheet. The $57,480 is entered directly in the Income Statement Credit column since it is a deduction from the cost of goods available for sale when computing the cost of goods sold. The ending inventory amount is also entered in the Balance Sheet Debit column because the ending inventory is on hand and, thus, is an asset to the firm at year-end, and it is necessary to enter an equal debit to maintain the equality of debits and credits in the worksheet. In other words, the ending inventory is reported in two statements: (1) in the income statement (a credit balance) as a subtraction from cost of goods available for sale, and (2) in the balance sheet (a debit balance) as a current asset. Journal entries made to enter the balances in the general ledger Merchandise Inventory account are discussed in the next section. The inventory balances, purchases, and purchases-related accounts enter into the computation of cost of goods sold for Educational Software, Inc., as shown in the income statement in Figure 6-8 on page 250.

COMPLETION OF THE ACCOUNTING CYCLE

Although not shown here, the worksheet is used as a basis for preparing the balance sheet, retained earnings statement, and the adjusting entries in the general journal. In addition, the worksheet is used for preparing closing entries.

Closing Entries

Information needed to prepare the closing entries is available in the Income Statement columns of the worksheet. The process is similar to that illustrated in Chapter 5 for a service firm. As shown in Figure 6-7, closing entries are made (1) to close the temporary accounts with debit balances, (2) to close the temporary accounts with credit balances, (3) to close the balance in the Income Summary account, and (4) to close the balance in the Dividends Declared account. In addition, it is necessary to remove the beginning inventory balance and record the ending inventory in the Merchandise Inventory account.

The closing entries reduce all the temporary accounts to a zero balance. In addition, the entries accomplish the following:

1. The credit of $52,560 to the Merchandise Inventory account in the first closing entry removes the beginning balance from the account, and this amount plus the balances in the temporary accounts with debit balances is debited to the Income Summary account. After this entry is posted, the balance in the Merchandise Inventory account is zero as shown here.

Merchandise Inventory

1/1 Beg. Bal.	52,560	12/31 Clos. Ent.	52,560

2. In the second closing entry, the ending inventory balance of $57,480 is recorded as a debit to the Merchandise Inventory account, and this amount plus the balances in the temporary accounts with credit balances is credited to the Income Summary account. Before the second closing entry is made and posted, the ending inventory is not reported in any ledger account. The effect of these two closing entries on the Merchandise Inventory account is shown here.

Merchandise Inventory

1/1 Beg. Bal.	52,560	12/31 Clos. Ent.	52,560
12/31 Clos. Ent.	57,480		
Bal.	57,480		

Although both a debit and a credit are made to the Merchandise Inventory account as part of the closing process, the account is not closed because the account balance is an asset (a permanent account).

Figure 6-7
Closing Entries
for the Periodic
Inventory System

		Closing Entries		
Dec.	31	Income Summary	673,380	
		Merchandise Inventory (Beginning balance)		52,560
		Sales Returns and Allowances		19,250
		Sales Discounts		2,940
		Purchases		425,360
		Freight-in		5,120
		Sales Salaries and Commissions		54,930
		Delivery Expense		6,060
		Advertising Expense		9,980
		Bad Debts Expense		6,380
		Rent Expense		26,100
		Office Salaries Expense		44,330
		Income Tax Expense		9,200
		Interest Expense		900
		Depreciation Expense–Store Equipment		6,840
		Depreciation Expense–Office Equipment		2,880
		Insurance Expense		550
		To remove the beginning balance from the inventory account, close all temporary accounts with debit balances, and record the total in the Income Summary account.		
	31	Merchandise Inventory (Ending balance)	57,480	
		Sales	638,860	
		Purchases Returns and Allowances	12,130	
		Purchases Discounts	2,570	
		Rent Revenue	2,160	
		Income Summary		713,200
		To record the ending inventory balance, close all temporary accounts with credit balances, and record the total in the Income Summary account.		
	31	Income Summary	39,820	
		Retained Earnings		39,820
		To close the net income to retained earnings.		
	31	Retained Earnings	9,000	
		Dividends Declared		9,000
		To close dividends declared to retained earnings.		

3. The balances in the accounts that enter into the computation of cost of goods purchased are reduced to zero balances and the net effect is debited to the Income Summary account.

4. The net effect of including all the purchases-related accounts in the closing process is that the cost of goods sold for the period is included as a debit balance in the Income Summary account. Although the total debit of entry 1 and the total credit of entry 2 are posted to the Income Summary account, it may be helpful to understand the purpose of the entries and confirm the cost of goods sold amount

by separating the inventory and purchases-related accounts from the total debit and the total credit, as follows.

Income Summary

(From closing entry 1)		(From closing entry 2)	
12/31 Beg. Inv.	52,560	12/31 End. Inv.	57,480
Purchases	425,360	Purchases Ret.	
Freight-in	5,120	and Allow.	12,130
Balance	410,860	Purchases Disc.	2,570

Cost of goods sold
See computation in Figure 6-8.

INCOME STATEMENT FOR A MERCHANDISING FIRM

An income statement for Educational Software, Inc. is presented in Figure 6-8 to show how a merchandiser's income statement accounts are reported. The company uses a periodic inventory system and reports a detailed cost of goods sold section. In practice, there is considerable variation in income statement formats. As a general rule, only the net sales and cost of goods sold amounts are reported in annual reports.

Objective 10: Multiple-step income statement

The format shown in Figure 6-8 is called a *multiple-step income statement* because it shows several subtotals to highlight significant relationships such as gross profit on sales. Note that in this format items that do not result from regular operations of the firm are reported near the bottom of the statement in a section called Other Revenue and Expense. In other words, other revenues and expenses result from transactions related to secondary or miscellaneous activities of the firm. Included in this category are items such as interest expense, dividend revenue, interest revenue, miscellaneous earnings from rentals, and gains and losses from the sale of nonmerchandise assets.

Also note that in this format, the expenses are classified by function, such as cost of goods sold, selling expenses, and administrative expenses. Operating expenses, which are often separated into selling expenses and administrative expenses, exclude cost of goods sold and other expenses. Some expenses, such as the rent expense of $26,100, may need to be allocated between selling expenses ($18,200) and administrative expenses ($7,900). Several methods can be used to allocate an expense. The allocation should be based on a logical relationship between the expense to be allocated and the benefits from the expense. For example, rent could be allocated on the basis of the number of square feet occupied by each department. Allocation methods are covered in more detail in a managerial accounting course.

SUMMARY

This chapter focused on the accounting for and the reporting of transactions of a merchandising firm. A merchandising firm is one that purchases finished products (called merchandise inventory) for sale to its customers as a means of earning revenue. Accounting for inventory involves measuring the cost of the inventory and allocating the cost between the inventory on hand and the inventory that was sold during the accounting period. The cost of inventory on hand is reported as a current asset, whereas the cost of goods sold is an expense matched against sales in the income statement.

EDUCATIONAL SOFTWARE, INC.
Income Statement
For the Year Ended December 31, 1992

Gross sales			$638,860
Less: Sales returns and allowances		$ 19,250	
Sales discounts		2,940	22,190
Net sales			$616,670
Cost of goods sold:			
Merchandise inventory–1/1		52,560	
Purchases	$425,360		
Less: Purchases returns and allowances	$12,130		
Purchases discounts	2,570	14,700	
Net purchases		410,660	
Add: Freight-in		5,120	
Cost of goods purchased		415,780	
Cost of goods available for sale		468,340	
Less: Merchandise inventory–12/31		57,480	
Cost of goods sold			410,860
Gross profit on sales			205,810
Operating expenses:			
Selling expenses:			
Sales salaries and commissions expense		54,930	
Delivery expense		6,060	
Advertising expense		9,980	
Bad debts expense		6,380	
Rent expense–store space		18,200	
Depreciation expense–store equipment		6,840	
Total selling expenses		102,390	
Administrative expenses:			
Office salaries expense		44,330	
Rent expense–office space		7,900	
Depreciation expense–office equipment		2,880	
Insurance expense		550	
Total administrative expenses		55,660	
Total operating expenses			158,050
Income from operations			47,760
Other revenue and expense:			
Add: Rent revenue			2,160
Less: Interest expense			(900)
Income before income taxes			49,020
Income tax expense			9,200
Net income for the year			$ 39,820
Earnings per share			$ .40

Figure 6-8
Income Statement for a Merchandising Firm

Either the perpetual or the periodic inventory system is used to account for inventory costs. The basic differences between the two systems are illustrated in Figure 6-5 on page 243. Under a perpetual inventory system, inventory purchases are recorded in the Merchandise Inventory account. Each time a sale is made, two entries are made: one to record the sale, and the other to reduce the Merchandise Inventory account and record the cost of goods sold. Thus, the perpetual inventory system provides a current record of goods on hand and cost of goods sold. This system provides useful information to management for controlling inventory costs, but requires more clerical effort to operate than the periodic system.

In contrast, under the periodic inventory system, the cost of inventory purchases is recorded in the Purchases account. A physical count must be taken to determine the goods on hand. The cost of goods can then be determined as follows:

$$\begin{array}{ccc} \text{Cost of} & \text{Cost of} & \text{Cost of goods} \\ \text{beginning inventory} + & \text{purchases} = & \text{available for sale} \end{array}$$

$$\begin{array}{ccc} \text{Cost of goods} & \text{Cost of} & \text{Cost of goods} \\ \text{available for sale} - & \text{ending inventory} = & \text{sold} \end{array}$$

The two systems should produce approximately the same results.

SELF-TEST

Test your understanding of the chapter by selecting the best answer for each of the following.

1. If net sales are $120,000, sales discounts are $5,000, and sales returns and allowances are $9,000, what is the amount of gross sales?
   a. $106,000.
   b. $134,000.
   c. $120,000.
   d. $115,000.

2. If goods are sold FOB destination, the party to the transaction responsible for the freight costs is:
   a. the seller of the goods.
   b. the trucking company.
   c. the buyer of the goods.
   d. the bank from which the cash was borrowed to make the purchase.

3. Sedona Company made a sale of merchandise for $4,000, terms 2/10, n/30. The entry to record the receipt of cash to settle the account assuming that the receipt was within the discount period and that sales are recorded using the gross invoice method should be:
   a. debit Cash, $4,000 and credit Accounts Receivable, $4,000.
   b. debit Cash, $3,920 and Sales Discounts, $80, and credit Accounts Receivable $4,000.
   c. debit Cash, $3,920 and credit Accounts Receivable, $3,920.
   d. debit Cash, $3,920 and credit Sales Discounts, $80 and Accounts Receivable, $4,000.

4. Laramie Company buys merchandise with an invoice price of $10,000. Terms of sale are 2/10, n/30, FOB shipping point. Freight charges on this shipment were $100. If Laramie Company uses the gross invoice method to record purchases and uses the periodic inventory system, it should debit which of the following?
   a. Merchandise Inventory, $9,800.
   b. Purchases, $10,000; Freight-in, $100.
   c. Purchases, $9,800; Freight-in, $100.
   d. Purchases, $9,800.

5. Dysan Company returned to Kodak Company, for credit on account, unsatisfactory merchandise that cost Dysan Company $200. Dysan Company uses a periodic inventory system and records purchases and sales using the gross invoice method. The entry to record the return on Dysan Company's books is:

a.	Sales Returns and Allowances	200	
	Accounts Receivable		200
b.	Accounts Payable	200	
	Sales Returns and Allowances		200
c.	Purchases Returns and Allowances	200	
	Accounts Receivable		200
d.	Accounts Payable	200	
	Purchases Returns and Allowances		200

6. Beginning inventory was $20,000. Purchases during the period were $54,000 and purchases discounts were $4,000. Freight on purchases paid by the buyer was $2,000. Ending inventory at cost is $22,000. Compute the cost of goods sold.
   a. $50,000.
   b. $46,000.
   c. $58,000.
   d. $52,000.

7. An item that cost $60 is sold for $100. The following entry is made to record the sale.

Cash (or Accounts Receivable)	100	
Sales		100

   Under the perpetual inventory system, which additional entry is also necessary?

a.	Merchandise Inventory	60	
	Cost of Goods Sold		60
b.	Cost of Goods Sold	60	
	Merchandise Inventory		60
c.	Purchases	60	
	Merchandise Inventory		60
d.	No second entry is necessary.		

8. Which of the following accounts *does not appear* in the ledger of a company that utilizes the perpetual inventory system?
   a. Merchandise Inventory.
   b. Cost of Goods Sold.
   c. Sales Returns and Allowances.
   d. Purchases.

9. The Purchases Discounts account:
   a. will normally have a credit balance.
   b. is a contra account to Purchases.
   c. is closed at the end of the accounting period.
   d. All of the above are correct.

10. For a company using a periodic inventory system, the merchandise inventory amount appearing in the Unadjusted Trial Balance columns of a year-end worksheet is the amount of:
    a. merchandise purchased during the year.
    b. merchandise on hand at the end of the year.
    c. merchandise on hand at the beginning of the current year.
    d. merchandise sold during the year.

REVIEW PROBLEM

Plaza Business Equipment opened for business on May 1, 1992. The transactions below were completed during May. Credit terms are 2/15, n/30 for purchases on account and 3/10, n/30 for sales on account. Plaza uses a periodic inventory system, and the gross method of recording purchases.

May	1	Purchased merchandise inventory on account for $8,000.
	3	Made sales on account, $2,200.
	5	Returned $500 of inventory purchased on May 1.
	8	Made sales on account, $1,150.
	14	Customer returned items sold for $150 on May 8.
	15	Purchased merchandise inventory on account for $6,000.
	18	Received payment for sales made on May 8.
	20	Purchased merchandise inventory on account for $800.
	22	Paid freight bill for inventory purchased, $230.
	23	Made sales on account, $3,400.
	30	Paid for inventory purchased on May 15.
	30	Paid for inventory purchased on May 1.
	31	Made sales on account, $12,620.
	31	Received payment for sales made on May 3.

Required:
A. Prepare journal entries for the May transactions.
B. Set up T accounts for the following accounts.

Cash	Sales Discounts
Accounts Receivable	Sales Returns and Allowances
Accounts Payable	Purchases
P. Mason, Capital	Purchases Discounts
Sales	Purchases Returns and Allowances
	Freight-in

Cash and P. Mason, Capital should have a beginning balance of $15,000 each; all other accounts have a zero beginning balance.

C. Post the May journal entries to the T accounts.
D. Prepare a partial income statement for May. The statement should begin with Gross Sales and end with Gross Profit on Sales. (Additional information: the value of inventory on hand at May 31 was $2,500.)

ANSWER TO REVIEW PROBLEM

A.

May	1	Purchases		8,000	
		Accounts Payable			8,000
	3	Accounts Receivable		2,200	
		Sales			2,200
	5	Accounts Payable		500	
		Purchases Returns & Allowances			500
	8	Accounts Receivable		1,150	
		Sales			1,150
	14	Sales Returns and Allowances		150	
		Accounts Receivable			150
	15	Purchases		6,000	
		Accounts Payable			6,000
	18	Cash		970	
		Sales Discounts		30	
		Accounts Receivable ·			1,000
	20	Purchases		800	
		Accounts Payable			800
	22	Freight-in		230	
		Cash			230
	23	Accounts Receivable		3,400	
		Sales			3,400
	30	Accounts Payable		6,000	
		Purchases Discounts			120
		Cash			5,880
	30	Accounts Payable		7,500	
		Cash			7,500
	31	Accounts Receivable		12,620	
		Sales			12,620
	31	Cash		2,200	
		Accounts Receivable			2,200

B. and **C.**

Cash				
5/1 Bal.	15,000	5/22	230
5/18	970	5/30	5,880
5/31	2,200	5/30	7,500
5/31 Bal.	4,560		

Accounts Payable				
5/5	500	5/1	8,000
5/30	6,000	5/15	6,000
5/30	7,500	5/20	800
		5/31 Bal.	800

Accounts Receivable				
5/3	2,200	5/14	150
5/8	1,150	5/18	1,000
5/23	3,400	5/31	2,200
5/31	12,620		
5/31 Bal.	16,020		

P. Mason, Capital				
		5/1 Bal.	15,000

Sales				
		5/3	2,200
		5/8	1,150
		5/23	3,400
		5/31	12,620
		5/31 Bal.	19,370

Purchases				
5/1	8,000		
5/15	6,000		
5/20	800		
5/31 Bal.	14,800		

Sales Discounts		
5/18	30	

Purchases Discounts		
	5/30	120

Sales Returns & Allowances		
5/14	150	

Purchases Returns & Allowances		
	5/5	500

Freight-in		
5/22	230	

D.

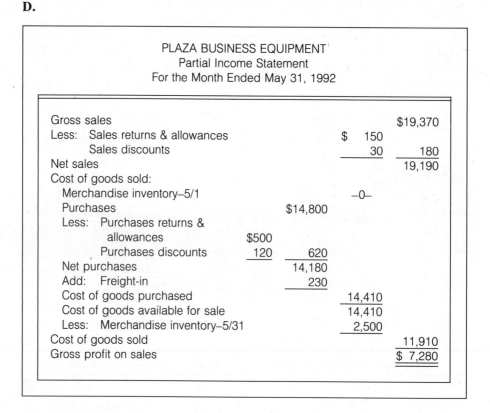

PLAZA BUSINESS EQUIPMENT
Partial Income Statement
For the Month Ended May 31, 1992

Gross sales			$19,370
Less: Sales returns & allowances		$ 150	
Sales discounts		30	180
Net sales			19,190
Cost of goods sold:			
Merchandise inventory–5/1		–0–	
Purchases	$14,800		
Less: Purchases returns & allowances	$500		
Purchases discounts	120	620	
Net purchases		14,180	
Add: Freight-in		230	
Cost of goods purchased		14,410	
Cost of goods available for sale		14,410	
Less: Merchandise inventory–5/31		2,500	
Cost of goods sold			11,910
Gross profit on sales			$ 7,280

ANSWERS TO SELF-TEST

1. b **2.** a **3.** b **4.** b **5.** d **6.** a **7.** b **8.** d
9. d **10.** c

APPENDIX: AN ALTERNATIVE METHOD FOR CLOSING ACCOUNTS—PERIODIC INVENTORY SYSTEM

**Objective 11:
Alternative
end-of-period
process—periodic
inventory system**

When using the periodic inventory system, journal entries made to transfer the beginning balance in the Merchandise Inventory account to the Income Summary account and record the ending balance, per the physical count, contain elements of an adjusting entry and some of a closing entry. Some accountants prefer to record the ending inventory and determine the cost of goods sold for the period as an adjusting entry rather than as part of the closing process illustrated in this chapter. If this approach is used, an additional adjusting entry is needed for the Educational Software, Inc. (see page 245). The adjusting entry is:

Dec.	31	Cost of Goods Sold	410,860	
		Merchandise Inventory (12/31)	57,480	
		Purchases Returns and Allowances	12,130	
		Purchases Discounts	2,570	
		Purchases		425,360
		Freight-in		5,120
		Merchandise Inventory (1/1)		52,560

The debit to the Cost of Goods Sold account for $410,860 is a balancing amount in the above entry. The amount can be verified by checking the cost of goods sold reported in the income statement prepared in Figure 6-8 on page 250. In the worksheet, the balance reported for the cost of goods sold is extended to the Income Statement debit column as shown in Figure 6-9. The credit to the Merchandise Inventory account reduces the account to a zero balance. The debit to Merchandise Inventory establishes the ending inventory balance which is extended to the Balance Sheet debit column. The entries for the closing process become:

		Closing Entries		
Dec	31	Sales	638,860	
		Rent Revenue	2,160	
		Sales Returns and Allowances		19,250
		Sales Discounts		2,940
		Income Summary		618,830
		To close revenue and contra revenue accounts.		
	31	Income Summary	579,010	
		Sales Salaries and Commissions		54,930
		Delivery Expense		6,060
		Advertising Expense		9,980
		Bad Debts Expense		6,380
		Rent Expense		26,100
		Office Salaries Expense		44,330
		Income Tax Expense		9,200
		Interest Expense		900
		Depreciation Expense–Store Equipment		6,840
		Depreciation Expense–Office Equipment		2,880
		Insurance Expense		550
		Cost of Goods Sold		410,860
		To close expense accounts.		
	31	Income Summary	39,820	
		Retained Earnings		39,820
		To close the net income to retained earnings.		
	31	Retained Earnings	9,000	
		Dividends Declared		9,000
		To close dividends declared to retained earnings.		

Note that this approach results in the same net income and balance sheet amounts as determined in Figure 6-6. In the income statement, the cost of goods sold of $410,360 is reported as a single line item rather than preparing a detailed cost of goods sold section as in Figure 6-8.

Figure 6-9
Worksheet When the Periodic Inventory System Is Used

EDUCATIONAL SOFTWARE, INC.
Worksheet
For the Year Ended December 31, 1992

Account Title	Unadjusted Trial Balance Debit	Unadjusted Trial Balance Credit	Adjustments Debit	Adjustments Credit	Adjusted Trial Balance Debit	Adjusted Trial Balance Credit	Income Statement Debit	Income Statement Credit	Balance Sheet Debit	Balance Sheet Credit
Cash	47,050				47,050				47,050	
Accounts Receivable	91,620				91,620				91,620	
Merchandise Inv.–1/1	52,560		(f) 57,480	(f) 52,560	57,480				57,480	
Prepaid Insurance	1,720			(d) 550	1,170				1,170	
Store Equipment	64,800				64,800				64,800	
Acc. Depr.–Store Equip.		41,940		(b) 6,840		48,780				48,780
Office Equipment	23,760				23,760				23,760	
Acc. Depr.–Office Equip.		11,970		(c) 2,880		14,850				14,850
Accounts Payable		59,630				59,630				59,630
Notes Payable		50,000				50,000				50,000
Capital Stock		45,000				45,000				45,000
Retained Earnings		32,400				32,400				32,400
Dividends Declared	9,000				9,000				9,000	
Sales		638,860				638,860		638,860		
Sales Returns & Allow.	19,250				19,250		19,250			
Sales Discounts	2,940				2,940		2,940			
Purchases	425,360			(f) 425,360						
Freight-in	5,120			(f) 5,120						
Purchases Ret. & Allow.		12,130	(f) 12,130							
Purchases Discounts		2,570	(f) 2,570							
Sales Salaries and Commissions	52,950		(a) 1,980		54,930		54,930			
Delivery Expense	6,060				6,060		6,060			
Advertising Expense	9,980				9,980		9,980			
Bad Debts Expense	6,380				6,380		6,380			
Rent Expense	26,100				26,100		26,100			
Office Salaries Exp.	43,010		(a) 1,320		44,330		44,330			
Income Tax Expense	8,100		(e) 1,100		9,200		9,200			
Interest Expense	900				900		900			
Rent Revenue		2,160				2,160		2,160		
Totals	896,660	896,660								
Salaries Payable				(a) 3,300		3,300				3,300
Depreciation Expense–Store Equipment			(b) 6,840		6,840		6,840			
Depreciation Expense–Office Equipment			(c) 2,880		2,880		2,880			
Insurance Expense			(d) 550		550		550			
Income Taxes Payable				(e) 1,100		1,100				1,100
Cost of Goods Sold			(f) 410,860		410,860		410,860			
Totals			497,710	497,710	896,080	896,080	601,200	641,020	294,880	255,060
Net income for the period							39,820			39,820
Totals							641,020	641,020	294,880	294,880

GLOSSARY

ADMINISTRATIVE EXPENSE. Expense associated with the management of the business such as operations of the corporate accounting, personnel, and credit offices (p. 230).

BEGINNING INVENTORY. Merchandise on hand at the start of an accounting period that is available for sale to customers in the normal course of business (p. 236).

CASH DISCOUNT. An incentive offered to the buyer to induce early payment of a credit sale. Cash discounts are a reduction in the invoice price (p. 233).

CONTROL ACCOUNT. A general ledger account that is supported by the detail of a subsidiary ledger. The control account replaces accounts that have been removed from the general ledger and placed in a subsidiary ledger (p. 231).

COST OF GOODS AVAILABLE FOR SALE. The cost of beginning inventory plus the cost of net purchases (p. 239).

COST OF GOODS SOLD. An amount that is deducted from sales in the income statement and is a measure of the cost of the inventory sold during the accounting period (p. 230).

CREDIT MEMORANDUM (CREDIT MEMO). A business form prepared by the seller that contains information related to the receipt of returned goods or an adjustment to the sales price. The purpose of the memo is to inform customers that their account is being credited on the books of the firm preparing the credit memo (p. 232).

CREDIT PERIOD. The period of time granted for the payment of an account (p. 232).

CREDIT TERMS. The agreement made between buyer and seller concerning the sale of goods on credit (p. 232).

DEBIT MEMORANDUM (DEBIT MEMO). A business form prepared by the buyer that contains information related to the return of goods or an adjustment to the purchase price of inventory purchased. The purpose of the memo is to inform a supplier that the supplier's account is being debited on the books of the firm preparing the debit memo (p. 240).

DISCOUNT PERIOD. The period of time during which a cash discount may be taken if payment is made. The discount is subtracted from the invoice price (p. 233).

ENDING INVENTORY. Merchandise on hand at the end of an accounting period that is held for sale to customers in the normal course of the business (p. 238).

FOB DESTINATION. Shipping terms in which freight is paid by the seller and transfer of title to the buyer occurs when the goods arrive at the buyer's firm (p. 234).

FOB SHIPPING POINT. Shipping terms in which freight is paid by the buyer and transfer of title to the buyer occurs when the goods leave the seller's firm (p. 234).

GROSS INVOICE METHOD. A procedure in which sales revenue and purchases of inventory are recorded at the gross or full invoice price (p. 233).

MERCHANDISE INVENTORY (INVENTORY). Goods acquired by a merchandising firm for the purpose of resale in the normal course of business (p. 229).

PERIODIC INVENTORY SYSTEM. A system of accounting for inventory in which the goods on hand are determined by a physical count. Cost of goods sold is determined at the end of the accounting period and is equal to the cost of the beginning inventory plus the cost of purchases less the cost of the ending inventory (p. 236).

PERPETUAL INVENTORY SYSTEM. A system of accounting for inventory that provides a continuous and detailed record of the goods on hand and the cost of goods sold (p. 235).

PHYSICAL INVENTORY. The process of counting and pricing the goods on hand (p. 238).

PURCHASE DISCOUNT. A percentage reduction (cash discount) received when an account payable is settled within the discount period (p. 233).

PURCHASE INVOICE. A business form that contains the terms of a purchase transaction (p. 232).

SALES DISCOUNT. A percentage reduction (cash discount) in the gross invoice price granted to a customer to encourage early payment of the account receivable (p. 232).

SALES INVOICE. A business form prepared by the seller that contains the information relating to a sale (p. 232).

SELLING EXPENSE. Expense incurred in storing, promoting, and delivering the merchandise inventory to customers (p. 230).

SUBSIDIARY LEDGER. A group of individual accounts which have been removed from the general ledger. The sum of the individual account balances should equal the balance of a related control account which has replaced them in the general ledger (p. 231).

TRADE DISCOUNT. A reduction in the suggested list or catalog price granted to certain classifications of customers. Trade discounts are not recorded in the accounts (p. 234).

DISCUSSION QUESTIONS

1. Define the term ''merchandise inventory'' as the term is used in a merchandising operation.
2. Describe the normal operating cycle for a merchandising firm.
3. Explain how the matching principle is met by a merchandising concern.
4. What is cost of goods sold? Why is it important?
5. What is gross profit on sales? How is it computed and what does it tell the financial statement reader?
6. List the two functional classifications of operating expenses and explain the types of expenses that are included in each classification.
7. What is a control account? a subsidiary ledger? How are they related?
8. Define the term credit memo. Does the seller or buyer issue the credit memo?
9. What kind of account is the Sales Returns and Allowances? How is it shown on the financial statements?
10. Define the following:
    a. Credit period.
    b. Credit terms.
    c. Cash discount.
    d. Discount period.
11. Why do firms selling merchandise on credit offer cash discounts?
12. What is net sales and how is it calculated?
13. What is a trade discount? When are they used?
14. Discuss the significance of the terms ''FOB shipping point'' and ''FOB destination.''
15. Distinguish between a perpetual and a periodic inventory system and tell how each one works.

16. What kind of account is Purchases? What function does it serve in a periodic inventory system?

17. Define ''Cost'' in the context of accounting inventories. Conceptually, what items should be included in the computation of an inventory's cost?

EXERCISES

Exercise 6-1   Cost of Goods Sold
The following information is from the books of Top-notch Company.

Purchases	$150,200
Merchandise Inventory, January 1, 1992	9,200
Merchandise Inventory, December 31, 1992	42,670
Selling Expenses	25,000
Sales	163,740
Purchases Returns and Allowances	2,690
Sales Returns and Allowances	2,780
Administrative Expenses	9,800
Sales Discounts	976
Freight-in	2,246
Purchases Discounts	1,800

Required:
Use the preceding information to prepare a multiple-step income statement for the year ended December 31, 1992 for Top-notch Company.

Exercise 6-2   Effective Interest Rates of Cash Discounts
The following terms are offered to a purchaser of $100 in merchandise:

1. 1/10, n/30.
2. 2/15, n/60.
3. 3/10, n/45.
4. 2/EOM, n/45—Goods purchased on April 15.

Required:
A. Compute the effective annual interest rate if the discount is not taken and the invoice is paid when due.
B. Considering your results, discuss the desirability of short-term borrowing to allow a firm to take advantage of the cash discounts.

Exercise 6-3   Discounts and Returns
Karen Company sells merchandise with credit terms of 3/15, n/60. A trade discount of 20% is given to wholesalers. On June 2, 1992, Bridge Resales (a wholesaler) purchased merchandise with a list price of $1,500 from Karen Company.

Required:
1. How much is the trade discount?
2. On June 5, Bridge returned merchandise with an original list price of $400. Prepare the journal entries to record the return on both company's books. Assume that both companies use a periodic inventory system and the gross invoice method of recording cash discounts.

3. How long is the discount period? If Bridge pays on the last day of the discount period, how much is the sales discount recorded by Karen Company?

4. If Bridge does not remit payment within the discount period, when is the net amount due? What would be the effective annual yield?

Exercise 6-4 Recording Merchandise Transactions—Perpetual Inventory System

Below are listed merchandise transactions completed by Duncan Corporation during the months of January and February 1992.

January	3	Purchased 600 units of Product K at $5 per unit; terms 2/10, n/30; invoice dated January 3.
	4	Sold 400 units of Product K for $10 per unit; terms 1/15, n/30; FOB destination. Cost per unit of Product K is $5.
	5	Purchased 200 units of Product K at $5 per unit; terms 2/10, n/30; invoice dated January 5.
	7	Sold 600 units of Product K for $12 per unit; terms 1/15, n/30. Cost per unit of Product K is $5.
	7	Returned 75 damaged units of Product K purchased on January 3 to the supplier for credit.
	10	Received 50 units of Product K sold on January 4 from the customer. The units were not defective and were returned to stock.
	15	Paid for the January 5 purchase of Product K.
	22	Received payment from the customer for the January 7 sale of Product K.
February	2	Paid for the January 3 purchase of Product K.
	3	Received payment from the customer for the January 4 sale of Product K.

Required:

Prepare general journal entries to record the January and February transactions listed above for the Duncan Corporation. Duncan Corporation uses the perpetual inventory system.

Exercise 6-5 Recording Merchandise Transactions—Periodic Inventory System

Rosenberg Corporation engaged in the following transactions during April 1992.

April	1	Purchased merchandise on account. List price $10,500, trade discount 5%. Credit terms 2/10, n/30; FOB shipping point.
	3	Paid freight bill of $250 for the shipment made on April 1.
	6	Returned damaged merchandise received in the April 1 shipment for $425 credit on account.
	11	Paid the amount due for the merchandise purchased April 1.

Required:

Prepare general journal entries to record the transactions. Rosenberg Corporation uses the periodic inventory system.

Exercise 6-6 Recording Sales Transactions—Periodic and Perpetual

Lewis Company completed the following sales transactions during the months of September and October.

September	10	Sold 25 units at $125 per unit; terms n/45; FOB destination. Cost per unit is $75.

	12	Paid freight costs of $300 to ship units sold on September 10.
	14	Customer returned 3 units. The units were not defective and were returned to stock.
October	25	Received payment from customer for units sold in September.

Required:

In parallel columns prepare journal entries to record the transactions under both the periodic and the perpetual inventory systems.

Exercise 6-7   Recording Purchase Transactions—Periodic and Perpetual

Track Company completed the following purchase transactions during the months of March and April.

March	6	Purchased 60 units at $50 per unit; terms n/30; FOB shipping point.
	11	Returned 5 of the units purchased on March 6 because they were defective. Credit of $50 per unit was granted by the seller.
	15	Sold 20 units purchased on March 6 to Corso Company on account for $85 per unit.
April	5	Paid supplier for the units purchased in March.

Required:

In parallel columns prepare journal entries to record the transactions under both the periodic and the perpetual inventory systems.

Exercise 6-8   Recording Sales Transactions—Perpetual Inventory System

Dexter Company had the following transactions relating to the sales of their merchandise inventory during the months of July and August.

July	2	Sold 100 units of Product X at $50 per unit to Jacobs Company, terms 2/10, n/30. Cost per unit is $30.
	5	Sold 60 units of product Z at $60 per unit to A.B.C. Industries, terms 1/10, n/30. Cost per unit is $25.
	10	A.B.C. Industries returned 10 units of Product Z purchased on July 5. The units were not defective and were returned to stock.
	12	Received payment from Jacobs Company for the July 2 sale.
August	5	Received payment from A.B.C. Industries for the July 5 sale less the units returned on July 10.

Required:

Prepare journal entries to record the transactions. Assume a perpetual inventory method.

Exercise 6-9   Recording Purchase Transactions—Periodic Inventory System

Peter Company had the following transactions relating to their merchandise acquisition activities during the months of May and June.

May	4	Purchased 100 units of Product X at $40 per unit from Stone Enterprises, terms 2/10, n/30.
	7	Purchased 120 units of Product Z at $25 per unit from Lantern Company, terms 1/10, n/30.
	9	Returned 15 units of the goods purchased from Stone Enterprises.
	14	Paid the amount owed to Stone Enterprises for the May 4 purchase less the returned goods.
June	7	Paid the amount owed to Lantern Company for the May 7 purchase.

Required:
Prepare journal entries to record the transactions. Assume a periodic inventory system.

Exercise 6-10   Short-answer and Fill-in-the-Blank Questions
Complete the following statements by filling in the blanks.

1. The account _____ is debited when merchandise is purchased and a perpetual inventory is used.
2. Goods shipped FOB shipping point indicates that title passes to the buyer _____ and the _____ pays the freight costs.
3. Credit terms 1/15, n/30 means that _____ .
4. When a credit sale is made and the perpetual inventory system is used, _____ entry(ies) is/are required to record the event.
5. Freight-out is part of _____ on the income statement.
6. Cash discounts are normally given to encourage _____ .
7. The accounts _____ and _____ are debited to record a credit sale when using the perpetual inventory system.
8. A _____ percent trade discount on a list price of $500 means the qualified buyer will pay $425.
9. A customer's payment for a prior sale received within the discount period when the gross invoice method is used requires debits to the accounts _____ and _____ .
10. A purchase with an invoice amount of $200 that is paid in full by remitting $198 means a _____ percent cash discount was offered.
11. The balance in the account "Freight-in" is _____ to the net purchases in the _____ section of the income statement.
12. An _____ must be maintained for each different inventory item when the perpetual inventory system is used.
13. Costs of items returned to the supplier are credited to the Purchases Returns account instead of the Purchases account because _____ .
14. A purchases allowance occurs when _____ .

Exercise 6-11   Income Statement Through Gross Profit
Information for three independent cases is shown below:

	Case 1	Case 2	Case 3
Gross sales	$150,000	$ (g)	$ (k)
Sales discounts	(a)	8,000	5,000
Sales returns and allowances	6,000	10,000	10,000
Net sales	138,000	378,000	(l)
Inventory—January 1	80,000	(h)	110,000
Purchases	115,000	240,000	(m)
Purchases discounts	3,100	5,000	4,000
Purchases returns and allowances	(b)	12,000	10,000
Net purchases	100,000	(i)	170,000
Transportation-in	(c)	15,000	10,000
Cost of goods purchased	110,000	238,000	(n)
Cost of goods available for sale	(d)	353,000	290,000
Inventory—December 31	(e)	120,000	(o)
Cost of goods sold	100,000	(j)	200,000
Gross profit	(f)	145,000	100,000

Required:
Complete the schedules by calculating the missing information.

Exercise 6-12 Closing Entries for Merchandise Related Accounts

The following selected accounts with their related balances were taken from Taylor Company's December 31, 1992 adjusted trial balance.

Cash	$ 48,860
Accounts Receivable	156,240
Purchases	650,000
Sales Returns and Allowances	8,650
Merchandise Inventory, January 1, 1992	110,000
Sales Discounts	1,890
Accounts Payable	38,915
Purchases Discounts	4,250
Freight-in	6,830
Sales	872,490
Retained Earnings	430,735
Purchases Returns and Allowances	8,300
Capital Stock	400,000
Merchandise Inventory, December 31, 1992	152,600

Required:
Prepare the closing entries to close all appropriate accounts listed above relating to the merchandise operations of Taylor Company.

Exercise 6-13 Completion of Worksheet—Periodic Inventory System

Select accounts and a partial worksheet are shown here.

Account Title	Adjusted Trial Balance		Income Statement		Balance Sheet	
	Debit	Credit	Debit	Credit	Debit	Credit
Merchandise Inventory	?					
Sales		102,000				
Sales Returns and Allowances	4,600					
Sales Discounts	2,800					
Purchases	85,000					
Purchases Returns and Allowances		1,800				
Purchases Discounts		1,200				
Freight-in	800					

Required:
The beginning and ending merchandise inventory were $20,000 and $24,000, respectively. You are to enter the beginning and ending inventory amounts in the proper columns and extend the other account balances listed to their proper columns.

Exercise 6-14 Worksheet for a Merchandising Company—Periodic Inventory System

The unadjusted trial balance for Shelley's Shoes, Inc., is shown on the following page.

SHELLEY'S SHOES, INC.
Unadjusted Trial Balance
January 31, 1992

Account Title	Debit	Credit
Cash	$ 15,700	
Merchandise Inventory	42,900	
Prepaid Insurance	4,800	
Store Equipment	26,000	
Accumulated Depreciation—Store Equipment		$ 6,000
Payables		6,300
Capital Stock		50,000
Retained Earnings		13,830
Sales		151,870
Sales Returns and Allowances	3,890	
Purchases	70,680	
Purchases Returns and Allowances		3,250
Purchases Discounts		1,040
Freight-in	3,800	
Expenses	64,520	
Totals	$232,290	$232,290

Required:

Prepare a worksheet for the year ended January 31, 1992. The following information is available to make the year-end adjustments. Make all adjustments to the account titles listed in the trial balance.

a. 60% of the prepaid insurance has expired.
b. The store equipment has an estimated 13-year life with no residual value.
c. The unpaid income tax expense for the period is $520.
d. The ending merchandise inventory, as determined by a physical count of the goods on hand, is $38,300.

Exercise 6-15 Completion of Worksheet—Perpetual Inventory System

Select accounts and a partial worksheet are shown here.

Account Title	Adjusted Trial Balance Debit	Adjusted Trial Balance Credit	Income Statement Debit	Income Statement Credit	Balance Sheet Debit	Balance Sheet Credit
Merchandise Inventory	?					
Sales		78,000				
Sales Returns and Allowances	3,000					
Cost of Goods Sold	51,000					
Selling Expenses	10,000					
Administrative Expenses	7,500					

Required:
The beginning and ending merchandise inventory were $8,000 and $10,500, respectively. You are to enter the proper inventory amount in the trial balance column and extend the other account balances to the proper columns.

Exercise 6-16 Worksheet for a Merchandising Company—Perpetual Inventory System
The unadjusted trial balance for Marcia's Fashion Source is shown below.

MARCIA'S FASHION SOURCE
Unadjusted Trial Balance
October 31, 1992

Account Title	Debit	Credit
Cash	$ 25,200	
Merchandise Inventory	66,600	
Prepaid Insurance	5,500	
Store Equipment	31,500	
Accumulated Depreciation—Store Equipment		$ 18,900
Payables		21,730
Capital Stock		25,000
Retained Earnings		55,150
Dividends Declared	10,000	
Sales		212,600
Sales Returns and Allowances	4,080	
Cost of Goods Sold	98,400	
Expenses	92,100	
Totals	$333,380	$333,380

Required:
Prepare a worksheet for Marcia's Fashion Source for the year ended October 31, 1992. The following information is available to make the year-end adjustments. Make all adjustments to the account titles listed above.

a. Insurance expired during the year is $4,400.
b. The store equipment has an estimated 10-year life with no residual value.
c. The income tax expense for the year is $3,200.

Exercise 6-17 Multiple Choice—Inventory Concepts
Choose the best answer for the following questions.

1. The account Sales Returns and Allowances is:
   a. an asset.
   b. a liability.
   c. part of stockholder's equity.
   d. a contra account to Sales.
2. Which of the following items should be included in the cost of inventory?
   a. Invoice price.
   b. Storage costs.

    c. Freight charges.

    d. All of the above are part of inventory cost.

3. Under the periodic inventory system, when merchandise is returned to a supplier, which of the following accounts is credited?

    a. Merchandise Inventory.

    b. Purchases.

    c. Purchases Returns and Allowances.

    d. Purchases Discounts.

4. FOB shipping point means:

    a. Title passes to the buyer upon delivery of the goods to the buyer's warehouse.

    b. Title passes to the buyer when the goods are paid for.

    c. The seller pays the freight.

    d. The buyer pays the freight?

5. Gross profit on sales is computed as:

    a. net sales minus purchases.

    b. net sales divided by cost of goods sold.

    c. net sales minus cost of goods sold.

    d. net sales divided by operating expenses.

6. Which of the following accounts is not used in a perpetual inventory system?

    a. Sales.

    b. Cost of Goods Sold.

    c. Purchases.

    d. Sales Discounts.

7. The normal operating cycle for a firm is:

    a. one year.

    b. the time it takes for a firm to acquire and sell inventory.

    c. the financial statement period.

    d. the time it takes for a firm to acquire inventory, sell it, and collect cash from the sale.

8. If a purchaser may subtract 2% from the cost of her purchases if she pays within 15 days of the invoice date, and the total cost must be paid in 60 days, the credit terms are:

    a. 2/15, n/60.

    b. 2/15, EOM.

    c. 1/10, n/30

    d. n/60.

9. Under which of the following methods are purchases and sales recorded at the full invoice price?

    a. Allowance method.

    b. Gross invoice method.

    c. Full cost method.

    d. Net invoice method.

10. A physical inventory:

    a. is required to determine cost of goods sold if a company uses a perpetual inventory system.

    b. is not required if a company uses a periodic inventory system.

    c. should be taken once a year, regardless of the inventory system used.

    d. is never required.

PROBLEMS

Problem 6-1 Journal Entries for Both Buyer and Seller—Periodic Inventory System

The following transactions occurred between Joe's Wholesales and Knotty Furniture during the months of March and May.

Mar. 2 Joe's Wholesales sold merchandise with a total price of $58,000 to Knotty Furniture. Terms 2/15, n/45; FOB destination. Knotty Furniture qualifies for a 15% trade discount.

2 Joe's Wholesales paid $3,100 in freight charges to ship the merchandise to Knotty Furniture.

8 Knotty Furniture returned merchandise that had a list price (before trade discount) of $7,500.

17 Knotty Furniture paid for the merchandise.

20 Joe's Wholesales sold merchandise to Knotty Furniture for $50,000. Terms 2/15, n/45; FOB destination; 15% trade discount.

May 4 Knotty Furniture paid for the merchandise.

Required:

Prepare general journal entries for both companies to record the transactions. Assume that both companies use a periodic inventory system.

Problem 6-2 Journal Entries—Perpetual Inventory System

The following transactions related to product item NC-8A occurred in November. The beginning inventory on November 1 consisted of 11 units at $125 each.

Nov. 2 Purchased 5 units for $125 each, on credit.

11 Returned 2 units to the manufacturer for credit on account.

13 Sold 10 units for $300 each, on account. Terms, FOB shipping point.

17 The customer returned 2 units. The units were not defective and were returned to stock.

28 Sold 3 units for $300 each, on account.

Required:

A. Prepare journal entries to record the transactions, assuming that a perpetual inventory system is used.

B. The company closes its books each month. Prepare entries to close the income statement accounts for November, based on the data provided, and assuming that operating expenses for the month were $1,460, and according to a physical inventory count on November 30, 3 units are on hand at a total cost of $375.

Problem 6-3 Cash Discounts and Effective Interest Rates

Wayne Corporation operates a chain of retail stores in southern Arizona. Business is seasonal with summer being the slowest time of the year. Sales in the winter are high due in part to the large number of winter visitors escaping the colder weather in other parts of the United States and Canada. Because of the high winter demand, Wayne must order its merchandise in July and take delivery in October, the times that business is the slowest and cash flow is negative.

During 1992, Wayne placed two large orders for merchandise of $250,000 and $500,000 respectively. The credit terms offered by the suppliers were 2/15, n/60 on the $250,000 purchase and 3/10, n/30 on the $500,000 purchase. Wayne was unable to pay within the discount period, thus they had to pay the full invoice price for the goods.

Required:

A. Compute the dollar amount of the lost discounts on the two purchases described above.

B. Compute the effective annual rate of interest Wayne paid for the additional 45 days and 20 days they took to pay for the merchandise purchased.

C. Assuming Wayne could have borrowed the money needed to pay for the purchases within the discount period from the local bank at a 20% annual rate with the notes being short-term and open-ended (i.e., 30 to 60 days, repayment can take place any time after the 30th day), how much money would Wayne have saved if they had borrowed the money from the bank to pay for the purchases within the discount period?

Problem 6-4 Recording Merchandise Transactions— Perpetual Inventory System

Stacey Company, a merchandise retailer, uses the perpetual inventory system. Listed below are merchandise transactions that occurred during August, 1992.

August	3	Sold 50 units of Product B to Newark Corporation at $80 per unit; terms 1/10, n/30. Cost per unit is $50.
	4	Purchased 325 units of Product F from Georgia Industries at $50 per unit; terms 2/10, n/30; invoice dated August 3.
	7	Returned 30 damaged units of product F from the August 4 purchase to Georgia Industries for credit.
	12	Sold 250 units of Product·J to Alison Corp. at $60 per unit; terms 2/10, n/30. Cost per unit is $20.
	17	Received 40 units of Product J sold to Alison Corporation on August 12. The units were not defective and were returned to stock.
	20	Sold 600 units of Product R to Saturn, Inc., at $75 per unit; terms 3/10, n/20. Cost per unit is $40.
	22	Received payment from Alison Corp. for the August 12 sale less merchandise return and applicable cash discount.
	22	Purchased 600 units of Product B at $50 per unit from Ashley Corporation; terms 3/10, n/30; invoice dated August 21.
	24	Received notification from Saturn, Inc., that 200 units of Product R sold on August 20 were slightly damaged but could still be sold. Granted Saturn, Inc., a $25 per unit sales allowance on the 200 damaged units.
	27	Notified Ashley Corp. that 100 units of Product B, purchased August 22 were of a lower quality than those ordered. Ashley Corp. granted a $15 per unit allowance on these 100 units.
	30	Received payment from Saturn Inc., for the August 20 sale less allowance granted for damaged merchandise and applicable cash discount.
	31	Paid Ashley Corp. for the August 22 purchase less allowance granted for inferior units and applicable cash discount.
Sept.	2	Received payment from Newark Corporation for the August 3 sale.
	3	Paid Georgia Industries for the August 4 purchase less returned merchandise.

Required:
Record the August transactions of the Stacey Company in the general journal.

Problem 6-5 Journal Entries—Periodic Inventory System
The following transactions related to Product K-9 occurred in February. The beginning inventory on February 1 consisted of 110 units at $10 each.

February 1 Purchased 445 units for $10 each on credit.
7 Returned 25 units, which were defective.
12 Sold 250 units on account for $18 each.
24 A customer returned 8 units. The units were not defective and were returned to stock.
25 Sold 68 units on account for $18 each.

Required:
A. Prepare journal entries to record the transactions, assuming that a periodic inventory system is used.
B. The company closes its books each month. Prepare entries to close the income statement accounts for February, based on the data just given, and assuming that operating expenses for February were $1,800, and a physical inventory count on February 28 shows 220 units at a total cost of $2,200.

Problem 6-6 Recording Merchandise Transactions— Periodic and Perpetual Inventory Systems
The following merchandise transactions were completed by Big & Little, Inc., a merchandise retailer, during the month of August, 1992.

August 2 Purchased 2,000 units of inventory for $10 per unit; terms 2/10, n/30; invoice dated August 2, 1992.
3 Sold 1,700 units of inventory with a unit cost of $6 for $10 per unit; terms 2/10, n/30.
5 Returned 200 damaged inventory units purchased on August 2 for credit.
7 Purchased 3,000 units of inventory for $5 per unit; terms 2/10, n/30; invoice dated August 7, 1992.
8 Customer returned 200 units from August 3 sale. The original order was for 1,500 units and was misread by the shipping clerk. The units were returned to the inventory.
11 Sold 2,500 units of inventory with a unit cost of $10 for $15 per unit; terms 2/10, n/30.
17 Paid for August 7 purchase and took the discount.
21 Received payment from the customer for the August 11 sale. Customer took the cash discount.

Required:
A. Prepare general journal entries to record the August transactions of Big & Little, Inc., under both the periodic and perpetual inventory systems. All purchases and sales were on credit.
B. Prepare partial income statements, through gross profit on sales, for both the periodic and perpetual inventory systems. As per physical inventory counts, the beginning and ending inventory balances were $60,000 and $58,700, respectively.
C. Prepare the closing entries, as of August 31, 1992, for both the periodic and perpetual inventory systems.

D. Compare the following balances for both the periodic and perpetual inventory systems:
1. ending inventory
2. cost of goods sold
3. gross profit on sales

Are they the same? If so, explain why. If not, explain why.

Problem 6-7 Worksheet and Completion of Accounting Cycle— Periodic Inventory System

The unadjusted trial balance of Herman's Doors & Locks is shown below.

HERMAN'S DOORS & LOCKS
Trial Balance
December 31, 1992

Account Title	Debit	Credit
Cash	$ 23,470	
Accounts Receivable	31,210	
Merchandise Inventory	59,300	
Prepaid Insurance	3,400	
Office Equipment	77,460	
Accumulated Depreciation—Office Equipment		$ 12,600
Delivery Truck	16,500	
Accumulated Depreciation—Truck		4,280
Accounts Payable		36,400
Note Payable, due June, 1996		18,000
Capital Stock		70,000
Retained Earnings		32,000
Dividends Declared	18,000	
Sales		389,480
Sales Returns and Allowances	7,300	
Sales Discounts	1,150	
Purchases	204,300	
Purchases Returns and Allowances		6,400
Purchases Discounts		980
Freight—in	4,350	
Freight—out	2,000	
Salaries Expense—Sales	36,000	
Sales Commissions Expense	11,000	
Rent Expense—Store	46,500	
Salaries Expense—Administrative	19,500	
Interest Expense	1,700	
Income Tax Expense	7,000	
Totals	$570,140	$570,140

Required:

A. Prepare a worksheet for Herman's Doors & Locks. Use the following information to make year-end adjustments.
   a. $2,400 of the prepaid insurance has expired during the year.
   b. Depreciation on the office equipment was $3,960 for the year.

c. Depreciation on the delivery truck was $2,010 for the year.

d. Accrued interest on the note payable is $535.

e. Income taxes of $3,200 are unrecorded.

Use the following additional accounts for making adjustments.

    Interest Payable
    Income Taxes Payable
    Depreciation Expense—Office Equipment
    Depreciation Expense—Truck
    Insurance Expense

The ending merchandise inventory determined by a physical count was $47,390.

B. Prepare an income statement, a retained earnings statement, and a classified balance sheet for the year ended December 31, 1992. Expired insurance is reported as an administrative expense.

C. Prepare adjusting and closing entries.

 Problem 6-8 Worksheet and Completion of Accounting Cycle for a Merchandising Company Using a Periodic Inventory System

The unadjusted trial balance for Karen's Kraft Kottage is shown below.

KAREN'S KRAFT KOTTAGE
Unadjusted Trial Balance
December 31, 1992

Account Title	Debit	Credit
Cash	$ 28,200	
Accounts Receivable	90,600	
Merchandise Inventory	110,210	
Prepaid Insurance	4,800	
Store Equipment	78,120	
Accumulated Depreciation—Store Equipment		$ 23,120
Delivery Trucks	19,600	
Accumulated Depreciation—Delivery Trucks		8,200
Accounts Payable		30,180
Notes Payable—Current		30,000
Capital Stock		100,000
Retained Earnings		78,810
Dividends Declared	42,000	
Sales		803,470
Sales Returns and Allowances	21,220	
Sales Discounts	11,600	
Purchases	440,280	
Purchases Returns and Allowances		20,800
Purchases Discounts		7,290
Freight-in	8,240	
Operating Expenses	221,450	
Income Tax Expense	21,000	
Interest Expense	4,550	
Totals	$1,101,870	$1,101,870

The following account titles were included in the chart of accounts.

Interest Payable   Income Taxes Payable

Required:

A. Prepare a worksheet for Karen's Kraft Kottage. The following information is available to make the year-end adjustments:

    a. Prepaid insurance in the amount of $1,200 is unexpired at the end of the year. Charge to operating expenses.

    b. Depreciation on the store equipment for the year is $5,780; depreciation on the delivery trucks for the year is $4,100. Charge to operating expenses.

    c. Accrued interest on the note payable is $1,800.

    d. Total income tax expense for the year is $25,000.

    e. The ending merchandise inventory as determined by a physical count of the goods on hand is $92,120.

B. Prepare an income statement, retained earnings statements, and a balance sheet for the year ended December 31, 1992.

C. Prepare the adjusting entries in general journal form.

D. Prepare the closing entries in general journal form.

Problem 6-9 Worksheet and Completion of Accounting Cycle— Merchandising Company—Perpetual Inventory System

The unadjusted trial balance of Al's Electronics Emporium is shown on the next page.

The following account titles were included in the chart of accounts.

Inventory Loss	Insurance Expense
Office Supplies Expense	Depreciation Expense—Building
Depreciation Expense—Store Equipment	Depreciation Expense—Office Equipment
Interest Payable	Salaries Payable
Income Taxes Payable	

Required:

A. Prepare a worksheet for Al's Electronics Emporium. The following information is available for the year-end adjustments.

    a. A physical count of the ending inventory showed $96,400 of merchandise on hand.

    b. Insurance expired during the year is $4,000.

    c. Office supplies on hand have a cost of $1,000.

    d. The building is depreciated over 25 years (70% is related to selling activities).

    e. The store equipment is depreciated over 10 years.

    f. The office equipment is depreciated over 8years.

    g. Accrued interest on the notes and mortgage is $2,250.

    h. Accrued salaries on January 31, 1992 are $3,300.

    i. Income taxes in the amount of $1,570 are unpaid.

B. Prepare an income statement, a retained earnings statement, and a balance sheet for the year ended January 31, 1992.

C. Prepare the adjusting entries in general journal form.

D. Prepare the closing entries in general journal form.

AL'S ELECTRONICS EMPORIUM
Unadjusted Trial Balance
January 31, 1992

Account Title	Debit	Credit
Cash	$ 36,060	
Marketable Securities	30,000	
Merchandise Inventory	97,100	
Prepaid Insurance	5,600	
Office Supplies On Hand	1,800	
Land	80,000	
Building	155,000	
Accumulated Depreciation—Building		$ 31,000
Store Equipment	66,000	
Accumulated Depreciation—Store Equipment		33,000
Office Equipment	24,000	
Accumulated Depreciation—Office Equipment		6,000
Accounts Payable		46,800
Notes Payable—Current		30,000
Mortgage Payable—Long-term		92,410
Capital Stock		100,000
Retained Earnings		135,780
Dividends Declared	20,000	
Sales		571,510
Sales Returns and Allowances	23,110	
Sales Discounts	9,480	
Cost of Goods Sold	241,550	
Salaries Expense—70% selling	192,000	
Utilities Expense—70% selling	22,800	
Interest Expense	14,400	
Other Operating Expenses—30% selling	24,600	
Income Tax Expense	3,000	
Totals	$1,046,500	$1,046,500

Problem 6-10   Reconstructing an Annual Income Statement from Financial Records

David Cross opened an art supplies store during 1992 under the name Cross Art Supplies. On January 20, 1992, David invested the following assets in the business in return for all of the capital stock in the corporation: $10,000 cash, $15,000 of inventory, and $30,000 of store equipment. During 1992, David made the following cash disbursements: $140,000 for inventory purchases and $80,000 for operating expenses.

The following balance sheet was prepared on December 31, 1992.

CROSS ART SUPPLIES
Balance Sheet
December 31, 1992

Assets

Current Assets:		
Cash		$108,000
Accounts receivable		32,000
Merchandise Inventory		22,000
Total Current Assets		162,000
Property, Plant and Equipment:		
Store equipment	$ 30,000	
Less: Accumulated depreciation	5,000	25,000
Total Assets		$187,000

Liabilities and Stockholders' Equity

Current Liabilities:		
Accounts payable (for inventory)		$ 14,000
Wages payable		5,000
Total Current Liabilities		19,000
Stockholders' Equity:		
Capital stock	$ 55,000	
Retained earnings	113,000	
Total Stockholders' Equity		168,000
Total Liabilities and Stockholders' Equity		$187,000

Required:

A. Using the information given above, prepare an income statement for the year ended December 31, 1992 in the following format. Show supporting schedules for the computations of: net income, cost of goods sold, operating expense, and sales.

Sales	$ _____
Cost of goods sold	_____
Gross profit on sales	_____
Operating expenses	_____
Net income	$ _____

B. Prepare schedules that explain the changes in each of the balance sheet account balances between the starting date of the business, January 20, 1992, and the end of the operating year, December 31, 1992.

Problem 6-11 **Comprehensive**

Linda Hill and her daughter, Ashley, opened an antique and gift shop called Heart's Desire. The business was organized as a corporation. To provide timely information, they elected to prepare monthly financial statements. They were advised that the periodic inventory system should be used to account for inventory. All sales are for cash and most purchases qualify for a cash discount, which are accounted for using the gross invoice method. During February, each owner invested $5,000 cash in the business and was issued 500 shares of capital stock. The business received $13,200 in merchandise inventory that was purchased on account.

A chart of accounts for the business is given below.

100 Cash	400 Sales
110 Prepaid Rent	410 Sales Returns and Allowances
111 Prepaid Insurance	500 Purchases
130 Merchandise Inventory	501 Purchases Discounts
150 Equipment	502 Purchases Returns and
151 Accumulated Depreciation—	Allowances
Equipment	515 Depreciation Expense
200 Accounts Payable	520 Insurance Expense
210 Accrued Expenses Payable	525 Interest Expense
250 Notes Payable	530 Rent Expense
300 Capital Stock	535 Utilities Expense
310 Retained Earnings	540 Wages Expense
311 Dividends Declared	570 Income Tax Expense
350 Income Summary	

The owners opened for business on March 1. Transactions for the month are given below in summary form. Numbers, rather than dates, are used to identify the transactions since they are in summary form.

1. Linda and Ashley each invested an additional $10,000 in the business and received 1,000 additional shares of capital stock.
2. Early on the morning of March 1, display and office equipment was delivered that was purchased for $22,000. The corporation paid $10,000 cash and financed the rest with a 14% note payable.
3. Space for the store was rented in a shopping center for $1,200 a month. The business was required to pay six month's rent in advance. The rent is for the period March 1 through August 31.
4. On March 1, a 12-month insurance policy was purchased for $2,400.
5. Sales for the first half of the month were $10,200.
6. Purchased $29,000 in merchandise inventory on terms 2/10, n/30.
7. Paid for $20,000 (list price before cash discount) of the merchandise within the discount period.
8. Paid $440 to employees for wages earned during the first half of the month.
9. Sales for the second half of the month were $9,700.
10. A $1,000 cash dividend was paid to each stockholder.

Required:
A. Open T accounts for each account listed in the chart of accounts. Leave 18 lines for the Cash account and 6 lines for each of the other accounts. Enter the March 1 beginning balances.
B. Prepare general journal entries to record the summary transactions.
C. Post the journal entries to the general ledger.
D. Prepare a worksheet as of March 31, 1992. Include all balance sheet accounts in the trial balance even though some have a zero balance. Leave four lines for the Accrued Expenses Payable account. Enter adjusting entries based on the following information.
   1. The equipment has a useful life of ten years and is estimated to have a $1,000 residual value. The equipment was used a full month during March.
   2. March utility bill for $680 was received, but had not been recorded.
   3. Unpaid wages as of March 31 amounted to $470.

4. Income taxes for the month are estimated to be $1,940.
5. Enter other adjusting entries based on information provided in the transactions.

A physical count of the inventory showed that $32,480 was on hand on March 31.
E. Prepare an income statement and retained earnings statement for the month of March and an unclassified balance sheet on March 31.

Problem 6-12 Continuation of Problem 6-11

This problem is a continuation of the information given in Problem 6-11. Transactions for the month of April are given below in summary form. Note that the adjusting entries for March were not entered in the accounts.

1. Paid $980 to employees for wages earned during March and April.
2. Paid the March utility bill.
3. Sales for the first half of the month were $12,830.
4. Purchased $7,720 in merchandise inventory on terms 2/10, n/30.
5. Paid $9,000 for merchandise purchases made in March that did not qualify for a cash discount.
6. A $1,500 cash dividend was paid to each stockholder.
7. Sales for the second half of the month were $13,150.
8. Customers returned items for $630 cash refunds.
9. Returned $2,000 (list price) of merchandise for credit on account.

Required:
A. Prepare journal entries to record the April summary transactions.
B. Post the journal entries to the T accounts prepared in Problem 6-11.
C. Prepare a worksheet as of April 30, 1992. List all balance sheet accounts leaving four lines for the Accrued Expenses Payable account. (Recall that the adjusting entries for March were not entered in the accounts.) The inventory on hand, per a physical count taken on April 30, is $25,420. Unpaid wages of $560 and a utility bill for April in the amount of $760 were unrecorded. Income taxes for the first two months of operations are estimated to be $3,800. Other adjustments for April should be made based on the information given in Problem 6-11.
D. Assume now that the accounting cycle is to be completed at the end of April.
    1. Enter the adjusting entries in the general journal and post them to the general ledger.
    2. Enter the closing entries in the general journal and post them to the general ledger. For cross reference purposes number the closing entries from 1 through 4.
    3. Prepare a post closing trial balance.

CASE

Case 6-1 Discussion Case

Ashland Furniture retails home furnishings. The firm stocks about 850 different items ranging in retail price from $25 to $2,500. The inventory balance throughout the year is maintained at approximately $350,000. The company orders large ticket items four times a year, but places 10 to 15 orders per month for the lower-priced accessories from 30 different manufacturers. Sales are about 25% cash and credit card, 25% n/30, 40% n/90 with no interest, and 10% are financed over periods longer than 90 days. The financing contracts for these sales are sold to finance companies within five days of the sale.

Forty to sixty sales are made on a typical day. The sales volume is not seasonal although volume does increase before Christmas and Father's Day. The store's volume is affected by the general economic conditions of the area.

Required:

A periodic inventory system has been used since the firm began operations, but management is considering changing to the perpetual inventory system. Management believes a perpetual system will enable them to prepare monthly financial statements more easily and might assist with the monthly ordering.

In the position of a consultant that was hired by management, write a report to the store's management explaining the advantages and disadvantages of each inventory system. Complete your report by recommending one system for them to use and listing the reasons for your recommendation.

7

ACCOUNTING CONTROLS AND SYSTEMS

CHAPTER OVERVIEW AND OBJECTIVES

This chapter describes accounting systems and general internal control concepts. When you have completed the chapter, you should understand:

1. The basic structure of an accounting system.
2. How data are transformed into information within an accounting system.
3. The impact of the Foreign Corrupt Practices Act on an accounting system.
4. General internal control concepts.
5. The distinction between administrative controls and accounting controls.
6. The key features of any good internal control system.
7. The development of an accounting system with systems analysis, systems design, and systems implementation.
8. How control accounts and subsidiary ledgers are used in a manual accounting system.
9. The need for electronic data processing.
10. The impact of microcomputers on accounting.
11. How a computer can be used in an accounting system.
12. The advantages of special journals: Appendix.
13. The formats of and procedures used with a sales journal, purchases journal, cash receipts journal, and cash disbursements journal: Appendix.

In previous chapters, we saw that the effects of various business transactions are collected, processed, and reported within the framework of a firm's accounting system. An **accounting system** is a collection of business forms (also called source documents), records, procedures, management policies and controls, and data-processing methods used to transform economic data into useful information. Accounting systems range from simple manual systems to sophisticated computerized systems. Regardless of its form, the dual purpose of any accounting system is to keep track of a firm's business transactions and report their effects on the operating performance and financial position to anyone who may be interested. An essential feature of a good accounting system is strong internal control. It provides reasonable assurance that the business transactions are authorized, recorded, and reported properly and that assets are safeguarded.

Previously, we have limited the consideration of an accounting system to one that is both *simple* and *manually operated* so that we could introduce basic accounting procedures. Such a system may be satisfactory for a small business with a limited number of transactions. In most cases, however, even relatively small businesses require a more sophisticated accounting system for two reasons.

1. The procedures described earlier may be too time-consuming for rapid data processing and timely reporting. The volume of transactions may be so great that the accounting staff cannot process the data manually at a reasonable cost and on a sufficiently prompt basis.
2. Many transactions will be so repetitive that they can be handled more efficiently with more specialized treatment than the general procedures so far discussed. Special journals can be used for sales, purchases, cash receipts, and cash disbursements, instead of the less efficient general journal.

This chapter begins by considering the fundamental concepts associated with any accounting system. It also describes accounting systems and internal control procedures as they are designed and installed for efficient, dependable processing of financial data. This chapter also covers special journals, which are used to record such repetitive transactions as sales, purchases, cash receipts, and cash disbursements more efficiently than the general journal. The use of special journals is described in the Appendix to this chapter.

OPERATION OF AN ACCOUNTING SYSTEM

The operation of an accounting system consists of three basic phases:

**Objective 1:
Basic structure
of an accounting
system**

1. The *input* phase. Transactions are recorded as they occur on various business forms (such as sales invoices, purchase invoices, checks, bank deposit tickets, and payroll cards). An example of a sales invoice is shown in Figure 7-1. These forms serve as input that is entered into some type of journal as a chronological record of the transactions.
2. The *processing* phase. This phase occurs when the debits and credits in the journal are classified as assets, liabilities, owners' equity, revenues, and expenses and posted to the general ledger.
3. The *output* phase. Financial reports, such as an income statement and balance sheet, and other special reports prepared from the data in the general ledger represent output from the system. This material provides useful information concerning the operating results and financial position of the firm for both outside parties (such as creditors and taxing authorities) and insiders (such as members of the management team). Consequently, both financial and managerial accounting information is produced with the same system.

Figure 7-1
Example of a Source
Document

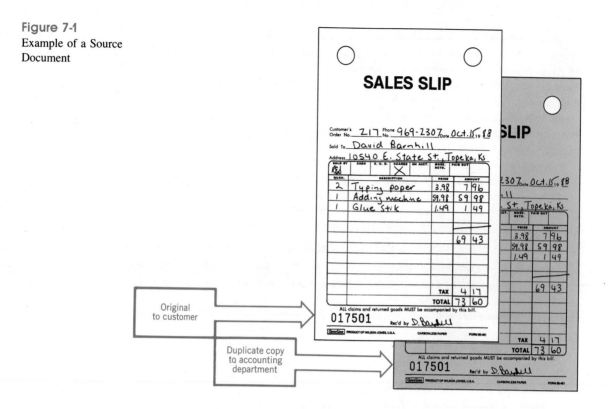

Original
to customer

Duplicate copy
to accounting
department

**Objective 2:
Comparing data
and information**

In the conversion of input to output, data are transformed into information. While the terms "data" and "information" are often used synonymously in practice, a useful distinction can be made: *Data* are recorded facts; *information* is data that has been processed in some prescribed manner to be more useful to a potential user. For example, the amount of each sale is collected on individual invoices chronologically, processed through the accounting system, and the aggregate amount reported as revenue from sales in the income statement. The development of information from data in an accounting system can be diagramed as:

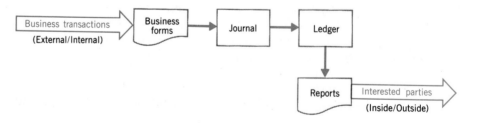

THE FOREIGN CORRUPT PRACTICES ACT

**Objective 3:
The Foreign Cor-
rupt Practices
Act**

During the 1970s, several large corporations admitted to making payments to foreign officials to obtain or retain business. Although these payments were not necessarily illegal under the laws of the countries in which the payments were made, they were considered illegal, or at least unethical, in the United States. Payments were often made from secret funds that did not appear in the company's records, and top executives of some companies maintained that they were not even aware that the payments were being made.

In an effort to halt these practices, the U.S. Congress passed the Foreign Corrupt Practices Act, (the Act) in 1977. The Act contains antibribery and accounting standards provisions. The ***antibribery provisions*** apply to all American businesses and individuals. They prohibit the offer, payment, promise to pay, or authorization of payment of anything of value to a foreign official or foreign political party for the purpose of obtaining or retaining business. The Act also makes it illegal to make such a payment to any person while knowing or having reason to believe that the person will offer, give, or promise an item of value to a foreign official.

The ***accounting standards provisions*** require that all publicly held corporations keep reasonably detailed and accurate accounting records. Under these provisions, such corporations must also maintain internal controls sufficient to provide reasonable assurance that transactions are properly authorized and are recorded in accordance with generally accepted accounting principles and that assets are used only in compliance with management's authorization. These accounting standards provisions apply to all companies that must file annual reports with the Securities and Exchange Commission (SEC), even if they are not operating in a foreign country. Violators are subject to severe penalties, including prison terms and fines.

A major impact of the Act is the recognition that management is solely responsible for maintaining an adequate internal control system and for the accuracy of the financial statements. As a result, top corporate managements have directed much more attention to strengthening their corporations' internal control systems. Corporate boards of directors now regularly assure compliance with the Act by obtaining written evidence of management's primary responsibility for the content of financial statements, as well as adequacy of internal controls. An example of this involvement, taken from an annual report of Smith International, Inc., is presented in Figure 7-2.

INTERNAL CONTROL

Assets are valuable to a business because they represent scarce resources that will be used by the business in future operations. The efficient use and protection of these resources is a primary management function. Management needs an organized way of dealing with this function, particularly when a business grows and the owners delegate much of their hands-on control. An accounting system designed to aid managers in controlling operations is called an internal control system. All of the measures employed by a business to (1) safeguard its resources against waste, fraud, and inefficiency, (2) to promote the reliability of accounting data, and (3) to encourage compliance with company policies and governmental regulations are part of the system.

Objective 4:
Internal control concepts

ADMINISTRATIVE CONTROLS AND ACCOUNTING CONTROLS

Two types of internal control measures are used by a business: administrative controls and accounting controls. Internal control systems consist of administrative controls and accounting controls. Administrative controls are controls established to maintain an efficient operation and ensure adherence to prescribed company policies. Examples of administrative controls include: written directives to the personnel department iden-

Objective 5:
Administrative and accounting controls

Figure 7-2
Management Report

Report of Management

The accompanying consolidated financial statements have been prepared in conformity with generally accepted accounting principles and, as such, include amounts that are based on our best estimates and judgments, giving due consideration to materiality. Financial information included elsewhere in this Annual Report is consistent with that in the financial statements.

The integrity and objectivity of data in these financial statements are the responsibility of management. To this end management maintains a system of accounting and controls, which includes an internal audit function. The system of controls includes a careful selection of people, a division of responsibilities, and the application of formal policies and procedures that are consistent with high standards of accounting and administrative practices. Management is continually reviewing, modifying and improving its system of accounting and controls in response to changes in business conditions and operations. We believe our controls provide reasonable assurance that assets are safeguarded against loss from unauthorized use or disposition and that accounting records are reliable for preparing financial statements.

The independent public accountants, recommended by the Audit Committee of the Board of Directors and selected by the Board of Directors and the shareholders at the annual meeting, are engaged to express an opinion on our financial statements. Their opinion is based on procedures performed in accordance with generally accepted auditing standards, including tests of the accounting records and such other auditing procedures as they considered necessary in the circumstances.

The Board of Directors, acting through the Audit Committee composed solely of outside directors, is responsible for determining that management fulfills its responsibilities in the financial control of operations and preparation of financial statements. The Committee meets regularly with management, the internal auditors and the independent public accountants to discuss the Company's system of accounting and controls and financial reporting matters. The independent public accountants have full and free access to the Audit Committee.

Management has long recognized its responsibility for conducting the Company's affairs in a manner which is responsive to the ever increasing complexities of the business environment. The responsibility is reflected in key Company policies regarding, among other things, potential conflicting outside business interests of Company employees, proper conduct of domestic and international business activities and compliance with anti-trust laws.

JERRY W. NEELY
Chairman of the Board,
President and Chief Executive Officer

FRED J. BARNES
Group Vice President
and Chief Financial Officer

tifying hiring standards for new employees; manuals identifying purchasing and sales procedures; and various performance reports required from employees.

Accounting controls are the methods and procedures used to protect assets and ensure that accounting information is reliable. They include procedures used to authorize various business transactions and to separate recordkeeping duties from the custody of a company's assets. For example, in the control of cash, the person receiving the cash from customers should not post amounts received to the Accounts Receivable account, nor should the person authorizing payment of an account payable be the same person writing the check. Accounting controls are designed to provide reasonable assurance that

1. Transactions are executed in accordance with management's general or specific authorization.
2. Transactions are recorded as necessary (a) to permit preparation of financial statements in conformity with generally accepted accounting principles and (b) to maintain accountability for assets.
3. Access to assets is permitted only in accordance with management's authorization.
4. The recorded accountability for assets is compared with the existing assets at reasonable intervals and appropriate action is taken with respect to any differences.[1]

Although each business must design an internal control system to meet its own specific needs, several general elements of internal control can be identified.

CLEARLY ESTABLISHED LINES OF RESPONSIBILITY

Control ultimately involves people. Individuals initiate business transactions, record the transactions, and handle the assets resulting from the transactions. Thus, the cornerstone of a good internal control system is the employment of competent personnel. The level of responsibility assigned to personnel should be commensurate with their ability and authority. If employees are to operate effectively, they must have a clear understanding of their responsibilities: two employees must not have areas of overlapping authority; there must not be any undefined areas. If two or more employees share a specific area of responsibility and something goes wrong, it is difficult to determine who is at fault. This can impede the taking of corrective action.

Objective 6: Features of an internal control system

Responsibilities and duties should be rotated among employees periodically so that they can become familiar with the entire system. Rotation of duties also tends to discourage deviation from prescribed procedures since employees know that other employees may soon be taking over their duties and reviewing their activities.

SEPARATION OF RECORDKEEPING AND CUSTODIANSHIP

To help avoid the misappropriation or misuse of assets, responsibility for initiating business transactions and for custody of the business' assets should be separate from responsibility for maintaining the accounting records whenever possible. Under these circumstances, the person with custody of an asset is unlikely to misappropriate or misuse it when a record of the asset is being kept by another employee. The employee maintaining the records has no reason to falsify them because he or she has no access to the asset. A theft of the asset and falsification of records to cover up the theft would, therefore, require collusion between the two employees.

To minimize the possibility of errors, fraud, and theft, responsibility for a series of related transactions should be divided among two or more employees or departments so that each employee's work acts as a check on the work of another. For example, if one employee was permitted to order the goods, receive the goods, and pay the

---

[1]Professional Standards No. 1, "Auditing, Management Advisory Services, Tax Practice, and Accounting and Review Services," (Commerce Clearing House, Inc., Chicago, June, 1980), Sec. AU 320.28.

supplier, that employee might be tempted to order goods for personal use, have the goods delivered to his or her home, and pay for them from business funds. Or, an employee might be tempted to place an order with a personal friend, rather than seek the best quality items at the lowest price.

To avoid such potential abuses, authority for ordering goods should be assigned to a purchasing department, the goods should be physically received by a receiving department, and payment for the order should be performed by a third employee or department. Source documents (such as purchase orders, receiving reports, and invoices) showing the work done by each department or employee are then sent to the accounting department for recording purposes. In this way, the work of each employee acts as a check on the work performed by others.

MECHANICAL AND ELECTRONIC DEVICES

Mechanical and electronic devices designed to protect assets and to improve the accuracy of the accounting process should be used wherever feasible. Cash registers are used to provide an accurate record of cash sales, produce a receipt for the customer, and protect the cash received. A safe or vault may be provided for the protection of cash on hand and important documents. Measuring devices, such as time clocks for recording hours worked by employees, coin machines in a subway system, meters on gasoline pumps in a service station, and check protectors that perforate the amount of a check on its face, are other examples of devices that strengthen internal control. Many retail stores even attach sensors to merchandise to reduce losses from shoplifting. If the sensors are not removed when the merchandise is paid for, an alarm goes off as the customer leaves the store with the goods.

ADEQUATE INSURANCE AND BONDING OF EMPLOYEES

Another element of good internal control is the provision of adequate insurance on business assets to protect against loss, theft, or casualty. In addition, employees having access to cash and negotiable instruments should be bonded by coverage with fidelity insurance to insure against losses by fraud on the part of those employees. Bonding companies generally investigate an employee's background before issuing a bond on the employee. Bonding also serves as a deterrent to misappropriation of funds because employees are aware that they are bonded and will have to deal with the bonding company if a shortage is discovered. Bonding companies generally will not cover a loss unless the employer is willing to prosecute employees who misappropriate funds.

INTERNAL AUDITING

Many companies have internal auditors who are responsible for a continuous review and analysis of the internal control system. Both administrative and accounting controls are studied by internal auditors to identify weaknesses that can develop over time. Deviations from established procedures and suggestions for improving the system are reported to top management. Internal auditors often aid the independent Certified Public Accountant (CPA) who conducts the annual audit by preparing schedules and worksheets or performing some of the tests required by the independent CPA. In the course of an audit, it is common for the independent auditor to make suggestions to management concerning improvements to the company's accounting system. Internal auditors are likely to follow up on those suggestions to determine whether they have been implemented.

DEVELOPMENT OF AN ACCOUNTING SYSTEM

One of the first steps in starting a new business is developing a dependable accounting system. In many instances, the system is designed and implemented by a member or members of the firm's own accounting department. If the employees lack the skills needed to do so, the system may be developed by an outside source such as a CPA firm. In either case, the development of an accounting system must be based on a thorough understanding of both the business and the industry in which it operates.

Objective 7: Development of an accounting system

As the business grows and engages in different activities, the accounting system must be revised frequently to accommodate both a larger volume of transactions and changes in the nature of those transactions. For example, as a business grows and adds employees, one employee can be assigned the task of handling cash and another employee can be responsible for maintaining the accounting records. A firm that manufactures a product for sale to retailers may eventually establish its own retail outlets, and therefore, must revise its accounting system to accommodate retail sales transactions. Expanding and revising the chart of accounts is just one of the changes that is required in an accounting system. In addition, the increase in the volume of transactions may require conversion from a primarily manual system to a computerized system. Therefore, the design of an accounting system is not a one-time process: it requires continuous refinement to ensure that the system's capability is compatible with the changing needs of the business it serves. Many large firms have a separate systems department that has responsibility for continuously reviewing the accounting system to determine whether portions or all of it require revision. The installation or revision of an accounting system consists of three phases: systems analysis; systems design; and systems implementation.

SYSTEMS ANALYSIS

The objective of **systems analysis** is to gather facts that provide a thorough understanding of both a business's information requirements and the sources of that information. Systems analysis may be performed when a new system is installed or when an existing system is evaluated. Systems analysis is a study of how the organization's business functions are performed in order to determine the best combination of personnel, forms, records, procedures, and equipment. Questions that must be considered include:

- How is the business organized?
- What is its history?
- What type of business is involved?
- What activities are performed?
- Who is responsible for the activities?
- What decisions must be made to properly manage the business?
- What needs to be reported, to whom, and for what purposes?
- How often is information required?
- How much money will be devoted to the development and operation of the system?
- What is the projected growth and direction of the firm?
- What are the strengths and weaknesses of the business?
- What are management's plans for future changes in operations?
- What business forms, records, procedures, reports, and equipment are currently being used?

In existing systems, much of the information required for systems analysis may be available in the form of an **operating manual**. An operating manual is a detailed description of how the organization's accounting system should function. It is developed and put together under the supervision of the firm's top accounting management. If the system is computerized, the computer department personnel are also involved. The operating manual is distributed to the various departments and employees who provide input into the accounting system to ensure that each party providing this input is performing his or her job correctly, thus allowing for reliable and accurate output. The manual is updated when the accounting system changes for whatever reason—for example, management may change its information requirements from the system or, perhaps, the equipment used to process data may change.

A major consideration in such cases is an evaluation of how closely the instructions in the manual are followed in the actual operation of the accounting system. Any deficiencies in procedures and data processing methods currently in use should be corrected with the analysis. In the installation of a new system or in the revision of an existing system, many of the facts gathered during the systems analysis phase are used later in the preparation of an operating manual.

SYSTEMS DESIGN

Based on the facts gathered through systems analysis, a new system is developed or improvements are made to an existing system in the systems design   A team approach using accountants, managers, engineers, computer experts, and other specialists is often required in the design of an accounting system. The specific means to be used for input, processing, and output must be selected in terms of the information requirements of the business.

The design must include a consideration of the *personnel* required to operate the system, the *business forms* needed to document transactions, the *accounting records* and *procedures* to be used to process data, the *reports* to be prepared for interested parties, and *any automated features* of the system. The basic concern in the design phase is to develop an accounting system with the most efficient flow of information, given the funds committed to the system and the information requirements involved. Development of reliable internal control is a fundamental part of the design phase.

The guiding principle in the choice of output in the form of reports is that the benefits from each must exceed the costs. Some reports, such as financial statements and tax returns, are mandatory but should still be produced at a reasonable cost. The value of other reports, such as those prepared for management, must be compared continuously with the preparation cost. To be beneficial to users, the information in these reports must be accurate, timely, and relevant. In most cases, the ultimate measure of the benefits from the information is the quality of the decision-making based on it. Cost/benefit analysis of accounting information is particularly important when a large investment of funds is required in a computer and other electronic equipment.

SYSTEMS IMPLEMENTATION

Systems implementation is the final phase in the development or revision of an accounting system. This step involves the implementation of the decisions made during the design stage. In other words,

- The business forms, records, and equipment chosen must be purchased.
- The personnel needed to operate the system must be selected, trained, and supervised closely to assure that they understand how the system should function.
- An operating manual should be prepared as a formalized description of the procedures required to transform economic data into useful information.

When an existing system is being revised, the old system often is operated parallel to the new one until management is certain that the new system is reliable. Major revisions are usually accomplished gradually rather than all at once to aid in ensuring reliable data flows. Any new accounting system should be tested thoroughly to be certain that its output is compatible with the desired results. For example, in the conversion of a manual payroll system to a computerized system, the payroll would be calculated both manually and by the computer for a period of time. The output from both systems would be compared and any discrepancies investigated to determine that the new computerized system is operating correctly. Modifications should be made whenever necessary. For instance, in the payroll example above, the government may increase the amount of employees' earnings subject to social security tax. This change would require a modification in the payroll system which produces the payroll checks and the payroll information used in the various documents filed with governmental agencies.

REFINEMENTS TO A MANUAL ACCOUNTING SYSTEM

As discussed earlier, one element of a good internal control system is the division of responsibilities for a series of related transactions among two or more employees or departments. In addition, as the volume of transactions grows, firms require more sophisticated accounting systems than the one illustrated in earlier chapters in which an entry is made in the general journal for each transaction and each debit and credit is posted to an appropriate account in the general ledger. To provide for a division of labor and responsibilities, and to make the manual accounting system more efficient, firms use subsidiary ledgers and special journals.

Objective 8:
Using control accounts and subsidiary ledgers

The use of special journals is discussed in the Appendix to this chapter. Subsidiary ledgers were introduced in Chapter 6 and are discussed in detail in the next section. Similar subsidiary ledgers and special journals are used in computer accounting systems; therefore, it is important that you learn how they function in a manual system, where it is easier to visualize them.

SUBSIDIARY LEDGERS AND CONTROL ACCOUNTS

So far, the coverage of a ledger as an essential part of an accounting system has been limited primarily to a general ledger. For more timely and efficient processing, however, most firms use control accounts and subsidiary ledgers. For example, assume that a business sells merchandise on credit to 5,000 customers. If the firm used only one Accounts Receivable account—as we have done for illustrative purposes so far—adequate detail would not be provided concerning the amount of merchandise sold to individual customers, the amount of money received from them, or the amount still owed by them. Consequently, a firm generally establishes a separate Accounts Receivable account for each customer. If this were done in the general ledger, 5,000 accounts would have to be established and combined with the other assets, liabilities, owners' equity, revenues, and expenses. As a result, the general ledger would be unwieldy and the likelihood of errors would be high. The trial balance prepared from such a large general ledger would also be very long and difficult to work with. This situation is complicated further by the fact that other general ledger accounts, such as Accounts Payable, require the same detailed information.

Therefore, when a large amount of detailed information must be kept about a certain general ledger account, a separate record called a *subsidiary ledger* is used. The detailed information is thus recorded outside the general ledger. For example, one Accounts Receivable account can be used in the general ledger and an Account Receivable account can be established for each customer (5,000 in the case above) in the subsidiary ledger.

The Accounts Receivable account in the general ledger is called a ***control account***. Such a general ledger account is supported by the detail of a subsidiary ledger. A subsidiary ledger consists of a group of individual accounts, the total of which should equal the balance of the related control account in the general ledger after all accounting is completed. Control accounts and subsidiary ledgers are used for a number of general ledger accounts such as Accounts Receivable, Accounts Payable, Merchandise Inventory, Marketable Securities, and Plant Assets.

To illustrate the relationship between Accounts Receivable as a control account and its subsidiary ledger, assume that Jewels Records employs a general journal and operates a manual accounting system. Two journal entries, which summarize the sales and cash receipts with three customers, and the posting of the transactions to the general and subsidiary ledger are shown in Figure 7-3. It is assumed that the beginning-of-the month account receivable balances totaled $13,000. The postings and relationship between the control account and subsidiary ledger accounts are summarized in tabular form below.

	Beginning Balance	Debit for Sales	Credit for Cash Receipts	Ending Balance
H. Johnson	$ 6,400	$ 3,600	$ 6,400	$3,600
L. Mayberry	2,200	4,800	2,200	4,800
J. Vella	4,400	1,800	5,200	1,000
Accounts Receivable control account	$13,000	$10,200	$13,800	$9,400

The Posting Reference column for the Accounts Receivable shows (130/√). Such a reference is used to indicate that the amount has been posted two places (in this case, to account number 130 in the general ledger and to the individual accounts in the subsidiary ledger which is indicated by a check mark).

The accounts receivable subsidiary ledger is an alphabetical file with a separate account for each customer. Note that at the beginning of May and after the two transactions are posted the totals of the subsidiary ledger accounts are in agreement with the Accounts Receivable control account in the general ledger. The use of a subsidiary ledger has three major advantages: (1) it relieves the general ledger of a mass of detail; (2) it allows a division of labor in maintaining the ledgers; and (3) it provides effective internal control. Similar subsidiary ledgers are used in a computerized accounting system.

THE IMPACT OF DATA PROCESSING EQUIPMENT ON ACCOUNTING

To process data accurately and rapidly, most businesses use some type of equipment. Even in the manual accounting applications discussed earlier, equipment such as calculators, typewriters, cash registers, and copy machines are used to reduce the work load and errors. A wide range of additional equipment that can be adapted to satisfy the information requirements and operating conditions of a firm is available. The most modern and sophisticated type of automated accounting system involves

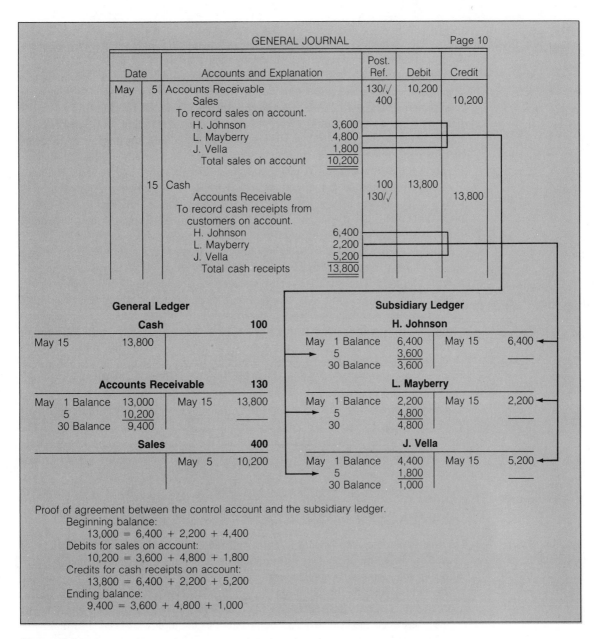

Figure 7-3
Posting to a Subsidiary Ledger

electronic computers. While a detailed description of a computer accounting system is beyond the scope of this book, an overview of how a computer operates and the importance of its role in the accounting function follows.

ELECTRONIC DATA PROCESSING

The terms **electronic data processing (EDP)** and **computer data processing** are often used interchangeably. They refer to the use of a computer and its peripheral equipment to process data. The primary advantages of a computer as a data-processing

Objective 9:
Electronic data
processing

device are its accuracy, speed, storage capacity, and versatility for performing analytical operations. As a firm grows in size and complexity, the volume of paperwork from transactions to be processed increases significantly.

At some point, the cost, inaccuracy, and time delays of a manual system force a business to contemplate using a computer. Consider, for example, the data-processing requirements of a medium-sized commercial bank with assets of $150 million. The bank must have an accounting system to process data related to revenue and expense transactions, as well as its balance sheet accounts. It also must maintain detailed records concerning such functions as credit card activity, installment loans, business loans, real estate loans, check processing, customer deposits, and savings accounts. Hundreds of thousands of transactions are involved, and a computerized operation of some sort is required to cope with the volume of data. Similar situations are confronted by a variety of other operations such as airlines, retail-store chains, stock brokerage firms, hospitals, hotel chains, and manufacturing companies.

The increasing popularity of minicomputers, microcomputers, and time-sharing services have made EDP affordable even for small businesses. As its name suggests, a *minicomputer* is a small, low-cost machine capable of performing many of the operations of a large computer, although on a more limited scale. A *microcomputer* is even smaller than a minicomputer; it can have most of its essential components on a single silicon chip smaller than a key on a pocket calculator. A *time-sharing application* exists when one business shares a computer's time with other users, as happens when time is rented from a service bureau specializing in data processing.

The computer system of a large business may consist of a number of microcomputers that have access to a larger computer (often called the mainframe) that is located at a central processing site. A mainframe computer can both store and process large amounts of data at very high speed and support a number of auxiliary systems. The ability to transfer programs and data between the mainframe and a microcomputer enables many users with smaller computers to share the resources of a larger, much more expensive computer.

THE IMPACT OF MICROCOMPUTERS ON ACCOUNTING

Objective 10:
Microcomputers
and accounting

The microcomputer explosion has been well recognized because of the publicity it has received, the number of microcomputers sold, its use in education, and the versatility of microcomputer applications.

The field of accounting has been widely affected by the dramatic impact of the microcomputer. Computerized accounting is found in businesses that previously could not have afforded the cost of larger computers or the employees needed to make the computer work. It is no longer uncommon to see managers prepare their own sales forecasts or budgets on microcomputers located in their offices. Furthermore, the microcomputer may be portable so that the manager can take it away from the office to do his or her work. Operating a simple program on a microcomputer usually requires only a minimum amount of training—even a noncomputer-oriented person can feel comfortable operating the machine after a short period of time. Popular models of microcomputers are the IBM Personal Computer (which is being used to write this book), the Apple Macintosh, the Hewlett Packard Touchscreen Personal Computer, the TRS-80, and the Compac Portable Computer.

One of the major advantages of a microcomputer is its flexibility. This flexibility, made possible by recent technological advances, permits the microcomputer to perform increasingly sophisticated functions. A microcomputer can be used to perform virtually every accounting function, including processing accounts receivable, accounts payable, payroll, inventory control, and general ledger. Software is readily available for these accounting functions to avoid the need for specialized programming. In addition, electronic spreadsheet programs are sold that support many important accounting applications. An **electronic spreadsheet** is a versatile computer program that can be utilized to perform numerous types of financial analysis on a microcomputer. Electronic spreadsheets are similar to the worksheets you have been exposed to in manual form in this book, in that they consist of a matrix display of cells organized into rows and columns. These can be used to electronically manipulate accounting data.

A spreadsheet program permits a business to perform calculations that would be impossible using a manual system because of the time involved. For example, using a computer, the impact on net income over the next 10 years of an annual sales increase of 8% combined with an annual manufacturing cost increase of 6% can be quickly evaluated during a management meeting. Names of popular electronic spreadsheets used today are VisiCalc, SuperCalc, and Lotus 1-2-3. These spreadsheets provide the means of electronically applying many of the accounting topics developed in this book. Software called a **database management system** is also available to efficiently create and maintain files of accounting data (defined in the next section) that can easily be converted into a variety of financial reports with the microcomputer. Names of some database management systems are dbase III, PC/FOCUS, and REVELATION.

INTERNAL CONTROL OF MICROCOMPUTERS

Controlling the microcomputer presents a challenge to management, however. One control problem is physically protecting the equipment. As mentioned previously, microcomputers are quite small, lightweight, and sometimes portable. The diskettes which contain the programs and data are likewise lightweight and portable. Furthermore, microcomputers, which may be shared and used by several employees, are generally located in various offices in the firm, rather than in a central location. All of these factors suggest that microcomputers are susceptible to theft and other abuses. This could represent a loss of expensive equipment as well as a loss of important, perhaps highly confidential data.

For these reasons it is best not to have a microcomputer located in open work areas where many employees and visitors have access to it. Furthermore, it may be desirable to permanently attach the microcomputers to larger, heavier pieces of furniture such as desks or tables and to require users to log in when they wish to use it. Regardless of the precautions taken, there is bound to be some loss and damage to the equipment.

The more serious control problems involved with microcomputers are those of data security and data integrity. A manager, for example, may need to obtain a current listing of accounts receivable. If the microcomputer is hooked up to the mainframe, the list can easily be retrieved. When the microcomputer is used this way, however, it poses a security problem. It provides an access point to data that did not exist before; control is needed to prevent unauthorized personnel from obtaining entry into data which may be very sensitive or confidential.

Passwords are frequently employed for this purpose. In order for users to obtain access to data, the correct password, usually just a single word or a combination of letters and numbers typed on the keyboard, must be given. If the password is not correct, access is denied. Passwords should be changed frequently because the longer any one password is in use, the more likely it becomes that unauthorized personnel will learn it.

Data integrity refers to maintaining the accuracy of data. As mentioned above, the microcomputer may be tied into the organization's mainframe. Furthermore, depending upon how the organization's computer system is set up, the manager's microcomputer may have the ability to change the data "residing" in the mainframe. In other words, the mainframe has no way of detecting whether the person gaining access to the data is authorized to make changes or not; it cannot tell whether a change is being initiated by the accounts receivable clerk, who is authorized to make such changes, or the manager, who is not. Hardware is becoming increasingly more sophisticated, however, to permit entry to data for retrieval purposes only without allowing that user to initiate any changes to them.

COMPUTERIZED ACCOUNTING SYSTEMS

**Objective 11:
Using computers
in an accounting
system**

It is important to note the similarities between a manual accounting system and a computerized accounting system. Each involves *input, processing,* and *output.* The integration of a computer into an accounting system is, therefore, a relatively simple task. Remember, a manual accounting system consists of business forms, journals, ledgers, and reports. A computerized accounting system uses basically the same business forms converted into a machine-readable format to be accepted as input to the computer. Business transactions are recorded on coding forms similar to the special journals discussed in the Appendix to this chapter. The data are then put into the computer through some device, such as a keyboard, which is similar to an ordinary typewriter.

The programs supporting a particular accounting application are moved into the primary storage area of the computer, that is, the work area of the CPU. Input, programs, and output are moved in and out of the primary storage area as the computer processes data according to well-defined instructions. Files, which are ordered sets of accessible records, are used to process the accounting data. For example, the accounts receivable master file (consisting of a record for each customer) at the beginning of an accounting period can be updated by the computer to record credit sales billed to customers as follows.

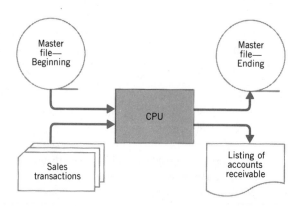

In this simple case, there are two sources of input and output. The input consists of the accounts receivable file (a master file) at the beginning of the period and the sales transactions (called a transaction file) required to update the beginning balances.

On the output side, an updated accounts receivable master file and a listing of accounts receivable billed are produced through the computer processing. In general, the transformation of data into information with a computer accounting system can be diagrammed as:

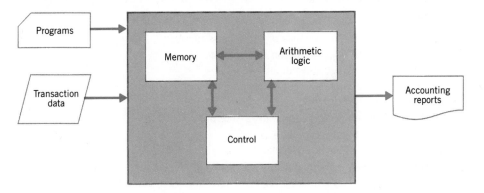

SUMMARY

This chapter contains a discussion of the development of an accounting system. The development of a system consists of three phases: (1) system analysis; (2) system design; and (3) system implementation. Most businesses incorporate some type of data processing equipment in their accounting system, particularly when the volume of transactions makes a manual system too time-consuming for rapid data processing and timely reporting. A fundamental part of the design phase is the development of reliable internal control to safeguard the firm's resources, promote the reliability of accounting data, and encourage compliance with company policies and governmental regulations. There are two types of internal controls:

1. Administrative controls established to provide operational efficiency and adherence to prescribed company policies; and
2. Accounting controls used to protect assets and ensure the reliability of accounting records.

Several general elements of internal accounting controls are:

- Clearly established lines of responsibility;
- Separation of recordkeeping and custody of the firm's assets;
- Division of responsibility for related transactions;
- Use of mechanical and electronic devices designed to protect assets and to improve the accuracy of the accounting process;
- Adequate insurance on business assets and bonding of employees having access to cash and negotiable instruments; and
- Establishment of an internal audit staff.

A subsidiary ledger contains the detailed information about a certain general ledger account. The use of a subsidiary ledger eliminates the need for a large number of individual accounts in the general ledger that are related to the same type of transaction. The account in the general ledger is called the control account. The balance in the control account should be equal to the sum of the individual account balances in the subsidiary ledger. A separate subsidiary ledger is established when a large amount of detailed information about a certain general ledger account must be kept.

SELF-TEST

Test your understanding of the chapter by selecting the best answer for each of the following.

1. An accounting system consists of three basis phases:
   a. Input, source documentation, and output.
   b. Input, processing, and output.
   c. Input, processing, and subsidiary ledgers.
   d. Input, output, and financial reports.
2. An example of an accounting control (internal control) is:
   a. a sales procedures manual.
   b. a purchases procedure manual.
   c. a job qualifications manual.
   d. the separation of handling cash and maintaining accounting records.
3. Which of the following is not an element of good internal control?
   a. Clearly established lines of authority.
   b. Use of electronic devices.
   c. Continuous internal auditing.
   d. A person receiving cash from the collection of accounts receivable who also maintains the accounts receivable records.
4. The proper sequence of steps to be followed in the installation or revision of an accounting system is:
   a. systems design, systems analysis, and systems implementation.
   b. systems analysis, systems design, and systems implementation.
   c. internal auditing, systems analysis, and systems design.
   d. systems analysis, systems design, and installation of a computer.
5. The Sellit Company sells merchandise to 420 customers and purchases merchandise from 32 suppliers. The correct number of control accounts and subsidiary ledger accounts for the firm's accounts receivable are:
   a. one control account and 32 subsidiary ledger accounts.
   b. thirty-two control accounts and one subsidiary ledger account.
   c. one control account and 420 subsidiary ledger accounts.
   d. two control accounts and 452 subsidiary ledger accounts.

REVIEW PROBLEM

George Crumbly works as a cashier four hours a day, five days a week at a convenience market franchised by a national chain. George purposely obscures the customer's view of the cash register window with various posters of charitable organizations. George has established a procedure whereby each hour of his shift he fails to register an average of three $.70 sales of soda. George appears to ring up the sales, and makes change when he receives more than $.70. He accomplishes this either by ringing up a $0.00 sales or by pressing the "no sale" key which will cause the register to sound like a sale has been rung up. The cash drawer opens in both cases. A $0.00 sale or "no sale" is recorded on an internal tape in the cash register. George keeps track of the unrecorded sales and pockets the cash at the end of his shift.

Liza Taysom also works for the same convenience store. Liza prepares all nonin-ventory purchase orders for the store. She also approves payment of all vendors' invoices, writes and signs all checks in payment of the invoices, and mails payment to the vendor. An investigation revealed that several large payments were made to one company for purchases of office equipment that could not be found on the premises.

Required:

A. How much money is George stealing each day? Each week? Each year (George takes a two-week vacation)?

B. How might the owner of the store prevent George from engaging in his scheme?

C. Describe the internal control procedures that should be established for ordering equipment.

ANSWER TO REVIEW PROBLEM

A. $.70 × 3 times per hour = $2.10 per hour
$2.10 per hour × 4 hours = $8.40 per day
$8.40 per day × 5 days = $42.00 per week
$42.00 per week × 50 weeks = $2,100 per year

B. The store is using the cash register to protect the firm's assets and to improve the accuracy of the accounting process. With this device, there are several pre-cautions that the store owner can take to thwart George's stealing.

1. The customer should have a clear view of the cash register and the amount of the sale being rung up. As it is now, because the display is hidden from the customer's view, he or she has no way of knowing if the sale is rung up.

2. Customers should be encouraged to ask for sales receipts, perhaps by telling customers their purchases are free if they are not offered a receipt.

3. The owner may periodically, on a surprise basis, count the cash in the cash drawer. If George waits until the end of his shift to remove the money from the drawer, there would consistently be an overage in the drawer and this would be detected by a surprise count.

4. The cash register tape should be removed by someone other than George (separation of recordkeeping from custodianship), and the total sales as shown on the tape should be compared to the cash in the cash drawer which should be counted by George. The tape should also be reviewed for the number of $0.00 sales or "no sale" rung up during each shift.

5. A log of errors, shortages, and overages on the register should be kept for each employee. A consistent number of errors, shortages, and overages may indicate that the employee is doing something fraudulent. At a minimum, it would indicate that the employee is not being careful in recording and han-dling cash.

C. The ordering of goods, authorizing payment for goods, preparing checks, and signing checks should not be the responsibility of a single person. Liza could easily order items for her own use and pay for them with company funds (and this she has apparently done). These functions should be divided among different personnel. For example, one employee should be given authority for ordering goods (clearly established lines of responsibility), the goods should be physically received by another employee, and payment for the order should be made by a third employee (division of responsibility for related transactions). Source documents (such as purchase orders, receiving reports, and invoices) showing the work done by each employee are then sent to the accounting department for recording purposes (separation of recordkeeping and custodianship). In this way, the work of each employee acts as a check on the work performed by others.

ANSWERS TO SELF-TEST

1. b   **2.** d   **3.** d   **4.** b   **5.** c

APPENDIX: PROCESSING OF REPETITIVE TRANSACTIONS IN A MANUAL SYSTEM

Objective 12:
Special journals

As the name suggests, a manual accounting system is operated by human effort. Clerical personnel or bookkeepers prepare business forms, make journal entries, post to ledger accounts, and prepare financial reports. Many small businesses are able to satisfy their information requirements with a manual system, although the number has decreased significantly in recent years because of the increasing popularity and decreasing cost of computers.

In earlier chapters, we illustrated basic accounting procedures by recording each transaction with an entry in a general journal and later posting each debit and credit to an appropriate account in the general ledger. For most firms, many of the transactions are so repetitive that they can be handled more efficiently with more specialized treatment than the general procedures discussed so far. To process a large number of repetitive transactions, the basic version of a manual accounting system can be streamlined and made more efficient by incorporating subsidiary ledgers and special journals into the accounting system. Special journals and subsidiary ledgers similar to those discussed below are used in computer accounting systems and it is important that you learn how they function in a manual system where it is easier to visualize them.

SPECIAL JOURNALS

The general journal described in earlier chapters can be used to record all types of transactions—sales, purchases, cash receipts, cash disbursements, sales returns and allowances, and purchase returns and allowances. The universal nature of the general journal imposes some limitations that adversely affect the efficiency of processing data.

- Each debit and credit recorded in the general journal must be posted individually, requiring a large amount of posting time. As the number of transactions increases, this inefficiency can make it difficult to provide accounting information on a timely basis.
- Only one person at a time can record the effects of transactions and post debits and credits to the ledger accounts, since all of the entries are recorded in one journal.

To avoid the limitations of using only a general journal, transactions are grouped into like categories and a special journal is set up for each category. Most of a typical firm's transactions fall into four categories, which in turn require four special journals:

Category of Transaction	Special Journal
Sales of merchandise on credit	Sales journal
Purchases of merchandise on credit	Purchases journal
Receipts of cash	Cash receipts journal
Disbursements of cash	Cash disbursements journal

The general journal is retained for recording transactions other than those in these four categories. For example, sales returns and allowances, purchase returns and allowances, adjusting entries, and closing entries are recorded in the general journal. If the sales returns and allowances or the purchase returns and allowances occur frequently, special journals may also be designed for them. The combination of the five journals represents a much more efficient way to process data than the use of a general journal alone. As will be seen later, the time required to journalize entries under this system will be less, and totals, rather than individual entries, can be posted to ledger accounts in many cases. Also, an efficient division of labor can be achieved by assigning different journals to different employees so work can be performed concurrently—at a reduced cost of accounting labor.

Several selected transactions involving the Baldwin Video Equipment Store during the month of January illustrate the four special journals. The formats used for the four special journals are typical. The nature of a given business determines the exact formats required; additional columns can be added to each of the special journals to accommodate other repetitive transactions that are not illustrated here.

SALES JOURNAL

A **sales journal**, such as the one shown in Figure 7-4, is used solely for recording *sales of merchandise on credit*. (Cash sales are recorded in the cash receipts journal, as will be shown later.) As each credit sale occurs, several copies of a sales invoice are prepared to document the transaction. The information shown on a sales invoice includes the customer's name, date of sale, invoice number (usually prenumbered), amount of sale, and the credit terms. One copy of the sales invoice is used by the seller to record the sale in the sales journal.

Objective 13: Format and procedures used with special journals

In Figure 7-4, eight sales to five different customers have been recorded. All credit sales are made on the basis of 2/10, n/30 terms. Other columns can be added to the sales journal to satisfy the needs of a specific business. If credit terms vary among customers, an additional column can be added to the sales journal to identify the terms of each sale. In addition, a sales tax payable column can be used to record the amount of sales tax to be collected from customers when a business is required to do so for state or local taxing authorities.

Advantages of a Sales Journal

The sales journal shown in Figure 7-4 has these time-saving advantages:

1. Each sales transaction is recorded on a single line. All credit sales are alike in that they result in a debit to Accounts Receivable and a credit to Sales. Record-keeping efficiency is achieved by simply identifying the customer who is the debtor instead of entering the account titles—Accounts Receivable and Sales—for each transaction.

2. The entries in the sales journal do not require an explanation because (a) all the transactions involved are the same, as previously discussed and (b) the detailed

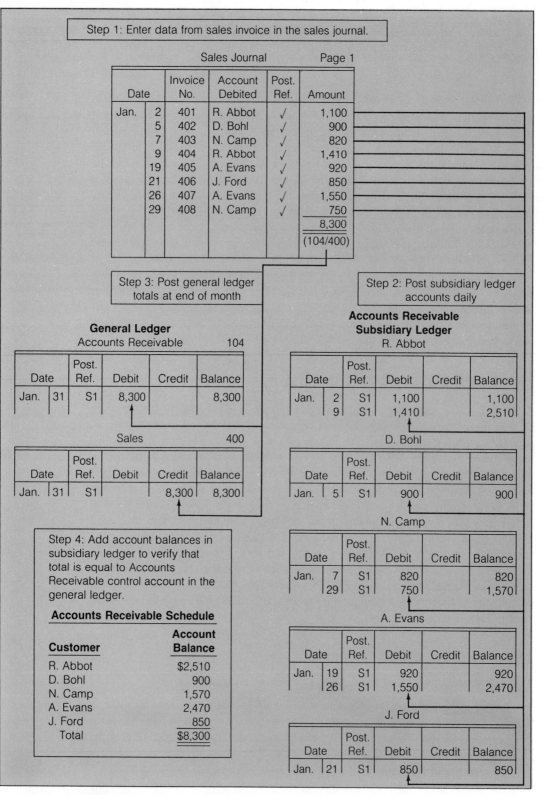

Figure 7-4
Relationship of Sales Journal and Ledger Accounts

information related to each sale is documented on a sales invoice that is referenced in the second column of the sales journal. If additional information concerning a particular sale is required, the interested party can simply identify the invoice number and refer to the details of the sales invoice.

3. Posting efficiency is achieved with the sales journal since only one amount, the total credit sales for the month, is posted to the general ledger. Note that in Figure 7-4, the total sales on account ($8,300) is posted twice—once to the Accounts Receivable control account and once to the Sales account. This procedure eliminates posting separate debits and credits during the month. In addition, the sales information needed for each customer in the accounts receivable subsidiary ledger is posted daily from the line items of the sales journal.

A check mark is recorded in the Post. Ref. (Posting Reference) column to indicate that each sale has been posted to the subsidiary ledger. The account numbers for Accounts Receivable (104) and Sales (400) are entered below the total credit sales for the month, to show that the general ledger accounts have been posted. A Posting Reference column is also included in the ledger accounts to indicate the source of the entries posted for cross-referencing purposes. S1 refers to the first page of the sales journal. Note that we can use the Posting Reference columns of the journal and the ledger to go back and forth easily between the two accounting records.

Summary of Sales Journal Procedures

The procedures used with the sales journal illustrated in Figure 7-4 can be summarized as follows:

1. From each sales invoice, enter the date of the sale, invoice number, customer's name, and amount of sale on a line of the sales journal.
2. At the end of each day, post each sale to the related customer's account in the subsidiary ledger. Place a check mark in the Posting Reference column of the sales journal and S1 in the Posting Reference column of the customer's account.
3. At the end of each month, total the Amount column of the sales journal and post the total amount as a debit and credit to the two general ledger accounts, Accounts Receivable and Sales, respectively. Place the general ledger account numbers involved (104/400) below the Amount column total and S1 in the Posting Reference columns of the two general ledger accounts.
4. Add the account balances of the accounts receivable subsidiary ledger to verify that the total is equal to the Accounts Receivable control account balance in the general ledger. In Figure 7-4, the amount involved is $8,300 (the same as the balance of the Accounts Receivable control account), as shown in the following accounts receivable schedule.

Accounts Receivable Schedule

Customer	Amount
R. Abbot	$2,510
D. Bohl	900
N. Camp	1,570
A. Evans	2,470
J. Ford	850
Total	$8,300

PURCHASES JOURNAL

The **purchases journal** can be set up as either a single-column or a multicolumn journal. In either case, the purchases of merchandise must be recorded separately from the acquisition of other assets because, as seen earlier, the total purchases of merchandise for a period are used to compute cost of goods sold. A single-column purchases journal, such as that shown in Figure 7-5, is used solely for recording the purchases of merchandise on credit with a periodic inventory system. Cash purchases of merchandise are recorded in the cash disbursements journal, as discussed later. Other purchases, such as the acquisition of an automobile or an office machine, will be recorded in some other journal, determined by the means of payment involved. If such assets are acquired for cash, the transactions are recorded in the cash disbursements journal; if purchased on credit, they are recorded in the general journal.

Advantages of a Purchases Journal

The advantages of and procedures required for a single-column purchases journal are similar to those described earlier for a sales journal. Recall from the discussion in Chapter 6 that the purchase of merchandise on credit with a periodic inventory system (as we are assuming here) is recorded with a debit to Purchases and a credit to Accounts Payable. If a perpetual inventory system is used, the debit is to the Merchandise Inventory account. The account credited on each line item of a purchases journal is an account payable with a particular creditor to whom the business has an obligation. A subsidiary ledger is maintained to provide the detailed information concerning each individual account payable. An Accounts Payable control account also is established in the general ledger. The procedures used with a single-column purchases journal are illustrated in Figure 7-5.

CASH RECEIPTS JOURNAL

The **cash receipts journal** is used to record all transactions involving the receipt of cash (a debit to Cash). Typical sources of cash are the sale of merchandise for cash, the collection of accounts receivable from customers, investments by owners, and bank loans. A multicolumn cash receipts journal is necessary because of the numerous sources of cash possible. Two debit columns are required—one for the actual cash collected and the other for sales discounts. To keep the required number of columns manageable but at the same time achieve efficient processing, three credit columns often are used to separate the sources of cash in the journal. The headings on the three credit columns as shown in Figure 7-6 are Sales, Accounts Receivable, and Other Accounts. The first two credit columns are used to record collections from cash sales and accounts receivable. All other sources of cash are entered in the third credit column.

The following cash receipts transactions for the Baldwin Video Equipment Store provide the basis for the entries in Figure 7-6.

1. The owner of the business, Betty Baldwin, invested $10,000 of her own cash on January 3 through the purchase of capital stock.
2. Video equipment was sold for $285 cash on January 8.
3. Received payment from Robert Abbot for an eight-day-old account receivable of $1,100 less a 2% sales discount of $22 on January 10. Therefore, $1,078 cash was received. Credit terms are 2/10, n/30 and the cash was received within 10 days.

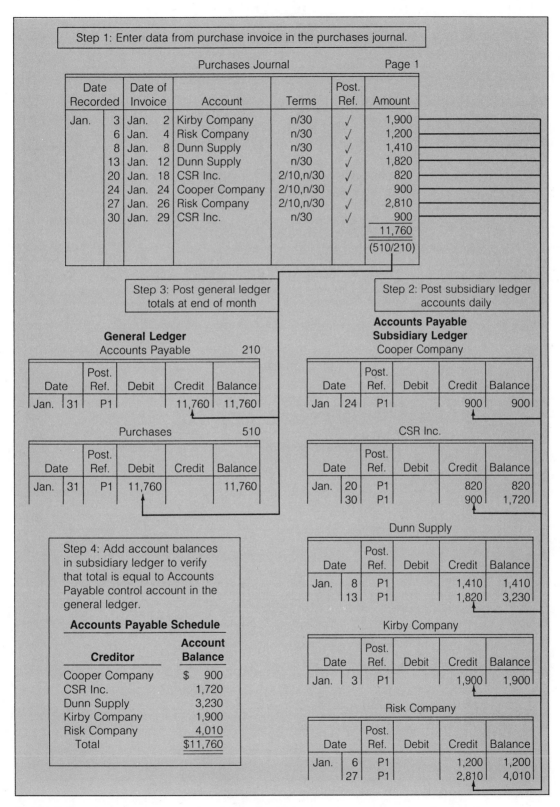

Figure 7-5
Relationship of Purchases Journal and Ledger Accounts

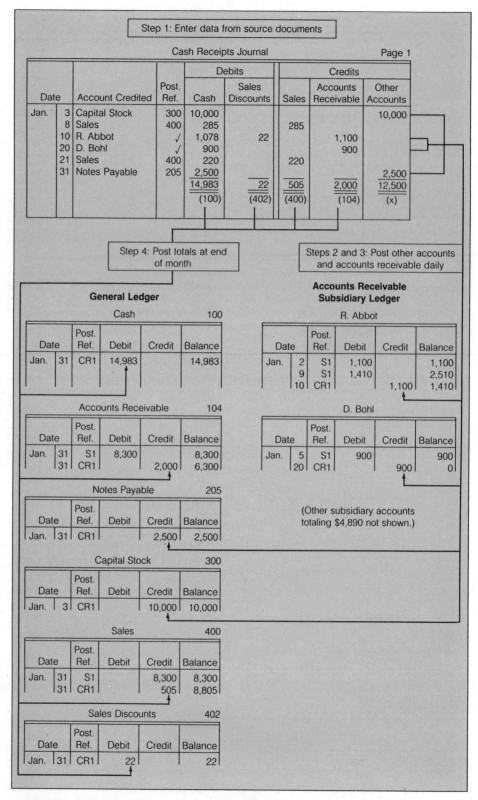

Figure 7-6
Relationship of Cash Receipts Journal and Ledger Accounts

4. Received payment from Don Bohl for a 15-day-old account receivable of $900 on January 20. No discount was involved since the cash was not received within 10 days.
5. Video equipment was sold for $220 cash on January 21.
6. A bank loan of $2,500 was received on January 31.

The two debit columns and three credit columns of the cash receipts journal shown in Figure 7-6 are used as follows.

Debits

Cash. The Cash column is used in every entry because only cash receipt transactions are recorded in the cash receipts journal.

Sales Discounts. This column is used to record all sales discounts allowed customers for prompt payment. Note that on January 10, the 2% discount (2% × $1,100 = $22) given to R. Abbot was recorded because the payment was made within 10 days. The total debits to Cash ($1,078) and Sales Discounts ($22) are equal to the $1,100 credit to Accounts Receivable, all of which are recorded on one line.

Credits

Sales. All cash sales are recorded in the Sales column. Most firms use cash registers to account for daily cash sales. At the end of a day, a sales tape showing the total cash sales is removed from the cash register and used to make the entry in the Sales column.

Accounts Receivable. This column is used to record the collections on accounts from customers. The name of the customer is written in the Account Credited column to identify the proper account to be credited in the subsidiary ledger.

Other Accounts. This column is used for all cash collections other than from cash sales and accounts receivable. The title of the specific account to be credited is identified in the Account Credited column. For example, the Capital Stock account is credited on January 3 for the $10,000 investment.

Summary of Cash Receipts Journal Procedures

The procedures required to record and post the entries in the cash receipts journal can be summarized as follows.

1. Data from source documents are entered in the cash receipts journal.
2. The entries in the Accounts Receivable column should be posted daily to the subsidiary ledger. A check mark is placed in the Posting Reference column of the cash receipts journal, and CR1 (indicating page one of the cash receipts journal) is entered in the Posting Reference columns of the subsidiary ledger accounts. Note that by posting the receipts daily (along with the accounts receivable recorded in the sales journal), balances in the customers' subsidiary Accounts Receivable accounts are up-to-date.
3. The credits in the Other Accounts column should be posted when it is convenient but no later than at the end of the month. The number of the account involved is recorded in the Posting Reference column as the entries are posted to show that the posting has been accomplished. In addition, CR1 is entered in the Posting Reference column of each account to indicate the source of each entry.
4. At the end of the month, the entries in each column should be totaled. The sum

of the debit columns should be compared with the sum of the credit columns to verify that the debits and credits are equal. This procedure is called *crossfooting*, which gives the following results, using the totals of the journal columns.

Debit Columns		Credit Columns	
Cash	$14,983	Sales	$ 505
Sales Discounts	22	Accounts Receivable	2,000
		Other Accounts	12,500
Total debits	$15,005		$15,005
		Crossfooted	

After the totals have been crossfooted, the following four column totals are posted:

Cash debit column. Posted as a debit to the Cash account. The account number (100) is entered below the total to indicate that the posting has been done, and CR1 is recorded in the Posting Reference column of the Cash account.

Sales Discounts debit column. Posted as a debit to the Sales Discounts account. The account number (402) is placed below the total to show that the posting has been accomplished, and CR1 is entered in the Sales Discounts account.

Sales credit column. Posted as a credit to the Sales account. The account number (400) is entered below the total as an indication that the posting has taken place, and CR1 is recorded in the Sales account.

Accounts Receivable credit column. Posted as a credit to the Accounts Receivable control account. The account number (104) is recorded below the total, and CR1 is entered in the control account.

The total of the Other Accounts column *is not posted at the end of the month* because each entry is posted individually. Some accountants use a special symbol—such as (x)—at the bottom of the column to indicate that it is not posted as a total.

CASH DISBURSEMENTS JOURNAL

The **cash disbursements journal**, also called the **cash payments journal**, is used to record all transactions involving payments of cash—cash purchases of merchandise, payment of accounts payable to creditors, disbursements for operating expenses, and payment of bank loans. The multicolumn format of the cash disbursements journal is similar to the one described earlier for the cash receipts journal. Three debit columns (Purchases, Accounts Payable, and Other Accounts) are used along with two credit columns (Cash and Purchases Discounts), as illustrated in Figure 7-7. The following transactions for Baldwin Video Equipment Store illustrate the cash disbursements journal:

1. Merchandise costing $680 was purchased for cash on January 4.
2. Store rent of $325 was paid on January 7.
3. Store equipment costing $410 was purchased for cash on January 14.
4. Merchandise costing $840 was purchased for cash on January 28.
5. A one-year premium for an insurance policy amounting to $510 was paid on January 29.
6. The $1,900 account payable to the Kirby Company was paid on January 30.
7. The $900 account payable to Cooper Company was paid less a 2% discount of $18 on January 30. Therefore, $882 cash was paid.

The three debit columns and two credit columns of the cash disbursements journal shown in Figure 7-7 are used as follows.

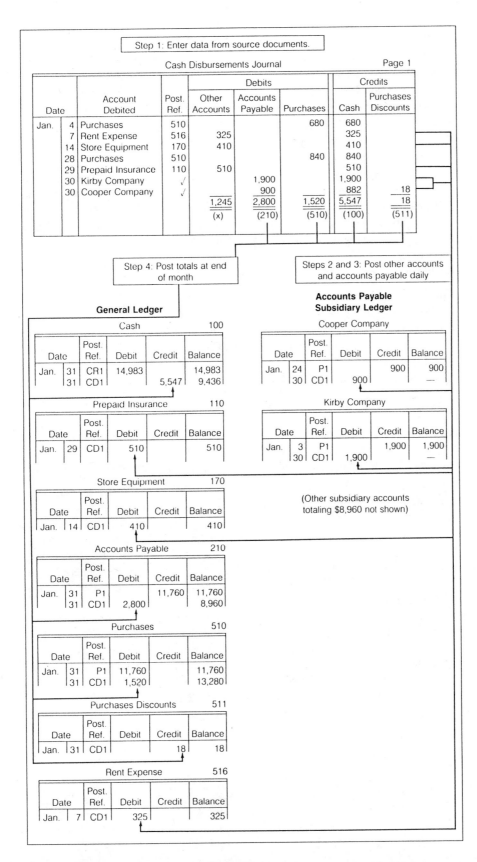

Figure 7-7
Relationship of Cash Disbursements Journal and Ledger Accounts

Debits

Purchases. The Purchases column is used to record all cash purchases of merchandise. The total of this column is posted to the Purchases account in the general ledger. When posted, the amount is added to the credit purchases posted from the purchases journal to determine the total purchases for the period.

Accounts Payable. Payments of accounts payable are entered in this column. The name of the supplier is written in the Account Debited column so the entry can be posted to the appropriate subsidiary ledger account.

Other Accounts. This column is used for all cash disbursements *except* cash purchases and payments of accounts payable. The title of the account to be debited is entered in the Account Debited column to identify a specific type of cash disbursement. In Figure 7-7, rent expense and prepaid insurance were paid for, along with the acquisition of store equipment.

Credits

Cash. The Cash column must be used for *each* transaction because *only* cash payments are recorded in the journal.

Purchases Discounts. Any purchases discounts taken for prompt payment are recorded in this column. Remember from Chapter 6 that purchases are recorded at either the gross invoice price or the net invoice price. We are assuming that the gross invoice price method is used in this illustration.

Summary of Cash Disbursements Journal Procedures

The recording and posting procedures required with the cash disbursements journal are the two types discussed earlier for the cash receipts journal—postings during the month and postings at the end of the month. The procedures can be summarized as:

1. Data from source documents are entered in the cash disbursements journal.
2. The entries in the Accounts Payable column should be posted *daily* to the subsidiary ledger. A check mark is placed in the Posting Reference column of the cash disbursements journal, and CD1 (representing page one of the cash disbursements journal) is entered in the Posting Reference columns of the subsidiary ledger accounts. By combining the daily postings of both the cash payments and the accounts payable recorded in the purchases journal, we have up-to-date balances of the amounts owed to suppliers.
3. The debits in the Other Accounts column should be posted when convenient but no later than at the end of the month. The number of each account involved is recorded in the Posting Reference column as the entries are posted to indicate that the posting has been done. CD1 is entered in the Posting Reference column of each account to show the source of each entry.
4. At the end of the month, the dollar amounts entered in each column should be totaled and crossfooted to verify that the debits and credits are equal, as follows.

Debit Columns		Credit Columns	
Other Accounts	$1,245	Cash	$5,547
Accounts Payable	2,800	Purchase Discounts	18
Purchases	1,520		
Total debits	$5,565	Total credits	$5,565
		Crossfooted	

The column totals for Accounts Payable, Purchases, Cash, and Purchases Discounts are posted at the end of the month to their respective accounts in the general ledger. The account numbers are entered below the column totals, and CD1 is recorded in the Posting Reference columns of the general ledger accounts. The total of the Other Accounts column is *not* posted at the end of the month because the individual entries were posted earlier. An (x) can be placed below the column total to indicate that it is not posted at the end of the month.

SELF-TEST

Test your understanding of the Appendix by selecting the best answer for each of the following.

1. The following type of transaction should not be recorded in the sales journal of a furniture store.
   a. Sales of office furniture (merchandise inventory) on credit.
   b. Sale of kitchen furniture (merchandise inventory) as an account receivable.
   c. Sale for cash of a chair that was used in the office.
   d. None of the above.
2. A sales return and allowance granted to a customer should be recorded in the:
   a. sales journal.
   b. cash receipts journal.
   c. purchases journal.
   d. general journal.
3. The process of checking to see if the sum of the debits and the sum of the credits in the cash receipts journal are equal is called:
   a. posting.
   b. crossfooting.
   c. posting reference.
   d. journalizing.
4. The column total in the cash disbursements journal that should not be posted at the end of a month is:
   a. purchases.
   b. accounts payable.
   c. cash.
   d. other accounts.

ANSWERS TO SELF-TEST

1. c   2. d   3. b   4. d

GLOSSARY

ACCOUNTING CONTROLS. Internal controls used to protect assets and ensure reliability of accounting records (p. 284).

ACCOUNTING SYSTEM. A collection of business forms, records, procedures, management policies and controls, and data-processing methods used to transform economic data into useful information (p. 280).

ADMINISTRATIVE CONTROLS. Internal controls used to provide operating efficiency and adherence to prescribed company policies (p. 283).

CASH DISBURSEMENTS JOURNAL (CASH PAYMENTS JOURNAL). A special journal used to record all cash payments (p. 306).

CASH RECEIPTS JOURNAL. A special journal used to record all cash receipts (p. 302).

DATABASE MANAGEMENT SYSTEM. A program developed for a computer that enables a business to efficiently develop data files and prepare financial reports (p. 293).

ELECTRONIC DATA PROCESSING (EDP; COMPUTER DATA PROCESSING). The use of a digital computer and its peripheral equipment to process data (p. 291).

ELECTRONIC SPREADSHEET. A versatile computer program that can be used to perform numerous types of financial analysis (p. 293).

FILE. An ordered set of records used to process data (p. 294).

INTERNAL CONTROL SYSTEM. The overall procedures adopted by a business to safeguard its assets, promote the reliability of accounting data, and encourage compliance with company policy (p. 283).

OPERATING MANUAL. A book containing a detailed description of how a firm's accounting system should function (p. 287).

PURCHASES JOURNAL. A special journal used to record all purchases of merchandise on credit (p. 302).

SALES JOURNAL. A special journal used to record all sales of merchandise on credit (p. 299).

SPECIAL JOURNALS. Books of original entry used for such repetitive transactions as sales, purchases, cash receipts, and cash disbursements (p. 298).

SYSTEMS ANALYSIS. The initial stage in the development of an accounting system through which an understanding of a business's information requirements and sources of information is provided (p. 287).

SYSTEMS DESIGN. The second stage in the development of an accounting system through which the specific means to be used for input, processing, and output are determined (p. 288).

SYSTEMS IMPLEMENTATION. The final stage in the development of an accounting system through which the system is made operational (p. 288).

DISCUSSION QUESTIONS

1. What is an accounting system and what is its ultimate goal?
2. Define the terms "input," "processing," and "output" as they relate to an accounting system.
3. Distinguish between the terms "data" and "information" as they are used in the accounting context. Give an example of an item that is data and one that is information.
4. List and describe the two types of provisions contained in the Foreign Corrupt Practices Act.
5. In a large corporation, who is responsible for the maintenance of an adequate internal control system and the accuracy of the financial statements?
6. What are the purposes of an internal control system?

7. List and describe the two types of internal controls.

8. What is the primary concern in the design phase of developing an accounting system?

9. What is a subsidiary ledger? What is a control account?

10. What is the relationship between the total of the accounts in a subsidiary ledger and the balance in the control account.

11. In a general journal, the Posting Reference column contains the following notation: $(201/\checkmark)$. On the same line in the Accounts and Explanation column appears Accounts Payable/Ajax Corp. $1,500 appears in the Credit column. What is the significance of the $(201/\checkmark)$ in the Posting Reference column?

12. What internal control problems result from the use of microcomputers?

13. How are the terms "input," "processing," and "output" related to both an accounting system and a computer?

14A. List the four special journals discussed in the chapter's Appendix and the type of transactions recorded in each.

15A. Why does a firm which uses special journals still need a general journal?

16A. Why are cash sales not recorded in the sales journal?

17A. Beneath the sales journal Amount column total of $48,300 for the month of April appears the notation (105/401). What is the significance of the (105/401)?

EXERCISES

Exercise 7-1   Diagram of a Basic Accounting System
Draw a diagram of an accounting system that features the three basic phases: input, processing, and output. After you draw the diagram, explain how the inputs (data) are transformed by the system into outputs (information).

Exercise 7-2   Responsibility for Internal Control
One of the main accomplishments of the Foreign Corrupt Practices Act has been the emphasis that maintenance of an adequate internal control system and the accuracy of financial statements are the responsibility of management.

Required:
Discuss the impact of the above statement on internal control systems since the Act was passed. Do you believe the Act has made the CPA's (auditor's) job easier or more difficult? Explain why.

Exercise 7-3   Evaluating Internal Control Procedures
John Rigner, the owner of a hardware store, has asked for your advice concerning the internal control of his business. In order to keep procedures simple, Rigner has assigned one employee the responsibility for ordering inventory, receiving goods, and paying suppliers. Another employee maintains the accounting records, collects cash from customers, and makes all bank deposits. Rigner notes that his system is not only simple, but that it also takes full advantage of specialization, because the two employees have been with the business for 15 years performing the same jobs.

Required:
Evaluate the internal control procedures of the hardware store.

Exercise 7-4 True/False Analysis of Internal Control and Accounting Systems

Indicate whether each of the following statements is true or false.

1. An accounting system consists of processing procedures and the output from them.
2. A fidelity bond would be a waste of money where a strong internal control system is in place.
3. Management's primary attention should be with accounting controls, because the administrative controls will take care of themselves.
4. A major impact of the Foreign Corrupt Practices Act has been an increased concern for sound internal control.
5. According to the Foreign Corrupt Practices Act, the CPA performing the audit for a publicly held company has the primary responsibility for sound internal control.
6. Custodianship of assets and recordkeeping should be combined in assigning responsibilities to employees in an efficient manner.
7. A major benefit of a subsidiary ledger is sound internal control.

Exercise 7-5 Controlling Accounts and Subsidiary Ledgers

Ebbets Company maintains an accounts receivable subsidiary ledger and an Accounts Receivable control account. The subsidiary ledger account balances on March 1 were as follows.

	Balance
C. Furillo	$820
G. Hodges	360
C. Labine	180
J. Robinson	425
D. Snider	670

Sales and cash receipts for the month of March were as follows.

	Sales	Cash Receipts
C. Furillo	$160	$780
G. Hodges	460	360
C. Labine	740	840
J. Robinson	475	480
D. Snider	210	770

Required:

A. Compute what the balance in the Accounts Receivable control account should be on March 1.
B. Prepare one general journal entry to record the total sales and one journal entry to record total cash collections during the month.
C. Set up T accounts for each customer in a subsidiary ledger and an Accounts Receivable control account. Enter the beginning balances in the accounts and post the general journal entries.
D. Verify the ending balance in the Accounts Receivable control account.

Exercise 7-6 Reconciling a Control Account and a Subsidiary Ledger

Assume that a retail store sold merchandise to three customers during April, as shown in the following Accounts Receivable account.

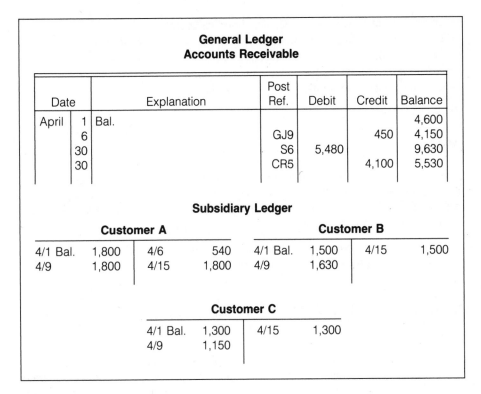

General Ledger
Accounts Receivable

Date		Explanation	Post Ref.	Debit	Credit	Balance
April	1	Bal.				4,600
	6		GJ9		450	4,150
	30		S6	5,480		9,630
	30		CR5		4,100	5,530

Subsidiary Ledger

Customer A

4/1 Bal.	1,800	4/6	540
4/9	1,800	4/15	1,800

Customer B

4/1 Bal.	1,500	4/15	1,500
4/9	1,630		

Customer C

4/1 Bal.	1,300	4/15	1,300
4/9	1,150		

Required:
Explain why the control account and related subsidiary ledger are not in balance, and what must be done to correct the situation. All postings to the subsidiary ledger were correct.

Exercise 7-7 Separation of Duties

Tyler Company, a client of your accounting firm, approaches you with the following problem. It has three employees who must perform the following functions:

1. Maintain general ledger.
2. Maintain accounts payable ledger.
3. Maintain accounts receivable ledger.
4. Prepare checks for signature.
5. Issue credit memos for sales returns.
6. Receive and deposit cash receipts.

All three employees have the ability to handle all six functions. Assume that except for the issuance of credit memos, all functions require the same amount of time. Also assume that these three employees will not perform any other accounting function; any accounting functions not listed above will be performed by other persons; and any four of the functions can be completed in an eight-hour day.

Required:
Assign the above functions to the three employees in a manner that achieves the highest degree of internal control. (CPA Exam Adapted.)

Exercise 7-8   Manual versus EDP Accounting Systems

Today, most firms, even the smallest, have access to some form of computer technology. Large firms possess the financial resources to acquire and operate one or more large mainframe computers. Smaller firms may utilize a minicomputer or microcomputer or may enter into a time sharing agreement.

Required:

Discuss the advantages an EDP accounting system has over a manual accounting system.

Exercise 7-9   Weaknesses in Internal Accounting Control Procedures

Below are listed six practices that weaken a company's internal accounting control system. For each practice listed: (a) explain what the weakness is, and (b) explain what steps the company should take to correct the weakness.

1. The employee who receives and opens incoming customers' mail receipts maintains the subsidiary accounts receivable ledger.
2. The same employee who prepares the payroll checks may add new employees to the payroll.
3. The employee who prepares checks for payments to creditors also approves and authorizes invoices for payment.
4. The individual responsible for maintaining the accounts receivable subsidiary ledger reconciles it to the general ledger control account only once a year.
5. The employee responsible for approving purchase requisitions and purchase orders is also responsible for approving creditor invoices for payment.
6. Invoices for purchased merchandise are not matched to purchase orders and receiving reports by the individual preparing the payment voucher. The person charged with approving the payment voucher does not request these supporting documents.

Exercise 7-10A   Matching Transactions and Special Journals

The following journals are used by a company:

Cash receipts	Purchases
Cash disbursements	Sales
General	

The company completed the following transactions during a recent month.

1. Sold merchandise on account.
2. Purchased merchandise on account.
3. Returned merchandise purchased on account and received a credit memo from the company indicating the reduced amount owed for the merchandise retained.
4. Sold capital stock for cash.
5. Sold merchandise for cash.
6. Purchased merchandise for cash.
7. Prepared adjusting entries at end of the month.
8. Purchased office equipment for cash.
9. Purchased land, signed a mortgage payable for the entire purchase price.
10. Received defective merchandise previously sold and shipped to a customer on account. Issued a credit memo to the customer.
11. Gave a cash refund to a customer for faulty merchandise previously sold to the customer in a cash sale.

12. Prepared closing entries.
13. Paid employees for the recent payroll period.
14. Sold marketable securities at a gain for cash.
15. Purchased for cash stock of another corporation as a short-term investment.

Required:
Match each of the above transactions to the journal in which it would be recorded. Do not make the entry.

Exercise 7-11A Special Journals, Transactions, and Accounts
The journals used by the Skelton Company are listed below coded by letter:

a. Cash disbursements journal   d. Purchases journal
b. Cash receipts journal   e. Sales journal
c. General journal

Skelton Company completed the following transactions during the last month of its fiscal year.

1. Sold merchandise for cash.
2. Purchased merchandise for cash. (The company uses a periodic inventory system.)
3. Recorded an adjusting entry to adjust the Prepaid Insurance account.
4. Recorded the entry to close the Sales account.
5. Sold merchandise on credit.
6. Purchased land giving a note payable for the entire purchase price.
7. Purchased merchandise on credit.
8. Returned merchandise previously purchased on credit. Received a credit memo from the creditor.
9. Declared and paid a cash dividend.
10. Issued a credit memorandum to a customer for merchandise sold and returned because it was defective.
11. Paid monthly utility bills.
12. Recorded payment for the purchase of merchandise on account. Payment was less than the invoice amount because of a cash discount that was taken.
13. Purchased prepaid insurance.
14. Recorded receipt of customers payment on account receivable. Amount received was less than recorded receivable because of an offered cash discount on the sale that was taken by the customer.
15. Recorded payment of the monthly advertising bill.
16. Paid monthly rent.

Required:
Prepare a form like the following.

Transaction	Journal	Account(s) Debited	Account(s) Credited

List the 16 transactions by number in the Transaction column. In the Journal column list the code letter of the journal in which the transaction would be recorded. List the names of the account(s) that would be debited and credited in recording the transactions in the last two columns.

Exercise 7-12A Accounting with Special Journals

The Dearborn Corporation uses a sales, purchases, cash receipts, cash disbursements, and general journal to record its accounting transactions. The following column totals were taken from the company's journals at the end of August:

1.	Sales journal		$45,000
2.	Purchases journal		36,000
3.	Cash receipts journal		
	a.	Cash	52,500
	b.	Sales Discounts	300
	c.	Sales	21,000
	d.	Accounts Receivable	29,000
4.	Cash disbursements journal		
	a.	Cash	48,300
	b.	Purchases Discounts	450
	c.	Accounts Payable	38,600
	d.	Purchases	9,200

The balance in the Accounts Receivable control account on August 1 was $8,250 and the Accounts Payable control account balance was $9,400.

Required:

A. At the end of August, the total of the sales journal should be posted to what account or accounts?

B. At the end of August, the total of the purchases journal should be posted to what account or accounts? The company uses a periodic inventory system.

C. For each column total in the cash receipts and cash disbursements journals, specify whether it would be posted to the proper general ledger account as a debit or a credit.

D. After the journals have been posted to the general ledger for August, what will be the balances in the Accounts Receivable and Accounts Payable control accounts?

E. By how much did cash increase or decrease during the month?

F. Why are the amounts listed above for the cash receipts and cash disbursements journals debit and credit columns not equal?

Exercise 7-13A Matching Ledger Accounts with Journals

The Wright Company has an accounting system that uses sales, purchases, cash receipts, cash disbursements, and general journals. Identify the journal that was most likely used for each posting to the following accounts.

Cash		Accounts Receivable		Accounts Payable	
(a) 11,900	(g) 8,740	(c) 21,000	(e) 10,000	(j) 8,000	(l) 12,000

Sales		Sales Discounts	
	(b) 21,000	(f) 100	
	(d) 2,000		

Purchases		Purchases Discounts		Purchases Allowances	
(h) 900			(i) 160		(m) 150
(k) 12,000					

Exercise 7-14A   Relating Special Journals to the Subsidiary Ledger

The sales and cash receipts journals of the Beta Company for the month of July are presented below. The company maintains an accounts receivable subsidiary ledger, which is balanced with the general ledger account each month. On July 1, the subsidiary ledger was comprised of four accounts: B. Allen—$180; J. Kline—$240; M. Feldman—$360, B. Lang—$150.

Sales Journal			P. 15		Cash Receipts			P. 11
Date	Invoice	Account	Amount	Date	Account	Cash	Accounts Receivable
July 2	503	R. Raman	130	July 5	B. Allen	75	75
6	504	B. Allen	60	10	J. Kline	200	200
7	505	J. Kline	125	23	M. Feldman	190	190
15	506	M. Feldman	100	27	B. Lang	125	125
25	507	K. Light	95				

Required:

A. Establish a T account for each customer's account in the subsidiary ledger and an Accounts Receivable control account. Post the amounts to the accounts receivable subsidiary ledger and the general ledger using the information in the journals shown.

B. Prepare a schedule of the accounts in the subsidiary ledger and compare its total to the balance in the control account.

PROBLEMS

Problem 7-1   Objectives of Internal Accounting Controls

Each of the following is a procedure commonly used as part of an internal accounting control system. For each procedure listed below, explain its objective.

1. A company uses a perpetual inventory method but spot checks certain high-priced items at irregular intervals throughout the year and takes an annual physical inventory at year-end.
2. All machinery repairs are approved by the purchasing department.
3. The vice president of operations approves all proposed acquisitions of machinery and equipment.
4. All supplies must be purchased through the purchasing department. A purchase requisition is required by the purchasing department before they prepare a purchase order.
5. All cash payments received from a customer require the preparation of a prenumbered receipt in duplicate.

Problem 7-2   Internal Control of Assets

For the following list of assets, describe a physical safeguard that may be used to protect the asset.

1. Cash on hand.
2. Magnetic computer tapes with accounts receivable files stored on them.

3. Cash received through the mail.
4. A portfolio of marketable securities.
5. Office supplies.
6. Typewriter, calculators, personal computers, and other movable office equipment.
7. An inventory held for resale of small, expensive precious gems.
8. Cash received by clerks in the retail operation.
9. An inventory of perishable goods held for resale.

Problem 7-3   Purpose of Accounting Controls

Following are five general elements of an internal accounting control system.

1. Clearly established lines of responsibility.
2. Separation of recordkeeping and custodianship.
3. Division of responsibility for related transactions.
4. Mechanical and electronic devices.
5. Adequate insurance and bonding of employees.

Required:

A. Explain the purposes of the five general elements.
B. Explain how each of the elements contributes to the overall goal of accounting controls to protect assets and ensure the reliability of the accounting records.
C. Give an example of two procedures typically used for each of the first four elements.

Problem 7-4   Development of an Accounting System

All businesses use an accounting system. Some are very simple; some are extremely complex. Most firms revise their system frequently to accommodate a larger volume of activity or for changes in the nature of their business.

Required:

Discuss the procedure followed to design and install an accounting system. Include in your discussion the following:

1. The three phases of installing an accounting system.
2. The critical factors to be considered within each phase and in general.
3. The types of accounting reports desired as output from the system.

Problem 7-5   Internal Control Procedures

Many fast-food chains and fast-food retail outlets use cash registers with programmed keys for high volume items and locked-in internal tapes. Some of these firms also prominently display a sign telling the customer that their purchase is free whenever a certain logo appears on their sales slip.

Required:

A. Discuss the effectiveness, for internal control procedures, of programmed cash registers and locked-in internal tapes.
B. Discuss how the logo can be used as an advertising technique.
C. Discuss how the logo can be used as an internal control procedure.

Problem 7-6   Internal Control of Payroll Deductions

Alicia Zurko had total responsibility for the payroll of Entec Industries, a company with 416 employees. The payroll system was computerized. Alicia wrote the computer program. Most of the employees were salaried and very little overtime was required of the employees. Employees were paid semi-monthly and received with each paycheck a stub showing gross pay, total deductions for the current pay period and net pay. No to-date totals were provided. In addition to performing all payroll duties, Alicia prepared the W-2's at year-end for the employees.

During Alicia's tenth year with the firm, a new CPA was hired as controller. At the end of the year when the new controller received his W-2, he compared the information on the W-2 to the sum of the amounts on his paycheck stubs. He found a discrepancy of $6 for the amounts of Federal income tax withheld with the W-2 reflecting a smaller amount than the sum of his stubs. The new controller has received 12 paychecks during the year.

The next day the new controller mentioned this to three other employees who had worked for Entec the entire year and asked them to make the same comparison. Each reported back on the following day that they had a $6 discrepancy in the same manner as the controller and one individual reported that he had gone over his records for the previous six years and for every year the amount reported on his W-2 for federal income tax withheld was $6 less than the total of his 24 payroll stubs.

The controller confronted Alicia with the information. Alicia stated there must be an error in the computer program because the W-2's were printed by the computer from the information contained on the payroll records. She told the new controller she would check it out and report back the next day. The next day Alicia called in sick and the following day did not report at all. Calls to her home went unanswered and a personal visit by the controller found an empty apartment and no forwarding address.

Required:
A. How was Alicia stealing money and from whom was she stealing?

B. Assuming Entec had an average of 386 employees over the past ten years, how much did Alicia steal?

C. What internal control procedures should the new controller implement to ensure this type of fraud cannot be duplicated in the future?

Problem 7-7 Administrative and Accounting Controls
An internal control system consists of administrative controls and accounting controls. Classify each of the following procedures as an administrative control or an accounting control.

1. All new employees must have a complete physical examination before they begin work.
2. The payroll records are maintained on a computer and the computer prepares all payroll checks.
3. The computer programmer is not allowed to operate the computer.
4. Employees who input data into the computer are not allowed to program or to change computer programs.
5. The cashier is not allowed access to the accounting records or the computer.
6. An independent CPA conducts an annual audit of the company records.
7. Job descriptions for each employee of the firm are in written format and given to all employees.
8. Company policies and procedures are maintained in a bound notebook. A copy is given to all new employees.
9. A record of employee absences is kept.

Problem 7-8 Relating Journals to Accounts Receivable Control Account

The William Company uses sales, cash receipts, and general journals in its accounting system. The company also maintains an accounts receivable subsidiary ledger, which contained the following five accounts on August 31.

L. Bird

Date		Explanation	Post. Ref.	Debit	Credit	Balance
Aug.	1	Balance				1,700
	7		GJ1		1,440	260

B. Cartwright

Date		Explanation	Post. Ref.	Debit	Credit	Balance
Aug.	5		GJ1	620		620
	15		GJ2	720		1,340
	21		GJ4		600	740

M. Johnson

Date		Explanation	Post. Ref.	Debit	Credit	Balance
Aug.	10		GJ1	600		600
	19		GJ2		360	240

D. Manning

Date		Explanation	Post. Ref.	Debit	Credit	Balance
Aug.	1	Balance				760
	11		GJ2		480	280
	22		GJ4	240		520

I. Thomas

Date		Explanation	Post. Ref.	Debit	Credit	Balance
Aug.	1	Balance				1,500
	20		GJ3		240	1,260
	30		GJ5		1,260	–0–

Required:

Establish a three column Accounts Receivable control account and post all entries for the month of August in chronological order with the necessary posting references.

Problem 7-9 Control Account and Subsidiary Ledger

Shoe Corporation maintains an accounts payable subsidiary ledger to provide the detail for the Accounts Payable control account (account number 200) in the general ledger. The balances in the subsidiary ledger accounts on November 1 and transactions that occurred during the month were as follows.

	Nov. 1 Balance	Nov. 15 Purchases on Account	Nov. 30 Cash Payments
A. Bolen	$ 400	$ 675	$ 400
J. Clark	275	160	275
F. Hunt	190	115	90
K. Mack	460	90	380
B. Ralston	365	220	365
Total	$1,690	$1,260	$1,510

Also, on November 11, Shoe Corporation returned merchandise to F. Hunt that was defective and was given credit on account in the amount of $75. Shoe Corporation uses a periodic inventory system to account for inventory costs.

Required:

A. Open T accounts for the Accounts Payable control account and for each account in the subsidiary ledger. Enter the beginning balance in each account.

B. Prepare general journal entries to record the transactions for the month. Use page 15 for the general journal.

C. Post the entries to the T accounts.

D. Verify the balance in the Accounts Payable control account.

Problem 7-10 Accounting Systems—Cost Benefit Analysis

Jerry Jackson started a metal fabricating and stamping firm in 1987. At that time an aunt who was a CPA established a manual accounting system for the new firm. Initially Jerry hired an accounting student, John Kolb, part time to handle the accounting work. Upon graduating from college in May, 1990, John began working full time because the firm had grown and needed more than a part-time accountant. All tax reports are prepared by Jerry's aunt and have been since the firm began operations. John believes he could prepare the reports, but he does not have time.

The firm initially had five employees; however, a strong market for the products and high quality work resulted in rapid growth. By December 31, 1988 the firm had 11 employees; by December 31, 1989, 19 employees; and by December 31, 1990, 35 employees.

John and Jerry have discussed the strain the rapid growth has placed on John. John believes if the firm buys a computer and hires one more employee in the accounting area, all the accounting work can be done on time. If the firm retains its manual system, John believes he needs three more employees.

Required:

A. Discuss the factors that must be considered in changing to a computerized accounting system for the firm.

B. Discuss the internal control considerations the firm has or will have:

    1. with only one employee in the accounting department;

    2. with four employees in the accounting department;

    3. with two employees and a computer in the accounting department.

Problem 7-11A Accounting with Sales and Purchases Journals

The Comp Company uses sales and purchases journals in its accounting system. The following transactions occurred during March 1992. (Sales discounts are not given by Comp Company.)

March 3 Purchased merchandise on account from the James Co., Invoice 307, $800, terms 2/10, n/30.
      7 Purchased merchandise on account from the Weiner Co., Invoice 737, $420, terms 2/10, n/30.
      10 Sold merchandise on account to the Blander Co., Invoice 126, $1,630.
      15 Sold merchandise on account to the Duton Co., Invoice 127, $990.
      17 Purchased merchandise on account from the Dale Co., Invoice 328, $300, terms, 2/10, n/30.
      25 Sold merchandise on account to the Giles Co., Invoices 128, $780.
      27 Sold merchandise on account to the Duton Co., Invoice 129, $750.

Required:

A. Establish all necessary general ledger accounts, accounts receivable subsidiary ledger accounts, and accounts payable subsidiary ledger accounts. Use the following account numbers: Accounts Receivable—105; Accounts Payable—200; Sales—400; Purchases—500.
B. Journalize the March transactions in the appropriate journals.
C. Post the data from the journals to the correct general ledger and subsidiary accounts.
D. Prepare a schedule of the accounts receivable subsidiary ledger and the accounts payable subsidiary ledger as of March 31, to prove that their totals are equal to the balances of the control accounts.

Problem 7-12A Accounting with Sales, Cash Receipts, and General Journals

The Blackwell Company uses a sales journal, a cash receipts journal, a general journal, and an accounts receivable subsidiary ledger. The terms of all credit sales are 2/10, n/30 and all accounts receivable balances as of October 1, 1992 were the result of transactions prior to September 15, 1992. The trial balance as of October 1 included the following accounts, among others.

Account Number	Account Title	Account Balance
100	Cash	$ 8,400
150	Accounts Receivable	7,360
400	Sales	96,000
410	Sales Discounts	960
420	Sales Returns and Allowances	1,200

The accounts receivable subsidiary ledger balances were:

P. Dickens	$ –0–
D. Fields	2,380
S. Lamb	460
R. Roberts	1,800
S. Sheets	1,640
J. Tinker	1,080
Total	$7,360

The following October transactions were recorded in the sales, cash receipts, or general journals.

October	1	Issued credit to J. Tinker for defective merchandise sold on account during September, $160.
	4	Sold merchandise on account to P. Dickens, $1,500. Invoice 324.
	8	Received a check from S. Lamb for payment of a September purchase, $280.
	9	Sold merchandise on account to R. Roberts, $160, Invoice 325.
	10	Sold merchandise on account to D. Fields, $260, Invoice 326.
	13	Received payment from P. Dickens for Invoice 324, less 2% discount.
	17	Received payment in full from J. Tinker.
	20	Borrowed $6,000 cash from the bank.
	21	Sold merchandise for cash, $180.
	27	Received a check from D. Fields, $2,420, for payment on his account.
	27	Sold merchandise on account to S. Lamb, $500, Invoice 327.
	30	Received payment from S. Lamb for Invoice 327 less 2% discount.

Required:

A. Record the October transactions in the appropriate journals. Establish all ledger accounts needed and make all postings to the proper general ledger accounts and to the accounts receivable subsidiary ledger.

B. Prepare a schedule of the accounts receivable subsidiary ledger to prove that the balance is equal to the balance in the control account.

Problem 7-13A Comprehensive Accounting System Problem

The RAB Company uses a sales journal, purchases journal, cash receipts journal, cash disbursements journal, and a general journal. The firm also maintains subsidiary accounts receivable and accounts payable ledgers, in addition to the control accounts. The relevant account balances as of January 1, 1992, were as follows.

Acct. No.	Account Title	Account Balance Debit	Account Balance Credit
100	Cash	$ 4,500	
110	Accounts Receivable	6,300	
130	Merchandise Inventory	10,000	
200	Plant and Equipment	110,000	
300	Accounts Payable		$ 5,300
330	Notes Payable		50,000
400	Capital Stock		75,500
500	Sales		
510	Sales Discounts		
520	Sales Returns & Allowances		
600	Purchases		
610	Purchases Discounts		
		$130,800	$130,800

The accounts receivable and accounts payable subsidiary ledger balances were as follows.

Accounts Receivable		Accounts Payable	
J. Dickson	$1,400	C.J. Inc.	$1,300
M. Moreau	900	Design Concepts	1,000
A. Piccioli	2,000	Williams Wholesale	3,000
L. Robbins	1,500	Total	$5,300
D. Roberge	500		
Total	$6,300		

The following transactions occurred during the first quarter.

Jan. 5 M. Moreau took advantage of the 2% sales discount and paid off her account with $882.

10 Sold a $1,000 couch to D. Roberge on account, Invoice 401.

15 Purchased $3,000 in inventory from Design Concepts on account. The terms were 2/10, n/30.

18 Received $500 from J. Dickson on his account. He has passed the discount period without paying.

20 Paid $700 to Design Concepts on account. No discount was taken.

24 Paid $2,940 to Design Concepts, taking advantage of the 2% discount. This reduced the balance on this account to zero.

Feb. 10 A cash sale of $2,000 was made to a new customer.

13 A. Piccioli paid $700 on his account. He missed the discount period.

23 Sold a $500 painting to D. Roberge on account, Invoice 402.

28 Paid $2,000 on the Williams Wholesale account. No discount was taken.

28 Borrowed $10,000 from United Bank by issuing a 12% note payable.

Mar. 4 Purchased $4,000 in inventory from C.J. Inc. on account. Terms were n/30.

16 Sold a $50 lamp to L. Robbins on account, Invoice 403.

22 Paid $2,000 on the C.J. Inc. account.

27 A $50 sales allowance was given to L. Robbins, due to a defective product.

28 Made $400 principal payment on notes payable.

Required:

A. Journalize the first quarter's transactions in the appropriate journals.

B. Open the necessary general ledger accounts, the accounts receivable subsidiary ledger accounts and the accounts payable subsidiary ledger accounts.

C. Post the data from the journals to the appropriate general ledger and subsidiary ledger accounts.

D. Prepare a schedule of accounts receivable and accounts payable as of March 31, 1992, to confirm the balance in the control accounts.

E. Prepare a trial balance like the one given in the problem, as of March 31, 1992.

Problem 7-14A Detecting Errors in an Accounting System

The James Company has an accounting system that uses sales, purchases, cash receipts, cash disbursements, and general journals. At various times during the year, the following errors have occurred. Specify a procedure that would detect each error.

1. An error was made in totaling the cash column in the cash receipts journal.

2. A customer's check, net of the applicable sales discount, was correctly entered in the cash column at the net amount and in the accounts receivable column at the gross amount. No entry was made in the Sales Discounts column.

3. The Amount column in the purchases journal was incorrectly totaled.
4. A subtraction error was made on a customer's account in the accounts receivable subsidiary ledger.
5. The amount of a bank loan entered in the Other column of the cash receipts journal was posted as a debit to Notes Payable.
6. A sales return, journalized in the general journal, was posted to the Accounts Receivable control account and to the Sales Returns and Allowances account but was not posted to the accounts receivable subsidiary ledger.
7. A credit sale for $850 was posted as $85 in the accounts receivable subsidiary ledger.
8. A purchase discount was not entered in the cash disbursements journal. The gross amount of supplier's invoice was entered in the Accounts Payable column and the net amount of the check was entered in the Cash column.
9. A purchase allowance for merchandise purchased on account was entered in the general journal. The entry was posted to only two accounts—the Accounts Payable subsidiary account and to Purchase Returns and Allowances.
10. The sales journal was incorrectly totaled.

Problem 7-15A   Comprehensive Accounting System Problem

The New River Company uses a sales journal, purchases journal, cash receipts journal, cash disbursements journal, and a general journal. The firm also maintains subsidiary accounts receivable and accounts payable ledgers in addition to the control accounts. The relevant account balances as of August 1, 1992, were as follows.

Acct. No.	Account Title	Account Balance Debit	Credit
100	Cash	$ 7,500	
110	Accounts Receivable	4,100	
135	Merchandise Inventory	25,000	
210	Plant and Equipment	78,000	
300	Accounts Payable		$ 5,300
320	Notes Payable		45,000
400	Capital Stock		62,000
500	Sales		10,300
510	Sales Discounts	200	
520	Sales Returns & Allowances	100	
600	Purchases	8,000	
610	Purchases Discounts		300
		$122,900	$122,900

The accounts receivable and accounts payable subsidiary ledger balances were as follows.

Accounts Receivable		Accounts Payable	
C. Clark	$1,400	Miller Company	$ 800
P. Hills	600	Royal Inc.	3,500
R. Kennison	900	Sterling Co.	1,000
B. Murray	1,200	Total	$5,300
Total	$4,100		

The following transactions occurred during August.

Aug.   2   Purchased merchandise from Sterling Co. for $1,800 on account. The terms were 2/10, n/30.
       3   Received $600 from P. Hills on his account.
       6   Paid $1,000 to Sterling Co. on its previous balance. No discount was taken.
       9   Sold merchandise to B. Murray on account for $500, Invoice 201.
       12 Paid $1,764 to Sterling Co., taking advantage of the 2% discount.
       13 Sold $1,500 in merchandise to P. Hills on account. The terms were 1/10, n/60. Invoice 202.
       14 Received $300 from R. Kennison on his account.
       15 Paid $2,000 on the Royal Inc. account.
       17 Purchased inventory for $1,000 from Miller Company on account. Terms were n/30.
       19 Sold merchandise for $500 in cash.
       21 Purchased equipment for $8,000 by issuing a 14% notes payable due in two years.
       23 Received $1,000 from C. Clark on her account. There was no discount.
       29 Purchased merchandise for $100 in cash.

Required:

A. Journalize August's transactions in the appropriate journals.

B. Open the general ledger accounts, the accounts receivable subsidiary ledger accounts, and the accounts payable subsidiary ledger accounts.

C. Post the data from the journals to the appropriate general ledger and subsidiary ledger accounts.

D. Prepare a schedule of accounts receivable and accounts payable as of August 31, 1992, to confirm the balance in the control accounts.

E. Prepare a trial balance like the one given in the problem, as of August 31, 1992.

CASE

CASE 7-1   Discussion Case   Internal Control Procedures

John Brown took over the management of his family's successful retail store upon graduation from college where he majored in foreign languages. Since he had little knowledge of business practices and internal control procedures, he relied heavily on the company's new accountant, Tom Krieder, to establish appropriate inventory control. Tom decided that the best way to operate was for him to have complete responsibility for ordering inventory, inspecting the goods when received, and making payments to the suppliers. Tom convinced John that this was the best approach because he knew all the suppliers personally and could get good service from them.

When inventory is purchased, Tom prepares a purchase order and sends it to the supplier. Frequently, he phones an order into a supplier to save time and does not prepare a purchase order, since the supplier does not require one. When the inventory is received by the store, it is left on the receiving dock until Tom has a chance to inspect it and record it in the accounting system. Usually, the inspection is done at night after the store is closed so that Tom does not interfere with the regular business of the store while performing inspection. After inspecting the goods received, Tom initials the supplier invoice involved, attaches it to the purchase order (if one exists), and journalizes the transaction. On the due date, Tom prepares a check for payment to the supplier and mails it himself.

After several months, John Brown has become very concerned about the store's gross profits, which have steadily declined from their historical levels. When he mentioned his concern to Tom Krieder, the reply was "you should either raise prices or sell more inventory."

Required:

Evaluate the internal control procedures currently used by the store. What suggestions would you recommend to improve the situation?

CASE 7-2   Annual Report Analysis

Refer to the financial statements and related footnotes of BFGoodrich Company in the Appendix to this text and answer the following questions. Indicate the Appendix page number on which you found the answer.

1. The management of The BFGoodrich Company must take the responsibility for preparing the financial statements. Where is this disclosed in the annual report? What are the ramifications of these responsibilities for the firm's accounting system? Has the Foreign Corrupt Practices Act affected these responsibilities?
2. How does the Board of Directors pursue its responsibility for the company's financial statements?

8

CASH, MARKETABLE SECURITIES, AND RECEIVABLES

CHAPTER OVERVIEW AND OBJECTIVES

This chapter discusses cash control concepts and the nature of cash, marketable securities, and receivables. When you have completed the chapter, you should understand:

1. The nature of cash.
2. The procedures used to control cash receipts and cash disbursements.
3. The purpose and operation of a petty cash fund.
4. The purpose and preparation of a bank reconciliation.
5. How to account for temporary investments in marketable securities.
6. The different types of receivables.
7. The nature of and how to account for uncollectible accounts.
8. How to compute and account for interest.

Cash, temporary investments in marketable securities, and receivables are often called **liquid assets** because they are either in the form of cash or are easily convertible into cash in the near future. Because of their nature, they are all classified as current assets in the balance sheet. Knowledge of the amount and composition of these liquid assets is helpful to users of financial statements in evaluating the ability of the company to meet currently maturing obligations. This chapter discusses each of these three types of current assets.

CASH

Objective 1: Nature of cash

Cash is a term used to identify money and any other instrument, such as a check or money order, that a bank normally accepts as a deposit to the depositor's bank account. Cash does not include postdated checks, IOUs, or postage stamps. Although companies may have several bank accounts as well as cash on hand, the sum of all the cash items is reported as a single item in the current asset section of the balance sheet.

Practically every business transaction eventually results in an inflow or outflow of cash. Cash is an unproductive asset because it produces no revenue directly. Therefore, any cash accumulated in excess of that needed for current use should be invested, even temporarily, in some type of revenue-producing investment. Excess cash is often invested in short-term, highly liquid investments such as treasury bills and money market funds. Because they can be converted into cash on very short notice, they are sometimes called *cash equivalents*.

Perhaps most importantly, cash is the asset that is most easily subject to misappropriation. Therefore, it must be adequately protected by controlling access to and use of it. Thus, the control and proper use of cash is an important management function. The techniques used to accomplish this constitute the internal control system for cash.

INTERNAL CONTROL OF CASH

A good internal control system for handling cash and cash transactions is vital. Such a system must contain procedures for protecting cash on hand as well as for handling both cash receipts and cash disbursements. Three particularly important elements of the internal control system for cash are:

Objective 2:
Cash control
procedures

1. The separation of responsibility for cash handling and custodianship from responsibility for maintaining cash records. This element prevents the misappropriation of cash and corresponding falsification of accounting records without collusion among employees.
2. The deposit of each day's cash receipts intact. This element prevents the cash custodian from "borrowing" the funds until the next deposit date.
3. Making all cash payments by check. This element, in combination with item (2), allows the business to use the bank's record of cash transactions as a cross-check of its internal cash records.

Because the details of a system of internal control over cash vary with the size and type of business, only a general system will be considered here. Procedures used to build an internal system of cash control can be illustrated best by considering cash receipts and cash disbursements separately.

Control of Cash Receipts

Cash receipts normally consist of two types: (1) over-the-counter receipts from cash sales and (2) cash received through the mail from customers making payments on charge accounts. Different control procedures are needed for each type.

Receipts from Cash Sales. Cash received over the counter from cash sales should be rung up on a cash register. The cash register should be located in a position that permits the customer to see the amount recorded. The receipt printed by the register should be given to the customer. However, each register also has a locked-in tape on which each cash sale is recorded, thereby keeping an accurate running total of cash sales.

The basis for internal cash control is the principle of separation of recordkeeping from custodianship. The salesclerk who collects the cash should not have access to the tape in the register.

At the end of each business day, the salesclerk should be required to count the cash in the register and record the amount on a business form that is sent to the accounting department. An employee other than the salesclerk should be responsible for removing the tape and cash from the register, counting the cash, comparing the count with that of the salesclerk, and noting any discrepancies. The cash is then forwarded to the cashier (the employee responsible for accumulating and depositing cash) for deposit. The tape, along with any discrepancy noted, is sent to the accounting department, where it is used to prepare appropriate accounting entries. In this way, neither the salesclerk nor the cashier has access to the accounting records, and the accounting department personnel have no access to cash.

Cash Received Through the Mail. Procedures for the control of mail receipts are also based on the separation of recordkeeping and custodianship. The employee who opens the mail prepares a multicopy list of the amounts received. One copy is sent to the cashier along with the receipts (usually checks or money orders). The receipts are combined with those from the cash registers in preparing the daily bank deposit. Another copy of the list is forwarded to the accounting department for use in preparing entries in the cash receipts journal and the customers' accounts. Again, neither the mail clerk nor the cashier has access to the accounting records, and accounting department personnel have no access to cash. Thus, fraud is generally avoided unless there is collusion.

Control of Cash Disbursements

Just as an adequate system of internal control must contain procedures for controlling cash receipts, it must also provide for the protection of cash balances and procedures for the control of cash disbursements. A safe or vault is generally provided for the protection of cash on hand. The daily deposit of cash receipts provides additional protection for cash balances.

Control over cash disbursements centers on the policy of making all cash disbursements by check. Checks should be prenumbered so they can be easily accounted for.

These procedures are supported by a division of responsibility among employees for the approval and payment of invoices. The employee designated to approve invoices for payment should have no checkwriting or accounting responsibility. Before authorizing payment, the employee should be required to verify that the goods or services represented by the invoice were properly ordered and actually received. Approval of the invoice for payment is generally indicated by placing an approval stamp on its face.

The employee responsible for signing checks should have no invoice-approval or accounting responsibilities. Checks presented for signature should be signed only upon receipt of a properly approved invoice indicating that payment is justified. At the time the check is signed, the related invoice should be canceled by either perforating it or stamping it ''paid.'' Either of these tactics prevent the possibility of having the invoice presented for payment a second time. The approved invoice and a copy of the check should be forwarded to the accounting department, where the appropriate entry is made to record the payment.

The combination of these procedures makes it difficult for a fraudulent disbursement to be made without collusion by two or more employees. Internal control of cash disbursements can be strengthened further by use of a voucher system. A description of a voucher system and its use is presented in Chapter 11.

THE PETTY CASH FUND

**Objective 3:
Petty cash fund**

To avoid the expense and inconvenience of writing many small checks for minor expenditures, such as for postage stamps and miscellaneous supplies, a petty cash fund is established. A **petty cash fund,** which is a specified amount of cash placed under the control of a particular employee (the petty cash fund cashier) for use in making small payments, should be the sole exception to the policy of making all cash disbursements by check.

Establishing the Petty Cash Fund

The petty cash fund is established by writing a check to the petty cash fund cashier. The amount is generally a round amount, such as $100 or $200. The amount should only be expected to handle petty cash payments for a relatively short period, such as a month. The petty cash fund cashier then cashes the check and places the proceeds in a locked box to which only he or she has access.

The check is recorded by a debit to a Petty Cash account and a credit to the Cash account. For example, assuming a fund of $200 is established on January 2, the journal entry is:

Jan.	2	Petty Cash	200	
		Cash		200

Making Disbursements from the Fund

As cash payments are made from the fund, the recipient should be required to sign a **petty cash receipt** prepared by the petty cash fund cashier. The receipt should show the amount paid, the purpose of the payment, and the date paid. A receipt must be prepared for every payment made from the fund. It should also be stamped "paid," and then placed in the petty cash fund box. Thus, the total of the receipts plus the cash in the fund should always be equal to the amount originally placed in the fund ($200 in our illustration).

Replenishing the Petty Cash Fund

The petty cash fund must be replenished periodically. Every paid receipt in the fund should be sent to the accounting department to serve as a basis for the entry needed to record the replenishment. Then a check should be issued in an amount sufficient to restore the fund to its original amount ($200). The check should be cashed by the petty cash fund cashier and the proceeds placed in the petty cash box.

The petty cash fund is always replenished at the end of an accounting period, even when the fund is not running low on cash, so that the expenses represented by the receipts in the fund can be recorded during the current accounting period. If the fund is not replenished at the end of each period, cash will be overstated on the balance sheet and expenses will be understated on the income statement.

On occasion, the custodian of the fund may forget to obtain a signed receipt for a payment from the fund, in which case cash in the fund will be short. When this occurs, the Cash Short and Over account (explained in the next section) is debited for the shortage when the fund is replenished.

Various expense accounts are debited as indicated by the petty cash receipts, and cash is credited for the amount needed to replenish the fund. For example, assume that the petty cash box contained the following receipts and cash at the end of the first month of operations:

Receipt Nos.	Purpose	Amount
1, 2, 6	Office supplies	$ 24.70
3, 7	Postage stamps	60.00
4	Gasoline	30.44
5, 8, 9	Delivery expense	52.94
	Total receipts in the box	168.08
	Cash in the box	31.92
	Total	$200.00

Because the cash in the fund is low, the fund is replenished and the following journal entry is prepared:

Jan.	31	Postage Expense	60.00	
		Office Supplies Expense	24.70	
		Auto Expense	30.44	
		Delivery Expense	52.94	
		Cash		168.08

Since the petty cash receipts are supplementary records, this entry is needed so that the expenses are properly recorded in the journal and general ledger accounts. Thus, expense accounts are debited when the fund is replenished.

Note that the Petty Cash account is not affected by the replenishing entry. The Petty Cash account is debited only when the fund is initially established, and no other entries are made to the account unless a decision is made to increase or decrease the size of the fund. The petty cash fund amount is normally included with other cash amounts and reported as a single amount on the balance sheet.

CASH SHORT AND OVER

When numerous individual cash sales are recorded, it is inevitable that some errors will be made (e.g., some customers might be given the wrong change). As a result, when the actual cash in the cash register is compared with the cash register tape, there will be a cash shortage or overage.

For example, assume that the cash register tape shows that total sales recorded were $1,908, and the cash in the register amounted to $1,903. The cash shortage is recorded as follows when the daily sales are recorded:

May	6	Cash	1,903	
		Cash Short and Over	5	
		Sales		1,908

If the cash count exceeds the amount of sales recorded, the Cash Short and Over account is credited for the difference. The Cash Short and Over account is closed to the Income Summary account at year-end as part of the normal closing process. If the account has a debit balance (shortages exceed overages), it will be reported as miscellaneous expense on the income statement. If the account has a credit balance (overages exceed shortages), it is normally reported as an item of other income on the income statement.

BANK CHECKING ACCOUNTS

As mentioned earlier, an important element of internal control of cash is the requirement that each day's cash receipts be deposited intact into a bank checking account and that all disbursements be made by check. Internal control is strengthened because the bank record of deposits received and checks paid provides a cross-check on the internal cash records of the business.

Deposits of cash receipts are made by preparing a deposit ticket (Figure 8-1) that includes the amount of currency and coin and a list of the checks included with the deposit. Each check deposited is identified by the code number of the bank on which the check is drawn. The deposit ticket is prepared in duplicate; one copy is sent to

Figure 8-1
Deposit Ticket

UNITED AMERICAN BANK		
Century City, California		

Date November 6, 1992

Depositor: American Precision Metals

8590 S. Strane Avenue

Century City, California

0542-87-1156

CASH	Currency	189	00
	Coin	11	70
CHECKS:	56-231	129	35
	56-233	321	23
	58-45	111	84
	56-231	474	65
	22-12	156	42
Total		1,394	19
Less Cash Received		—0—	
Net Deposit		1,394	19

the bank with the deposit and the other copy is retained by the depositor.

Disbursements from the checking account are authorized by checks written by the depositor. **Checks** are legal instruments signed by the depositor ordering the bank to pay a specified amount of money to the person or company identified on the check.

The Bank Statement

Each month the bank sends the depositor a **bank statement**. The bank statement is a monthly report detailing the activity that has taken place in the depositor's account. The statement contains the following information:

1. The balance in the account at the beginning of the month;
2. Each deposit received during the month;
3. A list of all checks written by the depositor and paid by the bank during the month (**canceled checks**);
4. Debit and credit memoranda identifying miscellaneous charges and credits made to the account; and
5. The account balance at month-end.

If the depositor elects not to leave the canceled checks on file at the bank, the bank statement will also include the depositor's canceled checks.

The depositor's cash balance in the account represents a liability on the bank's part. It is therefore shown on the bank's books by a credit balance.

Debit and Credit Memos. Debit memos identify charges (debits or decreases) in the depositor's account during the month. Items such as bank service charges, check-printing charges, and **nonsufficient funds (NSF) checks** (checks that were included in a depositor's deposit and recorded by the bank but not paid by the check writer's bank because of the lack of sufficient funds to cover the checks) are debit memo items. NSF checks are subtracted from the depositor's account and the depositor is notified by a debit memo.

Credit memos identify credits (increases) made to the depositor's account by the bank. For example, the bank may have collected a note receivable for the depositor, at the depositor's request, and placed the proceeds in the depositor's account.

Debit and credit memos are also used by the bank to correct errors made by the bank in previous months. An example of a bank statement is shown in Figure 8-2.

Reconciling the Bank Account

Objective 4:
Bank reconciliation

The cash balance as reported on the closing date of the bank statement seldom agrees with the balance shown in the depositor's general ledger Cash account. As a result, a **bank reconciliation** (Figure 8-3) is prepared by the accounting department for each bank account. The goal of the reconciliation is to reconcile the cash balance reported on the bank statement with the adjusted balance according to the depositor's records. The purpose is to verify the accuracy of both records.

The bank statement balance may differ from the depositor's records for several reasons:

1. Cash shown as deposited in the depositor's books has not yet been added to the bank account by the bank. Such deposits generally reflect what are called **deposits in transit** (deposits that were either deposited late in the day on the last day of the month or mailed to the bank but not recorded by the bank at the time the bank statement was prepared).
2. Amounts deducted from cash on the depositor's books have not yet been deducted from the bank account balance by the bank. The most common example is **outstanding checks** (checks written by the depositor that have not yet cleared the bank).
3. Amounts added to the depositor's bank account by the bank and not yet recorded on the depositor's books, for example, a note or other receivable collected by the bank on behalf of the depositor and credited directly to the depositor's bank account.
4. Amounts deducted from the depositor's account by the bank but not yet recorded on the depositor's books, for example, service charges, check-printing charges, and NSF checks.
5. Either the depositor or the bank (or both) might make errors in recording cash transactions or in the running balance.

Procedures for Locating Reconciling Items. The following steps are generally followed in order to locate reconciling items, such as those listed above, and determine the correct cash balance:

1. The individual deposits listed on the bank statement are compared with those recorded on the depositor's books. Any errors are identified and listed for cor-

Figure 8-2
Bank Statement

UNITED AMERICAN BANK
Century City, California

STATEMENT OF ACCOUNT WITH:

American Precision Metals
8590 S. Strane Avenue
Century City, California

Account No.

0542-87-1156

Page

1

Period Covered

6/1/92 to 6/30/92

| Date | Checks/Debits | | Deposits/Credits | Balance |
	Check No.	Amount		
5/31				6,391.23
6/2	2016	489.75		
	2017	328.77		
	2018	274.44	1,459.28	6,757.55
6/5	2019	741.33		
	2020	576.90	927.63	6,366.95
6/9	2021	99.65		
	2022	297.59		
	2023	1,147.20	1,299.51	6,122.02
6/15	2024	55.08		
	2025	176.72		
		134.67 NSF	816.81	6,572.36
6/22	2026	191.91		6,380.45
6/27	2028	469.95		
	2030	185.47	922.32	6,647.35
6/29	2033	296.31		6,351.04
6/30		12.75 SC	1,800.00 CM	8,138.29

| Beginning Balance | Debits | | Credits | | Current Balance |
	No.	Amount	No.	Amount	
6,391.23	16	5,478.49	6	7,225.55	8,138.29

SYMBOLS:	DM = Debit Memo	CM = Credit Memo
	NSF = Nonsufficient Funds	SC = Service Charge

rection. Any deposits unrecorded by the bank are listed so they can be added to the bank statement balance on the reconciliation.

2. The amounts of the individual checks paid by the bank as listed on the bank statement are compared with the amounts listed on the depositor's records. (If the canceled checks are returned to the depositor, they may be placed in numerical order and their amounts compared with the amounts listed on the depositor's records.) Any errors are identified and listed for correction. Issued checks that have not yet cleared the bank are listed so they can be deducted from the bank balance on the reconciliation as outstanding checks.

3. Any debit or credit memos included with the bank statement are identified so they can be deducted from or added to the book balance as reconciling items. (The depositor must also prepare journal entries that correspond to these items.)

4. The bank is notified of errors in its records so that bank employees can make appropriate adjustments to the bank account. Errors discovered in the depositor's own records are corrected by preparing appropriate journal entries.

Bank Reconciliation Illustration. To illustrate the bank reconciliation process, assume that American Precision Metals received the bank statement presented in Figure 8-2. The bank statement shows a bank balance of $8,138.29 on June 30, 1992. Assume the cash balance shown on American Precision's books is $6,323.76. The following differences between the bank statement and American Precision's cash records were identified while applying the procedures for locating reconciling items described earlier.

1. A deposit in the amount of $820.31 was placed in the night depository at the bank by American Precision's cashier on the evening of June 30. (This was not shown on the bank statement because it was received too late.)
2. Checks issued and recorded by American Precision that were not returned with the bank statement were:

Check No.	Amount
2027	$142.00
2029	262.25
2031	153.93
2032	59.37
2034	324.71
Total	$942.26

(These checks were not returned with the bank statement because the bank had not yet received them.)
3. Two debit memos were included with the bank statement:
    a. One debit memo, in the amount of $134.67, represented a check received from a customer (Jerry Franklin) and deposited by American Precision that was returned for lack of sufficient funds in Jerry Franklin's account.
    b. The second debit memo, amounting to $12.75, represented bank service charges for the month of June.
4. A credit memo included with the bank statement indicated that the bank had collected a noninterest-bearing note receivable for American Precision in the amount of $1,830. The bank charged a collection fee of $30 and credited the remaining $1,800 to American Precision's account.
5. Comparison of the checks clearing the bank with the accounting records showed that check number 2024 in the amount of $55.08, in payment for the purchase of office supplies, had been incorrectly entered in the cash disbursements journal as $95.08, thereby producing an understatement of the Cash account of $40.

The bank reconciliation for American Precision Metals as of June 30 is shown in Figure 8-3.

Note that the correct cash balance of $8,016.34 is different from both the balance on the bank statement and the balance in American Precision's general ledger Cash account. After the bank records the deposit in transit and the outstanding checks clear, the bank records will show the correct balance of $8,016.34. In order to adjust American Precision's cash balance to the correct amount, either several individual journal entries or one composite entry must be prepared for those reconciling items made to

Figure 8-3
Bank Reconciliation

```
                        AMERICAN PRECISION METALS
                            Bank Reconciliation
                              June 30, 1992


Balance per bank statement                                    $8,138.29
Add: Deposit in transit (Item 1)                                 820.31
                                                               8,958.60
Deduct: Outstanding checks (Item 2)                              942.26
Adjusted Bank Balance                                         $8,016.34


Balance per books                                             $6,323.76
Add: Proceeds from note collected, less
        collection fee ($1,830 − $30) (Item 4)   $1,800.00
     Error in recording Check No. 2024 (Item 5)      40.00     1,840.00
                                                               8,163.76


Deduct: NSF check–Jerry Franklin (Item 3a)         134.67
        Bank service charge (Item 3b)               12.75       147.42
Adjusted Book Balance                                         $8,016.34
```

the book balance on the bank reconciliation. Individual entries might be made as follows:

June	30	Cash	1,800.00	
		Miscellaneous Expense	30.00	
		Notes Receivable		1,830.00
		To record the collection of a note by the		
		bank, less collection fee.		
	30	Cash	40.00	
		Office Supplies Inventory		40.00
		To record correction of Check 2024.		
	30	Accounts Receivable–J. Franklin	134.67	
		Cash		134.67
		To set up NSF check as a receivable.		
	30	Miscellaneous Expense	12.75	
		Cash		12.75
		To record bank service charge for June.		

However, the adjustments to the accounting records are generally accomplished by one combined entry such as the following:

June	30	Cash	1,692.58	
		Miscellaneous Expense	42.75	
		Accounts Receivable–J. Franklin	134.67	
		Notes Receivable		1,830.00
		Office Supplies Inventory		40.00
		To record bank reconciliation items for		
		June.		

After this entry has been posted, the Cash account will have a balance of $8,016.34 as indicated below:

Cash

Balance before adjustment	6,323.76
Adjustment	1,692.58
6/30 Balance	8,016.34

The account balance now agrees with the adjusted book balance on the bank reconciliation. This balance, plus the balance in the petty cash fund, is the amount that should be reported as cash in the June 30, 1992 balance sheet.

TEMPORARY INVESTMENTS IN MARKETABLE SECURITIES

**Objective 5:
Accounting for
temporary marketable securities**

Companies often have cash that is not needed immediately but will be needed later for current operating purposes. To obtain revenue from dividends, interest, and market appreciation, this excess cash may be invested in marketable securities, such as stocks and bonds of corporations, U.S. government securities (U.S. treasury bills or treasury bonds), or bank certificates of deposit.

Marketable securities held as investments are classified as either temporary (short-term) investments or as long-term investments. Classification is determined on the basis of marketability and the length of time management intends to hold the securities. To be classified as temporary, the securities must be both readily marketable and intended to be held for a short time.

Marketability means that the security is traded regularly on an organized market, such as the New York Stock Exchange, so that there is a continuous market available. The holding period is short-term if management intends to convert the securities into cash within the normal operating cycle or one year, whichever is longer. If management intends to hold the securities for a long period, then the securities are considered long-term investments. Long-term investments are discussed in Chapter 14.

Securities may be purchased directly from the issuer (e.g., when an investor purchases a new issue of treasury bills from the U.S. government). However, many securities are purchased from other investors through brokers who charge a commission (generally some percentage of the value of the transaction) for their services. Brokers are normally employees of brokerage firms such as Merrill Lynch or Paine Webber. Brokers act as agents since they buy and sell stocks and bonds for their clients through securities exchanges such as the New York and American Stock Exchanges.

Millions of securities are traded each weekday. A record of these transactions is reported daily in the financial pages of many newspapers. Stock prices are quoted in terms of dollars and fractions of dollars, with 1/8 of a dollar normally being the minimum fraction. Thus, a quote of 35 3/8 means that the security has a value of $35.375 per share and a stock quoted at 102 1/2 means the security has a price of $102.50. Bond prices are quoted as a percentage of the bond's par value. Therefore, a quote of 98 1/4 means that a $1,000 par value bond has a market value of $982.50 ($1,000 × 98.25%).

REPORTING TEMPORARY INVESTMENTS IN MARKETABLE SECURITIES

Since temporary securities are readily marketable, they can be converted to cash on short notice and are often considered to be as liquid as cash itself. Consequently, they are reported on the balance sheet as current assets included with cash or immediately after cash. For example, the 1989 annual report for General Mills, Inc. shows cash and short-term investments as follows:

(Millions of Dollars)

Current Assets:
   Cash and short-term
     investments $10.6

In contrast, Ford Motor Company reports its temporary investments separately in its 1989 annual report as:

(Millions of Dollars)

Current Assets:
   Cash and cash equivalents $4,045.3
   Marketable securities, at cost
     which approximates market   1,680.2

ACCOUNTING FOR MARKETABLE SECURITIES PORTFOLIOS

As mentioned earlier, marketable securities may be equity securities (capital stock of other companies), or debt securities (bonds and notes payable of other companies or governmental bodies). When a company holds shares of stock or debt securities in one or more companies, the group of equity securities is called an **equity securities portfolio,** and the group of debt securities is called a **debt securities portfolio.**

Temporary Investments in Equity Securities

A temporary investment in marketable equity securities (stocks) is recorded initially at its cost. For example, if American Precision Metals purchased as a temporary investment 7,400 shares of Crane Company capital stock for $69,000, including broker's fees, the purchase would be recorded as follows:

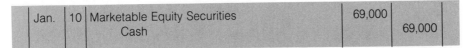

| Jan. | 10 | Marketable Equity Securities | 69,000 | |
| | | Cash | | 69,000 |

Dividends are recorded as revenue when declared since the investor has a legal claim as of the declaration date. For example, if Crane Company declared a dividend of $1 per share on August 15, American Precision would record the dividend as:

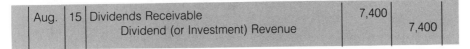

| Aug. | 15 | Dividends Receivable | 7,400 | |
| | | Dividend (or Investment) Revenue | | 7,400 |

When the dividends are received, Cash is debited and Dividends Receivable is credited. If the dividends are declared and paid during the same accounting period, many companies do not make an entry on the dividend declaration date and simply debit Cash and credit Dividend Revenue when the dividend check is received.

If all or part of the investment is sold, the cost of the shares sold is removed from the Marketable Equity Securities account and the difference between this cost and the selling price of the securities is recognized as a realized gain or loss. For example, if

American Precision sold one-half of the Crane Company shares for $42,500 (net of broker's fees), the following entry would be made:

Oct.	9	Cash	42,500	
		Marketable Equity Securities		
		(1/2 × $69,000)		34,500
		Gain on Sale of Investments		8,000

Lower of Cost or Market for Marketable Equity Securities

The temporary equity securities portfolio is reported on the balance sheet at the lower of its aggregate cost or aggregate market value at the balance sheet date.[1] For example, assume that American Precision Metals had the following temporary stock portfolio on December 31, 1992:

Stock Investment	Cost	Market
Blair Company	$ 33,000	$ 27,000
Crane Company	69,000	73,500
Even Company	52,500	52,500
Grow Company	121,500	105,000
Totals	$276,000	$258,000

Because the market value of the portfolio is $18,000 less than its cost, an $18,000 loss has been incurred and the portfolio must be reported in the balance sheet at its lower market value of $258,000. To record the loss and reduce the marketable securities to their market value, an entry is made as follows:

Dec.	31	Unrealized Loss on Marketable Equity		
		Securities	18,000	
		Allowance to Reduce Marketable Equity		
		Securities to Market Value		18,000

Although the loss is unrealized because the securities have not been sold, it must be deducted on the income statement. Large losses are reported as a separate item in determining income from operations. Small losses are normally included in the "other expense" category.

The Allowance to Reduce Marketable Equity Securities to Market Value is a contra asset account. It is deducted from the cost of the marketable securities on the balance sheet as follows:

Current Assets:
Cash $187,500
Marketable equity securities $276,000
Less: Allowance to reduce marketable
        equity securities to market value   18,000   258,000

Reporting in this way discloses both the cost of the marketable equity securities and their current market value to statement users.

If the market value of the portfolio is greater than cost, the unrealized gain is not

---

[1]Statement of Financial Accounting Standards No. 12, "Accounting for Certain Marketable Securities" (Stamford, Conn.: FASB, 1975), par. 8.

recorded and the marketable securities are reported at their cost with market value disclosed parenthetically or in a footnote. This treatment is consistent with the accounting convention of ***conservatism***, under which gains are not recognized until realized by a sale but losses are recognized when there is evidence of probable incurrence.

If the portfolio's total market value in a subsequent period is higher than its carrying value (cost minus Allowance account), an unrealized loss recovery (sometimes called "unrealized gain") is recognized up to the amount in the Allowance account and included in net income of that period. Thus, when the temporary marketable equity securities portfolio has been written down to its market value, it may be written back up to its original cost only. In other words, the Allowance account is adjusted upward and downward so that the Allowance account balance equals the excess of cost over market value of the portfolio on the balance sheet date. For example, if the portfolio had a market value of $270,000 at the end of 1993, the following entry would be made:

| Dec. | 31 | Allowance to Reduce Marketable Equity Securities to Market Value | 12,000 | |
| | | Unrealized Loss Recovery | | 12,000 |

Note that the lower of cost or market method is applied using the portfolio's total cost and total market value rather than on an item-by-item basis. It is also important to understand that a portfolio of temporary equity securities may be on hand at the end of every fiscal period. However, the individual securities held in the portfolio change over time as some are sold to obtain cash and others are purchased later as temporary cash investments.

Temporary Investments in Debt Securities

A temporary investment in debt securities is recorded at its cost, including broker's fees. For example, the purchase of U.S. Treasury Notes for $52,600 plus a broker's fee of $700 is recorded as follows:

| Jan. | 9 | Temporary Investment in Debt Securities | 53,300 | |
| | | Cash | | 53,300 |

These securities are normally reported on the balance sheet at their cost. However, some companies report them at the lower of cost or market for consistency with accounting for equity securities. In any event, if the market value of the securities is substantially less than their cost and the decline in market value is not due to a temporary condition, the investment should be reported at its market value.[2]

The write-down to market value is recorded by a debit to a Loss on Temporary Investments account, which is reported as a loss in the income statement, and a credit to the Temporary Investment in Debt Securities account. Later recoveries in market value are not recognized, because the balance remaining in the account is considered to be a new substituted cost. Interest revenue on debt securities is accrued as earned (discussed later in this chapter in the section on notes receivable).

---

[2]Accounting Research Bulletin No. 43, "Restatement and Revision of Accounting Research Bulletins" (New York: AICPA, 1953), Ch. 3A, par. 9.

RECEIVABLES

Receivables are amounts due from other persons or businesses. Although arising from various business transactions, receivables most often result from the sale of goods or services on credit. There are two main kinds of receivables:

- **Accounts receivable:** When credit is extended to customers on open account, which means that the buyer has a specified length of time such as 30 or 60 days before payment is due, the receivables are called accounts receivable.
- **Notes Receivable (promissory notes):** Sometimes credit is granted only upon receipt of a formal legal instrument such as a promissory note. A promissory note is a negotiable instrument. A **negotiable instrument** is a legal document that can be transferred to a third party by endorsement. An **endorsement** is a signature on the back of the instrument that assigns the rights therein to another party. To the grantor of credit, the promissory note is a note receivable. Creditors often favor promissory notes because (1) they are generally interest-bearing (thereby producing interest revenue) and (2) they are more easily converted into cash than are accounts receivable before their maturity date by transferring them by endorsement to a bank or finance company. Promissory notes are often demanded by creditors when customers request extensions of payment of open accounts receivable.

CLASSIFICATION OF RECEIVABLES

Objective 6: Types of receivables

Accounts and notes receivable that arise from the sale of merchandise or services in the normal course of business are called **trade receivables**. They are normally classified as current assets on the balance sheet because they are scheduled for collection in cash within the normal operating cycle. Other receivables, such as those from officers and employees for loans or salary advances, and from the sale of nonmerchandise assets, are called *nontrade receivables*. They are considered current assets if they are to be collected within one year or within the normal operating cycle; otherwise they are classified as noncurrent assets.

To facilitate the proper classification of receivables, a general ledger account should be used for each type. Subsidiary ledgers should be provided where needed.

ACCOUNTS RECEIVABLE

Accounts receivable arise from the sale of goods or services on open account. Although businesses would prefer to collect the sales price at the time of sale, experience has shown that extending credit can sometimes significantly increase revenue and net income. To accomplish an increase in net income, however, the additional gross profit generated by credit sales must exceed the additional expenses incurred in extending credit. These expenses include investigation of the creditworthiness of prospective customers, additional recordkeeping, and a provision for uncollectible accounts.

No business wants to extend credit to a customer who is unlikely to pay the account when due. Therefore, most large companies maintain a credit department. The credit department has responsibility for investigating the credit history and determining the debt-paying ability of customers who apply for credit. If the customer is a business, the credit department normally requests a set of its audited financial statements for use in judging its ability to pay. If the customer is an individual, the credit department will ask for information about current earnings, outstanding debts, and general financial position. In addition, the credit department normally obtains a credit report from a local or national credit-rating agency, such as Dun and Bradstreet, that accumulates data on the credit history of individuals and businesses.

Uncollectible Accounts

Regardless of the diligence exercised in extending credit, there are always some customers who do not pay their accounts. Business managers know that some of the resulting accounts receivable eventually will prove to be uncollectible when they make the decision to sell goods and services on credit. These uncollectible accounts (often called **bad debts**) are considered an expense of doing business on a credit basis.

The *matching principle* requires that the expense of uncollectible accounts be deducted in the same accounting period in which the credit sales were recognized. This is difficult because receivables recorded in one accounting period may not become uncollectible until a later accounting period. Since there is no way of telling in advance which accounts will become uncollectible, bad debts expense is estimated at the end of the accounting period by the allowance method of accounting for uncollectible accounts.

Allowance Method of Accounting for Uncollectible Accounts

At the end of the accounting period, before the books are closed and the financial statements prepared, an estimate is made of the amount of accounts receivable expected to become uncollectible. An adjusting entry is prepared with a debit to Bad Debts Expense and a credit to Allowance for Uncollectible Accounts.

To illustrate, assume that Dome Company began operations in January 1992, made credit sales amounting to $600,000 during 1992, and collected $450,000 of these accounts during the year. The balance in the Accounts Receivable account at the end of the year is therefore $150,000. After a careful review of the accounts receivable, management of Dome Company estimated that $8,000 of the accounts will be uncollectible. An adjusting entry is made on December 31, 1992, the end of the fiscal year for Dome Company, as follows:

| Dec. | 31 | Bad Debts Expense | 8,000 | |
| | | Allowance for Uncollectible Accounts | | 8,000 |

This entry serves two important purposes: (1) It records the estimated bad debts of $8,000 as an expense of the period in which the revenue from credit sales was recognized. Thus, bad debts expense will be deducted in the income statement for 1992, thereby properly matching expenses and revenues. (2) The entry establishes an Allowance account that is deducted from Accounts Receivable on the balance sheet in order to report accounts receivable at their estimated collectible (realizable) value.

Rather than crediting Accounts Receivable directly when recording the entry for estimated bad debts, the Allowance account is credited. This is because the general ledger Accounts Receivable account is a control account supported by a subsidiary ledger that identifies the amounts owed by individual customers. Any debit or credit to the Accounts Receivable control account requires a like debit or credit to one of the subsidiary-ledger accounts. But it is impossible to determine in advance which specific accounts will prove uncollectible. A direct credit to the Accounts Receivable control account would produce an imbalance between it and the accounts receivable subsidiary ledger, thereby destroying an important element of internal control. The alternative is to credit an Allowance account (contra asset account) that is subtracted from accounts receivable on the balance sheet. This results in the reporting of accounts receivable at the estimated amount expected to be collected (the expected realizable value of accounts receivable) as shown below:

Current Assets:		
Cash		$ 97,450
Accounts receivable	$150,000	
Less: Allowance for uncollectible accounts	8,000	142,000
Inventory		106,500
Total current assets		345,950

Estimating the Amount of Bad Debts Expense

The estimate of the amount of bad debts is generally based on a combination of past experience and best-guess forecast of future economic and business conditions. Considerable personal judgment is involved. The goal is to produce a reasonable estimate of the amount of accounts receivable that eventually will be collected in cash.

Two methods are widely used to estimate bad debts expense. One method determines the amount as a percentage of net credit sales for the period. Because the net credit sales amount is used as a base, it is sometimes called the *income statement method*. The method places emphasis on the relationship between credit sales and uncollectible accounts. Therefore, it is more in accordance with the *matching principle*.

The second method analyzes the age and probability of collection of the individual accounts and is called *aging the accounts receivable*. Since this method bases bad debts expense on an analysis of accounts receivable, it is often called the *balance sheet method*. Emphasis is placed on the realizable value of accounts receivable on the balance sheet. Most firms will use either of these two methods, but not both.

Estimate Based on the Income Statement Method. An analysis of past accounting data usually shows some predictable percentage relationship between the amount of bad debts and the amount of net credit sales. This percentage is then applied to net credit sales for the period to estimate the amount of bad debts expense. The logic of this method is that credit sales produce the accounts receivable that may become uncollectible in the future. For example, assume that past experience shows that about 1% of net credit sales each year have been uncollectible and that net credit sales for the year amounted to $986,000. The year-end adjustment to recognize bad debts expense would be:

Dec.	31	Bad Debts Expense	9,860	
		Allowance for Uncollectible Accounts		9,860

Under this method, any existing balance in the Allowance for Uncollectible Accounts is ignored in computing the amount of bad debts expense. Basically, this method answers the question, "How much of this year's net credit sales is expected to be uncollectible?" The Allowance for Uncollectible Accounts is then adjusted by that amount.

Estimate Based on the Balance Sheet Method. If the estimate of bad debts expense is based on an analysis of accounts receivable, the estimate is normally derived from a schedule that classifies and analyzes accounts receivable by age. The older an account receivable, the greater the probability that it will be uncollectible. Past accounting records are therefore analyzed to determine the approximate percentage of each age group that will become uncollectible. For example, assume that an analysis of past accounting records shows the following percentages of accounts receivable that were written off as uncollectible:

Age Category	Percent
Not yet due	1%
1 to 30 days past due	4%
31 to 90 days past due	10%
91 to 180 days past due	40%
Over 180 days past due	70%

An aging of the December 31, 1992 balance in Accounts Receivable produced the following results:

Accounts Receivable Balance	Not Yet Due	Number of Days Past Due			
		1–30	31–90	91–180	Over 180
$92,100	$72,500	$9,700	$4,600	$3,200	$2,100

With these data, the balance needed in the Allowance for Uncollectible Accounts to reduce the accounts receivable to their estimated realizable value is computed as follows:

Age Category	Accounts Receivable Amount	Estimated Uncollectibles	
		Percent	Amount
Not yet due	$72,500	1%	$ 725
1–30 days past due	9,700	4%	388
31–90 days past due	4,600	10%	460
91–180 days past due	3,200	40%	1,280
Over 180 days past due	2,100	70%	1,470
Totals	$92,100		$4,323

The total determined ($4,323) is the balance needed in the Allowance for Uncollectible Accounts. Consequently, any existing balance in the Allowance account must be taken into consideration in determining the amount of the year-end adjustment. For example, if the Allowance for Uncollectible Accounts has a $1,215 credit balance before adjustment, Bad Debts Expense must be charged for the difference of $3,108 ($4,323 − $1,215) and the following adjusting entry prepared:

Dec.	31	Bad Debts Expense	3,108	
		Allowance for Uncollectible Accounts		3,108

After this entry is posted, the Accounts Receivable and Allowance for Uncollectible Accounts will appear as follows:

Accounts Receivable

12/31 Balance	92,100	

Allowance for Uncollectible Accounts

		12/31 Balance before adjustment	1,215
		12/31 Adjustment	3,108
		12/31 Balance	4,323

The Allowance for Uncollectible Accounts may sometimes have a debit balance at year-end because more accounts than estimated actually became uncollectible. If the Allowance for Uncollectible Accounts had a debit balance (for example, $365) before adjustment, that balance would be added to the $4,323 and the total of $4,688 would be debited to Bad Debts Expense and credited to Allowance for Uncollectible Accounts to produce the desired balance of $4,323 in the Allowance account.

Short-Cut Balance Sheet Approach. Rather than preparing an aging schedule, some companies simply analyze past data to determine a percentage relationship between uncollectible accounts and accounts receivable. This percentage is multiplied times the balance in Accounts Receivable at the end of the year to determine the balance needed in the Allowance for Uncollectible Accounts. The Allowance account is then adjusted to that balance by an entry debiting Bad Debts Expense and crediting Allowance for Uncollectible Accounts.

Writing Off an Uncollectible Account

When an account receivable is determined to be uncollectible, it is written off against the Allowance for Uncollectible Accounts by debiting the Allowance account and crediting Accounts Receivable. The related account in the accounts receivable subsidiary ledger is also credited. For example, assume that after an extended effort to collect, the $524 account of B.C. Craft is determined to be uncollectible. The following entry would be made:

Dec.	31	Allowance for Uncollectible Accounts	524	
		Accounts Receivable—B.C. Craft		524

Two important things should be noted concerning this entry: (1) The write-off is debited to the Allowance for Uncollectible Accounts rather than to Bad Debts Expense. Expense was recognized on an estimated basis in the year in which the sale was made. To charge an expense account again at the time the account is written off would result in a double recording of expense. (2) The net amount of accounts receivable is unchanged by the entry to write off an uncollectible account. After the write-off entry is posted, the general ledger accounts would appear as follows:

Accounts Receivable

12/31 Balance before write-off	92,100	12/31 Write-off	524
Balance	91,576		

Allowance for Uncollectible Accounts

12/31 Write-off	524	12/31 Balance before write-off	4,323
		Balance	3,799

Note that the estimated realizable value of accounts receivable is the same both before and after the write-off:

	Before Write-off	After Write-off
Accounts receivable	$92,100	$91,576
Less: Allowance for uncollectible accounts	4,323	3,799
Estimated realizable value	$87,777	$87,777

The fact that the write-off did not change the net amount of accounts receivable clearly demonstrates that no expense results from the write-off of an account receivable. The expense from uncollectible accounts is properly charged to the period in which the credit sale was made rather than to the period in which the account is written off.

NOTES RECEIVABLE

Sometimes, credit is extended only upon receipt of a promissory note, often referred to simply as a *note*. A **promissory note** is an unconditional written promise to pay a sum of money on demand or at a future determinable date. The person making the promise to pay by signing the note is called the **maker** of the note. The person to whom payment is to be made is called the **payee**.

If the note bears interest, it is called an *interest-bearing note*. The interest rate must be stipulated. If no interest rate is stipulated, the note is called a *noninterest-bearing note*. **Interest** is a charge made for the use of money. To the payee, interest is revenue; to the maker of the note it is an expense. The amount printed on the note is called its **principal** or **face value**. The amount due on the maturity date of the note is called the **maturity value**. The maturity value of a short-term interest-bearing note is the sum of its principal plus interest. The maturity value of a noninterest-bearing note is its face value.

Computing the Amount of Interest

The formula for computing the amount of interest is:

Principal × Rate × Time = Interest

Objective 8:
Computing and accounting for interest

Interest rates are normally stated in terms of a period of one year. Thus, a $1,000, 14% note receivable would earn interest of $140 each year. If the term of the note is expressed in days, the exact number of days should be used to compute interest. For convenience, however, it is generally assumed that a year contains 360 days. Thus, if the $1,000 note above was a 90-day note, interest would be:

$1,000 × 14% × 90/360 = $35

On the maturity date of the note, the payee would receive $1,035.

If the term of the note is expressed in months, each month (regardless of the number of days in it) is considered to be 1/12 of a year. Thus, a three-month note dated June 6 is due on September 6, and a four-month note dated February 28 is due on June 30. Interest on a $3,000, 12%, three-month note is $90 ($3,000 × 12% × 3/12).

Accounting for Notes Receivable

Some companies, particularly manufacturing and wholesale firms that sell in large quantities, often request a note from a buyer who asks for credit. Other companies, such as retail firms, may receive notes only occasionally. However, some retailers, for example, those selling high-priced items on an installment plan under which the buyer makes a down payment and gives a note (or a series of notes with different maturity dates) for the balance, use notes on a regular basis. Firms that regularly sell goods on open account are sometimes asked for an extension of credit beyond the normal due date. In these cases, the company often requires that the customer give it an interest-bearing note to replace the account receivable.

To illustrate the accounting for a note receivable, assume that Blair Company sold merchandise to Dix Company for $6,000 and received a 14%, 60-day note in payment. Blair Company would make the following entry:

| Mar. | 16 | Notes Receivable | 6,000 | |
| | | Sales | | 6,000 |

If the note had been received to extend the payment of an open account receivable, the credit in the entry above would have been to Accounts Receivable rather than Sales.

On the due date, when Dix Company paid the note, Blair Company would make the following entry:

May	15	Cash	6,140	
		Notes Receivable		6,000
		Interest Revenue		140
		($6,000 × 14% × 60/360 = $140)		

If the maturity date of the note extended beyond the end of Blair Company's fiscal year, an adjusting entry to accrue interest revenue would be needed at year-end as explained in Chapter 4.

Dishonored Note Receivable

If the maker of a note fails to pay on the maturity date, the note is said to have been dishonored and the maker is said to have *defaulted* on the note. Because the maturity date has passed, the note is no longer negotiable. The maker, however, is not relieved from legal responsibility for the debt, and the payee will make the normal effort to collect.

The payee generally transfers the claim, including any interest due, to an Accounts Receivable account. For example, if Dix Company failed to pay the above note on its maturity date, the entry on Blair Company's books would be:

May	15	Accounts Receivable	6,140	
		Notes Receivable		6,000
		Interest Revenue		140

This entry removes the note from the Notes Receivable account and establishes an account receivable from Dix Company. The Notes Receivable account will then contain only those notes that have not yet matured. Note that the account receivable includes the interest on the note, which was credited to Interest Revenue even though it has not yet been collected. Dix Company's obligation to Blair Company is for the maturity value of the note—principal and interest—and its account should contain the full amount owed.

Discounting a Note Receivable

One of the positive features of a note receivable is its relative ease of conversion to cash before its maturity date. The note may be endorsed by the payee and sold to a bank in exchange for cash. The bank then holds the note until its maturity date when it expects to collect the maturity value from its maker.

This process is called *discounting a note receivable* because the bank will deduct in advance an interest charge called a **discount.** The discount is based on the maturity value of the note for the period the bank will hold the note (the **discount period** The discount period is the time between the date the note is transferred to the bank and its due date. The maturity value of the note less the discount deducted are the **proceeds.** The proceeds are paid to the endorser by the bank.

The bank normally computes discount to the nearest day, including the day of maturity, but excluding the date the note is discounted. Thus, the Dix Company note dated March 16 would have a maturity date of May 15 computed as follows:

Term of note in days		60
Number of days in March	31	
Date of note, March 16	16	
Number of days outstanding in March		15
Days remaining		45
Number of days in April		30
Due date in May		15

Assuming the note is discounted at a bank on April 5, the discount period is computed as follows:

Days remaining in April (30 − 5)	25
Days in May to maturity date	15
Discount period in days	40

To illustrate, assume that the $6,000, 14%, 60-day note received from Dix Company was held by Blair Company until April 5 when it was sold to a bank at a discount rate of 16%. The bank will charge interest (discount) at 16% on the maturity value of the note. Thus, the bank will charge 16% interest for 40 days, and give Blair Company the cash proceeds computed as follows:

Face value of the note	$6,000
Interest at 14% for 60 days ($6,000 × 14% × 60/360)	140
Maturity value	6,140
Less: Discount at 16% for 40 days ($6,140 × 16% × 40/360)	109*
Proceeds	$6,031

*Rounded to the nearest dollar.

The sale of the note is recorded by Blair Company as follows:

Apr.	5	Cash	6,031	
		Notes Receivable		6,000
		Interest Revenue		31

The excess of the proceeds received over the face value of the note is recorded as interest revenue. It represents the amount of interest Blair Company would have earned if it had held the note to maturity ($140) less the amount deducted as discount by the bank when it purchased the note ($109). In this case, the proceeds exceed the face value of the note, resulting in interest revenue. If the proceeds are less than the face value, the difference is debited to Interest Expense.

Contingent Liability. A discounted note must be endorsed by the payee. The payee then becomes contingently liable for payment of the note unless the endorsement is made without recourse—that is, contains the words "without recourse" as part of the endorsement. *Without recourse* means that the endorser cannot be held liable if the maker of the note defaults. Because banks will seldom accept without recourse notes, the payee-endorser of most discounted notes has a contingent liability.

Contingent liability means that the endorser (Blair Company in our illustration) must pay the maturity value of the note on its maturity date if the maker (Dix Company) fails to do so. The discounting of the note therefore creates a contingent liability for Blair Company that continues until the due date of the note. If the maker pays the note, the contingent liability ceases. If the maker defaults, the contingent liability becomes an actual, that is, real liability for Blair Company, and Blair Company must pay the note.

The nature and amount of any contingent liability must be disclosed in the financial statements. Consequently, the contingent liability for notes receivable discounted must be disclosed if a balance sheet is prepared earlier than the maturity date of the notes. Disclosure is normally made in a "contingencies" footnote to the financial statements that explains the nature of various contingent liabilities. For example, PepsiCo, Inc. included the following footnote in its 1989 annual report:

Contingencies

PepsiCo is involved in various claims and legal proceedings, the resolution of which management believes will not have a material effect on PepsiCo's business or financial condition. PepsiCo intends to prosecute or defend vigorously, as the case may be, all such matters.

At year-end 1989 PepsiCo was contingently liable under direct and indirect guarantees aggregating $65 million.

SUMMARY

In this chapter, the nature and balance sheet reporting of liquid assets, such as cash, temporary investments in marketable securities, and receivables, have been discussed. Because cash is the asset most subject to manipulation, it is important to provide a good internal control system for handling cash and cash transactions. Adequate control includes (1) the control of both cash receipts and cash disbursements, (2) the separation of responsibility for handling and custodianship of cash from the responsibility for maintaining cash records, (3) the use of bank reconciliations, and (4) the use of a petty cash fund.

Wise cash management includes the temporary investment of excess cash in marketable securities. Marketability and management's intent to hold the securities for a short time are the requirements for reporting the investments as temporary ones in the current asset section of the balance sheet. Temporary securities are usually grouped into an equity securities portfolio and a debt securities portfolio. The equity securities portfolio is accounted for at the lower of its aggregate cost or aggregate market value. The debt securities portfolio is accounted for at either its cost or the lower of aggregate cost or aggregate market value.

Receivables include trade receivables (notes and accounts receivable arising from normal operating activities) and nontrade receivables (receivables due from officers and employees, and from the sale of nonmerchandise assets). Trade receivables are reported at their estimated realizable (collectible) value by subtracting the Allowance for Uncollectible Accounts from the gross amount of trade receivables. Bad debts expense is estimated and charged to expense in the same accounting period that the credit sales are recognized.

Notes receivable, generally earning interest, are often obtained by businesses from credit sales or from the extension of the due date of an open account receivable. These notes may be held to maturity or, alternatively, they may be discounted (sold) at a bank to receive cash. Discounted notes represent contingent liabilities until they are settled.

SELF-TEST

Test your understanding of the chapter by selecting the best answer for each of the following.

1. Barney Company uses the allowance method of accounting for bad debts. Writing off an uncollectible account receivable will:
   a. increase the net account receivable balance.
   b. decrease the net account receivable balance.
   c. have no effect on the net account receivable balance.
   d. increase bad debts expense for the current accounting period.
2. The Allowance for Uncollectible Accounts should be reported on the balance sheet as a(an):
   a. liability.
   b. asset.
   c. contra-asset.
   d. contra-liability.
3. A temporary marketable equity securities portfolio should be reported on the balance sheet at the:
   a. higher of total portfolio cost or total portfolio market value.
   b. lower of total portfolio cost or total portfolio market value.
   c. market value of the portfolio.
   d. cost of the portfolio.
4. Baker corporation had the following balances at year-end:

Checking account balance	$17,600
Cash on hand	2,100
Petty cash	500

   What amount of cash should be reported on the year-end balance sheet?
   a. $2,600.
   b. $18,100.
   c. $19,700.
   d. $20,200.

5. Which of the following bank reconciliation items requires a journal entry on the books of the depositor?
   a. Bank service charge.
   b. Deposit in transit.
   c. Outstanding checks.
   d. Recording error by the bank.

6. Which of the following statements is true regarding a petty cash system?
   a. The petty cash account is debited only when the fund is replenished.
   b. The cash account is debited only when the fund is established.
   c. Small payments are made out of cash receipts before they are deposited.
   d. No entry is made in the petty cash account when the fund is replenished unless the size of the fund is increased or decreased.

7. If the stated rate of interest on a note is less than the market rate of interest, the face amount of the note will be:
   a. equal to the present value of the note.
   b. less than the present value of the note.
   c. greater than the present value of the note.
   d. equal to the fair value of the goods or services given or received in the exchange transaction.

8. A bank statement shows a cash balance of $1,000. The company's cash account for the same date shows a balance of $886. The following information is needed to reconcile the bank statement:

Deposit in transit	$200
Outstanding checks	350
NSF check	30
Service charge for the month	6

What is the correct balance for cash to be reported in the balance sheet?
   a. $820.
   b. $850.
   c. $856.
   d. $886.

9. An NSF check returned by the bank should be recorded on the depositor's books as a:
   a. debit to Cash.
   b. debit to Accounts Receivable.
   c. debit to Cash Short and Over.
   d. credit to Cash Short and Over.

REVIEW PROBLEM

Karen Industries, a calendar year corporation, follows a policy of investing idle cash in equity securities as short-term investments. A cash budget, prepared monthly, provides information that Karen's management uses to ascertain the amount of cash available and the time period for which it will be available to use for short-term investments in marketable equity securities.

On January 1, 1992, Karen Industries had no short-term investments. Transactions completed during 1992 and 1993 by Karen's management regarding their investments in marketable equity securities were:

<u>1992</u>

Mar. 2 Purchased 5,000 shares of Brady Company capital stock for $12 per share, plus a broker's fee of $1,800.

May 4 Purchased 10,000 shares of Warwick Corporation capital stock for $4 per share, plus a broker's fee of $1,200.

June 15 Sold the Brady Company capital stock for $15 per share less a broker's fee of $2,000.

July 10 Received a $.40 per share dividend on the Warwick Corporation capital stock.

Aug. 3 Purchased 15,000 shares of Sherman Company capital stock for $5 per share plus a broker's fee of $1,500.

Sept. 1 Purchased 8,000 shares of Lancaster Industries capital stock for $10 per share, plus a broker's fee of $2,400.

Oct. 30 Received a $.50 per share dividend on the Sherman Company capital stock.

Dec. 15 Received a $1 per share dividend on the Lancaster Industries capital stock.

31 At year-end, the market prices of the securities in Karen's portfolio of marketable equity securities were:

Warwick Corporation	$3 per share
Sherman Company	6 per share
Lancaster Industries	8 per share

<u>1993</u>

Jan. 4 Sold the Warwick Corporation capital stock for $3 per share, less a broker's fee of $800.

29 Sold the Sherman Company capital stock for $7 per share, less a broker's fee of $1,500.

Mar. 3 Purchased 6,000 shares of Newton Corporation capital stock for $15 per share, plus a broker's fee of $2,500.

June 24 Received a $.50 per share dividend on the Lancaster Industries capital stock.

Aug. 2 Purchased 20,000 shares of Royal Industries capital stock for $7 per share, plus a broker's fee of $3,500.

Sept. 15 Received a $1 per share dividend on the Newton Corporation capital stock.

Oct. 31 Sold the Lancaster Industries capital stock for $10 per share, less a broker's fee of $1,800.

Dec. 12 Purchased 3,000 shares of Baker Enterprises capital stock for $20 per share, plus a broker's fee of $1,500.

30 Received a $.35 per share dividend on the Royal Industries capital stock.

31 At year-end, the market prices of the securities in Karen's portfolio of marketable equity securities were:

Newton Corporation	$12 per share
Royal Industries	8 per share
Baker Enterprises	21 per share

Required:

A. Prepare journal entries to record the transactions for 1992 and 1993, including any entry at year-end to reflect the difference between the cost and market value of the marketable equity securities portfolio.

B. Show how the marketable equity securities would be reported on Karen's 1992 and 1993 balance sheets.

C. Explain what would appear on Karen's 1992 and 1993 income statements as a result of these investments in marketable equity securities.

ANSWER TO REVIEW PROBLEM

A.

1992				
Mar.	2	Marketable Equity Securities	61,800	
		Cash		61,800
		[(5,000 × $12) + $1,800]		
May	4	Marketable Equity Securities	41,200	
		Cash		41,200
		[(10,000 × $4) + $1,200]		
June	15	Cash*	73,000	
		Marketable Equity Securities		61,800
		Gain on Sale of Securities		11,200
		*[(5,000 shares × $15) − $2,000]		
July	10	Cash	4,000	
		Dividend (or Investment) Revenue		4,000
		(10,000 × $.40)		
Aug.	3	Marketable Equity Securities	76,500	
		Cash		76,500
		[(15,000 × $5) + $1,500]		
Sept.	1	Marketable Equity Securities	82,400	
		Cash		82,400
		[(8,000 × $10) + $2,400]		
Oct.	30	Cash	7,500	
		Dividend (or Investment) Revenue		7,500
		(15,000 × $.50)		
Dec.	15	Cash	8,000	
		Dividend (or Investment) Revenue		8,000
		(8,000 × $1)		
	31	Unrealized Loss on Marketable Equity Securities	16,100	
		Allowance to Reduce Marketable Equity Securities to Market Value		16,100

Stock Investment	Shares	Cost	Market	Unrealized Gain (Loss)
Warwick Corporation	10,000	$ 41,200	$ 30,000	$(11,200)
Sherman Company	15,000	76,500	90,000	13,500
Lancaster Industries	8,000	82,400	64,000	(18,400)
Totals		$200,100	$184,000	$(16,100)

Because the market value of the portfolio is $16,100 less than its cost and the balance in the Allowance account prior to the journal entry is zero, a $16,100 unrealized loss has been incurred during 1992. The portfolio must be reported in the balance sheet at its lower market value of $184,000. The unrealized loss will be reported on the 1992 income statement.

1993					
Jan.	4	Cash*		29,200	
		Loss on Sale of Securities		12,000	
		Marketable Equity Securities			41,200
		*[(10,000 × $3) − $800]			
	29	Cash*		103,500	
		Marketable Equity Securities			76,500
		Gain on Sale of Securities			27,000
		*[(15,000 × $7) − $1,500]			
Mar.	3	Marketable Equity Securities		92,500	
		Cash			92,500
		[(6,000 × $15) + $2,500]			
June	24	Cash		4,000	
		Dividend (or Investment) Revenue			4,000
		(8,000 × $.50)			
Aug.	2	Marketable Equity Securities		143,500	
		Cash			143,500
		[(20,000 × $7) + $3,500]			
Sept.	15	Cash		6,000	
		Dividend (or Investment) Revenue			6,000
		(6,000 × $1)			
Oct.	31	Cash*		78,200	
		Loss on Sale of Securities		4,200	
		Marketable Equity Securities			82,400
		*[(8,000 × $10) − $1,800]			
Dec.	12	Marketable Equity Securities		61,500	
		Cash			61,500
		[(3,000 × $20) + $1,500]			
	30	Cash		7,000	
		Dividend (or Investment) Revenue			7,000
		(20,000 × $.35)			
	31	Allowance to Reduce Marketable Equity Securities to Market Value		13,600	
		Recovery of Unrealized Loss on Marketable Equity Securities			13,600
		($16,100 − $2,500)			

Investment	Shares	Cost	Market	Unrealized Gain (Loss)
Newton Corporation	6,000	$ 92,500	$ 72,000	$(20,500)
Royal Industries	20,000	143,500	160,000	16,500
Baker Enterprises	3,000	61,500	63,000	1,500
Totals		$297,500	$295,000	$ (2,500)

Because the market value of the portfolio is $2,500 less than its cost, the portfolio must be reported in the balance sheet at its lower market value of $295,000. The balance needed in the Allowance account is the difference between the total cost and the total market value of the portfolio, in this case, $2,500. Since the Allowance account already has a balance of $16,100—established at the end of 1992—the procedure required at the end of 1993 is to reduce the balance from $16,100 to $2,500. Therefore, the journal entry accomplishes two things: (1) It establishes the proper balance in the Allowance account at the end of 1993, and (2) It reflects the recovery in 1993 of $13,600 of the $16,100 unrealized loss, which occurred in 1992.

B.

	1992		1993	
Current Assets:				
Marketable equity securities	$200,000		$297,500	
Less: Allowance to reduce marketable equity securities to market value	16,100	$184,000	2,500	$295,000

C.

Karen Industries' 1992 income statement would contain the following items:

Other Revenue and Expense:	
Gain on sale of securities	$11,200
Dividend (or Investment) revenue	19,500
Unrealized loss on marketable equity securities	16,100

Karen's 1993 income statement would contain the following items:

Other Revenue and Expense:	
Gain on sale of securities	$10,800*
Dividend (or Investment) revenue	17,000
Recovery of unrealized loss on marketable equity securities	13,600

*Gain of $27,000 minus losses of $16,200 ($12,000 + $4,200)

ANSWERS TO SELF-TEST

1. c   **2.** c   **3.** b   **4.** d   **5.** a   **6.** d   **7.** c   **8.** b
9. b

GLOSSARY

ACCOUNT RECEIVABLE.   Amount due from a customer for sales or services performed on credit (p. 342).

BAD DEBTS.   An expense arising from an estimate of the accounts receivable that will be uncollectible (p. 343).

BANK RECONCILIATION.   A form prepared to reconcile the cash balance reported on the bank statement with the adjusted cash balance per the depositor's records (p. 334).

BANK STATEMENT.   A report prepared by the bank that provides the detail of activity that has taken place in a checking account for a period (p. 333).

CANCELED CHECK.   Check written by the depositor and paid by the bank (p. 333).

CASH.   Money and any instrument such as a check or money order that a bank will accept for immediate deposit in a bank account (p. 328).

CHECK.   Legal instrument signed by the depositor ordering the bank to pay a specified amount of money to the person or company identified on the check (p. 333).

CONTINGENT LIABILITY.   A possible liability that may become actual if certain future events occur (p. 350).

CREDIT MEMO.   A document that identifies a credit (increase) made to the depositor's account by the bank (p. 334).

DEBIT MEMO.   A document that identifies a debit (decrease) made to the depositor's account by the bank (p. 334).

DEBT SECURITIES PORTFOLIO.   A group of debt securities held by an investor (p. 339).

DEPOSITS IN TRANSIT.   Deposits recorded on the depositor's books but not yet recorded on the bank's records (p. 334).

DISCOUNT.   Interest deducted in advance (p. 349).

DISCOUNT PERIOD.   The period of time for which a bank will charge interest on a discounted note (p. 349).

DISHONORED NOTE.   A note that the maker has failed to pay on its maturity date (p. 348).

ENDORSEMENT.   A signature on the back of a negotiable instrument that assigns the rights therein to another party (p. 342).

EQUITY SECURITIES PORTFOLIO.   A group of equity securities held by an investor (p. 339).

INTEREST.   A charge made for the use of money; computed as Principal $\times$ Rate $\times$ Time (p. 347).

LIQUID ASSETS.   Assets that are in the form of cash or easily converted into cash in the near future (p. 328).

MAKER.   The person who promises to pay a note on its maturity date (p. 347).

MATURITY VALUE.   The amount due on the maturity date of a note; it includes principal and interest (p. 347).

NEGOTIABLE INSTRUMENT.   A legal document that can be transferred to another party by an endorsement (p. 342).

NONSUFFICIENT FUNDS (NSF) CHECK.   A check that was included in a depositor's deposit, but was not paid by the maker's bank because of insufficient funds (p. 334).

NOTE RECEIVABLE. A receivable evidenced by a formal written promise to pay (p. 342).

OUTSTANDING CHECK. Check written by a depositor that has not yet cleared the bank (p. 334).

PAYEE. The person to whom a promissory note (or other negotiable instrument) is made payable (p. 347).

PETTY CASH FUND. A specified amount of cash placed under the control of an employee for use in making small cash payments (p. 330).

PETTY CASH RECEIPT. A form used as a receipt for payments from a petty cash fund (p. 331).

PRINCIPAL (FACE VALUE). The face amount of a note (p. 347).

PROCEEDS. The maturity value of a note less discount (p. 349).

PROMISSORY NOTE. An unconditional written promise to pay a sum of money on demand or at a future determinable date (p. 347).

TRADE RECEIVABLES. Accounts and notes receivable that arise from the sale of merchandise or services in the normal course of business (p. 342).

DISCUSSION QUESTIONS

1. Define "cash" in the accounting sense. What items are included and excluded in the cash amount on the balance sheet?

2. Why is an internal control system for cash essential? List the three elements of an internal control system for cash and briefly discuss their purposes.

3. Discuss the internal control procedures normally used for cash sales and cash received through the mail.

4. What is meant by a division of responsibility among employees in the context of an internal control system?

5. Outline an internal control system for cash disbursements.

6. A firm's employee has the responsibility for opening all incoming invoices, approving the invoices for payment, and preparing the checks for the treasurer's signature. Discuss the weaknesses of the system. How could the employee embezzle money from the firm?

7. What kinds of accounts are debited to record a petty cash fund reimbursement?

8. Explain the function of the Cash Short and Over account. How is it reported on the income statement?

9. Why is a petty cash fund always replenished at the end of the fiscal period regardless of the amount of cash in the fund?

10. Explain how the use of bank checking accounts strengthens the internal control system for cash.

11. Define the following terms as they relate to a bank statement:
    a. Debit memo.
    b. Deposit in transit.
    c. Canceled checks.
    d. Credit memo.
    e. NSF check.
    f. Outstanding checks.

12. What is a bank reconciliation? What is its purpose?

13. What reconciling items on a bank reconciliation require a journal entry on the company's books?

14. What two criteria must be met to classify securities held as investments as current assets?

15. What is an investment portfolio?

16. What procedure is followed when a temporary investment in debt securities suffers a permanent decline in value that is below the cost of the securities?

17. What value is used to account for a temporary stock portfolio? Explain the accounting process when the portfolio's market value is less than total cost.

18. Define an account receivable and a note receivable. What is the difference between the two types of assets?

19. List three examples of nontrade receivables.

20. Receivables are reported on the balance sheet at their expected realizable value. Define expected realizable value and explain how it is calculated.

21. Why is the contra asset account Allowance for Uncollectible Accounts credited instead of Accounts Receivable when recording the entry to estimate bad debts?

22. Name and explain the two methods used to estimate bad debts expense.

23. What accounts are debited and credited when an account receivable is considered uncollectible and written off the books?

24. What impact does the writing off of an uncollectible account receivable have on the net amount of accounts receivable? Explain.

25. Define the following terms as they relate to promissory notes:
    a. Face value.
    b. Interest-bearing note.
    c. Interest.
    d. Maker.
    e. Maturity value.
    f. Noninterest-bearing note.
    g. Payee.

26. What is the due date and the amount of interest on a four-month, 15%, $5,000 note dated June 26, 1992?

27. What is a dishonored note?

28. What is the process called when the payee of a note sells the note to a bank?

29. A 90-day note dated April 20, 1992 is sold to a bank on May 27. What is the due date and what is the discount period of the note?

30. How are contingent liabilities for discounted notes receivable normally reported on the financial statements?

EXERCISES

Exercise 8-1 Composition of Cash

Several items that might be considered components of cash follow:

Item	Included in Cash Balance	Excluded from Cash Balance	
		Account Title	Balance Sheet Classification
1. Cashier's check from a customer			
2. NSF check returned by bank			
3. Cash on hand			
4. Cash register change fund			
5. Traveler's checks in firm's name			
6. IOUs from employees			
7. Money orders received from customers			
8. Certificates of deposit with the firm's bank			
9. Deposits in transit			
10. Postage stamps			
11. Promissory note received from the company president			
12. Customer's check dated 5 days after the balance sheet date			
13. Petty cash fund			

Required:

Indicate for each item whether it should be included or excluded from the cash balance reported on the balance sheet. If it should be excluded, write the name of the account in which it should be recorded and the account's classification on the balance sheet.

Exercise 8-2 Internal Control of Cash

Marvin Smith's gambling habit resulted in his owing $3,200 to certain individuals who demanded payment within two days. Having no sources from which to obtain the money, Marvin decided to ''borrow'' the needed cash from the company for which he works as a bookkeeper. Marvin ''borrowed'' the money by undertaking the following procedures:

1. On March 5, Marvin removed $3,200 in cash from the daily cash receipts while preparing the daily cash sales summary.
2. Luckily, a customer's check for $3,200 from Sara Miller as payment on account was received that day in the mail. Marvin included the check in the deposit ticket as part of the daily cash sales. No journal entry was made to record the customer's payment.

3. On March 8, Marvin made a general journal entry debiting Sales Returns and Allowances and crediting Accounts Receivable–Sara Miller. Marvin posted the entry to the two general ledger accounts affected and to Miller's account in the subsidiary accounts receivable ledger. Thus, when Ms. Miller's statement was mailed at the end of the month, it reflected the correct balance due.

Required:
A. What are the weaknesses in this company's internal control procedures that allowed Marvin to steal the money?
B. What procedures should be implemented to prevent any future thefts of this type?
C. Is the general ledger in balance after these actions of Marvin Smith? What accounts, if any, have an incorrect balance? Will the total of the accounts receivable subsidiary ledger accounts equal the balance in the control account? Why or why not?

Exercise 8-3   **Establishing and Replenishing Petty Cash**

Gentry Company established a petty cash fund for $300 on April 14. On June 6, the petty cash fund cashier submitted the following report:

Type of Expenditure	Amount
Postage and delivery costs	$ 46.40
Office supplies	32.80
Taxi, bus and subway fares	58.85
Newspapers and magazines	21.60
Birthday party for office manager	29.10
United Way contribution	50.00
Soda pop for pop machine	52.25
Total expenditures	291.00
Cash in fund	9.00
Total	$300.00

The company's chart of accounts contains the following relevant account titles: Postage Expense, Office Supplies, Transportation Expense, Miscellaneous Expense, and Charitable Contributions.

Required:
Prepare journal entries to record the establishment and replenishment of the petty cash fund.

Exercise 8-4   **Petty Cash—Cash Short and Over**

On December 31, the end of Taylor Company's fiscal year, the petty cash fund contained the following:

Expense Receipts	Amount
Postage	$ 26.40
Delivery expenses	28.20
Bus, subway, and taxi fares	37.30
Freight-in	31.60
Total receipts	123.50
Cash in the fund	124.15
Total	$247.65

The Petty Cash general ledger account shows a $250 balance.

Required:

Make the journal entry to record the replenishment of the petty cash fund on December 31.

Exercise 8-5 Bank Reconciliation

The following information was taken from the bank statement and the accounting records of Styler Corporation for the month of July 1992.

1.	Balance per books, 7/31/92	$12,293.82
2.	Balance per bank statement, 7/31/92	11,675.30
3.	Bank service charge for July 1992	18.00
4.	Deposit in transit on 7/31/92	4,360.40
5.	NSF check returned with bank statement	183.87
6.	Outstanding checks on 7/31/92	2,908.75
7.	Note collected by the bank	1,000.00
8.	Interest on the above note	50.00
9.	Note collection fee	15.00

Required:

A. Prepare a bank reconciliation for the month of July 1992.
B. Prepare the journal entries indicated by the bank reconciliation.

Exercise 8-6 Bank Reconciliation from Incomplete Data

The following information is available concerning the Kegen Company for the month of August 1992:

1.	Cash balance per books, 8/31/92	$?
2.	Balance per bank statement, 8/31/92	?
3.	Corrected book balance	9,624.20
4.	Bank service charge	12.00
5.	Customer's NSF check returned by bank	107.05
6.	Deposit in transit on 8/31/92	3,375.65
7.	Outstanding checks	1,554.45
8.	Net proceeds of note collected by bank	546.30

Required:

Prepare a bank reconciliation for the month of August 1992.

Exercise 8-7 Temporary Investments in Equity Securities

Pitre Company accumulated excess cash which will not be needed for operations for 9 to 10 months. To use the idle cash profitably, Pitre's management decided to invest the cash in equity securities as a short-term investment. Pitre Company entered into the following transactions during 1992 with respect to its temporary equity securities portfolio:

May   11   Purchased 20,000 shares of Carter Corporation capital stock for $342,600 including broker's fees.

Sept. 22   Received a $1.70 per share cash dividend from Carter Corporation.

Dec.   31   At the end of Pitre's fiscal year, Carter Corporation capital stock was selling at $16.60 per share.

Required:

A. Prepare the journal entries needed to record the purchase of the stock, the receipt of the cash dividend, and any necessary year-end adjustment.

B. Show how the investment would be reported on Pitre's December 31, 1992 balance sheet.

C. Explain what would appear on Pitre's 1992 income statement as a result of this investment.

Exercise 8-8 Temporary Investment in Equity Securities

Sutton Corporation uses the calendar year as its fiscal year. Profitable operations resulted in Sutton accumulating excess cash. To put the cash to work temporarily, Sutton entered into the following transactions during 1992:

Jan.	6	Purchased 6,000 shares of Riley Corporation capital stock at a total cost of $94,200.
Mar.	20	Purchased 10,000 shares of Delmont Company capital stock for $26 per share plus broker's fees and transfer costs of $13,800.
June	12	Sold 3,000 shares of Riley Corporation capital stock for $21 per share less broker's fees of $4,500.
Oct.	29	Received a $2.25 per share cash dividend on the Delmont Company capital stock.
Dec.	31	On December 31, Riley Corporation capital stock was selling at $26.50 per share and the Delmont Company capital stock was selling at $19.50 per share.

Required:

A. Prepare journal entries to record these transactions, including any adjustment needed on December 31. Sutton Corporation had no temporary investments in stock prior to January 6, 1992.

B. Show how the effects of these transactions would be reported on Sutton's 1992 income statement and balance sheet.

Exercise 8-9 Temporary Investments in Debt Securities

The following transactions were completed by Marco Company during the fiscal year ended October 31, 1992 with respect to its temporary investments in debt securities:

March	16	Purchased debt securities as a temporary investment at a cost of $280,000, plus a broker's commission of $7,500.
April	10	Purchased debt securities as a temporary investment at a cost of $225,000, plus a broker's commission of $6,250.
June	30	Received interest on temporary investments in debt securities, $18,600.
Sept.	10	Sold debt securities with a cost of $260,000 for $305,000.
Oct.	31	Accrued interest on debt securities of $3,400. The market value of the debt security portfolio is $220,000. The decline in value is not due to a temporary condition.

Required:

A. Prepare journal entries to record the transactions.

B. Prepare the income statement and balance sheet presentations that result from these transactions. Prior to March 16, the company had no investments in debt securities.

Exercise 8-10 Trade and Nontrade Receivables

In reviewing the accounting records of the Vinco Corporation, you discover that all receivables are recorded in a single account titled "Receivables." An analysis of the account provided the following results of its contents:

Accounts receivable, trade	$165,300
Notes receivable, trade	28,000
Notes receivable from officers	15,000
Travel advances to salesperson	4,500
Gas company utilities deposit	500
Notes receivable from employees	3,000
Deposit made to Baker Company for a machine to be delivered later	20,000
Accounts receivable from sale of plant asset	2,600
Total	$238,900

Required:

Explain where each of the above items would be presented in Vinco's balance sheet.

Exercise 8-11 Estimating Bad Debts Expense

Sigma Company began operations on January 10, 1992. During 1992, total sales were $860,000 of which $726,000 were on account. At year-end, the balance in Accounts Receivable was $82,060. An aging schedule of the accounts receivable showed the following:

Age Category	Amount	Estimated Percent Uncollectible
Not yet due	$50,000	1%
1 to 30 days past due	17,500	4%
31 to 90 days past due	9,860	10%
91 to 180 days past due	4,700	40%

Required:

A. Prepare the journal entry to record 1992 estimated bad debts expense if .5% of the credit sales are estimated to be uncollectible.

B. Prepare the journal entry to record 1992 estimated bad debts expense assuming the estimate is based on the aging of accounts receivable. No accounts were written off during the year.

C. If management wishes to present accounts receivable on the balance sheet at their estimated realizable value, which of the two methods above should be used?

Exercise 8-12 Accounting for Uncollectible Accounts Receivable

On January 1, 1992, Durham Company had the following general ledger accounts and balances: Accounts Receivable, $380,000; Allowance for Uncollectible Accounts, $11,400. During 1992, Durham had sales on account of $5,260,000; collections on account of $5,165,000; and accounts receivable written off as uncollectible of $14,250. An aging schedule prepared on December 31, 1992 showed the following:

Age Category	Amount	Estimated Percent Uncollectible	
Not yet due	$292,000	.5%	1460
1 to 30 days past due	61,500	3.0%	1845
31 to 60 days past due	43,000	6.5%	2745
61 to 90 days past due	32,250	10.0%	32.25
91 to 180 days past due	20,000	25.0%	5000
Over 180 days past due	12,000	80.0%	9600

460,750   *23,925   expect it to be bad*

Required:

A. Prepare summary 1992 journal entries to record the credit sales, collections of accounts receivable, and the write-offs of accounts receivable.
B. Prepare the entry on December 31, 1992 to record bad debts expense based on the aging schedule.
C. Compute the expected realizable value of accounts receivable on January 1, 1992 and on December 31, 1992.

Exercise 8-13   Analyzing Accounts Receivable

Relevant data pertaining to transactions affecting sales and accounts receivable for the Baxter Company during 1992 are:

Cash sales	$400,000
Net credit sales	612,000
Accounts receivable, January 1, 1992	92,000
Accounts receivable, December 31, 1992	98,000
Allowance for uncollectible accounts, January 1, 1992	3,960
Allowance for uncollectible accounts, December 31, 1992, before adjustment	440 (Debit)

Required:

A. Compute the dollar amount of accounts receivable written off as uncollectible during 1992.
B. Compute the dollar amount of accounts receivable collected during 1992.
C. Compute the expected realizable value of the accounts receivable as of January 1, 1992.

Exercise 8-14   Comparison of Bad Debt Estimation Methods

Relevant data pertaining to transactions affecting sales and accounts receivable of Brown Corporation during 1992 are:

Cash sales	$900,000
Net credit sales	740,000
Accounts receivable, January 1, 1992	89,500
Accounts receivable, December 31, 1992	111,000
Allowance for uncollectible accounts, January 1, 1992	6,650
Allowance for uncollectible accounts, December 31, 1992, before adjustment	590 (Debit)

An aging schedule of accounts receivable prepared on December 31, 1992 showed:

Age Category	Amount	Estimated Percent Uncollectible
Not yet due	$69,000	1%
1 to 30 days past due	24,200	5%
31 to 60 days past due	7,200	8%
61 to 120 days past due	6,100	30%
121 to 180 days past due	4,500	60%

Required:

A. Assuming Brown uses the income statement method and past experience shows 1% of net credit sales each year have been uncollectible, prepare the journal entry to record bad debts expense.

B. Assuming Joiner uses the balance sheet method, prepare the entry to record bad debts expense.

C. Explain why the amounts calculated for requirements A and B are not the same.

Exercise 8-15 Estimating Bad Debts

During 1992, Lark Corporation had sales revenue of $960,000, of which $700,000 were credit sales. On January 1, 1992, accounts receivable were $85,000 and the Allowance for Uncollectible Accounts had a credit balance of $11,330. Collections of accounts receivable during 1992 were $620,000, and $17,600 of accounts receivable were written off as uncollectible. For 1992, management decided to continue the accounting policy of basing bad debts expense on 2% of credit sales for the year.

Required:

A. Prepare journal entries to record the 1992 accounting transactions pertaining to the events described above.

B. Show how the Accounts Receivable, Allowance for Uncollectible Accounts, and Bad Debts Expense accounts would appear on Lark's 1992 income statement and December 31, 1992 balance sheet.

C. On the basis of the data given, discuss the adequacy of using 2% of credit sales as the basis for estimating bad debts expense.

Exercise 8-16 Accounting for Notes Receivable

Pace Equipment Company sells farm machinery. Credit terms are customary with down payments between 15% and 30%. Credit terms usually involve promissory notes for the balance of the sales price. Pace's annual fiscal year ends on October 31. Following are transactions entered into by Pace during its 1992 fiscal year.

Jan. 15 Sold equipment to J.B. Short for $160,000; received a 25% down payment and a six-month, 10%, interest-bearing note for the balance.

June 30 Sold equipment to Charles Cossell for $300,000; received a 30% down payment and a six-month, 12%, interest-bearing note for the balance.

July 15 J.B. Short paid his note and interest.

Required:

Prepare journal entries to record the transactions, including the October 31 accrual of interest on the Cossell note.

Exercise 8-17   Interest-Bearing and Noninterest-Bearing Notes

Hank Sackton recently spent a weekend at a gambling resort. He obtained his gambling money by taking out cash advances on his bank credit cards. Hank had a run of bad luck, and lost $7,000. Because the banks charge 21% interest on bank cards, Hank contacted two local banks in an attempt to borrow $7,000 at a lower interest rate to pay off his credit card debt. He has received the following terms from two banks:

1. Bank A will lend Hank $7,000 for one year at an annual interest rate of 16%.
2. Bank B will lend Hank $7,000 for one year. Hank will receive $7,000 and give the bank a $8,274 note, payable in one year.

Hank is unsure which bank has offered him the best terms and has come to you for help.

Required:
A. What is the dollar amount of interest Hank will pay to Bank A? To Bank B?
B. What is the face value of the note from Bank A? From Bank B?
C. What is the maturity value of the note from Bank A? From Bank B?
D. What is the effective interest rate for the loan from Bank A? From Bank B?
E. Which bank is giving Hank the better terms?

Exercise 8-18   Note Receivable Defaulted

Lasiter Company sells approximately 70% of its merchandise on credit with terms of n/30. If an open account becomes delinquent, Lasiter requires the customer to replace the open account with a promissory note. Lasiter's fiscal year ends on December 31. Following is a series of transactions relating to one of Lasiter's sales for 1992.

Jan.	28	Sold merchandise on account for $11,000 to James Carter.
Mar.	15	Received a three-month, 14% note from James Carter in settlement of his overdue account.
June	15	James Carter defaulted on his note.
Aug.	15	James Carter paid his dishonored note plus interest at 14% on the defaulted amount since the due date.

Required:
Prepare all journal entries on the books of Lasiter Company. (Round to the nearest dollar.)

Exercise 8-19   Note Receivable Discounted

Foster Company sells approximately 80% of its merchandise on credit and requires customers to sign a promissory note for their credit purchase. Foster routinely discounts the notes at a local bank. The company's fiscal year ends on December 31. Following is a series of transactions relating to one of Foster's sales during 1992.

Feb.	10	Sold merchandise for $25,000 to Rossler Corporation, a new customer. Received a 20% down payment and a 120-day, 12% promissory note for the balance.
Mar.	12	Sold the Rossler Corporation note to the bank. The bank charges a 15% discount rate.
June	11	The bank notified Foster that Rossler Corporation paid the note on its due date.

Required:
Prepare all journal entries on the books of Foster Company.

Exercise 8-20 **Discounting Notes Receivable**
The following notes receivable were sold (discounted) during 1992:

1. A $3,000, 180-day, 12% note dated January 16 is sold to the bank at a discount rate of 15% on March 17.
2. A $2,000, 60-day, 15% note dated March 10 is sold to the bank at a discount rate of 18% on March 20.
3. A $6,000, 60-day, 12% note dated May 17 is sold to the bank at a discount rate of 16% on July 6.

Required:
Prepare journal entries to record the discounted notes. Round amounts to the nearest dollar.

PROBLEMS

Problem 8-1 **Petty Cash**
On January 5, 1992, Baxter Company established a petty cash fund for $500 by writing a check to "Jerry Barber, Petty Cash Fund Cashier." Jerry was designated the custodian of the fund. On March 31, the end of the first quarter, $87 remained in the fund. Signed receipts for cash expenditures during the three-month period are summarized as follows: Postage, $65; Freight costs on purchased merchandise, $85; Office supplies, $51; Taxi, bus, and subway fares, $49; Retirement party for an employee, $74; and Newspapers and magazines, $54.

Required:
A. Prepare the journal entry to establish the fund on January 5, 1992.
B. Prepare the journal entry to replenish the fund on March 31, 1992.
C. What balance should appear in the Petty Cash account in the general ledger on January 31, February 28, and March 31? Explain.
D. How should Petty Cash be reported on the quarterly balance sheet prepared as of March 31, 1992?
E. What is the impact of the petty cash fund activities on the first quarter's income statement?
F. Assume on April 3, 1992, management decides to reduce the petty cash fund to $200. Prepare the journal entry to record the reduction.

Problem 8-2 **Petty Cash Fund Transactions**
Foxcraft Corporation established a petty cash fund on May 8, 1992 for $200 and appointed Amanda Everly as cashier. Following are the transactions completed through the petty cash fund for the remainder of May.

Date	Amount Paid	Petty Cash Receipt #	Purpose of Expenditure
May 8	$ 40	1	Purchase of postage stamps
12	38	2	C.O.D. charges on merchandise purchased for resale
14	55	3	Purchase of janitorial supplies
15	36	4	Repair of office copier
18	23	5	Purchase of newspapers and magazines
19			Replenished fund; cash in the fund was $8. Increased the fund to $400
20	77	6	Pay overnight delivery service for delivery of an important contract
21	65	7	Repair of air-conditioner thermostat
22	115	8	Cleaning of office carpet
26	21	9	Purchase of coffee and supplies for employees' lounge
28	14	10	Flowers for secretary's birthday
29	95	11	Washing of office windows
29			Replenished fund; cash in fund was $10

Required:

Prepare journal entries to:

A. Establish the fund on May 8.
B. Replenish the fund and increase its size on May 19.
C. Replenish the fund on May 29.

Problem 8-3 Bank Reconciliation

The bookkeeper for Prestige Company is on vacation. In her absence, you have been asked to prepare the monthly bank reconciliation. Following are the June 1992 bank statement, the Cash in Bank, Cash on Hand, and Petty Cash general ledger accounts, all in summarized form:

Bank Statement

	Debits	Credits	Balance
Balance, June 1, 1992			$ 47,100
June deposits		$72,000	119,100
Note collected for customer–principal amount $2,000; interest $180		2,180	121,280
Checks paid	$88,600		32,680
NSF check–Jim Candy	280		32,400
Bank service charge	30		32,370
Master card usage charge	30		32,340
Balance, June 30, 1992			32,340

Cash in Bank

June 1 Balance	45,500	June checks written	89,500
June cash deposits	84,000		

Cash on Hand

June 30 Balance	200

Petty Cash

June 30 Balance	400

Outstanding checks on May 31 were $1,600. All of these checks were cleared by the bank during June. There were no deposits in transit on May 31, but a deposit was in transit on June 30. The Cash on Hand account represents the amount of cash maintained as a change fund.

Required:

A. Prepare a bank reconciliation for June 1992.

B. Prepare any journal entries indicated by the bank reconciliation.

C. What amount should be reported as Cash on the June 30, 1992 balance sheet?

Problem 8-4 **Bank Reconciliation**

The September 1992, bank statement for Compuco Company and the general ledger accounts for Cash and Petty Cash are given below:

Bank Statement

Date	Debits			Credits	Balance
Sept. 1					$ 82,000
1	800	300		32,000	112,900
2	14,000	160			98,740
4	240	360	3,000		95,140
7	1,800	2,400	180	44,000	134,760
9	900	1,400	3,800		128,660
10	34,000	4,000			90,660
14	80	47,000		53,000	96,580
17	3,600	5,300			87,680
18	4,400	9,600			73,680
21	26,000	3,780		39,000	82,900
23		600 NSF			82,300
25	1,000	36 CC			81,264
28				16,000	97,264
30	2,300	2,400	20 SC	15,610 CM	108,154

Beginning Balance	Debits		Credits		Ending Balance
	No.	Amount	No.	Amount	
$82,000	29	$173,456	6	$199,610	$108,154

Symbols	CC = Check Charge	CM = Credit Memo
	NSF = Nonsufficient funds	SC = Service Charge

Cash

Sept. 1 Balance	111,700	Checks Written During September		
Deposits:		80	14,000	5,300
Sept. 4	44,000	26,000	9,600	1,000
11	53,000	1,400	3,780	2,300
18	39,000	8,800	3,000	4,400
25	16,000	2,400	240	14,000
30	41,000	360	160	300
		34,000	47,000	900
		180	1,600	4,000
		3,600	2,400	3,800
Sept. 30 Balance	110,100			

Petty Cash

Sept. 30 Balance	400

The NSF check is from Bostwick Company and was a payment on their open account. The credit memo relates to a note receivable from Nygard Corporation with a face value of $15,000.

A review of the August 1992, bank reconciliation provides the following information: The adjusted bank balance on August 31, was $111,400; a deposit in transit on August 31 was $32,000; outstanding checks on August 31 were $2,600, composed of two checks for $800 and $1,800.

Compuco Company maintains a $300 change fund on its premises. This $300 is included in the Cash account.

Required:

A. Compute the amount of the deposit in transit on September 30, 1992.
B. Compute the amount of outstanding checks on September 30, 1992.
C. Prepare a bank reconciliation for September 1992.
D. Prepare the journal entries resulting from the bank reconciliation.
E. What amount should be reported for cash on a balance sheet prepared as of September 30, 1992?
F. Comment on Compuco Company's efficient use of cash. Might some of their cash be invested in income-producing assets? If so, what types of assets might be acquired?

Problem 8-5   Temporary Investments in Equity Securities

Donelan Company uses its idle cash to buy securities as short-term investments. Following are the transactions completed by Donelan during 1992. The annual accounting period ends December 31.

Feb.	10	Purchased the following capital stocks as short-term investments

      Baker Corp.   300 shares $20 per share
      Cedar Corp.   650 shares   22 per share
      Manko Corp. 1,000 shares   12 per share

May	21	Received a $3 per share cash dividend on the Baker Corp. stock.
June	11	Received a $1.50 per share cash dividend on the Cedar Corp. stock.
Aug.	27	Sold the Manko Corp. stock for $10 per share, net of broker fees.
Oct.	26	Purchased 500 shares of Tamco Corp. stock for $41 per share.
Dec.	31	Closing market prices were: Baker Corp., $27; Cedar Corp., $19; Manko Corp., $9; and Tamco Corp., $42.

Required:

A. Prepare journal entries to record the transactions.

B. Prepare the journal entry on December 31, if necessary, to reflect the portfolio at lower of cost or market. Donelan Company had no transactions in marketable equity securities prior to 1992.

C. Prepare the 1992 income statement and balance sheet presentations resulting from these transactions.

Problem 8-6 Temporary Investments in Marketable Equity Securities

The following presentation appeared on the balance sheet for a public corporation in its 1992 annual report:

	1992	1991
Current Assets:		
Marketable equity securities, at cost in 1992		
and at market in 1991 (Note 1)	$27,350	$30,200

Note 1—Marketable Equity Securities

Marketable equity securities are carried at the lower of cost or market at the balance sheet date; that determination is made by aggregating all current marketable equity securities. Marketable equity securities included in current assets had a market value at December 31, 1992 of $27,600 and a cost at December 31, 1991 of $31,150.

At December 31, 1992, there were gross unrealized gains of $1,000 and gross unrealized losses of $750 pertaining to the current portfolio. A net realized loss of $150 on the sale of marketable equity securities was included in the determination of net income for 1992. The cost of the securities sold was based on the first-in, first-out method for 1992. A reduction of $1,200 in the valuation allowance for net unrealized losses was included in income during 1992. The valuation allowance was established in 1991 by a charge against income of $1,200.

Required:

A. By how much was pretax income increased or decreased for 1992 as a result of the transactions regarding marketable equity securities?

B. Prepare the journal entries that were made on December 31, 1991 and December 31, 1992 with respect to the difference between the cost and market value of the portfolio.

C. By how much would the combined pretax income for 1991 and 1992 have been different if the cost method rather than the lower of cost or market method had been used to account for the marketable equity securities? Explain.

Problem 8-7 Temporary Investments in Equity Securities—Covering Two Years

Taylor Corporation began operations in January 1991, and ends its fiscal year on December 31. Management adopted a policy of investing excess cash in equity securities as short-term investments. Transactions completed during the first two years of operations follow:

1991

Stock Purchased:		
Kay Corporation	1,000 shares	$18 per share
Lee Corporation	600 shares	25 per share
Cash Dividends Received:		
Kay Corporation		$2.50 per share

Market Value–December 31:

Kay Corporation	$17 per share
Lee Corporation	23 per share

1992

Stock Purchased:

Leming Corporation	1,200 shares	$24 per share
Stanford Corporation	2,000 shares	18 per share
Veland Corporation	900 shares	12 per share

Cash Dividends Received:

Kay Corporation	$2 per share
Leming Corporation	3 per share
Veland Corporation	1 per share

Stock Sold:

Kay Corporation	1,000 shares	$22 per share
Lee Corporation	600 shares	17 per share

Market Value–December 31:

Leming Corporation	$25 per share
Stanford Corporation	16 per share
Veland Corporation	14 per share

Required:

A. Prepare summary journal entries, by year, to record the transactions.

B. Compute the realized and unrealized gains and losses that would be reported on the 1991 and 1992 income statements.

C. Prepare the 1991 and 1992 balance sheet presentations for the temporary marketable equity securities portfolio.

Problem 8-8 Estimating Bad Debt Percentage and Determining Annual Expense

In 1992, the fifth year of operations, Swenter Company is preparing an analysis of its bad debts in order to more accurately estimate its annual bad debts expense. During the first four years of operations, Swenter followed the policy of charging uncollectible accounts to bad debts expense in the period in which the accounts became uncollectible. In order to better match revenues and expenses, however, Swenter is changing to the allowance method for 1992. The following information has been accumulated from the accounting records:

	1988	1989	1990	1991	1992
Credit Sales	$186,000	$316,000	$422,000	$490,000	$610,000
Collections on Accounts Receivable:					
From 1988 sales	162,000	16,000	400	–0–	–0–
From 1989 sales		270,000	28,600	4,800	–0–
From 1990 sales			364,500	39,500	4,100
From 1991 sales				426,200	48,300
From 1992 sales					528,900
Accounts Receivable Written Off:					
From 1988 sales	5,000	2,000	600	–0–	–0–
From 1989 sales		8,200	2,800	1,600	–0–
From 1990 sales			9,300	3,100	1,500
From 1991 sales				9,300	2,300
From 1992 sales					9,800

Required:

A. Using the years for which all receivables have been collected and/or written off (1988 through 1990), compute the average bed debt loss rate for that period.

B. Calculate the amount of bad debt expense Swenter reported on its 1988 through 1991 income statements and the balance in the Bad Debts Expense account at the end of 1992 which is based on the direct write-off method.

C. Using the rate computed in requirement A, calculate what the bad debts expense for 1988 through 1992 should be. Compare your answers with those in requirement B.

D. What is the balance needed in the Allowance for Uncollectible Accounts on December 31, 1992?

Problem 8-9 Estimating Bad Debts Expense

Clarkson Corporation opened for business on January 20, 1991. A calendar year corporation, Clarkson had credit sales during 1991 of $93,500, of which $77,000 were collected by December 31. Prior to preparing the 1991 financial statements, Clarkson's management decided that $500 of the accounts receivable were uncollectible and wrote them off. Because Clarkson was a new company, management decided to use the industry average of 2% of credit sales to estimate bad debts expense for 1991.

Credit sales during 1992 were $146,000. Accounts receivable of $138,600 were collected during the year and $3,600 of accounts receivable were written off as uncollectible. Clarkson again used the industry average of 2% of credit sales to estimate bad debts expense for 1992.

Required:

A. Prepare journal entries for 1991 to:
    1. Record the credit sales
    2. Record collection of accounts receivable
    3. Record the write-offs of uncollectible accounts
    4. Record bad debts expense
    5. Close the bad debts expense account

B. Prepare T accounts for three general ledger accounts—Accounts Receivable, Allowance for Uncollectible Accounts, and Bad Debts Expense and post the relevant portions of the journal entries to the three T accounts.

C. Repeat requirements A and B for 1992.

D. Prepare the 1991 and 1992 balance sheet presentations for accounts receivable and the related contra account.

E. Does the balance in the Allowance for Uncollectible Accounts on December 31, 1992 appear adequate based on the evidence presented in the problem? Why or why not?

Problem 8-10 Discounting Notes Receivable

Wally Furniture sells merchandise for cash and credit. For credit sales, Wally requires a promissory note from the buyer. Wally generally sells (discounts) its notes receivable to a local bank within 5 to 10 days of receipt. Following is information for some transactions occurring during the last quarter of Wally's 1992 fiscal year.

Oct. 6 Sold merchandise for $4,000 to J.D. Cobble. Accepted a 150-day, 12% note for the full amount.

16 Sold the Cobble note to a local bank; the bank's discount rate was 14%.

21 Sold merchandise to Alice Lavel for $6,500. Accepted a 90-day, 14% note for the full amount.

26 Sold the Lavel note to a local bank which charged a 15% discount rate.

Nov. 4 Sold merchandise to Traveler's Rest Motel for $22,000. Received a $7,000 down payment and accepted a 120-day, 14% note for the remainder.

14 Sold the Traveler's Rest Motel note to a local bank which charged a 16% discount rate.

Required:

A. Prepare journal entries to record the transactions. (Round to the nearest dollar.)

B. If Alice Lavel defaults on her note on the due date, what must Wally do, and what journal entry will be made?

Problem 8-11   Notes Receivable

Transactions involving notes receivable received by Cutter Company, an equipment manufacturer, during 1992 follow (Cutter's year-end is December 31).

Jan. 15 Sold equipment for $150,000 to Henry Baxter. Received a $50,000 down payment and an 18-month, 12% note receivable for the balance. Interest is to be paid every six months; the principal is due on the note's maturity date.

Apr. 1 Sold equipment for $80,000 to Kelter Company. Accepted a 12-month, 15% note for the full sales price. One-fourth of the principal plus accrued interest on the full remaining principal is due July 1 and October 1, 1992, and January 1 and April 1, 1993.

June 1 Sold equipment to Stevens Company for $40,000. Accepted a 12-month, 15% note for the full sales price. Principal and interest are due on June 1, 1993.

Sept. 30 Sold equipment for $150,000 to Jones Company. Received a $50,000 down payment and accepted a six-month, 15% note for the balance. Interest is to be paid monthly on the principal balance on the last day of the month. The principal is due in two equal installments on December 31, 1992, and March 31, 1993.

Required:

Prepare all necessary journal entries for 1992.

CASE

CASE 8-1   Internal Control of Cash

The following problem is based on an actual situation. Unfortunately, many businesses experience similar conditions.

George Kurtz works part-time as business manager for a medical clinic. In addition to George, the clinic employs three doctors, three nurses, one laboratory technician, one X-ray technician, one receptionist, and one office manager. All employees are salaried except George, who is paid an hourly rate. George maintains a time card on which he records the hours he works. Occasionally a salaried employee will work overtime. When that happens, the employee will fill out a time card and give it to George before the next payroll date. Employees are paid on the 5th and the 20th of each month for the previous one-half month.

The head nurse does all the ordering of medical supplies; the laboratory technician orders all laboratory supplies; and the X-ray technician orders all X-ray supplies. They are supposed to give all purchase orders to George—but he only receives about 70% of them.

The office manager orders all office supplies, opens the incoming mail, prepares and deposits the daily cash receipts, and records all daily charges and collections to patients' accounts. The office manager is also in charge of collecting delinquent accounts. Accounts over 120 days past due are given to a collection agency. The agency charges a fee of 50% of the amount collected. The collection agency remits a monthly statement of accounts collected plus a check for the clinic's 50% share.

George performs the following duties: (1) maintains all time cards and prepares the semi-monthly payroll and payroll tax reports; (2) maintains the accounts payable ledger and writes all checks to pay suppliers and other creditors; (3) prepares the monthly bank reconciliation; and (4) prepares monthly financial statements.

The medical clinic utilizes a computerized accounting system via a time-sharing plan with a local bank. Each day, the office manager enters the medical services performed and unpaid amounts via a telephone modem. A monthly report, the service analysis, is prepared by the bank and mailed directly to the clinic. Patient statements are prepared by the bank at the end of each month and mailed directly to the patients. George uses the service analysis to prepare the monthly financial statements because it contains all revenues earned during the period. Each month he prepares a cash disbursements journal, a cash receipts journal, a payroll journal, and a general journal on coded paper and mails them to the bank. The bank prepares the monthly statements and sends them to George at the clinic.

The medical clinic is incorporated as a family owned corporation. One of the doctors owns the clinic. He signs all checks and briefly scans the monthly reports.

A petty cash fund of $100 is maintained by the office manager. It is improperly used because cash receipts from the pop machine are added to the petty cash on hand each time the machine is filled. The clinic also pays all insurance premiums for the doctors and their medical and dental bills. The owner-doctor does not cross reference the checks written by George to the invoices and statements they are paying.

Required:
A. Discuss the weaknesses of the medical clinic's internal control procedures. Make suggestions to correct those weaknesses within the personnel constraints of the clinic's staff.
B. Which employees are in the best position to steal from the clinic? Describe how a dishonest employee might do so.

INVENTORY COSTING METHODS

CHAPTER OVERVIEW AND OBJECTIVES

This chapter describes various methods used to assign cost to ending inventory and cost of goods sold. When this chapter is completed, you should understand:

1. How to determine when the title to inventory transfers.
2. How to allocate the total inventory cost between ending inventory and cost of goods sold using four different costing methods when the periodic inventory system is used.
3. How to determine inventory values by applying the lower of cost or market rule.
4. How to compute the net realizable value of an inventory item.
5. How to allocate the total inventory cost between ending inventory and cost of goods sold using four different costing methods when the perpetual inventory system is used.
6. The effects of inventory errors on the balance sheet and income statement.
7. How to estimate a value for the ending inventory using the retail inventory and gross profit methods.

The term *inventory* is used to describe the tangible assets of a firm that (1) are held for sale in the normal course of the business, (2) are in the process of being produced for sale but not as yet completed, or (3) are materials being held for future use in producing goods or services. The accounts used to record inventory costs depend upon the firm's normal activity:

● For a merchandising firm, the term *merchandise inventory* is used to designate all goods owned and held for future sale to the firm's customers in the normal course of the business.
● For a manufacturing firm, the term *finished goods inventory* designates units that are completed and ready for sale, the term *raw materials inventory* indicates materials and component parts that are to be used in the manufacturing process, and the term *work-in-process inventory* refers to units that are in the course of production but not yet completed.

This chapter begins with a discussion of how to identify the units to be included in inventory. The perpetual and periodic inventory systems described and illustrated in Chapter 6 assumed that the cost per unit was the same for both the beginning inventory and all purchases made during the year. However, in today's markets, the prices of most goods change frequently during the accounting period. When prices change, the firm is confronted with an accounting problem of determining what portion of the total cost of goods available for sale should be assigned to ending inventory and what portion to cost of goods sold. This chapter considers four alternative methods used to assign the cost of goods available for sale to ending inventory and cost of goods sold when prices are changing.

Although cost is the primary basis for measuring inventory values, there are circumstances under which it is appropriate to value inventory at less than its historical cost. Several of these situations are discussed in this chapter. In addition, the effects of inventory errors on the company's financial statements are discussed. The chapter concludes with a discussion of two methods that are used to estimate ending inventory values.

DETERMINING THE INVENTORY ON HAND

TAKING A PHYSICAL INVENTORY

When a periodic inventory system is maintained, the cost of inventory purchased during the period is recorded in the Purchases account, as seen in Chapter 6. The balance in the Merchandise Inventory account is the cost of the inventory on hand at the beginning of the period. To determine the cost of the ending inventory, the units on hand must be counted and priced. The ending inventory is then reported as a current asset in the balance sheet. It is also deducted from the cost of goods available for sale in the income statement to determine the cost of goods sold. Although the inventory on hand and the cost of goods sold balances are available in the accounts when a perpetual inventory system is used, a physical inventory is also taken at least once a year to verify the balances reported.

Before conducting the actual physical count of units on hand—commonly referred to as *taking an inventory*—and pricing the units, the entire process must be carefully planned. The procedures established for the counting process must be supervised to ensure that all units owned by the firm are properly counted. Although the specific details vary from firm to firm, this is a typical approach:

1. A prenumbered inventory ticket is issued for each type of item in stock and distributed to each department. The ticket provides space to record (a) a description or code number of the item, (b) the number of units counted, (c) the initials of the person making the count, and (d) the initials of the person verifying the count.
2. An employee counts the units, enters the number of units on hand on the inventory ticket, and initials the ticket to identify the person performing the count. The inventory ticket is then attached to the units counted.
3. A supervisor recounts a sufficient number of items to ensure the accuracy of the recorded count and initials the inventory ticket.
4. A supervisor examines the inventory in each department to be sure that an inventory ticket has been attached to all items. Any group of like items without a ticket attached has not been counted.
5. The inventory tickets are collected and forwarded to the accounting department, where the prenumbered tickets are all accounted for. The information on the inventory tickets is summarized on an inventory summary sheet.
6. The unit cost of each individual item in stock is determined from purchase invoices or other supplementary records.

7. The number of units of the various individual items is multiplied by their unit cost and added together to compute the total ending inventory value.

Because conducting the physical count is often difficult, this step is frequently performed outside of business hours.

TRANSFER OF OWNERSHIP

During an inventory count, care must be exercised to assure that all goods legally owned by the firm on the inventory date are counted and included in the ending inventory, regardless of where the inventory is located. Transfer of ownership normally depends on the terms of the shipment. When goods are sold **FOB** (*free on board*) *shipping point,* freight is paid by the buyer. Title ordinarily transfers when the goods are delivered to the transportation company by the seller. If the terms are **FOB destination,** the seller is responsible for paying the freight, and title usually does not transfer until delivery is made to the buyer.

Objective 1:
Transfer of title

From an accounting point of view, the seller should record a sale and the buyer should record a purchase when title to the goods transfers. In practice, however, sales are normally recorded when shipment is made and purchases are recorded when the inventory is received irrespective of the shipping terms.

To increase the accuracy of the financial statements at year-end, purchases and sales invoices for both the last week or two of the current accounting period and for the first week or two of the next period should be reviewed to determine whether there were units in transit on the date of the physical inventory count that should be included with the units counted. For example, goods purchased with the terms FOB shipping point and in transit at year-end should be recorded as a purchase and included in the physical count even though they were not physically there when the actual count was made. Although exclusion of this inventory will have no effect on net income (purchases, goods available for sale, and ending inventory will each be understated by an equal amount), total assets and total liabilities will each be understated if the purchase is not recorded. Similarly, goods sold with the terms FOB destination should be included in the seller's ending inventory if in transit at year-end since title to the goods has not been transferred. The sale and related cost of goods sold are transactions to be recorded in the succeeding period.

In some cases, the seller may have received orders for goods, but shipment may not have been made. In such situations, a sale is *not* recorded because the revenue has not been earned. However, an exception is made when (1) an order for goods has been received, (2) the goods are ready for shipment, and (3) the buyer has requested that the goods be held for later delivery. Such items should be excluded from the seller's inventory and included in the buyer's inventory. In some cases, however, it may not be clear whether title has transferred. The accountant must then use his or her best judgment to assess when the parties to the transaction intended the title to transfer.

GOODS ON CONSIGNMENT

Another problem sometimes encountered in taking an inventory is the treatment of goods held on **consignment**. A consignment is a marketing arrangement whereby a business (the **consignor**) ships goods to a dealer (the **consignee**) who agrees to sell the goods for a commission. Although a physical transfer of goods has taken place, title to the goods remains with the consignor. It does not transfer.

Since title to the goods has not transferred, the shipment of consigned goods is not considered a sale/purchase transaction. Therefore, goods out on consignment are part of the consignor's inventory, even though physical possession of the goods is with the consignee. The goods are excluded from the consignee's inventory since they remain the consignor's property.

ALLOCATION OF INVENTORY COST BETWEEN ENDING INVENTORY AND COST OF GOODS SOLD

In Chapter 6, it was assumed that the unit cost was the same for all units acquired. However, units purchased on different dates often have different unit costs. When this happens, management is confronted with the problem of selecting the unit costs to be matched against sales. Assume that the following purchases of the same model of personal computer were made.

January 15	$480
February 10	560
March 8	600

If one unit is sold for $900 on March 25, which unit cost is charged to cost of goods sold to be matched against the revenue of $900? Whichever unit is selected means that the other two units will be reported in the inventory on hand. Gross profit could vary by as much as $120, depending on which item is assumed sold.

To implement the matching principle, the allocation of total inventory cost between ending merchandise inventory and cost of goods sold is based on some cost-flow assumption. The flow of inventory cost through a firm refers to the assignment of cost to the units that were sold and to those on hand. Intuitively, we may expect to be able to match precisely the identified cost of specific units with the revenues derived from their sale. However, there are limited cases in which this is practical. These include situations in which each item in inventory is unique, such as automobiles on a car dealer's lot and works of art held by an art gallery. In many instances, it is impossible, or it may not be practical because of the clerical cost involved, to identify each unit in inventory with its original cost. For example, the cost of a gallon of gasoline sold cannot be identified with its original cost because a new delivery of gasoline mixes with the gallons already in the storage tank. Other examples include units of inventory that are identical, such as textbooks at the campus bookstore and hand tools at a hardware store. Therefore, an assumed flow of cost is necessary to implement the matching principle when prices are changing.

The flow of cost assumed does not have to conform to the actual physical movement of goods. A firm may rotate its stock so that the oldest units are sold first. However, in determining the cost of units sold, the cost of the most recent purchases may be assigned to cost of goods sold. All that generally accepted accounting principles require is that the method selected be used consistently and that the cost allocation be systematic and rational. Although a switch in cost-flow assumption may occur occasionally, such a change is infrequent in the life of most firms.

Four methods are commonly used to allocate cost: (1) specific identification; (2) first-in, first-out (FIFO); (3) last-in, first-out (LIFO); and (4) average cost. The average cost method is called the weighted average method when a periodic inventory system is used. It is called the moving average method when a perceptual system is used. All four methods are considered acceptable for accounting purposes, but, when prices are changing, each will produce different ending inventory and cost of goods sold amounts. LIFO, FIFO, and average cost are the most commonly used methods, as shown by a survey of 600 companies, reported in Figure 9-1. As noted in Figure

Figure 9-1
Inventory Cost
Methods Used by
600 Companies

Costing Method	Number
FIFO	379
LIFO	396
Average cost	213
Other	50
Total	1,038

The total exceeds 600 companies because a company may adopt a different method for different types of inventory held.

Source: Accounting Trends and Techniques, 1989 edition (New York: AICPA, 1989), p. 119.

9-1, a company does not have to use a single inventory method for all its inventory items.

To illustrate the effects of the four inventory costing methods on the allocation of the total cost of goods available for sale to ending inventory and cost of goods sold, the inventory record in Figure 9-2 of a computer game will be assumed for the fiscal period.

PERIODIC INVENTORY SYSTEM

With a periodic inventory system, the number of units on hand at the end of the period must be determined by taking a physical inventory. In this illustration, it is assumed that 38 units were counted on December 31. The total cost of these units must then be determined from invoices or other inventory records. When prices are changing, the cost assigned to the ending inventory depends on the cost flow assumption that the firm adopts. Once the cost of the ending inventory is determined, the cost of goods sold is computed by deducting the ending inventory cost from the cost of goods available for sale of $824.

Objective 2:
Allocation of inventory costs—periodic inventory system

Figure 9-2
Inventory Record for
a Computer Game

Date		Number of Units	Unit Cost	Total Cost
Jan. 1	Beginning merchandise inventory	20	$10	$200.00
	Purchases made during the current period:			
April 15	Purchase	24	11	$264.00
July 7	Purchase	30	12	360.00
	Total purchases	54		624.00
	Goods available for sale	74		824.00
Dec. 31	Ending merchandise inventory	38		?
	Sales made during the current period	36*		$?

? Dollar amount will be computed later.

*Sales made during the current period:

	Units
April 20 Sales	16
August 12 Sales	20
Total unit sales	36

SPECIFIC IDENTIFICATION METHOD

The **specific identification method** requires that the cost of each unit sold and each unit on hand be identified with a particular purchase invoice. To do this, the firm must use some form of identification such as serial numbers.

To illustrate, assume that the 38 units in the ending inventory can be separately identified as 20 units from the July 7 purchase and 18 units from the beginning inventory. Costs are assigned as follows.

Cost of goods available for sale—74 units				$824.00

Less: Cost of 38 units in the ending merchandise inventory

Date	Units	Unit Cost	Total Cost	
1/1	18	$10	$180.00	
7/7	20	12	240.00	
Cost of ending merchandise inventory—38 units				420.00
Cost of goods sold—36 units				$404.00

As can be seen, the cost of goods sold is a residual amount, but the $404 figure can be verified as follows.

Cost of goods sold—36 units
2 units from the beginning inventory at $10 per unit	$ 20.00
24 units from the April 15 purchase at $11 per unit	264.00
10 units from the July 7 purchase at $12 per unit	120.00
Total cost of goods sold	$404.00

Using the amounts computed for the specific identification method, the cost allocation procedure is diagrammed as follows.

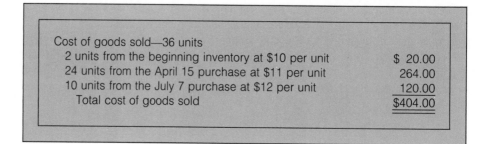

Under a periodic inventory system, the ending inventory ($420) is reported as a current asset in the balance sheet and as a deduction from cost of goods available for sale in the income statement. As shown in Chapter 6, these amounts may be entered in the ledger accounts as part of the closing or adjusting process. Recall that Merchandise Inventory is credited for $200 to remove the beginning inventory balance from the account and Merchandise Inventory is debited for $420 to record the ending inventory. These procedures are the same for the three other costing methods, but the amounts will vary with the costing method used.

FIRST-IN, FIRST-OUT (FIFO) METHOD

The **FIFO method** of determining the cost of goods sold is based on the assumption that the first units acquired (first-in) are the first units sold (first-out). In other words, the cost of the oldest units in the inventory are charged to the cost of goods sold to be matched against revenue. Therefore, the cost of the units on hand is that of the most recent units purchased. Once again, this is a cost flow assumption and need not represent the actual physical movement of goods.

It should be emphasized that the name of the inventory method, for example, FIFO, refers to the flow of cost and the determination of cost of goods sold and not to the ending inventory. That is, under FIFO, the cost of goods sold is made up of the beginning inventory and the first units purchased, while the ending inventory is made up of the last units purchased.

In the periodic inventory system, the ending inventory is computed first and is subtracted from the cost of goods available for sale to compute the cost of goods sold as follows.

Cost of goods available for sale—74 units $824.00
Less: Cost of 38 units in ending merchandise inventory

Date	Units	Unit Cost	Total Cost
7/7	30	$12	$360.00
4/15	8	11	88.00

Cost of ending merchandise inventory—38 units   448.00
Cost of goods sold—36 units $376.00

Note that the 38 units in the ending inventory are associated with the last two purchases. In a periodic inventory system, the cost of goods sold is a residual amount, but in this example it can be verified as follows.

Cost of goods sold—36 units
20 units from the beginning inventory at $10 per unit $200.00
16 units from the April 15 purchase at $11 per unit   176.00
Total cost of goods sold $376.00

The cost of the 36 units sold in this period consists of the 20 units from the beginning inventory and 16 units from the first purchase made on April 15. The other eight units from the April 15 purchase were assumed to be on hand as of December 31.

LAST-IN, FIRST-OUT (LIFO) METHOD

Under the **LIFO method,** the last units purchased (last-in) are assumed to be the first units sold (first-out). Consequently, the costs of the most recent purchases are matched with sales revenue in the income statement. The cost of the ending inventory consists of the costs of the beginning inventory and the earliest purchases. The cost allocation is:

Cost of goods available for sale—74 units			$824.00
Less: Cost of 38 units in the ending merchandise inventory			

Date	Units	Unit Cost	Total Cost
1/1	20	$10	$200.00
4/15	18	11	198.00

Cost of ending merchandise inventory—38 units	398.00
Cost of goods sold—36 units	$426.00

The cost of goods sold can be verified as follows.

Cost of goods sold—36 units	
30 units from the July 7 purchase at $12 per unit	$360.00
6 units from the April 15 purchase at $11 per unit	66.00
Total cost of goods sold	$426.00

Note that when the LIFO method is used with a periodic inventory system, no attempt is made to compare the dates of sales with those of purchases. Units on hand at the end of the period are assigned the cost of the beginning inventory and the earliest purchases. Thus, units sold during the period are assigned the cost of the most recent purchases. In other words, it is possible to expense the cost of units sold, even though they were not on hand at the time of sale. For example, in applying the LIFO method, if a purchase had been made after August 12 (the date of the last sale), those units would be considered sold first.

WEIGHTED AVERAGE METHOD

Under the **weighted average method**, an average cost per unit is computed by dividing the total cost of goods available for sale, including the cost of the beginning inventory and all purchases made during the accounting period, by the total number of units available for sale. This weighted average is then multiplied by the number of units on hand to determine the cost of the ending inventory as follows.

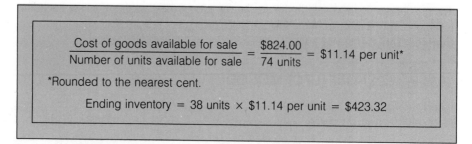

$$\frac{\text{Cost of goods available for sale}}{\text{Number of units available for sale}} = \frac{\$824.00}{74 \text{ units}} = \$11.14 \text{ per unit*}$$

*Rounded to the nearest cent.

Ending inventory = 38 units × $11.14 per unit = $423.32

The cost of goods sold is:

Cost of goods available for sale—74 units	$824.00
Less: Cost of ending merchandise inventory—38 units	423.32
Cost of goods sold—36 units	$400.68

The cost assigned to cost of goods sold is confirmed as follows:

$$36 \text{ units} \times \$11.14 \text{ per unit} = \$401.04$$
(The difference is due to rounding the unit cost.)

The use of this method results in all units sold and on hand being priced at the average cost of $11.14 per unit.

COMPARISON OF COSTING METHODS

The preceding sections examined the procedural aspects of each costing method. This section discusses the justifications, features, advantages, and disadvantages of each method. In doing so, the effects of each of the four methods on the firm's financial statements are compared, and the results are illustrated in Figure 9-3. It is assumed that the 36 units were sold for a total of $720, operating expenses totaled $180, and the average income tax rate was 30%. The sales and operating expenses are the same in all cases because the inventory method used does not affect those income statement items. The beginning inventory in each case was assumed to be 20 units costing a total of $200. In the next period, the beginning inventory value will vary, depending on the costing method selected, and will be equal to the ending inventory computed in the current period.

Figure 9-3
Comparison of Four Costing Methods

Periodic Inventory System				
	Specific Identification	FIFO	LIFO	Weighted Average
Sales—36 units	$720	$720	$720	$720
Beginning inventory	$200	$200	$200	$200
Add: Purchases	624	624	624	624
Goods available for sale	824	824	824	824
Less: Ending inventory	420	448	398	423
Cost of goods sold	404	376	426	401
Gross profit on sales	316	344	294	319
Less: Operating expenses	180	180	180	180
Income before taxes	136	164	114	139
Less: income taxes—30%*	41	49	34	42
Net income	$ 95	$115	$ 80	$ 97
Ending inventory	$420	$448	$398	$423

*Income taxes are rounded to the nearest dollar.

Note that the computations in Figure 9-3 are based on the assumption that the unit cost increased steadily from $10 to $12 during the period. If the unit cost had not changed during the period, cost of goods sold, net income, and ending inventory values would be the same for all four methods. When costs change during a period, the costing method selected can have a significant effect on the firm's reported assets and net income figure. Even in this simple example, with increasing prices and only one inventory item held for sale, FIFO net income was almost 45% greater than the LIFO net income. However, keep in mind that all four methods are based on the cost concept. Although cost of goods sold and net income may vary between accounting periods (remember that sales revenue is unaffected by the cost method used), the total cost of goods sold and total net income reported over the life of the firm is the same using all four methods, because only the actual cost incurred for inventory can be expensed.

SPECIFIC IDENTIFICATION METHOD

Under the specific identification method, when a sale is made, the item sold is identified and the cost of that item is matched against revenues. Thus, the method is based on the actual physical flow of goods.

Use of this method is primarily limited to businesses that sell easily identified items with a high unit cost (e.g., automobile dealerships and jewelry stores). Most other firms find this method impractical because it is both costly and time-consuming. Another disadvantage of the method is that if the inventory units are identical and have different costs, it is possible for management to manipulate income by choosing to sell a unit with a low or a high cost.

FIRST-IN, FIRST-OUT METHOD

The FIFO method is widely used because it is easy to apply. When stock is rotated so that the oldest units are sold first, the method's cost flow assumption approximates the actual physical flow of goods. The method does not permit manipulation of income, since management is not free to pick the cost of a certain item to be matched with revenue. Instead, it must expense the oldest unit cost available for sale.

As can be seen in Figure 9-3, during periods of rising unit cost, this method results in reporting a lower cost of goods sold and higher net income than either the LIFO or weighted average methods. On the balance sheet, the ending inventory reflects the higher cost of the most recent purchases—a more realistic measure of the inventory's value than is provided by the other methods. However, during a period of declining unit cost, FIFO will produce the highest cost of goods sold, the lowest net income, and the lowest ending inventory values.

Many accountants argue that using FIFO during periods of rising prices results in an overstatement in real net income. To illustrate this point, consider the data used in our previous illustration.

January 1	Beginning inventory	20 units @ $10
April 15	Purchase	24 units @ $11
April 20	Sales	16 units @ $20
July 7	Purchase	30 units @ $12
August 12	Sales	20 units @ $20

On April 20, the firm sold 16 units for $20 per unit. Under FIFO, the company charged $10 per unit to cost of goods sold, which resulted in a gross profit of $10 per unit. However, these units were replaced on July 7 with units costing $12 each. Therefore, $2 of the gross profit per unit ($12 replacement cost less historical cost of $10) was used to replace the units sold, and only $8 per unit represents the distributable gross profit of the firm. Inclusion of the $2 in gross profit is considered misleading because it cannot be distributed to the owners or reinvested in other aspects of the business without reducing the firm's ability to replace units sold. For this reason, it is sometimes called "phantom profit" or "illusory profit." The same line of reasoning applies to the units sold on August 12, which, if prices continue to rise, must be replaced with higher cost units.

LAST-IN, FIRST-OUT METHOD

The basic assumption of the LIFO method is that the firm must maintain a certain level of inventory to operate. When inventory is sold, it must be replaced at its current replacement cost. Income is not considered earned unless the sales price exceeds the cost to replace the units sold. Although the cost of goods sold does not always equal the cost to replace the unit sold because of price changes after the sale, it is frequently argued that LIFO provides the best measure of net income because it matches the more recent costs with current revenues. Since prices have generally moved upward, the effect of this method is to produce (1) a higher cost of goods sold and (2) a lower net income than the other methods (see Figure 9-3).

However, balance sheet values soon become outdated under LIFO because the oldest unit costs remain in the inventory. To illustrate, assume that during the next five years the unit cost increased to $20 and that in each year the firm sold the same number of units that were purchased. In this case, using the LIFO cost flow assumption, the cost of goods sold will be equal to the cost of the units purchased each year; the ending inventory each year will continue to be the 38 units at a total cost of $398. However, the cost to replace these units is now $760 (38 × $20). This understatement in the value of the inventory creates a problem in evaluating the working capital position of a firm. In addition, if the number of units on hand falls below the 38 units, there is a matching of old costs with current revenues, which distorts income in the year of the inventory decrease. To continue the illustration, assume that five years from now the sales price is $40 per unit and the unit cost is $20. If the number of units sold is greater than the number of units purchased in the fifth year, part of the beginning inventory is accounted for as sold. The gross profit per unit on current purchases and the beginning inventory purchased on April 15 is compared here.

	Current Purchases	Beginning Inventory
Sales price	$40	$40
Cost of goods sold	20	11
Gross profit	$20	$29

Inclusion of the $29 gross profit in the current period's income statement may distort comparison of the performance of the company to other periods. For this reason, a material effect on income from a reduction in the LIFO beginning inventory should be disclosed.

Another disadvantage of LIFO is that the possibility exists for management to manipulate net income by buying or not buying goods at the end of the period. If management wants to increase net income, for example, it could delay the purchase made on July 7 until the next fiscal period. In this case the cost of the 36 units sold is:

24 units from the April 15 purchase at $11 per unit	$264.00
12 units from the beginning inventory at $10 per unit	120.00
Cost of goods sold	$384.00

Thus, under this assumption the cost of goods sold is $42 ($426 − $384) less than if the July 7 purchase is made. As a result, net income is $42 higher.

Note that in Figure 9-3 the income tax expense under LIFO is the lowest of the four methods ($34). Thus, although all four methods are acceptable for computing taxable income, using LIFO during periods of rising prices produces a tax benefit in the current period. The reduced cash outflow for taxes makes more cash available for use in the firm's operations. However, as noted earlier, only the actual cost incurred is deductible as an expense. Thus, if the beginning inventory is eventually sold or if prices decline, the total cost of goods sold will be lower and taxable income will be greater under LIFO. Over the life of the firm, however, these items will be the same for all four methods.

Despite the tax benefit, some firms have been reluctant to switch to LIFO because current tax laws require that if LIFO is used for tax purposes, it must also be used for financial reporting purposes.[1] This means that firms using LIFO must report lower earnings, and such a report may have an unfavorable effect on investors.

WEIGHTED AVERAGE METHOD

The weighted average cost method is usually justified because the method is simple to apply and is less subject to income manipulation. In applying this method, the average unit cost is affected by (1) the number of units and cost of units in the beginning inventory and (2) by all purchases made during the year. As a result, the cost of goods sold, net income, and ending inventory amounts reported under the weighted average cost method falls between the extremes produced by FIFO and LIFO when prices are dropping or rising. Thus, the use of the weighted average cost method tends to smooth out net income and inventory values with neither the cost of goods sold nor the ending inventory reported at current values.

Since purchases made at the end of the year are included in the weighted average unit cost, it is possible for management to affect net income by making or delaying purchases at the end of the year. However, the impact is usually not significant because of the averaging effect. Although the average cost method is not used as frequently as FIFO and LIFO, it is sometimes employed when the inventory units involved are homogeneous in nature and it is difficult to establish a physical-flow assumption. Examples of such inventory are grain in a grain elevator or gasoline in a storage tank. It is not possible to identify each unit with its original cost because a new delivery mixes with the units on hand. Remember, however, that although the physical flow is on an average basis, the owner may elect to use the FIFO or LIFO cost-flow assumption.

---

[1] A company may use an inventory method other than LIFO in reports submitted as a supplement to, or as an explanation of, a primary presentation of financial income. For example, in a supplemental section of the annual report, management may discuss the effect of using the LIFO method instead of another accounting method. Prentice-Hall, Inc., *Federal Taxes 2nd*, 33,264-33,265.

WHICH METHOD TO SELECT?

The selection of the cost method to use for a particular type of inventory depends upon many factors, including the effect on the firm's financial statements, income tax considerations, the information needs of management and statement users, and the clerical cost of applying the method. In practice, more than one of the methods may be considered appropriate in accounting for the same type of inventory. That is, generally accepted accounting standards do not prescribe the use of a specific costing method as being "best" for a particular set of inventory conditions. It is up to management and to the firm's accountant to decide which method provides both the most useful information to its statement users and satisfies other needs as well.

CONSISTENCY IN USING A COSTING METHOD

Clearly, the inventory costing method selected can have a significant impact on the firm's reported net income and asset amounts. For this reason, the method used to assign cost to inventory and cost of goods sold should be disclosed in the financial statements.

Once a costing method has been selected, management cannot indiscriminately switch to another. When alternative accounting methods or procedures are considered acceptable in a given situation, the *principle of consistency* requires that a firm apply the same method from one accounting period to the next. If switching accounting methods between periods were permitted, the accounting data produced in different accounting periods would not be comparable.

The consistency principle does not completely rule out changing to an acceptable alternative method if the new method results in improved financial reporting. However, for tax purposes, a change in inventory costing methods, except a switch to LIFO, can only be made with the consent of the Internal Revenue Service. Generally, the approval to switch is automatic. A firm can switch to LIFO by merely using the method in the tax return and including a required form. Once a change is made, the nature of the change, the effect of the change on the financial statements, and the reasons the newly adopted method is preferred must be fully disclosed in the notes accompanying the financial statements. Such disclosure is illustrated in Figure 9-4. Without such disclosure, the statement reader may assume that no material changes in accounting methods were made during the period.

Effective January 1, 1990, the Company changed its method of determining the cost of its inventories from the first-in, first-out (FIFO) method to the last-in, first-out (LIFO) method. The Company believes the LIFO method will more fairly present results of operations by reducing the effect of inflationary cost increases in inventories and thus match current cost with current revenues. The 1989 results of operations do not reflect this accounting change. Pro-forma effects of retroactive application of LIFO to prior years are not determinable, and thus there is no cumulative effect on retained earnings at the beginning of the year. Thus, the December 31, 1989, inventories valued at FIFO are the opening LIFO inventories. The effect of the change in 1990 was to reduce inventory and net earnings by $1,262,000.

Figure 9-4
Illustration of Reporting Change in Inventory Costing Methods

THE LOWER OF COST OR MARKET RULE

Objective 3:
Lower of cost or
market rule

Cost is the primary basis for recording and reporting most assets. The four inventory costing methods previously discussed are alternatives for arriving at the cost of inventory when the unit cost fluctuates during an accounting period. However, when the value of inventory or the cost to replace the inventory decrease, it is sometimes considered appropriate to report inventory at an amount below its cost. The decline in value could result from obsolescence, damage, deterioration, or a decline in unit costs caused by supply and demand factors. If at the end of the period, the cost of replacing the inventory is less than its historical cost, the inventory is written down to the lower replacement cost and a loss is reported. This valuation approach is referred to as the lower of cost or market (LCM) rule. Market, as the term is used here, is *the cost to replace* the inventory in the quantities typically purchased through the usual sources of supply.

Using a valuation figure that is lower than cost is justified by the convention of conservatism. Under this convention, a decrease in value is recorded in the accounts in the period in which the decrease occurs. Thus, application of the LCM rule results in a loss in inventory value being recorded (matched against revenue) in the period in which the decline in value occurs, rather than in a subsequent period when the inventory is sold. Increases in the cost to replace inventory are not recorded because they have not yet been realized by a sale (revenue principle).

To illustrate, if the ending inventory has a cost of $140,000 and a replacement cost of $138,500, a loss of $1,500 is recognized in the current period. Under a periodic inventory system, the ending inventory amount to be subtracted from the cost of goods available for sale is $138,500. As a result, cost of goods sold is increased by the $1,500. This approach is acceptable if the loss is not material in relation to the cost of goods sold. If the loss is material, it should be reported as a separate item in the income statement, since it is not related to selling goods. On the other hand, if the inventory had a cost of $140,000 and the replacement cost was $142,000, the increase in value is not recognized.

Methods of Applying the LCM Rule

The LCM rule may be applied using three alternative approaches. Any of these approaches is acceptable for accounting, but once selected the method should be used consistently. The LCM rule may be applied as follows:

1. To each inventory item, such as a particular model of tapedeck.
2. To each major inventory category, such as all tapedecks or all electronics stocked by a department store.
3. To the total inventory.

Computing the ending inventory value using each of these approaches is illustrated in Figure 9-5. The three approaches result in an ending inventory value of $5,860 when applied to each inventory item, $6,070 when applied to major categories, and $6,280 when applied to the total inventory. Whichever approach is used, the ending inventory value computed is reported on the balance sheet and subtracted from the cost of goods available for sale in the income statement. Also, the approach used must be applied consistently.

Several modifications to the LCM rule as illustrated above are used in practice to determine the market value to be compared to historical cost. These modifications and other issues related to applying the LCM rule are discussed in Intermediate Accounting.

| Item | Unit Price | | | Total Cost | LCM | | | |
	Quantity	Cost	Market Price		Total Market	Item	Major Category	Total Inventory
Computers:								
IT3	4	$400	$250	$1,600	$1,000	$1,000		
IT35	6	600	620	3,600	3,720	3,600		
				5,200	4,720		$4,720	
Printers:								
PRT5	3	150	120	450	360	360		
Prt18	4	225	300	900	1,200	900		
				1,350	1,560		1,350	
				$6,550	$6,280	$5,860	$6,070	$6,280

Figure 9-5
Applying LCM Rule

NET REALIZABLE VALUE

The inventory of a retail or wholesale business often contains units that have been used or that are obsolete, shop-worn, or damaged. Such inventory items are generally reported at **net realizable value**—the anticipated sales price in the normal course of the business, less the estimated cost of selling and disposal. To illustrate, assume that a company is holding a tape deck that cost $340 and normally sells for $415. Because the unit was used as a demonstrator, however, it is estimated that it could be sold for $310 after the unit is reconditioned for a cost of $45. A sales commission on the unit is expected to be $31. The value of the unit is computed for inventory purposes as follows:

Objective 4:
Computing net realizable value

Estimated sales value	$310
Estimated selling and reconditioning cost	76
Estimated net realizable value	$234

Since the estimated net realizable value is below the historical cost of $340, the unit should be carried in the ending inventory at $234. This results in a loss of $106 ($340 − $234) being reported in the period in which the decrease in value occurs, rather than in the period in which the unit is sold. Under a periodic inventory system, the loss becomes a part of the cost of goods sold. (If a perpetual inventory system is used, the inventory card is adjusted to reflect the lower value, and an entry is made to reduce the Merchandise Inventory account and recognize a loss.)

If the net realizable value is greater than the historical cost, the inventory is not written up to reflect the higher value. Again, the historical cost of the unit is the upper value to be used in valuation. In addition, if inventory is written down to net realizable value or replacement cost, the new value substitutes for the original cost figure for computations in future periods.

PERPETUAL INVENTORY SYSTEMS

This part of the chapter illustrates the application of the four cost flow methods— specific identification, FIFO, LIFO, and weighted average—with a perpetual inventory system. Under the perpetual system, the inventory records are updated at the time of purchase or sale. This involves a great deal of time and, consequently, money. The

Objective 5:
Allocation of inventory cost— perpetual inventory system

availability of more versatile and less costly computers, however, has allowed more companies to adopt the perpetual inventory system—and thus achieve better inventory control.

In a perpetual inventory system, an inventory card is maintained for each item in stock and an inventory control account is kept in the general ledger. To provide a continuous and current record of inventory transactions, the appropriate inventory card and the Merchandise Inventory account are adjusted as purchases and sales transactions occur. Inventory purchases are recorded at cost in the Merchandise Inventory account and in the individual inventory cards. Chapter 6 showed that the following two entries are made at the time of sale:

Mar.	15	Accounts Receivable (or Cash)	20	
		Sales		20
		Sold one unit of inventory for $20.		
	15	Cost of Goods Sold	10	
		Merchandise Inventory		10
		Transferred cost of unit sold to Cost of		
		Goods Sold account.		

The dollar amount of the first entry is based on the sales price. If the per-unit cost varies, the dollar amount recorded in the second entry depends on the cost flow method used.

SPECIFIC IDENTIFICATION METHOD

The computations for the specific identification method would be the same as those described earlier for a periodic inventory system. They will not be repeated here. The only difference between the two methods is that under the perpetual system an entry is made at the time of sale to record the transfer of cost from the Merchandise Inventory account to the Cost of Goods Sold account.

FIRST-IN, FIRST-OUT METHOD

A perpetual inventory card using the same data presented earlier for the periodic inventory system is shown in Figure 9-6. Note that the perpetual inventory record shows the units and dollar amounts on a continuous basis for goods on hand, goods purchased, and goods sold.

Under the FIFO method, the cost of units removed from inventory is assumed to be from the first units available for sale at the time of each sale. The cost of the units on hand is composed of the most recent purchases. Thus, in Figure 9-6, the cost of the 16 units sold ($160) on April 20 is computed from the unit cost of the earliest units available, which are those in the beginning inventory. The 28 remaining unsold units are identified as (1) four units from the beginning inventory and (2) 24 units from the April 15 purchase.

The identification of units from separate purchases results in what are frequently called "inventory cost layers." For the next sale, the cost of four units from the beginning inventory ($40) and 16 units from the first purchase ($176) are transferred to cost of goods sold. This leaves an ending inventory of 38 units valued at $448. Thus, at the end of the period, the Cost of Goods Sold account will show a balance of $376 ($160 + $216).

Item: Computer Software—Bridge for the Novice — Minimum Stock: 10
Code: CS115 — Location: Store Display — Maximum Stock: 60

Date	Explanation	Purchases Units	Unit Cost	Total Cost	Cost of Goods Sold Units	Unit Cost	Total Cost	Balance Units	Unit Cost	Total Cost
1/1	Beginning balance							20	10.00	200.00
4/15	Purchases	24	11.00	264.00				20	10.00	200.00
								24	11.00	264.00
4/20	Sales				16	10.00	160.00	4	10.00	40.00
								24	11.00	264.00
7/7	Purchases	30	12.00	360.00				4	10.00	40.00
								24	11.00	264.00
								30	12.00	360.00
8/12	Sales				4	10.00	40.00	8	11.00	88.00
					16	11.00	176.00	30	12.00	360.00

Figure 9-6
Inventory Card Perpetual Inventory System—FIFO Cost Flow Method

LAST-IN, FIRST-OUT METHOD

When the LIFO method (see Figure 9-7) is used in conjunction with a perpetual inventory system, the cost of goods sold is determined at the point of each sale based on the assumption that the last units acquired are the first ones sold. Thus, the cost of the 16 units sold on April 20 consists of the cost of the most recent units purchased

Figure 9-7
Inventory Card Perpetual Inventory System—LIFO Cost Flow Method

Item: Computer Software—Bridge for the Novice — Minimum Stock: 10
Code: CS115 — Location: Store Display — Maximum Stock: 60

Date	Explanation	Purchases Units	Unit Cost	Total Cost	Cost of Goods Sold Units	Unit Cost	Total Cost	Balance Units	Unit Cost	Total Cost
1/1	Beginning balance							20	10.00	200.00
4/15	Purchases	24	11.00	264.00				20	10.00	200.00
								24	11.00	264.00
4/20	Sales				16	11.00	176.00	20	10.00	200.00
								8	11.00	88.00
7/7	Purchases	30	12.00	360.00				20	10.00	200.00
								8	11.00	88.00
								30	12.00	360.00
8/12	Sales				20	12.00	240.00	20	10.00	200.00
								8	11.00	88.00
								10	12.00	120.00

on April 15. The inventory balance of 28 units consists of two inventory cost layers—20 units from the beginning inventory and eight units from the April 15 purchase. Similarly, the 20 units sold on August 12 are identified with the most recent units acquired on July 7. The cost of goods sold for the period is $416 ($176 + $240). The ending inventory is $408 ($200 + $88 + $120).

MOVING AVERAGE METHOD

Under the **moving average method** (see Figure 9-8), a new average cost per unit is computed after each purchase, rather than simply computing a weighted average at year-end. The moving average cost is used to compute the cost of goods sold and inventory on hand until additional units are acquired at a different unit price. It is computed as follows.

$$\frac{\text{Cost of goods available for sale currently}}{\text{Total number of units available for sale currently}} = \text{Moving average cost}$$

In our illustration, the average cost per unit after the April 15 purchase is:

$$(\$200 + \$264)/(20 \text{ units} + 24 \text{ units}) = \$10.55 \text{ per unit}$$

Since there were no additional purchases made before the sale of the 16 units on April 20, the cost of the units sold is $168.80 (16 units × $10.55 per unit). The 28 units on hand are valued at $295.20 ($464.00 − $168.80). As a result of rounding, the cost of the units on hand is approximately equal to the 28 units times the $10.55 per unit. This average $10.55 cost would be used to cost additional units sold until another purchase is made, at which time a new moving average cost is computed, as shown in Figure 9-8.

Figure 9-8
Inventory Card Perpetual Inventory System—Moving Average Cost Flow Method

Item: Computer Software—Bridge for the Novice   Minimum Stock: 10
Code: CS115   Location: Store Display   Maximum Stock: 60

		Purchases		Cost of Goods Sold			Balance		
Date	Explanation	Units	Unit Cost	Total Cost	Units	Unit Cost	Total Cost	Units	Unit Cost	Total Cost
1/1	Beginning balance							20	10.00	200.00
4/15	Purchases	24	11.00	264.00				44	10.55	464.00
4/20	Sales				16	10.55	168.80	28	10.55	295.20
7/7	Purchases	30	12.00	360.00				58	11.30	655.20
8/12	Sales				20	11.30	226.00	38	11.30	429.20

Computations
4/15 ($200.00 + $264.00)/(20 units + 24 units) = $10.55 per unit*
7/7 ($295.20 + $360.00)/(28 units + 30 units) = $11.30 per unit*
   *Rounded to the nearest cent.

COMPARISON OF COSTING METHODS

The justifications and disadvantages of using each method are the same as those discussed earlier for the periodic inventory system and will not be repeated here. The relative dollar amounts of cost of goods sold, net income, and ending inventory produced by the four methods would also be the same. That is, in periods of rising prices, LIFO will produce a higher cost of goods sold, a lower net income, and a lower ending inventory than the FIFO or average cost methods.

COMPARISON OF THE PERPETUAL AND PERIODIC INVENTORY SYSTEMS

Application of the four alternative cost flow assumptions has been illustrated using the same data for both the periodic and perpetual inventory systems. For comparison, the results obtained for both systems are presented in Figure 9-9. Figure 9-9 assumes that the 36 units are sold for a total of $720. Operating expenses are $180, and the average income tax rate is 30%.

Figure 9-9
Comparison of Inventory Systems and Four Costing Methods

Perpetual Inventory System

	Specific Identification	FIFO	LIFO	Moving Average
Sales—36 units	$720	$720	$720	$720
Less: Cost of goods sold	404	376	416	395
Gross profit on sales	316	344	304	325
Less: Operating expenses	180	180	180	180
Income before taxes	136	164	124	145
Less: Income taxes—30%*	41	49	37	43
Net income	$ 95	$115	$ 87	$102
Ending inventory	$420	$448	$408	$429

Periodic Inventory System (From Figure 9-3)

	Specific Identification	FIFO	LIFO	Weighted Average
Sales—36 units	$720	$720	$720	$720
Beginning inventory	200	200	200	200
Add: Purchases	624	624	624	624
Goods available for sale	824	824	824	824
Less: Ending inventory	420	448	398	423
Cost of goods sold	404	376	426	401
Gross profit on sales	316	344	294	319
Less: Operating expenses	180	180	180	180
Income before taxes	136	164	114	139
Less: Income taxes—30%*	41	49	34	42
Net income	$ 95	$115	$ 80	$ 97
Ending inventory	$420	$448	$398	$423

*Income taxes are rounded to the nearest dollar.

Specific Identification and FIFO Methods

Under either inventory system, both the specific identification and FIFO methods assign the same amount of cost to the ending inventory and to cost of goods sold. The values obtained with the specific identification method are the same because the units identified as sold are the same under both inventory systems. Using FIFO, the same amounts are obtained because the cost of goods sold is computed assuming that the oldest units available for sale are always sold first.

LIFO METHOD

When the LIFO method is used, both the ending inventory and cost of goods sold dollar amounts may vary between the perpetual and periodic systems. The periodic system with LIFO produced a cost of goods sold of $426 and an ending inventory of $398. The amounts for a perpetual inventory system were $416 and $408, respectively. The two methods produce different results because of the timing of the computation of cost of goods sold.

Under the periodic system, the cost of goods sold is computed at the end of the period and the dates of sale are ignored. Under the perpetual system, the cost of goods sold is computed at the time of each sale. The cost of goods sold and ending inventory computations for both inventory systems are:

Periodic Inventory System (See page 384) (LIFO)				Perpetual Inventory System (See Figure 9-7) (LIFO)			
Cost of Goods Sold							
Date Acquired	Units	Unit Cost	Total	Date Acquired	Units	Unit Cost	Total
4/15	6	$11	$ 66	4/15	16	$11	$176
7/7	30	12	360	7/7	20	12	240
Cost of goods sold			426	Cost of goods sold			416
Ending Inventory							
1/1	20	$10	$200	1/1	20	$10	$200
4/15	18	11	198	4/15	8	11	88
–	–	–	–	7/7	10	12	120
Ending inventory			398	Ending inventory			408
Total cost of goods available for sale			$824	Total cost of goods available for sale			$824

Under a periodic system with LIFO, the last units purchased with a higher unit cost were included in the cost of goods sold computation; the lower cost units in the beginning inventory and first purchase are considered to be on hand in the ending inventory.

When the perpetual system is used and prices are rising, units with a lower cost (i.e., the more recent purchases at the time of each sale) are charged to cost of goods sold. As a result, ten units of the last purchase on July 7 are included in the ending inventory.

Average Cost Method

Although the computation of average cost is essentially the same under both systems, each system produces different results when prices change during the reporting period. This difference occurs because: (1) under the periodic system, one weighted average cost is used to cost all goods sold during the entire period. When a periodic weighted average is computed (at the end of the period), it is affected by the higher unit cost of purchases made late in the period. (2) Under the perpetual system, the cost transferred to cost of goods sold each time a sale is made is based on a moving average. The moving average is unaffected by price changes that occur after the sale. When prices increase, a moving average will yield a lower cost of goods sold and a higher ending inventory than a periodic weighted average.

When prices are changing, the periodic and perpetual systems will produce different net income figures under the LIFO and average costing methods. The extent of the variation is determined primarily by the rate of change in prices during the period and the frequency with which the inventory is purchased and sold.

INVENTORY ERRORS

The cost of goods sold is the largest expense for many firms. The inventory balance of unsold goods is often the largest current asset reported in the balance sheet. Therefore, determination of correct dollar amounts to be reported for these two financial statement items is very important. Because of the large volume of inventory transactions and the necessity of making numerous computations, errors can occur at various stages in accounting for inventory.

Objective 6:
Effects of inventory errors

PERPETUAL INVENTORY SYSTEM

If a perpetual inventory system is maintained, a physical count is taken at the end of the period to verify the balances shown on the individual inventory cards. Even if the inventory records and the physical count are in agreement, there may still be errors in the accounts.

A common error is the failure to record goods in transit owned by the firm at the end of the period. As discussed earlier, such errors have no effect on net income, but inventory and accounts payable are both understated by the same amount.

Another common error is the failure to observe a proper cut off for recording sales and the related cost of goods sold. For example, a sale made after the year-end may have been recorded before the year-end. If the inventory, which was still on hand at year-end, is isolated and not counted, sales, cost of goods sold, gross profit, and net income are overstated. In the balance sheet, accounts receivable are overstated and inventory is understated—resulting in a net overstatement in total assets and owners' equity equal to the amount of the gross profit on the sale.

PERIODIC INVENTORY SYSTEM

Under a periodic inventory system, errors may occur in counting and pricing the inventory and in the failure to use the proper cut off dates for recording purchases and sales. To illustrate the effects of errors in a periodic inventory system, it is helpful to reconsider the calculation of cost of goods sold.

In Figure 9-10, it is assumed that a $20,000 understatement in the ending inventory occurred while taking the physical inventory at the end of 1991. Comparison with the "correct" column shows that this error resulted in an overstatement in the cost of

	1991			1992	
	With a Correct Ending Inventory	With an Understated Ending Inventory		With an Understated Beginning Inventory	With a Correct Beginning Inventory
Sales revenue	$600,000	$600,000		$600,000	$600,000
Cost of goods sold:					
Beginning inventory	100,000	100,000		100,000	120,000
Purchases	380,000	380,000		400,000	400,000
Goods available for sale	480,000	480,000		500,000	520,000
Less: Ending inventory	120,000	100,000		160,000	160,000
Cost of goods sold	360,000	380,000	(Ending inventory for one period becomes beginning inventory for next period.)	340,000	360,000
Gross profit on sales	240,000	220,000		260,000	240,000
Operating expenses	140,000	140,000		150,000	150,000
Net income	$100,000	$ 80,000		$110,000	$ 90,000

Total net income for two periods:	Correct	Incorrect	Difference
1991	$100,000	$ 80,000	($20,000)
1992	90,000	110,000	20,000
Totals	$190,000	$190,000	–0–

Figure 9-10

Comparative Income Statements Showing Effects of Inventory Errors in Two Operating Periods (all amounts are assumed)

goods sold and an understatement in both gross profit and net income. Since the ending inventory is also reported as a current asset, this error causes current assets, total assets, and owners' equity all to be understated by $20,000. The opposite occurs if the ending inventory is overstated rather than understated.

Failure to discover the error in the ending inventory also causes the income statement for the next period to be incorrect, since the ending inventory for one period becomes the beginning inventory for the next period. Thus, in the next year, cost of goods sold is understated by $20,000 and both gross profit and net income are overstated by $20,000. The opposite is true if the beginning inventory was overstated.

It is assumed that the physical count taken at the end of 1992 is correct. Thus, the balance sheet amounts will be correct at the end of 1992. This results because inventory errors offset one another over two consecutive periods. That is, the net income in 1991 is understated by $20,000, but the net income in 1992 is overstated by $20,000. Thus, although each year is in error, the total net income for the two periods of $190,000 is correct and owners' equity at the end of 1992 is also correct as long as the ending inventory for 1992 is computed and recorded correctly.

If the errors are discovered after 1992 and comparative financial statements are prepared, the appropriate amounts reported in the financial statements should be corrected, even though the errors are offsetting. Failure to do so will distort the trend of the firm's earnings. For example, in Figure 9-10 the correct inventory amounts yielded a declining earnings trend, whereas the incorrect amounts show increasing net income amounts. Finally, if the error is discovered before the close of the 1992 year-end, a correcting entry should be made to increase the inventory account. The offsetting credit is made to retained earnings because the net income closed to retained earnings was understated by $20,000 at the end of 1991.

The effects of inventory errors in various financial statement items can be summarized as follows:

	Income Statement		Balance Sheet	
	Cost of Goods Sold	Net Income	Inventory Balance	Owners' Equity
Year 1—Ending inventory is understated	overstated	understated	understated	understated
Year 2—Beginning inventory is understated	understated	overstated	correct	correct
Year 1—Ending inventory is overstated	understated	overstated	overstated	overstated
Year 2—Beginning inventory is overstated	overstated	understated	correct	correct

ESTIMATING INVENTORIES

When a perpetual inventory accounting system is used, the cost of goods sold and the dollar amount of the inventory on hand is readily determinable throughout the period from the accounting records. However, under a periodic inventory system a physical inventory must be taken to determine the ending inventory balance.

Taking a physical inventory is so time-consuming and expensive that it is usually performed only at the end of the fiscal period. However, management and other statement users often want interim financial statements at regular intervals during the accounting period so they can assess the firm's performance. If a periodic inventory system is used, the preparation of the income statement requires that the inventory on hand be determined for the computation of the cost of goods sold.

The *retail inventory method* and the *gross profit method* are two approaches commonly used to estimate the dollar amount of unsold goods without taking a physical count. The two methods are also useful to test the reasonableness of a physical inventory taken by the firm's employees, to provide some insights into the dollar amount of inventory shortages from such causes as theft and damage, and to compute an estimate of the goods on hand when a physical inventory cannot be taken (e.g., when the inventory has been destroyed by a fire or a flood). The retail method is also used by a retail business to convert a physical inventory taken at retail prices to an estimated cost amount.

RETAIL INVENTORY METHOD

To use the **retail inventory method**, the firm must maintain records of the beginning inventory and purchases made during the period both at cost and retail price. The cost of goods available for sale is divided by the retail price of goods available for sale to calculate a relationship between cost and selling price. This amount is called the *ratio of cost to retail* or simply the *cost ratio*. An estimate of the inventory at retail is then determined by subtracting the sales recorded during the period from the goods available for sale at retail. The ending inventory at retail is multiplied by the cost ratio to arrive at an estimate of the ending inventory at cost. To illustrate, assume that the following information was accumulated in the accounts and supplementary records:

Objective 7: Methods used to estimate ending inventory values

	Cost	Retail
Beginning inventory	$ 49,000	$ 80,000
Net purchases to date	71,000	120,000
Net sales	–	160,000

The ending inventory at cost is estimated as follows.

	Cost	Retail
Beginning inventory	$ 49,000	$ 80,000
Net purchases	71,000	120,000
Goods available for sale	$120,000	200,000

Ratio of cost to retail:

$$\frac{\$120,000}{\$200,000} = 60\%$$

Less: Net sales	160,000
Estimate of ending inventory at retail	40,000
Cost ratio	x 60%
Estimate of ending inventory at cost	$ 24,000

The cost of goods sold can now be determined as $96,000 ($120,000 cost of goods available for sale minus $24,000 ending inventory at cost). The ending inventory, as computed above, is an estimate acceptable for interim statements. The firm should still conduct a physical inventory at least once a year for control purposes and to assure a proper measurement of the cost of goods sold.

The retail inventory method is also a convenient means to convert a physical inventory taken at retail to a cost amount. In other words, in a retail store each item for sale is generally marked to indicate the sales price. Consequently, during a physical inventory the units are listed at current retail prices as they are counted. This procedure eliminates the need to look up purchase invoices to determine the unit cost of each item. The retail dollar value of the ending inventory is converted to cost by applying the cost ratio calculated as shown above. Remember that the inventory value determined by a physical count is multiplied by the cost ratio. An estimate of the ending inventory at retail is still calculated as a control measure, because significant differences between the actual retail value and the estimate may indicate problems in the accounting system or excessive losses from theft or other causes.

The accuracy of the ending inventory, determined by the retail inventory method, depends on the mix or composition of goods in the ending inventory in relation to the mix of goods used to compute the cost ratio. The method assumes that the ending inventory consists of the same mix of goods at various cost percentages as was contained in the goods available for sale.

In practice, the originally established sales prices of many items do not remain constant during the period. Instead, they change frequently during the year as prices are reduced for special sales or are increased as the market value of the items increase. Frequent changes in the original selling prices make the calculation of a cost ratio actually more complicated than illustrated here. Modifications needed to adjust the retail inventory method for price changes are covered in Intermediate Accounting.

GROSS PROFIT METHOD

Some businesses do not maintain a record of the retail price of beginning inventory and purchases. If this information is not available, the retail inventory method cannot be used. However, the goods on hand may be estimated without taking a physical count by applying the **gross profit method**. This method is based on the assumption that the gross profit percentage remains approximately the same from period to period.

To illustrate, assume that the inventory of a business was totally destroyed by fire. A review of the last two years' operations revealed that the gross profit percentage was 40%. On the date of the fire, the ledger, which was locked in a fireproof safe every night after closing, was posted up to date. Selected account balances were:

	Dr. (Cr.) Balance
Sales	($210,000)
Sales returns and allowances	12,000
Purchases	124,650
Inventory—Beginning balance	24,450
Purchases returns and allowances	(3,750)
Freight-in	1,050

The inventory on hand on the date of the fire can be estimated for insurance purposes by completing a partial section of the income statement for the known amounts. An estimate of the cost of goods sold and gross profit can be made by multiplying the net sales by the cost percentage of 60% and 40%, respectively. An estimate of the cost of the ending inventory can now be made as shown here.

Sales		$210,000	
Less: Sales returns and allowances		12,000	
Net sales		198,000	(100%)
Cost of goods sold:			
Beginning inventory		$ 24,450	
Purchases	$124,650		
Less: Purchases returns and allowances	(3,750)		
Add: Freight-in	1,050		
Net purchases		121,950	
Goods available for sale		146,400	
Less: Estimated ending inventory		?	
Estimated cost of goods sold			
($198,000 × .60)		118,800	(60%)
Estimated gross profit on sales			
($198,000 × .40)		$ 79,200	(40%)

It can be determined from the records that the company had $146,400 of goods available for sale up to the date of the fire. By applying the cost percentage of 60% to the net sales, the cost of goods sold is estimated to be $118,800. The goods that were available for sale but had not been sold must have been on hand. Their cost is the difference between the estimated cost of goods sold ($118,800) and the cost of goods available for sale ($146,400). In this case, the result is $27,600.

PRESENTATION IN FINANCIAL STATEMENTS

The method used to account for inventory can significantly affect a firm's financial position and results of operations. Because of the importance of inventory, additional information is provided in footnotes to the financial statements. The disclosure commonly contains:

1. The composition of the inventory (e.g., raw materials, work in process, or finished goods).
2. The cost flow method that is used.
3. Whether that method is applied to all of the inventory.

4. The method of valuing the inventory (cost or lower of cost or market).
5. Whether the cost flow method was used consistently from one period to another.

Figure 9-11 shows an example of the disclosure provided. Other examples are contained in the Appendix to the text.

Figure 9-11
Illustration of Inventory Disclosures in Financial Statements

K MART CORPORATION
Consolidated Balance Sheets

($ millions)	January 31, 1990	January 25, 1989
Assets		
Current Assets:		
Cash (includes temporary investments of $35 and $594, respectively)	$ 353	$ 948
Merchandise inventories	6,933	5,671
Accounts receivable and other current assets	698	527
Total current assets	7,984	7,146
Investments in Affiliated Retail Companies	512	506
Property and Equipment—net	3,850	3,896
Other Assets and Deferred Charges	799	578
	$13,145	$12,126

Notes to Consolidated Financial Statements

(A) Summary of Significant Accounting Policies

Inventories: Merchandise inventories are valued at the lower of cost or market, using the retail method, on the last-in, first-out basis for substantially all domestic inventories and the first-in, first-out basis for the remainder.

(G) Merchandise Inventories

A summary of inventories by method of pricing and the excess of current cost over stated LIFO value follows.

(Millions)	January 31, 1990	January 25, 1989
Last-in, first-out (cost not in excess of market)	$6,288	$5,090
Lower of cost (first-in, first-out) or market	645	581
Total	$6,933	$5,671
Excess of current cost over stated LIFO value	$ 988	$ 898

Source: K mart Corporation 1989 annual report.

SUMMARY

Merchandise inventory is generally accounted for in accordance with the cost principle. Cost generally includes all expenditures incurred in bringing the inventory to (1) a saleable condition and (2) its existing location. Usually, the unit cost of an item changes during the accounting period. When prices change, management must select a cost flow method to use in allocating the cost of goods available for sale between the cost of goods sold and ending inventory.

Four alternative methods—specific identification, FIFO, LIFO, and average cost—were illustrated first for the periodic inventory system and then the perpetual inventory system. The specific identification method allocates costs by identifying the unit cost of specific units sold and on hand. FIFO assumes that the earliest units purchased are the first units sold, whereas LIFO assumes that the most recent units purchased are the first sold. The average cost method has two variations, weighted and moving, each of which allocates cost based on the average cost per unit. It was shown that each of these methods produces different amounts for cost of goods sold and ending inventory when prices are changing. As a result, income taxes, net income, total assets, and owners' equity are also affected by the cost flow method used.

Although cost is the primary basis of accounting for inventory, it is sometimes considered appropriate to write the inventory down to a lower value. This happens when the inventory's replacement cost or net realizable value is less than historical cost.

In some cases, it may be necessary or more convenient to estimate the ending inventory cost. Two approaches were illustrated for doing so: (1) The retail inventory method estimates the ending inventory by using the current relationship between cost and retail price. (2) The gross profit method is based on the assumption that the gross profit rate of prior years can be applied to current period sales to estimate the cost of goods sold. This estimate is then subtracted from cost of goods available for sale to provide an estimate of ending inventory.

SELF-TEST

Test your understanding of the chapter by selecting the best answer for each of the following.

1. If goods are in transit as of the end of the year and the terms of the sale are FOB shipping point, the goods should be shown as a part of the inventory of:
   a. the seller of the goods.
   b. the common carrier.
   c. the buyer of the goods.
   d. the consignor.
2. Micro Company holds goods on consignment from Software Company. Thirty percent of the units were sold by Micro during the period. Which of the following statements is true?

a. Software Company is the consignee and owns the goods.
b. Micro Company is the consignee and owns the goods since the company has physical possession.
c. Software Company is the consignor and should not include the unsold units in its ending inventory since the company does not hold the goods.
d. Software Company is the consignor and should include the unsold units in its ending inventory.

Use the following information for Questions 3, 4, and 5.
Inventory and purchases data for a certain inventory item are as follows.

	Number of Units	Unit Cost
Beginning inventory	10	$5
Purchases:		
March 8	15	6
November 6	8	7

Sales for the year occurred as follows.

8 units were sold on July 18.
9 units were sold on October 7.

The ending inventory contains 16 units. The company uses a periodic inventory system.

3. If the company uses the FIFO cost flow method, cost of goods sold would be:
   a. $104.
   b. $92.
   c. $110.
   d. $86.
4. If this company uses the weighted average cost flow method, what would ending inventory be? (Round your answer to the nearest dollar.)
   a. $104.
   b. $110.
   c. $101.
   d. $95.
5. If this company uses the LIFO cost flow method, cost of goods sold would be:
   a. $104.
   b. $92.
   c. $110.
   d. $86.
6. In a period of rising prices, which inventory method would tend to give the highest reported net income?
   a. Weighted average.
   b. FIFO.
   c. LIFO.
   d. Net income will be the same for all three methods.
7. The lower of cost or market rule is primarily supported by:
   a. the cost principle.
   b. the going concern principle.
   c. conservatism.
   d. consistency.

Use the following information for Questions 8, 9, and 10.
Inventory and purchases data for a certain inventory item are as follows.

	Number of Units	Unit Cost
Beginning inventory	10	$5
Purchases:		
March 8	15	6
November 6	8	7

Sales for the year occurred as follows.

8 units were sold on July 18.
9 units were sold on October 7.

The ending inventory contains 16 units. The company uses a perpetual inventory system.

8. If this company uses the FIFO cost-flow method, the debit to Cost of Goods Sold for the July 18 sale would be for:
   a. $40.
   b. $48.
   c. $56.
   d. $86.

9. If this company uses the LIFO cost-flow method, the debit to Cost of Goods Sold for the October 7 sale would be for:
   a. $62.
   b. $63.
   c. $54.
   d. $52.

10. If this company uses the moving average cost-flow method, the moving average cost per unit after the March 8 purchase is:
    a. $5.00.
    b. $6.00.
    c. $5.60.
    d. None of the above.

11. Net income for the period was reported to be $30,000. Later it was discovered that the beginning inventory was overstated by $2,000 and ending inventory understated by $1,500. The correct net income for the period is:
    a. $29,500.
    b. $33,500.
    c. $30,500.
    d. $25,500.

12. Given the following information, compute the estimated ending inventory.

	Cost	Retail
Beginning inventory	$ 45,000	$ 75,000
Net purchases	105,000	150,000
Net sales		180,000

   a. $24,000.
   b. $30,000.
   c. $42,000.
   d. $45,000.

REVIEW PROBLEM

Neal, Inc., a merchandising concern, engaged in the following transactions during the month of March 1992 with respect to their inventory.

Merchandise Purchases

Date	Units	Unit Cost
March 4	6,000	$5.00
March 11	16,000	5.10
March 18	20,000	5.20
March 25	7,000	5.30
Total	49,000	

Merchandise Sales

Date	Units	Sales Price per Unit
March 6	8,000	$10.00
March 13	12,000	10.00
March 20	18,000	10.50
March 27	7,000	10.50
Total	45,000	

Neal, Inc., uses a periodic inventory system. The March 1, 1992 beginning inventory consisted of 6,000 units at a cost of $4.80 per unit.

Required:

A. Compute the March 31, 1992 ending inventory in units.

B. Compute the ending inventory and cost of goods sold, in dollars, for the following cost flow assumptions:
  1. FIFO.
  2. LIFO.
  3. Weighted average.

C. Prepare an income statement through gross profit for the three inventory cost flow assumptions:
  1. FIFO.
  2. LIFO.
  3. Weighted average.

ANSWER TO REVIEW PROBLEM

A. The ending inventory is composed of 10,000 units. The following schedule can be used to calculate the number of units in the ending inventory.

	Units
Beginning inventory	6,000
Add: Purchases	49,000
Total units available	55,000
Less: Sales	45,000
Ending inventory	10,000

B. 1. Using FIFO, the ending inventory is $52,700 and the cost of goods sold is $228,800. Calculations are shown below:

Ending Inventory:
7,000 units from March 25 purchase at $5.30 per unit =	$ 37,100
3,000 units from March 18 purchase at $5.20 per unit =	15,600
Total	$ 52,700

Cost of Goods Sold:
6,000 units from beginning inventory at $4.80 per unit =	$ 28,800
6,000 units from March 4 purchase at $5.00 per unit =	30,000
16,000 units from March 11 purchase at $5.10 per unit =	81,600
17,000 units from March 18 purchase at $5.20 per unit =	88,400
Total	$228,800

2. Using LIFO, the ending inventory is $48,800 and the cost of goods sold is $232,700. Calculations are shown below:

Ending Inventory:
6,000 units from beginning inventory at $4.80 per unit =	$ 28,800
4,000 units from March 4 purchase at $5.00 per unit =	20,000
Total	$ 48,800

Cost of Goods Sold:
7,000 units from March 25 purchase at $5.30 per unit =	$ 37,100
20,000 units from March 18 purchase at $5.20 per unit =	104,000
16,000 units from March 11 purchase at $5.10 per unit =	81,600
2,000 units from March 4 purchase at $5.00 per unit =	10,000
Total	$232,700

3. Using weighted average, the ending inventory is $51,200 and the cost of goods sold is $230,300. Calculations are shown below:

Weighted Average Cost per Unit:

$$\frac{\text{Cost of goods available for sale}}{\text{Number of units available for sale}} = \frac{\$281,500^*}{55,000 \text{ units}} = \underline{\$5.12 \text{ per unit}^{**}}$$

*Cost of goods available for sale is computed as follows:
Beginning inventory ——	6,000 units at $4.80 per unit =	$ 28,800
March 4 purchase ——	6,000 units at $5.00 per unit =	30,000
March 11 purchase ——	16,000 units at $5.10 per unit =	81,600
March 18 purchase ——	20,000 units at $5.20 per unit =	104,000
March 25 purchase ——	7,000 units at $5.30 per unit =	37,100
Total		$281,500

**Rounded to nearest cent.

Ending Inventory:
10,000 units × weighted average cost per unit ($5.12) =	$51,200

Cost of Goods Sold:
Cost of goods available for sale ——	$281,500
Less: Cost of ending inventory ——	51,200
Cost of goods sold	$230,300

C. The income statements through gross profit for each of the three inventory cost flow assumptions are presented below.

	FIFO (1)	LIFO (2)
Sales*	$462,500	$462,500
Cost of goods sold:		
Beginning inventory	$ 28,800	$ 28,800
Add: Purchases	252,700	252,700
Cost of goods available for sale	281,500	281,500
Less: Ending inventory	52,700	48,800
Cost of goods sold	228,800	232,700
Gross profit on sales	$233,700	$229,800

	Weighted Average (3)
Sales	$462,500
Cost of goods sold:	
Beginning inventory	$ 28,800
Add: Purchases	252,700
Cost of goods available for sale	281,500
Less: Ending inventory	51,200
Cost of goods sold	230,300
Gross profit on sales	$232,200

*Calculation of Sales:
8,000 units from March 6 sale at $10.00 per unit = $ 80,000
12,000 units from March 13 sale at $10.00 per unit = 120,000
18,000 units from March 20 sale at $10.50 per unit = 189,000
7,000 units from March 27 sale at $10.50 per unit = 73,500
Total $462,500

ANSWERS TO SELF-TEST

1. c **2.** d **3.** b **4.** d **5.** c **6.** b **7.** c **8.** a
9. d **10.** c **11.** b **12.** b

GLOSSARY

CONSIGNEE. A firm or individual holding goods on consignment. The consignee does not own the goods held on consignment (p. 379).

CONSIGNMENT. A marketing arrangement whereby physical control of merchandise, but not title, is transferred from one business (the consignor) to another (the consignee) (p. 379).

CONSIGNOR. A firm or individual that ships goods on consignment. Title to the goods is retained by the consignor until the goods are sold by the consignee (p. 379).

FIRST-IN, FIRST-OUT (FIFO) METHOD. An inventory costing method that assumes the first units available for sale were the first units sold. The ending inventory consists of the cost of the most recently purchased units (p. 383).

GROSS PROFIT METHOD. A method used to estimate ending inventory value based on the assumption that the gross profit percentage is approximately the same from period to period (p. 401).

LAST-IN, FIRST-OUT (LIFO) METHOD. An inventory costing method that assumes the most recent units available for sale were the first units sold. Ending inventory consists of the cost of the earliest units purchased (p. 383).

LOWER OF COST OR MARKET (LCM) RULE. An inventory valuation method by which inventory is valued at the lower of original cost or market on the financial statement date (p. 390).

MOVING AVERAGE METHOD. An inventory costing method by which an average unit cost is computed after each purchase and used to compute the cost of goods sold for each sale occurring until the next purchase occurs (p. 394).

NET REALIZABLE VALUE. The anticipated sales price of an item less the estimated cost of selling and reconditioning (p. 391).

RETAIL INVENTORY METHOD. A method used to estimate the ending inventory value based on the relationship of cost to retail prices (p. 399).

SPECIFIC IDENTIFICATION METHOD. An inventory costing method by which the cost of a specific item sold can be separately identified from the cost of other units held in the inventory (p. 382).

WEIGHTED AVERAGE METHOD. An inventory costing method by which an average cost per unit is computed by dividing the total cost of the units available for sale by the total number of units available for sale (p. 384).

DISCUSSION QUESTIONS

1. Define the term "inventory." What is the difference between merchandise inventory, finished goods inventory, raw materials inventory, and work-in-process inventory?
2. Why is the control and safeguarding of inventory so essential? Explain.
3. When a periodic inventory system is maintained, how is the ending inventory determined?
4. Explain the terms "FOB shipping point" and "FOB destination." If goods are shipped FOB shipping point at a cost of $800, which party to the transaction must pay the freight bill? When does title to goods sold FOB destination normally transfer to the buyer?
5. Explain how a consignment arrangement works. Which party in a consignment arrangement should include the consigned goods in its inventory on the balance sheet date? Why?
6. Does the inventory costing method adopted by a company have to conform to the actual physical movement of the goods? Explain why or why not.
7. If a company uses the LIFO method, are the most recent costs of inventory on the balance sheet or on the income statement?
8. What is meant by "phantom profit?" Explain.
9. Explain why use of the LIFO method may have a tax advantage. Why would a company be reluctant to switch to LIFO?
10. What accounting principle requires that a firm apply the same inventory costing method from one accounting period to the next.
11. Define the term "market" as used in the phrase "lower-of-cost-or-market." What accounting principle justifies the use of the lower of cost or market rule?

12. Define net realizable value.
13. Differentiate between the weighted average cost method and the moving average cost method.
14. Explain why the LIFO method used with a periodic inventory system will generally produce results different from when it is used with a perpetual system.
15. What uses can be made of the retail inventory method and the gross profit method of estimating the cost of inventory?
16. What records must be maintained to use the retail inventory method?
17. What assumption does the retail inventory method make about the mix of goods in the ending inventory?

EXERCISES

Exercise 9-1 Determining Ending Inventory

General Sales Company has just completed a physical inventory count at year-end, December 31, 1992. The cost assigned to the inventory was $150,000. During the audit, the CPA discovered the following additional information:

1. On December 31, General Sales Company recorded goods purchased for $4,000 in the Purchases account. The terms were FOB shipping point. The goods were delivered by the seller to the transportation company on December 27. The goods were not included in the physical inventory since they had not arrived.
2. General Sales Company sells goods that it does not own on a consignment basis. Consigned goods on hand at year-end were included in the inventory at a cost of $2,200.
3. A purchase of goods worth $1,900 was made in December but was not recorded in the Purchases account until January. The goods were received on December 28, and included in the physical inventory.
4. A sale of goods costing $3,800 was made and recorded in December. The buyer requested that the goods be held for later delivery; the items were on hand and included in inventory at year-end.
5. General Sales Company sold goods costing $1,400 for $2,600 on December 26. The terms were FOB destination. The goods were shipped in December and arrived at the destination in January. The sale was recorded in 1992 and the goods were excluded from the ending inventory count.

Required:
Determine the correct ending inventory balance for 1992. All purchases and sales were made on credit.

Exercise 9-2 First-In, First-Out, Periodic Inventory System

Titan Sporting Goods Store sells cans of tennis balls. During 1992, Titan Sporting Goods sold 9,000 cans of tennis balls at $3.00 per can. Purchases of the product were made at the following times during the year:

January 1	Beginning Inventory	1,400 cans at $1.25
March 4	Purchase	2,000 cans at 1.35
May 11	Purchase	3,600 cans at 1.40
July 10	Purchase	2,400 cans at 1.50
September 1	Purchase	2,100 cans at 1.65
December 15	Purchase	1,500 cans at 1.75

Titan Sporting Goods uses a periodic inventory system and the first-in, first-out method to cost the ending inventory.

Required:
A. Determine the cost of the ending inventory at December 31, 1992.
B. Determine the cost of goods sold for the year ending December 31, 1992.
C. What are the advantages of the FIFO method?

Exercise 9-3   Last-In, First-Out, Periodic Inventory System
Wildcat Oil Company entered into the following transactions related to its synthetic oil inventory during 1992.

		Number of Cases	Price Per Case
January 1	Beginning Inventory	250	$50
February 8	Sales	140	75
April 15	Purchases	400	54
June 18	Sales	320	75
July 20	Purchases	500	55
August 18	Purchases	280	57
September 11	Sales	560	75
November 19	Sales	170	75

Wildcat Oil Company uses a periodic inventory system and the last-in, first-out method to assign a cost to the ending inventory.

Required:
A. Determine the cost of inventory on hand on December 31, 1992.
B. Determine the cost of goods sold for 1992.
C. What was the gross profit on sales for 1992?
D. Management considered making a purchase of 300 cases at $60 each on December 31, 1992. Determine the new cost of ending inventory, cost of goods sold, and gross profit on sales for 1992 if the purchase had been made. Comment on your results.

Exercise 9-4   Weighted Average, Periodic Inventory System
Keeley Petroleum Company purchases unleaded gasoline from producers and resells the gasoline to independent service stations. Due to the nature of its inventory, Keeley uses a periodic inventory system and the weighted average method to determine the cost of goods sold and ending inventory. The beginning inventory on July 1, 1991 consisted of 40,000 gallons at a cost of $.60 per gallon. The following gasoline purchases took place during the fiscal year that ended June 30, 1992.

September 12	60,000 gallons at $0.63 = $37,800
October 25	30,000 gallons at 0.64 = 19,200
December 10	50,000 gallons at 0.70 = 35,000
March 5	20,000 gallons at 0.72 = 14,400
May 20	80,000 gallons at 0.75 = 60,000

An inspection of the storage facilities on June 30, 1992 indicates that 60,000 gallons of gasoline are in the ending inventory.

Required:
A. Prepare the journal entry to record the purchase of the gasoline on September 12 by Keeley Petroleum Company.
B. How many gallons of gasoline were sold to service stations by Keeley Petroleum during the fiscal year ending June 30, 1992?

C. What is the cost assigned to the ending inventory on June 30, 1992?

D. Compute the cost of goods sold for the fiscal year ended June 30, 1992.

E. Why would Keeley Petroleum Company prefer to use the weighted average inventory method over other inventory costing methods?

Exercise 9-5 Comparison of Inventory Costing Methods

The beginning inventory and the transactions related to the inventory of the Helmuth Company during March 1992 follow.

			Units	Unit Cost	Total Cost
March	1	Beginning inventory	200	$10	$2,000
	3	Purchase	300	14	4,200
	8	Sale	220		
	15	Purchase	100	18	1,800
	22	Purchase	200	22	4,400
	29	Sale	280		

The Helmuth Company uses the periodic inventory system.

Required:

A. Compute the cost of goods available for sale, the ending inventory, and cost of goods sold for March 1992, using each of the following inventory costing methods.
1. FIFO.
2. LIFO.
3. Weighted average.
4. Specific identification. The sale on March 8 was identified with the March 3 purchase; 100 units of the March 29 sales were identified with the beginning inventory and the remainder was identified with the March 22 purchase.

B. Which inventory costing method resulted in:
1. the largest dollar amount for ending inventory?
2. the smallest dollar amount for ending inventory?
3. the largest net income?
4. the smallest net income?

Exercise 9-6 Inventory Cost Flow Methods—Period of Declining Prices

The following information was taken from the inventory records of Amity Supply Company.

			Units	Unit Cost	Total Cost
Jan.	1	Beginning inventory	500	$7.00	$3,500
Mar.	21	Purchase	600	6.75	4,050
May	13	Purchase	900	6.40	5,760
Sept.	24	Purchase	300	6.35	1,905
Dec.	6	Purchase	400	6.25	2,500

The ending inventory on December 31 was 600 units. All units were sold for $9.00 each. Amity Supply Company uses the periodic inventory system.

Required:

A. Before doing any computations, determine which inventory costing method, LIFO or FIFO, would result in:
1. the largest dollar value for ending inventory.
2. the smallest dollar value for ending inventory.
3. the highest net income.
4. the lowest net income.

B. Determine the value of the ending inventory, cost of goods sold, and gross profit for the following inventory methods.
  1. FIFO.
  2. LIFO.
C. Comment on your results.

Exercise 9-7 Consistency in Application of Inventory Costing Methods

Royal Mattress Corporation reported the following summarized financial data at the end of 1992.

	Millions
Sales revenue	$538
Cost of goods sold*	303
Gross margin	235
Operating expenses	145
Pretax income	$ 90

*Based on ending FIFO inventory of $120 million. On a LIFO basis this ending inventory would have been $55 million.

Before issuing the financial statements from which the summarized financial data above was selected, the company decided to change from FIFO to LIFO for 1992 because: "LIFO better matches expenses to revenues." The company has always used FIFO.

Required:
A. Restate the summarized income statement on a LIFO basis.
B. How much did the pretax income change as a result of the decision to switch from FIFO to LIFO? What caused the change?
C. Discuss probable stockholder reactions.

Exercise 9-8 Lower-of-cost-or-market

The Sewing Shoppe classifies its inventory into two departments. Its inventory on December 31, 1992, contained the following items.

Sewing Machine Department	Quantity	Unit Cost	Market Price Per Unit
Model 517	10	$260	$240
Model 312	5	225	230
Model 430	7	230	210

Fabric Department	Number of Bolts	Cost per Bolt	Market Price Per Bolt
Cotton	20	$140	$130
Polyester blend	15	150	170
Velvet	5	120	110

Required:
A. Compute the value of the inventory on December 31, 1992, applying the LCM rule to each individual inventory item.
B. Compute the value of the inventory applying the LCM rule on a departmental basis.
C. Compute the value of the inventory applying the LCM rule on a storewide basis.
D. Assume that at the end of 1993, the market price for model 517 was $250 and that eight units were on hand. How would this increase in the market price affect the inventory value of the eight units?

Exercise 9-9 Net Realizable Value

Empire Computer Sales has two personal computers that have been used as demonstration models. The first computer cost $800 and would normally sell for $1,180. The second computer cost $500 and would normally sell for $750. Empire estimates that each set will require $100 in repairs and then the computers can be sold for $900 and $600, respectively. Empire pays a 15% sales commission to all its salespeople.

Required:
A. Calculate the net realizable value of each personal computer.
B. Assume that Empire Computer Sales uses a perpetual inventory system. Prepare the journal entry to record the write-down of the inventory items.

Exercise 9-10 Calculating Ending Inventory and Cost of Goods Sold

Vista Appliance Company sells only one make and type of microwave ovens. It uses the specific identification method to account for its inventory. As of November 30, 1992, the company had 23 microwaves in inventory, which were acquired on the following dates.

August 15	5 at $290 each
September 8	10 at $320 each
October 29	8 at $340 each

Vista held a clearance sale in December and sold 14 microwaves for $440 each. There were no additional purchases made in December.

Required:
A. Calculate the ending inventory and gross profit on sales for December assuming that Vista identified the microwave sales with the purchases that would maximize reported gross profit.
B. Repeat requirement A, assuming that Vista identified the microwave sales with the purchases that would minimize reported gross profit.
C. From your results, what seems to be the disadvantage(s) of using the specific identification method? How could Vista Appliance Company overcome some of these objections?

Exercise 9-11 Perpetual Inventory Method and FIFO Costing

The Lucille Mitchell Corporation uses a perpetual inventory system and FIFO. The inventory records for June, 1992 are shown below.

Transactions	Units	Unit Cost
Beginning Inventory, June 1	200	$8.00
Purchase, June 10	500	8.60
Sale, June 12 (at $15 per unit)	330	
Purchase, June 18	400	9.20
Sale, June 30 (at $16 per unit)	540	

Required:
A. Prepare an inventory card for the month of June.
B. Prepare journal entries for the inventory transactions given above. Assume all purchases and sales are made on account.
C. Prepare a partial income statement through gross profit on sales for the month of June, 1992.

Exercise 9-12   Perpetual Inventory Method and LIFO Costing

Use the information contained in Exercise 9-11 and assume that Lucille Mitchell Company uses a perpetual inventory system and LIFO.

Required:
A. Prepare an inventory card for the month of June.
B. Prepare journal entries for the inventory transactions. Assume all purchases and sales are made on account.
C. Prepare a partial income statement through gross profit on sales for the month of June 1992.

Exercise 9-13   Perpetual Inventory Method and Moving Average Costing Method

Griff Enterprises uses a perpetual inventory system and the moving average costing method. During 1992 the following inventory transactions occurred.

Transactions	Units	Unit Cost
Beginning inventory, January 1	50	$20.00
Purchase, February 4	200	22.00
Sale, March 9 (at $30 per unit)	160	
Purchase, May 13	90	23.00
Sale, July 18 (at $30 per unit)	40	
Sale, August 22 (at $30 per unit)	110	
Purchase, October 27	150	25.00

Required:
A. Prepare an inventory card for 1992.
B. Prepare journal entries for the inventory transactions given above. Assume all purchases and sales are made on account.
C. Prepare a partial income statement through gross profit on sales for the year ended December 31, 1992.

Exercise 9-14   Perpetual Inventory System Comparing FIFO and LIFO

Medtech Industries uses a perpetual inventory system to account for its inventory of scientific instruments. The beginning inventory was 100 units with a cost of $45 each. During March, 1992, the following transactions occurred with respect to the instruments.

March	7	Sold 25 at $70 each.
	12	Purchased 50 units at $48 each.
	18	Sold 90 units at $70 each.
	20	Purchased 120 units at $50 each.
	28	Sold 30 units at $75 each.

Required:
A. Compute the cost of goods sold for March and the ending inventory on March 31 on:
    1. a FIFO basis.
    2. a LIFO basis.
B. Give the journal entry for each basis for the purchase on March 12. Assume all purchases are made on account.

C. Give the entries for each basis for the sale on March 18. Assume all sales are for cash.

D. Complete the following financial statements.

	March	
Income Statement	**FIFO**	**LIFO**
Sales revenue	$	$
Cost of goods sold		
Gross margin		
Expenses	1,725	1,725
Pretax income		
Balance Sheet		
Current Assets:		
Merchandise inventory	$	$

E. Which inventory method results in the higher net income? When would the other method result in the higher net income?

F. Assume a 40 percent tax rate. Which method would provide the more favorable cash position? By how much? Explain how this happens.

G. Which inventory method assumption would you recommend Medtech Industries to use? Explain your recommendation.

Exercise 9-15 LIFO Inventory Costing Method with Periodic and Perpetual Records

At the end of December, 1992, the inventory records for Spotless Mirror and Glass Company reflected the following for its inventory of wall mirrors.

Transaction	Units	Unit Cost
Beginning inventory, December 1	75	$35
Purchase, December 5	90	39
Sale, December 10 (at $60 each)	110	
Purchase, December 18	125	42
Sale, December 24, (at $64 each)	70	

Required:

A. Compute the goods available for sale in units and dollars.

B. Compute: (a) cost of ending inventory, and (b) cost of goods sold, using the LIFO inventory costing method and a *periodic* inventory system.

C. Compute: (a) cost of ending inventory, and (b) cost of goods sold, using the LIFO inventory costing method and a *perpetual* inventory system.

D. Compare the results of requirements (B) and (C) and explain why the amounts computed for ending inventory and cost of goods sold are different between the periodic and perpetual inventory systems.

Exercise 9-16 Inventory Errors

The president of Whitmire Company likes the trend of the gross profit percentage reflected in the following income statements.

WHITMIRE COMPANY
Income Statement
For the Years Ended December 31, 1990, 1991 and 1992

	1990		1991		1992	
Sales		$300,000		$380,000		$500,000
Cost of goods sold:						
Beginning inventory	$ 50,000		$ 40,000		$ 70,000	
Purchases	200,000		290,000		315,000	
Goods available for sale	250,000		330,000		385,000	
Ending inventory	40,000		70,000		60,000	
Cost of goods sold		210,000		260,000		325,000
Gross profit on sales		$ 90,000		$120,000		$175,000
Gross profit percentage		30%		32%		35%

The following errors were discovered after the books had been closed at the end of 1992.

1. Ending inventory for 1990 was understated by $8,000.
2. Ending inventory for 1992 was overstated by $15,000.

Required:

A. What effect did these errors have on the gross profit for 1990? for 1991? for 1992? What effect did the first error have on the combined gross profit for 1990 and 1991? Explain.

B. Prepare a new three-year schedule for Whitmire Company using the format above.

C. Recompute the gross profit percentages for each year. Will the president be as happy with these percentages as he was with the original ones? Explain.

Exercise 9-17 Retail Inventory Method

Delta Corporation uses the retail inventory method to estimate ending inventory in the preparation of quarterly financial statements. The following information is available for the second quarter of 1992.

	Cost	Retail
Beginning inventory	$ 94,000	$127,000
Purchase (net)	560,000	745,000
Net sales		692,000

Required:

Calculate an estimate of the cost of the ending inventory for the second quarter financial statements. Round the cost ratio to the nearest whole percent.

Exercise 9-18 Gross Profit Estimation of Inventory

The following information is available for Costumes Unlimited for the six months ended June 30, 1992.

Merchandise inventory, January 1, 1992	$ 65,000
Purchases (net of returns and allowances)	
February 2	24,000
March 15	36,000
May 24	48,000
Freight-in (January 1–June 30)	5,000
Net sales	192,000

The gross profit margin was 35% of sales.

Required:
Use the gross profit method to estimate the cost of the inventory on June 30, 1992.

Exercise 9-19 **Financial Statement Disclosure**
Polin Corporation has provided you with the following information related to the ending inventory for 1992.

Inventory, January 1, 1992	$ 912,000
Inventory, December 31, 1992	1,037,000
Cost flow method used in 1992	Last-in, first-out
Method of valuing the inventory	Lower-of-cost-or-market

Required:
Prepare the appropriate footnote to the financial statements prepared on December 31, 1992.

PROBLEMS

Problem 9-1 **Determining Ending Inventory**
A. H. Ramsey Company took a physical inventory count on December 31, 1992 and determined the cost to be $340,000. The accounts payable balance on December 31 was $120,000, and sales in 1992 were $750,000.
Additional information:

a. Goods held by Ramsey on consignment with a total cost of $8,100 were included in the physical count.
b. The company shipped goods with a cost of $6,900 for $12,300 on December 31, 1992, FOB shipping point. The buyer received the goods on January 8, 1993, at which time the sale was recorded. The goods were excluded from the December 31 physical inventory count.
c. A. H. Ramsey Company purchased goods with a cost of $3,200. The goods were shipped by the supplier on December 23, 1992, FOB shipping point. The goods were in transit and excluded from the physical count on December 31, and the purchase was recorded when the invoice was received in January.
d. The company recorded a $4,800 invoice from a supplier for goods shipped FOB destination on December 28, 1992. The goods were not included in the physical count because they had not yet arrived.
e. Goods with a cost of $2,400 were sold for $3,700 and shipped on December 29, 1992, FOB destination. A. H. Ramsey Company recorded the sale in December and excluded the goods from the December 31 physical inventory count.
f. All sales and purchases were made on account.

Required:
Complete the following schedule of adjustments. Show the effect of each transaction separately. If any transaction would have no effect on the initial balances shown, state "none."

	Merchandise Inventory	Accounts Payable	Sales
Initial balances, December 31, 1992	$340,000	$120,000	$750,000
Adjustments:			
Adjusted balances, December 31, 1992			

Problem 9-2 Calculating Ending Inventory and Cost of Goods Sold Using the Specific Identification Method

The Starlight Jewelry Store specializes in the sale of gold chains of various styles. The inventory on April 1, 1992 was composed of the following chains.

Identification	Unit Cost	Quantity
GC 1A76	$ 45	4
GC 1A78	50	5
GC 2B81	70	6
GC 4X83	150	4
GC 5Z84	300	3

During April the store purchased the following chains.

GC 1A78	50	4
GC 2B81	70	3
GC 3C87	100	2

A review of sales tickets indicates that during April the following chains were sold:

Identification Number	Quantity
GC 1A76	1
GC 1A78	6
GC 2B81	4
GC 4X83	2
GC 5Z84	1
GC 3C87	1

Required:
A. Compute the cost of goods sold for the month of April using the specific identification costing method.
B. Compute the cost of inventory on hand on April 30, 1992.

Problem 9-3 Use of Alternative Cost Flow Assumptions

The beginning inventory and inventory transactions for the single product of the Goodfriend Sales Company are shown below. Goodfriend uses the periodic inventory system.

Beginning inventory, January 1, 1992	1,000 units at $15.00 each
Purchases:	
January 5	2,000 units at $15.50 each
March 22	3,000 units at $16.50 each
August 23	3,000 units at $17.00 each
November 15	1,000 units at $18.50 each

A physical inventory on December 31, 1992, showed 2,400 units on hand.

Required:
Calculate the cost of the ending inventory and cost of goods sold under each of the following inventory costing methods.

1. FIFO.
2. LIFO.
3. Weighted average.

Problem 9-4 Use of Alternative Cost Flow Assumptions

The following data relate to the Doyle Company for September, 1992.

Merchandise Purchased

Date	Units	Unit Cost
September 7	400	$250
September 14	320	260
September 26	640	270
September 30	360	275
Total	1,720	

Merchandise Sold

Date	Units
September 8	240
September 15	200
September 20	200
September 29	400
Total	1,040

The company uses a periodic inventory system and there was no beginning inventory.

Required:
A. Compute the (a) goods available for sale, (b) cost of goods sold, and (c) cost of the ending inventory for both the FIFO and LIFO costing methods.
B. Prepare an income statement through gross profit on sales and explain why the FIFO and LIFO ending inventory, cost of goods sold, and gross profit amounts are different. Assume that all the merchandise had a selling price of $335 per unit.
C. Doyle's income tax rate is 40%. Determine which inventory method may be preferred for income tax purposes.

Problem 9-5 Comparison of FIFO and LIFO

Griggins Company sells a single product. The 1992 beginning inventory consisted of 100 units at a cost of $10 per unit. Sales and purchases of the product for a three-year period are presented below. Due to the declining demand for its product, Griggins Company decided to discontinue operations in 1994. Operating expenses each year totaled $200.

	Sales	Purchases
1992	100 @ $15	70 @ $14
1993	70 @ $20	50 @ $17
1994	50 @ $25	—

Griggins Company uses the periodic inventory system.

Required:

A. Compute the cost of goods sold, net income, and ending inventory for each year using the FIFO cost flow method.

B. Repeat requirement (A), using the LIFO cost flow method.

C. Compute the total sales, total cost of goods sold, and total net income for the three years under both FIFO and LIFO.

D. Compute the return on sales (net income divided by sales) for each year under both FIFO and LIFO.

E. Explain why net income under the LIFO method increased or decreased in 1994 when compared to 1993.

Problem 9-6 Use of Alternative Inventory Systems and Cost Flow Assumptions

The following data relate to the merchandise transactions of Adair Company for the month of October, 1992, its first month of operations.

Merchandise Purchased

Date	Units	Unit Cost
October 5	7,000	$6.00
October 12	6,400	6.20
October 21	9,800	6.80
October 29	5,200	7.30
Total	28,400	

Merchandise Sold

Date	Units	Selling Price Per Unit	Total
October 7	4,800	$ 9.00	$ 43,200
October 14	3,000	9.40	28,200
October 19	4,500	10.20	45,900
October 27	7,000	10.60	74,200
Total	19,300		$191,500

Required:

A. Assume Adair uses a periodic inventory system:
   1. Compute the (a) goods available for sale, (b) cost of goods sold, and (c) ending inventory for both the FIFO and LIFO costing methods.
   2. Prepare an income statement through gross profit on sales for both the FIFO and LIFO costing methods, and explain why the amounts are different for the two methods.

B. Assume Adair uses a perpetual inventory system:
   1. Compute the (a) goods available for sale, (b) cost of goods sold, and (c) ending inventory for both the FIFO and LIFO costing methods.
   2. Prepare an income statement through gross profit on sales for both the FIFO and LIFO costing methods, and explain why the amounts are different for the two methods.

C. Refer to your answers in requirements (A) and (B).
   1. Why are the FIFO results the same for both (A) and (B)?
   2. Why are the LIFO results different for (A) and (B)?

Problem 9-7 Lower-Of-Cost-Or-Market Rule

Ending inventory for Midtown Home Entertainment Sales is shown below.

	Item	Quantity	Unit Cost	Unit Market
Televisions:				
	T25	20	$100	$ 80
	T55	5	175	190
	T120	12	250	280
VCR:				
	V15	10	125	140
	V35	14	150	120
	V75	8	240	230

Required:

A. Compute the value of the ending inventory applying the LCM rule to:
  1. individual inventory items.
  2. major categories of televisions and VCRs.
  3. total inventory.
B. What happens as the pool of inventory to which LCM is applied is broadened from individual items to major categories to total inventory?

Problem 9-8 Lower-Of-Cost-Or-Market Rule

Banner Company prepared its annual financial statements dated December 31, 1992. The company uses a periodic inventory system and the FIFO costing method. The summarized income statement for 1992 is presented below.

BANNER COMPANY
Income Statement
For the Year Ended December 31, 1992

Sales		$462,000
Cost of goods sold:		
Beginning inventory	$ 72,000	
Purchases	270,000	
Goods available for sale	342,000	
Ending inventory (FIFO Cost)	90,000	
Cost of goods sold		252,000
Gross profit		210,000
Operating expenses		116,000
Pretax income		94,000
Income tax expense (30%)		28,200
Net Income		$ 65,800

The company's accountant forgot to apply the LCM rule to the ending inventory. You have been asked to restate Banner Company's 1992 financial statement, incorporating the LCM rule, and using the following data:

Item	Quantity	Acquisition Cost Unit	Acquisition Cost Total	Current Replacement Unit Cost (Market)
W	1,800	$ 4	$ 7,200	$ 4
X	2,700	12	32,400	10
Y	3,600	8	28,800	10
Z	900	24	21,600	20
			$90,000	

Required:

A. Restate the 1992 income statement of Banner Company to reflect the LCM valuation of the 1992 ending inventory. Apply the LCM on an item-by-item basis and show computations.

B. What is the accounting justification for applying LCM to inventories?

 Problem 9-9   **Net Realizable Value**

Oleta Manufacturing Company wants to determine the net realizable value of its inventory for valuation purposes. The following information is available to you.

Inventory Item	Number of Units	Unit Cost	Estimated Selling Price	Estimated Unit Cost to Dispose
1	225	$10.40	$10.95	$ .75
2	180	5.50	8.60	1.20
3	270	8.40	9.15	.85
4	90	4.00	5.20	.40
5	320	1.50	2.10	.30
6	135	2.40	4.75	.55

Required:

A. Determine the net realizable value of the inventory. Prepare a schedule with the following headings: Inventory Item, Number of Units, Unit Cost, Total Cost, Per Unit Net Realizable Value, and Total Estimated Net Realizable Value.

B. Which inventory items need to be written down?

C. Compute the value of the inventory that should be reported on the balance sheet.

Problem 9-10   **Perpetual Inventory System—FIFO**

Trane Company uses a perpetual inventory system and applies FIFO inventory costing. The data provided below comes from the 1992 accounting records for inventory.

Transactions		Units	Unit Cost	Total Cost
January 1	Beginning inventory	175	$ 8.60	$1,505
April 15	Purchase	425	10.00	4,250
July 17	Sales at $17 each	(350)		
October 19	Purchase	700	11.25	7,875
December 21	Sales at $18 each	(550)		
	Ending Inventory	400		

Required:

A. Compute the dollar amount of (1) the cost of goods sold, and (2) the ending inventory, assuming the FIFO inventory costing method.

B. Give the journal entries to record the April 15 and July 17 transactions assuming:
  1. a perpetual inventory system.
  2. a periodic inventory system.

C. Explain why the entries are different for requirements (B.1) and (B.2).

Problem 9-11   Perpetual Inventory System—FIFO and LIFO

Patterson Distributing Company uses a perpetual inventory system. This problem deals with one particular inventory item stocked by Patterson Distributing Company and the transactions affecting that item during June, 1992. The beginning inventory was 9,000 units with a cost of $2 each. The June transactions are as follows:

June	9	Sold 3,500 units at $3.50 per unit.
	14	Purchased 7,000 units at $2.25 each.
	20	Sold 10,600 units at $3.50 per unit.
	22	Purchased 12,000 units for a total purchase price of $31,200.
	28	Sold 8,200 units at $4.00 per unit.

Required:

A. Compute the cost of goods sold for June and the ending inventory on June 30, assuming:
  1. a FIFO basis.
  2. a LIFO basis.

B. Prepare the journal entry for each basis for the purchase on June 14.

C. Prepare the journal entries for each basis for the sale on June 20.

D. Compute the gross profit for the month of June for each basis. Which method results in the higher gross profit? Under which conditions would the comparison be the opposite of the results in this problem?

Problem 9-12   Perpetual Inventory System and Moving Average

Mueller Corporation uses the moving average cost flow assumption to account for inventory costs. The inventory transactions for the month of January, 1992 are given below.

Transactions	Units	Unit Cost
Beginning inventory	100	$22.00
January 8 Sale at $35 per unit	80	
11 Purchase	200	24.30
19 Sale at $36 per unit	160	
23 Purchase	220	27.00
30 Sale at $40 per unit	130	

Required:

A. Prepare a perpetual inventory card for January on a moving average basis. Round all calculations to the nearest cent.

B. Complete the following partial financial statements:

Income Statement	
Sales	$ _____
Cost of goods sold	_____
Gross profit	_____
Operating expenses	2,780
Pretax income	_____
Income tax expense (25%)	_____
Net income	$ _____

Balance Sheet	
Merchandise inventory	$ _____

Problem 9-13 Effects of Inventory Errors

Fairwell Corporation discovered in 1992 that the following inventory errors had occurred.

	INCOME STATEMENT			BALANCE SHEET	
	Cost of Goods Sold	Gross Profit	Net Income	Inventory Balance	Retained Earnings
1. 1990 ending inventory is overstated	_____	_____	_____	_____	_____
2. 1991 beginning inventory is overstated	_____	_____	_____	_____	_____
3. 1991 ending inventory is understated	_____	_____	_____	_____	_____
4. 1992 beginning inventory is understated	_____	_____	_____	_____	_____

Required:
Indicate the impact of these errors on the respective year's financial statement items shown above by using the following symbols: O for overstated, U for understated, and NE for no effect.

Problem 9-14 Effects of Inventory Errors

You have examined the records of the Dorsett Company as of June 30, 1992 (the end of the fiscal year), and have discovered the following with respect to the merchandise inventory for the prior four years.

a. June 30, 1988, inventory was correct.
b. June 30, 1989, inventory was understated $15,000.
c. June 30, 1990, inventory was overstated $9,000.
d. June 30, 1991, inventory was understated $22,000.

The June 30, 1992, inventory was correct. The reported net income for each year, before any corrections for inventory errors, was as follows.

Year Ended

June 30, 1989	$ 98,000
June 30, 1990	141,500
June 30, 1991	234,200
June 30, 1992	279,000

Required:
A. What is the correct net income for each year, 1989 through 1992.
B. What errors would have been included in each June 30 balance sheet?
C. Compare the total reported net income for the four years with the total corrected net income. Explain your results.

Problem 9-15 Retail Inventory Method

Beal's Department Store maintains separate accounting records for its home furnishings department. A summary of various inventory data for the month of October follows.

	Home Furnishings Department		All Other Departments	
	Cost	*Retail*	*Cost*	*Retail*
Beginning inventory	$64,300	$102,000	$250,000	$420,000
Net purchases	21,500	30,000	86,000	140,000
Net sales		56,000		245,000

Required:
A. Compute the estimated cost of the ending inventories for October.
B. Compute the total cost of goods sold for October.

Problem 9-16 Gross Profit Method of Inventory Estimation

On March 31, 1992, Coulter Company suffered major storm damage to its entire merchandise inventory. Coulter Company had casualty insurance to cover the damages. The accounting records were saved and the following information for the period January 1 to March 31, 1992 is available.

Inventory, December 31, 1991	$ 56,200
Sales	329,600
Sales returns	9,600
Purchases	214,000
Purchase returns	7,400
Freight-in	2,200

Coulter Company has experienced a 30 percent gross profit rate on net sales during the last two years. The damaged inventory can be sold for a salvage value of approximately $4,500.

Required:
Determine the amount of the inventory loss to be submitted to the insurance company as a claim for the damaged inventory.

CASE

CASE 9-1   Discussion Case

The financial statements of the Arden Group, Inc., contained the following footnote:

Note 3 (in part): During the year, the Company adopted the last-in, first-out (LIFO) method of determining the cost of its nonperishable grocery merchandise. Perishable merchandise and all other inventory is valued at the lower of first-in, first-out (FIFO) cost or market. The Company believes that the use of the LIFO method for nonperishable grocery merchandise results in a better matching of costs and revenues. At December 31, inventories valued by the LIFO method would have been $637,445 higher if they had been stated at the lower of FIFO cost or market. The effect on net income and income per share for the fifty-two weeks ended December 31 was a decrease of approximately $562,000 ($.20 per share). The results of prior operations do not reflect this accounting change. Pro-forma effects of retroactive application of LIFO to prior years are not determinable, and thus there is no cumulative effect on retained earnings at the beginning of the year.

Required:

A. What arguments must have been used in support of LIFO for Arden's management to accept a reduction in net income of $562,000?

B. What disadvantages may result from the adoption of LIFO?

C. Why do the results of prior operations not reflect the accounting change?

CASE 9-2   Annual Report Analysis Case

Refer to the financial statements and related footnotes of BFGoodrich Company in the appendix and answer the following questions. Indicate the appendix page number on which you found the answer.

1. What inventory costing method is used by the company?

2. What is the percentage of cost of sales to sales in 1989?

3. What is the balance reported for inventories in the December 31, 1989 balance sheet?

4. What percent of total current assets are the inventories as of December 31, 1989?

5. What are the major classes of inventories that make up the December 31, 1989 balance?

6. What is the replacement cost of inventories at December 31, 1989?

10

OPERATING ASSETS

CHAPTER OVERVIEW AND OBJECTIVES

This chapter discusses the nature of operating assets (i.e. plant assets, intangibles, and natural resources), the components of their cost, and the methods used to allocate their cost to expense. When you have completed the chapter, you should understand:

1. The distinction between plant assets, intangible assets, and natural resources.
2. The nature of depreciation, amortization, and depletion.
3. How the cost of operating assets is determined.
4. The factors that should be considered in determining a plant asset's useful life.
5. How to calculate depreciation expense under each of the commonly used depreciation methods.
6. The difference between capital expenditures and revenue expenditures.
7. How to account for the disposition of operating assets.
8. How to account for intangible assets.
9. How to account for natural resources.

Objective 1: Distinguishing among plant assets, intangibles, and natural resources

Operating assets are noncurrent, long-lived assets acquired by a business for use in operations rather than for resale to customers. These assets have value in use. Therefore, they are said to contain future service benefits for the business. Examples of operating assets are **plant assets**, including *tangible assets* (such as land, buildings, equipment, and machinery), *intangible assets* (such as patents and leaseholds), and *natural resources* (such as coal or oil deposits).

Management's intention to use these assets for the future production of goods or services over several accounting periods distinguishes operating assets from other assets. For example, buildings contain future housing services for the company's operations, automobiles contain future transportation services, and computers contain future data processing services. Operating assets are expected to be used in the future to sell goods or to produce goods and services for sale to customers.

Objective 2: What depreciation, amortization, and depletion represent

Because the service benefits contained in operating assets will be used over more than one accounting period, the cost of the assets is allocated in a systematic manner to the accounting periods that benefit from their use. As the assets are used to produce goods or services, their cost is transferred to expense to match it with the revenue earned from the sale of the goods or services (*matching principle*). The cost of operating assets allocated to expense is called *depreciation* for plant assets, *amortization* for intangible assets, and *depletion* for natural resources.

Operating assets are often the most costly assets acquired by a firm, and the depreciation, amortization, and depletion expenses may be very large. For example, General Electric Company reported depreciation and amortization expense for 1989 in excess of $2.25 billion. Accounting for operating assets involves four phases, which will be discussed in this chapter.

1. Determining and recording acquisition cost.
2. Allocating acquisition cost to expense.
3. Accounting for expenditures related to operating assets after acquisition.
4. Accounting for the disposition of operating assets.

DETERMINING THE ACQUISITION COST OF OPERATING ASSETS

The cost of an operating asset includes all reasonable and necessary expenditures incurred to obtain the asset and get it ready for the use intended by the purchaser. An **expenditure** is either a cash payment or an incurred liability to acquire a good or service. For example, the cost of acquiring a machine includes its invoice price (minus any cash discounts), sales taxes, freight, installation expenditures (such as power hook up), and any initial adjustments needed to make the machine function properly. To illustrate, the cost of a machine purchased on January 2, 1992 may be computed as follows:

Objective 3:
Determining the cost of operating assets

List price of the machine	$50,000
Less: Cash discount (3% × $50,000)	1,500
Net cash price	48,500
Sales tax (6% × $48,500)	2,910
Freight	1,450
Installation	940
Total	$53,800

The acquisition is recorded by the following entry:

Jan.	2	Machinery	53,800	
		Cash		53,800

The cost of an asset should not exceed the amount for which it could be acquired in a cash transaction plus the other expenditures necessary to get the asset ready for use. Consequently, if the consideration given in the acquisition is other than cash, the acquisition cost of the asset should be limited to its cash price—that is, its **fair market value**. Cost is measured by the fair market value of the consideration given. If the fair market value of the consideration given is not determinable, cost is measured by the fair market value of the asset received.

When a company constructs an asset, for example, a building, for its own use, the cost includes:

- All expenditures made directly for construction (e.g., labor, materials, and insurance premiums paid during construction);
- Architectural fees;
- Engineering fees;
- Building permits;

- A reasonable amount of general overhead for such things as power, management supervision during construction, and depreciation on machinery used for construction; and
- Interest incurred on borrowed money during the construction period.

Note that only interest incurred during the construction period is included in the cost of the asset.[1] Interest incurred after the building is ready for use is expensed.

The cost of the land the building is built on includes the price paid to the seller, the broker's commission, and other necessary expenditures such as title-search and survey fees. If the buyer pays delinquent taxes on the property, such taxes should also be included in the cost of the land. If the land contains a building that is to be demolished in order to construct a new building, the total purchase price plus the cost of removing the old building (less amounts received from the sale of salvaged materials) is included in the cost of the land. The cost of removing the old building is considered part of the land cost because it was incurred to get the land into condition for its intended use (the construction of a new building).

Although land cost is not depreciable because it has an unlimited life, some expenditures related to its acquisition and use, such as driveways, fences, and parking lots, do have limited lives and are properly depreciated. Consequently, these items are normally charged to a separate Land Improvements account and depreciated over their estimated useful lives.

APPORTIONING THE COST OF A LUMP-SUM ACQUISITION

Several assets may be acquired for a single lump-sum payment without the cost of each asset being identified separately. In such cases, the total cost must be allocated systematically to the assets purchased because they may have different depreciable lives or may not be depreciable at all.

The most common method is to allocate total cost on the basis of the fair market values of the acquired assets. Fair market values may be either current selling prices as shown in catalogs of prices for used assets, or appraised values determined by an appraisal firm. For example, assume that a building, land, and office equipment were acquired for a lump-sum payment of $960,000. Fair market values of the assets were determined by an independent appraisal as follows:

	Fair Market Value
Building	$ 714,000
Land	204,000
Office equipment	102,000
Total fair market value	$1,020,000

The total cost of $960,000 is allocated to each asset on the basis of these fair market values by using the following formula:

$$\frac{\text{Fair market value of specific asset}}{\text{Total fair market value}} \times \text{Cost} = \frac{\text{Cost allocated to the}}{\text{specific asset}}$$

[1]Statement of Financial Accounting Standards No. 34, "Capitalization of Interest Cost" (Stamford, Conn.: FASB, 1979), par. 6.

Thus, the allocation is as follows:

```
Building    ($714,000/$1,020,000) × $960,000 = $672,000
Land        ($204,000/$1,020,000) × $960,000 =  192,000
Equipment   ($102,000/$1,020,000) × $960,000 =   96,000
       Total                                   $960,000
```

The acquisition is recorded by the following entry:

Jan.	3	Buildings	672,000	
		Land	192,000	
		Office Equipment	96,000	
		Cash		960,000

ALLOCATING ACQUISITION COST TO EXPENSE

As explained earlier, operating assets contain service benefits a business intends to use over the life of the assets in the production and sale of goods or services. All operating assets except land have limited useful lives, and their service benefits will be consumed by the end of their useful lives. The cost of the service benefits is therefore assigned to expense as the benefits are used. The service benefits of plant assets, intangible assets, and natural resources are called *depreciation, amortization*, and *depletion*, respectively. Accounting for depreciation is discussed below. Amortization and depletion will be treated in later sections on intangible assets and natural resources.

NATURE OF DEPRECIATION

Depreciation is the allocation of the cost of plant assets to the accounting periods benefiting from their use. The meaning of depreciation is sometimes misunderstood because the term is often used by nonaccountants to refer to the decline in the market value of assets. Although plant assets are subject to changes in market values, accountants generally are not concerned with recognizing these changes because plant assets are acquired for use, not for sale. Depreciation is therefore a cost allocation process, rather than a valuation process.

Factors needed to determine the amount of periodic depreciation for a plant asset are its cost, its estimated useful life, and its estimated residual value. Determination of the cost of assets was discussed earlier. Estimated useful life and estimated residual value are discussed below.

Estimated Useful Life

A plant asset's **useful life** is the time period during which the asset is expected to be used by the purchaser in the production and sale of goods or services. This period is generally much shorter than the asset's physical life. For example, the physical life of an automobile may be eight to ten years or longer. Its useful life, however, may be only three years because it will require more maintenance and operate less efficiently after that. The purchaser may decide that it is more economical to trade in the automobile for a new one after three years. If that is the case, the cost of the automobile, less the estimated residual value, should be charged to depreciation expense over the three-year period.

Objective 4:
Determining a plant asset's useful life

Three major factors are considered in estimating the useful life of a plant asset:

1. **Physical wear and tear**, which is affected by such things as frequency of use, climatic conditions under which the asset is used, and the frequency of expected maintenance.
2. **Obsolescence**, which results when technological advances produce new assets that can provide the same service more efficiently than existing assets, thereby causing them to become out of date. For example, rapid improvements made in the design and performance of computers generally make them obsolete long before they wear out physically.
3. **Inadequacy**, which refers to the inability of an asset to meet the increasing needs of the user caused by growth of the firm.

When a company acquires plant assets, it generally attempts to acquire those that will provide adequate capacity to meet foreseeable operating needs. When demand for the company's products increases more rapidly than anticipated, the plant assets may not have the capacity to meet that demand and the assets are said to have become inadequate. Because obsolescence and inadequacy cannot be easily predicted, business managers often are conservative in estimating the useful lives of plant assets that are most affected by these factors.

Estimated Residual Value

The **residual value** of a plant asset is the amount expected to be received from the sale or other disposition of the asset at the end of its useful life. Assets such as automobiles and trucks may have significant resale values. Other assets, such as specifically designed machinery and equipment, may have value only as scrap metal at the end of their useful lives.

The cost of an asset less its residual value is called the asset's **depreciable cost**. It is the amount that should be charged to depreciation expense over the asset's useful life. When residual value is expected to be an immaterial amount in relation to the asset's cost, it is often ignored in computing depreciation. Residual value is sometimes also called **salvage value** or **trade-in value**.

DEPRECIATION METHODS

Objective 5: Calculating depreciation expense by different methods

Several methods can be used to allocate the cost of an asset over its useful life. The four most frequently used methods are the straight-line, units-of-production, sum-of-years'-digits, and declining balance methods. The sum-of-years'-digits and declining balance methods are called **accelerated depreciation methods** because they charge greater depreciation expense in the early years of a plant asset's life than in later years. All four methods are generally accepted in accounting because they result in a systematic and rational allocation of the cost of a plant asset to the periods that benefit from its use.

A company does not have to use a single depreciation method for all of its depreciable assets. The methods chosen will vary with management's expectations about the way the service benefits incorporated in the assets are to be used. In addition, the methods adopted by management for use in the financial statements may differ from those used in the preparation of income tax returns. That is, neither accounting rules nor income tax laws require that the same depreciation methods be used for both financial reporting and income tax reporting.

Straight-Line Method

The **straight-line method** allocates an equal amount of depreciation to each full accounting period in the asset's useful life. The amount of depreciation for each period is determined by dividing the cost of the asset minus its residual value by the number of periods in the asset's useful life. For example, assume a machine has a cost of $66,000, a residual value of $6,000, and a useful life of five years. Depreciation for each full year is computed as follows:

$$\frac{\text{Cost} - \text{Residual value}}{\text{Useful life}} = \frac{\$66,000 - \$6,000}{5 \text{ years}} = \$12,000$$

The adjusting entry to record depreciation, assuming the machine was purchased at the beginning of the year, is:

Dec.	31	Depreciation Expense	12,000	
		Accumulated Depreciation—Machinery		12,000

The straight-line method produces uniform charges to depreciation expense over the life of the asset. Under the straight-line method, depreciation is considered a function of time. Thus, this method is appropriate where the service benefits in the asset are received evenly throughout the asset's useful life. A depreciation schedule covering the life of the machine in the above example might appear as follows:

				Year-end Balances	
Year	Cost Less Residual Value	Depreciation Expense	Cost	Accumulated Depreciation	Book Value
1	$60,000	$12,000	$66,000	$12,000	$54,000
2	60,000	12,000	66,000	24,000	42,000
3	60,000	12,000	66,000	36,000	30,000
4	60,000	12,000	66,000	48,000	18,000
5	60,000	12,000	66,000	60,000	6,000

Note that the depreciation expense each year is constant. Each year, accumulated depreciation increases by the same amount. Each year, the **book value** (cost minus accumulated depreciation) of the machine decreases by the same amount. The straight-line method is simple to apply and is widely used, as shown in Figure 10-1, taken from the 1989 edition of *Accounting Trends & Techniques*, an annual survey of 600 companies conducted by the American Institute of Certified Public Accountants (AICPA).

Units-of-Production Method

The **units-of-production method** relates depreciation to use rather than to time. Therefore, this method is particularly appropriate for assets whose use varies significantly from one period to another because it results in a better matching of expenses with revenues. Accounting periods with greater production from the asset will be charged with a greater amount of depreciation expense.

Figure 10-1
Depreciation
Methods Used

Depreciation Method	No. of Companies*
Straight-line	563
Declining balance	44
Sum-of-years'-digits	11
Accelerated method (method not specified)	70
Units-of-production	53

*The number of companies exceeds 600 because some companies use more than one method.
Source: *Accounting Trends & Techniques*, 1989 edition (New York: AICPA, 1989), p. 279.

A disadvantage of the method is that it requires additional recordkeeping to determine the units produced during each period by each asset. It also requires an estimate of the total expected production of each asset over its useful life.

Under the units-of-production method, the cost of the asset minus its residual value is divided by the estimated number of production units expected from the asset during its estimated life. Production units might be expressed in several ways—for example, miles, operating hours, or units of product. The result of the division is an estimated depreciation rate per production unit. The amount of depreciation for the period is then determined by multiplying the depreciation rate per production unit times the number of production units used or produced during the period.

To illustrate, assume that a machine with a cost of $66,000 and an estimated residual value of $6,000 is estimated to have a useful life of 20,000 operating hours. The depreciation rate per operating hour is:

$$\frac{\text{Cost} - \text{Residual value}}{\text{Operating hours}} = \text{Depreciation per operating hour}$$

$$\frac{\$66,000 - \$6,000}{20,000} = \$3.00 \text{ per operating hour}$$

If the machine were operated for 3,000 hours the first year and 4,200 hours the second year, the depreciation entries for each year would be:

Year 1			
	Depreciation Expense	9,000	
	Accumulated Depreciation—Machinery		9,000
Year 2			
	Depreciation Expense	12,600	
	Accumulated Depreciation—Machinery		12,600

Note that the amount of depreciation expense charged each year is directly proportionate to the number of hours the machine was operated each period.

ACCELERATED DEPRECIATION METHODS

As mentioned earlier, accelerated depreciation methods charge relatively large amounts of depreciation to the first year of an asset's life and decreasing amounts thereafter. Although depreciation is considered a function of time, the benefits received from the use of the asset are expected to be greater in the early years of use. When an asset is new, maintenance and repair expenses are expected to be low. As the asset ages, relatively higher maintenance and repair expenses are incurred. However, the combination of decreasing depreciation expense and increasing repair and maintenance expense tends to equalize the total periodic expense of the asset, as illustrated in Figure 10-2. Thus, a better matching of expenses with revenues is achieved. Although there are several variations of accelerated depreciation, the two most common methods are the sum-of-years'-digits method and the declining balance method.

Sum-of-Years'-Digits Method

The sum-of-years'-digits method results in a decreasing depreciation charge over the useful life of the asset. Depreciation for each period is determined by multiplying the cost less residual value by successively smaller fractions. The fraction's denominator, which is constant, is determined by adding the years in the asset's useful life. For example, the denominator for an asset with a six-year life is 21 (1 + 2 + 3 + 4 + 5 + 6). The fraction's numerators, which change each year, are the years remaining in the asset's life at the beginning of the period. For example, the numerator for the third year of an asset's six-year life would be four.

To illustrate, assume that the sum-of-years'-digits method is used to allocate depreciation on a machine with a cost of $66,000, a residual value of $6,000, and an estimated useful life of five years. The sum of the years' digits (the denominator) is computed as:

$$1 + 2 + 3 + 4 + 5 = 15$$

The depreciation charge for each full year is then calculated as shown in the following depreciation schedule:

Year	Cost Less Residual Value		Fraction		Depreciation Expense	Year-end Balances		
						Cost	Accumulated Depreciation	Book Value
1	$60,000	×	5/15	=	$20,000	$66,000	$20,000	$46,000
2	60,000	×	4/15	=	16,000	66,000	36,000	30,000
3	60,000	×	3/15	=	12,000	66,000	48,000	18,000
4	60,000	×	2/15	=	8,000	66,000	56,000	10,000
5	60,000	×	1/15	=	4,000	66,000	60,000	6,000

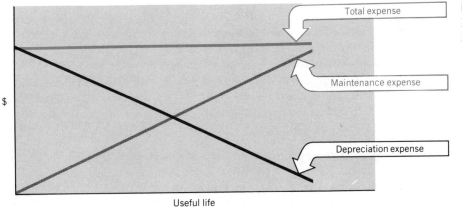

Figure 10-2
Depreciation and Maintenance Expense

Note that the method results in a book value equal to the asset's residual value at the end of its useful life. The charge to depreciation expense decreases each year by a constant amount ($4,000 in our example).

When the asset has a long life, the sum of the years' digits can be calculated by using the formula: $S = n\left(\dfrac{n + 1}{2}\right)$, where S equals the sum of the years' digits and n equals the number of years in the asset's life. The sum of the years' digits for an asset with a 10-year life is therefore $10\left(\dfrac{10 + 1}{2}\right) = 55$.

Declining Balance Method

Under the **declining balance method**, depreciation expense for each period is determined by multiplying a fixed depreciation rate times the declining undepreciated cost (book value) of the asset as of the beginning of the year. The depreciation rate is some multiple of the straight-line rate. Although this multiple can be several different numbers as computed by a formula discussed in more advanced accounting courses, it is often two. Thus, the method is often called the **double declining balance method**. (This book uses a multiple of two for purposes of illustration.)

To illustrate, assume that an asset has a cost of $66,000, an estimated residual value of $6,000, and a useful life of five years. The straight-line rate is determined by dividing 100% by the useful life (five years) of the asset. This rate (20%) is then multiplied by the multiple (2) to determine the depreciation rate, in this case 40%. The depreciation rate is then applied to the book value of the asset at the beginning of the year to compute depreciation expense for the period. The following depreciation schedule shows this:

Year	Book Value at Beginning of Year	Rate	Annual Depreciation Expense	Cost	Year-end Balances Accumulated Depreciation	Book Value
1	$66,000	× .40 =	$26,400	$66,000	$26,400	$39,600
2	39,600	× .40 =	15,840	66,000	42,240	23,760
3	23,760	× .40 =	9,504	66,000	51,744	14,256
4	14,256	× .40 =	5,702	66,000	57,446	8,554
5	8,554		2,554	66,000	60,000	6,000

Three things should be specifically noted in the above schedule:

1. The 40% depreciation rate is applied to the beginning of the year *book value*. Estimated residual value is *not* deducted under the declining balance method.
2. The amount of depreciation expense declined each year.
3. Depreciation for the last year was *not* determined by multiplying $8,554 times 40% because that would have resulted in a book value lower than the asset's residual value. Depreciation expense of $2,554 was computed for the last year by simply subtracting the residual value of $6,000 from the book value at the beginning of the year, $8,554.

Figure 10-3 compares the periodic depreciation charges under the straight-line, units-of-production, and accelerated depreciation methods for a machine with a cost of $66,000, a residual value of $6,000, and a useful life of five years.

Figure 10-3
Comparison of De-
preciation Methods

Year	Straight-Line	Units-of-Production (Amounts Assumed)	Sum-of-Years'-Digits	Double Declining Balance
1	$12,000	$ 9,000	$20,000	$26,400
2	12,000	12,600	16,000	15,840
3	12,000	13,800	12,000	9,504
4	12,000	14,100	8,000	5,702
5	12,000	10,500	4,000	2,554
Total	$60,000	$60,000	$60,000	$60,000

DEPRECIATION FOR PART OF A YEAR

Preceding illustrations assumed that the asset was purchased at the beginning of the year. Thus, a full year's depreciation was recorded.

If the asset is acquired during a fiscal period, only part of the depreciation assignable to a full year's use should be recorded. For example, if the annual depreciation amount is $12,000, the asset was acquired on April 1, and the firm's fiscal year ends on December 31, depreciation taken for the first year should be $9,000 (9/12 × $12,000). The same concept is followed in the preparation of interim reports (i.e., reports for periods of less than a year). Thus, a quarterly income statement would report $3,000 (3/12 × $12,000) depreciation expense.

Although depreciation could be computed to the exact day when an asset is acquired during a month, computation to the nearest month is generally sufficient. A full month's depreciation is taken on an asset acquired during the first half of a month, and no depreciation is taken for the month if the asset is acquired during the last half of the month. In fact, because depreciation is an estimate, many companies compute depreciation only to the nearest full year.

DEPRECIATION FOR INCOME TAX PURPOSES

Accelerated depreciation methods (for example, declining balance and sum-of-years'-digits) were widely used for income tax purposes for property acquired before 1981. The Economic Recovery Act of 1981 established the accelerated cost recovery system (ACRS), which provided new depreciation rules for income tax purposes. The new rules provided for more rapid depreciation than was allowed under previous tax laws. This was accomplished by a significant reduction in the number of years over which property was depreciated. ACRS depreciation rules were modified for property placed in service after December 31, 1986.

The modified rules provide for six classes of personal property: (1) a three-year class; (2) a five-year class; (3) a seven-year class; (4) a ten-year class; (5) a fifteen-year class; and (6) a twenty-year class. All personal property is assigned to one of these six classes. For example, automobiles and light trucks are assigned to the five-year class. The rules provide for rapid depreciation of personal property by applying the double declining balance method to the three- five-, seven-, and ten-year classes. The 150 percent declining balance method is applied to the other classes. Real property is depreciated using the straight-line method over 27.5 years for residential rental property and 31.5 years for nonresidential property.

Depreciable lives of asset categories are set arbitrarily under ACRS. Sometimes they do not reflect actual useful lives. Consequently, ACRS often may not be appropriate for financial accounting purposes, because it may not result in an appropriate matching of expenses and revenues. Thus, different useful lives and depreciation methods may be used for financial reporting purposes than for tax purposes. Accounting for the differences arising from the use of different useful lives and depreciation methods for book and tax purposes is discussed in Chapter 11.

REVISION OF DEPRECIATION ESTIMATES

Two of the factors used to determine periodic depreciation—residual value and useful life—are based on estimates, either of which is subject to misestimation. Small misestimates occur frequently and are often ignored because their effect is not material. Large misestimates, however, should be revised when discovered. When it becomes known that an estimate should be revised, the generally accepted accounting procedure is to spread the remaining undepreciated cost (less revised residual value) over the asset's remaining useful life.[2] Annual depreciation is increased or decreased enough in the current and future periods to offset the effect of the misestimate in prior periods. For example, assume the following:

Asset cost	$76,000
Estimated useful life	6 years
Estimated residual value	$16,000
Accumulated depreciation at the end of four years	40,000

Early in the fifth year, it is decided that the asset will last for four more years, at which time its residual value is estimated to be $8,000. The amount of depreciation to be recognized in the fifth year and each of the remaining years is $7,000, as computed below:

Undepreciated cost of the asset at the end of the 4th year ($76,000 − $40,000)	$36,000
Less: Estimated residual value	8,000
Remaining cost to be depreciated	$28,000
Useful life remaining	4 years
Revised annual depreciation ($28,000/4 years)	$ 7,000

DEPRECIATION AND CASH FLOW

A common misunderstanding of those who are not well informed about accounting is that accumulated depreciation represents cash that can be used to replace the assets when they wear out. The informed user knows, however, that accumulated depreciation represents nothing more than the portion of an asset's cost that has been transferred to depreciation expense since the asset was acquired. The Cash account is not affected by the periodic entries made to transfer the asset's cost to depreciation expense.

---

[2]Opinions of the Accounting Principles Board No. 20, ''Accounting Changes'' (New York: AICPA, July, 1971), par. 31.

This misunderstanding probably occurs because depreciation expense, unlike most other expenses, does not require a cash outlay in the same period in which the expense is deducted from revenue. As a result, most companies have a net cash inflow from operations (cash receipts from revenues less cash payments for expenses) in excess of reported net income.

To illustrate, assume that Rox Company sells services only in exchange for cash and pays cash for all expenses with the exception of depreciation in the same period in which the expense is incurred. During 1992, Rox Company made cash sales of $276,000, paid cash expenses, other than income tax expense, of $204,000, paid income tax expense of $12,000, and recognized depreciation expense of $20,000 on equipment purchased with cash in 1990. A comparison of cash flow from operations with net income reported for 1992 is:

	1992 Cash Flow		1992 Net Income	
Cash receipts from sales		$276,000		$276,000
Cash expenses, before tax	$204,000		$204,000	
Depreciation expense	–0–	204,000	20,000	224,000
Net		72,000		52,000
Less: Income tax		12,000		12,000
Net cash flow/income		$ 60,000		$ 40,000

Rox Company had a $20,000 greater net cash flow from operations than the amount of net income reported. This results because the depreciation expense deducted in arriving at net income did not require a cash payment in 1992.

But, isn't the $20,000 cash in the bank account? Couldn't it be used to replace the equipment when it wears out? The answer is that the $20,000 may or may not be in the bank. It may have been used already, or will be used before the equipment needs replacement, for any of the purposes for which a company normally uses cash. It may be used to pay cash expenses or to pay off long-term debt, for example, or it may have been distributed to the stockholders as dividends.

ACCOUNTING FOR EXPENDITURES AFTER ACQUISITION

Expenditures made to acquire, improve, and maintain plant assets are either capital expenditures or revenue expenditures. **Capital expenditures** are those that add to the utility or usefulness of a plant asset for more than one accounting period either by lengthening the asset's useful life or by increasing its capacity. Examples include expenditures made for building additions, extraordinary repairs, or the replacement of a major component of a machine. Capital expenditures are debited to asset accounts and allocated to the current and future periods through depreciation.

Objective 6: Capital expenditures vs. revenue expenditures

Revenue expenditures are those that benefit only the current accounting period and are debited to expense accounts when incurred. They are called revenue expenditures because they are matched against revenues in the period in which they are made. Examples include ordinary recurring repairs and maintenance costs.

It is important to distinguish carefully between capital and revenue expenditures because improper treatment affects both the determination of periodic income and balance sheet values. For example, if the cost of equipment (a capital expenditure) is charged to expense when purchased, the net income of the current period will be understated and the net income of future periods will be overstated because of the absence of depreciation expense. In addition, plant assets, as well as retained earnings, will be understated on the balance sheet until the asset is either disposed of or reaches the end of its useful life. The accounting for the different kinds of repairs and maintenance demonstrates the distinction between capital and revenue expenditures.

REVENUE EXPENDITURE—ORDINARY REPAIRS AND MAINTENANCE

Ordinary repairs and maintenance are those relatively small recurring outlays necessary to keep a plant asset in good operating condition. Buildings need painting and minor repairs to their electrical and plumbing systems. Machines must be lubricated, cleaned, and reconditioned on a regular schedule. Engines require tune-ups and the replacement of small parts.

Expenditures for these purposes do not materially add to the economic value or useful life of the asset. Rather, they are made to assure the obtaining of benefits from the asset over its original estimated useful life. Ordinary repairs and maintenance expenditures therefore are matched against revenues of the current period by charging them to expense.

CAPITAL EXPENDITURE—EXTRAORDINARY REPAIRS

Extraordinary repairs are major reconditioning and overhaul expenditures made to extend a plant asset's useful life beyond the original estimate. For example, assume a delivery truck was purchased for $21,000 and was estimated to have a useful life of five years (straight-line method) with a residual value of $3,000. At the end of the truck's fourth year its book value is $6,600, as shown below:

Cost	$21,000
Accumulated depreciation (4/5 × $18,000)	14,400
Book value	$ 6,600

At the beginning of the fifth year, it is decided to replace the truck's engine at a cost of $6,300, after which the truck will last for three more years and have a residual value of $3,000. The entry to record this capital expenditure is:

Jan.	2	Delivery Truck	6,300	
		Cash		6,300

Depreciation expense for each of the remaining three years of the truck's life is computed as follows:

Total cost ($21,000 + $6,300)	$27,300
Accumulated depreciation	14,400
Book value after installing new engine	12,900
Less: Estimated residual value	3,000
New depreciable amount	$ 9,900
New annual depreciation expense ($9,900/3 years)	$ 3,300

ACCOUNTING FOR THE DISPOSITION OF OPERATING ASSETS

Objective 7: Disposal of operating assets

When an operating asset is no longer useful, it is discarded, sold, or traded in on a new asset. The entry to record the disposal varies with the nature of the disposal. In all cases, however, it is necessary to remove the book value of the asset from the records. This is accomplished by debiting the appropriate accumulated depreciation (amortization, depletion) account for the amount of depreciation (amortization, depletion) accumulated on the asset to the date of its disposal and crediting the asset account for its cost. If operating assets are disposed of during the year, an entry should be made to record depreciation, amortization, or depletion expense for the fractional portion of the year prior to disposal.

DISCARDING OPERATING ASSETS

When an operating asset is no longer useful to the business and has no sales value, it is discarded or scrapped. If the asset is fully depreciated (amortized, depleted), there is no loss on disposal because the book value of the asset is zero. If the asset is discarded before it is fully depreciated, a loss on disposal will be recognized in the amount of the asset's book value. For example, if a machine with a cost of $10,000 and accumulated depreciation to the date of disposal of $9,400 is discarded, the following entry is made:

Dec.	31	Accumulated Depreciation—Machinery	9,400	
		Loss on Disposal of Assets	600	
		Machinery		10,000

SALE OF OPERATING ASSETS

A second means of disposing of an operating asset is to sell it. If the selling price is equal to book value, there is no gain or loss. If the selling price exceeds the asset's book value on the date of sale, there is a gain on disposal. Conversely, if the selling price is less than the book value, there is a loss on disposal. Gains and losses on the disposal of assets should be reported on the income statement as part of income from operations.

To illustrate the various possibilities for reporting a gain or loss, assume that a machine with a cost of $33,000, an estimated residual value of $4,200, and a useful life of eight years was acquired on January 2, 1987, and sold on July 1, 1992. After the adjusting entry is made to record depreciation expense for six months on July 1, 1992, the book value of the machine is:

Machinery cost	$33,000
Accumulated depreciation–machinery	19,800*
Book value	$13,200

*($33,000 − $4,200)/8 = $3,600
 $3,600 × 5.5 years = $19,800

Entries to record the sale under three different assumptions as to selling price follow:

1. The machine is sold for $13,200.

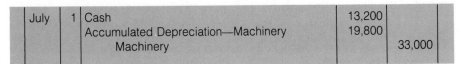

July	1	Cash	13,200	
		Accumulated Depreciation—Machinery	19,800	
		Machinery		33,000

Because the machine was sold for its book value, no gain or loss is recognized. The cash received is recorded and the cost of the machine and its related accumulated depreciation are removed from the accounts.

2. The machine is sold for $14,000.

July	1	Cash		14,000	
		Accumulated Depreciation—Machinery		19,800	
		Machinery			33,000
		Gain on Disposal of Assets			800

Since the machine was sold for more than its book value, a gain is recognized equal to the difference between the selling price ($14,000) and the book value ($13,200) of the machine.

3. The machine is sold for $11,500.

July	1	Cash		11,500	
		Accumulated Depreciation—Machinery		19,800	
		Loss on Disposal of Assets		1,700	
		Machinery			33,000

Because the machine was sold for less than its book value, a loss is recognized equal to the difference between the selling price ($11,500) and the book value ($13,200) of the machine.

EXCHANGING OPERATING ASSETS

Another means of disposing of an operating asset is to trade it for another asset. Such exchanges occur frequently with machinery, automobiles, and equipment. A trade-in allowance for the old asset is deducted from the price of the new asset, and the balance is paid in accordance with the normal credit terms. Accounting procedures used for the exchange of assets depend upon whether the assets exchanged are similar or dissimilar.

Exchanging Similar Assets

Similar assets are those that are of the same general type and that perform the same function in a business. The exchange of a truck for another truck or a typewriter for another typewriter are examples. The entry to record an exchange of similar assets varies according to whether there is a gain or a loss on the exchange.

When the trade-in allowance exceeds the book value of the asset traded in, a gain results. If the trade-in allowance is less than the book value of the asset traded in, a loss results. Losses on an exchange of similar assets are recognized immediately. Gains are not recognized, and the recorded value of the new asset is decreased by the amount of the unrecognized gain.[3]

---

[3]Opinions of the Accounting Principles Board No. 29, "Accounting for Nonmonetary Transactions" (New York: AICPA, May, 1973), par. 22.

Recognition of a Loss. To illustrate the recognition of a loss on an exchange, assume that a machine with a cost of $33,000 and accumulated depreciation to date of exchange of $22,000 is traded for a new machine with a cash price of $45,000. A trade-in allowance of $6,000 is received and the remaining $39,000 is paid in cash. The excess of the book value of the old machine ($11,000) over the trade-in allowance received ($6,000) results in a loss of $5,000 and the exchange is recorded as follows:

Jan.	2	Machinery	45,000	
		Accumulated Depreciation—Machinery	22,000	
		Loss on Disposal of Assets	5,000	
		Machinery		33,000
		Cash		39,000

This entry records the new machine at its cash price of $45,000. That is the amount that would have been paid in a straight cash transaction. Therefore, it is the maximum amount that should be debited to the asset account. The entry also removes the old machine and its related accumulated depreciation from the accounts and recognizes a loss on the exchange. The immediate recognition of losses on exchanges of similar assets is justified under the accounting convention of *conservatism*.

Nonrecognition of a Gain. When there is a gain on the exchange of similar assets, accounting rules require that the gain *not* be recognized at the time of the exchange. The amount of the gain serves to reduce the recorded value of the asset received, and the new asset is recorded at its cash price less the nonrecognized gain. Another way of viewing this is that the new asset is recorded at the book value of the old asset plus cash paid in acquiring the new asset. To illustrate, assume that a trade-in allowance of $14,000 rather than $6,000 was received for the old machine in the preceding illustration and the balance of $31,000 was paid in cash. Although the exchange results in a gain of $3,000 ($14,000 trade-in allowance minus $11,000 book value), the gain is not recognized and the exchange is recorded as follows:

Jan.	2	Machinery	42,000	
		Accumulated Depreciation—Machinery	22,000	
		Machinery		33,000
		Cash		31,000

The recorded amount of the new machine is its cash price of $45,000 less the unrecognized gain of $3,000. Looked at another way, the recorded amount is equal to the book value of the old machine ($11,000) plus the amount of cash paid in the exchange ($31,000). The recorded amount of $42,000 is the new machine's "cost." As such, it is the amount that will be used in recording depreciation over its useful life. The nonrecognition of the gain at the time of exchange is actually a postponement of the gain. Total depreciation expense over the life of the new machine will be $3,000 less and net income $3,000 greater than if depreciation were based on the $45,000 cash price of the machine. Thus, the gain is recognized gradually over the life of the new machine in the form of lower annual depreciation expense.

Two important facts support the nonrecognition of a gain. First, the amount of the gain is difficult to measure objectively. The price of the new asset may have been set higher than the amount of cash the seller could realistically expect to receive in a cash sale in order to offer an inflated trade-in allowance. Anyone who has traded in an automobile on a new one is aware of this practice. Second, as expressed by the Accounting Principles Board, "revenue should not be recognized merely because one productive asset is substituted for a similar productive asset but rather should be considered to flow from the production and sale of the goods or services to which the substituted productive asset is committed."[4] Thus, the exchange is considered a continuation of a past transaction in which production capacity was acquired.

Exchanging Dissimilar Assets

When assets that perform different functions in a business are exchanged, both gains and losses are recognized immediately. For example, when machinery is exchanged for land or a building is exchanged for equipment, both gains and losses are recognized. Each of these exchanges is considered a new transaction in the sense that they are unrelated to the continuation of the same prior production capacity. To record the exchange:

- The asset and related accumulated depreciation, amortization, or depletion accounts for the old asset are removed from the books;
- The asset received is recorded at its fair market value; and
- Gain or loss is recognized for the difference between the book value and the fair market value of the asset given.

To illustrate, assume that Rox Company exchanged a building with a cost of $250,000, accumulated depreciation of $120,000, and a fair market value of $180,000 for construction equipment. The exchange would be recorded as follows:

Jan.	2	Construction Equipment	180,000	
		Accumulated Depreciation—Buildings	120,000	
		Buildings		250,000
		Gain on Disposal of Assets		50,000

Note that the construction equipment received is recorded at the fair market value of the building given ($180,000); the cost of the building ($250,000) and its related accumulated depreciation ($120,000) are removed from the accounts; and a gain is recognized in the amount of $50,000, which is the difference between the fair market value ($180,000) and the book value of the building given ($130,000).

If the fair market value of the building is $100,000 rather than $180,000, a $30,000 loss is recognized. The loss results because the fair market value of the building ($100,000) is less than its book value ($130,000).

INTANGIBLE ASSETS

**Objective 8:
Accounting for
intangible assets**

Long-term operating assets that are useful to a business but have no physical substance are called **intangible assets**. Their value is derived from the long-term legal and economic rights obtained from ownership. Examples of intangible assets include patents, copyrights, leaseholds, franchises, and goodwill. Short-term assets that lack

[4]Ibid., par. 16.

physical substance, such as accounts receivable and prepaid expenses, are not classified as intangible assets.

The accounting principles followed for intangible assets are similar to those used
to account for plant assets. Accounting for intangibles is somewhat more difficult,
however, because the lack of physical substance makes the identification, valuation,
and estimation of useful lives more difficult.

Intangible assets are recorded initially at their acquisition cost. Some intangibles,
for example, trademarks and trade names, may have been acquired without incurring
any cost. Although they may be extremely valuable—even essential—to profitable
business operations, they should not be included in the balance sheet because they do
not have an acquisition cost. Intangible assets are generally reported at the portion of
their cost that has not yet been amortized and either shown in a separate section of
the balance sheet immediately after the plant asset section, or included in the "other
assets" category.

AMORTIZATION

The allocation of the cost of intangible assets to the periods benefiting from their use
is called **amortization**. Amortization is similar to depreciation of plant assets. Unlike
depreciation, however, an accumulated amortization account often is not used. Instead, the amortization entry consists of a debit to amortization expense and a credit
directly to the intangible asset account.

Accounting standards require that all intangible assets be amortized over the lesser
of their legal or useful lives, with a maximum amortization period of 40 years.[5]
Significant changes in estimated useful lives are accounted for by spreading the unamortized cost of the intangible assets over their remaining useful lives. The straight-
line method of amortization is generally used to account for intangible assets.

PATENTS

A **patent** is an exclusive right, granted by the federal government, to produce and
sell a particular product or to use a specific process for a period of 17 years. The
reason for issuing patents is to encourage the invention of new machines, processes,
and mechanical devices.

American businesses spend billions of dollars yearly on research and development
for new products and new processes. These expenditures are a vital contribution to
the nation's economic growth and increased productivity. Because of the difficulty in
relating research and development expenditures to specific patents, accounting
standards require that all research and development expenditures not reimbursable
from government agencies or other parties must be charged to expense in the period
incurred.[6]

Since research and development expenditures are charged to expense as incurred,
the only additional costs involved in an internally developed patent are the legal and
filing fees paid to obtain it. Because these legal fees are usually small, they are often
also charged to expense as incurred based on the materiality concept. When a patent

[5]Opinions of the Accounting Principles Board No. 17, "Intangible Assets" (New York: AICPA, August,
1970), par. 27, 29.

[6]Statements of Financial Accounting Standards No. 2, "Accounting for Research and Development Costs"
(Stamford, Conn., FASB, October 1974), par. 12.

is purchased from an inventor or patent holder, instead of developed internally, the purchase price should be debited to the Patents account. In addition, any legal costs involved with the successful defense of a patent (which occurs quite frequently) should also be debited to the Patents account. To illustrate, assume that a patent was purchased for $120,000. The entry is:

Jan.	2	Patents	120,000	
		Cash		120,000

Although a patent grants exclusive rights to the holder for 17 years, new inventions often make the patent obsolete sooner. The cost of a patent should therefore be amortized over its estimated useful life with a maximum period of 17 years. If the patent recorded above is expected to have a useful life of 10 years, the following adjusting entry is made to record each full year's amortization expense:

Dec.	31	Amortization Expense	12,000	
		Patents		12,000

Some firms use an Accumulated Amortization account rather than crediting the Patents account directly.

COPYRIGHTS

A copyright is an exclusive right, granted by the federal government, to reproduce and sell an artistic or published work. The exclusive right exists for the life of the creator plus 50 years. If a copyright is purchased, the purchase price is debited to the Copyrights account and amortized over its useful life, not to exceed 40 years. Because it is difficult to determine how long benefits will be received, the costs of most copyrights are amortized over a relatively short period.

TRADEMARKS AND TRADE NAMES

The exclusive right to trademarks and trade names can be obtained by registering them with the federal government. The main cost of developing trademarks and trade names lies in advertising, which is normally charged to expense in the period incurred. Other costs, such as registration fees and design costs, should be capitalized and amortized if their amount is material. Because these costs are often small, they are generally charged to expense when incurred. If a trademark or trade name is purchased, however, the purchase price may be material. If it is, its cost should be debited to the appropriate intangible asset account and amortized over its useful life, not to exceed 40 years.

LEASEHOLDS

Many companies rent property under a contract called a lease. The owner of the property is the lessor and the person or company obtaining the rights to possession and use of the property is the lessee. The rights of possession and use granted to the lessee by the contract are called a leasehold.

Some leases provide for regular monthly rent payments. The lease generally can be canceled at any time by either the lessor or the lessee, as long as a specified amount of notice is given. In these cases, a leasehold account is not used, and the monthly rent payments are debited to Rent Expense.

Sometimes a lease agreement provides that the rent for the entire period of the lease must be paid in advance or a lump-sum cash payment is made in advance in addition to periodic rental payments. In these cases, it is necessary to allocate the payments to the proper accounting periods. If the lease covers a short time period, the prepayments are debited to a current asset account, Prepaid Rent, and transferred to rent expense as discussed in earlier chapters. If the lease covers a long time period, the prepayment is debited to a Leasehold account and is generally classified on the balance sheet as an intangible asset. The prepayment is then allocated to rent expense as the lease benefits are received.

As an example, assume an agreement was made to lease a portion of a building from Layton Realty for four years beginning on January 1, 1992. The lease agreement requires a prepayment of $60,000 plus an annual payment of $30,000 on December 31 of each year. The prepayment is recorded as follows:

Jan.	1	Leasehold	60,000	
		Cash		60,000

On December 31 of each year the additional payment is recorded and the Leasehold (prepayment) amortized as follows:

Dec.	31	Rent Expense	45,000	
		Leasehold		15,000
		Cash		30,000

At times, the life of the lease covers 75% or more of the useful life of the leased property. For example, a company may sign an eight-year noncancelable lease for a machine with a useful life of 10 years. In these cases, the lease is treated as the equivalent of an installment purchase of property and the lessee records both the leased asset (such as Leased Machinery) and an equal lease liability. Both the asset and the liability are recorded at the discounted present value of the future lease payments required under the lease contract. Accounting for this type of lease is discussed further in Chapter 11.

LEASEHOLD IMPROVEMENTS

Long-term leases often require that special improvements to the leased property must be paid for by the lessee. Examples include partitions and permanent store fixtures installed in a leased building. These **leasehold improvements** become a permanent part of the property and cannot be removed by the lessee at the end of the lease. As a result, the cost of these improvements is debited to a Leasehold Improvements account and amortized to expense over the life of the improvements or the life of the lease, whichever is shorter. The amortization entry consists of a debit to Rent Expense and a credit to Leasehold Improvements.

FRANCHISES

A franchise is a right granted by a company or governmental body to an individual or company to conduct business at a specified location or in a specific geographical area. Examples of franchises include the right to operate a retail computer store, such as a ComputerLand or MicroAge, Inc., and the right to operate a municipal bus line or private water company.

The initial cost of a franchise may be substantial and should be capitalized and amortized over the term of the franchise. If the franchise is perpetual, it should be amortized over a period not to exceed 40 years. Periodic annual payments, such as those based on a percentage of gross or net revenue, required by a franchise agreement should be expensed by a debit to Franchise Expense and a credit to Cash.

GOODWILL

The term goodwill is used by accountants and the public to mean various things. It is often thought of as the favorable reputation of a business among its customers. From an accounting standpoint, however, goodwill has a special meaning not limited to good customer relations. Goodwill is the business's potential to earn a rate of return in excess of the normal rate of return in the industry in which the business operates. It arises from many factors, including customer confidence, superior management, favorable location, manufacturing efficiency, good employee relations, and other competitive advantages.

A successful business continually builds goodwill as it develops these factors, but the expenditures made in doing so generally cannot be specifically identified with the development of goodwill. Thus, goodwill is often called the "unidentifiable" intangible represented by the overall ability of a business to earn above normal profits.

Goodwill is recorded in the accounts only when it has been purchased. Because goodwill cannot be purchased or sold separately, this occurs only when a business is purchased in its entirety. The purchaser is often willing to pay a price in excess of the sum of the fair market values of a successful business's net assets (assets minus liabilities). This excess payment represents goodwill. Thus, the purchase price of the business is assigned first to the fair market values of the identifiable assets purchased and liabilities assumed, and any remainder of the purchase price is recorded as goodwill.

Many businesses have goodwill that has been developed internally by establishing good customer relations, acquiring or training superior management, and obtaining the other factors that contribute to above-normal earnings. This internally developed goodwill is not recorded in the accounts, however, because the expenditures made to develop it have been charged to expense in the periods incurred.

As with other intangible assets, goodwill must be amortized to expense over its useful life, not to exceed a maximum period of 40 years. For example, in their 1989 annual report, General Mills, Inc. reports Intangible assets, principally goodwill, of $57.2 million and notes that the goodwill is being amortized over periods of 40 years or less.

NATURAL RESOURCES

Natural resources are assets, such as mineral deposits, oil and gas reserves, sand and gravel, and standing timber, that are physically consumed as they are used. Thus, they are often called wasting assets.

In their natural state, these assets represent inventories that will be consumed in the future by mining, pumping, or cutting to convert them into various products. For example, a copper mine is a deposit of unmined copper ore, an oil field is a pool of unpumped oil, and standing timber is an inventory of uncut lumber. When mined, pumped, or cut they are converted into products for sale to customers.

Until converted, natural resources are noncurrent assets generally reported on the balance sheet after plant assets and intangible assets, with such descriptive titles as Mineral Deposits, Oil and Gas Reserves, and Timberlands. For example, St. Regis Corporation reports timberlands in a recent annual report under the category of "Property, Plant, and Equipment" as follows:

	(in Thousands)
Property, Plant, and Equipment, at cost:	
Timberlands	$316,372
Less accumulated depletion	92,895
Timberlands, net	223,477

Natural resources are recorded in the accounts at their cost, which may include costs of exploration and development in addition to the purchase price. As the resource is converted by mining, pumping, or cutting, the asset account must be reduced proportionately. The carrying value of a copper mine, for example, is reduced for each ton of copper ore mined. As a result, the original cost is gradually transferred from the asset account to a depletion account to be matched against the revenue earned from the copper that is produced and sold.

DEPLETION

The periodic allocation of the cost of natural resources to the units removed is called depletion. Depletion is computed in the same way depreciation is under the units-of-production method. The cost of the natural resource (minus residual value) is divided by the estimated number of units available (such as tons of copper ore or barrels of oil) to arrive at a depletion rate per unit. This depletion rate is then multiplied by the number of units removed during the period to determine the total depletion charge for the period. If a copper mine is purchased for $15 million, has an estimated residual value of $1 million, and contains an estimated 7 million tons of copper ore, the depletion rate per ton is $2 [($15,000,000 − $1,000,000)/7,000,000 tons].

If 450,000 tons of ore are mined during the first year, the depletion charge for the year is $900,000. It is recorded as follows:

Dec.	31	Depletion of Copper Mine	900,000	
		Copper Deposits		900,000

Some firms may use an Accumulated Depletion account instead of crediting the natural resource asset account directly.

Depletion represents a part of the cost of the resource extracted or product produced. It is possible that a natural resource extracted in one year may not be sold until a later year. In that case, the unsold portion represents inventory and should be reported as a current asset on the balance sheet. For example, if only 300,000 tons of the copper ore in the illustration were actually processed and sold during the year, $600,000 would be reported on the income statement as depletion (included in cost of goods sold), and the remaining $300,000 would be shown as Inventory of Copper Ore on the balance sheet.

In other words, depletion is recorded in the year in which the copper ore is mined. It is then allocated to (1) cost of goods sold and (2) inventory based on the number of units sold and the number of units retained in inventory. The following entry shows how this is done.

Dec.	31	Cost of Goods Sold	600,000	
		Inventory of Copper Ore	300,000	
		Depletion of Copper Mine		900,000

SUMMARY

This chapter discussed the nature of operating assets and the procedures followed in accounting for them. Operating assets are noncurrent assets held for use rather than for sale. They include plant assets (i.e., tangible assets such as land, buildings, and machinery), intangible assets (e.g., patents and leaseholds) and natural resources (e.g., coal deposits and oil deposits). Operating assets are recorded initially at their cost, which includes all reasonable and necessary expenditures made to obtain the assets and get them ready for the use intended by the purchaser.

As operating assets are used to produce goods and services, their cost (less residual value) is transferred to expense to be matched against the revenue earned from the sale of the goods or services. The cost of operating assets allocated to expense is called *depreciation* for plant assets, *amortization* for intangible assets, and *depletion* for natural resources. Amortization and depletion are usually allocated on a straight-line basis and unit-of-production basis, respectively. However, four different depreciation methods are used to allocate the cost of plant assets: straight-line, units-of-production, sum-of-years'-digits, and declining balance. The latter two methods are called accelerated methods because they allocate larger amounts to the early years of the asset's use and smaller amounts to later years.

Capital expenditures and revenue expenditures are made to improve or maintain plant assets after they are acquired. Capital expenditures are those that add to the utility or usefulness of a plant asset for more than one accounting period. They are debited to asset accounts when they are incurred. Examples are building additions and the replacement of a major component of a machine. Revenue expenditures are those that benefit the current accounting period only and are therefore debited to expense accounts when incurred. Ordinary recurring repairs and maintenance are examples.

When operating assets are no longer useful, they are disposed of by scrapping them, selling them, or trading them in for new assets. Regardless of the method of disposal, the cost and related accumulated depreciation (amortization, depletion) of the asset disposed of should be removed from the accounts. Losses may be recognized when operating assets are scrapped if they are not fully depreciated. If operating assets are sold, gains or losses are recognized for the difference between the selling price and the book value of the assets sold. Losses on the exchange of similar assets are recognized immediately, but gains are not recognized, and the recorded value of the new asset is decreased by the amount of the unrecognized gain. However, both losses and gains are recognized immediately on the exchange of dissimilar assets.

SELF-TEST

Test your understanding of the chapter by selecting the best answer for each of the following.

1. Expenditures that benefit the current accounting period only are:
    a. capital expenditures.
    b. revenue expenditures.
    c. disposal expenditures.
    d. purchase expenditures.

2. Which of the following depreciation methods produces a constant annual depreciation expense?
    a. Sum-of-years'-digits.
    b. Straight-line.
    c. Units of production.
    d. Double declining balance.

3. In the financial statements prepared at the end of an accounting period, the item "Accumulated depreciation" should appear:
    a. on the income statement as an expense.
    b. on the balance sheet as a long-term liability.
    c. on the balance sheet as a subtraction from a related asset.
    d. on both the income statement and the balance sheet.

4. Rayburn Company purchased land and an office building for $560,000. The fair market values of the building and land were $300,000 and $700,000, respectively. At what amount should the building be recorded?
    a. $300,000
    b. $240,000
    c. $168,000
    d. $392,000

5. Equipment was purchased on January 1, 1992, for $30,000. The equipment had an estimated useful life of five years and a residual value of $6,000. What will be the depreciation expense charge for the year ending December 31, 1994, under the sum-of-years'-digits depreciation method?
    a. $8,000
    b. $10,000
    c. $6,000
    d. $4,800

6. On July 1, 1992, Baxter Company purchased a patent for $45,000. The patent had a remaining legal life of sixteen years but an estimated useful life of nine years. The amortization expense charge for the year ending December 31, 1992, is:
    a. $2,500.
    b. $5,000.
    c. $45,000.
    d. None of the above.

7. Sullivan Company had the following expenditures related to the purchase of equipment:

Gross invoice price (including sales tax of $2,400)	$32,000
Preparation of a base to hold the equipment	500
Freight charges	2,000

At what amount should the equipment be recorded?
   a. $32,000
   b. $34,000
   c. $29,600
   d. $34,500

8. A dying machine with a book value of $2,250 was traded for a new dying machine priced at $11,400, less a $3,000 trade-in allowance. The cost that should be recorded for the new machine is:
   a. $20,250.
   b. $8,400.
   c. $10,650.
   d. $11,400.

9. Depletion of natural resources is generally recorded by using the:
   a. straight-line method.
   b. sum-of-years'-digits method.
   c. double declining balance method.
   d. units of production method.

REVIEW PROBLEM

Wharton Corporation began operations on January 3, 1992. On that date, Wharton purchased several operating assets, as follows:

Asset	Quantity	Cost	Estimated Residual Value	Useful Life
Delivery van	1	$ 9,000	$ 1,000	4 years
Used computer	1	3,000	300	3 years
Printing press	1	18,000	2,000	8 years
Photo-enlarger	1	4,500	500	8 years

Wharton Corporation uses the straight-line depreciation method and calculates depreciation to the nearest month. Depreciation is recorded for the partial year at the time of disposition for any asset exchanges, sales, or disposals occurring during the year.

During 1992 and 1993, the following events took place with respect to these assets:
1992

Recorded depreciation on the assets on December 31.
1993

Because of a lack of demand for its use, management decided to sell the photo-enlarger. It was sold on August 31 for $3,500.

The delivery van had experienced significant mechanical problems throughout 1992 and 1993. On October 3, it was traded in for a new delivery van having a cash price of $9,500. Wharton gave $5,000 plus the old delivery van for the new van. The new van had a $1,100 estimated residual value and an estimated useful life of four years.

Because Wharton grew faster than was originally anticipated, the computer's capacity was insufficient by December 1. On December 1, a new computer costing

$6,600 was purchased for cash. The new computer had an estimated residual value of $600 and an estimated useful life of five years. Since there was no market for the old computer, it was given to one of the employee's children.

Required:
Prepare journal entries to record the purchase of the assets on January 3, 1992 and the other events listed.

ANSWER TO REVIEW PROBLEM

1992			
Jan.	3	Delivery Van	9,000	
		Computer	3,000	
		Printing Press	18,000	
		Photo-enlarger	4,500	
		Cash		34,500
		To record the purchase of operating assets.		
Dec.	31	Depreciation Expense	2,000	
		Accumulated Depreciation—Delivery Van		2,000
		To record one year's depreciation on the delivery van [($9,000 − $1,000)/4 years].		
	31	Depreciation Expense	900	
		Accumulated Depreciation—Computer		900
		To record one year's depreciation on the computer [($3,000 − $300)/3 years].		
	31	Depreciation Expense	2,000	
		Accumulated Depreciation—Printing Press		2,000
		To record one year's depreciation on the printing press [($18,000 − $2,000)/8 years].		
	31	Depreciation Expense	500	
		Accumulated Depreciation—Photo-enlarger		500
		To record one year's depreciation on the photo-enlarger [($4,500 − $500)/8 years].		
1993			
Aug.	31	Depreciation Expense—Photo-enlarger	333	
		Accumulated Depreciation—Photo-enlarger		333
		To record 8 months' depreciation ($500 × 8/12).		
	31	Cash	3,500	
		Accumulated Depreciation—Photo-enlarger	833	
		Loss on Disposal of Plant Assets	167	
		Photo-enlarger		4,500
		To record the sale of the photo-enlarger.		

Oct.	3	Depreciation Expense	1,500	
		Accumulated Depreciation—Delivery Van		1,500
		To record 9 months' depreciation on the		
		delivery van ($2,000 × 9/12).		
	3	Delivery Van	9,500	
		Accumulated Depreciation–Delivery Van	3,500	
		Loss on Exchange of Assets	1,000	
		Delivery Van		9,000
		Cash		5,000
		To record the exchange of similar assets		
		and record a loss for the excess of the		
		book value of the old van ($5,500) over		
		the trade-in allowance received ($4,500).		
Dec.	1	Depreciation Expense	825	
		Accumulated Depreciation—Computer		825
		To record 11 months' depreciation on the		
		computer ($900 × 11/12).		
	1	Accumulated Depreciation—Computer	1,725	
		Loss on Disposal of Plant Assets	1,275	
		Computer		3,000
		To record the disposal of the computer.		
	1	Computer	6,600	
		Cash		6,600
		To record the purchase of a new computer.		
	31	Depreciation Expense	2,000	
		Accumulated Depreciation—Printing		
		Press		2,000
		To record one year's depreciation on the		
		printing press.		
	31	Depreciation Expense	525	
		Accumulated Depreciation—Delivery Van		525
		To record 3 months' depreciation on the		
		delivery van [($9,500 − $1,100)/4 years		
		× 3/12].		
	31	Depreciation Expense	100	
		Accumulated Depreciation—Computer		100
		To record 1 month's depreciation on the		
		computer [($6,600 − $600)/5 years ×		
		1/12].		

ANSWERS TO SELF-TEST

1. b   **2.** b   **3.** c   **4.** c   **5.** d   **6.** a   **7.** d   **8.** c
9. d

GLOSSARY

ACCELERATED DEPRECIATION METHOD. A depreciation method that results in greater depreciation expense in the early years of a plant asset's life than in later years (p. 432).

AMORTIZATION. The allocation of the cost of intangible assets to the periods that benefit from their use (p. 445).

BOOK VALUE. The cost of a plant asset minus its accumulated depreciaton (p. 433).

CAPITAL EXPENDITURE. Expenditure that adds to the utility or usefulness of an operating asset for more than one accounting period (p. 439).

COPYRIGHT. An exclusive right granted by the federal government to reproduce and sell an artistic or published work (p. 446).

DECLINING BALANCE METHOD (DOUBLE DECLINING BALANCE METHOD). A depreciation method under which a multiple of the straight-line rate is applied to the book value of a plant asset to arrive at the annual depreciation charge (p. 436).

DEPLETION. The periodic allocation of the cost of natural resources to the units removed (p. 449).

DEPRECIABLE COST. The cost of a plant asset less its residual value (p. 432).

DEPRECIATION. The allocation of a plant asset's cost to the periods benefiting from its use (p. 431).

EXPENDITURE. A cash outlay or an incurred liability to acquire a good or service (p. 429).

FAIR MARKET VALUE. The current cash equivalent value (p. 429).

FRANCHISE. A right granted by a company or governmental body to conduct business at a specified geographical area (p. 448).

GOODWILL. The ability of a business to earn a rate of return in excess of the normal rate of return in an industry. It is recorded as an intangible asset when a business is purchased for an amount in excess of the value of the net identifiable assets of that business (p. 448).

INADEQUACY. The inability of a plant asset to meet current demand for its product (p. 432).

INTANGIBLE ASSET. Noncurrent asset that is useful to a business but has no physical substance (p. 444).

LEASE. A contract for the rental of property (p. 446).

LEASEHOLD. The rights of possession and use of property granted under a lease contract (p. 446).

LEASEHOLD IMPROVEMENT. Permanent improvement to leased property made by the lessee (p. 447).

LESSEE. The person or company obtaining the rights to possession and use of leased property (p. 446).

LESSOR. The owner of property leased to others (p. 446).

NATURAL RESOURCE (WASTING ASSET). Asset that is physically consumed as it is used. (p. 448).

OBSOLESCENCE. A condition under which a plant asset is out of date and can no longer produce on a competitive basis (p. 432).

OPERATING ASSET. Noncurrent asset acquired by a business for use in operations rather than for resale to customers (p. 428).

PATENT. An exclusive right granted by the federal government to produce and sell a particular product or process for a period of 17 years (p. 445).

PHYSICAL WEAR AND TEAR. One of the factors determining an operating asset's useful life. It is affected by frequency of use, climatic conditions, and maintenance and repair policies (p. 432).

PLANT ASSET. Tangible operating asset such as land, building, and machinery (p. 428).

RESIDUAL VALUE (SALVAGE VALUE; TRADE-IN VALUE). The estimated value of an operating asset at the end of its useful life (p. 432).

REVENUE EXPENDITURE. An expenditure that benefits the current accounting period only (p. 439).

STRAIGHT-LINE METHOD. A method that allocates an equal amount of an operating asset's cost to each period benefiting from its use (p. 433).

SUM-OF-YEARS'-DIGITS METHOD. A depreciation method under which the cost of a plant asset is allocated to depreciation on a fractional basis. The denominator of the fraction is the sum of the digits in the asset's useful life. The numerators of the fractions are the years remaining in the asset's useful life at the beginning of the period (p. 435).

UNITS-OF-PRODUCTION METHOD. A method under which the cost of an operating asset is allocated to expense based on the number of production units produced or used during the period (p. 433).

USEFUL LIFE. The time period an operating asset is expected to be used to produce goods or services (p. 431).

DISCUSSION QUESTIONS

1. What are operating assets? What factor distinguishes operating assets from other assets?
2. Why is the cost of an operating asset allocated over two or more accounting periods?
3. What expense term is used when the cost of a plant asset is allocated to expense? When an intangible is allocated? When a natural resource is allocated?
4. In general, what costs should be included in the acquisition cost of an operating asset?
5. Which of the following should be included in the cost of equipment?
   a. Sales tax.
   b. Installation costs.
   c. Freight charges.
   d. Cost of a permanent foundation.
   e. New parts to replace those damaged while unloading.
6. A $20,000, 12%, six month note was exchanged for machinery with a fair market value of $20,000 on January 2, 1992. What entry should be made to record the cost of the machinery? Assuming that a $21,200, six month noninterest-bearing note was exchanged for machinery having a fair market value of $20,000, what entry should be made to record the purchase?
7. When a company constructs an asset for its own use, what expenditures should be included in the cost of the asset?

8. When several assets are acquired for a single lump-sum payment, a portion of the total cost must be allocated to the individual assets acquired. Why? What is the most common allocation method?

9. Rey Company acquired a piece of land, a building, and some equipment for a total purchase price of $400,000. Fair market value of the land was $240,000, the building $192,000, and the equipment $48,000. How much of the total payment should be allocated to each asset?

10. What does the term ''depreciation'' mean as used in accounting?

11. Suppose that the market value of a building increased during the fiscal year. Should depreciation expense on the building be recorded for the fiscal year?

12. What factors determine the amount of periodic depreciation for a plant asset? Explain estimated useful life and estimated residual value.

13. What is the difference between ''obsolescence'' and ''inadequacy'' as related to plant assets?

14. What are the four most frequently used depreciation methods for financial accounting purposes? Which ones are accelerated depreciation methods?

15. Why are some depreciation methods termed ''accelerated''? Why are they sometimes used?

16. An asset with a cost of $22,000, residual value of $2,000, and an estimated life of four years was purchased at the beginning of Year 1. What is the amount of depreciation expense for Years 1 and 2 if the sum-of-years'-digits method is used?

17. What would be the amount of depreciation for Years 1 and 2 for the asset purchased in question 16 if the double declining-balance method were used?

18. What is represented by the balance in the Accumulated Depreciation–Building account? How is it reported on the financial statements?

19. How are changes in estimated useful life or estimated residual value accounted for?

20. What is the difference between a revenue expenditure and a capital expenditure? Give an example of each.

21. What are intangible assets? What are the most common types?

22. What is amortization? In general, what should be the length of the amortization period? What amortization method is generally used?

23. What are leasehold improvements? Over what time period should they be amortized? Why?

24. What is goodwill, from an accounting standpoint? When and in what amount is it recorded in the accounts? Is it necessary to amortize goodwill?

25. At what amount are natural resources recorded in the accounts? What is the expense from the extraction of natural resources called? How is it computed?

EXERCISES

Exercise 10-1 **Measuring Acquisition Cost**

Metro Flight Service purchased a new airplane. The invoice price of the airplane was $760,000. A 2% cash discount was available if the invoice was paid within 10 days. Delivery charges were $2,100 and Metro Flight Service incurred $4,500 in initial testing costs to assure itself that the plane was operating properly.

Required:

What cost should be recorded for the new airplane by Metro Flight Service's accountant?

Exercise 10-2 Lump-Sum Purchase

Sunnyside Farming purchased a fenced piece of land with a crop growing on it for $320,000. An independent appraisal indicated the following fair market values: land, $230,000; crop, $150,000; and fence, $20,000.

Required:

How should the purchase price of $320,000 be allocated among the three assets?

Exercise 10-3 Allocating Acquisition Cost to Expense

Cost allocation methods and several types of assets are presented below:

A – Amortization	C – Depreciation
B – Depletion	N – None of these

_____	1. Timber tract	_____	11. Land
_____	2. Leasehold improvement	_____	12. Cash
_____	3. Investment in common stock	_____	13. Trademark
_____	4. Tools	_____	14. Franchise
_____	5. Goodwill	_____	15. Land investment
_____	6. Inventory of goods	_____	16. Leasehold
_____	7. Gold mine	_____	17. Copyright
_____	8. Patent	_____	18. Oil well
_____	9. Office equipment	_____	19. Gravel Pit
_____	10. Building	_____	20. Machinery

Required:

Place the appropriate letter code on the line preceding each asset type.

Exercise 10-4 Depreciation Calculations

Valley Company purchased a machine at the beginning of Year 1 at a cost of $4,100. The estimated useful life is four years, and the estimated residual value is $500. Assume that the estimated productive life of the machine is 75,000 units and the production for each year was as follows: Year 1, 30,000 units; Year 2, 22,500 units; Year 3, 13,500 units; and Year 4, 9,000 units.

Required:

Complete the following table. Show computations and round to the nearest dollar.

Year	Depreciation Expense			
	Straight-Line	Units-of-Production	Sum-of-Years'-Digits	Double Declining Balance
1				
2				
3				
4				
Total				

Exercise 10-5   Depreciation and Book Value Computations

Sullivan Company purchased a machine that cost $72,000 at the beginning of Year 1. The estimated useful life is 10 years and the estimated residual value is $12,000. Assume the estimated useful life in productive units is 100,000. In Year 1, 20,000 units were actually produced, and 22,000 units were produced in Year 2.

Required:
Complete the table below for Years 1 and 2. Show computations and round to the nearest dollar.

	Depreciation Expense		Book Value at End of	
	Year 1	Year 2	Year 1	Year 2
Straight-line	____	____	____	____
Units-of-production	____	____	____	____
Sum-of-years'-digits	____	____	____	____
Double declining balance	____	____	____	____

Exercise 10-6   Effect of Depreciation Methods on Net Income

Acme Company acquired a machine that cost $24,000 on January 2, 1992. The machine's estimated useful life is four years and the estimated residual value is zero.

Required:
A. Compute annual depreciation for 1992 and 1993 assuming the use of (1) the straight-line method and (2) the double declining balance method.
B. Assume cash revenues of $140,000 and cash expenses of $90,000 for the year 1992 and an income tax rate of 20%. Complete the following table:

	Straight-Line	Double Declining Balance
Revenues	____	____
Expenses	____	____
Depreciation expense	____	____
Pretax income	____	____
Income tax expense	____	____
Net income	____	____

C. Which depreciation method produced the higher net income? By how much? Explain.

Exercise 10-7   Comparison of Depreciation Methods

Risky Corporation acquired a machine on January 2, 1992 at a cost of $85,000. The machine has an estimated useful life of seven years with an estimated residual value of $1,000. It is estimated that the machine can produce 1,400,000 units during its life. In 1992, the machine produced 350,000 units and in 1993, 300,000 units.

Required:
A. Prepare the entry on December 31, 1992 to recognize depreciation expense, assuming the straight-line method is used. What is the book value of the machine after this entry?

B. Prepare the entry on December 31, 1993 to recognize depreciation expense, assuming the units-of-production method is used. What is the balance in the Accumulated Depreciation–Machinery account after this entry?

Exercise 10-8 Part-Year Depreciation

Curtis Corporation acquired a building on May 1, 1992, at a cost of $264,000. The building has an estimated useful life of 25 years and an estimated residual value of $15,000. Curtis Corporation's accounting year ends on December 31, and depreciation is calculated to the nearest month.

Required:

A. Prepare the entries to record depreciation expense on December 31, 1992, using the straight-line and double declining balance methods.

B. Compute Curtis Corporation's depreciation expense for 1993 using the straight-line and double declining balance methods.

Exercise 10-9 Revised Depreciation Methods

Sweep Company purchased a machine with a cost of $90,000 on January 2, 1991. The machine had an estimated useful life of 20 years, a residual value of $1,000, and was depreciated by the straight-line method.

Required:

A. Show how the machine would be reported on the December 31, 1994 balance sheet.

B. During January, 2001, Sweep Company determined that the total estimated useful life of the machine should be changed to 14 years (instead of 20) and that the residual value would remain at $1,000. Give the adjusting entry for depreciation expense at the end of 2001.

C. Ignoring the information in part B, assume that in January 1996 Sweep Company determined that the remaining useful life of the machine was five years and that at the end of five years the machine would not have any residual value. Calculate depreciation expense for 1996.

Exercise 10-10 Accounting for Expenditures After Acquisition

Given below are several expenditures and codes for types of expenditures.

C – Capital expenditure

R – Revenue expenditure

N – Neither capital nor revenue expenditure

_____ 1. Routine maintenance: cost of $1,000; on credit.
_____ 2. Paid cash dividends to stockholders, $45,000.
_____ 3. Purchased a machine for $18,000; gave a long-term note.
_____ 4. Paid $1,500 for ordinary repairs to machinery.
_____ 5. Paid $32,000 for monthly salaries.
_____ 6. Purchased a patent for $10,000 cash.
_____ 7. Paid $6,000 for leasehold improvements.
_____ 8. Paid $18,000 for extraordinary repairs to building.
_____ 9. Addition to old building; paid $30,000 cash.

Required:

Enter the appropriate letter to the left of the expenditure to indicate its type.

Exercise 10-11   Accounting for Disposal of Assets

Rachel Company sold office furniture that had been used in the business for four years. The records showed the following on the date of sale:

Office Furniture	$7,800
Accumulated Depreciation–Office Furniture	3,120

Required:
Give the journal entry to record the sale assuming the sales price was:

A. $4,680.
B. $5,280.
C. $4,380.

Exercise 10-12   Disposal of Operating Assets

The records of Myer Company showed the following on December 31, 1992:

Pumping Machine, original cost	$20,000
Accumulated Depreciation–Pumping Machine	12,000

The machine has a $2,000 estimated residual value and is being depreciated by the straight-line method over a six-year life. On October 1, 1993, the machine was sold for $6,100 cash. Myer's fiscal year is the calendar year.

Required:
A. How old was the machine on January 1, 1993?
B. Prepare the journal entry or entries necessary to record the sale.
C. Assume the machine was determined to be obsolete on October 1, 1993, and had no residual value. Prepare the journal entry to record the scrapping of the machine.

Exercise 10-13   Exchange of Similar Assets

Moonbeam Company owned Machine B which no longer met its production needs. On December 31, 1992, the accounting records showed the following:

Machine B:	
Cost	$70,000
Accumulated Depreciation	36,000

On January 2, 1993, Machine B was traded for Machine C. The fair market value of Machine C was $39,000. Machines B and C perform similar functions.

Required:
A. Give the journal entry to record the exchange in each of the following independent cases:
   1. The machines were exchanged on an even basis with no cash exchanged.
   2. Moonbeam paid an additional $5,000 in cash.
   3. Moonbeam paid an additional $7,000 in cash.
B. For each case, explain how you determined the amount recorded as the cost of Machine C.

Exercise 10-14   Exchange of Dissimilar Assets

Greco Products Company acquired a new asset by trading in a dissimilar asset and paying $28,000 in cash. At the time of the trade, the old asset had an acquisition cost of $20,000 and accumulated depreciation of $15,000.

Required:
Prepare the journal entry to record the trade assuming that the fair value of the old asset was:

A. $5,000.
B. $7,000.
C. $2,000.

Exercise 10-15 Accounting for Intangible Assets
Parker Company had the following three intangible assets at the end of the accounting year, December 31, 1992:

1. Patent purchased from Bill Company on January 2, 1992, for $90,000. The patent had a remaining legal life of 15 years and an estimated economic life of 6 years.
2. A franchise acquired from the state to provide services to customers for five years starting January 1, 1992. The franchise cost of $12,500 was paid on January 2, 1992.
3. A parking lot constructed for employees on leased property adjacent to the manufacturing plant. Cost of the parking lot was $18,750 and it has an expected life of five years. The lease on the property expires on December 31, 2000. The construction was completed on January 2, 1992.

Required:
A. Prepare the journal entry to record the acquisition of each intangible.
B. Prepare the adjusting entry on December 31, 1992, to record the yearly amortization of each intangible. Credit the asset account directly.
C. Indicate how the assets and related expenses are reported on the 1992 financial statements.

Exercise 10-16 Accounting for Intangible Assets
Jameson Company has four different intangible assets at the end of 1992. The facts concerning each are:

1. A copyright purchased on January 3, 1992, for $85,000. Its remaining legal life at that time was 24 years and it is expected to have a useful life of 17 years with no residual value.
2. A franchise purchased on April 2, 1992 to distribute a new product for a nine-year period with no right of renewal. Cost was $40,500.
3. A patent purchased on July 1, 1992 from Beech Company for $144,900. The patent was initially registered on January 1, 1987, and is expected to be useful to Jameson Company until the end of its legal life.
4. Jameson Company began operations on January 2, 1987, by purchasing another company for $510,000. Included in the purchase price was a payment of $70,000 for goodwill. The management of Jameson Company believes that the "goodwill is such an important asset of the company that it will last for 200 years."

Required:
A. Prepare journal entries to record the acquisition of the intangible assets acquired during 1992.
B. Prepare journal entries for each intangible asset to record amortization expense on December 31, 1992, the end of the fiscal year. Jameson Company does not use accumulated amortization accounts.
C. Determine the balance in each intangible asset account on December 31, 1992.

Exercise 10-17 **Accounting for Intangibles**

Mendoza and Sedillo, a law firm, moved into a suite of offices in a high-rise professional office complex on January 2, 1992. The lease required an initial advance payment of $137,500, which was applicable to the entire lease term, and additional monthly rental payments of $8,500. The lease term is five years.

Required:
A. Compute the rent expense for Mendoza and Sedillo for a full year's use.
B. Prepare the journal entry to record amortization of the leasehold at the end of 1992.
C. How would the leasehold be reported on the Mendoza and Sedillo balance sheet prepared on December 31, 1992?

Exercise 10-18 **Accounting for Natural Resources**

On May 1, 1992, PD Mining Co. paid $875,000 for a copper mine containing an estimated 1 million tons of copper ore. By December 31, 1992, the end of the fiscal year, PD Mining had extracted 75,000 tons of ore. Of this, 60,000 tons were sold during the year and the remaining 15,000 tons are in the December 31 inventory.

Required:
Prepare journal entries for 1992.

PROBLEMS

Problem 10-1 **Acquisition Cost and Depreciation**

Long and Farow, Attorneys, purchased an office building at a cost of $290,000. Transfer fees were $6,300. Before occupying the building, Long and Farow had the floors replaced at a cost of $48,000 and incurred major plumbing repairs amounting to $43,000.

Required:
A. What amount should Long and Farow record as the cost of the building?
B. The office building had an estimated useful life of 30 years and an estimated residual value of $30,000. Calculate annual depreciation expense if Long and Farow use the straight-line depreciation method.
C. Assuming Long and Farow occupied the building on January 2, 1992, what is the balance in the Accumulated Depreciation–Building account on December 31, 1994? What is the book value of the building on December 31, 1996?

Problem 10-2 **Acquisition Cost of Operating Assets**

On January 2, 1992, Bander Company purchased, for $97,000, a piece of land to be used as a plant site. The property had an old building on it that was demolished. A new building was constructed on the land and completed on June 1, 1992. Costs incurred were:

Demolition of the old building	$ 9,000
Architect's fees	13,000
Legal fees for title investigation and contract preparation	2,500
Construction costs paid to contractor	850,000

Materials salvaged from the demolished building were sold for $3,200.

Required:

Determine the cost of the land and the cost of the new building.

Problem 10-3 Lump-Sum Purchase of Assets

Wilson Company paid $640,000 to purchase land, a building, and equipment. The company then paid $12,000 for an appraisal of the assets acquired. The appraised values were as follows:

Land	$177,840	169 520
Building	424,080	404 240
Equipment	82,080	78 240
	684,000	652,000

Required:

Determine the cost that should be allocated to the land, building, and equipment.

Problem 10-4 Depreciation Methods

On January 1, 1992, Jefferson Company purchased a machine at a cost of $77,500. The machine's estimated useful life is 15 years or 297,000 units; its estimated residual value is $3,250. The machine produced 29,000 units in 1992 and 22,400 units in 1993.

Required:

A. Complete the following table.

	Depreciation Expense		Book Value at End of	
	1992	**1993**	**1992**	**1993**
Depreciation Method				
Straight-line	_____	_____	_____	_____
Units-of-production	_____	_____	_____	_____
Sum-of-years'-digits	_____	_____	_____	_____
Double declining balance	_____	_____	_____	_____

B. Prepare the entries to record depreciation expense for 1992 and 1993 assuming use of the sum-of-years'-digits method.

Problem 10-5 Depreciation Calculations

The following information is available concerning a machine purchased by Globe Company:

Paid to seller	$67,000
Installation cost	3,000
Estimated residual value	10,000
Estimated useful life	5 years
Estimated total units of output	25,000 units

The machine was put into service on April 1, 1992. Actual output for 1992 was 2,875 units.

Required:

A. Compute straight-line and units-of-production depreciation for 1992.

B. If output is 3,000 units in 1993, compute straight-line and units-of-production depreciation for 1993.

C. What is the book value of the machine on December 31, 1993 under each of the depreciation methods given in requirement (B)?

Problem 10-6 Revised Estimate of Useful Life and Residual Value

Center Company purchased a building on January 2, 1982 for $375,000. It has been depreciated over an estimated useful life of 25 years using the straight-line method and an estimated residual value of $75,000. In January 1992, management decided that a total estimated useful life of 35 years and an estimated residual value of $54,000 was more realistic. Center's fiscal year ends on December 31.

Required:
A. Compute depreciation expense for 1991.
B. Determine the book value of the building on December 31, 1991.
C. Compute depreciation expense for 1992.
D. Prepare the entry to record depreciation expense for 1992.

Problem 10-7 Accounting for Post Acquisition Expenditures

Gilbert Company owns a building purchased on January 2, 1982 at a cost of $525,000. The building is depreciated on a straight-line basis using an estimated useful life of 30 years with no residual value. During 1992, the following transactions related to the building occurred:

1. Ordinary repairs and maintenance costs were incurred in the amount of $1,700.
2. Extraordinary repairs to the roof cost $33,750. These repairs were completed on June 30, 1992, and extended the estimated useful life of the building by five years.
3. A new wing was added to the building at a cost of $264,000. Construction was completed on June 30, 1992. The new wing's useful life is limited by the new remaining useful life of the original building.

Required:
A. Prepare journal entries for each of the transactions occurring in 1992.
B. Prepare the journal entry to record depreciation expense on December 31, 1992, the end of the fiscal year. Record to the nearest month.
C. Show how the building would be reported on the December 31, 1992 balance sheet.

Problem 10-8 Disposal of Plant Assets

Spic and Span Laundry and Dry Cleaning disposed of three operating assets as shown below. On January 1, 1992, prior to disposal, recorded information showed:

Asset	Original Cost	Residual Value	Estimated Life	Accumulated Depreciation (Straight-Line)
Dry cleaning machine	$3,000	$200	5 years	$1,680
Presser	2,200	100	7 years	1,500
Washer	900	–0–	3 years	525

Spic and Span, whose fiscal year ends on December 31, disposed of these assets as follows:

Dry cleaning machine—Sold on January 2, 1992 for $900 cash.
Presser—Sold on April 1, 1992 for $700. The buyer paid 20% of the sales price in cash and signed a 10%, six-month note for the balance.

Washer—On October 2, 1992, the washer would not operate properly. Because the washer required extensive repairs, management decided to discard it rather than repair it. A salvage company removed the washer from the premises at no charge to Spic and Span.

Required:

Prepare journal entries to record the disposals. Explain the rationale for the way you recorded each disposal.

Problem 10-9   Sale of Operating Assets

Marlboro Company purchased a cutting machine on January 2, 1987, at a cost of $26,750. The machine had an estimated useful life of 10 years and an estimated residual value of $1,750. Marlboro Company adopted the straight-line method of depreciation.

Required:

Prepare the journal entry to record the sale of the cutting machine under each of the following independent assumptions. (The accounting year ends on December 31.)

A. The machine was sold on March 31, 1992, for $13,625.
B. The machine was sold on June 30, 1992, for $11,500.
C. The machine was sold on September 30, 1992, for $12,525. The purchaser paid $7,525 in cash and signed a 12-month, 12%, interest-bearing note for $5,000.

Problem 10-10   Exchange of Similar Assets

Curtis Company acquired a machine worth $69,000 by paying $54,000 cash and giving a similar machine, which had originally cost $72,000 and had accumulated depreciation of $55,000 on the date of exchange.

Required:

A. Compute any gain or loss resulting from the exchange.
B. Prepare the journal entry to record the exchange.
C. Repeat (A) and (B) assuming the new machine was worth $74,000.

Problem 10-11   Accounting for Intangible Assets

Salem Company entered into the following transactions involving intangible assets during 1992.

1. A trademark was purchased on January 2, 1992, for $59,000. According to management, the trademark has an indefinite life.
2. A three-year-old patent was acquired on July 1, 1992 at a cost of $36,000. The estimated useful life of the patent to Salem Company is six years.
3. A franchise granting exclusive distribution rights for the state of Nevada for a new skin care product made from mink oil was obtained at a cost of $45,000 on September 1, 1992. The franchise is effective for three years.
4. Shelving and storage cabinets were constructed and permanently attached to the walls of a building being leased from another firm. These improvements were completed on October 1, 1992, at a cost of $84,000. The physical life of the shelving and cabinets is 18 years; at the time of installation, there were 12 years remaining on the building lease.

Required:
A. Prepare journal entries to record the transactions.
B. Record amortization expense for Salem Company whose fiscal year ends on December 31. Accumulated amortization accounts are not used.

Problem 10-12 Accounting for Intangible Assets
Parker Company engaged in the following transactions during 1992:

1. Developed a process, at a cost of $140,000, for making dripless ice cream bars. Legal costs to apply for a patent on the process were $20,000. The patent was granted on October 1, 1992.
2. On January 2, 1992, $14,000 in legal fees were paid to successfully defend a copyright acquired four years earlier at a cost of $25,000. The original copyright was being amortized over a life of 20 years.
3. Paid $90,000 to have the company's name displayed on the local bank's outdoor electronic display board showing local time and temperature.

Required:
A. Prepare journal entries to record the transactions.
B. Prepare the journal entry to record amortization expense on December 31, 1992, the end of the fiscal year. Accumulated amortization accounts are not used.

Problem 10-13 Computing and Recording Goodwill
Bay Company purchased Minute Company for $400,000. On the purchase date the fair values of Minute Company's assets and liabilities were $1,100,000 and $760,000 respectively.

Required:
A. How much goodwill should Bay Company record as a result of the purchase of Minute Company?
B. How will the goodwill be reported on the financial statements of Bay Company?
C. Over what period of time should the goodwill be amortized?
D. Assuming goodwill is amortized over the maximum allowable period, prepare the journal entry to record a full year's amortization.

Problem 10-14 Natural Resources and Depletion
Sebring Sand and Gravel Company purchased a gravel pit containing an estimated 1.5 million tons of high grade gravel. The following costs were incurred to get the gravel pit into operation:

Purchase price of the pit	$500,000
Legal fees	7,000
Grading and leveling	63,000

When all the gravel has been extracted, the gravel pit site is expected to have a sales value of $15,000.

Required:
A. Assuming 125,000 tons of gravel are mined the first year, prepare the journal entry to record depletion of the gravel pit.
B. Assuming that 95,000 tons of gravel were sold and 30,000 tons remain in inventory at year-end, prepare the journal entry to record cost of goods sold and ending inventory of gravel.

Problem 10-15 Natural Resources and Depletion

Petro Oil Company acquired an oil field in 1992 at a cost of $20 million. The field is expected to produce 4 million barrels of oil and it is estimated that the field can be sold for $4 million after the oil is removed. Production and sale of oil during 1992 and 1993, in barrels, were:

	1992	1993
Production	410,000	500,000
Sales	300,000	520,000

Required:

A. Compute the oil depletion rate per barrel.
B. Prepare the journal entries for 1992 and 1993 to record depletion of the oil field and to allocate depletion to cost of goods sold and ending inventory.

CASE

CASE 10-1 Annual Report Analysis

Refer to the financial statements and related footnotes of BFGoodrich Company in the Appendix to this text and answer the following questions. Indicate the page number on which you found the answer.

A. How much was depreciation and amortization expense for the year ended December 31, 1989?
B. What depreciation and amortization method(s) is used?
C. What was the amount of goodwill reported as of December 31, 1989? What does the goodwill represent? Over what time period is it being amortized?
D. What items make up the property amount of $991.5 million on December 31, 1989?

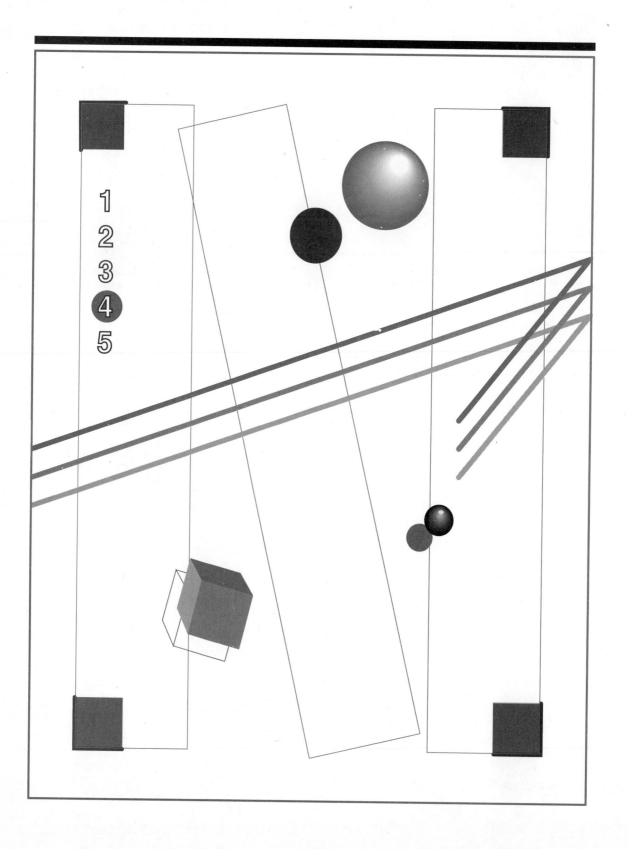

PART 4

ACCOUNTING FOR LIABILITIES AND OWNERS' EQUITY

11

LIABILITIES AND THE TIME VALUE OF MONEY

CHAPTER OVERVIEW AND OBJECTIVES

This chapter contains two parts. Part I describes the accounting treatment of liabilities except for bonds and mortgage notes payable, which are covered in Chapter 12. Part II discusses the time value of money concept. When you have completed the chapter, you should understand:

1. The different types of liabilities and how to account for them.
2. The differences in accounting for interest-bearing and noninterest-bearing notes payable.
3. How to account for payroll liabilities.
4. The accounting for lease obligations, pension liabilities, and deferred income taxes.
5. The meaning and importance of the time value of money concept.
6. How control over cash disbursements is enhanced by the use of a voucher system: Appendix.

PART I. LIABILITIES

Today's U.S. economy is essentially a credit economy. The willingness of businesses to extend credit and of financial institutions to lend money is an important factor in the significant growth of our economy. Most businesses borrow money and acquire various types of goods and services on credit, thereby incurring significant amounts of liabilities. Liabilities are generally classified into two broad groups: current liabilities and long-term liabilities.

CURRENT LIABILITIES

Current liabilities are those obligations that must be settled within one year or the normal operating cycle, whichever is longer. Generally, they are expected to be paid with assets that are classified as current assets on the same balance sheet. This relationship between current assets and current liabilities is often expressed in the form of a ratio called the current ratio. The current ratio is computed by dividing total current assets by total current liabilities. Thus, a firm with total current assets of $250,000 and total current liabilities of $100,000 has a current ratio of 2.5 to 1, which means that on the balance sheet date, there are $2.50 in current assets for each $1 of current liabilities. The current ratio is often used by creditors as one means of judging the ability of a firm to pay its short-term obligations.

Objective 1:
The different
types of liabilities

Among the common current liabilities are accounts payable, short-term notes payable, accrued expenses (including wages payable, taxes payable, and rent payable), and unearned revenues (revenues collected in advance). Most current liabilities result from the acquisition of goods and services that are either used or sold in conducting normal operations. They are generally settled by cash payment. Controlling these cash payments by the use of a voucher system is discussed in an Appendix to this chapter.

ACCOUNTS PAYABLE

Accounts payable are amounts owed to creditors for the purchase of merchandise, supplies, and services in the normal course of business. Because they are not evidenced by a formal debt instrument such as a note, they are often referred to as open accounts or open payables. Each time merchandise, supplies, or services are acquired on open account, the appropriate asset, purchases, or expense account is debited and Accounts Payable is credited.

SHORT-TERM NOTES PAYABLE

Notes payable differ from accounts payable in that the liability is evidenced by a *promissory note*, which is an unconditional promise to pay a sum of money on demand or at a future determinable date. Promissory notes are often issued when a business borrows money from a bank or finance company. In some industries, if the credit term is more than 30 or 60 days it is normal practice for the buyer of merchandise to give a note payable to the seller at the time of purchase. Other examples of transactions that result in notes payable include purchases of relatively high-cost items of machinery or equipment and the substitution of a note payable for a past-due open account payable.

Note Issued for a Bank Loan

Interest-Bearing Note.   When money is borrowed from a bank, the borrower often issues an interest-bearing note payable to the bank under which the borrower agrees to repay the amount of the note, plus interest, on its maturity date. For example, assume that Braxton Company borrowed $30,000 from a bank on June 1 and signed a six-month note for $30,000 at an interest rate of 14%. The journal entry to record the note on Braxton's books is:

Objective 2:
Interest-bearing
vs. noninterest
bearing notes
payable

June	1	Cash	30,000	
		Notes Payable		30,000

Assuming that adjusting entries are made only on December 31, no interest is recorded on the note until it is paid on December 1, when the entry is:

Dec.	1	Notes Payable	30,000	
		Interest Expense	2,100	
		Cash		32,100
		($30,000 × 14% × 6/12 = $2,100)		

In this example, the note provided for the payment of its face value plus interest at a stipulated rate. The borrower received the face amount of the note at the time it was given to the bank. On the note's maturity date, the borrower repaid that amount plus interest.

Noninterest-Bearing Note. As an alternative, banks sometimes have the borrower sign a so-called noninterest-bearing note for the amount to be paid at maturity. In reality, *such a note does bear interest, but the interest is deducted in advance.* That is, the borrower receives the difference between the face value of the note and the amount of interest deducted; this amount is called the proceeds. This practice is called *discounting a note payable* because the proceeds represent the discounted present value of the note. (The concept of present value is discussed later in this chapter.) If this practice were followed for the note in the preceding example, it would be recorded by Braxton Company as follows:

June	1	Cash	27,900	
		Discount on Notes Payable	2,100	
		Notes Payable		30,000

The Discount on Notes Payable is deducted as a contra liability in the current liability section of the balance sheet as shown below:

Current Liabilities:		
Accounts payable		$57,800
Notes payable	$30,000	
Less: Discount on notes payable	2,100	27,900
Accrued expenses		13,600
Total current liabilities		99,300

Because the discount on notes payable represents interest deducted in advance, it is transferred to interest expense over the term of the note. In the example above, the maturity date of the note falls within the same year as the issue date. Thus, the discount is charged to interest expense when the note is paid on December 1 as follows:

Dec.	1	Notes Payable	30,000	
		Interest Expense	2,100	
		Discount on Notes Payable		2,100
		Cash		30,000

Both an interest-bearing and a discounted noninterest-bearing note have the same amount of interest. However, the effective annual interest rate is higher under the discounted method because the borrower has the use of less money. For example, if the effective interest rates for each method are compared for a $30,000, one-year,

14% note, the following results are obtained:

	Annual Interest Amount	Amount Borrowed	Effective Interest Rate
Interest-bearing note	$4,200	$30,000	14.0%
Discounted note	4,200	25,800	16.3%

$4,200/$30,000 = 14.0%
$4,200/$25,800 = 16.3%

End-of-Period Adjustments for Interest

When a note payable is issued in one accounting period and matures in another, an adjusting entry must be made at the end of the first period to allocate interest expense properly. For example, assume that Braxton Company's $30,000, six-month, 14% note was issued on November 1 rather than on June 1. Regardless of whether the note is interest-bearing or noninterest-bearing, the amount of interest expense allocated to each accounting period is the same—$700 to the period in which the note was issued and $1,400 to the following period. However, the actual accounting procedure differs.

If the note is an interest-bearing one, an adjusting entry is needed on December 31 to accrue interest expense for two months as follows:

Dec.	31	Interest Expense	700	
		Interest Payable		700
		($30,000 × 14% × 2/12)		

When the note is paid on May 1, the following entry is made:

May	1	Notes Payable	30,000	
		Interest Payable	700	
		Interest Expense	1,400	
		Cash		32,100

The adjustment process is slightly different if the note had been discounted at 14% on November 1. The year-end adjustment is:

Dec.	31	Interest Expense	700	
		Discount on Notes Payable		700
		($2,100 × 2/6)		

The entry to record payment of the note and interest expense on May 1 is then:

May	1	Notes Payable	30,000	
		Interest Expense	1,400	
		Discount on Notes Payable		1,400
		Cash		30,000

Note Issued in Exchange for Plant Assets

When a plant asset is purchased on credit, a note is often given in exchange. The note may or may not contain a specific interest rate.

If a current market interest rate is stated, the face value of the note will be equal to the cash price of the asset. For example, if a $40,000, 15%, nine-month note is exchanged for a machine that could be purchased for $40,000 cash, the transaction is recorded as follows:

Jan.	2	Machinery	40,000	
		Notes Payable		40,000

When the note is paid on its maturity date, the entry is:

Oct.	2	Notes Payable	40,000	
		Interest Expense	4,500	
		Cash		44,500
		($40,000 × 15% × 9/12 = $4,500)		

Note that the Machinery account is debited only for the cash purchase price of the asset. Interest on the note is not a part of the asset's cost, and is therefore debited to interest expense when accrued or paid.

If no interest rate is specified on the note, or if the specified rate is unreasonable, a portion of the face value of the note must be assumed to represent interest. The asset acquired with the note is recorded at either the asset's cash value or the note's market value, whichever is more clearly determinable. The difference between the face value of the note and the recorded value of the asset is considered interest. This process is called *imputing interest* on a note.[1] To illustrate, assume that a nine-month, $44,500 noninterest-bearing note was exchanged for a machine with a cash value of $40,000. The transaction would be recorded as follows:

Jan.	2	Machinery	40,000	
		Discount on Notes Payable	4,500	
		Notes Payable		44,500

Note that the machine is recorded at its cash value of $40,000 rather than at the face value of the note. The cash value is the machine's cost; the remaining $4,500 represents interest (generally recorded as discount) on the note that will be recognized as expense over the term of the note.

ACCRUED EXPENSES

Although most operating expenses are recorded at the time they are paid, some are recorded as accrued. Accrued expenses (sometimes called accrued liabilities) are expenses that have been incurred but not yet paid.

At the end of the accounting period, there are usually some incurred expenses that have not been recorded because they have not yet been paid. These expenses should be recognized in the period they were incurred (under the matching principle). The obligations to pay for them should be recorded and reported as current liabilities in the balance sheet. For example, wages due employees at the end of the period are recorded through an adjusting entry debiting Wages Expense and crediting Wages

[1]Opinions of the Accounting Principles Board No. 21, "Interest on Receivables and Payables" (New York: AICPA, 1971), par. 12.

Payable. Other kinds of accrued expenses include interest, utilities, and commissions as discussed and illustrated in Chapter 4.

UNEARNED REVENUES

Unearned revenues (often called **deferred revenues** or **revenues received in advance**) are advance payments received from customers for goods or services to be delivered or performed in the future. Until the goods are delivered or the services performed, the firm has a liability equal to the amount of the advance payment. The liability is generally settled by the future delivery of goods or performance of services, at which time the liability is transferred to revenue. That is, recognition of the revenue is deferred until the earning process is complete.

To illustrate unearned revenue, assume that Rox Company rented some excess warehouse space to Dade Company for a three-month period beginning on December 1 at a rental of $3,000, all received in advance. On December 1, Rox Company records the receipt of cash as follows:

Dec.	1	Cash	3,000	
		Unearned Rent Revenue		3,000

On December 31, the end of the fiscal year for Rox Company, the following adjusting entry is made:

Dec.	31	Unearned Rent Revenue	1,000	
		Rent Revenue		1,000

This entry recognizes $1,000 as rent revenue for December and adjusts the Unearned Rent Revenue account to a balance of $2,000, which will be reported on the December 31 balance sheet as a current liability. It will be recognized as revenue during the next fiscal period, when it is earned.

PAYROLL LIABILITIES

As discussed and illustrated in Chapter 4, when employees have performed services by the end of the accounting period that have not been paid or recorded, the employer must make an adjusting entry to recognize the expense for the period and to record the liability to employees. The effects of payroll taxes and payroll deductions, which were ignored in previous chapters for the purpose of simplification, will be discussed here as they relate to the reporting of current liabilities.

In addition to the liability for accrued salaries and wages, the employer normally has two other types of payroll-related liabilities. The first liability is for amounts withheld from employees wages or salaries for taxes and other types of deductions; the second is for payroll taxes levied against the employer. These liabilities will also be discussed here.

Objective 3: Accounting for payroll liabilities

Withholdings from Employee Earnings

In computing the amount to be paid to an employee for a given payroll period, the employee's gross earnings in the form of wages or salary must first be determined. The term *wages* is used for compensation paid to an employee on the basis of either an hourly rate or piecework (i.e., the number of pieces or units produced by the employee). *Salary* refers to compensation paid on a weekly, biweekly, or monthly basis.

To arrive at the employee's ***take-home-pay***, certain required or voluntary deductions are made from the gross earnings. Required deductions are those for federal and state income taxes and for social security taxes (FICA taxes). In addition, employees may have voluntary deductions made for such things as life insurance premiums, health insurance premiums, and union dues. The employer is required to pay these withheld amounts to the appropriate government agency or other organization. Until payment is made, they represent current liabilities of the employer.

Income Taxes.

The federal income tax system of the United States is on a "pay-as-you-go" basis. This means that an employer must withhold certain amounts of federal income tax from each employee's wages or salary based on (1) the amount of gross earnings and (2) the number of exemptions for the employee and his or her dependents.

Withholding tables are provided by the Internal Revenue Service. These tables are based on the amount of earnings and number of exemptions. The employer uses them to determine the amount of tax to be withheld. The amount of tax withheld must be paid to the federal government periodically, accompanied by a form identifying the employees, their gross earnings, and the amount withheld from each. Until payment is made, the amount withheld constitutes a current liability on the part of the employer. In addition to withholding for federal income taxes, some states also require withholding of state income taxes.

FICA Taxes.

The Social Security System was created by the Federal Insurance Contributions Act (FICA) of 1935. The system's main purpose is to provide qualified workers with a basic amount of continuing income during their retirement years. Certain medical, disability, and survivorship benefits also are provided.

The funds required to finance the system are provided by a tax on wages and salaries. The tax is imposed equally on the employee and the employer. Self-employment income is taxed according to a separate schedule established by Congress. Although most sources of compensation are subject to FICA taxes, special rules apply to some types of employment such as agricultural labor, domestic laborers, and government employees.

The FICA tax schedule includes a tax rate on compensation up to a maximum or ceiling amount of earnings. Although the schedule is subject to change by congressional action, the effective rate as of January 1, 1990, is 7.65% on the first $50,400 paid to each employee during the year.

By January 31 of every year, an employer must provide each employee several copies of a **Wage and Tax Statement (Form W-2)**, for the preceding calendar year. The Form W-2 furnishes information needed by the employee to file his or her income tax returns, including

- Total gross earnings of the employee;
- Amount of federal income taxes withheld;
- Amount of state income taxes withheld;
- Earnings subject to FICA taxes; and
- FICA taxes withheld.

A copy of the form must be attached to each return filed (i.e., federal, state, and local). The employer also must send a copy of each employee's Form W-2 to the

Social Security Administration, which processes the information so that it can pay benefits to employees when appropriate. The Social Security Administration then sends the Internal Revenue Service the income tax related information it requires from the form.

Like federal income taxes, FICA taxes withheld from employees must be paid periodically to the federal government. Until they are paid, they are reported as current liabilities on the balance sheet.

Voluntary Deductions. In addition to the mandatory deductions for income and FICA taxes, employees often request that other deductions be made from gross earnings. Examples of such deductions include union dues, insurance premiums, retirement plan contributions, savings bond purchases, uniform allowances, and charitable contributions. These deductions are taken out of the employees' paychecks by the employer and later remitted to the appropriate organization. Until remitted, they represent current liabilities to the employer.

To illustrate the accounting for employee payroll deductions, assume that Rox Company obtained the following data from its detailed payroll records for the month of August:

Gross salaries and wages	$120,000
Employee withholdings:	
Federal income tax	26,700
FICA taxes ($120,000 × 7.65%)	9,180
Medical insurance premiums	1,500
Union dues	900
United Way contributions	1,100

The entry to record salaries and wages expense and employee deductions is:

Aug.	31	Salaries and Wages Expense	120,000	
		Employee Income Taxes Payable		26,700
		FICA Taxes Payable		9,180
		Insurance Premiums Payable		1,500
		Union Dues Payable		900
		United Way Contribution Payable		1,100
		Cash		80,620

Note that all the liabilities recorded in the entry represent either taxes levied on the employees or voluntary deductions authorized by the employees. No expense was recorded except for the gross salaries and wages earned by employees. Thus, the employer acts as a collection agency, withholding both mandatory and voluntary deductions from the gross payroll.

Employer Payroll Taxes

Payroll taxes are paid by both employees and employers. As indicated earlier, employers must match the amount of the employee's deduction for FICA taxes. In addition, employers must make payments for federal and state unemployment taxes. The *Federal Unemployment Tax Act (FUTA)* provides certain benefits for a limited period to employees who lose their jobs through no fault of their own. FUTA is a joint federal and state unemployment program that is part of the Social Security System. It establishes certain minimum standards that must be complied with by each state.

The major portion of the tax (generally 2.7%) is levied by the states and a minor portion (.7%) by the federal government. Actual unemployment benefits are paid from the state's share, while administrative expenses are paid from the federal portion. Although the amount of the FUTA tax can be changed by Congress, the recent state and federal rate for most states amounted to 3.4% of the first $6,000 earned by each employee.

By law, the federal unemployment tax is 3.4%, but a 2.7% credit is granted for the state portion of the tax. A particular employer may actually pay a lower rate to a state if that employer has had a sufficiently low unemployment record in the past. For example, while the federal rate always remains a constant .7%, the employer's state rate may be reduced to say 2.2%—thereby making the total tax rate 2.9% (2.2% state tax plus .7% federal tax).

The following illustrations and problems assume that the employer must pay the full 3.4% (i.e., .7% to the federal government and 2.7% to the state). To illustrate the accounting for employer payroll taxes, assume the data used in the preceding illustration of employee deductions for Rox Company. The entry to record employer's payroll taxes for August would be:

Aug.	31	Payroll Tax Expense	13,260	
		FICA Taxes Payable (1)		9,180
		State Unemployment Tax Payable (2)		3,240
		Federal Unemployment Tax Payable (3)		840
		(1) $120,000 × 7.65%		
		(2) $120,000 × 2.7%		
		(3) $120,000 × .7%		

Note that these taxes are levied against the employer and are, therefore, debited to Payroll Tax Expense since they represent operating expenses of the business. When these liabilities (as well as those recorded for employee payroll deductions) are paid, the individual liability accounts are debited and cash is credited.

Current liabilities are reported as the first category under the "Liabilities and Stockholders' Equity" section of the balance sheet. The amount of detail provided varies from company to company. An example from a recent annual report of St. Regis Corporation is presented below:

Current Liabilities:	(In Thousands)
Notes payable	$ 8,106
Accounts payable	143,012
Current portion of long-term debt	51,018
Accrued wages and interest	56,070
Other accrued taxes	27,141
Other accrued liabilities	72,445
Total	$357,792

Note that the current liabilities category also includes the current portion of long-term debt, that is, the portion of long-term debt that is payable within the following year.

LONG-TERM LIABILITIES

Long-term liabilities are those obligations that are due beyond one year from the balance sheet date or the operating cycle, whichever is longer. In other words, when the operating cycle is less than one year, a one-year period is used to classify liabilities as current or long-term. When the operating cycle is longer than one year, the length of the operating cycle is used. The main types of long-term liabilities (other than bonds and mortgage notes payable) are lease obligations, pension obligations, and deferred income taxes. Accounting for these types of liabilities is complex and is, therefore, covered in detail in more advanced accounting courses. Our discussion here is limited to the fundamentals.

Objective 4:
Leases, pensions,
and deferred
income taxes

Lease Obligations

A **lease** is a rental agreement in which the lessor (the owner) transfers to the lessee (the user) the right to use property for a specified period of time in return for periodic rental payments. Many companies obtain much of their equipment by lease rather than by purchase for one or more of the following reasons:

1. Leasing permits 100% financing rather than making a substantial down payment as required in most credit purchases.
2. The full lease payment, even for land, is deductible for tax purposes.
3. Lease contracts may be more flexible and contain fewer restrictions than most debt agreements.

Because of these advantages, the use of leasing has grown rapidly. As a result, the accounting profession has devoted a great deal of effort to establish accounting standards for lease reporting.

Capital Leases.   For accounting purposes, there are two types of leases: *capital leases* and *operating leases*. Leases that transfer substantially all the benefits and risks of ownership to the lessee are installment purchases in substance and are called capital leases. Lease terms vary widely. Often, it is difficult to distinguish between a capital lease and an installment purchase. In an effort to clarify this, the Financial Accounting Standards Board ruled[2] that a lease is a capital lease if it is noncancelable **and** meets one or more of the following four criteria:

1. The lease transfers ownership of the property to the lessee by the end of the lease term;
2. The lease permits the lessee to acquire the property at the end of the lease for a bargain price;
3. The length of the lease (lease term) is equal to 75% or more of the estimated economic life of the leased property; and
4. The present value of the lease payments at the beginning of the lease term equals or exceeds 90% of the fair value of the leased property.

To illustrate, assume that a major airline entered into an equipment lease to acquire its airplanes. The lease has a fixed noncancelable term of eight years. The estimated economic life of the airplanes is 10 years. Because the lease satisfies criterion 3 (8/10 = 80%), the airline would account for the lease as a capital lease.

Capital leases are accounted for as if they were installment purchases. The lessee records the leased property as a plant asset and credits a long-term liability for the future lease payments. Both the asset and liability are recorded at an amount equal to the present value of the future lease payments. Part of each lease payment is recorded as interest expense, and the remainder is a reduction in the principal balance. In addition, the leased asset is depreciated over the period it is expected to be used.

Assume, for example, that the lease contract for the airplanes mentioned earlier

[2]Statement of Financial Accounting Standards No. 13, "Accounting for Leases" (Stamford, Conn.: FASB, 1976), par. 7.

required a $1 million payment at the end of each of the eight years and provides for an interest rate of 12%. The present value of the lease payments is $4,967,600. Both the leased asset and the lease obligation are recorded at this amount. (The calculation of the present value of future cash payments is discussed in Part II of this chapter.) The accounting is as follows:

At the Inception of the Lease

| Jan. | 1 | Leased Airplanes | 4,967,600 | |
| | | Lease Obligation | | 4,967,600 |

To Record First Lease Payment

Dec.	31	Interest Expense	596,112	
		Lease Obligation	403,888	
		Cash		1,000,000
		($4,967,600 × 12% = $596,112)		

To Record Depreciation on Leased Asset

Dec.	31	Depreciation Expense	620,950	
		Accumulated Depreciation–		
		Leased Airplanes		620,950
		($4,967,600/8 years)		

Accounting in the remaining seven years would be similar to that above except that the portion of the $1 million lease payment pertaining to interest will decrease each year (since the lease obligation is decreasing), and the portion pertaining to the lease obligation will increase.

Operating Leases.   Leases that do not meet at least one of the four criteria for a capital lease are classified as operating leases. Operating leases are generally either short-term or cancelable, and the lessor retains the usual risks and rewards of ownership. For example, a company that leases delivery trucks on a weekly basis during its peak demand periods accounts for the truck lease as an operating lease. The lease payments are accounted for by the lessee as an expense. Neither the leased asset nor the related lease obligation is recorded on the lessee's books. However, if the amounts involved are significant, the minimum future rental payments for each of the next five years and the total rental expense included in each income statement presented must be disclosed in a footnote to the financial statements.

Pension Plans

Most firms have pension plans to provide payments to eligible employees when they retire. The company normally appoints a trustee, such as an insurance company, to administer the plan. It satisfies its pension obligation by making regular payments to the trustee. The trustee then invests the funds and uses the fund earnings and contributions to pay benefits to retired employees. This type of plan is called a funded plan.

The amount to be paid into the fund is determined jointly by the policies of the company, the trustee, and the provisions of the Pension Reform Act of 1974. Measurement of the pension expense is complex and beyond the scope of our coverage here. However, the amount reported as expense in the income statement is determined independently of the cash contribution. Payments to the pension fund are recorded by a debit to Pension Expense and a credit to Cash. If payments to the pension fund are equal to the pension expense computed each period, a liability will not appear on the balance sheet. A liability will arise, however, if payments to the fund are less than the pension expense recognized. Therefore, the liability that often appears in the balance sheet represents the accumulated excess of pension expense over the cash paid into the pension fund.

Deferred Income Tax Liability

Permanent Differences.   There are differences in the recognition of revenues and expenses between tax law and generally accepted accounting principles (GAAP) that result in differences between accounting income and taxable income. An item that enters into the computation of either taxable income or accounting income, but not both, creates a **permanent difference**. For example, interest received on a bond issued by a state government is reported on the books as income, but such income is not taxable. Consequently, accounting income in the year the interest is accrued is greater than taxable income. In other cases, the differences cause taxable income to exceed accounting income. For example, legally imposed fines and penalties are not deductible in computing taxable income, but such payments are expensed for accounting purposes. When a difference between the amount of taxable income and accounting income is the result of a permanent difference, the income tax expense reported in the income statement will be equal to the income tax liability.

Timing Differences.   In contrast with permanent differences, other differences between taxable income and accounting income, called **temporary** or **timing differences,** arise when an item of revenue or expense enters into the computation of both taxable and accounting income, but during different periods. A timing difference may result because the timing of certain revenues and expenses, as required by tax law, differs from the timing of revenues and expenses in accordance with generally accepted accounting principles. For example, the tax law specifies that an advance receipt of rent is fully taxable in the year received, but accounting principles recognize it as revenue as it is earned. Although the rent is reported earlier for tax purposes, the total revenue will be the same over the rental period for both tax and financial reporting. The only difference is the pattern of recognizing the annual income amounts.

In addition, for some items, the tax law requires accounting methods that may be different from those used for financial reporting purposes. For example, tax rules effective for years beginning after December 31, 1986 use an accelerated depreciation method to compute depreciation on personal property for tax purposes, whereas many firms often use the straight-line method to compute depreciation for accounting income. In this case, the total depreciation recognized over the useful life of the asset will be the same for financial reporting and tax purposes, but the amount computed for each purpose for each year will not be equal.

As mentioned in Chapter 10, the Economic Recovery Act of 1981 established the *accelerated cost recovery system* (ACRS), which provided new depreciation rules for income tax purposes. The new rules allow more rapid depreciation than previously by reducing the number of years over which property is depreciated combined with the use of the declining balance depreciation method. ACRS depreciation rules were modified for property placed in service after December 31, 1986.

The modified rules provide for six classes of personal property: (1) a three-year class; (2) a five-year class; (3) a seven-year class; (4) a ten-year class; (5) a fifteen-year class; and (6) a twenty-year class. All personal property is assigned to one of these six classes. Depreciation is computed by the double declining-balance method for the three-, five-, seven-, and ten-year classes, and 150% declining-balance method for the fifteen- and twenty-year classes. The half-year convention is used, which means that one-half of a full year's depreciation is taken in the year of purchase, regardless of when purchased. This has the effect of extending each class life by one year. Residual value is ignored. The Internal Revenue Service provides appropriate depreciation tables showing the depreciation percentages for each year for each class life. For example, the table for the three-year class is as follows:

Year	Percent
1	33.3
2	44.5
3	14.8
4	7.4

When the use of alternative accounting methods or different useful lives results in a temporary difference, a financial accounting problem arises as to the proper measurement of income tax expense. Accounting standards generally require that income tax expense should be based on accounting income rather than on taxable income. Of course, income tax payable is based on taxable income. Since the depreciation expense for tax purposes and book purposes differs, income tax expense does not equal the tax liability. Therefore, an account called Deferred Income Tax Liability is created to balance the two as shown in the following illustration.

Assume that Rox Company purchased an asset for $120,000 that had a four-year useful life and a zero residual value. The company reported accounting income of $100,000 before taxes and depreciation on the new asset in each of four years. The company elected to use the straight-line depreciation method for book purposes. The asset falls into the three-year class under the ACRS. To simplify the tax computations, a fixed corporate income tax rate of 30% is assumed. Depreciation expense for both book and tax purposes is as follows:

Year	Income Tax Purposes Computation	Amount	Book Purposes $120,000/4 = $30,000
1	$120,000 × .333 =	$ 39,960	$ 30,000
2	120,000 × .445 =	53,400	30,000
3	120,000 × .148 =	17,760	30,000
4	120,000 × .074 =	8,880	30,000
Total		$120,000	$120,000

Using these figures, the income tax expense, income tax payable, and the change in deferred income tax liability are recognized each year as follows:

Year 1

Income Tax Expense	21,000	
Income Tax Payable [.3($100,000 − $39,960)]		18,012
Deferred Income Tax Liability [.3($39,960 − $30,000)]		2,988

Year 2

Income Tax Expense	21,000	
Income Tax Payable [.3($100,000 − $53,400)]		13,980
Deferred Income Tax Liability [.3($53,400 − $30,000)]		7,020

Year 3

Income Tax Expense	21,000	
Deferred Income Tax Liability [.3($30,000 − $17,760)]	3,672	
Income Tax Payable [.3($100,000 − $17,760)]		24,672

Year 4

Income Tax Expense	21,000	
Deferred Income Tax Liability [.3($30,000 − $8,880)]	6,336	
Income Tax Payable [.3($100,000 − $8,880)]		27,336

Note that the total depreciation computed over the life of the asset is the same for tax and accounting purposes. However, more depreciation is deducted for tax purposes in the early years of the asset's useful life—resulting in lower taxable income than accounting income. In later years, this reverses because less depreciation is deducted for tax purposes than for accounting purposes and taxable income exceeds accounting income.

At the end of the four-year period, the Deferred Income Tax Liability account appears as follows:

Deferred Income Tax Liability

		Year 1	2,988
		Year 2	7,020
Year 3	3,672		
Year 4	6,336		
Balance	–0–	Balance	–0–

The credit balance in the Deferred Income Tax Liability account at the end of Years 1, 2, and 3 is reported as a liability because the balance in the account represents an obligation for taxes that will be paid in future years when taxable income exceeds accounting income. The classification of the account balance as current or long-term depends on the expected reversal date. The portion that is expected to reverse within the next year or normal operating cycle, whichever is longer, is classified as a current liability. The remainder is classified as long-term. For example, assuming an operating cycle of less than one year, at the end of year 2, $3,672 of the Deferred Income Tax Liability would be reported as a current liability; the remaining $6,336 would be reported as a long-term liability.

PART II. THE TIME VALUE OF MONEY

As previously discussed, interest is the payment made for the use of money. As such, it is the measure of the time value of money. A dollar expected to be received sometime in the future is not equivalent to a dollar held today because of the time value of money. Today's dollar can be invested to earn interest so it will be worth more than one dollar in the future. Therefore, we would rather receive $1 now than $1 in the future—even if we are certain of receiving it at the later date. Businesses often invest and borrow large sums of money, so the time value of money is very important. The dramatic increase in interest rates in some years has a corresponding impact on the time value of money. For example, the average interest rates on short-term bank loans between 1965 and 1970 ranged from 5% to 9%. By the mid-1970s, the rate averaged as high as 14%. During the early 1980s, the interest rate on short-

Objective 5:
The time value of money concept

term loans exceeded 20% at times. Although current interest rates are lower, they still have a significant effect on the time value of money. We begin the examination of the time value of money with a discussion of simple and compound interest.

SIMPLE AND COMPOUND INTEREST

Simple interest is interest earned on an original amount invested (the ***principal***). The amount of principal and the interest payments remain the same from period to period since interest is computed on the amount of principal only as follows:

Interest (in dollars) = Principal (in dollars) × Rate (% per year) × Time (in years)

To illustrate the computation of simple interest, assume that Carter Company sells merchandise in exchange for a $4,000 two-year note receivable bearing simple interest of 12% per year. The amount of interest due Carter Company at the end of two years is:

$$\text{Interest} = \text{Principal} \times \text{Rate} \times \text{Time}$$

$$= \$4,000 \times 12\% \times 2$$

$$= \$960$$

Compound interest is interest earned on the original amount invested (principal) plus previously earned interest. As interest is earned during any period, it is added to the principal; interest is computed on the new balance (often called the ***compound amount***) during the next period. Interest can be compounded in a number of ways, such as daily, monthly, quarterly, semiannually, or annually. As an illustration of compound interest, assume the note receivable held by Carter Company is the same except that interest is compounded annually. The total interest for the two-year period can be computed as:

(1) Year	(2) Beginning Balance	(3) Compound Interest [Column (2) × 12%]	(4) Ending Balance
1	$4,000.00	$480.00	$4,480.00
2	4,480.00	537.60	5,017.60

Note that the total interest here is $1,017.60 compared with the $960 computed at simple interest. The $57.60 difference represents interest earned in the second year on the first year's interest ($480 × 12%) and is the product of using compound rather than simple interest.

The time value of money is used in a wide variety of accounting applications, including the valuation of bonds, the valuation of notes receivable and notes payable, the determination of amounts to contribute to pension plans, the valuation of capital leases, and capital budgeting. In most cases involving the time value of money, compound interest is applicable, so we will consider only compound interest in the discussion that follows. Four cases must be considered in developing an understanding of the time value of money.

Case I —Future value of a single amount

Case II —Future value of an ordinary annuity

Case III —Present value of a single amount

Case IV —Present value of an ordinary annuity

CASE I—FUTURE VALUE OF A SINGLE AMOUNT

As we have seen earlier, an amount of money invested today will have a higher future value than the original principal because of interest earned. The future value of a single amount invested today can be computed as follows:

$$FV = PV(1 + i)^n$$

where:

> FV = Future value
> PV = Present value of single amount invested (principal)
> i = Interest rate per period
> n = Number of periods

Schematically, the future-value computation can be shown as:

$$\text{Present value (principal invested)} \longrightarrow \text{Compounded at } i \text{ interest rate for } n \text{ periods} \longrightarrow \text{Future value (accumulated amount)}$$

Normally, the interest rate is expressed as an annual rate. However, interest often is compounded more frequently—for example, daily, monthly, quarterly, or semiannually. In such cases, the interest rate and number of periods must coincide with the compounding schedule. For example, if 12% per year interest is earned over a two-year period with quarterly compounding, the interest rate and number of periods used in the future-value formula are 3% and eight, respectively. This means that the annual interest rate (12%) is divided by the number of times compounding takes place (four) within a year, which is 3%, and the number of years (two) is multiplied by the number of compounding periods (four), for a total of eight periods.

To illustrate the use of the future value formula with annual compounding, consider again the Carter Company 12%, $4,000 note receivable, with compound interest. The future value of the note receivable is found as follows:

$$FV = \$4,000(1 + .12)^2$$
$$= \$4,000(1.2544)$$
$$= \$5,017.60$$

As we see, the total amount due Carter Company at maturity ($5,017.60) is the same as we computed earlier by adding the compound interest to the principal. If the note receivable involves quarterly compounding, we must revise the formula by dividing the 12% interest rate by four and multiplying two years by four to give:

$$FV = \$4,000(1 + .03)^8$$
$$= \$4,000(1.2668)$$
$$= \$5,067.20$$

The amount of interest earned with quarterly compounding will be $49.60 more than it was with annual compounding. Note that the mathematics involved with the future-value formula becomes more tedious as the number of periods involved increases. Fortunately, tables have been developed for various combinations of interest rates and periods to avoid the necessity of using the formula each time a future value of a single amount of money must be computed. Table 11-1 shows the future value of $1 for various interest rates and various periods.

Suppose we want to know how much a dollar invested today at 12% interest compounded annually will be worth 10 years from now. We simply find the amount (called a *factor*) in the 12% column and 10-period row of Table 11-1—3.1058. Thus, the dollar invested now will be approximately $3.11 in 10 years because of the compound interest earned. Note that the left-hand column of Table 11-1 (and Table 11-3) refers to periods instead of years. This enables us to use the table even if interest is compounded more frequently than once a year.

As noted earlier for such cases, the number of years is multiplied by the number of times compounding occurs to determine the number of periods that must be considered. In addition, an annual interest rate is divided by the number of compounding periods per year to convert it to the appropriate interest rate. For example, assume the dollar invested earlier will earn 12% interest compounded semiannually over a 10-year period. We need to multiply 10 years by two (20 periods) and divide 12% by two (6%) to determine the appropriate factor in Table 11-1. The factor is 3.2071—located in the 6% interest rate column and the 20-period row. Therefore, the dollar will grow to approximately $3.21 over the 10-year period. This same adjustment is required with the later tables whenever interest is compounded more frequently than once a year.

Table 11-1

Future Value of $1 $FV = (1 + i)^n$

Periods	2%	3%	4%	5%	6%	8%	10%	12%	16%	20%
1	1.0200	1.0300	1.0400	1.0500	1.0600	1.0800	1.1000	1.1200	1.1600	1.2000
2	1.0404	1.0609	1.0816	1.1025	1.1236	1.1664	1.2100	1.2544	1.3456	1.4400
3	1.0612	1.0927	1.1249	1.1576	1.1910	1.2597	1.3310	1.4049	1.5609	1.7280
4	1.0824	1.1255	1.1699	1.2155	1.2625	1.3605	1.4641	1.5735	1.8106	2.0736
5	1.1041	1.1593	1.2167	1.2763	1.3382	1.4693	1.6105	1.7623	2.1003	2.4883
6	1.1262	1.1941	1.2653	1.3401	1.4185	1.5869	1.7716	1.9738	2.4364	2.9860
7	1.1487	1.2299	1.3159	1.4071	1.5036	1.7138	1.9487	2.2107	2.8262	3.5832
8	1.1717	1.2668	1.3686	1.4775	1.5938	1.8509	2.1436	2.4760	3.2784	4.2998
9	1.1951	1.3048	1.4233	1.5513	1.6895	1.9990	2.3579	2.7731	3.8030	5.1598
10	1.2190	1.3439	1.4802	1.6289	1.7908	2.1589	2.5937	3.1058	4.4114	6.1917
11	1.2434	1.3842	1.5395	1.7103	1.8983	2.3316	2.8531	3.4785	5.1173	7.4301
12	1.2682	1.4258	1.6010	1.7959	2.0122	2.5182	3.1384	3.8960	5.9360	8.9161
13	1.2936	1.4685	1.6651	1.8856	2.1329	2.7196	3.4523	4.3635	6.8858	10.6993
14	1.3195	1.5126	1.7317	1.9799	2.2609	2.9372	3.7975	4.8871	7.9875	12.8392
15	1.3459	1.5580	1.8009	2.0789	2.3966	3.1722	4.1772	5.4736	9.2655	15.4070
16	1.3728	1.6047	1.8730	2.1829	2.5404	3.4259	4.5950	6.1304	10.7480	18.4884
17	1.4002	1.6528	1.9479	2.2920	2.6928	3.7000	5.0545	6.8660	12.4677	22.1861
18	1.4282	1.7024	2.0258	2.4066	2.8543	3.9960	5.5599	7.6900	14.4625	26.6233
19	1.4568	1.7535	2.1068	2.5270	3.0256	4.3157	6.1159	8.6128	16.7765	31.9480
20	1.4859	1.8061	2.1911	2.6533	3.2071	4.6610	6.7275	9.6463	19.4608	38.3376
25	1.6406	2.0938	2.6658	3.3864	4.2919	6.8485	10.8347	17.0001	40.8742	95.3962
30	1.8114	2.4273	3.2434	4.3219	5.7435	10.0627	17.4494	29.9599	85.8499	237.3763

The factors in Table 11-1 were determined by using the future-value formula with a principal of $1. By multiplying a specific factor found in the table for the appropriate combination of interest rate and number of periods by the single amount of money involved, the future value of that amount can be calculated. To illustrate the use of Table 11-1 when the amount involved is more than $1, assume again that the two-year, $4,000 note receivable of Carter Company has a 12% interest rate compounded annually. The factor in Table 11-1 for 12% interest and two periods is 1.2544, so the note's future value is:

$$FV = \$4,000(1.2544)$$
$$= \$5,017.60$$

This is the same result we obtained earlier with the future-value formula. If interest is compounded quarterly, the factor from the table is 1.2668 (3% and eight periods) so the future value is

$$FV = \$4,000(1.2668)$$
$$= \$5,067.20$$

Again, the future value is the same as the one computed earlier with the formula approach.

CASE II—FUTURE VALUE OF AN ORDINARY ANNUITY

In contrast to the single amount of money considered in Case I, an annuity consists of a series of equal payments (or receipts to the one receiving the payments) over a specified number of periods, with compound interest on the payments. An ordinary annuity is a series of equal payments that occur at the end of each time period involved. Here, we will consider only ordinary annuities and defer the subject of *annuities due* (in which the payments occur at the beginning of the time periods) to more advanced courses.

The future value of an ordinary annuity is the sum of all payments plus the compound interest accumulated on each. For example, if a company makes a payment of $10,000 to a savings program at the end of three consecutive years with each payment earning 12% interest compounded annually, the total amount accumulated over the three-year period is the future value of an ordinary annuity. One way to calculate the future value of the series of payments is to treat each payment separately and determine the amount of interest earned:

(1) Year	(2) Beginning Balance	(3) Annual Interest [Column (2) × 12%]	(4) Payment	(5) Ending Balance
1			$10,000	$10,000
2	$10,000	$1,200	10,000	21,200
3	21,200	2,544	10,000	33,744

It can be seen from these calculations that interest is earned for only two periods even though three payments were made. As the number of payments increases, this approach obviously becomes more time-consuming.

A formula can be used also to calculate the future value of an ordinary annuity. The formula is more complicated than the one used for the future value of a single amount, however, so it is not normally used. Instead, a table such as Table 11-2 is used because it contains factors for various combinations of interest rates and number of payments as computed with a future value of an ordinary annuity formula when payments of $1 are involved.

To illustrate the use of Table 11-2, consider the previous example in which the company makes three annual payments of $10,000 at the end of each year and earns 12% interest, compounded annually. In Table 11-2, the factor for 12% interest and three payments is 3.3744. Since the factor represents the future value of three payments of $1 at 12% interest, it is used to determine the future value of the actual payments made as:

$$FV = \$10,000(3.3744)$$

$$= \$33,744$$

This is the same answer we found earlier by treating each payment separately. The three payments of $10,000 (total of $30,000) will increase in value to $33,744 over the three-year period. The difference between the $33,744 future value and the payments totaling $30,000 is interest amounting to $3,744. If semiannual payments of $5,000 were involved during the three-year period, the appropriate factors from Table 11-2 would be for six payments and 6%. Again, this adjustment is required because

Table 11-2

Future Value of an Ordinary Annuity of $1 $FV = \dfrac{(1 + i)^n - 1}{i}$

Payments	2%	3%	4%	5%	6%	8%	10%	12%	16%	20%
1	1.0000	1.000	1.0000	1.0000	1.0000	1.0000	1.0000	1.0000	1.0000	1.0000
2	2.0200	2.0300	2.0400	2.0500	2.0600	2.0800	2.1000	2.1200	2.1600	2.2000
3	3.0604	3.0909	3.1216	3.1525	3.1836	3.2464	3.3100	3.3744	3.5056	3.6400
4	4.1216	4.1836	4.2465	4.3101	4.3746	4.5061	4.6410	4.7793	5.0665	5.3680
5	5.2040	5.3091	5.4163	5.5256	5.6371	5.8666	6.1051	6.3528	6.8771	7.4416
6	6.3081	6.4684	6.6330	6.8019	6.9753	7.3359	7.7156	8.1152	8.9775	9.9299
7	7.4343	7.6625	7.8983	8.1420	8.3938	8.9228	9.4872	10.0890	11.4139	12.9159
8	8.5830	8.8923	9.2142	9.5491	9.8975	10.6366	11.4359	12.2997	14.2401	16.4991
9	9.7546	10.1591	10.5828	11.0266	11.4913	12.4876	13.5795	14.7757	17.5185	20.7989
10	10.9497	11.4639	12.0061	12.5779	13.1808	14.4866	15.9374	17.5487	21.3215	25.9587
11	12.1687	12.8078	13.4864	14.2068	14.9716	16.6455	18.5312	20.6546	25.7329	32.1504
12	13.4121	14.1920	15.0258	15.9171	16.8699	18.9771	21.3843	24.1331	30.8502	39.5805
13	14.6803	15.6178	16.6268	17.7130	18.8821	21.4953	24.5227	28.0291	36.7862	48.4966
14	15.9739	17.0863	18.2919	19.5986	21.0151	24.2149	27.9750	32.3926	43.6720	59.1959
15	17.2934	18.5989	20.0236	21.5786	23.2760	27.1521	31.7725	37.2797	51.6595	72.0351
16	18.6393	20.1569	21.8245	23.6575	25.6725	30.3243	35.9497	42.7533	60.9250	87.4421
17	20.0121	21.7616	23.6975	25.8404	28.2129	33.7502	40.5447	48.8837	71.6730	105.9306
18	21.4123	23.4144	25.6454	28.1324	30.9057	37.4502	45.5992	55.7497	84.1407	128.1167
19	22.8406	25.1169	27.6712	30.5390	33.7600	41.4463	51.1591	63.4397	98.6032	154.7400
20	24.2974	26.8704	29.7781	33.0660	36.7856	45.7620	57.2750	72.0524	115.3797	186.6880
25	32.0303	36.4593	41.6459	47.7271	54.8645	73.1059	98.3471	133.3339	249.2140	471.9811
30	40.5681	47.5754	56.0849	66.4388	79.0582	113.2832	164.4940	241.3327	530.3117	1181.8816

of semiannual compounding. The factor for six payments and 6% from Table 11-2 is 6.9753, so the future value of the ordinary annuity is:

$$FV = \$5,000(6.9753)$$
$$= \$34,876.50$$

As we see, the future value of $34,876.50 with semiannual compounding is higher than the $33,744 computed with annual compounding because additional interest is earned.

CASE III—PRESENT VALUE OF A SINGLE AMOUNT

In Case I, we were concerned with the determination of the future value of a single amount of money. Many accounting applications of the time value of money involve the reverse of the future value consideration—that is, the concern is with computing the present value of some future amount of money. As noted earlier, money held today is worth more than the same amount of money received in the future because of the time value of money. In other words, the present value of a given amount to be received in the future is less than the future value. To determine the present value of a specific future amount, the future value must be discounted (reduced for the effect of interest) with an appropriate interest rate. The interest rate involved is generally called a **discount rate**. Future value and present value have a reciprocal relationship, as can be seen by comparing the formulas for the future value and present value of a single amount of money. Recall that the future value is computed as:

$$FV = PV(1 + i)^n$$

In contrast, the present value of a single amount of money is calculated as:

$$PV = \frac{FV}{(1 + i)^n}$$

where:

PV = Present value
FV = Future value of amount to be accumulated
i = Interest rate per period
n = Number of periods

Schematically, the present value computation can be shown as:

Present value   Discounted at   Future value
(amount to be ⟵ i interest rate ⟵ (amount to be
invested now)   for n periods   accumulated)

To illustrate the use of the present value of a single amount of money formula, consider again the note receivable held by Carter Company. We determined earlier that the future value of the $4,000 note was $5,017.60 when interest was compounded annually. By discounting the $5,017.60 for two years at 12%, we can determine its present value, which should be $4,000, as:

$$PV = \frac{\$5,017.60}{(1 + .12)^2}$$
$$= \$5,017.60/1.2544$$
$$= \$4,000$$

As calculated earlier, if the interest is compounded quarterly, the future value of the note is $5,067.20. However, the present value of the note should remain at $4,000 when it is discounted for eight periods at 3% interest per period, or:

$$PV = \frac{\$5,067.20}{(1 + .03)^8}$$

$$= \$5,067.20/1.2668$$

$$= \$4,000$$

As another example of calculating the present value of a single amount of money to be accumulated, assume that Holmes Company has a liability of $23,958 that must be paid in three years. The company wants to know how much it must invest today to have $23,958 in three years if the amount invested earns 10% interest, compounded annually. The amount to be invested would be determined as:

$$PV = \frac{\$23,958}{(1 + .10)^3}$$

$$= \$23,958/1.331$$

$$= \$18,000$$

The $18,000 (present value) will increase in value to $23,958 (future value) by the end of the third year because interest amounting to $5,958 will be earned. Like the future-value formulas, the math involved with the computation of present value with a formula can be tedious, so a table is normally used. Table 11-3 shows factors for various combinations of interest rates and number of periods when the present value of $1 is computed. By multiplying an appropriate factor from the table by the single amount of money involved, its present value can be determined. For example, in the Carter Company case with annual compounding, a value of .7972 is found in Table 11-3 for 12% interest and two periods. The present value of the note receivable is therefore:

$$PV = \$5,017.60(.7972)$$

$$= \$4,000$$

With quarterly compounding, the value in Table 11-3 is found for 3% interest and eight periods (.7894) and used as follows:

$$PV = \$5,067.20(.7894)$$

$$= \$4,000$$

Table 11-3 also can be used to determine the amount Holmes Company must invest today to have $23,958 three years later if the amount earns 10% interest. The factor in Table 11-3 for 10% interest and three periods is .7513, so the present value of $23,958 is:

$$PV = \$23,958(.7513)$$

$$= \$18,000 \text{ (rounded)}$$

Each of the factors shown in Table 11-3 for a particular combination of interest rates and number of periods is one (1) divided by the corresponding factor found in Table 11-1. This is true because of the reciprocal relationship between the formulas for future value and present value of a single amount. For example, the factor in

Table 11-3

Present Value of $1 $PV = \dfrac{1}{(1 + i)^n}$

Periods	2%	3%	4%	5%	6%	8%	10%	12%	16%	20%
1	0.9804	0.9709	0.9615	0.9524	0.9434	0.9259	0.9091	0.8929	0.8621	0.8333
2	0.9612	0.9426	0.9246	0.9070	0.8900	0.8573	0.8264	0.7972	0.7432	0.6944
3	0.9423	0.9151	0.8890	0.8638	0.8396	0.7938	0.7513	0.7118	0.6407	0.5787
4	0.9238	0.8885	0.8548	0.8227	0.7921	0.7350	0.6830	0.6355	0.5523	0.4823
5	0.9057	0.8626	0.8219	0.7835	0.7473	0.6806	0.6209	0.5674	0.4761	0.4019
6	0.8880	0.8375	0.7903	0.7462	0.7050	0.6302	0.5645	0.5066	0.4104	0.3349
7	0.8706	0.8131	0.7599	0.7107	0.6651	0.5835	0.5132	0.4523	0.3538	0.2791
8	0.8535	0.7894	0.7307	0.6768	0.6274	0.5403	0.4665	0.4039	0.3050	0.2326
9	0.8368	0.7664	0.7026	0.6446	0.5919	0.5002	0.4241	0.3606	0.2630	0.1938
10	0.8203	0.7441	0.6756	0.6139	0.5584	0.4632	0.3855	0.3220	0.2267	0.1615
11	0.8043	0.7224	0.6496	0.5847	0.5268	0.4289	0.3505	0.2875	0.1954	0.1346
12	0.7885	0.7014	0.6246	0.5568	0.4970	0.3971	0.3186	0.2567	0.1685	0.1122
13	0.7730	0.6810	0.6006	0.5303	0.4688	0.3677	0.2897	0.2292	0.1452	0.0935
14	0.7579	0.6611	0.5775	0.5051	0.4423	0.3405	0.2633	0.2046	0.1252	0.0779
15	0.7430	0.6419	0.5553	0.4810	0.4173	0.3152	0.2394	0.1827	0.1079	0.0649
16	0.7284	0.6232	0.5339	0.4581	0.3936	0.2919	0.2176	0.1631	0.0930	0.0541
17	0.7142	0.6050	0.5134	0.4363	0.3714	0.2703	0.1978	0.1456	0.0802	0.0451
18	0.7002	0.5874	0.4936	0.4155	0.3503	0.2502	0.1799	0.1300	0.0691	0.0376
19	0.6864	0.5703	0.4746	0.3957	0.3305	0.2317	0.1635	0.1161	0.0596	0.0313
20	0.6730	0.5537	0.4564	0.3769	0.3118	0.2145	0.1486	0.1037	0.0514	0.0261
25	0.6095	0.4776	0.3751	0.2953	0.2330	0.1460	0.0923	0.0588	0.0245	0.0105
30	0.5521	0.4120	0.3083	0.2314	0.1741	0.0994	0.0573	0.0334	0.0116	0.0042

Table 11-3 for 12% interest and two periods is .7972, which is the same as one (1) divided by 1.2544 (Table 11-1). Consequently, the appropriate Table 11-3 factor can always be determined from Table 11-1 and vice versa.

CASE IV—PRESENT VALUE OF AN ORDINARY ANNUITY

In Case II, we considered how to determine the future value of an ordinary annuity (i.e., a series of equal payments made at the end of each time period involved). Our final concern with the time value of money is the reverse of Case II (i.e., the present value of a series of equal future payments representing an ordinary annuity). The present value of an ordinary annuity is the amount that would have to be invested today at a certain compound interest rate in order to make a series of future payments over a specified period of time. Assume that at the beginning of the current year the Briden Company has obligations of $6,000 that must be repaid at the end of each of the next three years, including the current year. The firm wants to know how much it would have to invest today to repay each of the obligations if the amount invested earns 10% compounded annually. One way to determine the amount of the required investment is to treat each $6,000 payment as a single amount. Using Table 11-3, each payment is discounted to its present value, and the results are added to determine the total amount needed to be invested. If this approach is taken, the calculations are as follows:

(1) Year	(2) Payment	(3) Factor (Table 11-3—10%)	(4) Present Value [Column (2) × Column (3)]
1	$6,000	.9091	$ 5,454.60
2	6,000	.8264	4,958.40
3	6,000	.7513	4,507.80
Total present value			$14,920.80

The firm would have to invest $14,920.80 today to have the money available to make payments of $6,000 at the end of each of the next three years. If numerous payments are involved, this approach is quite time-consuming. Since the $6,000 payments can be viewed as an annuity, an easier way to discount them to their present value is to use Table 11-4. The factors in Table 11-4 were derived from a formula representing the present value of a $1 annuity. In the table, factors for various combinations of interest rates and number of payments are presented for the determination of the present value of an annuity of $1. Again, a given factor must be multiplied by

Table 11-4

Present Value of an Ordinary Annuity of $1 $PV = \dfrac{1 - \dfrac{1}{(1 + i)^n}}{i}$

Payments	2%	3%	4%	5%	6%	8%	10%	12%	16%	20%
1	0.9804	0.9709	0.9615	0.9524	0.9434	0.9259	0.9091	0.8929	0.8621	0.8333
2	1.9416	1.9135	1.8861	1.8594	1.8334	1.7833	1.7355	1.6901	1.6052	1.5278
3	2.8839	2.8286	2.7751	2.7232	2.6730	2.5771	2.4869	2.4018	2.2459	2.1065
4	3.8077	3.7171	3.6299	3.5460	3.4651	3.3121	3.1699	3.0373	2.7982	2.5887
5	4.7135	4.5797	4.4518	4.3295	4.2124	3.9927	3.7908	3.6048	3.2743	2.9906
6	5.6014	5.4172	5.2421	5.0757	4.9173	4.6229	4.3553	4.1114	3.6847	3.3255
7	6.4720	6.2303	6.0021	5.7864	5.5824	5.2064	4.8684	4.5638	4.0386	3.6016
8	7.3255	7.0197	6.7327	6.4632	6.2098	5.7466	5.3349	4.9676	4.3436	3.8372
9	8.1622	7.7861	7.4353	7.1078	6.8017	6.2469	5.7590	5.3282	4.6065	4.0310
10	8.9826	8.5302	8.1109	7.7217	7.3601	6.7101	6.1446	5.6502	4.8332	4.1925
11	9.7868	9.2526	8.7605	8.3064	7.8869	7.1390	6.4951	5.9377	5.0286	4.3271
12	10.5753	9.9540	9.3851	8.8633	8.3838	7.5361	6.8137	6.1944	5.1971	4.4392
13	11.3484	10.6350	9.9856	9.3936	8.8527	7.9038	7.1034	6.4235	5.3423	4.5327
14	12.1062	11.2961	10.5631	9.8986	9.2950	8.2442	7.3667	6.6282	5.4675	4.6106
15	12.8493	11.9379	11.1184	10.3797	9.7122	8.5595	7.6061	6.8109	5.5755	4.6755
16	13.5777	12.5611	11.6523	10.8378	10.1059	8.8514	7.8237	6.9740	5.6685	4.7296
17	14.2919	13.1661	12.1657	11.2741	10.4773	9.1216	8.0216	7.1196	5.7487	4.7746
18	14.9920	13.7535	12.6593	11.6896	10.8276	9.3719	8.2014	7.2497	5.8178	4.8122
19	15.6785	14.3238	13.1339	12.0853	11.1581	9.6036	8.3649	7.3658	5.8775	4.8435
20	16.3514	14.8775	13.5903	12.4622	11.4699	9.8181	8.5136	7.4694	5.9288	4.8696
25	19.5235	17.4131	15.6221	14.0939	12.7834	10.6748	9.0770	7.8431	6.0971	4.9476
30	22.3965	19.6004	17.2920	15.3725	13.7648	11.2578	9.4269	8.0552	6.1772	4.9789

the actual amount of each payment involved. The factor is 2.4869 for 10% and three payments. Therefore, the present value of the three $6,000 payments can be calculated as:

$$PV = \$6,000(2.4869)$$

$$= \$14,921.40$$

As we see, the results are essentially the same as those obtained by discounting each payment and adding the individual present values. If semiannual payments of $3,000 were made to satisfy the firm's obligations, the present-value calculation would require an adjustment of the number of payments and the annual interest rate. Six payments (3 years $\times$ 2) and an interest rate of 5% (10%/2) would be used to determine the factor of 5.0757 from Table 11-4, and the present value of the annuity would be:

$$PV = \$3,000(5.0757)$$

$$= \$15,227.10$$

Note that the present value with semiannual payments is more than it was with annual payments. This is because the amount invested does not have as much time to earn interest because payments are made every six months instead of at the end of the year.

SUMMARY

This chapter consists of two parts. Part I contains a discussion of the accounting treatment of current and long-term liabilities other than bonds payable and mortgage notes payable. Included are accounts payable, short-term notes payable, accrued expenses, unearned revenues, payroll liabilities, lease obligations, pension obligations, and deferred income taxes. There are generally two types of employer liabilities related to employee payroll deductions: required deductions for income and FICA taxes and voluntary deductions for such items as insurance premiums and union dues. These liabilities are settled periodically throughout the year and, until settled, represent current liabilities. In addition, employers must pay FICA and unemployment taxes on their total payroll. Since these taxes are levied against the employer, they are operating expenses and are current liabilities until paid.

Long-term, noncancelable lease contracts that meet certain specified criteria must be treated as capital leases; the leased asset and lease obligation are both recorded on the lessee's books at the present value of the future lease payments. Lease payments represent both interest expense and a reduction in the lease obligation.

Many companies report a pension obligation for the cumulative excess of amounts charged to expense over amounts of cash deposited with the pension trustee. Many companies also have a deferred income tax liability reported in their balance sheets because the cumulative amounts they have debited to income tax expense under GAAP exceed the cumulative amounts of tax paid or accrued under income tax laws.

Part II of the chapter consists of a discussion of the time value of money, which means that there is a cost (interest) for the use of money. Interest may be computed on the basis of either simple or compound interest. Simple interest is earned on the original investment (principal), and the amount of principal and interest payments remain the same from period to period because interest is computed on the amount of principal only. Compound interest is interest earned on the original amount invested plus previously earned interest. The time value of money is used in many accounting applications, which generally involve four basic situations: (1) future value of a single amount; (2) future value of an ordinary annuity; (3) the present value of a single amount; and (4) the present value of an ordinary annuity.

SELF-TEST

Test your understanding of the chapter by selecting the best answer for each of the following.

1. When a company receives services from employees, but has not yet paid the employees, the obligations should be recorded and classified as:
   a. unearned revenues.
   b. accrued liabilities.
   c. contingent liabilities.
   d. trade accounts payable.

2. Which of the following entries is appropriate for recording the payment of payroll?
   a. Payroll Expense
      Cash
   b. Cash
      Payroll Expense
   c. Payroll Expense
      Wages Payable
      Income Taxes Withheld
      FICA Tax Withheld
   d. Payroll Expense
      FICA Tax Withheld
      Income Taxes Withheld
      Cash

3. Carson Company purchased automotive equipment for $20,000 and gave a non-interest-bearing note. Carson could have purchased the equipment for $15,000 in cash after borrowing the money at 10%. At what amount should Carson record the equipment?
   a. $20,000.
   b. $16,000.
   c. $16,528.
   d. $15,000.

4. One of the four criteria for a capital lease compares the lease term to the estimated economic life of the leased property. In order for a lease to be classified as a capital lease, the lease term should be what percent of the economic life of the property?
   a. 65%.
   b. 75%.
   c. 85%.
   d. 90%.

5. Which of the following would cause a deferred tax liability?
   a. Interest on municipal bonds.
   b. Fines imposed for pollution.
   c. Different depreciation schedules for accounting and tax purposes.
   d. None of the above.

6. Payments made on a capital lease should be recorded as follows:
   a. Lease Obligation
      Cash
   b. Lease Obligation
      Interest Expense
      Cash

    c. Cash
          Lease Payment
    d. Lease Payment
          Cash

7. Which of the following is a measure of the time value of money?
    a. An annuity.
    b. Interest.
    c. Present value.
    d. Future value.

8. In the determination of a future value, which of the following relationships is true?
    a. The higher the interest rate and the longer the interest period, the lower the future value.
    b. The higher the interest rate and the shorter the interest period, the higher the future value.
    c. The lower the interest rate and the shorter the interest period, the lower the future value.
    d. The lower the interest rate and the longer the interest period, the lower the future value.

9. Nash Company purchased equipment on January 1, 1992, by making a down payment of $10,000 and agreeing to pay $50,000 on December 31, 1993. What is the present value of the payable if the borrowing rate for such equipment purchases is 8%?
    a. $42,865.
    b. $52,000.
    c. $52,865.
    d. $60,000.

REVIEW PROBLEM

Secor Corporation, a manufacturing concern, frequently engages in transactions that involve the use of notes payable. Below are transactions of Secor, which occurred during 1992. Each resulted in a note being signed by Secor's management.

Mar. 2 Borrowed $40,000 from First National Bank and signed a six-month note at an interest rate of 14%.

May 1 Purchased plant machinery from Allister Equipment Company at a total cost of $360,000. Paid $60,000 in cash and signed a one-year note at an interest rate of 12% for the remainder. The principal and interest are due on May 1, 1993.

Aug. 3 Borrowed $20,000 from Citizens Bank and received $19,200 in cash. Signed a four-month noninterest-bearing note for $20,000.

Sept. 2 Paid the six-month note dated March 2, 1992 plus interest for the six-month period.

Nov. 2 Purchased office equipment with a cash price of $20,000 from Setton Office Supply. Signed a six-month noninterest-bearing note for $21,500.

Dec. 3 Paid the four-month note dated August 3.
    31 End of Secor's fiscal year.

Required:

A. Prepare all journal entries related to these transactions.

B. Prepare the December 31, 1992 balance sheet presentations resulting from the 1992 transactions.

C. Compute the effective interest rates for the notes to Citizens Bank and Setton Office Supply.

ANSWER TO REVIEW PROBLEM

A.

Mar.	2	Cash	40,000	
		Notes Payable		40,000
May	1	Machinery	360,000	
		Cash		60,000
		Notes Payable		300,000
Aug.	3	Cash	19,200	
		Discount on Notes Payable	800	
		Notes Payable		20,000
Sept.	2	Notes Payable	40,000	
		Interest Expense	2,800	
		Cash		42,800
		($40,000 × 14% × 6/12 = $2,800)		
Nov.	2	Office Equipment	20,000	
		Discount on Notes Payable	1,500	
		Notes Payable		21,500
Dec.	3	Notes Payable	20,000	
		Interest Expense	800	
		Discount on Notes Payable		800
		Cash		20,000
	31	Interest Expense	24,000	
		Accrued Interest Payable		24,000
		(Interest on Allister Equipment note. $300,000 × 12% × 8/12)		
	31	Interest Expense	500	
		Discount on Notes Payable		500
		(Amortize discount on the Setton note for 2 months. $1,500/6 = $250 × 2)		

B.

Current Liabilities:		
Interest payable		$ 24,000[1]
Notes payable	$321,500[2]	
Less: Discount on notes payable	1,000[3]	320,500

[1]Accrued interest on Allister Equipment note.
[2]Allister Equipment note for $300,000 plus Setton note for $21,500.
[3]Remaining discount on Setton note.

C.

Citizens Bank Note–Effective Interest Rate
  ($800/$19,200) × 12/4 = 12.5%
Setton Office Supply Note–Effective Interest Rate
  ($1,500/$20,000) × 12/6 = 15%

ANSWERS TO SELF-TEST

1. b **2.** d **3.** d **4.** b **5.** c **6.** b **7.** b **8.** c
9. a

APPENDIX: CONTROLLING LIABILITIES AND CASH DISBURSEMENTS WITH A VOUCHER SYSTEM

A **voucher system** consists of the procedures used to obtain control over liabilities and cash expenditures from the time an obligation is incurred for goods or services received until the obligation is settled by the payment of cash. Under a voucher system, the incurrence of a liability and the payment of cash to settle the liability are considered separate, independent transactions. Four relatively distinct steps make up the cycle involved in ordering, receiving, and paying for goods and services:

Objective 6:
Controlling cash disbursements with a voucher system

1. Orders are placed;
2. Goods or services are received;
3. The accuracy of invoices is verified and the invoices are approved for payment; and
4. Checks are written in payment of approved invoices.

A major ingredient of control with a voucher system is assigning responsibility for these steps to specific individuals or departments. One or more source documents are prepared at each step to provide verification that the step was completed properly. Although the same general procedures are followed for the acquisition of both goods and services, the following description concentrates on the acquisition of goods, that is, merchandise or other physical assets.

PLACING ORDERS

Operating department managers are normally prohibited from placing orders directly with suppliers; to permit them to do so would prohibit effective centralization of the control of the total goods ordered and the resulting liabilities. Operating managers, who have reponsibility for determining the goods needed by their departments, prepare a **purchase requisition** (Figure 11-1) that lists the items needed by the department. The purchase requisition is sent to a central purchasing department (which has responsibility for placing orders) and a copy is forwarded to the accounting department. Purchasing department personnel determine the appropriate source of supply, negotiate the terms of the purchase with the supplier, and place the order by preparing a **purchase order**. The purchase order is a business form that authorizes a supplier to ship specific goods (Figure 11-2). The original of the purchase order is sent to the supplier, a copy is sent to the requisitioning department to inform the manager that the order has been placed, and another copy is forwarded to the accounting department which will eventually approve payment for the order.

Figure 11-1
Purchase Requisition

PURCHASE REQUISITION

No. _____ 269 _____

Data Company

Date _____ August 6, 1992 _____

From: Assembly Department
To: Purchasing Department

Please place the following order:

Quantity	Number	Description
200	142 JX	J-type Gear Boxes
400	142 JY	Gear Box Brackets

For Purchasing Department Use:
  Date Ordered _____ August 9, 1992 _____

Paula Jones
Approved

  Purchase Order No. _____ 348 _____

Figure 11-2
Purchase Order

PURCHASE ORDER

No. _____ 348 _____

Data Company
1842 Elm Street
New York, New York 10156

To: Croyden Gear Supply, Inc.
     1487 Lancer Avenue
     San Diego, California 92478

Date _____ August 9, 1992 _____
Terms _____ 2/10, n/30 _____

Please ship the following:

Quantity	Description	Price	Total
200	142 JX J-type Gear Boxes	$4.95	$990.00
400	142 JY Gear Box Brackets	.78	312.00

Data Company
By

J. P. Dee

RECEIPT OF GOODS

When goods are shipped, the supplier prepares a document called an **invoice** or **bill** (Figure 11-3) that itemizes the goods shipped, the price charged for each item, the terms of the sale, and the total amount of the invoice. A copy of the invoice is mailed to the purchaser. When the invoice is received, it is sent to the accounting department, where it is held until the goods are received and inspected by the receiving department. The receiving department prepares a **receiving report** (Figure 11-4), which lists the type and quantity of goods received. Copies are sent to the requisitioning department

INVOICE

No. _2416_

Croyden Gear Supply, Inc.
1487 Lancer Avenue
San Diego, California 92478

Sold to Data Company   Invoice Date   8/15/92
         1842 Elm Street   Your Order No.   348
         New York, New York 10156   Terms   2/10, n/30

Quantity	Description	Price	Amount
200	142 JX J-type Gear Boxes	$4.95	$ 990.00
400	142 JY Gear Box Brackets	.78	312.00
			$1,302.00

Figure 11-3
Invoice

RECEIVING REPORT

No. _694_

Data Company

To: Accounting Department   Date Received   8/19/92
From: Receiving Department   Purchase Order No.   348
                              Supplier   Croyden Gear Supply, Inc.

The following items have been received:

Description	Quantity	Condition
142 JX J-type Gear Boxes	200	Good
142 JY Gear Box Brackets	400	Good

Andy Poe
Signed

Figure 11-4
Receiving Report

and the purchasing department to serve as notification that the goods have been received, and a copy is sent to the accounting department for comparison with the purchase requisition, purchase order, and invoice.

The flow of documents in the acquisition of goods is depicted as follows:

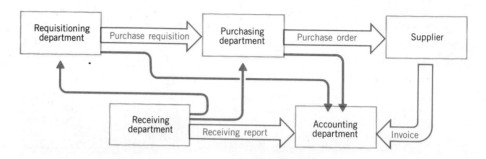

The large arrows represent the transfer of the original documents; the single lines show the transfer of copies of the various documents.

VERIFICATION OF THE ACCURACY OF INVOICES AND APPROVAL OF PAYMENT

The accounting department receives copies of all of the source documents relating to each specific purchase—the purchase requisition, purchase order, invoice, and receiving report. Accounting department personnel then perform the following verification procedures, after which the invoice is approved for entry into the accounting records and for payment:

1. Items on the purchase order are compared with those listed on the purchase requisition to verify that the goods ordered were properly requisitioned.
2. Items on the invoice are compared with those listed on the purchase order to verify that the goods shipped are the same as those ordered.
3. Items listed on the invoice are compared with those listed on the receiving report to verify that the goods billed by the supplier were actually received.
4. Additional verification is performed on the invoice to assure that prices charged and credit terms are those agreed upon and that computations and price extensions are accurate.

The Voucher

A document called a **voucher** (Figure 11-5) is attached to each purchase order when it is received by the accounting department. As the other related documents (purchase order, receiving report, and invoice) are received, they too are attached to the voucher. A voucher typically contains the types of information shown in the sample voucher in Figure 11-5.

The voucher contains the following categories of information:

1. The name of the creditor, the date the voucher is prepared, and the last date on which payment can be made to obtain cash discounts or the date on which payment is otherwise due.
2. General invoice data such as the date of the invoice, payment terms, the amount of the invoice, and the net amount due after allowing for cash discounts, if any.

Figure 11-5
Voucher

Voucher No. ___341___

DATA COMPANY
New York, New York

Pay to   Reardon Wholesale   Date ___Sept. 1, 1992___
            224 W. Oak
            Phoenix, Arizona 85042   Due Date ___Sept. 11, 1992___

Date of Invoice	Sept. 1, 1992	Invoice Amount	$2,147.80
Invoice Number	2163	Cash Discount	42.97
Payment Terms	2/10, n/30	Net Amount	2,104.83

Verification of: Approved by
   Proper Purchase Requisition   _R.S._
   Quantities on Purchase Order with Invoice   _R.S._
   Quantities on Receiving Report with Invoice   _R.S._
   Prices on Purchase Order with Invoice   _R.S._
   Credit Terms in Agreement with Purchase Order   _R.S._
   Invoice Extensions and Footings
Approved for Payment   _J. Ahren_

Account Distribution	Amount
Advertising	
Freight-in	
Office Salaries	
Office Supplies	
Purchases	$2,147.80
Sales Salaries	
Utilities	
Miscellaneous Expense	
Total Vouchers Payable Credit	$2,147.80

Payment Record:
   Date Paid ___9/10/92___   Check No. ___260___   Amount ___$2,104.83___

3. The initials of the person performing the verification steps and of the employee authorized to approve payment of the invoice.
4. Amounts to be debited to identified general ledger accounts by the accounting department and the total amount to be credited to Vouchers Payable.
5. Payment data identifying the date paid, the check number, and the amount of the check.

Every cash payment, including reimbursement of the petty cash fund, requires a voucher regardless of whether the payment is for services, merchandise, equipment, or a mortgage payment. Even the receipt of a bill that is to be paid immediately (such as a utility bill) must first be vouchered. Probably the greatest benefit received from use of a voucher system is the assurance that every cash expenditure has been thoroughly reviewed and amounts verified before payment is made.

The Voucher Register

After the voucher is prepared it is recorded in a **voucher register** a book of original entry that takes the place of the purchases journal described in the Appendix to Chapter 7. It is used in combination with a check register which, under the voucher system, takes the place of the cash disbursements journal also described in the Appendix to Chapter 7. The function of the check register is described later in this chapter. An example of a voucher register is shown in Figure 11-6.

Under the voucher system, a Vouchers Payable account takes the place of the Accounts Payable account. Every voucher is entered in the voucher register with a debit to various asset, expense, liability, or owners' equity accounts and a credit to Vouchers Payable. All information in the voucher register is entered from the voucher at the time it is approved for recording with the exception of the payment information, which is entered as each voucher is paid.

The posting of the voucher register follows the same general procedures used to post the other special journals. Columns are totaled and crossfooted at the end of the month to verify the equality of debits and credits. The total of all debit columns, including the Other Debits column, must equal the total of the Vouchers Payable column. The total of each column, with the exception of the Other Debits column, is posted as a debit or credit to the appropriate account listed in the column heading. Evidence of the posting is indicated by placing the general ledger account number in parentheses just below the column total. Entries in the Other Debits column are posted individually as debits to the account listed and the account number is entered in the Posting Reference column.

The Unpaid Vouchers File

Some vouchers—particularly those prepared for the payment of ongoing expenses such as sales salaries, office salaries, and utilities—are often paid on the date they are recorded in the voucher register. With other payments, however, there may be a

Figure 11-6
Voucher Register

Date 1992	Voucher No.	Payee	Payment Date	Chk. No.	Vouchers Payable Credit	Purchases Debit	Freight-in Debit	Advertising Debit	Sales Salaries Debit	Office Salaries Debit	Other Debits Account	P/R	Amount
9/1	341	Reardon Wholesale	9/10	260	2,147 80	2,147 80							
9/1	342	Daly Freight Co.	9/3	251	122 50		122 50						
9/4	343	Haried Insurance Co.	9/5	253	347 80						Prepaid Insurance	136	347 80
9/6	344	Acme Office Supply	9/12	263	89 40						Office Supplies	124	89 40
9/6	345	The Leader	9/11	261	138 00			138 00					
9/7	346	Doug Johnson	9/7	256	236 50				236 50				
9/7	347	Rick Burdick	9/7	257	149 30					149 30			
9/7	348	Charles Myler	9/7	258	220 00				220 00				
9/8	349	Zylon Equipment Co.	9/20	284	370 00						Office Equipment	158	370 00
9/30	382	United Bank	9/30	349	2,060 00						Notes Payable / Interest Expense	210 / 535	2,000 00 / 60 00
9/30	383	Turner Supply Co.			896 22	896 22							
9/30	384	Adventure Travel	9/30	350	384 50						Travel Expense	574	384 50
9/30	385	The Leader			74 90			74 90					
					18,249 24	6,483 94	286 89	399 40	1,839 42	597 20			8,642 39
					(202)	(533)	(520)	(504)	(562)	(572)			(X)

VOUCHER REGISTER — Page 17

time lag between the receipt of an invoice and its due date. In those cases, the voucher is prepared and filed in an *unpaid vouchers file.* To protect the company's credit rating and to assure the payment of invoices in time to obtain cash discounts, the vouchers are filed under the dates on which payment is due. The unpaid vouchers file constitutes a subsidiary ledger of vouchers payable and, under a voucher system, takes the place of the accounts payable subsidiary ledger described in Chapter 7. The elimination of the accounts payable subsidiary ledger often results in a considerable cost savings to the business. At the end of the month, after month-end posting has taken place, the total of all vouchers in the unpaid voucher file should be equal to the balance in the Vouchers Payable account in the general ledger.

The Check Register

On each business day, the vouchers in the unpaid vouchers file under that date are removed and sent to the employee authorized to approve vouchers for payment. The employee reviews the vouchers to assure that all verification steps have been completed; initials the voucher to signify approval for payment; prepares a check; fills in the payment-record section of the voucher; and forwards the check and voucher to the person authorized to sign checks, usually the company's treasurer. The treasurer then reviews the voucher for proper authorization of payment, signs the check and mails it to the creditor, and sends the voucher to the accounting department.

When the voucher is received by the accounting department, an entry is made in the Payment column of the voucher register to indicate that the voucher has been paid. The check is then recorded in a *check register* (Figure 11-7), which serves as a record of all cash disbursements, and the paid voucher is filed in numerical order in a *paid vouchers file*.

Because checks are written only in payment of specific vouchers, every check drawn is recorded as a debit to Vouchers Payable and a credit to Cash, with the exception

Figure 11-7
Check Register

Date 1992		Check No.	Payee	Voucher No.	Vouchers Payable Debit		Purchase Discounts Credit		Cash Credit	
Sept.	1	251	Daly Freight Co.	342	122	50			122	50
	3	252	Haried Insurance	343	347	80			347	80
	5	254	Reardon Wholesale	335	1,246	00	24	92	1,221	08
	6	255	Batho Company	334	1,322	80	26	46	1,296	34
	7	256	Doug Johnson	346	236	50			236	50
	7	257	Rick Burdick	347	149	30			149	30
	7	258	Charles Myler	348	220	00			220	00
	30	349	United Bank	382	2,060	00			2,060	00
	30	350	Adventure Travel	384	384	50			384	50
					18,629	90	193	48	18,436	42
					(202)		(534)		(101)	

CHECK REGISTER — Page 12

of cases where a check is drawn in payment of a voucher on which a cash discount is taken. In those cases, the entry in the check register results in a debit to Vouchers Payable for the gross amount, a credit to Purchase Discounts, and a credit to Cash for the net amount paid. At the end of the month, the columns of the check register are footed and crossfooted, and the column totals are posted to the general ledger accounts specified in the column headings. As with the posting of other special journals, the general account ledger numbers are written in parentheses at the bottom of each column to indicate that the total has been posted.

GLOSSARY

ACCOUNTS PAYABLE (OPEN ACCOUNTS; OPEN PAYABLES). Amounts owed to creditors for the purchase of merchandise, supplies, and services in the normal course of business (p. 473).

ACCRUED EXPENSES (ACCRUED LIABILITIES). Expenses that have been incurred but not yet paid (p. 476).

ANNUITY. A series of equal payments or receipts per period for a specified number of periods (p. 489).

CAPITAL LEASE. A lease that is in substance an installment purchase of property (p. 481).

COMPOUND INTEREST. Interest earned on both an original amount invested plus previously earned interest (p. 486).

CURRENT RATIO. Total current assets divided by total current liabilities (p. 473).

FUNDED PLAN. A pension plan in which deposits are made to an outside agency appointed to manage the fund (p. 482).

INVOICE (BILL). A document, prepared by a supplier, that itemizes the goods shipped, prices charged, terms of the sale, and total amount due (p. 501).

LEASE. A rental agreement in which the lessor transfers to the lessee the right to use property for a specified period of time in return for periodic rental payments (p. 481).

NOTE PAYABLE. An obligation evidenced by a promissory note (p. 473).

OPERATING LEASE. A lease that is not a capital lease. In an operating lease, the lessor retains the risks and rewards of ownership (p. 482).

ORDINARY ANNUITY. A series of equal payments or receipts that occur at the end of each time period involved (p. 489).

PENSION PLAN. A plan established to provide payments to eligible employees when they retire (p. 482).

PERMANENT DIFFERENCE. An item that enters into the computation of accounting income or taxable income but not both (p. 483).

PROCEEDS. The difference between the face value of a note payable and interest that has been deducted therefrom (p. 474).

PURCHASE ORDER. A business form that authorizes a supplier to ship specific goods (p. 499).

PURCHASE REQUISITION. A business form used by operating managers to request the purchasing department to place orders for goods and services (p. 499).

RECEIVING REPORT. A business form prepared by the receiving department that lists the type and quantity of goods received (p. 501).

SIMPLE INTEREST. The interest earned on an original amount (principal) invested (p. 486).

TEMPORARY (TIMING) DIFFERENCE.   A revenue or expense item that enters into the determination of both accounting income and taxable income but in different periods (p. 483).

UNEARNED REVENUES (DEFERRED REVENUES; REVENUES RECEIVED IN ADVANCE).   A liability for goods and services to be delivered or performed in the future for which advanced payments were received from customers (p. 477).

VOUCHER.   A business form used to summarize a purchase transaction and approve the invoice for recording and payment (p. 502).

VOUCHER REGISTER.   A book of original entry in whch all vouchers prepared are listed in numerical order (p. 505).

VOUCHER SYSTEM.   The procedures used to obtain control over liabilities and cash expenditures from the time an obligation is incurred for goods or services received through the payment of cash to settle the obligation (p. 499).

WAGE AND TAX STATEMENT (FORM W-2).   A form furnished by an employer to every employee showing gross earnings and certain tax information for a particular year (p. 478).

DISCUSSION QUESTIONS

1. What are current liabilities?
2. What is the "current ratio"?
3. What information does a current ratio give to a firm's creditors?
4. When a firm borrows money and signs a noninterest-bearing note, it pays no interest for the use of the money. Do you agree or disagree with this statement? Explain.
5. Does an interest-bearing or noninterest-bearing note generally contain the best terms for the borrower? Explain.
6. Compute the effective interest rates on the two following notes:
   a. $50,000, one-year, 15% interest-bearing note.
   b. $50,000, one-year, noninterest-bearing note discounted at 15%.
7. Define the term "accrued interest expense."
8. When plant assets are purchased on credit and a note payable is given for the purchase price, the interest paid on the note is not considered in determining the assets' cost. Explain.
9. Explain what is meant by "imputed interest." When is it necessary to impute interest?
10. What significance does the "completion of the earning process" have to an Unearned Revenue account?
11. What items typically explain the difference between an employee's gross earnings and his or her take-home pay?
12. Distinguish among (a) withholdings from employee earnings, (b) voluntary deductions, and (c) employer payroll taxes.
13. Why should an employer try to have a low unemployment record?
14. What is meant by the "current portion of long-term debt" and how is it classified on a balance sheet?
15. What are three major advantages of leasing assets instead of purchasing them?
16. What are the two main types of leases for accounting purposes?
17. What are the four criteria used to identify capital leases?
18. What is meant by a "funded pension plan"?

19. Explain the terms "permanent difference" and "temporary difference" as they relate to accounting income and taxable income.
20. Why do accountants apply income tax allocation procedures?
21. How is the decision made to classify deferred income taxes as either current or long-term on the balance sheet?
22. What is meant by the time value of money?
23. What is the difference between future value and present value?
24. What is the difference between simple interest and compound interest?
25. Which of the following is the greatest amount:
    a. Future value of $5,000 for 4 periods compounded at 16%, or
    b. Future value of $5,000 for 16 periods compounded at 4%? Why?
26. How many payments and how many interest periods are there in the future value of an ordinary annuity with five years compounding at 12% annually?
27. Which amount is smaller, the present value of an amount of $10,000 for five periods discounted at 10% or the present value of an ordinary annuity of $10,000 for five periods discounted at 10%? Why?
28A. What is a voucher system and what is the primary reason a business would use it.
29A. Describe the verification procedures accounting department personnel would follow before recording a purchase and approving the payment to a supplier when a voucher system is used.
30A. What is a voucher register? What journal does it replace in an ordinary accounting system?
31A. When a voucher is entered in a voucher register, what account is credited? What kinds of accounts are debited?

EXERCISES

Exercise 11-1   Recognition of Current Liabilities
Below are 10 types of current liabilities often found on balance sheets.

1. Amounts of money, based on a percentage of sales prices, earned but not yet received by firm employees for sales they made during the current month.
2. An amount of money owed to the local gas company for gas consumed but not yet paid for.
3. An amount of money owed to a creditor for the use of borrowed money.
4. An amount of money owed to creditors for the acquisition of merchandise, supplies, and services in the normal course of business.
5. An amount of money withheld from employees' paychecks, which is matched by the employer and remitted to the federal government to provide retirement income for qualified individuals.
6. An amount of money received from a customer for advertising services to be provided in the future.
7. Amounts of money withheld from employees' paychecks to be remitted to the federal government based on gross earnings and personal exemptions.
8. An amount of money withheld from an employee's paycheck, which will be paid in the future to a medical insurance company.
9. An amount of money owed to a creditor on a note.

10. An amount of money to be paid to the state government, which will use the fund to provide certain benefits for a limited time period to individuals who lose their jobs through no fault of their own.

Required:
For each type, give the account title normally used to record the activity.

Exercise 11-2   Interest-Bearing Notes Payable

Following are descriptions of three notes payable transactions entered into by the Lucky Company during its 1992 fiscal year, which ends on December 31.

Note A: A six-month note dated April 20, for $2,000, with an annual interest rate of 14%.

Note B: A four-month note dated November 1, for $5,000, with an annual interest rate of 10%.

Note C: A 60-day note dated December 1, for $9,000, with an annual interest rate of 8%.

All of these notes plus interest were paid on their due dates.

Required:
A. Prepare journal entries on Lucky's books for 1992 and 1993 with respect to the notes. (Round amounts to the nearest dollar.)
B. Show the income statement and balance sheet presentations as of December 31, 1992 with respect to the notes.

Exercise 11-3   Interest-Bearing and Noninterest-Bearing Notes

On September 1, 1992, Crosby Company borrowed $120,000 by signing a one-year note payable at 16% interest. Crosby's fiscal year ends on December 31.

Required:
A. Assuming the note is interest-bearing, compute the following.
   1. Cash received.
   2. Interest expense for 1992.
   3. Effective interest rate for the life of the note.
B. Assuming the note is noninterest-bearing, compute the following.
   1. Cash received.
   2. Interest expense for 1992.
   3. Effective interest rate for the life of the note.
C. Show the December 31, 1992 balance sheet presentation for this note assuming:
   1. The note is interest-bearing.
   2. The note is noninterest-bearing.

Exercise 11-4   Note Issued for Operating Assets

On May 1, 1992, Cresenta Company purchased machinery with a cash price of $160,000. Cresenta Company signed a one-year note at 10% interest. (Round answers to the nearest dollar.)

Required:
A. Prepare the journal entry to record the machinery purchase assuming the note payable is:
   1. Interest-bearing with a face value of $160,000.
   2. Noninterest-bearing with a face value of $195,122.

B. Prepare the adjusting entry on December 31, 1992, the end of Cresenta's fiscal year, assuming the note is:
   1. Interest-bearing.
   2. Noninterest-bearing.
C. Compute the following:
   1. Cash interest for the life of the note if the note is interest-bearing.
   2. Cash interest for the life of the note if the note is noninterest-bearing.
   3. Effective interest rate if the note is interest-bearing.
   4. Effective interest rate if the note is noninterest-bearing.

Exercise 11-5 Payroll and Payroll Taxes
The payroll of the Alpine Company on December 31, 1992, for the month of December is as follows:

1. Gross wages, $850,000.
2. Gross wages to employees who have earned in excess of $50,400; $130,000.
3. Gross wages to employees who have earned in excess of $6,000; $760,000.
4. Federal income taxes withheld, $172,600.
5. Union dues withheld, $1,600.
6. Pension plan contributions withheld from employees, $28,600.
7. Tax rates are: FICA, 7.65%; SUTA, 2.7%; and FUTA, .7%.

Required:
A. Prepare the journal entries to record Alpine's payroll and payroll taxes.
B. Compute the total labor cost for Alpine Company for December.
C. What percent of the payroll was take-home pay?

Exercise 11-6 Payroll and Payroll Taxes
Totals of the June 15, 1992 payroll for Boxlite Company follow:

Gross salaries and wages	$274,000
Federal income tax withheld	52,850
State income tax withheld	8,124
FICA taxes withheld	16,380
Medical insurance premiums withheld	910
Union dues withheld	650
Savings plan deposits withheld	9,050

Gross wages subject to unemployment taxes were $90,000.

Required:
A. Prepare the journal entries to record the payroll and Boxlite's payroll taxes.
B. Compute Boxlite's total labor cost for this period.
C. What portion of the gross salaries and wages were subject to FICA taxes?
D. What was the average tax rate for the federal income taxes?
E. What percent of the payroll was take-home pay?

Exercise 11-7 Leases
Answer the following questions relating to the general characteristics of leases:

1. What are capital leases?
2. Explain the balance sheet impact of capital leases and operating leases.
3. What are the two accounts debited when a lease payment is made on a capital lease?

4. At the inception of a capital lease, two balance sheet accounts are created. What are these accounts and what is the relationship between the account balances at the inception of the lease?

5. What two expense accounts related to capital leases appear on the income statement of a lessee?

Exercise 11-8 Accounting for a Capital Lease

Genro Company entered into an equipment lease for factory equipment on January 2, 1992. The lease has a fixed, noncancelable term of 12 years, which is the same as the expected useful life of the equipment. The lease contract requires an annual payment of $350,000 on December 31 of each year for 12 years starting December 31, 1992. The lease provides for 12% interest. The present value of the lease payments is $2,168,040. Genro Company uses straight-line depreciation for all depreciable assets.

Required:
Prepare all journal entries on Genro's books for 1992.

Exercise 11-9 Deferred Income Taxes

Summarized, comparative income statements for Carlyle Industries for the years ended December 31, 1991 and 1992 follow:

	1991	1992
Revenues	$170,000	$200,000
Expenses	110,000	130,000
Pretax income	$ 60,000	$ 70,000

Included in revenues on the 1991 income statement is an item amounting to $20,000 that was not included on the tax return until 1992. Assume an average income tax rate of 20 percent.

Required:
Prepare the journal entry for each year to record the income tax expense, income tax payable, and deferred income tax.

Exercise 11-10 Deferred Income Taxes

Summarized, comparative income statements for Winslow Company for the years ended December 31, 1992 and 1993 follow:

	1992	1993
Revenues	$800,000	$920,000
Expenses	600,000	650,000
Pretax income	$200,000	$270,000

Winslow Company had two items causing temporary differences during this two-year period:

1. A revenue item amounting to $50,000 on the 1992 income statement was included on the tax return in 1993.

2. An expense item amounting to $25,000 on the 1993 income statement was included on the tax return in 1992.

Assume an average income tax rate of 30%.

Required:

Prepare the journal entries for each year to record income tax expense, income tax payable, and deferred income tax.

Exercise 11-11 Time Value of Money

Several situations involving the time value of money follow:

1. The amount a $12,000 deposit on January 1, 1992 will be worth on January 1, 1997, assuming an annual interest rate of 16% compounded
   a. Annually.
   b. Semiannually.
   c. Quarterly.
2. The amount to be deposited on January 1, 1992, to accumulate a balance of $50,000 on January 1, 1997, assuming the deposit will earn 12% interest compounded
   a. Annually.
   b. Semiannually.
   c. Quarterly.
3. The amount eight equal deposits of $2,000 made at the end of each year for eight years will be worth immediately after the eighth deposit is made if the invested money earns
   a. 10% compounded annually.
   b. 20% compounded annually.
   Is the answer to item 3b twice as much as the answer to item 3a? Why or why not?
4. The quarterly payment needed to repay a $5,000 loan over a four-year period if the annual interest rate is 16%. How much interest will be paid on this loan?

Required:

Make the computations for each situation.

Exercise 11-12 Time Value of Money

Ben Company plans to deposit $75,000 today in a special building fund account, which will be needed at the end of five years. A financial institution will pay 16% interest on the fund balance.

Required:

How much will be in the fund at the end of the fifth year assuming:

A. Annual compounding.
B. Semiannual compounding.
C. Quarterly compounding.

Exercise 11-13 Time Value of Money

South Company desires to accumulate a plant expansion fund over the next eight years. The company will make equal annual deposits to the fund of $130,000 starting December 31, 1992. The fund will earn interest at an annual rate of 10%.

Required:

What will be the balance in the fund on December 31, 1999, after the deposit on that date has been made?

Exercise 11-14 **Time Value of Money**

Myer Company estimates it will need $900,000 cash to renovate an old plant five years from now. They have reached an agreement with a financial institution whereby the institution will pay them 12% interest on invested money if the entire amount is invested today.

Required:

How much money must Myer Company deposit today to meet the estimated need in five years if the interest is compounded

A. Annually.
B. Semiannually.

Exercise 11-15 **Time Value of Money**

Joan Wilson is the beneficiary of a trust fund established by her aunt. The aunt has given Joan two options to choose from with respect to how she wishes to receive the money. Joan can elect to receive either $7,500 per year for the next nine years or $5,600 per year for the next 15 years. Joan can invest the proceeds at an annual rate of 10%.

Required:

If the trust fund monies will be received at the end of each year, which method should Joan choose in order to maximize her income from the trust? Show your computations.

Exercise 11-16 **Time Value of Money**

Following are various situations requiring the use of time value of money analysis techniques:

1. Joe Curlack deposited $1,500 on January 1, 1971 in a savings account. Interest at 6% was credited to the account yearly through 1981. Starting January 1, 1982, the interest rate was raised to 10%, and has been credited yearly through December 31, 1992. What is the balance in the savings account on January 1, 1993?
2. Clara Clortly has received $30,087.44 per year for the past 10 years on the last day of the year. If the fund paid 12% interest on the remaining balance, what amount did Clara deposit 10 years ago if the fund was depleted after the tenth payment?
3. Orland Breisweig deposited $3,000 into a savings account on January 1, 1983. Interest at 10% per year has been credited to the account semiannually through June 30, 1992. What is the amount in the savings account on June 30, 1992?
4. Siegfried Asbornson wants to accumulate $15,000 by December 31, 1999 in order to take a trip to his native Norway. If he can earn 10% on his savings, how much must be deposited each December 31, 1991 through 1999 in order to have the $15,000 on the date needed?

Required:

Compute the amounts requested in each situation. Show your computations.

Exercise 11-17A **Recording Transactions in a Voucher System**

Secor Company completed the following transactions during July 1992. Secor uses a voucher system.

July   1   Prepared voucher No. 788 payable to Jackson Company for merchandise purchased, $2,800; invoice dated June 3; terms, n/30.

         2   Prepared voucher No. 789 payable to Ajax Insurance for one year insurance premium, $800.

3 Issued check No. 4803 in payment of voucher No. 788.

6 Prepared voucher No. 790 for sales salaries, $1,340, and administrative salaries, $2,200.

6 Issued check No. 4804 to payroll bank account in payment of voucher No. 790.

8 Issued check No. 4805 in payment of voucher No. 789.

10 Prepared voucher No. 791 payable to Kent Corp. for merchandise purchased, $2,400; invoice dated July 6, terms, 2/10,n/30.

14 Prepared voucher No. 792 payable to Furniture Warehouse for office furniture, $5,000, invoice dated June 20 terms, n/30.

15 Issued check No. 4806 in payment of voucher No. 791.

17 Prepared voucher No. 793 payable to Searer Power Company, $580, for monthly electric bill.

20 Issued check No. 4807 in payment of voucher No. 793.

20 Issued check No. 4808 in payment of voucher No. 792.

24 Prepared voucher No. 794 for sales salaries, $1,480, and administrative salaries, $2,200.

24 Issued check No. 4809 to payroll bank account in payment of voucher No. 794.

27 Prepared voucher No. 795 payable to Lincoln Company for merchandise purchased, $900, invoice dated July 17 terms, n/30.

29 Prepared voucher No. 796 payable to Strick Telephone Company for telephone bill, $350.

31 Prepared voucher No. 797 payable to Needles Company for merchandise purchased, $2,548, invoice dated July 27 terms, 2/10,n/30.

Secor Company uses the gross invoice method for recording merchandise purchases on credit.

Required:

A. Prepare a voucher register and check register similar to those illustrated in the chapter and record the transactions in the registers. Set up separate debit columns for Purchases, Sales Salaries Expense, Administrative Salaries Expense, and Utilities Expense. Record amounts to the nearest dollar.

B. Foot the voucher register and check register and post the appropriate amounts from both registers to a Vouchers Payable general ledger account (no. 336).

C. Reconcile the Vouchers Payable general ledger account balance with the unpaid vouchers file at the end of July.

PROBLEMS

Problem 11-1 **Current Assets, Current Liabilities, and Current Ratio**

The following selected accounts appeared on the 1992 balance sheet of Videos Unlimited:

Allowance for doubtful accounts	$ 14,760
Accounts payable	130,900
Accounts receivable	166,900
Accumulated depreciation–automobiles	16,875
Accumulated depreciation–office equipment	6,375
Automobiles	48,000
Cash	38,260

FICA taxes payable	1,084
FUTA taxes payable	150
Income taxes payable	67,040
Interest payable	2,500
Interest receivable	1,850
Inventory of video tapes and discs	113,820
Marketable securities, at cost	45,200
Notes payable–current	40,000
Notes payable, 12%, due June 30, 1995	100,000
Notes receivable–current	38,000
Office equipment	28,800
Prepaid insurance	7,500
Supplies	2,380
SUTA taxes payable	570
Trademarks, net of amortization	34,650
Utilities payable	886
Wages payable	14,578

Required:

A. Prepare the 1992 balance sheet presentation for the current assets and current liabilities.

B. Compute the amount of working capital and the current ratio.

Problem 11-2 **Notes and Interest Payable**

On May 1, 1992, Custom Builders borrowed $50,000 from First State Bank to improve their working capital position during the high-activity summer months. Custom Builders signed a nine-month, 14% promissory note. Custom Builders ends its fiscal year on October 31.

Required:

A. Prepare the journal entry to record the receipt of the loan on May 1, 1992.

B. Prepare any needed adjusting entry on October 31, 1992.

C. Prepare the October 31, 1992 balance sheet presentation for the note and any related accounts.

D. Prepare the entry on the maturity date of the note to record payment of principal and interest.

Problem 11-3 **Interest-Bearing and Noninterest-Bearing Notes**

Alpha Company found itself short of cash and approached a local bank to borrow exactly $90,000 for a one-year period. The bank charges 12% interest on such loans. (Round answers to the nearest dollar.)

Required:

A. What will be the face amount of the note if the bank agrees to an interest-bearing note?

B. What will be the face amount of the note if the bank requires a noninterest-bearing note?

C. What is the effective interest rate if the money is borrowed on a noninterest-bearing note?

D. Prepare journal entries on the following dates assuming (1) the note is interest-bearing, and (2) the note is noninterest-bearing.

1. September 1, 1992, the date the loan is received.
2. December 31, 1992, the end of Alpha's fiscal year.
3. September 1, 1993, the due date of the note.

Problem 11-4 Notes Payable

Terms of four separate notes follow:

Note A: $60,000 borrowed for 60 days on May 26, 1992, with a stated interest rate of 10%.

Note B: A $100,000 note discounted at a discount rate of 12% by the lending institution. The note is dated February 10, 1992, and is for nine months.

Note C: A 90-day, 14% stated interest rate, for $60,000 dated August 12, 1992.

Note D: A three-month noninterest-bearing note dated June 10, 1992. The discount rate was 12%; the borrower received $87,300.

Required:

A. Calculate the face value of each of the four notes.

B. Calculate the total amount due on the maturity date of each of the four notes.

C. For each of the four notes, calculate the cash interest paid at maturity.

D. Calculate the effective interest rate for each of the four notes.

Problem 11-5 Note Issued for an Operating Asset

On September 30, 1992, Webster Company purchased factory equipment with a cash price of $500,000. A down payment of $140,000 was made and a one-year, 12% note for $360,000 was given for the balance. The note principal and accrued interest is due in two equal installments on March 31 and September 30, 1993. Webster's fiscal year ends on December 31.

Required:

A. Prepare all journal entries with respect to the note from its inception through its maturity date. Webster does not use reversing entries.

B. Show how the note and accrued interest will be presented on Webster's December 31, 1992 balance sheet.

Problem 11-6 Payroll

James Henry is employed by a state government agency. For a one-half month period, his payroll check stub contained the following information:

Gross pay	$1,360
Mandatory deductions:	
FICA tax	7.65% of gross pay
Federal income tax	14.3% of gross pay
State income tax	20% of federal income tax withheld
Retirement contribution	7.0% of gross pay
Voluntary deductions:	
U.S. Savings Bonds	$128.00
Life insurance premiums	5.14
Health insurance premiums	10.50
Dental insurance premiums	4.30

Additional information: The state for which Mr. Henry works requires a 7% contribution by all employees to a retirement plan. The state matches the employee's contribution. The state pays, each month, $64 toward its employees' health insurance and $8.70 for dental insurance.

Required:
A. Compute the following:
   1. FICA tax withheld.
   2. Federal income tax withheld.
   3. State income tax withheld.
   4. Retirement contribution withheld.
   5. James Henry's take-home pay.
B. What percent of gross pay is Mr. Henry's take-home pay?
C. Compute the payroll tax expense the state will recognize for Mr. Henry's semi-monthly payroll. State employees are not eligible for Federal or State unemployment compensation.
D. What percent of gross pay is the semi-monthly payroll tax expense?

Problem 11-7 Leases
Mundell Company entered into a five-year lease on January 2, 1992 for the use of a cargo ship. The lease contract requires five annual payments of $250,000 starting December 31, 1992. The lease provides for 10% interest. The present value of the lease payments is $947,700. Mundell Company uses straight-line depreciation for all depreciable assets.

Required:
A. Assuming the lease is an operating lease, prepare all journal entries for 1992 and 1993 on Mundell's books.
B. Assuming the lease is a capital lease, prepare all journal entries for 1992 and 1993 on Mundell's books.

Problem 11-8 Deferred Income Tax
Harris Company reported the following summarized income statements for the years ended December 31, 1991, 1992, and 1993.

	1991	1992	1993
Revenues	$600,000	$710,000	$800,000
Expenses	440,000	490,000	560,000
Income before tax	$160,000	$220,000	$240,000

Harris experienced the following temporary differences between accounting income and taxable income for the three-year period:

1. Machinery purchased on January 2, 1991 for $60,000 was depreciated over four years for accounting purposes at $15,000 per year. The following depreciation expenses were deducted for tax purposes: 1991, $15,000; 1992, $22,800; 1993, $22,200.
2. Installment sales revenues of $40,000 were reported on the 1991 income statement for accounting purposes. For tax purposes, $15,000 was reported in 1991 and $25,000 was reported in 1992.

Harris's average income tax rate is 20%.

Required:
A. Prepare journal entries for each year to record income tax expense, income tax payable, and deferred income tax.
B. To what assets is the deferred income tax balance as of December 31, 1993 related? When will it reverse?

Problem 11-9 Time Value of Money—Annuities

Following are various situations requiring the use of annuity time value of money techniques:

1. Joe Blackburn entered into an annuity plan whereby he invests $2,000 per year at the end of each year for 20 years. How much will Joe have in the fund after he makes the twentieth payment if the fund earns
    a. 12% interest compounded annually:
    b. 16% interest compounded annually:
2. Billy Went died leaving his wife Sheila an insurance policy that provides for the following choices of payment:
    a. $50,000 cash immediately.
    b. $3,300 at the end of each quarter for five years.
    c. $15,000 immediately and $2,800 at the end of each quarter for four years.
    If interest is 3% per quarter, compounded quarterly, which option should Sheila select if she wishes to maximize the proceeds from the policy?
3. Bill Taylor is 68 years old. He has available cash of $60,000. If he buys a 10-year annuity that earns 12% interest each year, what amount of money will Bill receive each year if the money is paid out at the end of the year?

Required:

Compute the amounts requested in each situation. Show all computations.

Problem 11-10 Time Value of Money—Amounts

Following are several situations requiring the use of time value of money techniques:

1. Rachelle Kyson invests $2,000 at 12% interest compounded annually. She leaves the money invested without drawing out any of the interest for eight years. How much will Rachelle have at the end of the eighth year?
2. Mannett Company plans to deposit $120,000 today in a special building fund which will be needed at the end of four years. A bank will pay them 16% on the fund balance. How much will the fund be worth at the end of the fourth year assuming:
    a. Annual compounding
    b. Semiannual compounding
    c. Quarterly compounding
3. Under the terms of his salary agreement, the president of Carlotti Company has an option of receiving either an immediate bonus of $75,000 or a deferred bonus of $110,500 payable in four years. Ignoring income tax considerations and assuming a relevant interest rate of 10%, which settlement should the president select?
4. On January 1, 1988, Betsy Bucks deposited $5,000 in a savings account. How much will she have on January 1, 1994, if the money earns a 12% interest rate compounded:
    a. Annually.
    b. Semiannually.
5. Ted Jung wishes to take a trip to Australia in January 1998. To do this, he needs $8,000. How much must he deposit on January 1, 1992, in order to have the $8,000 he needs on January 1, 1998? Ted can earn 10% interest compounded annually.

Required:

Compute the amounts requested in each situation. Show your computations.

Problem 11-11 Time Value of Money

Following are various situations requiring the use of time value of money techniques:

1. Fletcher Company recently issued a $20 million, 20-year bond issue. To retire the bonds when due, Fletcher has established a bond redemption fund. Deposits of $275,000 will be made each year on the last day of the year. The funds assets will earn a 12% return, compounded annually.
   a. Will the fund be sufficient to pay off the bonds at the end of 20 years? If not, how much is the deficiency?
   b. Given a 12% annual rate of interest, how much should Fletcher deposit each year for 20 years in order to have $20 million in the fund on the date the bonds become due?
2. James Cox owes a Las Vegas casino $700,000. The casino has offered James two methods of payment: $700,000 now or $105,000 a year for 11 years with payments to be made at the end of each year. Which plan is most advantageous to James assuming a 10% interest rate?
3. Sandra Brown has saved $150 each month since January 1, 1986. Every six months, Sandra deposits the amount she has accumulated for the past six months in her credit union, which pays 8% annual interest compounded twice a year. How much will Sandra have in her account on July 1, 1993, after she makes her July 1 deposit?
4. When Clayton Newsom retired, his retirement fund had $1,650,000 in it. Clayton decided to withdraw the money in 15 annual installments starting one year from the date of his retirement. If the fund earning 10% compounded annually, how much will Clayton receive in each installment?

Required:
Compute the amount requested in each situation. Show your computations.

Problem 11-12 Time Value of Money

Alicia Brown has just become a grandmother. She has decided to establish a savings account for her new grandchild's education.

Required:
A. If Alicia deposits $750 now (on her grandchild's date of birth) and on each of her grandchild's birthdays until she is 18, how much will be in the fund after the deposit on the grandchild's 18th birthday if the fund earns 12% compounded annually?
B. If Alicia wants to have $60,000 in the fund after the deposit on her grandchild's 18th birthday, how much must she deposit each time?

Problem 11-13 Time Value of Money

Mark Cox has just purchased a new car and is trying to determine how to pay for it. He can pay the cash price of $15,195 now, or finance the car over 36 months at an annual interest rate of 16%. If he finances the car, he will make payments every three months with the first payment due three months following the purchase date. Interest starts accruing on the purchase date. If he finances the car, the bank requires a $12.40 process fee for each payment.

Required:
A. Compute the total payment Mark will make every three months if he finances the car.
B. What is the total amount Mark will pay over the life of the financial agreement if he finances the car? How much of this total will be interest?

Problem 11-14 Current Assets, Current Liabilities, and General Review
Griffin Company applied to First State Bank for a two-year loan of $150,000 to finance
an expansion of its sales office. As required by the application, Griffin provided the
following balance sheet:

GRIFFIN COMPANY
Balance Sheet
December 31, 1992

Assets

Current Assets:

Cash		$ 12,000
Accounts receivable		33,000
Inventory		98,000
Prepaid insurance		15,000
Office supplies		6,800
Total Current Assets		164,800

Property, Plant & Equipment:

Land		$ 40,000	
Buildings	$160,000		
Less: Accumulated depreciation	45,000	115,000	
Equipment	68,000		
Less: Accumulated depreciation	42,000	26,000	
Total Property, Plant & Equipment			181,000
Other Assets			6,300
Total Assets			$352,100

Liabilities and Owners' Equity

Current Liabilities:

Accounts payable		$ 28,000
Short-term notes payable		15,000
Income taxes payable		17,500
Rent payable		4,000
Total Current Liabilities		64,500

Long-term Liabilities:

Long-term notes payable	$100,000	
Mortgage payable	80,300	
Total Long-term Liabilities		180,300
Total Liabilities		244,800

Stockholders' Equity:

Capital stock	40,000	
Retained earnings	67,300	
Total Stockholders' Equity		107,300
Total Liabilities and Stockholders' Equity		$352,100

After reviewing the balance sheet, First State Bank officials agreed that Griffin's
current ratio met the bank's minimum criterion of 2:1 for making loans. Concerned
about other balance sheet items, however, bank officials required an independent audit
of Griffin's financial records to ascertain their accuracy. The audit revealed the following deficiencies:

1. $8,000 of the accounts receivable are over one year old and considered uncollectible. Griffin uses the direct write-off method for bad debt expense. Thus, no provision exists for other possible uncollectible accounts. The auditor believes 5% of the remaining receivables is a reasonable estimate of those that will become uncollectible.

2. Inventory with a book value of $42,000 is either damaged or obsolete and has an estimated net realizable value of $5,000.

3. No interest has been accrued on either the current or long-term notes payable. The current note is at 15% and is dated July 1, 1992 and no interest has been paid on the note; the long-term note is at 12% and interest was last paid on August 31, 1992.

4. Accrued wages and payroll taxes of $5,800 have not been recorded.

5. The prepaid insurance was purchased June 1, 1992. It is a two-year policy on the building and equipment.

6. A physical count revealed only $940 of office supplies on hand.

7. An advertising bill for $1,700 dated December 4, 1992, was not recorded and is unpaid.

Required:

A. Prepare journal entries to account for the financial information discovered by the auditor. Since the books are closed, all expense and revenue items should be debited or credited to the Retained Earnings account.

B. Prepare a new balance sheet as of December 31, 1992. T accounts may be helpful.

C. Compute Griffin's old and new working capital and current ratio.

D. If you were the bank's loan officer, would you approve the $150,000 two-year loan? Why or why not?

Problem 11-15A Recording Transactions in a Voucher System

Collins Company completed the following transactions during February 1992. Collins uses a voucher system and records merchandise purchases using the gross invoice method.

<u>1992</u>

Feb. 4 Prepared voucher No. 104 payable to Sebac Co. for merchandise purchased, $485; invoice dated February 3; terms, 3/10, n/60.

6 Prepared voucher No. 105 payable to High Country Realty for February rent, $1,600.

10 Prepared voucher No. 106 payable to Drummond Company for office equipment, $2,550; invoice dated February 9; terms, n/20.

10 Prepared voucher No. 107 for employee wages, $1,480.

11 Issued check No. 346 to payroll bank account in payment of voucher No. 107.

13 Issued check No. 347 in payment of voucher No. 104.

16 Issued check No. 348 in payment of voucher No. 105.

17 Prepared voucher No. 108 payable to Brock Company for merchandise purchased, $1,764; invoice dated February 16; terms 2/10,n/30.

20 Prepared voucher No. 109 payable to Gothic Press for advertising, $710; invoice dated February 16; terms, n/30.

20 Prepared voucher No. 110 payable to Southern Power Company, $327 for monthly utility bill.

23 Issued check No. 349 in payment of voucher No. 110.

24 Prepared voucher No. 111 for employee wages, $1,810.

24 Issued check No. 350 to payroll bank account in payment of voucher No. 111.

26 Issued check No. 351 in payment of voucher No. 108.
27 Prepared voucher No. 112 payable to Brown Company for merchandise purchased, $931; invoice dated February 25; terms, 2/10, n/30.
27 Issued check No. 352 in payment of voucher No. 106.

Required:

A. Prepare a voucher register and a check register similar to those illustrated in the chapter and record the transactions in the registers. Set up separate debit columns for Purchases, Wages Expense, and Utilities Expense.

B. Foot the voucher register and check register and post the appropriate amounts from both registers to the Vouchers Payable general ledger account (No. 222).

C. Reconcile the Vouchers Payable general ledger account balance with the unpaid vouchers file at the end of February. No vouchers payable were outstanding at the end of January.

CASE

CASE 11-1 Annual Report Analysis Case

Refer to the financial statements and related footnotes of BFGoodrich Company in the Appendix to this text and answer the following questions. Indicate the page number on which you found the answer.

A. What is the total amount of accrued expenses on December 31, 1989? What is the largest item included in accrued expenses?

B. How much interest expense was incurred during 1989?

C. What was the total long-term debt on December 31, 1989? How much of this amount represented capital lease obligations?

D. How much long-term debt was due within one year on December 31, 1989?

E. Does BFGoodrich Company appear to have (in dollar amount) more operating leases or capital leases?

F. Does BFGoodrich Company have a pension plan(s) for its employees? If so, what was the net pension cost for 1989?

ACCOUNTING FOR LONG-TERM BONDS PAYABLE

CHAPTER OVERVIEW AND OBJECTIVES

This chapter describes accounting for bonds payable and long-term notes payable. When you have completed the chapter, you should understand:

1. How to define a bond and describe its major characteristics.
2. Why a firm obtains funds by long-term borrowing.
3. The features commonly included in a bond issue.
4. How to record the issuance of bonds at par value, at a discount, and at a premium.
5. The relationship between bond prices and interest rates.
6. How bond prices are determined.
7. How to amortize a bond discount or premium by the straight-line method of amortization.
8. How to account for bonds issued between interest payment dates.
9. Why an adjusting entry is needed to accrue bond interest expense and how to prepare the entry.
10. How to record the retirement of bonds.
11. How to record the conversion of bonds into capital stock.
12. The purpose of a bond sinking fund and how to account for one.
13. How to amortize a bond discount or premium by the effective interest method of amortization.

Firms obtain some of the funds needed for operating a business from a variety of lending sources. In securing such financing, it is sound financial practice to match the maturity of the debt with the cash flow produced by the assets acquired with the borrowed funds. Inventories that will be sold in the near future, for example, are usually financed through short-term credit such as accounts and notes payable. Cash needed to finance seasonal activities is generally borrowed on short-term notes because current operations are expected to produce sufficient cash to repay the loans.

When a firm needs large amounts of financing for long-term purposes, however, such as for the acquisition of plant assets, the funds are often obtained by issuing long-term bonds or notes. Deferring the payment for an extended period allows time for the acquired assets to generate sufficient cash to cover interest payments and accumulate the funds needed to repay the loan. Also, because the interest rate is often fixed for the life of the note, the lender is able to lock in this rate and avoid the effects of interest rate fluctuations.

Chapter 11 dealt with current liabilities and certain long-term liabilities. This chapter discusses long-term financing through the issuance of bonds payable. For reporting purposes, a liability is reported as long-term if it is due beyond one year of the balance sheet date or the operating cycle, whichever is longer. The repayment of long-term debt is often deferred for a period of 30 years or more. The agreement between the lender and the borrower usually provides for periodic interest payments on specified dates, as well as for the repayment of the amount borrowed on specified dates.

The borrower receives current dollars in exchange for a promise to make payments to the lender at specific times in the future. Dollars received and paid at different times are made comparable by considering the time value of money. To understand accounting for long-term notes and bonds, one should be familiar with the concept of present value. Part II of Chapter 11 contains concepts and computations pertinent to that topic.

To focus on the fundamentals of accounting for bonds and to provide flexibility in assigning topics, this chapter is divided into two parts as follows.

Part I.   Characteristics and Fundamentals of Accounting for and Reporting Bonds Payable

Part II. Other Issues Related to Accounting for Bonds Payable

PART I. CHARACTERISTICS AND FUNDAMENTALS OF ACCOUNTING FOR AND REPORTING BONDS PAYABLE

BONDS PAYABLE

Objective 1:
Define a bond

When a large amount of long-term financing is needed, one—or even a few—lenders may not be able or willing to lend the total amount of money needed. In such situations, long-term funds may be obtained by issuing bonds to many investors. A bond is a written promise to pay a sum of money on a specified date and to pay interest each period as specified in the debt instrument. Thus, a bond is essentially a form of a promissory note, and the issuer has certain responsibilities.

PAR VALUE OF THE BONDS

Bonds are generally issued in denominations of $1,000, which is called the par value, face value, principal, or maturity value. On the maturity date the borrower must pay the par value to the bondholders. Maturity dates vary, but terms of 20 to 30 years are common for corporate bonds. A total bond issue of $2 million generally consists of 2,000 individual bonds of $1,000 par value each. The division of the total issue into relatively small units permits more investors to participate in the issue.

A specified annual rate of interest is paid on the par value throughout the life of the bonds. The rate, called the coupon rate, contract rate, nominal rate, or stated is expressed as a percentage of par value. Interest payments are normally made semiannually, although the stated rate of interest is expressed as an annual rate.

Default (i.e., failure to make payment when due) on either the amount borrowed or the interest commitment could result in the bondholders taking legal action against the firm to enforce their claims. Such action could force the borrower into declaring bankruptcy. In bankruptcy, creditors must be paid in full before any asset distribution is made to the stockholders.

WHO ISSUES THE BONDS?

Bonds are issued by corporations and other entities (e.g., federal and state governments, school districts, cities, and universities). Bonds may be sold by the issuing company directly to investors, but normally the issuer sells them to an investment firm called an underwriter. The underwriter then attempts to sell the bonds to investors at a higher price, thereby earning a profit.

THE BOND INDENTURE

A bond certificate is given to the buyer as evidence of the firm's indebtedness. The terms of the agreement constitute a contract called the bond indenture. The bond indenture indicates the interest rate to be paid, the dates on which interest is to be paid, the maturity date, the principal amount, and other features, such as the bondholder's right to convert the bonds into capital stock. An example of a bond certificate is shown in Figure 12-1.

Figure 12-1
Example of a Bond Indenture

THE FUNCTION OF THE TRUSTEE

Because the bonds may be held by numerous individual investors, a third party, called a **trustee**, is appointed by the issuing company to represent the bondholders. In most cases, the trustee is a large bank or trust company with the primary duty of assuring that the issuing company fulfills the terms of the bond indenture. The issuing company pays the trustee's expenses.

SELLING EXISTING BONDS

Bond prices are quoted as a percentage of par value. For example, the price of a $1,000 par value bond quoted at 104 is $1,040 ($1,000 × 104%). The minimum variation in a bond price is ⅛ of a dollar. Thus a $1,000 bond quoted at 83⅝ would sell for $836.25 ($1,000 × 83.625%).

Bonds may be sold at par, which means that the bond price was 100. If the bond price is below 100, the bonds sell at a **discount**; if the bond price is above 100, the bonds sell at a **premium**. The amount of the discount or premium is the difference between the issue price and the par value of the bond. For example, a bond quoted at 104 is selling at a $40 ($1,040 − $1,000) premium. Alternatively, if the firm received $920 for a bond, there is an $80 discount.

After the bonds are issued, they are usually listed on one of the securities exchanges. Thus, they can be bought or sold through brokers, who charge a commission for their services. Information related to bond prices is found in the financial section of most newspapers. Several bond listings taken from the *Wall Street Journal* are shown below.

Bonds	Current Yield	Volume	Close	Net Change
ATT 8¾ 00	9.0	138	97⅜	+ ¼
GM 8⅛ 91	8.1	10	100¼	+ ⅜
Mobil 14.4 04	13.3	21	108¼	− ¼

This information reports that for the ATT bonds, the issue had a stated interest rate of 8¾% and matures in the year 2000. The closing price of 97⅜ and net change of + ¼ are stated as a percentage of par value. During the day, 138 of the bonds were traded. The last bond traded for $973.75 ($1,000 × 97.375%) and this price was $2.50 ($1,000 × .25%) higher than that of the previous day. Based on the closing price of the day, the current yield is 9.0% (stated interest of $87.50 per bond ÷ the closing price of $973.75).

THE ADVANTAGES OF DEBT FINANCING

Objective 2: Why borrow long-term?

Firms obtain most long-term resources by either issuing long-term notes or bonds or by selling additional shares of capital stock. Selecting the most advantageous types of financing is a management function, and there are several reasons why management opts to issue bonds:

1. As a creditor, the bondholder does not hold an ownership interest in the firm and, accordingly, does not have a voting right. As a result, the issuance of bonds does not dilute the control of the existing owners.
2. Net income available to the capital stockholders can be increased through the use of financial leverage. **Financial leverage** is the borrowing of funds with the

expectation of investing the funds in such a way as to earn a return greater than the rate paid for the use of the funds. For example, if funds borrowed at an interest rate of 12% are used to earn an 18% return, the additional 6% earnings accrue to the stockholders.

3. Interest charges are an expense that is deductible from revenue in computing taxable income, whereas dividends on capital stock are not.

COMPARISON OF DEBT FINANCING AND EQUITY FINANCING

To illustrate the effect of *debt financing* (raising capital by selling bonds or long-term notes) versus *equity financing* (raising capital by selling stock), assume that a firm with 240,000 shares of $10 par value capital stock outstanding is currently earning $480,000 a year before income taxes. The firm needs to raise $1,200,000 in additional funds to finance a planned plant expansion. Management estimates that after the expansion the firm will earn $840,000 annually before interest and income taxes.

The $1,200,000 can be obtained from one of two plans that are proposed for consideration: (1) issue 120,000 shares of $10 par value capital stock; and (2) issue 12% bonds. It is assumed that each security is issued at its total par value of $1,200,000 and that income taxes are 40% of income. The effect of these two plans on the net income available to stockholders is shown in Figure 12-2.

Using earnings per share as the sole criterion for making the decision, Plan 2 is clearly the most attractive to the existing stockholders despite the payment of $144,000 in interest each period. Two factors cause this result. First, the firm is predicting that the expansion will increase earnings $360,000, which results in an increase in after-tax net income of $216,000 [$360,000 − (40% × $360,000)]. Second, because interest is a tax-deductible expense, the cost of borrowing is considerably less than the $144,000 paid to the bondholders. In other words, the after-tax cost of borrowing is $86,400, which is the $144,000 expense minus the $57,600 (40% × $144,000)

Figure 12-2
Illustration of Two Plans to Finance Expansion

	Before Expansion	Plan 1 Capital Stock	Plan 2 Bonds
		Plans to Finance Expansion	
Capital Stock:			
Shares currently outstanding	240,000	240,000	240,000
Additional shares issued	—	120,000	—
Totals	240,000	360,000	240,000
Income before bond interest and income taxes	$480,000	$840,000	$840,000
Less: Interest expense	—	—	144,000
Income before income taxes	480,000	840,000	696,000
Less: Income taxes (40%)	192,000	336,000	278,400
Net Income available to stockholders	$288,000	$504,000	$417,600
Number of shares of capital stock outstanding	240,000	360,000	240,000
Net income (earnings) per share of capital stock	$1.20	$1.40	$1.74

reduction in income tax expense. The after-tax cost of borrowing can also be computed as follows:

$$\text{After tax cost of borrowing} = \text{Interest expense} \times (1.0 - \text{tax rate})$$
$$= \$144,000 \times (1.0 - .40)$$
$$= \$86,400$$

The net increase in earnings of \$129,600 (\$216,000 − \$86,400) accrues to the existing stockholders, a favorable use of financial leverage. Although Plan 1 shows a higher net income than the other plan, it is divided over 120,000 more shares, resulting in a lower earnings per share than Plan 2.

SUCCESSFUL USE OF FINANCIAL LEVERAGE

This analysis shows that borrowing money may be advantageous to a firm. However, the illustration was based on the effect of the alternative plans on earnings per share and on a favorable leverage assumption. If the rate earned on the funds borrowed is less than the interest rate—unfavorable financial leverage—the earnings per share is reduced. In other words, the use of financial leverage is only successful when the earnings from using the borrowed funds is greater than the fixed charges paid to the investors.

Furthermore, there is a limit to the amount of new funds a firm can obtain by borrowing. The use of increasing amounts of debt increases the firm's fixed interest costs. At lower levels of net income, the firm may be unable to generate sufficient cash from operations to satisfy the periodic interest payments and could be forced into bankruptcy. In other words, because the bondholders are creditors, the interest payments must be made regardless of the firm's income level. Because the risk of default increases as the amount borrowed increases, the interest rate required by investors increases to reflect this added risk. The rate increases slowly for moderate amounts of debt, but at some level investors consider any new debt excessive and the market rate increases rapidly. At some point, the interest rate will exceed the rate that management is willing to incur. Determination of a favorable balance between debt and equity financing is discussed in more detail in finance courses.

TYPES OF BONDS ISSUED

Objective 3: Features of a bond issue

A bond indenture is written to satisfy the financial needs of the borrower, but the agreement must also be attractive to a sufficient number of investors. Consequently, individual bond issues with a variety of features have been created. Some of the more common features are presented here.

1. Bond Features Related to the Underlying Security
   a. Secured Bonds or Mortgage Bonds. A secured bond is backed by the specific physical assets of the firm which serve as collateral for the bond. Collateral is something of value (i.e., specific assets) acceptable to the lender that can be converted into cash to satisfy the debt if the borrower defaults. If the firm fails to make payments as specified in the bond indenture, the specific assets may be sold and the proceeds used to pay the bondholder.
   b. Debenture Bonds or Unsecured Bonds. Holders of debenture bonds rely on the general credit standing of the issuing firm for their security. As a result, debenture bonds are generally issued by financially strong companies. De-

benture bonds may be *subordinated* or *junior* to other types of debt. This means that in the event of bankruptcy the claims of subordinated debenture holders to the firm's assets are met only after higher priority claims, called senior debt, have been satisfied.

2. Bond Features Related to Evidence of Ownership and Payment of Interest

   a. **Registered Bonds.** The names and addresses of all holders of registered bonds must be on file with either the issuing company or the trustee. This file is called the *bond register*. Interest payments are made by check to the currently registered owners. If ownership of the bond is transferred, the issuing company must be notified so that the new owner can be entered in the bond register.

   b. **Coupon Bonds** or **Bearer Bonds.** These bonds have a printed coupon attached to the bond for each interest payment. The amount of interest due and interest payment date are specified on each coupon. When interest is due, the bondholder detaches the proper coupon, endorses it, indicates his or her address, and then presents it to a bank for collection. Neither the issuing company nor the trustee normally maintains a record of coupon bondholders. The title to the bond is assumed to be with the holder or bearer.

3. Bond Features Related to the Maturity Date

   a. **Term Bonds.** The principal of term bonds is paid in full on a single specified date. That is, the entire issue—no matter how many bondholders there are or when they purchased the bonds—matures on the same date.

   b. **Serial Bonds.** The principal of serial bonds matures in installments on a series of specified dates. For example, $100,000 of a $1 million bond issue may mature at the end of each year for a period of 10 years.

4. Bond Features Related to Potential Early Retirement

   a. **Callable Bonds.** Some bonds can be called in by the issuing company before they mature. The price that the issuer must pay, called the *call price,* is stipulated in the indenture and is usually slightly higher than the par value of the bonds. Most bonds issued today are callable bonds.

   b. **Convertible Bonds.** These are bonds that can be exchanged for capital stock at the bondholder's option.

A bond issue may contain other special features. For example, the agreement may prohibit a corporation from paying dividends to stockholders unless a stipulated level of working capital is maintained, or it may require that the issuing company make periodic deposits to a bond retirement fund (called a bond sinking fund) to accumulate the cash needed to retire the bonds when they mature.

Since most bonds are issued with a fixed coupon rate for the life of the bond issue, accounting and reporting for fixed interest rate bonds are illustrated in this chapter. However, during periods of high, unstable interest rates, and during periods of high inflation, other forms of debt instruments are often used. An example is the issuance of variable interest rate debt for which the interest is tied to the prevailing market rate. As an example, the interest rate paid by USX on one of its bond issues is tied to the interest rate of U.S. Treasury bills. Variable interest rate mortgages on real estate offered by lending institutions serves as another example of variable rate lending.

Another type of financing is *zero coupon bonds*. With zero coupon bonds, the semiannual interest on the bonds is added to the principal and both the interest and maturity value are paid at maturity. Because periodic interest is not paid, zero coupon bonds sell for much less than their par values.

FINANCIAL STATEMENT DISCLOSURES

Although bond issues may contain different features, accounting for the various issues is similar. Because the features of long-term debt are important to potential investors, they are disclosed in a footnote to the financial statements. This disclosure usually contains the interest rate, maturity date, and any special features related to the debt issue. Such disclosure is illustrated in Figure 12-3.

Figure 12-3
Illustration of
Long-term Debt
Disclosures

Note 5—Long-Term Debt

Long-term debt and capital lease obligations outstanding were as follows:

	March 31,	
(Dollars in thousands)	1990	1989
7¼% Convertible Subordinated Debentures due 1995	$11,188	$11,188
Mortgage notes payable	10,429	
Revolving Credit Loans from banks		64,600
Capital lease obligations (Note 6)		9,076
Other	9,196	9,392
Total debt	30,813	94,256
Less current portion	4,724	43,279
Long-term debt and capital lease obligations	$26,089	$50,977

The 7¼% Debentures due 1995 are convertible at an effective conversion price of $52.56 per share. The effective conversion price is subject to adjustment for anti-dilution provisions contained in the debt agreement. The debt indenture contains restrictive covenants, which among other things restrict the amount of dividends that the Company may pay.

Mortgage notes payable are collateralized by property and equipment. The notes are payable at annual interest rates from 4.5% to 7.2%.

The Company has an agreement with four banks to provide up to $100,000,000 in revolving credit loans at the banks' prime rate or at the prevailing London interbank rate plus ⅜ percent. No debt was outstanding under this arrangement at March 31, 1990.

In addition, the Company has an agreement with a bank to borrow up to the equivalent of $40,000,000 in the United States and four foreign countries at the prevailing Eurocurrency rate plus ½ percent. At March 31, 1990, no debt was outstanding under this arrangement.

Capital leases, primarily redundant data processing equipment, acquired through the merger with Cullinet were disposed of during fiscal 1990.

The maturities of long-term debt outstanding for the five fiscal years noted are as follows: 1991—$4,724,000; 1992—$2,493,000; 1993—$1,683,000; 1994—$605,000; 1995—$11,475,000.

Interest expense for the years ended March 31, 1990, 1989 and 1988 was $8,048,000, $12,372,000 and $10,689,000, respectively, and is netted against interest income.

Source: Computer Associates International, Inc., 1990 Annual Report.

ACCOUNTING FOR BONDS ISSUED AT PAR VALUE

To illustrate the accounting for bonds issued at par value, assume that Hayden Corporation's board of directors authorized the issuance of $100,000 par value, 10%, five-year bonds dated July 1, 1992. (For illustrative purposes, the bonds are issued for an unusually small amount and are assumed to be outstanding for a relatively short period of time.) Interest is payable semiannually on June 30 and December 31. No other special features are contained in the bond indenture. Assuming that the entire bond issue is sold at par value on July 1, the entry to record the issue is as follows.

Objective 4:
Recording the issue of bonds

July	1	Cash	100,000	
		Bonds Payable		100,000
		Issued 10%, 5-year bonds at par value.		

The bonds are reported as a long-term liability until the maturity date is within a year or the next operating cycle, whichever is longer. They are then switched to the current liability classification. An exception to reporting the liability as being current is made when the bondholders are to be paid from resources classified as noncurrent assets, such as when a bond sinking fund is established. If noncurrent assets are specifically identified as available to retire the debt, the current maturity is reported as a long-term liability.

In this case, interest of $5,000 ($100,000 × 10% × 6/12) is due each June 30 and December 31 until the bonds mature. The entry to record the first semiannual interest payment is as follows.

Dec.	31	Interest Expense	5,000	
		Cash		5,000
		Paid semiannual interest on 10% bonds.		

This entry is made every June 30 and December 31 until the bonds mature. Upon maturity, the entries to record the last interest payment and bond retirement are:

1993				
June	30	Interest Expense	5,000	
		Cash		5,000
		Paid semiannual interest on 10% bonds.		
	30	Bonds Payable	100,000	
		Cash		100,000
		To record bond retirement.		

Once the bonds are issued, they may be traded on the open market. Depending on a number of factors, such as current interest rates and the financial position of the borrower, the market price of the bonds will fluctuate above or below their par value. Changes in the market price are not entered in the firm's books because such changes do not alter the firm's commitment to make the stated semiannual interest payments and to pay the par value when the bonds mature.

THE EFFECT OF MARKET INTEREST RATES ON BOND PRICES

In the previous example, Hayden Corporation received the $1,000 par value for each bond. However, a company may not receive the par value. Given the maturity date for a bond set forth in the bond indenture, the issue price depends on the relationship between the stated interest rate and the prevailing rate of return required by investors, sometimes called the *market rate of interest.*

The market rate of interest for a particular bond is determined in the money markets, and influenced by several different factors such as general economic conditions, the demand for the bonds, and the current financial position and expected future earnings of the issuing company. The market rate tends to fluctuate daily as economic conditions and investors' perceived risk of an investment change. The greater the risk associated with an investment, the greater the rate of return required by investors. Because securities vary in risk, no single market rate of interest exists. Instead, there is a schedule of rates corresponding to the risk associated with a particular security. For example, on July 25, 1990, the interest rate on U.S. Treasury bonds due in one year was 7.9%, while bonds of Stone Container Corp. due in 1995 were selling to yield 13.4%. Obviously, the treasury bonds were considered less risky than the corporate bonds.

The stated rate of interest establishes the amount of interest to be paid annually by the issuing company. An attempt is made to set the stated rate approximately equal to the market rate for similar securities. However, to allow sufficient time for drafting a bond indenture, printing the certificates, arranging underwriters, obtaining approvals from state and federal securities agencies (such as the Securities and Exchange Commission), and performing an audit, if needed, the stated rate must be determined in advance of the issue date.

From the time that the terms of a bond issue are established and the bonds are issued, economic conditions and expectations for a given company may change. As a result, the market rate for a given bond on the date of issue is often not equal to the stated rate. Because the stated rate, interest payments dates, the maturity date, and the maturity value are all fixed by contract, the market price of a bond must adjust if the bonds are to be marketable. In other words, since the bond contract is fixed, the market price of a bond will adjust so that the bond will yield a rate (the market rate) that is currently required by investors. The market price of a bond will be equal to the present value of the future cash payments. The discount rate used to discount the cash payments is the market rate of interest.

The actual rate at which a bond is issued is called the **effective rate** or **yield rate**. That is, the effective rate is the rate of interest an investor will earn (and the issuer will pay) if bonds purchased at a certain price are held to maturity.

In the case of the 10% Hayden Corporation bonds, the firm will receive the $100,000 par value for the bonds only if the market rate of interest for comparable alternative investments equals the stated rate of 10% on the bonds. If the market rate of interest is higher on other investments of similar risk, investors will offer less than the par value (i.e., the bonds will be issued at a discount) so that they can earn the prevailing market rate of interest. Investors will not pay $1,000 for a Hayden Corporation bond and get $100 interest per year if another comparable investment would yield 12%, or $120 annually. Conversely, if other investments of similar risk are selling to yield 8%, or $80 per year, investors will bid up the price of Hayden Corporation's bonds (i.e., the bonds will be issued at a premium) paying $100 per year until a price is reached that will result in an 8% return.

Note that there is an inverse relationship between the price of a bond and the market rate as diagrammed below.

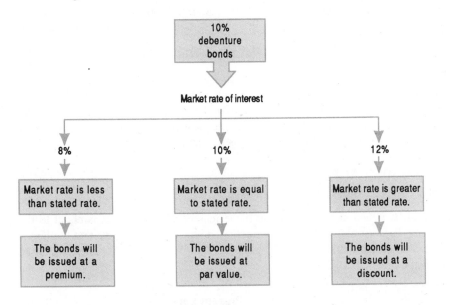

In effect, a discount results because the market rate of interest is higher than the stated rate and a premium results when the market rate is less than the stated rate. Thus, a discount should be thought of as additional interest expense and a premium as a reduction in interest expense.

DETERMINING THE ISSUE PRICE OF A BOND

Computing bond prices involves using present value concepts and computing present values using compound interest tables. Thus, this section relies heavily on the reader's understanding of the present value concepts presented in part II of Chapter 11.

Objective 6: Computing bond prices

The issue price of a bond is the present value of its future cash payments. A bond usually requires that two different types of cash payments be made to the bondholders: (1) an annuity for the cash interest payments made every six months, and (2) a single payment of the par value at maturity. The interest rate used to compute the present value is the market rate of interest on the date of issue. Recall that the effective rate of interest is the rate of interest that an investor will earn if bonds purchased at a certain price are held to maturity. The market rate and the effective rate are the same at the date of issue. Using the market rate will derive the bond price that an investor would be willing to pay for the bonds to earn the market rate.

To illustrate the computation of a bond price, the Hayden Corporation's 10%, five-year bonds will be used. Hayden Corporation will pay $1,000 per bond in five years when the bonds mature, and an interest payment of $50 every six months for the next five years. It is assumed that the bonds are issued in three independent cases to yield a rate of 10%, 12%, and 8%. Because the interest is paid twice a year, there are 10 compounding periods (5 years × 2 periods per year) during the life of the bonds. It is then necessary to convert the annual interest rate to a semiannual rate by dividing the annual rate by two. A time scale showing the cash flows may appear as follows:

```
7/1  12/31/92 6/30  12/31/93 6/30  12/31/94 6/30  12/31/95 6/30  12/31/96 6/30
|——|——|——|——|——|——|——|——|——|——|
     $50   $50   $50   $50   $50   $50   $50   $50   $50   $50
                                                              $1,000

     <————————————————10 semiannual periods————————————————>
```

Given the prevailing market rate of interest on July 1, 1992, the issue price of the bond can be calculated. The issue price per bond is the present value of the interest payments of $50 per period (an annuity) plus the present value of the $1,000 maturity value (a single amount). The discount rate is the market rate on July 1, 1992.

BONDS ISSUED AT PAR VALUE— MARKET RATE EQUALS STATED RATE

Bonds will be issued at their par value if the market rate of interest is equal to the stated rate. To illustrate the steps in computing the issue price, assume that the bonds are issued when the market rate of interest is 10% (5% per period). The issue price is computed here.

Type of Cash Flow	Present Value Table	Present Value Factor— 5%, 10 Periods*	Amount	Present Value
Single payment	11–3, page 493	.6139	$1,000	$613.90
Annuity payment	11–4, page 494	7.7217	50	386.09
Present value of future cash flows discounted at 5% per discount period				$999.99**

*Note that 10 interest periods are used for both types of cash flows.
**The $.01 difference from par value is due to rounding.

The issue price is composed of the sum of the present value of the maturity payment and the present value of the semiannual interest payments. This computation shows that an investor seeking a return of 10% (5% per semiannual period) would be willing to pay $1,000 per bond.

BONDS ISSUED AT A DISCOUNT— MARKET RATE IS GREATER THAN STATED RATE

Assume now that the bonds are issued at a price to yield a return of 12% (6% per period). The two separate cash flows are discounted using the market rate of interest as shown below.

Type of Cash Flow	Present Value Table	Present Value Factor— 6%, 10 Periods	Amount	Present Value
Single payment	11–3, page 493	.5584	$1,000	$558.40
Annuity payment	11–4, page 494	7.3601	50	368.01
Present value of future cash flows discounted at 6% per discount period				$926.41

Note that the cash flows specified in the bond indenture (a single payment of $1,000 and an annuity of $50) do not change with a change in the market rate to 12%. However, the present value factors do change, as they are based on the market rate of 6% per period.

Because the market rate of interest is higher than the fixed stated rate, the bonds will be issued at a discount. An investor paying $926.41 for a bond and holding it until maturity will earn a return of 6% per period on the bonds.

BONDS ISSUED AT A PREMIUM— MARKET RATE IS LESS THAN STATED RATE

To illustrate the computation of the bond price when the bonds are issued at a premium, assume that the market rate of interest is 8% (4% per semiannual period) when the bonds are issued. The issue price per bond is computed as follows.

Type of Cash Flow	Present Value Table	Present Value Factor— 4%, 10 Periods	Amount	Present Value
Single payment	11–3, page 493	.6756	$1,000	$ 675.60
Annuity payment	11–4, page 494	8.1109	50	405.55
Present value of future cash flows discounted at 4% per discount period				$1,081.15

The bonds will be issued for a premium because the market rate of interest is lower than the stated rate.

Note that bond prices move in an opposite direction to the market rate of interest. If the market rate of interest increases, the price of a bond will decline. Conversely, if the market rate of interest decreases, the price of a bond will increase. These relationships are summarized in Figure 12-4.

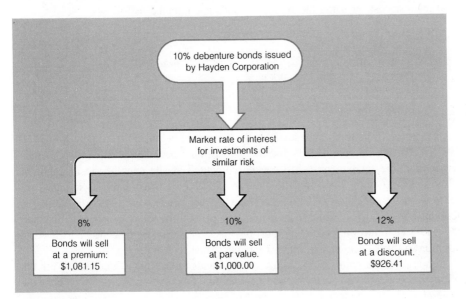

Figure 12-4
Relationship of Market Rate to Issue Price of Bonds

ACCOUNTING FOR BONDS ISSUED AT A DISCOUNT

Objective 7:
Amortization of
bond discount
or premium—
straight-line
method

To illustrate accounting for bonds issued at a discount, assume that Hayden Corporation issued its $100,000, 10%, five-year bonds on July 1 for $92,641 to yield the market rate of interest of 12%. The issuance of the bonds is recorded as follows.

July	1	Cash	92,641	
		Discount on Bonds Payable	7,359	
		Bonds Payable		100,000
		Issued 10%, 5-year bonds at a discount.		

In recording the issue of bonds, Cash is debited for the amount received, Bonds Payable is credited for the par value of the bonds, and Discount on Bonds Payable is debited for the difference between the two.

In a balance sheet prepared immediately after the bonds are issued, the bonds will be reported in this manner.

Long-term Liabilities:		
10% Bonds payable, due 6/30/97	$100,000	
Less: Unamortized discount on bonds payable	7,359	$92,641

The discount is deducted from the par value of the bonds to show the carrying value of the debt. On the date of issuance, the carrying value is equal to the amount borrowed. In subsequent periods, the debit balance in the discount account is amortized to interest expense over the life of the bonds, which results in a gradual increase in the carrying value from period to period. When the bonds mature, the discount will be fully amortized and the carrying value of the bonds will equal their par value.

COMPUTING THE TOTAL INTEREST COST

Because the par value, rather than the amount received, must be paid to the bondholders at the maturity date, the discount is an increased interest cost to the firm. The total interest cost for using the borrowed funds is computed as follows.

Cash to be paid to the bondholders:	
Principal at maturity	$100,000
Interest payments ($100,000 × 10% × 5 years)	50,000
Total cash paid to bondholders	150,000
Cash received when the bonds were issued	92,641
Total interest cost	$ 57,359

As can be seen, the total interest cost is the difference between the amount borrowed ($92,641) from the bondholders and the amount paid back to them ($150,000). Alternatively, the total interest cost can be computed as the sum of the discount of $7,359 paid when the bonds mature plus the $50,000 total cash interest payments. In other words, the amount of cash received when the bonds were issued ($92,641) is less than the cash to be paid back at maturity ($100,000) by the amount of the discount ($7,359). Therefore, the company must pay back $7,359 more than was borrowed in addition to the 10 semiannual interest payments that total $50,000.

Although the discount is not paid until the bonds mature, it is amortized over the life of the bonds because each period benefits from the use of the money. Thus, the amount of the discount increases the cost of borrowing and, as shown later, amortization of the discount results in an interest expense each period that is greater than the semiannual cash payment. The effect of the discount is to increase the stated rate of interest of 10% to the effective rate of 12% required by the investors.

Two methods may be used to amortize a discount or premium: the ***straight-line method*** and the ***effective-interest method***. The straight-line method is easier to apply because it allocates the interest cost evenly over the life of the bonds. However, the method is conceptually deficient because it does not report interest at the effective rate. The effective-interest method (described in a later section of this chapter) is theoretically preferred. However, a discount or premium may be amortized using the straight-line method if the results obtained from using the method are not materially different from those obtained using the effective-interest method.[1]

Amortizing the Bond Discount—Straight-line Method

An amortization table based on the straight-line method is prepared in Figure 12-5. The straight-line method allocates an equal amount of the discount to bond interest expense each interest period. In our illustration, the bonds were issued for $92,641. The amount of the $7,359 discount amortized each period is computed as follows.

$$\frac{\text{Discount Amortization}}{\text{per Interest Period}} = \frac{\text{Total Discount}}{\text{Number of Interest Periods Bonds are Outstanding}}$$

$$= \frac{\$7,359}{\text{10 six-month periods}}$$

$$= \$736 \text{ per six-month period}$$

The cash interest payment is:

$$\text{Interest} = \text{Par Value} \times \text{Rate} \times \text{Time}$$
$$= \$100,000 \times 10\% \times 6/12$$
$$= \$5,000$$

The entry to record the first semiannual interest payment is[2]

Dec.	31	Interest Expense	5,736[3]	
		Discount on Bonds Payable		736
		Cash		5,000
		Paid semiannual interest and amortized discount on 10%, 5-year bonds.		

[1]"Interest on Receivables and Payables," *Opinions of the Accounting Principles Board No. 21* (New York: AICPA, 1971), par. 15.

[2]In this chapter, one compound journal entry is made to amortize any discount or premium on bonds payable. Making one entry emphasizes that the interest expense for the period consists of the cash paid plus the discount amortization. However, it is sometimes easier to see the effects of amortization on the accounts if two entries are made: (1) to record the payment of interest and (2) to record the amortization of the discount or premium. Those entries would be made as follows.

Dec.	31	Interest Expense	5,000	
		Cash		5,000
		To record the payment of semiannual interest.		
	31	Interest Expense	736	
		Discount on Bonds Payable		736
		To record the amortization of discount.		

Both the compound journal entry and the two entries above are considered acceptable alternatives.

[3]When the straight-line method of amortization is used, the bond interest expense can be verified by dividing the total interest cost of $57,359 by the 10 semiannual interest periods.

Semiannual Interest Periods	(A) Semiannual Cash Payment ($100,000 × 5%)	(B) Discount Amortization ($7,359*/10)	(C) Semiannual Interest Expense (Col. A + Col. B)	(D) Par Value	(E) Bond Discount Balance (Col. E for previous period − Col. B)	(F) Carrying Value—End of Period (Col. D − Col. E)
7/1/92				$100,000	$7,359	$ 92,641
12/31/92	$ 5,000	$ 736	$ 5,736	100,000	6,623	93,377
6/30/93	5,000	736	5,736	100,000	5,887	94,113
12/31/93	5,000	736	5,736	100,000	5,151	94,849
6/30/94	5,000	736	5,736	100,000	4,415	95,585
12/31/94	5,000	736	5,736	100,000	3,679	96,321
6/30/95	5,000	736	5,736	100,000	2,943	97,057
12/31/95	5,000	736	5,736	100,000	2,207	97,793
6/30/96	5,000	736	5,736	100,000	1,471	98,529
12/31/96	5,000	736	5,736	100,000	735	99,265
6/30/97	5,000	735*	5,735	100,000	—	100,000
Totals	$50,000	$7,359	$57,359			

*Unamortized bond discount balance (Column E).

Figure 12-5
Amortization Table for Bonds Issued at a Discount—Straight-line Amortization

Note that interest expense of $5,736 is reported, although cash of only $5,000 is paid. The added expense of $736 does not involve cash until the par value is paid when the bonds mature. The Bonds Payable and Discount on Bonds Payable accounts will appear as follows after the December 31 entry is posted.

Bonds Payable		**Discount on Bonds Payable**		
	6/30 100,000	6/30 7,359	12/31 736
		12/31 Bal. 6,623	

The credit of $736 to the contra liability account, Discount on Bonds Payable, results in an increase of $736 in the carrying value of the bonds. The bonds are reported as follows in the December 31 balance sheet.

Long-term Liabilities:
  10% Bonds payable, due 6/30/97 $100,000
  Less: Unamortized discount on bonds payable   6,623 $93,377

In each subsequent six-month period, the carrying value will increase $736 as the discount is amortized. The amortization of the discount will increase the carrying value of the bonds payable to its par value of $100,000 on its maturity date as shown in Figure 12-6.

ACCOUNTING FOR BONDS ISSUED AT A PREMIUM

Bonds will be issued at a premium if the stated rate of interest on them is greater than the market rate of interest at the time of issue. For example, assume that the 10%, five-year bonds of the Hayden Corporation are issued for $108,115 to yield the market

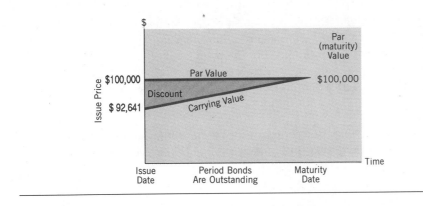

Figure 12-6
Effect of Discount
on Carrying Value
of Bonds Payable

rate of interest of 8% at the time of issue. The entry to record the issue on July 1 is as follows.

July	1	Cash	108,115	
		Premium on Bonds Payable		8,115
		Bonds Payable		100,000
		Issued 10%, 5-year bonds at a premium.		

In this entry, Cash is debited for the amount received, Bonds Payable is credited for the par value of the bonds, and Premium on Bonds Payable is recorded for the difference between the two.

The bonds would be shown in a balance sheet prepared immediately after their issue as

Long-term Liabilities:
10% Bonds payable, due 6/30/97 $100,000
Add: Unamortized premium on bonds payable   8,115 $108,115

Both the Premium on Bonds Payable and Bonds Payable accounts have a credit balance, so they are added together to derive the carrying value of the debt. In subsequent periods, the premium is allocated over the life of the bonds as a reduction in interest expense to reflect that the actual rate of borrowing is less than the stated rate. By the time the bonds mature, the premium account will be reduced to a zero balance, leaving a carrying value of $100,000, the amount due the bondholders at that time.

COMPUTING THE TOTAL INTEREST COST

Because the bonds were issued at a premium, the total cost of borrowing is $41,885, as computed below.

Cash to be paid to the bondholders:
   Principal at maturity $100,000
   Interest payments ($100,000 × 10% × 5 years)   50,000
Total cash paid to bondholders   150,000
Cash received when the bonds were issued   108,115
Total interest cost $ 41,885

The total interest cost is equal to the sum of the periodic interest payments, less the amount of the premium. That is, the amount of cash received when the bonds were issued ($108,115) is greater by the amount of the premium ($8,115) than the amount to be paid back at maturity ($100,000). The premium received over the cash to be paid back reduces the total cost of borrowing and is amortized over the life of the bonds because each period benefits from the lower interest cost. Amortization of the premium results in an interest expense each period that is less than the semiannual cash payment.

The bond premium may be amortized using the straight-line method of amortization or the effective interest method of amortization, although the latter is preferred on conceptual grounds.

Amortizing the Bond Premium— Straight-line Method of Amortization

An amortization table for these bonds using the straight-line method of amortization is prepared in Figure 12-7. If the straight-line method is used to amortize a premium, an equal amount is amortized as a reduction in interest expense each period. Thus the amortization per period is $812 as computed here.

$$\frac{\text{Premium Amortization}}{\text{per Interest Period}} = \frac{\text{Total Premium}}{\substack{\text{Number of Interest Periods Bonds} \\ \text{Are Outstanding}}}$$

$$= \frac{\$8,115}{10 \text{ six-month periods}}$$

$$= \$812 \text{ per six-month period}$$

The entry to record the first interest payment on December 31 is[4]

Dec.	31	Interest Expense	4,188	
		Premium on Bonds Payable	812	
		Cash		5,000
		Paid semiannual interest and amortized the premium on 10%, 5-year bonds.		

This entry is the same in each interest period. Note that the interest expense is less than the cash payment by the amount of the premium amortization. The interest expense is less because the actual cost of borrowing (8%) is less than the 10% stated rate.

[4]Alternatively, the payment and amortization may be recorded by making two entries each period, as follows.

Dec.	31	Interest Expense	5,000	
		Cash		5,000
		To record the payment of semiannual interest.		
	31	Premium on Bonds Payable	812	
		Interest Expense		812
		To record the amortization of premium.		

Semiannual Interest Periods	(A) Semiannual Cash Payment ($100,000 × 5%)	(B) Premium Amortization ($8,115*/10)	(C) Semiannual Interest Expense (Col. A − Col. B)	(D) Par Value	(E) Bond Premium Balance (Col. E for previous period − Col. B)	(F) Carrying Value—End of period − (Col. D + Col. E)
7/1/92				$100,000	$8,115	$108,115
12/31/92	$ 5,000	$ 812	$ 4,188	100,000	7,303	107,303
6/30/93	5,000	812	4,188	100,000	6,491	106,491
12/31/93	5,000	812	4,188	100,000	5,679	105,679
6/30/94	5,000	812	4,188	100,000	4,867	104,867
12/31/94	5,000	812	4,188	100,000	4,055	104,055
6/30/95	5,000	812	4,188	100,000	3,243	103,243
12/31/95	5,000	812	4,188	100,000	2,431	102,431
6/30/96	5,000	812	4,188	100,000	1,619	101,619
12/31/96	5,000	812	4,188	100,000	807	100,807
6/30/97	5,000	807*	4,193	100,000	—	100,000
Totals	$50,000	$8,115	$41,885			

*Unamortized bond premium balance (Column E).

Figure 12-7
Amortization Table for Bonds Issued at a Premium—Straight-line Amortization

After the December 31 entry is posted, the Bonds Payable and Premium on Bonds Payable accounts will appear as follows.

Bonds Payable		Premium on Bonds Payable			
	6/30 100,000	12/31	812	6/30	8,115
				12/31 Bal.	7,303

These accounts will be reported in the December 31 balance sheet as shown here.

Long-term Liabilities:
10% Bonds payable, due 6/30/97 .... $100,000
Add: Unamortized premium on bonds payable .... 7,303 .... $107,303

Note that the carrying value of $107,303 is $812 less than the carrying value of $108,115 on June 30, the date of issue. In each subsequent interest period, the carrying value will decrease $812 until the bonds mature, at which time the carrying value will be equal to the par value of the bonds, as shown in Figure 12-8.

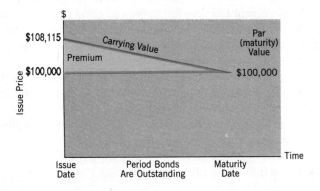

Figure 12-8
Effect of Premium on Carrying Value of Bonds Payable

Conceptual Problem With the Straight-line Method

When the straight-line method is used, total interest cost is allocated equally to each period over the life of the bonds. When bond discount is amortized, the carrying value increases each period, and interest expense, as a percentage of the carrying value of the debt, will decrease over time. Conversely, the straight-line amortization of a bond premium results in a decreased carrying value for the bonds, and interest, as a percentage of carrying value, will increase. Since the effective rate of interest is a fixed rate, using the straight-line method distorts the actual cost of borrowing. For this reason, the APB and its successor, the FASB, have required the use of the effective-interest method of amortization. Although the effective interest method is required, the straight-line method of amortization is permitted if the results obtained are not materially different from those resulting from the effective-interest method (materiality convention).

PART II: OTHER ISSUES RELATED TO ACCOUNTING FOR BONDS PAYABLE

Accounting for bonds is a complex topic. To focus on the basic issues of accounting for bonds payable, the previous section of this chapter assumed the following.

1. The bonds were sold on their issue date.
2. One of the interest payment dates coincided with the fiscal year-end.
3. The bonds were outstanding to maturity.

Accounting for a bond issue when these assumptions are *not* valid is discussed and illustrated in this section, along with the following related topics.

1. Accounting for bonds issued between interest payment dates.
2. Year-end adjusting entry for bond interest expense.
3. Retirement of bonds before maturity.
4. Conversion of bonds into common stock.
5. Accounting for a bond sinking fund.
6. The effective-interest method of amortization.

BONDS ISSUED BETWEEN INTEREST PAYMENT DATES

Objective 8:
Issue of bonds between interest payment dates

The Hayden Corporation example used in previous sections assumed that the bonds were issued on an interest payment date and were outstanding for a full six months before the first semiannual interest payment was made. However, bonds are frequently issued between interest payment dates. In such cases, the buyer must pay the issuing company the interest accrued from the last interest payment date to the date of issue, plus the issue price of the bonds. On the first interest payment date, a full six months' interest is paid on the bonds outstanding regardless of when they were issued. Thus, in the first payment, the accrued interest collected from the buyer is returned along with the payment for the interest accrued after the date of issue. If the firm did not collect accrued interest at the time of issue, it would be necessary to maintain a record of each bondholder and of the dates the bonds were issued. At the first interest payment date, interest due each bondholder would have to be computed separately—resulting in increased recordkeeping costs.

If a bond is later sold by an investor, the buyer must pay the seller accrued interest from the last payment date to the sales date. The holder of the bond then receives a full six months' interest on the next interest payment date.

To illustrate, assume that the 10% bonds of Hayden Corporation dated July 1 are issued on September 1 for $93,620 plus two months' accrued interest. The entry to record the issue is as follows.

Sept.	1	Cash	95,287	
		Discount on Bonds Payable	6,380	
		Bonds Payable		100,000
		Interest Payable		1,667
		Issued 10%, 5-year bonds at $93,620 plus		
		accrued interest for 2 months.		

Interest Payable = $100,000 × 10% × 2/12 = $1,667
Cash Received = $93,620 + $1,667 = $95,287

On December 31, the first semiannual interest payment date, a full six months' interest is paid to the bondholders even though the bonds were not issued until September 1. The entry is as follows.

Dec.	31	Interest Expense	3,773	
		Interest Payable	1,667	
		Cash		5,000
		Discount on Bonds Payable		440
		Paid semiannual interest and amortized		
		discount on 10% bonds issued two		
		months after date of issue.		

$$\text{Discount Amortization} = \frac{\$6,380}{58 \text{ months*}} = \$110 \text{ per month}$$

$110 per month × 4 months = $440

*Number of months bonds are outstanding.

Interest Expense = $100,000 × 10% × 4/12 = $3,333
$3,333 + $440 = $3,773

YEAR-END ADJUSTING ENTRY FOR BOND INTEREST EXPENSE

A company's fiscal year-end often does not correspond with an interest-payment date. In such cases, an adjusting entry must be made at year-end to record the interest accrued on the bonds and to amortize any discount or premium from the last interest payment date to the fiscal year-end. For example, assume that Mann Corporation's 12%, five-year $100,000 par value bonds were issued for $103,900 on May 1, 1992. Interest is paid on April 30 and October 31. The entry to record the first interest payment on October 31, 1992, using straight-line amortization is as follows.

Objective 9: Accruing bond interest expense

Oct.	31	Interest Expense	5,610	
		Premium on Bonds Payable	390	
		Cash		6,000
		Paid semiannual interest and amortized the		
		premium on 12%, 5-year bonds. ($3,900/		
		10 periods = $390 per 6 month period)		

If Mann has a December 31 fiscal year-end, an adjusting entry must be made on December 31, to accrue two months' interest and to amortize two months' bond premium. The entry is:

Dec.	31	Interest Expense	1,870	
		Premium on Bonds Payable	130	
		Accrued Interest Payable		2,000
		To accrue interest and amortize premium for		
		two months on 12% bonds.		
		$6,000 × 2/6 = $2,000		
		$390 × 2/6 = $130		

On December 31, 1992, the Interest Expense account would appear as follows:

Interest Expense

1992		
10/31	5,610	
12/31	1,870	
12/31 Bal.	7,480	

The $7,480 balance in the account is closed to the Income Summary account as part of the closing process.

When interest is paid on April 30, 1993, the following entry is made.

April	30	Interest Expense	3,740	
		Premium on Bonds Payable	260	
		Accrued Interest Payable	2,000	
		Cash		6,000
		Paid semiannual interest, a portion of which		
		was accrued at fiscal year-end, and		
		amortized premium for 4 months on		
		12% bonds.		

In this entry, the interest expense and premium amortization for the remaining four months is recorded and the accrued liability recorded at December 31 is paid. If bonds are issued at a discount, the accrual of interest and amortization of the discount is recorded in a similar manner.

RETIREMENT OF BONDS BEFORE MATURITY

Objective 10: Recording the retirement of bonds

As mentioned earlier, most bond issues are callable by the issuing company if it pays the bondholders a price specified in the bond indenture. Bonds are made callable to enable the company to retire the bonds and issue new ones at a lower effective interest rate. Bonds may also be retired if the issuer purchases them on the open market.

In accounting for the early retirement of bonds, called an *early extinguishment of debt*, a material difference between the price paid and the bonds' carrying value is reported separately in the income statement as an extraordinary gain or loss.[5] An extraordinary gain results if the purchase price of the bonds is less than their carrying value, and an extraordinary loss is incurred if the purchase price is greater than their carrying value.

To illustrate, assume that bonds issued by Marcos Corporation for $103,860 ($100,000 par value) contained a provision that the bonds could be called at 104 on any interest date after June 30, 1993. The company exercised its call option on June 30, 1994, after the June 30 interest payment had been made. The unamortized bond premium was $1,544 on June 30. The entry is:

1994					
June	30	Bonds Payable	100,000	
		Premium on Bonds Payable	1,544	
		Extraordinary Loss on Retirement of Bonds	2,456	
		Cash ($100,000 × 104%)		104,000

A gain would result if the company were able to purchase the bonds for a price less than the carrying value of $101,544.

CONVERSION OF BONDS INTO CAPITAL STOCK

A convertible bond permits the bondholder to exchange the bond for capital stock of the issuing company at the option of the bondholder. The terms of conversion, such as the *conversion ratio* (i.e., the number of shares received for each bond converted) and the conversion period or dates, must be specified in the bond agreement.

Objective 11: Recording the conversion of bonds

Convertible bonds are popular because they offer advantages to both issuer and investor. From the point of view of the investor, a convertible bond provides a fixed rate of return and the security of being a creditor of the firm, while at the same time allowing the option of converting the bonds into stock should conversion become attractive. The conversion option also gives the investor the opportunity to benefit from the price appreciation of the stock because the price of a convertible bond increases with increases in the market price of the underlying stock. To illustrate, assume that a firm issued a convertible bond, which can be exchanged for 50 shares of stock. If the market value of the firm's stock is $15 per share, the conversion feature makes the bonds worth $750 (50 shares × $15). However, the bond value may be more than $750. As a straight bond (i.e., without the conversion feature) it has a value equal to the present value of the future cash flows. If the market price of the stock increases to $25 per share, the bond would have a market price of approximately $1,250 since it could be converted into 50 shares of stock with a total market value of $1,250. An advantage to the issuing company is that the effective rate of interest is generally lower for convertible bonds than for nonconvertible bonds.

Up to the date of conversion, convertible bonds are accounted for in the same way as nonconvertible bonds. If the bonds are converted, the carrying value of the debt is transferred to paid-in capital accounts. For example, assume that $100,000 par value bonds were issued by Mountain Corporation, and that each $1,000 bond is convertible into 30 shares of $10 par value capital stock. Bondholders elect to convert 50 bonds

[5]*Statement of Financial Accounting Standards No. 4*, "Reporting Gains and Losses from Extinguishment of Debt" (Stamford, Conn.: FASB, 1975), par. 8.

after the interest payment has been made on June 30, 1994. The unamortized premium on this date is $1,544. The portion related to the converted bonds is $772 ($1,544 × 50%). Fifteen hundred shares of capital stock are issued as computed here.

$$\begin{aligned} \text{Shares issued} &= \text{Conversion rate} \times \text{Number of bonds converted} \\ &= 30 \text{ shares per bond} \times 50 \text{ bonds} \\ &= 1{,}500 \text{ shares} \end{aligned}$$

The entry for the conversion is:

1994					
June	30	Bonds Payable ($100,000 × 50%)	50,000	
		Premium on Bonds Payable	772	
		Capital Stock — $10 par value		15,000
		Paid-in Capital in Excess of Par Value		35,772

Note that there *is no gain or loss recognized* on the transaction. The essence of this entry is to recognize the carrying value of the debt as the payment for the stock. Accordingly, the excess of the carrying value of the bonds ($50,772) over the par value of the capital stock ($15,000) is credited to Paid-in Capital in Excess of Par Value.

BOND SINKING FUND

Objective 12: Accounting for a bond sinking fund

When bonds mature, the issuing company must have sufficient cash available to pay their maturity value. Bond indentures often provide that periodic deposits must be made to a ***bond sinking fund*** during the life of the bonds. In other cases, management may decide to make voluntary deposits to accumulate the cash needed at the maturity date. Sinking fund deposits are usually made to a trustee, who invests the cash in income-earning securities. The periodic deposits, plus the earnings on the investments, accumulate until the bonds mature, at which time the trustee sells the investments and uses the proceeds to retire the bonds. Any deficiency in the fund is made up by an additional deposit by the issuing company. If there is an excess of cash in the fund, it is returned to the issuing company.

The amount of each periodic deposit depends on the rate of return earned from the investments. For example, assume that on January 1, 1992, Kline Corporation issued $2 million of five-year bonds and agreed to deposit with a trustee at the end of each year for the next five years $400,000 less the earnings made on the fund investments during the year. The initial deposit is recorded as follows.

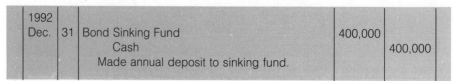

1992				
Dec.	31	Bond Sinking Fund	400,000	
		Cash		400,000
		Made annual deposit to sinking fund.		

Although the assets in the sinking fund are physically held by the trustee, they are still the property of Kline Corporation. The Bond Sinking Fund account is reported in Kline Corporation's balance sheet as a long-term investment, because the funds are not available for use in current operations.

The trustee will report the earnings on the investments each period to Kline Corporation. The entries at the end of 1993, assuming that earnings of $36,000 were reported by the trustee, are as follows.

1993				
Dec.	31	Bond Sinking Fund	36,000	
		Sinking Fund Revenue		36,000
		To record revenue earned from sinking fund investments.		
	31	Bond Sinking Fund	364,000	
		Cash		364,000
		Made annual deposit to sinking fund.		

Revenue earned from sinking fund investments is reported in the income statement in the Other Revenue and Expense section.

Similar entries are made at the end of each year for the remainder of the accumulation period. As the maturity date approaches, the trustee will sell the investments and will inform the company of any final deposit required to bring the accumulated balance up to the $2 million needed to retire the debt. The entry to record the bond retirement is:

1993				
Jan.	1	Bonds Payable	2,000,000	
		Bond Sinking Fund		2,000,000
		To record the payment of bonds at maturity.		

EFFECTIVE-INTEREST METHOD OF AMORTIZATION

As noted earlier, the effective-interest method is the preferred method for computing interest expense. However, the straight-line method is considered an acceptable alternative when the difference between the amortization amounts computed with both methods is not material. In order to contrast the two methods, the same data used earlier to illustrate the straight-line method of amortizing a discount or premium will now be used to illustrate the effective-interest method.

Objective 13: Amortization of bond discount or premium—effective interest method

AMORTIZATION OF A DISCOUNT: EFFECTIVE-INTEREST METHOD

The following facts are assumed for the bond issue of Hayden Corporation.

Date of issue	July 1, 1992
Par value	$100,000
Stated rate of interest	10%
Interest payment dates	June 30, December 31
Term to maturity	5 years
Date of maturity	June 30, 1997
Effective rate of interest	12%
Issue price to yield 12%	$ 92,641

The journal entry to record the bond issue is:

1992					
July	1	Cash		92,641	
		Discount on Bonds Payable		7,359	
		Bonds Payable			100,000
		Issued 5-year, 10% bonds at a discount.			

A discount amortization table for the Hayden Corporation bonds is presented in Figure 12-9. Amounts have been rounded to the nearest dollar. Under the effective-interest method, interest expense for each period (Column B) is computed as follows.

$$\begin{matrix} \text{Interest} \\ \text{Expense} \\ \text{per Period} \\ \text{(Column B)} \end{matrix} = \begin{matrix} \text{Carrying Value of} \\ \text{the Bonds at the} \\ \text{Beginning of the} \\ \text{Period} \\ \text{(Column A)} \end{matrix} \times \begin{matrix} \text{Effective} \\ \text{Rate} \\ \text{of} \\ \text{Interest} \end{matrix}$$

In this illustration, since interest is paid semiannually, a period is equal to six months. Since the bonds were issued to yield 12% annually, the semiannual effective interest rate is 6%. The semiannual interest payment (Column C), which remains constant over the life of the bonds, is.

$$\begin{aligned} \text{Cash Interest Payment} &= \text{Par Value} \times \text{Stated Interest Rate Per Period} \\ \$5,000 &= \$100,000 \times (10\% \div 2 \text{ periods per year}) \end{aligned}$$

The amount of the discount amortized each period (Column D) is

$$\begin{matrix} \text{Discount} \\ \text{Amortization} \\ \text{(Column D)} \end{matrix} = \begin{matrix} \text{Interest} \\ \text{Expense} \\ \text{(Column B)} \end{matrix} - \begin{matrix} \text{Semiannual Cash} \\ \text{Interest Payment} \\ \text{(Column C)} \end{matrix}$$

During the first six-month period (July 1–December 31, 1992), interest expense is $5,558 ($92,641 × .06), but only $5,000 was paid to the bondholders. The difference of $558 is the amount of the discount amortization for the period. The entry to record the payment and discount amortization is as follows.

Dec.	31	Interest Expense	5,558	
		Discount on Bonds Payable		558
		Cash		5,000
		Paid semiannual interest and amortized discount on 10% bonds.		

For the second six-month period, interest expense is the net liability at the beginning of the period (January 1, 1993) of $93,199 multiplied by 6%, or $5,592. Because the carrying value of the liability increased during the first period, the interest cost is greater in the second period. In subsequent periods, the interest expense increases as the carrying value increases.

Note that interest expense (Column B), as a percentage of the beginning carrying value (Column A), is a constant 6% each period. Although the bond indenture requires

Semiannual Interest Periods	(A) Carrying Value Beginning of Period (Col. G for previous period)	(B) Effective Semiannual Interest Expense (Col. A × .06)	(C) Semiannual Cash Payment ($100,000 × .05)	(D) Discount Amortization (Col. B − Col. C)	(E) Par Value	(F) Bond Discount Balance (Col. F for previous period − Col. D)	(G) Carrying Value—End of Period (Col. E − Col. F)
7/1/92					$100,000	$7,359	$ 92,641
12/31/92	$92,641	$ 5,558	$ 5,000	$ 558	100,000	6,801	93,199
6/30/93	93,199	5,592	5,000	592	100,000	6,209	93,791
12/31/93	93,791	5,627	5,000	627	100,000	5,582	94,418
6/30/94	94,418	5,665	5,000	665	100,000	4,917	95,083
12/31/94	95,083	5,705	5,000	705	100,000	4,212	95,788
6/30/95	95,788	5,747	5,000	747	100,000	3,465	96,535
12/31/95	96,535	5,792	5,000	792	100,000	2,673	97,327
6/30/96	97,327	5,840	5,000	840	100,000	1,833	98,167
12/31/96	98,167	5,890	5,000	890	100,000	943	99,057
6/30/97	99,057	5,943*	5,000	943	100,000	—	100,000
Totals		$57,359	$50,000	$7,359			

*In the last period, interest expense is equal to the semiannual interest paid plus the remaining balance in the bond discount column ($5,000 + $943 = $5,943). The carrying value at the beginning of the tenth interest period times 6% may not exactly equal this amount due to the accumulated effects of rounding errors.

Figure 12-9
Amortization Table for Bonds Issued at a Discount—Effective-Interest Method of Amortization

a semiannual interest payment of $5,000, the interest expense reported each period reflects the effective interest rate incurred by the firm.

AMORTIZATION OF A PREMIUM: EFFECTIVE-INTEREST METHOD

To illustrate the amortization of a bond premium, we assume that the Hayden Corporation bonds were issued for $108,115 to yield an effective annual interest rate of 8%, 4% per semiannual period. A premium amortization table for the Hayden Corporation bonds under the effective-interest method is given in Figure 12-10. The computations are based on the same concepts discussed earlier for the amortization of a discount. Note, however, that the amount of premium amortized each period decreases interest expense. Interest expense reported each period is the effective semiannual rate of 4% times the carrying value of the bonds at the beginning of the period.

The first interest payment is recorded as follows:

Dec.	31	Interest Expense	4,325	
		Premium on Bonds Payable	675	
		Cash		5,000
		Paid semiannual interest and amortized premium on 10% bonds.		

Over the life of the bonds, the interest expense debit decreases with a corresponding increase in the debit to the premium account. This results because the carrying value of the bonds is decreasing each period as the premium is reduced through amortization.

Semiannual Interest Periods	(A) Carrying Value Beginning of Period (Col. G for previous period)	(B) Effective Semiannual Interest Expense (Col. A × .04)	(C) Semiannual Cash Payment ($100,000 × .05)	(D) Premium Amortization (Col. B − Col. C)	(E) Par Value	(F) Bond Premium Balance (Col. F for previous period − Col. D)	(G) Carrying Value—End of Period (Col. E + Col. F)
7/1/92					$100,000	$8,115	$108,115
12/31/92	$108,115	$ 4,325	$ 5,000	$ 675	100,000	7,440	107,440
6/30/93	107,440	4,298	5,000	702	100,000	6,738	106,738
12/31/93	106,738	4,270	5,000	730	100,000	6,008	106,008
6/30/94	106,008	4,240	5,000	760	100,000	5,248	105,248
12/31/94	105,248	4,210	5,000	790	100,000	4,458	104,458
6/30/95	104,458	4,178	5,000	822	100,000	3,636	103,636
12/31/95	103,636	4,145	5,000	855	100,000	2,781	102,781
6/30/96	102,781	4,111	5,000	889	100,000	1,892	101,892
12/31/96	101,892	4,076	5,000	924	100,000	968	100,968
6/30/97	100,968	4,032*	5,000	968	100,000	—	100,000
Totals		$41,885	$50,000	$8,115			

*In the last period, interest expense is equal to the semiannual interest paid less the remaining balance in the bond premium account ($5,000 − $968). The carrying value at the beginning of the tenth period times 4% may not exactly equal this amount due to the accumulated effects of rounding errors.

Figure 12-10
Amortization Table for Bonds Issued at a Premium—Effective Interest Method of Amortization

LONG-TERM NOTES PAYABLE

Companies often issue long-term notes payable to obtain resources to finance the acquisition of operating assets. As defined in Chapter 11, a note payable is an unconditional promise to pay a sum of money on demand or at a future determinable date. Long-term unsecured notes and mortgages are normally issued when money is borrowed from one or a few lending institutions, such as banks or insurance companies. Long-term notes are also frequently issued for a shorter period of time and/or issued to borrow smaller amounts of money than when bonds are issued. Smaller companies generally use notes rather than bonds whereas a large company may issue both.

Long-term notes may take various forms. In one common form, the note requires periodic interest payments with the principal payable in full at maturity. Another common form provides that both the interest and principal must be paid in installments. This latter type of note is often used by consumers to finance the purchase of a home or an automobile. Both types of notes may be unsecured, but frequently, when a company borrows money to finance the purchase of plant assets, a promissory note secured by a legal document, called a mortgage, is given to the lender or seller. The **mortgage** is a secured claim against specific property of the borrower. The promissory note given is called a **mortgage note payable**. If the debt is not paid, the mortgage holder may have the specific property sold and the proceeds applied to payment of the debt. An **unsecured note payable** is a promissory note that is backed by a legal claim against the borrower's general assets.

Long-term notes are generally accounted for using the effective-interest method. Thus, their accounting is essentially the same as illustrated above for bonds payable.

COMPREHENSIVE ILLUSTRATION OF REPORTING LIABILITIES

In this and the preceding chapters, various types of current and long-term liabilities were discussed. Although the terminology used and the amount of detail provided vary considerably in practice, Figure 12-11 shows one possible presentation of the liability section of the balance sheet. Additional information, such as interest rates, maturity dates, minimum cash payments, and restrictions, is presented in footnotes. The annual reports presented in an Appendix to this book contain illustrations of such footnote disclosures.

SUMMARY

Accounting for bonds payable and long-term notes payable was discussed in this chapter. One reason a firm issues long-term debt is to increase the return to its stockholders by earning a return on the funds borrowed that is greater than the fixed interest paid to the debtholders. Debt also has an advantage over stock because interest paid is tax deductible.

Long-term debt is measured by the present value of the future cash outflows. The issue price of a bond varies inversely with changes in the market interest rate as

Figure 12-11
Liability Section of Balance Sheet

Liabilities and Stockholders' Equity	
Current liabilities:	
Notes payable to banks	$100,000
Accounts payable	62,000
Current maturities of long-term liabilities	10,000
Bank overdraft	4,500
Accrued liabilities:	
Salaries, wages, and employee benefits	10,200
Property and payroll taxes	4,800
Interest	5,400
Other	2,500
Federal and state income taxes payable	6,700
Cash dividends payable	4,300
Advance deposits received from customers	2,800
Total current liabilities	213,200
Long-term liabilities:	
Notes and bonds payable, net of current maturities	140,000
7% convertible subordinated debentures	100,000
Obligations under capital leases	31,500
Deferred income taxes	18,400
Accrued pension costs, not to be funded currently	7,200
Total long-term liabilities	297,100
Total liabilities	510,300
Stockholders' Equity	

summarized below:

Issue Price	Relationship of Stated Rate to Market Rate
Bond issued at par value	Stated rate = market rate
Bond issued at a discount	Stated rate < market rate
Bond issued at a premium	Stated rate > market rate

A discount or premium is amortized as an adjustment to interest expense over the life of the debt instrument. As a result, the carrying value of the liability in the balance sheet will approach its face value as the maturity date approaches.

There are two methods used to amortize a premium or discount: straight-line and the effective-interest method. The effective-interest method is preferred because the interest expense reported each period is based on the constant rate of interest applied to the carrying value of the debt.

A number of other issues related to the accounting for bonds and long-term notes were also addressed, including:

1. Accounting for bonds issued between interest payment dates;
2. Year-end adjusting entry for bond interest expense;
3. Retirement of bonds before maturity;
4. Conversion of bonds into capital stock;
5. Accounting for a bond sinking fund; and
6. The effective interest method of amortization.

SELF-TEST

Test your understanding of the chapter by selecting the best answer for each of the following.

1. A 10% bond is sold at a price that will result in an 11% effective (market) rate. Therefore, we can conclude that the price at which the bond was sold was:
   a. greater than par value.
   b. less than par value.
   c. equal to par value.
   d. not determinable from the above information.

2. In computing the market price of a bond, the future cash payments are discounted using the:
   a. stated rate of interest.
   b. the rate of interest printed on the bond certificate.
   c. effective (yield) rate desired by investors.
   d. coupon rate.

3. The account "Discount on Bonds Payable" appears:
   a. on the income statement as an expense.
   b. on the balance sheet as an asset.
   c. on the balance sheet as a reduction of a liability.
   d. on the balance sheet as an increase of a liability.

Use the following information for the next two questions. Myler Corporation issued $100,000, 6%, 10-year bonds for $112,000. The bonds are dated March 1, 1992, and were issued on March 1, 1992. Interest payment dates are August 31 and February 28.

4. The entry to record the issuance of the bonds would include:
   a. a credit to Bonds Payable for $112,000.
   b. a credit to Cash for $112,000.
   c. a credit to Premium on Bonds Payable for $12,000.
   d. a debit to Discount on Bonds Payable for $12,000.

5. On August 31, 1992, the entry to record the payment of interest (assuming straight-line amortization) would include:
   a. a debit to Interest Expense for $2,400.
   b. a debit to Premium on Bonds Payable for $1,200.
   c. a credit to Premium on Bonds Payable for $600.
   d. a credit to Cash for $3,600.

6. A bond is purchased at a discount. What will happen to the net carrying value of the bond on the balance sheet as its maturity date approaches?
   a. Increases.
   b. Stays the same.
   c. Decreases.
   d. Cannot be determined from the data given.

7. The interest rate that determines the amount of interest paid periodically over the life of the bond to the bondholders is called:
   a. the market rate.
   b. the stated rate.
   c. the coupon rate.
   d. both b and c.

8. Debenture bonds are the same as:
   a. registered bonds.
   b. secured bonds.
   c. unsecured bonds.
   d. term bonds.

9. If a company sells bonds at a discount instead of at par, the interest expense is:
   a. increased.
   b. reduced.
   c. unaffected.
   d. none of the above.

10. When a long-term liability matures in the next accounting period:
    a. the amount of the debt must be switched to the current liabilities category.
    b. footnote disclosure is required indicating that the long-term liability matures in the next period.
    c. the amount of the debt is reported as a long-term liability.
    d. the amount of the debt is switched to the current liability category unless the bondholders are to be paid from assets classified as noncurrent assets.

11. For the issuer of a 10-year bond, the amount of amortization using the effective-interest method would increase each year if the bond were sold at a:

	Discount	Premium
a.	No	No
b.	Yes	Yes
c.	No	Yes
d.	Yes	No

12. When using the effective-interest method of amortizing a bond discount or premium, the periodic interest expense is equal to:
    a. the stated rate of interest multiplied by the carrying value at the beginning of the period.
    b. the effective interest rate multiplied by the carrying value at the beginning of the period.
    c. the stated rate of interest multiplied by the par value of the bonds.
    d. the effective interest rate multiplied by the par value of the bonds.

REVIEW PROBLEM

In order to raise funds to construct a new plant, Magill Corporation's management decided to issue bonds. The proposed bond indenture was submitted to the board of directors and approved. The provisions of the bond indenture specified the issuance of $5 million par value bonds dated March 1, 1992. The bonds contain a stated interest rate of 10% per annum and pay interest semiannually on August 31 and February 28 of each year. The bonds are 10-year bonds and mature on March 1, 2002.

The bonds were sold on July 1, 1992 at 88.864 plus accrued interest. This price approximates a 12% rate of return for the bond investors. Magill Corporation's annual accounting period ends on December 31.

Required:

A. How much cash did Magill Corporation receive on July 1, 1992 from the sale of the bonds?
B. How much is the discount on the bonds payable. Over how many months should it be amortized?
C. Using straight-line amortization, compute the amount of the discount amortization per month and for each six-month interest period.
D. Prepare the journal entry on July 1, 1992 to record the sale and issuance of the bonds payable.
E. Prepare the journal entry on August 31, 1992 to record the first interest payment and amortization of the discount.
F. Prepare the required adjusting journal entry on December 31, 1992, the end of the accounting period.
G. Prepare the journal entry on February 28, 1993 to record the second interest payment and amortization of the discount.
H. Show how the bond interest expense, bond interest payable and the bonds payable would be reported on Magill's financial statements at December 31, 1992.

ANSWER TO REVIEW PROBLEM

A.　　Cash received by Magill Corporation on July 1, 1992.
　　　Sale price of bonds:
　　　　($5,000,000 × 88.864%)　　　　　　　　　　　　　　　$4,443,200
　　　Add accrued interest for four months
　　　　(March 1 to June 30) ($5,000,000 × 10% × 4/12)　　　　166,667*
　　　　　Total cash received for bonds　　　　　　　　　　　$4,609,867

　　　*Rounded to nearest dollar

B. Discount to be amortized:
  ($5,000,000 − $4,443,200) $ 556,800
  Months to amortize discount:
  (12 months × 10 years)–4 months   116 months

C. Discount amortization per month:
  ($556,800/116 months) $ 4,800
  Discount amortization per six-month interest
  period: ($4,800 × 6 months) $ 28,800

D. Journal entry on July 1, 1992 to record sale and issuance of bonds payable:

July	1	Cash–(from requirement A)	4,609,867	
		Discount on Bonds Payable (from		
		requirement B)	556,800	
		Interest Expense (from requirement A)		166,667
		Bonds Payable		5,000,000

E. Journal entry on August 31, 1992 to record first interest payment:

Aug.	31	Interest Expense	259,600	
		Discount on Bonds Payable		
		($4,800 × 2 months)		9,600
		Cash ($5,000,000 × 10% × 6/12)		250,000

F. Adjusting entry on December 31, 1992:

Dec.	31	Interest Expense	185,867	
		Discount on Bonds Payable		
		($4,800 × 4 months)		19,200
		Interest Payable		
		($5,000,000 × 10% × 4/12)		166,667*
		*Rounded to nearest dollar		

G. Journal entry on February 28, 1993 to record second interest payment:

Feb.	28	Interest Expense	92,933	
		Interest Payable	166,667	
		Discount on Bonds Payable		
		($4,800 × 2 months)		9,600
		Cash ($5,000,000 × 10% × 6/12)		250,000

H. Income Statement for 1992:

  Other revenue and expense:
  Interest expense $ 278,800

  Balance Sheet as of December 31, 1992:

  Current liabilities:
  Interest payable $ 166,667

  Long-term liabilities:
  Bond payable, 10% (due March 1, 2002) $5,000,000
  Less: Unamortized discount on bonds
  payable   528,000 $4,472,000

ANSWERS TO SELF-TEST

1. b   **2.** c   **3.** c   **4.** c   **5.** a   **6.** a   **7.** d   **8.** c
9. a   **10.** d   **11.** b   **12.** b

GLOSSARY

BOND (BOND PAYABLE).   A certificate containing a written promise to pay the principal amount at a specified time plus interest on the principal at a specified rate per period (p. 524).

BOND SINKING FUND.   An investment fund established to provide for the retirement of bonds (p. 529).

CALLABLE BOND.   A bond that may be purchased before the bond matures at the option of the issuing company for a specified price stated in the indenture (p. 529).

CARRYING VALUE.   The par value of a bond issue less any unamortized discount or plus any unamortized premium (p. 536).

COLLATERAL.   Something of value that is acceptable to a lender as security for a loan (p. 528).

CONVERTIBLE BOND.   A bond that may be converted into capital stock of the issuing company (p. 529).

COUPON BOND (BEARER BOND).   A bond that has a printed interest coupon attached for each interest payment date. Title is assumed to be with the holder of the bond (p. 529).

COUPON RATE (NOMINAL RATE; CONTRACT RATE; STATED RATE). The interest rate stated as a percentage of par value and used to determine the amount paid periodically to the bondholder (p. 524).

DEBENTURE BOND (UNSECURED BOND).   A bond backed only by the general credit rating of the issuing company (p. 528).

DISCOUNT.   The excess of the par value of a bond over its sale price (p. 526).

EFFECTIVE RATE (YIELD RATE).   The actual rate of interest an investor will earn if bonds are purchased at a certain price and held to maturity (p. 532).

FINANCIAL LEVERAGE.   The use of borrowed funds to earn a higher rate of return than paid on the borrowed funds for the purpose of increasing the earnings of the owners (p. 526).

INDENTURE.   The terms of a bond agreement contained in a contract between the borrower and the bondholder (p. 525).

MATURITY DATE.   The date on which the borrower must pay the maturity value of a note or bond (p. 524).

MORTGAGE.   A legal document setting forth the specific assets serving as collateral for a loan (p. 550).

MORTGAGE NOTE PAYABLE.   A form of a promissory note in which specific property of the borrower serves as collateral for a loan (p. 550).

PAR VALUE (FACE VALUE; PRINCIPAL; MATURITY VALUE).   The amount due to a lender when a debt matures (p. 524).

PREMIUM.   The excess of the sale price of a bond over its par value (p. 526).

REGISTERED BOND.   A bond whose owner's name is on file with the issuing firm (p. 529).

SECURED BOND (MORTGAGE BOND).   A bond secured by a prior claim against specific property of the issuing company (p. 528).

SERIAL BONDS.   A bond issue that matures in installments (p. 529).
TERM BONDS.   A bond issue in which all of the bonds mature on one date (p. 529).
TRUSTEE.   A third party appointed to represent the bondholders (p. 526).
UNDERWRITER.   An investment firm that markets a bond issue (p. 525).
UNSECURED NOTE PAYABLE.   A promissory note backed by a legal claim against the general assets of the borrower (p. 550).

DISCUSSION QUESTIONS

1. What is a bond? Who normally issues bonds?
2. What terms can be used to describe the specified rate of interest paid on the par value of bonds? How often are bond interest payments normally made?
3. What is default as it relates to bonds payable? What could happen to a borrower as a result of the issuing company defaulting on a bond issue?
4. Explain the role an underwriter plays in the sale of bonds. What evidence does an investor have of ownership of a bond?
5. What is a bond indenture? What types of information are found in a bond indenture?
6. How are bond prices quoted on the stock exchanges? If a $1,000 bond is quoted at 99⅜, what amount is it selling for? If the same bond was later quoted at 103¾, what is its selling price? Which bond is selling at a premium? a discount? What is the amount of the premium in dollars? What is the amount of the discount in dollars?
7. Define financial leverage. When is debt financing advantageous to a firm? Under what conditions is debt financing unfavorable?
8. Explain the difference between:
    a.   secured (mortgage) bonds and debenture (unsecured) bonds.
    b.   term bonds and serial bonds.
9. Generally, bonds are reported as a long-term liability until the maturity date is within one year or the next operating cycle. What conditions result in an exception to this reporting rule?
10. An issuer of bonds generally establishes a stated rate of interest approximately equal to the market rate when the bonds will be issued. Why are bonds then issued at a premium or a discount?
11. Define amortization of discount or premium on bonds payable. What effect does amortization of a discount have on interest expense? What is the effect of amortization of a premium on interest expense? Explain why the amortization of a premium or discount affects interest expense.
12. What must a company that issues bonds do at the end of its fiscal year if its fiscal year-end and the interest payment date on the bonds do not coincide? Why?
13. Why would a company that has issued bonds want to call them in for redemption before their maturity date? If there is a material difference between the call price of the bonds and the bonds' carrying value, how is this difference reported on the financial statements?
14. Where would the owner of a bond look to determine if the bond he/she owns is convertible? Why is the conversion feature of a bond a desirable feature for the investor? What advantage does a convertible bond give to the issuer?
15. What is a mortgage?

EXERCISES

(For the exercises and problems in this chapter, round all computations to the nearest dollar.)

Exercise 12-1 Fill in the Blank—Terms and Concepts
A number of statements are given below.

1. On the _____ _____ the issuer of a bond must pay the par value of the bonds to the bondholders.
2. A $1,000 par value bond with a stated rate of interest of 12% will pay $_____ semiannually for the term of the bond.
3. The terms of the agreement between the issuer and the holder of a bond are contained in a certificate or document called the bond _____ .
4. Bonds are quoted on the securities exchanges as a percentage of par value. A bond that is issued at par value is quoted at _____ .
5. A $1,000 face value bond quoted at 103⅝ is selling for $ _____ .
6. The amount of the issue price in excess of the par value is called a _____ .
7. If the market interest rate is 12% and the bond's stated interest rate is 10%, the bonds will be issued at a _____ .
8. The amount of unamortized discount is reported in the _____ _____ as a(n) _____ from the par value of the bonds to show the _____ value of the debt.
9. The carrying value of bonds issued at a premium will (increase or decrease) _____ over the life of the bonds.

Required:
Complete each statement by entering a word in the blank space which will make the statement a true statement.

Exercise 12-2 Alternative Financing Arrangements
Pinewood Company was formed by the issuance of 100,000 shares of $5 par value capital stock for $500,000. Annual earnings before income taxes average $100,000. The firm needs to raise $600,000 to finance a planned plant expansion. Management estimates that after the expansion the firm will have average earnings, before any new interest and income taxes of $170,000. Two alternatives are being discussed: (1) issue 60,000 shares of $5 par value capital stock, or (2) issue 10% bonds. The bonds are expected to be issued at par value, but the company's capital stock is currently selling for $10 per share. The relevant income tax rate is 40%.

Required:
A. Prepare a schedule that shows:
   1. the current net income and earnings per share, and
   2. the net income and earnings per share that would result under each of the alternatives being considered.
B. Which alternative would probably be preferred by the current stockholders? Why?

Exercise 12-3 Matching—Bond Features and Definitions
A list of types of bond indentures is given next.

1. Mortgage bonds
2. Coupon bonds
3. Term bonds
4. Callable bonds
5. Registered bonds
6. Debenture bonds
7. Serial bonds
8. Convertible bonds

Each of the following statements describe a type of bond issue.

_____ **A.** Bearer paper where the bondholder detaches a coupon, endorses it, and presents it to a bank for collection.
_____ **B.** Matures in installments on a series of specified dates.
_____ **C.** May be canceled before maturity by the issuing company by paying a call price.
_____ **D.** Specific assets of the firm serve as collateral for the bond.
_____ **E.** The bondholder's name and address is on file with the issuing company or the trustee.
_____ **F.** Bondholders rely on the general credit rating of the issuing company.
_____ **G.** The bond may be exchanged for common stock at the option of the bondholder.
_____ **H.** The entire bond issue matures on one date.

Required:
Match the type of bond with its description by placing the code number in the blank preceding the description.

Exercise 12-4   Matching Terms with Definitions
A number of terms or concepts discussed in this chapter are given below followed by a list of statements describing each term.

Terms and Concepts

1. Amortization of bond discount or premium
2. Bond indenture
3. Carrying value
4. Discount
5. Effective-interest method
6. Market or effective rate of interest
7. Mortgage
8. Premium
9. Stated rate
10. Straight-line method
11. Maturity date

Statements

_____ **A.** The par value of a bond issue less any unamortized discount or plus any unamortized premium.
_____ **B.** A promissory note that is backed by a legal claim against the borrower's specific assets.
_____ **C.** The excess of the issue price of a bond over its par value.
_____ **D.** The actual rate of interest an investor will earn if bonds are purchased at a certain price and held to maturity.
_____ **E.** The process of allocating a bond discount or premium to interest expense over the period the bonds are outstanding.
_____ **F.** A method for amortizing a bond discount or premium in which an equal amount of discount or premium is allocated to interest expense each period.
_____ **G.** The amount by which the par value of a bond exceeds its issue price.
_____ **H.** The date on which the borrower must pay the par value of a bond to a bondholder.

_____ **I.** The interest rate stated as a percentage of par value and used to determine the amount paid periodically to a bondholder.

_____ **J.** A contract between the issuer of a bond and the bondholder.

_____ **K.** A method for amortizing a bond discount or premium in which the amount of the amortization is the difference between the stated interest and the effective-interest computed by multiplying the carrying value of the bonds by the market rate of interest at the time of issue.

Required:
Match the appropriate term or concept to its description by placing the code number in the blank preceding each statement.

Exercise 12-5 Bonds Issued at Par

On July 1, 1992, Nelson Corporation issued $100,000 par value, five-year, 11% bonds at 100. Nelson's fiscal year-end is December 31.

Required:
A. Prepare the journal entry on July 1, 1992 to record the issue of the bonds.

B. Compute the total interest expense to be recognized over the period the bonds are outstanding.

C. Assuming interest is paid semiannually on June 30 and December 31, prepare the journal entry that will be made each June 30 and December 31 during the period the bonds are outstanding.

D. Prepare the journal entry to record the retirement of the bonds on their maturity date.

Exercise 12-6 Determination of Selling Price of Bonds

Management of KC Company is considering the issue of $300,000 face value, 8%, five-year bonds. The bonds are to be dated July 1, 1992, and provide for semiannual interest payments.

Required:
Assuming that the bonds are issued on July 1, compute the issue price of the bonds for each of the following three situations.

1. The market rate of interest is 8%.
2. The market rate of interest is 10%.
3. The market rate of interest is 6%.

Exercise 12-7 Bonds Issued at a Discount—Straight-line Method of Amortization

The following information relates to a bond issue of Rupp Company dated January 1, 1992.

Date issued	January 1, 1992
Par value	$300,000
Stated interest rate	9%
Interest payment dates	June 30 and December 31
Term to maturity	10-year
Cash received for the issue	$287,400

The company's fiscal year-end is December 31 and it uses the straight-line method to amortize bond discounts and premiums.

Required:

A. Prepare journal entries to record:
  1. the issuance of the bonds.
  2. the June 30, 1992 interest payment.
  3. the December 31, 1992 interest payment.
B. Compute the interest expense to be reported in the income statement for the year ended December 31, 1992, and prepare the entry to close the Interest Expense account to the Income Summary account.
C. Compute the total interest expense to be reported over the life of the bonds. Use this information to verify the amount computed in requirement (B).
D. Show how the bonds will be reported on a balance sheet prepared January 1, 1992 and one prepared December 31, 1992.
E. What is the relationship (less than, greater than, or equal to) between the stated interest rate and the effective rate of interest?

Exercise 12-8   Bonds Issued at a Premium—Straight-line Method of Amortization

Use the information given in Exercise 12-7 except that the bonds were issued by Rupp Company for $323,600.

Required:

Complete requirements (A) through (E) as given in Exercise 12-7.

Exercise 12-9   Bonds Issued Between Interest Payment Dates

On April 1, 1992, Foxfire Corporation issued $300,000 face value, ten-year, 9% bonds, dated January 1, 1992. The bonds were issued for $296,490 plus accrued interest. Interest is paid semiannually on June 30 and December 31. The company's fiscal year ends on December 31 and it uses the straight-line method to amortize bond discounts and premiums.

Required:

A. Prepare the journal entry on April 1, 1992 to record the issue of the bonds.
B. Prepare the journal entries on June 30 and December 31, 1992 to record the interest payments.
C. Open an Interest Expense account and post the entries to the account.
D. Prepare a schedule to verify the interest expense for 1992.
E. Compute the carrying value of the debt to be reported on the December 31, 1992 balance sheet.

Exercise 12-10   Adjusting Entry to Accrue Bond Interest Expense

On April 1, 1992, Spencer Company issued $1,000,000 of 8%, 10-year bonds for $1,050,000. The bonds are dated April 1, 1992. Interest is payable on March 31 and September 30. The fiscal year of the company is the calendar year, and the company uses the straight-line method of amortization.

Required:

Prepare journal entries to record the following transactions.

1. Issue of the bonds on April 1, 1992.
2. The interest payment on September 30, 1992.
3. Accrual of interest and amortization of the premium on December 31, 1992.
4. Payment of interest and amortization of the premium on March 31, 1993.

Exercise 12-11   Early Retirement and Conversion of Bonds Payable

The long-term liabilities section of Kingston Company's December 31, 1992 balance sheet appears as follows.

Long-term liabilities:		
9% Convertible bonds		$400,000
Less: Unamortized discount		7,200
		$392,800

Required:

A. Assume that on January 1, 1993, Kingston Company retires the bonds by purchasing them on the open market for $376,200. Prepare the journal entry to record the early retirement of the bonds.

B. Assume instead, that on January 1, 1993, the bondholders elect to convert their bonds to Kingston's capital stock. Each $1,000 bond may be converted to 50 shares of $5 par value capital stock. Prepare the journal entry to record the conversion of the bonds to stock.

Exercise 12-12   Accounting for a Bond Sinking Fund

Eden Corporation has a $500,000 par value bond issue outstanding that is due on December 31, 1995. On December 31, 1992, Eden Corporation decides to establish a bond sinking fund by making four equal deposits of $110,960 to a savings account. The first deposit is to be made on December 31, 1992. It is expected that the fund will earn 8% interest, which will be added to the fund balance at each year-end.

Required:

A. Complete the following bond sinking fund accumulation schedule based on an 8% rate of return. Round all calculations to the nearest dollar.

Date	Cash Deposit	Interest Revenue	Sinking Fund Increase	Accumulated Sinking Fund Balance
12/31/92	$110,960	$_____	$_____	$_____
12/31/93	_____	_____	_____	_____
12/31/94	_____	_____	_____	_____
12/31/95	_____	_____	_____	_____

B. Prepare journal entries to record each of the following transactions.
  1. The first deposit made to the sinking fund on December 31, 1992.
  2. On December 31, 1993, it is determined that the sinking fund investments earned $8,877 during the year.
  3. The second deposit made to the sinking fund on December 31, 1993.
  4. On December 31, 1995, the accumulated balance in the sinking fund is $501,750. The money is used to retire the bonds and the balance is returned to the Cash account.

C. How was the annual deposit amount of $110,960 computed?

D. Discuss how the bonds should be reported in the balance sheet prepared on December 31, 1993.

Exercise 12-13   Effective-Interest Method of Amortizing a Discount

The Davison Corporation issued $100,000 par value, 3-year, 10% bonds on January 1, 1992 for $95,087. Interest is paid on June 30 and December 31. The market rate of interest is 12%. Davison uses the effective-interest method to amortize bond discounts and premiums and its fiscal year ends on December 31.

Required:
A. Verify the issue price of the bonds.
B. Prepare the journal entry to record the issue of the bonds on January 1, 1992.
C. Prepare an amortization table.
D. Prepare the general journal entry to record the payment of interest and the amortization of the discount on June 30, 1992.

Exercise 12-14   Effective-Interest Method of Amortizing a Premium
Use the information given in Exercise 12-13, except that the bonds were issued for $105,241 to yield 8%.

Required:
Complete requirements as given in Exercise 12-13.

Exercise 12-15   Long-term Notes Payable—Principal Paid at Maturity
SIU Company borrowed $100,000 from a local bank on March 1, 1992. Interest, at an annual rate of 10%, is payable semiannually on August 31 and February 28, with the principal amount due on February 28, 1995. The company's fiscal year ends on December 31.

Required:
A. Prepare the journal entry on March 1, 1992 to record the borrowing.
B. Prepare the journal entry on August 31, 1992 to record the first interest payment.
C. Prepare the adjusting entry on December 31, 1992.
D. Assume the Company does not prepare reversing entries. Prepare the journal entry to record the interest payment on February 28, 1993.

PROBLEMS

Problem 12-1   Alternative Financing Options
Charger Corporation was formed by the issuance of 200,000 shares of $5 par value capital stock. The company's net income before taxes has averaged $300,000 during the last three years and it has incurred no interest cost. The company recently purchased land for development of a truck stop. After the purchase of the land, a government agency announced the construction of an interstate highway that will be adjacent to the company's property and will link two major cities. The price of the company's capital stock increased to $10 per share as a result of the increase in value of the property and expectations regarding the activities of the truck stop. Because of the freeway, management decided to expand the project and exercise an option on adjacent property. To do so, the company needs $1,000,000 additional cash. Management estimates that annual average earnings after the truck stop is operating will be $500,000 before interest and income taxes. The $1,000,000 can be raised from one of two plans currently under consideration: (1) sell 100,000 shares of its $5 par value capital stock for $10 per share; or (2) issue 1,000 bonds with a face value of $1,000 and an interest rate of 12%, the expected market rate of interest. The company's effective income tax rate is 30%.

Required:

A. Compute the earnings per share on the current level of net income.

B. Assuming management is able to achieve its estimated level of income, prepare a schedule illustrating the effects of the two plans on the company's:

    1. net income, and

    2. earnings per share.

C. If you currently own shares of the company's capital stock, which plan would you prefer? State the reasons for your answer.

D. Now assume that after the cash was received from the new financing, the country entered into a recessionary period. As a result the company was able to produce income of $200,000 before interest and taxes. Repeat requirement (B) for this level of income.

Problem 12-2 **Computing the Issue Price of Bonds and Recording the Issue**

A company plans to issue $100,000 of par value bonds on January 1, 1992. The stated rate of interest is 10% payable semiannually on June 30 and December 31. The bonds mature in 10 years. Management received three forecasts of the market rate of interest. These forecasted rates were 10%, 12%, and 8%.

Required:

A. For each of the forecasted rates:

    1. Compute the issue price of the bonds.

    2. Record the issuance of the bonds.

    3. Show how the bonds will be reported on the balance sheet at the date of issue.

    4. Compute the total interest expense for the 10-year period.

    5. Assuming the straight-line method of amortization, compute the interest expense for each annual period.

B. Assuming that the bonds were issued for $70,541, compute the market rate of interest.

Problem 12-3 **Bonds Issued at a Discount—Straight-line Method of Amortization**

On January 1, 1992, Parker Corporation issued $400,000 in par value, 12%, 10-year bonds for $394,600. Interest is paid semiannually on June 30 and December 31. Parker's fiscal year also ends on December 31.

Required:

A. Prepare the journal entry to record the sale of the bonds.

B. Show how the bonds would be presented on a balance sheet prepared immediately after the bonds were issued.

C. Prepare the journal entry that will be made each June 30 and December 31 to record payment of the semiannual bond interest. The company uses the straight-line method to amortize bond discounts and premiums and records the amortization each interest payment date.

D. Show how the bonds would be presented on the December 31, 1992 balance sheet. Why is this presentation different from the one prepared in requirement (B)?

E. Prepare the journal entry on December 31, 2001 to record the semiannual interest payment and retirement of the bonds.

F. What is the total cash interest paid over the 10-year life of the bonds?

G. What is the total interest expense reported over the 10-year life of the bonds?

H. Why are the answers to requirements (F) and (G) different? What is the dollar amount of the difference? What is the dollar difference between the total cash interest paid and the total interest expense equal to?

Problem 12-4   Bonds Issued at a Premium—Straight-line Method of Amortization

Use the information given in Problem 12-3 except that the bonds were issued for $405,400.

Required:

Complete the requirements as given in Problem 12-3.

Problem 12-5   Bonds Issued at a Discount—Straight-line Method of Amortization

On January 1, 1992, Stevens Corporation issued a five-year bond indenture with a par value of $700,000, and a stated interest rate of 9%. The bonds were sold for $672,964 to yield a return of 10% to the investors. The bonds pay interest semi-annually on June 30 and December 31, which also is the end of Steven's fiscal year. Stevens Corporation uses the straight-line method to amortize bond discounts and premiums.

Required:

A. Verify the selling price of the bond issue.

B. Prepare the journal entries to:
1. record the sale and issuance of the bonds.
2. record the bond interest payment and amortization of the bond discount on June 30, 1992.
3. record the bond interest payment and amortization of the bond discount on December 31, 1992.

C. Compute the interest expense to be reported in the income statement for the year ended December 31, 1992, and prepare the entry to close the Interest Expense account to the Income Summary account.

D. Compute the total cash interest Stevens will pay over the five-year life of the bonds.

E. Compute the total interest expense Stevens will recognize over the five-year life of the bonds. Use the information to verify the interest expense recorded in requirement (C).

F. Explain the reason for the difference between your answers for requirements (D) and (E) above.

G. Show how the bonds would be presented on a balance sheet prepared on December 31, 1992 and one prepared on December 31, 1993.

Problem 12-6   Impact of Alternative Selling Price on Bonds Payable

Becker Corporation authorized an $800,000, 10-year bond issue dated July 1, 1992. The stated rate of interest on the bond issue is 9%. Interest is paid semiannually on June 30 and December 31. Becker ends its fiscal year on December 31. Assume the bonds were issued on July 1, 1992, for the three different prices listed below.

1. Bonds were issued at par value.
2. Bonds were issued at 97.
3. Bonds were issued at 103.

Required:

Complete the schedule shown below for the three different assumptions relating to the issue price of the bonds. Assume straight-line amortization of the premium or discount. Show supporting computations in good form.

95 %

		Case 1 Par	Case 2 97	Case 3 103
760,000	1. Total cash received on the date of issue.	$ 800000	$ 776000	$ 824000
40,000	2. Amount of premium or discount on the date of issue.	0	24000 Disc.	24000 PREM
760000	3. Carrying value on the date of issue.	800000	776000	824000
9b	4. Stated interest rate (annual).	9 %	9 %	9 %
36000	5. Cash interest paid during 1992.	$ 36000	$ 36000	$ 36000
38000	6. Interest expense reported on the 1992 income statement.	36000	37200	34800
2000	7. The amount of discount or premium amortized during 1992.	0	1200	1200
800,000	8. The balance reported in the Bonds Payable account on December 31, 1992.	800000	800000	800000
38000	9. The unamortized premium or discount on December 31, 1992.	0	22,800	22800
762000	10. Carrying value on December 31, 1992.	800000	777,200	822800
2000	11. Change in the carrying value between July 1 and December 31.	0	1200	1200

Problem 12-7 Bonds Issued Between Interest Payment Dates and Accrual of Interest Expense

Dobson Corporation was authorized to issue $500,000, 9%, five-year bonds dated February 1, 1992. Interest is payable on January 31 and July 31. On March 1, 1992, Dobson Corporation issued $300,000 of the par value bonds at 98 plus accrued interest. On April 1, 1992, $200,000 of the bonds were issued at 96 plus accrued interest. The fiscal year-end for Dobson Corporation is December 31, and the company uses the straight-line method to amortize a bond discount or premium.

Required:

A. Compute the amount that the company will receive on March 1 and April 1.
B. Compute the discount amortization per month for each of the issues.
C. Prepare general journal entries to record the following transactions.
   1. Issuance of the bonds on March 1.
   2. Issuance of the bonds on April 1.
   3. First interest payment on July 31.
   4. Accrued interest on December 31, 1992.
   5. The interest payment on January 31, 1993.
D. Compute the amount of interest expense to be reported in the income statement for the 1992 fiscal year.
E. Compute the carrying value of the debt to be reported on the December 31, 1992 balance sheet.

Problem 12-8 Issue of Bonds Between Interest Payment Dates, Accrual of Interest Expense, Conversion of Bonds Into Capital Stock, and Retirement Before Maturity

The Third Edition Company issued $3,000,000 of 9% debenture bonds on September 30, 1992, at 96 plus accrued interest. The bonds were dated June 30, 1992; they mature in 10 years; interest is payable semiannually on June 30 and December 31; they are redeemable after June 30, 1997 and to June 30, 1998, at 104, and thereafter until maturity at 102; and convertible after June 30, 1998, into $100 par value capital stock at the rate of 5 shares for each $1,000 bond. The company closes its books on December 31 of each year.

The following transactions occurred in connection with the bonds:

July 1, 1998	$500,000 par value were converted into stock.
July 1, 1998	The remaining bonds were called. For purposes of obtaining funds for redemption and business expansion, a $4,000,000 issue of 7% bonds were issued at 101¾. These bonds were dated July 1, 1998.

Required:
You are to prepare the entries necessary for the company in connection with the above transactions, including the year-end adjustments where appropriate, as of each of the following dates.

1. September 30, 1992.
2. December 31, 1992.
3. July 1, 1998.

Problem 12-9 Early Retirement and Conversion of Bonds Into Capital Stock

Software Company issued five-year, 10%, $400,000 par value, convertible bonds on January 1, 1992 for $420,000. Each $1,000 bond is convertible into 80 shares of $5 par value capital stock. Interest is paid semiannually on June 30 and December 31 and the premium is amortized using the straight-line method.

Required:
A. Prepare the journal entry on December 31, 1995, to record the payment of the semiannual interest and amortize the bond premium.
B. Assume that after the interest payment on December 31, 1995, that Software Company retires the bonds by purchasing them on the open market for 99.
C. How is the gain or loss, if any, on the retirement reported in the financial statements?
D. Assume instead, that on December 31, 1995, the bondholders elect to convert their bonds into capital stock. Prepare the journal entry on December 31, 1995 to record the conversion of the bonds. How is the gain or loss, if any, from the conversion reported in the financial statements?

Problem 12-10 Bond Sinking Fund

On January 1, 1992, Lund Corporation issued $5,000,000 of 10-year bonds. The bond indenture contained a clause requiring Lund to establish a bond sinking fund with a trustee. At the end of each year for 10 years, Lund must deposit with the trustee the amount of $500,000 reduced by the earnings made on the fund's investments during the year.

Required:

Part I

A. Prepare the journal entry to record the initial deposit to the fund on December 31, 1992.

B. At the end of 1993, the trustee reports earnings on the fund during 1993 of $54,350. Prepare the journal entry on December 31, 1993 to:
   1. recognize the earnings on the fund.
   2. record the deposit to the fund.

C. At the end of 2001 the trustee reports earnings on the fund during 2001 of $441,000. Prepare the journal entry on December 31, 2001 to:
   1. recognize the earnings on the fund.
   2. record the deposit to the fund.

D. Prepare the journal entry on December 31, 2001 to record the bond retirement.

Part II

Assume the bond indenture does not contain provisions for required annual deposits. Lund Corporation decides it wants to deposit an equal amount each year, at the end of the year, so that the fund will have $5,000,000 on December 31, 2001 after the last deposit is made.

Required:

If the fund can earn a 12% return each year on the monies in the fund, compute the annual required deposit.

Problem 12-11   Bonds Issued at a Discount—Effective-Interest Method of Amortization

The Newark Company is expanding its operations. To finance the expansion, the company was authorized to issue $900,000, 10% bonds dated January 1, 1992. The bonds mature in three years and pay interest on June 30 and December 31. The bonds were issued on January 1, 1992 when the market rate of interest was 12%. The company uses the effective-interest method to amortize bond discounts and premiums and has a December 31 year-end.

Required:

A. Compute the issue price of the bonds.

B. Prepare a bond amortization table for this bond issue for the period it will be outstanding.

C. Prepare the journal entries to:
   1. record the issue of the bonds.
   2. record the bond interest payment and amortization of the bond discount on June 30, 1992.
   3. record the bond interest payment and amortization of the bond discount on December 31, 1992.

D. Show how the bonds would be presented on the December 31, 1992 balance sheet.

E. Compute the total cash interest that will be paid over the life of the bonds.

F. Answer the following questions.
   1. What amount of bond interest is reported in 1992?
   2. What amount of bond interest is reported in 1993?
   3. Is the 1993 interest expense the same as, greater than, or less than the amount reported in 1992? If they are different, explain why.

G. Assuming that the straight-line method of amortization is used rather than the effective-interest method, compute the following.
  1. The total interest expense over the life of the bonds.
  2. The interest expense reported for each semiannual interest period.
  3. The carrying value of the bonds on December 31, 1992.
H. For the two amortization methods:
  1. Compare the total interest expense over the life of the bonds. Are they the same?
  2. Compare the interest expense for the first two semiannual interest payments. Which method results in the greatest interest expense for the first year that the bonds are outstanding?
  3. Compare the interest expense for the last two interest payments. Which method reports the highest interest expense?
  4. Compare the carrying value of the debt on December 31, 1992. Which method produces the highest carrying value?

Problem 12-12 Bonds Issued at a Premium—Effective-interest Method of Amortization

On January 1, 1992, Canton Corporation issued three-year bonds with a par value of $500,000, and a stated interest rate of 12%. The bonds were issued to yield a return of 10% to the investors. The bonds pay interest semiannually on June 30 and December 31. The company's fiscal year ends on December 31 and it uses the effective-interest method to amortize bond premiums and discounts.

Required:
A. Compute the issue price of the bonds.
B. Prepare a bond amortization table for this bond issue for the period it will be outstanding.
C. Prepare the journal entries to:
  1. record the issue of the bonds.
  2. record the bond interest payment and amortization of the bond premium on June 30, 1992.
  3. record the bond interest payment and amortization of the bond premium on December 31, 1992.
D. Show how the bonds would be presented on the December 31, 1992 balance sheet.
E. Compute the total cash interest that will be paid over the life of the bonds.
F. Answer the following questions.
  1. What amount of bond interest is reported in 1992?
  2. What amount of bond interest is reported in 1993?
  3. Is the 1993 interest expense the same as, greater than, or less than the amount reported in 1992? If they are different, explain why.
G. Assuming that the straight-line method of amortization is used rather than the effective-interest method, compute
  1. the total interest expense over the life of the bonds.
  2. the interest expense reported for each semiannual interest period.
  3. the carrying value of the bonds on December 31, 1992.
H. For the two amortization methods:
  1. Compare the total interest expense over the life of the bonds. Are they the same?

2. Compare the interest expense for the first two semiannual interest payments. Which method results in the greatest interest expense for the first year that the bonds are outstanding?
3. Compare the interest expense for the last two interest payments. Which method reports the highest interest expense?
4. Compare the carrying value of the debt on December 31, 1992. Which method produces the highest carrying value?

Problem 12-13 Comprehensive Bonds Payable Problem

Light Company was authorized to issue $500,000 par value, 12%, 15-year, convertible bonds, dated June 1, 1992. Each $1,000 bond is convertible into 40 shares of $10 par value capital stock. Interest payments are made on May 31 and November 30 of each year. The fiscal year of Light Company ends on December 31, and it uses the straight-line method to amortize bond premiums and discounts. Light Company completed the following transactions related to this bond issue during its fiscal years 1992 and 1993.

August 31, 1992	Issued the entire bond issue for cash for $510,620 plus accrued interest.
November 30, 1992	Paid the semiannual interest payment.
December 31, 1992	Prepared the adjusting entry to record the accrued interest on the bonds.
May 31, 1993	Paid the semiannual interest payment. The company does not prepare reversing entries.
May 31, 1993	Bondholders converted $300,000 of the bonds into capital stock at the stipulated conversion rate.
November 30, 1993	Paid the semiannual interest payment.
December 31, 1993	Prepared the adjusting entry to record the accrued interest on the bonds.

Required:
A. Prepare all necessary journal entries to record the transactions.
B. Prepare the December 31, 1992 and December 31, 1993 balance sheet presentations for the bond issue.

CASE

CASE 12-1 Annual Report Analysis

Refer to the financial statements and related footnotes of BFGoodrich Company in the Appendix to this text and answer the following questions. Indicate the Appendix page number on which you found the answer.

1. What is the amount of long-term debt, less unamortized discount, on December 31, 1989?
2. As reported in the balance sheet, what is the amount of long-term debt and capital lease obligations due within one year of December 31, 1989?
3. What is the amount of the aggregate maturities of long-term debt, exclusive of capital lease obligations, for the years 1991 and 1994?
4. Which note or bond issue has the highest interest rate?

5. What is the amount of interest expense reported in 1989?

6. Did the Company retire any of its long-term debt before its scheduled maturity? If so, describe the debt that was retired early. What is the amount of gain or loss for each issue that was retired early? How is any gain or loss associated with the retirement reported?

7. Many long-term debt instruments contain restrictive covenants that place limitations on a company. What restrictions are placed on the BFGoodrich Company by certain of its debt agreements?

13

ACCOUNTING FOR OWNERS' EQUITY AND SPECIAL INCOME STATEMENT ITEMS

CHAPTER OVERVIEW AND OBJECTIVES

This chapter discusses the way corporations are organized, the types of stock they issue, and accounting procedures for stockholders' equity. When you have completed the chapter, you should understand:

1. What a corporation is.
2. The management structure of a corporation.
3. The rights attached to stock ownership.
4. Why a distinction is made between paid-in capital and retained earnings.
5. The difference between authorized, issued, and outstanding stock.
6. How to record the issuance of corporate stock.
7. The effect of dividends on assets and stockholders' equity.
8. The differences between common and preferred stock.
9. What treasury stock is and how to account for it.
10. The nature of stock dividends and stock splits and how to account for them.
11. How to report the effects of discontinued operations, extraordinary items, and changes in accounting principles.
12. The meaning of retained earnings restrictions.
13. How to account for owners' equity in proprietorships and partnerships: Appendix.

Owners' equity is the owners' interest in the firm's assets. It is measured by the excess of total assets over total liabilities; thus, owners' equity equals the net assets (assets − liabilities) of the business. Because of legal differences, the terminology used and the way owners' equity is reported on the balance sheet varies somewhat for proprietorships, partnerships, and corporations. Regardless of how they are organized, all businesses follow the same basic procedures to record most business transactions and adhere to generally accepted accounting principles (GAAP). The main difference in accounting for the three forms of organization is in the recording and reporting of owners' equity.

Although there are fewer corporations than proprietorships and partnerships in the United States, corporations transact about six times more business than the other two types of entities combined and control vast amounts of resources. Because of the dominant role they play in our economy and because many of you will at some time either work for or own shares in a corporation, it is important to have an understanding of corporations and their accounting practices. Thus, in this chapter we will concentrate on accounting for owners' equity (stockholders' equity) of a corporation. The primary differences in accounting for owners' equity of proprietorships and partnerships is covered in an Appendix to this chapter.

CORPORATION DEFINED

Probably the most widely quoted definition of a corporation is that given by Chief Justice John Marshall in the Dartmouth College Case in 1819, in which he described a corporation as "an artificial being, invisible, intangible, and existing only in contemplation of law." A corporation is a legal entity or artificial person separate and distinct from its owners. As a separate legal entity, it has many of the rights and responsibilities of a person, including:

Objective 1: What a corporation is

- The right to buy, own, and sell property in its own name through its agents;
- The right to enter into contracts with others;
- The right to sue and be sued in a court of law;
- The responsibility for its liabilities; and
- The responsibility to pay income taxes.

TYPES OF CORPORATIONS

Corporations may be classified in several ways. They may be organized for profit or for nonprofit purposes. A **profit corporation** is one that engages in business activity with the goal of earning a profit for its owners. Its continued existence is dependent upon profitable operations. **Nonprofit corporations** are organized to engage in educational, charitable, health research, and other society-benefiting activities and generally depend upon public contributions for their continued existence.

Corporations are also often classified as public corporations and nonpublic corporations. **Public corporations** are those whose shares of stock are widely held and traded through national stock exchanges. Corporations whose shares of stock are held by a small group, often by the members of a single family, and are not publicly traded are called **nonpublic** (or **closely held**) **corporations**.

ADVANTAGES OF THE CORPORATE FORM

The corporate form has several main advantages as discussed below.

Limited Liability

Owners of corporations (stockholders) are not personally liable for corporate debts. Thus, the maximum amount they can lose if the corporation encounters financial difficulty is the amount of their equity in the corporation.

Broad Source of Capital

By dividing ownership into transferable shares of stock with relatively low values per share, corporations permit both large and small investors to participate in the ownership of the business. Most large corporations can therefore draw upon the savings of many investors to obtain the capital they need.

Ready Transferability of Shares

Corporate shares may be transferred easily without disrupting the activities of the corporation. Shares in public corporations can be bought and sold on practically every weekday through one of the national or regional stock exchanges. Thus, a stockholder can readily convert his or her investment into cash if the need arises.

Continuity of Existence

A corporation has an indefinite life and continues in existence even if its ownership changes. The transfer of shares from one owner to another has no effect on a corporation. In contrast, the death, incapacity, or withdrawal of an owner often terminates a proprietorship or a partnership.

DISADVANTAGES OF THE CORPORATE FORM

Corporations also have some main disadvantages which are:

Heavier Tax Burden

Corporations are generally subject to federal and state income taxes, the total of which often exceeds 40% of corporate income. When a corporation's after-tax income is distributed to its stockholders as dividends, the income (with some minor exceptions) is taxed again as personal income to the stockholders receiving the dividends. Thus, it is often said that corporate income is subject to *double taxation*.

Greater Governmental Regulation

Because corporations are created under state and federal laws, they are subject to a much greater degree of control and supervision than are proprietorships or partnerships. In addition, public corporations must file periodic reports with the Securities and Exchange Commission and the stock exchanges on which their shares are traded. Meeting these additional reporting requirements often can be very costly.

Separation of Ownership and Management

The use of professional managers to manage the corporation may be a disadvantage because they sometimes operate corporations for their own benefit rather than for the benefit of the stockholders. Considerable harm may be done before stockholders become aware of the condition and take action to change management.

FORMING A CORPORATION

Some corporations, such as national banks and savings and loan associations, are formed under federal laws. The majority of corporations, however, are created by obtaining a charter from one of the 50 states. To form a corporation, states require that individuals called **incorporators** must sign an application for a corporate charter and file it with the appropriate state official. Although state laws vary, the application generally must include:

1. The name, address, and purpose of the proposed corporation;
2. A description of the different classes of stock and their par or stated value per share, if any;
3. The number of shares of each class of stock authorized;
4. A description of the rights, preferences, and restrictions of each class of stock; and
5. The names and addresses of the original subscribers to shares of stock and the amount of each subscription.

If the application is approved, a legal contract between the state and the incorporators, called a **corporate charter**, is entered into and the corporation is authorized to conduct business. The incorporators hold an initial meeting to adopt the bylaws to be followed in conducting corporate affairs and to elect a board of directors. The board of directors then meets to appoint the president and other officers who will manage the company. After capital is raised through the issuance of shares of stock, the corporation is ready to begin operating activities.

MANAGING THE CORPORATION

Although control of a corporation ultimately rests with its stockholders, that control is exercised only indirectly. Stockholders elect a board of directors, which sets overall corporate policies. The board, in turn, appoints a president and other officers to manage the corporation's day-to-day affairs and carry out the policies established by the board.

Objective 2: Management structure of corporations

The Stockholders

Stockholders are not directly involved in the daily management of the corporation unless they have been elected to serve on the board of directors or have been appointed as officers or managers. Stockholders generally are involved only in electing the board of directors and voting on certain important corporate actions specified in the corporate bylaws. For example, corporate bylaws often provide that stockholders must approve such actions as the merger with or acquisition of another company and changes in the capital structure of the corporation.

Stockholders receive a **stock certificate**, a legal document that provides evidence of ownership and contains the basic provisions of the stock ownership agreement. An example of a stock certificate is shown in Figure 13-1.

Figure 13-1
Stock Certificates

Objective 3:
Stock ownership
rights

Ownership of stock usually carries certain rights and privileges that can be modified only by a specifically worded contract at the time the shares are issued. These basic rights are:

1. The right to vote for both directors and on matters described in the corporate bylaws. (We will see later that this right is generally eliminated for preferred stockholders.)

2. The right to share in profits by receiving dividends declared by the board of directors.

3. The right to share in the distribution of the corporation's assets if it is liquidated. When a corporation is liquidated, creditors must be paid first, and any remaining assets are distributed to the stockholders in proportion to the number of shares held.

4. The right to purchase a portion of any additional stock issued by the corporation. This right, called the **preemptive right**, permits stockholders to maintain their percentage interests in a corporation by purchasing new shares in proportion to their current holdings. For example, if a stockholder owns 4,000 of the 40,000 outstanding shares of a corporation, the stockholder has a 10% interest. If the corporation issues 10,000 additional shares, the stockholder has the right to purchase 10% of them, or 1,000 shares, so that he or she will maintain a 10% interest in the corporation after the issuance of the additional shares. This right may unduly restrict the actions of management of widely held corporations, by hindering the

timely issuance of new shares. Consequently, the preemptive right is frequently waived by stockholders in the bylaws.

Stockholders generally meet once a year to elect directors and to conduct other business as provided by the corporate bylaws. Each share of stock is entitled to one vote. A stockholder who owns more than 50% of a corporation's stock can thus elect the board of directors and control the corporation. Because many of the stockholders of a widely held company do not attend the annual meeting, however, a corporation can often be controlled through the ownership of a much smaller percentage of stock. Stockholders who do not attend the annual meeting may delegate their voting right to an agent by signing a legal document called a **proxy statement**. Often the voting right is delegated to the current management in order to permit them to continue in control.

The Board of Directors

Although the board of directors has final responsibility for managing the corporation, it normally restricts its role to formulating the major business policies of the company and appointing the officers who will have responsibility for carrying out those policies. Duties of the board are normally identified in the corporate bylaws and generally include such things as (1) taking responsibility for protecting the rights of stockholders and creditors, (2) setting officers' salaries, (3) declaring dividends, (4) authorizing long-term borrowing, additional stock issues, and major expansion projects and (5) reviewing the system of internal control. The board of directors normally includes officers of the corporation and holders of large blocks of corporate stock. In addition, the board often has several outside directors to ensure a more objective evaluation of management performance.

Official actions of the board are recorded in the minutes of their meetings. The *minutes book* is important to the accountant because it contains board decisions that serve as the basis for the authorization of certain transactions and the preparation of many accounting entries.

The Corporate Officers

A corporation's chief executive is usually the president. The president manages and controls the business activities and is responsible to the board of directors. The president is normally supported by one or more vice-presidents, who are responsible to the president for managing specific functional areas. For example, a corporation may have a vice-president of finance, a vice-president of production, and a vice-president of marketing.

Other officers are the controller, the treasurer, and the secretary. The *controller* is the chief accounting officer and is generally responsible for maintaining the accounting records and an adequate internal control system, preparing financial statements, tax returns, other reports, and developing the budget. The controller also advises the board of directors about the accounting and tax consequences of proposed corporate actions. The *treasurer* is responsible primarily for managing cash. He or she normally has custody of the company's funds and is responsible for planning and controlling the company's cash position. The *secretary* maintains the minutes of meetings of the directors and stockholders, and represents the corporation in many legal and contractual matters. In a small corporation, the secretary often also maintains the records of stockholders and the amount of their stock interests. Large corporations use outside registrars and transfer agents to perform this stockholder-record function. Some corporations, particularly smaller ones, combine the positions of secretary and treasurer.

The following diagram illustrates a typical corporate organization chart. Lines of authority extend from the stockholders to the board of directors to the president to other officers.

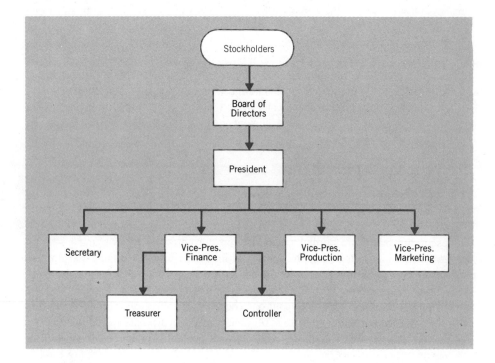

CORPORATE CAPITAL

The owners' equity section of a corporation's balance sheet is called ***stockholders' equity*** or ***shareholders' equity*** since owners' equity is evidenced by shares of stock. The stockholders' equity section of a typical corporate balance sheet might appear as follows:

Stockholders' Equity

Paid-in capital:	
Preferred stock, $100 par value, 10,000 shares authorized,	
7,000 shares issued and outstanding	$ 700,000
Common stock, $5 par value, 600,000 shares authorized,	
300,000 shares issued and outstanding	1,500,000
Paid-in capital in excess of par value–preferred	50,000
Paid-in capital in excess of par value–common	2,100,000
Total paid-in capital	4,350,000
Retained earnings	920,000
Total stockholders' equity	$5,270,000

Objective 4: Difference between paid-in capital and retained earnings

    State incorporation laws generally require that stockholders' equity must be separated into paid-in capital and retained earnings. **Paid-in capital** represents the amount of assets invested in the corporation by its stockholders or sometimes donated to the corporation. When stockholders invest cash or other assets in a corporation, they are given shares of the corporation's stock as evidence of their investments. The paid-in capital section includes information about the types of stock, their par values, and the number of shares authorized and outstanding. We will discuss these concepts later in the chapter.

Retained earnings represent the interest of the stockholders in the amount of income (assets) earned by the corporation and retained in the business. As shown in previous chapters, when a corporation's income statement accounts are closed at year-end, the Income Summary account is closed to retained earnings. If the Income Summary account has a credit balance, the corporation has earned net income and retained earnings will increase. If the Income Summary account has a debit balance, a net loss has been incurred, and retained earnings will decrease. A debit balance in retained earnings is called a **deficit** and is deducted in arriving at total stockholders' equity.

AUTHORIZED CAPITAL STOCK

When a corporation is formed, its charter indicates the maximum number of shares of stock it is permitted to issue and the par or stated value per share, if any. This maximum number of shares is called **authorized stock**. A corporation may be authorized to issue only one type of stock, called **common stock**, or it may be authorized to issue both common stock and *preferred stock*. (Preferred stock is discussed later in this chapter.)

Objective 5: Authorized, issued, and outstanding stock

The corporation normally obtains permission to issue more stock than it plans to sell immediately. This allows the corporation to raise additional capital in the future without asking the state to authorize more stock each time it wishes to issue additional shares. For example, a corporation may be authorized to issue 1 million shares of common stock even though it intends to issue only 400,000 shares initially to raise the capital needed to begin operations. The remaining 600,000 shares may then be issued in the future if additional capital is needed.

Par Value

The par value of stock is an arbitrary amount per share placed on the stock by the incorporators at the time they apply for the corporate charter. They may select any value they wish, and par values per share of $1, $5, and $10 are common. For example, St. Regis Corporation's common stock has a par value of $5, Holiday Corporation's is $1.00, General Electric Company's is $1.25 per share, and Springs Industries, Inc.'s is $.50. Most corporations set a par value substantially below the value at which the stock is initially issued because most states prohibit the issue of stock for less than its par value. In states that permit the issue of stock below par value, if the market price of the stock drops below its par value, the corporation is unable to issue additional stock, except at a discount—and the discount may carry a liability for stockholders, as discussed later. Establishing a relatively large spread between the initial issue price of the stock and its par value minimizes the possibility of its market price dropping below par value.

If a corporation issues par value stock, the par value is printed on each stock certificate and is the amount recorded in the capital stock accounts. The only significance of par value is that it establishes a minimum amount of capital, called *legal capital*, which provides an element of protection for creditors. That is, a corporation's creditors have claims only against the assets of the corporation, additional protection is provided them by maintaining a minimum amount of assets equal to legal capital. This minimum amount of assets cannot be returned to the stockholders until all creditors' claims have been paid. Legal capital cannot be reduced except by operating losses or legal action initiated by a majority vote of the stockholders. Total legal capital of a corporation issuing par value stock is equal to the number of shares outstanding times par value per share.

The par value of stock has no relationship to its worth or market value. Par value is a fixed amount per share; market value generally fluctuates daily. For example, the market value of Holiday Corporation's common stock ranged from about $41 to $57 per share during 1989; its par value remained at $1.00 per share.

OUTSTANDING STOCK

The outstanding stock of a corporation consists of the shares held by stockholders at any given time. As authorized stock is issued, it becomes outstanding stock. If one million shares are authorized and 400,000 shares have been issued, the remaining 600,000 shares are called *unissued stock* and contain no rights until they are issued. The holders of the 400,000 shares own 100% of the corporation. At times, a corporation's issued stock may exceed the number of shares outstanding because some of the shares may have been repurchased by the corporation. Accounting for these repurchased shares, called *treasury stock,* is discussed later in this chapter.

ISSUING COMMON STOCK

Objective 6:
Recording the
issuance of cor-
porate stock

When common stock is issued for cash, the Cash account is debited, the Common Stock account is credited for the par value of the shares issued (legal capital), and a separate account called Paid-in Capital in Excess of Par Value is credited for the excess of the selling price over the par value. For example, if 20,000 shares of $5 par value common stock are issued at $25 per share, the entry is:

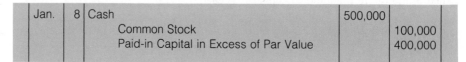

Jan.	8	Cash	500,000	
		Common Stock		100,000
		Paid-in Capital in Excess of Par Value		400,000

Paid-in capital in excess of par value is sometimes called *contributed capital in excess of par value* or *premium on common stock*. It is important to recognize that this premium on common stock does not constitute income to the corporation. It is a part of total paid-in capital that is reported on the balance sheet as a separate element of paid-in capital because it is not legal capital.

A few states permit the issue of stock for less than its par value, in which case a Discount on Common Stock account is debited for the difference between the issue price and the par value of the stock. If stock is issued at a discount, the purchasers of the stock may be liable to the corporation's creditors for the amount of the discount. Consequently, issuing of stock at a discount is rare.

Issuing Stock for Assets Other Than Cash

Corporations normally issue their stock for cash and use the cash to acquire needed goods and services. At times, however, the stock may be issued directly for assets such as land, buildings, or equipment. When this occurs, the assets received are recorded at the fair market value of the stock issued or the fair market value of the assets received, whichever is more objectively determinable. If the stock is publicly traded, the market value of the shares given is often a better measure of value than the appraised value of the assets received. If 4,000 shares of common stock are exchanged for a parcel of land and the stock has a current market value of $20 per share, it is reasonable to record the cost of the land at $80,000 (4,000 × $20) since the stock could have been sold for $80,000 and the cash used to purchase the land. For a newly formed corporation, or a closely held one, the market value of the stock is often unknown and the fair value of the assets received must be determined. For example, assume a new corporation issued 10,000 shares of $5 par value common stock to one of the incorporators in exchange for land with an appraised value of $80,000 and a building appraised at $250,000. The issuance of the stock is recorded as follows:

Jan.	8	Land	80,000	
		Building	250,000	
		Common Stock		50,000
		Paid-in Capital in Excess of Par Value		280,000

Because the fair value of the stock is unknown, the land and buildings are recorded at their appraised values. Common Stock is credited for the par value of the shares issued and the difference between the fair value of the assets and the par value of the stock is credited to Paid-in Capital in Excess of Par Value.

NO-PAR STOCK

In the early history of American corporations, all stock was required to have a par value. Today, however, all states permit the issuance of no-par stock. In some states, the entire proceeds from the sale of no-par stock must be credited to the capital stock account as legal capital. This type of stock is referred to as **_straight no-par stock_**. In other states, the board of directors may assign a stated value per share to their no-par stock. From an accounting standpoint, stated value and par value are the same thing in that they both identify the amount that must be recorded as legal capital in the Capital Stock account.

To illustrate the accounting for no-par stock, assume that a corporation issues 10,000 shares of no-par common stock at $30 per share. If the stock does not have a stated value, the entire proceeds are recorded in the no-par common stock account as follows:

| Jan. | 8 | Cash | 300,000 | |
| | | Common Stock—No Par Value | | 300,000 |

If the board of directors has assigned a stated value of $5 to the no-par stock, the difference between the issue price and the stated value is credited to Paid-in Capital in Excess of Stated Value as follows:

Jan.	8	Cash	300,000	
		Common Stock—No Par Value		50,000
		Paid-in Capital in Excess of Stated Value		250,000

CASH DIVIDENDS

Many corporations distribute part of their earnings periodically to their stockholders by declaring a dividend. A **dividend** is a distribution of cash, other assets, or a corporation's own stock to its stockholders. The authority to declare dividends rests solely with the board of directors, which is responsible for determining both the legality of the dividend and the corporation's ability to pay it. In other words, the corporation must have sufficient retained earnings (or, in some states, additional paid-in capital) and cash or other assets to distribute to stockholders without putting an undue strain on the corporation's ability to continue to operate efficiently. The board of directors must therefore determine the wisdom of distributing assets to stockholders rather than retaining them for operating activities or for financing growth. Once the board has declared a dividend, the obligation to pay it becomes a current liability and cannot be rescinded.

Cash dividends are the most common form of dividend, and they will be discussed here. Distributions of other assets are quite rare, and accounting for them is covered in more advanced accounting courses. Dividends of corporate stock are discussed later in this chapter.

LIQUIDATING DIVIDENDS

Most states prohibit the payment of dividends in excess of retained earnings, although some states permit the payment of dividends as long as legal capital is not infringed. When a dividend in excess of retained earnings is declared, the corporation is returning to its stockholders a portion of their paid-in capital. These dividends are called **liquidating dividends** because they do not represent income to the stockholders. That is, liquidating dividends represent a return of stockholders' investments rather than a return on their investments.

Cash dividends on common stock are stated in terms of so many dollars or cents per share. For example, a corporation may declare a dividend of $.50 per share on outstanding stock and a stockholder owning 1,000 shares will receive a dividend check for $500.

DIVIDEND DECLARATION AND PAYMENT

A corporation's stockholders change as shares are traded on the market. To assure that dividends are paid to the rightful owner of the shares, dividends are declared on one date, payable on some future date to the stockholders of record on some date between the declaration date and the payment date. For example, the board may declare a dividend on August 25 (the *declaration date*) to be paid on September 20 (the *payment date*) to the stockholders of record on September 10 (the *date of record*). Investors buying stock between August 25 and September 10 will therefore have time to get the ownership of their shares recorded before payment of the dividend.

To illustrate, assume that on August 25 the board of directors declared a $.50 per-share dividend on 300,000 outstanding shares of common stock to be paid on September 20 to stockholders of record on September 10. Because a dividend liability is created on the declaration date that will not be settled until the payment date, two journal entries are required. The entry on the declaration date is:

Aug.	25	Dividends Declared	150,000	
		Dividends Payable		150,000

This entry recognizes the reduction of owners' equity and a dividend liability, which is reported as a current liability on the August 31 balance sheet if one is prepared. The entry to record payment of the dividend is:

Sept.	20	Dividends Payable	150,000	
		Cash		150,000

No entry is required on the date of record since that date is used only to determine the owners of the stock who are to receive the dividend checks.

The Dividends Declared account is a temporary account that is closed to Retained Earnings at the end of the year. If a company declares dividends on both common and preferred stock, it may use a separate Dividends Declared and Dividends Payable account for each type of stock. Regardless of the procedures followed, the net effect of a cash dividend is to reduce both retained earnings and cash by the amount of the dividend.

PREFERRED STOCK

In addition to common stock, many corporations issue one or more types of **preferred stock**. Preferred stock receives its name from the fact that preferred stockholders receive preferential treatment over common stockholders in one or more respects. Common stock is the residual equity in a corporation, which means that common stockholders are the last to receive asset distributions if the corporation is liquidated. Common stockholders take the greatest risk of loss if the corporation is unsuccessful— but they also have the greatest potential for gain if the company is profitable. As a result, the market value of common stock is closely related to profitability and generally increases and decreases as stockholders' expectations about future profits rise and fall.

Preferred stock is normally given one or more preferences over common stock. The most common are preferences as to dividend distributions and asset distributions if the corporation is liquidated. In addition, preferred stock is generally callable at the option of the corporation and is sometimes convertible into common stock at the option of the preferred stockholders. In exchange for these preferences, preferred stockholders normally relinquish the right to vote. Preferences and other special features of preferred stock vary widely. Consequently, the preferred stock contract must be read carefully to determine its specific provisions.

Objective 8:
Distinction between common stock and preferred stock

DIVIDEND PREFERENCE

If stock is preferred as to dividends, its stockholders are entitled to some specified dividend before any dividend is paid to common stockholders. The annual dividend is usually stated as a dollar amount per share or as a percentage of the stock's par value. For example, Oak Industries' balance sheet includes $5 stated value convertible cumulative preferred stock with a $1.75 annual dividend per share, and Tenneco Inc.'s balance sheet shows 8.52%, $100 par value preferred stock, which means that $8.52 must be paid yearly on each share of preferred stock before a dividend can be paid to common stockholders.

Because the obligation to pay a dividend arises only if the board of directors declares one, preferred stockholders are not assured of receiving an annual dividend. Although dividends must be paid on preferred stock before any are paid on common stock, the board of directors may decide not to declare a dividend on either preferred or common stock because of a lack of retained earnings, a shortage of cash, or both.

The dividend preference on most preferred stock is **cumulative**, which means that undeclared dividends accumulate and the accumulated amount plus the current year's preferred dividend must be paid before any dividend can be paid to common stockholders. Dividends that are not declared in the year they are due are called **dividends in arrears**. Current accounting standards require disclosure of dividends in arrears. Generally, disclosure is made in a footnote to the financial statements. To illustrate cumulative dividends, assume that Baker Corporation has stockholders' equity as shown below. Assume also that dividends are in arrears for the previous year.

Stockholders' Equity

Paid-in capital:	
$5 Cumulative preferred stock, $50 par value, 100,000 shares authorized, 60,000 shares issued and outstanding	$ 3,000,000
Common stock, $50 par value, 500,000 shares authorized, 180,000 shares issued and outstanding	9,000,000
Retained earnings	4,000,000
Total stockholders' equity	$16,000,000

If the board of directors declares an $800,000 dividend, it will be distributed to preferred and common stockholders as follows:

	Preferred	Common
Dividends in arrears (60,000 × $5)	$300,000	
Current year's dividend	300,000	$200,000
Totals	$600,000	$200,000

If the board declared a $400,000 dividend, it would all be distributed to preferred stockholders; common stockholders would receive no dividends, and dividends in arrears on preferred stock would still exist in the amount of $200,000.

If preferred stock is **noncumulative**, any undeclared dividends at the end of the year are lost. Because investors are hesitant to purchase such stock, very few noncumulative preferred stocks are issued.

Sometimes preferred stockholders are not limited to a fixed amount of dividends for the current year, but are permitted to participate with common stockholders in dividends above a specified amount. This type of preferred stock is called **participating preferred stock**. The stock may be *fully participating*, which means that preferred stockholders will share in all dividends paid in excess of (1) dividends in arrears, (2) the current fixed dividend on preferred stock, and (3) a specified amount of dividends to common stockholders. For example, the par value of the preferred and common stock in the previous example was $50 per share, and the preferred stock is cumulative and participates fully with common stock after common stockholders have received dividends for the current year at the same rate as preferred stockholders. Since the preferred dividend rate is 10% ($5/$50), a $1,900,000 dividend would be distributed as follows:

	Preferred	Common
Dividends in arrears	$300,000	
Current year's preferred dividend	300,000	
Current year's common dividend (10% × $9,000,000)		$ 900,000
Participation in ratio of total par values ($3,000,000 to $9,000,000, or 1 to 3)	100,000	300,000
Totals	$700,000	$1,200,000

At times, participating preferred stock is limited as to the total amount of dividends it can receive for the current year and is called *partially participating preferred stock*. For example, if the preferred stock above is limited to a 12% current dividend, the $1,900,000 total dividend is distributed as follows:

	Preferred	Common
Preferred dividend in arrears	$300,000	
Current year's dividend on preferred	300,000	
Current year's dividend on common		$ 900,000
Participation feature (2% × $3,000,000)	60,000	
Residual to common stock		340,000
Totals	$660,000	$1,240,000

ASSET PREFERENCE

In addition to a dividend preference, most preferred stocks include a preference as to assets if the corporation is liquidated. If the corporation is terminated, the preferred stockholders are entitled to receive payment (after creditors have been paid) up to the par value of their stock—or a higher liquidation value if a specified liquidation value is included as part of the preferred stock contract—before common stockholders receive any portion of the corporation's assets. This preference also includes any dividends in arrears on cumulative preferred stock.

CALLABLE PREFERRED STOCK

Preferred stock contracts usually include a **call provision**, which gives the corporation the right to repurchase the stock from the stockholder at a predetermined call price. The call price (sometimes called *redemption price*) is often higher than par value. For example, General Motor's no-par, $100 stated value preferred stock has a redemption price of $120 per share. When preferred stock is called, the stockholder is paid the call price plus any dividends in arrears and a pro rata portion of the current year's dividend. A call provision gives the corporation some flexibility in structuring its equity. A preferred stock may be called and retired, for example, in order to distribute greater dividends to common stockholders. Or a preferred stock may be retired and replaced with another preferred stock with a lower dividend rate.

CONVERTIBLE PREFERRED STOCK

Some preferred stock is *convertible,* which permits the preferred stockholder to convert the stock into common stock at a predetermined exchange ratio. For example, each share of Oak Industries' $1.75 preferred stock referred to earlier is convertible at the option of the holder into 6.51 shares of common stock. The conversion privilege is an attractive feature to investors. If the corporation is successful and the market price of its common stock rises, the market price of the preferred stock will also increase since it is convertible into common stock. If the market price of the common stock does not increase, the preferred stock still has its preference as to regular fixed dividends.

When the market price of the common stock increases, some preferred stockholders may convert their preferred stock into common stock. For example, assume that a corporation has 20,000 shares of 8%, $100 par value convertible preferred stock outstanding. The stock was issued several years ago at par value. Each preferred share is convertible into three shares of the corporation's $10 par value common stock at any time. If the holders of 5,000 of the preferred shares converted their stock, the entry is:

Jan.	6	Preferred Stock		500,000	
		Common Stock			150,000
		Paid-in Capital in Excess of Par Value			350,000

This transfers the stockholders' equity associated with the preferred shares converted to appropriate common stockholders' equity accounts. The Preferred Stock account is reduced by $500,000 (5,000 shares × $100 par value per share) and the Common Stock account is credited for the par value of the common stock issued (15,000 shares × $10). The difference between the par value of the preferred stock retired and the par value of the common stock issued is credited to Paid-in Capital in Excess of Par Value.

TREASURY STOCK

**Objective 9:
Accounting for
treasury stock**

Treasury stock is a corporation's own stock that has been issued and reacquired but not retired or reissued. Treasury stock may be either preferred or common stock, but when preferred stock is reacquired, it is normally retired and will not be reissued. Most treasury stock is therefore common stock. Among the most common reasons a corporation reacquires its own common stock are: (1) to support the current market price of the stock, since stockholders often judge management performance on the basis of the market value of the stock; (2) to have stock available for issue to employees and officers under stock purchase or stock option plans; and (3) to have stock available for use in acquiring other companies. For these reasons, many large corporations reacquire and reissue their own shares on a fairly regular basis.

Most treasury stock is acquired by cash purchase on the open market and therefore results in a corresponding decrease of both the corporation's assets and stockholders' equity. The treasury shares may be held for an indefinite period, reissued at any time, or retired. While held by the corporation, treasury stock is similar to unissued stock in that it contains none of the stockholder rights. Thus, treasury stock is not entitled to vote, receive dividends, receive assets if the corporation is liquidated, or exercise the preemptive right.

Treasury stock is different from unissued stock, however, in one important respect. Remember, if par value stock is originally issued at a price below its par value, the original purchasers of the stock may be liable to the corporation's creditors for the amount of the discount. However, if stock was originally issued at an amount in excess of its par value and later purchased as treasury stock, it can be reissued (sold) for less than its par value without incurring a discount liability.

PURCHASE OF TREASURY STOCK

Purchases of treasury stock are normally recorded at cost by debiting a Treasury Stock account and crediting Cash. For example, assume Rox Corporation purchased 4,000 shares of its own $10 par value common stock at $35 per share. The entry would be:

June	4	Treasury Stock		140,000	
		Cash			140,000

Note that the Treasury Stock account is debited for the total cost of the shares acquired.

The par or stated value and the original issue price of the stock have no effect on the entry.

When treasury stock is purchased, the corporation essentially pays off some of its stockholders, thereby reducing both stockholders' equity and corporate assets. Because the stock may be reissued later, it is recorded in a Treasury Stock account, which is a contra stockholders' equity account that is subtracted from the total of paid-in capital and retained earnings in the stockholders' equity section of the balance sheet as follows.

Stockholders Equity

Paid-in capital:	
Common stock, $10 par value, 100,000 shares authorized,	
50,000 shares issued, 46,000 shares outstanding	$500,000
Paid-in capital in excess of par value	275,000
Total paid-in capital	775,000
Retained earnings	221,000
Total paid-in capital and retained earnings	996,000
Less: Treasury stock, 4,000 shares at cost	140,000
Total stockholders' equity	$856,000

The stockholders' equity section of the balance sheet shows that 50,000 shares of common stock were issued, of which 4,000 are held as treasury stock. The number of shares outstanding is therefore 46,000, which constitutes the total ownership of the corporation.

REISSUE OF TREASURY STOCK

When treasury stock is reissued, Cash (or other assets received) is debited, the Treasury Stock account is credited for the cost of the shares reissued, and any difference between cost and the reissue price is credited or debited to Paid-in Capital from Treasury Stock Transactions. To illustrate, assume that Rox Corporation reissues, for $45 per share, 2,000 of the 4,000 treasury shares acquired on June 4. The reissue entry is:

Oct.	10	Cash	90,000	
		Treasury Stock		70,000
		Paid-in Capital from Treasury Stock		
		Transactions		20,000

If treasury stock is reissued at a price below its cost, Paid-in Capital from Treasury Stock Transactions is debited. If there is no paid-in capital from previous treasury stock transactions, or if the balance in that account is insufficient to cover the excess of cost over the reissue price, the debit is made to Retained Earnings.

Note that the difference between the reissue price and cost of the treasury stock is credited or debited to paid-in capital rather than to a gain or loss account. Corporations earn profits or incur losses from the sale of goods or services to customers, not from the retirement or reissue of capital stock.

STOCK DIVIDENDS

A **stock dividend** is a pro-rata distribution of additional shares of a corporation's stock to its stockholders. It normally consists of the distribution of additional shares of common stock to common stockholders. Stock dividends should be clearly distinguished from cash dividends. Unlike cash dividends, which reduce corporate assets

Objective 10: Accounting for stock dividends and stock splits

and stockholders' equity, stock dividends have no effect on corporate assets or on total stockholders' equity. The only effect of a stock dividend is a transfer of retained earnings to paid-in capital.

Stock dividends often are declared by successful companies that have used their earnings to expand operations. These companies use their cash earnings to acquire additional plant and equipment in order to grow and therefore generally declare only minimal cash dividends.

The declaration of a stock dividend gives stockholders some additional shares as evidence of the increase in their equity in the corporation without distributing cash or other assets to them. Stock dividends also result in a permanent transfer of retained earnings to paid-in capital, thereby removing the amount of retained earnings transferred from dividend availability. Another reason for stock dividends is to reduce the market price of the common stock by increasing the number of shares outstanding. When a corporation grows, the market price of its common stock tends to increase. By reducing the market price of its shares, the corporation can encourage a broader ownership by both small and large investors in the hope that these stockholders would be inclined to purchase the corporation's goods and services. To accomplish this objective, the stock dividend must be a relatively large one. As an alternative, the corporation may undertake a stock split, which is described later.

When stock dividends are declared, retained earnings are transferred to paid-in capital. As discussed earlier, state incorporation laws generally require the maintenance of legal capital at an amount equal to the number of shares outstanding times par or stated value per share. Consequently, a minimum amount equal to the par or stated value of the additional shares issued must be transferred from Retained Earnings to the Common Stock account. Accounting rules, however, distinguish between small and large stock dividends. *Small stock dividends* (defined as about 20% or less of outstanding shares) are often perceived by stockholders to have little immediate effect on the market price of the stock; some investors therefore consider them to be distributions of earnings. Accounting rules provide that retained earnings should be transferred to paid-in capital in an amount equal to the number of additional shares issued times the market price per share.

Large stock dividends (those in excess of about 20% of shares outstanding) generally have the effect of an immediate and proportionate reduction in the market price of the stock. For example, if the market price of the stock was $70 before a stock dividend, the declaration of a 100% stock dividend would reduce the market price immediately to about $35 per share, since there would be twice as many shares outstanding. Because stockholders observe that the total market value of their shares remains unchanged after a large stock dividend, they do not tend to view it as a distribution of earnings. As a result, accounting rules require the transfer of retained earnings in an amount sufficient only to comply with state laws, which is the par or stated value of the additional shares issued.

To illustrate a small stock dividend, assume that Lerner Corporation has the following stockholders' equity:

Stockholders' Equity

Paid-in capital:	
Common stock, $5 par value, 100,000 shares authorized, 60,000 shares issued and outstanding	$300,000
Paid-in capital in excess of par value	214,000
Total paid-in capital	514,000
Retained earnings	380,000
Total stockholders' equity	$894,000

Assume further that the board of directors declares a 5% stock dividend on December 20, distributable on January 10 to stockholders of record on December 31. The market price of the stock was $25 per share on December 20. The entry to record the declaration of the stock dividend is:

Dec.	20	Retained Earnings	75,000	
		Stock Dividend Distributable		15,000
		Paid-in Capital in Excess of Par Value		60,000

Like cash dividends, stock dividends are declared on outstanding shares only. Because this is a small stock dividend, the Retained Earnings account is debited for the market value of the shares to be distributed, computed as follows:

$$60,000 \times 5\% = 3,000 \text{ shares} \times \$25 = \$75,000$$

The Stock Dividend Distributable account is credited for the par value of the shares to be issued (3,000 × $5 = $15,000), and the excess of the total market value over par value is credited to Paid-in Capital in Excess of Par Value [3,000 × ($25 − $5) = $60,000]. The Stock Dividend Distributable account is reported as a separate item of paid-in capital on the December 31 balance sheet. Note that it is *not* a liability because there is no obligation to distribute corporate assets.

When the shares are distributed on January 10, the entry is:

Jan.	10	Stock Dividend Distributable	15,000	
		Common Stock		15,000

The net effect of the entries on December 20 and January 10 is to decrease retained earnings by $75,000 and to increase paid-in capital by the same amount, of which $15,000 is an increase in legal capital and $60,000 increases Paid-in Capital in Excess of Par Value. Thus, total stockholders' equity remains unchanged by the stock dividend as demonstrated below:

	Before Stock Dividend	After Stock Dividend
Common stock	$300,000	$315,000
Paid-in capital in excess of par value	214,000	274,000
Retained earnings	380,000	305,000
Total stockholders' equity	$894,000	$894,000

Because total stockholders' equity remained unchanged, each stockholder's interest in total stockholders' equity also would remain unchanged. For example, assume that Paula Darling owned 6,000 shares (10%) of Lerner Corporation before the distribution of the stock dividend. Her share of the stockholders' equity before and after the dividend would be:

$$\text{Before } \frac{6,000 \text{ shares}}{60,000 \text{ shares}} = 10\% \times \$894,000 = \$89,400$$

$$\text{After } \frac{6,300 \text{ shares}}{63,000 \text{ shares}} = 10\% \times \$894,000 = \$89,400$$

STOCK SPLITS

Many investors prefer to spread their investment risk by purchasing stock in several corporations. Since stock is normally traded in 100-share lots, the purchase of 100 shares of a stock with a market price of $100 per share requires a $10,000 investment, which may prohibit small investors from diversifying their holdings. Consequently, as mentioned earlier, a company may want to reduce the market price of its stock in order to make it available to a wider range of investors. One method of accomplishing this objective is to declare a large stock dividend. An alternative is to *split the stock* by decreasing the par or stated value of the stock and increasing the number of shares proportionally.

To illustrate, assume that Draydon Corporation's stockholders' equity is:

Stockholders' Equity

Paid-in capital:	
Common stock, $5 par value, 100,000 shares	
authorized, 60,000 shares issued and outstanding	$300,000
Paid-in capital in excess of par value	200,000
Total paid-in capital	500,000
Retained earnings	400,000
Total stockholders' equity	$900,000

Assume further that the common stock has a current market price of $120 per share. In order to reduce the market price, the board of directors votes to split the stock 4 for 1, which should reduce the market price per share to about $30. When the stock is split, the par value per share is decreased to $1.25 ($5/4) and the number of authorized shares is increased to 400,000. Outstanding stock is recalled and new stock certificates are issued, four new shares given for each share recalled.

A stock split does not change the balance of any of the stockholders' equity accounts. Legal capital remains the same ($300,000) since 240,000 shares are outstanding with a par value of $1.25 each. Thus, all that is necessary is a memo entry in the journal and Common Stock account indicating that the par value has been reduced and the number of shares increased.

COMPARISON OF LARGE STOCK DIVIDENDS AND STOCK SPLITS

Large stock dividends are sometimes mistakenly called stock splits. Although both have the same effect on the market price of the stock—so that a 2-for-1 stock split and a 100% stock dividend both result in a doubling of the number of shares outstanding and a market price of about one-half of the previous market price—they are legally different. All stock dividends result in an increase in the amount of legal capital and a decrease in retained earnings; stock splits do not.

SPECIAL INCOME STATEMENT ITEMS AND RETAINED EARNINGS

Retained earnings often are a major portion of total stockholders equity. For example, General Electric Company's 1989 annual report shows total stockholder's equity of $20.89 billion, of which $20.35 billion is retained earnings. Retained earnings increase primarily from earnings as reported on the income statement. Thus, the way net income is determined has an effect on the amount of retained earnings reported.

Determining periodic net income is one of the primary functions of accounting. The amount of net income earned, as well as the trend of earnings over time, are important to users of accounting information because they serve as measures of management efficiency, of creditworthiness, and as factors in the prediction of future earnings. Earnings from normal, recurring operating activities are presumed to be more useful in predicting future earnings. Thus, as explained in Chapter 2, earnings from normal operations are separated on the income statement from those resulting from unusual transactions not expected to recur on a regular basis. Three categories of unusual transactions are identified by current accounting practice: discontinued operations, extraordinary gains and losses, and changes in accounting principles. These special components of income are illustrated in Figure 13-2 and discussed following a brief discussion of net-of-tax reporting.

NET-OF-TAX REPORTING

The special components of income are reported in the income statement on a net-of-tax basis. That is, the increase or decrease in income from the special component is reported net of its income tax effect. For example, in Figure 13-2 the income tax effects on discontinued operations are reported parenthetically and both the operating income from the discontinued segment and the gain on sale of the discontinued segment are added to income at their net-of-tax amounts. Thus, the pretax gain on the sale of the segment was $1,067,000 and the net-of-tax gain was $800,000 ($1,067,000 − $267,000).

Figure 13-2
Special Income
Statement Items

DRAKE COMMUNICATIONS, INC.
Partial Income Statement
For the Year Ended December 31, 1992

Income from continuing operations before tax		$1,050,000
Income tax expense		320,000
Income from continuing operations		730,000
Discontinued operations:		
Operating income of discontinued segment		
(Net of $29,000 income tax)	$ 60,000	
Gain on sale of discontinued segment		
(Net of $267,000 income tax)	800,000	860,000
Income before extraordinary item		1,590,000
Extraordinary item: Earthquake loss		
(Net of $240,000 income tax savings)		600,000
Income before effect of accounting change		990,000
Cumulative effect on prior years' income of a		
change in depreciation method		
(Net of $36,000 income tax)		84,000
Net income		$1,074,000
Earnings (loss) per common share for:		
Income from continuing operations		$1.83
Discontinued operations		2.15
Extraordinary loss		(1.50)
Cumulative effect of accounting change		.21
Net income		$2.69

The earnings per share data are based on the assumption that Drake Communications, Inc. capital stock consists of 400,000 shares of outstanding common stock.

The use of net-of-tax reporting avoids distorting the income (loss) from the continuing operations figure that would result if the entire net tax expense of $412,000 ($320,000 + $29,000 + $267,000 − $240,000 + $36,000) in Figure 13-2 were deducted from income from continuing operations before tax. In addition, the special components of income would also be distorted since they would be reported at their pretax amounts. Instead, the total tax expense is allocated to income from continuing operations and the special components of income. We will see later that this net-of-tax approach is also used to report prior period adjustments (discussed later in this chapter).

DISCONTINUED OPERATIONS— DISPOSAL OF A BUSINESS SEGMENT

Objective 11: Reporting Discontinued Operations, Extraordinary Items, and Changes in Accounting Principles

Most large corporations have several business segments. For the purpose of reporting discontinued operations, a segment of a business is defined as "a component of an entity whose activities represent a separate major line of business or class of customer."[1] For example, assume that Drake Communications, Inc. has four segments— newspaper publishing, magazine publishing, radio, and television. If one segment is sold, the income statement for the year will not be comparable with those of other years. Current accounting standards require that for the segment sold, the gain or loss on sale and the operating net income or loss of the current year to the date of sale must be presented in a separate section of the income statement after income from continuing operations.

Assume that Drake Communications, Inc. sold its radio stations on August 1, 1992, at an after-tax gain of $800,000. Prior to August 1, the radio stations had earned $60,000 net income after taxes. The sale is reported in a separate discontinued operations section of the income statement as shown in Figure 13-2.

EXTRAORDINARY ITEMS

Some gains and losses result from events so unusual and occur so infrequently that they are reported separately on the income statement to distinguish them from the results of normal operating activities. The events, called extraordinary items, are relatively rare, because they must be material in amount, unusual in nature, and occur infrequently. Unusual and infrequent events are described in APB Opinion No. 30 in the following way.

Unusual Nature—the underlying event or transaction should possess a high degree of abnormality and be of a type clearly unrelated to, or only incidentally related to, the ordinary and typical activities of the entity, taking into account the environment in which the entity operates.

Infrequency of Occurrence—the underlying event or transaction should be of a type that would not reasonably be expected to recur in the foreseeable future, taking into account the environment in which the entity operates.[2]

The environment includes such factors as the characteristics of the industry in which the firm operates, the geographical location of its operations, and the nature and extent of governmental regulations.

A given event may be unusual in nature for one firm but not for another because

[1]Opinions of the Accounting Principles Board No. 30, "Reporting the Results of Operations" (New York: AICPA, June 1973), par. 13.

[2]Ibid., par. 20.

of differences in their environments. For example, an earthquake loss in Minnesota (where earthquakes rarely occur) would be unusual, whereas one in California may not be. Past experience of a company may be used to determine the probability of recurrence of an event, but is not sufficient, by itself, to satisfy the criterion of infrequency of occurrence. If the event occurs frequently in the environment in which the firm operates, it is not extraordinary.

When an event qualifies as an extraordinary item, it is reported on the income statement after discontinued operations (if any) under the caption of "Extraordinary Items." To illustrate, assume that Drake Communications, Inc. has a television station damaged by an earthquake in an area where no quake has ever occurred before. The loss is reported on the income statement as shown in Figure 13-2. Note that, as with the disposal of a segment, the extraordinary loss is reported net of its related tax effect. That is, we have assumed an $840,000 pretax earthquake loss, of which $240,000 reduces income tax expense, thereby producing a tax savings.

Sometimes events occur that meet only one of the criteria for extraordinary items. In those cases, any material gain or loss resulting should be reported as a separate item in the determination of income from continuing operations. These gains or losses are generally reported under the "Other revenue and expense" caption. Extraordinary items are closed to the Income Summary account.

CHANGE IN ACCOUNTING PRINCIPLES

As discussed in earlier chapters, alternative methods may be used to account for some types of transactions. For example, several methods are acceptable in accounting for inventory and for depreciation. Different methods may result in material differences in income statement and balance sheet amounts.

The *consistency principle* in accounting generally requires that once an accounting method is adopted, it must be used consistently to provide comparable data from one accounting period to another. However, an exception to the consistency principle is permitted and an accounting method may be changed if a new method is preferable to the old one. A company may change from the straight-line method to an accelerated depreciation method for depreciating equipment, for example, because the service benefits incorporated in the equipment are actually being used on an accelerated basis.

When an accounting principle is changed, a description of the change, the reason for it, and its effect on net income for the period must be disclosed in a footnote to the financial statement. In addition, the change in principle is assumed to have been made at the beginning of the year of change, and the cumulative effect of the change to the beginning of the year generally must be reported on the income statement immediately after extraordinary items (if any). The *cumulative effect* is the total effect the new method would have had on retained earnings if it had been applied in past periods instead of the old method.[3]

To illustrate, assume that Drake Communications, Inc. uses the sum-of-years'-digits depreciation method for its printing equipment. In 1992, management decides to change to the straight-line method, because it more closely reflects the true pattern of asset use. The cumulative effect of the change to the beginning of 1992 was computed as $120,000.

The cumulative effect of the change, assuming a 30% income tax rate, is reported on the income statement as shown in Figure 13-2. Again, note that it is reported net

---

[3]Some changes in accounting principles are disclosed by restating the financial statement of prior years. For a complete discussion of accounting changes, see APB Opinion No. 20, Accounting Changes (New York: AICPA, 1972).

of its related tax effect. Because it is an income statement account, the Cumulative Effect of Accounting Change account is closed to the Income Summary account at year-end.

RETAINED EARNINGS STATEMENT

In addition to a balance sheet, income statement, and statement of cash flows, corporations also prepare a retained earnings statement either as a separate statement or as part of a combined statement of income and retained earnings. The retained earnings statement summarizes the changes that have taken place in the Retained Earnings account during the year, as illustrated in Figure 13-3.

PRIOR PERIOD ADJUSTMENTS

Generally, all items that affect retained earnings during a period, with the exception of dividends, must be included in the determination of net income of that period. A major exception to this general policy is the correction of a material error in the financial statements of a prior period.[4]

Errors result from mathematical mistakes, mistakes in the application of accounting principles, or oversights or misuse of facts that existed at the time the financial statements were prepared. Errors discovered in the same period in which they occurred are corrected in the current period's financial statements. Errors in net income not discovered until a later accounting period are excluded from the current year's income statement to avoid distorting the net income of the current period. Because net income is closed to retained earnings, the correction of an error in a prior year's net income is adjusted to the beginning balance of retained earnings in the year in which the error is discovered. These adjustments, which are made net of income tax effects, are called **prior period adjustments**.

To illustrate, assume that in the process of preparing closing entries at the end of 1992 the accountant discovered that the company failed to record depreciation of $125,000 on machinery acquired at the beginning of 1991. Therefore, 1991 net income

Figure 13-3
Retained Earnings
Statement

DRAKE COMMUNICATIONS, INC.
Statement of Retained Earnings
For the Year Ended December 31, 1992

Retained earnings balance, January 1	$ 485,000
Prior period adjustment:	
Correction of error in prior years' depreciation	(75,000)
Retained earnings balance, January 1 as adjusted	410,000
Net income for 1992	1,074,000
Total	1,484,000
Less: Cash dividends	(502,000)
Retained earnings balance, December 31	$ 982,000

[4]Statement of Financial Accounting Standards Board No. 16, "Prior Period Adjustments" (Stamford, Conn.: FASB, 1977), par. 11.

before taxes was overstated by $125,000. If we assume an income tax rate of 40%, income tax expense of 1991 was also too high by $50,000 ($125,000 × 40%). As a result of these two items, 1991 net income after taxes, and retained earnings, were overstated by $75,000 ($125,000 − $50,000). The 1991 income tax return is amended and a claim for the $50,000 refund is filed. To correct the records in 1992, the following journal entry is made:

Dec.	31	Receivable for Tax Refund	50,000	
		Retained Earnings Prior Period Adjustment	75,000	
		Accumulated Depreciation		125,000

The Prior Period Adjustment is shown in the statement of retained earnings as illustrated in Figure 13-3.

RETAINED EARNINGS RESTRICTIONS

Restrictions are often placed on retained earnings so that the retained earnings reported in the balance sheet are not entirely available for dividend declarations. Some restrictions are legal requirements. For example, most states restrict the availability of retained earnings for dividends to the extent of the cost of treasury stock purchased. To protect creditors, most states limit the distribution of assets to stockholders to the amount of retained earnings. If a corporation were to declare dividends in the amount of its total retained earnings, and also acquire treasury stock, it would distribute assets in excess of retained earnings, thereby reducing creditors' protection.

Some retained earnings restrictions are contractual. For example, bond indentures and other borrowing agreements often include a restriction on the amount of dividends that can be paid until the debt is repaid. The purpose of such a restriction is to provide additional protection to the lenders, since corporate assets not distributed as dividends are more likely to be available for interest payments and debt retirement. Other retained earnings restrictions are made voluntarily by the board of directors. For example, many corporations have contingent liabilities such as lawsuits in process.

Regardless of the nature of the restriction—legal, contractual, or voluntary—its purpose is to retain assets in the business rather than distribute them as dividends. Restrictions on the payment of dividends are normally disclosed in footnotes to the financial statements. For example, a recent annual report for International Multifoods Corporation included the following footnote:

Retained earnings are restricted as to payment of cash dividends and other stock payments by terms of long-term debt indentures unless certain financial tests are met. Under the most restrictive of these tests, approximately $25,700,000 of retained earnings was free from such restrictions.

BOOK VALUE PER SHARE OF COMMON STOCK

Common stockholders' equity is often reported in statistical summaries in annual reports and in the financial press as an amount per share, generally called **book value per share of common stock**. It is computed by dividing total common stockholders' equity by the number of common shares outstanding. If a corporation has only one type of stock, book value per share is determined by dividing total stockholders' equity by the number of shares outstanding. For example, assume a corporation has

Objective 12:
The nature of retained earnings restrictions

the following stockholders' equity:

Common stock, $5 par value, 100,000 shares authorized,	
60,000 shares issued and outstanding	$ 300,000
Paid-in capital in excess of par value	550,000
Retained earnings	722,000
Total stockholders' equity	$1,572,000

Book value per share of common stock is $26.20 ($1,572,000/60,000 shares).

When a corporation has both preferred and common stock outstanding, total stockholders' equity must be allocated to the two classes of stock. Because book value per share is reported for common stock only, the approach is to subtract from total stockholders' equity the amount that would be distributed to preferred stockholders if the corporation were liquidated. Thus, the equity allocated to preferred stock is its call price plus any dividends in arrears. To illustrate, assume a corporation has the following stockholders' equity:

8% Cumulative preferred stock, $100 par value, 5,000	
shares issued and outstanding, callable at $105	$ 500,000
Common stock, $5 par value, 100,000 shares	
authorized, 60,000 shares issued and outstanding	300,000
Paid-in capital in excess of par value	550,000
Retained earnings	722,000
Total stockholders' equity	$2,072,000

Assume further that there were no dividends in arrears for prior years, but that the current year's preferred dividend has not yet been declared. Book value per common share is computed as follows:

Total stockholders' equity		$2,072,000
Allocated to preferred stock:		
Call price (5,000 × $105)	$525,000	
Preferred dividends (8% × $500,000)	40,000	
Total		565,000
Allocated to common stock		$1,507,000
Book value per share of common stock		
($1,507,000/60,000 shares)		$25.12

The main purpose of including the book value per share of common stock in statistical summaries is to give some indication to readers of financial statements of the effect of the retention of earnings on growth of the corporation. For example, the book value per common share of BFGoodrich Company increased from $30.43 to $46.07 during a recent five-year period, reflecting the effect of the retention of earnings.

Book value should not be confused with liquidation value. If the corporation were liquidated, its assets would probably be sold at prices quite different from their book values. In addition, book value normally has little relationship to a stock's market value. The level of current earnings, earning capacity, and dividend policy are more important factors affecting the market value of common stock.

SUMMARY

In this chapter, we discussed how corporations are organized, the types of stock they issue, accounting procedures for stockholders' equity and the reporting of special income statement items. Corporations may be organized for profit or nonprofit purposes. Profit corporations may be either public corporations whose stock is widely held or nonpublic corporations whose stock is held by a relatively small group. Corporate stockholders elect a board of directors which has final responsibility for managing the corporation. Boards of directors often restrict their activity to formulating broad major policies and appointing corporate officers who are responsible for carrying out those policies. Corporate officers generally consist of a president, one or more vice-presidents, a controller, a treasurer, and a secretary.

Corporate capital is classified by source into two major types: paid-in capital and retained earnings. Paid-in capital shows the interest of the stockholders in the amount of assets invested in the corporation by them. Retained earnings represents the stockholders interest in the amount of income earned by the corporation and retained in the business. Paid-in capital is subclassified into legal capital (par value or stated value) and other types of paid-in capital such as paid-in capital in excess of par or stated value.

Corporations may often issue both common stock and preferred stock. Stock that has been issued and not reacquired is called outstanding stock, which are the only shares containing the normal stock rights. Stock that has been issued and reacquired but not formally retired is called treasury stock. Earnings that are not retained in the business are distributed to the stockholders as dividends. Dividends may be cash dividends which reduce corporate assets and stockholders equity by equal amounts. In contrast, stock dividends do not result in a change in total assets or total stockholders' equity; rather, they result in a transfer of retained earnings to paid-in capital. Corporations sometimes also split their stock by increasing the number of shares and decreasing the par or stated value per share proportionately. The main objective of a stock split is to reduce the market value per share to make the shares available to a broader range of investors.

Special income statement items, such as the effects of discontinued operations, extraordinary items, and changes in accounting principles, are reported in separate sections of the income statement on a net-of-tax basis.

SELF-TEST

Test your understanding of the chapter by selecting the best answer for each of the following.

1. Shares of common stock that have been issued and not repurchased are called:
    a. outstanding stock.
    b. treasury stock.
    c. authorized stock.
    d. unissued stock.
2. The preemptive right of common stockholders is the right to:
    a. share in dividend distributions.
    b. vote for directors and on other matters.
    c. share in the distribution of assets on liquidation of the company.
    d. purchase shares of new common stock issues on a pro rata basis.
3. The par value of common stock is the:
    a. book value of the common stock.
    b. present value of the common stock.
    c. market value of the common stock.
    d. legal value assigned to the stock.

4. Declaration of a cash dividend:
   a. reduces cash.
   b. increases the number of shares outstanding.
   c. reduces legal capital.
   d. reduces retained earnings.
5. When holders of preferred stock have a right to current year dividends and dividends in arrears before any dividend payment can be made to the holders of common stock, they have:
   a. participating preferred stock.
   b. cumulative preferred stock.
   c. noncumulative preferred stock.
   d. voting preferred stock.
6. A stock split:
   a. reduces total stockholders' equity.
   b. reduces legal capital.
   c. reduces the par value of par value stock.
   d. increases an investor's ownership percentage.
7. Small stock dividends are recorded at the number of shares issued times the:
   a. market price per share.
   b. book value per share.
   c. par value per share.
   d. average issue price per share.
8. The difference between the cost of treasury stock and its reissue price is reflected in the following accounts:
   a. Paid-in capital.
   b. Retained earnings and paid-in capital.
   c. Retained earnings and income.
   d. Retained earnings, income, and paid-in capital.

REVIEW PROBLEM

The stockholders' equity section of the December 31, 1992 balance sheet for Forgy Steel Corporation is shown below:

Stockholders' Equity

Paid-in Capital:	
Capital stock:	
Preferred stock, 6%, cumulative $50 par value, 50,000 shares authorized, 20,000 shares issued	$1,000,000
Common stock, $5 par value, 200,000 shares authorized, 150,000 shares issued, 123,500 shares outstanding	750,000
Other paid-in capital:	
Paid-in capital in excess of par value–preferred	85,000
Paid-in capital in excess of par value–common	2,100,000
Paid-in capital from treasury stock transactions	75,000
Total paid-in capital	4,010,000
Retained Earnings	1,420,000
Total paid-in capital and retained earnings	5,430,000
Less: Treasury stock, common, 26,500 shares at cost	609,500
Total Stockholders' Equity	$4,820,500

Required:
Using the data contained in the stockholders' equity presented above for Forgy Steel Corporation, complete the following requirements:

A. How many shares of commons stock are outstanding?
B. What was the average price at which the common stock was originally issued?
C. What is the cost per share of the treasury stock?
D. Assuming all the treasury stock was purchased at one time, and that 28,000 shares were originally purchased, what was the average price received for the 1,500 shares of the treasury stock that were resold?
E. Assume 1,000 shares of the treasury stock are sold for $50 per share. Make the journal entry to record the sale.
F. Assume 1,000 shares of the treasury stock are sold for $8 per share. Make the journal entry to record the sale.
G. Forgy's board of directors declared a 5% common stock dividend. The market value of the stock on the declaration date was $33 per share.
   1. How many shares of common stock will be issued in the stock dividend?
   2. At what value per share should retained earnings be transferred to paid-in capital? Why.
   3. Prepare the journal entry to record the declaration of the stock dividend.
   4. Prepare the journal entry to record the distribution of the stock dividend.

ANSWER TO REVIEW PROBLEM

A. 150,000 shares issued minus 26,500 treasury shares = 123,500 shares outstanding.
B. $750,000 par value plus $2,100,000 paid-in capital in excess of par value = $2,850,000/150,000 shares = $19 per share.
C. $609,500/26,500 = $23 per share.
D. Since there is paid-in capital from treasury stock transactions amounting to $75,000, the treasury stock must have been sold for $23 per share plus $75,000. Thus, [($23 × 1,500) + $75,000 = $109,500/1,500 shares = $73 per share.
E.

Cash	50,000	
Treasury Stock		23,000
Paid-in Capital from Treasury Stock		
Transactions		27,000

F.

Cash	8,000	
Paid-in Capital from Treasury Stock		
Transactions	15,000	
Treasury Stock		23,000

G. 1. 123,500 shares outstanding × 5% = 6,175 shares
    2. Market value per share ($33) since it is a small stock dividend.
    3.

Retained Earnings	203,775	
Stock Dividends Distributable		30,875
Paid-in Capital in Excess of Par Value		172,900

    4.

Stock Dividends Distributable	30,875	
Common Stock		30,875

ANSWERS TO SELF-TEST

1. a   **2.** d   **3.** d   **4.** d   **5.** b   **6.** c   **7.** a   **8.** b

APPENDIX: ACCOUNTING FOR OWNERS' EQUITY OF NONINCORPORATED BUSINESSES

Objective 13: Accounting for owners' equity in proprietorships and partnerships

Nonincorporated businesses consist of two types, proprietorships and partnerships. A *proprietorship* is a business owned by one person. The owner usually maintains two owners' equity accounts, a Capital account (e.g. Brent Jones, Capital), and a Drawing account (such as Brent Jones, Drawing). The Capital account is used to record investments of cash and other assets by the owner and to accumulate periodic net income or net loss. Thus, the Income Summary account is closed to the Capital account at the end of the accounting period.

The Drawing account is used to record the withdrawal of assets, usually cash, from the business by the owner. The owner of a proprietorship often establishes a fixed amount to be withdrawn from the business periodically for personal living expenses. Although the owner may think of these withdrawals as a salary, neither law nor tax codes recognize a proprietor as an employee of the business because the owner cannot hire himself. Consequently, recurring withdrawals made in anticipation of earnings are not considered a salary nor an expense of the business. Sometimes personal expenses of the owner may be paid directly from the cash of the business. Such payments should be debited to the Drawing account since they are not expenses of doing business.

The Drawing account is closed to the Capital account at the end of the accounting period as part of the closing process. Thus, on a cumulative basis, the Capital account contains all investments by the owner plus all earnings of the business less all business losses and withdrawals of assets by the owner.

The following transactions and journal entries illustrate the normal accounting for owner's equity of a proprietorship.

Jan.	1	Brent Jones invested $100,000 cash from his personal savings to start an appliance repair business.		
Jan.	1	Cash	100,000	
		Brent Jones, Capital		100,000
Jan.	31	Brent Jones established a policy of withdrawing $1,200 at the end of each month to be used for personal expenses. The first withdrawal was made.		
Jan.	31	Brent Jones, Drawing	1,200	
		Cash		1,200
Dec.	31	The balances of $32,500 in the Income Summary account and $14,400 in Brent's Drawing account are closed to the Capital Account.		

Dec.	31	Income Summary	32,500	
		Brent Jones, Capital		32,500
Dec.	31	Brent Jones, Capital	14,400	
		Brent Jones, Drawing		
		($1,200 × 12 months)		14,400

The owner's equity portion of the balance sheet on December 31 would be as follows:

Owner's Equity:
Brent Jones, capital, January 1 $100,000
Add: Net Income for the year   32,500
    Total   132,500
Less: Withdrawals during the year   14,400
Brent Jones, capital, December 31 $118,100

There is one other major difference between accounting for a corporation and accounting for a proprietorship: proprietorships are not taxable entities. The net income (or loss) of the proprietorship must appear on the personal income tax return of the owner. Consequently, the financial statements for the proprietorship will not contain an income tax expense amount in the income statement nor an income tax liability in the balance sheet.

PARTNERS' OWNERSHIP EQUITY ACCOUNTS

A *partnership* is defined by the Uniform Partnership Act (which has been adopted in most states) as "an association of two or more persons to carry on as co-owners a business for profit." A written agreement is not necessary to form a partnership; thus, it is sometimes difficult to determine if a partnership in fact exists. Three attributes are necessary for a partnership:

1. There must be an agreement between two or more legally competent persons;
2. The business must be operated for the purpose of earning a profit; and
3. Members of the firm must be co-owners of the business.

Co-ownership involves the right of each partner to share in the profits of the firm, to participate with the other partners in the management of the firm, and to own jointly with the other partners the property of the partnership. The right to participate in management is sometimes limited by an express agreement among the partners. The partnership contract or agreement should contain such important matters as how profits and losses will be split among the partners, responsibilities and duties of the partners, and procedures to be followed upon dissolution of the partnership.

Partnerships have certain advantages and disadvantages when compared to corporations. The primary advantages are ease of formation and the lack of income tax on the income of the partnership as an entity. (Partners report their share of partnership income or loss on their personal tax returns.) The main disadvantage is that each partner is personally liable for the obligations of the partnership, which means that if the creditors of the partnership are not paid from the assets of the partnership, they can look to an individual partner's personal assets for recovery of unpaid claims.

Accounting for owners' equity of a partnership is similar to accounting for a proprietorship except that separate Capital and Drawing accounts are maintained for each partner. Investments of assets by individual partners are credited to their separate Capital accounts; withdrawals by each partner are debited to their respective Drawing accounts. The Income Summary account is closed to the partners' Capital accounts in accordance with the profit and loss sharing agreement. Like proprietors, partners' drawing accounts are closed to their respective Capital accounts.

The following transactions and journal entries illustrate the normal accounting for owners' equity in a partnership.

Jan. 1 A partnership was formed by Brent Jones and Sally Deal to operate a real estate office. Brent Jones invested $65,000 and Sally Deal invested $35,000; they agreed to share profits and losses in the ratio of 70% and 30%, respectively. The journal entry to record the investment is:

Jan.	1	Cash	100,000	
		Brent Jones, Capital		65,000
		Sally Deal, Capital		35,000

Jan. 31 It was agreed that Brent Jones and Sally Deal would withdraw $1,000 and $700 per month respectively to cover personal expenses. The entry for January and for each month thereafter would be:

Jan.	31	Brent Jones, Drawing	1,000	
		Sally Deal, Drawing	700	
		Cash		1,700

Dec. 31 After all revenue and expense accounts have been closed, the credit balance in the Income Summary account was $47,000. The Income Summary and individual Drawing accounts are closed as follows:

Dec	31	Income Summary	47,000	
		Brent Jones, Capital (70% × $47,000)		32,900
		Sally Deal, Capital (30% × $47,000)		14,100
	31	Brent Jones, Capital ($1,000 × 12)	12,000	
		Sally Deal, Capital ($700 × 12)	8,400	
		Brent Jones, Drawing		12,000
		Sally Deal, Drawing		8,400

Financial statements for the partnership are similar to those of a proprietorship except that the allocation of profit or loss is often indicated at the bottom of the income statement and the individual partners' Capital accounts are shown in owners' equity, as shown below:

Partial Income Statement

Net Income	$47,000
Allocation of Net Income:	
Brent Jones, 70%	$32,900
Sally Deal, 30%	14,100
Total	$47,000

Partial Balance Sheet

Partners' Equity:		
Brent Jones, Capital	$85,900	
Sally Deal, Capital	40,700	
Total Partners' Equity		$126,600

In addition, a statement of changes in partners' capital is often prepared as a supplement to the balance sheet:

Jones and Deal Partnership
Statement of Changes in Partners' Capital
For the Year Ended December 31, 1992

	B. Jones	S. Deal	Total
Investment, January 1	$65,000	$35,000	$100,000
Add: Net income for the year	32,900	14,100	47,000
Total	97,900	49,100	147,000
Less: Withdrawals during the year	12,000	8,400	20,400
Partners' capital, December 31	$85,900	$40,700	$126,600

GLOSSARY

AUTHORIZED STOCK.   The maximum amount of stock a corporation is permitted to issue under the terms of its charter (p. 579).

BOOK VALUE PER SHARE OF COMMON STOCK.   The amount of common stockholders' equity related to each share of common stock (p. 595).

CALL PROVISION.   The right of a corporation to repurchase preferred stock from its stockholders at a predetermined price (p. 585).

COMMON STOCK.   Stock of a corporation having only one class of stock; if there is more than one class, the class that has no preferences relative to the other classes of stock (p. 579).

CORPORATE CHARTER.   The legal contract between the state and the incorporators (p. 575).

CUMULATIVE PREFERRED STOCK.   Preferred stock on which undeclared dividends accumulate and must be paid before any dividend can be paid to common stockholders (p. 584).

DEFICIT.   A negative (debit) balance in retained earnings (p. 579).

DIVIDEND.   A distribution of cash, other assets, or a corporation's own stock to its stockholders (p. 582).

DIVIDENDS IN ARREARS.   Dividends on cumulative preferred stock that are not declared in the year in which they are due (p. 584).

EXTRAORDINARY ITEM.   An event that is unusual in nature and occurs infrequently, considering the environment in which a firm operates (p. 592).

INCORPORATORS.   Individuals who form a corporation and sign the application for a corporate charter (p. 575).

LIQUIDATING DIVIDEND.   A dividend declared in excess of retained earnings. It is a return of capital rather than a return on capital (p. 582).

NONCUMULATIVE PREFERRED STOCK.   Preferred stock on which the right to receive dividends is lost in any year in which dividends are not declared (p. 584).

NONPROFIT CORPORATION.   A corporation organized for nonprofit purposes; it generally depends upon public contributions for its continued existence (p. 573).

NONPUBLIC CORPORATION (CLOSELY HELD CORPORATION).   A corporation whose shares are not publicly traded (p. 573).

PAID-IN CAPITAL.   The capital invested in the corporation by its stockholders or donated by nonstockholders (p. 578).

PARTICIPATING PREFERRED STOCK.   Preferred stock that participates in dividends declared in excess of any dividends in arrears and current required dividends (p. 584).

PREEMPTIVE RIGHT.   The right that permits stockholders to maintain their percentage interest in a corporation by purchasing new shares in proportion to their current holdings (p. 576).

PREFERRED STOCK.   A type of stock that has certain preferences, such as a preference in dividend distributions or in asset distributions if the corporation is liquidated (p. 583).

PRIOR PERIOD ADJUSTMENT.   Direct adjustment to retained earnings to correct an error in the net income of a prior period (p. 594).

PROFIT CORPORATION.   A corporation organized with the goal of earning a profit for its stockholders (p. 573).

PROXY STATEMENT.   A legal document under which a stockholder assigns his or her vote to an agent (p. 577).

PUBLIC CORPORATION.   A corporation whose shares are widely held and traded through national stock exchanges (p. 573).

RETAINED EARNINGS.   The interest of stockholders in the earnings of a corporation that have been retained in the business rather than distributed to them (p. 579).

SEGMENT OF A BUSINESS.   A component of an entity whose activities represent a separate major line of business or class of customer (p. 592).

STOCK CERTIFICATE.   A legal document providing evidence of the number of shares owned and containing the provisions of stock ownership (p. 575).

STOCK DIVIDEND.   A pro-rata distribution of additional shares of a corporation's own stock to its stockholders (p. 587).

TREASURY STOCK.   A corporation's own stock that has been issued and reacquired but not retired or reissued (p. 586).

DISCUSSION QUESTIONS

1.   What is the difference between public corporations and nonpublic corporations?

2.   What are the main advantages of the corporate form of business organization? What are the main disadvantages?

3.   What are the general rights of common stockholders?

4.   What is a proxy statement?

5.   Distinguish between paid-in capital and retained earnings.

6.   Bee Corporation has retained earnings at the beginning of the year of $200,000. The only entry affecting this account during the year was the entry to close the $220,000 debit balance in the Income Summary account. What is the balance in the Retained Earnings account at year-end? What is this balance called?

7.   What is legal capital? What does it consist of?

8.   What entry would be made to record the issuance of 10,000 shares of $2 par value common stock for $20 per share? How much (if any) of the amount received represents income to the corporation?

9.   When stock is issued for assets other than cash, accountants must determine the amount at which to record the transaction. What is the rule generally followed?

10. What accounts are involved when recording the declaration of a cash dividend? What accounts are involved when recording payment of the cash dividend?

11. Define each of the following terms in the context of their application to preferred stock:
    a. Cumulative.
    b. Dividends in arrears.
    c. Call provision.
    d. Convertible.

12. What is treasury stock? For what purposes might a corporation reacquire its own shares?

13. A corporation purchased 1,000 shares of its own $1 par value common stock at a price of $20 per share. What is the entry to record the purchase? What kind of account is the Treasury Stock account? How is this account reported on the balance sheet?

14. What is a stock dividend? What effect do stock dividends have on corporate assets and on total stockholders' equity?

15. What is a stock split? What effect does a stock split have on total stockholders' equity?

16. What is the purpose of the retained earnings statement?

17. XYZ Corporation has retained earnings of $480,000 and holds treasury stock purchased at a cost of $180,000. In most states, what is the maximum amount of retained earnings that could be declared as a dividend? Why? Where is information regarding restrictions on retained earnings disclosed?

18. How is book value per share of common stock determined when a corporation has both common stock and preferred stock outstanding?

19. What relationship is there between book value per share of common stock and the market price of the common stock?

20A. What is the form of business owned by one person? What owner's equity accounts are used for this form of business? Describe the type of transactions recorded in each of these accounts.

21A. Define a "partnership." What attributes are necessary for a partnership to exist?

22A. Identify the advantages and disadvantages of a partnership form of business as compared to a corporation. Is the accounting for owners' equity in a partnership more like accounting for a corporation or a proprietorship?

EXERCISES

Exercise 13-1 Preparing a Stockholders' Equity Section of a Balance Sheet
Following are several general ledger accounts of Vulcan Company:

Cash	$ 457,540
Retained earnings	42,165,600
Land	6,000,000
Paid-in capital in excess of par value–preferred	365,000
Bonds payable	5,000,000
Preferred stock, $100 par value, 6% cumulative, 100,000 shares authorized, 40,000 shares issued and outstanding	4,000,000
Paid-in capital in excess of par value–common	21,120,000
Common stock, $1 par value, 10,000,000 shares authorized, 6,780,000 shares issued and outstanding	6,780,000

Required:

Prepare the stockholders' equity section of Vulcan Company's balance sheet.

Exercise 13-2 Issuance of Common Stock

Treadway Company recently received a corporate charter which included authorization to issue 500,000 shares of common stock.

Required:

A. Prepare the journal entry to record the sale of 50,000 shares of common stock at $20 per share assuming:
1. The stock has a par value of $1 per share.
2. The stock is straight no-par stock.
3. The stock is no-par stock with a stated value of $9 per share.
B. Prepare the journal entry to record the issue of 40,000 shares of common stock in exchange for land and a building with appraised values of $50,000 and $350,000 respectively. The stock has a par value of $4 per share and a current market price of $11.25 per share. (Record the transaction at the fair value of the stock given.)

Exercise 13-3 Declaration and Payment of Dividends

Clatten Corporation has 20,000 shares of 6% cumulative, $100 par value preferred stock and 400,000 shares of $1 par value common stock outstanding. On December 10, 1992, Clatten declared the annual dividend on preferred stock and a $.25 per share dividend on common stock. The dividend is to be paid on December 30, 1992, to stockholders of record on December 23, 1992.

Required:

Prepare the journal entries to record the declaration and payment of the dividends.

Exercise 13-4 Dividend Distributions

Felix Company has 20,000 shares of 6% cumulative, $100 par value preferred stock and 400,000 shares of $1 par value common stock outstanding. All the stock was issued during January, 1991, the first month of the company's operations. Felix declared and paid dividends during the first four years as follows:

1991	$120,000
1992	150,000
1993	90,000
1994	130,000

Required:

Prepare a schedule showing (A) the total dividends paid each year, (B) the total dividends paid to each class of stock each year, (C) the amount of preferred dividends in arrears (if any) at the end of each year, and (D) the total dividends paid to each class of stock during the entire four-year period.

Exercise 13-5 Preferred Stock Dividends

The stockholders' equity of Armstrong Company on December 31, 1992 consisted of:

Preferred stock, 8%, $20 par value, 40,000 shares outstanding	$ 800,000
Common stock, $10 par value, 320,000 shares outstanding	3,200,000
Retained earnings	940,000

The board of directors declared a dividend in the amount of $463,000. (One year's dividends on preferred stock are in arrears.)

Required:

Determine the amount of dividends each class of stock will receive under each of the following conditions:

A. The preferred stock is noncumulative and nonparticipating.
B. The preferred stock is cumulative and nonparticipating.
C. The preferred stock is cumulative and fully participating.
D. The preferred stock is cumulative and participating, but limited to a total 10% dividend for the current year.

Exercise 13-6   Treasury Stock Transactions

On January 27, 1992, Cedar Hills Company purchased, on the open market, 7,000 of its own shares of $2 par value common stock for $18 per share. Cedar Hills was incorporated in 1962 and engages in several transactions of this kind each year.

Required:

A. Record the journal entry to record the purchase of the stock.
B. Prepare the journal entry on June 18, 1992, to record the resale of 1,000 shares of the stock assuming it is resold for:
    1. $20 per share.
    2. $18 per share.
    3. $16 per share.

Exercise 13-7   Stock Dividends

Rockwell Corporation has the following balances in its stockholders' equity accounts on December 1, 1992:

Common stock, $2 par value, 400,000 shares authorized,	
200,000 shares issued and outstanding	$ 400,000
Paid-in capital in excess of par value	3,350,000
Retained earnings	1,135,000

On December 17, 1992, the board of directors declared an 8% stock dividend, distributable on January 8, 1993, to stockholders of record on December 31, 1992. The market price of the stock on December 17, 1992, was $14 per share; on December 31, 1992, it was $16 per share; on January 8, 1993, it was $13 per share.

Required:

A. Prepare the journal entry on December 17, 1992, to record the dividend declaration.
B. Assuming net income for 1992 was $363,000, prepare the stockholders' equity section of the December 31, 1992 balance sheet.
C. Prepare the journal entry on January 8, 1993 to record the distribution of the dividend.

Exercise 13-8   Stock Splits

On June 1, 1992, Taylor Corporation had 180,000 shares of $8 par value common stock outstanding. The board of directors is considering a stock split. It is deciding among the following splits:

1. Four for one.
2. Eight for one.
3. Five for two.
4. Two for three.

Required:

Compute the number of shares outstanding, the par value per share, and the total par value of the common stock outstanding for each of the splits under consideration.

Exercise 13-9 Income Statement Classification

Selected transactions and events of Hoosier Corporation follow:

1. An earthquake in Hardenburg, where the company's largest plant is located, resulted in an uninsured loss of $3.6 million. Earthquakes have never occurred before in the Hardenburg area.
2. Long-term investments were sold at a loss of $700,000.
3. A strike at the Evansville plant by the machinists' union resulted in a loss to the corporation of $4.6 million.
4. Excess machinery was sold at a gain of $480,000.
5. The company disposed of its entire meat packing operation, incurring a loss of $2.2 million.
6. The meat packing operation had incurred a loss of $210,000 up to the date of sale.
7. The company sold one of its shoe manufacturing factories at a gain of $1,178,000.

Required:

Indicate in which section of the income statement each of the transactions or events should be reported. Your choices are:
A. Income from continuing operations.
B. Disposal of a segment of the business.
C. Extraordinary item.

Exercise 13-10 Cumulative Effect of Accounting Change

Arthur Company had revenues and operating expenses for the year 1992, as follows:

Sales	$850,000
Cost of goods sold	390,000
Administrative expenses	95,000
Selling expenses	110,000
Depreciation expense	14,630

During 1992, the depreciation method used on two machines was changed from the straight-line method to the double declining-balance method. (The $14,630 depreciation expense shown above was computed under the new method.) Relevant data for the two machines is presented here.

	Cost	Date of Purchase	Estimated Useful Life	Estimated Residual Value
Machine A	$90,000	1/1/90	10 years	$6,000
Machine B	36,000	1/1/89	5 years	2,500

Assume an income tax rate of 40%.

Required:

A. Prepare the journal entry needed to record the effect of the change in depreciation method.
B. Prepare an income statement for the year ended December 31, 1992 for Arthur Company.

Exercise 13-11 Retained Earnings and Stockholders' Equity

The following data were taken from the records of More Company on December 31, 1992. All year-end adjusting entries have been journalized and posted.

Common stock, $10 par value, 200,000 shares authorized,	
140,000 shares issued, 139,100 shares outstanding	$1,400,000
Paid-in capital in excess of par value	628,000
Bond sinking fund	100,000
Dividends declared	83,460
Retained earnings, January 1, 1992	197,000
Treasury stock–900 shares at cost	10,800
Income summary (credit balance)	62,000
Correction of prior period accounting error (debit)	17,000

There is a restriction on retained earnings in an amount equal to the cost of the treasury stock, as required by state law.

Required:
A. Prepare a retained earnings statement for the year ended December 31, 1992.
B. Prepare the stockholders' equity section of the balance sheet as of December 31, 1992.

Exercise 13-12 Book Value per Share of Common Stock

Paxton Corporation has the following stockholders' equity on December 31, 1992.

Stockholders' Equity

Paid-in capital:	
Preferred stock, $100 par value, 8% cumulative, 100,000	
shares authorized, 30,000 shares issued and outstanding	$ 3,000,000
Common stock, $5 par value, 800,000 shares authorized,	
400,000 shares issued and outstanding	2,000,000
Paid-in capital in excess of par value–preferred	600,000
Paid-in capital in excess of par value–common	4,000,000
Total paid-in capital	9,600,000
Retained earnings	2,230,000
Total Stockholders' Equity	$11,830,000

Required:
Calculate the book value per share of common stock under each of the following independent situations:

A. No dividends are in arrears on the preferred stock and the current year's preferred stock dividend has been declared and paid. The preferred stock is callable at par value.
B. No dividends are in arrears on the preferred stock, but the current year's preferred stock dividend has not yet been declared. The preferred stock is callable at par value.
C. No dividends are in arrears on the preferred stock, the current year's preferred stock dividend has been declared and paid, and the preferred stock has a call price of $106 per share.
D. The preferred stock has a call price of $105 per share, and no dividends have been declared on preferred stock in 1990, 1991, or 1992.

Exercise 13-13 Stockholders' Equity Analysis

Following are the components of stockholders' equity of Thompson Corporation:

Cumulative, 10% preferred stock, $100 par value, callable at $106	$ 250,000
Common stock, $4 par value, 300,000 shares authorized, 170,000 shares issued and outstanding	680,000
Paid-in capital in excess of par value–common	2,560,000
Retained earnings deficit	(311,700)

Dividends are in arrears in the amount of $90,000.

Required:

A. Compute the net assets of Thompson Corporation.

B. Compute the number of shares of preferred stock outstanding.

C. Compute the book value per share of preferred stock.

D. Compute the book value per share of common stock.

PROBLEMS

Problem 13-1 Preparing Retained Earnings Statement and Stockholders' Equity Section of Balance Sheet

Following are selected general ledger data of Ripley Corporation on December 31, 1992, after adjusting entries have been prepared and posted and revenue and expense accounts closed to the Income Summary account:

Bond sinking fund	$ 725,000
Cash dividends declared–common stock	362,000
Cash dividends declared–preferred stock	160,000
Common stock, $5 par value, 500,000 shares authorized, 200,000 shares issued, 192,000 shares outstanding	1,500,000
Common stock dividends declared	132,480
Common stock dividends distributable	132,480
Paid-in capital in excess of par value–preferred	240,000
Paid-in capital in excess of par value–common	3,600,00
Paid-in capital from treasury stock transactions	71,800
Dividends payable	136,000
Income Summary (credit balance)	624,700
Long-term investments in equity securities	175,000
Preferred stock, $100 par value, 8% cumulative, 100,000 shares authorized, 20,000 shares issued and outstanding	2,000,000
Retained earnings 1/1	1,621,400
Treasury stock–8,000 common shares at cost	184,000

There is a restriction on dividends equal to the cost of treasury stock as required by state law.

Required:

A. Prepare a retained earnings statement for the year ended December 31, 1992.

B. Prepare the stockholders' equity section of Ripley's December 31, 1992 balance sheet.

Problem 13-2 Stock Transactions and Dividends

Styler Corporation received its corporate charter on January 7, 1992. The charter authorized the following classes of capital stock:

Preferred stock, $40 par value, 10% cumulative, 100,000 shares authorized
Common stock, $1 par value, 1 million shares authorized.

During 1992, the following transactions occurred:

Jan. 7 Issued 8,000 shares of common stock to each of the four corporate organizers at $6 per share. Cash was collected in full from three of the organizers; the other organizer contributed a patent in exchange for her shares.

21 Sold 3,000 shares of preferred stock at $50 per share.

Mar. 20 Sold 50,000 shares of common stock at $9 per share and 1,000 shares of preferred stock at $63 per share.

Aug. 6 Sold 10,000 shares of common stock at $11 per share.

Dec. 28 Declared the annual dividend on preferred stock.

31 Closed the $74,000 credit balance in the Income Summary account.

Required:

A. Prepare journal entries to record the transactions.

B. Prepare the stockholders' equity section of the December 31, 1992 balance sheet.

C. Compute the weighted average issuance price of the:
   1. Common stock.
   2. Preferred stock.

D. Explain how you determined the value to assign to the patent received in the January 7 transaction.

Problem 13-3 Par Value and No-par Value Stock Transactions

Trimore Corporation received its corporate charter authorizing 800,000 shares of common stock on January 16, 1992. During 1992, the following transactions occurred.

Jan. 22 Sold 20,000 shares of common stock at $25 per share.

June 10 Issued 8,000 shares of common stock in exchange for land and a building. The land was appraised at $50,000; the building at $190,000. Trimore Corporation's stock is not traded on an organized market, and no common stock had been sold since the January 22 transaction.

Dec. 21 Declared a $.30 per share dividend on the common stock to be paid on January 14, 1993.

31 The Income Summary account had a credit balance of $49,000.

Three independent cases exist with respect to the common stock:

Case A: The common stock has a par value of $7 per share.
Case B: The common stock is straight no-par stock.
Case C: The common stock is no-par and the board of directors has assigned a $10 per share stated value.

Required:

A. For each of the three cases, prepare journal entries to record the four transactions or events and prepare the stockholders' equity section of the December 31, 1992 balance sheet.

B. Explain why the total stockholders' equity is the same under each case.

C. Explain why you recorded the land and building the way you did.

Problem 13-4 Preferred and Common Cash Dividends

Archer Company had the following stockholders' equity on December 31, 1992:

Preferred stock, $60 par value, 10%, 20,000 shares issued and outstanding	$1,200,000
Common stock, $6 par value, 300,000 shares issued and outstanding	1,800,000
Retained earnings	4,380,000

The board of directors is considering the distribution of a cash dividend to stockholders. No dividends were declared or paid in 1991. Assume three independent cases for the preferred stock as follows:

Case A: The preferred stock is noncumulative and nonparticipating.
Case B: The preferred stock is cumulative and nonparticipating.
Case C: The preferred stock is cumulative and fully participating.

Required:
Prepare schedules showing the amounts to be received by each class of stockholders if the total dividends declared and paid are:

A. $130,000.
B. $220,000.
C. $340,000.
D. $450,000.

Problem 13-5 Stock Dividends

On December 31, 1992, Barker Company's balance sheet reported the following stockholders' equity:

Common stock, $10 par value, 200,000 shares authorized, 30,000 shares issued and outstanding	$300,000
Paid-in capital in excess of par value	180,000
Retained earnings	290,500

On March 12, 1993, the board of directors declared a 10% stock dividend to be distributed on April 3, 1993. The market value of the stock on March 12 was $14 per share.

Required:
A. Prepare journal entries to record the declaration and distribution of the stock dividend.
B. Prepare comparative stockholders' equity sections of Barker's balance sheet on:
  1. March 11, 1993, before the declaration of the stock dividend.
  2. March 12, 1993, after the declaration of the stock dividend.
  3. April 3, 1993, after the distribution of the stock dividend.
  Use three side-by-side columns for the comparative presentation.
C. Explain the effect of this stock dividend on the assets, liabilities, and stockholders' equity of Barker Company.
D. Compute the book value per share of common stock before and after the stock dividend. Why did book value per common share change?

Problem 13-6 Treasury Stock, Dividends, and Retained Earnings

On December 31, 1991, Tyler Company reported the following stockholders' equity on its balance sheet:

Common stock, $2 par value, 600,000 shares authorized,	
200,000 shares issued and outstanding	$400,000
Retained earnings	298,000

During 1992, Tyler completed the following transactions:

Jan.   15   Purchased, for $16 per share, 4,000 shares of common stock to be held as treasury stock.

Mar.   25   Resold, for $17 per share, 1,000 of the treasury shares purchased on January 15.

May   20   Sold 20,000 shares of common stock at $18 per share.

June   30   Declared a $.25 per share dividend on the common stock payable to stockholders of record on July 14, to be paid on July 28.

July   28   Paid the dividend declared on June 30.

Sept.   9   Resold, for $15.50 per share, 1,000 of the treasury shares purchased on January 15.

Nov.   10   Resold, for $14 per share, 1,000 of the treasury shares purchased on January 15.

Dec.   31   Closed the credit balance of $65,000 in the Income Summary account.

Required:

A. Prepare journal entries to record the transactions.

B. Prepare a retained earnings statement for the year ended December 31, 1992.

C. Prepare the stockholders' equity section of Tyler's December 31, 1992 balance sheet.

D. Compute the amount of retained earnings available for dividends on December 31, 1992.

Problem 13-7   Income Statement with Special Items

Lampert Inc. had revenues and expenses for the year ended December 31, 1992, as follows:

Sales revenues	$5,290,000
Cost of goods sold	3,685,000
Administrative expenses	410,000
Selling expenses	380,000
Interest expense	160,000

Other events affecting 1992 net income were:

1. Lampert sold its food processing division on May 31, 1992, at a pretax gain of $254,000. Operating income before tax for the division to the date of sale was $23,500, which is not included in the data given previously.

2. A mining venture in Central America, partially owned by Lampert in a joint venture with other firms, was expropriated by the foreign government. Lampert's share of the loss amounted to $350,000 before tax effects.

Required:

Prepare an income statement for Lampert Inc. for the year ended December 31, 1992. Assume an income tax rate of 40% on all items. Include earnings per share data under the assumption that Lampert had 200,000 shares of common stock outstanding throughout the year.

Problem 13-8 Income Statement and Special Items

Wayland Company earned revenues and incurred expenses for the year ended December 31, 1992, as follows:

Sales revenues	$3,570,000
Cost of goods sold	2,382,000
Administrative expenses	318,000
Selling expenses	556,500
Interest expense	108,000

Other events affecting 1992 income were:

1. An extraordinary loss of $217,500 before tax was incurred when a tornado severely damaged one of Wayland Company's warehouses.
2. Wayland sold its fast-food division on July 31, 1992, at a pretax gain of $252,000. An operating loss of $108,000 before tax was incurred by the division to the date of sale.
3. Wayland changed from the double declining-balance method to the straight-line method of depreciation. The cumulative effect of the change to the beginning of 1992 was $78,000 (credit) before tax.

Required:

Prepare an income statement for Wayland Company for the year ended December 31, 1992. Assume an income tax rate of 30% on all items. Include earnings-per-share data under the assumption that Wayland had 120,000 shares of common stock outstanding throughout the year.

Problem 13-9 Corporate Income Statement

Information about the operations of Herringbone Corporation during 1992 follow:

Administrative expenses	$ 200,000
Cost of goods sold	700,000
Cumulative effect of change in depreciation methods that increased income (net of $40,000 tax)	84,000
Extraordinary item, earthquake loss (net of $70,000 tax)	120,000
Net sales	1,600,000
Selling expenses	160,000
Income taxes on income from continuing operations	206,000

Required:

Prepare the company's income statement for the year ended December 31, 1992, including earnings per share information, assuming a weighted average of 100,000 common stock shares outstanding during the year.

Problem 13-10 Stockholders' Equity Analysis

The stockholders' equity section of the December 31, 1992 balance sheet of Ivor Company follows:

Stockholders' Equity

Paid-in capital:	
Preferred stock, 6%, $50 par value, cumulative and fully participating, 50,000 shares authorized, 20,000 shares issued	$1,000,000
Common stock, $5 par value, 200,000 shares authorized, 180,000 shares issued	900,000
Paid-in capital in excess of par value–preferred	85,000

Paid-in capital in excess of par value–common	1,800,000
Paid-in capital from donated plant site	400,000
Paid-in capital from treasury stock transactions	5,000
Total paid-in capital	4,190,000
Retained earnings	1,540,000
Total paid-in capital and retained earnings	5,730,000
Less: Common treasury stock at cost, 26,500 shares	662,500
Total stockholders' equity	$5,067,500

Required:

A. How many shares of common stock are outstanding?

B. What was the average issue price of the common stock?

C. What is the cost per share of the treasury stock?

D. Assuming all the treasury stock was purchased at one time, and that 28,000 shares were originally purchased, what was the average price received for the 1,500 shares of treasury stock that have been resold?

E. Assuming 1,000 shares of the treasury stock are sold for $27 per share, prepare the journal entry to record the sale.

F. Assuming 1,000 shares of the treasury stock are sold for $10 per share, prepare the journal entry to record the sale.

G. Refer to the original data, if Ivor's board of directors declared a 5% common stock dividend when the market price of the stock was $33 per share,
   1. How many shares of common stock will be issued?
   2. At what value should the stock dividend be recorded?
   3. Prepare the journal entry to record the declaration.
   4. Prepare the journal entry to record the issue of the stock.

H. Refer to the original data. Cash dividends of $200,000 are declared; there are no dividends in arrears. How much of the total dividend will be paid to the preferred and common stockholders?

I. Refer to H. Assuming one year's dividends on preferred stock are in arrears, how much of the total dividend will be paid to the preferred and common stockholders?

Problem 13-11   Callable and Convertible Preferred Stock

Velder Company had the following stockholders' equity on December 31, 1992:

Convertible preferred stock, 8% cumulative, $100 par value,	
4,000 shares authorized, issued, and outstanding	$ 400,000
Common stock, $5 par value, 1,000,000 shares authorized,	
750,000 shares issued and outstanding	3,750,000
Paid-in capital in excess of par value–preferred	10,000
Paid-in capital in excess of par value–common	1,675,000
Retained earnings	498,500
Total stockholders' equity	$6,333,500

Each share of preferred stock is convertible into three shares of common stock. On January 1, 1993, all of the preferred stock was converted into common stock.

Required:

A. Prepare the journal entry to record the conversion of the preferred stock into common stock.

B. Prepare the stockholders' equity section of the balance sheet immediately after the conversion.

Problem 13-12 Stock Dividends and Stock Splits

The stockholders' equity section of Braxton Company's June 30, 1992 balance sheet showed:

Common stock, $10 par value, 500,000 shares authorized,	
60,000 shares issued and outstanding	$ 600,000
Paid-in capital in excess of par value	300,000
Retained earnings	600,000
Total stockholders' equity	$1,500,000

Required:

A. Prepare journal entries for each of the three independent cases below:
1. Braxton declared and issued a 15% stock dividend when the market price of its shares was $20.
2. Braxton declared and issued a 60% stock dividend when the market price of its shares was $17.
3. Braxton declared a 2 for 1 stock split.

B. Prepare the stockholders' equity section of Braxton's balance sheet immediately after the stock dividend or stock split for each case.

Problem 13-13 Retained Earnings Statement with Prior Period Adjustment and Dividend Restrictions

Morgan Company had retained earnings of $370,000 on December 31, 1992. During 1993, Morgan reported net income of $200,000 and declared and paid cash dividends of $70,000. Other events and information about Morgan Company are:

1. While counting the inventory on December 31, 1993, employees discovered that the inventory on December 31, 1992 was understated by $40,000. The correct beginning inventory amount was used to calculate the 1993 net income.
2. Morgan Company's income tax rate is 40%.
3. During 1993, Morgan Company acquired 5,000 shares of its own common stock to be held as treasury stock at a cost of $15 per share.

Required:

Prepare, in good form and with an appropriate footnote, Morgan Company's retained earnings statement for the year ended December 31, 1993.

Problem 13-14A Alternative Forms of Business Ownership

Part I

Following are three independent cases regarding ownership forms of a business. Assume, for each case, that the accounting period ends on December 31, 1992, and that the Income Summary account (after closing revenue and expense accounts) has a credit balance of $75,000.

Case 1: The company is a proprietorship owned by Susan Blakemore. Prior to the closing entries, her capital account had a balance of $59,000 and her drawing account a balance of $26,000.

Case 2: The company is a partnership owned by John Bloom and Darla Moore, who share profits and losses 30% and 70%, respectively. Prior to the closing entries, the owners' equity accounts had the following balances:

John Bloom, Capital	$35,000 credit
John Bloom, Drawing	14,000 debit
Darla Moore, Capital	72,000 credit
Darla Moore, Drawing	21,000 debit

Case 3: The company is a corporation. Prior to the closing entries, the stockholders' equity accounts were:

Common stock, $3 par value, 100,000 shares authorized, 50,000 shares issued and outstanding	$150,000
Paid-in capital in excess of par value	397,850
Retained earnings	262,500

Required:

A. Prepare journal entries to close the Income Summary account for each of the three cases.

B. Prepare the owners' equity section of the December 31, 1992 balance sheet for each case.

Part II

Assume the same facts as in Part I, except that the Income Summary account has a debit balance of $25,000.

Required:

A. Prepare journal entries to close the Income Summary account for each case.

B. Prepare the owners' equity section of the December 31, 1992 balance sheet for each case.

CASE 13-1

CASE 13-1 Annual Report Analysis Case

Refer to the financial statements and related footnotes of BFGoodrich Company in the Appendix to this text and answer the following questions. Indicate the page number on which you found the answer.

A. How much were cash dividends per share in 1989? in 1988?

B. BFGoodrich Company reports two classes of capital stock outstanding as part of stockholders' equity.

    1. What are the names of the two classes of stock?

    2. What is the par value of each class of stock?

    3. How many shares of each class of stock were authorized as of December 31, 1989?

    4. How many shares of each class of stock were issued as of December 31, 1989?

    5. How many shares of each class of stock were outstanding as of December 31, 1989?

C. What account title does BFGoodrich use for its retained earnings?

D. How much is total stockholders' equity on December 31, 1989?

E. How many shares of common stock were purchased as treasury stock during 1989? What total price was paid for the treasury stock held on December 31, 1989?

F. Did BFGoodrich have any income or loss from activities other than continuing operations during the years reported on? If so, what was the nature of the activity?

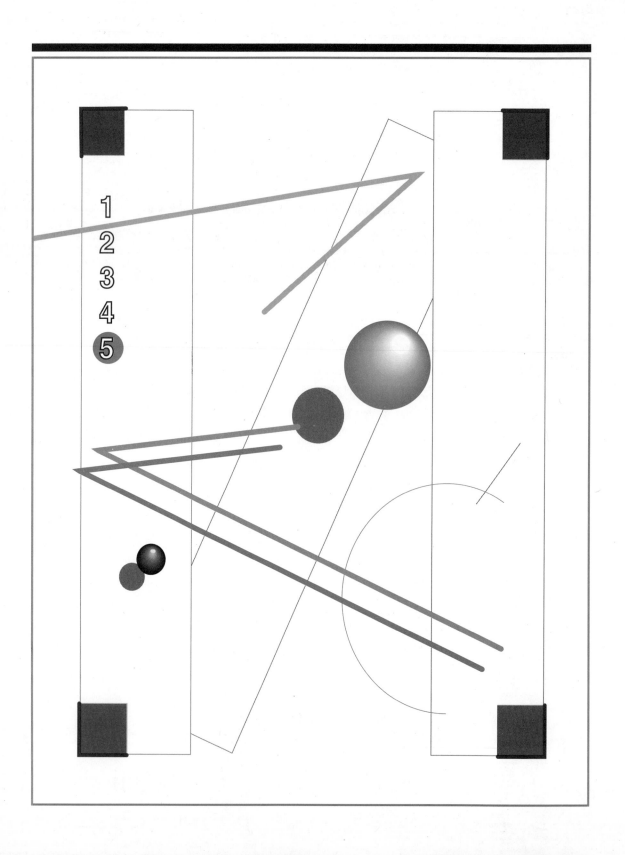

PART 5

OTHER ISSUES

14

LONG-TERM INVESTMENTS, CONSOLIDATED FINANCIAL STATEMENTS, AND INTERNATIONAL ACCOUNTING

CHAPTER OVERVIEW AND OBJECTIVES

This chapter consists of two parts. Part I describes the accounting and reporting procedures followed in accounting for long-term investments, primarily investments in debt and equity securities. Part II covers the preparation of consolidated financial statements. Accounting for receivables and payables to be settled in a foreign currency and the translation of a foreign subsidiary's financial statements into U.S. dollars are discussed in an Appendix. When you have completed the chapter, you should understand:

1. The reasons for holding long-term investments in securities.
2. How to account for long-term investments in bonds.
3. The difference between the cost and equity methods of accounting for long-term investments in equity securities.
4. The purpose of consolidated financial statements.
5. The conditions that must be met before a subsidiary is included in the consolidated financial statements.
6. Limitations in the use of information contained in consolidated financial statements.
7. Accounting for the effects of changes in foreign exchange rates on receivables and payables settled in foreign currency: Appendix.
8. How to translate a foreign subsidiary's financial statements into U.S. dollars: Appendix.

PART I. ACCOUNTING FOR LONG-TERM INVESTMENTS

In preceding chapters we discussed accounting for the issuance of securities and payment of dividends and interest from the viewpoint of the issuing corporation. We now turn our attention to the accounting procedures followed by the investors who purchase these securities with the intention of holding them for a long time. Investors may be individuals, mutual funds, pension funds, or other corporations.

Temporary (short-term) investments were defined in Chapter 8 as investments that are readily marketable and that management intends to convert to cash as needed within one year or the normal operating cycle, whichever is longer. Long-term investments are not intended to be converted into cash for normal operating activities. In other words, long-term investments are those investments that do not meet the criteria necessary for classification as temporary. Like temporary investments, they may consist of either equity securities or debt securities. Long-term investments also include funds set aside for special purposes, such as a bond sinking fund, and land or other assets owned by a company but not used in normal operations. Although representing long-term investments, these two latter items often are classified under the caption of "Other Assets."

Objective 1:
Why long-term investments are made in corporate securities

This chapter focuses on accounting for long-term investments in debt and equity securities of other corporations. Although there are several reasons a company makes long-term investments in the securities of other companies, the primary objective is often to increase net income. Net income is increased by (1) the receipt of interest or dividends, (2) market appreciation of securities (which is recognized when the securities are sold), and (3) expansion of operations.

When a company wants to expand, it generally has two alternatives. First, it can expand either by enlarging existing facilities or by purchasing or building new facilities in various locations. This process requires large amounts of capital and produces results rather slowly. Second, a company can expand its operations by acquiring sufficient voting capital stock of another company to influence or control its operations by electing members of its board of directors. The company acquiring the stock is called the **investor company** and the company whose stock is acquired is called the **investee company**. Many companies choose the second alternative because

- Expansion is accomplished rapidly since the investee company already has operating facilities, customers, and suppliers;
- The investee company may own natural resources needed for the investor company's operations; and
- By acquiring slightly more than 50% of the voting stock of another company, the investor can control the investee with a much smaller investment than would be required to build or buy new equivalent facilities.

ACCOUNTING FOR LONG-TERM INVESTMENTS IN BONDS

Accounting for a long-term investment in another company's bonds is essentially the reverse of the issuing company's accounting for the bonds. The bond investment is recorded at its cost, including any broker's fees. Since interest on bonds accrues over time, the purchaser must also pay interest accrued between the date of the last interest payment and the purchase date. The amount paid for accrued interest is normally debited to Interest Revenue so that it will be offset against the credit to Interest Revenue when the first interest payment is received. Alternatively, the debit can be to Interest Receivable, which is then credited when the interest is received. The

Objective 2:
Accounting for long-term bond investments

Figure 14-1
Effect of Premium
and Discount
Amortization on
Carrying Value of a
Bond Investment

balancing credit would be to Interest Revenue for the portion earned by the purchaser since acquisition of the bonds.

The amount paid for bonds is often more or less than par value; that is, the bonds are purchased at a premium or a discount. As explained in Chapter 12, if the market rate of interest is less than the stated rate on the bonds, the bonds will sell at a premium. If the market interest rate is more than the stated rate, the bonds will sell at a discount. A premium or a discount represents an adjustment to interest revenue and, therefore, must be amortized over the remaining life of the bonds.

The premium or discount on a bond investment normally is not recorded in a separate account as is done for bonds payable. Instead, the bonds are recorded at their cost, and the difference between cost and the par value of the investment is amortized by direct entries to the Investment in Bonds account. Consequently, on each balance sheet date the Investment in Bonds account will contain the carrying value of the investment, which is equal to cost plus amortized discount or cost minus amortized premium. The amortization of a discount will increase the carrying value of the bond investment to its maturity (par) value on its maturity date as shown in Figure 14-1. Conversely, the amortization of a premium will decrease the carrying value.

BONDS PURCHASED AT A PREMIUM—STRAIGHT-LINE AMORTIZATION

To illustrate bonds purchased at a premium, assume that on May 1, 1992, Rox Company purchased 400, $1,000 par value, 12% bonds of Dolly Corporation on the open market at 105 plus accrued interest of $12,000 and broker's fees of $2,500. The bonds pay interest semiannually on July 31 and January 31. They mature on January 31, 1996, and thus have 45 months remaining to maturity date. The entry to record the purchase is:

May	1	Investment in Dolly Corp. Bonds		422,500	
		Interest Revenue		12,000	
		Cash			434,500

The investment account is debited for the total cost of the bonds [(400 × $1,000 × 105%) + $2,500 broker's fee] and Interest Revenue is debited for the three months' accrued interest of $12,000 ($400,000 × 12% × 3/12). Note, as mentioned earlier, that a separate premium account for the investment is not used.

The receipt of the first semiannual interest payment and amortization of premium for three months are recorded as follows:

July	31	Cash	24,000	
		Investment in Dolly Corp. Bonds*		1,500
		Interest Revenue		22,500
		*3 months × $500 per month		

Because there are 45 months between the purchase of the bonds and their maturity date, amortization per month under the straight-line method is computed as follows:

Cost of the investment	$422,500
Par value of the bonds	400,000
Amount to be amortized	$ 22,500
Amortization per month ($22,500/45 months)	$ 500

The debit to cash represents the amount received for the semiannual period ($400,000 × 12% × 6/12). The credit to the investment account reflects the amortization of premium for the months of May, June, and July (3 × $500).

The amount of interest earned each month can be computed as follows:

Amount to be received by the investor:	
Maturity value	$400,000
Interest for 45 months ($400,000 × 12% × 45/12)	180,000
Total	580,000
Less: Cost of the investment	422,500
Total interest revenue	$157,500
Interest revenue per month ($157,500/45 months)	$ 3,500

After the interest entry above is posted, the Investment in Dolly Corporation Bonds account and the Interest Revenue account will appear as follows:

Investment in Dolly Corporation Bonds

5/1	422,500	7/31	1,500

Interest Revenue

5/1	12,000	7/31	22,500

The $10,500 ($22,500 − $12,000) balance in the Interest Revenue account represents the correct amount of interest earned for the three months from May 1 to July 31 ($3,500 × 3).

On December 31, the end of the fiscal year, interest is accrued and amortization for five months is recorded as follows:

Dec.	31	Interest Receivable[a]	20,000	
		Investment in Dolly Corp. Bonds[b]		2,500
		Interest Revenue[c]		17,500
		[a]$400,000 × 12% × 5/12		
		[b]$500 × 5 months		
		[c]$3,500 × 5 months		

The amortization process will reduce the investment account to the par value of the bonds ($400,000) by their maturity date, at which time Rox Company will receive the maturity value and make the following entry:

<u>1996</u>

Jan.	31	Cash			400,000	
		Investment in Dolly Corp. Bonds				400,000

BONDS PURCHASED AT A DISCOUNT—STRAIGHT-LINE AMORTIZATION

If the bonds are purchased at a discount rather than at a premium, the amount of periodic amortization is debited (rather than credited) to the investment account. In this way the investment account is gradually increased over time and will be equal to the maturity value of the bonds on their maturity date.

For example, assume that the Dolly Corporation bonds in the previous example were purchased for $391,000 (including broker's fees) plus accrued interest. Thus, the bonds were purchased at a $9,000 discount ($400,000 − $391,000), and the monthly amortization of bond discount is $200 ($9,000/45 months). During the first year, the investment in bonds would be accounted for as follows:

May	1	Investment in Dolly Corp. Bonds	391,000	
		Interest Revenue	12,000	
		Cash		403,000
		To record the purchase of bonds.		
July	31	Cash	24,000	
		Investment in Dolly Corp. Bonds*	600	
		Interest Revenue		25,000
		To record the receipt of interest and		
		amortization of discount.		
		*$200 × 3 months		
Dec.	31	Interest Receivable	20,000	
		Investment in Dolly Corp. Bonds	1,000	
		Interest Revenue		21,000
		To accrue interest for five months and		
		amortize discount.		

RECORDING THE SALE OF BOND INVESTMENTS

When bond investments are sold, the procedure is similar to that for the sale of any asset. Cash is debited for the amount received, the investment account is credited for the carrying value of the investment sold, and a gain or loss is recognized for the difference. In addition to the selling price of the bonds, the seller also receives any interest accrued since the last interest-payment date. Before recording the sale, amortization of the premium or discount on the investment to the date of sale should be recorded.

To illustrate, assume that Rox Company sold one-half of its Dolly Corporation bonds on April 1, 1994 for $216,000 (net of broker's fees) plus accrued interest of $4,000. Assume also that the bonds were purchased at a premium as illustrated previously. Before recording the sale, amortization should be recorded from the last interest-payment date to the date of sale as follows:

Apr.	1	Interest Revenue	1,000	
		Investment in Dolly Corp. Bonds		1,000
		To record amortization for February and		
		March at $500 per month.		

After this entry is posted, the Investment in Dolly Corporation Bonds account will appear as follows:

Investment in Dolly Corporation Bonds

5/1/92	422,500	7/31/92 Amortization	1,500
		12/31/92 Amortization	2,500
		1/31/93 Amortization	500
		7/31/93 Amortization	3,000
		12/31/93 Amortization	2,500
		1/31/94 Amortization	500
		4/1/94 Amortization	1,000
4/1/94 Balance	411,000		

The sale of the bonds can now be recorded by the following entry:

Apr.	1	Cash	220,000	
		Interest Revenue		4,000
		Investment in Dolly Corp. Bonds		205,500
		Gain on Sale of Investments		10,500
		To record the sale of one-half of the Dolly		
		Corporation bonds.		

Cash is debited for the proceeds from the sale of $216,000 plus $4,000 accrued interest ($200,000 × 12% × 2/12), the Investment in Dolly Corporation Bonds account is credited for half its carrying value (1/2 × $411,000) since only half the bonds were sold, and a gain on the sale of $10,500 is recorded. The gain can be verified as follows:

Selling price	$216,000
Carrying value of the bonds sold (1/2 × $411,000)	205,500
Gain on sale of investment	$ 10,500

Since half the bonds were sold, interest received on each following July 31 and January 31 will be $12,000 ($200,000 × 12% × 6/12), and amortization of premium will be $250 per month rather than $500.

Effective Interest Method of Amortization

The straight-line method of amortizing discounts or premiums on bond investments is often used by companies that make only incidental investments in long-term bonds because it is easy to apply and interest revenue constitutes only a small part of their total income. Consequently, the difference between the straight-line and effective-interest methods of amortization is an immaterial amount. When the difference between the straight-line and effective-interest methods of amortization is material, however, the effective-interest method of amortization is required. The effective-interest method of amortization is conceptually superior because annual interest is based on the effective interest rate, which produces a better measure of both income and the carrying value of the bond investment.

To illustrate the effective-interest method, assume that on January 1, 1992 Rox Company purchased 50, $1,000 par value, 10% bonds of Lode Company. Interest is payable annually on December 31, and the bonds mature on December 31, 1995. Based on a 12% market rate of interest, the purchase price of the bonds is $46,962, which involves a discount of $3,038. Given the effective interest rate of 12%, the purchase price of the bonds is determined by computing the present value of the future cash flows as follows:

Present value of the maturity value, four periods @ 12%:	
Table 11-3 = .6355 × $50,000 =	$31,775
Present value of interest annuity, four periods @ 12%:	
Table 11-4 = 3.0373 × $5,000 =	15,187
Total present value (purchase price)	$46,962

Rox Company records the acquisition of the bonds as follows:

Jan.	1	Investment in Lode Company Bonds	46,962	
		.Cash		46,962

An effective interest method amortization schedule is shown in Figure 14-2. Note that the computation of interest revenue is based on the yield rate of 12% rather than the nominal rate of 10%.

Figure 14-2
Effective-Interest Method Amortization Schedule

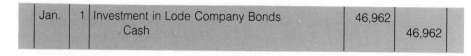

Col. 1	Col. 2	Col. 3	Col. 4	Col. 5
	Cash	Interest	Amortization to Increase	Investment
	Interest	Revenue	Investment Account	Carrying
Date	Received	(12% × Col. 5)	(Col. 3 − Col. 2)	Value
1/1/92				$46,962
12/31/92	$ 5,000	$ 5,635	$ 635	47,597
12/31/93	5,000	5,712	712	48,309
12/31/94	5,000	5,797	797	49,106
12/31/95	5,000	5,894[a]	894	50,000
Totals	$20,000	$23,038	$3,038	

[a]$1 rounding error

Column 2 of Figure 14-2 shows the amount of cash interest received each year at the nominal interest rate of 10%. Column 3 shows the amount of interest revenue to be reported in the income statement each year based on the effective interest method. It is computed by multiplying the Column 5 amount on the preceding line times the effective (yield) rate (e.g., $46,962 × 12% = $5,635). Column 4 reflects the amount of discount on the investment to be amortized each year measured as the difference between the amount of interest revenue recognized and the amount of cash interest received. Column 5 shows the carrying value at the end of each year to be reported in the balance sheet. Note that when the bonds are purchased at a discount, the amounts of interest revenue, discount amortization, and the investment carrying value all increase during the remaining life of the bonds. If the investment is purchased at a premium, interest revenue and the investment carrying value will decrease over time. However, premium amortization will increase each year.

Entries to record the receipt of cash, the recognition of interest revenue, and amortization of discount each year is:

	1992		1993		Etc.
Cash	5,000		5,000		
Investment in Lode Co. Bonds	635		712		
Interest Revenue		5,635		5,712	

ACCOUNTING FOR LONG-TERM INVESTMENTS IN EQUITY SECURITIES

Objective 3:
Cost method vs. equity method for stock investments

Investments in equity securities generally consist of preferred stock, common stock, stock rights, and stock options. Stock rights and stock options represent the right to purchase stock for a fixed period at a preestablished price. Long-term investments in preferred stock, stock rights, and stock options are all initially recorded at their cost and thereafter included in the long-term equity securities portfolio, which is accounted for at the lower of cost or market as explained later. Long-term investments in common stock are also recorded initially at their cost. Accounting for the investment in common stock after acquisition, however, depends upon whether the investor owns enough common stock to exercise significant influence over the investee's operating and financing activities. If the investor can exercise significant influence over the investee, the investment is accounted for by the **equity method**; otherwise, it is accounted for by the **cost method**.

In order to provide a reasonable degree of uniformity in practice, current accounting standards state that unless there is evidence to the contrary the ownership of 20% or more of the voting common stock of a corporation provides presumptive evidence of the ability to exercise significant influence.[1] Common stock investments of 20% through 50% are normally accounted for by the equity method. (If the ownership level is over 50% of the voting stock, the investment usually must be included as a consolidated subsidiary, as explained in Part II of this chapter.) Common stock investments of less than 20% are included in the long-term marketable equity securities portfolio and are accounted for by the cost method.

THE COST METHOD

When less than 20% of a corporation's common stock is purchased and held as a long-term investment, the investment is recorded at its cost, including any broker's commission. For example, assume that Rox Company purchased 10,000 (10%) of Lum Corporation's 100,000 outstanding common shares as a long-term investment at 22 1/4 plus a broker's commission of $2,000. The investment is recorded as follows:

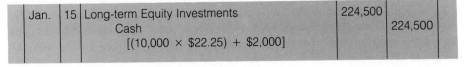

Jan.	15	Long-term Equity Investments	224,500	
		Cash		224,500
		[(10,000 × $22.25) + $2,000]		

[1]Opinions of the Accounting Principles Board No. 18, ''The Equity Method of Accounting for Investments in Common Stock'' (New York: AICPA, 1971), par. 17.

Because less than 20% of Lum Corporation's common stock was acquired, the investment is included in the long-term marketable equity securities portfolio and accounted for by the cost method. Under the cost method, dividends are recognized as dividend revenue on the date they are declared. For example, if Lum Corporation declared a $.75 per share dividend, the entry would be:

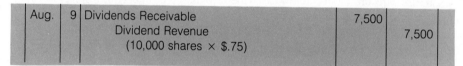

Aug.	9	Dividends Receivable	7,500	
		Dividend Revenue		7,500
		(10,000 shares × $.75)		

When the dividends are received, Cash is debited and Dividends Receivable is credited as follows:

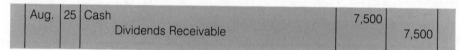

| Aug. | 25 | Cash | 7,500 | |
| | | Dividends Receivable | | 7,500 |

(In order to avoid making two entries for dividends, in future illustrations and examples we will assume that the dividends were declared and paid on the same day and will record them, therefore, as a debit to Cash and a credit to Dividend Revenue.)

Lower of Cost or Market Procedures

Long-term common stock investments, each less than 20% of the outstanding common stock of the respective investee company, plus investments in preferred stock, stock rights, and stock options constitutes the investor's long-term marketable equity securities portfolio. Like the temporary marketable equity securities portfolio (discussed in Chapter 8), lower of cost or market procedures must also be applied to the long-term marketable equity securities portfolio. Thus, the aggregate cost of the portfolio is compared with the aggregate market value at the end of each accounting period.

If aggregate market value is less than aggregate cost, an Unrealized Loss on Long-term Investments account is debited and an Allowance to Reduce Long-term Investments to Market Value account is credited. Accounting procedures are the same as those used for the temporary marketable equity securities portfolio with one major exception—*the Unrealized Loss on Long-term Investments account is reported as a contra stockholders' equity item rather than as a deduction in the income statement.* Thus, the Unrealized Loss account is not closed at the end of the period. In subsequent periods, both the Unrealized Loss account and the Allowance account are adjusted by an amount sufficient to report the long-term marketable equity securities portfolio at the lower of its cost or market. Any balance in the Unrealized Loss account is deducted from total stockholders' equity and the Allowance account is deducted as a contra to Long-term Investments.

The loss in value of temporary investments is reported on the income statement because the loss is more likely to be realized since management intends to sell the investment in the near future. Consequently, the reduction in market value is charged to income. Because management intends to hold the long-term equity investments for several years, during which time the market value of the equity investments may rise again, the FASB decided that these fluctuations in stock values should not be reflected in net income.

To illustrate, assume that Drake Company has the following long-term marketable equity securities portfolio on December 31, 1992:

Investee	Type of Security	Cost	Market
Abe Company	Common stock	$26,000	$28,000
Baker Company	Preferred stock	15,000	14,000
Cox Company	Common stock rights	44,000	36,000
Totals		$85,000	$78,000

Because aggregate market value of the portfolio is $7,000 less than aggregate cost, the following entry is made:

Dec.	31	Unrealized Loss on Long-term Investments		7,000	
		Allowance to Reduce Long-term			
		Investments to Market Value			7,000

The Unrealized Loss and Allowance accounts are reported on the December 31, 1992 balance sheet as follows:

Assets
Current assets		$278,000
Operating assets (net of depreciation)		312,000
Long-term equity investments	$85,000	
Less: Allowance to reduce long-term		
investments to market value	7,000	78,000
Total assets		$668,000

Liabilities		$120,000

Stockholders' Equity
Common stock, $5 par value	$150,000	
Retained earnings	405,000	
Total	555,000	
Less: Unrealized loss on long-term		
equity investments	7,000	548,000
Total liabilities & stockholders' equity		$668,000

Selling Long-term Securities.

When any of the long-term equity securities are sold, the difference between the cost of the securities and their selling price is recognized as a realized gain or loss. For example, if during 1993 Drake Company sold one-half of its shares in Abe Company for $14,500, the sale would be recorded as follows:

June	12	Cash		14,500	
		Long-term Equity Investments			13,000
		Gain on Sale of Investments			1,500

Note that the Long-term Equity Investments account is credited for one-half of the original cost ($26,000) of the Abe Company shares. *The Unrealized Loss and Allowance accounts are not affected by the sale of securities.* As noted earlier, those accounts will simply be adjusted sufficiently at the end of 1993 to report the long-term equity securities portfolio at the lower of its then aggregate cost or aggregate market value. For example, assume that the long-term marketable securities portfolio has cost and market values on December 31, 1993 as follows:

Investee	Type of Security	Cost	Market
Abe Company	Common stock	$13,000	$14,000
Baker Company	Preferred stock	15,000	12,000
Cox Company	Common stock rights	44,000	42,000
Totals		$72,000	$68,000

Since the aggregate cost of the portfolio is now $72,000 and aggregate market value is $68,000, aggregate market value is $4,000 lower than aggregate cost; thus, the Unrealized Loss and Allowance accounts should be adjusted to that balance through the following entry:

Dec.	31	Allowance to Reduce Long-term Investments to Market Value	3,000	
		Unrealized Loss on Long-term Investments		3,000

After this entry is posted, the Allowance account and the Unrealized Loss account appear as follows:

Allowance to Reduce Long-Term Investments to Market Value

12/31/93	3,000	12/31/92	7,000
		12/31/93 Balance	4,000

Unrealized Loss on Long-Term Investments

12/31/92	7,000	12/31/93	3,000
12/31/93 Balance	4,000		

To assist in identifying the differences in accounting and reporting, a comparison of accounting for temporary and long-term equity investments under the lower of cost or market method is presented in Figure 14-3.

The Equity Method

As mentioned earlier, when a company acquires 20% to 50% of the voting common stock of a corporation, the investment is normally accounted for by the equity method. When the stock is acquired, the investment is recorded at its cost, just as it is with the cost method. However, two main features distinguish the equity method from the cost method. Under the equity method:

1. The investor company recognizes its proportional share of the investee's income as an increase in the Investment account and as revenue for the period. If the investee reports a loss for the period, the investor decreases the Investment account for its proportional share and recognizes a loss. When the investor has significant influence over the policies of the investee, the investor can influence the timing of investee dividends. Since, under the cost method, the investor recognizes dividend revenue when the dividends are declared, the investor could

Figure 14-3
Accounting for
Temporary and
Long-term Equity
Investments under
the Lower of Cost or
Market Method

Item	Equity Investments Temporary	Long-term
Balance sheet location	Current assets	Investments
Allowance to reduce to lower of cost or market	Deducted from the cost of investment	Same as temporary
Unrealized loss	Subtracted in the income statement	Subtracted from stockholders' equity
Recovery of market value	Adjusted through Recovery account in income statement	Adjusted through the Unrealized Loss account in stockholders' equity
Sale of investment	Results in realized gain or loss in the income statement	Same as temporary
Dividends declared	Reported as revenue in the income statement	Same as temporary

manipulate the timing of its revenue by influencing the investee's dividend policy. The equity method was established to prevent investors from engaging in such potential income manipulation.

2. The investor's share of cash dividends declared is credited to the Investment account rather than to dividend revenue.

To illustrate, assume that on January 2, 1992, Drake Company purchased 30,000 (30%) of the 100,000 outstanding shares of Lox Corporation at 21½ plus a broker's commission of $3,000. On September 1, Lox Corporation declared a $.75 per share dividend and on December 31 reported net income of $300,000. To record the effects of these events, Drake Company would make the following entries:

Jan.	2	Investment in Lox Corporation	648,000	
		Cash		648,000
		[(30,000 × $21.50) + $3,000]		
Sept.	1	Cash	22,500	
		Investment in Lox Corporation		22,500
		(30,000 × $.75)		
Dec.	31	Investment in Lox Corporation	90,000	
		Investment Revenue		90,000
		(30% × $300,000)		

The investment is recorded initially at its cost. The distribution of the dividend on September 1 reduced Lox Corporation's stockholders' equity by $75,000 and reduced Drake Company's share of Lox Corporation's stockholders' equity by $22,500 (30% × $75,000). Consequently, the dividend is credited to the investment account to reflect the decrease in Drake's share of Lox's equity. Because Drake Company can influence significantly the operating policies of Lox Corporation, Drake Company recognized its share of Lox Corporation's net income for the period. Lox Corporation's stockholders' equity increased by the amount of income earned during the year ($300,000), and Drake Company's share of $90,000 (30% × $300,000) is added to the investment account. The investor's share of the increases and decreases in the investee's stockholders' equity are thus recorded as increases and decreases in the investment account. After recording these transactions, the Investment account appears as follows:

Investment in Lox Corporation

1/2 Purchase	648,000	9/1 Dividends	22,500
12/31 Income	90,000		
12/31 Balance	715,500		

The balance in the Investment account ($715,500) is reported as a long-term investment in the December 31, 1992 balance sheet, and investment revenue of $90,000 is reported in the 1992 income statement. A comparison of accounting for long-term equity investments under the cost method and equity method is shown in Figure 14-4.

PART II. CONSOLIDATED FINANCIAL STATEMENTS

Objective 4:
Purpose of consolidated financial statements

Corporations often own all or a majority (i.e., more than 50%) of the voting stock of other corporations. The company owning the stock is called the **parent company**, and the company whose stock is more than 50% owned is called a **subsidiary**. Thus, if Platt Company owns more than 50% of the voting stock of Swab Company, Platt Company is the parent company and Swab Company is the subsidiary. By owning more than 50% of the voting stock, Platt Company can elect the majority of the board of directors of Swab Company and thereby control its activities and resources.

Each company is a separate legal entity, so each maintains its own accounting records and prepares separate financial statements. In the separate financial statements of Platt Company, the Investment in Swab Company will appear in the balance sheet as an investment accounted for at its cost, and the income statement will include dividend revenue received from Swab Company.

Because the parent company controls the activities and resources of the subsidiary, the two companies effectively function as a *single economic entity*. Investors in the parent company want financial information about the entire resources, obligations, and operations under the control of the parent company. Consequently, the separate financial statements of the parent company and its subsidiary (or subsidiaries) are combined into a single set of financial statements called **consolidated financial statements**.

The preparation of consolidated financial statements is complex and is normally the subject of an advanced accounting course. However, because most publicly held

Figure 14-4
Comparison of Cost
and Equity Methods

Item	Cost Method	Equity Method
Acquisition of investment	Recorded at acquisition cost (Investment account remains unchanged).	Same as cost, but balance changes each year.
Revenue from investment	Recorded only when dividends are declared.	Investment account increased by investor's share of earnings.
Dividends declared by investee	Revenue recognized.	No revenue recognized. Credit investment account.
Use of lower of cost or market method	Compare total cost and total market value of long-term equity securities portfolio. Write down in a contra account if market is lower than cost.	Investment account not written down unless market decline is material and permanent.

corporations consist of a parent company owning one or more subsidiary companies, it is important to understand the basic principles followed in the preparation of consolidated financial statements.

PRINCIPLES OF CONSOLIDATION

Consolidated financial statements are prepared by combining the individual account balances of the parent company with those of the subsidiary in order to report them as single amounts. For example, the cash balance of the parent company is combined with the cash balance of the subsidiary; the parent company's accounts payable are combined with the subsidiary's accounts payable; and the parent company's sales are combined with those of the subsidiary. Before combining account balances, however, certain duplicate items must be eliminated so that the combined amounts are not overstated from a single-entity standpoint. Three basic types of eliminations must be made:

1. Elimination of the Investment account and subsidiary stockholders' equity;
2. Elimination of intercompany receivables and payables; and
3. Elimination of intercompany revenues and expenses.

The first two types are discussed in the section on the preparation of the consolidated balance sheet. Elimination of intercompany revenues and expenses will be discussed in a later section on the preparation of the consolidated income statement.

CRITERIA FOR THE PREPARATION OF CONSOLIDATED FINANCIAL STATEMENTS

Objective 5: Criteria for inclusion of a subsidiary in consolidated financial statements

When certain conditions are met, a given subsidiary usually must be included in a corporation's consolidated financial statements. The most important condition is that the parent company must actually control the subsidiary by owning more than 50% of its voting stock. In addition, the management of the parent company should actively exercise control of the subsidiary and expect to continue to do so in the future. A parent company should not consolidate a subsidiary that it expects to sell in the near future, or one that is in legal reorganization or in bankruptcy.

Even though control conditions are met, there is one additional case where the subsidiary should be excluded from consolidation. That occurs when the subsidiary operates under foreign exchange restrictions, controls, or other governmentally imposed uncertainties so severe that they cast significant doubt on the parent company's ability to control the subsidiary. When a subsidiary is excluded from consolidation, it is generally reported in the financial statements as an investment accounted for by the cost method.

CONSOLIDATED BALANCE SHEET

The consolidated balance sheet shows the total assets under control of the parent company's board of directors, the total debts owed by the consolidated entity to outsiders, and stockholders' equity in the consolidated assets. To illustrate the preparation of a consolidated balance sheet, assume that Platt Company and Swab Company had the following balance sheets on January 1, 1992.

	Platt Company	Swab Company
Assets:		
Cash	$240,000	$ 36,750
Note receivable from Swab Company	22,500	–0–
Accounts receivable (net)	60,000	39,000
Inventory	93,750	53,250
Plant assets (net)	297,000	57,000
Total assets	$713,250	$186,000
Liabilities and Stockholders' Equity:		
Accounts payable	$ 64,500	$ 36,000
Note payable to Platt Company	–0–	22,500
Common stock, $10 par value	375,000	75,000
Retained earnings	273,750	52,500
Total liabilities and stockholders' equity	$713,250	$186,000

On January 2, 1992, Platt Company purchased 70% of the outstanding common stock of Swab Company for $89,250 on the open market. Late in 1991, Platt Company had loaned Swab Company $22,500, obtaining a note receivable as evidence of the loan. To record the purchase of Swab Company's stock, Platt Company made the following entry:

Jan.	2	Investment in Swab Company	89,250	
		Cash		89,250

Note that the purchase price of the stock is equal to the book value of Swab Company's

net assets acquired [70% × ($75,000 + $52,500)]. The total purchase price of the
stock is often greater (or less) than the book value of the net assets purchased. Accounting for those cases is discussed later in this chapter.

Data for the preparation of consolidated statements are normally accumulated on a
worksheet similar to that in Figure 14-5. Because no operating activity has yet taken
place, the only consolidated financial statement prepared on the date of stock acquisition is a consolidated balance sheet. Notice that Platt Company's balance sheet on
the worksheet includes cash of $150,750, since $89,250 was used to buy Swab Company's stock, and also includes its investment in Swab Company. The $89,250 cash
was paid to Swab Company's stockholders, and, therefore, is not included in Swab
Company's balance sheet.

When a parent company acquires less than 100% of the subsidiary's voting stock,
the subsidiary has stockholders other than the parent company. These other stockholders are called minority stockholders and their interest in the net assets of the
subsidiary is called a **minority interest**. Since the parent company purchased 70% of
the subsidiary's voting stock, the minority interest in the net assets of Swab Company
amounts to 30%.

The theory of consolidated statements is that the parent company and its subsidiary

Figure 14-5
Worksheet for Consolidated Balance Sheet—Minority Interest

PLATT COMPANY AND SUBSIDIARY
Worksheet for a Consolidated Balance Sheet
January 2, 1992

	Platt Company	Swab Company	Eliminations Dr.	Eliminations Cr.	Consolidated
Cash	150,750	36,750			187,500
Notes receivable from Swab Company	22,500			(2) 22,500	
Accounts receivable	60,000	39,000			99,000
Inventory	93,750	53,250			147,000
Investment in Swab Company	89,250			(1) 89,250	
Plant assets	297,000	57,000			354,000
Totals	713,250	186,000			787,500
Accounts payable	64,500	36,000			100,500
Note payable to Platt Company		22,500	(2) 22,500		
Common stock:					
Platt Company	375,000				375,000
Swab Company		75,000	(1) 75,000		
Retained earnings:					
Platt Company	273,750				273,750
Swab Company		52,500	(1) 52,500		
Minority interest				(1) 38,250	38,250
Totals	713,250	186,000	150,000	150,000	787,500

(1) To eliminate the investment in Swab Company.
(2) To eliminate intercompany note receivable and note payable.

are viewed as a single economic entity. Thus, before the accounts of Platt Company and Swab Company are combined, it is necessary to prepare the two types of balance sheet eliminating entries mentioned earlier. *The elimination entries are worksheet entries only—they are not made on either the parent company's or subsidiary company's books.*

Eliminating entry (1) in Figure 14-5 is made to eliminate the Investment in Swab Company and Swab Company's stockholders' equity. When Platt Company purchased the stock of Swab Company, it effectively acquired 70% of Swab Company's net assets, which were recorded in the Investment in Swab Company account. Because Swab Company's assets and liabilities will be combined with those of Platt Company, failure to eliminate the net assets included in the Investment account would result in a double counting.

Note that all of the subsidiary's assets and liabilities are included in the consolidated balance sheet in order to show the total resources and obligations under control of the parent company's board of directors. However, since only 70% of the stock was purchased, a minority interest in the net assets of Swab Company exists in the amount of $38,250 [30% × ($75,000 + $52,500)]. This minority interest is entered on the last line of the worksheet as part of eliminating entry (1) and is reported as a separate item on the consolidated balance sheet. Most companies report minority interest between liabilities and stockholders' equity on the consolidated balance sheet as shown in Figure 14-6.

Eliminating entry (2) is made to eliminate the intercompany note receivable and note payable. Failure to eliminate them would result in an overstatement of both assets and liabilities since the receivable and payable result from the transfer of funds within the consolidated entity—that is, no outside party is involved. Since a company cannot owe money to itself, the intercompany note receivable and note payable are eliminated.

Figure 14-6
Consolidated Balance Sheet

PLATT COMPANY AND SUBSIDIARY
Consolidated Balance Sheet
January 2, 1992

Assets

Current assets:	
Cash	$187,500
Accounts receivable (net)	99,000
Inventory	147,000
Total current assets	433,500
Plant assets (net)	354,000
Total assets	$787,500

Liabilities and Stockholders' Equity

Current liabilities:	
Accounts payable	$100,500
Minority interest	38,250
Stockholders' Equity:	
Common stock, $10 par value	375,000
Retained earnings	273,750
Total liabilities and stockholders' equity	$787,500

After the eliminating entries have been made on the worksheet, the remaining balance sheet accounts are combined and carried into the consolidated column as assets, liabilities, and stockholders' equity of the consolidated entity. The consolidated column is then used to prepare the consolidated balance sheet as shown in Figure 14-6. Note that the stockholders' equity of the consolidated entity is the same as Platt Company's since Swab Company's stockholders' equity was eliminated.

PURCHASE OF STOCK FOR MORE (OR LESS) THAN BOOK VALUE

In the preceding example, we assumed that the parent company purchased its shares in the subsidiary company at a price equal to their book value. That assumption was made to simplify the example and concentrate attention on the fundamentals followed in the preparation of a consolidated balance sheet. When a company purchases stock in another company, it must pay the market price of the shares, which will normally be more or less than their book value. In the preparation of consolidated statements, this difference between the cost of the investment and the book value of the subsidiary's equity acquired must be reported properly.

If the parent company pays more than book value for the shares, an excess of cost over book value will remain when the Investment account is eliminated against the subsidiary's stockholders' equity. There are several reasons why a company may pay more than book value for the shares:

1. The fair values of the subsidiary's assets may be greater than their book values. The application of conservative accounting procedures such as the use of accelerated depreciation and the LIFO inventory method often produces book values for plant assets and for inventory that are less than their fair values. Or some subsidiary assets such as land may have appreciated in value.
2. Long-term subsidiary liabilities may be overvalued as a result of an increase in general market interest rates.
3. The subsidiary may have unrecorded goodwill as evidenced by its above-normal earnings.
4. The parent company may be willing to pay a premium for the right to acquire a controlling interest in the subsidiary and the economic advantages it expects to obtain from integrated operations.

The Accounting Principles Board (APB) identified the standards to be followed in assigning the cost of shares in a subsidiary company as follows: First, all identifiable assets acquired—and liabilities assumed—whether or not shown in the financial statements of the acquired company, should be assigned a portion of the cost of the acquired company, normally equal to their fair values at date of acquisition. Second, the excess of cost over the sum of the amounts assigned to identifiable assets acquired less liabilities assumed should be recorded as goodwill.[2]

To illustrate, assume that Platt Company and Swab Company had balance sheets on January 1, 1992, as shown on page 634. On January 2, 1992, Platt Company purchased all (rather than 70%) of Swab Company's outstanding stock for $165,000. Since the book value of Swab Company's net assets (stockholders' equity) is $127,500, there is an excess of cost over book value of $37,500 ($165,000 − $127,500). Assume further that $25,000 of this excess relates to an undervaluation of Swab Company's plant assets and the remaining $12,500 represents consolidated goodwill. (Although a more descriptive phrase such as "Excess of cost over the fair

[2]Opinions of the Accounting Principles Board No. 16, "Business Combinations" (New York: AICPA, 1970), par. 87.

value of subsidiary net assets acquired" is often used in annual reports, we will use the shorter term "goodwill.") A worksheet for the preparation of a consolidated balance sheet on the date of acquisition is shown in Figure 14-7.

Platt Company's cash balance on January 2 is $75,000 because $165,000 was used to acquire Swab Company stock. Note that when the Investment account is eliminated against Swab Company's stockholders' equity, a $37,500 excess of cost over equity acquired remains, $25,000 of which is added to plant assets and the remaining $12,500 shown as consolidated goodwill. The $25,000 must be charged to depreciation expense on the worksheet over the remaining life of the plant assets in determining consolidated net income. Likewise, consolidated goodwill is amortized to expense on the worksheet over its estimated life, not to exceed 40 years. Note also that there is no minority interest because Platt Company purchased 100% of Swab Company's stock.

Sometimes the parent company pays less than book value for the subsidiary company's shares because the fair values of the subsidiary's assets are less than their book values, its liabilities are understated, or it has incurred operating losses that have decreased the market value of its shares. If this occurs, accounting standards provide that the excess of book value over cost should be allocated to reduce the values assigned to noncurrent assets in determining their fair values.[3]

Figure 14-7
Worksheet for Consolidated Balance Sheet—Excess Cost

PLATT COMPANY AND SUBSIDIARY
Worksheet for a Consolidated Balance Sheet
January 2, 1992

	Platt Company	Swab Company	Eliminations Dr.	Eliminations Cr.	Consolidated
Cash	75,000	36,750			111,750
Note receivable from Swab Company	22,500			(2) 22,500	
Accounts receivable	60,000	39,000			99,000
Inventory	93,750	53,250			147,000
Investment in Swab Company	165,000			(1) 165,000	
Plant assets	297,000	57,000	(1) 25,000		379,000
Goodwill			(1) 12,500		12,500
Totals	713,250	186,000			749,250
Accounts payable	64,500	36,000			100,500
Note payable to Platt Company		22,500	(2) 22,500		
Common stock:					
Platt Company	375,000				375,000
Swab Company		75,000	(1) 75,000		
Retained earnings:					
Platt Company	273,750				273,750
Swab Company		52,500	(1) 52,500		
Totals	713,250	186,000	187,500	187,500	749,250

(1) To eliminate the investment in Swab Company.
(2) To eliminate intercompany note receivable and note payable.

[3]Ibid., par. 91.

CONSOLIDATED INCOME STATEMENT

The consolidated income statement is prepared by combining the individual revenue and expense accounts of the parent company and its subsidiaries. Before combining the accounts, however, any intercompany revenues and expenses must be eliminated so that the consolidated income will reflect the results of operations from transactions with parties outside the affiliated group. Examples of intercompany items that must be eliminated are intercompany sales and purchases, intercompany rent revenue and rent expense, and intercompany interest revenue and interest expense.

To illustrate, assume that Platt Company and Swab Company had revenues and expenses during 1992 as shown in Figure 14-8. Assume also that Platt Company sold $60,000 worth of merchandise to Swab Company during the year, and that Swab Company paid $1,800 in interest to Platt Company on the note payable to Platt Company. Swab Company sold all of the merchandise purchased from Platt Company during the year. A worksheet for the preparation of a consolidated income statement is shown in Figure 14-8.

Eliminating entry (1) eliminates intercompany sales and purchases (included here in cost of goods sold) by eliminating the $60,000 sales of Platt to Swab and, at the same time, eliminating the $60,000 cost of goods sold recorded by Swab on sales to outsiders. The cost of goods sold recorded by Platt and the sales to outsiders recorded by Swab are included in the consolidated income statement, which is correct.

Eliminating entry (2) eliminates intercompany interest revenue and interest expense since the intercompany note receivable and note payable were eliminated on the consolidated balance sheet. In addition, the interest payment resulted in a cash transfer within the consolidated entity since no outside party was involved.

The preparation of a consolidated income statement is normally much more complex than illustrated here. The consolidated financial statements would also include a consolidated retained earnings statement and a consolidated statement of cash flows. Their preparation is reserved for a more advanced accounting course.

Figure 14-8
Worksheet for Consolidated Income Statement

PLATT COMPANY AND SUBSIDIARY
Worksheet for a Consolidated Income Statement
For the Year Ended December 31, 1992

	Platt Company	Swab Company	Eliminations Dr.		Eliminations Cr.		Consolidated
Sales	481,500	280,500	(1)	60,000			702,000
Interest revenue	1,800		(2)	1,800			
Total revenue	483,300	280,500					702,000
Cost of goods sold	282,000	156,000			(1)	60,000	378,000
Operating expenses	126,750	91,500					218,250
Interest expense		1,800			(2)	1,800	
Total expenses	408,750	249,300					596,250
Net income	74,550	31,200		61,800		61,800	105,750

(1) To eliminate intercompany sales and purchases.
(2) To eliminate intercompany interest revenue and interest expense.

PURCHASE VERSUS POOLING OF INTERESTS

When a corporation and one or more other companies are brought together (i.e., become affiliated) into one economic unit, the transaction is called a **business combination**. Both the purchase method and the pooling of interests method of accounting for business combinations are acceptable under generally accepted accounting principles (GAAP), but not as alternatives for the same business combination.

THE PURCHASE METHOD

In preceding examples we assumed that Platt Company acquired its controlling interest in Swab Company by purchasing the subsidiary's shares for cash. This is called the **purchase method** of acquisition and the consolidated financial statements are prepared under the purchase method of accounting. Rather than using cash, the parent company could acquire the shares purchased with other assets, debt securities, equity securities, or a combination of these.

As mentioned earlier, under the purchase method the investment in the subsidiary is recorded at its cost, which is assigned to the assets acquired and liabilities assumed in an amount equal to their fair values. Any excess of cost over the fair value of the net assets acquired is recorded as consolidated goodwill. Under the purchase method, the former stockholders of the subsidiary sell their shares to the parent company in exchange for the cash, other assets, or securities received. Consequently, none of the subsidiary's stockholders' equity is included in consolidated stockholders' equity.

THE POOLING OF INTERESTS METHOD

If the parent company exchanges its voting stock for essentially all (defined as 90% or more) of the voting stock of a subsidiary and certain other specific conditions are met, the business combination must be accounted for as a **pooling of interests**.[4] Because the former stockholders of the subsidiary become stockholders in the combined or consolidated entity, and because no resources are distributed, the business combination is viewed as a transaction under which the stockholders of the combining companies pool their resources and stockholder interests to form a new company. In other words, no purchase and sale of the subsidiary's stock occurs.

Based on this reasoning, the market price of the shares given and the fair values of the subsidiary's assets and liabilities are ignored. The assets and liabilities of the subsidiary are not revalued in the consolidated balance sheet. Rather, the *book values* of the subsidiary's assets and liabilities are combined with those of the parent company in the consolidated balance sheet and no excess of cost over book value (or excess of book value over cost) exists. As a consequence, no consolidated goodwill exists in a pooling of interests.

Under the pooling of interests method, the investment in a subsidiary is normally recorded at an amount equal to the par or stated value of the parent company shares issued. The investment account is then eliminated on the consolidated worksheet in a manner similar to that under the purchase method.

As mentioned earlier, the pooling method ignores the revaluation of assets and liabilities to their fair values and no consolidated goodwill exists. Thus, consolidated net income in the future will be greater under the pooling method than under the purchase method because there will be no depreciation of the $25,000 increment in plant assets and no amortization expense for goodwill.

[4]Ibid, par. 45–48.

Another important difference between the purchase and pooling of interests methods is the treatment of the subsidiary's earnings in the year of combination. If the business combination occurs during the subsidiary's fiscal year, under the purchase method only that portion of the net income earned by the subsidiary after the date of combination is included in consolidated net income. Under the pooling of interests method, the subsidiary's net income for the full year is included in consolidated net income even though the business combination may occur late in the year. Also, if prior years' comparative statements are presented, the subsidiary's net income for those years would be included in consolidated net income in a pooling but not in a purchase.

In summary, a business combination that meets the specific conditions for pooling must be accounted for by the pooling of interests method. All other business combinations must be accounted for by the purchase method. A comparison of the primary differences between the purchase and pooling of interests methods is given in Figure 14-9.

LIMITATIONS OF CONSOLIDATED FINANCIAL STATEMENTS

Consolidated financial statements are prepared primarily for use by management, stockholders, and creditors of the parent company. They are of limited use to minority stockholders and creditors of the subsidiary companies because they contain no detailed information about the individual subsidiaries. Creditors and minority stockholders of a subsidiary have legal claims only against the resources of that subsidiary and, thus, must rely on the individual financial statements of the subsidiary to assess the safety and earning potential of their investments.

Information in consolidated financial statements of highly diversified companies that operate in several industries is often of limited use to investors and prospective

Objective 6:
Limitations of consolidated financial statements

Figure 14-9
Comparison of Purchase and Pooling of Interests

Purchase	Pooling of Interests
1. The investment is recorded at its cost. Subsidiary assets and liabilities are adjusted to their fair values in the consolidated balance sheet and any excess of cost over the fair value of the subsidiary's net assets is consolidated goodwill.	The investment is recorded at the par or stated value of the parent company's shares issued. Subsidiary assets and liabilities are included in the consolidated balance sheet at their book values. No excess of cost over book value exists.
2. Subsidiary retained earnings do not become a part of consolidated retained earnings	Subsidiary retained earnings are included in consolidated retained earnings.
3. The excess of cost over book value assigned to depreciable assets and goodwill is amortized to reduce consolidated net income.	No excess of cost over book value exists; thus, there is no amortization expense.
4. Subsidiary earnings are included in consolidated net income only from the date of combination.	Subsidiary earnings for the full year of combination, and prior years if presented, are included in consolidated net income.

investors of the parent company. Financial position and the results of operations of these companies cannot be compared with industry standards or with other companies since they may operate in several different industries. To partially counter this deficiency, accounting standards require that diversified companies must report certain information by segments of the business. Specific requirements of segment reporting are contained in *Statement of Financial Accounting Standards No. 14*, "Financial Reporting for Segments of a Business Enterprise," and are explored in more advanced accounting courses.

SUMMARY

Part I of this chapter describes the accounting for long-term investments in debt securities (primarily bonds of other companies) and equity securities. Initially, long-term investments in debt securities are accounted for at their cost. Any discount or premium on the investment represents an adjustment to interest revenue and is, therefore, amortized over the remaining life of the investment. The amortization of discount gradually increases the carrying value of the debt investment to its maturity (par) value on its maturity date. (Amortization of a premium causes a decrease.) Gains and losses on the sale of long-term investments in debt securities are recognized for the difference between the selling price of the securities and their carrying value on the date of sale.

Long-term investments in equity securities may consist of preferred stock, common stock, stock rights, and stock options. Investments in these equity securities are generally included in the long-term equity securities portfolio and accounted for by the cost method, applying the lower of cost or market procedures. The aggregate market value of the portfolio on a balance sheet date is compared with the portfolio's aggregate cost and, if lower, the portfolio is valued downward to its lower market value. The excess of the portfolio's aggregate cost over its aggregate market value is debited to an Unrealized Loss account and credited to an Allowance to Reduce Long-term Investments to Market Value account. The Unrealized Loss Account is reported as a contra to stockholders' equity and the Allowance account is reported as a contra to the Long-term Investments account. In subsequent periods, both the Unrealized Loss account and the Allowance account are adjusted by an amount sufficient to report the long-term equity securities portfolio at the lower of its aggregate cost or aggregate market value at the balance sheet date.

Accounting for long-term investments in common stock depends upon whether the investor owns enough stock to exercise significant influence (20% or more of the investee's common stock) over the investee's operations. If the investor cannot exercise significant influence, the common stock investment is included in the long-term equity securities portfolio and accounted for by the cost method. If the investor can exercise significant influence, the equity method is used. Under the equity method, the investor recognizes its share of the investee's earnings or losses as an increase or decrease in the investment account. Dividends received from the investee are credited to the investment account. Accounting in this way prevents the investor from possibly manipulating its income by influencing the timing of investee dividends.

Part II describes the necessary criteria for and procedures used in the preparation of consolidated financial statements. The primary criterion is the existence of control, ownership of over 50% of another company's common stock. Consolidated financial statements are prepared by combining the individual account balances of a parent company with those of its subsidiaries in order to report them as single amounts. In this way, investors and creditors of the parent company are given financial information about the entire resources, obligations, and operations under control of the management of the parent company. Consolidated financial statements may be prepared under two different accounting methods, the purchase method and the pooling of interests method. The primary difference between the methods is that, under the purchase method the fair values of the assets and liabilities of the subsidiary are combined with the book values of the assets and liabilities of the parent company. Under the pooling of interests method, the book values of the subsidiary's assets and liabilities are combined with those of the parent company.

SELF-TEST

Test your understanding of the chapter by selecting the best answer for each of the following.

1. Interest-bearing bonds purchased as long-term investments have the highest income if purchased at:
   a. a discount.
   b. par value.
   c. a premium.
   d. face value.

2. When applying the lower of cost or market procedures for valuation of long-term equity securities investments, the unrealized loss is reported as a:
   a. component of operating expenses in the income statement.
   b. component of other expenses in the income statement.
   c. contra to long-term investments in the balance sheet.
   d. contra to stockholders' equity in the balance sheet.

3. If a long-term bond was purchased at a premium and sold at a discount, the loss on the sale would be the:
   a. discount amount on sale.
   b. premium amount on purchase.
   c. premium amount on purchase plus the discount amount on sale minus the premium amortized till the date of sale.
   d. premium amount on purchase plus the discount amount on sale minus the discount amortized till the date of sale.

4. For bonds purchased at a discount, the amortization process will:
   a. increase the investment account to the par value of the bond.
   b. decrease the investment account to the par value of the bond.
   c. increase the par value of the bond.
   d. decrease the par value of the bond.

5. Under the equity method of accounting for long-term investments, the dividends declared by the investee and received by the investor should be treated as:
   a. dividend revenue.
   b. an increase in the long-term investment account.
   c. a decrease in the long-term investment account.
   d. a decrease in a stockholders' equity account.

6. A subsidiary may be acquired by paying cash in a purchase transaction. The assets and liabilities of the subsidiary are combined with those of the parent company at:
   a. fair values.
   b. book values.
   c. cost at which the assets were acquired and liabilities incurred by the subsidiary.
   d. original cost minus accumulated depreciation (if any).

7. Preparation of consolidated financial statements involves elimination entries. These entries are recorded on:
   a. the subsidiary company's books only.
   b. the parent company's books only.
   c. both the parent company's and the subsidiary company's books.
   d. the consolidated worksheet only.
8. Which of the following items is recorded and reported at the same amount regardless of whether the pooling of interests method or the purchase method is used as the accounting method for a business combination?
   a. Assets and liabilities.
   b. Retained earnings.
   c. Minority interest.
   d. Goodwill.

REVIEW PROBLEM

Ling Corporation initiated a new company policy in 1992 of investing excess cash in equity securities of other corporations. The company had accumulated a sizable amount of cash because of profitable operations in preceding years. The following long-term equity securities transactions were completed by Ling Corporation during 1992.

Jan.   5 Purchased 60,000 of the 200,000 outstanding shares of Gardner Company common stock at a total cost of $23.60 per share.

      14 Purchased 100,000 of the 400,000 outstanding shares of Houser Company common stock at a total cost of $37.80 per share.

      20 Purchased 40,000 of the 100,000 outstanding shares of Bradley Company common stock at a total cost of $4.30 per share.

Mar. 18 Received a quarterly dividend of $.60 per share on the Gardner Company stock.

June 18 Received a quarterly dividend of $.60 per share on the Gardner Company stock.

      25 Received a semiannual dividend of $2 per share on the Houser Company stock.

Sept. 18 Received a quarterly dividend of $.80 per share on the Gardner Company stock.

Dec. 18 Received a quarterly dividend of $.80 per share on the Gardner Company stock.

      29 Received a semiannual dividend of $2 per share on the Houser Company stock.

      31 Gardner, Houser, and Bradley Companies reported net income (loss) for 1992 as follows: Gardner Company, $900,000; Houser Company, $2,520,000; Bradley Company, ($250,000).

Required:
A. Explain which accounting method Ling Corporation should use to account for each stock investment.
B. Prepare the necessary journal entries to record 1992 transactions.

C. Show how the investments will be reported on Ling's December 31, 1992 balance sheet, and how the revenue or loss on the investments will be reported on Ling's 1992 income statement.

ANSWER TO REVIEW PROBLEM

A. Ling Corporation should use the equity method to account for each of the stock investments because they purchased more than 20 percent of each company. Percent of ownership is: Gardner, 30%; Houser, 25% and Bradley, 40%.

B.

Jan.	5	Investment in Gardner Company		1,416,000	
		Cash			1,416,000
		(60,000 × $23.60)			
	14	Investment in Houser Company		3,780,000	
		Cash			3,780,000
		(100,000 × $37.80)			
	20	Investment in Bradley Company		172,000	
		Cash			172,000
		(40,000 × $4.30)			
Mar.	18	Cash		36,000	
		Investment in Gardner Company			36,000
		(60,000 × $.60)			
June	18	Cash		36,000	
		Investment in Gardner Company			36,000
		(60,000 × $.60)			
	23	Cash		200,000	
		Investment in Houser Company			200,000
		(100,000 × $2)			
Sept.	18	Cash		48,000	
		Investment in Gardner Company			48,000
		(60,000 × $.80)			
Dec.	18	Cash		48,000	
		Investment in Gardner Company			48,000
		(60,000 × $.80)			
	29	Cash		200,000	
		Investment in Houser Company			200,000
		(100,000 × $2)			
	31	Investment in Gardner Company		270,000	
		Investment Revenue			270,000
		($900,000 × 30%)			
	31	Investment in Houser Company		630,000	
		Investment Revenue			630,000
		($2,520,000 × 25%)			
	31	Investment Revenue		100,000	
		Investment in Bradley Company			100,000
		($250,000 × 40%)			

C.

Balance Sheet:
Long-term investments in common stock $5,600,000*

*Gardner Company	$1,518,000
Houser Company	4,010,000
Bradley Company	72,000
Total	$5,600,000

Income Statement:
Other revenues and expenses:
Investment revenue $ 800,000*

*Gardner Company	$270,000
Houser Company	630,000
Bradley Company	(100,000)
Total	$800,000

ANSWERS TO SELF-TEST

1. a   **2.** d   **3.** c   **4.** a   **5.** c   **6.** a   **7.** d   **8.** c

---

APPENDIX: ACCOUNTING FOR FOREIGN TRANSACTIONS AND TRANSLATION OF FOREIGN FINANCIAL STATEMENTS

Growth is a major objective of many businesses. To increase revenues, business managers often search for ways to expand existing markets or enter into new markets for their products and services. They also continually look for new, more economical sources of supply as a means of helping to control costs. In their search for these new markets and sources of supply, managers naturally consider expansion into other countries. Today, many large businesses, called **multinational corporations**, operate throughout the world. Foreign operations often make up a significant part of their total operations.

Multinational companies engage in two broad types of foreign activities: (1) import/ export transactions, and (2) ownership activities (i.e., the complete or partial ownership of foreign companies). Accounting problems are encountered when transactions with a foreign company are to be settled in a foreign currency. In addition, companies normally record transactions in their books in the currency of the country they operate in. Consequently, the financial statements of foreign companies must be translated into U.S. dollars before they can be consolidated with U.S. companies or before the equity method can be applied to common stock investments.

EXCHANGE RATES—TRANSLATION

Sale and purchase contracts (transactions) between firms in different countries specify the currencies to be used to settle the transactions. For example, a U.S. firm that purchases goods from a French firm may have to pay in francs and, therefore, have to exchange dollars for francs to pay for the goods. The number of dollars to be exchanged for the specified number of francs is determined by the exchange rate between dollars and francs. The **exchange rate** is the ratio between a unit of one currency and the amount of another currency for which that unit can be exchanged at a particular time. Exchange rates change continually to reflect changes in the demand for and supply of different currencies.

Transactions that are to be settled in a foreign currency, and the financial statements of foreign subsidiaries or investees, are translated into U.S. dollars by multiplying the number of units of foreign currency by a direct exchange rate. Thus, *translation* is the process of expressing monetary amounts that are stated in terms of a foreign currency in the currency of the reporting company.

A direct exchange rate is the ratio of the number of units of the domestic currency that can be converted into *one unit of foreign currency.* For example, a direct exchange rate between U.S. dollars and British pounds of 1.711 means that $1.711 can be exchanged for one British pound. To translate 100 pounds into dollars, the 100 pounds is multiplied by the direct exchange rate of $1.711. Figure 14-10 shows the direct exchange rate of selected currencies in terms of U.S. dollars.

Country	Prices in U.S. Dollars
Britain (Pound)	$1.711
Canada (Dollar)	.833
Denmark (Krone)	.1552
France (Franc)	.17635
Israel (Shekel)	.5383
Japan (Yen)	.006892
Mexico (Peso)	.0003662
West Germany (Mark)	.5993

Source: The Wall Street Journal, February 21, 1990.

Figure 14-10
Selected Foreign Currency Exchange Rates

ACCOUNTING FOR IMPORT AND EXPORT TRANSACTIONS

A common activity for many U.S. companies engaged in international business is the purchase and sale of goods and services. Accounting for the resulting accounts payable and accounts receivable depends on whether the transactions are to be settled in U.S. dollars or in the currency of the foreign country.

Objective 7:
Effect of changes in exchange rates on foreign receivables and payables

IMPORTING TRANSACTIONS

When a U.S. company purchases goods and services from a foreign company, the contract may specify payment in either U.S. dollars or the foreign country. If payment is to be made in dollars, no accounting problem arises. For example, assume that a U.S. company purchases $80,000 worth of goods from a French company on December 1, 1992. Payment is to be made in U.S. dollars on February 28, 1993. The accounting entries are the same as those illustrated in earlier chapters.

1992					
Dec.	1	Purchases		80,000	
		Accounts Payable, French Company			80,000
1993					
Feb.	28	Accounts Payable, French Company		80,000	
		Cash			80,000

If the transaction is to be settled in francs, however, the U.S. company must purchase francs for payment to the French company. Since exchange rates change daily, the U.S. company may incur an exchange gain or loss between the December 1, 1992 purchase date and the February 28, 1993 payment date.

Three dates are important in accounting for transactions to be settled in a foreign currency. These dates and the appropriate exchange rate to use for translation are as follows.

1. **The transaction date.** Each element (asset, liability, etc.) is measured and recorded in dollars by multiplying the units of foreign currency by the direct exchange rate in effect on that date.
2. **Each balance sheet date between the transaction date and the settlement date.** Balance sheet amounts to be settled in a foreign currency are adjusted to reflect the current exchange rate at the balance sheet date and an exchange gain or loss may be recognized at that time.
3. **The settlement date.** In the case of a foreign currency payable, the U.S. company must exchange U.S. dollars for foreign currency to settle the account. Foreign currency units received in settlement of a foreign currency receivable will be exchanged for dollars. An exchange gain or loss is recognized if the number of dollars paid or received does not equal the balance of the payable or receivable.

To illustrate the application of these rules, assume the previous example (the purchase by a U.S. company of $80,000 worth of goods from a French company), except that payment for the purchase is to be made by paying the French company 400,000 francs. Assume, further, that the exchange rate for the franc is as follows.

Date	Rate
December 1, 1992	$.200
December 31, 1992	.210
February 28, 1993	.205

Journal entries are:

1992 Dec.	1	Purchases		80,000	
		Accounts Payable, French Company			80,000
		(400,000 × $.200)			

On December 31, 1992, at the balance sheet date, the payable due in foreign currency is adjusted using the exchange rate in effect at that time. The entry is as follows:

Dec.	31	Exchange Loss	4,000	
		Accounts Payable, French Company		

12/31 payable (400,000 × $.210)	$84,000
Recorded payable	80,000
Exchange loss	$ 4,000

On February 28, the U.S. company must purchase 400,000 francs to settle the transaction. Since the exchange rate on this date is $.205, the company must pay $82,000 (400,000 × $.205) to acquire the necessary francs. The journal entry to record the settlement is:

1990				
Feb.	28	Accounts Payable, French Company	84,000	
		Cash		82,000
		Exchange Gain		2,000

Over the course of the entire transaction, the U.S. company has incurred a $2,000 net exchange loss, because it agreed to pay a fixed number of French francs, and before payment was made the cost to acquire each franc increased from $.20 to $.205. This net loss is recorded as an exchange loss of $4,000 in 1992 and an exchange gain of $2,000 in 1993.

REALIZED VERSUS UNREALIZED EXCHANGE GAINS AND LOSSES

Note in the example just used that an exchange loss on the account payable was recognized on the balance sheet date, December 31. The loss is unrealized, because the account has not yet been settled. When an account payable (or receivable) is settled, an exchange gain or loss on the settlement is considered realized. The Financial Accounting Standards Board believes that users of financial statements are served best by reporting the effects of the exchange rate changes in the period in which they occur, even though they are unrealized and may reverse or partially reverse in a later period. This procedure is criticized, however, because under generally accepted accounting principles gains are not normally reported until realized, and the recognition of unrealized gains and losses results in increased earnings volatility.

EXPORTING TRANSACTIONS

Since sale transactions are the opposite of purchase transactions, the same general logic discussed in the previous section applies to them, except that the relationship of exchange gains and losses to changes in the exchange rate is reversed. For example, assume that the U.S. company in the previous example sold $80,000 of merchandise to the French company. As before, if the transaction is to be settled in U.S. dollars, no accounting problem exists and the journal entries are:

1992				
Dec.	1	Accounts Receivable, French Company	80,000	
		Sales		80,000
1993				
Feb.	28	Cash	80,000	
		Accounts Receivable, French Company		80,000

If the agreement is that the French company will pay for the goods in francs, however, the U.S. company will incur an exchange gain or loss if the exchange rate for the franc changes between the date of sale and the settlement date. The entries on the U.S. company's books in this case are as follows:

1992				
Dec.	1	Accounts Receivable, French Company	80,000	
		Sales		80,000
		(400,000 × $.20)		

Dec.	31	Accounts Receivable, French Company	4,000	4,000
		Exchange Gain		

Receivable value, 12/31 (400,000 × $.21)	$84,000
Recorded receivable	80,000
Exchange gain	$ 4,000

1993				
Feb.	28	Cash (400,000 × $.205)	82,000	
		Exchange Loss	2,000	
		Accounts Receivable, French Company		84,000

A comparison of the entries to record an exporting transaction with those for an importing transaction reveals that the same movement in the exchange rate has an opposite effect on the company's reported income. That is, the increase in the exchange rate from $.20 to $.205 results in a net $2,000 exchange loss in the case of a foreign currency payable, whereas a net exchange gain of $2,000 is reported in the case of a foreign currency receivable.

TRANSLATION OF FOREIGN FINANCIAL STATEMENTS

**Objective 8:
Translating a foreign subsidiary's financial statements into U.S. dollars**

As mentioned earlier, multinational corporations often engage in international business activity by owning all or part of foreign companies. Financial statements expressed in foreign currencies must be translated into U.S. dollars before the equity method of accounting can be applied or a foreign subsidiary can be consolidated with its U.S. parent company. Because we are interested only in the general principles of translation, discussion is limited to the translation of the financial statements of a foreign subsidiary. Although two different translation methods might be used, the *current rate method* is the more widely used and, therefore, the one examined here.

CURRENT RATE TRANSLATION METHOD

Under the current rate method, revenue and expense accounts (and gains and losses) are translated into U.S. dollars using the exchange rate in effect when those items were recognized during the period. Because individual translation of numerous revenue and expense transactions is impractical, an appropriate average exchange rate for the period normally is used.

In the balance sheet, all assets and liabilities are translated into U.S. dollars using the exchange rate at the balance sheet date. Common stock and other paid-in capital accounts are translated using the historical exchange rate—that is, the exchange rate existing on the date that the subsidiary was acquired.

TRANSLATION ILLUSTRATION

As an illustration of the translation of a foreign subsidiary's financial statements, assume that Cook Company has a 100% owned subsidiary in West Germany, named Werner Company. Before year-end consolidated financial statements can be prepared, Werner Company's financial statements must be translated into U.S. dollars. Assume the following exchange rates for the West German mark.

1. When the subsidiary was acquired, $.34.
2. Average for 1993, $.63.
3. December 31, 1993, $.64.
4. When dividends were paid, $.62.

The December 31, 1993, balance sheet and the 1993 income statement for Werner Company are shown in Figure 14-11 in both West German marks and U.S. dollars.

The translation adjustment (sometimes called a translation gain or loss) is the amount needed to balance the total debits and credits in the balance sheet after the individual accounts have been translated. It results because some items are translated at current rates and others are translated at historical rates.

Figure 14-11
Translation of Foreign Subsidiary's Financial Statements

WERNER COMPANY
Balance Sheet
December 31, 1993

	Marks	Exchange Rate	Dollars
Cash	50,000	$.64	$ 32,000
Accounts receivable (net)	130,000	.64	83,200
Inventory	110,000	.64	70,400
Plant and equipment (net)	470,000	.64	300,800
Total Assets	760,000		$486,400
Accounts payable	45,000	.64	$ 28,800
Notes payable	100,000	.64	64,000
Common stock	300,000	.34	102,000
Retained earnings	315,000	Assumed Amount	260,900
Translation adjustment	–0–	Balancing Amount	30,700
Total Liabilities and Stockholders' Equity	760,000		$486,400

WERNER COMPANY
Income Statement
For the Year Ended December 31, 1993

	Marks	Exchange Rate	Dollars
Sales	800,000	$.63	$504,000
Cost of goods sold	360,000	.63	226,800
Gross profit	440,000		277,200
Expenses	240,000	.63	151,200
Net income	200,000		126,000
Dividends declared and paid	(50,000)	.62	(31,000)
Increase in retained earnings	150,000		$ 95,000

A MOVE TOWARD UNIFORM INTERNATIONAL ACCOUNTING STANDARDS

The growth in international business and an increased interest in international companies by investors emphasize the need for developing international accounting standards. Currently, no accounting standards are required worldwide. Progress toward development of international accounting standards is slow, primarily because different countries often have fundamentally different business practices, legal and regulatory constraints, and economic environments. However, several supranational organizations—such as the International Accounting Standards Committee (IASC), the European Economic Community, and the United Nations—are attempting to harmonize international accounting and reporting standards. The most active of these organizations is the IASC.

The IASC was established in 1973 to develop accounting standards to be followed in the preparation of financial statements, and to promote the worldwide acceptance and observance of those standards. The committee's objective is not to adopt any particular country's accounting principles as the only acceptable ones, but to improve and harmonize accounting standards globally.

The International Accounting Standards (IAS) issued by the IASC have no formal authority. However, member organizations of the IASC, such as the AICPA in the United States, have agreed to use their "best efforts" to ensure that published financial statements in their countries comply with the IAS in all material respects. Some countries, such as Singapore, have adopted these standards as part of their generally accepted accounting principles. Others have encouraged their use. For example, the stock exchange regulatory body in Italy has recommended that listed companies follow these standards in areas where no local standards or laws apply.

Since its inception, the IASC has issued more than 25 standards, covering topics ranging from the general principles of revenue recognition to the standards to be followed in accounting for leases and the capitalization of interest charges. To obtain greater international comparability, an increasing acceptance of IAS by multinational companies is needed.

GLOSSARY

BUSINESS COMBINATION. A transaction under which a corporation and one or more other companies are brought together into one economic unit (p. 640).

CONSOLIDATED FINANCIAL STATEMENTS. The financial statements of a parent company and its subsidiaries in which the assets and liabilities of the affiliates are combined into a consolidated balance sheet and the revenues and expenses are combined into a consolidated income statement (p. 632).

COST METHOD. An accounting method under which the investment is recorded at its cost with lower of cost or market adjustments. Income is recognized on the investment as dividends are declared by the investee (p. 627).

DIRECT EXCHANGE RATE. The ratio of the number of units of a domestic currency that can be converted into one unit of a foreign currency (p. 647).

EQUITY METHOD. An accounting method under which the investor recognizes its share of the investee's earnings or losses as they are reported by the investee. The investor increases or decreases the investment account for its share of the investee's earnings or losses and decreases the investment account for dividends received (p. 627).

EXCHANGE RATE. The ratio between a unit of one currency and the amount of another currency for which that unit can be exchanged at a particular time (p. 646).

INVESTEE COMPANY. A corporation whose stock is owned by another company (p. 621).

INVESTOR COMPANY. A company that owns stock in another company (p. 621).

LONG-TERM INVESTMENTS. Investments that are not intended to be converted into cash for normal operating needs (p. 621).

MINORITY INTEREST. The minority stockholders' interest in the net assets of a subsidiary company (p. 635).

MULTINATIONAL CORPORATIONS. Corporations that operate in different countries throughout the world (p. 646).

PARENT COMPANY. A company that owns more than 50% of the voting stock of a corporation (p. 632).

POOLING OF INTERESTS. A method of accounting for a business combination in which the parent company exchanges its voting stock for essentially all of the voting stock of a subsidiary and certain other specific conditions are met. The assets and liabilities of the separate companies are combined at their book values (p. 640).

PURCHASE METHOD. A method of accounting for a business combination in which the stockholders of the subsidiary company sell their shares to the parent company. Assets and liabilities of the subsidiary are reported at their fair values as measured by the total cost of the shares (p. 640).

SUBSIDIARY. A corporation whose voting shares are more than 50% owned by another company (p. 632).

DISCUSSION QUESTIONS

1. What is the distinction between temporary investments and long-term investments?

2. Why does the purchaser of a bond pay accrued interest to the seller?

3. See Company purchased five, $1,000, 12% bonds as a long-term investment. The purchase price was $5,075 including a broker's fee of $50. What amount should be recorded in the investment account?

4. Under what circumstances will a company's bonds sell on the market at
   a. Par value.
   b. A premium.
   c. A discount.

5. Why is it necessary to amortize a discount or premium that arises from the purchase of a long-term investment in bonds? Over what period of time should the discount or premium be amortized?

6. Gordon Company purchased a $1,000 par value, 12% bond on July 1, 1992 for $1,083. The bond matures on December 31, 1997. How much interest revenue should be reported by Gordon for the year ended December 31, 1992, assuming straight line amortization.

7. What are the two methods of amortizing discounts and premiums on bond investments? Which method is superior conceptually? Why?

8. On January 1, 1992, Smith Company purchased a $1,000 par value, 10% bond when the market rate of interest for such bonds was 12%. Was the bond purchased at a discount or a premium?

9. On January 1, 1992, Byer Company purchased 100, $1,000 par value, 12% bonds of Cellar Company. Interest is paid annually on December 31, and the bonds mature on January 1, 1997. Based on a 10% market interest rate, use present-value tables to determine the purchase price of the bonds.

10. Explain how the sale of a long-term investment in bonds is accounted for.

11. Long-term investments in equity securities are recorded initially at cost. After acquisition, they are accounted for by one of two methods. Name each method and explain when the use of each is appropriate.

12. Explain briefly how the use of the cost method of accounting for long-term investments in common stock differs from the accounting procedures used for temporary investments in common stock.

13. East Company purchased 20,000 of the 80,000 outstanding common shares of West Company on January 2, 1992, paying $10 per share. During 1992, West Company declared a dividend of $90,000 and reported earnings for the year of $200,000. The market value of West's stock was $9 per share on December 31, 1992. What is the balance in the Investment in West Company account to be reported on the December 31, 1992 balance sheet?

14. Why is interest revenue accrued on a long-term investment in bonds but dividend revenue is not accrued on a long-term investment in stock?

15. What are consolidated financial statements? What is their purpose?

16. What are the three basic types of eliminations that must be made in the preparation of consolidated financial statements?

17. Why are the investment account and the subsidiary's stockholders' equity eliminated on a worksheet for the preparation of a consolidated balance sheet?

18. What is meant by the term "minority interest"? Where is this item generally reported on a consolidated balance sheet?

19. Briefly explain when a business combination must be accounted for as a pooling of interests. Why is consolidated goodwill never recognized in a business combination accounted for as a pooling of interests?

20. Why might consolidated net income be greater using the pooling of interests method than when using the purchase method to account for a business combination?

21. What are the main limitations of consolidated financial statements?

22A. What is meant by a direct exchange rate?

23A. Explain what causes an unrealized foreign exchange gain or loss and tell when such gains and losses are recognized. Why has the FASB been criticized for its requirements regarding this question?

EXERCISES

Exercise 14-1 Long-Term Bond Investments

On July 1, 1992, Acker Company purchased at par 600, $1,000 par value, 8% bonds of Holly Corporation as a long-term investment. The bonds pay interest annually on June 30 and mature on June 30, 2001. Acker's fiscal year ends on December 31.

Required:

A. Prepare journal entries required on the following dates:
   1. July 1, 1992.
   2. December 31, 1992.
   3. June 30, 1993.
   4. June 30, 2001.
B. Prepare the December 31, 1992 balance sheet presentation for Acker's long-term investment in bonds.

Exercise 14-2 Long-Term Bond Investment

On May 1, 1992, Orr, Inc., purchased at par value plus acrued interest 300, $1,000 par value, 12% bonds of Rodgers Corporation to hold as a long-term investment. The bonds are dated January 1, 1987, mature on January 1, 1997, and pay interest semi-annually on July 1 and January 1. Orr's fiscal year ends on December 31.

Required:

A. Prepare journal entries on the following dates:
   1. May 1, 1992 to record the purchase.
   2. July 1, 1992 to record the receipt of interest.
   3. December 31, 1992 to record the accrual of interest.
   4. January 1, 1993 to record the receipt of interest.
   5. January 1, 1997 to record the receipt of maturity value.
B. Compute the amount of interest revenue Orr will show on its income statement for 1992, 1993, and 1996.

Exercise 14-3 Long-Term Bond Investments

On October 1, 1992, Astor Company purchased as long-term investments, bonds of two companies. Data with respect to the bond purchases follow:

Company	Total Par Value of Bonds Purchased	Stated Interest Rate	Maturity Date of Bonds	Interest Payment Dates	Price Paid (Net of Accrued Interest)
Kelly	$200,000	12%	1/1/95	6/30 and 12/31	$200,000
Moore	800,000	8%	10/1/98	3/31 and 9/30	740,000

Required:

A. Prepare the journal entries to record separately the purchase of each bond investment.
B. Prepare journal entries on December 31, 1992 to record the receipt of interest and to accrue interest. Use straight-line amortization.
C. Prepare the March 31, 1993 journal entry to record the receipt of interest.

Exercise 14-4 Purchase and Sale of Long-Term Bond Investments

On July 1, 1992, Jennings Company purchased 800, $1,000 par value, 12% bonds of Carson Corporation to hold as a long-term investment. The bonds are dated January 1, 1987, mature on January 1, 1997, and pay interest semiannually on June 30 and December 31. Jennings Company paid $787,720 plus a broker's fee of $3,640, and uses the straight-line method to amortize discounts and premiums. On September 30, 1994, Jennings sold the entire bond investment for $821,500, including accrued interest.

Required:

A. Prepare journal entries for the following dates:
   1. July 1, 1992.
   2. December 31, 1992.
   3. June 30, 1993.
   4. September 30, 1994.
B. Calculate the amount of interest revenue Jennings will report on its 1992, 1993, and 1994 income statements.

Exercise 14-5 Bond Investment—Effective Interest Amortization

On July 1, 1992 Bradford Company purchased $300,000 par value, 10% bonds of Temple Company to be held as a long-term investment. The bonds pay interest on June 30 and December 31, and mature on December 31, 1997. Bradford Company paid $228,867 for the bonds, which will produce a 16% annual yield, and uses the effective interest amortization method for all long-term bond investments.

Required:

A. Prepare an interest amortization table like that shown in Figure 14-2 through July 1, 1994.
B. Prepare journal entries on Bradford Company's books for 1992 and 1993.

Exercise 14-6 Long-term Investments in Equity Securities

At the beginning of 1992, Seko Company had no long-term investments in equity securities. During 1992, Seko completed the following transactions with respect to long-term investments in equity securities:

Jan.	10	Purchased 20,000 shares of AZK common stock for $7 per share plus a broker's fee of $3,000.
Mar.	14	Purchased 12,000 shares of Booker Company common stock for $14 per share plus a broker's fee of $4,200.
Apr.	15	Received notification that AZK had declared a $.30 per share cash dividend on its common stock, payable May 3.
May	3	Received the dividend on AZK common stock.
June	18	Purchased 10,000 shares of Pronton Company common stock for $21 per share plus a broker's fee of $5,800.
July	10	Received a $1 per share dividend on the Booker Company common stock.
Aug.	3	Sold 5,000 shares of the AZK common stock for $10 per share less a broker's fee of $1,300.
Nov.	4	Purchased 10,000 shares of Atwood Company, 8%, $100 par value preferred stock for $88 per share plus a broker's fee of $8,000.
Dec.	31	Seko's fiscal year-end. Market prices of the stock were:

AZK common stock	$ 9 per share
Booker common stock	12 per share
Pronton common stock	16 per share
Atwood preferred stock	89 per share

Each of the purchases of common stock represented less than 20% of the outstanding stock of the related company.

Required:

A. Prepare journal entries to record the transactions and any year-end adjustment.

B. Prepare the 1992 balance sheet and income statement presentations resulting from Seko's investments in long-term equity securities.

Exercise 14-7 Long-term Investments in Equity Securities

Landon Company began 1992 with the following investments in long-term equity securities:

Investment	Shares	Cost
Milton Company common stock	20,000	$ 62,500
Alpine Corporation common stock	10,000	144,200
Acquire Industries common stock	15,000	323,700
Burton Company 8%, $100 par preferred stock	10,000	898,000

During 1992, Landon completed the following transactions in long-term equity securities:

Feb. 16 Received an $.80 per share dividend on the Acquire stock.

Mar. 17 Received a $.20 per share dividend on the Milton stock.

May 26 Sold 5,000 shares of the Alpine stock for $10.50 per share less a broker's fee of $1,300.

June 19 Received a $.20 per share dividend on the Milton stock.

Aug. 25 Sold the Milton Company stock for $9 per share less a broker's fee of $4,000.

Nov. 6 Purchased 7,000 shares of Applied Electronics common stock for $7 per share plus a broker's fee of $1,800.

Dec. 22 Received the annual dividend on the Burton preferred stock.

31 Landon's fiscal year-end. The market prices of the stock in the long-term equity investments portfolio were:

Alpine common	$10 per share
Acquire common	21 per share
Burton preferred	90 per share
Applied Electronics common	8 per share

Each of the ownership levels of common stock represents less than 20% of the outstanding common stock of the respective companies.

Required:

A. Prepare journal entries to record the transactions of Landon Company, including any necessary year-end adjustment. (The Allowance to Reduce Long-term Investments to Market Value had a $6,700 balance on January 1, 1992.)

B. Prepare the 1992 balance sheet and income statement presentations related to Landon's long-term equity investment portfolio.

Exercise 14-8 Long-Term Investments in Equity Securities

Central Company began operations in 1986. During 1992, profitable operations enabled Central to engage in the acquisition of other corporations' stock as long-term investments. The 1992 transactions were:

Jan. 3 Purchased 45,000 of the 125,000 outstanding shares of Muro Corporation's common stock for $22 per share plus a broker's fee of $9,200.

Apr. 23 Received a $.70 per share dividend on the Muro Corporation stock.

May 7 Purchased 50,000 of the 800,000 outstanding shares of Pullen Company's common stock for $8 per share plus a broker's fee of $7,200.

July 17 Received a $.70 per share dividend on the Muro stock and a $.30 per share dividend on the Pullen stock.

Oct. 26 Received a $.70 per share dividend on the Muro stock and a $.50 per share dividend on the Pullen stock.

Dec. 31 Muro Corporation reported net income of $600,000 and Pullen Company reported net income of $1,630,000 for the year ended December 31, 1992. The market price per share of the stock on December 31, 1992 was: Muro Corp., $24.25; Pullen Co., $8.

Required:

A. Prepare journal entries to record the transactions, including necessary year-end adjustments.

B. Show how the investments will be presented on the December 31, 1992 balance sheet.

C. Show how the revenue earned will be shown on the 1992 income statement.

Exercise 14-9 Investments in Equity Securities—Equity Method

Baker Company began operations in 1987. Profitable operations resulted in Baker's acquiring excess cash, which management decided to invest in the common stock of other companies. During 1992, Baker completed the following transactions with respect to its long-term equity securities investments:

Jan. 5 Purchased 70,000 of the 280,000 outstanding common shares of Sagebrush Industries for $7 per share plus a broker's fee of $10,400.

12 Purchased 100,000 of the 250,000 outstanding common shares of DCA Corporation for $2 per share plus a broker's fee of $8,000.

June 18 Received an $.80 per share dividend on the Sagebrush stock, and a $.10 per share dividend on the DCA Corporation stock.

Dec. 15 Received an $.80 per share dividend on the Sagebrush stock.

31 Sagebrush reported net income for 1992 of $800,000; DCA Corp. reported a net loss for 1992 of $155,000. The closing market price of the Sagebrush and DCA stock on December 31, 1992, was $8 and $2.90 respectively.

Required:

A. Prepare journal entries to record the transactions.

B. Show how the investments will be presented on Baker Company's December 31, 1992 balance sheet.

C. Show how the revenue (loss) on the investments will be shown on Baker's income statement for the year ended December 31, 1992.

Exercise 14-10 Consolidated Balance Sheet—100% Ownership

On January 2, 1992, Riley Company purchased all of the outstanding common stock of Straw Company for $25 per share. Immediately after the purchase, the balance sheets of the two companies were as follows:

	Riley	Straw
Cash	$ 87,000	$ 50,000
Accounts receivable	280,000	110,000
Inventory	300,000	210,000
Investment in Straw Company	1,000,000	–0–
Property, plant, and equipment (net)	865,000	400,000
Total assets	$2,532,000	$770,000

Accounts and notes payable	$ 960,000	$200,000
Common stock, $5 par value	400,000	200,000
Retained earnings	1,172,000	370,000
Total liabilities and stockholders' equity	$2,532,000	$770,000

The fair value of Straw's property, plant and equipment on the date of acquisition was $615,000.

Required:

A. Prepare the journal entry on Riley's books to record the acquisition of Straw's stock.

B. Prepare a consolidated balance sheet workpaper on the date of acquisition.

Exercise 14-11   Consolidated Balance Sheet—90% Ownership

On January 5, 1992, Post Company purchased 90% of the outstanding common stock of Salem Company for $1,350,000. Immediately after the purchase, the balance sheets of the two companies were as follows:

	Post	Salem
Cash	$ 400,000	$ 450,000
Accounts receivable	1,200,000	400,000
Inventory	800,000	375,000
Investment in Salem Company	1,350,000	–0–
Property, plant and equipment (net)	5,000,000	1,275,000
Totals	$8,750,000	$2,500,000
Accounts payable	$ 400,000	$ 100,000
Notes payable, long-term	800,000	300,000
Mortgage payable, long-term	1,400,000	600,000
Common stock, $5 par value	3,000,000	600,000
Retained earnings	3,150,000	900,000
Totals	$8,750,000	$2,500,000

The book values of Salem's assets and liabilities were equal to their fair values on the date of acquisition.

Required:

A. Prepare the journal entry on Post's books to record the acquisition of Salem's stock.

B. Prepare a consolidated balance sheet on the date of acquisition.

Exercise 14-12   Consolidated Income Statement

Silex Company is a wholly owned subsidiary of Proctor Company. The income statements for the two companies for the year ended December 31, 1992 follow:

	Proctor	Silex
Sales	$900,000	$300,000
Interest revenue	24,500	2,000
Total revenue	924,500	302,000
Cost of goods sold	375,000	125,000
Operating expenses	120,000	63,600
Interest expense	6,250	3,000
Total expenses	501,250	191,600
Net income	$423,250	$110,400

During 1992, Proctor made sales of merchandise to Silex totaling $85,000. All of the merchandise was sold by Silex Company during 1992. The $3,000 of interest expense on Silex's income statement was paid to Proctor during the year on a note payable to Proctor.

Required:

Prepare a consolidated income statement workpaper for the year ended December 31, 1992.

Exercise 14-13 Business Combination—Purchase versus Pooling

On January 2, 1992, Pritchard Company acquired all of the outstanding common stock of Switzer Company. On the acquisition date, Switzer's balance sheet showed the following book values:

Total assets	$890,000*
Total liabilities	310,000
Stockholders' equity:	
Common stock, $6 par value	360,000
Retained earnings	220,000

* The market value of the assets was $960,000.

Assume two separate, independent alternatives exist with respect to the method Pritchard used to acquire Switzer's stock:

Alternative 1: Pritchard issued two shares of its own common stock (par value $3 per share) for each share of Switzer's common stock.

Alternative 2: Pritchard paid $13 cash for each share of Switzer's common stock.

Required:

Complete the following requirements for each alternative:

A. Is the acquisition more likely a purchase or a pooling of interests? Explain.

B. Prepare the journal entry on Pritchard's books to record the stock acquisition. If none is required, explain why.

C. Compute the amount of goodwill Pritchard will recognize on the January 2, 1992 consolidated balance sheet. If none, explain why.

D. On what basis (book value or market value) will Switzer's assets be valued on the January 2, 1992 consolidated balance sheet?

Exercise 14-14A Import and Export Transactions

The following transactions were entered into by Diamond Empire, a jewelry company.

Feb. 1 Purchased watches from a French manufacturer for 145,000 francs. The exchange rate was $.13.

15 Sold merchandise to a British company for 57,000 pounds. The exchange rate was $1.20.

24 Purchased necklaces from a Japanese manufacturer for 2,400,000 yen. The exchange rate was $.005.

Mar. 2 Paid one-half of the amount owed to the French company when the exchange rate was $.15. (Payment was made in francs.)

7 Received 57,000 British pounds from the British company in settlement of the transaction of February 15. The exchange rate was $1.27.

11 Paid 2,400,000 yen to settle the February 24 purchase from the Japanese manufacturer. The exchange rate was $.0045.

Apr. 1 Paid the remainder of the amount owed the French company when the exchange rate was $.13. (Payment was made in francs.)

Required:
Prepare journal entries to record the transactions.

Exercise 14-15A Import and Export Transactions

Best Company, a furniture dealer, entered into the following transactions. Best's fiscal year ends on December 31.

1992

Dec.   1   Purchased cabinets from a Denmark manufacturer. The invoice price was 135,000 kroner, and the exchange rate was $.0846. The contract calls for payment in kroner.

     10   Sold an assortment of lamps to a Canadian firm. The invoice price was 8,000 Canadian dollars, and the exchange rate was $.74. The contract calls for payment in Canadian dollars.

1993

Jan.   30   Paid the Denmark company 135,000 kroner when the exchange rate was $.09.

Feb.   10   Received 8,000 Canadian dollars from the Canadian firm when the exchange rate was $.79. The Canadian dollars were immediately converted into U.S. dollars.

Required:

A. Prepare journal entries to record the 1992 transactions.

B. Prepare journal entries to adjust the account payable and account receivable at December 31. The exchange rates on December 31, 1992 were:

Kroner	$.091
Canadian dollar	.81

C. Prepare journal entries to record the settlement transactions in 1993.

PROBLEMS

Problem 14-1 Long-term Bond Investments—Straight-Line Amortization

During 1992, Slate Company purchased the following bonds as long-term investments:

Apr.   1 $900,000 par value, 10% bonds of Clay Corporation. The bonds pay interest on March 31 and September 30, are dated April 1, 1985, and mature on April 1, 2000. The purchase price was $876,000.

July   1 $600,000 par value, 14% bonds of Lucon Company. The bonds pay interest on June 30 and December 31, are dated January 1, 1983, and mature on January 1, 1997. The purchase price was $629,700.

Required:

A. Prepare all journal entries related to these bond investments for 1992 and 1993. Slate uses the straight-line method to amortize bond discounts and premiums.

B. Prepare the balance sheet and income statement presentations resulting from these bond investments for 1992 and 1993. Slate's fiscal year ends on December 31.

C. Assume Slate Company sold the Lucon Company bonds on April 1, 1994 for $622,000 plus accrued interest. Prepare journal entries to:

1. Bring amortization up to date.

2. Record the sale of the bond investment.

Problem 14-2 Long-term Bond Investments—Straight-Line Amortization

During 1992, Vizon Company purchased the following bonds as long-term investments:

May 1 $800,000 par value, 8% bonds of Foxhill Corporation. The bonds pay interest on June 30 and December 31, are dated January 1, 1980, and mature on January 1, 2000. Vizon paid $772,400 plus accrued interest.

Nov. 1 $500,000 par value, 15% bonds of Karkill Company. The bonds pay interest on March 31 and September 30, are dated April 1, 1977, and mature on April 1, 1997. Vizon paid $523,055 plus accrued interest.

Required:

A. Prepare all journal entries related to these bond investments for 1992 and 1993. Vizon uses the straight-line method to amortize bond discounts and premiums.

B. Prepare the 1992 and 1993 balance sheet and income statement presentations resulting from these investments. Vizon's fiscal year ends on December 31.

Problem 14-3 Long-term Bond Investments—Effective-Interest Amortization

During 1992, Ramsey Company purchased two long-term investments as follows:

Jan. 1 $200,000 par value, 8% bonds of Carter Corporation for $169,367. The bonds pay interest semiannually on June 30 and December 31, mature on January 1, 1998, and were purchased to yield 12%.

July 1 $300,000 par value, 14% bonds of Olphant Corporation for $343,714. The bonds pay interest semiannually on June 30 and December 31, mature on January 1, 2000, and were purchased to yield 12%.

Ramsey Company uses the effective-interest method to amortize bond discounts and premiums.

Required:

A. Prepare amortization schedules for 1992 and 1993 for the two bond investments.

B. Prepare all journal entries for the bond investments for 1992 and 1993.

C. Prepare the presentations of the bond investments on Ramsey's December 31, 1992 and 1993 balance sheets.

Problem 14-4 Long-term Bond Investments—Effective-Interest Amortization

During 1992, Great Plains Company purchased the following two bond issues as long-term investments:

Jan. 1 $500,000 par value, 14% bonds of Green Valley Company. The bonds pay interest annually on December 31, mature on January 1, 1999, and were purchased to yield 12%.

July 1 $100,000 par value, 8% bonds of Giger Company. The bonds pay interest semiannually on June 30 and December 31, mature on January 1, 1995, and were purchased to yield 12%.

Great Plains uses the effective-interest method to amortize bond premiums and discounts.

Required:

A. Prepare an amortization schedule for 1992 and 1993 for the investment in Green Valley bonds.

B. Prepare all journal entries for 1992 and 1993 for the Green Valley bond investment.

C. Prepare an amortization schedule for the remaining life of the Giger bonds.

D. Prepare all journal entries for 1992 and 1993 for the Giger bond investment.
E. Show how the two bond investments will be presented on Great Plains' December 31, 1992 balance sheet.
F. Prepare the journal entry on Great Plains' books on January 1, 1995, the maturity date of the Giger bonds.

Problem 14-5 Long-term Bond Investment Analysis

On January 1, 1992, Colton Company purchased, as a long-term investment, $500,000 par value, 14% bonds of Neeter Company. The bonds pay interest annually on December 31, and mature on January 1, 2003. Colton Company uses the effective-interest method to amortize discounts and premiums. To facilitate the accounting for the investment, an effective-interest amortization schedule was prepared, the first five years of which are shown below:

Date	Interest Received	Interest Revenue	Amortization Amount	Investment Carrying Value
1/2/92				$449,702
12/31/92	$70,000	$71,952	$1,952	451,654
12/31/93	70,000	72,265	2,265	453,919
12/31/94	70,000	72,627	2,627	456,546
12/31/95	70,000	73,047	3,047	459,593
12/31/96	70,000	73,535	3,535	463,128

Required:
A. What was the purchase price of the bonds?
B. Were the bonds purchased at a discount or a premium? Explain.
C. How much was the initial discount or premium?
D. What is the rate of return being earned by Colton on this investment?
E. If the bonds are held to maturity, what is the total cash outflow for Colton over the life of the investment? What is the total cash inflow? What does the difference represent?
F. What is the total cash interest Colton will receive over the life of the investment? What is the total interest revenue Colton will recognize over the life of the investment? What is the reason for the difference?
G. How much interest revenue will be recognized on Colton's income statement for 1994 and for 1997?
H. What amount will appear in the bond investment account on Colton's December 31, 1995 balance sheet?
I. Show how the four amounts on the line dated 12/31/95 were computed.
J. Show how the bond purchase price was computed.

Problem 14-6 Long-term Investments in Equity Securities

On January 2, 1992, Almond Company purchased, as a long-term investment, common stock of Litzler Corporation at $23 per share. Litzler had 300,000 shares of $5 par value common stock outstanding for the entire year. For the year ended December 31, 1992, Litzler reported net income of $600,000 and paid dividends of $80,000. The market value of Litzler's common stock on December 31, 1992 was $23.60 per share.

Required:
A. Recopy the following schedule on a separate sheet of paper and complete the schedule. Show calculations where appropriate.

	Reporting Method	
Question	**Cost**	**Equity**
1. What level of ownership in Litzler should Almond possess to use the method?	%	%
Assume the Following Ownership Levels	30,000 Shares	120,000 Shares
2. On January 2, 1992, for how much should Almond debit the investment account?		
3. For the year ended December 31, 1992, what amount of revenue should Almond recognize?		
4. What will be the balance in the investment account on Almond's books on December 31, 1992?		
5. What amount of unrealized gain or (loss) should Almond report for 1992 with respect to this investment?		

B. Explain when, how, and why Almond should recognize revenue earned on this investment if it uses the:
   1. Cost method.
   2. Equity method.

Problem 14-7   Long-Term Equity Securities Investments

Reynolds Company regularly invests in equity securities of other companies on a long-term basis. During 1992, and 1993, Reynolds completed the following transactions:

1992

Stock purchased:		
Kylon Company common stock	15,000 shares	$ 8 per share
Murton Company common stock	10,000 shares	19 per share
Cash dividends received:		
Murton Company		$2.50 per share
Market value on December 31:		
Kylon Company		$ 6 per share
Murton Company		20 per share

1993

Stock purchased:		
Alwast Company common stock	28,000 shares	$ 5 per share
Norton Company common stock	5,000 shares	25 per share
Cash dividends received:		
Kylon Company		$ .50 per share
Murton Company		2.50 per share
Norton Company		5.00 per share
Market value on December 31:		
Alwast Company		$ 4 per share
Kylon Company		8 per share
Murton Company		20 per share
Norton Company		25 per share

Each stock investment represents less than 20% of the outstanding common stock of the related company.

Required:
A. Prepare journal entries, including any necessary year-end adjustments.
B. Prepare the 1992 and 1993 balance sheet presentations related to the long-term equity security investments.

Problem 14-8 Long-term Equity Securities Investments

During January 1992, Tremont Company purchased the stocks listed below as long-term investments:

Corporation	Type of Stock	Number of Shares		Cost per Share
		Purchased	Outstanding	
Prost	Common	30,000	400,000	$10
Jaspar	Preferred	15,000	40,000	75
Emerson	Common	40,000	100,000	20

The fiscal year for all corporations ends on December 31. Data concerning the investments for 1992 and 1993 follow:

	1992	1993
Net income reported:		
Prost	$300,000	$350,000
Jaspar	800,000	900,000
Emerson	600,000	400,000
Dividends declared and paid per share:		
Prost	$1	$1
Jaspar	4	4
Emerson	5	3
Market value per share on December 31:		
Prost	$ 9	$12
Jaspar	76	76
Emerson	24	20

Required:
A. What accounting method should Tremont use for each investment? Why?
B. Prepare the journal entries Tremont should make for 1992 and 1993 (in parallel columns) for each of the following:
   1. Purchase of the investments.
   2. Net income reported by the corporations.
   3. Dividends received from the corporations.
   4. Market value effects at year-end.
C. Show how the investments and related accounts would be presented on Tremont's 1992 and 1993 balance sheets and income statements.

Problem 14-9 Accounting for Long-Term Equity Securities

During January 1992, Nelson Company began a policy of investing in equity securities of other companies on a long-term basis. Investments during 1992 were:

Jan.   5 40,000 of the 100,000 shares of Axlerod Company's common stock at a cost of $15.50 per share.
      12 40,000 of the 1,000,000 shares of Holton Company's common stock at a cost of $9.75 per share.

19 120,000 of the 2,000,000 shares of Gabaldon, Inc.'s common stock at a cost of $5.60 per share.
26 40,000 of the 125,000 shares of Montoya Company's common stock at a cost of $12.20 per share.
30 25,000 of the 100,000 shares of Nesbitt Company's common stock at a cost of $3.40 per share.

All companies end their fiscal years on December 31. The following data are available for 1992 and 1993:

	1992	1993
Net income (loss) reported:		
Axlerod	$ 330,000	$ 370,000
Holton	4,400,000	4,100,000
Gabaldon	6,200,000	6,300,000
Montoya	625,000	375,000
Nesbitt	(400,000)	60,000
Dividends declared and paid per share:		
Axlerod	$1.40	$1.60
Holton	1.00	.80
Gabaldon	.60	.70
Montoya	1.10	.50
Market value per share on December 31:		
Alxerod	$16.10	$16.30
Holton	9.20	8.20
Gabaldon	5.70	5.95
Montoya	12.50	9.10
Nesbitt	1.60	1.80

Required:
A. What accounting method should be used by Nelson for each investment? Why?
B. Prepare journal entries for 1992 and 1993 (in parallel columns) for each of the following:
    1. Purchase of the investments.
    2. Net income reported by the companies.
    3. Dividends received.

Problem 14-10 Consolidated Balance Sheet

On January 2, 1992, Par Company acquired all of the outstanding common stock of Share Company on the open market for $180,000 cash. On that date (prior to acquisition), the separate balance sheets of the two companies were as follows:

	Par	Share
Cash	$200,000	$ 30,000
Accounts receivable	90,000	20,000
Receivable from Par	–0–	4,000
Property, plant and equipment (net)	160,000	126,000
Totals	$450,000	$180,000
Accounts payable	$ 56,000	$ 60,000
Payable to Share	4,000	–0–
Common stock, $5 par value	200,000	100,000
Retained earnings	190,000	20,000
	$450,000	$180,000

The fair value of Share's property, plant, and equipment on the acquisition date was $154,000.

Required:

A. Is this business combination a purchase or a pooling? Explain.
B. Prepare the journal entry on Par's books to record the acquisition of Share's stock.
C. Is there any goodwill from this stock acquisition? If so, how much?
D. Prepare a worksheet for a consolidated balance sheet as of the date of acquisition.
E. Prepare a consolidated balance sheet as of January 2, 1992.

Problem 14-11 **Consolidated Balance Sheet**

Assume the same data as in Problem 14-10, except that Par Company acquired only 90% of the common stock of Share for $140,000.

Required:

A. Is this business combination a purchase or a pooling? Explain.
B. Prepare the journal entry on Par's books to record the acquisition of Share's common stock.
C. Is there any goodwill from this acquisition? If so, how much?
D. Prepare a worksheet for a consolidated balance sheet as of the date of acquisition.
E. Prepare a consolidated balance sheet as of January 2, 1992.

Problem 14-12 **Consolidated Income Statement**

Income statements for the year ended December 31, 1992 for Park Company and its 100% owned subsidiary, Sare Company, follow:

	Park	Sare
Sales	$1,800,000	$1,100,000
Cost of goods sold	(700,000)	(500,000)
Gross profit	1,100,000	600,000
Operating expenses:		
Administrative expenses	(375,000)	(190,000)
Selling expenses	(450,000)	(180,000)
Other revenue and (expense):		
Interest revenue	105,000	10,000
Interest expense	(45,000)	(18,000)
Investment revenue	38,000	6,000
Gain (loss) on sale of investments	(12,000)	3,000
Net income	$ 361,000	$ 231,000

During 1992, Park sold $300,000 worth of merchandise to Sare, and Sare sold $100,000 worth of merchandise to Park. All the merchandise was sold to outside parties by the end of 1992. On July 1, 1992, Sare borrowed $300,000 from Park on a six-month, 10% note. The principal and interest were paid on December 31, 1992.

Required:

A. Prepare a worksheet for a consolidated income statement for the year ended December 31, 1992.
B. Prepare a consolidated income statement for the year ended December 31, 1992.

Problem 14-13A **Import and Export Transactions**

The Honey Company, a U.S. firm, engaged in the following transactions with foreign companies.

Date	Transaction	Billing Amount	Direct Exchange Rate
1992			
11/10	Purchased inventory from a Japanese firm, Mushi Company	2,800,000 Yen	$.0039
12/18	Sold merchandise to Thomas Company, a British firm	50,000 Pounds	$1.27
12/29	Paid one-half of the amount due Mushi Company.		$.0037
12/31	Close of Honey Company's fiscal year		
1993			
1/7	Purchased goods from a West German company	43,000 Marks	$.337
3/18	Paid the remainder of the amount due Mushi Company		$.0045
3/19	Received payment in full from Thomas Company		$1.19
4/4	Paid the West German company		$.336

Required:

A. Prepare general journal entries for Honey Company for 1992.

B. Adjust the accounts at year-end, December 31, 1992. Year-end exchange rates were:

> Japanese yen $.0044
> British pound $1.22

C. Assuming Honey Company engaged in no other foreign transactions during 1993, prepare journal entries for 1993 and compute the net exchange gain or loss for 1993.

Problem 14-14A   Foreign Operations

On January 1, 1992, a U.S. parent company formed a wholly owned subsidiary, Sherwood, Inc., located in England. Sherwood, Inc.'s financial statements for 1992 in British pounds follow:

SHERWOOD, INC.
Statement of Income and Retained Earnings
For the Year Ended December 31, 1992
(in British pounds)

Sales revenues	170,000
Cost of goods sold	50,000
Gross profit on sales	120,000
Operating expenses	40,000
Net income	80,000
Less dividends paid	72,000
Increase in retained earnings	8,000

SHERWOOD, INC.
Balance Sheet
December 31, 1992
(in British pounds)

Cash	22,000
Accounts receivable (net)	41,000
Inventory	51,000
Plant and equipment (net)	72,000
Total Assets	186,000
Accounts and notes payable	88,000
Common stock	90,000
Retained earnings	8,000
Total Equities	186,000

Relevant exchange rates for the British pound are:

	U.S. Dollars per Pound
January 1, 1992	$1.16
December 31, 1992	1.27
Average for 1992	1.20
Dividend payment date	1.25

Required:

Translate the year-end balance sheet and income statement of Sherwood, Inc. into U.S. dollars so that it can be included in the consolidated financial statements.

Problem 14-15A Foreign Operations

Forest Company has a 100% owned West German subsidiary, Dorsch Corporation, located in Buchholz, West Germany. The West German mark is the currency used by Dorsch in its accounts and financial reports. Dorsch's financial statements for 1992, in West German marks, follow.

DORSCH COMPANY
Income Statement
For the Year Ended December 31, 1992
(in West German marks)

Sales	1,655,000
Cost of goods sold	660,000
Gross profit	995,000
General and administrative expenses	293,000
Net income before income taxes	702,000
Income tax expense	175,000
Net Income	527,000

DORSCH COMPANY
Balance Sheet
December 31, 1992
(in West German marks)

Assets	
Cash	50,000
Accounts receivable (net)	90,000
Inventory	75,000
Property, plant, and equipment (net)	375,000
Total Assets	590,000
Liabilities and Stockholders' Equity	
Accounts payable	120,000
Taxes payable	14,000
Common stock	289,000
Retained earnings	167,000
Total Liabilities and Stockholders' Equity	590,000

On December 31, 1991, the translated retained earnings balance was $23,000. Assume the following exchange rates for the West German mark.

Historical	$.20
January 1, 1992	.33
Average for 1992	.30
December 31, 1992	.32

Required:

Translate Dorsch Corporation's financial statements into U.S. dollars. (*Hint:* Translate the income statement first and use net income plus the December 31, 1991 translated retained earnings of $23,000 to find the correct ending retained earnings for the balance sheet.)

CASE

CASE 14-1 Annual Report Analysis

Refer to the financial statements and related footnotes of BFGoodrich Company in the Appendix to this text and answer the following questions. Indicate the page number on which you found the answer.

A. Are the financial statements of BFGoodrich Company consolidated or nonconsolidated?

B. Does BFGoodrich have any nonconsolidated long-term investments in equity securities of other corporations? If so, what method is used to account for these investments?

C. What does the balance sheet account "Goodwill" represent? Over what period, and by what method is goodwill amortized?

D. Did BFGoodrich acquire any businesses during 1989? If so, how many, and what method of accounting was used?

E. With reference to foreign operations:

    1. Does BFGoodrich enter into transactions with foreign companies? If so, in what country does most of the activity occur?

    2. Does BFGoodrich consolidate any foreign subsidiaries? How can you tell?

15

STATEMENT OF CASH FLOWS

OVERVIEW AND OBJECTIVES

This chapter discusses the preparation and uses of a statement of cash flows. When you have completed the chapter, you should understand:

1. The purpose and use of cash flow information.
2. The classification of cash receipts and cash payments by operating, investing, and financing activities.
3. The content and form of the statement of cash flows.
4. The difference between the direct and indirect approach to reporting net cash flow from operating activities.
5. How to report the effects of exchanges of noncash items.

As discussed earlier, a complete set of financial statements includes a balance sheet, an income statement, a retained earnings statement, and a statement of cash flows (SCF). Details of the first three have been presented in the preceding chapters. The fact that the SCF is discussed last does not imply that it is any less important than the others, however. It is a very useful statement for investors, creditors, and managers because it identifies the activities related to the receipt of cash and the purposes for which cash was used during a period.

BRIEF HISTORY OF THE DEVELOPMENT OF THE SCF

The operating, financing, and investing activities of a company are of considerable interest to users of financial statements because those activities change the financial position of a business. An analysis of comparative balance sheets for successive periods helps identify the total changes that have taken place in asset, liability, and owners' equity accounts, but does not give a ready explanation of what caused those changes. The income statement and retained earnings statement do give a partial explanation by giving a summary of the effects of operating activities, the amount of earnings distributed as dividends, and the amount of earnings retained for other uses. Neither statement, however, gives a full report of the financing activities nor the investing activities involving financial resources.

For many years, the financing and investing activities of a firm were reported in a financial statement called a Statement of Changes in Financial Position (SCFP). That statement was used to report the sources and uses of financial resources (funds) for a specified time period. Funds were defined as either cash (or cash and cash equivalents) or working capital. Firms were required to present a cash basis or working capital basis SCFP whenever financial statements purporting to present both financial position and results of operations were issued. Although most firms initially prepared their SCFP on a working capital basis, increasing requests for cash flow information by users of financial information produced a gradual shift from a working capital basis SCFP to a cash basis SCFP. Over time, the cash basis was used by a majority of firms as shown by surveys of 600 companies conducted by the American Institute of Certified Public Accountants.

	1986	**1980**
Number of companies reporting:		
Changes in working capital	202	541
Changes in cash	398	59
Total companies	600	600

Because of the increased emphasis on the usefulness of cash flow information to statement users, the Financial Accounting Standards Board (FASB) issued SFAS No. 95, "Statement of Cash Flows," in November 1987. SFAS 95 requires the preparation of a Statement of Cash Flows (SCF) rather than a SCFP.

PURPOSE OF THE SCF

As stated by the FASB, "the primary purpose of a statement of cash flows is to provide information about the cash receipts and cash payments of an entity during a period."[1] The statement of cash flows also provides information about the investing and financing activities of the firm. Cash flow information, used with information contained in the other financial statements, should help investors, creditors, and other users to assess:

Objective 1: Purpose and uses of SCF

1. The firm's ability to generate positive net cash flows in the future;
2. The firm's ability to meet its obligations and pay dividends;
3. The firm's needs for external financing;
4. The reasons for differences between net income and related cash receipts and payments; and
5. Both the cash and noncash aspects of the firm's investing and financing transactions during the period.

To provide information useful to investors, creditors, and others in making these assessments, the SCF should report the cash effects during a period related to operating activities, investing activities, and financing activities. In addition to providing information for use by external users, the SCF also provides important information for use by managers in planning and controlling operations.

CONCEPT OF CASH

In the preparation of the SCF, cash is defined as those items a bank would normally accept for deposit to the firm's checking account (this is the concept of cash discussed in Chapter 8) plus cash equivalents. Thus, cash flow statements should explain the

[1]Statement of Financial Accounting Standards No. 95, "Statement of Cash Flows" (Stamford, Conn.: FASB, 1987), par. 4.

change during the period in cash and cash equivalents. **Cash equivalents** are short-term, highly liquid investments such as Treasury bills, commercial paper, and money market funds. Investing temporarily excess cash in such investments is considered part of a firm's cash management rather than part of its operating, investing, and financing activities. Consequently, this temporary investment activity should not be reported in the statement of cash flows. In addition, gross amounts of both cash receipts and cash payments normally should be presented for each of the firm's operating, investing, and financing activities.

CLASSIFICATION WITHIN THE SCF

Objective 2: Classification in the SCF

Classification in accounting facilitates the use of accounting information by grouping items with similar characteristics and separating items with different characteristics. In the statement of cash flows, cash receipts and payments are classified by business activities into three types: operating, investing, and financing. A basic description of each of these activities follows.

OPERATING ACTIVITIES

Operating activities involve the production or delivery of goods for sale and the providing of services. Cash flows from operating activities generally represent the effects of transactions that enter into the determination of net income. Cash inflows from operating activities include (1) collections from customers for the cash sale of goods and services or the collection of accounts receivable, (2) interest receipts for loans made, and (3) dividend receipts from equity investments.

Cash outflows for operating activities result from cash payments for the acquisition of inventory, to employees, to governments for taxes, to lenders for interest, and to other suppliers for other types of expenses. The cash outflows may represent payments for goods and services acquired currently, or for the settlement of obligations incurred for goods or services charged to operations of prior periods.

INVESTING ACTIVITIES

Investing activities generally include those transactions involving (1) lending money and collecting the principal, and (2) acquiring and selling (a) securities that are not cash equivalents, and (b) productive assets that are expected to produce revenues over several periods. Cash inflows from investing activities include receipts from:

1. Principal repayments by borrowers; (Note that interest receipts on the loans are included in operating activities.)
2. The sale of loans (receivables) made by the firm; and
3. The sale of assets such as (a) debt or equity securities of other firms (other than cash equivalents), and (b) property, plant, and equipment.

   Cash outflows for investing activities include:

1. Loans made or purchased by the firm; and
2. Payments to acquire assets such as (a) debt or equity securities of other firms (other than cash equivalents), and (b) property, plant, and equipment.

Cash inflows from the sale of loans, and cash outflows for loans made or purchased by the firm relate primarily to financial institutions such as finance companies and banks.

FINANCING ACTIVITIES

Financing activities generally include obtaining resources (1) from owners and providing them with a return on and a return of their investment, and (2) from creditors and repaying the amounts borrowed or otherwise settling the obligation. (Again, note that interest payments are included as outflows from operating activities.) Cash inflows from financing activities include:

1. Proceeds from the issuance of equity securities; and
2. Proceeds from the issuance of bonds, mortgages, notes, and other short-term or long-term borrowings.

Cash outflows for financing activities result from:

1. The payment of dividends;
2. Outlays to repurchase the firm's shares of stock (to be retired or held as treasury stock); and
3. Outlays for repayments of amounts borrowed.

Most borrowing and repayment of amounts borrowed are financing activities. However, the settlement of liabilities, such as accrued expenses and accounts payable incurred to acquire inventory and supplies, is considered an operating activity.

The classification of some items depends upon the nature of the firm's operations. For example, there is a presumption that the acquisition and sale, or other disposal, of long-lived assets are investing activities. However, if long-lived assets are acquired or produced to be rented to others for a short period and then sold, the acquisition or production of those assets should be considered an operating activity. In addition, some gains and losses that are normally included in the income statement relate to investing or financing activities rather than to operating activities. For example, a gain or loss from the sale of plant assets or from the disposal of discontinued operations is generally a part of cash inflow from investing activities, and a gain or loss on the extinguishment of debt is generally part of a cash outflow from financing activities. Thus, considerable judgment must be exercised in the preparation of the SCF.

CONTENT AND FORM OF THE SCF

The SCF should report net cash provided or used by operating, investing, and financing activities and the aggregate effect of those flows on cash and cash equivalents during the period. Some flexibility is permitted in the form of the statement. For example, cash flow from operating activities might be presented either directly or indirectly.

Objective 3:
Format of SCF

CASH FLOW FROM OPERATING ACTIVITIES

As just mentioned, cash flow from operating activities may be reported either directly or indirectly. However, SFAS 95 encourages the use of the direct method.

Direct Method of Reporting Cash Flow from Operating Activities

Under the **direct method**, major classes of operating revenues are shown as cash inflows from operations. For example, cash inflows may be reported for cash collected from customers and for cash received from interest and dividends. Conversely, cash payments and expenses are reported by major class such as cash paid to suppliers for goods and services, cash paid to employees, cash paid to creditors for interest, and

Objective 4:
Direct vs. indirect method

cash paid to governments for taxes. The difference between the cash inflows from operations and cash payments for expenses represents the net cash flow from operating activities. The main advantage of the direct method is that it shows the operating cash receipts and payments. Knowledge of where operating cash came from and how cash was used in operations in past periods may be useful in estimating future cash flows.

To illustrate the direct method of presenting net cash flow from operating activities, assume that PMX Corporation's income statement for 1992 and selected comparative balance sheet data were as follows:

PMX CORPORATION
Income Statement
For the Year Ended December 31, 1992

Sales revenues		$694,000
Cost of goods sold		316,000
Gross profit on sales		378,000
Operating expenses:		
Advertising expense	$ 48,600	
Depreciation expense	69,300	
Insurance expense	4,200	
Repairs and maintenance expense	26,800	
Salaries and wages expense	112,600	
Total operating expenses		261,500
Net income before income tax		116,500
Income tax expense		21,000
Net income		$ 95,500

Selected comparative balance sheet data for 1992 and 1991 were:

	December 31	
	1992	1991
Accounts receivable	$169,400	$147,300
Inventory	101,600	109,500
Prepaid insurance	6,800	9,400
Accounts payable	74,200	81,600
Accrued salaries and wages payable	24,900	21,400
Accrued income taxes payable	9,300	–0–

In computing cash provided by operating activities, the normal approach is to convert the accrual basis net income to a cash basis income. To make this conversion, the relationship between the effects of operating transactions on accrual income and cash movements within the company must be considered. Thus, the different classes of accrual basis revenues are adjusted to show cash inflows from operations. Conversely, accrual basis expenses are adjusted to report cash outflows for various classes of expenses. The difference between cash inflows from operations and cash outflows for expenses represents the net cash flows from operating activities. The conversion process is presented in the following sections.

Cash Received from Customers

Under accrual accounting, sales on account are recognized by a debit to Accounts Receivable and a credit to Sales at the time each sale is made. Under the cash basis, revenue is not recognized until cash is received. The conversion of accrual basis sales revenues to cash basis sales revenues is made by considering the beginning and ending balances in accounts receivable, as follows:

$$\begin{matrix} \text{Accrual} \\ \text{basis} \\ \text{sales} \end{matrix} \begin{Bmatrix} + \text{ beginning accounts receivable} \\ - \text{ ending accounts receivable} \end{Bmatrix} = \begin{matrix} \text{Cash received} \\ \text{from customers} \end{matrix}$$

PMX Corporation's comparative balance sheet data show that accounts receivable on 12/31/91 and 12/31/92 were $147,300 and $169,400, respectively. Thus, cash received from customers may be computed as follows.

Accrual basis sales from the income statement	$694,000
Add: Beginning accounts receivable	147,300
Total cash collectible from customers	841,300
Less: Ending accounts receivable	169,400
Cash received from customers	$671,900

The beginning balance of accounts receivable is added to accrual basis sales. The total shows the amount of cash that could have been collected during the current period, including collections of sales recognized in prior years. The ending accounts receivable balance is subtracted because it represents sales that have not yet been collected. The result is cash collected from customers during the current period.

Cash Payments to Suppliers for Purchases

Under accrual accounting, purchases of merchandise on account are recognized when made by a debit to Purchases (in a periodic system) and a credit to Accounts Payable. Under the cash basis, purchases are not recognized until cash is paid. Thus, to convert from accrual basis cost of goods sold to cash basis cost of goods sold, adjustments must be made for the changes during the year in inventory and in accounts payable as follows:

$$\begin{matrix} \text{Accrual basis} \\ \text{cost of} \\ \text{goods sold} \end{matrix} \begin{Bmatrix} - \text{ beginning inventory} \\ + \text{ ending inventory} \end{Bmatrix} = \begin{matrix} \text{Accrual} \\ \text{basis} \\ \text{purchases} \end{matrix}$$

$$\begin{matrix} \text{Accrual} \\ \text{basis} \\ \text{purchases} \end{matrix} \begin{Bmatrix} + \text{ beginning accounts payable} \\ - \text{ ending accounts payable} \end{Bmatrix} = \begin{matrix} \text{Cash paid} \\ \text{for} \\ \text{purchases} \end{matrix}$$

PMX Corporation's comparative balance sheet data show that on December 31, 1991, and December 31, 1992, (1) inventory balances were $109,500 and $101,600, respectively, and (2) accounts payable balances were $81,600 and $74,200, respectively. Thus, cash paid to suppliers for purchases during 1992 can be computed as follows.

Accrual basis cost of goods sold (from income statement)	$316,000
Less: Beginning inventory	(109,500)
Add: Ending inventory	101,600
Accrual basis purchases for the year	308,100
Add: Beginning accounts payable	81,600
Less: Ending accounts payable	(74,200)
Cash paid to suppliers for purchases	$315,500

The amount of purchases made during the year is computed first by deducting the beginning inventory balance from accrual basis cost of goods sold and adding the ending inventory balance to accrual basis cost of goods sold. After the amount of purchases for the year is determined, the amount of cash paid to suppliers for purchases can be computed. This is done by adding beginning accounts payable (goods purchased last year are paid for during the current year) and deducting ending accounts payable (goods purchased this year have not yet been paid for).

Cash Paid for Expenses

Under accrual accounting, expenses are recognized when resources are used to earn revenues. Some expenses are prepaid, some are paid during the current period as incurred, and some are accrued at the end of the period. Under the cash basis, expenses are recognized when they are paid for. The relationship between various expenses and cash payments depends upon the related changes in prepaid expenses and/or accrued expenses. Thus, the conversion of an accrual basis expense to a cash basis expense may be made as follows:

$$\begin{matrix} \text{Accrual} \\ \text{basis} \\ \text{expense} \end{matrix} \left\{ \begin{matrix} - \text{ beginning prepaid expense} \\ + \text{ ending prepaid expense} \\ \text{or} \\ + \text{ beginning accrued expense} \\ - \text{ ending accrued expense}^2 \end{matrix} \right\} = \begin{matrix} \text{Cash payment} \\ \text{for} \\ \text{expense} \end{matrix}$$

PMX Corporation's comparative balance sheet data show that the December 31, 1991, and December 31, 1992, balances in the Prepaid Insurance account were $9,400 and $6,800, respectively. Thus, the conversion of accrual basis insurance expense to cash basis insurance expense is:

Accrual basis insurance expense from income statement	$4,200
Less: Beginning prepaid insurance	(9,400)
Plus: Ending prepaid insurance	6,800
Cash paid for insurance	$1,600

Beginning prepaid insurance is deducted from accrual basis insurance expense to remove the amount paid for in prior years. Ending prepaid insurance is then added to show insurance paid for this year that will not be charged to insurance expense until later years.

Reference to the comparative balance sheet data of PMX Corporation shows liabilities for two accrued expenses: salaries and wages payable and income taxes payable. Accrued salaries and wages payable on December 31, 1991, and December 31, 1992, amounted to $21,400 and $24,900, respectively; the amounts of accrued income taxes payable on those dates were $–0– and $9,300, respectively. Thus the conversion

---

[2]If total accrual basis expenses are converted to cash basis expenses, noncash expenses (such as amortization and depreciation) also must be deducted.

of accrual basis salaries and wages expense and income tax expense to cash basis expenses is made as follows.

	Salaries and Wages Expense	Income Tax Expense
Accrual basis expense from the income statement	$112,600	$21,000
Add: Beginning accrued expense	21,400	–0–
Less: Ending accrued expense	(24,900)	(9,300)
Cash paid during the year	$109,100	$11,700

Beginning accrued expenses are added to accrual basis expenses, since they were paid for this year, even though they were recognized as expenses last year. Ending accrued expenses are then deducted, because they were charged to expenses this year but will not be paid for until next year.

Using the cash basis information determined in the preceding paragraphs, we can prepare the cash flow from operating activities section of the SCF by the direct method as shown in Figure 15-1.

Note that the cash paid for advertising expense and for repairs and maintenance expense equals the amounts in the respective accounts, since there are no related prepaid or accrued amounts. In addition, fewer classes of expense payments might be used, that is, several of the expenses might be grouped together as one item. For example, advertising, insurance, and repairs and maintenance might be grouped and listed as "cash paid to suppliers for other services."

A summary of the computation of cash flows from operating activities and the conversion of accrual basis income to cash basis income are presented in Figure 15-2.

Indirect Method of Reporting Cash Flow from Operating Activities

Rather than showing the major classes of operating cash receipts and cash payments, the same amount of net cash flow from operating activities may be reported by the **indirect method**. Under the indirect method accrual basis net income is adjusted to

Figure 15-1
Statement of Cash Flows—Direct Method

PMX CORPORATION
Statement of Cash Flows
For the Year Ended December 31, 1992

Cash flow from operating activities:		
Cash received from customers		$671,900
Less cash paid:		
To suppliers for purchases	$315,500	
To employees for salaries and wages	109,100	
For insurance	1,600	
For advertising	48,600	
For repairs and maintenance	26,800	
For income taxes	11,700	
Total cash paid for operating activities		513,300
Net cash flow from operating activities		$158,600

a cash basis net income by making adjustments to convert accrual net income to net cash flow from operating activities. Items that were deducted in arriving at accrual net income, such as expense incurred but not yet paid, and expenses paid for in prior periods and expensed in the current period, like depreciation and amortization, are added back to accrual income. Items that were added in determining accrual net income, such as interest earned but not yet received and sales revenues recorded but not yet received, are deducted from accrual income. The main advantage of the indirect method is that it focuses attention on the differences between income and cash flow from operating activities. An understanding of the differences may be important to investors, creditors, and others who wish to use assessments of income as an intermediate step in assessing future cash flows.

Analyzing Changes in Balance Sheet Accounts. The amounts needed to adjust accrual income to cash income are normally derived by analyzing changes in balance sheet accounts during the period that relate to items of revenue or expense. The analysis of account changes is much the same as that discussed earlier when using the direct method. For example, accounts receivable are recorded as accrual sales are made and reduced as cash is collected. Consequently, an increase in the Accounts Receivable account means that sales recorded during the period exceeded collections from customers by the amount of the increase (sales revenues recorded but not yet received). To adjust to a cash basis, the increase in accounts receivable is deducted from accrual income on the SCF. Conversely, a decrease in accounts receivable during the period has the reverse effect and, therefore, is added to accrual basis net income on the SCF.

Changes in some other current assets, such as inventory and prepaid expenses, relate to expenses but have a similar effect on net income. For example, a decrease in the Inventory account during the period means that the firm sold more merchandise than it purchased. Thus, cost of goods sold is higher under accrual accounting than it would have been on a cash basis (expenses paid for in prior periods and expensed in the current period). As a result, the decrease in inventory is added back to accrual basis income on the SCF. Again, an increase in inventory has the reverse effect and is, therefore, deducted from accrual net income. A similar analysis can be applied to changes in prepaid expenses. For example, an increase in prepaid expenses means that the firm paid more cash than there are expenses recorded (expenses paid for this period but not yet charged to an expense account). Thus, the increase is deducted to adjust accrual income to cash basis income on the SCF.

The amount of revenues and expenses recognized on an accrual basis also may be related to changes in liability accounts, particularly current liabilities. For example, accounts payable generally relate to the purchase of merchandise inventory. A decrease in the Accounts Payable account means that the firm paid for more purchases than it made during the period. As a result, cash paid for purchases is higher than purchases recorded on an accrual basis. To adjust accrual income to cash income, the decrease in accounts payable is deducted on the SCF. Of course, an increase in accounts payable is added back on the statement.

Accrued liabilities (expenses) relate to the recognition of accrual basis expenses. For example, an increase in accrued salaries and wages payable means that more salaries and wages expense was recorded than was paid for during the period. The increase, therefore, is added back to accrual basis income to convert to cash basis income on the SCF. As before, a decrease in an accrued liability has the opposite effect.

In addition to the items discussed previously, expenses paid for in prior periods and related to long-term assets, such as depreciation, amortization, and depletion expenses, were deducted during the current period in computing accrual basis income. Since no cash outlay was made in the current period, these expenses are added back to accrual basis income on the SCF to adjust to cash basis income.

An example of the indirect approach, based on the income statement and comparative balance sheet data presented earlier for PMX Corporation, is shown in Figure 15-3.

RECONCILIATION OF NET INCOME TO NET CASH FLOW FROM OPERATING ACTIVITIES

SFAS 95 requires the preparation of a reconciliation of net income to net cash flow from operating activities. The reconciliation should report, separately, all major classes of reconciling items. If the direct method of reporting net cash flow from operating activities is used, the reconciliation must be provided in a separate schedule. The format of the reconciliation is the same as that in Figure 15-3. If the indirect method of reporting net cash flow from operating activities is used, no separate reconciliation is needed since the format of the indirect method constitutes a reconciliation.

In addition to reporting cash flows from operating activities, the SCF reports, separately, the gross inflows and outflows of cash from investing activities and financing activities.

Figure 15-3
Statement of Cash
Flows—Indirect
Method

PMX CORPORATION
Statement of Cash Flows
For the Year Ended December 31, 1992

Net income	$ 95,500
Adjustments to convert net income to net cash flow from operating activities:	
Increase in accounts receivable (1)	(22,100)
Decrease in inventory (2)	7,900
Decrease in prepaid insurance (3)	2,600
Decrease in accounts payable (4)	(7,400)
Increase in accrued salaries and wages payable (5)	3,500
Increase in accrued income taxes payable (6)	9,300
Depreciation expense (given)	69,300
Net cash flow from operating activities	$158,600

(1) $169,400—$147,300
(2) $109,500—$101,600
(3) $9,400—$6,800
(4) $81,600—$74,200
(5) $24,900—$21,400
(6) $9,300—$-0-

CASH FLOWS FROM INVESTING ACTIVITIES

As mentioned earlier, investing activities involve both outflows and inflows of cash from transactions generally considered as investing activities. Investing activities generally include (1) lending money and collecting on the loans, and (2) acquiring and selling, or otherwise disposing of (a) securities that are not cash equivalents and (b) productive assets that are expected to generate revenue over a long period of time.

Cash outflows for investing activities are made primarily for the acquisition of productive assets (such as plant and equipment and natural resources), and for the purchase of securities of other entities that are not cash equivalents. (Recall that readily marketable securities representing temporary investments of excess cash are considered a component of cash rather than cash investments.) Cash outflows for investing activities also include loans made or purchased by the firm.

Cash inflows from investing activities result essentially from events opposite those producing cash outflows for investing activities. Thus, cash inflows include receipts from the sale of productive assets (such as plant and equipment and natural resources), and from the sale of securities of other entities that are not cash equivalents. Cash inflows from investing activities also include receipts from loans by either principal repayments by borrowers or by the sale of loans made by the entity. Note that interest receipts are not treated as investing activities, but are included as interest revenue in operating activities.

Cash inflows and cash outflows should be shown individually by activity at their gross amounts. For example, the total receipts from the sale of productive assets during the period should be reported as a cash inflow, and the total payments for new productive assets reported as a cash outflow. An example of the cash flows from investing activities section of the SCF follows:

Cash flows from investing activities:

Purchases of property, plant, and equipment	$(365,000)	
Proceeds from the disposal of property, plant, and equipment	106,000	
Purchases of investment securities	(235,000)	
Proceeds from the sale of investment securities	68,000	
Loans made	(55,000)	
Collections on loans	42,000	
Net cash used by investing activities		$(439,000)

CASH FLOWS FROM FINANCING ACTIVITIES

Financing activities involve both outflows and inflows of cash from transactions normally considered as financing activities of the firm. These activities generally include (1) obtaining resources from owners and providing them with a return on their investments as well as a return of their investments, and (2) obtaining resources from creditors and repaying the amounts borrowed or otherwise settling the obligations.

Cash inflows from financing activities include the proceeds received from the issuance of equity securities and from debt securities, such as bonds, notes, mortgages and other short- or long-term borrowings. Cash outflows from financing activities generally represent events opposite those producing cash inflows. Thus, cash outflows from financing activities include payments (1) for the reacquisition of the entity's equity securities (either for retirement or to be held as treasury shares); (2) dividend payments; and (3) repayments of amounts borrowed. Note that payments representing interest on borrowings are not included in financing activities, but are included as interest expense in operating activities.

As with investing activities, cash inflows and outflows from financing activities should be shown individually at their gross amounts. For example, the total receipts from long-term borrowing during the period should be shown separately from total payments to settle long-term debt. An example of the cash flows from financing activities section of the SCF follows:

Cash flows from financing activities:

Proceeds from issuing short-term debt	$124,500	
Payments to settle short-term debt	(86,000)	
Proceeds from issuing long-term debt	800,000	
Payments to settle long-term debt	(350,000)	
Proceeds from the issuance of capital stock	500,000	
Payments for the purchase of treasury stock	(240,000)	
Cash dividends paid	(130,000)	
Net cash provided by financing activities		$618,500

NONCASH EXCHANGE TRANSACTIONS

Firms sometimes engage in significant financing and investing transactions that do not directly affect cash, such as the exchange of a long-term note payable or capital stock for plant assets. In some cases, these transactions are consummated by giving part cash (a down payment) and a debt or equity security for the remainder of the purchase price. In these cases, only the cash portion is reported in the body of the SCF. Since the noncash portion of exchange transactions represents a combination of investing (the acquisition of plant assets) and financing (the issuance of debt or equity securities) activities, accounting standards require that these transactions be disclosed. Disclosure

Objective 5:
Reporting non-cash exchange transactions

may be either narrative in form or summarized in a schedule. In either case, the disclosure should clearly relate the cash and noncash aspects of transactions involving similar items.[3]

Other noncash transactions include the conversion of debt securities into equity securities and the acquisition of plant assets through capital leases. These transactions often involve little or no cash inflows and outflows in the period in which they occur, but generally have a significant effect on the future cash flows of a company. Examples of the treatment of noncash exchange transactions are given in Figure 15-5.

PREPARING THE SCF—AN EXTENDED ILLUSTRATION

The comparative balance sheets and statement of income and retained earnings of Apex Corporation presented in Figure 15-4 are used to illustrate the preparation of the SCF. During 1992, Apex Corporation entered into the following transactions relevant to the SCF:

1. A new wing was added to the building at a cost of $600,000 cash.
2. New equipment was purchased at a cost of $337,000; cash of $87,000 and a note payable for $250,000 due January 2, 1995, were given in exchange.
3. Equipment with a book value of $100,000 was sold for $92,000 cash.
4. Long-term stock investments were sold for $274,000.
5. Bonds payable of $150,000 were issued for cash at par.
6. An additional 30,000 shares of $5 par value common stock were issued for $259,500.
7. Cash dividends of $174,000 were declared and paid.

Figure 15-4
Apex Corporation
Financial Statements

APEX CORPORATION
Comparative Balance Sheets

	December 31	
	1992	1991
Assets		
Current assets:		
Cash and cash equivalents	$ 482,000	$ 318,000
Accounts receivable (net)	246,500	189,000
Inventory	471,000	483,000
Prepaid expenses	54,000	21,000
Total current assets	1,253,500	1,011,000
Operating assets:		
Buildings	1,800,000	1,200,000
Accumulated depreciation—buildings	(522,000)	(472,500)
Equipment	1,011,000	774,000
Accumulated depreciation—equipment	(400,500)	(348,000)
Land	350,000	350,000
Total operating assets	2,238,500	1,503,500
Long-term stock investments (at cost, which is less than market value)	250,000	400,000
Total assets	$3,742,000	$2,914,500

[3]SFAS No. 95, par. 32.

Liabilities and Stockholders' Equity

Current liabilities:		
Accounts payable	$ 450,000	$ 478,500
Accrued expenses	31,500	24,000
Total current liabilities	481,500	502,500
Long-term liabilities:		
Notes payable, due January 2, 1995	250,000	–0–
Bonds payable, due July 1, 2005	900,000	750,000
Total long-term liabilities	1,150,000	750,000
Stockholders' equity:		
Common stock, $5 par value	975,000	825,000
Paid-in capital in excess of par value	448,500	339,000
Retained earnings	687,000	498,000
Total stockholders' equity	2,110,500	1,662,000
Total liabilities & stockholders' equity	$3,742,000	$2,914,500

APEX CORPORATION
Statement of Income and Retained Earnings
For the Year Ended December 31, 1992

Net sales		$6,930,000
Cost of goods sold		3,660,000
Gross profit on sales		3,270,000
Operating expenses other than depreciation	$2,625,000	
Depreciation expense	102,000	
Total operating expenses		2,727,000
Operating income		543,000
Other revenues, gains, expenses, and losses:		
Dividend and interest revenue	36,000	
Gain on sale of investments	124,000	
Interest expense	(92,000)	
Loss on sale of equipment	(8,000)	
Net other revenues and gains		60,000
Net income before income tax		603,000
Income tax expense		240,000
Net income		363,000
Retained earnings, January 1		498,000
Total		861,000
Less: Cash dividends		174,000
Retained earnings, December 31		$ 687,000

Reference to the comparative balance sheets shows that cash and cash equivalents increased by $164,000 ($482,000 − $318,000) during 1992. Thus, the SCF should show the operating, investing, and financing activities that caused the increase in cash and cash equivalents. An SCF, using the direct method of reporting cash flows from operating activities, is presented in Figure 15-5.

Figure 15-5
Statement of Cash
Flows—Direct
Method

APEX CORPORATION
Statement of Cash Flows
For the Year Ended December 31, 1992

Cash flows from operating activities:		
Cash received from customers (1)		$6,872,500
Cash received from interest and dividends		36,000
Cash provided by operating activities		6,908,500
Less cash paid:		
To suppliers for purchases (2)	$3,676,500	
To suppliers for operating expenses (3)	2,650,500	
For interest and taxes (4)	332,000	
Cash disbursed for operating activities		6,659,000
Net cash flow from operating activities		249,500
Cash flows from investing activities:		
Purchase of building and equipment (5)	(687,000)	
Proceeds from the sale of equipment	92,000	
Proceeds from the sale of investments	274,000	
Net cash used by investing activities		(321,000)
Cash flows from financing activities:		
Proceeds from the issuance of bonds payable	150,000	
Proceeds from the issuance of common stock	259,500	
Cash dividends paid	(174,000)	
Net cash provided by financing activities		235,500
Net increase in cash and cash equivalents		$ 164,000
Schedule of noncash investing and financing activities:		
Notes payable given in exchange for equipment		$250,000
(1) Accrual basis sales		$6,930,000
Add: Beginning accounts receivable		189,000
Less: Ending accounts receivable		(246,500)
Cash received from customers		$6,872,500
(2) Accrual basis cost of goods sold		$3,660,000
Less: Beginning inventory		(483,000)
Plus: Ending inventory		471,000
Plus: Beginning accounts payable		478,500
Less: Ending accounts payable		(450,000)
Cash paid to suppliers for purchases		$3,676,500
(3) Operating expenses other than depreciation		$2,625,000
Less: Beginning prepaid expenses		(21,000)
Plus: Ending prepaid expenses		54,000
Plus: Beginning accrued expenses		24,000
Less: Ending accrued expenses		(31,500)
Cash paid to suppliers for operating expenses		$2,650,500

(4)	Interest expense	$ 92,000
	Income tax expense	240,000
	Cash paid for interest and taxes	$ 332,000
(5)	Building addition	$ 600,000
	Cash paid for equipment purchase	87,000
	Cash payments for building and equipment	$ 687,000

In Figure 15-5, cash flows from operating activities are presented by the direct method. In order to contrast the direct and indirect methods, Figure 15-6 presents the SCF of Apex Corporation with cash flows from operating activities presented by the indirect method.

Figure 15-6
Statement of Cash Flows—Indirect Method

APEX CORPORATION
Statement of Cash Flows
For the Year Ended December 31, 1992

Net cash flow from operating activities:		
Net income		$363,000
Adjustments to convert net income to net cash flow from operating activities:		
Depreciation expense		102,000
Increase in accounts receivable		(57,500)
Decrease in inventory		12,000
Increase in prepaid expenses		(33,000)
Decrease in accounts payable		(28,500)
Increase in accrued expenses		7,500
Gain on sale of investments		(124,000)
Loss on sale of equipment		8,000
Net cash flow from operating activities		249,500
Cash flows from investing activities:		
Purchase of building and equipment	$(687,000)	
Proceeds from the sale of equipment	92,000	
Proceeds from the sale of long-term investments	274,000	
Net cash used by investing activities		(321,000)
Cash flows from financing activities:		
Proceeds from the issuance of bonds payable	150,000	
Proceeds from the issuance of capital stock	259,500	
Cash dividends paid	(174,000)	
Net cash provided by financing activities		235,500
Net increase in cash		$164,000
Schedule of noncash investing and financing activities:		
Note payable given for equipment		$250,000

SUMMARY

This chapter described the preparation and uses of the statement of cash flows (SCF). The SCF is intended to provide users of financial statements with information about the cash receipts and cash payments of an entity during a period. The concept of cash used in the SCF is that of cash and cash equivalents. Cash equivalents are investments in short-term highly liquid securities that the firm intends to convert to cash when needed for normal operations. The statement also provides information about the investing and financing activities of the firm. This information, which is not readily available in the other financial statements, is considered important to users who are interested in projecting the future cash flows of the business.

The SCF classifies cash flows into three types of business activities: (1) operating activities, (2) investing activities, and (3) financing activities. Operating activities involve the production or delivery of goods for sale or the providing of services. Cash flows from operating activities generally summarize the effects of transactions that enter into the determination of net income.

Gross cash inflows and gross cash outflows are reported for each of investing and financing activities. Investing activities generally include transactions involving (1) lending money and collecting on the loans, and (2) acquiring and selling (a) securities that are not cash equivalents, and (b) productive assets that are expected to produce revenues over several periods. The net effect on cash of the gross inflows and outflows from investing activities is reported as net cash received or used in investing activities. Financing activities generally include the obtaining of resources (1) from owners and providing them with a return of and a return on their investments, and (2) from creditors and repaying the amounts borrowed. Interest revenue and expense related to investing and financing activities are reported as a part of operating activities.

Net cash flow from operating activities may be reported by the direct method or the indirect method. Under the direct method, major classes of operating revenues are shown as cash inflows from operations, and major classes of expenses are reported as cash outflows from operations. The difference between cash inflows and cash outflows from operations is reported as the net cash flow from operating activities. Under the indirect method, net cash flow from operations is reported by adjusting accrual basis net income to cash basis net income. Accrual net income is adjusted for noncash expenses, revenues, gains, and losses. Noncash items that were deducted in arriving at accrual net income are added back to accrual net income; conversely, noncash items that were added in determining accrual net income are deducted.

Direct exchange (noncash) transactions representing significant investing and financing activities must be disclosed either in narrative form or in a separate schedule.

SELF-TEST

Test your understanding of the chapter by selecting the best answer for each of the following:

1. The primary purpose of a statement of cash flows is to provide investors, creditors, and others information about:
    a. the financial position of an entity.
    b. the entity's current cash balance.
    c. the entity's assets.
    d. the entity's cash receipts and payments.

2. An increase or decrease in which of the following investments should be included in the statement of cash flows?
   a. Money market funds.
   b. Commercial paper.
   c. Long-term bonds of another company.
   d. U.S. Treasury bills.

3. The direct method of preparing the statement of cash flows differs from the indirect method in that the direct method contains:
   a. the major classes of operating cash receipts and payments.
   b. the cash flows from investing activities.
   c. the cash flows from financing activities.
   d. a reconciliation of accrual basis income to cash flow from operating activities.

4. A decrease in accounts payable should be reported in a statement of cash flows (indirect method) as:
   a. a cash outflow in operating activities.
   b. a cash inflow in operating activities.
   c. a cash outflow in investing activities.
   d. should not be included in the statement of cash flows.

5. Dividends declared and not yet paid by an entity should be shown in a statement of cash flows as:
   a. a cash outflow in operating activities.
   b. a cash outflow in investing activities.
   c. a cash outflow in financing activities.
   d. should not be included in the statement of cash flows.

6. Depreciation expense for the current period:
   a. increases cash flow from operating activities.
   b. decreases cash flow from operating activities.
   c. decreases cash flow from investing activities.
   d. does not affect cash flow.

7. Which of the following is not a financing activity?
   a. Cash dividends paid.
   b. Common stock issued.
   c. Cash dividends received.
   d. Long-term bonds issued.

8. A loss on the sale of equipment should be presented in a statement of cash flows (indirect method) as a(n):
   a. deduction from net income in operating activities.
   b. outflow of cash in investing activities.
   c. addition to net income in operating activities.
   d. inflow of cash from investing activities.

REVIEW PROBLEM

Weaver Brothers, Inc., a merchandising concern, was organized in 1987. Because it is located in a rapidly growing area, it has enjoyed rapid growth as well. Presented on the following page are comparative balance sheets and a statement of income and retained earnings prepared on January 31, 1992, the end of Weaver Brothers' fiscal year. Its statement of cash flows has not yet been prepared.

WEAVER BROTHERS, INC.
Comparative Balance Sheets

	January 31	
	1992	**1991**
Assets		
Current assets:		
Cash and cash equivalents	$ 334,000	$ 455,000
Accounts receivable (net)	523,000	385,000
Notes receivable	–0–	40,000
Interest receivable	–0–	2,000
Merchandise inventory	1,312,000	816,000
Prepaid expenses	67,000	46,000
Total current assets	2,236,000	1,744,000
Investments:		
Long-term investments in equity securities (at cost, which approximates market value)	30,000	185,000
Property, plant, and equipment:		
Land	40,000	40,000
Buildings	1,925,000	650,000
Accumulated depreciation—buildings	(152,000)	(85,000)
Equipment	1,040,000	415,000
Accumulated depreciation—equipment	(275,000)	(184,000)
Total property, plant, and equipment	2,578,000	836,000
Total assets	$4,844,000	$2,765,000
Liabilities and Stockholders' Equity		
Current liabilities:		
Notes payable	$ 220,000	$ 400,000
Accounts payable	415,000	280,000
Income taxes payable	41,000	64,000
Interest payable	12,000	26,000
Accrued expenses payable	65,000	143,000
Total current liabilities	753,000	913,000
Long-term liabilities:		
Notes payable, due August 31, 1995	700,000	300,000
Bonds payable, due June 30, 2010	800,000	–0–
Total long-term liabilities	1,500,000	300,000
Stockholders' equity:		
Common stock, $2 par value	900,000	600,000
Paid-in capital in excess of par value	950,000	500,000
Retained earnings	741,000	452,000
Total stockholders' equity	2,591,000	1,552,000
Total liabilities & stockholders' equity	$4,844,000	$2,765,000

WEAVER BROTHERS, INC.
Statement of Income and Retained Earnings
For the Year Ended January 31, 1992

Net sales revenues		$4,735,000
Cost of goods sold		2,246,600
Gross profit on sales		2,488,400
Operating expenses other than depreciation	$1,747,400	
Depreciation expense	158,000	
Total operating expenses		1,905,400
Operating income		583,000
Other revenues, gains, expenses, and losses:		
Dividend and interest revenue	14,000	
Gain on sale of investments	27,000	
Interest expense	(69,000)	
Net other expense		28,000
Net income before income tax		555,000
Income tax expense		166,000
Net income		389,000
Retained earnings, February 1, 1991		452,000
Total		841,000
Less: Cash dividends paid		100,000
Retained earnings, January 31, 1992		$ 741,000

Additional information:

1. Long-term investments in equity securities with a cost of $155,000 were sold during the year for $182,000.
2. A new building was purchased during the year at a total cost of $1,275,000. A cash payment of $875,000 plus a long-term note payable for $400,000 were given to cover the cost of the purchase.
3. Additional equipment was purchased for $625,000 cash.
4. Bonds payable of $800,000 were issued for cash at par value.
5. An additional 150,000 shares of the $2 par value common stock were issued for $5 per share.

Required:
A. Prepare a cash flow statement for the year ended January 31, 1992, for Weaver Brothers, Inc. Use the direct method of presenting the net cash flow from operating activities.
B. Verify the amount of net cash flow from operating activities using the indirect method.

ANSWER TO REVIEW PROBLEM

A.

WEAVER BROTHERS, INC.
Statement of Cash Flows
For the Year Ended January 31, 1992

Cash flows from operating activities:		
Cash received from customers (1)		$4,637,000
Cash received from dividends and interest (2)		16,000
Cash provided by operating activities		4,653,000
Less cash paid:		
To suppliers for purchases (3)	$2,607,600	
To suppliers for operating expenses (4)	1,846,400	
To creditors for interest (5)	83,000	
To governments for taxes (6)	189,000	
Cash paid for operating activities		4,726,000
Net cash flow from operating activities		(73,000)
Cash flows from investing activities:		
Purchase of building and equipment (6)	(1,500,000)	
Proceeds from the sale of investments	182,000	
Net cash used by investing activities		(1,318,000)
Cash flows from financing activities:		
Proceeds from the issuance of bonds payable	800,000	
Proceeds from the issuance of common stock	750,000	
Payments to settle short-term notes payable	(180,000)	
Cash dividends paid	(100,000)	
Net cash provided by financing activities		1,270,000
Net decrease in cash and cash equivalents		$ 121,000
Schedule of noncash investing and financing activities:		
Note payable given in exchange for a building		$400,000

(1)	Net sales revenue	$4,735,000
	Add: Beginning accounts and notes receivable	425,000
	Less: Ending accounts and notes receivable	(523,000)
	Cash received from customers	$4,637,000
(2)	Dividend and interest revenue	$ 14,000
	Add: Beginning interest receivable	2,000
	Less: Ending interest receivable	–0–
	Cash received from dividends and interest	$ 16,000
(3)	Cost of goods sold	$2,246,600
	Less: Beginning merchandise inventory	(816,000)
	Add: Ending merchandise inventory	1,312,000
	Add: Beginning accounts payable	280,000
	Less: Ending accounts payable	(415,000)
	Cash paid to suppliers for purchases	$2,607,600

(4)	Operating expenses other than depreciation	$1,747,400
	Less: Beginning prepaid expenses	(46,000)
	Add: Ending prepaid expenses	67,000
	Add: Beginning accrued expenses payable	143,000
	Less: Ending accrued expenses payable	(65,000)
	Cash paid to suppliers for operating expenses	$1,846,400
(5)	Interest expense	$ 69,000
	Add: Beginning interest payable	26,000
	Less: Ending interest payable	(12,000)
	Cash paid to creditors for interest	$ 83,000
(6)	Income tax expense	$ 166,000
	Add: Beginning income taxes payable	64,000
	Less: Ending income taxes payable	(41,000)
	Cash paid to governments for taxes	$ 189,000

B. Net Cash Flow from Operating Activities—Indirect Method

Net income	$389,000
Adjustments to convert net income to net cash flow from operating activities:	
Increase in accounts receivable	(138,000)
Decrease in notes and interest receivable	42,000
Increase in inventory	(496,000)
Increase in prepaid expenses	(21,000)
Increase in accounts payable	135,000
Decrease in income taxes payable	(23,000)
Decrease in interest payable	(14,000)
Decrease in accrued expenses payable	(78,000)
Depreciation expense	158,000
Gain on sale of investments	(27,000)
Net cash flow from operating activities	$ (73,000)

ANSWERS TO SELF-TEST

1. d   **2.** c   **3.** a   **4.** a   **5.** d   **6.** d   **7.** c   **8.** c

GLOSSARY

CASH EQUIVALENTS.   Short-term, highly liquid investments such as Treasury bills, commercial paper, and money market funds (p. 674).

DIRECT METHOD.   A method of reporting cash flow from operating activities by which major classes of operating revenues and expenses are shown as cash inflows and cash outflows from operations (p. 675).

NONCASH EXCHANGE TRANSACTIONS. Transactions that represent joint investing and financing activities with no direct affect on cash, such as the exchange of common stock for a plant asset (p. 684).

FINANCING ACTIVITIES. Activities involving the acquisition of resources from (1) owners and providing them with a return on and a return of their investments, and (2) creditors and repaying the amounts owed or otherwise settling the obligation (p. 675).

INDIRECT METHOD. A method of reporting cash flow from operating activities by which accrual basis net income is adjusted to cash basis net income by adjusting accrual income for noncash expenses, revenues, losses, and gains (p. 679).

INVESTING ACTIVITIES. Activities involving (1) lending money and collecting on the loans, and (2) acquiring and selling (a) securities that are not cash equivalents, and (b) productive assets that are expected to produce revenues over several periods (p. 674).

OPERATING ACTIVITIES. Activities involving the production or delivery of goods for sale and the providing of services (p. 674).

STATEMENT OF CASH FLOWS (SCF). A financial statement that reports cash receipts and cash payments for a firm for a time period (p. 673).

DISCUSSION QUESTIONS

1. What are the purposes of the statement of cash flows (SCF)?
2. What is the concept of cash used in the preparation of the SCF?
3. What are the three main parts of the SCF?
4. Explain what is meant by:
   a. Operating activities.
   b. Investing activities.
   c. Financing activities.
5. List three examples of investing activities and three examples of financing activities.
6. What is the direct method of reporting cash flows from operating activities?
7. What is the indirect method of reporting cash flows from operating activities?
8. Do all revenues in the income statement represent an increase in cash? Explain.
9. Colin Company sold a piece of undeveloped land for $75,000 that had cost $50,000 five years ago. What effect does this transaction have on the current year's income statement? What effect does the transaction have on the current year's SCF?
10. Do all expenses on the income statement represent a decrease in cash? If not, identify some expenses that do not reduce cash during the current period.
11. A company reported a net loss of $40,000 on its income statement and a $20,000 positive net cash flow from operating activities. How could this happen?
12. Indicate how the following are computed from the information found in accrual basis financial statements:
    a. Cash received from customers.
    b. Cash paid for purchases.
    c. Cash paid for operating expenses.
13. Total sales revenue for 1992 was $450,000, of which one-fourth was on account. The balances in Accounts Receivable were $22,000 at the end of 1992 and $34,000 at the end of 1991. How much was cash received from customers during 1992?

14. How are dividends and interest earned from investment activities treated on the SCF?
15. What are noncash exchange transactions? How are they treated on the SCF?
16. Give three examples of noncash exchange transactions.
17. Dee Company's fiscal year ends on December 31. Dee's board of directors declared a cash dividend on December 20 of the current year, payable on January 15 to stockholders of record on December 31. What effect would the declaration of the dividend have on the SCF for the current year? What would be the effect on the SCF for the following year?

EXERCISES

Exercise 15-1 Effects of Account Changes on Cash Fl⌐

Following is a list of changes in balance sheet accounts for a period:

1. Increase in accounts payable.
2. Decrease in accounts receivable.
3. Increase in inventory.
4. Increase in accumulated depreciation.
5. Decrease in property, plant and equipment.
6. Decrease in dividends payable.
7. Decrease in interest receivable.
8. Increase in prepaid expenses.

Required:

Indicate the effect that each of these changes would normally have on the cash flows of an entity. (Use increase, decrease, or no effect.)

Exercise 15-2 Effect of Transactions on Cash Flows

Following is a list of transactions undertaken by a business during a period.

1. Manufacturing equipment was sold for cash.
2. Merchandise was purchased for cash.
3. Cash dividends were received on investments.
4. Long-term bonds payable were issued.
5. Cash sales were made to customers.
6. Paid cash to purchase preferred stock of another company.
7. Paid income taxes.
8. Issued common stock for cash.
9. Paid cash dividends on common stock.
10. Purchased common stock as treasury stock.
11. Received interest on a loan made to another company.
12. Received a principal payment on a loan made to another company.

Required:

For each transaction, indicate whether the effect would be reported as operating, investing, or financing activities. Assume the use of the indirect method of reporting cash flows from operating activities.

Exercise 15-3 Conversion from Accrual Basis to Cash Basis

The following information was taken from the general ledger accounts of Cox Company, which uses the accrual basis of accounting.

	December 31	
	1992	**1991**
Accounts receivable	$ 46,700	$ 30,200
Inventory	40,200	42,100
Prepaid insurance	1,800	2,200
Accounts payable	24,100	30,400
Wages payable	2,600	3,800
Sales	107,000	
Cost of goods sold	59,600	
Operating expenses (including $17,000 depreciation expense)	35,400	

Required:

A. Compute:
1. The amount of cash collected from customers during 1992.
2. The amount of cash paid for purchases during 1992.
3. The amount of cash paid for operating expenses during 1992.
B. Prepare a schedule to compute net cash flow from operating activities during 1992 using the direct method.

Exercise 15-4 Net Cash Flow from Operating Activities—Indirect Method

Assume the same information as given in Exercise 15-3.

Required:

Prepare the cash flow from operating activities section of the SCF using the indirect method.

Exercise 15-5 Net Cash Flow from Operating Activities—Indirect Method

Assume you are preparing an SCF and have the following information.

Net income (accrual basis)		$145,000
Depreciation expense	$54,000	_____
Decrease in accounts payable	7,700	_____
Amortization of goodwill	19,000	_____
Gain on sale of plant assets	21,300	_____
Increase in inventories	7,500	_____
Decrease in accounts receivable	14,800	_____
Net cash flow from operating activities		$ _____

Required:

Prepare the cash flow from operating activities section of the SCF using the indirect method.

Exercise 15-6 Computing Net Cash Flow from Operating Activities— Indirect Method

The following information was taken from the comparative financial statements of Volga Company, which were prepared on an accrual basis.

	December 31	
	1992	**1991**
Net sales	$392,000	$360,000
Cost of goods sold	172,000	142,000
Operating expenses (including depreciation expense of $32,000 each year)	148,000	136,000
Net income	72,000	82,000
Accounts receivable (net)	74,000	68,000
Inventory	55,000	60,000
Accounts payable	34,000	31,000
Wages payable	12,000	16,000

Required:
Prepare a schedule to compute the net cash flow from operating activities using the indirect method.

Exercise 15-7 Cash Flow from Operating Activities—Direct Method
An income statement and selected comparative balance sheet information for Century Company follow:

CENTURY COMPANY
Income Statement
For the Year Ended June 30, 1992

Sales revenue		$467,200
Cost of goods sold		288,000
Gross profit		179,200
Operating expenses:		
Advertising expense	$16,400	
Depreciation expense	19,000	
Salaries and wages expense	46,000	
Utilities expense	29,600	
Total operating expenses		111,000
Net income before income tax		68,200
Income tax expense		13,600
Net income		$ 54,600

Selected balance sheet data:

	June 30	
	1992	**1991**
Accounts receivable	$81,400	$91,000
Inventory	62,000	56,300
Accounts payable	29,400	22,700
Income taxes payable	4,800	5,600

Required:
Prepare the cash flow from operating activities section of the SCF for Century Company for the year ended June 30, 1992, using the direct method.

Exercise 15-8 Cash Flow from Operating Activities—Indirect Method

Assume the same data as given in Exercise 15-7.

Required:

Prepare the cash flow from operating activities section of the SCF using the indirect method.

Exercise 15-9 Cash Flow from Operating Activities

Following are descriptions of changes in balance sheet accounts and other selected events for Favor Company:

1. Increase in interest receivable	_____
2. Loss on sale of equipment	_____
3. Depreciation expense	_____
4. Cash dividends paid	_____
5. Increase in inventory	_____
6. Increase in accounts payable	_____
7. Decrease in accrued expenses	_____
8. Decrease in accounts receivable	_____
9. Gain on sale of securities included in cash equivalents	_____
10. Amortization of discount on bonds payable	_____

Required:

Indicate whether each of the items should be added or subtracted from net income using the indirect method of determining net cash flow from operating activities. If the item should be neither added nor subtracted, so indicate.

Exercise 15-10 Cash Flow from Operating Activities

Following are three items that have an effect on the computation of cash flow from operating activities. None of these were specifically discussed or illustrated in the chapter, but you should be able to "reason" the appropriate treatment.

1. Earnings on a long-term investment in common stock accounted for by the equity method amounted to $42,000.
2. Premium amortization on a long-term investment in bonds amounted to $3,550.
3. Discount amortization on bonds payable amounted to $7,900.

Required:

Explain how each item is treated in the preparation of the cash flow from operations section of the SCF using the indirect method.

Exercise 15-11 Effect of Transactions on SCF

Following is a list of transactions completed by Ace Company during 1992:

Transaction	(a) Section of SCF	(b) Amount	(c) Amount added (+) or deducted (−)
1. Accounts payable decreased by $12,500 during the year.	_____	_____	_____
2. Paid a long-term note payable of $100,000.	_____	_____	_____

3. Purchased a plant asset for $67,000, giving $17,000 cash and a $50,000 note payable. _____ _____ _____

4. Declared and paid a $42,000 dividend. _____ _____ _____

5. Purchased treasury stock for $60,000 cash. _____ _____ _____

6. Accounts receivable decreased by $48,000 during the year. _____ _____ _____

7. Borrowed $36,000 with a six-month note payable. _____ _____ _____

8. Exchanged 10,000 shares of common stock for land with a fair value of $75,000. _____ _____ _____

9. Issued common stock for cash, $60,000. _____ _____ _____

10. Sold for $21,000 a plant asset with a book value of $10,000. _____ _____ _____

Required:
For each transaction, indicate (a) the section (i.e., operating, investing, or financing) of the SCF in which the cash effect is reported (if the effect is not reported in any of the sections, place NA on the line); (b) the amount; and (c) whether the amount is added ($+$) or deducted ($-$) in that section.

Exercise 15-12   Cash Flow from Investing Activities
The following transactions were undertaken by Corona, Inc., during 1992:

1. Sold for $93,000 used machinery with a book value of $64,000.
2. Issued capital stock for cash, $120,000.
3. Purchased land to be held for future expansion, $220,000.
4. Paid off a long-term $90,000 note payable plus interest of $7,500.
5. Purchased machinery, giving $25,000 cash and a two-year, 12% note payable for $100,000.
6. Purchased Corona, Inc., common stock to be held as treasury stock paying $106,000.
7. Sold a long-term bond investment, with a book value of $96,000, for $102,000, including $5,000 accrued interest.
8. Purchased common stock of Duper Company to be held as a long-term investment, paying $190,000.
9. Issued bonds payable at par value for $400,000.
10. Declared and paid cash dividends of $60,000.
11. Purchased and retired 5,000 shares of Corona, Inc., $10 par value preferred stock for $57,000.

Required:
Prepare the net cash flow from investing activities section of the SCF.

Exercise 15-13   Cash Flow from Financing Activities
Refer to the transaction data given in Exercise 15-12.

Required:
Prepare the net cash flow from financing activities section of the SCF.

Exercise 15-14   Preparing an SCF

An income statement for the year ended December 31, 1992, and comparative balance sheets for 1992 and 1991 for Jackson Company follow:

JACKSON COMPANY
Income Statement
For the Year Ended December 31, 1992

Sales revenue		$720,090
Cost of goods sold		291,400
Gross profit on sales		428,690
Operating expenses:		
Advertising expense	$ 26,880	
Depreciation expense	33,400	
Salaries and wages expense	149,600	
Utilities expense	42,300	
Total operating expenses		252,180
Net income before income tax		176,510
Income tax expense		44,128
Net income		$132,382

JACKSON COMPANY
Comparative Balance Sheets

	December 31	
	1992	1991
Cash	$102,822	$ 40,320
Accounts receivable (net)	71,200	79,800
Inventory	312,000	268,000
Prepaid expenses	32,000	16,000
Plant assets	376,000	232,000
Accumulated depreciation—plant assets	(73,720)	(40,320)
Total assets	$820,302	$595,800
Accounts payable	$117,120	$115,000
Income taxes payable	21,200	12,800
Accrued salaries and wages payable	10,400	13,800
Long-term notes payable	56,000	80,000
Common stock, $5 par value	260,000	220,000
Paid-in capital in excess of par value	180,000	20,000
Retained earnings	175,582	134,200
Total liabilities and stockholders' equity	$820,302	$595,800

An inspection of the general ledger accounts produced the following additional information:

1. New equipment was purchased during the year for $144,000 cash.
2. A long-term note payable of $24,000 was paid off.
3. Eight thousand shares of common stock were issued during the year at an issue price of $25 per share.
4. Cash dividends of $1.75 per share were declared and paid on outstanding shares, including those issued during the year.

Required:
Prepare an SCF. Use the indirect method of reporting net cash flow from operating activities.

PROBLEMS

Problem 15-1 Analyzing Transactions

Several transactions of Piper Company follow:

1. Sold land for more than its book value.
2. Exchanged common stock for convertible bonds.
3. Sold treasury stock for more than its cost.
4. Paid a long-term note payable.
5. Declared and paid a cash dividend.
6. Depreciation expense was recorded for the year.
7. Sold long-term investments for less than book value.
8. Merchandise inventory decreased during the year.
9. Accrued interest payable increased during the year.
10. Borrowed money using a four-year note payable.
11. Sold securities classified as cash equivalents.
12. Sold unissued common stock for cash.
13. Sold used machinery for cash equal to its book value.
14. Paid cash for new office furniture.
15. Exchanged common stock for a building.

Required:
For each of the transactions, indicate the section (operating, investing, financing) of the SCF in which the cash effect of the transaction would be reported assuming use of the indirect method. If the transaction is not reported in the body of the statement, indicate so.

Problem 15-2 Preparing a SCF—Direct Method

Comparative balance sheet information for 1992 and 1991 and income statement data for 1992 for McDowell Company follow:

	1992	1991
Cash	$ 19,600	$ 22,400
Accounts receivable	26,900	24,900
Inventory	32,700	34,800
Property, plant and equipment	72,000	50,000
Accumulated depreciation	(30,000)	(27,000)
Total assets	$121,200	$105,100
Accounts payable	$ 23,400	$ 22,100
Accrued expenses	12,900	13,600
Long-term note payable	15,000	–0–
Common stock	20,000	20,000
Retained earnings	49,900	49,400
Total liabilities and stockholders' equity	$121,200	$105,100
Sales	$ 98,700	
Cost of goods sold	60,200	
Gross profit on sales	38,500	
Operating expenses, including depreciation	32,400	
Net income	$ 6,100	

Property, plant, and equipment assets were purchased during the year, but none was sold. Dividends were declared and paid during December of 1992.

Required:

Prepare an SCF for McDowell Company. Use the direct method of reporting net cash flow from operating activities. (You will need to analyze changes in balance sheet accounts to determine the effects of investing and financing activities.)

Problem 15-3 **Preparing a SCF—Indirect Method**

Comparative balance sheets for 1992 and 1991 and a 1992 income statement for Rocky Company follow:

	1992	1991
Cash	$ 34,800	$ 47,200
Accounts receivable (net)	67,600	62,400
Inventory	93,400	99,200
Property, plant and equipment	232,000	160,000
Accumulated depreciation	(80,000)	(68,000)
Patents	21,000	28,000
Total assets	$368,800	$328,800
Accounts payable	$ 53,600	$ 46,400
Accrued expenses payable	3,600	7,600
Long-term notes payable	20,000	–0–
Long-term mortgage payable	32,000	36,000
Common stock	40,000	40,000
Retained earnings	219,600	198,800
Total liabilities and stockholders' equity	$368,800	$328,800

Sales	$345,800
Cost of goods sold	226,400
Gross profit	119,400
Operating expenses (including depreciation expense and patent amortization expense)	98,400
Net income	$ 21,000

Property, plant and equipment assets were purchased during the year, but none was sold. Dividends were declared and paid in October 1992.

Required:
Prepare an SCF. Use the indirect method of reporting net cash flow from operating activities.

Problem 15-4 **Preparing an SCF—Indirect Method**

Box Company had balance sheets on December 31, 1992 and 1991 as follows:

	1992	1991
Cash	$ 454,000	$ 240,700
Accounts receivable (net)	356,000	399,000
Inventory	1,612,200	1,340,000
Prepaid expenses	260,000	40,000
Property, plant and equipment	1,780,000	1,160,000
Accumulated depreciation	(336,000)	(201,600)
Total assets	$4,126,200	$2,978,100
Short-term notes payable	$ 106,000	$ 65,000
Accounts payable	585,600	550,000
Accrued expenses payable	52,000	52,100
Long-term notes payable	280,000	440,000
Common stock, $5 par value	1,400,000	1,100,000
Paid-in capital in excess of par value	700,000	100,000
Retained earnings	1,002,600	671,000
Total liabilities and stockholders' equity	$4,126,200	$2,978,100

An investigation of the firm's 1992 income statement and the general ledger accounts produced the following information:

1. Net income for 1992 was $541,600.
2. Depreciation expense of $154,400 was recorded; a fully depreciated machine with a cost of $20,000 was discarded and its cost and accumulated depreciation were removed from the accounts.
3. New equipment costing $640,000 was purchased during the year with cash.
4. A long-term note payable of $160,000 was paid off.
5. Sixty thousand shares of common stock were issued during the year at a price of $15 per share.
6. Cash dividends of $.75 per share were declared and paid on the outstanding common stock, including those issued during the year.

Required:

Prepare an SCF for Box Company for the year ended December 31, 1992. Use the indirect method of reporting net cash flow from operating activities.

Problem 15-5 Preparing a SCF—Direct Method

Comparative balance sheets for 1992 and 1991 and the 1992 income statement for Nifty Company follow:

| | December 31 | |
	1992	1991
Cash	$ 75,600	$ 89,600
Accounts receivable (net)	76,000	63,000
Merchandise inventory	31,000	46,200
Property, plant and equipment (net)	301,000	280,000
Patents	17,900	21,000
Total	$501,500	$499,800
Accounts payable	$ 61,500	$ 77,000
Accrued expenses payable	9,000	20,000
Income taxes payable	13,500	2,800
Long-term notes payable	15,000	50,000
Common stock, $5 par value	315,000	294,000
Retained earnings	87,500	56,000
Total	$501,500	$499,800
Sales revenue	$420,000	
Cost of goods sold	230,000	
Gross profit	190,000	
Expenses (including depreciation of $26,000 and patent amortization of $3,100)	111,500	
Net income before income tax	78,500	
Income tax expense	17,500	
Net income	$ 61,000	

Additional information:

1. Property, plant, and equipment was purchased for $47,000 cash.
2. A $35,000 note payable was paid off during the year.
3. Common stock was sold for $21,000 cash.
4. Cash dividends of $29,500 were declared and paid.

Required:

Prepare an SCF for Nifty Company for the year ended December 31, 1992. Use the direct method of reporting net cash flow from operating activities.

Problem 15-6 Preparing an SCF—Direct Method

Comparative balance sheets for 1992 and 1991 and the statement of income and retained earnings for the year ended December 31, 1992, for Kingsford Company follow:

KINGSFORD COMPANY
Comparative Balance Sheets

	December 31	
	1992	**1991**
Current assets:		
Cash	$ 201,000	$ 268,000
Marketable securities, at cost	155,000	150,000
Accounts receivable (net)	585,000	515,000
Notes receivable	160,000	80,000
Interest receivable	8,000	4,000
Merchandise inventory	981,000	1,040,000
Prepaid expenses	41,000	78,000
Total current assets	2,131,000	2,135,000
Investments:		
Long-term investments in equity securities at cost, which is less than market value	450,000	420,000
Property, plant and equipment:		
Land	600,000	400,000
Buildings	3,000,000	2,400,000
Accumulated depreciation—buildings	(1,420,000)	(1,100,000)
Equipment	1,550,000	1,200,000
Accumulated depreciation—equipment	(640,000)	(480,000)
Total property, plant and equipment	3,090,000	2,420,000
Intangible assets:		
Patents	250,000	300,000
Total assets	$5,921,000	$5,275,000
Current liabilities:		
Notes payable	$ 300,000	$ 600,000
Accounts payable	735,000	560,000
Income taxes payable	130,000	110,000
Interest payable	15,000	53,000
Salaries and wages payable	254,000	304,000
Total current liabilities	1,434,000	1,627,000
Long-term liabilities:		
Notes payable, due April 30, 1996	350,000	–0–
Bonds payable, due November 30, 2000	1,000,000	800,000
Mortgage note payable, due January 1, 1996	125,000	–0–
Total long-term liabilities	1,475,000	800,000
Stockholders' equity:		
Common stock, $2 par value	1,100,000	1,000,000
Paid-in capital in excess of par value	870,000	860,000
Retained earnings	1,042,000	988,000
Total stockholders' equity	3,012,000	2,848,000
Total liabilities and stockholders' equity	$5,921,000	$5,275,000

KINGSFORD COMPANY
Statement of Income and Retained Earnings
For the Year Ended December 31, 1992

Net sales		$11,650,000
Cost of goods sold		5,995,000
Gross profit on sales		5,655,000
Operating expenses:		
Advertising expense	$ 306,000	
Amortization expense	50,000	
Depreciation expense	480,000	
Salaries and wages expense	2,794,000	
Other operating expenses	1,473,000	
Total operating expenses		5,103,000
Operating income		552,000
Other revenues, expenses, gains, and losses:		
Interest and dividend revenue	64,000	
Interest expense	(188,000)	
Loss on sale of investments	(60,000)	
Net other expenses and losses		(184,000)
Net income before income tax		368,000
Income tax expense		144,000
Net income		224,000
Retained earnings, January 1, 1992		988,000
Total		1,212,000
Less: Cash dividends		170,000
Retained earnings, December 31, 1992		$ 1,042,000

Additional information:

1. Land was purchased during the year for $200,000. A long-term mortgage note was given for $125,000.
2. A building was purchased for $600,000 cash.
3. Equipment was purchased at a total cost of $350,000. A note payable due April 30, 1996, was given for the entire purchase price.
4. Bonds payable of $200,000 were issued at par value for cash.
5. Long-term investments in equity securities with a cost of $210,000 were sold for $150,000. Additional long-term investments in equity securities were purchased at a cost of $240,000.
6. 50,000 shares of $2 par value common stock were issued for $110,000.
7. Marketable securities are cash equivalents.
8. Notes receivable are from customers.

Required:
Prepare an SCF for Kingsford Company for the year ended December 31, 1992. Use the direct method of reporting net cash flow from operating activities.

Problem 15-7 Preparing an SCF—Indirect Method
Comparative balance sheets for 1992 and 1991 and the statement of income and retained earnings for 1992 for Sphinx Company follow:

SPHINX COMPANY
Comparative Balance Sheets

	December 31 1992	December 31 1991
Current assets:		
Cash and cash equivalents	$ 568,000	$ 745,000
Accounts receivable (net)	891,300	812,700
Loans receivable	240,000	160,000
Interest receivable	22,000	10,000
Merchandise inventory	2,510,000	2,640,000
Prepaid expenses	105,000	197,000
Total current assets	4,336,300	4,564,700
Investments and funds:		
Long-term investments in equity securities		
(at cost, which is less than market value)	363,000	486,000
Bond sinking fund	485,000	350,000
Total investments and funds	848,000	836,000
Property, plant, and equipment:		
Land	500,000	380,000
Buildings	3,400,000	2,100,000
Accumulated depreciation—buildings	(1,165,000)	(945,000)
Equipment	2,420,000	1,650,000
Accumulated depreciation—equipment	(890,000)	(630,000)
Total property, plant, and equipment	4,265,000	2,555,000
Intangible assets:		
Patents	410,000	400,000
Trademarks	115,000	120,000
Total intangible assets	525,000	520,000
Total assets	$9,974,300	$8,475,700
Current liabilities:		
Short-term notes payable	$ 600,000	$1,200,000
Accounts payable	825,000	648,000
Income taxes payable	–0–	120,000
Interest payable	27,000	16,000
Salaries payable	63,000	77,000
Mortgage payable, current portion	12,000	–0–
Other accrued expenses	293,000	183,000
Total current liabilities	1,820,000	2,244,000
Long-term liabilities:		
Notes payable, due September 30, 1997	800,000	400,000
Bonds payable, due December 31, 2021	1,000,000	–0–
Mortgage payable	108,000	–0–
Total long-term liabilities	1,908,000	400,000
Stockholders' equity:		
Common stock, $10 par value	2,200,000	2,000,000
Paid-in capital in excess of par value	2,400,000	2,150,000
Retained earnings	1,846,300	2,081,700
Treasury stock, at cost	(200,000)	(400,000)
Total stockholders' equity	6,246,300	5,831,700
Total liabilities and stockholders' equity	$9,974,300	$8,475,700

SPHINX COMPANY
Statement of Income and Retained Earnings
For the Year Ended December 31, 1992

Net sales		$14,658,000
Cost of goods sold		8,928,400
Gross profit on sales		5,729,600
Operating expenses:		
Other than depreciation and amortization	$5,169,000	
Depreciation expense	530,000	
Amortization expense	20,000	
Total operating expenses		5,719,000
Operating income		10,600
Other revenues, expenses, gains, and losses:		
Gain on sale of investments	54,000	
Bond sinking fund revenue	35,000	
Loss on sale of equipment	(115,000)	
Net other expense and loss		(26,000)
Net loss		15,400
Retained earnings, January 1		2,081,700
Total		2,066,300
Less: Cash dividends paid		220,000
Retained earnings, December 31		$ 1,846,300

Additional information:

1. Land was purchased on July 1, for $120,000. A 10-year mortgage note was given for the entire purchase price. The mortgage is payable in 10 equal annual payments of $12,000 plus interest on the unpaid balance. The annual payment is due each June 30.
2. A building was purchased for $1,300,000. Cash of $900,000 plus a long-term note payable of $400,000 was given in exchange.
3. Equipment was purchased for $1,070,000 cash.
4. Equipment with an original cost of $300,000 and accumulated depreciation of $50,000 was sold for $135,000 cash.
5. A patent was purchased for $25,000 cash.
6. Long-term investments in equity securities with a cost of $123,000 were sold for $177,000.
7. A $100,000 deposit was made to the bond sinking fund during 1992. In addition, the fund earned $35,000, which was debited to the bond sinking fund.
8. Bonds payable of $1,000,000 were issued for cash at par value.
9. An additional 20,000 shares of $10 par value common stock were issued for $18 per share.
10. Treasury stock costing $200,000 was sold for $290,000. The excess of the selling price over cost was credited to Paid-in Capital in Excess of Par Value.
11. Cash dividends of $220,000 were declared and paid.
12. Depreciation expense was $220,000 on the building and $310,000 on the equipment. Amortization expense was $15,000 on patents and $5,000 on trademarks.

13. Loans made during the year amounted to $800,000, and loans receivable collected during the year were $720,000.
14. Cash paid to reduce short-term notes payable amounted to $600,000.

Required:
Prepare a SCF for Sphinx Company for the year ended December 31, 1992. Use the indirect method of reporting net cash flow from operating activities.

CASE

CASE 15-1 Annual Report Analysis
Refer to the financial statements and related footnotes of BFGoodrich Company in the Appendix to this text and answer the following questions. Indicate the page number on which you found the answer.

A. Does BFGoodrich use the direct or indirect method to report cash flows from operating activities?   *INDIRECT*   *BIGGEST*
B. How much cash was provided by operating activities during 1989? *275.3*
C. Did BFGoodrich have a net inflow or a net outflow of cash during 1989: *NEGATIVE*
   1. From investing activities? How much?
   2. From financing activities? How much? *NEGATIVE 108.2*
D. What activity produced the largest inflow of cash from investing activities during 1989?   *SOLD BUILD.*
E. What activity resulted in the largest outflow of cash from financing activities during 1989? *DIVIDENDS*
F. With reference to cash flows from operating activities, can you explain why the $23.9 million provision for deferred income taxes was added back to net income in 1989? Even if you say "no," try.

even though we wanted to slow the expense we had to added up.

15.1 36 POINTS
15.1 28
MULT. CH. 9
BONDS   9
PROBLEM 12.6

16

ANALYSIS OF FINANCIAL STATEMENTS AND ACCOUNTING FOR CHANGING PRICES

CHAPTER OVERVIEW AND OBJECTIVES

This chapter contains two parts. Part I describes some of the techniques used to analyze a firm's financial statements. Part II examines the effect of changing prices on financial reporting. When this chapter is completed, you should understand:

1. The objectives of financial statement analysis.
2. How to perform horizontal analysis, trend analysis, and vertical analysis.
3. How to compute and use ratios to analyze a firm's profitability.
4. How to compute and use ratios to analyze a firm's liquidity.
5. How to compute and use ratios to analyze a firm's use of financial leverage.
6. The limitations of financial statement analysis.
7. The nature of inflation.
8. The difference between general price level changes and specific price changes.
9. The distinction between constant dollar accounting and current value accounting.

PART I. ANALYSIS OF FINANCIAL STATEMENTS

A firm's financial statements are used by various external parties to evaluate the firm's financial performance. The preceding chapter demonstrated how the statement of cash flows is used by an investor to supplement the balance sheet and income statement in analyzing a firm's financing and investing activities. This chapter focuses on the basic techniques commonly employed to analyze a firm's balance sheet and income statement.

SOURCES OF FINANCIAL INFORMATION

PUBLISHED FINANCIAL REPORTS

The firm's financial statements contained in the annual report are the end products of the accounting process. To report on the progress of a firm during the year, most publicly held companies also issue interim reports each quarter. (Recall that an interim report covers a period of less than 12 months.) Interim reports focus primarily on the income statement and contain summary data rather than a full set of financial statements. Still, they provide additional information for evaluating the financial position and profitability of the firm's operations. Unlike the annual report, however, interim reports are unaudited.

Annual and interim reports are two of the primary means by which management communicates information about the firm to interested outside parties. In addition to the financial statements, these reports generally contain the auditors' report, schedules and explanatory notes, and a discussion and analysis of the firm's operations by management. An analysis of the published reports should include, at a minimum, a review of these components. For example, the auditors' report tells the reader that the statements were audited and whether the statements are fairly presented in accordance with generally accepted accounting principles. Major concerns of the auditors will also be discussed in the report. A review of the notes will indicate the accounting policies followed by the company.

REPORTS FILED WITH THE SEC

Probably the most detailed information available on publicly held companies is contained in the reports that must be filed with the Securities and Exchange Commission (SEC). These reports include the following:

1. Form S-1. A report that must be filed when a firm wishes to offer securities for sale to the public. Form S-1 contains financial information about the company, its management, and management's plan for the use of the money received from the sale of the proposed securities.
2. Form 10-K. An annual report that is more detailed than the published annual report provided to stockholders.
3. Form 10-Q. A quarterly report of summarized financial information.
4. Form 8-K. A special report filed whenever any significant event occurs, such as a change in top management.

These reports are available to the public on request.

ADVISORY SERVICES AND FINANCIAL PUBLICATIONS

Financial advisory services, such as Moody's Investors Service and Standard and Poor's Corporation, also publish financial data about both publicly and privately owned companies. These are normally not as detailed as the SEC reports or the company reports. The advantage of advisory service reports is their accessibility since they are found at most public and university libraries.

A comparison of the company under study with firms in a similar line of business and with industry norms is also useful. Industry data are available from a number of financial services. For example, Robert Morris Associates' *Annual Statement Studies* provides income statement and balance sheet data and 16 financial ratios for many industries. Dun & Bradstreet publishes *Industry Norms and Key Business Ratios,* which contains typical balance sheets, income statements, and 14 selected financial ratios for over 800 different lines of business. The 14 ratios for the most recent year by industry groups are also reported in *Key Business Ratios* published by Dun & Bradstreet. Individual company and industry analyses are also available from stock brokerage firms. An abundance of useful information is found in various economic and financial newspapers and magazines such as the *Wall Street Journal, Forbes, Fortune, Business Week,* and *Barron's.*

In making comparisons with other companies, an analyst must recognize that the company under review may not be similar to other companies because of diversification into other product lines. Also, because of diversification, industry data may not clearly resemble the company under study. In such cases, the analyst attempts to identify the industry that the company best fits and uses that industry data and companies in that industry group for comparison.

NEED FOR ANALYTICAL TECHNIQUES

Information contained in the various sources of financial data is expressed primarily in monetary terms. When the absolute dollar amounts for most items reported in the financial statements are considered individually, they are generally of limited usefulness. Significant relationships may not be apparent from a review of absolute dollar amounts because no indication is given whether that absolute dollar amount is good or bad for a firm. For example, merely knowing that a company reported earnings of $100,000 for the current year is of limited use unless the amount is compared to other information, such as last year's earnings, the amount invested, the current year's sales, the earnings of other companies in the same business, or some predetermined standard established by the statement user.

To simplify the identification of significant changes and relationships, the dollar amounts reported in the financial statements are frequently converted into percentages or ratios by the statement user. Some commonly recognized percentages are sometimes shown in supplementary schedules to the financial statements as part of the annual report. The analysis of relationships between dollar amounts of each item to some base amount is referred to as *horizontal analysis* and *vertical analysis*. *Ratio analysis* is the interpretation of the relationship between two items, such as current assets to current liabilities.

OBJECTIVES OF FINANCIAL STATEMENT ANALYSIS

Objective 1: Objectives of financial statement analysis

Percentage analysis and *ratio analysis* were developed to provide an efficient means by which a statement user can identify (1) important relationships between items in the same statement and (2) trends in financial data. Percentages and ratios simplify the evaluation of financial conditions and past operating performance.

The information is used primarily to forecast a firm's ability to pay its debts when due and to operate at a satisfactory profit level. However, because the analytical techniques are almost limitless—and so are the users' special interests and objectives—the choice of proper ratios and percentages must fit their purpose. For example, some users of financial data are concerned with evaluating the firm's ability to meet its current obligations and still have sufficient cash left to carry out its other activities. In other words, they are concerned about the firm's liquidity. The focus of this type of investigation is generally on the firm's current assets and current liabilities.

Other users, such as long-term creditors and stockholders, want to know about a firm's liquidity, but are also interested in the business' ability to pay its long-term obligations. In this analysis, the statement user assesses the financial structure of the firm and its use of financial leverage. The objective is to evaluate the prospects for operating at an earnings level adequate to provide sufficient cash for the payment of interest, dividends, and debt principal.

To serve as a basis for the discussion of percentage and ratio analysis, balance sheets and income statements for the Wesley Corporation during a two-year period are presented in the first two columns of Figures 16-1 and 16-2. In order to show the computations of ratios for two periods, a December 31, 1990 balance sheet is also included in Figure 16-1. The statements in Figures 16-1 and 16-2 are not in a format that would appear in an annual report. For example, the Change during the Year and the Common Size Statement columns are not part of an annual report presentation. These computations must be made by the analyst, as discussed later in this chapter.

It cannot be emphasized too strongly that for the statement analysis of an individual company to be useful, the relationships must be compared to other data or standards. Comparisons of the company under study may be made to industry averages, to the past performance of the company, and to the performance of individual companies in the same industry. (In the following discussion, rather than stating the need for comparison every time a particular analysis is performed, it will be assumed that this additional step is taken by the statement user.)

PERCENTAGE ANALYSIS

HORIZONTAL ANALYSIS

An analysis of the change from year to year in individual statement items is called **horizontal analysis**. Horizontal analysis of the preceding year's financial statements is generally performed as a starting point for forecasting future performance. Most firms' annual reports include financial statements for the two most recent years and selected summary data for five to ten years. Financial statements presented for the same company for two or more years are called **comparative statements**. (See pages A24–A27 of the Appendix to the text for an example of this disclosure.)

In horizontal analysis, the individual items or groups of items on comparative financial statements are generally first placed side by side, as in the first columns of Figures 16-1 and 16-2. Because it is difficult to compare absolute dollar amounts, the difference between the dollar amount of one year and the next is computed in both dollar amount and percentage change. In computing the increase or decrease in dollar amount, the earlier year is used as the base year. The percentage change is computed by dividing the increase or decrease from the base year in dollars by the base year amount. For example, from 1991 to 1992 the Cash account of the Wesley Corporation increased by $140,000, from $450,000 to $590,000 (Figure 16-1). The percentage change is 31.1%, computed as follows.

Objective 2: Performing horizontal, trend, and vertical analysis

$$\text{Percentage increase} = \frac{140{,}000}{450{,}000} = 31.1\%$$

A percentage change can only be computed when a positive amount is reported in the

WESLEY CORPORATION
Comparative Balance Sheets
December 31, 1992, 1991, and 1990
(000's omitted)

	Year Ended December 31			Change during the Year 1991–1992		Common Size Statements*	
	1992	1991	1990	Dollar Amount	Percent	1992	1991
Assets							
Current Assets:							
Cash	$ 590	$ 450	$ 430	$ 140	31.1	5.2	4.7
Marketable securities	570	660	690	(90)	(13.6)	5.1	6.9
Accounts receivable (net)	2,190	1,960	1,980	230	11.7	19.4	20.4
Inventory	3,040	2,680	2,790	360	13.4	27.0	27.9
Prepaid expenses	200	200	200	–0–	–0–	1.8	2.1
Total Current Assets	6,590	5,950	6,090	640	10.8	58.5	62.0
Long-term investments	600	750	750	(150)	(20.0)	5.3	7.8
Plant and equipment	3,870	2,700	2,650	1,170	43.3	34.4	28.1
Other assets	200	200	200	–0–	–0–	1.8	2.1
Total Assets	$11,260	$9,600	$9,690	$1,660	17.3	100.0	100.0
Liabilities							
Current Liabilities:							
Notes payable	$ 940	$ 920	$1,130	$ 20	2.2	8.4	9.6
Accounts payable	1,570	1,370	1,550	200	14.6	13.9	14.3
Accrued expenses	160	160	160	–0–	–0–	1.4	1.6
Total Current Liabilities	2,670	2,450	2,840	220	9.0	23.7	25.5
Long-term liabilities—11%	2,900	2,550	2,700	350	13.7	25.8	26.6
Total Liabilities	5,570	5,000	5,540	570	11.4	49.5	52.1
Stockholders' Equity							
Preferred stock, 10%	450	450	450	–0–	–0–	4.0	4.7
Common stock ($10 par value)	2,400	2,000	2,000	400	20.0	21.3	20.8
Additional paid-in capital	622	500	500	122	24.4	5.5	5.2
Retained earnings	2,218	1,650	1,200	568	34.4	19.7	17.2
Total Stockholders' Equity	5,690	4,600	4,150	1,090	23.7	50.5	47.9
Total Liabilities and Stockholders' Equity	$11,260	$9,600	$9,690	$1,660	17.3	100.0	100.0

*Computations are explained on page 717.

Figure 16-1
Comparative Balance Sheets, Change during the Year, and Common Size Statements

base year; the amount of change cannot be stated as a percentage if the item in the base year was reported as a negative or a zero amount.

Analysts must also be careful when the dollar amount in the base year is small because a small absolute change can result in substantial percentage change. For example, assume that net income was $100 last year and increased to $300 in the current year. This is an increase of only $200 in net income, but is a 200% in-

	Year Ended December 31		Change During the Year		Common Size Statements	
	1992	1991	Dollar Amount	Percent	1992	1991
Sales	$15,480	$14,395	$1,085	7.5	100.0	100.0
Less: Cost of goods sold	11,560	10,462	1,098	10.5	74.7	72.7
Gross profit on sales	3,920	3,933	(13)	(0.3)	25.3	27.3
Expenses:						
Selling expense	1,495	1,162	333	28.7	9.6	8.1
Administrative expense	895	984	(89)	(9.0)	5.8	6.8
Interest expense	415	370	45	12.2	2.7	2.6
Income tax expense	250	382	(132)	(34.6)	1.6	2.6
Total expenses	3,055	2,898	157	5.4	19.7	20.1
Net Income	865	1,035	(170)	(16.4)	5.6	7.2
Preferred stock cash dividends	45	45	–0–	–0–	0.3	0.3
Net income available to common stockholders	$ 820	$ 990	$ (170)	(17.2)	5.3	6.9

WESLEY CORPORATION
Comparative Income Statements
For the Years Ended December 31, 1992 and 1991
(000's omitted)

Figure 16-2
Comparative Income Statements, Change During the Year, and Common Size Statements

crease in percentage terms. Such a large percentage change may create a misleading impression.

A review of the percentage increases or decreases reveals the items that show the most significant change between the periods under study. Important and unusual changes, such as a significant percentage change in sales, should be investigated further by the analyst. The objectives of the investigation are:

- To determine the cause of the change;
- To determine whether the change was favorable or unfavorable; and
- To attempt to assess whether a trend is expected to continue.

The analyst must also consider changes in other related items. For example, when reviewing the percentage changes in the balance sheet accounts included in Figure 16-1, attention is directed to the change in plant and equipment because of the size of the change (a 43.3% increase). The cause of the change is an expansion in the firm's operations. In assessing whether the change is favorable or unfavorable, an analyst would seek further answers to such questions as:

- How is the added investment being financed?
- Is expansion going to cause severe cash flow problems?
- Are sales markets adequate to support the additional output?
- What is the impact of the expansion on income?

Answers to these questions, and announcements made by management, will assist the analyst in determining whether the expansion is expected to continue. The analyst may look to the balance sheet, the income statement, the supplementary disclosures, and the statement of cash flows for additional data in answering these questions.

In Figure 16-2, sales increased 7.5%—by itself a favorable trend. However, the rate of increase in cost of goods sold was 10.5%, and selling expenses increased by 28.7%. Thus, the firm was unable to maintain its profit margin percentage [(sales − cost of goods sold)/sales] during the period. It appears that the increase in sales was at least partially the result of an increased sales effort. An analyst who is concerned with the profitability and long-term future of the firm should investigate further. In this case, the analyst should try to determine whether inventory costs are continuing to increase, the extent of competitive pressures on the revenues of the firm, and the effect of the increased selling expenses on future sales.

TREND ANALYSIS

Trend analysis is commonly employed when financial data are presented for three or more years (See annual report on page A27). In this analysis, the earliest period is the base period. Each financial statement item of the base year is set equal to 100. In subsequent years, statement items are stated as a percentage of their value in the base year as follows.

$$\text{Index} = 100 \left(\frac{\text{Dollar amount in index year}}{\text{Dollar amount in base year}} \right)$$

For example, assume that sales and net income were reported for the last five years as follows.

(In dollars)	(Base Year) 1988	1989	1990	1991	1992
Sales	$1,000,000	$1,050,000	$1,120,000	$1,150,000	$1,220,000
Net income	200,000	206,000	218,000	222,000	232,000

It is clear that the dollar amounts of both sales and net income are increasing. However, the relationship between the change in sales and the change in net income can be interpreted more easily if the changes are expressed in percentages. By dividing the amount reported for each subsequent year by the base-year amount, the appropriate percentages are:

(%)	1988	1989	1990	1991	1992
Sales	100	105	112	115	122
Net income	100	103	109	111	116

Now it can be seen that net income is increasing more slowly than sales.

The relationship between sales and net income is only one trend that should be reviewed. The trend in other accounts should also be investigated, particularly since the level of net income is affected by the firm's expenses as well as its sales. In this case, it is possible that the firm's inventory costs are increasing faster than selling prices. Or the increase in sales may be the result of granting liberal credit terms which are resulting in larger bad debt expenses. The point is that other related operating data must also be reviewed before drawing conclusions about the significance of one particular item. The overall objective is to evaluate various related trends and attempt to assess whether the trends can be expected to continue.

VERTICAL ANALYSIS

Horizontal analysis compares the proportional changes in a specific item from one period to the next. **Vertical analysis** involves restating the dollar amount of each item reported on an individual financial statement as a percentage of a specific item on the same statement. This specific item is referred to as the "base amount." For example, on the balance sheet, individual components are stated as a percentage of total assets or total liabilities and stockholders' equity. On the income statement, net sales or total revenue are usually set equal to a base of 100%, with each income statement item expressed as a percentage of the base amount. Such statements are often called **common size statements**, since all items are presented as a percentage of some common base amount.

Vertical analysis for the Wesley Corporation is presented in the last two columns of Figures 16-1 and 16-2 (pages 714–715). Vertical analysis is useful for identifying the relative importance of items to the base used. For example, it can be readily observed that the cost of goods sold as a percentage of sales increased from 72.7% to 74.7%. Vertical analysis is also an important tool for comparing data to other standards such as the past performance of the firm, the current performance of competing firms, and averages developed for the industry in which the firm operates.

RATIO ANALYSIS

A financial statement **ratio** is computed by dividing the dollar amount of one item reported in the financial statements by the dollar amount of another item reported. The purpose is to express a relationship between two relevant items that is easy to interpret and compare with other information. For example, the relationship of current assets to current liabilities—called the *current ratio*—is of interest to most statement users. For a firm reporting current assets of $210,000 and current liabilities of $120,000, the current ratio is 1.75 ($210,000/$120,000). This means that the company has $1.75 in current assets for every $1 of its current liabilities.

The relationship could be converted to a percentage (175%) by multiplying the ratio by 100. Whether in ratio form or as a percentage, the relationship between the two items can be more easily compared to other standards, for example, the current ratio of other companies in the industry in which the firm operates.

Relevant relationships can exist between items in the same financial statement or between items reported in two different financial statements, so there are many ratios that can be computed. The analyst must give careful thought to which ratios best express the relationships relevant to the area of immediate concern. The user must keep in mind that a ratio shows a significant relationship that may have little significance when used alone. Consequently, to evaluate the adequacy of a certain relationship, the ratio should be compared to other standards, such as industry averages and the historical record of the company under study.

Ratios are classified according to their evaluation of a firm's *profitability*, *liquidity*, and use of *financial leverage*. Unless otherwise noted, the computations in the remainder of this section are based on the financial statements presented for the Wesley Corporation in Figures 16-1 and 16-2. A summary of the ratios discussed in this chapter is presented in Figure 16-3.

Ratio	Method of Calculation	Significance of Each Ratio
Profitability Ratios		
Return on total assets	$$\frac{\text{Net income} + \text{Interest expense (net of tax)}}{\text{Average total assets}}$$	A measure of the rate of return earned on total assets provided by both creditors and owners.
Return on common stockholders' equity	$$\frac{\text{Net income} - \text{Preferred stock cash dividend requirements}}{\text{Average common stockholders' equity}}$$	A measure of the rate of return earned on assets provided by owners.
Return on sales	$$\frac{\text{Net income}}{\text{Net sales}}$$	A measure of the net profitability of each dollar of sales.
Earnings per share	$$\frac{\text{Net income} - \text{Preferred stock cash dividend requirements}}{\text{Weighted average number of common shares outstanding}}$$	A measure of net income earned on each share of common stock.
Price-earnings ratio	$$\frac{\text{Market price per share of common stock}}{\text{Earnings per share}}$$	A measure of the amount investors are paying for a dollar of earnings.
Dividend yield	$$\frac{\text{Annual dividend per share of common stock}}{\text{Market price per share of common stock}}$$	A measure of the rate of return to stockholders based on current market price.
Dividend payout	$$\frac{\text{Total dividends to common stockholders}}{\text{Net income} - \text{Preferred stock cash dividend requirements}}$$	A measure of the percentage of income paid out to common stockholders.
Liquidity Ratios		
Current Ratio	$$\frac{\text{Current assets}}{\text{Current liabilities}}$$	A measure of short-term liquidity. Indicates the ability of a firm to meet its short-term debts from its current assets.
Quick ratio	$$\frac{\text{Cash} + \text{Marketable securities} + \text{Net receivables}}{\text{Current liabilities}}$$	A more rigorous measure of short-term liquidity. Indicates the ability of the firm to meet unexpected demands from the liquid current assets.
Receivable turnover	$$\frac{\text{Net sales}}{\text{Average receivable balance}}$$	A measure of the effectiveness of collections; used to evaluate whether receivable balance is excessive.
Inventory turnover	$$\frac{\text{Cost of goods sold}}{\text{Average inventory balance}}$$	Measures the number of times inventory was sold on the average during the period.
Financial Leverage Ratios		
Debt to total assets	$$\frac{\text{Total liabilities}}{\text{Total assets}}$$	A measure of the percentage of assets provided by creditors and extent of using leverage.
Times interest earned	$$\frac{\text{Net income} + \text{Interest expense} + \text{Income tax expense}}{\text{Interest expense}}$$	A measure of the ability of the firm to meet its interest payments out of current earnings.

Figure 16-3
Summary of Ratios

RATIOS TO ANALYZE PROFITABILITY

Objective 3: Using ratios to analyze profitability

Profitability analysis consists of tests used to evaluate a firm's earning performance during the year. The results are combined with other data to forecast the firm's potential earning power. Potential earning power is important to long-term creditors and stockholders because, in the long run, the firm must earn a satisfactory income to survive. Potential earning power is also important to statement users, such as suppliers and labor unions, who are interested in maintaining a continuing relationship with a financially sound company. A firm's financial soundness depends on its future earning power.

Adequacy of income is measured in terms of the relationship between income and either total assets or common stockholders' equity, the relationship between income and sales, and the availability of income to common stockholders. If income appears to be inadequate, the next step is to determine whether the sales volume is too low. Are the cost of goods sold and/or other expenses too high? Is the investment in assets excessive in relation to the firm's sales?

Rate of Return on Total Assets

Rate of return on total assets is a measure of how well management utilized all of the company's assets to generate income. The ratio is computed by dividing the sum of net income plus after-tax interest expense by average total assets for the year.[1]

$$\text{Return on total assets} = \frac{\text{Net income} + \text{Interest expense (net of tax)}}{\text{Average total assets}}$$

Interest expense (net of tax) is computed as:

$$\text{Interest expense} \times (1.0 - \text{Income tax rate})$$

Interest is added back to net income (it was deducted to derive net income) in the numerator to derive the total return earned on the total assets regardless of how they were financed. In other words, interest is a return to the creditors for the use of money to finance the acquisition of assets. Dividends paid to stockholders are not added back to net income because they were not an expense that was subtracted in deriving net income. The net of tax interest expense is used, because that is the net cost to the firm for using borrowed funds. Since the interest is tax deductible, a tax savings results that is equal to the amount of interest times the tax rate.

Average total assets is used in the denominator because the income was produced by using the resources throughout the period. The sum of the beginning and ending total assets is divided by two to compute average total assets used during the period to produce the reported income. If sufficient information were available, a monthly or quarterly average would be preferred to minimize the effects of seasonal fluctuations.

The management of the Wesley Corporation produced a return on average total assets of 11.40% in 1992 and 13.53% in 1991, as computed below assuming the tax rate was 22% and 27%, respectively.

$$\underline{1992}$$
$$\frac{865 + 415\,(1.0 - .22)}{(9,600 + 11,260)/2} = 11.40\%$$

$$\underline{1991}$$
$$\frac{1,035 + 370\,(1.0 - .27)}{(9,690 + 9,600)/2} = 13.53\%$$

[1]There are variations in the way analysts compute the same ratios. For example, some analysts prefer to compute the return on total assets using one of the following alternatives for the numerator in the ratio.

1. Net income + Interest expense.
2. Net income before interest expense and income taxes.
3. Net income.

The various approaches to computing the same ratio points out the need for an analyst to exercise care when comparing ratios computed by different individuals.

During 1992, management produced approximately 11.4 cents in profit for every dollar of assets invested, compared with 13.5 cents for every dollar in 1991. The decrease in rates between the two years is significant and results from decreased net income combined with an increased investment base. Such a decrease highlights the need for further investigation by the analyst.

Rate of Return on Common Stockholders' Equity

The return on total assets does not measure the return earned by management on the assets invested by the common stockholders. The return to the common stockholders may be more or less than the return on total assets because of the firm's use of financial leverage. *Financial leverage* is the use of debt securities or other financial sources, such as preferred stock, to earn a return greater than the interest and dividends paid to the creditors or preferred stockholders (see Chapter 12). If a firm is able to earn more on the borrowed funds than the amount that must be paid to the creditors and preferred stockholders, the return to the common stockholders will be greater than the return on total assets. If the amount earned on the borrowed funds is less than the fixed interest and preferred stock dividend, the return to the common stockholders will be less than the return on total assets. The rate of return to common stockholders may be computed as:

$$\frac{\text{Return on common}}{\text{stockholders' equity}} = \frac{\text{Net income} - \text{Preferred stock cash dividend requirements}}{\text{Average common stockholders' equity}}$$

The preferred dividend requirement is subtracted from net income to yield the portion of net income allocated to the common stockholders' equity. The denominator excludes the preferred stockholders' equity in the firm. The computations for the Wesley Corporation are:

	December 31		
	1992	*1991*	*1990*
Common stock	$2,400	$2,000	$2,000
Additional paid-in capital	622	500	500
Retained earnings	2,218	1,650	1,200
Total common stockholders' equity	$5,240	$4,150	$3,700

$$\underline{1992} \qquad \qquad \underline{1991}$$

$$\frac{865 - 45}{(4,150 + 5,240)/2} = 17.47\% \qquad \frac{1,035 - 45}{(3,700 + 4,150)/2} = 25.22\%$$

Note that these rates are approximately 6% (17.47% − 11.40%) and 12% (25.22% − 13.53%) higher than the corresponding returns computed on total assets, because the company earned a return on the assets financed by the creditors and preferred stockholders greater than the interest or dividends paid to them. In other words, the return earned on the total assets of 11.40% in 1992 and 13.53% in 1991 was greater than the net of tax rate paid to the preferred stockholders and bondholders, respectively.

The income earned in excess of the fixed amounts increases the common stockholders interest. However, the percentage decreased from 25.22% to 17.47%, a decrease worthy of further investigation.

Return on Sales

The return on sales—also called the profit margin—is calculated during a vertical analysis of the income statement. It reflects the portion of each dollar of sales that represents income. Return on sales is computed by dividing net income by net sales, as follows.

$$\text{Return on sales} = \frac{\text{Net income}}{\text{Net sales}}$$

For the Wesley Corporation, the rates are:

1992	1991
$\frac{865}{15{,}480} = 5.59\%$	$\frac{1{,}035}{14{,}395} = 7.19\%$

For 1992, each dollar of sales produced 5.59 cents in income. Consistent with the other rates computed, this ratio indicates a declining profitability trend for the firm. To be more useful, the rates should be compared to other standards. If the return on sales for competing firms is 5%, for example, the 5.59% appears favorable. Even so, other data, such as increases in major expenses, should be investigated further because other problem areas or poor management practices could be discovered to explain the decline between the two years.

Earnings Per Share

The earnings per share (EPS) of common stock is widely used in evaluating the performance of a firm. The ratio is commonly used to compile earnings data for the press and for statistical services. It is a widely publicized ratio because it converts the absolute dollar amount of net income to a per share amount. That is, the EPS ratio is the amount of net income earned on one share of stock. It is computed as follows.

$$\text{EPS} = \frac{\text{Net income} - \text{Preferred stock cash dividend requirements}}{\text{Weighted average number of common shares outstanding}}$$

In the Wesley Corporation illustration, the calculations are:

1992	1991
$\frac{865 - 45}{240} = \$3.42$	$\frac{1{,}035 - 45}{200} = \$4.95$

The average number of outstanding common shares is computed on a *weighted average basis*. The weighted average is based on the number of months that the shares were outstanding. For the Wesley Corporation, the average number of shares for 1991 and 1992 is computed on the assumption that there were 200,000 shares outstanding during all of 1991 and that 40,000 additional shares were issued at the beginning of 1992. Generally accepted reporting standards require that EPS be disclosed on the face of the income statement.

The computation of EPS can be much more complex than shown here, especially if a company has issued securities that are convertible into common stock. These complexities are discussed in detail in more advanced accounting courses.

Price-Earnings Ratio

The price-earnings ratio (P/E ratio) indicates how much investors are currently paying for each dollar of earnings. It enhances a statement user's ability to compare the market value of one common stock, relative to earnings, to that of other companies.

This ratio is computed by dividing the current market price of a share of common stock by the earnings per share, as follows.

$$\text{P/E ratio} = \frac{\text{Market price per share of common stock}}{\text{Earnings per share}}$$

Assuming a market price of $40 per share for the Wesley Corporation's common stock on December 31, 1992, the P/E ratio is:

$$\frac{40.00}{3.42} = 11.70 \text{ times}$$

In other words, the common stock of the Wesley Corporation is said to be selling for 11.7 times its earnings.

Price-earnings ratios vary widely between industries since they represent investors' expectations about the future earnings power of a company. Thus, high P/E stocks are associated with companies with prospects of high earnings growth, whereas more stable firms have lower P/E stocks. For example, in the early part of 1989, companies associated with high-technology generally had a high P/E ratio (such as Apple Computer, Inc. with a P/E ratio of approximately 27). On the other hand, companies in the auto industry had low P/E ratios (e.g., Ford Motor Company and General Motors had P/E ratios of 5 and 7, respectively).

Dividend Yield

The dividend yield is normally computed by investors who are investing in common stock primarily for dividends, rather than for appreciation in the market price of the stock. The percentage yield indicates a rate of return on the dollars invested and permits easier comparison to returns from alternative investment opportunities. The dividend yield is computed as:

$$\text{Dividend yield} = \frac{\text{Annual dividend per share of common stock}}{\text{Market price per share of common stock}}$$

Cash dividends of $252,000 ($1.05 per share) were paid during 1992 to the common stockholders of the Wesley Corporation.[2] Assuming a market price of $40 per share, the dividend yield is computed as follows.

$$\frac{1.05}{40.00} = 2.63\%$$

[2]The $252,000 can be verified as follows:

Retained earnings, 1/1/92 (Figure 16-1)		$1,650,000
Add: Net income (Figure 16-2)		865,000
Less: Cash dividends:		
Preferred stock	$ 45,000	
Common stock	252,000	(297,000)
Retained earnings, 12/31/92 (Figure 16-1)		$2,218,000

Dividends per share is computed as follows:

$$\text{Dividends per share} = \frac{\text{Dividends to common stockholders}}{\text{Number of common shares outstanding}}$$

$$= \frac{\$252,000}{240,000}$$

$$= \$1.05 \text{ per share}$$

Dividend Payout Ratio

Investors interested in dividend yields may also compute the percentage of common stock earnings distributed as dividends to the common stockholders each period. This ratio is referred to as the dividend payout ratio.

$$\text{Dividend payout} = \frac{\text{Total dividends to common stockholders}}{\text{Net income} - \text{Preferred stock cash dividend requirements}}$$

For the Wesley Corporation, the 1992 ratio is:

$$\frac{252}{865 - 45} = 30.73\%$$

This ratio provides an investor with some insights into management's policy of distributing dividends as a percentage of net income available to the common stockholders. A low payout ratio indicates that management is reinvesting earnings internally. Investing in such a company is desirable for someone looking for growth in the market price of the shares. However, an investor who depends on dividends as a source of current income (e.g., a retired individual) would probably seek a company with a consistently high payout ratio.

Some recent dividend payout percentages for selected companies are given in Figure 16-4. Over the years, the aggregate dividend payout ratio for U.S. corporations has averaged about 40% to 60%.

RATIOS TO ANALYZE LIQUIDITY

Liquidity—that is, the firm's ability to meet its short-term obligations—is an important factor in financial statement analysis. After all, a firm that cannot meet its short-term obligations may be forced into bankruptcy and, therefore, will not have the opportunity to operate in the long run. The focus of this aspect of analysis is on working capital or some component of working capital.

Objective 4: Using ratios to analyze liquidity

Current Ratio

Perhaps the most commonly used measure of a firm's liquidity is the current ratio, which is computed as:

$$\text{Current ratio} = \frac{\text{Current assets}}{\text{Current liabilities}}$$

Company	Dividend Payout Ratio (%)
Compaq Computers Corporation	0.0
Dupont	45
Eli Lilly and Company	46
General Electric Company	42
International Paper	33
K Mart Corporation	34
Microsoft Corporation	0.0
RJR Nabisco, Inc.	37
Wal-mart Stores, Inc.	11

Source: Computed from annual reports by authors.

Figure 16-4
Dividend Payout Ratio for Selected Companies

The current ratio, a measure of the firm's liquidity, measures the creditors' margin of safety in being paid. It indicates the relationship of current assets to current liabilities on a dollar-per-dollar basis. A low ratio may indicate that the firm will be unable to meet its short-term debt in an emergency. A high ratio is considered favorable to creditors, but may indicate excessive investment in working capital items, such as holding slow-selling inventory, that may not be producing income for the firm.

Analysts often contend that the current ratio should be at least 2:1. In other words, a firm should maintain $2 of current assets for every $1 of current liabilities. Although such a rule is one standard of comparison, it is arbitrary and subject to exceptions and numerous qualifications in the modern approach to statement analysis. Deviations from the 2:1 rule nevertheless indicate an area in which additional tests are needed to evaluate the firm's liquidity. For example, a firm with a ratio of 1:1 may have a difficult time meeting its short-term commitments. Therefore, to assess its liquidity, the quick ratio and turnover ratios discussed below and the cash flow should be carefully investigated.

The current ratios for the Wesley Corporation for 1992 and 1991 are:

$$\underline{1992} \qquad \underline{1991}$$

$$\frac{6,590}{2,670} = 2.47 \qquad \frac{5,950}{2,450} = 2.43$$

Wesley Corporation shows a slight improvement in the relationship between current assets and current liabilities and, in the absence of other information, would be considered liquid, at least in the short run. However, a ratio of 2.4 or higher may signify excessive investments in current assets that may not be producing revenue.

Quick Ratio (Acid Test Ratio)

One of the limitations of the current ratio is that it includes inventory and prepaid expenses in the numerator. However, these items are not as liquid as cash, marketable securities, notes receivable, or accounts receivable. In the normal course of business, inventories must first be sold, and then the cash collected, before cash is available. Also, most prepaid expenses, such as prepaid insurance and office supplies, are to be consumed and cannot be readily converted into cash. The *quick ratio* or *acid test ratio* is often used to supplement the current ratio because it provides a more rigorous measure of liquidity. The quick ratio is computed by dividing the sum of the most liquid current assets—generally, cash, short-term marketable securities, and net accounts receivables—by total current liabilities.

$$\text{Quick ratio} = \frac{\text{Cash} + \text{Marketable securities} + \text{Net receivables}}{\text{Current Liabilities}}$$

The higher the ratio, the more liquid the firm is considered. A lower ratio may indicate that the company would be unable to meet its immediate obligations in an emergency.

The quick ratio for the Wesley Corporation is computed as:

	1992	1991
Cash	$ 590	$ 450
Marketable securities	570	660
Accounts receivable (net)	2,190	1,960
Total quick assets	$3,350	$3,070

$$\underline{1992} \qquad\qquad \underline{1991}$$

$$\frac{3,350}{2,670} = 1.25 \qquad \frac{3,070}{2,450} = 1.25$$

A ratio of 1.25:1 in both years indicates that the firm is highly liquid. However, this observation is somewhat dependent on the collectibility of the receivables included in the numerator.

The current ratio and quick ratio are used to measure the adequacy of the firm's current assets to satisfy its current obligations as of the balance sheet date. However, these ratios ignore how long it takes for a firm to collect cash—an important aspect of the firm's liquidity. Since receivables and inventories normally make up a large percentage of a firm's current assets, the quick ratio and current ratio may be misleading if there is an extended interval between purchasing inventory, selling it, and collecting cash from the sale. Thus, the receivable turnover and inventory turnover ratios are two other measures of liquidity that are often used to yield additional information. These turnover ratios are sometimes called *activity ratios*.

Receivable Turnover Ratio

The receivable turnover ratio is a measure of how many times the average receivable balance was converted into cash during the year. It is also considered a measure of the efficiency of the firm's credit-granting and collection policies. It is computed as follows.

$$\text{Receivable turnover} = \frac{\text{Net sales}}{\text{Average receivable balance}}$$

The higher the receivable turnover ratio, the shorter the time period between recording a sale and collecting the cash. To be competitive, the firm's credit policies are influenced by industry practices. Comparison of this ratio to industry norms can reveal deviations from competitors' operating results.

In computing this ratio, credit sales should be used in the numerator whenever the amount is available. However, such information is normally not available in financial statements, so net sales is used as a substitute. An average of monthly receivable balances should be used in the denominator. In the absence of monthly information, the year-end balance, an average of the beginning of the year and end of the year balances, or averages of quarterly balances are used in the calculation. The average of the receivable balances is used, because net sales are earned over a period of time. Therefore, the denominator should approximate what the receivable balance was throughout the period. The computations for the Wesley Corporation are:

$$\underline{1992} \qquad\qquad \underline{1991}$$

$$\frac{15,480}{(1,960 + 2,190)/2} = 7.46 \qquad \frac{14,395}{(1,980 + 1,960)/2} = 7.31$$

Frequently, the receivable turnover is divided into 365 days to derive the average number of days it takes to collect receivables from sales on account.

$$\underline{1992} \qquad\qquad \underline{1991}$$

$$\frac{365 \text{ days}}{7.46} = 48.93 \text{ days} \qquad \frac{365 \text{ days}}{7.31} = 49.93 \text{ days}$$

During 1992, the Wesley Corporation collected the average accounts receivable balance 7.46 times. Expressed another way, it took an average of 48.93 days to collect sales on account, an improvement of one day over 1991. These measures are particularly useful if one knows the credit terms granted by the firm. Assuming credit terms of 60 days, the average 49-day collection period provides some indication that the firm's credit policy is effective and that the firm probably is not burdened by excessive amounts of uncollectible accounts that have not been written off. A collection period significantly in excess of 60 days indicates a problem with either the granting of credit, collection policies, or both.

Inventory Turnover Ratio

The control of the amount invested in inventory is an important aspect of managing a business. The size of the investment in inventory and inventory turnover are dependent upon such factors as type of business and time of year. A grocery store has a higher turnover than an automobile dealership; the inventory level of a seasonal business is higher at certain times in the operating cycle than at others.

The inventory turnover ratio is a measure of the adequacy of inventory and how efficiently it is being managed. The ratio is an expression of the number of times the average inventory balance was sold and then replaced during the year. The ratio is computed as follows:

$$\text{Inventory turnover} = \frac{\text{Cost of goods sold}}{\text{Average inventory balance}}$$

Cost of goods sold, rather than sales, is used in the numerator because (1) it is a measure of the cost of inventory sold during the year, and (2) the cost measure is consistent with the cost basis of the denominator. Ideally, an average of monthly inventory balances should be computed, but this information is generally not available to external parties in published reports. A quarterly average can be computed if quarterly interim reports are published by the firm.

The inventory turnover for the Wesley Corporation is based on the average of the beginning of year and end of the year balances:

$$\frac{1992}{} \qquad \frac{1991}{}$$

$$\frac{11,560}{(2,680 + 3,040)/2} = 4.04 \qquad \frac{10,462}{(2,790 + 2,680)/2} = 3.83$$

The average days per turnover can be computed by dividing 365 days by the turnover ratio:

$$\frac{1992}{} \qquad \frac{1991}{}$$

$$\frac{365 \text{ days}}{4.04} = 90.35 \text{ days} \qquad \frac{365 \text{ days}}{3.83} = 95.30 \text{ days}$$

The 1992 turnover ratio indicates that the average inventory was sold 4.04 times during the year as compared to 3.83 times in 1991. In terms of days, the firm held its inventory approximately 90 days in 1992 before it was sold, as compared to about 95 days in 1991.

The increased turnover in 1992 is generally considered a favorable trend. Inventory with a high turnover is less likely to become obsolete and decline in price before it is sold. A higher turnover also indicates greater liquidity, since the inventory will be converted into cash in a shorter period of time. However, given the nature of the firm's business, a very high turnover may indicate that the company is carrying insufficient inventory and is losing a significant amount of sales.

RATIOS TO ANALYZE THE USE OF FINANCIAL LEVERAGE

A firm is using financial leverage whenever it finances a portion of its assets by borrowing. Issuing bonds to finance the purchase of plant assets is an example of financial leverage. Debt of the firm carries two obligations, one to make interest payments on specified dates and the other to repay the principal when it matures. If a firm fails to meet these commitments, the bondholders can force the firm into bankruptcy. Thus, borrowing increases the risk of default. The advantage to the common stockholders is that their return may be increased if the return earned on the funds borrowed is greater than the cost of the debt. As a result, long-term creditors, short-term creditors, and stockholders are all concerned with the amount of leverage a firm employs.

Objective 5:
Using ratios to
analyze financial
leverage

Several ratios are used to analyze the firm's use of leverage. One approach focuses on the firm's ability to meet its interest commitments as indicated by the income statement, while a second ratio considers the firm's ability to carry debt as indicated by the balance sheet.

Debt to Total Assets Ratio (Debt Ratio)

The percentage of total assets financed by creditors indicates the extent to which the firm uses **debt financing**. The ratio of debt to total assets, also called the **debt ratio**, is a measure of the relationship between total liabilities and total assets.[3] It is computed as follows:

$$\text{Debt to total assets} = \frac{\text{Total liabilities}}{\text{Total assets}}$$

A high debt to total assets ratio indicates a greater risk of default and less protection for the creditors. This percentage is important to long-term creditors and stockholders, since the creditors have a prior claim to assets in the event of liquidation—that is, the creditors must be paid in full before assets are distributed to stockholders. The greater the percentage of assets invested by stockholders, the greater the protection to the creditors.

For the Wesley Corporation the ratio is:

1992	*1991*
$\frac{5,570}{11,260} = 49.47\%$	$\frac{5,000}{9,600} = 52.08\%$

Thus, for both years, approximately 50% of the assets were provided by the firm's creditors.

Because of the trade-off between increased risk for potentially greater returns to common stockholders, there is no one percentage that is considered better than another. Other things being equal, firms with stable income can issue a greater percentage

---

[3]Some analysts include preferred stock with the total debt rather than with equity on the basis that it has a preference to assets in liquidation and that it is often used to obtain financial leverage for the common stockholders. Preferred stock is not included here because it does not have a maturity date and because dividends do not have to be paid.

of debt than firms with volatile income. Stable income levels enable statement users to better predict the level of debt costs that can be covered from cash generated by operations from period to period. Some selected examples of debt to total assets ratios computed from recent balance sheets are shown in Figure 16-5.

Times Interest Earned Ratio

The times interest earned ratio is an indication of the firm's ability to satisfy periodic interest payments from current earnings. The rough rule of thumb is that the company should earn three to four times its interest requirement. Since current interest charges are normally paid from funds provided by current operations, analysts frequently compute the relationship between earnings and interest.

$$\text{Times interest earned} = \frac{\text{Net income} + \text{Interest expense} + \text{Income tax expense}}{\text{Interest expense}}$$

Interest expense and income taxes are added back to net income in the numerator because the ratio is a measure of income available to pay the tax deductible interest charges. For the Wesley Corporation, the ratio is:

1992

$$\frac{865 + 415 + 250}{415} = 3.69$$

1991

$$\frac{1,035 + 370 + 382}{370} = 4.83$$

In 1991, earnings before interest and income taxes were 4.83 times interest expense. This ratio declined to 3.69 in 1992. The 1992 result is marginal but it still is an adequate coverage according to the rule of thumb. However, the result should be considered in relation to other trends in the company's financial status, especially the trend in this ratio, and in comparison with other standards, such as industry averages.

LIMITATIONS OF FINANCIAL ANALYSIS

Objective 6: Limitations of financial statement analysis

The analytical techniques introduced in this chapter are useful for providing insights into the financial position and results of operations of a particular firm. However, financial statement users must be careful in interpreting trends and ratios computed from reported financial statements because there are certain intrinsic limitations. Several of these limitations are:

Figure 16-5
Debt to Total Assets Ratio for Selected Companies

Company	Debt to Total Assets Ratio (%)
Compaq Computers Corporation	56
Cincinnati Gas & Electric	62
General Electric	58
K Mart Corporation	60
Pfizer, Inc.	44
Union Pacific	62
Winnebago Industries	32

Source: Computed from annual reports by authors.

1. Financial analysis is performed on historical data primarily for the purpose of forecasting future performance. However, these historical relationships may not continue because of changes in:
   a. The general state of the economy;
   b. The business environment in which the firm must operate;
   c. Management; and
   d. Policies established by management.

2. The measurement base used in computing the analytical measures is historical cost. Failure to adjust for price changes may result in some computations providing misleading information on a trend basis and in any comparison between companies. For example, the return on total assets includes net income in the numerator, which is affected by the current year's sales and current operating expenses measured in current dollars. However, plant assets and inventory are measured in historical dollars—which are not adjusted to reflect current price levels. Thus, the ratio divides items primarily measured in current dollar amounts by a total measured primarily in terms of historical dollars. As discussed in Part II of this chapter, this limitation may be partially overcome by reporting inflation-adjusted data as supplementary information to the historical dollars.

3. Year-end data may not be typical of the firm's position during the year. Knowing that certain ratios are computed at year-end, management may improve a ratio by entering into certain types of transactions near the end of the year. For example, the current ratio can be improved by using cash to pay off short-term debt. To illustrate, assume that the Wesley Corporation reported current assets of $200,000 and current liabilities of $100,000 before paying $50,000 on accounts payable. The payment will increase the current ratio, as follows:

	Before Payment	Payment	After Payment
Current assets	$200,000	$50,000	$150,000
Current liabilities	100,000	50,000	50,000

$$\text{Current ratio} = \frac{200,000}{100,000} = 2 \qquad \text{Current ratio} = \frac{150,000}{50,000} = 3$$

A firm usually establishes a fiscal year-end that coincides with the low point of activity in its operating cycle. Therefore, account balances such as receivables, accounts payable, and inventory, may not be representative of the balances carried in these accounts during the year.

4. Companies may not be comparable. Despite the fact that this chapter has emphasized such comparisons, data among companies may not provide meaningful comparisons because of factors such as the use of different accounting methods, the size of the companies, and the diversification of product lines.

The selection of a particular accounting method or estimate can have a significant effect on net income and the financial position of a firm. Using accounting methods or making estimates that result in reporting the lowest net income in the current period is considered a conservative approach to income measurement. For example, in a period of increasing inventory prices, the LIFO inventory method results in the lowest net income, so it is conservative. FIFO is the least conservative inventory method when prices are increasing. To use a five-year period to amortize an intangible asset rather than a 40-year period is another example of conservatism. Financial analysts carefully review such policies to assess what is called the *quality of earnings*. A firm that follows more conservative policies is considered to have a higher quality of earnings.

PART II. EFFECTS OF INFLATION

Objective 7:
The nature of
inflation

In the United States, money (the dollar) is used as both a medium of exchange and as a measure of "real" value as determined by the amount of goods and services for which it can be exchanged. The amount of goods or services for which a dollar can be exchanged is called the purchasing power of the dollar. Although the price of some goods (e.g., calculators, digital watches, and computers) has decreased in recent years, the economy of the United States and of most other countries has been characterized by increasing prices of most goods and services. The general increase in prices results in inflation, which can be defined as a decrease in the purchasing power of the dollar or as an increase in the general price level. The general price level is the weighted average price of all goods and services in the economy.

Objective 8:
General price
level changes vs.
specific price
changes

Price changes are of two types: *specific price changes* and *general price level changes*. It is important to distinguish between these two types because they reflect quite different things.

Specific price changes are changes in the prices of individual goods or services such as bread, computers, or medical services. The prices of specific items may increase or decrease from one period to another. As just indicated the prices of calculators and digital watches, for example, have been decreasing, whereas the prices of gasoline, foods, and medical services have been increasing.

General price level changes are changes in the weighted average of all goods and services in the economy. Therefore, a general price level change represents a change in the value of money in all its uses. Specific price changes affect the general price level because the prices of specific goods and services constitute the items used to determine the general price level. Although the general price level may decrease (deflation), such a decrease is rare. Since the 1930s it has occurred only once in the United States—in 1949. The more common occurrence is inflation—an increase in the general price level (inflation).

When the general price level increases, it takes more dollars to acquire a given amount of goods or services. Stated another way, with an increased general price level, a dollar will buy a smaller amount of goods or services. The general price level is expressed in the form of an index number with a specific base year set equal to 100. Although agencies of the United States government publish several general price indexes, the most widely recognized is the *Consumer Price Index* (CPI), which is published monthly by the Bureau of Labor Statistics.

The CPI measures the average change in the prices of a "market basket" of goods and services purchased by families living in cities. The Financial Accounting Standards Board (FASB) recommends that this index be used to restate financial statements for general price level changes because it is readily available in the news media, timely, and produces results that are comparable to other general price indexes. A partial listing of the CPI and the yearly inflation rate are shown in Figure 16-6.

As can be seen in Figure 16-6, the general price level increased by approximately 50% from 1980–1989; that is, the 1989 dollar purchased about 50% fewer goods and services than the 1980 dollar. Stated another way, it would have taken $124.00 in 1989 to purchase the same goods and services that could have been purchased in 1980

Figure 16-6
Consumer Price In-
dex for All Urban
Consumers

Year	Average Index* (1982–84 = 100)	Year-End Index	Yearly Inflation Rate
1980	82.4	86.3	
1981	90.9	94.0	10.3
1982	96.5	97.6	6.2
1983	99.6	101.3	3.2
1984	103.9	105.3	4.3
1985	107.6	109.3	3.6
1986	109.6	110.5	1.9
1987	113.6	115.4	3.7
1988	118.3	120.5	4.1
1989	124.0	126.1	4.8

*Source: U.S. Department of Labor, Bureau of Labor Statistics.

for $82.40. The inflation rate is determined on the basis of the change in the average index for the year. For example, the inflation rate for 1985 was computed as $(107.6 - 103.9)/103.9 = 3.6\%$.

REPORTING THE EFFECTS OF INFLATION

As discussed in previous chapters, accountants prepare financial statements based on historical cost under the *stable-dollar assumption*. These historical cost financial statements consist of aggregated amounts of dollars from different years. In each of these years, the dollar has a different purchasing power. As a result, the impact of inflation is difficult to assess by statement users. Because of the persistent nature of inflation, however, some accountants and users of financial information question the usefulness of the dollar measurements in the traditional historical cost statements. They disagree, however, on what should be done to make the financial statements more useful.

Although several approaches have been suggested, only two primary methods of reporting the effects of inflation have received relatively wide support: (1) **constant dollar accounting** (i.e., restating the historical cost financial statements for changes in the general price level); and (2) **current value accounting** (i.e., preparing the financial statements on the basis of current prices).

CONSTANT DOLLAR ACCOUNTING

The objective of constant dollar accounting is to state all amounts in dollars of the same current purchasing power. To do this, the historical cost figures in the financial statements are converted through the use of a general price level index such as the CPI to the number of current dollars representing an equivalent amount of purchasing power. This is accomplished by multiplying the historical cost amounts by a fraction. The numerator of the fraction is the general price level index number at the current balance sheet date.[4] The denominator is the general price level index number at the date the transaction occurred. For example, assume that land was purchased on December 31, 1980 for $100,000. The land would be restated to an equivalent number of end of 1989 dollars as follows:

Objective 9:
Distinction be-
tween constant
dollar accounting
and current value
accounting

[4]Companies are permitted to use either average-for-the-year index or year-end index as illustrated here.

$$\frac{\text{Index at end of year}}{\text{Index at transaction date}} \times \text{Historical cost} = \text{Restated constant dollar cost}$$

$$\frac{126.1}{86.3} \times \$100,000 = \$146,118$$

If additional land was purchased for $50,000 on December 31, 1985, it would be converted to end of 1989 purchasing power dollars as:

$$\frac{126.1}{109.3} \times \$50,000 = \$57,685$$

Land would be reported on the 1989 constant dollar balance sheet at $203,803 ($146,118 + $57,685).

Restatement for general price level changes is not considered a departure from the cost principle because costs are merely restated to a constant 1989 measuring unit. Thus, the restated amount for land of $203,803 does not represent the current market value of the land. The restatement does, however, represent a departure from the stable-dollar assumption.

Monetary Items

When preparing constant dollar financial statements, monetary and nonmonetary items must be distinguished because they are treated differently **Monetary items** are money and those assets and liabilities that represent either claims to receive or obligations to pay a fixed number of dollars. The number of dollars to be received or paid is fixed in amount, regardless of changes that may occur in the purchasing power of the dollar. Such items are already stated in terms of current purchasing power and, therefore, do not need to be restated. Thus, cash, accounts receivable, and notes receivable are *monetary assets*. Most liabilities are monetary because they represent obligations to pay fixed amounts of dollars.

Purchasing power gains and losses result from holding monetary items over time. Holding monetary assets during a period of rising prices results in a loss in purchasing power since the value of money is falling. Conversely, owing money (i.e., holding monetary liabilities) during a period of rising prices results in a purchasing power gain since the debts can be paid in the future with dollars of smaller purchasing power.

To illustrate a purchasing power loss, assume that Bray Company held $40,000 in cash throughout 1989. The loss in purchasing power would be:

Number of year-end dollars needed to maintain purchasing power.	
$40,000 \times \dfrac{126.1}{120.5} =$	$41,859
Actual number of dollars held at year-end	40,000
Purchasing power loss	$ 1,859

If Bray Company also held a $60,000 note payable throughout 1989, the gain in purchasing power would be:

Number of year-end dollars representing the same purchasing power as the amount owed at the beginning of the year:	
$60,000 \times \dfrac{126.1}{120.5} =$	$62,788
Number of dollars actually owed	60,000
Purchasing power gain	$ 2,788

Nonmonetary Items

Nonmonetary items are those items that are not monetary in nature. Examples are inventory, plant assets, intangibles, service obligations, and stockholder's equity. Since these items do not represent claims to fixed amounts of cash, no purchasing power gain or loss results and the nonmonetary items must be restated in terms of constant dollars. By restating them, recognition is given to the effect of changes in the general price level from the time the items were originally acquired.

Use of an Average Index

Constant dollar accounting restates all nonmonetary items by multiplying the historical cost amount by a fraction consisting of the general price index at the balance sheet date over the price index when the transaction originated. However, some business activities, such as sales transactions and certain expense incurrences, occur throughout the year. Application of the basic conversion procedure would require that each individual sale or expense incurrence be restated by multiplying the dollar amount times a fraction consisting of the index at the balance sheet date divided by the index when the transaction occurred. Price indexes are not available on a daily basis and the restatement of a particular type of transaction that occurs continuously throughout the year is impractical. Therefore, to approximate the constant dollar amount that would have resulted had each transaction been restated, an average CPI for the year is used in the denominator to translate such transactions. This procedure assumes that the sale or expense activity occurred relatively evenly throughout the period. For example, if sales were $450,000 during the calendar year 1989, the sales amount would be converted for a constant dollar income statement as follows:

$$\$450,000 \times \frac{126.1}{124.0} = \$457,620$$

The average for the year should be based on the values that existed throughout the period. Often, the average used is either an average of the beginning and ending general price index or is an average of the monthly indexes.

Constant Dollar Financial Statements

To illustrate the preparation of constant dollar financial statements, we will make the following assumptions for the Flint Company.

1. Flint Company was formed on January 1, 1988. Capital stock was issued and all plant, equipment, and land were acquired at that time.
2. Ending inventory was acquired evenly throughout 1992.
3. Beginning inventory was acquired evenly throughout 1991.
4. Plant and equipment are depreciated by the straight-line method and have a 10-year useful life with no residual value.
5. Sales were made and other expenses (except for depreciation) were incurred evenly throughout the year.
6. Purchases were made evenly throughout the year.
7. A $50,000 cash dividend was paid on December 31, 1992.
8. The beginning constant dollar retained earnings balance is assumed to be $140,559.
9. The company began the year with monetary assets of $164,000 and monetary liabilities of $148,000. These amounts would be derived from the December 31, 1991 balance sheet.

10. To restate the historical cost financial statements to constant dollar amounts, the CPI at various relevant dates was as follows.

Date	CPI
January 1, 1988	104
Monthly average for 1991	148
December 31, 1991	150
Monthly average for 1992	155
December 31, 1992	160

Constant Dollar Balance Sheet. To illustrate the preparation of a constant dollar balance sheet, the historical cost balance sheet, restatement computations, and constant dollar balance sheet for the Flint Company, adjusted to year-end dollars, are shown in Figure 16-7. Note that the monetary assets and liabilities are not restated. Nonmonetary assets and capital stock are restated on the basis of the index at the balance sheet date over the index at the time the nonmonetary assets were acquired and capital stock issued (January 1, 1988). The retained earnings figure is an amount that is entered to bring the constant dollar balance sheet into balance.

Constant Dollar Combined Income and Retained Earnings Statement.
A historical cost combined income and retained earnings statement, restatement computations, and a constant dollar combined statement for Flint Company is given in Figure 16-8. Note that sales, purchases, and other expenses are converted on the basis

Figure 16-7
Constant Dollar Balance Sheet

FLINT COMPANY
Constant Dollar Balance Sheet
December 31, 1992

	Historical Cost	Restatement Factor	Constant Dollar
Assets			
Cash	$ 71,000	Monetary—not restated	$ 71,000
Accounts receivable	114,000	Monetary—not restated	114,000
Inventory	120,000	(160/155) × $120,000	123,871
Plant and equipment	300,000	(160/104) × $300,000	461,538
Accumulated depreciation	(150,000)	(160/104) × $150,000	(230,769)
Land	100,000	(160/104) × $100,000	153,846
Total	$555,000		$693,486
Liabilities			
Accounts payable	$ 79,000	Monetary—not restated	$ 79,000
Notes payable, due 1993	60,000	Monetary—not restated	60,000
Stockholders' Equity			
Capital stock	270,000	(160/104) × $270,000	415,385
Retained earnings	146,000	From Figure 16-8*	139,101
Total	$555,000		$693,486

*Also is the amount needed to balance liabilities and stockholders' equity with total assets.

FLINT COMPANY
Constant Dollar Combined Income and Retained Earnings Statement
For the Year Ended December 31, 1992

	Historical Cost	Restatement Computation	Constant Dollar
Sales	$591,000	(160/155) × $591,000	$610,065
Cost of Goods Sold:			
Beginning inventory	100,000	(160/148) × $100,000	108,108
Purchases	381,000	(160/155) × $381,000	393,290
Goods available for sale	481,000		501,398
Less: Ending inventory	120,000	(160/155) × $120,000	123,871
Cost of goods sold	361,000		377,527
Depreciation expense	30,000	(160/104) × $30,000	46,154
Other expenses	130,000	(160/155) × $130,000	134,194
Total expenses	521,000		557,875
Net income	70,000		
Net income before purchasing power loss			52,190
Purchasing power loss		From Figure 16-9	3,648
Constant dollar net income			48,542
Beginning retained earnings balance	126,000	Assumed amount	140,559
	196,000		189,101
Less: Cash dividends	50,000	(160/160) × $50,000	50,000
Ending retained earnings balance	$146,000	To Figure 16-7	$139,101

Figure 16-8
Constant Dollar Combined Income and Retained Earnings Statement

of the end-of-year CPI over the average CPI for the year. Depreciation and the beginning and ending inventory balances are converted on the basis of the CPI that existed when the respective assets were acquired. Computation of the purchasing power loss is discussed in the next section. The cash dividend paid on December 31 is stated in terms of year-end dollars.

Computation of Purchasing Power Gain or Loss.

In Figure 16-8, a purchasing power loss of $3,648 is reported in the constant dollar income statement. The purchasing power loss is computed in Figure 16-9. The first step in computing the loss is to identify net monetary items at the beginning and end of the period. Net monetary items are monetary assets less monetary liabilities. The Flint Company started the period in a $16,000 net monetary asset position and ended the period with $46,000 in net monetary assets. In the second step, transactions that changed net monetary items are identified. The first column reconciles historical cost net monetary assets at the beginning of the year to the net monetary assets at the end of the year. During the period, net monetary assets were increased $591,000 by sales (i.e., cash or accounts receivable were received) and were decreased $561,000 by purchases of inventory, incurring other expenses, and the payment of cash dividends (i.e., cash paid or liabilities incurred).

FLINT COMPANY
Computation of Purchasing Power Gain or Loss
For the Year Ended December 31, 1992

	Historical Cost	Restatement Factor	Constant Dollar
Beginning net monetary items:*			
Cash and accounts receivable	$164,000		
Accounts and notes payable	148,000		
Net monetary assets	$ 16,000	(160/150) × $16,000	$ 17,067
Add: Transactions that increase net monetary items:			
Sales	591,000	(160/155) × $591,000	610,065
	607,000		627,132
Less: Transactions that decrease net monetary items:			
Purchases	381,000	(160/155) × $381,000	393,290
Other expenses	130,000	(160/155) × $130,000	134,194
Cash dividends	50,000	(160/160) × $50,000	50,000
	561,000		577,484
Net monetary items restated			49,648
Ending net monetary items:*			
Cash and receivables	185,000		
Accounts and notes payable	139,000		
Net monetary assets	$ 46,000		
Less: Ending net monetary items—historical cost			46,000
Purchasing power loss (To Figure 16-8.)			$ 3,648

*Monetary items at the beginning of the period are the ending monetary items of the last period. Here the monetary items are assumed as given in No. 9 on page 733. Ending monetary items are determined from the balance sheet in Figure 16-7.

Figure 16-9
Computation of Purchasing Power Gain or Loss

The historical cost dollar amounts are then restated to constant dollars using the appropriate general price level restatement factor. Beginning net monetary items are restated to year-end constant dollars using the index on January 1 as the denominator in the restatement fraction. The denominator in the fraction to restate each type of transaction that changed the beginning net monetary items is the index at the date of the transaction, or an average index is used where appropriate. The net monetary items restated (constant dollar) is compared to the actual amount of ending net monetary items on hand to determine the purchasing power gain or loss.

The net monetary items restated amount shows that the company needed net monetary assets of $49,648 to maintain its purchasing power. Since its actual net monetary assets were $46,000, the company had a loss in purchasing power of $3,648. The purchasing power loss resulted because Flint Company carried an excess of monetary assets over monetary liabilities throughout the year during which prices increased.

The need for constant dollar financial statements is an unsettled issue. Those who support their preparation argue that the stable dollar assumption does not reflect reality, particularly when inflation rates are high. They believe that the aggregation of dollars with different purchasing power may mislead users of financial information and thereby cause poor decisions. In addition, they argue that the financial data in constant dollar financial statements are just as reliable and verifiable as historical cost data. Critics of constant dollar accounting argue that both historical cost and constant dollar financial statements are inadequate because they ignore real value changes. Consequently, most critics support the preparation of current value financial statements.

CURRENT VALUE ACCOUNTING

As explained earlier, constant dollar accounting does not depart from the historical cost concept. Rather, it merely restates historical costs in terms of the current purchasing power of money—that is, historical costs are adjusted only for general price level changes. Current value accounting, however, is a departure from historical cost because it gives effect to specific price changes.

There are two basic concepts of current value: (1) net realizable value and (2) current replacement cost (current cost). Net realizable value is an exit value, an estimate of the amount an asset could be sold for in its present condition minus disposal costs. Current replacement cost is an entry value, an estimate of the amount that would have to be paid currently to acquire an asset in its present condition. It is generally referred to simply as current cost.

Proponents of current value accounting tend to support the use of current cost rather than net realizable value, for two reasons. First, current costs are believed to be more objectively determinable by the use of current price lists of suppliers, prices in established markets for used assets, and specific price indexes. Second, most assets are held for use rather than for direct sale. Thus, the current cost to replace an asset being used is considered more relevant than an estimate of its sales value as provided by net realizable value. In addition, the FASB recommends the disclosure of selected current cost information, as discussed later. The following discussion, although limited, concentrates on current cost accounting.

In the preparation of current cost financial statements, income activities are divided into two elements.

1. **Current operating income** or **loss.** Current operating income or loss is the difference between revenues and current cost of the assets sold or used at the time of sale or use. Operating income is not recognized unless revenues exceed the cost to replace the assets sold or used to produce the revenue.
2. **Holding gain** or **loss.** Holding gain or loss is the change in the current cost of assets held during the period.

Holding Gain and Loss Illustrated

The profit-making activities of the firm are recognized as resulting from the production and sale of a product (operating activities) and from holding assets during a period in which their prices increase or decrease. To illustrate a holding gain or loss, assume that the land purchased by the Flint Company for $100,000 in 1988 had a replacement cost of $153,000 and $170,000 on January 1 and December 31, 1992, respectively.

A holding gain for 1992 of $17,000 is computed as follows.

Replacement cost—December 31	$170,000
Replacement cost—January 1	153,000
Holding gain	$ 17,000

Total holding gains of $53,000 ($153,000 − $100,000) would have been reported in prior years. In the historical cost accounting model, holding gains and losses are not recognized until the land is sold.

Realized and Unrealized Holding Gain or Loss

Holding gains and losses may be classified further into realized or unrealized categories.

Realized holding gains or **losses** relate to changes in the replacement cost of assets sold or used during the year.

Unrealized holding gains or **losses** relate to changes in the replacement cost of assets held at the balance sheet date.

For example, assume that a company purchased two units of inventory during a period for $50 per unit. One unit was sold for $100 when its replacement cost was $70. The other unit was held at the end of the period, at which time its replacement cost was $80. Holding gains are computed as follows.

	Historical Cost	Current Cost	Holding Gain (Loss)
Cost of goods sold	$50	$70	$20 realized
Ending merchandise inventory	50	80	30 unrealized

Historical cost accounting reports a realized gross profit of $50 ($100 − $50) in the year of the sale, and an ending inventory of $50 in the year-end balance sheet. Current cost accounting also reports realized income of $50, but separates it into operating income of $30 ($100 − $70) and a realized holding gain of $20. In addition, ending inventory of $80 is reported in the balance sheet with an unrealized holding gain of $30 reported on the unit still held.

Reporting Realized and Unrealized Holding Gain or Loss

There has been considerable discussion regarding the appropriate reporting of holding gains and losses. Two methods that are commonly proposed are: (1) including both realized and unrealized holding gains and losses in the income statement as an adjustment to current operating income and (2) including realized holding gains and losses in the income statement, but reporting unrealized holding gains and losses in the stockholders' equity section of the balance sheet. The first approach will be used in the illustration that follows and in the end of chapter material to this chapter.

To illustrate the preparation of current cost financial statements, assume that the replacement cost of Flint Company's nonmonetary assets on December 31, 1992 and the replacement cost of goods sold at the time they were sold were as follows.

Inventory	$134,000
Plant and equipment	500,000
Accumulated depreciation	(250,000)
Land	170,000
Cost of goods sold	388,000

Plant and equipment items are depreciated by the straight-line method and have a 10-year useful life with no residual value.

A balance sheet comparing historical cost with current cost is shown in Figure 16-10. In the current cost balance sheet, monetary assets (cash and accounts receivable) and monetary liabilities (accounts and notes payable) are not changed from their historical amounts because they already reflect current values. Nonmonetary assets are reported at the current cost to replace them in their present physical condition. Paid-in capital accounts are normally restated for general price-level changes and retained earnings are computed as a balancing amount.

Figure 16-11 shows an income statement comparing historical cost with current cost. In the current cost income statement, sales and those expenses resulting from current cash payments or current accruals are reported at their historical cost amounts. Historical costs are used because sales resulted in an increase in monetary assets (cash or accounts receivable) and cash type expenses resulted in a decrease in monetary assets (cash) or an increase in monetary liabilities (accrued expenses). Expenses related to nonmonetary assets (primarily cost of goods sold and depreciation) are reported at their current cost. Cost of goods sold is computed by multiplying the number of units sold by the replacement cost of the units at the time of sale. Depreciation expense is determined by applying the depreciation methods used to the plant assets' replacement costs at the balance sheet date ($500,000/10 year useful life). By reporting current costs, each company recognizes the effect of the specific price changes that effect the resources used by it. The holding gains and losses, both realized and unrealized, are included in the income statement in Figure 16-11. The amount of $73,000 is assumed. The computation is rather complex and is covered in more advanced accounting courses.

Proponents of current cost accounting argue that current cost information is much more realistic than historical cost or constant dollar information—and therefore more

Figure 16-10
Comparative Historical Cost and Current Cost Balance Sheet

FLINT COMPAMY
Balance Sheet
December 31, 1992

	Historical Cost	Current Cost
Cash	$ 71,000	$ 71,000
Accounts receivable	114,000	114,000
Inventory	120,000	134,000
Plant and equipment	300,000	500,000
Accumulated depreciation	(150,000)	(250,000)
Land	100,000	170,000
Total Assets	$555,000	$739,000
Accounts payable	$ 79,000	$ 79,000
Notes payable, due 1993	60,000	60,000
Capital stock [(160/104) × $270,000]*	270,000	415,385
Retained earnings (balancing amount)	146,000	184,615
Total Equities	$555,000	$739,000

*See Figure 16-7.

FLINT COMPANY Income Statement For the Year Ended December 31, 1992	Historical Cost	Current Cost
Sales	$591,000	$591,000
Expenses:		
Cost of goods sold	$361,000	388,000
Depreciation	30,000	50,000
Other expenses	130,000	130,000
Total expenses	521,000	568,000
Current operating income		23,000
Holding gains and losses	–0–	73,000
Net income	$ 70,000	$ 96,000

useful. They also believe that a company has net earnings only if it has recovered the replacement cost of resources used, thereby permitting it to maintain its productive capacity. Critics of current cost accounting maintain that replacement costs are too subjective and difficult to verify and may therefore mislead decision-makers. In addition, they believe that the use of the last-in, first-out costing method to determine cost of goods sold and the use of accelerated depreciation methods are objective and verifiable and will result in reported earnings that approach those that would be reported under current cost accounting. Consequently, they argue, essentially the same earnings results could be obtained without departing from the historical cost basis.

FASB RECOMMENDATIONS

The FASB has been concerned with the reporting problems created by inflation, but has had difficulty reaching an agreement as to the proper solution. Each reporting basis—historical cost, constant dollar, and current cost—has its advantages and disadvantages. Because decision-makers use financial information daily, a major change in the reporting basis has the potential of disrupting the decision-making process and, therefore, the allocation of resources within the economy.

In order to obtain experience in the preparation and use of different reporting bases, the FASB required that some companies present selected data on both a constant dollar and a current cost basis in supplementary schedules to the historical cost based financial statements. Specific reporting requirements were provided in *Statement of Financial Accounting Standards No. 33,* "Financial Reporting and Changing Prices" which was issued in 1979. Following an extended period of experimentation with reporting both constant dollar and current cost data, the FASB, in 1984, eliminated some constant dollar disclosure requirements as provided in *SFAS No. 82,* "Financial Reporting and Changing Prices: Elimination of Certain Disclosures." During 1986 the FASB issued *SFAS No. 89,* "Financial Reporting and Changing Prices" which superseded the prior standards related to this topic. *SFAS No. 89* encourages, but does not require the disclosure of supplementary information about the impact of inflation. Several reasons advanced for this change in position are (1) inflation is not the problem it was in the 1970s, (2) the conclusion of several empirical studies conducted to assess the usefulness of the required disclosure was that costs of providing the information exceeded its benefit, and (3) the disclosures were too complex and as a result were difficult to understand.

Statement No. 89 applies only to large publicly-held companies—that is, those with inventories and property, plant, and equipment (before deducting accumulated depreciation) of more than $125 million, or with total assets of more than $1 billion (after deducting accumulated depreciation). The main disclosures recommended for each of the five most recent years are:

1. Net sales and other operating revenues;
2. Income from continuing operations on a current cost basis;
3. Purchasing power gain or loss on net monetary items;
4. Increase or decrease in the current cost or lower recoverable amount of inventory and property, plant, and equipment, net of inflation;
5. Net assets at year-end on a current cost basis;
6. Income per common share from continuing operations on a current cost basis;
7. Cash dividends declared per common share;
8. Market price per common share at year-end; and
9. The average level of the Consumer Price Index.

SUMMARY

Part I of this chapter discussed three techniques—horizontal analysis, vertical analysis, and ratio analysis—that are commonly used in conducting an analysis of a firm's financial statements. The technique or techniques selected by statement users depends upon the nature of the decision. Short-term investors are normally interested in assessing the liquidity of a firm whereas long-term investors usually analyze a firm's use of financial leverage and profitability as well as its liquidity.

It was emphasized that the percentages and ratios computed for an individual firm should be compared to some other standards, such as the historical record of the firm under study, the performance of other firms, or some standard established by the analyst. The limitations of using historical cost data to predict the performance must also be recognized.

Part II of the chapter discussed the effects of price changes on financial statements. Price changes are of two types—specific and general. General price level changes are measured by changes in the prices of a large sample of goods or services. A specific price change is the change in the price of a particular good or service, such as the sales price of a textbook. General price changes are recognized by restating historical cost data into constant dollar data as follows:

$$\frac{\text{Current price index}}{\text{Historical cost price index}} \times \text{Historical cost} = \text{Restated cost}$$

Specific price changes, usually measured in terms of replacement cost, are reflected in current cost financial statements. In order to gain experience in the use of these two alternative methods of reporting financial data, the FASB required certain large publicly held companies to disclose constant dollar and current cost in supplementary schedules. Because empirical studies in general did not provide evidence of sufficient incremental information, supplementary disclosure of price changes is now recommended, but not required.

SELF-TEST

Test your understanding of the chapter by selecting the best answer for each of the following.

1. What type of analysis is indicated by the following?

	Amount	Percent
Current assets	$ 250,000	25
Long-term assets	750,000	75
Total assets	$1,000,000	100

   a. Vertical analysis.
   b. Horizontal analysis.
   c. Ratio analysis.
   d. Differential analysis.

2. Expressing financial data from two or more accounting periods in terms of a single designated base period is known as:
   a. vertical analysis.
   b. ratio analysis.
   c. horizontal (trend) analysis.
   d. percentage analysis.

3. The receivable and inventory turnover ratios are used to analyze:
   a. profitability.
   b. liquidity.
   c. long-term debt-paying ability.
   d. leverage.

4. Dickenson Company's inventory and other related accounts for 1992 were as follows.

Sales	$3,000,000
Cost of Goods Sold	2,200,000
Inventory balances:	
Beginning of the year	500,000
End of the year	600,000

   Purchases and sales were made evenly throughout the year. How many times did the inventory turnover during 1992?
   a. 4.00.
   b. 4.40.
   c. 5.00.
   d. 5.45.

5. The financial ratio that measures the ability of the firm to meet its interest payments out of current earnings is:
   a. return on sales.
   b. debt to total assets.
   c. times interest earned.
   d. quick ratio.

6. The current ratio is computed by dividing
   a. current assets by current liabilities.
   b. current assets by total liabilities.
   c. quick assets by current liabilities.
   d. total assets by total liabilities.
7. Inflation is the result of a(n):
   a. decrease in specific price.
   b. loss on monetary assets.
   c. increase in the purchasing power of the dollar.
   d. increase in the weighted-average price of all goods and services in the economy.
8. Which of the following is an example of a monetary asset?
   a. Land.
   b. Merchandise inventory.
   c. Accounts receivable.
   d. Patent.
9. In periods of increasing prices, purchasing power gains are caused by:
   a. holding monetary assets.
   b. holding monetary liabilities.
   c. holding nonmonetary assets.
   d. holding nonmonetary liabilities.
10. In a current cost balance sheet, plant assets are reported at:
    a. their original cost to purchase, less accumulated depreciation.
    b. the estimated amount for which they could be sold.
    c. the current cost of replacing them in their present condition.
    d. the purchasing power equivalent of new similar assets.

REVIEW PROBLEM

The comparative financial statements of the Marker Corporation are shown here.

MARKER CORPORATION
Comparative Income Statements
For the Years Ended December 31, 1992 and 1991

	1992	1991
Sales	$395,000	$386,500
Less: Cost of goods sold	247,000	228,000
Gross profit on sales	148,000	158,500
Operating expenses	110,000	120,500
Interest expense	7,500	7,000
Income tax expense (50%)	15,250	15,500
Total expenses	132,750	143,000
Net income	$ 15,250	$ 15,500

MARKER CORPORATION
Comparative Balance Sheets
December 31, 1992 and 1991

	1992	1991
Assets		
Current Assets:		
Cash	$ 10,000	$ 9,000
Marketable securities	10,500	12,500
Accounts receivable	39,500	37,000
Inventory	105,000	101,500
Prepaid expenses	2,000	2,500
Total Current Assets	167,000	162,500
Plant and equipment	80,000	70,500
Total Assets	$247,000	$233,000
Liabilities		
Current Liabilities:		
Accounts payable	$ 38,500	$ 32,000
Notes payable	20,000	15,000
Total Current Liabilities	58,500	47,000
Bonds payable	70,000	70,000
Total Liabilities	128,500	117,000
Stockholders' Equity		
Preferred stock	20,000	20,000
Common stock ($2.50 par value)	25,000	25,000
Additional paid-in capital	57,500	57,500
Retained earnings	16,000	13,500
Total Stockholders' Equity	118,500	116,000
Total Liabilities and Stockholders' Equity	$247,000	$233,000

During 1992, Marker Corporation declared and paid preferred stock cash dividends of $1,400 and common stock cash dividends of $11,350. On December 31, 1992, the market price of the common stock was $14 a share.

Required:

Compute the following ratios for 1992:

A. Return on total assets.
B. Return on common stockholders' equity.
C. Return on sales.
D. Earnings per share.
E. Price-earnings ratio.
F. Dividend yield.
G. Dividend payout.
H. Current ratio.
I. Quick ratio.
J. Receivable turnover.
K. Inventory turnover.
L. Debt to total assets.
M. Times interest earned.

ANSWER TO REVIEW PROBLEM

A. Return on total assets $= \dfrac{15,250 + 3,750}{(233,000 + 247,000)/2} = 7.92\ \%$

B. Return on common stockholders' equity $= \dfrac{15,250 - 1,400}{(96,000 + 98,500)/2} = 14.24\%$

C. Return on sales $= \dfrac{15,250}{395,000} = 3.86\%$

D. Earnings per share $= \dfrac{15,250 - 1,400}{10,000} = \$1.39$

E. Price/earnings ratio $= \dfrac{14}{1.39} = 10.07$

F. Dividend yield $= \dfrac{1.14}{14} = 8.14\%$

G. Dividend payout $= \dfrac{11,350}{15,250 - 1,400} = 81.95\%$

H. Current ratio $= \dfrac{167,000}{58,500} = 2.85$

I. Quick ratio $= \dfrac{10,000 + 10,500 + 39,500}{58,500} = 1.03$

J. Receivable turnover $= \dfrac{395,000}{(37,000 + 39,500)/2} = 10.33$

K. Inventory turnover $= \dfrac{247,000}{(101,500 + 105,000)/2} = 2.39$

L. Debt to total assets $= \dfrac{128,500}{247,000} = 52.02\%$

M. Times interest earned $= \dfrac{15,250 + 7,500 + 15,250}{7,500} = 5.07$

ANSWERS TO SELF-TEST

1. a   **2.** c   **3.** b   **4.** a   **5.** c   **6.** a   **7.** d   **8.** c
9. b   **10.** c

GLOSSARY

COMMON SIZE STATEMENT.   A financial statement in which the amount of each item reported in the statement is stated as a percentage of some specific base amount also reported in the same statement (p. 717).

COMPARATIVE STATEMENTS.   Financial statements for the current year and prior years presented together to facilitate the analysis of changes in account balances (p. 713).

CONSTANT DOLLAR ACCOUNTING. The restatement of historical cost financial statements for changes in the general price level (p. 731).

CURRENT OPERATING INCOME. Excess of current revenues over current cost to produce the revenues (p. 737).

CURRENT VALUE ACCOUNTING. The preparation of financial statements on the basis of current costs (p. 731).

CURRENT REPLACEMENT COST (CURRENT COST). The amount that would have to be paid currently to acquire an asset in its present condition (p. 737).

GENERAL PRICE LEVEL. The weighted average price of all goods and services in the economy (p. 730).

GENERAL PRICE LEVEL CHANGE. A change in the weighted average of the prices of all goods and services in the economy (p. 730).

HOLDING GAIN. A gain resulting from holding an asset when its replacement cost increases (p. 737).

HOLDING LOSS. A loss resulting from holding an asset when its replacement cost decreases (p. 737).

HORIZONTAL ANALYSIS. That part of an analysis based on the comparison of amounts reported for the same item in two or more comparative statements with an emphasis on the change from year to year (p. 713).

INFLATION. A decrease in purchasing power of money; also defined as an increase in the general price level (p. 730).

MONETARY ITEMS. Assets and liabilities that represent claims to fixed amounts of dollars established by contract or otherwise (p. 732).

NET MONETARY ITEMS. Monetary assets minus monetary liabilities (p. 735).

NET REALIZABLE VALUE. The amount an asset could be sold for less disposal costs (p. 737).

NONMONETARY ITEMS. All financial statement amounts that are not monetary in nature—that is, do not represent claims to fixed amounts of cash (p. 733).

PURCHASING POWER. The amount of goods or services for which a dollar can be exchanged (p. 730).

PURCHASING POWER GAIN. The gain from holding monetary liabilities during a period of rising prices (p. 732).

PURCHASING POWER LOSS. The loss from holding monetary assets during a period of rising prices (p. 732).

RATIO. Relationship of the amount reported for one financial statement item to the amount reported for another financial statement item. Ratio analysis is the evaluation of the relationship indicated by this division (p. 717).

REALIZED HOLDING GAIN OR LOSS. A gain or loss resulting from a change in the current cost of an asset sold or used during the period (p. 738).

SPECIFIC PRICE CHANGE. A change in the price of a particular good or service (p. 730).

TREND ANALYSIS. That part of statement analysis involved with comparing the changes in a particular item over a series of years. In trend analysis, a base year is selected. Statement items in subsequent statements are expressed as a percentage of their value in the base year (p. 716).

UNREALIZED HOLDING GAIN OR LOSS. A gain or loss resulting from a change in the current cost of an asset held at the balance sheet date (p. 738).

VERTICAL ANALYSIS. That part of an analysis in which the focus of the study is on the proportion of individual items expressed as a percentage of some specific item reported in the same statement (p. 717). (See also *Common Size Statement*.)

DISCUSSION QUESTIONS

1. What is the objective of financial statement analysis?
2. Differentiate between horizontal analysis, trend analysis, and vertical analysis.
3. What is the importance of the base year when using trend analysis with percentages?
4. Explain what is meant by the term "common size statements."
5. What is the purpose of computing ratios?
6. Name and define the three financial aspects of a firm that are analyzed using ratio analysis.
7. Explain the significance of the following profitability ratios.
   a. Rate of return on total assets.
   b. Rate of return on common stockholders' equity.
   c. Earnings per share.
   d. Price-earnings ratio.
8. How are the current ratio and the quick ratio similar? How do they differ?
9. A firm's receivable turnover ratio declined from 14.3 in 1991 in 12.7 in 1992, to 10.4 in 1993. If the firm's credit terms are 30 days, what problems may be indicated by the ratios?
10. What risk does a company assume as the inventory turnover increases?
11. How could earnings per share decrease even though net income has increased from the previous year?
12. Why is the debt to total assets ratio of importance to the firm's creditors?
13. What are the limitations of financial statement analysis?
14. Which ratio will help to answer each of the following questions?
    a. How effective are the credit policies of the firm?
    b. How much confidence do investors have in the firm?
    c. Are the assets being used effectively?
    d. How is the firm being financed?
    e. Are the firm's current earnings sufficient to meet the annual interest payments?
15. Explain how the following alternative accounting principles will affect a company's reported earnings.
    a. Use of an accelerated depreciation method rather than straight-line depreciation.
    b. Use of LIFO rather than FIFO inventory valuation in a period of inflation.
    c. Use of the equity method rather than the cost method in accounting for long-term investments in equity securities.
16. What is meant by "purchasing power of the dollar?" How is it affected by inflation? by deflation?
17. Explain the difference between specific price changes and general price level changes.
18. Identify and briefly define the two primary methods used to report the effects of inflation.
19. Define monetary and nonmonetary items. Explain how purchasing power gains and losses result from holding monetary items during a period of inflation.

20. Explain why monetary items are not restated when preparing a constant dollar balance sheet.

21. Explain why the current cost concept is preferred over net realizable value by proponents of current value accounting.

22. Explain how the current cost amount is calculated for cost of goods sold and depreciation expense.

EXERCISES

Exercise 16-1 Horizontal and Vertical Analysis—Income Statement

The 1991 and 1992 comparative income statements for Tubb Corporation follow:

TUBB CORPORATION
Comparative Income Statements
For the Years Ended December 31, 1992 and 1991

	1992	1991
Sales	$750,000	$680,000
Cost of goods sold	487,500	408,000
Gross profit	262,500	272,000
Selling expenses	82,500	81,600
Administrative expenses	67,500	51,000
Interest expense	22,500	17,000
Income tax expense	31,500	42,840
Net Income	$ 58,500	$ 79,560
Earnings per share	$.585	$.796

Required:

A. Prepare common size income statements for 1992 and 1991.

B. Compute the dollar and percent change in each item from 1991 to 1992.

C. Comment on any significant changes from 1991 to 1992 revealed by the horizontal analysis. Can you determine whether the changes are favorable or unfavorable? Can you determine any trends from the data?

D. Comment on any significant changes from 1991 to 1992 revealed by the vertical analysis. Can you determine whether the changes are favorable or unfavorable? Can you determine any trends from the data?

Exercise 16-2 Horizontal and Vertical Analysis—Balance Sheet

The 1991 and 1992 condensed comparative balance sheets for Cache Corporation are as follows:

CACHE CORPORATION
Balance Sheets
December 31, 1992 and 1991

	1992	1991
Assets:		
Current assets	$1,565,000	$1,400,000
Long-term investments	350,000	370,000
Plant and equipment (net)	3,420,000	2,680,000
Total Assets	$5,335,000	$4,450,000
Liabilities:		
Current liabilities	$ 670,000	$ 605,000
Long-term liabilities	2,145,000	1,935,000
Total Liabilities	2,815,000	2,540,000
Stockholders' Equity:		
Common stock	1,330,000	1,125,000
Paid-in capital in excess of par value	625,000	410,000
Retained earnings	565,000	375,000
Total Stockholders' Equity	2,520,000	1,910,000
Total Liabilities and Stockholders' Equity	$5,335,000	$4,450,000

Required:
A. Compute the dollar and percent change in each item from 1991 to 1992.
B. Prepare common size balance sheets for 1992 and 1991.
C. Comment on any significant changes from 1991 to 1992 revealed by the horizontal analysis. Can you determine whether the changes are favorable or unfavorable? Can you determine any trends from the data?
D. Comment on any significant changes from 1991 to 1992 revealed by the vertical analysis. Can you determine whether the changes are favorable or unfavorable? Can you determine any trends from the data?

Exercise 16-3   Trend Analysis
Blake Corporation reported the following financial data over a five-year period.

	1989	1990	1991	1992	1993
Sales	$2,100,000	$2,227,700	$2,310,000	$2,260,400	$2,430,000
Gross profit	882,000	944,500	990,000	986,700	993,400
Operating expenses	567,000	612,600	635,200	626,100	632,000
Interest expense	56,000	61,000	61,000	61,000	69,000

Required:
A. Prepare a trend analysis of the data. Use the trend analysis to determine any favorable and unfavorable trends and any changes in the direction of any items over the five-year period.
B. What overall conclusion, if any, can be reached by an analysis of the trend analysis?

Exercise 16-4 Trend Analysis

Below are the 1989 through 1993 income statements of Farnsbook Corporation expressed in percentages using 1988 as the base year:

	1989	1990	1991	1992	1993
Sales	100%	108%	117%	126%	136%
Cost of goods sold	100	109	119	133	144
Selling expenses	100	106	112	122	133
Administrative expenses	100	110	121	133	146
Interest expense	100	114	130	136	139
Net Income	100	107	114	122	130

Required:

A. Determine the favorable and unfavorable trends in the items listed above. Determine also any changes in the direction of any item over the five-year period.

B. What overall conclusion can be reached by an analysis of the data presented above?

Exercise 16-5 Ratio Calculations

A list of ratios is given below followed by the method of calculating each of the ratios.

Ratio

1. Earnings per share
2. Quick ratio
3. Times interest earned
4. Price-earnings ratio
5. Debt to total assets
6. Current ratio
7. Return on sales

8. Inventory turnover
9. Dividend payout
10. Return on common stockholders' equity
11. Receivable turnover
12. Dividend yield
13. Return on total assets

Method of Calculation

_____ A. $\dfrac{\text{Net income + Interest expense (net of tax)}}{\text{Average total assets}}$

_____ B. $\dfrac{\text{Net income − Preferred stock cash dividends requirements}}{\text{Average common stockholders' equity}}$

_____ C. $\dfrac{\text{Net income − Preferred stock cash dividends requirements}}{\text{Weighted average number of shares outstanding}}$

_____ D. $\dfrac{\text{Market price per share of common stock}}{\text{Earnings per share}}$

_____ E. $\dfrac{\text{Annual dividend per share of common stock}}{\text{Market price per share of common stock}}$

_____ F. $\dfrac{\text{Total dividends to common stockholders}}{\text{Net income − Preferred stock cash dividend requirement}}$

_____ G. $\dfrac{\text{Current assets}}{\text{Current liabilities}}$

_____ H. $\dfrac{\text{Cash + Marketable securities + Net receivables}}{\text{Current liabilities}}$

_____ I. $$\frac{\text{Net sales}}{\text{Average receivable balance}}$$

_____ J. $$\frac{\text{Cost of goods sold}}{\text{Average inventory balance}}$$

_____ K. $$\frac{\text{Total liabilities}}{\text{Total assets}}$$

_____ L. $$\frac{\text{Net income + Interest expense + income tax expense}}{\text{Interest expense}}$$

_____ M. $$\frac{\text{Net income}}{\text{Net sales}}$$

Required:

Match each ratio to its method of calculation by placing the ratio number on the blank preceding the formula.

Exercise 16-6 Ratio Significance

A list of ratios is given below followed by a list of statements describing the significance of a specific ratio.

Ratio

1. Debt to total assets
2. Earnings per share
3. Receivable turnover
4. Current ratio
5. Times interest earned
6. Return on total assets
7. Price-earnings ratio
8. Return on common stockholders' equity
9. Dividend payout
10. Return on sales
11. Quick ratio
12. Dividend yield
13. Inventory turnover

Ratio Significance

_____ A. Measures rate of return earned on total assets provided by both creditors and owners.

_____ B. Measures rate of return earned on assets provided by owners.

_____ C. Measures net profitability of each dollar of sales.

_____ D. Measures net income earned on each share of common stock.

_____ E. Measures the amount investors are paying for a dollar of earnings.

_____ F. Measures rate of return to stockholders based on current market price.

_____ G. Measures the percentage of income paid out to common stockholders.

_____ H. A measure of short-term liquidity. Indicates the ability of a firm to meet its short-term debts from its current assets.

_____ I. A more rigorous measure of short-term liquidity. Indicates the ability of the firm to meet unexpected demands from the liquid current assets.

_____ J. Measures effectiveness of collections; used to evaluate whether receivable balance is excessive.

_____ K. Indicates the liquidity of inventory. Measures the number of times inventory was sold on the average during the period.

_____ L. Measures the percentage of assets provided by creditors and the extent of using leverage.

_____ M. Measures the ability of the firm to meet its interest payments out of current earnings.

Required:

Match the appropriate ratio to the statement describing the significance of that ratio by placing the ratio number in the blank preceding each statement.

Exercise 16-7 Profitability Analysis

Brownly Corporation reported a net income of $910,000 for 1992. During the year, the company paid preferred stock cash dividends of $30,000 and common stock cash dividends of $400,000. Throughout the year, 400,000 shares of common stock were outstanding. The common stock is currently selling at $33 per share.

Required:
Compute the following ratios.

1. Earnings per share.
2. Price-earnings ratio.
3. Dividend yield.
4. Dividend payout.

Exercise 16-8 Liquidity Analysis

The following information was taken from the 1992 and 1991 financial statements of Gallico Corporation.

	1992	1991
Cash	$ 85,000	$ 135,000
Marketable securities	225,000	200,000
Accounts receivable	219,000	196,000
Inventory	617,000	602,000
Prepaid expenses	22,000	45,000
Plant and equipment (net)	1,052,000	1,033,000
Accounts payable	595,000	562,000
Wages payable	38,000	32,000
Sales	2,560,000	2,590,000
Cost of goods sold	1,554,000	1,570,000

Required:
A. Compute the following items for 1992 and 1991.
   1. Current ratio.
   2. Quick ratio.
B. Compute the following items for 1992.
   1. Receivable-turnover ratio.
   2. Average collection period of accounts receivable.
   3. Inventory-turnover ratio.
   4. Average days per inventory turnover.
C. Comment on any potential problems indicated by these items.

Exercise 16-9 Profitability and Financial Leverage

The following information is available for the Warbler Corporation.

	1992	1991
Sales	$1,800,000	$1,650,000
Interest expense	77,000	79,000
Income tax expense	140,100	122,700
Net Income	164,000	145,000
Preferred dividends paid	10,000	10,000
Total assets	1,460,000	1,380,000

Total liabilities	820,800	910,000
Preferred stock	169,000	169,000
Common stock	295,000	278,000
Retained earnings	175,200	23,000
Tax rate	40%	40%

Required:

A. Compute the following ratios for 1992.
  1. Return on total assets.
  2. Return on common stockholders' equity.
B. Compute the following ratios for 1992 and 1991.
  1. Return on sales.
  2. Debt to total assets.
  3. Times interest earned.
C. Comment on any potential problems and/or improvements indicated by these ratios.

Exercise 16-10   Analysis of Two Companies

Financial data for two companies engaged in the same line of business is presented below for 1992:

	Arlington Company	Brilliant Company
Sales (all on credit)	$4,000,000	$2,400,000
Total assets	2,000,000	800,000
Total liabilities	1,000,000	200,000
Average accounts receivable	500,000	200,000
Average inventory	500,000	300,000
Interest expense	–0–	–0–
Gross profit as a percentage of sales	50%	25%
Operating expenses as a percentage of sales	48%	21%
Net income as a percentage of sales	2%	4%

Required:

A. Compute the following items for each company.
  1. Net income.
  2. Return on total assets.
  3. Return on common stockholders' equity. Neither company had issued preferred stock.
  4. Accounts receivable turnover.
  5. Inventory turnover.
B. In which of the two companies would you buy stock? Explain your reasons.

Exercise 16-11   Constant Dollar Financial Statement Adjustments

Presented below are general price level indexes for specific dates or periods:

December 31, 1964	100	June 30, 1991	208
February 15, 1965	104	December 31, 1991	211
March 21, 1965	105	Average for 1991	210
May 1, 1980	154	June 19, 1992	218
September 23, 1984	182	December 31, 1992	225
December 31, 1987	190	Average for 1992	220

Presented below are transactions or account balances and their respective dates.

1. Cash on hand on December 31, 1992.
2. Equipment purchased on March 21, 1965.
3. Common stock issued on December 31, 1964.
4. Land purchased on February 15, 1965.
5. Preferred stock issued on September 23, 1984.
6. Accounts Receivable balance on December 31, 1992.
7. Inventory (LIFO—accumulated evenly throughout 1991).
8. Depreciation expense for 1992 on equipment purchased on March 21, 1965.
9. Sales made during 1992.
10. Investment in common stocks purchased on May 1, 1980.
11. Accounts Payable balance on December 31, 1992.
12. Bonds Payable issued on December 31, 1987, maturing on December 31, 2003.
13. Purchases made during 1992.
14. Interest Expense incurred evenly throughout 1992.
15. Allowance for Uncollectible Accounts balance on December 31, 1992.

Required:
Indicate what the numerator and denominator would be to adjust the above items for general price-level changes for presentation on the 1992 constant dollar financial statements. Sales are made and expenses were incurred evenly during 1992.

 Exercise 16-12 Purchasing Power Gain or Loss on Net Monetary Items
On January 1, 1992, Raist Corporation had net monetary assets of $145,000. During 1992, the following transactions increased or decreased this balance:

1. Equipment was purchased on May 31, 1992 for $25,000 and $10,000 in cash dividends were paid on December 31.
2. Sales of $450,000 were made evenly throughout the period.
3. Purchases of $320,000 were made evenly throughout the period.
4. Selling expenses (excluding depreciation) of $75,000 were incurred evenly throughout the period.

Assume that the Consumer Price Index for all Urban Consumers was as follows for 1992:

January 1, 1992	108
May 31, 1992	117
Average for 1992	125
December 31, 1992	132

Required:
Compute the purchasing power gain or loss on the net monetary items for 1992.

Exercise 16-13 Current Cost Income Statement
Palin Corporation adopted a current cost accounting system in its first year of operation, 1992. At the beginning of 1992, the corporation purchased $75,000 of inventory, and at the end of the year inventory on hand was $41,800 on an historical cost basis and $66,300 on a current cost basis. At the time the inventory was sold, the

current cost of the inventory was $35,100. Sales for the year were $80,000 and operating expenses, exclusive of depreciation were $24,900. Depreciation expense was $8,400 on an historical cost basis and $9,800 on a current cost basis. Holding gains were $42,000.

Required:
Prepare a current cost income statement for 1992 for Palin Corporation.

Exercise 16-14   Current Cost Income Statement and Balance Sheet

Realgar Company is considering the adoption of a current cost accounting system. Presented below is the company's balance sheet at the end of the first year of operations based on historical cost.

```
                    REALGAR COMPANY
                      Balance Sheet
                   December 31, 1992

  Cash        $ 90,000     Accounts payable   $ 68,000
  Inventory    115,000     Common stock        170,000
  Land          60,000     Retained earnings    27,000
              $265,000                        $265,000
```

The following additional information is also available:

1. The cost of goods sold on an historical cost basis is $210,000, on a current cost basis is $228,000.
2. No dividends were paid in 1992.
3. Ending inventory on a current cost basis is $123,000; land on a current cost basis is $80,000.
4. Operating expenses for 1992 were $84,000.
5. Sales for 1992 were $321,000.
6. Holding gains were $46,000.
7. The common stock adjusted for general price level changes is $186,000.

Required:
A. Prepare an income statement for 1992 on:
   1. an historical cost basis.
   2. a current cost basis.
B. Prepare a balance sheet as of December 31, 1992 on a current cost basis.

PROBLEMS

Problem 16-1   Horizontal and Vertical Analysis
The 1991 and 1992 comparative income statements and balance sheets for Nantucket Corporation are as follows:

NANTUCKET CORPORATION
Comparative Income Statements
For the Years Ended December 31, 1992 and 1991

	1992	1991
Sales	$2,619,200	$2,148,200
Less: Cost of goods sold	1,190,000	860,280
Gross Profit	1,429,200	1,287,920
Selling expenses	582,400	429,640
Administrative expenses	315,870	325,000
Interest expense	117,960	64,500
Income tax expense	93,891	140,644
Total Expenses	1,110,121	959,774
Net Income	$ 319,079	$ 328,146
Earnings per share	$ 2.58	$ 2.66

NANTUCKET CORPORATION
Comparative Balance Sheets
December 31, 1992 and 1991

	1992	1991
Assets		
Current Assets		
Cash	$ 728,500	$ 664,000
Marketable securities	487,300	1,344,700
Accounts receivable (net)	3,228,000	2,390,500
Inventory	4,081,000	2,656,200
Prepaid expenses	112,700	159,400
Total Current Assets	8,637,500	7,214,800
Long-term investments	682,000	1,294,900
Plant and equipment (net)	11,860,000	7,835,700
Other assets	285,000	255,600
Total Assets	$21,464,500	$16,601,000
Liabilities		
Current Liabilities		
Accounts payable	$ 3,474,500	$ 2,490,100
Notes payable	2,500,000	1,211,800
Accrued expenses	1,069,700	730,400
Total Current Liabilities	7,044,200	4,432,300
Long-term Liabilities		
Bonds payable	3,843,800	1,012,700
Mortgage payable	2,453,500	3,087,800
Total Long-term Liabilities	6,297,300	4,100,500
Total Liabilities	13,341,500	8,532,800

Stockholders' Equity		
Preferred stock, 5%, $200 par value	463,000	463,000
Common stock, $20 par value	2,290,600	2,290,600
Additional paid-in capital in excess of par value	2,144,400	2,144,400
Retained earnings	3,225,000	3,170,200
Total Stockholders' Equity	8,123,000	8,068,200
Total Liabilities and Stockholders' Equity	$21,464,500	$16,601,000

Required:

A. Prepare common size financial statements for 1992 and 1993.

B. Compute the dollar and percent change for each financial statement item from 1991 to 1992.

C. Comment on any significant changes from 1991 to 1992 revealed by the horizontal analysis. Can you determine whether the changes are favorable or unfavorable? Can you determine any trends from the data?

D. Comment on any significant changes from 1991 to 1992 revealed by the vertical analysis. Can you determine whether the changes are favorable or unfavorable? Can you determine any trends from the data?

Problem 16-2   **Ratio Analysis**

Use the financial data presented in Problem 16-1 to answer the questions and compute the items listed below.

1. Compute the average percentage markup on cost for 1992 and 1991.

2. Compute the average income tax rate for 1992 and 1991.

3. Compute the return on sales for 1992 and 1991.

4. What percent of the total resources available to Nantucket Corporation were invested in plant and equipment in 1992 and in 1991? Did the amount increase or decrease from 1991 to 1992?

5. Compute the debt to total assets ratios for 1992 and 1991. Do they look favorable or unfavorable? Explain.

6. Compute the times interest earned for 1992 and 1991. Does it look favorable or unfavorable? Explain.

7. Compute the 1992 and 1991 return on common stockholders' equity.

8. Compute the book value per share of the common stock at the end of 1992 and 1991.

Problem 16-3   **Ratio Analysis**

Use the financial data presented in Problem 16-1 to compute the ratios requested below.

A. Compute all ratios discussed in the chapter for 1992. Separate the ratios into the three categories: (1) profitability, (2) liquidity, and (3) use of financial leverage. The common stock's market value is $52 per share on December 31, 1992.

B. Comment on any ratios that point out abnormalities or possible danger signs.

Problem 16-4 Computation of Financial Statement Items Using Ratios

The information presented below relates to the Silvart Corporation for the year 1992.

Current assets, January 1, 1992	$ 300
Total assets, January 1, 1992	1,200
Long-term liabilities, January 1, 1992	380
Current ratio, January 1, 1992	3:1
Increase in working capital during 1992	$ 60
Net income as a percentage of ending asset balance for 1992	20%
Total assets, December 31, 1992	$1,500
Noncurrent assets, December 31, 1992	1,100
Long-term liabilities, December 31, 1992	460
Debt to total assets, December 31, 1992	40%

Required:

Calculate each of the missing items requested below. (*Hint:* Reconstruct the balance sheets at the beginning and end of the year to start your solution.)

1. Current liabilities, January 1, 1992.
2. Debt to total assets, January 1, 1992.
3. Net income for 1992.
4. Dividends declared during 1992.
5. Current liabilities, December 31, 1992.

Problem 16-5 Effect of Transactions on Ratios

The Cambridge Corporation completed the transactions listed below in the left-hand column.

Transaction	Ratio
1. Retired bonds payable by issuing common stock.	Return on common stockholders' equity
2. Purchased inventory on account.	Quick ratio
3. Sold inventory for cash.	Current ratio
4. Issued additional shares of common stock for cash.	Debt to total assets
5. Declared a cash dividend on common stock.	Dividend payout
6. Paid the cash dividend declared in No. 5.	Dividend yield
7. Wrote off an uncollectible account receivable to Allowance for Uncollectible Accounts.	Current ratio
8. Collected an account receivable.	Receivable turnover
9. Paid an account payable.	Return on total assets
10. Sold obsolete inventory at cost.	Return on sales
11. Issued a stock dividend on common stock.	Earnings per share
12. Sold inventory on account.	Inventory turnover
13. Purchased machinery on account.	Debt to total assets
14. Retired bonds payable with cash.	Debt to total assets
15. Issued common stock in exchange for land.	Return on common stockholders' equity
16. Paid an account payable.	Quick ratio
17. Declared a cash dividend on common stock.	Current ratio
18. Sold inventory on account.	Quick ratio

19. Collected an account receivable.	Current ratio
20. Sold inventory for cash.	Receivable turnover
21. Paid a cash dividend previously declared.	Current ratio
22. Recorded accrued interest on notes payable.	Return on sales
23. Issued bonds payable for cash.	Return on total assets
24. Issued additional shares of stock for cash.	Earnings per share

Required:
State whether each transaction listed above would cause the ratio listed opposite it to increase, decrease, or remain unchanged.

Problem 16-6   Financial Statement Analysis of Two Companies

The 1992 financial statements of Tucker and Hamilton Companies are presented below in summary form:

	Tucker	Hamilton
Balance Sheet		
Cash	$ 165,000	$ 90,000
Accounts receivable (net)	200,000	140,000
Inventory	535,000	170,000
Plant and equipment (net)	835,000	2,500,000
Other assets	265,000	2,100,000
Total Assets	$2,000,000	$5,000,000
Current liabilities	$ 600,000	$ 335,000
Long-term debt (12%)	335,000	500,000
Capital stock, par $20	800,000	3,330,000
Additional paid-in capital	65,000	500,000
Retained earnings	200,000	335,000
Total Liabilities and Stockholders' Equity	$2,000,000	$5,000,000
Income Statement		
Sales revenue (on credit)	$4,200,000 − (1/3)	$7,500,000 − (1/8)
Cost of goods sold	(2,450,000)	(3,750,000)
Expense (including interest and taxes)	(1,435,000)	(3,000,000)
Net Income	$ 315,000	$ 750,000
Selected Information from the 1991 Balance Sheets		
Accounts receivable (net)	$150,000	$160,000
Inventory	510,000	195,000
Long-term debt	335,000	500,000
Other Relevant Financial Information		
Market price per share of common stock at end of 1992	$ 55	$ 31.50
Average income tax rate	40%	40%
Dividends declared and paid in 1992	$90,000	$765,900

Tucker and Hamilton Companies are in the same line of business and directly compete with each other in a large metropolitan area. They each have been in operation for approximately ten years, and each has experienced a relatively steady growth. The management styles of the two companies differ significantly. Hamilton is an extremely conservative company and Tucker tends to be more progressive and risky in its activities. Neither company is publicly held. Tucker Company has an annual audit performed by an independent CPA firm, but Hamilton does not.

Required:

A. Prepare a schedule that reflects a ratio analysis of each company. Compute as many of the ratios discussed in the chapter as possible. Where information is not provided, use end-of-year balances as estimates of the average balances maintained throughout the year.

B. Prepare common size balance sheets and income statements for 1992 for both companies.

C. A friend of yours has decided to invest in either Tucker or Hamilton Company and will purchase 15% of the common stock of the company she decides to purchase. Prepare a comparative evaluation of the ratio analyses you prepared in requirement (A), and any other information you consider important, to assist your friend in making a decision. She will pay the market price listed above. Also, give your recommendation regarding which stock you think she should purchase, stating the reasons for your choice.

Problem 16-7 Effect of Inventory Valuation Method on Ratio Analysis

Recker Company uses the FIFO method to cost its inventory and Image Company uses the LIFO method. The two companies are *exactly alike* except for the difference in the inventory costing methods used. Costs of inventory for both companies have been rising steadily in recent years and each company has increased its inventory each year. Each company has paid its tax liability in full for the current year and for all previous years. Each company uses the same accounting methods for both financial reporting and income tax reporting.

Required:

For each ratio listed below, indicate which company will report the higher (or better) ratio. If it is not possible to determine this from the information given above, explain why.

1. Current ratio.
2. Quick ratio.
3. Inventory turnover.
4. Debt to total assets.
5. Return on common stockholders' equity.
6. Earnings per share.
7. Times interest earned.
8. Return on sales.

Problem 16-8 Limitations of Ratio Analysis

Todd Company and Brass Company both began operation on January 1, 1992. For illustrative purposes, assume that at that date their financial positions were identical and that their operations during 1992 were also identical. The only difference between the two companies is that they elected to use different accounting methods as shown below:

	Todd Company	Brass Company
Inventory valuation	FIFO	LIFO
Plant and equipment depreciation methods	Straight-line	Accelerated

Financial statements for the two companies prepared at the end of 1992 follow:

Income Statements

	Todd Company	Brass Company
Revenues	$480,000	$480,000
Cost of goods sold	288,000	316,000
Gross profit	192,000	164,000
Interest expense	(18,000)	(18,000)
Depreciation expense	(36,000)	(72,000)
Other expenses	(18,000)	(38,000)
Income tax expense (25%)	(30,000)	(9,000)
Net Income	$ 90,000	$ 27,000

Balance Sheets

	Todd Company	Brass Company
Cash	$ 58,000	$ 58,000
Accounts receivable	146,000	146,000
Inventories	102,000	74,000
Plant and equipment (net)	150,000	114,000
	$456,000	$392,000
Current liabilities	$ 74,000	$ 74,000
Long-term liabilities	110,000	110,000
Common stockholders' equity	272,000	208,000
	$456,000	$392,000

Required:

A. Compute the following ratios for each company.
  1. Return on total assets.
  2. Return on common stockholders' equity.
  3. Return on sales.
  4. Current ratio.
  5. Receivable turnover.
  6. Inventory turnover.
  7. Debt to total assets.
B. Comment on the differences in the ratios caused by the two companies using different accounting methods.

Problem 16-9   Financial Statement Analysis of Two Companies

The 1992 financial statements of Ricter and Staten Companies are presented below in summary form:

	Ricter	Staten
Balance Sheet		
Cash	$ 24,000	$ 46,000
Accounts receivable (net)	72,000	12,000
Inventory	142,000	34,000
Plant & equipment (net)	595,000	174,000
Other assets	184,000	62,000
Total Assets	$1,017,000	$328,000

Current liabilities	$ 140,000	$ 22,000
Long-term debt (15%)	240,000	60,000
Capital stock, $8 par value	575,000	230,000
Paid-in capital in excess of par value	28,000	2,000
Retained earnings	34,000	14,000
Total Liabilities and Stockholders' Equity	$1,017,000	$328,000

Income Statement

Sales revenue (on credit)	$1,100,000(1/3)	$350,000(1/4)
Cost of goods sold	(638,000)	(210,000)
Expenses (including interest and taxes)	(357,000)	(98,000)
Net Income	$ 105,000	$ 42,000

Selected Information from the 1991 Balance Sheets

Accounts receivable (Net)	$ 50,000	$18,000
Long-term debt (15% interest rate)	240,000	60,000
Inventory	120,000	45,000

Other Relevant Financial Information

Market price per share of common stock at end of 1992	$10.50	$8.50
Average income tax rate for 1992	30%	20%
Income tax expense for 1992	$45,000	$10,500
Dividends declared and paid in 1992	$45,000	$12,000

Ricter and Staten Companies operate in the same line of business and in the same state, but in different cities. Each company was founded ten years ago. Both firms have an audit of their financial records by an independent CPA each year. Ricter is audited by a large national accounting firm, while Staten is audited by a local CPA firm located in the city where Staten is located. Both companies have received unqualified opinions for the last five years. Ricter Company wants to borrow $90,000 and Staten Company wants to borrow $35,000. The loans are two-year loans and will be used for "working capital purposes."

Required:
A. Prepare a schedule that reflects a ratio analysis of each company. Compute as many of the ratios discussed in the chapter as possible. Where information is not provided, use end-of-year balances to approximate the average balances maintained throughout the year.
B. Prepare common size balance sheets and income statements for 1992 for both companies.
C. Assume you are the manager of the loan department of a bank located in one of the cities in the state where the two firms operate. You have been given the task of analyzing the situations of the two firms and recommending which loan is preferable. Based on the data given in the problem, and any other financial information you consider important, state your choice between the two companies for the loan and give your reasons.

Problem 16-10 Using Ratios to Analyze Financial Performance

Pleasant Corporation commenced operations on January 2, 1990. Presented next is selected financial information from financial statements prepared at the end of the fiscal years (December 31) 1990, 1991, 1992, and 1993.

	1990	1991	1992	1993
Accounts receivable (net) (credit terms, n/30)	$150,000	$ 190,000	$ 300,000	$ 420,000
Inventory	190,000	225,000	375,000	460,000
Net Sales (2/3 on credit)	750,000	1,125,000	1,875,000	2,250,000
Cost of goods sold	485,000	675,000	1,200,000	1,500,000
Net Income (Loss)	(185,000)	110,000	260,000	185,000

Required:
A. Complete the tabulation format given below. Use end-of-year balances to approximate the average balances maintained throughout the year.
B. Evaluate the results of the first three related ratios identifying the favorable and unfavorable items. Give your recommendations to improve Pleasant's performance.
C. Evaluate the results of the last four related ratios identifying the favorable and unfavorable items. Give your recommendations to improve Pleasant's performance.

Items	1990	1991	1992	1993
1. Return on sales				
2. Gross profit percentage on sales				
3. Expenses, excluding cost of goods sold, as a percent of sales				
4. Inventory turnover				
5. Day's supply in inventory				
6. Receivable turnover ·				
7. Average number of days to collect accounts receivable				

Problem 16-11 Financial Analysis Using Ratios
Below are several financial ratios for the Crispie Company for the three years ended December 31, 1991, 1992, and 1993.

Ratio	1991	1992	1993
1. Current ratio	4:1	3:1	1.5:1
2. Accounts receivable turnover	12.0	9.9	5.8
3. Inventory turnover	3.0	5.5	4.1
4. Return on sales	18.0%	16.0%	12.0%
5. Return on total assets	22.4%	19.6%	17.8%
6. Return on common stockholders' equity	25.0%	27.2%	26.5%
7. Debt to total assets	.162	.357	.378
8. Times interest earned	19.1	6.3	5.4
9. Earnings per share	$.35	$.60	$.75
Additional Data:			
1. Net income	$43,750	$75,000	$93,750
2. Interest expense	6,000	30,000	48,000
3. Tax rate	40%	40%	40%
4. Total assets	$270,000	$600,000	$850,000

5. No dividends were paid during the three-year period.
6. No stock was sold during the three-year period.
7. There is no preferred stock outstanding.
8. The data are based on a 360-day year.
9. Interest is computed at 10% on all liabilities.

Required:

A. Using the data above, compute the following.

    1. Sales for 1991, 1992, and 1993.

    2. Number of shares of common stock outstanding.

    3. The increase in debt in 1992 and 1993.

    4. The average number of days the accounts receivable were outstanding in 1991, 1992, and 1993.

B. Based on the ratios given and computed in requirement (A), evaluate Crispie Company with respect to: liquidity, profitability, and use of financial leverage.

C. In your opinion, what are the two main problems facing Crispie Company in the future? Be specific.

Problem 16-12 Constant Dollar Balance Sheet

Presented below is the December 31, 1992 historical cost post-closing trial balance for Downing Industries, Inc. The company began operations on January 2, 1992. General price level indexes for 1992 are given below.

January 2, 1992	198
February 1, 1992	201
September 1, 1992	207
December 31, 1992	218
Average for 1992	206

DOWNING INDUSTRIES, INC.
Post-Closing Trial Balance
December 31, 1992

Accounts	Debits	Credits
Cash	$ 60,000	
Accounts receivable (net)	140,000	
Long-term investments in equity securities, purchased September 1, 1992	41,000	
Land, purchased February 1, 1992	50,000	
Equipment, purchased January 2, 1992	320,000	
Accumulated depreciation		$ 40,000
Accounts payable		58,000
Notes payable, dated January 2, 1992, due January 2, 1995		138,000
Common stock, no par, sold January 2, 1992		350,000
Retained earnings		25,000
Totals	$611,000	$611,000

A cash dividend of $20,000 was declared and paid on December 31, 1992.

Required:

A. Prepare a December 31, 1992 balance sheet on a constant dollar basis for Downing Industries, Inc.

B. Compute the 1992 constant dollar net income. How does this compare to the 1992 historical cost net income?

Problem 16-13   Current Cost Income Statement and Balance Sheet

Presented below are the 1992 income statement and balance sheet for Majere Corporation prepared on an historical cost basis.

MAJERE CORPORATION
Income Statement
For the Year Ended December 31, 1992

Sales		$924,000
Less: Cost of goods sold		554,000
Gross Profit		370,000
Operating expenses	$200,000	
Depreciation expense	45,000	245,000
Net Income		$125,000
Earnings per share		$1.25

MAJERE CORPORATION
Balance Sheet
As of December 31, 1992

Assets

Current Assets:			
Cash			$ 90,000
Accounts receivable (net)			142,000
Inventory			160,000
Total Current Assets			392,000
Property and Equipment:			
Land		$200,000	
Plant & equipment	$362,000		
Less: Accumulated depreciation	149,000	213,000	
Total Property & Equipment			413,000
Total Assets			$805,000

Liabilities

Current Liabilities:			
Accounts payable			$ 82,000
Wages payable			15,000
Accrued liabilities			8,000
Total Current Liabilities			105,000
Notes payable, due in 1997			80,000
Total Liabilities			185,000

Stockholders' Equity

Common stock, no par, 100,000 shares, issued			
on June 1, 1984		$350,000	
Retained earnings		270,000	
Total Stockholders' Equity			620,000
Total Liabilities and Stockholders' Equity			$805,000

The following information relating to the replacement cost of Majere's assets and the 1992 expenses is available:

Inventory, December 31, 1992	$192,000
Plant and equipment (net)	475,000*
Land	380,000
Cost of goods sold for 1992	627,000
Holding gains for 1992	130,000
Consumer Price Index for All Urban Consumers:	
June 1, 1984 (Date company was formed)	178.2
December 31, 1992	238.6

*Plant and equipment items are depreciated by the straight-line method and have a ten-year remaining life.

Required:
Prepare a 1992 current cost income statement and balance sheet for Majere Corporation.

Problem 16-14 Constant-dollar and Current Cost Financial Statements
An income statement for the year ended December 31, 1992, and a balance sheet on December 31, 1992, for Hawk Company are presented here.

Income Statement

Net sales		$1,400,000
Cost of goods sold		1,050,000
Gross profit		350,000
Expenses:		
Depreciation	$ 24,000	
Other expenses	296,000	320,000
Net Income		$ 30,000

Balance Sheet

Assets		Liabilities & Owners' Equity	
Cash	$104,000	Accounts payable	$137,000
Accounts receivable	160,000	Notes payable	225,000
Inventory	220,000	Common stock	250,000
Plant and equipment (net)	381,000	Retained earnings	253,000
Total	$865,000	Total	$865,000

Hawk Company was formed in 1982, at which time the common stock was issued and the plant and equipment were purchased. Inventory was purchased evenly throughout 1992, and sales were made and cost of goods sold and expenses (other than depreciation) were incurred evenly throughout the year. Additional information:

1. Depreciation expense computed on the basis of plant asset replacement cost is $50,000.
2. The replacement cost of goods sold during 1992 was $1,155,000.
3. A purchasing power gain of $12,000 was computed for 1992.
4. The replacement cost of the December 31, 1992 inventory was $250,000.
5. The replacement cost of plant and equipment on December 31, 1992 was $602,000.

6. Assumed price indexes:

When the company was formed	126
December 31, 1992	190
Average for 1992	184

7. Holding gains were $180,000 in 1992.

Required:
A. Prepare a constant-dollar and a current cost income statement for Hawk Company for the year ended December 31, 1992.
B. Prepare a constant-dollar and a current cost balance sheet at December 31, 1992.

CASE

CASE 16-1   Annual Report Analysis
Refer to the financial statements and related footnotes of BFGoodrich Company in the Appendix to this text.

Required:
A. Compute, or determine from the information provided, the following ratios for 1989.
  1. Return on total assets.
  2. Return on sales.
  3. Earnings per share on net income.
  4. Current ratio.
  5. Inventory turnover.
B. Compute inventories as a percentage of total assets on December 31, 1989 and 1988.
C. Compute the percentage change in sales and net income from 1988 to 1989.

17

INCOME TAXES: AN OVERVIEW

CHAPTER OVERVIEW AND OBJECTIVES

This chapter contains two parts. Part I provides an introduction to the tax system and an overview of federal income tax laws as they pertain to individual taxpayers. Part II discusses the computation of a corporation's income tax liability and the impact of income taxes on business decisions. When completed, you should understand:

1. Some basic features of the federal income tax system.
2. The importance of tax planning.
3. The major components of an individual tax return, such as gross income, deductions from gross income, itemized deductions, personal exemptions, and tax credits.
4. How to compute the tax liability for an individual using the tax rate schedules.
5. The computation of taxable income and income tax liability for a corporation.

Tax payments to various governmental bodies are a significant part of the cost of doing business. Corporations may report a federal income tax expense of up to 34% of income. Because of the magnitude of taxes, few business decisions are made without first considering their tax effect.

The various taxes levied by federal, state, and local governments also have a significant effect on individuals. Federal income tax rates vary according to income. The highest effective tax rate for individuals is 28%. Therefore, planning to minimize the legal tax liability is as vitally important for individuals as it is for businesses.

Because of the complexity of tax rules and regulations, tax specialists are often engaged to determine the tax consequences of various alternatives. To benefit fully from the advice of specialists, decision makers must understand the basic structure of the tax system so that they will be aware of the tax consequences of their decisions.

The basic provisions of the federal income tax laws that affect individuals are discussed in Part I. Part II addresses the income tax laws that affect corporations. The aspects of the federal tax laws covered include the provisions of the Tax Reform Act of 1986. Federal income tax laws are emphasized because they have the greatest impact on both personal and business income. Although state and local tax laws are not covered in this chapter, they should not be ignored in tax planning. They also increase the total tax burden—even though their tax rates are lower than federal rates.

Some provisions of the Tax Reform Act of 1986 are being phased in during the period 1987 through 1991. Thus, the tax rates and the amount of certain items that may be deducted will depend on the tax year. Computations in the illustrations in this chapter and solutions to end-of-chapter materials are prepared based on the tax rates and scheduled amounts provided for use in determining the tax liability in a recent year. Various items are scheduled for change because of indexing for inflation. Because the amounts to be changed are not known, the indexing provisions are ignored.

PART I. INTRODUCTION TO THE FEDERAL TAX SYSTEM AND TAX CONSIDERATIONS FOR INDIVIDUALS

A BRIEF HISTORY OF FEDERAL INCOME TAXATION

Federal income taxes were first collected in this country to help finance the American Civil War. In the late 1800s, however, the Supreme Court ruled the income tax unconstitutional, because it was levied in proportion to the income of individuals, rather than in proportion to a census, as permitted by the Constitution. In 1913, Congress enacted the first permanent income tax law after the Sixteenth Amendment to the Constitution was ratified. The Sixteenth Amendment gave Congress the power to levy and collect taxes on individual incomes without regard to a census. Since then, Congress has enacted numerous other tax laws, most of which are compiled in the **Internal Revenue Code**.

The U.S. Treasury Department, operating through an agency called the Internal Revenue Service (IRS), is responsible for administering and enforcing the income tax laws. The IRS periodically issues regulations that reflect its interpretations of income tax laws. The ultimate interpretation of the tax laws, however, lies with the federal court system, which handles disputes between the IRS and taxpayers.

The original purpose of the income tax was to raise revenue. Although that is still its primary purpose, Congress has also used its taxing authority to accomplish other economic and social goals, such as attaining full employment, providing an incentive to small businesses, offering economic stimulation to certain industries or to the national economy, redistributing national income, and controlling inflation.

SOURCES AND USES OF FEDERAL GOVERNMENT FUNDS

For 1991, the federal government budgeted receipts of $1,170.2 billion, excluding borrowing, and outlays of $1,233.3 billion. The income tax on individuals is the primary source of funds for the U.S. government. It is expected to account for 43 cents of every dollar of receipts for the 1991 fiscal year (see Figure 17-1). Another 11 cents comes from corporate income taxes. The major budget outlays are direct benefit payments to individuals, national defense, and interest payments, in that order.

Figure 17-1
The Budget Dollar

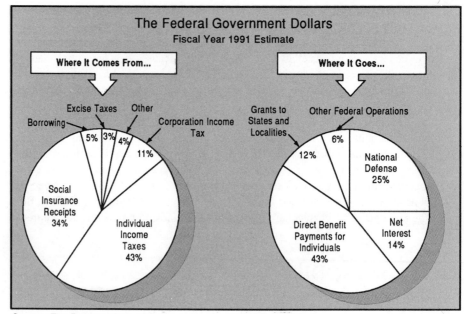

The Federal Government Dollars
Fiscal Year 1991 Estimate

Where It Comes From...

Where It Goes...

Source: The Budget of the U.S. Government—Fiscal Year 1991

SOME FEATURES OF THE FEDERAL INCOME TAX SYSTEM

**Objective 1:
Features of the
federal tax
system**

Before discussing some specific tax provisions related to computing taxable income for individuals and businesses, it is helpful to discuss some basic features of the federal income tax system.

CLASSIFICATIONS OF TAXABLE ENTITIES

For purposes of federal income tax, there are four classifications of taxable entities: individuals, corporations, estates, and trusts. Each must file a tax return and pay taxes on taxable income. Discussion is limited here to individual and corporate taxes. Taxation of estates and trusts is covered in more advanced courses.

Proprietorships and partnerships are recognized as separate business entities for accounting purposes, but they are not subject to tax as separate taxable entities. Instead, a proprietor must include the income or loss from a business in his or her individual tax return. A partnership must file an information return showing the results of operations and a computation of how the income or loss is allocated to each partner. In turn, the partners must include their share of the income or loss in their respective individual tax returns. Remember that the income of a proprietorship or the allocable share of partnership income is taxed directly to the individual owners whether or not it is actually withdrawn from the business.

A corporation, on the other hand, is a separate taxable entity, which must file a tax return and pay a tax on its taxable income. When after-tax income is distributed to stockholders, dividends must be included as income in the stockholders' individual tax returns. This taxing of income when it is earned by the corporation and again when it is distributed to the stockholders has led to the assertion that corporate income is subject to double taxation.

Corporations that satisfy certain criteria can avoid the direct tax on corporate income by electing to be considered an **S corporation** (previously called a Subchapter S

Corporation). An S corporation is treated similarly to a partnership for tax purposes. That is, stockholders report their share of the corporation's income on their individual tax return, whether or not it is distributed to them. However, unlike a partnership, there are limited situations in which an S corporation may be subject to taxation at the corporate level. An S corporation still offers limited liability and other nontax benefits of the corporate form to its stockholders.

An S corporation may have one stockholder, but one of the basic conditions for S corporation treatment is that the number of stockholders cannot exceed a specified maximum (currently 35). Thus, the option generally is available only to relatively small businesses. The requirements to elect and continue to qualify as an S corporation are enforced very literally. It is essential that advice be sought from a tax specialist before deciding to be taxed as an S corporation.

RELATIONSHIP OF TAX LAW TO GENERALLY ACCEPTED ACCOUNTING PRINCIPLES

To accomplish the purposes of raising revenue and implementing certain economic and social policies, Congress has enacted an increasingly complex and ever-changing set of tax laws. Under these laws, taxable income is based on objectives and rules that are sometimes different from the generally accepted accounting principles applied in determining accounting income. Furthermore, a taxpayer is often permitted or required to use one accounting method for tax purposes and another for accounting purposes. For example, a corporation may use the straight-line depreciation method in computing accounting income but an accelerated depreciation method in computing taxable income. As another example, the tax law specifies that an advance receipt of rent is fully taxable in the year of receipt, but for financial reporting purposes rent revenue is reported when it is earned.

In addition, certain types of income are included in accounting income but are excluded from income for tax purposes. For example, interest received on an obligation of a state government and 80% of dividends received from a U.S. corporation are excluded from taxable income of a corporation. Consequently, taxable income often does not equal accounting income.

THE ROLE OF TAX PLANNING

The potential effect of income taxes is usually a significant factor in evaluating alternative courses of action. **Tax planning** or **tax avoidance** involves evaluating the impact of alternative courses of action on taxable income. The objective of tax planning is to structure business and personal transactions in such a way that the tax liability resulting from them is legally minimized.

Objective 2:
The importance
of tax planning

In contrast, **tax evasion** is the deliberate misstatement of a tax liability by failing to report income received or by claiming fraudulent deductions. For example, taxes are evaded when interest, tips, and gains on the sale of investments are not reported, when excessive depreciation is deducted, and when a contribution to a charitable organization is deducted but not made. Tax evasion is illegal, and carries severe penalties.

In most business decisions, however, the tax factor is only one variable and should be considered in the light of other objectives. For example, the tax consequences of incorporating a business will be different from those of forming a partnership, since each alternative will have a different effect on the amount of taxable income allocable to the owners. In addition, the cost of incorporating, the fact that partners have unlimited liability, and the amount of funds needed should also be considered—and may ultimately be more important than the tax implications of the decision. Nevertheless, regardless of other considerations, the goal of tax planning is to choose and implement the alternative that produces the lowest legal tax liability.

THE CHOICE OF ACCOUNTING METHODS

The taxable year in which an item is reported as income or is reported as expense depends on the accounting method adopted—accrual basis or cash basis. Most individual taxpayers use the cash basis of accounting. A taxpayer who engages in a business and also has other sources of income such as salaries, rental income, and interest may elect to report the business income on the accrual basis, but report other income and deductions on a cash basis. The tax law now requires the accrual method to be used by most corporations (other than S corporations) with average annual gross receipts in excess of $5 million.

Accrual Basis

The *accrual basis* of accounting described throughout the preceding chapters is used by many businesses in computing taxable income. In general, for tax purposes, revenues are recognized when a sale is made or when services are rendered, and expenses are recognized when resources are used in the production of revenue, regardless of when cash is received or paid. Any taxpayer (other than an individual whose only income is salary) who maintains a set of accounting records can elect to use the accrual basis for tax purposes. When inventories are a significant factor in the calculation of net income, the accrual basis is required for purchases and sales figures.

Cash Basis

The *cash basis* of accounting—that is, revenues recognized when cash is received and expenses or deductions claimed when cash is paid—is used by most individuals not engaged in a business and by businesses that do not have significant inventories. Therefore, this method is widely used by service businesses.

For income tax purposes, the cash basis is modified in two major ways.

1. Revenue is reported as income when it is available to the taxpayer. In tax terms, this is called **constructive receipt**. For example, interest credited to a savings account is taxable even though it was not withdrawn by the taxpayer.
2. In general, the cost of a depreciable asset is depreciated in accordance with the tax laws.

The cash basis of accounting is simple to use and requires a minimum of record-keeping. For tax purposes, a major advantage is that it gives a taxpayer limited control over the timing of receipts for services performed and payments for deductible items. For example, a doctor may purposely delay billing patients until after year-end, or reasonable amounts of office supplies may be purchased in advance and deducted in the current tax year. Thus, taxable income is reduced in the current period, which results in a lower income tax liability.

Most transactions for a service firm are in cash. However, receipt of noncash items for services rendered must be included at their fair value for income tax purposes. For example, if an accountant agrees to maintain the accounting records and prepare the tax returns for a dentist in exchange for dental care for the accountant's family, both the accountant and the dentist have taxable income resulting from their arrangement. This is measured by the fair value of the services received by each party. The dentist also has a deduction for the accounting services received. If either the dentist or the accountant fails to report the value of the services received, he or she could be charged with income tax evasion and be subject to possible penalties.

TAX CONSIDERATIONS FOR INDIVIDUAL TAXPAYERS

FILING A FEDERAL INCOME TAX RETURN

In general, every U.S. citizen or resident who earns taxable income in excess of some specified amount must file a return. An individual who had income tax withheld from his or her salary, but whose income was not enough to be required to file a return, should file a return to get a refund of the tax withheld.

When to File

Ordinarily, tax returns for individuals must be filed within 3½ months after the close of the tax year. Most individuals are on a calendar year basis, and therefore must file their individual returns by April 15. However, any taxpayer who keeps adequate records may request to be on a fiscal year.

Filing Status

The filing status is one of the first things a taxpayer must determine. There are five possibilities.

1. Single.
2. Married filing jointly.
3. Married filing separately.
4. Head of household.
5. Qualifying widows or widowers (technically, surviving spouse).

The first three categories are self-explanatory. In general, a head of household is an unmarried taxpayer who provides more than half the cost of maintaining a home for certain qualified persons such as an unmarried child or any dependent of the taxpayer. The home may be a separate residence if provided to a dependent parent of the taxpayer. A qualifying widow or widower may always file a joint return in the year of death of a spouse and may be able to use joint return tax rates for up to two years following the date of death if a dependent child lives with the widow or widower.

The filing status determines the amount of certain deductions from income and the tax rate schedule for computing the correct tax. A taxpayer should normally select the appropriate filing status that results in the least amount of tax.

Basic Format for Computing Income Tax Liability

Tax returns are filed on forms provided by the federal government. Although the listing of specific data on a tax form varies from time to time, the general approach to computing taxable income for an individual taxpayer is shown in Figure 17-2.

Objective 3: Components of a tax return

Conceptually, the Internal Revenue Code defines gross revenue and deductions as shown in Figure 17-2. That is, revenues are defined as gross income, and expenses incurred to produce the gross income are subtracted to arrive at adjusted gross income. On the tax forms, however, some revenue and related expenses are reported on separate schedules and the net income or loss is carried forward in the computation of

Figure 17-2
Determining Taxable
Income for an Indi-
vidual Taxpayer

Income from all sources		$44,670
Less: Exclusions from income		5,070
Gross income for tax purposes		39,600
Less: Deductions from gross income		4,000
Adjusted gross income		35,600
Less: Deductions from adjusted gross income		
Itemized deductions	$16,228	
Exemptions ($2,000 × 4)	8,000	24,228
Taxable income		$11,372
Gross tax liability from tax rate schedules		
(or tax table)		$ 1,706
Less: Tax credits	$ 100	
Tax prepayments	1,750	1,850
Net tax liability (or refund)		$ (144)

adjusted gross income. For example, expenses of a trade or business operated by an individual taxpayer are subtracted from revenues earned from the trade or business in Schedule C, and rent and royalty income and related expenses are reported in Schedule E.

Note that Figure 17-2 shows three types of subtractions in deriving the net tax liability: exclusions, deductions, and credits. Exclusions are items omitted by law from the tax computation. In most cases, exclusions are not listed in the tax return because they are not part of the tax concept of income. Deductions are items that reduce the amount of income subject to tax. Tax credits are direct reductions in the amount of tax liability.

INCOME, EXCLUSIONS, AND GROSS INCOME

The starting point for computing an individual's tax liability is the identification of all income, from any source, that is associated with the current tax year. Not all income is included in the tax concept of gross income. For tax purposes, gross income is defined as all income not specifically excluded by statutory law. An item of income that is not included in gross income is called an exclusion. Figure 17-3 lists examples of items to be included in gross income and items excluded from gross income.

DEDUCTIONS FROM GROSS INCOME

There are two types of deductions in Figure 17-2: (1) deductions from gross income to arrive at adjusted gross income, and (2) deductions from adjusted gross income to arrive at taxable income (i.e., the amount taxes are paid on). This distinction is important because certain deductions made from adjusted gross income are limited to the amount in excess of a percentage of adjusted gross income. Such deductions are also deductible only if the total of all allowable deductions exceeds a certain specified amount, as discussed later in this chapter.

An item can be deducted from gross income only if it is specifically authorized by the Internal Revenue Code. In addition, a taxpayer must maintain adequate records to support any deduction claimed. Tax rules require the maintenance of adequate

These items represent general rules and are subject to certain exceptions.

Items Excluded from Gross Income	**Items Included in Gross Income**
Interest on state and municipal bonds	Wages and salaries
Certain life insurance proceeds	Bonuses
Scholarship for tuition and course-required equipment	Interest on savings account
Group health and accident insurance premiums paid by an employer	Severance pay
	Gambling gains
	Corporate cash dividends
	Tips for services rendered
Gifts	Rents received on rental property
Inheritance	Royalties
Accident and disability benefits	Vacation payments
Return of capital, as opposed to income	Business income from sole proprietorship
Dividends paid entirely in stock of the corporation.	Allocable share of partnership or S corporation income
	Prizes
	Proceeds from lotteries
	Gains from sale or exchange of real estate, investments, and other property
	Unemployment compensation
	Social security benefits in excess of limit
	Retirement pay in excess of cost

Figure 17-3
Examples of Items Excluded and Included in Income

written records to support business-related deductions. Failure to keep them will result in the disallowance of the deduction by the IRS. The major authorized deductions from gross income to arrive at adjusted gross income are:

1. **Expenses of a trade or business.** All ordinary and necessary expenses paid or incurred during the taxable year in carrying on a trade or business are deductible. In general, the expenses included in this category are those that appear on the income statement of a business prepared in accordance with generally accepted accounting principles.
2. **Expenses for the production of rental and royalty income.** A taxpayer may deduct ordinary and necessary expenses associated with producing rental and royalty income. For example, although the expenses incurred in the management and maintenance of a single rental property are not deductible from gross income as a business expense—because such limited activity does not constitute a trade or business—they are deductible if related to producing rental income.
3. **Contributions to retirement accounts.** An individual can accumulate funds for retirement in several types of retirement plans. Two common plans are Individual Retirement Accounts (IRAs) and Keogh plans.

    IRA—An individual can make a deductible contribution of the lesser of $2,000 or 100% of compensation if one of the following two tests are met.

a. The individual, or neither spouse in the case of filing a joint return, is not a participant in an employer maintained pension plan, or

b. Adjusted gross income does not exceed $40,000 for a married couple filing a joint return or $25,000 for a single taxpayer.

The maximum deduction is $2,250 if a spousal IRA is established for a non-working spouse.

Under the second test, the deductible IRA contribution is phased out for joint filers with adjusted gross income between $40,000 and $50,000 ($25,000 and $35,000 for a single taxpayer). No deduction is allowed if adjusted gross income exceeds $50,000 ($35,000). The deduction limit is computed by the following formula.

$$\frac{\$10,000 - \text{Excess Adjusted Gross Income}}{\$10,000} \times \begin{array}{l}\text{Maximum} \\ \text{Allowable} \\ \text{Deduction}\end{array}$$

The results may be rounded to the next highest $10. To illustrate, assume that a married couple files jointly and has an adjusted gross income of $46,380. Each spouse earns more than $2,000 and one is a participant in a pension plan at work. The deduction for each spouse is computed as follows.

$$\frac{\$10,000 - (\$46,380 - \$40,000)}{\$10,000} \times \$2,000 = \$724 \ (\$730 \text{ rounded})$$

Taxpayers can make nondeductible IRA contributions up to the deduction limits to the extent they are not eligible to make deductible contributions. In the case above, each spouse could make a nondeductible contribution of $1,270 ($2,000 − $730). Earnings on such accounts are not taxed until withdrawn.

Keogh plan—A self-employed individual can contribute a limited amount of his or her income to a Keogh plan. The deduction is 25% of self-employment income after deducting the Keogh contribution, up to a maximum contribution of $30,000. This amount is now indexed for inflation. This deduction is available to the self-employed, as well as to an employee who receives outside income from moonlighting, such as providing consulting, computer programming, and freelance writing services.

4. **Other deductions.** Deductions are permitted for losses from the sale or exchange of property used in a trade or business or for the production of income, alimony payment, and disability income. Generally, each item must satisfy some criterion before it is deductible, and limits are usually placed on the amount of each item that can be deducted.

DEDUCTIONS FROM ADJUSTED GROSS INCOME

The two categories of allowable deductions from adjusted gross income are deductions for (1) specified expenses and (2) personal and dependent exemptions. In the case of specified expenses, taxpayers have the option of reducing their adjusted gross income by either (1) the amount of a specified standard deduction, or (2) the amount of their itemized deductions. The taxpayer should elect whichever alternative produces the greatest deduction.

Standard Deduction

Deductions for personal, living, or family expenses are disallowed except those expressly provided for in the Internal Revenue Code. Taxpayers are permitted to deduct a specific **standard deduction** for personal expenses—that is, an amount of income on which no tax will be paid. The standard deduction amounts scheduled in a recent year are as follows.

Married persons filing a joint return	$5,000
Married person filing a separate return	2,500
Single individual	3,000
Head of household	4,400

The standard deduction is now indexed for inflation.

A married individual who is age 65 or older or is blind is allowed an additional standard deduction of $600 ($1,200 for an individual who is 65 or older and blind). An additional standard deduction of $750 is allowed for an unmarried individual who is age 65 or older or blind ($1,500 if both).

Itemized Deductions

Certain categories of expenses, called **itemized deductions**, are deductible by law. If the total of a taxpayer's itemized deductions is in excess of the applicable standard deduction, the taxpayer should itemize. If deductions are itemized, adequate records must be maintained to support them.

The tax laws specify the circumstances under which an item qualifies as an itemized deduction and any limitations of the amount that may be deducted. The categories of itemized deductions are presented here.

1. **Medical and dental expenses.** Medical and dental expenses of the taxpayer and his or her dependents that exceed 7.5% of adjusted gross income are deductible.
2. **Taxes.** Federal taxes do not qualify as an itemized deduction, but many state and local taxes do. For example, state and local income taxes, real estate taxes, and personal property taxes based on the value of the property are deductible. However, state and local taxes on sales, gasoline, liquor, tobacco, and most types of license fees (such as marriage, driver's, and pet licenses) are not deductible.
3. **Interest.** Generally, interest paid on debt secured by a principal home or second home is deductible. This includes first and second mortgages, home equity loans, and lines of credit. Consumer interest, sometimes called personal interest, related to purchases using credit cards and nonbusiness auto loans, is not deductible. Elimination of interest on consumer loans is being phased in over five years as shown in the following schedule.

Year	% of consumer interest disallowed
1987	35
1988	60
1989	80
1990	90
1991	100

   Interest incurred to acquire or continue to carry property held for investment purposes is deductible only to the extent of net income generated from investment activities. Treasury regulations provide for detailed tracking of the use of loan proceeds to determine the nature of the interest payment.
4. **Charitable contributions.** Cash contributions to public charities, such as religious, educational, scientific, or literary organizations, are deductible with a maximum deduction of 50% of adjusted gross income. Noncash gifts are subject to other limitations and substantiation of the value claimed as a deduction.

5. **Casualty or theft losses.** Uninsured casualty and theft losses in excess of $100 per loss are deductible to the extent they exceed, in the aggregate, 10% of adjusted gross income. A casualty loss is the damage, destruction, or loss of property resulting from an identifiable event that is sudden and either unexpected or unusual, such as a hurricane, flood, tornado, fire, lightning, or earthquake. Automobile accidents also qualify. However, gradual damage to property caused by termites, moths, or other insects does not qualify as a casualty loss. To illustrate the computation of the deductible loss, assume that a taxpayer with an adjusted gross income of $22,800 had uninsured stocks and bonds that originally cost $9,000, but now had a current value of $8,000, stolen. (For personal use property, the loss is limited to the lesser of the taxpayer's basis or fair market value.) The theft deduction is computed as follows.

Amount of loss	$8,000
Nondeductible amount	100
	7,900
Less: Limitation ($22,800 × .10)	2,280
Deduction	$5,620

6. **Moving expenses.** Expenses incurred to move in connection with beginning a new job are deductible to the extent not reimbursed by the employer. The move must result in the distance from the old residence to the new job site exceeding the distance from the old job site to the old residence by at least 35 miles. If the move is for a first job, the job site must be at least 35 miles from the old residence. In addition, the taxpayer must generally be employed for a minimum of 39 of the first 52 weeks following the move. Certain limitations apply to expenses other than for moving personal effects and travel costs for the taxpayer and his or her family.

7. **Miscellaneous deductions.** This category is a catchall for all allowable expenses related primarily to a taxpayer's employment or the management of income-producing assets. With limited exceptions, only the aggregate amount of the deductions in excess of 2% of adjusted gross income is deductible. Miscellaneous deductions include:

Employee business expenses, for example, travel, entertainment, and meals (meals and entertainment expenses are generally limited to 80% of actual expenses).

Union dues.

Safety equipment and protective clothing such as hard hats.

Small tools and supplies needed on the job.

Uniforms which are not suitable for every day use, but are required by an employer.

Physical examinations required by an employer.

Educational expenses required by an employer or by law or to improve skills in an existing trade or business (not to prepare for a new job).

Rental charges on a safety deposit box used to keep records of income-producing properties.

Fees paid to have a tax return prepared and for income tax advice.

Subscriptions to professional journals.

IRA custodian fees.

Legal and accounting fees related to management of income-producing assets.

Dues to professional organizations.

Investment counseling fees.

Exemptions

A taxpayer is entitled to deduct $2,000 (the $2,000 is now adjusted for inflation) from adjusted gross income for each personal exemption claimed. A separate **exemption** is allowed for the taxpayer, for his or her spouse if a joint return is filed, and for each dependent. An exemption cannot be claimed by a dependent child on the child's return if the child is eligible to be claimed as a dependent on the parent's return. A taxpayer claiming a dependent who is over five years old must report the dependent's Social Security number on his or her return.

To qualify as a dependent, a person must satisfy all of the following tests.

1. Has received over half of his or her support from the taxpayer.
2. Is closely related (relations are explicitly defined in the tax law) to the taxpayer or has been a member of the taxpayer's household for the entire year.
3. Has less than $2,000 in gross income for the year. (This test does not have to be satisfied if a taxpayer's child was under 19 at the end of the year or was under 24 and a full-time student for some part of each of five calendar months during the year.)
4. Is a citizen of the United States or a resident of the United States, Canada, or Mexico.
5. Has not filed a joint return with his or her spouse, if married, unless the sole purpose of filing is to receive a refund of withheld tax.

COMPUTING THE TAX LIABILITY

Once the taxpayer's income is computed, the next step is to compute the gross tax liability from the tax rate schedule. Tax rate schedules are provided for a single taxpayer, married taxpayers filing joint returns (including surviving spouses), married taxpayers filing separate returns, and a head of household.

**Objective 4:
Computing the
tax liability for
an individual**

Tax Rate Schedule

The appropriate tax rate schedule used to determine the gross tax liability depends on the taxpayer's filing status and the amount of taxable income. Tax rate schedules for a recent year are shown in Figure 17-4.

To illustrate the use of the tax rate schedules, assume that Bill and Susan Johnson, who have two children, filed a joint return for 1992. Their taxable income was computed as follows.

Adjusted gross income		$73,020
Itemized deductions	$14,600	
Personal exemptions (4 × $2,000)	8,000	22,600
Taxable income		$50,420

Figure 17-4
Tax Rate Schedules

Single taxpayers

Taxable Income	Tax Liability
$–0– to $17,850	15% of taxable income
17,850 to 43,150	$2,677.50 + 28% of amount over $17,850
43,150 to 89,560	$9,761.50 + 33%* of amount over $43,150
89,560 to —	28% of taxable income†

Married taxpayers filing jointly

Taxable Income	Tax Liability
$–0– to $29,750	15% of taxable income
29,750 to 71,900	$4,462.50 + 28% of amount over $29,750
71,900 to 149,250	$16,264.50 + 33%* of amount over $71,900
149,250 to —	28% of taxable income†

*Includes surtax of 5% designed to phase out the benefit of the 15% bracket for high income taxpayers.
†Personal exemptions are phased out for income in excess of $89,560 ($149,250 married filing jointly) by applying a 5% surtax until all of the benefits of personal exemptions have been totally offset.

From married taxpayer filing jointly data in Figure 17-4, the Johnson's gross tax liability is computed as follows.

Tax on first $29,750	$ 4,463
Tax on the remaining income ($50,420 − $29,750 = $20,670;	
$20,670 × .28)	5,788
Gross tax liability	$10,251

The maximum percentage paid by the taxpayer—28% in this case—is referred to as the **marginal tax rate** because it is the rate applied on the next dollar of income. The marginal tax rate is often used by taxpayers to identify their income tax bracket. However, because lower income levels are taxed at lower rates, the effective or average tax rate for the Johnsons is 20.3% ($10,251 ÷ $50,420).

One can see the progressive nature of the income tax rates from the tax rate schedules. A progressive tax is one in which the tax rate becomes higher as the amount of taxable income increases.

Surtax

The rate schedules include a 5% surtax on high income taxpayers. High income taxpayers are defined as married couples filing a joint return with taxable income over $71,900 and single taxpayers reporting over $43,150 of taxable income. The rationale for the surtax is that high income taxpayers do not need the benefit of the lower tax rate (15%) on the lower bracket of taxable income. For a married couple, the tax benefit from use of the lower tax bracket is equal to 13% (28% − 15%) of $29,750, or $3,868. The 5% surtax will apply to taxable income in excess of $71,900, but is phased out at $149,250. Applying a 5% surtax to this $77,350 income range will increase the tax liability by $3,868, exactly offsetting the benefit of the 15% bracket.

The appearance is that the top rate is 33%. However, as a practical matter, the effective tax rate will not exceed 28%. To illustrate, assume that a married couple reported taxable income of $149,250. The tax from the schedule is as follows.

Tax on first $71,900	$16,265
Excess over $71,900 [($149,250 − $71,900) × .33]	25,526
Tax liability	$41,791

The effective tax rate is then computed as follows.

$$\frac{\$41,791}{\$149,250} = 28\%$$

There is also an additional 5% adjustment related to the deduction for personal exemptions on taxable income in excess of $149,250 for a married couple filing a joint return ($89,560 for a single taxpayer). This surtax is designed to eliminate the tax benefit realized from claiming a personal exemption deduction. Discussion of this provision is beyond the scope of this text.

TAX CREDITS

A tax credit is a reduction in the amount of tax liability computed on taxable income. A tax credit is more beneficial to a taxpayer than a deduction, because it is a direct dollar-for-dollar reduction in the tax liability. In contrast, a deduction reduces the amount of income subject to tax resulting in a tax reduction equal to the amount of the deduction times the taxpayer's marginal tax rate. Income tax credits are available to the elderly, for child care while the taxpayer or spouse is at work, for payments of income taxes to foreign countries, and for taxpayers who have earned income below $17,000. Generally, specific limitations apply to each of these income tax credits.

TAX PREPAYMENTS

During the tax year, income tax is withheld by employers from the salaries and wages paid to employees, as noted in Chapter 11. The amount withheld is based on the employee's earnings for the year, his or her marital status and the number of exemptions claimed by the employee. The amount withheld must be reported to an employee on a Form W-2 by January 31 for the preceding calendar year.

Taxpayers who receive income not subject to withholding generally must estimate their tax for the year and make quarterly installment payments to the IRS. The sum of the amounts are subtracted from the gross tax liability to determine the amount of unpaid taxes due or the refund claimed at the time a tax return is filed. Failure to make estimated tax payments can result in the assessment of a nondeductible penalty. The penalty may be avoided if the taxpayer has withholdings and estimated payments equal to the lesser of 90% of the current year or 100% of the prior year tax liability.

THE IMPORTANCE OF THE MARGINAL TAX RATE

When considering the various alternatives affecting taxable income, it is important for individual taxpayers and other taxable entities to use their marginal tax rates in assessing the impact of taxes on their decisions. Assume, for example, that a married couple with a taxable income of $54,620 is considering whether to invest $10,000 in a municipal bond paying 9% nontaxable interest or a corporate bond paying 12% interest. The after-tax cash flow from each investment can be computed as follows.

	Invest in Municipal Bonds	Invest in Corporate Bonds
Cash flow from interest	$900	$1,200
Less: Increase in cash outflow for taxes*	–0–	336
Net after-tax cash flow	$900	$ 864

$$\begin{array}{ccc} \text{*Marginal} & \text{Increase in} & \text{Increase in cash} \\ \text{tax} \times & \text{taxable} = & \text{outflow of taxes} \\ \text{rate} & \text{income} & \end{array}$$

Investment in municipal bonds	Investment in corporate bonds
Interest of $900 is nontaxable income (28% × –0–) = –0–	Interest of $1,200 is taxable income (28% × $1,200) = $336

(The marginal tax rate for a married couple filing jointly with taxable income between $29,750 and $71,900 is 28% from Figure 17-4.)

Although the interest rate is higher on the corporate bonds, the after-tax cash flow is greater when the $10,000 is invested in municipal bonds. The increase in taxes of $336 is verified here.

	No Additional Investment	Invest in Corporate Bonds	Difference
Taxable income before interest	$54,620	$54,620	$ –0–
Taxable interest	–0–	1,200	1,200
Taxable income	$54,620	$55,820	$1,200
Income tax			
Income tax on first $29,750 (from Figure 17-4)	$ 4,463	$ 4,463	$ –0–
Income tax on amount over $29,750			
($54,620 – $29,750) × 28%	6,964		
($55,820 – $29,750) × 28%		7,300	+ 336
Total income taxes	$11,427	$11,763	+$ 336

A similar analysis can be performed in assessing the net cost of a tax deduction that results in a decrease in taxable income. For example, the net cost of a $10,000 contribution is $7,200 for a married couple with taxable income over $149,250 when the marginal tax rate is 28% as shown in Figure 17-4.

Because of the existence of complex phase-in provisions of the 1986 Tax Reform Act, it is generally advisable to compute the tax liability with and without incremental income or deductions to determine the marginal tax liability. A variety of provisions can result in an effective marginal tax rate other than 28%.

CAPITAL GAINS AND LOSSES

Capital gains or losses are recognized gains or losses on the sale of capital assets. **Capital assets** are defined in the Internal Revenue Code as any item of property *except* the following items.

1. Inventories. (This includes any property held primarily for sale to customers in the ordinary course of a trade or business.)
2. Trade accounts and notes receivable.
3. Land, buildings, and equipment used in a trade or business.
4. Certain intangible assets such as copyrights and literary works or artistic compositions held by the individual whose efforts created the work.

Thus, most property held for personal use or investment is a capital asset. Stock and bond investments, a personal residence, an automobile, and a coin collection are examples of capital assets that may be held by an individual. Although depreciable and real property used in a trade or business (item 3) are not capital assets, gains from the sale of such assets may be treated as capital gains under certain conditions.

When a capital asset is sold, the capital gain or loss reported is the difference between the selling price and the basis of the asset. Determining the basis of the asset for tax purposes may be complex, but, in general, it is the asset's cost adjusted for depreciation taken on the asset in computing taxable income.

A gain or loss on the sale of a capital asset is classified as short term or long term. The classification depends on the date that the asset was acquired and the length of the time it was held. Before 1976, if a capital asset was held for longer than six months, the gain or loss was classified as a **long-term capital gain** or a **long-term capital loss**. A gain or loss from the sale of a capital asset held less than six months was classified as a **short-term capital gain** or a **short-term capital loss**. In 1976, the holding period for long-term capital gains treatment was extended from six months to twelve months. As part of the 1984 Tax Reform Act, the holding period was reduced to six months for assets acquired after June 22, 1984. The holding period is twelve months for assets purchased after 1987.

A detailed discussion of the different tax treatments that may apply to the sale of a capital asset is beyond the scope of this book. However, in tax planning, an individual taxpayer should recognize that the tax consequences are significantly affected by the classification of a gain or loss as short term or long term. Capital gains are fully taxable as ordinary income, whereas capital losses are offset against capital gains or ordinary income dollar for dollar. A maximum of $3,000 of capital losses can be offset against income in any one year. Any remaining losses may be carried forward to offset income in future years. A complex procedure of netting gains and losses determines whether a net gain or loss exists for a taxable year. Year-end tax planning often includes triggering capital gains and losses to take maximum advantage of the netting rule. With the enactment of the Tax Reform Act of 1986, net capital gains are now taxed the same as ordinary income. However, Congress specifically retained the definitions of capital assets and classifications as long or short term to permit favorable treatment for long-term gains to be reinstated if marginal tax rates are raised in the future.

COMPUTATION OF INCOME TAX FOR A JOINT RETURN

To illustrate the computation of the federal income tax, assume that Jenny and Harry Matheson, ages 34 and 32, respectively, file a joint tax return. They have two children who qualify as dependents. Jenny Matheson, a real estate agent, earned commissions of $6,000 and made quarterly estimated federal income tax payments totaling $900 during the year. Jenny's employer does not have a retirement plan established for employees. Harry Matheson earned $25,000 during the year working as an accountant and had $950 withheld from his salary for federal income taxes. Even though his employer has a retirement plan for employees, they each contributed $2,000 to an individual retirement account. (Because their adjusted gross income is below $40,000, the IRA contributions are fully deductible.) During the year, the Mathesons sold a coin collection for a $10,000 gain, which they had held for five years, and also disposed of a common stock investment at a $5,000 loss, which they had held for five months. Dividends in the amount of $2,900 were received on a jointly owned stock investment. Interest of $1,070 on municipal bonds was received during the year and interest of $700 was credited to their savings account and was available for withdrawal. The itemized deductions and computation of tax shown in Figure 17-5 are determined on the basis of our previous discussion. In Figure 17-5, the information is presented in condensed form. In practice, some of the information would have been shown in more detail and on separate schedules.

PART II. TAX CONSIDERATIONS FOR CORPORATIONS

Objective 5: Computing the tax liability for a corporation

A corporation is a separate taxable entity that must file tax returns and pay taxes on its taxable income. Corporate returns are due within 2½ months after the close of the corporation's fiscal year. Some corporations, such as S corporations and charitable organizations organized as corporations, are generally exempt by law from taxation. Other corporations, such as banks and insurance companies, are subject to special tax regulations. For corporations without special regulations, the computation of taxable income centers around an income statement similar to the one prepared for external reporting. However, computing taxable income can still be very complex. For this reason, only some of the major distinguishing features of the corporate tax system are discussed here.

Fewer steps are involved in determining the taxable income of a corporation than in determining that of an individual, because there is no distinction between gross income and adjusted gross income for a corporation. Furthermore, a tax return for a corporation does not contain itemized deductions or personal exemptions, and there is no deduction for corporations comparable to the standard deduction. The steps for determining the corporate tax liability are shown in Figure 17-6.

Gross income:			
Salary			$25,000
Real estate commissions			6,000
Dividend income			2,900
Capital gains:			
Net long-term capital gains		$10,000	
Net short-term capital losses		(5,000)	
Net long-term capital gain			5,000
Interest received or credited to account:			
Savings accounts			700
(Interest on municipal bonds of $1,070 is excluded.)			
Gross income for tax purposes			39,600
Deductions from gross income:			
IRA contributions			4,000
Adjusted gross income			35,600
Deductions from adjusted gross income:			
Itemized deductions:			
Medical and dental expenses (doctors' fees, dentists' fees, nursing services, hospital care, X-rays, medical insurance premiums, prescription drugs, eyeglasses, ambulance service, lab fees, crutches, and physical therapist)	$4,750		
Less: 7.5% of adjusted gross income	2,670	2,080	
Taxes: Real estate		2,750	
State and local income taxes		1,180	
Personal property		510	
Interest on home mortgage		6,910	
Charitable contributions		2,790	
Miscellaneous (dues to professional organizations and safety deposit box rental)	720		
Less: 2% of adjusted gross income	712	8	
Total itemized deductions		16,228	
Personal exemptions (4 × $2,000)		8,000	
Total deductions from adjusted gross income			24,228
Taxable income			$11,372
Computation of federal income tax (see Figure 17-4 for tax rate schedules) $11,372 × .15 =			$ 1,706
Less: Prepayments—Federal income tax withheld		$ 950	
Estimated quarterly tax payments		900	1,850
Refund due to taxpayer			$ 144

Figure 17-5

Computation of Federal Income Tax—Jenny and Harry Matheson, Joint Return

Figure 17-6
Steps in Computing
Corporate Tax Lia-
bility

Total revenues	$892,000
Less: Exclusions from revenue	38,000
Gross income	854,000
Less: Deductions from gross income	718,000
Taxable income	$136,000
Tax liability computed from tax rate schedule (Figure 17-7)	
First $100,000	$ 22,250
($136,000 − $100,000) × .39	14,040
Total tax	36,290
Less: Tax credits	200
Net tax liability	$ 36,090

TOTAL REVENUES AND EXCLUSIONS

The first step in the computation of taxable income for a corporation is determining the corporation's total revenue and gains recognized during the year. Examples are revenues from the sale of goods or the performance of services, interest and dividends on investments, gains from the sale of assets, rental receipts, and royalties. In most cases, revenues recognized for accounting purposes are also considered revenues for tax purposes. There are, however, some exceptions. For example, interest on obligations of state and local governments and life insurance proceeds received by the corporation on the death of an insured employee or officer are reported in the income statement but are excluded from gross income for tax purposes.

DEDUCTIONS FROM GROSS INCOME

Most deductions from gross income are the usual expenses incurred in operating the corporation and producing revenue. These include cost of goods sold, selling expenses, and administrative expenses. Certain other deductions and limitations on some expenses are specified by law and result in a difference between accounting income and taxable income. Some of the more common differences are as follows.

1. **Capital gains and losses.** A corporation's capital losses cannot be offset against ordinary income; capital losses can be used to offset capital gains only. The unused portion of the loss can be carried back to the three years preceding the year of the loss and carried forward five years following the loss year. However, the loss carryback and carryforward can be offset against capital gains only. If carried back, the tax liability for that year is recomputed and a refund claim filed with the IRS for the difference between the original tax and the recomputed tax. Short-term capital gains are included in taxable income and subject to taxation at the regular tax rates. Long-term capital gains are taxed at the regular corporate rate or 34%, whichever is lower.

2. **Dividends-received deduction.** A corporation is permitted a deduction of 80% of dividends received from shares of stock in other U.S. corporations. The intent

of this deduction is to reduce the effects of taxing three entities for the same income. That is, if the deduction were not permitted, the distributing corporation would have already paid a tax on its net income, the dividend would be taxed to the receiving corporation, and when distributed to the stockholders of the receiving corporation would have another layer of tax imposed. There is a 100% dividend-received deduction for dividends received from a member of a corporation's affiliated group.

3. **Net operating loss.** Subject to certain restrictions, a corporation is permitted to offset losses of a particular year against income of other years. Losses may be carried back to the three preceding years. The tax is recomputed and the difference between this amount and the original tax is refunded to the corporation. Any unused loss may be carried forward successively to the next 15 years following the loss year and deducted from income. A corporation may elect to forgo the carryback and only carry the loss forward.

4. **Charitable contributions.** A corporation may deduct charitable contributions but the amount that can be deducted is limited to 10% of taxable income before deducting any contributions and the 80% dividend-received deduction. Contributions in excess of the 10% limitation may be carried forward to the five succeeding years, subject to the 10% limitation in each year.

5. **Expenses not deductible.** Premiums paid for employees' life insurance policies under which the corporation is the named beneficiary and the amortization of goodwill are not deductible for tax purposes. (Goodwill is not deductible by other taxable entities either, because it has no ascertainable useful life.)

COMPUTING THE TAX LIABILITY

The tax liability is computed by applying the appropriate tax rate to the taxable income. The current corporation income tax rate structure is shown in Figure 17-7. The corporate tax is also a progressive tax. To illustrate the use of this schedule, a corporation with reported taxable income of $80,000 in 1990 would compute its tax liability as follows.

Tax on first $75,000	$13,750
Tax on excess ($80,000 − $75,000 = $5,000 × 34%)	1,700
Total tax liability	$15,450

Figure 17-7
Tax Rate Schedule for Corporations

Tax Years Beginning After July 1, 1987

Taxable Income	Tax Liability
$–0– to $50,000	15% of taxable income
50,000 to 75,000	$ 7,500 + 25% of amount over $50,000
75,000 to 100,000	$13,750 + 34% of amount over $75,000
100,000 to 335,000	$22,250 + 39%* of amount over $100,000
335,000 to—	34% of taxable income

*Includes surtax of 5% designed to phase out the benefit of lower bracket taxation.

Like individuals, a corporation may qualify for certain tax credits to be deducted from the gross tax liability and must pay estimated taxes in quarterly installments.

TAX PLANNING AND BUSINESS DECISIONS

As noted before, income taxes have a significant effect on most business decisions and are often the most influential factor in a business decision. Because of the complexity of the tax laws, most firms engage a tax specialist to review the tax implications of alternative courses of action and provide guidance in arranging business transactions so that taxes are minimized legally. The following are some examples of the tax impact on alternative approaches to various business problems.

TAX IMPLICATIONS OF THE CHOICE OF BUSINESS ORGANIZATION

One of the first decisions an owner or owners of a business must make at the time of organization is whether to operate as a corporation, an S corporation, a proprietorship, or a partnership. Because of the difference between individual and corporate tax rates and because other tax provisions vary with the legal form of business, the tax consequences should be carefully considered in making this decision. The three types of businesses are taxed as follows.

Corporations. A corporation is a separate taxable entity and must report and pay taxes on its taxable income at a maximum rate of 34%. Dividends paid are not a tax-deductible business expense. Furthermore, dividend distributions are taxed again to the individual stockholders when received. Corporations may deduct reasonable salaries paid to stockholders who also work for the corporation as a business expense from gross income.

S Corporations. An S Corporation normally doesn't pay corporate income taxes. Instead, stockholders include their share of the corporation's income in their individual tax return, whether or not it was paid to them. Thus, by making the election to be taxed as an S Corporation, a corporation's income can be taxed at the lower individual rate for shareholders and also avoid the double taxation. Distributions of corporate income are generally tax free since shareholders have already included this income on their tax returns. An S corporation is organized as a corporation under state law. The election to be taxed as an S corporation is valid only for tax purposes and does not affect the entity's legal status. Also, some state taxing authorities do not recognize S corporation status and will require the corporation to pay state income taxes.

Partnerships or Proprietorships. Partners or proprietors must report business income on their individual returns when it is earned whether it is withdrawn for personal use or left in the business. A partnership will never be subject to income taxes provided it is recognized as a valid partnership.

To illustrate the impact of taxes on the form of business organization, assume that Mary Tyler is going to form a business, which she expects will produce an annual income of about $100,000 before deducting her own salary of $60,000. That salary is considered reasonable for the services she performs. There will be no other withdrawals from the business. The corporate tax and individual tax for Tyler are compared under a corporation and proprietorship (or an S corporation) in Figure 17-8.

Under these assumed conditions, her combined tax burden is $5,705 lower ($19,598 − $13,893) if she incorporates than if she operates as a proprietor or elects an S corporation status. This is a result of the fact that the full $100,000 of income is included on her individual tax return when operating as a proprietorship or an S corporation. Her marginal tax rate on the $100,000 is higher (33%) than the marginal tax rate used to compute the corporate tax on the $40,000 (15%). If a part or all the $34,000 corporate net income is distributed in subsequent periods, the dividends are taxable to Tyler as ordinary income. Should the dividends not be withdrawn and she is later able to sell the capital stock at an increased price that reflects the retained earnings, the gain will be reported in the year of sale. In either case, she is able to postpone the tax on the portion of earnings retained by the corporation. A corporation, however, may be subject to a penalty tax on accumulated earnings deemed excessive and retained for the purpose of avoiding the tax on dividends.

Unfortunately, determining the tax advantage of one form of organization over

Figure 17-8
Comparison of Tax Impact on Forms of Business Organizations

	Legal Form of Business Organization	
	Corporation	S Corporation or Proprietorship
Business income excluding salary to owner	$100,000	$100,000
Less: Salary to owner	60,000	—
Taxable income	40,000	—
Corporate tax expense:		
$40,000 × .15	6,000	–0–
Net income	$ 34,000	$100,000
Tax paid by business	$ 6,000	$ –0–
Individual tax*	7,893	19,598
Combined tax	$ 13,893	$ 19,598
Individual income	$ 60,000	$100,000
Less: Itemized deductions and personal exemptions	(18,000)	(18,000)
Taxable income	$ 42,000	$ 82,000
Income tax liability:*		
First $29,750	$ 4,463	
First $71,900		$ 16,265
Excess ($42,000 − $29,750) × .28	3,430	
($82,000 − $71,900) × .33		3,333
Total tax liability	$ 7,893	$ 19,598

*From tax rate schedule in Figure 17-4, assuming a joint return and total deductions and exemptions of $18,000.

another is not as straightforward as it appears from this illustration. The apparent tax advantage can vanish with a change in such variables as the individual's and the corporation's marginal tax rates, the level of income, what constitutes a reasonable salary, and the amount of earnings retained in the business. If the business is operated as a proprietorship or an S corporation, Tyler is entitled to receive the $34,000 income (after the salary payment) without further tax effect. If she desired to receive the $34,000 income from the corporation, the result would not be as favorable. To illustrate, the combined corporate and individual income tax is computed here, assuming that all the corporate net income is distributed to Tyler.

Taxable income:	
Salary	$60,000
Dividends of $34,000 (see Figure 17-8)	34,000
Total	94,000
Less: Deductions	18,000
Taxable income	$76,000
Income tax liability:	
Individual tax:	
Tax on first $71,900	$16,265
Excess ($76,000 − $71,900) × .33 =	1,353
	17,618
Plus the corporate tax	6,000
Combined tax liability	$23,618

The combined tax liability is $23,618 when all the corporate net income is distributed. The change in assumption does not affect the combined tax liability when a proprietorship is operated; it remains the same at $19,598, as computed in Figure 17-8. Thus, when all the corporate net income is distributed, the lowest combined tax liability is incurred when the proprietorship (or S corporation) form of organization is adopted ($19,598 compared to $23,618).

Thus, the deferral of tax is achieved at the cost of a deferral of the receipt of the corporate income. Note that the same problem may occur if Tyler were a minority shareholder in an S corporation. She is required to include an allocable share of corporate income on her return although the majority shareholders may elect not to distribute profits. Tyler then incurs a tax liability with no cash to pay the tax.

CHOICE OF FINANCING METHODS

When a corporation seeks additional funds for long-term purposes, it may obtain them by retaining earnings generated from operations, by issuing additional shares of capital stock, or by issuing long-term debt. As discussed in Chapter 12, we must consider a number of factors when making financing decisions. A significant factor is the overall tax effect on the business and stockholders. The tax impact of the various forms of financing varies, because interest on debt is a tax-deductible expense, whereas a dividend paid on capital stock is not. To illustrate this point, assume that a firm needs to raise $500,000 for plant expansion, on which a return of 18% is expected.

Management is considering whether to issue shares of 12% preferred stock or to borrow at a 14% rate of interest. The firm is in the 34% marginal tax bracket. The after-tax results for the two alternatives are shown here.

	Issue Stock	Issue Bonds
Increase in earnings ($500,000 × 18%)	$90,000	$90,000
Interest expense ($500,000 × 14%)	–0–	70,000
Taxable income	90,000	20,000
Income tax expense:		
$90,000 × 34%	30,600	
$20,000 × 34%		6,800
Net income before dividends	59,400	13,200
Preferred dividends ($500,000 × 12%)	60,000	
Net income available to common stockholders	$ (600)	$13,200

Clearly in certain situations, the tax advantage of debt encourages its use to finance a business.

OPERATING A BUSINESS

Once the business is organized, management should use its marginal tax rate to assess the impact of taxes on alternative decisions, as illustrated earlier for an individual. There are also many ways that transactions can be arranged so that a favorable tax treatment is obtained legally. Primarily, these relate to the timing of transactions and the choice of accounting methods.

The *timing of business transactions* is one of the simplest tax-planning techniques available. A company seeking to reduce taxable income can move discretionary expenses (such as routine plant and equipment maintenance) planned for the next year into the current year. Charitable contributions are another example of a discretionary expense. In addition, sales transactions near the end of the current year may be deferred until the next year.

SUMMARY

This chapter has presented an overview of the federal tax laws as they pertain to individual taxpayers and corporations. For an individual, the steps in the computation of taxable income are shown in Figure 17-9.

The description of the nature of the deductions, exclusions, and credits is by necessity brief—remember that most of these items are subject to limits or restrictions on the amount deductible.

A corporation is a separate taxable entity. Provisions of the corporate tax law differ significantly from those of individual tax law. For example, a corporation cannot reduce its gross income for itemized deductions or personal exemptions. Furthermore, a corporation is permitted to exclude from income 80% of dividends received from other U.S. companies. However, an income statement similar to the one prepared for external reporting purposes serves as a basis for computing the taxable income of a corporation.

Figure 17-9
Steps in Computation of Taxable Income

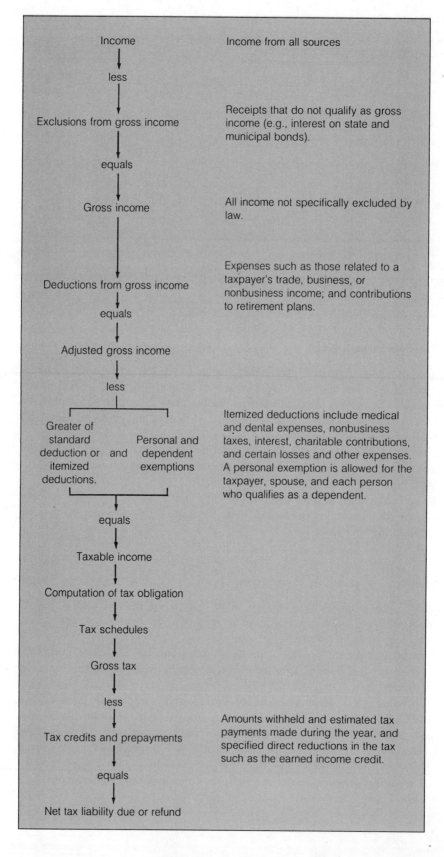

SELF-TEST

Test your understanding of the chapter by selecting the best answer for each of the following.

1. Which of the following is not required to file a separate federal income tax return?
    a. S corporation.
    b. Proprietorship.
    c. Partnership.
    d. Corporation.

2. Which of the following is true?
    a. Tax avoidance can never result in the assessment of penalties by the tax authorities.
    b. A physician who provides services to a lawyer in exchange for the preparation of a will and does not include the value of the services received in taxable income is practicing tax avoidance.
    c. Tax avoidance requires that the position claimed on the taxpayer's return be guaranteed to be correct if ever challenged by the IRS.
    d. Tax avoidance involves structuring a taxpayer's affairs to take maximum advantage of existing laws and interpretations of the laws while tax evasion is knowingly understating a tax liability.

3. A taxpayer would prefer to claim a deduction from gross income rather than an itemized deduction because:
    a. deductions from gross income provide a dollar-for-dollar tax benefit.
    b. a deduction from gross income may permit larger deductions for certain itemized deductions.
    c. many taxpayers will receive no tax benefit for itemized deductions because the total deductions are less than the standard deduction.
    d. both a and b are correct.
    e. both b and c are correct.

4. The standard deduction represents:
    a. a deduction the taxpayer is entitled to even if possessing no qualified deductions.
    b. a base amount the taxpayer must exceed before being able to receive a benefit for any deductions.
    c. the amount the taxpayer can deduct for each individual qualifying as a dependent.
    d. the sum of withholdings and estimated tax payments made during the tax year.

5. For decision making purposes, the relevant tax rate is:
    a. the average tax rate.
    b. the marginal tax rate.
    c. the effective average tax rate.
    d. the rate of tax for the highest tax bracket.

6. Which of the following items would be included in the federal taxable income of the recipient?
    a. An inheritance.
    b. A gift.
    c. State lottery winnings.
    d. Employer provided health insurance coverage.

7. Which of the following taxpayers would be entitled to the maximum IRA deduction ($4,000 married filing jointly or $2,000 single)?

   a. Married taxpayers filing a joint return with adjusted gross income of $120,000 (each earned $60,000). Each spouse is a participant in a qualified retirement plan.

   b. Married taxpayers filing a joint return with adjusted gross income of $50,000. One spouse is a participant in a qualified retirement plan.

   c. A single taxpayer with adjusted gross income of $30,000 who is a participant in a qualified retirement plan.

   d. A single taxpayer with adjusted gross income of $20,000 who is not a participant in a qualified retirement plan.

8. Compute the allowable casualty loss deduction for a taxpayer who has an item of personal property stolen. The cost of the item is $8,000 and its fair market value is $16,000. The taxpayer's adjusted gross income is $54,000.

   a. $2,400.

   b. $2,500.

   c. $8,000.

   d. $7,900.

9. Which of the following is true?

   a. An S corporation is not really a corporation under state law.

   b. A proprietorship is a separate legal entity.

   c. A partnership is taxed as a separate taxable entity.

   d. The partners in a partnership must pay tax on their share of the entity's income even if they receive no cash distribution.

REVIEW PROBLEM

Ross and Ellen Spencer are a married couple in their twenties. They have three children and support Ross's 17-year-old sister, who lives with them. Ross is an engineer and Ellen is a lawyer. Their records contain the following information, which may be used in preparing their joint return.

Ross's salary	$22,800
Ellen's salary	29,360
Interest on savings account	170
Dividends	210
Sold a painting purchased eight years ago for $3,000	6,800
Sold stock purchased four months ago for $2,600	1,950
Sales tax paid	550
Medical and dental expenses	5,140
Uninsured loss from automobile accident	780
Alimony payments to Ross's first wife	4,350
Subscriptions to professional journals	80
Property tax	660
Interest on home mortgage	11,900
Income tax withheld from Ellen's salary	2,125
Income tax withheld from Ross's salary	1,805

Required:

Compute the Spencer's taxable income, gross tax liability, and amount of unpaid taxes due or refund to be received.

ANSWER TO REVIEW PROBLEM

Gross income:		
Ellen's salary		$29,360
Ross's salary		22,800
Interest on savings		170
Dividends		210
Capital gains:		
Net long-term capital gain	$ 3,800	
Net short-term capital loss	(650)	3,150
Gross income		55,690
Deductions from gross income:		
Alimony payments		4,350
Adjusted gross income		51,340
Deductions from adjusted gross income:		
Itemized deductions:		
Medical and dental expenses	$5,140	
Less: 7.5% of adjusted gross income	3,851	1,289
Property tax		660
Interest on home mortgage		11,900
Loss on automobile accident (doesn't exceed 10% of AGI)		–0–
Miscellaneous—Subscriptions (doesn't exceed 2% of AGI)		–0–
Total itemized deductions		13,849
Personal exemptions (6 × $2,000)		12,000
Total deductions from adjusted gross income		25,849
Taxable income		$25,491
Tax from tax rate schedule:		
Tax ($25,491 × .15)		$ 3,824
Less: Prepayments—Income tax withheld ($2,125 + $1,805)		3,930
Refund due to taxpayers		$ 106

Sales tax of $550 is not deductible.

ANSWERS TO SELF-TEST

1. b **2.** d **3.** e **4.** a **5.** b **6.** c **7.** d **8.** b
9. d

GLOSSARY

ADJUSTED GROSS INCOME. Gross income less ordinary and necessary business expenses and other deductions permitted by law (p. 774).

CAPITAL ASSET. Any item of property except (1) inventories, (2) trade accounts and notes receivable, (3) land, building, and equipment used in a trade or business, and (4) certain intangible assets (p. 783).

CONSTRUCTIVE RECEIPT. The point in time when a cash receipt is taxable because it is controlled by a taxpayer even though it is not actually received (p. 772).

DEDUCTION. An item that reduces an amount subject to tax (p. 774).

EXCLUSION. An item omitted from gross income as provided by the tax laws (p. 774).

EXEMPTION. A deduction from adjusted gross income for each dependent claimed by a taxpayer. A separate exemption is allowed for the taxpayer, the taxpayer's spouse, and each qualified dependent (p. 779).

GROSS INCOME. All income not specifically excluded by statutory law, IRS regulation, or court decision (p. 774).

INTERNAL REVENUE CODE. A compilation of current federal income tax laws (p. 769).

ITEMIZED DEDUCTIONS. Expenses permitted by law to be deducted from adjusted gross income in computing taxable income. Should be utilized whenever the total is greater than the allowable standard deduction (p. 777).

LONG-TERM CAPITAL GAIN. A gain from the sale of a capital asset held longer than a specified period (p. 783).

LONG-TERM CAPITAL LOSS. A loss from the sale of a capital asset held longer than a specified period (p. 783).

MARGINAL TAX RATE. The tax rate applied to the next dollar of taxable income (p. 780).

S CORPORATION. A corporation that elects to be taxed similar to a partnership, which can be done when certain criteria are satisfied (p. 770).

SHORT-TERM CAPITAL GAIN. A gain from the sale of a capital asset held less than a specified period (p. 783).

SHORT-TERM CAPITAL LOSS. A loss from the sale of a capital asset held less than a specified period (p. 783).

STANDARD DEDUCTION. A deduction for personal expenses permitted in lieu of itemized deductions (p. 776).

TAXABLE INCOME. The amount of income on which the gross tax liability is computed (p. 774).

TAX CREDIT. An item that is a direct reduction in the amount of tax liability (p. 774).

TAX EVASION. The deliberate misstatement of taxable income, tax credits, prepayments, and/or other taxes (p. 771).

TAX PLANNING (TAX AVOIDANCE). A legal means of reducing or deferring an income tax liability (p. 771).

DISCUSSION QUESTIONS

1. What are the four classifications of taxpayers for federal income tax purposes?
2. The income of a proprietorship is $63,000, and the owner withdrew $35,000 during the year. How much business income must the owner report on his income tax return?
3. Explain the meaning of the expression double taxation of corporate income.
4. Why would a firm elect to be considered an S corporation?
5. Define tax planning and tax evasion.
6. How is the cash basis of accounting modified for income tax purposes?
7. What are the advantages of using the cash basis of accounting for income tax purposes?
8. What is the tax treatment for capital gains and losses?

9. Define the following terms:
    (a) Exclusion.
    (b) Deduction.
    (c) Tax credit.
10. Arrange the following items in the correct order to arrive at the net tax liability or refund due for an individual taxpayer.
    (a) Tax credits.
    (b) Exclusions from income.
    (c) Deductions from gross income.
    (d) Exemptions.
    (e) Adjusted gross income.
    (f) Taxable income.
    (g) Total income.
    (h) Itemized deductions.
    (i) Tax prepayments.
    (j) Gross income.
    (k) Gross tax liability.
11. Does it make any difference if an item is deducted to arrive at adjusted gross income or deducted from adjusted gross income? Why?
12. A married couple filing a joint return has taxable income of $52,000.
    (a) What is their gross tax liability?
    (b) What is the marginal tax rate?
    (c) What is their effective or average tax rate?
13. List, in order, the steps used to compute corporate net tax liability.
14. What are some ways in which the treatment of corporate capital gains and losses differs from that of the capital transactions of individual taxpayers?
15. Differentiate between the tax treatment of the owners' salaries for a corporation and for a partnership.
16. What is the tax advantage of financing with debt, rather than with stock?

EXERCISES

(For the exercises and problems in this chapter, round all computations to the nearest dollar.)

Exercise 17-1 Identifying Items of Income and Expense

Possible sources of income for an individual taxpayer are listed below.

1. Lottery winnings.
2. Tips.
3. Royalties.
4. Scholarship received for academic achievement.
5. Profit from a proprietorship.

Possible expenses incurred by an individual taxpayer are listed next.

6. Alimony payments.
7. Contribution to the Salvation Army.
8. Fee paid to CPA to have tax return prepared.
9. Cost of marriage license.

10. Payments to an individual retirement account.
11. Interest paid on credit cards used for personal use.

Required:

A. Determine whether each source of income should be included in gross income or excluded from gross income for tax purposes.
B. Determine whether each expense is deductible to arrive at adjusted gross income, deductible from adjusted gross income, or not deductible.

Exercise 17-2   Matching
Match the term on the left with its definition on the right.

1. Marginal tax rate	_____ **A.** An item that is a direct reduction in the amount of tax liability.
2. Itemized deductions	
3. Tax credit	_____ **B.** The deliberate misstatement of taxable income, tax credits, prepayments, and/or other taxes.
4. Tax avoidance	
5. Exclusion	
6. Constructive receipt	_____ **C.** An item omitted from gross income as provided by the tax laws.
7. Deduction	
8. Tax evasion	_____ **D.** A deduction from adjusted gross income for each dependent claimed by a taxpayer.
9. Standard deduction	
10. Exemption	

_____ **E.** Expenses that are permitted by law to be deducted from adjusted gross income in computing taxable income.

_____ **F.** A deduction for personal expenses permitted in lieu of itemized deductions.

_____ **G.** The point in time when a cash receipt is taxable because it is controlled by a taxpayer even though it is not actually received.

_____ **H.** The tax rate applied to the next dollar of taxable income.

_____ **I.** An item that reduces an amount subject to tax.

_____ **J.** A legal means of reducing or deferring an income tax liability.

Exercise 17-3   Multiple Choice
Select the best answer choice for each of the following.

1. Which of the following is a capital asset?
   a. Copyright.
   b. Personal residence.
   c. Inventory.
   d. Land used in a trade or business.
2. Which of the following must be included in gross income?
   a. Inheritance.
   b. Interest on municipal bonds.

    c. Disability benefits.

    d. Unemployment compensation.

3. What is the maximum Keogh contribution allowed for self-employed individuals?

    a. $4,000.

    b. $2,250.

    c. $30,000.

    d. $5,000.

4. Matthew is 70 years old, and his wife Joan is 67 years old and blind. They will file a joint return and do not itemize deductions. How much is their standard deduction?

    a. $5,000.

    b. $6,800.

    c. $6,500.

    d. $6,200.

5. A single taxpayer had adjusted gross income of $45,000 in 1990. She had $3,000 in medical bills and $500 in consumer interest. How much are her allowable itemized deductions?

	Medical and Dental Expenses	Consumer Interest
a.	–0–	$ 50
b.	–0–	$500
c.	$3,000	$325
d.	$ 750	$ 50

6. How many years can a corporation's net operating losses be carried back and carried forward?

	Carryback	Carryforward
a.	3	5
b.	3	15
c.	5	3
d.	15	3

Exercise 17-4   Computation of Tax Liability for an Individual

Sherry Gatewood is single with no dependents. She compiled the following tax-related information.

Total income	$38,200
Income tax withheld from salary	5,735
Itemized deductions	4,320
Exclusions from income	2,800
Deductions from gross income	1,000

Required:

Determine the following.

1. Taxable income.

2. Gross tax liability. (Use the Tax Rate Schedule in Figure 17-4.)

3. Net tax liability or refund.

4. Average tax rate.

Exercise 17-5 Computation of Tax Liability for a Married Couple

Tom and Joyce Nelson have two children. In preparing to file their tax return, the Nelson's compiled the following information:

Total income from all sources	$52,800
Itemized deductions	3,958
Inheritance from Grandpa Nelson	6,000
Income tax withheld from salaries	5,425
Alimony payments to Tom's first wife	2,250

Required:

Determine the following.

1. Taxable income.
2. Gross tax liability.
3. Net tax liability (refund).
4. Marginal tax rate.
5. Average tax rate.

Exercise 17-6 IRAs

ABC Accounting has the following clients:

a. David and Susan L. are both participants in their respective employers' pension plans. Together their adjusted gross income was $48,000.
b. Steven M.'s employer does not have a pension plan available. Steven's wife, Patty, is a student and unemployed. Steven and Patty's adjusted gross income was $32,000.
c. Marcia C. is a participant in her employer's pension plan, while her husband, Wayne, is not a participant in a pension plan. Their adjusted gross income was $65,000.
d. Both Mark and Ann G. are participants in pension plans. Their adjusted gross income was $39,000.
e. Gary R. is single, had an adjusted gross income of $29,000, and is a participant in his employer's pension plan.

Required:

For each of the above clients, determine the maximum IRA deduction allowed.

Exercise 17-7 Casualty Losses

Brian Luckless, who does not carry any insurance, has had a few unfortunate years. In 1990, lightning struck his garage and it was destroyed by fire. It cost $9,000 to rebuild. In 1991, jewelry costing $2,500, but with a fair market value of $3,900, was stolen. In 1992, Brian's automobile was involved in an accident and could not be repaired; the car was purchased for $10,000 two years ago but at the time of the accident was valued at $5,000. In 1993, Brian discovered termites in his home. The exterminator and repair bill totaled $6,000. Brian had an adjusted gross income of $40,000 each year.

Required:

Assuming the tax laws do not change, determine the deductible casualty or theft loss for each year.

Exercise 17-8 Moving Expenses and Miscellaneous Deductions

Charles Hoskins moved this year because of a job promotion. The old job site was 15 miles from his old home, while the new job site is 10 miles from his new home and 60 miles from his old home. Total moving expenses were $800. Charles also incurred unreimbursed employee travel expenses of $900, and he paid $320 for entertainment and meals while on the business trips. Charles subscribed to professional journals ($110), rented a safety deposit box ($30), and paid $200 to have his tax return prepared. Charles purchased $500 worth of business suits and paid $400 in investment counseling fees. Charles' adjusted gross income was $70,000.

Required:
A. Determine whether Charles can deduct any moving expenses.
B. Determine how much Charles can deduct for miscellaneous deductions.

Exercise 17-9 Surtax

Sheila Crenshaw, a single taxpayer, reported taxable income of $89,560.

Required:
A. Determine Sheila's tax liability for the year.
B. What is Sheila's marginal tax rate?
C. What is Sheila's effective tax rate?
D. What is the purpose of the 5% surtax?

Exercise 17-10 Investment Choices

A taxpayer with $5,000 to invest is considering the following investments.

a. Savings account paying 8% interest.
b. Municipal bond paying 7% interest.
c. Corporate stock paying a 9% dividend.

Required:
A. Determine which investment will result in the highest after-tax cash flow assuming the taxpayer has a marginal tax rate of 28%.
B. Repeat requirement (A), assuming the taxpayer has a marginal tax rate of 15%.
C. Repeat requirement (A), assuming the taxpayer is a corporation with a marginal tax rate of 34%. (*Hint:* Don't forget the dividends-received deduction.)

Exercise 17-11 Computation of Tax Liability for a Corporation

The records of the Serrano Corporation contain the following information.

Operating revenue	$733,000
Dividends from U.S. corporations	30,000
Net short-term capital gain	15,000
Net short-term capital loss	20,000
Operating expenses	596,000

Required:
Compute the tax liability of the Serrano Corporation.

Exercise 17-12 Computation of Tax Liability for a Corporation

The records of the Keystone Corporation contain the following information.

Sales revenue	$565,000
Dividends from U.S. corporations	9,000
Net operating loss carried forward from prior years	35,000
Interest revenue	16,000
Operating expenses	447,000
Charitable contributions	25,000

Required:
Compute the tax liability of the Keystone Corporation.

Exercise 17-13   Tax Effects of Financing Decisions

Heritage Company needs to raise $150,000 for plant expansion on which a return of 18% is expected. Management is considering whether to issue shares of 8% preferred stock or borrow at a 10% rate of interest. The corporation is in the 34% tax bracket.

Required:

Calculate the effect of each proposal on the firm's net income available to the common stockholders.

PROBLEMS

Problem 17-1   Computation of Tax Liability for a Married Couple

Donald and Kristen Turner are married and have one dependent child. They are both in their thirties. Donald is a consultant with his own private practice. Kristen heads the marketing department of a large firm. They plan to file a joint return, and they compiled the following information to give to their accountant.

Gross revenue from Donald's practice	$102,300
Expenses of Donald's practice	74,050
Estimated tax paid by Donald	7,600
Kristen's salary	41,200
Income tax withheld from Kristen's salary	6,760
Interest earned on savings in the bank	1,020
Sales tax	710
Property tax	900
Inheritance received	2,500
Medical and dental expenses	5,825
Net long-term capital gains	3,500
Net short-term capital losses	2,700
Interest on home mortgage	8,420
Theft loss	485
Dividends received	600

Required:

Compute the Turner's adjusted gross income, taxable income, and net income tax liability or refund due (use the tax rate schedule in Figure 17-4).

Problem 17-2   Computation of Tax Liability for a Married Couple

Frank and Erma Lindsey file a joint tax return. Frank is 64 and Erma is 60. They support their 21 year-old daughter who is a full-time student and who earned $1,500 during the summer. Frank is a photographer and participates in his employer's pension plan, while Erma works part-time as a salesclerk. Their records contain the following information.

Frank's salary	$36,800
Erma's salary	7,630
Received a gift of cash	3,000
Interest on savings account	220
Interest on City of Phoenix bonds	150
Sold stock purchased three years ago, cost $6,700	8,500
Sold gold coins purchased three months ago, cost $3,200	2,750

Tax return preparation fee	200
Charitable contributions	1,500
Home mortgage interest	5,400
Prescription drugs	915
Doctor and hospital payments	3,420
Uninsured loss from flood damage	7,630
Safe deposit box rental	45
Property tax	890
Unreimbursed photographic supplies needed on the job	695
Income tax withheld from Frank's salary	3,140
Income tax withheld from Erma's salary	480

Required:

Compute the Lindsey's taxable income, gross tax liability (use the tax rate schedule in Figure 17-4), and amount of unpaid taxes due or refund to be received.

Problem 17-3   **Computation of Tax Liability for a Married Couple**

Harry and Barbara Caplan are a married couple in their twenties. They have two children and support Harry's 17 year-old sister, who lives with them. Harry is an engineer. Barbara, who is blind, is a lawyer. Their records contain the following information, which may be used in preparing their joint return.

Barbara's salary	$32,800
Harry's salary	39,360
Interest on savings account	620
Dividends	1,140
Gambling gains	3,120
Sold a painting purchased eight years ago, cost $3,000	6,800
Sold stock purchased four months ago, cost $2,600	1,950
Dues to professional organizations	500
Educational expenses required by employer	2,300
Medical and dental expenses	5,140
Moving expenses (all qualifications were met)	900
Alimony payments to Harry's first wife	4,350
Subscriptions to professional journals	80
Property tax	1,260
Interest on home mortgage	10,900
Income tax withheld from Barbara's salary	4,795
Income tax withheld from Harry's salary	5,130

Required:

Compute the Caplan's taxable income, gross tax liability, and amount of unpaid taxes due or refund to be received. (Use the tax rate schedule in Figure 17-4.)

Problem 17-4   **Type of Business Organization**

Dean Bennett and Marilyn Carter plan on starting a business by investing equal amounts of money. They would like to organize the business as either a partnership or a corporation. They anticipate an annual net income of $80,000 before deducting their salaries of $18,000 each for services performed. Both Dean and Marilyn are single and have no dependents. Neither of them itemizes deductions. The business would be Dean's only source of income. Marilyn has yearly income from other sources of $12,000. For this problem, use the tax rate schedules in Figure 17-4 and Figure 17-7 to compute their individual income tax liability.

Required:

A. Assuming that the business is organized as a partnership, determine the income tax liability of both Dean and Marilyn. Profits of the partnership are shared equally.

B. Assume that the business is organized as a corporation and that no dividends are distributed. Allocate one-half of the corporate income tax to each owner, and determine the tax liability of both Dean and Marilyn.

C. Assume that a corporation is formed and that all the net income is distributed as dividends. Allocate one-half of the corporate income tax to each owner, and determine the tax liability of both Dean and Marilyn.

Problem 17-5 Computation of Tax Liability for a Corporation

The records of the Sigma Corporation contain the following information.

Sales revenue	$492,000
Interest on investments	5,000
Dividends from U.S. corporations	20,000
Cost of goods sold	305,000
Selling expenses	48,000
Administrative expenses	34,000
Net long-term capital loss	10,000
Net short-term capital gain	7,000
Goodwill amortization	7,500
Net operating losses carried forward from prior year	8,000
Premium for employees' life insurance policies (Sigma is the beneficiary)	6,500

Required:

Compute the tax liability of the Sigma Corporation.

Problem 17-6 Computation of Tax Liability for a Corporation

The records of Spartan Corporation contain the following information.

Interest received on state obligations	$ 12,500
Sales	840,000
Dividends from U.S. corporations	17,500
Dividends from foreign corporations	9,400
Life insurance proceeds (death of an insured officer)	75,000
Interest on investments	9,500
Cost of goods sold	475,000
Selling expenses	76,200
Administrative expenses	89,500
Tax credits	10,000
Goodwill amortization	15,000
Charitable contributions	50,000

Required:

Compute the tax liability of the Spartan Corporation.

Problem 17-7 Tax Effects on Financing Decisions

Advanced Systems Corporation needs $500,000 to introduce a new product line. The investment is expected to yield a return of 16% before taxes. Advanced's average net income before income taxes is $400,000. The following methods of raising the capital are being considered.

1. Issue $500,000 of 10-year, 11% bonds at par.
2. Issue 5,000 shares of 8.5%, cumulative, nonparticipating preferred stock for $100 a share.
3. Issue 20,000 shares of common stock for $25 a share. Advanced Systems Corporation currently has 50,000 shares of common stock outstanding. The firm has a 34% marginal tax rate.

Required:

Determine the effect of each of the three financing methods on the income tax expense, net income, net income available to common stockholders, and earnings per share on common stock.

CASE

CASE 17-1   Annual Report Analysis

Refer to the financial statements and related footnotes of BFGoodrich Company in the Appendix to this text and answer the following questions. Indicate the Appendix page number on which you found the answer.

1. What is the amount of income taxes reported in the income statements for 1989 and 1988?
2. What is the effective tax rate for 1989 and 1988?
3. What is the major reason that the effective tax rate for 1988 was lower than in 1989?
4. The Internal Revenue Service proposed an adjustment to the Company's federal income tax returns. What is the nature of the adjustment?

APPENDIX A
CONSOLIDATED FINANCIAL STATEMENTS

BFGoodrich Company

A2–A27

1989 Financial Report

Management's Responsibility for Financial Statements

The consolidated financial statements and notes to consolidated financial statements of The BFGoodrich Company and subsidiaries have been prepared by management. These statements have been prepared in accordance with generally accepted accounting principles and accordingly include amounts based upon informed judgments and estimates. Management is responsible for the fairness and integrity of such statements. Financial information appearing elsewhere in this annual report is consistent with these financial statements.

BFGoodrich maintains a system of internal controls designed to provide reasonable assurances that accounting records are reliable for the preparation of financial statements and for safeguarding assets. This system is augmented by the careful selection of people and by an internal auditing function.

Ernst & Young, independent auditors, were engaged to audit and to render an opinion on the consolidated financial statements of The BFGoodrich Company and subsidiaries. Their opinion is based on procedures believed by them to be sufficient to provide reasonable assurance that the financial statements are not materially misstated and do not contain material error. The report of Ernst & Young follows.

The Board of Directors has an Audit Committee consisting of Directors who are not employees of BFGoodrich. The Audit Committee meets regularly to review with management and Ernst & Young the Company's accounting policies, internal and external audit plans and results of audits. To ensure complete independence, the auditors have full access to the Audit Committee and meet with the Committee without the presence of management.

John D. Ong
Chairman and Chief
Executive Officer

D. Lee Tobler
Executive Vice President
and Chief Financial
Officer

Donald G. Barger Jr.
Vice President and
Controller

Report of Ernst & Young, Independent Auditors

To the Shareholders and Board of Directors of The BFGoodrich Company

We have audited the accompanying consolidated balance sheet of The BFGoodrich Company and subsidiaries as of December 31, 1989 and 1988, and the related consolidated statements of income, shareholders' equity and cash flows for each of the three years in the period ended December 31, 1989. These financial statements are the responsibility of the Company's management. Our responsibility is to express an opinion on these financial statements based on our audits.

We conducted our audits in accordance with generally accepted auditing standards. Those standards require that we plan and perform the audit to obtain reasonable assurance about whether the financial statements are free of material misstatement. An audit includes examining, on a test basis, evidence supporting the amounts and disclosures in the financial statements. An audit also includes assessing the accounting principles used and significant estimates made by management, as well as evaluating the overall financial statement presentation. We believe that our audits provide a reasonable basis for our opinion.

In our opinion, the financial statements referred to above present fairly, in all material respects, the consolidated financial position of The BFGoodrich Company and subsidiaries at December 31, 1989 and 1988, and the consolidated results of their operations and their cash flows for each of the three years in the period ended December 31, 1989, in conformity with generally accepted accounting principles.

As discussed in Note A to the consolidated financial statements, in 1988 the Company changed its method of accounting for income taxes.

Ernst & Young

Cleveland, Ohio
January 31, 1990

Consolidated Statement of Income

(Dollars in millions, except per share amounts)

See Note	Year Ended December 31	1989	1988	1987
D	**Sales**	**$2,419.7**	$2,326.4	$1,942.6
	Operating costs and expenses:			
	Cost of sales	**1,697.9**	1,619.5	1,379.9
	Selling and administrative expenses	**447.5**	414.2	365.6
		2,145.4	2,033.7	1,745.5
	Total Operating Income	**274.3**	292.7	197.1
	Interest expense	**(35.9)**	(44.4)	(54.0)
	Interest income	**30.8**	17.6	10.8
G	Other expense—net	**(25.0)**	(15.8)	(8.3)
	Income from continuing operations before income taxes	**244.2**	250.1	145.6
H	Income taxes	**(73.0)**	(45.0)	(64.8)
	Income from Continuing Operations	**171.2**	205.1	80.8
C	Income (loss) from discontinued operations—net	**1.2**	(12.1)	(1.6)
	Extraordinary items:			
N	Loss on extinguishment of debt, net of tax benefit	**—**	—	(3.3)
H	Tax benefit from utilization of loss carryforwards	**—**	—	29.1
A	Cumulative effect to January 1, 1988, of change in method of accounting for income taxes	**—**	2.7	—
	Net Income	**$ 172.4**	$ 195.7	$ 105.0
A	**Earnings (Loss) per Share:**			
	Continuing operations	**$ 6.43**	$ 7.80	$ 3.04
	Discontinued operations	**.05**	(.49)	(.07)
	Extraordinary items	**—**	—	1.09
	Cumulative effect of change in method of accounting	**—**	.11	—
	Net income	**$ 6.48**	$ 7.42	$ 4.06
	Earnings (Loss) per Share Assuming Full Dilution:			
	Continuing operations	**$ 6.23**	$ 7.49	$ 3.09
	Discontinued operations	**.04**	(.45)	(.06)
	Extraordinary items	**—**	—	1.00
	Cumulative effect of change in method of accounting	**—**	.10	—
	Net income	**$ 6.27**	$ 7.14	$ 4.03

See Notes to Consolidated Financial Statements.

Consolidated Balance Sheet

(Dollars in millions, except per share amounts)

December 31	1989	1988	*See* *Note*
Current Assets			
Cash and cash equivalents	$ **214.9**	$ 242.1	*A*
Short-term investments	**61.2**	71.5	*A*
Accounts and notes receivable	**317.0**	286.6	*J*
Inventories	**362.0**	356.3	*K*
Prepaid expenses	**10.9**	9.1	
Assets held for sale	**74.4**	37.7	
Total Current Assets	**1,040.4**	1,003.3	
Property	**991.5**	934.4	*L*
Goodwill	**108.4**	85.7	*A*
Intangible Pension Asset	**63.1**	—	*E*
Other Assets	**71.0**	49.6	
Total Assets	**$2,274.4**	$2,073.0	
Current Liabilities			
Short-term bank debt	$ **5.1**	$ 7.2	
Accounts payable	**233.6**	237.4	
Accrued expenses	**191.8**	180.1	*M*
Income taxes payable	**35.8**	33.7	
Current maturities of long-term debt and capital lease obligations	**19.7**	33.0	*N,O*
Total Current Liabilities	**486.0**	491.4	
Long-term Debt and Capital Lease Obligations	**289.0**	307.9	*N,O*
Deferred Income Taxes	**60.6**	34.4	
Other Non-current Liabilities	**150.3**	73.4	*P*
Redeemable Preferred Stock	**11.3**	11.3	*Q*
Shareholders' Equity			
$3.50 Cumulative Convertible Preferred Stock, Series D			
(stated at involuntary liquidation value of $50 per share)			
2,200,000 shares issued and outstanding	**110.0**	110.0	
Common Stock—$5 par value			
Authorized 100,000,000 shares; issued 25,554,627 shares	**127.8**	127.8	
Additional capital	**385.1**	382.9	
Income retained in the business	**662.1**	548.9	
Cumulative unrealized translation adjustments	**1.7**	(2.6)	
Amount related to recording minimum pension liability	**(1.7)**	—	
Common stock held in treasury, at cost (221,326 shares in 1989 and 352,396 shares in 1988)	**(7.8)**	(12.4)	
Total Shareholders' Equity	**1,277.2**	1,154.6	
Total Liabilities and Shareholders' Equity	**$2,274.4**	$2,073.0	

See Notes to Consolidated Financial Statements.

Consolidated Statement of Cash Flows

(Dollars in millions)

Year Ended December 31	1989	1988	1987
Cash Flows from Operating Activities			
Net income	**$172.4**	$195.7	$105.0
Adjustments to reconcile net income to net cash provided by operating activities:			
Cumulative effect of change in method of accounting	—	(2.7)	—
Loss on extinguishment of debt	—	—	5.5
Depreciation and amortization of property	**98.5**	95.9	87.4
Provision (credit) for deferred income taxes	**23.9**	(4.5)	6.2
Change in assets and liabilities, net of effects of acquisitions and dispositions of businesses:			
Receivables	**(6.6)**	(33.9)	(47.8)
Inventories	**(21.5)**	(54.1)	(24.6)
Accounts payable	**(.7)**	11.9	27.9
Accrued expenses	**(8.6)**	16.8	22.6
Income taxes payable	**(4.5)**	5.7	13.1
Non-current liabilities	**12.6**	20.2	(16.7)
Other	**9.8**	10.3	14.9
Net cash provided by operating activities	**275.3**	261.3	193.5
Cash Flows from Investing Activities			
Purchases of property	**(240.4)**	(180.5)	(142.6)
Proceeds from sale of property	**15.8**	8.1	10.3
Acquisitions less cash acquired	**(50.7)**	(70.2)	(3.2)
Sale of interest in accounts receivable—net	**(24.6)**	—	50.0
Proceeds from sale of investment in UGTC	—	225.0	—
Proceeds from sales of businesses and other investments	**96.0**	53.1	—
Decrease (increase) in short-term investments	**12.0**	(52.5)	(19.0)
Other transactions	**(4.0)**	3.9	1.6
Net cash provided (used) by investing activities	**(195.9)**	(13.1)	(102.9)
Cash Flows from Financing Activities			
Decrease in short-term debt	**(4.3)**	(18.7)	(8.0)
Proceeds from long-term debt	**4.0**	4.0	5.3
Repayment of long-term debt and capital lease obligations	**(36.2)**	(30.5)	(97.0)
Payment of deferred portion of 1988 acquisition cost	**(8.4)**	—	—
Proceeds from issuance of capital stock	**1.9**	.6	98.2
Dividends	**(59.2)**	(52.1)	(46.8)
Retirement of preferred stock	—	(3.1)	(3.0)
Net cash provided (used) by financing activities	**(102.2)**	(99.8)	(51.3)
Effect of Exchange Rate Changes on Cash	**(4.4)**	1.8	.7
Increase (Decrease) in Cash and Cash Equivalents	**(27.2)**	150.2	40.0
Cash and Cash Equivalents at Beginning of Year	**242.1**	91.9	51.9
Cash and Cash Equivalents at End of Year	**$214.9**	$242.1	$ 91.9

See Notes to Consolidated Financial Statements.

Consolidated Statement of Shareholders' Equity

(Dollars in millions, except per share amounts)

Year Ended December 31	1989	1988	1987	*See Note*
$3.50 Cumulative Convertible Preferred Stock, Series D	$ **110.0**	$ 110.0	$110.0	*Q*
Common Stock—$5 Par Value	**127.8**	127.8	127.8	*R*
Additional Capital				*R*
Balance at beginning of year	**382.9**	382.2	295.3	
Changes resulting from:				
Issuance of new Common Stock—net	—	—	86.5	
Reissuance of treasury shares	**2.2**	.7	1.5	
Federal tax assessment related to proceeds from warrants issued in 1972 and credited to additional capital	—	—	(1.1)	
Balance at end of year	**385.1**	382.9	382.2	
Income Retained in the Business				*N*
Balance at beginning of year	**548.9**	405.3	347.1	
Net income	**172.4**	195.7	105.0	
Dividends:				
Preferred Stock:				
Series A, $7.85 a share	**(.9)**	(1.0)	(1.0)	
Series B, $.975 a share annually	—	(.1)	(.2)	
Series D, $3.50 a share	**(7.7)**	(7.7)	(8.6)	
Common Stock—$2.00 a share in 1989; $1.72 a share in 1988 and $1.56 a share in 1987	**(50.6)**	(43.3)	(37.0)	
Total Dividends	**(59.2)**	(52.1)	(46.8)	
Balance at end of year	**662.1**	548.9	405.3	
Cumulative Unrealized Translation Adjustments				
Balance at beginning of year	**(2.6)**	(19.8)	(36.9)	
Aggregate adjustments for the year	**4.3**	17.2	17.1	
Balance at end of year	**1.7**	(2.6)	(19.8)	
Amount Related to Recording Minimum Pension Liability	**(1.7)**	—	—	*E*
Common Stock Held in Treasury, at Cost	**(7.8)**	(12.4)	(14.6)	*R*
Total Shareholders' Equity	**$1,277.2**	$1,154.6	$990.9	

See Notes to Consolidated Financial Statements.

Notes to Consolidated Financial Statements

(Dollars in millions, except per share amounts)

Note A: Significant Accounting Policies

Principles of Consolidation: The consolidated financial statements of The BFGoodrich Company ("BFGoodrich" or the "Company") include the accounts of the parent company and all subsidiaries. All significant intercompany accounts and transactions have been eliminated upon consolidation.

Cash and Cash Equivalents: Cash and cash equivalents include cash in banks and all highly liquid investments with a maturity of three months or less at the time of purchase.

Short-Term Investments: Short-term investments are those with maturities of more than three months when purchased and are valued at cost, which approximates market.

Inventories: Inventories are stated at the lower of cost or market. Most domestic inventories are valued by the last-in, first-out (LIFO) cost method. Inventories not valued by the LIFO method are valued principally by the average cost method.

Property and Depreciation: Property, plant and equipment is recorded at cost with depreciation and amortization thereof, including amounts recorded under capital leases, computed principally by the straight-line method. Property is generally depreciated on accelerated methods for income tax purposes. Repairs and maintenance costs are expensed as incurred, except for chemical plant turn-around costs, which are deferred and amortized over the period benefited.

Goodwill: Goodwill represents the excess of the purchase price over the fair value of the net assets of acquired subsidiary companies and is being amortized by the straight-line method, in most cases over 40 years. Goodwill as shown in the Consolidated Balance Sheet is net of accumulated amortization of $13.0 and $10.2 at December 31, 1989 and 1988, respectively.

Income Taxes: Effective January 1, 1988, the Company adopted Statement of Financial Accounting Standards No. 96—"Accounting for Income Taxes" (SFAS No. 96). This standard required, among other things, a change from the deferred to the liability method of computing deferred income taxes. As permitted by SFAS No. 96, consolidated financial statements of prior years have not been restated. The cumulative effect of this change in accounting to January 1, 1988, was $2.7, or $.11 per share.

Since it is BFGoodrich's intention to reinvest the undistributed earnings of its foreign subsidiaries, no provision is made for federal income taxes on these earnings. At December 31, 1989, the cumulative amount of undistributed earnings of foreign subsidiaries on which BFGoodrich has not provided deferred federal income taxes was $311.8. It is not practical to determine the amount of income tax liability that would result had such earnings actually been repatriated. On repatriation, certain foreign countries impose withholding taxes. The amount of withholding tax that would be payable on remittance of the entire amount of undistributed earnings would approximate $30.0.

Earnings Per Share: Earnings per share of common stock is computed after recognition of preferred stock dividend requirements, based on the weighted average number of common shares outstanding of 25,279,831 for 1989, 25,179,198 for 1988 and 23,650,701 for 1987. Earnings per share assuming full dilution gives effect to the assumed exercise of dilutive stock options in each year and the assumed conversion of Series D Cumulative Convertible Preferred Stock. The weighted average number of shares used for the fully-dilutive calculation is 27,351,650 for 1989, 27,247,334 for 1988 and 25,736,976 for 1987.

Reclassification: Certain amounts for 1988 and 1987 have been reclassified to conform to the 1989 presentation.

Note B: Acquisitions

During 1989, 1988 and 1987, BFGoodrich acquired several businesses, all of which were recorded using the purchase method of accounting. In the first quarter of 1989 the Company acquired JcAir Inc., a maker and seller of test equipment and related technical services to manufacturers of aircraft instruments and avionics; in the second quarter Foster Airdata Systems, Inc., a manufacturer of aircraft electronics equipment; in the third quarter the net operating assets, which include surface-mount technology and automatic assembly equipment, of Advanced Navigation, Inc.; and in the fourth quarter Arrowhead Industrial Water, Inc., ("Arrowhead") a provider of design, fabrication, installation and service of ultra-high-purity water systems. In the third quarter of 1988 the Company acquired Tramco, Inc., a provider of maintenance, repair and overhaul services for commercial airlines; and in the fourth quarter the remaining 50 percent interest in an Australian joint-venture—Pabco Holdings Pty. Limited. In 1987, four minor acquisitions were made. The cost of acquisitions amounted to $56.4 in 1989, $79.3 in 1988 and $3.4 in 1987.

The operating results of all of the above acquisitions are included in the consolidated financial statements from the dates acquired. Including the results of operations for these acquisitions on a pro forma basis would not have a material effect on the Company's reported results of operations.

Note C: Discontinued Operations

During 1989, BFGoodrich sold the elastomers business unit of its Specialty Chemicals segment and decided to sell the marine products and services business unit of its Aerospace Products segment.

In 1988, BFGoodrich sold its 50 percent interest in The Uniroyal Goodrich Tire Company ("UGTC") to UGTC Holding Corporation, a Delaware corporation formed by a group of investors organized by Clayton & Dubilier, Inc. UGTC had been formed on August 1, 1986, when BFGoodrich and Uniroyal Holdings, Inc. ("Uniroyal") combined their tire businesses (except aircraft tires) into a joint-venture partnership owned equally by subsidiaries of BFGoodrich and Uniroyal. In connection with the sale, BFGoodrich received $225.0 in cash, plus a warrant to purchase common stock of UGTC Holding Corporation representing 10 percent of its initial equity on a fully diluted basis, which effectively represents up to 7 percent of the equity of UGTC on a fully diluted basis. BFGoodrich has not recorded any value for the warrant. In September 1989, Groupe Michelin agreed to acquire UGTC, which agreement is subject to various conditions and government approvals. If the transaction is consummated as proposed, BFGoodrich expects to realize a pretax gain of approximately $30.0 from exercising or tendering the warrant.

Also during 1988, BFGoodrich sold substantially all of the assets and businesses of its Industrial Products business segment; sold its engineered rubber products business unit; and entered into an agreement to sell its aircraft tire business unit (such sale being consummated on January 24, 1989). The engineered rubber products and aircraft tire business units had been part of the Company's Aerospace Products business segment.

The results of operations of these businesses are accounted for as discontinued operations in the Consolidated Statement of Income. A summary of income statement information relating to discontinued operations is as follows:

	1989	1988	1987
Sales	$70.2	$193.6	$225.4
Costs and expenses	63.3	198.5	232.3
Operating income (loss)	6.9	(4.9)	(6.9)
Equity in earnings of UGTC	—	1.8	11.6
Other income (loss)—net	—	(.7)	—
Income (loss) from operations before income taxes	6.9	(3.8)	4.7
Income tax expense	(1.4)	(.3)	(1.6)
Income (loss) from operations	5.5	(4.1)	3.1
Loss on disposition of discontinued operations (net of income tax expense of $1.4 in 1989 and tax benefits of $3.7 in 1988 and $3.1 in 1987)	(4.3)	(8.0)	(4.7)
Income (loss) from discontinued operations—net	$ 1.2	$(12.1)	$ (1.6)

The loss on disposition of discontinued operations includes provisions of $4.0 ($3.2 net of income taxes) and $7.8 ($4.7 net of income taxes), in the second quarter of 1989 and in the fourth quarter of 1987, respectively, to cover estimated costs of environmental matters related to previously disposed discontinued operations.

Note D: Business Segment Information

The Company's continuing operations are classified in the following three business segments:

Geon Vinyl Products: This segment includes polyvinyl chloride (PVC) resins and compounds as well as the feedstocks and intermediate precursors to PVC—vinyl chloride monomer (VCM), chlorine and ethylene—and their by-products and co-products. External sales consist primarily of PVC resins and compounds but also include VCM and caustic soda. Intersegment sales are insignificant.

Specialty Chemicals: This segment consists of specialty chemicals such as hydrophilics, thermoplastic polyurethanes, low-combustibility/high-temperature plastics, reactive liquid polymers, rubber and plastic additives, specialty latexes, coatings, adhesives, sealants and roofing materials. It also provides design, fabrication, installation and service for ultra-high-purity water systems through Arrowhead, which was acquired in October 1989. Intersegment sales are insignificant.

Aerospace Products: This segment includes such products as aircraft wheels and brakes, emergency-evacuation systems, de-icing systems, specialty fasteners and related products for commercial and military markets. The segment has overhaul and service facilities certified by the Federal Aviation Administration for aviation instruments, flight control systems and avionics equipment and also provides maintenance, repair and overhaul services for commercial airlines. Intersegment sales are insignificant.

Segment operating income is total revenues less operating expenses. Corporate items include corporate general administrative and research expenses.

Assets of a business segment include both assets directly identified with those operations and an allocable share of jointly used assets. Corporate assets consist primarily of cash and cash equivalents, short-term investments, assets held for sale, intangible pension asset and other assets that cannot be directly associated with the operations of a business segment.

The net sales, operating income and certain other financial information by business segment and in total during the periods indicated are as shown below.

	1989	1988	1987
Sales to Unaffiliated Customers:			
Geon Vinyl Products	$1,241.8	$1,300.6	$1,056.5
Specialty Chemicals	734.8	695.5	617.8
Aerospace Products	443.1	330.3	268.3
Total	$2,419.7	$2,326.4	$1,942.6
Operating Income:			
Geon Vinyl Products	$ 183.3	$ 233.6	$ 143.5
Specialty Chemicals	77.3	69.0	62.1
Aerospace Products	56.5	41.4	30.3
Intersegment eliminations	1.1	(1.2)	(.9)
Business Segment Operating Income	318.2	342.8	235.0
Corporate Items	(43.9)	(50.1)	(37.9)
Total Operating Income	$ 274.3	$ 292.7	$ 197.1
Capital Expenditures:			
Geon Vinyl Products	$ 115.5	$ 88.2	$ 56.5
Specialty Chemicals	44.8	41.2	32.4
Aerospace Products	58.4	36.4	29.4
Depreciation and Amortization Expense:			
Geon Vinyl Products	$ 53.5	$ 50.2	$ 46.4
Specialty Chemicals	26.3	24.3	20.5
Aerospace Products	12.3	8.2	6.6
Assets:			
Geon Vinyl Products	$ 893.8	$ 815.6	$ 719.5
Specialty Chemicals	573.6	486.0	467.5
Aerospace Products	432.3	331.5	173.8
Intersegment eliminations	(2.1)	(3.2)	(2.0)
Identifiable Assets	1,897.6	1,629.9	1,358.8
Corporate, including discontinued operations	376.8	443.1	579.7
Total	$2,274.4	$2,073.0	$1,938.5

The following table sets forth certain financial information by geographic area for the years 1989, 1988 and 1987:

	1989	1988	1987
Sales to Unaffiliated Customers:			
United States	$1,774.1	$1,660.8	$1,415.9
Foreign:			
Canada	387.3	385.4	314.2
Other	258.3	280.2	212.5
Total	$2,419.7	$2,326.4	$1,942.6
Segment Operating Income:			
United States	$ 253.3	$ 269.2	$ 173.4
Foreign:			
Canada	33.2	53.2	44.1
Other	27.3	25.7	19.1
Interarea eliminations	4.4	(5.3)	(1.6)
Total	$ 318.2	$ 342.8	$ 235.0
Identifiable Assets:			
United States	$1,479.9	$1,262.4	$1,052.6
Foreign:			
Canada	237.5	196.1	165.4
Other	184.6	180.2	144.3
Interarea eliminations	(4.4)	(8.8)	(3.5)
	1,897.6	1,629.9	1,358.8
Corporate, including discontinued operations	376.8	443.1	579.7
Total	$2,274.4	$2,073.0	$1,938.5

United States sales to unaffiliated customers include export sales of $207.4 in 1989, $160.3 in 1988 and $131.5 in 1987. Intracompany transfers, which are made at prevailing market prices, from the United States to foreign operations amounted to $123.9, $164.1 and $95.6 for the years 1989, 1988 and 1987, respectively.

The net assets of consolidated foreign subsidiaries amounted to $376.3 in 1989, $322.0 in 1988 and $261.3 in 1987. Other than Canada, no single foreign geographic area is significant. Currency restrictions are not expected to have a significant effect on BFGoodrich's cash flow, liquidity or capital resources.

Note E: Pensions

BFGoodrich and its subsidiaries have several contributory and non-contributory defined-benefit pension plans covering substantially all employees. Plans covering salaried employees generally provide benefit payments using a formula that is based on employees' compensation and length of service. Plans covering hourly employees generally provide benefit payments of stated amounts for each year of service.

The Company's general funding policy for pension plans is to contribute amounts sufficient to satisfy regulatory funding standards. Provisions of the Omnibus Budget Reconciliation Act of 1987 allow additional tax deductible contributions for underfunded U.S. plans. In January 1990, the Company, under these provisions, made cash contributions of $26.2 for the 1989 plan year, $18.8 of which was not required under ERISA. After giving effect to these contributions, cumulative contributions made by the Company have exceeded the ERISA minimum funding requirements by $26.5. Plan assets for these plans consist principally of corporate and government obligations and commingled funds invested in equities, debt and real estate.

The components of net periodic pension cost for the Company's defined-benefit pension plans are as follows:

	1989	1988	1987
Service cost for benefits earned	$ 7.2	$ 7.4	$ 8.1
Interest cost on projected benefit obligation	46.6	45.7	40.9
Actual return on plan assets	(55.0)	(51.9)	(15.7)
Net amortization and deferral	16.1	18.4	(16.6)
Net pension cost	$ 14.9	$ 19.6	$ 16.7

Curtailment losses of $1.5 for 1989 and $5.2 for 1988, which resulted from dispositions of business units classified as discontinued operations, are not reflected in net pension cost in the preceding table, but are included in "Income (loss) from discontinued operations" in the Consolidated Statement of Income.

The following table sets forth the funded status (based principally on measurement dates of September 30, 1989 and 1988) of the Company's defined-benefit pension plans and amounts recognized in the Consolidated Balance Sheet at December 31, 1989 and 1988:

	1989		1988	
	Plans with Assets Exceeding Accumulated Benefit Obligation	Plans with Accumulated Benefit Obligation Exceeding Assets	Plans with Assets Exceeding Accumulated Benefit Obligation	Plans with Accumulated Benefit Obligation Exceeding Assets
Actuarial present value of accumulated benefit obligation:				
Vested	$ 43.2	$ 425.6	$38.0	$373.8
Non-vested	1.2	26.9	1.5	23.6
Accumulated benefit obligation	44.4	452.5	39.5	397.4
Plan assets at fair value	115.1	387.7	97.8	353.3
Plan assets in excess of (less than) accumulated benefit obligation	$ 70.7	$ (64.8)	$58.3	$ (44.1)
Projected benefit obligation	$ 61.7	$ 507.5	$57.2	$439.1
Plan assets at fair value	115.1	387.7	97.8	353.3
Plan assets in excess of (less than) projected benefit obligation	$ 53.4	$(119.8)	$40.6	$ (85.8)
Consisting of:				
Unrecognized transitional asset (liability)	$ 24.2	$ (72.2)	$25.9	$ (81.5)
Unrecognized prior service cost	(.5)	(39.7)	(.5)	(.2)
Unrecognized net gain (loss)	18.5	(7.9)	9.1	9.0
Adjustment required to recognize minimum liability	—	64.8	—	—
Contribution made subsequent to measurement date	—	(1.3)	—	—
Prepaid (accrued) pension cost recognized in the balance sheet	11.2	(63.5)	6.1	(13.1)
Total	$ 53.4	$(119.8)	$40.6	$ (85.8)

Commencing in 1989, Statement of Financial Accounting Standards No. 87—"Employers' Accounting for Pensions" requires recognition in the balance sheet of a minimum pension liability for underfunded plans. The minimum liability that must be recognized is equal to the excess of the accumulated benefit obligation over plan assets. A corresponding amount is recognized as either an intangible asset or a reduction of equity. Pursuant to this requirement, BFGoodrich has recorded, as of December 31, 1989, an additional liability of $64.8, an intangible pension asset of $63.1 and an equity reduction of $1.7.

General benefit improvements granted during 1989 in the Company's principal salary plan are reflected in the 1989 unrecognized prior service cost.

Major assumptions used in accounting for BFGoodrich's defined-benefit plans are as follows:

	1989	1988	1987
Discount rate for obligations	**9.25%**	9.75%	10.0%
Rate of increase in compensation levels	**6.0%**	6.0%	6.0%
Expected long-term rate of return on plan assets	**9.5%**	9.5%	9.25%

The Company also maintains a voluntary Retirement Plus Savings Plan for most U.S. salaried employees. Under provisions of this plan, eligible employees can receive Company matching contributions on up to the first 6 percent of their eligible earnings. For each of the three years in the period ended December 31, 1989, the Company matched fifty cents for each one dollar of employee contributions (up to six percent of earnings) invested in BFGoodrich common stock or twenty-five cents for each dollar of eligible employee contributions invested in other available investment options. For 1989, 1988 and 1987, Company contributions amounted to $4.7, $4.5 and $3.6, respectively. For 1990, the Company match has been increased to one dollar for each one dollar of employee contributions (up to six percent of earnings) invested in BFGoodrich common stock or fifty cents for each dollar of eligible employee contributions invested in other available investment options.

In addition to providing pension benefits, the Company and its subsidiaries provide certain health-care and life-insurance benefits for retired employees. Substantially all of the Company's employees in the United States as well as some employees in foreign countries may become eligible for those benefits if they reach retirement age while working for the Company. The cost of retiree health-care and life-insurance benefits is recognized as expense as claims or premiums are incurred. The cost of these benefits amounted to $24.0, $21.5 and $16.2 for the years ended December 31, 1989, 1988 and 1987, respectively. The increase in benefit costs in 1989 and 1988 resulted from escalating costs of health-care services coupled with an increase in the number of retirees.

Note F: Research and Development

Research and development expense for continuing operations amounted to $64.2, $54.9 and $45.6 for the years ended December 31, 1989, 1988 and 1987, respectively.

Note G: Other Expense—Net

"Other expense—net" as shown in the Consolidated Statement of Income comprises the following:

	1989	1988	1987
Cost of health care benefits for retirees not associated with current business segments	**$(10.6)**	$ (8.2)	$(6.4)
Exchange gain (loss)	**(11.4)**	(3.3)	.3
Discount on sale of trade receivables	**(3.2)**	(4.2)	(2.5)
Other—net	**.2**	(.1)	.3
	$(25.0)	$(15.8)	$(8.3)

Note H: Income Taxes

"Income from continuing operations before income taxes" as shown in the Consolidated Statement of Income comprises the following:

	1989	1988	1987
Domestic	**$176.2**	$166.2	$ 83.8
Foreign	**68.0**	83.9	61.8
Total	**$244.2**	$250.1	$145.6

Effective January 1, 1988, BFGoodrich changed its method of accounting for income taxes from the deferred method to the liability method (see Note A). The 1987 income tax amounts have not been restated.

Under the liability method adopted in 1988, the benefit of the operating loss carryforward is reflected as a reduction in income tax expense rather than as an extraordinary item, as was required under the deferred method used in 1987.

A summary of income tax (expense) benefit included in the Consolidated Statement of Income is as follows:

	1989	1988	1987
Continuing operations			
Current:			
Federal, including charge in lieu of tax	**$(20.7)**	$(41.8)	$(34.8)
Foreign	**(24.9)**	(42.1)	(22.4)
State	**(3.5)**	(2.2)	(1.4)
Reduction from utilization of loss carryforwards	**—**	36.6	—
	(49.1)	(49.5)	(58.6)
Deferred:			
Federal, including charge in lieu of tax	**(59.6)**	(5.6)	.3
Foreign	**(2.8)**	(.6)	(6.5)
Reduction from utilization of loss carryforwards	**—**	6.6	—
Reduction from utilization of credit carryforwards	**38.5**	4.1	—
	(23.9)	4.5	(6.2)
Tax expense—continuing operations	**(73.0)**	(45.0)	(64.8)
Discontinued operations	**(2.8)**	3.4	1.5
Extraordinary items:			
On extinguishment of debt	**—**	—	2.2
Reduction from utilization of loss carryforwards	**—**	—	29.1
	$(75.8)	$(41.6)	$(32.0)

At December 31, 1989, BFGoodrich and its domestic subsidiaries have available for federal income tax purposes a net operating loss carryforward of $122.9 that expires in the year 2000 and investment and other tax credit carryforwards of $42.7 that expire from 1994 to 2004. At December 31, 1989, the Company also has available an Alternative Minimum Tax (AMT) loss carryforward of $62.1 that expires in the year 2000 and an AMT credit of $8.2 that can be carried forward indefinitely.

During the fourth quarter of 1988, the Internal Revenue Service ("IRS") completed its examination of the Company's federal income tax returns for the years 1984 and 1985, and has proposed an adjustment. The proposed adjustment would disallow a $156.0 worthless-security deduction claimed by the Company. The Company is protesting the proposed adjustment through the IRS appeals process and believes that its position is supportable, although it is unable to predict the eventual outcome of this matter. Because of the uncertain outcome of this item, the Company has not recorded any of the potential $53.0 tax benefit related to the worthless-security deduction. If the Company had recorded a tax benefit related to this item for 1989, income tax expense would have been reduced by $16.4.

The income tax rate from continuing operations for the years ended December 31, 1989, 1988 and 1987 varied from the statutory federal income tax rate as set forth in the following table:

Percent of Pretax Income	**1989**	1988	1987
Statutory federal income tax rate	**34.0%**	34.0%	40.0%
Increases (decreases):			
Benefit of operating loss carryforwards	—	(16.8)	—
Benefit of tax credit carryforwards	**(9.0)**	(1.7)	—
Tax expense (benefit) on disposals of assets and investments	**2.2**	(3.0)	—
Difference in rates on consolidated foreign subsidiaries	**.6**	1.8	1.1
Foreign withholding taxes, net of federal benefit	**.8**	2.5	1.1
Other items	**1.3**	1.2	2.3
Effective income tax rate for the year	**29.9%**	18.0%	44.5%

Deferred income taxes result from the tax effect of transactions that are recognized in different periods for financial and tax reporting purposes. Significant components of deferred income taxes are as follows:

	1989	1988	1987
Reinstatement of previously recognized deferred tax liabilities	**$(21.1)**	$(2.3)	$ —
Sale of investment	—	7.4	—
Accelerated depreciation for tax purposes	**(2.3)**	(.6)	(15.1)
Capitalized and safe harbor leases	—	—	(6.5)
Net increase in financial accruals, not currently deductible	—	—	4.0
Elimination of deferred taxes due to loss carryforward	—	—	15.0
Other items	**(.5)**	—	(3.6)
Total	**$(23.9)**	$ 4.5	$ (6.2)

Note I: Supplemental Cash Flow Information

The following table sets forth non-cash financing and investing activities and other cash flow information:

	1989	1988	1987
Liabilities assumed or created in connection with acquisitions	**$17.1**	$15.3	$ .6
Treasury stock reissued in connection with an acquisition	**4.0**	—	—
Liabilities disposed in connection with sales of businesses	**4.7**	11.2	—
Interest paid (net of amount capitalized)	**37.3**	45.0	57.2
Income taxes paid	**45.6**	44.3	14.6

Note J: Accounts and Notes Receivable

"Accounts and notes receivable" as shown in the Consolidated Balance Sheet is net of allowances for doubtful receivables of $8.6 and $8.9 at December 31, 1989 and 1988, respectively. Receivables at December 31, 1989, include $.2 due from an employee relating to an indemnification in connection with the purchase of a business formerly owned by such employee. In 1987, BFGoodrich entered into a five-year arrangement under which the Company may receive up to a maximum of $50.0 on an ongoing basis for the sale of an undivided interest in a designated pool of trade accounts receivable. At December 31, 1989 and 1988, $25.4 and $50.0, respectively, in receivables had been sold pursuant to this arrangement. The discount on sales of receivables amounted to $3.2, $4.2 and $2.5 for the years ended December 31, 1989, 1988 and 1987, respectively, and is included in "Other expense—net."

Note K: Inventories

The major classes of inventories at December 31, 1989 and 1988 are as follows:

	1989	1988
Finished products	**$208.8**	$219.2
In process	**63.6**	67.8
Raw materials and supplies	**158.5**	150.8
	430.9	437.8
Reserve to reduce certain inventories to last-in, first-out (LIFO) basis	**(68.9)**	(81.5)
	$362.0	$356.3

At December 31, 1989 and 1988, approximately 69 percent and 72 percent, respectively, of the pre-LIFO inventory amounts have been valued by the LIFO method. The estimated replacement costs of inventories at December 31, 1989 and 1988 were $434.6 and $440.4, respectively.

Sales of businesses resulted in the liquidation of LIFO inventories. These liquidations benefited the income (loss) from discontinued operations in 1989 and 1988 by $2.5 ($2.0 net of income taxes) and $6.8 ($6.6 net of income taxes), respectively.

Note L: Property

Property, plant and equipment at December 31, 1989 and 1988 consisted of the following:

	1989	1988
Land	$ 19.0	$ 14.5
Buildings	294.2	267.5
Machinery and equipment	1,222.9	1,238.1
Construction	128.3	82.5
	1,664.4	1,602.6
Less allowances for depreciation and amortization	672.9	668.2
	$ 991.5	$ 934.4

Property includes assets acquired under capital leases, principally buildings and machinery and equipment, of $46.8 and $46.7 at December 31, 1989 and 1988, respectively. Related allowances for depreciation and amortization are $20.5 and $18.2, respectively. In 1989, interest costs of $4.9 were capitalized. Interest costs capitalized in 1988 and 1987 were insignificant.

Note M: Accrued Expenses

"Accrued expenses" as shown in the Consolidated Balance Sheet at December 31, 1989 and 1988, include the following:

	1989	1988
Wages, vacations, pensions and other employment costs	$ 76.0	$ 71.2
Taxes, other than federal and foreign taxes on income	31.4	27.2
Accrued environmental reserve	17.6	18.0
Other	66.8	63.7
	$ 191.8	$ 180.1

Note N: Financing Arrangements

BFGoodrich had available lines of credit and foreign overdraft facilities of $379.7 at December 31, 1989, of which $375.2 was unused. The total available lines of credit include $300.0 of domestic lines which are revolving credit arrangements entered into with certain banks during 1986, under which BFGoodrich could borrow at rates tied to the bank's certificates of deposit, Eurodollar, or prime rate. These are "evergreen" credit arrangements that require payment of a commitment fee of 1/4 of 1 percent per annum.

BFGoodrich also maintains uncommitted money market facilities with various banks. These facilities were typically the Company's lowest cost source of debt and were the primary vehicle for short-term borrowing during the past three years.

During 1987, BFGoodrich prepaid $50.0 of principal amount of 13 percent notes prior to their scheduled maturities. The $3.1 ($.13 per share) after-tax loss associated with the extinguishment is classified as an extraordinary item in the Consolidated Statement of Income. Also in 1987, BFGoodrich extinguished an Industrial Revenue Bond. The $.2 ($.01 per share) after-tax loss associated with the defeasance is also classified as an extraordinary item.

At December 31, 1989 and 1988, long-term debt and capital lease obligations payable after one year comprises the following:

	1989	1988
13.20% Notes, maturing in 1992	**$ 50.0**	$ 50.0
Adjustable Rate Notes, maturing to 1993	**19.2**	25.6
Floating Rate Notes, maturing in 1991	**50.0**	50.0
12.75% Notes, maturing 1990 to 2008	**23.7**	25.0
8.875% Notes, maturing to 1997	**16.3**	18.7
8.25% Debentures, maturing 1991 to 1994	**23.1**	23.1
7.00% Subordinated Debentures (effective interest rate of 7.85%), maturing to 1997	**9.1**	9.1
9.75% Notes, maturing to 1995	**14.3**	17.0
Other, maturing to 2012 (principally 6.20% to 14.50%)	**60.1**	63.6
Unamortized debt discounts	**(.6)**	(.7)
	265.2	281.4
Capital lease obligations (see Note O)	**23.8**	26.5
Total	**$289.0**	$307.9

Aggregate maturities of long-term debt, exclusive of capital lease obligations, during the five years subsequent to December 31, 1989, are as follows: 1990—$16.9; 1991—$70.8; 1992—$73.5; 1993—$24.8 and 1994—$16.8.

Certain of the Company's debt agreements contain restrictive covenants that, among other things, place limitations on the payment of cash dividends and the repurchase of the Company's capital stock. Under the most restrictive of these agreements, income retained in the business in the amount of $506.5 was free from such limitations at December 31, 1989.

Note O: Leasing Arrangements

The future minimum lease payments, by year and in the aggregate, under capital leases and under noncancelable operating leases with initial or remaining noncancelable lease terms in excess of one year, consisted of the following at December 31, 1989:

	Capital Leases	Noncancelable Operating Leases
1990	$ 5.0	$ 24.3
1991	4.9	20.4
1992	3.1	16.0
1993	5.1	13.2
1994	3.0	9.0
Thereafter	20.3	47.6
Total minimum payment due	41.4	$130.5
Amounts representing interest	(14.8)	
Present value of net minimum lease payments	26.6	
Less current portion of capital lease obligations	2.8	
Total	$23.8	

Net rent expense for continuing operations consisted of the following:

	1989	1988	1987
Minimum rentals	**$29.2**	$23.7	$20.2
Contingent rentals	**1.5**	.8	1.3
Sublease rentals	**(.9)**	(1.3)	(1.4)
Total	**$29.8**	$23.2	$20.1

Minimum future sublease rentals to be received on capital and operating leases amounted to $13.8 and $3.3, respectively, at December 31, 1989.

Note P: Other Non-current Liabilities

"Other non-current liabilities" as shown in the Consolidated Balance Sheet at December 31, 1989 and 1988 include the following:

	1989	1988
Accrued pension liability	**$ 56.1**	$ 2.1
Accrued environmental reserve	**33.0**	20.2
Other	**61.2**	51.1
	$150.3	$73.4

Note Q: Preferred Stock

There are 10,000,000 authorized shares of Series Preferred Stock—$1 par value. Shares of Series Preferred Stock which have been redeemed are deemed retired and extinguished and may not be reissued. As of December 31, 1989, 546,674 shares of Series Preferred Stock have been redeemed. The Board of Directors establishes and designates the series and fixes the number of shares and the relative rights, preferences and limitations of the respective series of the Series Preferred Stock.

Whenever dividends on Cumulative Series Preferred Stock are in arrears six quarters or more, holders of such stock (voting as a class) have the right to elect two Directors of the Company until all cumulative dividends have been paid.

Dividends on outstanding Series Preferred Stock must be declared and paid or set apart for payment, and funds required for sinking-fund payments, if any, on Series Preferred Stock must be paid or set apart for payment before any dividends may be paid or set apart for payment on the Common Stock.

Redeemable Preferred Stock—Series A (stated at involuntary liquidation value of $100 per share): BFGoodrich has issued 250,000 shares of $7.85 Cumulative Preferred Stock, Series A. In order to comply with sinking-fund requirements, each year on August 15, BFGoodrich must redeem 12,500 shares of the Series A Stock. The redemption price is $100 per share, plus dividends accrued at the redemption date. BFGoodrich may redeem, at such price, up to an additional 12,500 shares in each year. The sinking-fund requirements may also be satisfied with shares acquired on the open market. At December 31, 1988 and 1987, BFGoodrich held 12,050 and 12,500 shares, respectively, for future sinking-fund requirements. After giving effect to the shares held for future sinking-fund requirements, there were 112,500, 112,950 and 125,000 shares of Series A Stock outstanding at December 31, 1989, 1988 and 1987, respectively. The aggregate amount of redemption requirement for the Series A Stock is $1.3 in each of the years 1990 through 1994.

Redeemable Preferred Stock—Series B: BFGoodrich had issued 372,838 shares of $.975 Cumulative Preferred Stock, Series B. On July 15, 1988, BFGoodrich redeemed the then outstanding 192,838 shares of Series B Cumulative Preferred Stock at $10.24 per share plus accrued dividends.

Convertible Preferred Stock—Series D (stated at involuntary liquidation value of $50 per share): BFGoodrich has issued 2,200,000 shares of $3.50 Cumulative Convertible Preferred Stock, Series D. The Series D Stock is convertible into shares of BFGoodrich's Common Stock at a conversion rate, which is subject to certain anti-dilution provisions, of 0.909 shares of Common Stock for each share of Series D Stock. At BFGoodrich's option, the Series D Stock may be redeemed, in whole or in part, at any time on or after January 2, 1990. The redemption price, which decreases each January 2, is $52.45 a share until January 2, 1991, $52.10 a share until January 2, 1992 and $51.75 a share for the twelve months thereafter, plus accrued and unpaid dividends. At December 31, 1989, 1988 and 1987, there were 2,200,000 shares of Series D Stock outstanding.

Cumulative Participating Preferred Stock—Series E: On July 20, 1987, BFGoodrich declared a dividend distribution of one Right for each outstanding share of Common Stock of the Company to shareholders of record at the close of business on August 3, 1987. Each Right, when exercisable, entitles the registered holder thereof to purchase from BFGoodrich one one-hundredth of a share of Cumulative Participating Preferred Stock, Series E at a price of $200 per one one-hundredth of a share (subject to adjustment). The one one-hundredth of a share is intended to be the functional equivalent of one share of the Company's Common Stock. The Rights will not be exercisable or transferable apart from the Common Stock until a person, as defined in the Rights Agreement, as amended, without the proper consent of BFGoodrich's Board of Directors, acquires 20 percent or more of the voting power of the Company's stock or announces a tender offer that would result in 20 percent ownership. BFGoodrich will be entitled to redeem the Rights at five cents per Right any time before a 20 percent position has been acquired and in connection with certain transactions thereafter announced. Under certain circumstances, including the acquisition of 20 percent of the Company's stock, each Right not owned by a potential acquiror or related parties will entitle its holder to purchase, at the Right's then-current exercise price, shares of BFGoodrich's Series E Stock having a market value of twice the Right's exercise price. Holders of the Rights will be entitled to buy stock of an acquiror at a similar discount if, after the acquisition of 20 percent or more of the Company's voting power, BFGoodrich is involved in a merger or other business combination transaction with another person in which its common shares are changed or converted, or BFGoodrich sells 50 percent or more of its assets or earning power to another person. At December 31, 1989, 1988 and 1987, there were authorized 350,000 shares of open Series E Stock, of which 327,382, 328,038 and 328,604 shares, respectively, were reserved for future issuance in accordance with the above plan.

Note R: Common Stock

In October 1987, BFGoodrich, in a public offering, issued 1,800,000 shares of Common Stock for $99.0 in cash ($95.5 net of underwriting discount and issuance expenses). The par value of shares issued was added to the "Common Stock" account, and the excess of issue price over par value was added to the "Additional Capital" account.

BFGoodrich acquired 2,309, 4,002 and 14,155 shares of treasury stock in 1989, 1988 and 1987, respectively, and reissued 62,002, 69,117 and 166,073 shares, respectively, in connection with employee stock purchase and ownership plans. In 1989, BFGoodrich also reissued 71,377 shares of treasury stock as part payment for the acquisition of Foster Airdata Systems, Inc.

At December 31, 1989, 7,183,556 shares were reserved for future issuance as follows: 1,622,687 shares for the exercise of outstanding and the granting of future stock options; 3,415,700 shares for issuance to the Retirement Plus Savings Plan; 145,369 shares for issuance under the Tremco Stock Ownership Plan and 1,999,800 shares for conversion of Convertible Preferred Stock, Series D.

Note S: Stock Options

BFGoodrich's Key Employees' Stock Option Plan, which will expire on April 15, 1992, unless renewed, provides for the granting of options to purchase Common Stock of the Company. Options granted prior to 1988 generally became exercisable in two equal installments six months and twelve months from the date of the grant. Certain options granted in 1988 and 1989 become exercisable at the rate of 35 percent after one year, 70 percent after two years and 100 percent after three years. Certain options are fully exercisable immediately after grant. The term of each option cannot exceed 10 years from the date of the grant. All options granted under the Plan have been granted at not less than 100 percent of market value (as defined) on the date of grant. Certain options granted provide that the optionee, in lieu of exercise, can elect to surrender the option and receive, without payment to BFGoodrich, shares of Common Stock or a combination of Common Stock and cash equal to the appreciation on the option. Certain options granted after 1981 are incentive stock options for tax reporting purposes.

In 1989, $2.0 was credited to expense for the decrease in values of stock appreciation rights. In 1988 and 1987, $3.1 and $.7, respectively, was charged to expense for the increase in values and exercise of stock appreciation rights.

The following tabulation summarizes certain information relative to stock options:

	1989				1988			
	Number of Shares	Range	Option Price Per	Share	Number of Shares	Range	Option Price Per	Share
Outstanding at beginning of year (includes 375,223 in 1989 and 333,529 in 1988 with appreciation right alternative)	712,980	$17.75	to	$56.3125	595,758	$17.75	to	$56.3125
Granted (with appreciation right alternative)	91,100	52.625	to	54.6875	61,250	51.875		
Granted (without appreciation right alternative)	135,950	49.3125	to	56.625	133,400	51.875		
Exercised	25,395	17.75	to	56.3125	22,531	17.75	to	42.9375
Surrendered under appreciation right alternative	40,182	18.81	to	39.0625	34,147	17.75	to	39.8125
Terminated	16,305	32.875	to	56.3125	20,750	42.9375	to	56.3125
Outstanding at end of year (includes 420,511 in 1989 and 375,223 in 1988 with appreciation right alternative)	858,148	19.69	to	56.625	712,980	17.75	to	56.3125
Exercisable at end of year	674,930				604,180			
Reserved for future options	764,539				975,284			

The above table does not include options granted on January 2, 1990, for 231,500 shares at $42.125 per share.

Note T: Commitments and Contingencies

BFGoodrich and its subsidiaries have numerous purchase commitments for materials, supplies and energy incident to the ordinary course of business.

There are pending or threatened against BFGoodrich or its subsidiaries various claims, lawsuits and administrative proceedings, all arising from the ordinary course of business with respect to commercial, product liability and environmental matters, which seek remedies or damages for substantial amounts. BFGoodrich believes that either there are meritorious defenses to substantially all such actions or that any liability that may finally be determined, net of insurance, should not have a material effect on the Company's consolidated financial position.

The Company has been named a potentially responsible party for cleanup costs by the U.S. Environmental Protection Agency with respect to a number of sites. In addition, the Company initiates corrective and/or preventative environmental projects of its own to ensure the safe and lawful operations of its facilities. Based on estimates prepared by the Company's environmental engineers and consultants, the Company, at December 31, 1989, has accruals totaling $50.6 to cover such estimated future environmental expenditures.

At December 31, 1989, there were contingent liabilities with respect to guarantees of securities of other issuers of approximately $47.5 for which BFGoodrich would be reimbursed by Occidental Chemical Holding Corporation for any amounts paid under the guarantees.

BFGoodrich is contingently liable for approximately $18.2 of rental payments under leases that have been assigned to others.

On January 4, 1982, the Federal Trade Commission (''FTC'' or ''the Commission'') issued an administrative complaint challenging the acquisition by BFGoodrich of LaPorte Chemicals Corp., which consisted of a vinyl chloride monomer (VCM) plant and polyvinyl chloride (PVC) plant. On September 20, 1985, an Administrative Law Judge issued an Initial Decision upholding the Company's position and dismissing the complaint. The staff of the FTC appealed the decision to the Commission. On March 21, 1988, the FTC upheld the Administrative Law Judge's decision with respect to the PVC plant but reversed his decision with respect to the VCM plant and ordered a divestiture of the plant, with certain conditions, within 12 months after the order becomes final. The case was concluded with respect to the PVC plant and the Company appealed the divestiture order of the VCM plant to the U.S. Court of Appeals for the Second Circuit. Prior to the decision on the appeal, the Company entered into a settlement with the FTC which was approved by the U.S. Court of Appeals for the Second Circuit. The case is now concluded.

The settlement requires the Company to divest its ethylene dichloride (EDC) and VCM plants located at its Calvert City, Kentucky manufacturing facility by July 24, 1990. The divestiture is required to be made only to an acquiror and only in the manner that receives prior approval of the FTC. If the Company does not divest the Calvert City EDC and VCM plants by the above date, the FTC may appoint a trustee to effect the divestiture.

A definitive agreement has been signed with Westlake Monomers Corporation (Westlake) for the sale of these facilities subject to various conditions, including approval by the FTC. Upon divestiture of these facilities, the Company anticipates receiving cash, which will be available for general corporate purposes. Under proposed terms of a conversion agreement with Westlake, the Company would be unconditionally obligated to pay a fixed fee of $17.0 for the first year and $15.0 for the second year for converting ethylene and chlorine and/or EDC into VCM. In addition, the Company would also make payments that are based principally on Westlake's operating costs. The Company's cost to acquire a portion of its VCM requirements will be greater than before the divestiture.

Fourth Quarter Income Statement (Unaudited)

(Dollars in millions)

For the Quarter Ended December 31	1989	1988	1987
Sales	$573.7	$594.7	$509.2
Operating costs and expenses:			
Cost of sales	408.5	423.2	368.4
Selling and administrative expenses	112.7	111.9	89.0
	521.2	535.1	457.4
Total operating income	52.5	59.6	51.8
Interest expense	(8.1)	(10.9)	(12.0)
Interest income	9.6	7.8	2.2
Other expense—net	(7.6)	(6.1)	(1.8)
Income from continuing operations before income taxes	46.4	50.4	40.2
Income taxes	(18.3)	(10.3)	(17.8)
Income from continuing operations	28.1	40.1	22.4
Loss from discontinued operations—net	(1.1)	(2.9)	(6.7)
Extraordinary items:			
Loss on extinguishment of debt, net of tax benefit	—	—	(.2)
Tax benefit from utilization of loss carryforwards	—	—	5.0
Net income	$ 27.0	$ 37.2	$ 20.5

Quarterly Data (Unaudited)

(Dollars in millions, except per share amounts)

The quarterly results for 1989 and 1988, restated for discontinued operations, are set forth in the following table:

	1989 Quarters				1988 Quarters			
	First	Second	Third	Fourth	First	Second	Third	Fourth
Sales	**$615.9**	**$628.8**	**$601.3**	**$573.7**	$530.2	$583.4	$618.1	$594.7
Business segment sales:								
Geon Vinyl Products	**$347.4**	**$329.7**	**$299.7**	**$265.0**	$308.7	$327.9	$347.3	$316.7
Specialty Chemicals	**159.5**	**188.6**	**193.5**	**193.2**	149.1	180.5	185.7	180.2
Aerospace Products	**109.0**	**110.5**	**108.1**	**115.5**	72.4	75.0	85.1	97.8
Gross Profit	**$191.9**	**$193.7**	**$171.0**	**$165.2**	$158.8	$187.6	$189.0	$171.5
Business segment operating income:								
Geon Vinyl Products	**$ 68.1**	**$ 57.3**	**$ 30.1**	**$ 27.8**	$ 57.6	$ 62.1	$ 64.1	$ 49.8
Specialty Chemicals	**10.1**	**24.2**	**24.3**	**18.7**	6.0	24.1	24.9	14.0
Aerospace Products	**12.4**	**13.4**	**15.0**	**15.7**	7.7	9.7	10.1	13.9
Income from continuing operations	**$ 51.0**	**$ 53.0**	**$ 39.1**	**$ 28.1**	$ 39.8	$ 56.8	$ 68.4	$ 40.1
Income (loss) from discontinued operations	**$ 2.0**	**$ (.7)**	**$ 1.0**	**$ (1.1)**	$ (5.1)	$ 3.6	$ (7.7)	$ (2.9)
Net income	**$ 53.0**	**$ 52.3**	**$ 40.1**	**$ 27.0**	$ 37.4	$ 60.4	$ 60.7	$ 37.2
Earnings per share:								
Continuing operations	**$ 1.94**	**$ 2.01**	**$ 1.46**	**$ 1.03**	$ 1.49	$ 2.17	$ 2.63	$ 1.50
Net income	**2.02**	**1.98**	**1.50**	**.98**	1.40	2.31	2.32	1.39
Earnings per share assuming full dilution:								
Continuing operations	**$ 1.86**	**$ 1.93**	**$ 1.42**	**$ 1.02**	$ 1.45	$ 2.07	$ 2.50	$ 1.46
Net income	**1.94**	**1.90**	**1.45**	**.98**	1.36	2.20	2.22	1.36

1989: Income from continuing operations for the fourth quarter includes a $4.3 after-tax charge related to the planned disposition of the Company's Calvert City EDC/VCM facilities.

1988: Net income for the first quarter includes a benefit of $2.7 arising from the cumulative effect of the adoption of SFAS No.96—"Accounting for Income Taxes" as of January 1, 1988. Income from continuing operations for the fourth quarter includes a $6.6 after-tax charge related to the establishment of a charitable trust.

Common Stock Prices and Dividends

The table below lists dividend per share and quarterly price ranges for the common stock of The BFGoodrich Company, based on New York Stock Exchange prices as reported on the consolidated tape.

1989				1988			
Quarter	High	Low	Dividend	Quarter	High	Low	Dividend
First	$56⅜	$50⅜	$.50	First	$53⅜	$37½	$.43
Second	58⅝	51	.50	Second	57⅜	47¼	.43
Third	69	53⅞	.50	Third	60¾	44⅞	.43
Fourth	55⅞	38½	.50	Fourth	59	47½	.43

As of December 31, 1989, there were approximately 14,710 common shareholders of record.

Selected Five-Year Financial Data and Ratios

(Dollars in millions, except per share amounts)		1989	1988	1987	1986	1985
Statement	Sales from continuing operations	$2,419.7	$2,326.4	$1,942.6	$1,621.3	$1,489.3
of Income	Cost of sales	1,697.9	1,619.5	1,379.9	1,198.5	1,170.5
Data	Gross profit	721.8	706.9	562.7	422.8	318.8
	Selling and administrative expenses	447.5	414.2	365.6	303.6	252.2
	Charge related to restructuring	—	—	—	—	213.1
	Total operating income (loss)	274.3	292.7	197.1	119.2	(146.5)
	Interest expense	35.9	44.4	54.0	79.9	105.8
	Interest income	30.8	17.6	10.8	4.7	10.1
	Provision for income taxes	73.0	45.0	64.8	36.7	20.9
	Income (loss) from continuing operations	171.2	205.1	80.8	5.7	(259.2)
	Cumulative effect to January 1, 1988, of change in method of accounting for income taxes	—	2.7	—	—	—
	Net income (loss)	172.4	195.7	105.0	32.7	(354.6)
Balance	Current assets	$1,040.4	$1,003.3	$ 706.8	$ 611.7	$ 998.9
Sheet	Current liabilities	486.0	491.4	492.9	432.6	833.8
Data	Net working capital	554.4	511.9	213.9	179.1	165.1
	Net property	991.5	934.4	898.2	865.2	1,043.9
	Total assets	2,274.4	2,073.0	1,938.5	1,819.7	2,260.3
	Non-current long-term debt and capital lease obligations	289.0	307.9	340.8	427.2	536.5
	Redeemable preferred stocks	11.3	11.3	14.4	17.5	18.6
	Total shareholders' equity	1,277.2	1,154.6	990.9	814.7	690.1
Other	Total segment operating income (loss)	$ 318.2	$ 342.8	$ 235.0	$ 151.1	$ (117.6)
Financial	Depreciation and amortization	98.5	95.9	87.4	96.7	118.1
Data	Capital expenditures	240.4	180.5	142.6	144.0	202.3
	Dividends (common and preferred)	59.2	52.1	46.8	37.4	36.7
Per Share	Income (loss) from continuing operations	$ 6.43	$ 7.80	$ 3.04	$ .15	$ (11.56)
of Common	Net income (loss)	6.48	7.42	4.06	1.32	(15.79)
Stock	Dividends	2.00	1.72	1.56	1.56	1.56
	Book value	46.07	41.45	35.04	30.36	30.43
Ratios	As a percent of sales:					
	Gross profit (%)	29.8	30.4	29.0	26.1	21.4
	Selling and administrative expenses (%)	18.5	17.8	18.8	18.7	16.9
	Return on common shareholders' equity (%)	14.8	19.4	12.1	4.4	(40.2)
	Current ratio	2.1	2.0	1.4	1.4	1.2
	Debt-to-capital ratio (%)	19.6	23.0	28.2	37.0	53.3
	Dividend payout—Common Stock (%)	30.9	23.2	38.9	115.0	N.A.
Other Data	Number of common shareholders at end of year	14,710	15,628	15,244	16,670	18,766
	Common shares outstanding at end of year (millions)	25.3	25.2	25.1	23.2	22.7
	Number of employees at end of year	11,892	12,302	11,972	11,914	26,191

INDEX

Numbers in **boldface color** refer to pages in the glossary at the end of each chapter.

AAA, 7
Accelerated Cost Recovery System (ACRS), 437
Accelerated depreciation method:
　defined, 432, **455**
　illustrated:
　　double-declining balance, 436
　　sum-of-years'-digits, 435
Account:
　balance, 80
　closing of, 187–189
　contra account, 34, 138
　defined, 72, **103**
　permanent, 184
　T account, 80
　temporary, 184
Account balance:
　defined, 80, **103**
　normal, 83
Account form (balance sheet), 36
Accounting, 3, **23**
Accounting changes, *see* Change in accounting
　　principles
Accounting controls, 284, **309**
Accounting data processing cycle:
　complete cycle, 176
　defined, 78, **103**
　end of period, 176–178
　steps during period, 78
Accounting equation, 72
Accounting information:
　characteristics of, 3
　recording, 4
　using, 4–5
Accounting model (equation), 13–14, 72
Accounting period, 77, **103**
Accounting principle, *see* Generally accepted ac-
　　counting principles
Accounting Principles Board, 6. *See also* Opinions
　　of Accounting Principle Board
Accounting Research Bulletins, 6
　No. 43, 341
　No. 45, 128
Accounting Review, 7
Accounting system, 280, **309**
Account payable, 473, **506**

Account receivable:
　defined, 342, **357**
　uncollectible accounts, 343
Accrual accounting, 76, **103**
Accruals, *see also* Adjusting entries defined, 133,
　　155
Accrued expenses, 140, 476, **506**
Accrued liabilities, 476, **506**
Accrued revenue, 144
Accumulated depreciation, 138, 155, 431–437
Acid test ratio (quick ratio), 724
Adjusted gross income, 774, **795**
Adjusted trial balance, 145, **155**
Adjusting entries:
　accruals, 133
　accrued (unrecorded) expenses, 140
　accrued (unrecorded) revenue, 144
　deferrals, 133
　defined, 132, **155**
　prepaid expenses, 135
　unearned revenue, 139
　worksheet, 180
Administrative controls, 283, **310**
Administrative expenses, 36, **54**, 230, **259**
Aging of accounts receivable, 345
Allowance for Uncollectible Accounts, 343
American Accounting Association (AAA), 7
American Institute of Certified Public Accountants
　　(AICPA), 6
Amortization:
　bond investment, 622–627
　bonds payable, 537–541, 547–550
　defined, 445, **455**
　intangible assets, 445
Annual report, 42, **54**
Annuity, 489, **506**
Asset, 13, **23**
Audit, 8, **23**
Audit report, 43
Authorized capital, 579
Authorized stock, 581, **603**
Average cost:
　defined, 380
　periodic inventory system, 384
　perpetual inventory system, 394

Bad debts expense:
  accounting for, 343–347
  defined, 343, 357
Balance sheet:
  account form, 36
  consolidated, 634
  constant dollar, 734
  current cost, 739
  defined, 12, 23
  preparation from worksheet, 183
  report form, 36
Bank reconciliation, 334, 357
Bank statement:
  defined, 333, 357
  illustrated, 332–338
Beginning inventory, 236, 259
Board of directors, 577
Bonds:
  adjusting entries, 543
  bond sinking fund, 546
  computing issue price, 533
  conversion, 545
  defined, 524, 556
  effective interest method of amortization, 547
  issued at discount, 537
  issued between interest payment dates, 542
  issued at par value, 531
  issued at premium, 538
  retirement, 544
Bonds indenture, 525
Bonds investment:
  long-term, 621–627
  temporary, 341
Bonds sinking fund:
  defined, 529, 556
  illustrated, 546
Bookkeeping, 4
Book of original entry (journals), 84
Book value, 139, 155, 433, 455, 597, 603
Budgeting, 9, 23
Business combination:
  accounting for, 634–641
  defined, 640, 652
Business transactions, 3, 23

Calendar year firm, 77, 103
Callable bond, 529, 556
Callable preferred stock, 585
Call provision, 587, 603
Canceled check 333, 357
Capital, see Owner's equity
Capital asset, 783, 795
Capital expenditure, 439, 455
Capital gains and losses:
  corporations tax returns, 786
  individual tax returns, 783
Capital lease, 481, 506
Capital stock, see Common stock
Carrying value of bonds, 536, 556
Cash, defined, 328, 357

Cash basis of accounting, 126
Cash disbursements journal, 306, 310
Cash discount, 233, 259
Cash equivalents, 674, 693
Cash flow and depreciation, 438
Cash receipts journal, 302, 310
Cash short and over account, 332
Casualty or theft losses, itemized deductions, 778
Certified Public Accountant (CPA), 7, 23
Change in estimate, 438
Change in accounting principle, 593
Charge, 80, 103
Charitable contributions, itemized deductions, 777
Chart of accounts, 87, 103
Check, 333, 357
Check register, 505
Closing entries:
  defined, 184, 206
  illustrated, 183–190
  merchandising firm, 247
Collateral, 528, 556
Common size statements, 717, 745
Common stock:
  accounting for issue of, 579–582
  defined, 581, 603
  investment in, 627
Comparative statements, 713, 745
Completed contracts method, 128, 155
Compound interest, 486, 506
Compound journal entry, 86, 104
Computerized accounting, 290–295
Conservatism:
  applied to inventory, 391
  defined, 49, 54
  exchange operating assets, 443
  temporary investments, 340
Consignee, 379, 408
Consignment, 379, 408
Consignor, 379, 408
Consistency principle:
  accounting principle, 47, 54
  inventory methods, 389
Consolidated financial statements:
  balance sheet, 634
  defined, 632, 652
  criteria for preparation, 634
  income statement, 639
  purchase vs. pooling of interests, 640
Constant dollar accounting, 731, 746
Constructive receipt, 772, 795
Consumer Price Index, 730
Contingent liability, 350, 357
Contra account, 34, 54, 138, 155
Control account, 231, 259
Controller, 9, 23
Convertible bond, 529, 556, 545
Convertible preferred stock, 585
Copyright, 446, 455
Corporate charter, 577, 603
Corporation:
  accounting for, 572–597

book value, 595
defined, 11, 23
forming corporation, 575
nonprofit, 573
nonpublic (closely held), 573
paid-in capital, 578
public, 573
S corporation, 770, 788
Cost:
expired, 130
principle, 46
unexpired, 130
Cost accounting, 9, 23
Cost method:
defined, 627, 652
illustrated, 627
Cost of goods available for sale, 239, 259
Cost of goods sold, 34, 54, 230, 259
Cost principle, 46, 54
Coupon (bearer) bond, 529, 556
Coupon rate (nominal contract, or stated rate), 524, 556
CPA, see Certified Public Accountant
Credit, 30, 104
Credit memorandum, 232, 259, 334, 357
Creditor, 13
Credit period, 232, 259
Credit terms, 232, 259
Crossfooting, 180, 206
Cumulative preferred stock, 586, 603
Current assets, 38, 54
Current liabilities, 40, 54
Current operating income, 737, 746
Current ratio, 473, 506, 723
Current replacement cost (current cost), 737, 746
Current value accounting, 731, 746

Data processing, 291
Database management system, 293, 310
Debenture bond (unsecured bond), 528, 556
Debit, 80, 104
Debit memorandum, 240, 259, 334, 357
Debit securities portfolio, 339, 357
Debt to total assets, 727
Declining-balance method, 436, 455
Deduction, 774, 795
Deferrals, defined, 133, 155. See also Adjusting entries
Deferred revenues, 139, 200
Deficit, 581, 603
Dependent, 779
Depletion, 449, 455
Deposits in transit, 334, 357
Depreciable cost, 432, 455
Depreciation:
accelerated depreciation methods, 432, 434–437
adjusting entry, 137–139
defined, 137, 155, 431, 455
double declining-balance method, 436
income tax purposes, 437

revision of depreciation rates, 438
straight-line method, 433
sum-of-years'-digit method, 435
units of production method, 433
Direct exchange rate, 647, 652
Direct exchange (noncash) transactions, 684, 693
Direct method, 675, 694
Discontinued operations, 592
Discount bond:
amortization, 537, 547, 624
defined, 349, 357, 526, 556
Discount notes, 474
Discount period:
defined, 233, 259, 349, 357
notes, 349
Dishonored note, 348, 357
Disposal of operating asset, 440–444
Dividend:
cash, 583
defined, 584, 603
liquidating, 583
stock, 587
Dividend payout (ratio), 723
Dividends in arrears, 586, 603
Dividend yield (ratio), 722
Double declining-balance depreciation, 436, 455
Double-entry accounting, 76, 104
Drawing account, 600
Dun & Bradstreet, Inc., 712

Earnings, 16
Earnings per share:
computing, 720
defined, 36, 54
ratio to analyze profitability, 721
reporting of, 36
Effective interest method (bonds), 547, 625
Effective Rate (Yield Rate), 532, 556
Electronic data processing, 291, 310
Electronic spreadsheet, 293, 310
Ending inventory, 238, 259
Endorsement, 342, 357
Entity assumption, 44, 54
Equipment, 428–448
Equity method:
defined, 627, 652
illustrated, 631
Equity securities portfolio, 339, 357
Errors, discovery and correction of, 97–98
Estimated useful life, 431
Exchange rate, 646, 653
Exclusion, 774, 796
Exemptions, 779, 796
Expenditure, 429, 455
Expense:
accrual basis, 130
cash basis, 126
closing, 187–189
defined, 15, 23, 34
matching, 131–132

Expired cost, 130, 155
Exporting transactions, 649
External statements, 11, 23
External transactions, 3, 23
Extraordinary item, 36, 54, 594, 603

Face value, 524
Fair market value, 429, 455
FASB, 6, 23
Federal Insurance Contribution Act (FICA), 478
Federal Unemployment Tax Act (FUTA), 479
Federal unemployment taxes, 479
FICA taxes, 478
File, 294, 310
Financial Accounting Standards Board (FASB), 6,
    23. *See also* Statements of Financial
    Accounting Standards
Financial Executive Institute, 7
Financial leverage, 526, 556
Financial statement analysis, 710
Financial statements:
    defined, 5, 23
    general purpose, 34
Financing activities, 675, 694
Finished goods (inventory), 377
First-In, First-Out (FIFO):
    defined, 383, 408
    periodic inventory system, 382
    perpetual inventory system, 392
Fiscal year, 77, 104
Fixed assets, *see* Plant assets
FOB destination, 234, 259
FOB shipping point, 234, 259
Footing, 81, 104
Foreign Corrupt Practices Act, 282
Form W-2, 478
Franchise, 448, 455
Freight-In (Transportation-In), 244
Freight-Out (delivery expense), 234
Full disclosure principle, 48, 54
Funded plan, 482, 506
Future value:
    ordinary annuity, 489
    single amount, 487
    tables, 488, 490

GAAP, *see* Generally accepted accounting
    principles (GAAP)
Gains, 14, 23
General journal (two column journal), 85, 104
General ledger, 86, 104
Generally accepted accounting principles (GAAP):
    5, 23, 43
    conservatism convention, 49
    consistency principle, 47
    cost principle, 46
    defined, 5
    entity assumption, 44
    full-disclosure principle, 48

going concern assumption, 44
    matching principle, 47
    materiality convention, 48
    monetary unit assumption, 45
    objectivity principle, 46
    revenue principles, 47
    source of, 5–7
    stable dollar assumption, 45
    time period assumption, 45
General price level:
    constant dollar, 731–737
    defined, 730, 746
General price level change, 730, 746
General purpose financial statements, 34
Going concern assumption, 44, 54
Goods available for sale, 239
Goodwill, 448, 455
Government Accounting Standards Board
    (GASB), 7
Governmental accounting, 10
Gross income, 774, 796
Gross invoice method, 233, 259
Gross margin (gross profit) on sales, 34, 54, 230
Gross profit method, 401, 409

Head of household, 773
Holding gain (loss), 737, 746
Horizontal analysis, 713, 746

Importing transactions, 647
Imputing interest, 476
Inadequacy, 432, 455
Income statement:
    consolidated, 639
    constant dollar, 735
    current cost, 740
    defined, 14, 23
    merchandising firm, 229, 250
    multiple step, 34
    preparation from worksheet, 183
Income summary, 184
Income tax allocation, 483–485
Income taxes:
    cash basis *vs.* accrual basis, 773
    classification of taxable entities, 770
    corporations, 784–791
    income tax allocation, 483–485
    individuals, 770–784
    tax planning, 771
    timing difference, 483
Income tax expense, 36, 54
Incorporators, 577, 603
Indenture, 525, 556
Indirect method, 679, 694
Industry peculiarities exceptions, 49, 54
Inflation, 730, 746
Installment method, 129, 155
Intangible asset:
    accounting for, 444–450
    defined, 38, 54, 444, 455

Interest:
  adjusting entry, 142
  compound, 486
  computing, 347
  defined, 347, 357
  future value:
    of ordinary annuity, 489
    of single amount, 487
  imputing interest, 476
  present value:
    of ordinary annuity, 493
    of single amount, 491
  simple, 486
Interest, itemized deduction, 777
Interim statements, 78, 104
Internal auditing, 10
Internal control, 283, 310
Internal Revenue Code, 769, 796
Internal statements, 11, 23
Internal transactions, 3, 23
International accounting, 646–653
International Accounting Standards Committee
    (IASC), 7, 652
International Federation of Accountants (IFAC), 7,
    652
Inventory, *see* Merchandise inventory
Inventory turnover, 726
Investee company, 621, 653
Investing activities, 674, 694
Investments:
  bonds, 341
  classification of, 338
  consolidated statements, 632–642
  cost method, 627
  equity method, 631
  equity securities, 627–642
  long-term, 620–642
  temporary, 338–341
Investor company, 621, 653
Invoice, 501, 506
Itemized deductions, 777, 796

Journal (Books of Original Entry), 84, 104
Journal of Accountancy, 6
Journal entry, 85, 104
Journalizing, 85, 104

Last-In, First-Out (LIFO):
  defined, 383, 409
  periodic inventory system, 383
  perpetual inventory system, 393
LCM, *see* Lower of cost-or-market (LCM) rule
Lease:
  capital, 481
  defined, 446, 455, 481, 506
  operating, 482
Leasehold, 446, 455
Leasehold improvements, 447, 455
Ledger, *see* General ledger
Legal capital, 579

Lessee, 446, 455
Lessor, 446, 455
Leverage, *see* Financial leverage
Liabilities:
  accrued, 476
  classification, 40
  contingent, 350
  current, 473–480
  defined, 13, 23
  long-term, 480–485, 523–551
Liquid asset, 328, 357
Liquidating dividend, 584, 603
Liquidity, 38, 54
Long-term capital gain or loss, 783, 796
Long-term investments, defined, 39, 54, 621, 653.
    See also Investments
Losses, 15, 23
Lower of cost or market (LCM) rule:
  defined, 40, 55, 390, 409
  illustrated, 340, 390–391, 628
Lump-sum acquisition, 430

Maker, 347, 357
Management Accounting, 7
Management advisory services, 8
Marginal tax rate, 780, 796
Marketability, 338
Marketable securities, *see* Temporary investments
Market rate (effective rate, yield), 532
Marshall, John (Chief Justice), 573
Matching principle:
  accrual basis of accounting, 131
  defined, 47, 55, 127, 155
Materiality, 48, 55
Maturity date, 524, 556
Maturity value, 347, 357
Medical and dental expense itemized deduction,
    777
Merchandise inventory:
  accounting for, 228–251, 377–403
  consignment, 379
  defined, 229, 259
  periodic inventory system, 239–249
  perpetual inventory system, 235–239
Microcomputer, 292
Minicomputer, 292
Minority interest, 635, 653
Monetary items, 732, 746
Monetary unit assumption, 45, 55
Money, 3
Moody's Investors Service, 711
Mortgage, 550, 556
Mortgage note payable, 550, 556
Moving average, 394, 409
Multinational corporations, 646, 653
Multiple-step income statement, 34

National Association of Accountants (NAA), 7
Natural business year, 78
Natural resources, 448, 455

Negotiable instrument, 342, 357
Net income (earnings or profit), 14, 16, 23
Net loss, 14, 23
Net monetary items, 736, 746
Net realizable value:
  current value accounting, 737
  defined, 391, 409, 737, 746
  valuation of inventory, 391
Nominal accounts, 184
Nominal rate, 525
Noncumulative preferred stock, 586, 603
Nonmonetary items, 733, 746
Nonprofit corporation, 575, 603
Nonpublic (closely held) corporation, 575, 603
Nonsufficient funds check (NSF), 334, 357
Nontrade receivables, 342
No-par value stock, 581
Normal balance, 83, 104
Normal operating cycle, defined, 38, 55
Note payable:
  accounting for, 473–476
  defined, 473, 506
  long-term, 550
Note receivable:
  accounting for, 347–350
  defined, 342, 358

Objectivity principle, 46, 55
Obsolescence, 432, 455
Operating activities, 674, 694
Operating assets, 428, 455
Operating expenses, 36, 55
Operating income, 36, 55
Operating lease, 482, 506
Operating manual, 287, 310
Opinions of Accounting Principles Board:
  No. 10, 129
  No. 16, 637
  No. 17, 445
  No. 18, 627
  No. 20, 593
  No. 21, 476
  No. 29, 442
  No. 30, 593
Ordinary annuity, 489, 506
Ordinary repairs and maintenance, 440
Other assets, 40, 55
Outstanding checks, 334, 358
Outstanding stock, 580
Owners' equity, 13, 23

Paid-in capital, 14, 23, 580, 603
Paid vouchers file, 505
Parent Company, 632, 653
Participating preferred stock, 586, 604
Partnership:
  accounting for, 601–603
  defined, 11, 24
Par value (face value, maturity value):
  bonds issued at, 531
  capital stock, 579

defined, 524, 556
Patent, 445, 456
Payables, see Liabilities
Payee, 347, 358
Payout ratio, 723
Pension plan, 482, 506
Percentage-of-completion method, 128, 155
Periodic inventory system:
  defined, 236, 259
  illustrated, 239–249, 381
Permanent (real) accounts, defined, 184, 206
Permanent difference, 483, 506
Perpetual inventory system:
  defined, 235, 259
  illustrated, 235–239, 391
Petty cash fund, 330, 358
Petty cash receipt, 331, 358
Physical inventory, 239, 260, 378
Physical wear and tear, 432, 456
Plant assets:
  accounting for, 428–450
  defined, 428, 456
  depreciation, 431
Pooling of interests, 640, 653
Post-closing trial balance, 191, 206
Posting, 88, 104
Posting reference, 88
Preemptive right, 578, 604
Preferred stock:
  accounting for, 583–585
  defined, 585, 604
Premium, bond:
  amortizaton, 540, 549, 622
  defined, 526, 556
Prepaid expenses, 135, 199
Present value:
  ordinary annuity, 493
  single amount, 491
  tables, 493, 495
Price–earning ratio, 721
Principal, 347, 358
Prior period adjustment, 596, 604
Proceeds, 349, 358, 474, 506
Profit, 16
Profit corporation, 575, 604
Promissory note, 347, 358
Property, plant, and equipment, 39, 55
Proprietorship, 10, 24, 600
Proxy statement, 579, 604
Public accounting, 8–10
Public corporation, 575, 604
Purchase invoice, 232, 260
Purchase method, 640, 653
Purchase order, 499, 506
Purchase requisition, 499, 506
Purchases, 240–241
Purchases discounts, 233, 260
Purchases journal, 302, 310
Purchases returns and allowances, 240
Purchasing power, 730, 746
Purchasing power gain (loss), 732, 746

Quick ratio (acid test ratio), 724

Rate of return:
   on common stockholders' equity, 720
   on total assets, 719
Ratio, *see also specific ratios*
   analyze financial leverage, 727–728
   analyze liquidity, 723–727
   analyze profitability, 718–723
   defined, 717, 746
Rational, 131
Raw materials (inventory), 377
Real accounts, 184
Realized holding gain or loss, 738, 746
Receivables:
   accounting for, 342
   classification of, 342–347
   defined, 342
Receivable turnover ratio, 725
Receiving report, 501, 506
Registered bond, 529, 556
Replacement cost, 737
Report form (balance sheet), 36
Residual value, 138, 155, 432, 456
Retail inventory method, 399, 409
Retained earnings, 14, 24, 581, 594–595, 604
Retained earnings statement, 16, 24
Return on sales, 721
Revenue:
   accrual basis, 127–130
   cash basis, 126
   closing of, 187–189
   defined, 14, 34, 24, 74
Revenue expenditure, 439, 456
Revenue principle, 47, 55
Reversing entries, 178, 206
Robert Morris and Associates, 711

Sales discount, 232, 260
Sales invoice, 232, 260
Sales journal, 299, 310
Sales returns and allowances, 232
Salvage value, 432
S Corporation, 770, 796
Secured (mortgage) bond, 528, 556
Securities and Exchange Commission (SEC), 6,
   24, 711
Segment of a Business, 594, 604
Selling expenses, 36, 55, 230, 260
Serial bonds, 529, 557
Shareholders, *see* Stockholders.
Short-term capital gain or loss, 783, 796
Simple interest, 486, 506
Sinking fund, bond, 546
Source document, 71, 104
Special journals, 298, 310
Specific identification:
   defined, 382, 409
   periodic inventory system, 382
   perpetual inventory system, 392
Specific price change, 730, 746

Stable-dollar assumption, 45, 55
Standard & Poor's Corporation, 711
Standard deduction, 776, 796
Stated rate, 524
Statement of cash flows, 17, 24, 673, 694
Statement of retained earnings, 16, 40, 594
Statement of Financial Accounting Concepts:
   No. 1, 43
   No. 2, 43
   No. 3, 14
Statements of Financial Accounting Standards:
   No. 2, 445
   No. 4, 2, 545
   No. 12, 340
   No. 13, 481
   No. 16, 594
   No. 33, 740
   No. 34, 430
   No. 82, 740
   No. 89, 740
   No. 95, 673
Statements of International Accounting Standards,
   652
Stock, *see* Common stock; Preferred stock
Stock certificate, 577, 604
Stock dividend, 589, 604
Stockholders, 11, 24
Stockholders' equity, 40, 55
Stock split, 590
Straight-line amortization:
   bond investment, 622–624
   bonds payable, 537–542
Straight-line method, 433, 456
Subsidiary, 632, 653
Subsidiary ledger, 231, 260
Sum-of-year's-digits depreciation method, 435,
   456
Systematic, 131
Systems, *see* Accounting system
Systems analysis, 287, 310
Systems design, 288, 310
Systems implementation, 288, 310

T account, 80, 104
Taxable income, 774, 796
Tax accounting, 9
Tax credit, 774, 796
Tax evasion, 771, 796
Tax planning, 771, 796
Tax rate schedules, 780, 787
Temporary (nominal) accounts, 184, 206
Temporary investments:
   accounting for, 338–341
   defined, 338
Temporary (Timing) Difference, 483, 507
Term bonds (ordinary bonds), 529, 557
Time period assumption, 45, 55
Timesharing-computer, 292
Times interest earned, 728
Trade discounts, 234, 260
Trade-in value, 432

Trademark and trade names, 446
Trade receivables, 342, 358
Transactions, 3, 71
Translation:
  financial statements, 650–652
  transactions, 647–650
Treasury stock:
  accounting for, 586–587
  defined, 588, 604
Trend analysis, 716, 746
Trial balance, 88, 104
Trustee, 526, 557

Unadjusted Trial Balance, 134, 155
Uncollectible accounts, 343
Underwriter, 525, 557
Unearned revenue, 139, 477, 507
Unexpired cost, 130, 155
Units-of-production method, 433, 456
Unpaid vouchers file, 504

Unrealized holding gain (loss), 738, 746
Unsecured note payable, 550, 557
Useful life, 138, 155, 431, 456

Vertical analysis, 717, 746
Voucher, 502, 507
Voucher register, 505, 507
Voucher system, 499, 507

Wage and tax statement, 478, 507
Wasting asset, 449
Weighted average, 384, 409
Work in process (inventory), 377
Working capital, 40, 55
Worksheet:
  defined, 176, 206
  illustrated, 178–183
  merchandising firm, 245
W-2 form, 478